ICCA
CONGRESS SERIES NO. 18

INTERNATIONAL ARBITRATION CONGRESS
MIAMI, 6 - 9 APRIL 2014

INTERNATIONAL COUNCIL
FOR COMMERCIAL ARBITRATION

LEGITIMACY:
MYTHS, REALITIES, CHALLENGES

GENERAL EDITOR:
ALBERT JAN VAN DEN BERG

with the assistance of the
Permanent Court of Arbitration
Peace Palace, The Hague

ISBN 978-90-411-5944-1

Published by:
Kluwer Law International
PO Box 316
2400 AH Alphen aan den Rijn
The Netherlands
Website: www.kluwerlaw.com

Sold and distributed in North, Central and South America by:
Aspen Publishers, Inc.
7201 McKinney Circle
Frederick, MD 21704
United States of America
Email: customer.service@aspenpublishers.com

Sold and distributed in all other countries by:
Turpin Distribution Services Ltd.
Stratton Business Park
Pegasus Drive, Biggleswade
Bedfordshire SG18 8TQ
United Kingdom
Email: kluwerlaw@turpin-distribution.com

Printed on acid-free paper.

Printed and bound by CPI Group (UK) Ltd, Croydon, CR0 4YY, United Kingdom.

Preface

ICCA Congress Series no. 18 comprises the proceedings of the XXII ICCA Congress, organized by the ICCA Miami 2014 Host Committee in Miami, Florida, on 6-9 April 2014. We thank our hosts for their warm welcome, excellent organization and tireless efforts on behalf of ICCA and the Congress participants.

The theme of the Congress was Legitimacy: Myths, Realities, Challenges, and the innovative program was notable for its on-the-spot gathering of empirical data. The Opening Plenary began by identifying propositions relating to arbitral legitimacy and asked the question: Are these myths, reality or something else? The Congress sessions were divided into two streams which explored the twin pillars of arbitral legitimacy: (A) justice and (B) precision. The aim of each session was to identify specific propositions as myth or reality by exploring in depth the specific aspects contributing to both arbitral justice (A), in both procedure and outcome, and to precision (B) at every stage of the proceedings. A summary checklist of the Panels' conclusions is included as an Annex to the Report on the Opening Plenary Session (pp. 22-29).

I would like to extend my thanks to the Program Committee: Lucy Reed (Chair), John Barkett, Adriana Braghetta, Dushyant Dave, Meg Kinnear, Salim Moollan and Klaus Reichert SC. A futher word of thanks goes to the Session Chairs and Rapporteurs who provided invaluable assistance during all phases of the Congress. They are as follows:

Opening Plenary:
Lucy Reed and Meg Kinnear (chairs), James Freda and Tobias Lehmann (Rapporteurs)
Precision Stream
– A1: David Brynmor Thomas (Chair), Timothy L. Foden, (Rapporteur);
– A2: John Barkett (Chair), Natalie Reid, (Rapporteur);
– A3: Nathalie Voser (Chair), Nicholas Lingard, (Rapporteur);
– A4: Klaus Reichert SC (Chair), Elizabeth Karanja, (Rapporteur)
Justice Stream
– B1: Adriana Braghetta (Chair), Ricardo Dalmaso Marques, (Rapporteur);
– B2: Salim Moollan (Chair), Belinda McRae, (Rapporteur);
– B3: Anna Joubin-Bret (Chair), Neeti Sachdeva, (Rapporteur);
– B4: Dushyant Dave (Chair), Kathleen Claussen, (Rapporteur)
Plenary: Spotlight on International Arbitration in Miami and the United States
– John Barkett (Chair), Frank Cruz-Alvarez, (Rapporteur)
Breakout Sessions on Arbitral Legitimacy: The Users' and Judges' Perspectives
– José Astigarraga (Chair), Luis González García (Rapporteur);
– Melanie van Leeuwen (Chair), Amanda Lees (Rapporteur);
– Joseph Matthews (Chair), L Andrew S. Riccio (Rapporteur);
– Edna Sussman (Chair), Ruth Mosch (Rapporteur)
Lunch Seminar – Latin America: Hottest Issues, Country by Country
– R. Doak Bishop (Chair), Ricardo Dalmaso Marques (Rapporteur)
Lunch Seminar – Power of Arbitration to Fill Gaps in the Arbitration Agreement and Underlying Contract
– John H. Rooney, Jr. (Chair), Elodie Dulac (Rapporteur)

Closing Plenary
– Jan Paulsson and Albert Jan van den Berg (Chairs), James Freda and Tobias Lehmann (Rapporteurs).

The Miami Cogress was ICCA's largest Congress to date, with over 1,000 registered delegates. It was also the first Congress since ICCA opened its doors to general membership. Meetings by ICCA's newly formed interest and project groups complemented the formal progam.

Looking ahead, the next ICCA Congress will take place for the first time in Africa, on 8-11 May 2016 in Mauritius. Information on the Congress will be posted on the ICCA website <wwww.icca-arbitration.org> as it becomes available.

Once again, I wish to thank the Permanent Court of Arbitration and its Secretary-General, H.E. Hugo Hans Siblesz, for hosting the ICCA Editorial Staff at the headquarters of its International Bureau at the Peace Palace. The continued support of the entire administrative and technical staff of the PCA is much appreciated as well.

A final word of thanks to the Editorial Staff of ICCA Publications, in particular Ms. Alice Siegel, Assistant Managing Editor, for their invaluable assistance in preparing this volume for publication.

Albert Jan van den Berg
March 2015

23rd ICCA CONGRESS

8-11 May 2016

Mauritius

"International Arbitration and the Rule of Law:
Contribution and Conformity"

For program and registration information:

http://http://www.iccamauritius2016.com

www.arbitration-icca.org

For the Young ICCA Event:

www.arbitration-icca.org/YoungICCA/Home.html

TABLE OF CONTENTS

A-3 Matters of Evidence: Witness and Experts

Chair: Nathalie Voser
Rapporteur: Nicholas Lingard

A-4 Treaty Arbitration: Pleading and Proof of Fraud and Comparable Forms of Abuse

Chair: Klaus Reichert SC
Rapporteur: Elizabeth Karanja

Breakout Sessions on Arbitral Legitimacy: The Users' And Judges' Perspectives

Chairs: José Astigarraga, Melanie van Leeuwen, Joseph Matthews and Edna Sussman
Rapporteurs: Luis González García, Amanda Lees, Ruth Mosch and L Andrew S. Riccio

Lunch Seminar: Latin America: Hottest Issues, Country by Country

Chair: R. Doak Bishop
Rapporteur: Ricardo Dalmaso Marques

Lunch Seminar: Power of Arbitration to Fill Gaps in the Arbitration Agreement and Underlying Contract

Chair: John H. Rooney, Jr.
Rapporteur: Elodie Dulac

Closing Plenary

Rapporteurs: James Freda and Tobias Lehmann

Legitimacy: Examined Against Empirical Data

Chair: Jan Paulsson

Where We Have Been, Where We Should Go

Chair: Albert Jan van den Berg

Keynote Address:
In Defence of Bilateral Investment Treaties

*Judge Stephen M. Schwebel**

It is a pleasure and privilege to join in welcoming this distinguished audience to the opening of ICCA Miami.

Some sixty-three years ago, the Government of Iran, led by Prime Minister Mossadegh, expropriated the concession rights and installations of the Anglo-Iranian Oil Company. Anglo-Iranian had found, extracted and exported Iranian oil for decades. Its concession agreement was a template for oil and other concessions the world over. It provided for international arbitration of disputes and the application of international legal principles in the determination of those disputes. The Government of Iran refused to arbitrate pursuant to the concession agreement. By blocking access to the agreed forum, Iran thereby committed the international delict of a denial of justice. The concession agreement provided for default arbitral appointment by the President of the Permanent Court of International Justice (PCIJ). The President (or Vice President acting in his stead) of the International Court of Justice (ICJ) declined to exercise a power of appointment entrusted to the PCIJ President. Exercising its right of diplomatic espousal on behalf of Anglo-Iranian, the Government of the United Kingdom then brought proceedings against Iran in the ICJ. It alleged multiple violations of international law, including Iran's refusal to arbitrate pursuant to the concession agreement. Iran successfully challenged the treaty bases of jurisdiction invoked by the United Kingdom, so the Court was not empowered to pass upon the merits of the dispute. Anglo-Iranian sought to interdict the sale of oil from the concession areas through "hot oil" suits, with a measure of success. The Mossadegh Government was eventually overthrown; the Shah, who had fled abroad, returned; and it is accepted that in the overthrow of Mossadegh, the intelligence services of the United States and the United Kingdom had a hand. Thereafter the Iranian Oil Consortium Agreement was negotiated, on the one part between Anglo-Iranian and a group of the major international oil companies, and on the other part the Iranian Government. The export of Iranian oil resumed unhindered. That regime flourished until the Iranian revolution of 1979. The Consortium Agreement was ruptured in its wake. But, as an element of the release of the American diplomats taken hostage by Iran, the claims of the American members of the Consortium were remitted to arbitration before the Iran-United States Claims Tribunal, a Tribunal that over the last thirty-four years has amassed a body of valuable jurisprudence. The claims of the successor to Anglo-Iranian, British Petroleum, went to *ad hoc* arbitration. The BP case was eventually settled, while claims of the American oil companies before the Tribunal were adjudicated and paid.

---

* Former Judge and President, International Court of Justice. In preparing these remarks, the author has particularly benefitted from writings of Professors José Alvarez, Andrea K. Bjorklund and Susan D. Franck.

Why do I recall these events in these summary terms? I do so because they suggest that if, in 1951, the then Iranian Government had abided by its contractual, and international legal, obligation to arbitrate disputes arising under the Anglo-Iranian Concession, much that is deplorable that has taken place since very probably would not have happened. Foreign subversion would not have occurred. The position of secular and democratic elements of Iranian society, and Iran's national and international policies and relations, would be very different. For these and others reasons, the history of the Anglo-Iranian Oil Company expropriation is an object lesson demonstrating that the displacement of gunboat diplomacy by international arbitration is a very real achievement.

Today that achievement is under attack. That attack is not mounted by advocates of *realpolitik* but by those who profess to be progressives. My purpose in today's remarks is to examine whether the criticism directed at arbitration between investors and States is well founded.

But before I address these critical contentions, permit me to place international investment arbitration, and the treaties from which its jurisdiction and substantive legal principles largely derive, in historical context. The value of investment arbitration can only be understood in that context.

At the time of the expropriation of the Anglo-Iranian Oil Company, the middle of the twentieth century, there was a longstanding legal as well as economic gulf between capital-importing and capital-exporting States. There was a great gulf on the substance of the governing international law – if any. There was a great gulf on international legal process – if any.

The depth of that gulf was certified by the Supreme Court of the United States in the *Sabbatino Case* when it observed in 1964 that: "There are few if any issues in international law today on which opinion seems to be so divided as the limitations on a state's power to expropriate the property of aliens."[1]

On one side of that divide, capital-exporting States expounded a minimum standard of customary international law for the treatment of foreigners and their property. They could not be denied justice; they were entitled not merely to national treatment but to a minimum standard of treatment that included observance of contracts and, in the event of a taking of their investments, to prompt, adequate and effective compensation.

On the other side of the divide, capital-importing States adhered to the Calvo doctrine of national treatment. The alien and his property were subject to national law and national courts and were entitled to no more than was afforded to nationals of the host State, however little that might be. Customary international law governing the treatment of alien property did not exist.

All this was well rehearsed by the Russian Revolution, where foreign property was impartially expropriated with the same compensation as that afforded to Russian nationals, that is, none; by the Mexican nationalization of oil; and, after the Second World War, by the takings in a number of instances of which the Anglo-Iranian expropriation was perhaps the most notable.

The divide early manifested itself in the United Nations under the banner of "permanent sovereignty over natural resources". In 1962, after a decade of preparation, a resolution of that title came up for negotiation and adoption. The result was a reaching

---

1. 376 U.S. 398, 428 (1964).

across the divide that achieved a constructive accommodation of positions. UN General Assembly Resolution 1803 (XVII) repeatedly affirmed the permanent sovereignty of a State over its natural resources. But these recitals were balanced by a recognition that "capital imported ... shall be governed by the terms thereof, by the national legislation in force, and by international law". Expropriation required "appropriate compensation" in accordance with national and international law. Moreover, Resolution 1803 (XVII) strikingly provided that "Foreign investment agreements freely entered into by or between sovereign States shall be observed in good faith" – thus requiring the observance of contracts with foreign investors. In all, this was a proportionate resolution which recognized that foreign investment was governed by international as well as national law.

But soon after, confrontation displaced accommodation. Subsequent General Assembly resolutions on "permanent sovereignty over natural resources" excluded the governance, even the relevance, of international law. With the oil crisis of 1973, and the pain engendered by the immense surge in the price of oil, especially felt in the developing world, the UN Group of seventy-seven developing countries was led by OPEC to maintain that international economic problems were all the fault of the West. What was needed was a "New International Economic Order". North/South dispute came to a head in 1974 with the General Assembly's adoption of the "Charter of Economic Rights and Duties of States".[2] That Charter excluded international law in the treatment and taking of foreign property and asserted the sole governance of the domestic law of the host State as interpreted and applied by its courts. Key industrialized democracies voted against the Charter. At that juncture, the outlook for universal or even broad agreement in this sphere on either legal process or principle seemed remote.

This informed audience is familiar with two initiatives that changed that outlook to a presence far more beneficent. The first – the creation of the International Centre for Settlement of Investment Disputes (ICSID) – was one of process. The second – bilateral investment treaties (BITs) – was built on the first and successfully surmounted the divide not only over process but principle as well.

The then General Counsel of the World Bank, Aron Broches, saw in the 1960s at the time of the UN debates on permanent sovereignty over natural resources the difficulties of reaching meaningful and sustainable universal agreement on the principles at stake. His ingenious contribution was to sidestep what seemed to be a sterile substantive confrontation with procedural creativity. The Bank would not take sides between the developed and developing worlds. Rather it would create a facility for the impartial arbitral settlement of inevitable international investment disputes. Broches and his colleagues prepared the ground carefully in a series of regional conferences in which States and their legal advisers were fully consulted. He brought the persuasiveness of his vivacious personality to bear both with the legal advisers of governments and the Executive Directors of the Bank to put his insight across. The result was the conclusion in 1965 of the Washington Convention on Settlement of Investment Disputes between States and Nationals of Other States.

That Convention was and remains a remarkable achievement. Professors Dolzer and Schreuer in their valuable book, *Principles of International Investment Law,* offer this appraisal:

---

2. General Assembly Resolution 3281 (XXIX).

3

"At first sight, the Broches concept ('procedure before substance') seemed to be a limited and modest one.... In retrospect, it has become clear that the creation of ICSID amounted to the boldest innovative step in the modern history of international cooperation concerning the role and protection of foreign investment. This is so because of the combination of five pertinent features of ICSID: (a) foreign companies and individuals can directly bring suit against their host State; (b) state immunity is severely restricted; (c) international law can be applied to the relationship between the host State and the investor; (d) the local remedies rule is excluded in principle and (e) ICSID awards are directly enforceable within the territories of all states parties to ICSID."[3]

While ICSID got off to a slow start, as international institutions often do, today there are 150 States Parties to the Washington Convention. As of December 2013, ICSID has registered 459 cases. It currently is administering 183 arbitrations. Moreover, investor/State arbitration flourishes with the assistance of other institutions and rules, among them, the Permanent Court of Arbitration (PCA), the Stockholm Chamber of Commerce, the London Court of International Arbitration, the International Chamber of Commerce and the American Arbitration Association's International Center for Dispute Resolution. This year (2014) the PCA is administering nine arbitrations between States, fifty arbitrations between investors and States pursuant to bilateral investment treaties, and another thirty-one arbitrations founded in contracts between States and foreign investors. There are also numbers of *ad hoc* arbitrations between States and foreign investors, mostly applying the UNCITRAL Rules. The ICJ currently has eleven cases between States on its docket, and other international tribunals are not idle. In all, international litigation over international legal disputes is at the highest tide in history.

As for the legal principles applied in arbitrations between foreign investors and States, it may be recalled that, in 1959, Germany concluded the first bilateral investment agreement, with Pakistan. That treaty built upon the numbers of treaties of friendship, commerce and navigation. From that beginning, some 3,000 bilateral investment treaties – "BITs" – have sprung. The majority are in force, as are important multilateral treaties that incorporate essential elements of BITs, the Energy Charter Treaty, the North American Free Trade Agreement, and the Central American Free Trade Agreement. These three multilateral treaties in their provisions for arbitral recourse are equal to many bilateral treaties in force.

At the same time however, the European Union may be phasing out the BITs between its Members while, so far, maintaining those with other States and negotiating new BITs, such as one with Burma. Yet there are reports that the European Union, led by Germany, may favor excluding investor/State arbitration from the trade agreement under negotiation with the United States. Moreover, South Africa and Indonesia are reported to have decided not to renew their many BITs when they expire. Yet new BITs, such as that between Australia and the Republic of Korea, appear to be in the process of conclusion. Three Latin American States have withdrawn from ICSID. Since their withdrawal however ten States have ratified the ICSID Convention. So the prospects for the ubiquity of investor/State arbitration appear to be mixed.

3. Rudolf DOLZER and Christoph SCHREUER, *Principles of International Investment Law* (2008) p. 20.

Bilateral investment treaties bridge the substantive divide between the traditional positions of capital-exporting and capital-importing States in largely concordant terms designed to promote and protect foreign investment. Those terms are more precise and far-reaching than the content of customary international law earlier invoked by capital-exporting States. By the terms of typical BITs, foreign investment is assured of fair and equitable treatment, full security and protection, and no less than national and most-favored-nation treatment. The foreign investor is assured of management authority and control. The terms of commitments entered into in respect of foreign investment are to be observed. If there is a taking by the State of the foreign investment, by means direct or indirect, the host State is treaty-bound to pay prompt, adequate and effective compensation. Moreover, the great majority of BITs enable the foreign investor to require the host State to arbitrate treaty disputes, through ICSID or otherwise.

That entitlement to international arbitration is one of the most progressive developments in the procedure of international law of the last fifty years, indeed in the whole history of international law. It is consistent with the development of international human rights, including the right to own property, and with the dethroning of the State from its status as the sole subject of international law.

BITs now run not only between North and South but between East and West. There are more than 600 South/South BITs, that is, bilateral investment treaties between two developing States. The Russian Federation and other successor States of the Soviet Union, and the People's Republic of China, are parties to scores of BITs, as is Cuba. While early Chinese BITs were more limited than those pioneered by Western Europe, the cascade of Chinese BITs of recent years approach the norm, as China becomes not only a major capital importer but exporter.

There are few areas of international law and life that have been the subject of some 3,000 concordant treaties: most-favored nation provisions come to mind but it is not easy to call up another. In view of that immense number of treaties, the virtual universality of adherence to them, and the predominant consistency of their terms, there is room for the view that they have reshaped the body of customary international law in respect of the treatment and taking of foreign investment. That is to say, it may be argued that pervasive, core provisions of BITs, namely those providing for the international legal standards of fair and equitable treatment and prompt, adequate and effective compensation, by the fact of being prescribed in some 3,000 bilateral investment treaties and three multilateral treaties, have seeped into the corpus of customary international law, with the result that they are binding on all States, including those not parties to BITs. That arguable thesis has a measure of support in a few arbitral awards.[4] In any event, bilateral investment treaties have remarkably refashioned both the process and the principles of international law in respect of the treatment and taking of foreign property.

That development has produced diverse appraisals. I have just given a positive view. What are the elements of a negative view, of the claim that there is a "legitimacy crisis" affecting investor/State arbitration?

---

4. *Mondev International Ltd. v. United States of America* (ICSID Case No ARB(AF)/99/2), Award of 11 October 2002, and *CME Czech Republic B.V. v. Czech Republic,* Final Award of 14 March 2003, paras. 497-498.

The essential contentions advanced by the critics of international investment arbitration are these:

— International investment tribunals are biased in favor of multinational corporations and against defendant States, or in the least appear to be biased.
— They are or appear to be biased because international investment arbitrators are predominantly drawn from the ranks of commercial arbitration and from the West.
— They are or appear to be biased because investment arbitrators, many of whom have acted or continue to act as counsel, are or may be influenced by their desire for further appointments rather than only the merits of the case.
— Repeated appointments give rise to questions of "issue conflict" because such arbitrators pass upon questions on which they have passed upon earlier or have argued or written about as counsel or commentators.
— International investment arbitration is asymmetrical because investors can bring claims against States while States cannot bring claims against investors.
— Investors are placed on an equal plane with States, despite investors having their monetary interests in view whereas the State promotes the public interest.
— International investment encroaches upon the ability of States to regulate in the public interest, it constrains their "policy space".
— International arbitral awards repeatedly conflict with one another in the absence of an international appellate court that could impose order on disorder. A tenured international court, constituted only by States, should replace international investment arbitration. In the meantime, States that have suffered adverse arbitral awards are free to ignore them.

These criticisms are more colorful than they are cogent.

In point of fact, have international investment tribunals produced biased awards, biased in favor of investors and against States? The revealing research of Professor Susan Franck concludes that of 144 publicly available awards, as of January 2012, where arbitrators resolved a dispute arising under a treaty, States won 87 cases, awarding no damages to the investor, and investors won 57.[5] ICSID statistics show that of its disputes decided in 2013, jurisdiction was declined in 31%, the award dismissed all claims in 32%, and an award upholding claims in part or in full issued in 37%.[6] Those figures in the large hardly suggest bias against States.

Professor Franck, using data from published final awards, further shows that where the investors won damages, they won far less than claimed. That may suggest that investors tend to take an expansive view of their claims, but it hardly tends to show bias against States. The figures also show that about a quarter of investment claims are dismissed at the jurisdictional stage. If investment arbitrators were truly influenced by the prospect of remuneration for extended proceedings and the prospect of further appointments, why would they terminate so many arbitral proceedings at the jurisdictional stage? Moreover, the large majority of international arbitral awards are

---

5. Susan D. FRANCK, "Using Investor-State Mediation Rules to Promote Conflict Management: An Introductory Guide", 29 ICSID Review (2014, issue 1) p. 79.
6. The ICSID Caseload, Statistics (Issue 2013-2), Chart 7a, p. 28. See also p. 14.

unanimous, a fact that suggests that arbitrators are not unduly responsive to the interests of the party that appointed them.

Arbitrators of investment disputes may be predominantly drawn from those who act as commercial arbitrators, or even as practitioners, though in fact there are a number of leading international arbitrators who have been government officials or national or international judges or who are academics. International investment disputes tend to be substantial disputes. It is unsurprising that the parties tend to choose arbitrators of experience. Before a lawyer is chosen to be an arbitrator, he will need to have acquired a reputation, normally in the practice of law. If practitioners were to be excluded from international arbitral appointments, it is not apparent how arbitral tribunals would be composed of persons knowledgeable in the law and in the ways of adjudication. As for arbitrators continuing to act as counsel, the number of those who can make a living solely as arbitrator is not large. At this very gathering, which brings together the leading international arbitrators of the world, many also act as counsel. Some of the most distinguished arbitrators of our or any time were or remain practicing lawyers. Most of them may be from the West, a fact which is sustained by arbitral appointments by States, including non-Western States, as well as appointments by claimants and institutions, but there is a distinct and welcome trend towards diversity. There is room for many more female arbitrators, a development that will surely come as it has in the practice of law and in national and international courts.

Should arbitrators be subject to challenge because of "issue conflict", because, as arbitrator or counsel, or as a published commentator on the law, they have dealt with or passed upon a BIT provision that is at issue in the current case? Think of how many judges would be surprised to be asked to recuse themselves in a case in which a constitutional or statutory provision is at issue because, in a prior case, they had been required to pass on that provision. If the justices of the Supreme Court of the United States were required to interpret the commerce clause in one case, can it be seriously maintained that they cannot sit in another case where the commerce clause is in issue? Or is it rather and rightly presumed that a judge or arbitrator of integrity and ability will deal with the facts and law of each case on their merits?

Of course there is no such thing as perfect objectivity. Each of us sees the world through his or her own eyes, each of us is a prisoner of his or her own experience. But nevertheless the institutions of judging and arbitrating have long been accepted instruments of civilization. If international arbitrators who have dealt with a question of fair and equitable treatment, or the umbrella clause, or a security reservation, in one case are subject to challenge where that question is at issue in another case, will not the result be that novices will tend rule the roost, that the ranks of experienced arbitrators will be decimated?

As for the criticism that the international investment process is asymmetrical, that investors can bring claims against States but States cannot bring claims against investors, that is generally so though States can and have brought counterclaims. Arbitral rules, such as those of ICSID and UNCITRAL, expressly authorize counterclaims. In any event, any imbalance is exaggerated, because the State has not only police powers but the police. It can bring the weight of its bureaucracy to bear. The State has so many ways in which it can exert pressure upon the foreign investor; the ability of the investor to launch arbitration only mitigates that imbalance. And how is it that the NGOs who complain of asymmetry in investor/State arbitration make no such complaint about human rights courts, where only the alleged abused can bring a claim against the State? Nor does one hear that the United States Court of Claims is asymmetrical because it is the judicial forum for claims against the Government of the United States.

Moreover the critics of investor/State arbitration fail to weigh the importance of its substitution for diplomatic espousal. The exercise of diplomatic protection historically could produce pressure exerted by the more powerful State against the less powerful. Yet paradoxically it was replete with rules which allowed the government of the alien to escape the diplomatic burdens of espousal, such as the local remedies rule and that of continuity in the nationality of claims.

Naturally the investor and the State are on the same legal plane in proceedings in investor/State arbitration. Equality of arms is a fundament of legal proceedings. It is a norm that arbitral tribunals are bound to maintain. That is so whether or not governments are charged with acting in the public interest.

Do BITs invade the freedom of States to regulate, do they constrain the "policy space" of States? BITs are treaties. The very purpose of treaties is to constrain the freedom of States. As the PCIJ fundamentally held in its first judgment on the merits, in *The S.S. Wimbledon*,

> "The Court declines to see in the conclusion of any Treaty by which a State undertakes to perform or refrain from performing a particular act an abandonment of its sovereignty. No doubt any convention creating an obligation of this kind places a restriction on the exercise of the sovereign rights of the State, in the sense that it requires them to be exercised in a certain way. But the right of entering into international engagements is an attribute of State sovereignty."[7]

States that enter into international engagements in the form of BITs are free to confirm and specify their rights to regulate within their borders, as more recent model BITs and treaties of some States do. Legitimate questions may arise about how far BIT provisions bear upon those rights. If those questions have not been settled by the terms of the BIT, they can be through recourse to the treaty's machinery for dispute settlement. To cast aside investor/State arbitration because of unrealized apprehension that a few major cases which understandably arouse concern may – may – produce awards adverse to the State would be one of the profoundest misjudgments ever to afflict the procedures of peaceful settlement of international disputes.

Finally let's turn to the call for an appellate court to govern arbitral tribunals on the ground that arbitral awards conflict. In point of fact, there is a large measure of consistency in investment awards, both on jurisdiction and merits. But there have been conflicting interpretations of some comparable BIT provisions.

Conflicts in interpretation are undesirable. But in view of the decentralized, horizontal nature of the international system, they are not unusual. The international legal structure has never been neat. Even in the relatively centralized, hierarchical judicial systems of a State, conflicts among courts are frequent. In the United States, to take the example at hand, conflicts between state courts are common. Even in federal

---

7. *The S.S. Wimbledon, Judgment (Merits)*, 17 August 1923, Series A, No. 1, p. 25.

courts, conflicts are substantial. There are conflicts among Circuit Courts of Appeal that persist for years unsettled by a judgment of the Supreme Court.

Moreover much can be unduly made of investment arbitration conflicts that have occurred, as in the case of two awards in the so-called *Lauder* cases against the Czech Republic. The two decisions did not interpret the two concordant BITs conflictually. They rather interpreted the facts differently. Their difference was not of treaty interpretation but of factual causality. Moreover, counsel for the claimants had sought to have both actions joined or the same arbitrators appointed in both proceedings; counsel for the Czech Republic refused. Thus such conflict as there was between the outcome of the two cases was enabled by that decision of the Respondent.

In point of fact, the conflicts ascribed to interpretation of the same treaty provisions often do no such thing. Rather, as in the *Lauder* cases, the conflict derived from the differing facts of each case, or from differing treaty provisions. As an example of the latter, take the MFN provision in the *Maffezini* case and that at issue in the *Plama* case. Their differing wording goes far to explain the allegedly conflicting conclusions that were reached by the two tribunals . Still another such example is found in the differing terms of the umbrella clauses at issue in *SGS v. Philippines* and in *Salini v. Jordan*.

But insofar as there are cases in which there really have been conflicting interpretations of the same BIT provisions, should a tenured appellate court be established to resolve such conflicts?

In principle that proposal is appealing. A suitably composed and financed appellate court would not only provide review of the merits but should enhance confidence in the system, as the Appellate Body of the World Trade Organization has in its sphere. But to realize the creation of an appellate court for investor/State arbitration would present many difficulties, as ICSID may have found when it examined the possibility. If States wish to establish an appeals court, they can but they show little disposition to do so. When some fifty States concluded the Energy Charter Treaty after an extended, highly professional negotiation, they could have provided for a court but they opted for arbitration between investors and host States. Does that suggest that those States were unaware of their interests, that they overlooked their regulatory powers, that they were set on depreciating the currency of their courts? And the Parties to the Energy Charter Treaty appear to be satisfied with their choice. As the Deputy Director for Energy of the European Commission put it in an address to the 24th Meeting of the Energy Charter Conference, "This provision [the Energy Charter Treaty's dispute settlement mechanism providing for investor/State arbitration] is a jewel in the crown of the Treaty, and has over the past fifteen years proven its practical value. It gives investors a tool to enforce the rights provided by the Treaty."[8]

Furthermore, if there were to be an effort to achieve agreement on a worldwide multilateral treaty governing the treatment of foreign investment, the prospects of reaching and ratifying such a treaty would appear to be darker still than the outlook for establishing an appellate court. The failure to reach agreement in the OECD on a Multilateral Agreement on Investment should be instructive.

---

8. 24th Meeting of the Energy Charter Conference, Address by Mr. Fabrizio BARBASO, Deputy Director for Energy, European Commission.

In sum, can it really be supposed that States of North and South, East and West, developed and developing, of virtually all political complexions and economic models, some 180 countries, have been misguided in concluding some 3,000 investment treaties, and that it has taken a think tank here and a group of professors there, or labor union officials here, and environmental proponents there, to reveal to the world the error of their ways?

Many of the more than 600 South/South BITs running between developing States have been concluded with the benefit of careful preparation by the Asian-African Legal Consultative Organization. That Organization has strongly supported dispute settlement by ICSID and otherwise. Are we to believe that these pairs of developing States, contracting with each other in the light of advice of their Asian-African Legal Consultative Organization, acted not in their own interests but in the interests of multinational corporations?

What do critics of investor/State arbitration offer in place of investment arbitration? Primarily resort to tenured national courts to settle investor disputes, in the tradition of Calvo. Some national courts handle disputes with foreign investors competently and objectively, some do not. There are tenured courts in too much of the world that may find themselves constrained by state immunities, or which are incompetent, subject to political influence, corrupt, or just nationalistic in their perception of the facts and the law. All state courts in the United States cannot be said to have been uniformly free of such disabilities, as one NAFTA arbitral tribunal had compelling cause to find. It is perfectly reasonable and defensible for foreign investors to prefer international arbitration, just as many thousands of parties engaging in international commerce have for many years.

The processes of international arbitration can be improved. They are rife with tactical challenges to arbitrators. Perhaps arbitral tribunals or institutions should be empowered to impose sanctions on parties or their counsel who abuse the making of challenges.

Annulment proceedings in ICSID for a time seemed to have become reflexive rather than exceptional, though in the last few years the pace of resort to annulment has slowed. Sixty-five annulment proceedings were commenced as of 2013, resulting in the annulment of six awards in full and seven in part. Considering that 180 ICSID awards had been rendered as of that time, the rate of annulment has been low, but the processes have nevertheless been time-consuming and expensive. Some annulment committees, while proclaiming that they are not courts of appeal, proceeded to act as if they were.

Another reform that may merit consideration is institutionalizing security for costs. As it is, special purpose vehicles may bring a thin claim against a State which has the financial burden of defending itself; the State wins the arbitration and is awarded costs, but finds that the special purpose vehicle used by the claimant lacks the funds to pay costs.

It is to shortcomings such as these that reform efforts should be directed.

It is of course of capital importance that the awards of international arbitral tribunals be paid, promptly and in full, certainly once any legitimate legal recourse has been exhausted. It is extraordinary that a group of legal scholars has advocated violation of that

10

legal obligation.[9] International institutions, such as the World Bank and the International Monetary Fund, should threaten to suspend, and if needs be, actually suspend lending to States that willfully fail to pay international arbitral awards. When the World Bank, after years of indulging a State that evaded paying awards against it, finally indicated that fresh loans would not be forthcoming, that State made arrangements to pay outstanding awards – to the benefit of that State as well as the claimants whose awards were finally paid in some measure.

International lawyers have been long and rightly concerned with the progressive development of international law. Substitution of national adjudication for international investment arbitration would be a regressive development that is to be resisted rather than furthered. International investment law is a profoundly progressive development of international law which should be nurtured rather than restricted and denounced.

---

9. Public Statement on the International Investment Regime, 31 August 2010, para. 8:

"There is a strong moral as well as policy case for governments to withdraw from investment treaties and to oppose investor-state arbitration, including by refusal to pay arbitration awards against them where an award for compensation has followed from a good faith measure that was introduced for a legitimate purpose."

Opening Plenary Session

Setting The Scene:
What Are the Myths?
What Are the Realities?
What Are the Challenges?

Report on the Opening Plenary Session

*James Freda** and *Tobias Lehmann***

I.   INTRODUCTION TO THE CONGRESS

The Opening Plenary Session was designed to set the scene for the Congress on the Congress theme of "arbitral legitimacy and its myths, challenges and realities". Ms. Lucy Reed, Chair of the Congress' Program Committee and global head of the international arbitration group at Freshfields Bruckhaus Deringer, began the Plenary by introducing her fellow committee members: John Barkett, Adriana Braghetta, Dushyant Dave, Meg Kinnear, Salim Moollan and Klaus Reichert.

Ms. Reed continued her introduction by explaining the approach taken in organizing the Congress. Her hope was that the Congress would be focused and rigorous, learned and commercial, and conducted in an effort to scrutinize ideas about legitimacy in international arbitration. To do so, she stated, one must "return from the generalities to the pillars of legitimacy". Among those pillars are the Congress sub-themes of "Justice" and "Precision".

Ms. Reed defined "justice", the first pillar, as the "truism that arbitration must further justice and be seen to further justice". This topic included diversity, inclusiveness in arbitrator selection, the role of arbitral institutions, and equality of arms in investment treaty arbitration. The second pillar, Ms. Reed explained, was that for arbitration to have legitimacy, "the process must have legal precision at every stage". Arbitral "precision" included such issues as the burden and standard of proof, interim measures, witness protocols, and the challenge of pleading and proving fraud in investment treaty arbitration. The Congress focused each inquiry further into common propositions or

---

*   Panel Rapporteur; Senior Associate, Freshfields Bruckhaus Deringer US LLP.
**   Panel Rapporteur; Doctoral candidate, University of St. Gallen.

The following is their Report of the ICCA Opening Plenary session and any mistakes, misstatements or misimpressions should be attributed to them and not to the speakers. Please note that in some instances, for the sake of clarity, this Report does not follow the strict chronological order of the opening plenary session.

pieces of conventional wisdom, which would be judged as a myth, reality or something in between by Congress participants.

It was hoped that the ideas presented at the Congress and the papers produced by the various panel participants would be used by the legal community for years to come. Consequently, the Program Committee designed an integrated program to tie together and keep focused the intellectual energy and expertise drawn into the Congress. There were eight core panels based on the Congress subthemes of "Precision" and "Justice". Each of these panels produced propositions related to their panel's topic and enlisted its audience, as noted above, in determining whether those propositions were myths, realities or something else entirely. The responses to the panel propositions were given to the chair of four "Breakout" Sessions where users, judges and practitioners discussed them in more detail in a smaller setting to encourage group participation. The results of these panels were presented at the Congress' Closing Plenary.

Outside of the panel sessions, the Congress held luncheon seminars to discuss narrower substantive topics. ICCA Member Interest Groups also met to discuss the role of courts under the 1958 New York Convention, third-party funding, issue conflict in investment arbitration, the development of arbitration sourcebooks, and the launch of ICCA's academic interest group.

II.   THE "PRECISION STREAM" PANELS

With the roadmap for the Congress outlined, Ms. Reed introduced the chairs of the "Precision Stream" panels. It should be noted here that each panel chair for the "Precision" and "Justice" Streams, along with their respective panels, created a set of propositions and presented them at the Opening and Closing Plenary Sessions of the Congress. These panel propositions and conclusions are presented in slide format as an Annex to this Report. Readers should therefore consult the Annex for the propositions themselves. The main text of this Report only provides a brief introduction of the panel chairs and topics, along with a summary of the chairs' remarks.

The four "Precision Stream" panels were as follows.

Panel A-1, entitled **"Proof: A Plea for Precision"** was chaired by Dr. David Brynmor Thomas of Thirty-Nine Essex Street Chambers. Dr. Brynmor Thomas noted that although burden and standard of proof are fundamental in any arbitral proceeding, it was difficult for attorneys and clients to perceive how these concepts differed so profoundly across legal traditions and backgrounds. The panel would, therefore, explore whether arbitral tribunals should:

(i) address the burden and standard of proof with the parties early in the arbitration;
(ii) issue explicit directions regarding burden and standard of proof; and
(iii) describe the burden and standard of proof applied in the awards they render.

Panel A-2, entitled **"Early Stages of the Arbitral Process: Interim Measures and Document Production"** was chaired by Mr. John Barkett of Shook, Hardy & Bacon LLP. The panel was designed to explore the variability users face at the outset of an arbitration regarding these issues. Mr. Barkett recited the propositions of his panel to the audience.

Panel A-3, entitled **"Matters of Evidence: Witness and Experts"** was chaired by Dr. Natahalie Voser of Schellenberg Wittmer. Dr. Voser explained that her panel would discuss two forms of evidence: witness statements and expert reports. She noted that witnesses play a more important role in international arbitration than in many civil law jurisdictions and her panel would query whether this role is justified. She stated with regard to experts that her panel would also consider how useful party-appointed experts truly are. She then recounted her panel's propositions.

Panel A-4, entitled **"Treaty Arbitration: Pleading and Proof of Fraud and Comparable Forms of Abuse"** was chaired by Mr. Klaus Reichert SC of Brick Court Chambers. Mr. Reichert noted that the format of this panel would be that of a more traditional ICCA session, with the presentation of a major paper and commentary on the paper by the panelists. The panel paper is a survey of investment treaty law by Aloysius Llamzon and Anthony Sinclair, located at pp. 451-530 of this volume. That survey describes:

(i) what constitutes investor misconduct in investment treaty law;
(ii) the consequences for such misconduct; and
(iii) how one proves misconduct in an investment treaty proceeding.

After describing the paper, Mr. Reichert presented his panel's propositions.

III.   THE "JUSTICE STREAM" PANELS

Ms. Meg Kinnear, Secretary-General of the World Bank's International Centre for Settlement of Investment Disputes, introduced the "Justice Stream" panels. They were as follows.

Panel B-1, entitled **"Who Are the Arbitrators?"** was chaired by Ms. Adriana Braghetta of L.O. Baptista – SVMFA. She stated that her panel would discuss the notions of legitimacy and justice from the perspective of those making the decisions by asking "Who are the arbitrators?" She stated that research has shown that diverse groups outperform homogenous ones and that her panel would consider arbitrators' nationality, age, race, gender and other diversity factors. She then described the propositions of her panel for the audience.

Panel B-2, entitled **"Premise: Arbitral Institutions Can Do More to Further Legitimacy. True or False?"** was chaired by Salim Moollan of Essex Court Chambers. He stated that the rule of law is at the heart of justice and that arbitral institutions were key actors in international arbitration. Specifically, his panel was tasked with determining how these institutions perceive legitimacy. In that regard, he stated that his panel would present the results from a survey of twenty-four questions of nine arbitral institutions, all of which had been answered frankly, candidly, and in detail. He noted that the questionnaire was circulated to a representative sample of arbitral institutions including: the Cairo Regional Centre for International Commercial Arbitration; the International Chamber of Commerce; the Permanent Court of Arbitration; the International Centre for Settlement of Investment Disputes; the American Arbitration Association's International Centre for Dispute Resolution; the London Court of International Arbitration; the Center for Arbitration and Mediation of the Chamber of Commerce Brazil-Canada; the Kuala Lumpur Regional Centre for Arbitration; and the Bahrain Chamber for Dispute Resolution. The results of this survey are presented at pp. 667-752 of this volume. Mr. Moollan then presented his panel propositions.

Panel B-3, entitled **"Treaty Arbitration: Is the Playing Field Level and Who Decides Whether It Is Anyway?"** was chaired by Anna Joubin-Bret of Cabinet Joubin-Bret. Ms. Joubin-Bret noted that her panel would consider the question in depth. She also described its real-world importance using the specific examples of the European Union's public consultations on investor-state dispute settlement and popular protests in South Korea about similar dispute resolution systems. She then recounted her panel propositions.

Panel B-4, entitled **"Universal Arbitration: An Aspiration Within Reach or a Sisyphean Goal?"** was chaired by Dushyant Dave, Senior Advocate at the Supreme Court of India. He stated that the goal of international arbitration was to become universal with the aim of removing cultural clashes. He reflected on his experience of arbitration in India and the problems that can arise from legal and cultural divides. He then introduced his panel propositions and participants.

IV.   INSIDE THE ARBITRAL MIND

In between the presentation of the "Precision" and "Justice" Stream panel propositions, Ms. Reed introduced Professor Susan Franck of the Washington & Lee University School of Law, Professor Anne van Aaken of the University of St. Gallen, Dean Christopher Guthrie of Vanderbilt University Law School, James Freda of Freshfields Bruckhaus Deringer and Tobias Lehmann of the University of St. Gallen. Both an experimental study on arbitral decision-making and a thematic survey of Congress participants were conducted. The results of the survey are located at pp. 33-122 of this volume. The results of the study will be printed in a separate, forthcoming publication.

After a short break following the arbitral decision-making experiment and ICCA themed survey, Ms. Kinnear, reconvened the Plenary Session to place the questions given to the Congress participants into context. Ms. Kinnear then re-introduced Professor van Aaken. Professor van Aaken framed the experiment as forming part of the broader experimental-psychology literature on cognitive heuristics whose origins can be traced back to the work of Daniel Kahneman and Amos Tversky in the 1970s. She noted that this experimental work into decision-making, which tests the assumption of the rational or reasonable person, had already been performed with US judges by Dean Christopher Guthrie and Professor Jeffrey Rachlinski. She noted, however, that these developments had not yet reached international law. She hoped that the experiment would ultimately help improve the quality of international arbitral and judicial decision-making and thereby improve their legitimacy.[1] She then introduced Dean Guthrie to explain his work regarding judicial decision-making with US judges.

Dean Guthrie began his presentation by discussing the research he conducted on judges with two colleagues, Professor Rachlinski of Cornell University Law School and the Honorable Judge Andrew J. Wistrich of the United States Federal District Court for the Central District of California.[2] Their methodology is experimental; that is they present the judges with a fact pattern, assign a set of judges to a control group, and another set to a treatment or experimental group and determine whether there is any impact on the way the judges decide a question based on the fact pattern presented to each group. Although Dean Guthrie noted that this process was somewhat removed from the realities of day-to-day judicial decision-making, he stated that it had the benefit of internal statistical validity. He explained that he and his two colleagues have worked with 2,000-3,000 judges in the United States, France and Canada.

Dean Guthrie described the two dominant accounts of judicial decision-making, the formalist account and the realist account. However, he and his colleagues have advanced a third, which he termed the intuitive override/dual process model. This model recognizes that judges, like all human beings, have both intuitive and deliberative faculties. Trial judges rely heavily on intuition, but can and (sometimes) do override their intuition with deliberation.

He then described the cognitive reflection test (CRT), which was given as part of the Congress experiment. The CRT was developed by Shane Frederick of the Yale University School of Management.[3] Dean Guthrie described the CRT as a simple test that includes three questions, where each has an intuitive but wrong answer, but the right answer is easy to determine if one uses a deliberative thinking process. Although the CRT questions are straightforward, most judges who have taken the test get them wrong. Of those that get the questions wrong, most choose the intuitive answer and believe the questions are simplistic. Yet there are some judges who override this intuitive decision-making through deliberation, and perform well on the test.

Beyond the CRT, Dean Guthrie and his colleagues have used judicial decision-making studies. These studies have tested the effect of apologies on judges, their implicit racial attitudes, and their capacity to deliberately disregard relevant, but inadmissible evidence. Dean Guthrie's speech, however, focused on heuristics. Heuristics are cognitive shortcuts or intuitive rules of thumb. They happen quite quickly and unconsciously and we are often unaware that we are using these devices. Heuristics are often adaptive, so that individuals can get to a "good enough" response quickly. Yet they can lead to systematic and predictable errors that are described as "cognitive illusions". The

---

1. An example of Professor van Aaken's work in this area can be found in her article "Behavioral International Law and Economics", 55 Harv. Int'l L.J. (2014) pp. 421-481.
2. For a selection of their work, see, e.g., Chris GUTHRIE, Jeffrey J. RACHLINSKI and Andrew J. WISTRICH, "Inside the Judicial Mind", 86 Cornell L. Rev. (2001) p. 777; "Blinking on the Bench: How Judges Decide Cases", 93 Cornell L. Rev. (2007) p. 1; and most recently, "Contrition in the Courtroom: Do Apologies Affect Adjudication?", 98 Cornell L. Rev. (2013) p. 1189.
3. See Shane FREDERICK, "Cognitive Reflection and Decision Making", 19 J. Econ. Perspectives (2005, no. 4) p. 25.

remaining part of Dean Guthrie's presentation focused on three of these cognitive illusions: anchoring, framing and hindsight bias.

When we estimate the value of an item, we tend to rely disproportionately on the first number we encounter. Reliance on this heuristic, known as anchoring, can be desirable. For example, in an efficient housing market, list prices can be indicative of the value of a house. Yet anchoring can lead people astray because individuals also latch onto irrelevant numerical information. Dean Guthrie noted that with judges, experiments showed that irrelevant numbers could impact damages awards and criminal sentences in experimental conditions.

Framing, or loss aversion, is the concept that individuals tend to perceive numeric options as gains or losses from a *status quo*. This heuristic appears to indicate that individuals undertake relative valuations more than they do absolute valuations. It also suggests that losses are more unattractive than gains are attractive. Dean Guthrie gave examples of fact patterns where, in absolute economic terms, the results of a question were the same, but individuals judged outcomes framed as losses as more unfair than outcomes framed as gains. Dean Guthrie has examined this effect on judges and found that they also succumb to framing effects.

Hindsight bias describes the fact that people tend to overestimate the predictability of events that have already occurred. Dean Guthrie recounted Professor Rachlinski's research where two groups were given a foresight and hindsight condition in a tort case. The foresight group, who did not have the knowledge of an ensuing accident, refused to order that a precaution be taken to prevent the accident. In the hindsight condition, those with knowledge of the accident stated the defendants were negligent for not ordering the precaution and that damages should result from that negligence. Dean Guthrie mentioned how judges in a similar experiment were impacted by different assessments of an individual's wrongdoing in a case regarding whether a search was racially motivated.

Dean Guthrie concluded by summarizing his findings, stating that most judges are influenced by heuristics, which are often productive. However, these heuristics can still contain systematic cognitive illusions that compromise accuracy and justice in court. He also proposed several solutions to this problem, which included more time to process decisions, more frequent opinion writing, and group decision-making. At the end of his presentation, he then introduced Professor Franck.

In her brief remarks, Professor Franck noted that there was an ongoing debate as to whether arbitrators can or should be like judges. She noted that the questions in the experiment conducted at ICCA were substantially similar to those presented in the judicial decision-making studies. She stated that the research would attempt to identify if there are empirical differences between arbitrators and judges and how great any difference might be. She stressed that when considering international arbitrators (or arbitration in general) one should do so with data,[4] and that the international arbitration community should not be ashamed or nervous by this type of introspection.

Mr. Freda closed the introductory portion of the plenary session on arbitral decision-making.[5] He stated that international arbitration can be likened to a "shadow legal system" where billions of dollars and state policy may be impacted in what are often confidential proceedings. Mr. Freda stated that if arbitration is to be perceived as legitimate it must be understood and that empirical evaluation of arbitration was necessary for that understanding to reach the public.

V.   THE ICCA AWARD FOR "LIFELONG CONTRIBUTION TO THE FIELD OF INTERNATIONAL ARBITRATION"

During the Opening Plenary, ICCA President Jan Paulsson presented the ICCA Award for "Lifelong Contribution to the Field of International Arbitration" to Professor Eric E. Bergsten, Professor Emeritus at the Pace University School of Law. Professor Bergsten received the award for his work in creating the Willem C. Vis International Commercial Arbitration Moot. Professor Paulsson noted that by 2012 (the last year for which he had records), over 18,000 young people had participated in the Vis Moot. Indeed, in 2012 alone, 2,500 students participated on 285 teams hailing from 71 countries. Professor Paulsson, in presenting the award, described the Vis Moot as a "sociological phenomenon".

Upon receiving the award, Professor Bergsten addressed the plenary session. He stated that it was his impression that there were many international arbitration practitioners who were influenced by the Vis Moot. He described this as a "great joy". He concluded his remarks by stating that: "[a] student competition with the purpose of education is an endeavor that one hopes the academic community will have appreciated and they seemed to have. That the professional community, represented here by ICCA, should appreciate it in this way, is something I never expected and that means a great deal to me."

Following Professor Bergsten's remarks, Ms. Reed invited Mr. James Morrison of Allens to introduce a short video in celebration of Professor Bergsten, produced by Mr. Morrison and Young ICCA

Professor Paulsson then closed the Opening Plenary.

---

4. For examples of Professor Franck's empirical work, see, e.g., "Rationalizing Costs in Investment Treaty Arbitration", 88 Wash. U. L. Rev. (2011) p. 769; "Using Investor-State Mediation Rules to Promote Conflict Management: An Introductory Guide", 29 ICSID Rev. (2014) p. 66; "Conflating Politics and Development? Examining Investment Treaty Arbitration Outcomes" (forthcoming in the Va. J. Int'l L.); and *Investment Treaty Arbitration: Myths, Realities and Costs* (forthcoming Oxford University Press 2015).
5. See also James FREDA, "Heuristics and Arbitral Decision-Making: A Brief Discussion on How Arbitrators Make Decisions", Asian Disp. Rev. (2013) p. 50.

Annex

"Precision" and "Justice" Stream Panel Propositions

The following are the propositions presented by the "Precision" (A) and "Justice" (B) stream panels at the Opening Plenary Session of the XXII ICCA Congress. The conclusions reached by the panels on each proposition (i.e., whether a proposition was a "myth", "reality" or "other") are also included. For ease of use, the propositions and conclusions are reproduced in the same format in which they were presented at the closing plenary session of the Congress.[6]

A-1 Proof: A Plea for Precision

	Proposition	Myth?	Reality?	Other?
1.	It is universally accepted that each party must prove the facts upon which it relies in support of its case.		✔	
2.	Arbitral tribunals should, at the earliest opportunity, ensure that the parties understand the burden of proof and who carries it with respect to each issue.			✔
3.	In order to reflect the intent of the parties, the standard of proof to be applied should be determined as a matter of substantive law and articulated by the arbitral tribunal at the earliest opportunity.			✔

---

6. The final PowerPoint presentation was compiled with the assistance of Ms. Belinda McRae of 20 Essex Street Chambers, London.

A-1 Proof: A Plea for Precision (cont.)

	Proposition	Myth?	Reality?	Other?
4.	A tribunal should not depart from the standard of proof found in the substantive law when confronted with certain allegations, absent the consent of the parties.		✔	
5.	In using adverse inferences and other sanctions, a tribunal should always indicate its intent to make the adverse inference or sanction and explain clearly to the party receiving the benefit of the inference (or suffering as a result of the sanction) the precise consequences of the inference or sanction.		✔	
6.	A tribunal should always articulate the burden and standard of proof in the final award and explain (i) why a particular party carried the burden; and (ii) why the standard applied has been satisfied.			✔

A-2 Early Stages of the Arbitral Process: Document Production

	Proposition	Myth?	Reality?	Other?
1.	Document production in international arbitration is fair and not rife with gamesmanship to obtain tactical advantage or to avoid production of unfavorable information, in part because the IBA Rules on the Taking of Evidence in International Arbitration have eliminated concerns parties might have with the fairness of document production.	✔		
2.	Documents used for impeachment should never be required to be disclosed before being used.	✔		

A-2 Early Stages of the Arbitral Process: Document Production (cont.)

	Proposition	Myth?	Reality?	Other?
3.	It is unnecessary for a Tribunal to address confidentiality of non-public documents produced in international arbitration.	✔		
4.	Tribunals in international arbitration have the inherent power to sanction a party or a party's legal representative for abuse of the document production process and do so for failure to comply with an order of the Tribunal.	✔	✔	
5.	Where an attorney acts in bad faith in the document disclosure process, a Tribunal has a duty to report the attorney to the attorney's bar association.		✔	

	Proposition	Myth?	Reality?	Other?
6.	In a majority of cases, interim measures are sought by parties for tactical advantage or unmeritorious reasons.	✔		
7.	Interim measures are so rarely granted in international arbitration or fraught with enforcement difficulties that a party should seek an early hearing on the merits rather than spend the resources on seeking interim measures.		✔	
8.	There is no uniform standard in the international arbitration world when it comes to determine whether interim measures should be granted.		✔	

A-2   Early Stages of the Arbitral Process: Document Production (cont.)

	Proposition	Myth?	Reality?	Other?
9.	Assuming a likelihood of success on the merits, "balancing the conveniences" to each party, rather than requiring a finding of irreparable harm, is the appropriate test in evaluating whether to award interim measures.	✔		
10.	If interim measures are truly needed by a party, the solution is the use of an emergency arbitrator.	✔		

A-3   Matters of Evidence: Witness and Experts

	Proposition	Myth?	Reality?	Other?
1.	Written witness statements are useless because they have been drafted by the lawyers.	✔		
2.	Cross-examinations are useless for tribunals because the witnesses are too (well) prepared.	✔		
3.	It is for the parties alone to decide which witnesses will tell the story.	✔		
4.	Tribunals cannot do much about a no-show witness.			✔

A-3 Matters of Evidence: Witness and Experts (cont.)

	Proposition	Myth?	Reality?	Other?
5.	Arbitral tribunals always get it wrong: they will award too much or too little.	✔		
6.	Party appointed experts are partial and thus useless in determining complex technical or other issues which the arbitral tribunal cannot determine itself.	✔		
7.	The conduct of experts is a rule-free and sanction-free zone in arbitration.			✔

A-4 Treaty Arbitration: Pleading and Proof of Fraud and Comparable Forms of Abuse

	Proposition	Myth?	Reality?	Other?
1.	All investor wrongdoing is the same and it does not matter when it occurs.	✔		
2.	This is an appropriate maxim for all respondents: throw mud, it may stick, and if it does not, what matter (the arbitration equivalent of the "Garryowen").			✔
3.	No one really agrees as to what fraudulent misrepresentation means.		✔	

A-4 Treaty Arbitration: Pleading and Proof of Fraud and Comparable Forms of Abuse (cont.)

	Proposition	Myth?	Reality?	Other?
4.	The graver the charge, the more confidence there must be in the evidence relied on.			✔
5.	Tribunals and counsel are not properly equipped to address the issue of corruption (both as regards expertise, and the tools at their disposal).	✔		

B-1 Who Are the Arbitrators?

	Proposition	Myth?	Reality?	Other?
1.	There is a limited pool of arbitrators who share a common profile.		✔	
2.	This limited pool of arbitrators might jeopardize legitimacy of international arbitration.			✔
3.	There is a need for greater diversity.		✔	
4.	A pledge should be taken by responsible users.			✔

27

B-2   Arbitral Institutions Can Do More to Further Legitimacy. True or False?

	Proposition	Myth?	Reality?	Other?
1.	There is a pro-developed world bias in international arbitration to which arbitral institutions contribute.		✔	
2.	The internal workings of arbitral institutions are too opaque and assist in the maintenance of a mafia of arbitrators with repeat appointments and in a complacent attitude to increased delays and costs.	✔		
3.	Arbitration institutions focus on making money and gaining market share, instead of on their real role, which is to provide public services in the field of dispute resolution and to foster the rule of law.			✔

B-3   Treaty Arbitration: Is the Playing Field Level and Who Decides Whether It Is Anyway?

	Proposition	Myth?	Reality?	Other?
1.	Investment arbitration is inherently imbalanced and biased towards investors.	✔	✔	
2.	Investment case law has developed into an inconsistent and unpredictable body of "jurisprudence" that does not meet the expectations of end-users and other stakeholders.		✔	✔

B-3   Treaty Arbitration: Is the Playing Field Level and Who Decides Whether It Is Anyway? (cont.)

	Proposition	Myth?	Reality?	Other?
3.	End-users consider that investment arbitration is neither efficient nor economic and are being deterred by these disadvantages.		✔	
4.	Arbitrators and/or institutions should have a role in remedying this problem.		✔	

B-4   Universal Arbitration: An Aspiration Within Reach or a Sisyphean Goal?

	Proposition	Myth?	Reality?	Other?
1.	Arbitration is already universal.		✔	
2.	The users of the system have no interest in whether it enhances constitutional morality.			✔
3.	Universality will improve the effectiveness and enforceability of arbitral awards.		✔	
4.	Greater universality must be driven by arbitral institutions.			✔

Opening Plenary Session

Arbitration and Decision-Making: Live Empirical Study

International Arbitration:
Demographics, Precision and Justice

Susan D. Franck,* James Freda,** Kellen Lavin,*** Tobias Lehmann† and Anne van Aaken‡

*   Professor of Law, Washington & Lee University Law School.

**   Senior Associate, Freshfields Bruckhaus Deringer US LLP (New York). The views expressed within this Article are solely those of the author and not those of Freshfields Bruckhaus Deringer or its clients.

***   J.D. Washington & Lee University Law School (2013).

†   Ph.D. Candidate, University of St. Gallen; M.A. Economics, M.A. Law and Economics, University of St. Gallen.

‡   Professor of Law and Economics, Legal Theory, Public International Law and European Law, University of St. Gallen.

The authors express gratitude to the ICCA Miami 2014 Congress Host Committee, led by Burton Landy, for providing logistical and financial support to the research team. We must also thank the Congress's Program Committee for allowing us to perform our survey and experiment, especially Lucy Reed and Meg Kinnear, who both provided gracious assistance. We are especially thankful to all participants who took the research seriously and gave generously of their time. The authors deeply appreciate the diligent assistance of Washington & Lee University Law School students, namely George Mackie, Stephen Halpin, Krystal Swendsboe, Sharon Jeong, Trista Bishop-Watt, Rachael Kurzweil and Bret Marfut. Stephanie Miller and the Washington & Lee University Law Library also provided critical data transformation services. The Washington & Lee Administration, Frances Lewis Law Center, and Transnational Law Institute, as well as the University of St. Gallen Law School provided generous research support. We acknowledge the assistance of Catherine Rogers who offered us constructive comments, within a very tight timeframe, which permitted us to improve the quality of this Paper. Last but not least, we must thank John Barkett who provided us with the use of Shook, Hardy & Bacon's Miami office to compile our initial results; and we also thank Penny Perrin of Shook Hardy for her administrative support throughout the ICCA Congress.

I.   INTRODUCTION

In 2012, the International Council for Commercial Arbitration (ICCA) asked our research team to enter uncharted waters and provided us with unprecedented access to evaluate international arbitration empirically. We remain humbled by that trust and appreciate the opportunity. Our objective was to generate scientifically rigorous research to test others' theories and our own assumptions against verifiable data with the goal of improving international dispute settlement.

Two weeks before the conference and our planned "data collection exercise", V.V. Veeder asked the international arbitration community "to act now to regulate itself or risk 'reputational disaster'" and encouraged the use of data to begin that process.[1] At the outset of the Congress, Jan Paulsson reminded participants that ICCA should identify how to make international arbitration better. The twin observations of Veeder and Paulsson underscored both the importance and the risk of our research. While a daunting task, particularly given temporal restraints,[2] the effort to understand the international arbitration community more thoroughly and to identify areas for value-enhancing reforms warranted the risks.

We hope our data and analysis will further ICCA's broader institutional mission. When ICCA was formed in the early 1960s, the goal of its Congress was to bridge a number of divides. These included "the massive political divisions during the Cold War and the divide between academic, professional and state practitioners, both 'privatistes' and 'publicistes'; and both lawyers and non-lawyers".[3] By its fourth and fifth Congresses, ICCA had bridged gaps by holding meetings in Moscow (the Cold War east) and New Delhi (the non-aligned and developing world).[4] More recently, ICCA has developed a broader membership structure, which now includes mentoring programs for young professionals in international arbitration[5] and programs to train national judiciaries

---

1. Leo SZOLNOKI, "Veeder backs Paulsson's call to self-regulate", Global Arb. Rev., 27 Mar. 2014, at <http://globalarbitrationreview.com/journal/article/32528/london-veeder-backs-paulssons-call-self-regulate/> (last accessed 30 June 2014).
2. We note this is first generation research from the first dataset of its kind. While the data were initially entered within 36 hours of the survey in April 2014, Washington & Lee students recoded all of the data in May 2014. We note that there was 97% inter-coder reliability between the two coding rounds; and, for every divergence, we generated an agreed code upon consultation with the raw materials. Gathering the survey data and producing a report on a tight schedule for this Congress Paper was inevitably challenging. Given our timing constraints and the importance of transparency, we plan to make the dataset publicly available and welcome corrections, criticisms and insights others may have.
3. V.V. VEEDER, "Remarks on the 50th Anniversary of ICCA", 19 May 2011, p. 3 at <www.arbitration-icca.org/media/0/13087091952910/v.v._veeder_speach.pdf> (last accessed 30 June 2014).
4. *Ibid.*, pp. 6-7.
5. Information on the ICCA Mentoring Programme for young members is located at: <www.arbitration-icca.org/YoungICCA/Membership_and_mentoring.html> (last accessed 30 June 2014).

34

around the world.[6] One goal of our survey was to identify what divides still exist in international arbitration so that ICCA and the broader international legal community can engage constructively on those issues.

Whereas the divide between "east" and "west" dominated ICCA's early years, our survey indicates there are two remaining divisions within international arbitration related to development status and gender. Although the results identified areas for improvement, there were also bright spots. Even challenges generate an opportunity as international arbitration can engage in self-reflection and proactive improvement. In an effort to address the legitimacy of international arbitration, this Paper therefore provides information about the international arbitration community and assessments of the ICCA 2014 themes of justice and precision in international arbitration.

Part II of this Paper identifies the demographics of the respondents, with a specific focus on ICCA participants generally, the sub-set of arbitrators and the sub-set of arbitration counsel. Part III of this Paper examines the ICCA theme of legitimacy through the lens of precision, concentrating on issues involving burdens of proof, costs, document production, and arbitrator preparation for hearings. Part IV explores legitimacy by virtue of justice-related issues. These primarily relate to the prestige of international arbitration, issues of re-appointment and interaction with co-arbitrators, fraud and diversity within international arbitration. Part V acknowledges the limitations of the analyses. The Paper concludes that the data have identified areas that could benefit from improvement (whether structural or incremental). Efforts at improving quality will ultimately prove helpful in promoting both justice and precision.[7]

II.   DEMOGRAPHICS

In 1977, Oscar Schachter referred to "The Invisible College of International Lawyers" to describe the elite professional community of professors, students, government officials, civil servants and practitioners silently transforming international law.[8] At that moment in history, little was known about those involved in the "Invisible College" of the global international arbitration community. Yet with the classic socio-legal study by Dezalay and Garth,[9] tranches of discrete information published by arbitral institutions

---

6. For a listing of ICCA's New York Convention Road Shows, which have included locations such as Myanmar, Rwanda and Indonesia, see <www.arbitration-icca.org/NY_Convention_Roadshow .html> (last accessed 3 June 2014).

7. The "survey" also involved a psychological experiment related to cognition and decisionmaking. As that research is beyond the scope of this Paper, we anticipate publishing those results in due course.

8. Oscar SCHACHTER, "The Invisible College of International Lawyers", 72 N.W. L. Rev. (1977) p. 217; see also Diana CRANE, *Invisible Colleges: Diffusion of Knowledge in Scientific Communities* (University of Chicago Press 1972).

9. Yves DEZALAY and Bryant G. GARTH, *Dealing in Virtue: International Commercial Arbitration and the Construction of a Transnational Legal Order* (University of Chicago Press 1996); see also Thomas SCHULTZ and Robert KOVACS, "The Rise of a Third Generation of Arbitrators: Fifteen Years after Dezalay and Garth", 28 Arb. Int'l (2012) p. 161 (updating the scholarship of Dezalay and Garth); Maya STEINITZ, "Transnational Legal Process Theories", in Cesare P.R. ROMANO,

and the recent work of some empirical scholars, we have begun to uncover slowly a degree of information about key actors in international arbitration.[10] There is, however, still a dearth of systematically gathered scientific data that cut across arbitral institutions and subject matters and explore the identities of those involved in the "Invisible College" of international arbitration. In an effort to bring further transparency to the "Invisible College", this section addresses an existing gap within the literature and provides reliable data about demographic information of members of the global community of lawyers involved in international arbitration.[11]

The section first outlines the existing literature on the identities and demographics of those within the international arbitration community. It then provides basic background information on ICCA respondents, focusing on the prevalence of different experiences in international arbitration and identifies respondents' experiences. Next, it focuses upon demographic information including the gender, age, legal training, native language and

---

Karen J. ALTER and Yuval SHANY, eds., *The Oxford Handbook of International Adjudication* (Oxford University Press 2014) p. 339 at pp. 350-352 (discussing the "invisible college" of international arbitration); Daniel TERRIS, et al., *The International Judge: An Introduction to the Men and Women Who Decide the World's Cases* (Brandeis University Press 2007) (conducting a similar process to interview 30 international judges to offer a portrait of the public international law judiciary); but see Catherine A. ROGERS, "Gulliver's Troubled Travels, or the Conundrum of Comparative Law", 67 Geo. Wash. L. Rev. (1997) p. 149 at pp. 153, 166-168 (identifying concerns related to the methodology of Dezalay and Garth).

10. See José E. ALVAREZ, "The Democratization of the Invisible College", Transnational Dispute Management (2009) available at <www.transnational-dispute-management.com/article.asp?key=1365> (last accessed 30 June 2014) (identifying the "democratization of the invisible college"); see also David KENNEDY, "The Politics of the Invisible College: International Governance and the Politics of Expertise", 5 Eur. Hum. Rights L. Rev. (2001) p. 463 at <www.law.harvard.edu/faculty/dkennedy/publications/european.pdf> (last accessed 30 June 2014); Sergio PUIG, "Social Capital in the Arbitration Marketplace", 25 Eur. J. Int'l L. (2014) p. 387 (identifying a network effect among ICSID arbitrators).

11. In commercial arbitration, Queen Mary has worked with several partners to elucidate aspects of international arbitration through a series of surveys and interviews. See, e.g., Paul FRIEDLAND and Stavros BREKOULAKIS, "2012 International Arbitration Survey: Current and Preferred Practices in the Arbitral Process" (2012) at <http://bit.ly/Ps3inZ> (last accessed 30 June 2014) (henceforth White & Case/Queen Mary Survey); Paul FRIEDLAND and Loukas MISTELIS, "2010 International Arbitration Survey: Choices in International Arbitration" (2010) at <www.whitecase.com/files/upload/fileRepository/2010-International-Arbitration-Survey-Choices-International-Arbitration.PDF> (last accessed 30 June 2014); Gerry LAGERBERG and Loukas MISTELIS, "Corporate Choices in International Arbitration: Industry Perspectives" (2013) at <http://tinyurl.com/kwj8wpa> (last accessed 30 June 2014); see also Christopher R. DRAHOZAL and Richard W. NAIMARK, *Towards a Science of International Arbitration: Collected Empirical Research* (Kluwer Law 2005) (collecting empirical research related to commercial arbitration). Likewise, in treaty arbitration, there are a handful of studies and most focus on ICSID without demarcating between its ICA and ITA caseload. See Susan D. FRANCK, "Development and Outcomes in Investment Treaty Arbitration", 50 Harv. Int'l L.J. (2009) p. 438 (henceforth Development); PUIG, *op. cit.*, fn. 10; Michael WAIBEL and Yanhui WU, "Are Arbitrators Political?", Working Paper (December 2011) at <www.wipol.uni-bonn.de/lehrveranstaltungen-1/lawecon-workshop/archive/dateien/waibelwinter11-12> (copy on file with the authors) (last accessed 30 June 2014).

nationality of international arbitrators and counsel. It then discusses different ways to assess the development status of respondents' nationality to address claims of the lack of "western" arbitrators in international arbitration. Finally, it identifies the limitations of the demographic information and highlights the key findings.

1.   Existing Literature

There is an unfortunate lack of empirical evidence about the identity of actors in international arbitration, particularly those individuals who actually serve or might serve as arbitrators. Certain websites and organizations offer a degree of information about potential arbitrators. For example, the International Arbitration Institute[12] and Arbitral Women[13] offer a website where one can search through the biographies of registered arbitrators. Institutions like the American Arbitration Association's Centre for Dispute Resolution, the International Chamber of Commerce (ICC), London Court of International Arbitration (LCIA) and the International Centre for Settlement of Investment Disputes (ICSID) also maintain a general roster or database of people willing to serve as international arbitrators.[14] Other commercial services distribute lists of highly regarded arbitration experts.[15] Despite this general information on those who might – in theory – act as arbitrators, there is no central public repository providing information about individuals who have actually served as arbitrators that would permit one to identify and analyze core demographic information about international arbitrators.[16]

---

12. International Arbitration Institute, Search the IAI Directory, available at <www.iaiparis. com/drm_search.asp> (last accessed 8 June 2014).
13. Arbitral Women, Find a Practitioner, available at <www.arbitralwomen.org/index.aspx? sectionlinks_id=7&language=0&pageName=MemberSearch> (last accessed 30 June 2014).
14. Raymond G. BENDER, Jr., "Three Practical Steps to Avoid an Erroneous Arbitration", 30 Alternatives to High Cost of Lit. (Sept. 2012) p. 155.
15. For example, *Who's Who Legal* has a yearly compendium of Commercial Arbitration identifying the most highly regarded firms and individuals that requires participants to be nominated by peers. Who's Who Legal, Most Highly Regarded Firms: Commercial Arbitration 2013, available at <http://whoswholegal.com/news/analysis/article/30104/most-highly-regarded-firms-commercial-arbitration-2013/> (last accessed 30 June 2014). Similarly, Chambers & Partners identifies firms – and individuals within those firms – as having elite arbitration expertise and the Global Arbitration Review generates an index identifying top entities. Chambers & Partners, International Arbitration Worldwide, available at <www.chambersandpartners.com/ 12788/738/editorial/5/1> (last accessed 30 June 2014); Global Arbitration Review, GAR 100 – 7th Edition, at <http://globalarbitrationreview.com/gar100/> (last accessed 30 June 2014).
16. Catherine Rogers has suggested creating publicly available information about arbitrators, or what she identifies as "Arbitrator Intelligence". Catherine A. ROGERS, "Piloting Arbitrator Intelligence", Kluwer Arbitration Blog, 10 Apr. 2014, at <http://kluwerarbitrationblog.com/ blog/2014/04/10/piloting-arbitrator-intelligence/> (last accessed 3 July 2014); see also Catherine A. ROGERS, "Regulating International Arbitrators: A Functional Approach to Developing Standards of Conduct", 41 Stan. J. Int'l L. (2005) p. 53; Catherine A. ROGERS, "Fit and Function in Legal Ethics: Developing a Code of Conduct for International Arbitration, 23 Mich. J. Int'l L. (2002) p. 341; Catherine ROGERS, "The International Arbitrator Information Project: From an Ideation to Operation", Kluwer Arbitration Blog, 10 Dec. 2010, at <http://kluwerarbitrationblog.com/blog/2012/12/10/the-international-arbitrator-information-

Given the general lack of central information, it is perhaps unsurprising that the major multilateral arbitration institutions do not offer broad, public demographic data about their arbitrators. Where individual institutions have the internal capacity to gather and analyze the data on their own arbitrators, the data they publicize focuses nearly exclusively on basic information about arbitrator nationality; more systematic information is not available. Beyond individual stories published in *American Lawyer* or *Global Arbitration Review*,[17] there is little information available on the views, experience and identities of the international arbitration bar. As such, it is perhaps unsurprising that international arbitration functions essentially as a classic "invisible college".

Given the lack of a holistic analysis, understanding the baseline about who acts as counsel or arbitrator can be viewed by considering major international institutions on a case-by-case basis. The richest data come from information on arbitrators. This section therefore reviews information provided by institutions publicly offering information, including the ICC,[18] LCIA, Singapore International Arbitration Centre (SIAC) and ICSID.[19]

---

project-from-an-ideation-to-operation/> (last accessed 30 June 2014); see also Hans SMIT, "The Future of International Commercial Arbitration: A Single Transnational Institution?", 25 Colum. J. Transnat'l L. (1986) p. 9 at pp. 30-32.

17. See, e.g., The American Lawyer, "Arbitration Scorecard 2013", available at <www.americanlawyer.com/id=1202608198051/Arbitration-Scorecard-2013> (last accessed 30 June 2014); Global Arbitration Review, "GAR 45 Under 45 2011" at <http://globalarbitration review.com/surveys/article/29699/%20gar-45-45-2011-introduction/> (last accessed 30 June 2014); IA Reporter, "Arbitrator Profiles", available at <www.iareporter.com/categories/profiles> (last accessed 30 June 2014); see generally, Global Arbitration Review, "Portrait of the Arbitrator" (6 May 2014) at <http://globalarbitrationreview.com/news/article/32586/portrait-arbitrator/> (last accessed 30 June 2014); New York City Bar, "International Commercial Arbitration Practice", available at <www.nycbar.org/career-development/your-career-1/spotlight-on-careers/1464-lucy-reed> (last accessed 30 June 2014); see also Catherine ROGERS, "The Vocation of the International Arbitrator", 20 Am. U. Int'l L. Rev. (2005) p. 957.

18. In response to a separate questionnaire for another ICCA Congress session, the ICC reported that "[i]n 2002, there were 660 individuals from 62 countries fulfilling arbitral appointments in ICC arbitration, whereas in 2012 the numbers increased to 847 individuals from 72 countries". 2014 ICCA Congress, Panel B-2 Questionnaire, Draft Responses of John Beechey for the International Chamber of Commerce, Response to Question 2, this volume, pp. 667-752. The ICC also noted some demographic shifts in the location of parties and places of arbitration over the past decade, stating that "whereas the percentage of parties from Africa, Latin America, Central and East Europe and South East Asia increased from 38.3% to 46.9% between 2003 and 2012 (i.e., a 22% increase), the percentage of places of arbitration located in those regions within the same period increased from 15.6% to 25.3% (i.e., a 62% increase)". *Ibid.*, Response to Question 1.

19. We were unable to locate holistic demographic data on the websites or elsewhere from the following international arbitral institutions: American Arbitration Association's International Centre for Dispute Resolution (AAA-ICDR); Stockholm Chamber of Commerce (SCC); Hong Kong International Arbitration Centre (HKIAC); and Kigali International Arbitration Centre (KIAC). With the AAA-ICDR, for example, parties can pay US$750 for a list of five potential arbitrators, but we were unable to identify anywhere on the AAA-ICDR website where general demographic information about arbitrators (or some other list of arbitrators) was publicly available for free. American Arbitration Association, "Arbitrator and Mediator Section: Arbitrator Select", at <http://bit.ly/T2Zxxn> (last accessed 30 June 2014). Other regional arbitration institutions

Public LCIA reports indicate that, in 2012, the LCIA had 265 new international arbitrations. Of those cases, 52.6% of arbitrators were purely nationals from the United Kingdom.[20] As the 2005 rate of UK arbitrators at the LCIA was roughly 61% in 2005,[21] descriptively, this decrease in the proportion of British nationals is intriguing but could reflect the over 220% increase in the number of LCIA appointments.[22] Nevertheless, even recently, more than half of LCIA arbitrators were nationals of the United Kingdom.[23]

Other institutions have tended to have more than half of their arbitrator pool from the country where the institution's primary administrative office is located. SIAC's 2013 annual report, for example, indicated that – out of 56 new international arbitrations – around 51% of arbitrators were nationals from Singapore. Approximately 20% of the

---

failed to provide information on arbitrator demographics, including: the Australian Centre for International Commercial Arbitration (ACICA); Center for Arbitration and Mediation of the Chamber of Commerce Brazil-Canada (CAM-CCBC); Dubai International Arbitration Centre (DIAC); and Santiago Arbitration and Mediation Center (CAM Santiago). There is some data suggesting that the China International Economic and Trade Arbitration Commission (CIETAC) keeps track of the nationality of arbitrators, primarily by virtue of a listing process, albeit with mixed success in achieving diversity and results. Compare Jonathan H. ZIMMERMAN, "When Dealing with Chinese Entities, Avoid the CIETAC Arbitration Process", 53 Advocate (Feb. 2010) p. 23 at p. 23 ("CIETAC has been in existence since 1956, and boast that it has 274 foreign arbitrators (not Chinese Nationals) of its 969 listed arbitrators. Even with the foreign arbitrators, this method of arbitration is disagreeable prospect with foreign or North American companies; especially if you have experienced it.") with Sarah R. MACLEAN, "CIETAC, From Underdog to Role Model: Bringing the ICC Back to the Forefront in the Field of International Arbitration", 16 Gonz. J. Int'l L. (2012) p. 62 at pp. 72-73 (observing that CIETAC chairs are primarily Chinese nationals, US parties' win rates are roughly equal to cases lost and outcomes for parties involving other states – such as Germany and Australia – have been fairly similar).

20. See LCIA, *Registrar's Report* (2012) at p. 4, available at <www.lcia.org/LCIA/Casework_Report.aspx> (last accessed 30 June 2014) (observing that for the 344 total appointments in 2012, 181 were exclusively UK nationals, and of those UK nationals, parties appointed 84, the LCIA Court appointed 73 and co-arbitrators appointed 24); *ibid.* (observing that the remaining 144 appointments were "Australian; Austrian; Bahraini; Bangladeshi; Belgian; Brazilian; Canadian; Colombian; Czech; Dutch; Egyptian; French; German; Greek; Indian; Irish; Lebanese; Maltese; New Zealand; Nigerian; Peruvian; Portuguese; Russian; Singaporean; South African; Swedish; Swiss; and US"); but see *ibid.* (noting that 19 appointees were UK dual nationals, which means that 200 appointees were UK nationals or dual nationals for a total UK appointment rate of 58.1%).

21. See LCIA, *Director General's Report* (2005) p. 3, available at <www.lcia.org/LCIA/Casework_Report.aspx> (last accessed 30 June 2014) (observing that 57 arbitrators appointed by the parties were UK nationals, 36 nominated by the LCIA court were UK nationals, which indicates 93 of the 152 total appointments were UK nationals but failing to indicate whether any of the arbitrators appointed were dual nationals).

22. See *op. cit.,* fns. 20- 21 (reflecting the number of appointments in 2005 was 152 and the number in 2012 was 344).

23. But see *op. cit.,* fn. 21 (suggesting that "a higher percentage of party nominees than of LCIA Court nominees are of English nationality" means that "any English 'bias' in the nationality of arbitrators has very much to do with the pragmatic selection of arbitrators qualified in the most-commonly-applicable law(s) and nothing to do with the English origins of the institution").

arbitrators were from the United Kingdom. India and Malaysia were prominently represented at SIAC, with slightly less than 20% of appointments, demonstrating a degree of national diversity.[24]

ICSID, which has jurisdiction over cases arising under commercial contracts, national investment law and investment treaties, publishes summaries of ICSID tribunals and *ad hoc* committees. By the end of 2013, there were 459 registered cases. ICSID helpfully provides information both about individual countries and regions. By region, ICSID arbitrators, conciliators and *ad hoc* committee members came from seventy-seven different states; 49% were European nationals, 22% were from North America, 13% were from Central or South America, 10% were from Asia or the Pacific, and 6% were from Africa or the Middle East.[25] The most frequently appointed nationalities were the United States (163 appointments), France (155), the United Kingdom (133), Canada (97), Switzerland (93), Spain (52), and Australia (50).[26] Waibel and Wu's study of ICSID arbitrators similarly identified the dominance of developing-country arbitrators. For the 341 ICSID arbitrators sitting between 1978 and 2011, their data indicated 66% of arbitrators were nationals of OECD states.[27]

In investment treaty arbitration (ITA), scholars have used publicly available data to identify core arbitrator demographics. The first study of 101 ITA arbitration awards rendered prior to 2007 identified a pool of 145 ITA arbitrators; and of that group, 75% were from OECD states and 3.5% were women.[28] Expanded research from analyzing 252 ITA awards rendered by January 2012, identified a pool of 247 different arbitrators where 80.6% were from OECD states and only 3.6% were women. On the issue of gender, given repeated appointments of certain female arbitrators, at least one woman was present in 18.3% of the awards; but tribunals exclusively containing men generated the vast majority (81.7%) of awards.[29] Studies by other scholars have replicated the

---

24. SIAC, *Annual Report* (Singapore International Arbitration Centre, 2013) p. 10. These numbers were roughly stable over time. Previous annual reports are available at <www.siac.org.sg/>.

25. ICSID, *The ICSID Caseload – Statistics, Issue 2014-1* (2014) p. 18, available at <https://icsid. worldbank.org/ICSID/FrontServlet?requestType=ICSIDDocRH&actionVal=CaseLoadStatistics> (last accessed 30 June 2014).

26. *Ibid*, p. 20; see also Noah RUBINS and Anthony SINCLAIR, "ICSID Arbitrators: Is there a club and who gets invited?", 1 Global Arb. Rev. (Nov. 2006) at <http://globalarbitrationreview.com/ journal/article/16468/icsid-arbitrators-club-gets-invited/> (last accessed 30 June 2014) (exploring the nationality of ICSID arbitrators with pre-2007 data, identifying 279 individuals from 57 different countries who have served as arbitrators. with nationals from the United States having the largest number of appointments, followed by French, British, Swiss and Canadian nationals, but observing several Mexican arbitrators were appointed).

27. WAIBEL and WU, *op. cit.*, fn. 11, pp. 27 et seq.

28. Susan D. FRANCK, "Empirically Evaluating Claims about Investment Treaty Arbitration", 86 N.C. L. Rev. (2007) p. 1 at pp. 75-82 (henceforth Empirically Evaluating); see also FRANCK, Development, *op. cit.*, fn. 11, p. 459 (noting that, on the basis of World Bank classification of development status, for final awards, 74% of presiding arbitrators were from High Income states, 17% were from upper-middle income states, 11% were from lower-middle income states and there were no presiding arbitrators from low income states) and PUIG, *op. cit.*, fn. 10.

29. Susan D. FRANCK, *Investment Treaty Arbitration: Myths, Realities and Costs* (forthcoming Oxford University Press) (henceforth *Myths and Realities*).

findings about the lack of women arbitrators in ITA[30] and their representation within the caseload. Preliminary research by Waibel and Wu also indicated that, for ICSID arbitrators, 42% had the preponderance or all of their legal education in a common law jurisdiction, 26% were full-time academics.[31] This finding is not new as, in 2006, Rubins and Sinclair observed their analysis revealed that "[c]ertainly the data supports the view that ICSID belongs primarily to gentlemen".[32]

2.   ICCA Respondents

During the first plenary session, all ICCA Congress registrants in attendance were offered an opportunity to complete a survey voluntarily and confidentially. The survey materials relevant to this Paper included three pages of questions. One page asked demographic questions; and two other pages asked questions relevant to the ICCA themes of precision and justice.

Out of the 1,031 ICCA registrants,[33] 552 people completed the survey (the ICCA respondents).[34]

This Section presents the demographic characteristics of all ICCA respondents completing the survey.[35] While most respondents completed the entire questionnaire, given the voluntary nature of the survey, not all ICCA respondents completed all questions. For those who completed the materials, we distinguish between types of information provided. For example, we initially provide information on the

---

30. Research conducted by Waibel and Wu identified that 95% of their sample was male and 5% was female. WAIBEL and WU, *op. cit.*, fn. 11, pp. 27 et seq.; see also Lucy GREENWOOD and C. Mark BAKER, "Getting a Better Balance on International Arbitration Tribunals", 28 Arb. Int'l (2012) p. 653 at pp. 656, 663-665 (analyzing ICSID cases to identify that 5.6% of all arbitrator appointments were women and suggesting that, given statistics from the LCIA, SCC and American Lawyer that approximately 6% of ICA tribunals involve women); Gus VAN HARTEN, "The (Lack of) Women Arbitrators in Investment Treaty Arbitration", 59 Columbia FDI Perspectives, No. 59 (6 Feb. 2012) at <http://ccsi.columbia.edu/files/2014/01/FDI_59.pdf> (last accessed 30 June 2014) (observing that in 631 appointments in 249 known cases, only 41 of the appointments, namely 6.5% of appointments, were women).
31. WAIBEL and WU, *op. cit.*, fn. 11, pp. 27-29.
32. RUBINS and SINCLAIR, *op. cit.*, fn. 26.
33. Twelve of the registrants worked on the research team, and two people had reviewed earlier drafts of the material during beta-testing. As such, only 1017 of the registrants were capable of answering the survey. Any attendee who self-selected to attend the first plenary could voluntarily participate. This also meant that, out of the potential respondents, we obtained a 54.3% response rate. This was a reasonable response rate. See Edward K. CHENG, "Independent Judicial Research in the *Daubert* Age", 56 Duke L.J. (2007) p. 1264 at p. 1278 (identifying a response rate of approximately 60% of subjects in a judicial conference was "quite reasonable").
34. Only four of the 552 respondents objected to the use of their responses in published materials, which permitted us to analyze 548 respondents. As such, their contributions form no part in the analyses of these sections and the small size had a *de minimis* effect.
35. See Susan D. FRANCK, et al., "The Diversity Challenge: Exploring the 'Invisible College' of International Arbitration", Columbia J. Transnat'l L. (forthcoming 2015) (exploring aspects of this Paper involving demographics and diversity challenges in greater detail).

demographics of all ICCA respondents broken down by experience in international arbitration. Next, when we focus on arbitrators, we demarcate the general group of anyone who has served as an arbitrator and also include breakdowns for the subsets of individuals reflecting their experience in international commercial arbitration (ICA) or ITA. Similarly, we distinguish between response patterns for: (1) all ICCA respondents answering the relevant question(s); (2) the subset of respondents indicating they served as an international arbitrator; and (3) the subset of respondents indicating they served as counsel in international arbitration.[36]

a.   Experience related to international arbitration

Before turning to more specific analyses, we first identify the respondents' professional experiences. We hope that, moving forward, these demographics provide information to ICCA conference organizers for their consideration in connection with strategic outreach.

Overall, the data reflected that ICCA respondents tended to have experience either as counsel, experience as an arbitrator (whether in ICA or ITA) or a combination thereof. Table 1 indicates that most respondents acted as counsel in at least one international arbitration (87%). Each respondent serving as counsel was involved in an average of twenty-seven cases (median=15). International arbitrators were also prominent, with 60.4% of responding ICCA respondents indicating they had acted as arbitrator in at least one case. Sub-sect. II.2.b discusses the frequency of arbitral appointments in greater detail.[37] The data provide a counterpoint to claims that there are only between 100 and 200 practitioners worldwide with repeat appointments in arbitration.[38]

Experts in international arbitration were moderately well represented. Although it is not clear how many experts there are in international arbitration globally, our data indicated that one-third of ICCA respondents had been experts in at least one arbitration case. The experts at ICCA, however, were not heavy repeat players. Table 1 indicates both measures of central tendency suggested a low number of cases, with a mean of 3.6 and a median of two.

---

36. It is possible that there may be a response bias generated by those respondents who failed to answer all questions and those answers may have been meaningfully different from the answers that were provided. While we cannot eliminate the risk of response bias, the large number of respondents who answered the vast majority of questions (and the small number of respondents who failed to answer) attests to the underlying validity of the data. Nevertheless, replication is necessary to decrease the risk of error.

37. We recognize that the broader ICCA membership may contain more international arbitrators than were registered for the conference or participated in the survey. For the purposes of this Paper, references to ICCA arbitrators (or the subset of ICCA arbitrators) necessarily incorporate this limitation.

38. Christian BÜHRING-UHLE, et al., "The Arbitrator as Mediator: Some Recent Empirical Insights", 20 J. Int'l Arb. (2003) p. 81 at pp. 81-82. We cannot, however, discount that there may be distinctions in what role counsel plays in a particular case. On complex international cases, global law firms may employ "local counsel" to handle issues of domestic law while not relinquishing control of overall case strategy.

Table 1: Descriptive Data Identifying the Percentage and Frequency of Respondents' Professional Experience Related to International Arbitration for ICCA Respondents[39] and the Mean, Median and Maximum Number of Cases for ICCA Respondents with a Minimum of One Case in a Category of Professional Experience

Categories of Professional Experience in Arbitration[40]	Percentage (and Frequency) of Cases	Mean Number of Cases	Median Number of Cases	Maximum Number of Cases	Standard Deviation
Respondents Acting as Arbitration Counsel	87.3% (n=413)	27.3	15	501	46.9
All International Arbitrators	60.4% (n=262)	34.6	10	501	64.6
Expert	32.3% (n=126)	3.6	2	51	6.4
Judge in National Court	9.3% (n=35)	571.3	51	10001	1740.7
Adjudicator in Public International Law Dispute	4.6% (n=17)	27.8	2	301	76.4

39. Some ICCA respondents failed to provide information on their professional experiences. This may reflect their lack of experience or a possibility that the data underrepresent respondents' actual experience. Given the lack of clarity, respondents failing to answer were omitted from the percentage calculation. Of the 448 respondents analyzed, the following respondents expressly provided information about their appointments (or lack thereof): (1) counsel=473 responses (75 missing); (2) expert=390 responses (158 missing); (3) ICA arbitrators=432 responses (116 missing); (4) ITA arbitrators=386 responses (162 missing); (5) public international law adjudicators=368 responses (180 missing); (6) judges=376 responses (172 missing).

40. We based these categories on experiences we identified as typical gateway experiences to international arbitration. We did not focus on institutional appointments or tribunal secretaries as these individuals do not technically decide disputes. Nevertheless, we acknowledge that tribunal secretaries can play a critical part in the arbitration process. See Constantine PARTASIDES, "The Fourth Arbitrator? The Role of Secretaries to Tribunals in International Arbitration", 18 Arb. Int'l (2002) p. 147. At least two respondents volunteered they had served as tribunal secretaries. Although we did not code those appointments as arbitrators, future research should focus upon tribunal secretaries. Similarly, given methodological and timing constraints, we did not code for experience in academia, non-governmental organizations, policy think tanks, or labor unions. Future research might also explore representation of these groups at prominent international arbitration events.

There were at least two groups, however, that we were able to identify with minimal representation at ICCA.

First, few of the ICCA respondents had been judges in national courts. Table 1 indicates this was less than 10% of respondents. The wide standard deviation, however, reflects variation in responses; there was one group of respondents who had an extensive number of cases and a second group who had a smaller number. Consequently, for the thirty-five individuals who acted as judges, the mean number of proceedings was 571.3 but the median was fifty-one.

Second, independent of those respondents serving as ITA arbitrators, there were also only a few respondents with experience adjudicating public international law disputes.[41] Specifically, only thirty-five of respondents (9.3%) had served on at least one public international law proceeding. Of those respondents, there was a variation in relative levels of experience with respondents having an average of 27.8 cases and a median of two cases. This low level of representation at ICCA may, however, reflect the relatively small pool of public international adjudicators, such as the small number of elite adjudicators at institutions including the International Court of Justice and World Trade Organization (WTO).

ICCA Congresses therefore offer opportunities to interact with international arbitrators and counsel and, to a lesser degree, experts. Future ICCA Congresses may wish to expand existing outreach to national court judges and international law adjudicators. These latter groups represent potentially untapped groups that are affected by and interested in international arbitration. Continued outreach would also support ICCA's roadshows with domestic judiciaries that provide a venue for generating dialogue with national courts.[42]

b. Experience as international arbitrators

One critical question involved how frequently arbitrators exercised their adjudicative functions.[43] Our survey asked respondents to report how many times they acted as an arbitrator in ICA, and it separately asked how many times they served as an arbitrator in ITA. Overall, as Table 1 reflected, 262 of our respondents (or a little more than half) served as an arbitrator in at least one case. Yet these blunt figures lack a degree of nuance.

Table 2 reflects that, overall, those at ICCA who had acted as arbitrators reported being involved in an average of 34.6 cases; and the statistically "median arbitrator" arbitrated ten cases. The variation between those two measures of central tendency was

---

41. The survey and the data analysis differentiated between "public international law" and ITA cases. Respondents were therefore able to distinguish between traditional public international law cases and other cases.

42. See fn. 6 for a discussion of these roadshows.

43. See Daphna KAPELIUK, "The Repeat Appointment Factor: Exploring Decision Patterns of Elite Investment Arbitrators", 96 Cornell L. Rev. (2010) p. 47 (defining "elite" ITA arbitrators as those who have served on four or more cases); James CLASPER, "London's Arbitration Elite", 1 Global Arb. Rev. (Apr. 2006) at <http://globalarbitrationreview.com/journal/article/18197/londons-elite-arbitration-groups/> (last accessed 30 June 2014) (exploring elite arbitration practices, and arbitrators, in London).

driven by a small number of arbitrators sitting on a large number of cases. Twenty-five respondents sat on more than 100 arbitrations (whether ICA or ITA based), twelve respondents sat on more than 200 cases, and one arbitrator self-reported arbitrating more than 500 cases. Quartile breakdowns offer insight into how frequently people sit as arbitrators. Super-elite arbitrators in the top quartile arbitrated more than forty cases. Elite arbitrators in the second highest quartile arbitrated between 11-40 cases. Experienced arbitrators, with substantial but relatively less experience, were in the second lowest quartile and arbitrated between 4-10 cases. The least experienced arbitrators, namely those in the bottom quartile, arbitrated only 1-3 cases. See Table 2.

Table 2: Descriptive Data of the Frequency of Cases for All ICCA Respondents Reporting Service as an Arbitrator in at Least One Case and Subsets of ICA and ITA Arbitrators

Variables	All Arbitrators	ICA Arbitrators	ITA Arbitrators
Mean Number of Arbitration Cases	34.6	33.2	6.6
Appointment Quartiles 1st quartile (25th percentile)	3	3	1
2nd quartile (median)	10	10	2
3rd quartile (75th percentile)	40	30	6
Maximum Appointments	501	501	60
Standard Deviation	64.6	63.0	11.6
Total Respondents	262	260	67

While the data demonstrate that particularly elite arbitrators have more appointments than others, the sheer number of ICCA respondents with repeat experience as arbitrators reflects that the arbitrator bench is not necessarily as closed as one might initially perceive.[44] Acknowledging that this may be a by-product of the elite nature of ICCA conferences, these findings should be explored in other international arbitration venues.

The general patterns identified benefit from further analysis of individuals' specific experiences with ICA or ITA. Table 2 reflects that the general patterns of all arbitrators mirrors the pattern of arbitrators involved in ICA cases. Yet, there is a somewhat

---

44. See DEZALAY and GARTH, *op. cit.*, fn. 9 at pp. 34-41 (claiming that "key source of conflict" in international arbitration practice is the influx of newcomers); Catherine A. ROGERS, "The Vocation of the International Arbitrator", 20 Am. U. Int'l L. Rev. (2005) p. 957 at p. 968 (henceforth Vocation) (observing the "market for international arbitrators operates as a relatively closed system that is difficult for newcomers to penetrate".).

different facial pattern for ITA arbitrators. Specifically, more than half of the ITA arbitrators had only arbitrated 1-2 ITA cases. To be a super-elite arbitrator in ITA (i.e., in the top quartile), it was only necessary to have six or more cases. These figures for ITA may, however, reflect the recent and relatively small ITA caseload.

We note, however, that for the 67 ITA arbitrators, only two identified they had *not* also served as an ICA arbitrator. Put differently, it was highly unusual for ITA arbitrators at ICCA to have never sat on an ICA case. This provides evidence that acting as an ICA arbitrator may be a "gateway" experience or pre-requisite for serving as an ITA arbitrator,[45] but this is not conclusive as there may be alternative pathways to ITA appointments. Alternatively, the data may reflect that being appointed in ITA expands appointment opportunities in ICA.

c.   *Gender, age, legal training, native language and nationality of international arbitrators and counsel*

Existing literature on arbitrators offers some information on arbitrator background, but the information usually is institutition or subject matter specific. While difficult to prove a negative, we are unaware of any existing research that systematically explores the gender, age and nationality of international arbitrators across institutions and subject matter.[46] Likewise, we are unaware of any research on demographic information about the background of counsel in international arbitration. As such, this research provides a core baseline for future inquiries into the "invisible college" of international arbitration. While more is arguably known about the "invisible college" of ITA arbitration, the data is particularly valuable for ICA as those awards are confidential and minimal information is publicly available.[47] Although it also discusses counsel, this Section primarily focuses on international arbitrators.

There have been suggestions that international arbitrators tend to be "pale, male and stale".[48] The question is whether that narrative is empirically verifiable. Our research

---

45. This supports Anthea Robert's hypothesis that there is a public and private international law divide within ITA. Anthea ROBERTS, "Clash of Paradigms: Actors and Analogies Shaping the Investment Treaty System", 107 Am. J. Int'l L. (2013) p. 45; See also Bruno SIMMA, "Foreign Investment Arbitration: A Place for Human Rights?", 60 Int'l & Comp. L. Quart. (2011) p. 573.

46. There is an emerging literature related to the identity of ITA arbitrators including gender and nationality. See, e.g., fn. 11 and accompanying text; FRANCK, Empirically Evaluating, *op. cit.*, fn. 28, pp. 78-81 (exploring the gender and OECD status of arbitrators); PUIG, *op. cit.*, fn. 10, pp. 17-18 (collecting information on ICSID arbitrators related to name, gender and nationality); WAIBEL and WU, *op. cit.*, fn. 11 (collecting information on ICSID arbitrators only including gender, nationality, age and legal education). The limited quantitative data on ICA makes this research particularly critical. But see *op. cit.*, fn. 11 (identifying sources of empirical research on ICA).

47. See *op. cit.*, fn. 11 and accompanying text.

48. Michael D. GOLDHABER, "Madame La Présidente: A Woman Who Sits as President of a Major Arbitral Tribunal Is a Rare Creature. Why?", Am. Lawyer: Focus Europe (Summer 2004) at <https://fr.groups.yahoo.com/neo/groups/arbitrage-adr/conversations/messages/447> (last accessed 30 June 2014) ("Arbitration is dominated by a few aging men, many of whom pioneered the field. In the words of Sarah François-Poncet of Salans, the usual suspects are 'pale, male, and stale'.").

therefore explored the gender composition of ICCA respondents. It also investigated other aspects of diversity including age, legal training, linguistic capacity, nationality, and development status.

Given the existing literature reflecting questions about gender disparity in international arbitration, the basic descriptive data on gender composition is of interest. Table 3 reflects the gender distribution of all respondents, arbitrators and counsel. For all ICCA respondents and the subset of counsel, roughly three-quarters were men, and one quarter were women. The distribution shifted slightly, however, when evaluating those serving as arbitrators with the proportion of men becoming larger. Namely, 82.4% of respondents who had been arbitrators were men and 17.6% were women.[49]

The results also suggest that although all respondents were typically in the late 40s, the subset of arbitrators tended to be somewhat older. Table 3 indicates that the mean age of all respondents was 48 (median=47); and counsel age was similar with a mean age of 48 (median=46). In contrast, the mean age of responding arbitrators was 54 (median=53). This may not necessarily be unusual. Other research suggests the average age of an active member of the bar in California was 48 whereas the average of California judges was 60,[50] but that the age of median judges has been decreasing in several jurisdictions.[51]

---

49. As a caution, there is some evidence that, for the subset of arbitrators, the ICCA respondents had a disproportionately large number of women arbitrators. See infra fn. 244 and accompanying text.
50. Arden ROWELL and Jessica BREGANT, "Numeracy and Legal Decision Making", 46 Ariz. St. L.J. (2014) p. 191 at p. 225 n. 120.
51. See M. Margaret McKEOWN, "The Internet and the Constitution: A Selective Retrospective", 9 Wash. J.L. Tech. & Arts (2014) p. 135 at p. 142 ("the median age of active judges has declined: from 58 years old in 1990 to 50 years old in 2010"); Abhinav CHANDRACHUD, "Does Life Tenure Make Judges More Independent? A Comparative Study of Judicial Appointments in India", 28 Conn. J. Int'l L. (2013) p. 297 at pp. 305-306 (indicating the average age at appointment was 54 years for the Australian High Court, 56 years for the Canadian Supreme Court, and 64 years in the Supreme Court of Japan but noting that the average age at appointment was increasing in India and Japan).

Table 3: Descriptive Statistics of Gender and Age for All ICCA Respondents, the Subset of those Working as Arbitrators and the Subset of those Working as Counsel

Variables	All	Arbitrators	Counsel
Respondent Gender: Percentage and Frequency			
Women	25.5% (n=134)	17.6% (n=46)	24.0% (n=99)
Men	74.5% (n=392)	82.4% (n=216)	76.0% (n=314)
Total Respondents	*100% (n=526)*	*100% (n=262)*	*100% (n=413)*
Respondent Age:			
Mean	48.5	54.4	48.0
Median	47.0	53.0	46.0
Min	24.0	29.0	24.0
Max	85.0	85.0	85.0
Standard deviation	12.7	11.7	12.3
Total Respondents	514	253	406
Age as a Function of Gender:[52]			
Age of Women			
Mean	42.0	47.5	41.3
Median	40.0	45.0	40.0
Min	27.0	32.0	27.0
Max	71.0	68.0	65.0
Standard deviation	10.0	9.3	8.4
Total Number of Women	128	46	96
Age of Men			
Mean	50.6	55.8	50.0
Median	50.0	55.0	50.0
Min	24.0	29.0	24.0
Max	85.0	85.0	85.0
Standard deviation	12.8	11.7	12.5
Total Number of Men	386	216	310

---

52. When looking at age as a function of gender, there was a smaller number of respondents. Six men and six women identified their gender but not their age and, as such, could not be analyzed.

It is also noteworthy that the age difference between male and female respondents was statistically meaningful,[53] irrespective of whether all ICCA respondents ($t(512)=6.872$; $p<.001$; $r=.29$; $n=514$), counsel ($t(404)=6.385$; $p<.001$; $r=.30$; $n=406$) or arbitrators ($t(251)=4.337$; $p<.001$; $r=.26$; $n=253$) were analyzed. The effect sizes all suggested the size of the gender difference was statistically medium.[54] The direction was such that women attending ICCA, regardless of their arbitration experience, were reliably younger than the men. Table 3 indicates that for women arbitrators, the average age was 47.5 whereas the average age of male arbitrators was 57.8.

Another way to consider respondents' diversity is legal training. Table 4 reflects that ICCA respondents had a variety of training. For all ICCA respondents, common law was the dominant legal training, with 46% of the respondents exclusively trained in a common law jurisdiction. There was also a strong civil law component, with 30% of respondents trained exclusively as civil lawyers. There was also an intriguing hybrid as 24% of respondents had training from *both* common and civil law jurisdictions.[55] The dominance of common law training was also present in the subset of arbitrators but was not as facially prominent. More specifically, 38.5% of ICCA arbitrators had training exclusively in common law whereas 33.8% of ICCA arbitrators were exclusively trained as civil lawyers; and 27.7% of ICCA arbitrators were trained in both common and civil law.[56]

Language is another way to explore the diversity of international arbitration. Linguistically, ICCA respondents spoke fifty-eight different native languages. Although Chinese and Spanish are the two most prevalent languages in the world,[57] this dominance was not present in the ICCA respondents, the subset of counsel or the subset of arbitrators. For ICCA respondents generally and counsel, English, Spanish and Portuguese were most prevalent, together accounting for nearly 70% of the languages spoken. The proportions were slightly different for the subset of arbitrators, as the dominant languages were English, German and French (and accounted for over 60% of total language capacity). Only four arbitrators' native language was either Mandarin or Cantonese.[58]

---

53. Statistical significance "provides a measure to help us decide whether what we observe in our sample is also going on in the population that the sample is supposed to represent". Timothy C. URDAN, *Statistics in Plain English*, 3rd ed. (Routledge 2010) p. 62.

54. Because gender is a two-category variable, these analyses used independent samples t-tests to explore the potential gender variance in the continuous variable of age. See infra fn. 118 for a discussion of the underlying statistical tests.

55. These proportions were similar for the subset of those who have been arbitration counsel.

56. The results may be a function of a case selection effect. In theory, more US common-law trained lawyers attended as Miami was a geographically convenient forum. Future ICCA researchers may wish to explore this issue further to see, as the venue changes, whether this demographic aspect fluctuates or remains stable.

57. Paul LEWIS, et al., eds., *Ethnologue: Languages of the World*, 17th ed. (SIL International Online 2013) available at <www.ethnologue.com> (last accessed 30 June 2014).

58. This may reflect that the ICCA 2014 Congress in Miami occurred exclusively in English.

As regards geography, ICCA respondents and arbitrators appeared in proportions that did not reflect global population patterns.[59] For example, ranking continents from highest population to lowest yields: Asia; Africa; Europe; South America (including Central America and the Caribbean); North America and Oceania.[60] In contrast, Table 4 indicates that, irrespective of whether analyzing ICCA respondents or the subset of arbitrators, the trend was to have the greatest representation of nationals from Europe and North America and the lowest proportions came from Asia and Africa.[61]

For the subset of arbitrators, some states were underrepresented. Although highest in world population (60.27%), Asian arbitrators were the second least well represented (10%) of ICCA arbitrators. Ironically, although China and India together contain approximately 33% of the world's population, less than 3% of the ICCA arbitrators were from those states. Meanwhile, despite Africa's second highest population (15.41%), Africa exhibited the lowest level of representation (0.4%). Other states were arguably over-represented. Although Europe has 10.37% of the world's population, 48.2% of the arbitrators were European nationals. Similarly, North America has 4.93% of the world's population, but 27.9% of the ICCA arbitrators were from North America; and of the seventy arbitrators from North America, only one was from Mexico. Other states, however, were more balanced in their representation. For example, although Australia and New Zealand contain not quite 1% of world population, they represented 4.0% of ICCA arbitrators. The closest level of balance came from South America, with 8.49% of world population and 9.6% of ICCA arbitrators.[62]

---

59. For the purposes of this Paper, we used global population as a comparative baseline for basic demographic information. We acknowledge that better comparisons would evaluate the nationalities of the parties involved in international arbitration and/or the location of the subject matter of the dispute. As we are unaware of any such data on this topic gathered in a scientifically reliable and comparable manner, these comparisons are not currently possible. We encourage future research to identify whether the baselines identified in this Paper vary meaningfully from the nationality of those stakeholders actively using international arbitration.

60. STATISTA, Distribution of the global population mid-2013, The Statistics Portal, 2014, at <www.statista.com/statistics/237584/distribution-of-the-world-population-by-continent/> (last accessed 30 June 2014); NATIONS ONLINE, Current World Population, Nations online, at <www.nationsonline.org/oneworld/world_population.htm> (last accessed 30 June 2014).

61. Given our focus on nationality, there is a possible disjunction between where arbitrators reside and their nationality. Future research might also explore the variance generated by the distinction between where the international arbitration community originates from and with what countries they may currently have ties. In the interim, for a more nuanced discussion of the appropriate baselines regarding nationality in international arbitration, see FRANCK, et al., fn. 35.

62. Table 4 reflects that the strongest representation from Latin America came from the large contingent of Brazilians. In terms of ICCA-related outreach, it is possible that earlier ICCA Congresses and/or geographic proximity may affect participation in future Congresses and serve to grow the global arbitration community.

Table 4: Percentages and Frequency Distributions (in parentheses) of Legal Education, Native Language, Continent and Nationality for All ICCA Respondents, the Subset of those Working as Arbitrators and the Subset of those Working as Counsel

Variables	All	Arbitrators	Counsel
Legal Education			
Common Law	45.7% (n=237)	38.5% (n=100)	44.6% (n=184)
Civil Law	30.3% (n=157)	33.8% (n=88)	29.1% (n=120)
Both	24.1% (n=125)	27.7% (n=72)	26.4% (n=109)
Total Respondents	519	260	413
Mother Tongue			
English	48.6% (n=248)	43.3% (n=110)	47.4% (n=191)
Spanish	10.2% (n=52)	7.1% (n=18)	10.4% (n=42)
Portuguese	9.4% (n=48)	8.3% (n=21)	10.7% (n=43)
German	6.5% (n=33)	10.6% (n=27)	6.5% (n=26)
French	5.7% (n=29)	10.2% (n=26)	6.5% (n=26)
Dutch	2.2% (n=11)	3.5% (n=9)	2.7% (n=11)
Other languages	17.4% (n=89)	17.0% (n=43)	15.8% (n=64)
Total native languages	38	26	32
Total Respondents	510	254	403
Continent			
Europe	36.4% (n=183)	48.2% (n=121)	37.2% (n=148)
North America	33.6% (n=169)	27.9% (n=70)	31.4% (n=125)
South America	12.7% (n=64)	9.6% (n=24)	14.3% (n=57)
Asia	10.9% (n=55)	10.0% (n=25)	11.1% (n=44)
Australia / New Zealand	4.6% (n=23)	4.0% (n=10)	4.8% (n=19)
Africa	1.8% (n=9)	0.4% (n=1)	1.3% (n=5)
Total Respondents	503	251	398

Variables	All	Arbitrators	Counsel
Nationality			
United States	29.0% (n=145)	23.2% (n=58)	26.8% (n=106)
United Kingdom	10.6% (n=53)	9.6% (n=24)	10.4% (n=41)
Brazil	8.6% (n=43)	7.2% (n=18)	9.6% (n=38)
France	5.0% (n=25)	8.8% (n=22)	6.1% (n=24)
Australia	3.8% (n=9)	2.8% (n=7)	4.3% (n=17)
Germany	3.6% (n=18)	4.8% (n=12)	3.0% (n=12)
Canada	3.4% (n=17)	4.8% (n=12)	4.1% (n=16)
Switzerland	2.8% (n=14)	5.6% (n=14)	3.5% (n=14)
China	2.6% (n=13)	1.2% (n=3)	1.5% (n=6)
India	2.4% (n=12)	1.6% (n=4)	2.8% (n=11)
Sweden	2.4% (n=12)	2.8% (n=7)	2.8% (n=11)
Netherlands	1.8% (n=9)	2.4% (n=6)	2.3% (n=9)
Spain	1.8% (n=9)	2.4% (n=6)	2.0% (n=8)
South Korea	1.6% (n=8)	2.4% (n=6)	1.8% (n=7)
Italy	1.1% (n=6)	2.0% (n=5)	0.8% (n=3)
Argentina	1.0% (n=5)	0.4% (n=1)	1.0% (n=4)
Austria	1.0% (n=5)	2.0% (n=5)	1.0% (n=4)
Philippines	1.0% (n=5)	0.4% (n=1)	1.0% (n=4)
Portugal	1.0% (n=5)	1.2% (n=3)	1.3% (n=5)
Russia	1.0% (n=5)	1.6% (n=4)	0.5% (n=2)
Other Primary Nationalities	14.4% (n=82)[63]	12.8% (n=32)[64]	13.9% (n=53)[65]
Total Number of Different Primary Nationalities	58[66]	41	47
Total Respondents	500	250	395

63. This table reflects only those nationalities where, for all ICCA respondents, there were five or more nationals from the country. Thirty-eight other states had at least one but less than five respondents each, namely: Bahrain, Belgium, Bolivia, Colombia, Costa Rica, Cuba, Czech Republic, Denmark, Dominican Republic, Ecuador, Finland, Georgia, Ghana, Greece, Guatemala, Haiti, Ireland, Jamaica, Japan, Malaysia, Malta, Mexico, Morocco, New Zealand, Nigeria, Norway, Peru, Rwanda, Singapore, Slovakia, South Africa, Syria, Tanzania, Tunisia, Ukraine, Venezuela and Vietnam.
64. The other primary nationalities of arbitrators were Belgium, Bolivia, Chile, Czech Republic, Denmark, Finland, Georgia, Greece, Guatemala, Ireland, Japan, Malaysia, Mexico, New Zealand, Nigeria, Peru, Singapore, Slovakia, Ukraine, Venezuela and Vietnam.
65. The other primary nationalities of counsel were Belgium, Bolivia, Colombia, Cuba, Czech Republic, Denmark, Ecuador, Finland, Georgia, Greece, Guatemala, Jamaica, Japan, Malaysia, Malta, Mexico, Morocco, New Zealand, Nigeria, Peru, Singapore, Slovakia, South Africa, Ukraine, Venezuela and Vietnam.
66. For both primary and secondary nationalities, there were 60 different states.

Variables	All	Arbitrators	Counsel
Dual Nationals			
United States	17.6 (n=6)	--	19.4% (n=6)
Italy	14.7% (n=5)	10.0% (n=1)	16.1% (n=5)
United Kingdom	11.8% (n=4)	20.0% (n=2)	9.7% (n=3)
Germany	8.8% (n=3)	30.0% (n=3)	9.7% (n=3)
Australia	5.9% (n=2)	--	6.5% (n=2)
Brazil	5.9% (n=2)	10.0% (n=1)	3.2% (n=1)
Switzerland	5.9% (n=2)	20.0% (n=2)	6.5% (n=2)
Other Dual Nationalities	29.4% (n=10)[67]	10% (n=1)[68]	28.9% (n=9)[69]
Total Respondents	34	10	31

Historically, literature has focused upon the prevalence of "western" parties in international law;[70] yet, in a post-Cold War era with different policy concerns, this terminology is potentially arcane and not reflective of meaningful variance. As a final aspect for measuring the scope of diversity, we therefore explored the development status of respondents' nationality. Defining "Development Status" is challenging.[71] There is no consistent legal definition of this concept. Development is subtle and, at the margins, can mean different things to different people. For example, the World Trade Organization does not offer a precise measurement for development; rather, it permits member states to self-define development level.[72] As the lack of a consistent definition

---

67. This table reflects only dual nationals where there were two or more nationals for all ICCA respondents. There were also single dual nationals from Czech Republic, France, Ireland, Lebanon, New Zealand, Nigeria, Portugal, Spain, Uruguay and Venezuela.
68. This dual-national arbitrator was from Nigeria.
69. There were also dual nationals from the Czech Republic, France, Ireland, Lebanon, Nigeria, Portugal, Spain, Uruguay and Venezuela.
70. See, e.g., Kurt GAUBATZ and Matthew MACARTHUR, "How International Is 'International' Law?", 22 Mich. J. Int'l L. (2001) p. 239; see also PUIG, op. cit., fn. 10, p. 19 (identifying that, for only ICSID arbitration, "most arbitrators are from specific developed countries. Individuals of seven nations (New Zealand, Australia, Canada, Switzerland, France, the UK, and the US) represent almost half of total appointments").
71. Marc L. BUSH and Eric REINHARD, "Developing Countries and General Agreement on Tariffs and Trade/World Trade Organization Dispute Settlement", 37 J. of World Trade (2003) p. 719 at pp. 719, 723 (analyzing development dimensions in GATT disputes and observing the difficulty in making distinctions between developed and developing states).
72. See World Trade Organization, "Who Are the Developing Countries in the WTO?", at <www.wto.org/english/tratop_e/devel_e/d1who_e.htm> (last accessed 30 June 2014) ("There are no WTO definitions of 'developed' and 'developing' countries. Members announce for themselves whether they are 'developed' and 'developing' countries); Anu BRADFORD and Eric A. POSNER, "Universal Exceptionalism in International Law", 52 Harv. Int'l L.J. (2011) p.1 at n. 159 ("WTO rules do not contain a definition of a 'developing country.' Instead, states self-designate themselves as developed or developing countries as part of a political calculus.");

has caused confusion in international law,[73] it is appropriate to use measures based upon "judgments made for entirely different purposes by *other researchers*".[74]

We used three pre-existing measures to define development status. First, development was operationalized as a binary categorical variable – OECD Status – that derived from a state's membership in the Organisation for Economic Co-operation and Development (OECD). OECD membership is generally, but not always, associated with higher levels of development and therefore is a blunt proxy.[75] Second, development was also operationalized using a four-category variable – World Bank Status – that derived from a World Bank classification system grouping states as High Income, Upper-Middle Income, Lower-Middle Income and Low Income.[76] The World Bank's main criterion for classifying economies is gross national income (GNI) per capita.[77] Third, development status was operationalized using a continuous variable – HDI Status – derived from the United Nations Development Programme's Human Development Index (UNDP HDI). HDI evaluates elements including life expectancy, education and income. HDI is also a continuous variable and ranges from 0.0 (undeveloped) to 1.0 (completely developed).[78]

Regardless of the measure used, the results indicated that nationals from developed states dominated the roster of all ICCA respondents generally, and the subsets of counsel and arbitrators. Table 5 demonstrates that 75% (or more for the subset of arbitrators) of respondents were from an OECD and High Income state; and we observe that none of the ICCA respondents were arbitrators from low income states. There were similar results for dual nationals. HDI scores, however, make the point starkly for the subset of arbitrators. The median HDI score meant that half the arbitrators were from states the UNDP classified as having "very high human development" and reflected the top twelve most developed nations in the world. The mean also reflected that the statistically

---

Andrew D. MITCHELL and Joanne WALLIS, "Pacific Pause: The Rhetoric of Special & Differential Treatment, the Reality of WTO Accession", 27 Wisc. Int'l L.J. (2010) p. 663 at pp. 696-697.

73. Benjamin L. LIEBMAN, "Autonomy Through Separation?: Environmental Law and the Basic Law of Hong Kong", 39 Harv. Int'l L.J. (1998) p. 231 at pp. 261-262.

74. Gary KING, et al., *Designing Social Enquiry: Scientific Inference in Qualitative Research* (Princeton University Press 1994) p. 157 (emphasis in original); see also Susan D. FRANCK, et al., "Through the Looking Glass: Understanding Social Science Norms for Analyzing International Investment Law", 2010-2011 Y.B. on Int'l Investment Law & Pol'y (2011) p. 883.

75. Jan WOUTERS and Sven VAN KERCKHOVEN, "The OECD and the G20: An Ever Closer Relationship?", 43 Geo. Wash. Int'l L. Rev. (2011) p. 345.

76. The World Bank analytical classification is available at <http://goo.gl/LrGDO>. The Classifications used for coding were available at <http://bit.ly/907M8u>.

77. WORLD BANK, "Data: How We Classify Countries", at <http://bit.ly/cgOu7t> (last accessed 30 June 2014).

78. As the methodology for coding HDI changed in 2011 and was applied to all the data retroactively, previously published Human Development Reports were not used to code HDI levels. The research used data directly provided by Dr. Milorad Kovacevic, Chief Statistician at the Human Development Report Office of the United Nations Development Programme. All of the scores Dr. Kovacevic provided used the updated 2011 methodology to re-evaluate the historical and current rankings of states.

average arbitrator at ICCA came from a state with a HDI score in the top thirty most developed states.[79]

Table 5: Descriptive Statistics of the Development Status of All ICCA Respondents, the subset of Arbitrators and the Subset of Counsel as a Function of OECD Membership, World Bank Classification and the Human Development Index[80]

Variables	All	Arbitrators	Counsel
OECD Nationals: **Percentage** **(Frequency)**			
OECD national	74.6% (*n*=373)	82.4% (*n*=206)	75.2% (*n*=297)
Non-OECD national	25.4% (*n*=127)	17.6% (*n*=44)	24.8% (*n*=98)
Totals	100% (*n*=500)	100% (*n*=250)	100% (*n*=395)
OECD Dual Nationals: **Percentage** **(Frequency)**			
OECD national	79.4% (*n*=27)	80.0% (*n*=8)	80.6% (*n*=25)
Non-OECD national	20.6% (*n*=7)	20.0% (*n*=2)	19.4% (*n*=6)
Totals	100% (*n*=34)	100% (*n*=10)	100% (*n*=31)
World Bank Classification of Primary Nationality: **Percentage** **(Frequency)**			
High income	76.4% (*n*=382)	84.8% (*n*=212)	76.5% (*n*=302)
Upper-middle income	16.6% (*n*=83)	10.8% (*n*=27)	16.7% (*n*=66)
Lower-middle income	6.4% (*n*=32)	4.4% (*n*=11)	6.8% (*n*=27)
Low income	0.6% (*n*=3)	--	--
Totals	100% (*n*=500)	100% (*n*=250)	100% (*n*=395)
World Bank Classification of Secondary Nationality: **Percentage** **(Frequency)**			
High income	85.3% (*n*=29)	80.0% (*n*=8)	87.1%(27)
Upper-middle income	11.8% (*n*=4)	10.0% (*n*=1)	9.7%(3)
Lower-middle income	2.9% (*n*=1)	10.0% (*n*=1)	3.2%(1)
Low income	--	--	--
Totals	100% (*n*=34)	100% (*n*=10)	100% (*n*=31)

79. The results shifted only slightly for arbitrators who were dual nationals. Those respondents were classified as coming from states within "very high human development"; the median HDI score was in the top seventeen most developed states, and the mean HDI score placed respondents in the top thirty-five most developed states.
80. Forty-eight respondents did not provide nationality information.

Variables	All	Arbitrators	Counsel
HDI Classification of Primary Nationality			
Mean	0.859	0.874	0.860
Minimum	0.434	0.471	0.471
1st quartile	0.816	0.875	0.816
2nd quartile (median)	0.909	0.909	0.909
3rd quartile	0.937	0.937	0.937
Maximum	0.955	0.938	0.938
Standard deviation	0.105	0.086	0.102
Total Respondents	500	250	395
HDI classification of Secondary Nationality			
Mean	0.868	0.842	0.870
Minimum	0.471	0.471	0.471
1st quartile	0.875	0.839	0.875
2nd quartile (median)	0.883	0.897	0.885
3rd quartile	0.924	0.920	0.937
Maximum	0.938	0.920	0.938
Standard deviation	0.094	0.142	0.095
Total Respondents	34	10	31

As discussed in Sect. II.3, and as with any survey research, it is possible that the data did not reflect the global international arbitration community. Nevertheless, the data set an important initial baseline about the predominance of men (Table 3), particular nationalities (Table 4) and developed-world actors (Table 5). The data may reflect potential "pipeline" problems of capacity in law generally and international arbitration specifically. While a full analysis of the origins of diversity challenges in international adjudication is beyond the scope of this Paper, we note that not all states have the same level of legal infrastructure; and the men and women of states with less-developed legal education systems might be less well represented in international arbitration.[81]

As international law courts and tribunals generally exhibit diversity challenges,[82] the lack of representation by women and developing-country respondents could reflect broader diversity challenges in international law. International law is a creature of state practice and those who use it. As parties often control the selection of lawyers and core

---

81. See GREENWOOD and BAKER, *op. cit.*, fn. 30, pp. 654, 657 (stating "the additional obstacles which an international arbitrator must overcome in order to succeed may penalize women disproportionately" and discussing how "office climate, difficulties in managing dual careers, lack of female role models and mentors, lack of flexible work options and attitudes to flexible working" can contribute to a "pipeline leak").
82. See Nienke GROSSMAN, "Sex on the Bench: Do Women Judges Matter to the Legitimacy of International Courts", 12 Chi. J. Int'l L. (2012) p. 647 (identifying the lack of women on international courts and tribunals).

aspects of arbitrator appointment, variance could be a by-product of private choice. Irrespective of causal factors, these initial findings require replication to assess their ongoing value and to explore changes in the international arbitration community over time.[83] Diversity challenges are addressed in Sect. IV.4.[84]

3. Representativeness of ICCA Respondents

Inferences drawn from descriptive data are only as strong as the representativeness of the sample from which the data derive. Although the limitations will be discussed further in Sect. V,[85] it is important to acknowledge that should the respondents completing the survey not reflect the larger international arbitration community, the value of the inferences from the research decreases. Precisely capturing the "international arbitration community" is challenging as the community changes when people enter and exit the profession, individuals continue to age, and the spheres and cores of the community are in relatively constant motion.[86]

Our working supposition was that ICCA is an important group in the international arbitration community. As such, the ICCA Congress – given that it occurs biennially and is a prestigious event – is a critical event that international arbitration specialists will attend. While inevitably people will not attend the Congress or the initial plenary due to personal constraints or work obligations, our practical assessment was that if registrants were able to attend the first ICCA Plenary, they did.[87] We anticipated (but cannot scientifically confirm) that those registered for ICCA and taking the survey were representative of the international arbitration community and international arbitrators.

Selection effects, however, may impact the results in several ways. First, as the conference was in Miami, it is possible that respondents from the United States and/or North America were over-represented; this generates the possibility that the data may be systematically skewed. Second, the converse is that there was an under-representation of arbitrators from non-North American states even though there is a high concentration of international arbitration there. For example, CIETAC arguably has the largest international arbitration caseload in the world;[88] yet there were relatively few attendees

---

83. Greenwood and Baker suggested that the problems of international arbitration are beyond simply having sufficient women in the pipeline. They first concede that even though there are fewer men entering law firms in the United Kingdom than women, more men are making it to the partner position. Yet, they observe that, the "best estimates of 5% of women appointed as arbitrators on international arbitration tribunals is just over half the 11% figure for female partners on international arbitration teams". GREENWOOD and BAKER, *op. cit.*, fn. 30, p. 658.

84. See also FRANCK, et al., fn. 35.

85. The limitations of case selection effects are also an orienting principle of FRANCK, et al., fn. 35.

86. See DEZALAY and GARTH, *op. cit.*, fn. 9, pp. 12, 28, 61, 117, 157, 242, 248, 296 (discussing certain cores in international arbitration and the intersection spheres of related spheres); see also ROGERS, *op. cit.*, fn. 9, p. 167 (discussing "cores" in the international arbitration community).

87. ICCA Congress organizers also confirmed that, historically, the first plenary session is the most well-attended ICCA session.

88. Chi MANJIAO, "Drinking Poison to Quench Thirst: The Discriminatory Arbitral Award Enforcement Regime Under Chinese Arbitration Law", 39 Hong Kong L.J. (2009) p. 54 at pp. 557-559; Alexander ZESCH, "CIETAC's New Rules: A View Through the Critics' Lens", 16 Vindobona J. Int'l Comm. L. & Arb. (2012) p. 283.

from China.[89] To address those twin concerns and evaluate the value of the baseline descriptive data, over time, as ICCA Congresses rotate among venues, the demographic data collection could be replicated. The forthcoming conferences in Mauritius and Sydney, for example, provide a unique opportunity to assess differences at geographical venues that are proximate to continents with the two largest populations on the planet and presumably need international arbitration services. Third, as the ICCA proceedings were conducted in English, it is possible that those whose mother tongue is not English (particularly arbitration specialists speaking Chinese, Spanish, Hindi, Arabic, Japanese and French[90] which are among the most prevalent languages on the planet) were also under-represented.[91] Finally, to the extent that ICCA is a relatively expensive conference – in terms of the conference fee,[92] flight, hotel, and lost opportunity cost of being away from work – it is possible that those who are economically disadvantaged but nevertheless part of the international arbitration community, were systematically underrepresented in the analyses.

While we acknowledge the risk, we nevertheless believe our data offer a respectable, solid and representative sample of the international arbitration community and international arbitrators. The view, rightly or wrongly, of the research team was that an ICCA Congress is the elite "must go" event of the international arbitration community.[93] The Congress has both a historical pedigree, the substantive content exploring transnational legal innovations in arbitration, the scarcity of its programming (i.e., only every other year), and its transnational approach makes it a uniquely valuable event.[94]

---

89. We observe that, even though the most recent ICCA Congress was in Singapore, there was a relatively small number of Asian participants at the ICCA Miami Congress. It is uncertain whether this reflects saturation of the Asian arbitration market, the geographical distance, the finances related to travel, or some other variable(s).

90. We note that Africa is the continent with the most French speakers in the world. French is the second most common language in Africa with approximately 120 million people speaking French. Christian VALANTIN, et al., *La Francophonie dans le monde* (Nathan 2006).

91. ICCA has recognized the need for greater linguistic options at its Congresses and has pledged to have simultaneous translation in French, English and Portuguese at its Mauritius Congress in 2016. Salim MOOLLAN, Invitation to ICCA Mauritius 2016 (9 April 2014) available at <http://bit.ly/1o0sML3> at 7:24-35 (last accessed 1 July 2014).

92. Recognizing the costs, for ICCA's Mauritius Congress in 2016, participants from Africa will receive a 50% discount in their conference fees. See *ibid.*, 7:16-22.

93. New entrants to the international arbitration marketplace may, however, not necessarily use ICCA as their first "gateway experience" to the larger international arbitration community. As they may be more likely to attend local, regional or international conferences – particularly if conducted in their native language and in a nearby location at low cost – it is possible that our sample under-represents newer or non-elite entrants. Analyzing the international arbitration elites at the ICCA Miami Congress was an initial effort to identify those experts who were easily observable; but this necessarily means that there are untapped aspects of the "invisible college" of international arbitration. We hope that this initial data collection process is expanded to account for other core groups within the international arbitration community to have a more complete picture of the international arbitration community.

94. ICCA started in 1961 as a close-knit gathering of international arbitration experts. It was and is a unique group, as ICCA is a non-governmental organization untethered to any group or state. See, generally, V.V. VEEDER, "Gala Dinner Speech", ICCA 50th Anniversary Speech (2011) available at <http://www.arbitration-icca.org/media/0/13087091952910/v.v._veeder_speach.pdf"

Assessing ICCA attendees therefore provides a unique opportunity for "one-stop-shopping" of data collection on international arbitration. This high value was, in large part, why we selected the ICCA Congress as the forum for our research. Moreover, given that other empirical research designed to systematically study judges and the judiciary used an identical strategy of providing surveys to domestic court judges, the scientific methodology is sound.[95]

During a visual confirmation conducted while walking through the Plenary Session, many international arbitrators (including arbitrators with multiple appointments) completed the questionnaire. While we will *not* reveal the individual identities given our undertakings of confidentiality to all respondents, we observed that many of the individuals completing the survey had conducted international arbitrations.[96] In addition, while our survey did not reach 100% of the population of known-ITA arbitrators, there were responses from sixty-seven ITA arbitrators, which represents a healthy proportion (27%) of the arbitrators identified in Franck's most current research on ITA awards.[97]

As a final matter, we observe the potential risks related to language. English is a *lingua franca* in many worldwide contexts — irrespective of whether international arbitration is involved,[98] but English has also become dominant for those pursuing careers in international arbitration.[99] As such, it is possible that a conference conducted entirely in

---

www.arbitration-icca.org/media/0/13087091952910/v.v._veeder_speech.pdf> (last accessed 30 June 2014).

95. See, e.g., Chris GUTHRIE, et al., "Inside the Judicial Mind", 86 Cornell L. Rev. (2001) p. 777; Chris GUTHRIE, et al., "Blinking on the Bench: How Judges Decide Cases", 93 Cornell L. Rev. (2007) p. 1; Chris GUTHRIE, et al., "The 'Hidden Judiciary': An Empirical Examination of Executive Branch Justice", 58 Duke L.J. (2009) p. 1477.

96. We note that of the 1017 ICCA registrants capable of participating in the survey, see *op. cit.*, fn. 33, there is publicly available documentation confirming that 496 of those registrants served as international arbitrators in the past. We also observe that this means, given the 262 respondents expressly identifying their service as arbitrators, at a minimum, our respondents reflected at least 52.8% of the arbitrators attending ICCA. Given conference fees and others costs mentioned above, it is possible that we only sampled affluent senior counsel; and the broader population of counsel in international arbitration may be meaningfully different.

97. FRANCK, *Myths and Realities, op. cit.*, fn. 29 (coding arbitrators who were on tribunals rendering public awards); see also PUIG, *op. cit.*, fn. 10, p. 18 (coding arbitrator appointments at ICSID from its inception, including both ICA and ITA cases, and identifying 419 different arbitrators receiving appointments).

98. See, e.g., Timothy LAU, "Offensive Use of Prior Art to Invalidate Patents in the US and Chinese Patent Litigation", 30 UCLA Pac. Basin L.J. (2013) p. 201 at p. 250 (observing that, despite China's scientific advances and publications, "the prior art is indisputably in English, the lingua franca of the scientific and technical communities"); Ayelet SHACHAR and Ran HIRSCHL, "Recruiting 'Super Talent': The New World of Selective Migration Regimes", 20 Ind. J. Global Legal Stud. (2013) p. 71 at p. 97 (noting that the Max Planck Society "has adopted English as the lingua franca").

99. Roger P. ALFORD, "The American Influence on International Arbitration", 19 Ohio St. J. Disp. Resol. (2003) p. 69 at p. 86 ("English has become the lingua franca of international arbitration. One prominent arbitrator, Jan Paulsson, recently noted that that '[t]en years ago, half my cases were in French and half in English. Now, it's ninety percent English.'"); Stephan W. SCHILL, "W(h)ither Fragmentation? On the Literature and Sociology of International Investment Law", 22 Eur. J. Int'l L. (2001) p. 875 at p. 887 ("As was the case with most investment treaty arbitrations,

59

English generates a selection effect such that those without English language skills, but actively engaged with international arbitration, were not in attendance. The risk is noteworthy as those conducting international arbitrations in other regions (i.e., South America, francophone Africa, or Asia) may share a common non-English language.

4.   Key Findings

The data unsurprisingly reflect that counsel and arbitrators were the primary ICCA attendees and presumably the core members of the "invisible college" of international arbitration. The standard number of appointments for counsel ranged from a mean of thirty to a median of fifteen. For those appointed as arbitrators, individuals on average obtained 35 appointments but had only a median of ten appointments; and ICA arbitrators experienced facially larger numbers of appointments than ITA arbitrators. Although samples from other studies might demonstrate differently, we were unable to isolate large numbers of public international law and national court judges in the dataset.

On a positive note, ICCA respondents were representative of arbitration specialists from many continents, nationalities, languages and legal training. This reflects ICCA's historical achievements in bridging the east/west divide. Yet, within that breadth, there were notable concentrations that tended to be dominant in terms of sheer size; and the data confirmed narratives regarding a lack of diversity in the field of international arbitration. Counsel and arbitrators were primarily from developed-world states, with a higher concentration of developed-world respondents in the subset of arbitrators. Likewise, counsel and arbitrators were predominantly male, with somewhat higher proportions of men in the subset of arbitrators. Meanwhile, we identified a statistically meaningful gender difference between men and women, such that male arbitrators were older and female arbitrators were younger. We explore whether the demographics of international arbitration generate diversity concerns in Sect. IV.4.

Ultimately, the demographic data offer important, yet preliminary, information about the practitioners and adjudicators of international dispute settlement. Rather than perpetuating an "invisible college",[100] this information aids the demystification of international arbitration and offers rigorously gathered data about the international arbitration community.

English became the lingua franca of international investment law.").

100. See SCHACHTER, op. cit., fn. 8 at p. 217 ("the professional community of international lawyers ... though dispersed throughout the world and engaged in diverse occupations ... [is] a kind of invisible college dedicated to a common intellectual enterprise".); see also Tom DANNENBAUM, "Nationality and the International Judge: The Nationalist Presumption Governing the International Judiciary and Why It Must Be Reversed", 45 Cornell Int'l L.J. (2012) p. 77 at pp. 129-131 (discussing the "invisible college" involved in international dispute settlement that begins from legal education and grows through transnational legal dialogues amongst law firms and other networks); Harlan G. COHEN, "Lawyers and Precedent", 46 Vand. J. Transnat'l L. (2013) p. 1025.

III.   ICCA THEMES: LEGITIMACY AS PRECISION

One critical aspect of legitimacy relates to its procedural precision. Procedural integrity is crucial, as psychological research demonstrates people are more likely to defer to decisions and rules – and perceive the institutions as legitimate – when they view adjudicators as having provided procedural justice.[101] Such procedural justice includes, for example, following one's own internal rules, providing clear guidance about applicable standards, listening actively to parties, treating parties respectfully, offering procedural quality, and access to adverse information.[102]

In an effort to understand how norms of procedural precision affect international arbitration, we asked a series of questions related to burden of proof, advance notice of costs allocation rules, document withholding, and advance preparation by tribunals. This Section addresses each of those issues and then synthesizes the results. While there were meaningful differences in how common and civil law lawyers regarded procedural integrity related issues of proof and costs, there are several areas of procedural precision that could be improved to enhance arbitral legitimacy.

1.   Burden of Proof

Burden of proof is critical to any legal system. Proof affects case outcomes when the evidence on the record is equivocal or scant.[103] Burden of proof distributes risk between the parties, and the burden identifies what adjudicators must do in the absence of evidence. Arbitral rules generally give tribunals discretion about how to manage issues of evidence but without providing express standards on burden of proof;[104] yet the

---

101. Tom R. TYLER, *Why People Obey the Law* (Princeton University Press 2006); Tom R. TYLER, et al., "Legitimacy and Criminal Justice: International Perspectives" in Tom R. TYLER, ed., *Legitimacy and International Criminal Justice: International Perspectives* (Russell Sage 2007) pp. 9-10.

102. James L. GIBSON, "Institutional Legitimacy, Procedural Justice and Political Tolerance", 23 Law & Soc'y Rev. (1989) p. 469; Jerald GREENBERG and Robert FOLGER, "Procedural Justice, Participation and the Fair Process Effect in Groups and Organizations" in P.B. PAULUS, ed., *Basic Group Processes* (Springer 1983) p. 235; Tom R. TYLER, "Social Justice: Outcome and Procedure", 35 Int'l J. of Psych. (2000) p. 117; Alexandra D. LAHAV, "Portraits of Resistance: Lawyer Responses to Unjust Proceedings", 57 UCLA L. Rev (2010) p. 725 at pp. 777-779; Kristina MURPHY, et al., "Nurturing Regulatory Compliance: Is Procedural Justice Effective When People Question the Legitimacy of Law?", 3 Regulation & Governance (2009) p. 1; Andrea K. SCHNEIDER, "Bargaining in the Shadow of (International Law): What the Normalization of Adjudication in International Governance Regimes Means for Dispute Resolution", 4 N.Y.U. J. Int'l L. & Pol'y (2009) p. 789 at pp. 821-822.

103. Martin F. GUSY, et al., *A Guide to the ICDR International Arbitration Rules* (Oxford University Press 2011) p. 189; see also Christoph SCHREUER, *et al.*, *The ICSID Convention. A Commentary*, 2nd ed. (Cambridge University Press 2009) pp. 669-670 (discussing issues related to burden of proof); Andreas REINER, "Burden and General Standard of Proof", 10 Arb. Int'l (1994) p. 328 at p. 331.

104. Whereas UNCITRAL and ICDR have express provisions dealing with issues of evidence, whereas other institutions provide less particularized guidance. Compare U.N. Comm'n Int'l Trade [UNCITRAL] Arbitration Rules (revised 2010) 20 Aug. 2010, Art. 27(1), available at <http://bit.ly/1l6ndra> (last accessed 30 June 2014) (henceforth 2010 UNCITRAL Rules); Convention on the Settlement of Investment Disputes between States and Nationals of Other

general practice is to require each party to prove the facts upon which it relies to establish its case.[105] Commentators stress the importance of the parties having advance notice about who bears the burden of proof with respect to the issues in the case.[106] Policy justifications for this sensible rule include considerations of fairness, procedural justice, due process, efficiency and cost effectiveness.[107]

Beyond those common denominators, there is no other universal theory or treatment of burden of proof. The legal concept of burden of proof differs between civil and common law jurisdictions in at least three ways. First, in the civil law tradition, burden of proof and proof allocation is a matter of substantive law; whereas in common law, the same concepts traditionally fall into the concept of procedural law.[108] Second, in civil law countries, the burden of proof has only one meaning and refers to the duty of each party to prove their claims. In contrast, common law systems divide burden of proof into different concepts, namely: (1) a "burden of going forward", (2) the burden of evidence, and (3) the "burden of persuasion".[109] Third, there is a difference in when proof is required. In civil law countries, the burden is "frontloaded", and claimants detail the facts and offer proof in the initial statement of a claim; but in common law countries, both the facts and the law may not be particularly detailed in the initiating phase.[110] Yet, international arbitration involves a mixture of actors from different legal traditions and backgrounds.[111] It is therefore constructive to understand how the international arbitration community understands burden of proof issues.

We therefore asked two critical questions related to tribunals' activities related to proof, namely advance articulation of burden of proof issues and whether those burdens were outcome determinative. First, we asked, "In your experience as arbitrator or

---

States, opened for signature 18 Mar. 1965, 17 U.S.T. 1270, 575 U.N.T.S. 160 (henceforth ICSID Convention) Art. 43; with Int'l Ctr. For Dispute Resolution, International Dispute Resolution Procedures, Art, 19(1) (2010) available at <http://bit.ly/1lsFU8S> (last accessed 30 June 2014) (henceforth ICDR Rules); LCIA, LCIA Arbitration Rules (2010) Art. 22.1(f), at <http://bit.ly/1r74cx3> (last accessed 30 June 2014) (henceforth LCIA Rules); ICC, 2012 Arbitration Rules (2010), Art. 25, App. IV <http://bit.ly/1staN3O> (last accessed 30 June 2014) (henceforth ICC Rules).

105. Alan REDFERN, "Practical Distinction Between the Burden of Proof and the Taking of Evidence – an English Perspective", 10 Int'l Arb. (1994) p. 317 at p. 321; George M. VON MEHREN and Claudia T. SALMON, "Submitting Evidence in an International Arbitration: The Common Lawyer's Guide", 20 J. Int'l Arb. (2003) p. 284 at p. 291.

106. Richard KREINDLER, "Practice and Procedure Regarding Proof: The Need for More Precision," this volume, p. 156 et seq.

107. Michelle T. GRANDO, *Evidence, Proof, and Fact-Finding in WTO Dispute Settlement* (Oxford University Press 2009) p. 151; Edward EVELEIGH, et. al., "The Standards and Burden of Proof in International Arbitration", 10 Int'l Arb. (1994) pp. 317 et seq.

108. Anne Vernonique SCHLAEPFER, "The Burden of Proof in International Arbitration", this volume, p. 127; see also Restatement (First) of Conflict of Laws (1934) §§ 594-595; Restatement (Second) of Conflict of Laws (1971) Sects. 133-135.

109. GRANDO, *op. cit.*, fn. 107, p. 74 et seq.

110. KREINDLER, *op. cit.*, fn. 106, p. 159.

111. See Sect. II.2.c. Common and civil lawyers can differ in how they anticipate dividing responsibilities between the parties and the courts. This likely affects expectations related to burden of proof.

counsel, how often do tribunals articulate in advance what burden of proof they will require parties to meet?" Second, we asked, "In your experience as arbitrator or counsel, how often has the burden of proof been outcome determinative?"[112] For both questions, respondents then ranked their experience on a 1-5 ordinal scale of frequency, where: 1=never, 2=occasionally, 3=sometimes, 4=frequently, and 5=always.

For the first question, for those ICCA respondents who had served either as arbitrators and/or arbitration counsel, respondents tended to believe that tribunals rarely articulated the burden of proof and generally tended to not offer outcome determinative guidance. The median and mode response was that tribunals "occasionally" articulated the burden of proof in advance.[113] Specifically, (1) 25.8% stated tribunals "never" articulated the burden (n=114); (2) 36.9% stated tribunals "occasionally" articulated the burden (n=163); (3) 27.4% stated tribunals "sometimes" articulated the burden (n=121); (4) 8.4% stated tribunals "frequently" articulated the burden in advance (n=37); and (5) 1.6% stated tribunals "always" articulated the burden (n=7).[114] The dark gray bar in Figure 1 identifies the frequency of responses for those who have been counsel and/or arbitrators to the question of whether tribunals provide advance articulation of burden of proof.

For the second question related to whether proof was outcome determinative, for those serving as either arbitrators and/or counsel, the results were nearly a mirror image of the responses to the previous question. The most common response was that burden of proof was "frequently" outcome determinative.[115] More particularly, (1) 7.9% stated burden of proof was "never" outcome determinative (n=35); (2) 20.9% stated burden of proof was "occasionally" outcome determinative (n=93); (3) 31.8% stated burden of proof was "sometimes" outcome determinative (n=141); (4) 34.9% stated burden of proof was "frequently" outcome determinative (n=155); and (5) 4.5% stated proof was "always" outcome determinative (n=20).[116] The light gray bar in Figure 1 identifies the frequency of responses for those who have been counsel and/or arbitrators to the question of whether burden of proof is outcome determinative.

---

112. See Annex: Survey Materials, this volume, pp. 121-122.

113. The mean was 2.23 (SD=.979; n=442) indicating respondents "occasionally" experienced tribunals articulating the burden of proof in advance.

114. Eight respondents who were arbitrators or counsel did not answer the question. For the group of all ICCA respondents, 492 responded with similar results: (1) 24.4% stated tribunals "Never" articulated the burden (n=120); (2) 36% stated tribunals "occasionally" articulated the burden (n=177); (3) 27.2% stated tribunals "sometimes" articulated the burden (n=134); (4) 10.8% stated tribunals "frequently" articulated the burden in advance (n=53); and (5) 1.6% stated tribunals "always" articulated the burden (n=8).

115. The median was also 3 and the mean was 3.07 (SD=1.025; n=444), suggesting burden of proof was "sometimes" outcome determinative.

116. Six respondents who were arbitrators or counsel did not answer the question. The mirror image pattern, with respondents believing proof was outcome determinative but not articulated in advance, was also present in the group of all ICCA respondents. For the 493 respondents answering the question, (1) 7.3% stated burden of proof was "never" outcome determinative (n=36); (2) 20.3% stated burden of proof was "occasionally" outcome determinative (n=100); (3) 31.4% stated burden of proof was "sometimes" outcome determinative (n=155); (4) 36.1% stated burden of proof was "frequently" outcome determinative (n=178); and (5) 4.9% stated proof was "always" outcome determinative (n=24).

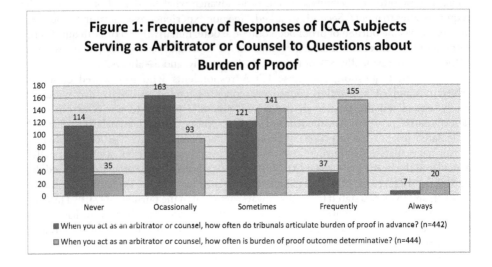

Figure 1: Frequency of Responses of ICCA Subjects Serving as Arbitrator or Counsel to Questions about Burden of Proof

■ When you act as an arbitrator or counsel, how often do tribunals articulate burden of proof in advance? (n=442)

▨ When you act as an arbitrator or counsel, how often is burden of proof outcome determinative? (n=444)

Overall, these two sets of results suggest an interesting contrast. Although respondents agreed proof issues were generally important, they also observed that tribunals did not generally articulate that burden in advance. Failure to articulate an outcome determinative burden in advance prevents parties from generating efficient and precise dispute resolution strategies and potentially generates a risk of party dissatisfaction. It also suggests that parties may wish to minimize this risk by requiring tribunals to provide advance articulation of proof issues. Meanwhile, the apparent disconnect between the importance of proof issues and lack of advance clarity generates a potentially constructive area for exploring how tribunals explain, address, and implement burdens of proof.

Despite efforts of the international law community to harmonize procedural traditions from common and civil law,[117] one might hypothesize that primary legal training might nevertheless anchor one's instinctive understanding of international proof issues. Given the different legal traditions, it is possible that variation in legal training generates divergent views on burden of proof questions. Analyses confirmed that there were statistically significant differences in survey responses depending upon a respondent's primary legal training.

Table 3 provides basic demographics about the legal training of respondents; yet Figure 1 reflects the composite responses for all arbitrators and counsel, irrespective of whether they have common and civil law legal training. The question remained, however, whether the answers of arbitrators and counsel varied meaningfully as a function of their legal education. To test whether responses on evidence issues were

---

117. International Bar Association Rules on the Taking of Evidence in International Arbitration (2010), available at <www.ibanet.org/ENews_Archive/IBA_30June_2010_Enews_Taking_of_Evidence_new_rules.aspx> (last accessed 30 June 2014) (henceforth IBA Rules).

meaningfully different, we used a one-way Analysis of Variance (ANOVA)[118] to isolate the effect of legal background. Our independent variable was therefore a three-category variable grouping respondents according to whether they were trained in common law, civil law, or both; the dependent variables were how respondents answered the proof questions using a 1-5 ordinal scale.

For the question related to whether tribunals indicated the burden of proof in advance, overall, there was a statistically significant relationship with legal training ($F(2,438)=5.060$; $p<.01$; $r=.15$; $n=441$).[119] Table 6 provides the mean responses for all respondents. The results suggest the overall effect was associated with different responses from common versus civil law lawyers; whereas those who were trained in both systems did not exhibit meaningful differences and tended to experience proof issues in international arbitration somewhere between the two poles exhibited by those with purely common law or civil law backgrounds.

Table 6: Mean Responses of ICCA Respondents Who Have Served as Arbitrators or Counsel to Question About Whether Tribunals Articulate Burdens of Proof in Advance

Legal Training	Mean Response	Standard Deviation	Total
Common Law	2.09	.911	202
Civil Law	2.44	.899	126
Both Common and Civil Law	2.23	1.134	113
Total	2.23	.979	441

---

118. In layman's terms, an independent samples *t*-test analyzes mean group differences in a continuous variable when there is one binary independent variable. That makes *t*-tests appropriate for a variable distinguishing between men and women. ANOVAs also analyze group differences in mean responses but explore differences in a variable with three or more categories. URDAN, *op. cit.*, fn. 53, pp. 53, 93-98, 105-113, 126-128. With statistics from a *t*-test (*t*-test statistic) or an ANOVA, using the sample size, degrees of freedom and degrees of freedom error, it is possible to calculate an *r*-statistic to identify the effect size of any group differences. See FRANCK, Development, *op. cit.*, fn. 11, pp. 457-458 (explaining effect sizes (*r*) and Cohen's conventions for understanding the relative size); Jacob COHEN, *Statistical Power Analyses for the Behavioral Sciences*, 2nd ed. (L. Erlbaum Associates 1988) at pp. 24-26, 115; see also URDAN, *op. cit.*, fn. 53, pp. 62, 68-71. The *r*-statistic reflects similar values to correlation coefficients calculated using Pearson's *r*.

119. Using a Kruskal-Wallis test to address the risk of a non-normal distribution across the three types of legal training likewise revealed a meaningful link between legal training and responses to advance articulation of proof ($X2=11.494$; $p<.01$; $r=.16$; $n=441$).

Follow-up analyses revealed that the facial trend in Table 6 was statistically significant. In other words, although respondents tended to identify that tribunals only "occasionally" (ranked "2") identified burden of proof in advance, lawyers with common law training were more likely to trend towards believing advance articulation occurred "occasionally" and bordered on "never". In contrast, civil lawyers tended to respond that tribunals "occasionally" articulated and bordering on "sometimes". Despite the statistically significant difference, the r-value bordered on the small-to-medium range, indicating that the meaningful difference was not large.

Although in theory there should be no difference since it is a factual question, perception did significantly vary, but not in a large scale. These results may reflect actual experience, namely that civil law lawyers had arbitral tribunals that actually articulated the burden in advance. The results may also reflect that civil law lawyers are used to addressing burden of proof independently and at the outset (without express specific guidance from the tribunal); as such, civil law lawyers may remember an "implicit" direction that may not have been either expressly stated by the tribunal or implicitly understood by all counsel involved. As such, civil law lawyers may be less focused on requiring direct guidance and precision from tribunals on proof matters.

Given earlier analyses, there was also a latent question as to whether the common/civil law divide also impacted how respondents viewed whether proof issues were outcome determinative. Since burden of proof is considered a matter of substantive law in civil law countries, the immediate importance to the outcome of the case may be more salient than in common law countries. An ANOVA explored the effect of legal background.

The results revealed, once again, that respondents with different legal training had different views as to whether proof questions were outcome determinative $(F(2,439)=10.281; p<.01; r=.21; n=442)$.[120] Table 7 provides the mean responses for all respondents to the question. The results suggest the overall effect was primarily attributable to differences in responses from common versus civil law lawyers; whereas those who were trained in both systems did not exhibit meaningful differences, but rather had experience somewhere between the two poles exhibited by the common law and civil law backgrounds.[121]

---

120. A Kruskal-Wallis test also revealed a meaningful link between the three types of legal training and responses to whether proof was outcome determinative $(X2=20.393; p<.01; r=.21; n=442)$.

121. Using a sensitive follow-up test (LSD), there was also a statistically significant difference whereas those trained in *both* common and civil law were less likely to believe than those trained wholly in civil law that proof issues were outcome determinative. The more conservative follow-up test (HSD) was non-significant $(p=.08)$.

Table 7: Mean Responses of ICCA Respondents Who Have Served as Arbitrators or Counsel to Question About Whether Burden of Proof Is Outcome Determinative Advance

Legal Training	Mean Response	Standard Deviation	Total
Common Law	2.86	1.082	201
Civil Law	3.38	.896	128
Both Common and Civil Law	3.10	.982	113
Total	3.07	1.027	442

These results suggest that civil law respondents believed more strongly that the burden of proof was outcome determinative in arbitration.

Further research is warranted to explore the issues related to proof. In spite of the divide of experience between common and civil lawyers about whether tribunals give parties advance guidance on burden of proof, all of those who had served as arbitrator or counsel generally found it lacking. Given that ICCA respondents who served as counsel and arbitrators also viewed proof issues as outcome determinative, it is reasonable to infer that there is a gap in precision of international arbitration. This, in turn, generates a problem with the legitimacy of how tribunals address burden of proof. The plea for more precision is therefore justified.

2.   Costs

Costs of adjudication are a subject of intense debate across dispute resolution systems. Costs implicate sensitive normative concerns about who should bear the risk of exposure to adjudication expenses and under which conditions, what is the appropriate legal basis and rationale for those assessments, and how costs affect the provision of and access to transnational justice. Costs have been described as a "hot issue" or "the sting in the tail".[122] This is perhaps unsurprising as arbitration costs can swell into millions of dollars, and even the *New York Times* has commented on the size of costs in international arbitration.[123]

---

122. Klaus REICHERT and James HOPE, "Costs – The Sting in the Tail", 1 Global Arb. Rev. (2006) p. 30; Chiara GEORGETTI, "Costs and their Apportionment in International Investment Arbitration", Int'l Disp. Resol. Q. (Fall 2009) p. 6; Sébastien MANCIAUX, *"Cirdi, Chronique des sentences arbitrales"*, 2012 J. Droit Int'l (2012) p. 265; Susan D. FRANCK, "Rationalizing Costs in Investment Treaty Arbitration", 88 Wash. U. L. Rev. (2012 p. 769 (henceforth Rationalizing Costs); John Y. GOTANDA, "Awarding Costs and Attorneys' Fees in International Commercial Arbitrations", 21 Mich. J. Int'l L. (1999) p. 1.

123. Elizabeth OLSON, "Growth in Global Disputes Brings Big Paychecks for Lawyers", *New York Times* (26 Aug. 2013) available at <http://dealbook.nytimes.com/2013/08/26/growth-in-global-disputes-brings-big-paychecks-for-law-firms/?_php=true&_type=blogs&smid=pl-share&_r=0> (last accessed 30 June 2014); see also FRANCK, *Myths and Relatiies, op. cit.*, fn. 29

Concerns implicate not merely fiscal exposure but also the ultimate liability for arbitration costs. National jurisdictions, however, have different normative baselines about whether (and how) costs should be shifted. Roughly speaking these approaches are: (1) complete cost shifting ("loser-pays"),[124] (2) no cost shifting ("pay-your-own-way"),[125] and (3) partial cost shifting derived from parties' relative success or other factors ("factor dependent").[126] Given international arbitration's transnational legal practice, one might reasonably conclude that – where millions of dollars of fiscal risk are involved – it might prove useful to manage potentially divergent party expectations on costs.

In an effort to manage these risks, several institutions have rules providing a degree of guidance about arbitration costs. UNCITRAL historically (and in its recent revisions)[127] provided costs guidance for international arbitration.[128] Even where rules provide initial baselines, they grant tribunals broad discretion to vary the rules' application. The question, therefore, is whether tribunals provide advance notice of whether they will adhere to (or vary) existing baselines and how tribunals will exercise that discretion.

Having a full appreciation of the potential economic risk aids parties and counsel in making strategically accurate risk assessments and decisions about the net value of international arbitration and specific procedural tactics. Existing empirical research in ITA indicates that tribunals rarely offer early guidance about cost assessments (for example at a jurisdictional phase or earlier);[129] and we are unaware of empirical evidence

---

(identifying that, on average, each party pays approximately US$5 million in legal fees); Susan D. FRANCK, "Using Investor-State Mediation Rules to Promote Conflict Management: An Introductory Guide", 29 ICSID Rev. (2014) p. 66 (same). Smaller ICA claims may, however, involve smaller arbitration costs; whereas large, complex ICA claims may be equivalent to or perhaps larger than ITA-related arbitration costs.

124. This is sometimes referred to as the "English" rule or the "costs-follow-the-event" rule. GOTANDA, op. cit., fn. 122; David P. REISENBERG, "Fee Shifting in Investor-State Arbitration: Doctrine and Policy Justifying Application of the English Rule", 60 Duke L.J. (2011) p. 977 at pp. 979, 989-990.

125. REISENBERG, op cit., fn. 124, pp. 989-990.

126. Some might combine categories one and three on the belief that these both reflect a "costs-follow-the-event" approach. See International Thunderbird Gaming Corp. v. Mexico, UNCITRAL, award (26 Jan. 2006) at 213, available at <www.italaw.com/sites/default/files/case-documents/ita0431.pdf> (last accessed 30 June 2014); Baiju S. VASANI and Anasttasiy UGALE, "Cost Allocation in Investment Arbitration: Back Toward Diversification", Columbia FDI Perspectives, No. 100 (29 July 2013) at <http://ccsi.columbia.edu/files/2014/01/FDI_100.pdf> (last accessed 30 June 2014). Doctrinally, the degree and basis of cost shifting is nuanced and deserves a thorough analysis.

127. 2010 UNCITRAL Arbitration Rules, op. cit., fn. 104, Art. 42(2).

128. See generally, UNCITRAL Arbitration Rules, G.A. Res. 31/98, arts. 38-41, U.N. GAOR, 31st Sess., Supp. No. 17, U.N. Doc. A/31/17 (15 Dec. 1976), at <http://bit.ly/Paq3vX> (last accessed 30 June 2014); 2010 UNCITRAL Rules, op. cit., fn. 104, Arts. 40-43; LCIA Rules, op. cit., fn. 104, Art. 28; ICC Rules, op. cit., fn. 104, International Chamber of Commerce, International Court of Arbitration Rules, Arts. 36-37; Stockholm Chamber of Commerce, Arbitration Rules (2007), Arts. 43-45, at <http://bit.ly/1cVU7t5> (last accessed 30 June 2014).

129. FRANCK, Rationalizing Costs, op. cit., fn. 122; see also FRANCK, Myths and Realities, op. cit., fn. 29.

identifying whether ICA exhibits similar challenges. We therefore explored respondents' experiences with tribunals' willingness to provide early articulation about how they anticipated exercising their cost-related discretion. Specifically, we asked, "In your experience as arbitrator or counsel, how often do tribunals indicate in advance how they will exercise their discretion to shift arbitration costs?"[130]

For those respondents who had served either as arbitrators and/or arbitration counsel, the responses tended to suggest that tribunals rarely articulated how they would articulate their cost shifting discretion. Respondents answered using a 1-5 ordinal scale. There was a tie for the most common response, where respondents said that tribunals either "never" or "occasionally" gave advance notice of how they would exercise their discretion to shift costs.[131] Table 8 provides the respondent answers.[132]

Table 8: Percentages and Frequency of Responses of ICCA Respondents Who Have Served as Arbitrators or Counsel to Question About Whether Tribunals Articulate in Advance How They Will Exercise Discretion on Costs

Answer	Response Percentage	Response Frequency
Never	33.2	147
Occasionally	33.2	147
Sometimes	23.0	102
Frequently	9.9	44
Always	0.7	3
Total	100.0	443

Much like the patterns related to the advance articulation of the burden of proof, the dominant trend was for respondents to experience tribunals either "never" or only "occasionally" identifying in advance how they would address cost shifting. Moreover, it was a rarity (slightly under 11%) for counsel and arbitrators to have tribunals "frequently" or "always" articulate an advance burden. These results supported Justice Menon's comments at the ICCA Singapore Congress in 2012 expressing concerns about the lack of a "coherent doctrine or approach to determining costs".[133] It would therefore

---

130. See Annex: Survey Materials, this volume, pp. 121-122.

131. The median was also "occasionally" (2), and the mean was 2.12 (SD=1.004; n=443).

132. Seven who were arbitrators or counsel did not answer the question. For the group of all ICCA respondents, 489 responded with somewhat similar results: (1) 31.5% stated tribunals "never" gave advance warning of how costs discretion would be exercised (n=154); (2) 33.1% stated "occasionally" (n=162); (3) 23.5% stated "sometimes" (n=115); (4) 10.8% stated "frequently" (n=53); and (5) 1% stated tribunals "always" gave advance notice of the exercise of costs discretion (n=5).

133. Sundaresh MENON, "International Arbitration: The Coming of a New Age for Asia (and Elsewhere)", Remarks Delivered at the ICCA Singapore 2012 Congress, para. 49 available at <www.arbitration-icca.org/media/0/13398435632250/ags_opening_speech_icca_

seem prudent for the international arbitration community to redress this so that parties (and counsel) have more advance warning about large fiscal components affecting decisionmaking.

Given the different jurisdictional traditions in cost shifting, it is an open question as to whether the experiences of arbitrators and counsel varied meaningfully as a function of their legal training. Given that most civil law jurisdictions follow the "loser-pays" model but prominent common law jurisdictions like the United States follow the "pay-your-own-way" model, this makes variation in experiences useful to identify. To test whether responses were meaningfully different, we used an ANOVA to isolate the effect of legal background. Our primary independent variable grouped respondents according to their common, civil, or mixed legal training; and the dependent variable was how respondents answered on the 1-5 scale.

Overall, there was a statistically significant relationship between legal training and respondents' experience with tribunal advance articulation of discretion for cost shifting ($F(2,438)=5.988$; $p<.01$; $r=.16$; $n=441$).[134] A t-test also revealed that whether or not the respondent was from the United States was linked with experience of advance articulation of cost shifting standards ($t(420)=2.016$; $p=.04$; $r=.10$; $n=422$). Although the effect was smaller than the overall results, US respondents less frequently experienced advance articulation of cost-shifting rules than non-US respondents. Table 9 provides the mean responses for all respondents to the question as a function of primary legal training.

Table 9: Mean Responses of ICCA Respondents Who Have Served as Arbitrators or Counsel to Question About Whether Tribunals Articulate in Advance How They Will Exercise Discretion on Costs

Legal Training	Mean Response	Standard Deviation	Total
Common Law	1.99	1.012	203
Civil Law	2.37	.971	128
Both Common and Civil Law	2.06	.984	111
Total	2.12	1.005	442

Follow-up analyses revealed that the facial trend in Table 9 was statistically significant. Although the respondents tended to experience tribunals only "occasionally" (ranked "2") addressing costs discretion in advance, lawyers with common law training were more likely to trend towards believing advance articulation occurred "occasionally" and bordered on "never" as compared to civil law lawyers. Similarly, even lawyers with *both* common and civil law training were more likely to have experienced relatively fewer

---

congress_2012.pdf> (last accessed 1 July 2014).

134. Non-parametric tests were unnecessary as the skewing of responses for experience of tribunals' advance articulation of cost was within acceptable levels (0.416; SE=0.110).

advance articulations as compared to lawyers with only civil law training. Despite the significant difference, the r-value bordered on the small-to-medium range, indicating that while there was a meaningful difference, the difference was not necessarily large.[135]

In any event, the analyses suggest that it is reasonable to conclude that there is a gap in precision of international arbitration for cost matters. This, in turn, generates a problem with the legitimacy of when and how tribunals address cost issues. The international arbitration community may therefore wish to explore ways to encourage greater precision for cost-related matters. Perhaps the most straightforward way is, for parties concerned about advance notice for cost-shifting, to draft those obligations directly into the arbitration agreement.

3. Withholding of Documents

Document disclosure in international arbitration poses a dilemma. On one hand "document production can be extremely useful to the parties and arbitrators" for the purposes of fact-finding, but on the other hand "document production is inherently subject to tactical abuse".[136] Even in the complete absence of tactical abuse, document production can be especially contentious between lawyers from different legal traditions where document production is either a frequent or a rare occurrence. Document disclosure is intended "to avoid unfair surprise at … [a] hearing and to discover the facts and get to the truth in order to create the record necessary for a just result".[137] Yet disclosure generates tension with other international arbitration values, including parties' desire for neutral procedural rules and the economical and expeditious resolution of disputes.

Regardless of the legal, practical and theoretical tensions, document production in international arbitration practice has become increasingly common. Gary Born explains, "[t]here is an emerging consensus among experienced arbitrators and practitioners that a measure of document disclosure is desirable in most international disputes".[138] Indeed, "[m]ost institutional rules provide arbitrators, in languages of varying degrees of clarity, with express authority to order discovery or disclosure by the parties [and] arbitral tribunals [have] consistently concluded that they have the authority to order disclosure from the parties to an arbitration".[139] Empirical data buttress this perception. The 2012 White & Case/Queen Mary University study identified that 62% of respondents stated that more than half of their arbitrations involved requests for document disclosure (although this answer was more typical of lawyers from a common law tradition).[140] Moreover, 59% responded, "that documents obtained through document production

---

135. For the ANOVA involving US and non-US respondents, the r-value was barely in the statistically small range.

136. James H. CARTER, "Five Fundamental Things about Document Production, and a Question" in *International Arbitration 2006: Back to Basics?*, ICCA Congress Series no. 13 (2008) (henceforth *ICCA Congress Series no. 13*) p. 592.

137. Robert H. SMIT and Tyler ROBINSON, "E-Disclosure in International Arbitration", 24 Arb. Int'l (2008) p. 105 at p. 126.

138. Gary B. BORN, *International Commercial Arbitration,* 2nd ed. (Wolters Kluwer 2014) at p. 2345.

139. *Ibid.*, p. 2336.

140. White & Case/Queen Mary Survey, *op. cit.*, fn. 11, p. 20.

materially affected the outcome of at least one-quarter of their arbitrations".[141] Document production is therefore a frequent and material part of international arbitral practice.

With the growth of document production in international arbitration has come the development of substantive legal standards to govern its use. Perhaps the most familiar to users are the International Bar Association's Rules on the Taking of Evidence in International Arbitration (2010) (IBA Rules),[142] which limits parties' request for production to a specific document or a narrow and specific category of documents that are both relevant and material to the outcome of a dispute.[143]

Yet even with governing standards, the fear of tactical misconduct related to document production looms large. Practitioners raise the specter of "guerrilla tactics" and the abuse of document production. "Guerilla tactics" involve "a range of behaviors and may include: late submission of evidence; expansive requests for document disclosure; [and] failure to produce documents, or to do so reasonably timely".[144] The IBA Rules have explicit sanctions for such misbehavior by a party[145] and the recently issued IBA Guidelines on Party Representation on International Arbitration (2013) (IBA Guidelines) now provide guidance to counsel on these matters as well.[146] Yet the concern over these tactics may not be unanimous. One prominent commentator stated that the IBA Guidelines only address "what in reality appears only as a marginal problem".[147] Whether the concern for procedural abuse is a myth or reality makes the issue ripe for empirical assessment.

To explore one type of procedural abuse, we asked a question related to document production. Specifically we asked, "[i]n your experience as arbitrator or counsel, how often have you believed one or both parties have withheld responsive documents?"[148] Respondents ranked their experiences on a 1-5 ordinal scale. Table 10 provides the distribution in responses.[149]

---

141. *Ibid.*

142. IBA Rules, *op. cit.*, fn. 117. The White & Case/Queen Mary survey noted that 53% of arbitrations used the IBA Rules as guidelines and 85% of survey participants responded that they found the IBA Rules useful. White & Case/Queen Mary Survey, *op. cit.*, fn. 11, p. 2.

143. IBA Rules, *op. cit.*, fn. 117, Art. 3(3); see also ICC Commission Report: Managing E-Document Production, para. 1.5 (2012) at <www.iccwbo.org/Advocacy-Codes-and-Rules/Document-centre/2012/ICC-Arbitration-Commission-Report-on-Managing-E-Document-Production/> (last accessed 30 June 2014) (noting there "is no automatic right to the production of documentary evidence in the possession or control of another party" in international arbitration).

144. R. Doak BISHOP and Magrete STEVENS, "Safeguarding the Fair Conduct of Proceedings – Report" in *International Arbitration: The Coming of a New Age*, ICCA Congress Series no. 17 (2013) p. 486.

145. IBA Rules, *op. cit.*, fn. 117, Arts. 9(5), (6), (7).

146. International Bar Association Guidelines on Party Representation in International Arbitration (2013), Guidelines 12-17, at <www.ibanet.org/LPD/Dispute_Resolution_Section/Arbitration/Default.aspx> (last accessed 30 June 2014).

147. Michael E. SCHNEIDER, "President's Message: Yet Another Opportunity to Waste Time and Money on Procedural Skirmishes: The IBA Guidelines on Party Representation", 31 ASA Bulletin (2013) p. 496.

148. See Annex: Survey Materials, this volume, pp. 121-122.

149. Six respondents failed to answer this question.

Table 10: Percentages and Frequency of Responses of ICCA Respondents Who Have Served as Arbitrators or Counsel to Question About Whether Parties Have Withheld Responsive Documents

Answer	Response Percentage	Response Frequency
Never	1.6	7
Occasionally	24.5	109
Sometimes	40.5	180
Frequently	30.6	136
Always	2.7	12
Total	100.0	444

Table 10 demonstrates the most common response to questions about document withholding was "sometimes".[150] Yet it also shows that 73% of respondents who had served as counsel and/or arbitrators believed withholding of responsive documents occurs either "sometimes" or more often, with 33.5% of respondents stating that the practice occurs "frequently" or "always". Given that document production may be an infrequent practice in many jurisdictions, we also queried whether a difference in legal training might result in different results to this question. Unlike responses related to burden of proof and cost issues, the 442 respondents analyzed did not permit us to identify a meaningful difference in responses to the question of document withholding as a function of respondents' legal training in common law, civil law or a combination thereof.[151]

Nearly seventy percent of sampled subjects believed that document withholding was occurring at least "sometimes" or "frequently" in international arbitration. The data reflect a meaningful concern about procedural impropriety in document disclosure by parties and counsel. This concern occurs despite the sanctions that arbitral tribunals can use to curb procedural misconduct. For example, the IBA Rules provide for costs sanctions for the failure to produce relevant documents,[152] a sanction enjoying broad support in the arbitration community.[153] The IBA Rules further provide that the failure to produce documentary evidence can lead an arbitral tribunal to draw adverse

---

150. The median was also "sometimes" (3), and the mean was 3.08 (SD=.847; $n=444$).

151. An ANOVA failed to reveal a meaningful difference ($F(2,439)=0.333$; $p=.72$; $r=.04$; $n=442$), and all follow-up comparisons were non-significant. Using a Kruskal-Wallis test to address the risk of a non-normal distribution across the three types of legal training also failed to reveal a statistically meaningful link between legal training and responses to withholding of documents ($X2=0.566$; $p=.75$; $r=.04$; $n=442$). Although we cannot rule out the possibility of a meaningful relationship as the sample was underpowered and exhibited an unacceptable probability of a Type II error, we note that any latent effect size was less than statistically small ($r<.10$) and *a priori* power analysis indicates need at least 1172 subjects in future to reliably rule out effect. Future research is therefore necessary before reaching a definitive conclusion about the lack of a meaningful relationship.

152. IBA Rules, *op. cit.*, fn. 117, Art. 9(7).

153. White & Case/Queen Mary Survey, *op. cit.*, fn. 11, pp. 5, 41.

inferences against a party who fails to produce a given document; however, the use of adverse inferences may be limited in practice.[154] The White & Case/Queen Mary study noted that tribunals have explicitly drawn adverse inferences only in a limited number of cases,[155] which suggests tribunal reluctance to take stringent measures against parties or perhaps the difficulty of crafting properly drawn adverse inferences (the latter also being an issue of precision). If tribunals are reluctant to take stiff measures against parties for withholding documents, it would seem unlikely for tribunals to admonish counsel, who often control arbitrator appointments, for the same behavior under the IBA Guidelines. Yet the data reflect, in our view, that the use of some form of sanction to ensure compliance with document production orders is necessary to guard the procedural integrity of an international arbitration.[156]

Perhaps the best remedy for document disclosure abuse is prevention. Parties should carefully structure document disclosure processes from the outset of arbitration – or require the tribunal to keep and fix firm guidelines – to reduce the risk of misconduct.[157] Such procedures signal a desire for active management and policing of document production procedures and also redress potential procedural deficiencies in arbitration. In turn, stronger case management and procedural control could reduce the perception of misconduct highlighted by our data and thereby minimize concerns related to the legitimacy of international arbitration.

4. Arbitrator Preparation for Hearings

At ICCA's Montreal Congress in 2006, Laurent Lévy and Lucy Reed described "[e]videntiary hearings [as] a most onerous part of arbitration, measured by time and expense".[158] Although writing from the perspective of arbitrators, their statement also holds true for parties. As a practical matter, sophisticated firms representing complex commercial and investment treaty cases engage in extensive mock hearings to prepare for real hearings. Given the substantial fiscal and temporal investment of their own preparation, parties rightfully expect their arbitrators to be fully prepared for hearings as well. Since arbitration also requires parties to pay non-trivial fees to arbitrators for

---

154. IBA Rules, *op. cit.*, fn. 117, Art. 9(5).
155. White & Case/Queen Mary Survey, *op. cit.*, fn. 11, p. 21; see also BORN, *op. cit.*, fn. 138, p. 2367 (noting "the only sanction for destruction of relevant evidence being the drawing of (often weak) adverse inferences").
156. While others might respectfully disagree with this view, the community as a whole may benefit from a considered debate on this topic. We nevertheless observe that the literature from Gary Born and Queen Mary demonstrate: (1) the arbitration community broadly supports costs as a sanction for document production abuse; (2) adverse inferences are often weak in practice; and (3) tribunals rarely use adverse inferences.
   So how does one reduce document production abuse? We give two ways, stricter sanction and more active document production management.
157. BISHOP and STEVENS, *op. cit.*, fn. 144, p. 486; ICC Commission Report: Managing E-Document Production, *op. cit.*, fn. 143, para. 51.
158. Laurent LÉVY and Lucy REED, "Managing Fact Evidence in International Arbitration" in *ICCA Congress Series no. 13* at p. 635; see also ICC Commission Report, "Controlling Time and Costs in Arbitration", para. 69 (2012) at <http://bit.ly/V3nUNe> (last accessed 30 June 2014) ("Hearings are expensive and time-consuming").

their arbitration services, arbitrators have legal duties (whether based in tort or contract) to provide parties devoted and expert attention.[159]

The benefits of a fully prepared arbitral panel at an evidentiary hearing are myriad. A fully prepared arbitral tribunal can manage hearings more efficiently, recognize important issues in a case more clearly and perhaps render their awards more efficiently.[160] A number of ideas have been advanced to improve an arbitrator's preparation prior to a hearing from checklists[161] to pre-hearing retreats.[162] Given preparation's intrinsic link to the theme of arbitral "precision," we explored how ICCA respondents viewed the preparation of their fellow arbitrators or the arbitrators before whom they appeared. Specifically, we asked, "In your experience as arbitrator or counsel, how often are all members of the tribunal fully prepared for a hearing?" Respondents could answer on an ordinal scale of 1-5 with 1 representing "never" and 5 representing "always".[163] The results focusing on the responses of those indicating they had served as either an arbitrator or as counsel are presented in Table 11.

159. John E. BEERBOWER, "International Arbitration: Can We Realise the Potential?", 27 Arb. Int'l (2011) p. 75 (describing the additional overhead costs of international arbitration); Susan D. FRANCK, "The Liability of International Arbitrators: A Comparative Analysis and Proposal for Qualified Immunity", 20 N.Y.L.S. J. Int'l & Comp. L. (2000) p. 1 at pp. 3-11 (describing the bases of arbitrator duties under contract and tort theory).

160. For example, David Rivkin has proposed a model of international arbitrators as "town elders" who manage and resolve disputes for parties accurately, fairly and expeditiously. In order to fulfill that role effectively, he states that "arbitrators must be more proactive and willing to assume control. *They must learn as much as they can about the case at an early stage.*" David W. RIVKIN, "Towards a New Paradigm in International Arbitration: The Town Elder Model Revisited", 24 Arb. Int'l (2008) p. 375 at p. 384 (emphasis added).

161. Michael J. MOSER, "The 'Pre-Hearing Checklist' – A Technique for Enhancing Efficiency in International Arbitral Proceedings", 30 J. of Int'l Arb. (2013) p. 155. A variety of other professional contexts (physicians, pilots, etc.) also recognize the value in generating simple checklists to reduce the probability of error and increase the likelihood of positive outcomes. Atul GAWANDE, *The Checklist Manifesto: How to Get Things Right* (Metropolitan Books 2009).

162. Lucy REED, "Arbitral Decision-Making: Art, Science or Sport?", 30 J. of Int'l Arb. (2013) p. 85 at pp. 94-95.

163. See Annex: Survey Materials, this volume, pp. 121-122.

Table 11: Percentages and Frequency of Responses of ICCA Respondents Who Had Experience as Arbitrator or Counsel to Question Regarding Full Preparation of Arbitrators for a Hearing

Answer	Response Percentage	Response Frequency
Never	1.1	5
Occasionally	14.8	66
Sometimes	31.9	142
Frequently	47.0	209
Always	5.2	23
Total	100.0	445

Table 11 reflects that both the median and the mode response was, for those with experience as counsel or arbitrators, to believe that all members of the tribunal were "frequently" fully prepared.[164] Specifically, a majority of ICCA respondents who were arbitrators or counsel (52.2%) stated that, in their experience, all members of arbitral tribunals were either "frequently" or "always" fully prepared for hearings. The mean answer was also 3.4 (SD=.84; n=445) reflecting that a more ordinal measure indicated full tribunal preparation was typical (bordering between "sometimes" and "frequently"); the data reflected that it was an outlier case for all members of the tribunal to be unprepared. Respondents were, therefore, generally positive in their views about levels of arbitrator preparation.[165]

Yet, given the expense and expectation of parties, one surmises that all members of arbitral tribunals ought to be fully prepared for their hearings on a frequent basis and that such a response, in an ideal world, would serve as a baseline and not as an achievement. Although not a majority view, the fact that 47.8% of qualifying respondents found that members of arbitral tribunals were only "sometimes" or less frequently fully prepared

---

164. For the subset of those who only acted as counsel and who never served as an arbitrator, the pattern of results was roughly equivalent. Namely 1.6% responded "never" (n=3), 20.8% responded "occasionally" (n=38), 30.1% responded "sometimes" (n=55), 42.6% responded "frequently" (n=78), and 4.9% (n=183) responded that members of the tribunal were "always" fully prepared.

165. Unlike responses related to burden of proof and cost issues, we were unable to identify a reliable difference in responses related to full tribunal preparation based upon respondents' legal training in common law, civil law or a combination thereof. An ANOVA failed to reveal a meaningful difference (F(2,440)=0.349; p=.71; r=.04; n=443), and all follow-up comparisons were non-significant. Using a Kruskal-Wallis test to address the risk of a non-normal distribution across the three types of legal training also failed to reveal a statistically meaningful link between legal training and responses to withholding of documents ($X2$=0.686; p=.71; r=.04; n=443). Although we cannot rule out the possibility of a meaningful link as the sample was underpowered and exhibited an unacceptable probability of a Type II error, any latent effect size was less than statistically small (r<.10) and *a priori* power analysis indicates a need for at least 1172 subjects in the future to reliably rule out effect. Future research is therefore necessary before reaching a definitive conclusion about the lack of a reliable effect.

for hearings signifies a potential source of discontent about arbitrator preparation despite respondents' generally positive responses.

Given its direct nature on a sensitive subject, it is possible that the question itself generated a self-serving bias where respondents answered more positively than their actual contemporaneous experiences might reflect.[166] Nevertheless, to the extent that the large constituents of arbitration counsel wanted to use the question to voice their displeasure with the lack of preparation by arbitrators in a confidential manner, this may negate response bias. In any event, the results offer an intriguing baseline for future research into the satisfaction of service providers and users within the international arbitration community.

5. *Key Findings*

The data reflected that, should the international arbitration community wish to continue to improve its legitimacy, there are several opportunities to enhance procedures and precision. Two areas – burden of proof and costs – could benefit from the international arbitration community or tribunals themselves providing clearer guidance.

On issues of proof, it was noteworthy that, although arbitrators and counsel reflected that tribunals were most likely to *not* provide advance notice of the burden of proof, arbitrators and counsel were more likely to view proof as outcome determinative. The disjunction between those two questions suggests that a degree of enhanced precision – perhaps by placing proof issues on a checklist tribunals use to give parties' early notice of procedures – would minimize the gap and also provide greater clarity. Focus on this issue may also either encourage tribunals to take initiative in encouraging earlier discussions about proof matters or that counsel may advocate addressing proof-related matters at an early phase.

On issues of cost, there was also a lack of advance notice on how tribunals would exercise their discretion on costs, with 66% of counsel and arbitrators saying that tribunals either "never" or only "occasionally" provided advance notice on costs; and the rarity (barely 10%) was for tribunals to "frequently" or "always" provide advance notice on costs. This may reflect a lack of precision or an underlying difficulty for tribunals in providing that advance notice themselves.[167]

A nuanced approach may be required when developing appropriate normative solutions on these two issues. Subtlety in addressing certain procedural matters is prudent, as responses were meaningfully different on matters related to burden of proof and cost questions; and responses varied depending upon whether a respondent was trained exclusively in common law or exclusively in civil law. For questions of procedure, common law lawyers were less likely to experience tribunal's advance articulation of burden of proof than their civil law colleagues; but common law lawyers were also less likely to say burden of proof was outcome determinative. Generating awareness of latent variations related to proof could also generate efficiencies. Given the reliable differences, arbitrators could strategically target burden of proof to understand

---

166. Fn. 220 also discusses self-serving biases and cognitive blind spots.
167. An early articulation of standards that tribunals will use in the exercise of discretion offers useful precision and prevents unfair surprise about ultimate liability for costs.

why and when guidance is necessary, and counsel may also better appreciate the expectations of the other side. On questions of costs, common law lawyers generally (and also US lawyers in some instances) were less likely to experience tribunals providing an advance articulation of how costs discretion would be exercised. While those group differences were relatively small, it does suggest that procedural reforms may require a degree of negotiation. In any event, should institutions not take an initiative to encourage tribunals to use a checklist or otherwise provide parties with guidance on key procedural issues, parties may wish to explore altering their arbitration agreements to require tribunals to provide parties with advance notice of applicable standards.

One other area raises procedural concerns. On issues of document production, approximately 70% of respondents identified that parties "sometimes" or "frequently" withhold documents. It is troubling for parties not to provide those documents for which there is a legal obligation to do so, as it both generates a risk of imprecision and inhibits accurate delivery of justice. Tribunals may therefore wish to become more proactive in their response to document production challenges so as to ensure, at the macro level, that arbitration is not viewed as a dispute resolution process where parties can skirt justice or hide relevant materials.

An area for cautious optimism, however, was the full preparation of tribunals. Nearly 79% of counsel and arbitrators indicated that tribunals were either "sometimes" or "frequently" fully prepared for hearings. It was rare for respondents to identify that tribunals were either "never" prepared or "occasionally" prepared. While Sect. 3.4 identified the possibility of skewed responses to this question, the results offer an intriguing baseline for future research into the internal satisfaction of service providers in international arbitration.

Nevertheless, the data reflect that there are at least three different subject areas within international arbitration – proof, costs, and document production – which could benefit from enhanced precision. By focusing on ways to generate that precision, those efforts stand to enhance the legitimacy of international arbitration as well as enhance its attractiveness to future users.

IV.   ICCA THEMES: LEGITIMACY AS JUSTICE

Legitimacy also relates to themes of substantive justice.

In an effort to understand how justice-related themes affect the legitimacy of international arbitration, we asked questions about the prestige of arbitration, the re-appointment of arbitrators and interaction with co-arbitrators, fraud, and diversity. This Section addresses each of those issues in turn. Overall, the data suggest that ICCA respondents identified areas of international arbitration where the arbitration community may wish to strategically address justice-related concerns to enhance legitimacy.

1.   Prestige of International Arbitration

Acting as an international arbitrator can be both prestigious and financially lucrative. Yet there has been little study of how pecuniary and non-pecuniary factors influence individuals to seek and obtain arbitral appointments.[168] While the literature on what motivates adjudicators is comparatively robust,[169] the literature is divided over whether individuals pursuing arbitration appointments are motivated by material gains, their personal prestige, or the pursuit of good policy and justice.[170]

There is undoubtedly a fiscal incentive to serve as an arbitrator and receive remuneration. In the context of ITA, historical data indicated tribunal and institutional costs were in order of US$600,000;[171] and tribunal costs in ICA cases can also be substantial.[172] As many respondents indicated that they served both as arbitrators and counsel,[173] their livelihoods were not exclusively dependent upon arbitration appointments.[174] Acting as counsel in an international arbitration may actually be more financially lucrative than acting as arbitrator. Non-pecuniary factors are therefore critical incentives.

One of the non-pecuniary factors that may lead arbitrators to seek appointments is prestige.[175] In the early 1990s, Judge Richard Posner of the United States Court of Appeals for the Seventh Circuit speculated that US federal judges, who are granted life tenure and whose salary cannot be diminished while in office, are motivated, in part, due

---

168. Some of the closest scholarship comes from Sergio Puig analyzing network effects of international arbitrators. PUIG, *op. cit.*, fn. 10. We also observe that re-appointment and positive interaction with one's colleagues are methods to generate prestige, gain goodwill, enhance one's reputation, and ultimately produce income. These issues will be addressed in the next Sub-section.

169. See, e.g., David E. KLEIN and Gregory MITCHELL, *The Psychology of Judicial Decision Making* (Oxford University Press 2010) pp. 4-14; Richard A. POSNER, *How Judges Think* (Harvard University Press 2008) (henceforth *How Judges Think*) p. 31 et seq.

170. See, e.g., Joshua KARTON, *The Culture of International Arbitration and the Evolution of Contract Law* (Oxford University Press 2013); Stavros BREKOULAKIS, "Systemic Bias and the Institution of International Arbitration: A New Approach to Arbitral Decision-Making", 4 J. Int'l Dispute Settlement (2013) p. 553. Compare Thomas J. STIPANOWICH, "Arbitration and the Multiparty Dispute: The Search for Workable Solutions", 72 Iowa L. Rev. (1987) p. 473 at p. 513 n. 220 ("While one would hope that arbitrators are primarily motivated by the desire to perform a service for the industry or the community and not by the need to generate an alternative source of income, there may be legitimate concerns regarding the ability of one or more arbitrators to address ... issue[s] free of self-interest.") with Alan REDFERN, "Opinions in International Commercial Arbitration: The Good, the Bad and the Ugly", 20 Arb. Int'l (2004) p. 223 at p. 224 ("Arbitrators in international arbitrations are expected to behave like judges, in the sense that they are expected to be impartial and independent of the parties").

171. FRANCK, Rationalizing Costs, *op. cit.*, fn. 122; see also FRANCK, *op. cit.*, fn. 123 (identifying average tribunal-related costs and expenses).

172. Louis FLANNERY and Benjamin GAREL, "Arbitration costs compared: the sequel", Global Arb. Rev. (15 Jan. 2013) at <http://globalarbitrationreview.com/news/article/31092/arbitration-costs-compared-sequel> (last accessed 1 July 2014) (exploring arbitration costs at a variety of international arbitration institutions).

173. Out of all 548 ICCA respondents, 225 respondents had experience as both counsel and international arbitrator.

174. Counsel practicing in large multinational law firms may experience disincentives in seeking appointments. Depending upon the applicable law, conflict of interest rules within a firm may prevent counsel from accepting arbitral appointments.

175. SCHULTZ and KOVACS, *op. cit.*, fn. 9, p. 162 (noting that "symbolic wealth" includes "prestige").

to prestige. Judge Posner asserted that "[t]he thirst for prestige [among US judges] is manifested primarily in opposition to any large increase in the number of judges, at least high-level judges, and to extending the title 'judge' to lower-level judicial personnel...".[176] Judge Posner surmises that judges maximize prestige by limiting the size of the federal judiciary. If prestige is a valuable commodity, presumably the difficulty in obtaining the position makes it more valuable; and those with access to the commodity have an incentive to keep it scarce.

For US judges, Judge Posner noted that, "there is little an individual judge can do to enhance his prestige as a judge".[177] The same is not necessarily true for an international arbitrator. Arbitrators can enhance prestige by both the number of appointments they take, the types of cases they arbitrate, and their role within a tribunal. One can hypothesize that international arbitrators not only compete with other arbitrators for monetary gain but also for other non-monetary goods like prestige and reputation.[178] Commentators observe that international arbitral appointments "are perceived as desirable personal benefits";[179] and others opine that appointments to ITA cases have particular "prestige and glamour".[180] Parties may also use perceived prestige as a proxy for influence and the desirability of appointing an individual to an arbitral tribunal,[181] so the loop becomes self-reinforcing.

Our survey was a first foray in evaluating the non-pecuniary factors that may motivate international arbitrators. As we hypothesized, that prestige might vary according to context, we asked multiple questions about arbitral prestige. We provided alternative frames that differentiated between ICA and ITA. The first question was: "How prestigious is it to have an appointment in *international commercial arbitration?*" The second related question was: "How prestigious is it to have an appointment in *investment treaty arbitration?*"[182] Respondents answered using a 1-5 ordinal scale with 1 representing "not prestigious" and 5 representing "very prestigious".

---

176. Richard A. POSNER, "What Do Judges and Justices Maximize? (The Same Thing Everybody Else Does)", 3 Sup. Ct. Econ. Rev. (1993) p. 1 at p. 13.

177. *Ibid.*, p. 14.

178. See Richard POSNER, "What Do Arbitrators Maximize?" in Peter NOBEL, et al., eds., *Law and Economics of International Arbitration, Series in Law and Economics, Fifth International Conference on Law and Economics at the University of St. Gallen* (Schulthess Verlag 2014) (henceforth What do Arbitrators Maximize?) p. 123 ("My conception of people including judges and arbitrators is that, in economic terms, everybody has a utility function. You have preferences and constraints and these will guide and influence your positions. I think there are no fundamental differences between judges, arbitrators, workers and politicians. They (or better we) all are self-interested, and I mean that not in any bad sense. It's human nature to think about one's life and an adequate income, to do a good job and to pursue, to a certain extent, also personal interests.").

179. BEERBOWER, *op. cit.*, fn. 159, p. 79.

180. Hans VAN HOUTTE and Maurizio BRUNETTI, "Investment Arbitration – Ten Areas of Caution for Commercial Arbitrators", 29 Arb. Int'l (2013) p. 553 at p. 554.

181. BEERBOWER, *op. cit.*, fn. 159, p. 78 ("[P]arties want only the most experienced arbitrators").

182. See Annex: Survey Materials, this volume, pp. 121-122 (emphasis in original). We are aware that issues of prestige and influence are complex. Future research should explore those concepts using refined methodological tools. In the interim, we seek to simplify these issues for the sake of tractability and generating information for preliminary dialogue.

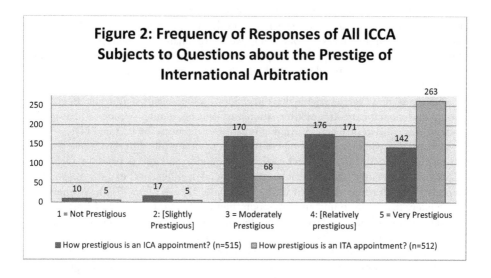

Figure 2: Frequency of Responses of All ICCA Subjects to Questions about the Prestige of International Arbitration

For both ICA and ITA, respondents did not indicate that international arbitration had low prestige. Rather, the vast majority of respondents identified both types of arbitration as – at a minimum – "moderately prestigious". While there was a degree of variation in how prestigious each type of arbitration was, the facial trend was for ICA to be equivalently prestigious across the most prestigious categories, whereas the perceived prestige of ITA was even higher and respondents tended to give it the most prestigious ranking. Figure 2 offers a frequency breakdown for how all ICCA respondents viewed the prestige of ICA (dark gray) and ITA (light gray).

For ICA, the median and the mode ranked ICA appointments between "moderately prestigious" and "very prestigious", indicating respondents felt ICA appointments were relatively prestigious.[183] This perception was widespread with 94.8% of ICCA respondents stating that an ICA appointment was, at a bare minimum, "moderately prestigious". More specifically, 27.6% (n=142) viewed appointments as "very" prestigious; 34.2% (n=176) ranked ICA as relatively prestigious; 33% (n=170) ranked ICA as "moderately prestigious"; 3.3% (n=17) identified ICA had slight prestige with a score of 2; and 1.9% (n=10) indicated ICA was "not prestigious" at all.

For ITA, by contrast, the means and mode were five, reflecting that ITA appointments were viewed with the highest level of prestige and considered "very prestigious".[184] Nearly 85% of all respondents gave ITA one of the two most prestigious rankings possible. More specifically, 51.4% (n=263) viewed ITA as "very prestigious"; 33.4% (n=171) viewed ITA appointments as relatively prestigious; 13.3% (n=68) indicated ITA appointments were "moderately prestigious"; 1% (n=5) indicated ITA had only slight prestige; and 1% (n=5) indicated ITA was "not prestigious".

---

183. The mean score for the prestige of ICA appointments was 3.82 (SD=.939).
184. The mean score for the prestige of ITA appointments was 4.33 (SD=.815).

It is not possible to eliminate the possibility that there was a difference in how arbitration specialists and non-specialists evaluate the prestige of ICA and ITA. Nevertheless, on the basis of our data, we were unable to identify a meaningful difference in patterns of perceived prestige when we looked at response patterns between those ICCA respondents who had either been an arbitrator or counsel and those who had not.[185]

There was, however, a variable that did generate a statistically significant effect in how groups evaluated the prestige of international arbitration, namely: gender.[186] The general pattern was consistent when examining prestige evaluations for ICA and ITA.

First, to test whether the prestige of ICA was meaningfully different across genders, a t-test analyzed the independent variable of gender and the dependent variable of relative ICA prestige. There was a reliable gender difference in how respondents perceived the prestige of ICA ($t(508)=2.491$; $p=.01$; $r=.11$; $n=510$). Women were more likely than men to find an ICA appointment prestigious.[187] Table 12 provides the mean responses of men and women and demonstrates that women were more likely to view ICA arbitration appointments as prestigious than their male counterparts.

Second, another t-test explored whether ITA prestige varied according to whether the respondent was a man or a woman. Those results also identified a meaningful gender difference in perceived prestige of ITA ($t(505)=-2.443$; $p=.02$;, $r=.11$; $n=507$).[188]

---

185. Using a Chi-square test of independence to evaluate a difference in response pattern in how respondents ranked the prestige of ITA depending on whether or not they had been arbitrator, counsel or both ($X2=3.940$; $p=.41$; $r=.09$; $n=481$). Similarly, a Chi-square test to identify response patterns related to the question of ITA prestige was unable to detect a meaningful relationship ($X2=5.107$; $p=.28$; $r=.10$; $n=478$). The null results, however, lack sufficient statistical power to definitively exclude the possibility that such a relationship exists. Particularly as ICCA respondents have a degree of sophistication and the fiscal cost of the conference suggests participants have more than a passing interest in arbitration, a lay audience with broader variance may generate different results.

186. As our results were somewhat mixed, it is possible that legal training may also generate a difference in perceived prestige of arbitration. For example, using ANOVAs, there was a statistically meaningful difference based upon legal training ($F(2,500=4.673$; $p=.01$; $r=.14$; $n=503$), such that civil lawyers found ICA more prestigious than their common law counterparts. Using a Kruskal-Wallis test to address the risk of a non-normal distribution across the three types of legal training also identified the same statistically meaningful link between legal training and responses to ICA prestige ($X2=10.782$; $p=.01$; $r=.15$; $n=442$). Using ANOVAs, we were unable to isolate any meaningful difference on the prestige of ITA, however ($F(2,497=.494$; $p=.61$; $r=.05$; $n=500$). A Kruskal-Wallis test also failed to identify a link between legal training and ITA prestige responses ($X2=3.076$; $p=.22$; $r=.08$; $n=439$). Why those with a civil law training background view commercial arbitration as more prestigious than common law counterparts is a puzzle that requires further investigation.

187. The skewness of responses for ICA prestige was within acceptable levels (-0.443; SE=0.108). Non-parametric tests also identified a meaningful difference in men's and women's perceived prestige of ICA (U=20738.5; $p=.02$). Although the median response for men and women was both 4, reflecting a relatively prestigious appointment, the mode for men was 4 but the mode for women was 5.

188. The skewness of responses for ICA prestige was beyond normally acceptable levels (-1.222; SE=0.108). A Mann-Whitney U test is therefore the preferred test for exploring group differences. The non-parametric test nevertheless also revealed a meaningful gender difference

Table 12 provides the mean responses and demonstrates that women reliably viewed ITA appointments as more prestigious than men.

Table 12: Descriptive Statistics, as a function of Gender, for ICCA Respondents Regarding Prestige of International Arbitration

Arbitration Type and Respondent Gender	Mean Response	Standard Deviation	Total
ICA			
Men	3.77	.946	386
Women	4.01	.870	124
Total	3.83	.933	510
ITA			
Men	4.29	.836	384
Women	4.50	.658	123
Total	4.34	.801	507

Previous studies suggested that fewer than 10% of ITA arbitrators were women, and Table 3 reflects that women arbitrators at ICCA comprised less than 20%. This suggests it is still a relatively rare achievement for women to break into the role of international arbitrator.[189] This may explain, in part, why women view international arbitral appointments as more prestigious than men. Perhaps women view scarce arbitral appointments as an even more valuable commodity on both a personal and financial level given the extreme scarcity. Breaking through the glass ceiling is, therefore, a measure of considerable professional success and thus particularly prestigious.

2.   Reappointment and Interaction with Co-Arbitrators

As explained earlier, international arbitration is prestigious, in part, because of the scarcity of appointments and competition in the arbitrator marketplace. The causal basis permitting entrance to the "invisible college" of arbitrators has been the subject of much speculation.[190] Irrespective of how one initially enters the arbitrator network,[191] it is

---

in perceived prestige of ITA appointments (U=20862.5; p=.03). The median response was 4 for men, but the median was 4.5 for women.

189. As noted in Section IV.4.c.i, for those women who had served as arbitrators, we were unable to detect a statistically meaningful difference between the number of appointments for men and women.

190. DEZALAY and GARTH, *op. cit.*, fn. 9; ROGERS, Vocation, *op. cit.*, fn. 44; see also David SCHNEIDERMAN, "Judicial Politics and International Arbitration: Seeking an Explanation for Conflicting Outcomes", 30 Nw. J. Int'l L. & Bus. (2010) p. 338 (expressing concern about the

unclear how one *stays* in the arbitrator marketplace and becomes a repeat player. The only way of remaining in the college of international arbitration is reappointment, which is driven by counsel, other arbitrators and professionals within arbitral institutions. Presumably, re-appointment is a complicated function involving one's current professional reputation and the quality of one's historical adjudicative skill.[192]

a.   Theoretical approaches to arbitral re-appointment
Beyond prestige, other non-pecuniary factors can motivate adjudicators. National court judges, for instance, can be influenced by various extra-legal factors including the desirability of collegial interactions with colleagues,[193] panel effects and group psychology,[194] popularity and public opinion.[195] Arbitrators, in many respects, are similar to judges in that they adjudicate disputes; and similar factors may therefore motivate international arbitrators. Several scholars and Judge Posner[196] suggest that supposition is correct. Mentschikoff and Haggard, for example, argued that "who the arbitrator is in terms of expertise and prior experience is the single most important factor in both decisional and the consensus processes" and influences the interactions with and decisions of other arbitrators.[197] Dezalay and Garth similarly identified the importance of arbitrator reputation on the arbitration process.[198] Yet, arbitrators are distinguishable from judges and instead similar to service providers and must compete in the arbitral marketplace for

---

closed "club" of ITA).

191. See Tom GINSBURG, "The Culture of Arbitration", 36 Vanderbilt J. Transnat'l L. (2003) p. 1337 (arguing arbitrators function as a network and identifying a "relatively closed world of international arbitration"); PUIG, *op. cit.*, fn. 10, pp. 22-26 (identifying a network effect in ICSID appointments).

192. See, e.g., GREENWOOD and Baker, *op. cit.*, fn. 30, p. 658 ("Previous service as an arbitrator is considered to be the 'pre-eminent qualification for an arbitrator-candidate'").

193. POSNER, *How Judges Think*, *op. cit.*, fn. 169; Lee EPSTEIN, et al., "Why (and When) Judges Dissent: A Theoretical Empirical Analysis", 3 J. Legal Analysis (2011) p. 101 at pp. 122 et seq.

194. Mark F. STASSON, "Group Consensus Processes on Cognitive Bias Tasks: A Social Decision Scheme Approach", 30 Japanese Psych. Research (1988) p. 68; see also KAPELIUK, *op. cit.*, fn. 43, p. 273 (observing collegial enterprises involve "dynamics by which each member has to consider and respond to her colleagues as she performs her task"); Lewis A. KORNHAUSER and Lawrence G. SAGER, "The One and the Many: Adjudication in Collegial Courts", 81 Cal. L. Rev. (1993) p. 1 at pp. 3-5 (1993) (identifying four varieties of collective enterprises: distributed, team, redundant and collegial).

195. Lee EPSTEIN and Jack KNIGHT, "Reconsidering Judicial Preferences", 16 Ann. Rev. Pol. Sci. (2013) p. 11 at p. 21.

196. See POSNER, What Do Arbitrators Maximize?, *op. cit.*, fn. 176, p. 123 (stating that "there are no fundamental differences between judges [and] arbitrators").

197. Soia MENTSCHIKOFF and Ernest A. HAGGARD, "Decision Making and Decision Consensus in Commercial Arbitration" in June Louin TAPP and Felice J. LEVINE, eds., *Law, Justice, and the Individual in Society: Psychological and Legal Issues* (1977) p. 295 at p. 307.

198. See DEZALAY and GARTH, *op. cit.*, fn. 9, p. 9 (suggesting that "the parties well understand that the 'authority' and 'expertise' of arbitrators determine their clout within the tribunal"); see also KAPELIUK, *op. cit.*, fn. 43, p. 277 ("prior experience, which, in effect, establishes an arbitrator's reputation, is considered an important attribute that plays a significant role in collegial dynamics"); MENTSCHIKOFF and HAGGARD, *op. cit.*, fn. 197, p. 305 (suggesting that "there is an implicit and relatively subtle struggle for dominance" among panel members).

appointments.[199] Arbitrators' hybrid characteristic –as both service provider paid by the parties and impartial adjudicator – generates a possibility that arbitrators' incentive structures are different from judges'.[200] As Judge Posner explained, arbitrators must "think very carefully about what impact their decision will have on their future employment. And that is what we particularly don't want judges to do (i.e., to be thinking about their future employment). That's the reason for life tenure in the judiciary."[201]

While two different schools of thought agree that international arbitrators strive to obtain repeat appointments and care deeply about how their peers perceive them, there is not uniform agreement about what reputational aspects arbitrators maximize to secure repeat appointments.

One group of theorists posit that arbitrators effectively function as partisans, irrespective of an obligation to remain impartial and independent, as they are seeking re-appointment and those derivative financial rewards.[202] As Kapeliuk explains, an "arbitrator motivated by creating a reputation for being impartial might decide the dispute differently than an arbitrator who has an incentive to be reappointed in future disputes by the appointing party".[203] Under this theoretical framework, providing repeat parties (and repeat counsel making arbitrator recommendations) with favorable outcomes enhances the "good" reputation that generates repeat appointments, fiscal remuneration and even more prestige. Decisionmaking therefore presumably involves treating arbitrators more as agents[204] making conscious choices to generate palatable results favoring a specific party, type of party or law firm.

---

199. Robert D. COOTER, "The Objectives of Private and Public Judges", 41 Pub. Choice (1983) p. 107 at p. 107 ("private judges have to attract business, so they are exposed to the same market pressures as anyone who sells a service").

200. This presumes, however, that the judicial appointments are stable. We note, however, that there are many jurisdictions in the United States where judges are not appointed for life or a fixed term, but rather those judges must stand for public election. The effect of a democratic electorate, which functions as public marketplace for adjudicators, is not wholly dissimilar to the private marketplace for arbitrators.

201. POSNER, "What Do Arbitrators Maximize?", *op. cit.*, fn. 178, p. 130.

202. KAPELIUK, *op. cit.*, fn. 43 at pp. 291-292; see also Yuval SHANY, "Squaring the Circle? Independence and Impartiality of Party-Appointed Adjudicators in International Legal Proceedings", 30 Loy. L.A. Int'l & Comp. L. Rev. (2008) p. 473 at p. 483 ("party-appointed adjudicators are pre-disposed to vote in favor of their appointing party").

203. KAPELIUK, *op. cit.*, fn. 43, pp. 294-295; see also Gilat LEVY, "Careerist Judges and the Appeals Process", 36 RAND J. of Econ. (2005) p. 275 at pp. 278-281 (modeling effect of reputation-seeking behavior on judicial decision-making); Catherine A. ROGERS, "The Politics of International Investment Arbitration", 12 Santa Clara J. Int'l L. (2014) (henceforth Politics) p. 223 at p. 226 ("Critics hypothesize that investment arbitrators favor their appointing party in a self-interest effort to increase the likelihood of future appointments").

204. Karen ALTER, "Agents or Trustees? International Courts in their Political Context", 14 Eur. J. Int'l Rel. (2008) p. 33; see also Paul B. STEPHAN, "Courts, Tribunals and Legal Unification – The Agency Problem", 2 Chi. J. Int'l L. (2002) p. 333 at p. 337 ("Knowing that they can be replaced, the members of the [international] tribunal have an incentive not to do anything that will upset the countries with nominating authority").

In contrast, others posit that the arbitrators are incentivized to be as neutral as possible.[205] In this context, a "good" reputation involves providing a portfolio of cases with balanced outcomes that favors neither one type of claimant nor respondent. As explained in recent scholarship by Klement and Neeman, "arbitrators want to increase their chances of being selected to decide future disputes and therefore want to acquire a good reputation for being unbiased".[206] Yet they caution that this approach generates a risk of negative externalities when arbitrators become overly focused on having a balanced record of outcomes that is unwarranted by underlying facts and law. As Klement and Neeman state, arbitrators "may decide incorrectly to avoid acquiring a bad reputation".[207] Under this paradigm, where facial adjudicative neutrality is the coin of the realm, arbitrators wishing to be perceived as neutral may make strategic decisions to appear balanced, decrease the risk of perceived bias and thereby enhance their reputation – even when the result is improper or may cause delay.

There may, however, be another narrative to explain what incentivizes arbitrators' decisionmaking. A third paradigm might involve arbitrators enhancing their professional reputations by acting as a "trustee" of the international arbitration system. As such, arbitrators maximize their reputations, and the possibility of reappointment, by being as neutral as possible on procedural matters to ensure all parties obtain equal treatment and have a chance to present their cases but, on substantive matters, take a firm stance on the basis of their independent evaluation when merited by the underlying facts and law.[208]

There is a reasonable possibility that these three different theories about what incentivizes arbitrators are not mutually exclusive. Arbitrators are not a purely homogeneous population. It is possible, if not probable, that different arbitrators within the international arbitration pool are incentivized differently and thereby decide cases

---

205. Alon KLEMENT and Zvika NEEMAN, "Does Information About Arbitrators' Win/Loss Ratios Improve their Accuracy?", 42 J. Leg. Stud. (2013) p. 369 at pp. 385-386; Charles N. BROWER and Stephan W. SCHILL, "Is Arbitration a Threat or a Boon to the Legitimacy of International Investment Law?", 9 Chi. J. Int'l L. (2009) p. 471 at p. 492 (arguing that arbitrators' self-interest is in developing reputations for impartiality); Alec Stone SWEET, "Investor-State Arbitration: Proportionality's New Frontier", 4 Law & Ethics Hum. Rts. (2010) p. 47 at p. 75 ("it seems suicidal for arbitrators to proceed ... with a very heavy thumb pressed permanently down on the investors' side in cases with very high political stakes").

206. KLEMENT and NEEMAN, *op. cit.*, fn. 205, pp. 385-386; Alan Scott RAU, "Integrity in Private Judging", 38 S. Tex. L. Rev. (1997) p. 485 at p. 522 ("An arbitrator may perceive that his award is likely to have an impact on his own acceptability, that is, on the probability of his being appointed again").

207. KLEMEN and NEEMAN, *op. cit.*, fn. 205, pp. 381-382, 385-386. In theory, legally incorrect outcomes might derive from "splitting the baby" within a single case when such conduct is unwarranted given the underlying facts or law; likewise, it might involve an arbitrator strategically pursuing a balanced overall adjudicative track record where, in some cases, arbitrators follow their independent judgment in one case but not another.

208. See ALTER, *op. cit.*, fn. 204; see also Anne van AAKEN, "Control Mechanisms in International Investment Law" in Zacharias DOUGLAS, Joost PAUWELYN and Jorge VINUALES, eds., *The Foundations of International Investment Law: Bringing Theory into Practice* (Oxford University Press 2014) pp. 409-435.

differently.[209] Some arbitrators may be more concerned with how their peers and parties perceive them because they wish to be viewed as service providers. Other arbitrators may eschew this approach and instead hone their reputation by appearing to be as neutral as possible – regardless of their independent evaluation of a case's merits. It is also possible that an individual arbitrator may adhere to different approaches when adjudicating different disputes or involving different subject matters. A classic example of that phenomenon might be an arbitrator who views his/her role through one lens in ICA but takes a different approach in ITA disputes. Given the possible variance, it is constructive to consider these dynamics carefully.

b.   *Empirically exploring dynamics related to re-appointment*
We are, unfortunately, unaware of any empirical scholarship that explores what factors incentivize international arbitrators generally or how those factors impact decisionmaking.[210] Presumably, arbitrator incentives and extra-legal factors affecting outcomes are complicated.[211] In an effort to begin a systematic assessment of those issues, we asked three questions designed to elucidate aspects of arbitrator collegiality and future appointments. While not directly addressing questions of incentives, it was an indirect effort to explore what factors, including co-arbitrator collegiality, might link to reappointment. As we anticipated that there may be differences in the incentives between ICA and ITA arbitrators we asked two separate questions. First, we asked, "When I am sitting as an international *commercial* arbitrator, I consider whether I will be appointed in the future." Second, we asked, "When I am sitting as an *investment treaty* arbitrator, I consider whether I will be appointed in the future." Finally, to explore how arbitrators evaluated the importance of collegiality and reputation, we asked, "When acting as arbitrator, I consider how I will interact with my co-arbitrators in future cases."[212] We then asked respondents to answer on a 1-5 ordinal scale with 1 representing "strongly disagree", 5 representing "strongly agree" and 3 representing "neither agree nor disagree".

For the subset of respondents who had served as ICA arbitrators, the tendency was for arbitrators to disagree with the idea that they considered future appointments. The most common answer was that respondents "strongly disagreed" with the idea that they considered future appointments in ICA. The median was "2" indicating that respondents somewhat disagreed with the proposition that they considered future appointments when arbitrating ICA disputes.[213] More specifically, 32.8% (n=84) strongly disagreed; 17.6% (n=45) somewhat disagreed; and 27.3% (n=70) neither agreed nor disagreed that they considered future appointments when arbitrating ICA disputes. There was a group that did indicate that they considered their future appointments, namely 14.5% (n=37)

---

209. The same arbitrator might also behave differently in different disputes or different subject matters (i.e., ICA and ITA disputes).
210. The scholarship of Kapeliuk (analyzing the effect of repeat arbitrators on ICSID outcomes), Waibel and Wu (isolating extra-legal factors like legal training, education and gender on ICSID outcomes), and Puig (exploring the web of relationships among ICSID arbitrators) comes the closest. KAPELIUK, *op. cit.*, fn. 43; WAIBEL and WU, *op. cit.*, fn. 11; PUIG, *op. cit.*, fn. 10.
211. ROGERS, Politics, *op. cit.*, fn. 203, p. 226-228.
212. See Annex: Survey Materials, this volume, pp. 121-122 (emphasis in original).
213. The mean response was 2.47 (SD=1.292; n=256).

indicated that they somewhat agreed with the idea that they considered future appointments, and the remaining 7.8% (n=20) indicated they strongly agreed with the idea that they considered future appointments when arbitrating ICA disputes. For the subset of ICA arbitrators, Figure 3 provides a percentage breakdown (in dark gray) of whether ICA arbitrators self-identified as considering the possibility of future appointments when resolving ICA disputes.

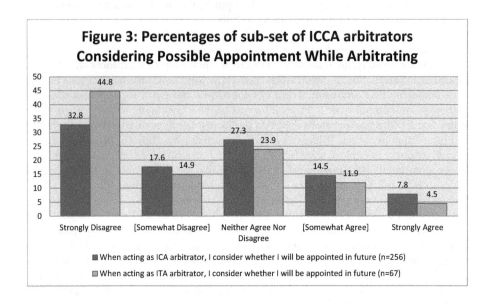

Figure 3: Percentages of sub-set of ICCA arbitrators Considering Possible Appointment While Arbitrating

For the smaller subset of respondents who served as ITA arbitrators, the dominant tendency was also for arbitrators to disagree strongly with the idea that they considered future appointments. Like ICA, the most common answer for ITA arbitrators was that respondents "strongly disagreed" with the idea that they considered future appointments in ITA; and the median was "2" indicating that respondents somewhat disagreed that they considered future appointments when arbitrating ITA disputes.[214] More specifically, 44.8% (n=30) strongly disagreed; 14.9% (n=10) somewhat disagreed; and 23.9% (n=16) neither agreed nor disagreed that they considered future appointments when arbitrating ITA disputes. There was a group that did indicate that they considered their future appointments, namely 11.9% (n=8) indicated that they somewhat agreed with the idea that they considered future appointments, and the remaining 4.5% (n=3) indicated they strongly agreed with the idea that they considered future appointments when arbitrating ITA disputes. For the subset of ITA arbitrators, Figure 3 provides a percentage breakdown (in light gray) of whether ITA arbitrators self-identified as considering the possibility of future appointments when resolving ITA disputes. The only

---

214. The mean response was 2.16 (SD=1.25; n=67).

noteworthy facial pattern was, when compared to their ICA colleagues, a greater proportion of ITA arbitrators "strongly" disagreed with the idea they considered future appointments.

Tests for both the subset of ICA[215] or ITA[216] arbitrators also failed to reveal any statistically meaningful difference in respondents' answer to the reappointment questions deriving from legal training or gender to the re-appointment questions.

To begin exploring the potential role of tribunal collegiality and its effects, we asked the subset of arbitrators whether arbitrators considered the possibility of future interaction with co-arbitrators. Recognizing the research was exploratory, the idea was to consider how the interconnectedness among arbitrators might impact group decisionmaking. The results focusing on the responses of respondents who indicated that they had served as an arbitrator are presented in Table 13.

---

215. We were unable to establish a reliable difference in responses for the ICA reappointment question based upon respondents' legal training in common law, civil law or a combination thereof. An analysis of mean differences was appropriate as skewness of responses was within acceptable levels (-0.240; SE=0.165). An ANOVA failed to reveal a meaningful difference ($F(2,253)=0.505$; $p=.60$; $r=.06$; $n=256$), and all follow-up comparisons were non-significant. We were also unable to identify a statistically meaningful link with gender and responses related to future appointments by ICA arbitrators ($t(254)=-0.496$; $p=.62$; $r=.03$; $n=256$). Although we cannot rule out the possibility of meaningful links as the sample was underpowered and exhibited an unacceptable probability of a Type II error, we note that latent effects were all less than statistically small, and *a priori* power analysis indicates a need for at least 1172 subjects in the future to reliably rule out effect. Future research is therefore necessary before reaching a definitive conclusion about the lack of a reliable effect.

216. We were unable to establish a reliable difference in responses for the ITA reappointment question based upon respondents' legal training. An analysis of mean differences was appropriate as skewness of responses was within acceptable levels (0.638; SE=0.293). An ANOVA failed to reveal a meaningful difference ($F(2,62)=0.532$; $p=.59$; $r=.12$; $n=65$), and all follow-up comparisons were non-significant. We were unable to identify a statistically meaningful link with gender and reappointment responses ($t(65)=.0136$; $p=.89$; $r=.02$; $n=67$). The non-significant facial trend was for, on average, women to be more likely to more strongly disagree that they considered the possibility of future ITA appointments. Although we cannot rule out the possibility of meaningful links as the sample was underpowered and exhibited an unacceptable probability of a Type II error, we note that latent effects were statistically small or less than small, and *a priori* power analysis indicates the need for at least 1172 subjects in the future to reliably rule out effect. Future research is necessary before definitively concluding there is no reliable relationship.

Table 13: Percentages and Frequency of Responses of ICCA Respondents Serving as Arbitrators to Question About Whether They Consider How They Will Interact with Co-arbitrators on Future Cases

Answer	Response Percentage	Response Frequency
1 – Strongly Disagree	27.3	71
2 – (Somewhat Disagree)	12.3	32
3 – Neither Agree nor Disagree	34.2	89
4 – (Somewhat Agree)	15.8	41
5 – Strongly Agree	10.4	27
Total	100.0	260

Overall, Table 13 demonstrates that both the median and mode were "3", namely that arbitrators neither agreed nor disagreed with the idea that they considered how they interact with co-arbitrators in future cases (34.2%; n=89).[217] The other common response was for respondents to disagree strongly with the idea that they considered how they would interact in the future with their co-arbitrators (27.3%; n=71). Barely one-quarter of respondents suggested they agreed in any way with the idea that they considered how they would interact with co-arbitrators in future cases. Qualifying respondents were therefore either ambivalent about the potential impact of collegiality or otherwise strongly disagreed that it affected their decisionmaking.

For the question related to considerations of future interactions with co-arbitrators, we were unable to identify any statistically reliable relationships, as a function of either the respondent's legal training or gender.[218] Similarly, using a Pearson's Product Moment Correlation Coefficient[219] to explore the possibility of a link between the number of a respondent's appointments and how they responded to the interaction with co-arbitrators, we were unable to identify any meaningful relationship ($r(262)=-.07$; $p=.26$). While we recognize the need for replication given the potentially underpowered

---

217. The mean was 2.7 (SD=1.305; n=260).

218. None of the tests were able to identify a reliable variation in the response pattern to the question of interaction with co-arbitrators irrespective of gender or legal training. An analysis of mean differences of future interaction of arbitrators was appropriate as skewness was within acceptable levels (-0.116; SE=0.151). For considerations of future interactions, we were unable to identify meaningful links in responses with either a respondent's legal training ($F(2,254)=0.425$; $p=.65$; $r=.06$; n=257) or gender ($t(258)=-.619$; $p=.54$; $r=.04$; n=258). Although we cannot rule out the possibility of meaningful links as the sample was underpowered and exhibited an unacceptable probability of a Type II error, we note that latent effects were all less than statistically small, and a priori power analysis indicates the need for at least 1172 subjects in the future to reliably rule out effect. Future research is therefore necessary before reaching a definitive conclusion about the lack of a reliable effect.

219. In layman's terms, this is a standard test to look only for a reliable statistical correlation. Stephen M. STIGLER, "Francis Galton's Account of the Invention of Correlation", 4 Statistical Sci. (1989) p. 73. Other analyses of correlation coefficients in this Paper use this test.

nature of the sample, we nevertheless observe that – even with a sample of more than 250 arbitrators – the potentially latent effect was less than statistically small.

c.   *Synthesis: Understanding the implications*

Overall, the general patterns of responses suggest that ICCA respondents serving as arbitrators did not tend to support the theory that arbitrators act as partisans. More particularly, there were strong disagreements, particularly in the context of ITA, that respondents were actively considering their re-appointment while involved in an international arbitration. Similarly, the evidence suggested that arbitrators were not necessarily interested in collegiality. The majority of respondents either expressed lack of concern about future interaction with co-arbitrators or disagreed that it was a meaningful consideration.

This provides initial, but non-conclusive, evidence that arbitrators associated with ICCA were more interested in models of adjudication that reflect arbitral neutrality. While they also respected the prestige of both ICA and ITA appointments, the arbitrators in our sample appeared to care less about potential reappointments or tribunal collegiality. While they might enjoy obtaining more appointments, which presumably would enhance their personal prestige and generate fiscal compensation, they expressed doubt that the possibility of a repeat appointment influenced their contemporaneous decisionmaking. Similarly, they did not self-report that they were impacted by potential future relationships with co-arbitrators.

Nevertheless, given the nature of the questions, it is possible that responses exhibited a self-serving bias. Rather than thinking of themselves as biased adjudicators, it is possible that respondents searched for responses that generated cognitive ease; alternatively, the responses may reflect introspective illusions, egocentrism biases, or blind spot biases where respondents were unaware of the impact of potential cognitive illusions on their responses.[220] In theory, one might have expected all reappointment and collegiality questions to have a "neither agree nor disagree" response if these aspects do not influence decisionmaking in any manner. Nevertheless, the expression of sharp disagreement, particularly in the context of ITA, indicates that exploring the impact of emotive responses is worthy of future research.

Future research is therefore necessary to explore these issues more thoroughly, perhaps in a more nuanced way, so as to avoid the risk of error generated by response bias. We welcome suggestions about how best to create an objective measure that does not involve self-assessment to assess how prestige, collegiality and re-appointment affect

---

220. In 2004, US Supreme Court Justice Antonin Scalia and Vice President Dick Cheney went on a duck-hunting trip together a few weeks before the Supreme Court agreed to take an appeal involving Cheney. Although Scalia stated, "I do not think my impartiality could reasonably be questioned," he ultimately (along with a majority of justices) voted in Cheney's favor. Scholars use this as an illustration of people tending to judge other people's biases according to their behavior but judge their own conduct according to internal feelings, thoughts and motivations. Sharot suggests Scalia experienced an introspection illusion whereby people strongly believe they have accurately identified their underlying mental state when, in fact, they have not. Tali SHAROT, *The Optimism Bias: A Tour of the Irrationally Positive Brain* (Random House 2011) pp. 16-18; see also Emily PRONIN, et al., "Objectivity in the Eye of the Beholder: Divergent Perceptions in Self versus Others", 111 Psych. Rev. (2004) p. 781.

international arbitrators. Presumably, future research might also usefully explore, in a more direct manner, what factors most motivate and impact the decisionmaking of international arbitrators as the rational actor model of economics suggests that arbitrators should be motivated to seek reappointment. Ultimately, it is worthwhile exploring sensitivities related to the claim that incentives to seek future appointments may affect decisionmaking in the present.

3.   *Fraud*

The presence of fraud, illegality or corruption in international arbitration – whether in the proceeding itself or in the underlying transaction – poses challenges to parties, arbitral tribunals, and courts tasked with enforcing arbitral awards. Since 1963, when Judge Gunnar Lagergren rendered the award in ICC Case No. 1110,[221] fraud and corruption have been serious concerns for the international arbitration community in light of their impact on the legitimacy of the international arbitral process. ICCA has explored the subject of fraud for well over a decade.[222] Fraud in international arbitration generates a series of concerns including arbitrability,[223] the burden and standard of proof,[224] the development of an international public policy dealing with fraud and corruption,[225] and the need to incorporate specific provisions for fraud in international investment agreements.[226]

---

221. See J. Gillis WETTER, "Issues of Corruption Before International Arbitral Tribunals: The Authentic Text and True Meaning of Judge Gunnar Lagergren's 1963 Award in ICC Case No. 1110", 10 Arb. Int'l (1994, no. 3) p. 277 (annexing text of award).

222. See, e.g., Karen MILLS, "Corruption and Other Illegality in the Formation and Performance of Contracts and in the Conduct of Arbitration Relating Thereto" in *International Commercial Arbitration: Important Contemporary Questions*, ICCA Congress Series no. 11 (2002) (henceforth *ICCA Congress Series no. 11*) p. 288; Peter V. TYTELL, "The Detection of Forgery and Fraud" in *ICCA Congress Series no. 11*, p. 314. More recently, a survey on investor misconduct in international treaty arbitration was presented by Anthony Sinclair and Aloysius Llamzon at the XXII ICCA Congress in Miami in April 2014 and is published in this volume, pp. 451-530.

223. Gary BORN, et al., "Bribery and an Arbitrator's Task", Kluwer Arbitration Blog, (11 October 2011) at <http://kluwerarbitrationblog.com/blog/2011/10/11/bribery-and-an-arbitrator%E2%80%99s-task/> (last accessed 16 June 2014); Cécilia A.S. NASARRE, "International Commercial Arbitration and Corruption: The Role and Duties of the Arbitrator", TDM 3 (2013) at <www.transnational-dispute-management.com/article.asp?key=1965> (last accessed 30 June 2014).

224. See, e.g., Michael HWANG and Kevin LIM, "Corruption in Arbitration – Law and Reality", 8 Asian Int'l Arb. J. (2012) p. 1 at pp. 21-36; Sophie NAPPERT, "Nailing Corruption: Thoughts For a Gardener" in Patrick WAUTELET, et al., eds., *The Practice of Arbitration: Essays in Honour of Hans van Houtte* (Hart Publishing 2012) p. 161; Constantine PARTASIDES, "Proving Corruption In International Arbitration: A Balanced Standard for the Real World", 25 ICSID Rev. (2010) p. 47.

225. Carolyn B. LAMM, et al., "Fraud and Corruption in International Arbitration" in Ángel FERNÁNDEZ-BALLESTEROS and David ARIAS, eds., *Liber Amicorum Bernardo Cremades* (Kluwer Law International 2010) p. 699 at pp. 705-718.

226. Jason Webb YACKEE, "Investment Treaties and Investor Corruption: An Emerging Defense for Host States?", 52 Va. J. Int'l L. (2012) p. 723 at pp. 742-743.

It is, of course, not the purpose of this Paper to survey the literature or arbitral jurisprudence relating to fraud, illegality and corruption. Rather, we sought to determine how the international arbitration community generally, and ICCA respondents specifically, perceived the prevalence of fraud issues in international arbitration. Some commentators posit that issues of fraud, illegality and corruption in international arbitration occur regularly.[227] To test the prevalence of this view and respondents' experiences, we asked: "How often do you believe issues of fraud – in the underlying dispute or the arbitration itself – are involved in international arbitration?" As with other questions, respondents were asked to judge frequency on an ordinal scale of 1-5 with 1 representing "never" and 5 representing "always".[228]

Table 14 offers those results.

Table 14: Percentages and Frequency of Responses of All ICCA Respondents in Response to Question About How Often Does Fraud Arise in International Arbitration

Answer	Response Percentage	Response Frequency
Never	3.6	18
Occasionally	53.9	268
Sometimes	31.2	155
Frequently	10.9	54
Always	0.4	2
Total	100.0	497

Table 14 shows the most common response to the question was that issues of fraud appear only "occasionally" in international arbitration – an answer that was selected by a clear majority of ICCA respondents.[229] Indeed, 88.7% of respondents stated that fraud occurs in international arbitration "sometimes" or less frequently. This result stands in contrast to the results of Sect. III.3 regarding document withholding, a form of procedural misconduct that arbitrators and counsel perceived to be more prevalent.

Table 14 also, however, refers to all ICCA respondents, including those who have never served as either counsel or arbitrator. One might rightfully ask whether the

---

227. Cecily ROSE, "Questioning the Role of International Arbitration in the Fight Against Corruption", 31 J. of Int'l Arb. (2014) p. 183 at p. 183 ("[I]nternational arbitral tribunals have had to consider allegations of corruption with increasing frequency"); PARTASIDES, *op. cit.*, fn. 224, at para. 7 ("It is against this backdrop that issues of illegality and corruption are featured in the landscape of international arbitration with greater regularity today than ever before."); LAMM, et al., *op. cit.*, fn. 225, p. 699 ("Allegations of fraud and corruption are *often* encountered in international arbitration")(emphasis added).

228. See Annex: Survey Materials, this volume, pp. 121-122.

229. The median and mode were both "occasionally" (2). The mean also tended in this direction (M=2.5; SD=.75; n=497) but suggested respondents experienced fraud issues in a range between "occasionally" and "sometimes".

responses of those experienced with international arbitration were markedly different from others. The answer is: yes, there were meaningful differences in response patterns, such that arbitration counsel and arbitrators were *less likely* to identify problems with fraud in international arbitration.

To test whether responses were meaningfully different, a t-test explored the effect of arbitration experience. For one test, our independent variable was whether the respondent had ever been arbitration counsel; and for the second test, the independent variable was whether the respondent ever served as an ICA and/or ITA arbitrator. The dependent variable was how respondents responded on the 1-5 ordinal scale. First, the results revealed that there was a link between experience as counsel and perceived issues with fraud in international arbitration ($t(453)=2.272$; $p=.02$; $r=.11$; $n=455$). For that subset, the mean score for those *without* arbitration counsel experience was 2.73 (SD$=.918$; $n=51$), whereas those *with* counsel experience was 2.46 (SD$=.733$; $n=404$). Second, there was also a statistically significant relationship between experience as an arbitrator and perceived fraud ($t(415)=2522$; $p=.01$; $r=.12$; $n=417$). For the subset of arbitrators, the mean score was 2.41 ($n=259$; SD$=.649$); whereas the non-arbitrators had a somewhat higher mean of 2.59 ($n=158$; SD$=.845$). Even for those respondents with some type of experience as either counsel or arbitrator, we were likewise unable to isolate any meaningful link between the number of those appointments and responses to the fraud question.[230]

The critical finding was that there were statistically significant gaps in perception with regard to fraud among arbitrators, counsel and those who had not acted in either role. For example, those who served as arbitrators responded that fraud occurred less frequently than those who had not served as arbitrators. This difference was statistically meaningful and there is minimal risk that the results were due to chance alone. Furthermore, those respondents who served as arbitrator or counsel believed fraud occurred less frequently in international arbitration than respondents who had not served in either of these roles.

The survey question, like any survey instrument designed to assess perceptions and personal views, gauges perceptions rather than verifiable objective frequency of fraud issues in international arbitration, through, for example, a review of arbitral decisions. While we would welcome such research using an archival data, one can nevertheless infer that it is possible that fraud in international arbitration does not occur sufficiently frequently so as to register markedly with respondents who have experience as arbitrators or counsel. If this inference is accurate, the difference in perception between those with arbitrator experience and those without is more concerning from a legitimacy perspective. It would mean that, at the very least, the international arbitral community

---

230. For subjects who had acted as counsel, a correlation coefficient was unable to identify a reliable linear relationship between the number of cases as counsel and responses to the question on fraud ($r(404)=.004$; $p=.95$). For those subjects who had acted as arbitrator, a correlation coefficient was unable to ascertain a reliable linear relationship between a respondent's total number of cases as an arbitrator and responses to the fraud question ($r(259)=-02$; $p=.76$). Given the risk of insufficient statistical power, it is possible that a larger sample of over 700 subjects could identify a link between relative arbitration experience and perceived experiences with fraud. Nevertheless, the effect sizes were less than statistically small and the p-values were far from significant.

should consider how to educate the public and arbitration users to allay concerns over systemic integrity.

4. *Issues of Diversity*

Several scholars identify that the diversity of those presiding over adjudicatory bodies, particularly international courts and tribunals, contributes meaningfully to those tribunals' legitimacy.[231] In a poignant example, Nienke Grossman argues that adjudicative bodies "where one sex is severely under- or over-represented lack normative legitimacy because they are normatively biased". She further posits that, even if men and women do not decide cases differently, "sex representation matters for sociological legitimacy because relevant constituencies believe they do" and "representativeness is an important democratic value".[232] As a result, concerns related to diversity in international arbitration impact its legitimacy and, more broadly, to that of international courts and tribunals.[233]

For ITA, as a hybrid creature involving public international law, concerns about sociological legitimacy, democratic legitimacy, and democracy deficits are poignant and arguably resonate strongly.[234] Yet, concerns about diversity also impact the legitimacy of ICA and disputes purely among private parties. Although the New York Convention[235] and the UNCITRAL Model Law[236] require domestic judiciaries to give arbitration awards

---

231. See generally GROSSMAN, *op. cit.*, fn. 82 (exploring how women's participation on international courts and tribunals affects their legitimacy); see also Leigh SWIGART, "The 'National Judge': Some Reflections on Diversity in International Courts and Tribunals", 42 McGeorge L. Rev. (2010) p. 223 at p. 224 ("Like their domestic counterparts, international courts and tribunals depend on public faith in their judges to inspire confidence in court decisions and in the judicial system more generally."); Sally J. KENNEY, "Breaking the Silence: Gender Mainstreaming and the Composition of the European Court of Justice", 10 Feminist Legal Studies (2002) p. 257 at pp. 265-266 (exploring whether the paucity of women on the European Court of Justice's bench affects its legitimacy and why).

232. GROSSMAN, *op. cit.*, fn. 82, p. 652.

233. See Shashank KUMAR and Cecily ROSE, "A Study of Lawyers Appearing before the International Court of Justice, 1999-2012", 25 (Eur. J. Int'l L. (2014) p. 893 (calling for empirical research comparing diversity imbalances at the ICJ with international arbitration).

234. See Nienke GROSSMAN, "The Normative Legitimacy of International Courts", 86 Temp. L. Rev. (2013) p. 61 (discussing a democratic theory of legitimacy); Nienke GROSSMAN, "Legitimacy and International Adjudicative Bodies", 41 Geo. Wash. Int'l L. Rev. (2009) p. 107 (discussing a sociological approach to legitimacy); Daniel BODANSKY, "The Legitimacy of International Governance: A Coming Challenge for International Environmental Law?", 93 Am. J. Int'l L. (1999) p. 596 at p. 601 (asserting that popular views about an authority comprise one dimension of that authority's legitimacy); Allen BUCHANAN and Robert O. KEOHANE, "The Legitimacy of Global Governance Institutions", 20 Ethics & Int'l Affairs (2006, no. 4) p. 405 at pp. 405-406 (suggesting that a global public standard of legitimacy can help citizens distinguish legitimate institutions from illegitimate ones).

235. Convention on the Recognition and Enforcement of Foreign Arbitral Awards, 330 U.N.T.S. No. 4739 at p. 3 (henceforth New York Convention).

236. UNCITRAL Model Law on International Commercial Arbitration (1985, as amended in 2006) at <www.uncitral.org/pdf/english/texts/arbitration/ml-arb/07-86998_Ebook.pdf> (last accessed 27 June 2014).

a degree of deference, that deference derives from trust in the integrity of arbitrators and the arbitral process. Consequently, domestic courts need not give international arbitration procedures or awards carte blanche but, instead, retain the power to oversee the parties, their lawyers and the arbitrators. Some jurisdictions have historically expressed a "judicial hostility" to arbitration, and others have perceived arbitration as an unwarranted intrusion into state authority.[237] States permit and honor arbitration proceedings, in part, because of their perceived utility; and should those actors believe that ICA is illegitimate or problematic, courts retain the capacity to re-absorb those cases into judicial dockets. There have, indeed, been calls to regulate international arbitration more closely regardless of whether a dispute involves a state or state-related entity.[238] Even private dispute resolution, therefore, is dependent on public trust and state regulation.[239] As Salim Moollan observed, there are risks when – rightly or wrongly – international arbitration is viewed as an imposed, an unwanted, foreign process.[240]

Diversity concerns are not unique to international arbitration.[241] As a report by Oxford Economics explains, "[e]mployee diversity – across lines of gender, ethnicity, country of birth, age and others – has become a hot boardroom topic across the globe. It is becoming not only a critical issue for human resources (HR) executives, but a major part of corporate strategy."[242] Some commentators argue that, "diversity should be considered both by policymakers and businesses when making investment and policy decisions as it can affect competitiveness which is key to economic growth and the quality of life of a nation's citizens".[243] The first Sub-section therefore first explores the basic demographics of international arbitration and then places those findings within a larger context. The next Sub-section then explores respondents' perceptions about potential

---

237. See, e.g., *Sherck v. Alberto-Culver Co.*, 417 U.S. 506 (U.S. Sp. Ct. 1974), at p. 511 (noting "centuries of judicial hostility to arbitration agreements"); BORN, *op cit.*, fn. 138, Sect. 1.01 (providing a brief history of international commercial arbitration).

238. See, e.g., MENON, *op. cit.*, fn. 133, para. 43 ("As we contemplate these problems of moral hazard, ethics, inadequate supply and conflicts of interests associated with international arbitrators, it seems surprising that there are no controls or regulations to maintain the quality, standards and legitimacy of the industry.").

239. Parties only have the right to choose arbitration, and choose their arbitrators, where states generate laws granting parties those rights. This reflects that, while party autonomy is a critical value in international arbitration, it is not the only value.

240. See MOOLLAN, *op. cit.*, fn. 91, at 2:12-3:16 (observing the disjunction between "the formal discourse repeated at every conference we go to emphasizing the inclusiveness of international arbitration" and "the perception of our field, in the developing world as predominantly Euro- and American-centric" and suggesting that this gives "rise to a risk of arbitration being perceived as a foreign process imposed from abroad, as an unwanted but inevitable corollary of trade and investment flows" but suggesting "the answer to this is to make sure that the developing world has its say in the process and in its development and for international arbitration progressively to become part and parcel of the legal culture of developing countries").

241. Other aspects of diversity that are worthy of exploration, which we did not have the time or space to explore, involved sexual orientation, religion, marital status, disability or medical condition.

242. Oxford Economics, "The Global Diversity Report: An Annual Guide to Measure Global Employee Diversity", at <http://bit.ly/1opaTao> (last accessed 30 June 2014).

243. *Ibid.*, p. 21.

diversity challenges within international arbitration. Finally, it contrasts this with respondents' actual experiences as with the diversity of international arbitrators.

a.   Contextualizing the demographics of diversity

Earlier, Sect.II.*2* and Tables 2-5 offered key descriptive data related to the diversity of the international arbitration community. Overall, the data suggested the "median" ICCA attendee and arbitration counsel was a male, 50 years of age, with some common law legal training and from a developed state. In slight contrast, the "median" arbitrator at ICCA was a male, 55 years of age, with some training from a common law jurisdiction and was a national of a developed state. For the subset of arbitrators, less than 18% were women,[244] 20% (or less) were from non-OECD or non-High Income states, and HDI scores reflected that the median arbitrator was from one of the top twelve most developed states in the world. Overall, these results suggest that: (1) women's presence in international arbitration was relatively small; and (2) the proportion of developing-world arbitrators was relatively small.

The data must, however, be viewed in context. Obtaining diversity in gender and race has been challenging for domestic dispute resolution; similarly, obtaining diversity in gender and nationality in international law adjudication has been complex. While there are contexts where diversity levels have become relatively more balanced, that is not a universal phenomenon. These premises raise the interesting questions of how the international arbitration community fares comparatively and whether it wishes to become a leader or a laggard in addressing diversity.

---

244. We would be remiss not to recall from Sect. II.*2.c* that women arbitrators were statistically younger (48 years old on average) than their male counterparts (56 years old on average). Given this possibility, one might expect a slightly lower representation of women with the need to achieve the requisite years of experience. Yet, Greenwood and Baker suggest that female partners make up about 11% of international arbitration teams; and when compared to their data on arbitrators, they infer that less than half of that 11% serve as arbitrators and thereby suffer from "more than the usual 'pipeline leak'". GREENWOOD and BAKER, *op. cit.*, fn. 30, p. 658. This creates three possibilities. First, Greenwood and Baker's extrapolation that women account for 6% of international arbitrators could be wrong, and their derivative inference is incorrect. Second, it means that the 17% proportion of women arbitrators in our sample was over-representative of women arbitrators. This could reflect that either women benefit from ICCA networking opportunities or women who have multiple appointments elect to attend ICCA Congresses. Third, as several studies identified that women accounted for 5-9% of the ITA arbitrator pool, there may be meaningful differences in the appointment of women in ICA and ITA arbitration and there may be comparatively more women acting as ICA arbitrators. At present, we believe the most plausible scenario is that our dataset reflects a slightly higher proportion of female arbitrators than the general population. For the subset of ITA arbitrators, there were nine female subjects (13.4%) and fifty-eight men (86.6%). This is facially distinguishable from recent research about ITA where, out of a pool of 248 arbitrators, there were nine women (3.6%) arbitrating cases generating a public award prior to 2012. FRANCK, *Myths and Realities, op. cit.*, fn. 29, ch. 8; see also FRANCK, Empirically Evaluating, *op. cit.*, fn. 28, p. 80 (identifying five women (3.5%) out of a pool of 145 arbitrators in pre-2007 awards). If the third possibility is also correct, however, the sample may simply be over-representative of ITA, rather than ICA, women arbitrators. This is a realistic possibility as, for our subset of ICA arbitrators, forty-five (17.3%) were women.

i.   More relative success at gender and racial diversity

There are a variety of professional contexts where women and minorities are represented reasonably well, albeit not perfectly. These areas typically involve the public sector, including domestic legislative and judicial branches, and some areas within the private sector.

Several national legislatures exhibited better diversity levels than international arbitration. For instance, as of 2013, the countries with the largest proportion of women serving as elected representatives included Sweden (47%), Iceland (43%), Argentina (43%), the Netherlands (42%), and Finland (42%).[245] Similarly, according to Women in National Parliaments' 2014 data, out of the 149 countries surveyed, thirty-five different countries (including Rwanda, Ecuador, Mexico, Serbia and Burundi) had more than 30% of women in their lower houses.[246]

Likewise, empirical research on national judiciaries offers instructive comparative information about diversity related to gender and race. Many – but not all – countries do better than international arbitration in having women in positions of key adjudicative responsibility. For example, several countries in the European Union have had respectable success in equalizing the representation of women in their domestic judiciaries.[247] Some European countries have more than fifty percent women in their judiciaries including, Bosnia and Herzegovina, Croatia, Czech Republic, France, Greece, Hungary, Latvia, Montenegro, Poland, Romania, Slovakia, and Slovenia;[248] and Israel has also experienced more than 50% of female judges.[249]

Not all countries experience perfect balance but exhibit relative success in diversifying their judiciaries. Although women have been nearly 50% of law school classes in the United States since 1992, women currently occupy only approximately 33% of positions within the federal judiciary;[250] and only roughly 23% of US federal district court judges

---

245. *Ibid.*, p. 10.

246. Women in National Parliaments, "World Classification: Situation as of 1st May 2014", at <www.ipu.org/wmn-e/classif.htm> (last accessed 1 July 2014). There were, however, 32 states where women in national legislatures accounted for less than 11%. *Id.* There was also wide variation in women's representation in upper houses.

247. See European Judicial Systems, European Commission for the Efficiency of Justice, available at <http://bit.ly/OGlJ7T> (last accessed 30 June 2014) (highlighting the achievements of several European Union judiciaries in having proportionate numbers of women in their judiciaries).

248. The percentages break down as follows: Bosnia and Herzegovina: 63.3%; Croatia: 67.4%; Czech Republic: 59.4%; France: 82.4%; Greece: 65.2%; Hungary: 68.8%; Latvia: 75.6%; Montenegro: 55%; Poland: 63.3%; Romania: 73%; Slovakia: 62.5%; Slovenia: 77.6%. See *ibid.* pp. 147-150, 275-281; see also Ulrike SCHULTZ and Gisela SHAW, eds., *Gender and Judging* (Hart Publishing 2013) (henceforth *Gender and Judging*) (exploring the experiences of women judges in nineteen different countries).

249. Eyal KATVAN, "The Entry and Integration of Women into Judicial Positions in Israel" in *Gender and Judging, op. cit.*, fn. 248, p. 83.

250. National Women's Law Center, "Women in the Federal Judiciary: Still a Long Way to Go", 30 May 2014, National Women's Law Center, at <http://bit.ly/1qn2SEv> (last accessed 30 June 2014); see also Jill D. WEINBERG and Laura B. NIELSEN, "Examining Empathy: Discrimination, Experience and Judicial Decisionmaking", 85 S. Cal. L. Rev. (2012) p. 313 at pp. 347-348. This is an improvement from 1977, when data suggested that women represented 1.4% and minorities represented 4.4% of the federal judiciary. Nancy SCHERER, "Diversifying

are minorities.[251] Similarly, within the United States, state courts experienced a range of gender diversity. Likewise, despite increases over time, recent data indicate women hold 29.2% of state judicial positions.[252] Similarly, despite increases over time, minorities hold approximately 12.6% of overall state judicial positions.[253] In Germany, in 2012, approximately 40% of national judges were women.[254] Likewise, Canada had a core proportion of female judges. Although women made up 51% of the Canadian population and 40% of practicing lawyers, only about 33% of judges were women. Canada, however, has had even weaker representation of minorities, with minorities comprising only 2.3% of federally appointed judges.[255] This suggests that, although these states did not exhibit perfect gender diversity, there were multiple instances where national judiciaries had proportionately better diversity levels than international arbitration. Nevertheless, given the difficulty of many states in reaching representative levels of gender and race, achieving diversity often requires long-term investments.

There were other states whose judiciaries did not exhibit gender balance but experienced better success in generating equilibrium than international arbitration. In 2010, for example, women made up approximately 36% of the judiciary in Venezuela, 35% in Costa Rica and 32% in Colombia.[256] In Kenya, although women lack representation on the court of appeal, approximately 35.5% of advocates are women and

---

the Federal Bench: Is Universal Legitimacy for the U.S. Justice System Possible?", 105 Nw. U. L. Rev. (2011) p. 587 at p. 588.

251. WEINBERG and NIELSEN, *op. cit.*, fn. 250, p. 347; see also Gregory L. ACQUAVIVA and John D. CASTIGLIONE, "Judicial Diversity on State Supreme Courts", 39 Seton Hall L. Rev. (2009) p. 1203 at pp. 1214, 1223.

252. The low was 5.6% in West Virginia and the high was 34.2% in Massachusetts.

253. Malia REDDIC, et al., "Racial and Gender Diversity on State Courts: An AJS Study", 48 Judges J. (2009) p. 31. The states with the lowest proportion of minority candidates were Maine, Montana, New Hampshire, Vermont and Wyoming (0%), with a high of 65.1% in Hawaii; the next states with the highest proportion of minority judges were Louisiana (20.6%) and New York (20.5%). *Ibid.* Research exploring women's variation in representation in US state courts also identified that the size of the court matters, and larger courts are more likely to have more women. Sally J. KENNY, "Choosing Judges: A Bumpy Road to Women's Quality and a Long Way to Go", 2012 Mich. St. L. Rev. (2012) p. 1499 at pp. 1520-1521; see also Margaret WILLIAMS, "Women's Representation on State Trial and Appellate Courts", 88 Soc. Sci. Quart. (2007) p. 1192 at p. 1199.

254. Bundesamt für Justiz, *"Zahl der Richter, Richterinnen, Staatanwälte, Staatanwältinnen und Vertreter, Vertreterinnen des öffentlichen Interesses in der Rechtspflege der Bundesrepublik Deutschland"* (31 December 2012) at <http://bit.ly/1mUKlON> (last accessed 30 June 2014). Scholars have identified, however, that women within the German judiciary "continue to be under-represented in leadership positions". Ulrike SCHULTZ, "'I was noticed and I was asked…' Women's Careers in the Judiciary: Results of an Empirical Study for the Ministry of Justice in Northrhine-Westfalia, Germany" in *Gender and Judging, op. cit.*, fn. 248, p. 145.

255. Meredith BACAL, "Diversity and the Judiciary: Who Is the Bench Representing Anyway?", The Court, 5 July 2012, at <http://bit.ly/1mltOEs> (citing Ryerson University Diversity Institute, "Improving Representation in the Judiciary: A Diversity Strategy" (27 June 2012) at <http://tinyurl.com/oyd5ork> (last accessed 30 June 2014).

256. Sital KALANTRY, "Women in Robes", 6 Americas Quart. (Summer 2012) p. 83 at p. 84 available at <http://tinyurl.com/lax56jv> (last accessed 30 June 2014).

women made up about 30% of the bench in 2010.[257] Even in Indonesia, in 2011, 23.4% of trial judges and 15.4% of appellate judges were women.[258]

Some countries, however, are laggards in terms of gender diversity.[259] In the United Kingdom, the Ministry of Justice reported that, in 2010, the levels of women finally rose to 20.6%, with only 4.8% minorities.[260] In Brazil, in 2010, 18% of the judges at its highest court were women but this was an increase from 0% in 1999.[261] In Malawi, approximately 17% of justices on the Malawi High Court and Supreme Court of Appeal were women.[262] In Japan, the percentage of women in the judiciary is relatively low (15%) but proportionate to the ratio of women lawyers (16%) generally.[263]

The private sector also exhibited a degree of success in putting women in elite positions and arguably better success than international arbitration. In some countries, there was better representation of women on corporate boards than in international arbitration. In the United States, for example, there is at least one woman on 97% of corporate boards.[264] Acknowledging that "there is a consistent deficit between the gender and ethnic diversity of mid-grade employees and their managerial counterparts within any given business",[265] an Oxford Economics Report observed that countries with the "highest female representation on corporate boards [were] Norway (36%), followed by Philippines (23%), Sweden (23%), Latvia (22%) and Slovakia (22%)".[266] Some of the

257. Winifred KAMAU, "Women Judges and Magistrates in Kenya: Challenges, Opportunities and Contributions" in *Gender and Judging, op. cit.*, fn. 248, p. 165 at pp. 170, 181.

258. Engy ABDELKADER, "To Judge or Not to Judge: A Comparative Analysis of Islamic Jurisprudential Approaches to Female Judges in the Muslim World", 37 Fordham Int'l L.J. (2014) p. 309 at p. 347.

259. These are, of course, countries that were sufficiently interested in issues of gender diversity that there is publicly available data identifying the scope of gender diversity; and it is possible that there are additional states with worse representation or states with no representation at all. Research on some Islamic law countries suggest this is the case. See ABDELKADER, *ibid.; Gender and Judging, op. cit.*, fn. 248, pp. 8-9 (observing that countries such as Egypt, Kuwait and the United Arab Emirates have female judges but noting that Saudi Arabia and Iran do not).

260. Mary L. CLARK, "Judicial Retirement and Return to Practice", 60 Catholic U. L. Rev. (2011) p. 841 at pp. 873-874 n. 216. More recent data also demonstrates low levels of women's representation as, in 2013, 24.3% of judges were women and 4.8% were black or ethnic minorities. Courts and Tribunals Judiciary, "Tribunals Diversity Breakdown 2012-13" (2014) available at <www.judiciary.gov.uk/publications/diversity-statistics-and-general-overview-2013> (last accessed 1 July 2014).

261. KALANTRY, *op. cit.*, fn. 256, p. 83.

262. Siri GLOPPEN and Fedelis E. KANYONGOLO, "Courts and the Poor in Malawi: Economic Marginalization, Vulnerability and the Law", 5 Int'l J. Const. L. (2007) p. 258 at p. 289.

263. David T. JOHNSON, "Japan's Prosecution System", 41 Crime & Just. (2012) p. 35 at p. 49 fn. 8.

264. Nizan Geslevich PACKIN, "It's (Not) All About the Money: Using Behavioral Economics to Improve Regulation of Risk Management in Financial Institutions", 15 U. Pa. J. Bus. L. (2013) p. 419 at pp. 453-455; but see *ibid.* (noting that women only make up 16% of the total number of directors and the average number of women on corporate boards is two).

265. Oxford Economics, *op. cit.*, fn. 242, p. 30.

266. *Ibid.*, p. 8; see also Kimberly GLADMAN, "2013 Women on Boards Survey", Harvard Law School Forum on Corporate Governance and Financial Regulation (20 May 2013) at <http://blogs.law.harvard.edu/corpgov/2013/05/20/2013-women-on-boards-survey/> (last

representation on European boards, however, may reflect that some countries enacted legislative mandates requiring women to be on corporate boards.[267]

ii.   Less relative or equal success at gender and racial diversity
Other contexts, however, suggest that international arbitration has low, but not necessarily unusual, levels of diversity and, in any event, diversity itself is a challenging concept. As indicated earlier, some national courts have experienced diversity challenges; and even where courts have been successful in increasing the level of women, they may have experienced challenges on issues of racial diversity or vice versa. Similarly, empirical research suggests, public international law courts and tribunals tend to be primarily populated by men from developed states; but some international tribunals have done comparatively better at promoting some aspect of diversity than others.

In terms of gender diversity, one study estimated women account for only about 5% of appointments in international courts and tribunals.[268] Grossman's earliest comprehensive study of international courts and tribunals in 2010 identified slightly higher proportions. Specifically, with only one outlier,[269] women have historically comprised less than 20% of international tribunals. Grossman identified that women made up only 19% of the World Trade Organization's Dispute Settlement Body; women comprised 18% of judges on the International Criminal Tribunal for Rwanda and the European Court of Human Rights; the International Criminal Tribunal for the Former Yugoslavia, and African Court on Human and People's Rights had 15% women; the Inter-American Court of Human Rights had 13%; the European Court of Justice had 7%; the International Court of Justice had 3%; and the International Tribunal for the Law of the Sea (ITLOS) had 0% women.[270] When surveyed in 2010, on average, women made up only about 21% of the judiciary of those international courts and tribunals (ranging from 0% at the ITLOS to 58% at the International Criminal Court).[271]

---

accessed 30 June 2014) (noting that "63% [of companies] have at least one female director" and "women make up a higher percentage of directors in developed markets"); European Commission, "Report on Women and Men in Leadership Positions and Gender Equality Strategy Mid-Term Review", MEMO/13/882 (14 October 2013) at <http://bit.ly/1rYZoaC> (last accessed 30 June 2014) (identifying within the EU that women accounted for 16.6%, or one in six, board members of the largest publicly listed company, including Finland (29.1%) and Latvia (29%), closely followed by France (26.8%) and Sweden (26.5%)).

267. See generally Fredrik ENGLESTAD and Mari TIEGEN, eds., *Firms, Boards and Gender Quotas: Comparative Perspectives* (Emerald Group Publishing 2012).
268. See Chiara GIORGETTI, "Who Decides Who Decides in International Investment Arbitration", 35 U. Penn. J. Int'l L. (2013) p. 431, at p. 459 fn. 99 (citing Lawyers Comm. for Hum. Rts., "LCHR's Chart Showing Gender and Regional Balance in Elections to International Courts and Tribunals", research by Lawyers Committee for Human Rights, at <http://bit.ly/1xie7QW> (last accessed 30 June 2014)).
269. The International Criminal Court was the one exception, with 44% women. GROSSMAN, *op. cit.*, fn. 82, pp. 652-654, 679-681.
270. *Ibid.*, pp. 679-680.
271. *Ibid.*, pp. 652-654, 679-681.

Beyond Grossman's research on women adjudicators, the Iran-U.S. Claims Tribunal (IUSCT) at The Hague currently has nine members, and only one is a woman.[272] Our historical research has only been able to identify one other woman – Gabrielle McDonald – serving on the IUSCT since its inception in 1981. Likewise, at present, only one of the seven members of the WTO Appellate Body is a woman.[273] Our research identified only one woman ever serving as a commissioner on the United Nations Claims Commission.[274]

Cecily Rose and Shashank Kumar's research confirms a similar lack of female counsel in public international law. More specifically, they identified that for all lawyers involved in contentious cases at the ICJ, female counsel only represented 11.2% of all advocates ($n=23$), and women only spoke 7.4% of the total time in ICJ proceedings.[275] For the subset of lawyers who were repeat ICJ counsel, women only represented 6.3% ($n=4$) of the pool, and women's speaking time decreased to 2.9% of all oral advocacy.[276] One intriguing contrast was that, in advisory proceedings, female advocates accounted for 19% of the population and 18% of total speaking time, but that these women tended to be government officials and state diplomats,[277] which suggests that having a healthy proportion of women in key domestic positions could generate a trickle-down effect in international law.

International law courts and tribunals also experience challenges with diverse representation of nationality and obtaining adjudicators from perspectives across a development dimension. One study observed, "the extent of the Western monopoly of international legal practice at the ICJ", and it argued that international law "is not as 'international' as the name implies".[278] The authors called into question the legitimacy of the ICJ given the lack of diversity in both the judiciary and counsel. For judges, their 2002 data indicated that all seven of the OECD judges received their education entirely in OECD states; and all but one of the non-OECD judges received the majority of his legal education in OECD states.[279] Similarly, they discovered a dearth of developing-world advocates.[280] Rose and Kumar replicated those findings with recent data. From 1999-2012, the vast majority of the 205 different lawyers appearing before the ICJ were

---

272. See Iran-United States Claims Tribunal, *Arbitrators*, at <http://bit.ly/1faG86s> (identifying Rosemary Barkett as the only female arbitrator currently on the Tribunal). Historically, Gabrielle McDonald was the only other woman and a US appointee.

273. Yuejiao Zhang is the current Chinese appointee. Other women include Merit Janow (US), Jennifer Hillman (US) and Lilia Bautista (Philippines). See World Trade Organization, *Dispute Settlement: Biography Appellate Body Members*, at <http://bit.ly/15Q2FCr> (last accessed 30 June 2014).

274. We were only able to identify Professor Dr. Nayla Comair-Obeid as a female Commissioner. See Reports and Recommendations of the Panel of Commissioners, <http://bit.ly/1koSNal> (showing several reports signed by "N. Comair-Obeid", including report [S/AC.26/2005/3;] 10 March 2005).

275. KUMAR and ROSE, *op. cit.*, fn. 233, p. 13.

276. *Ibid.*, pp. 13-14.

277. *Ibid.*, p. 25.

278. GAUBATZ and MACARTHUR, *op. cit.*, fn. 70, pp. 240-241.

279. *Ibid.*, pp. 261-263.

280. *Ibid.*, pp. 247, 251-253.

from the developed world. Specifically, 72.2% were nationals of OECD states, 71.5% were from states the World Bank classified as High Income, and 72.9% were from states with HDI scores that put them in the category of "very high human development"; and, for counsel who were repeat players at the ICJ, the balance was skewed towards representation by lawyers from developed states.[281]

The private sector also has its challenges. When power is concentrated into a single position, gender balance is not as prevalent. For example, the *Fortune 500* recently announced that women exhibited their best showing in history by comprising 4.8% of CEO positions in the top 500 corporations in the United States.[282] In contrast, when membership is more diffuse – such as when there are multiple positions on a corporate board – there is broader female representation as 63% of top corporations have one female member on their board.[283] This latter phenomenon might reflect the tendency for larger diffuse structures to generate greater opportunities for diversity, much like diversity in US state courts where larger courts exhibited larger proportions of women.[284] Meanwhile, large law firms also experience diversity struggles. Linklater's 2012 diversity statistics, for example, reflect that, globally, only 17% of its partners were female, with a high of 26% female partners in Asia and a low of 9% female partners in Europe; and 90% of UK partners were white.[285] Yet Linklater's experience is not unique given the dearth of women partners in US and UK law firms.[286] These potentially unrepresentative examples raise the possibility that the diversity data in arbitration reflects an international pipeline problem as not all countries have the same level of

---

281. KUMAR and ROSE, *op. cit.*, fn. 233, pp. 11-16; but see TERRIS, et al., *op. cit.*, fn. 9, p. 223 (concluding that "[t]here once was a time when the 'invisible college' of international judges consisted of a small band of men, principally Europeans, clustered tightly in The Hague" but then stating "[t]oday's more extensive network has much more diversity in terms of geography, race, and gender").

282. Caroline FAIRCHILD, "Number of Fortune 500 women CEOs reaches historic high", *Fortune 500*, 3 June 2014, at <http://bit.ly/1nLdkqE> (last accessed 18 June 2014).

283. GLADMAN, *op. cit.*, fn. 266 ("63% [of companies] have at least one female director, and 13% have at least three women"). Even with this historic success, the popular press nevertheless notes that those women CEOs are still likely to be paid less than their male counterparts and more likely to be fired. See Edward HELMORE, "The facts show it: female CEOs are more likely than men to be fired", The Guardian (17 May 2014) at <http://bit.ly/1o32V6x> (last accessed 30 June 2014); Claire Cain MILLER, "An Elusive Jackpot: Riches Come to Women as C.E.O.s, but Few Get There", New York Times (7 June 2014) at <http://bit.ly/1o32V6x> (last accessed 30 June 2014) (observing that women CEOs make $1.6 million less than male counterparts).

284. See *op. cit.*, fn. 253 and accompanying text.

285. Linklaters, "Diversity Statistics 2012", p. 1 at pp. 1-2, at <http://bit.ly/1vtOERM> (last accessed 1 July 2014).

286. See American Bar Association, "A Current Glance at Women in the Law 2013" (2013) at p. 2, at <http://bit.ly/1o0m06Q> (last accessed 1 July 2014) (identifying that women make up 19.9% of partners in the United States); Joanne Harris, "Diversity efforts fail to pay off at top end of profession", The Lawyer (5 August 2013) at <http://bit.ly/1iSQrzE> (last accessed 1 July 2014) (observing that The Lawyer's UK 200 indicated women made up 18.6% of all partners).

women or minority lawyers (to say nothing of women and minority lawyers who are interested in international arbitration).[287]

Nevertheless, it is worth observing that – by comparison to many (but not all) national judiciaries and legislatures – public international law courts and tribunals experience meaningful challenges about whether they are representative and thereby generate concerns about their institutional legitimacy. The question remains as to whether the international arbitration community wishes to find ways to be be viewed as a leader in promoting diversity in international law or is content with its current position.

b.   *Perceived problems of diversity*

Irrespective of the comparative baseline, the raw data reflected that there were diversity challenges within ICCA itself and within the ranks of counsel and arbitrators.[288] The question is whether, in light of the given demographic data, the international arbitration community considers the current state of diversity to be acceptable or worth addressing.

To explore issues about diversity from a broad perspective, we asked a wide-ranging question. Specifically, we asked respondents to respond to this statement: "International arbitration has diversity challenges related to gender, nationality, or age." Respondents then ranked their answer using a 1-5 ordinal scale, with 1 being "strongly disagree", 3 being "neither agree nor disagree" and 5 being "strongly agree".[289]

Overall, the responses reflected that ICCA respondents self-identified that international arbitration experiences diversity challenges. For the 513 ICCA respondents answering the question, both the most frequent answer and median answer was 4,[290] indicating that respondents somewhat agreed that there are diversity challenges in international arbitration related to gender, nationality or age. See Table 15.[291]

---

287. See also Sally J. KENNY, "Which Judicial Selection Systems Generate the Most Women Judges? Lessons from the United States", in *Gender and Judging, op. cit.*, fn. 248, p. 461 at pp. 462-469 (identifying various explanations for lack of female representation in judiciaries).

288. Arbitration's diversity concerns are somewhat reminiscent of commentary about the glass ceiling in transitioning to the judiciary. See KALANTRY, *op. cit.*, fn. 256, p. 85 ("Across the globe, women judges report that an 'old boys' club' mentality surround[s] judicial appointment [and] poses a crucial barrier to entry").

289. See Annex: Survey Materials, this volume, pp. 121-122.

290. Thirty-five respondents failed to answer this question. The mean response was 3.63 (SD=1.153).

291. For the subset of ICCA respondents who served as counsel or arbitrator, the 445 respondents yielded similar response patterns, with 6.3% strongly disagreeing (n=28); 10.3% somewhat disagreeing (n=46); 26.5% neither agreeing nor disagreeing (n=118); 30.1% somewhat agreeing (n=134); and 26.7% strongly agreeing (n=119) about international arbitration experiencing diversity concerns.

Table 15: Percentages and Frequency of Responses of All ICCA Respondents in Response to Question About Whether International Arbitration Has Diversity Issues Related to Gender, Nationality or Age

Answer	Response Percentage	Response Frequency
1 – Strongly Disagree	6.2	32
2 – (Somewhat Disagree)	9.2	47
3 – Neither Agree nor Disagree	27.1	139
4 – (Somewhat Agree)	30.8	158
5 – Strongly Agree	26.7	137
Total	100.0	513

There were also reliable gender differences in how respondents perceived diversity issues in international arbitration ($t(506)=6.189$; $p<.001$; $r=.27$; $n=508$).[292] For male respondents, the mean score was 3.46 (SD=1.13; $n=385$), indicating that the tendency overall was to neither agree nor disagree about the existence of a diversity problem in international arbitration but still, overall, reflective of a potential concern. In contrast, for female respondents the mean score was 4.17 (SD=1.05; $n=123$), indicating that the majority of women believed there was a problem and identified that they somewhat or strongly agreed with the possibility of diversity challenges related to gender, nationality or age. In addition, the r-value suggests that gender differences exhibited a medium-sized effect, suggesting the variation in experience was not trivial. Figure 4 reflects that men were more likely than women to either disagree with the idea that there are diversity challenges or not take a position on diversity challenges; by contrast, women were more likely than men to "strongly agree" that international arbitration experiences diversity challenges, with 50% of all women selecting that response.

---

292. The effect was also significant for the subset of ICCA respondents who were counsel and/or arbitrators ($t(443)=5.736$; $p<.001$; $r=.26$; $n=445$).

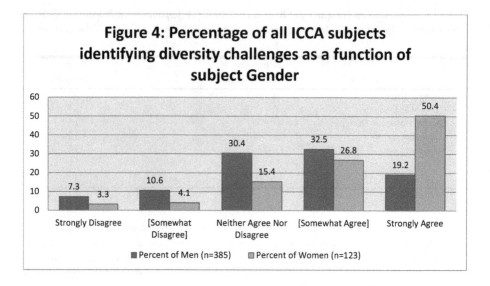

Figure 4: Percentage of all ICCA subjects identifying diversity challenges as a function of subject Gender

A correlation coefficient evaluated a possible relationship between age and perceived concerns about diversity and identified a statistically significant relationship ($r(497)=-.17$; $p<.001$). The reliable link was, as respondent age increased, respondents were *less* likely to identify a diversity problem in international arbitration. In contrast, as respondent age decreased, respondents were *more* likely to identify a diversity problem in international arbitration.

The results evaluating a relationship between respondents' development status, however, were more mixed. While one might hypothesize that, much like gender and age where women and younger practitioners were more sensitized to diversity concerns, this was not the case for development status. The results, however, suggested that respondents' development status was either irrelevant or operated in the *opposite* direction of that hypothesis.

Out of an abundance of caution, we analyzed respondents' primary nationality in three ways, namely: (1) OECD membership, (2) World Bank classification, and (3) HDI classification. The results generated a puzzle. First, using correlation coefficients[293] and ANOVAs,[294] it was not possible to identify a meaningful difference in responses to the

---

293. Using correlation coefficients, there was not a reliable linear relationship with respondents' development status using World Bank ($r(484)=-.05$; $p=.25$) or HDI status ($r(484)=.07$; $p=.15$). As any latent effect was less than statistically small, they are technically statistically underpowered and further research is necessary.

294. The ANOVA analyzed variation in the diversity question on the basis of the four-category variable of respondents' World Bank development status. There was no significant main effect for development ($F(3,480)=1.802$; $p=.15$; $r=.11$; $n=484$). Follow-up analyses using a conservative test also failed to identify any significant pairwise comparisons. Using a more liberal test, however, there was only one significant follow-up relationship where nationals of upper-middle income states expressed *lower* levels of concerns about diversity, whereas nationals of high income

diversity question using a respondent's World Bank or HDI classification. Nevertheless, the non-significant facial pattern was that respondents from countries with higher levels of development status were more likely to express concerns related to diversity.

There was, however, a reliable variation in answers to the diversity question based upon whether the respondent was from an OECD or a non-OECD country.[295] Yet, the difference was in an unexpected direction. Respondents who were from OECD countries were *more* likely to identify diversity issues; and, in contrast, respondents from non-OECD countries were *less* likely to identify diversity challenges. Nevertheless, even having identified the difference, the effect size was statistically small ($r=.10$), which indicates that the effect while reliably present was not large. Figure 5 reflects that non-OECD nationals were slightly more likely than OECD nationals to either disagree with the idea that there are diversity challenges or not take a position on diversity challenges. By contrast, OECD nationals were more likely than non-OECD nationals to either "somewhat" or "strongly agree" that international arbitration experiences diversity challenges.

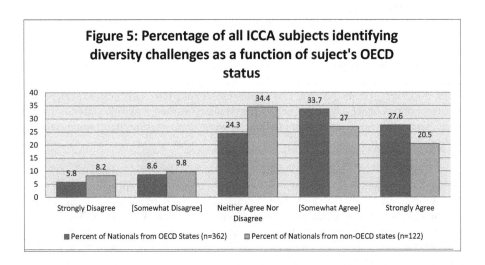

Figure 5: Percentage of all ICCA subjects identifying diversity challenges as a function of suject's OECD status

The results may, in part, reflect that in some national courts, there were low levels of diversity, and in public international law courts and tribunals, there were low levels of development status diversity. In these circumstances, it is possible that non-OECD nationals view arbitration as comparatively better at generating opportunities for a

---

states expressed *higher* level of concerns about diversity.
295. The relationship was significant using a correlation coefficient ($r(484)=.10$; $p=.03$) or a t-test ($t(482)=-2.255$; $p=.03$; $r=.10$; $n=484$). The mean response to the diversity question for OECD nationals was 3.69 (SD=1.14; $n=362$) and 3.42 (SD=1.16; $n=112$) for non-OECD nationals.

diverse range of arbitration specialists and thereby view the status quo as less problematic.

Overall, the general international arbitration community indicated there were concerns on issues of diversity related to gender, nationality or age. Women and younger respondents reliably identified the difference more distinctly. Although the results were mixed as regards a respondent's development status, which served as a proxy for nationality, there was some evidence suggesting that, for those attending the ICCA Miami 2014 Congress, the arbitration community from the developed world may perceive greater concerns than their counterparts. Yet, as demonstrated with respondents' actual experiences with diversity, these perceived concerns may need to be adjusted given the data.[296]

c.   *Actual experience with diversity in international arbitration*

Perception, however, can differ from reality. Scholarship in cognitive psychology reflects that assessments can be influenced by heuristics that make certain experiences seem more prevalent or generate selective perception.[297] For this reason, we tested the demographic data and perceptions against reported experiences in international arbitration.

This Sub-section first analyzes how frequently those acting as arbitrators receive appointments, both as a function of gender and development status. It then explores counsel's and arbitrators' experience with diverse appointments. To minimize response bias, we asked about respondents' experiences with international arbitration in a portion of the Survey that was separate from the demographic questions and the survey item about diversity. Specifically, we asked questions exploring – in their experience as arbitrator and counsel – how frequently respondents worked with tribunals comprised of at least one woman and/or tribunals with at least one developing-country arbitrator.[298]

i.   Gender and development: variations in frequency of arbitral appointments

Earlier, Tables 1 and 2 reflected that the average number of appointments for all types of arbitration was thirty-five; and given the variation in the number of appointments, the median number of total arbitration appointments (both in ICA and ITA) was ten. The question remained, however, whether the scope of those appointments varied according to arbitrators' gender or development status. For women, it was *not* possible to identify a meaningful difference in number of arbitral appointments; but for nationals of

---

296. Sect. IV.4.c.i-iii raises several questions, for example, as the data reflect a reliable pattern whereby developing-world arbitrators experienced lower numbers of appointments than their developed-world counterparts but were also likely to sit with other developing-world arbitrators; and we were unable to identify a meaningful difference between the appointment levels of men and women.

297. See, e.g., Christopher CHABRIS and Daniel SIMONS, *The Invisible Gorilla: How Our Intuitions Deceive Us* (Crown Publishing 2010); FRANCK, *Myths and Realities, op. cit.,* fn. 29, ch. 2 et seq.

298. If we had additional time and space, we could have explored other diversity aspects of international arbitrators and counsel. Methodological constraints related to timing and formatting, however, prevented us from doing so; and we were only in a position to ask those questions identified in the Annex : Survey Materials, this volume, pp. 121-122. Further research could consider a broader conception of diversity to explore other experiences.

developing countries, it *was* possible to identify a meaningful difference in the number of appointments.

For gender, we conducted two types of tests to assess meaningful differences between men and women in the number of arbitration appointments. First, a Mann-Whitney two-sample U-test failed to reveal a statistically significant difference in the median number of appointments (U=4564.5; p=.39).[299] The median number of appointments for women was 9 (IQR=3-22);[300] and the median for men was 10.5 (IQR=3-40). Similarly, an ANOVA failed to reveal any statistically significant difference in mean appointments (F(1,260)=0.086; p=.77; r=.01; n=262). The mean number of appointments for women was 32 (SD=79.39; n=46), and the mean number of appointments for men was 35 (SD=61; n=216). When we analyzed the separate subsets of ICA and ITA appointments, we were also unable to find a reliable gender difference in the number of appointments.[301]

For development status, we conducted a series of tests – using different constructs of development status – to assess whether there were meaningful differences between the appointment levels of developed and developing-world arbitrators.[302] First, a Mann-Whitney U-test identified a reliable difference in appointments between OECD and non-OECD nationals (U=3247.5; p<.01) such that OECD nationals reliably obtained more appointments. While the median number of appointments for arbitrators from non-OECD countries was 5 (IQR=2-19.25), the median number of appointments for arbitrators from OECD countries was 11.5 (IQR 4-40). Second, a Kruskal-Wallace test identified a reliable difference between World Bank classifications of an arbitrator's home state ($X2$=12.091; p<.01; r=.22; n=250) such that developing-world arbitrators obtained fewer appointments than their more developed-world colleagues. The median number of appointments for an arbitrator from a high-income state was 11 (IQR=4-40); the median number of appointments for arbitrators from an upper-middle income state was 8 (IQR=2-25); and the median number of appointments for arbitrators from a lower-middle income state was 2 (IQR=1-8). There were no arbitrators from low-income states. Third, a correlation coefficient identified a reliable difference between HDI classification of an arbitrator's home state and number of appointments (r(250)=.13; p=.04). The more developed the home state, the greater number of

---

299. Non-parametric tests of medians were necessary to evaluate group differences in appointments, as the mean number of arbitral appointments exhibited unacceptable levels of skewing (4.772; SE=.117).

300. IQR stands for an Inter Quartile Range, which reflects quartile breakdowns. See URDAN, *op. cit.*, fn. 53, pp. 19, 161-163 (describing IQRs, the Mann-Whitney U test, the Kruskal-Wallis test, and Chi-square tests of independence). In this case the 25th quartile is 3; the median was 9; and the 75th percentile was 22. For IQR=3-22, the three reflects the 25th quartile and the 22 reflects the 75th quartile.

301. Using a Mann-Whitney test, for example, we were unable to detect a reliable link between gender and number of arbitration appointments in either ICA (U=4511.5; p=.48) or ITA (U=3020.5; p=.23).

302. Different tests were necessary given different variable types. A Mann-Whitney test compares differences between two groups and a continuous variable; a Kruskal-Wallace test compares differences between multiple groups and a continuous variable; and correlations are used when there are two continuous variables, like HDI status and number of appointments.

appointments; and the less developed the arbitrator's home state, the fewer the number of appointments.

Overall, the results suggested that, for women, once they gain access to the arbitration "club" by having at least one appointment, the frequency of appointments was roughly equivalent to the appointment levels of their male colleagues. By contrast, for developing-world arbitrators, the number of their appointments was statistically lower than their developed-world counterparts.

This generates a rather interesting, and complex, puzzle. For women, it means that they were more likely to perceive diversity challenges, the diversity challenges being apparent in the small number of women acting as arbitrators (particularly when compared to women in positions of authority in national courts and legislatures). Once women joined the arbitrator pool, they obtained roughly equivalent levels of appointments. In other words, for women, the diversity challenge appears to involve obtaining initial access or breaking through the glass ceiling. For developing-world arbitrators, it means they were less likely to perceive diversity challenges, even though there were small numbers of developing-world arbitrators and they also received fewer appointments. Part of the explanation may be the contrast with the lower representation of developing-world adjudicators in international courts and tribunals, which is buttressed by the number of tribunals where developing-world arbitrators sat with other developing-world arbitrators. Nevertheless, in contrast to diversity challenges experienced by women, it suggests that developing-world arbitrators may require a different solution to achieving broader representation.

ii.   Experience of arbitrators

We asked respondents whether, in their experience as international arbitrators, they had served on a tribunal with a woman (or another woman). We then invited respondents to respond by ticking a box indicating that they had (1) never sat on a tribunal with a woman, (2) they had sat on such a tribunal 1-5 times, (3) they had sat on such a tribunal 6-10 times, or (4) they had sat on a tribunal with a woman more than 10 times.[303]

First, we adjusted responses to reflect women's self-reported arbitral appointments.[304] This made it possible to correct for potential under-reporting and identify the number of times ICCA arbitrators sat on tribunals with at least one woman. The mode and median response was two, reflecting that at least 1-5 arbitrations contained at least one woman. Table 16 provides a frequency breakdown of respondents responses, which indicates that a significant proportion of arbitrators reported they had "never" been on a tribunal with a woman and, overall, more than 75% of arbitrators indicated the absolute maximum number of times they had sat on a tribunal with a female co-arbitrator was five. A primary basis for there ever being a female arbitrator on

---

303. See Annex: Survey Materials, this volume, pp. 121-122.
304. For example, if a woman had indicated that she had "never" (=1) sat on a tribunal with a woman, but she sat on twenty cases, the response was re-coded as "more than ten times" (=4) to reflect her own appointments.

a tribunal resulted from ensuring that women's own appointment experience was reflected in the analysis.[305]

Table 16: Percentages and Frequency of Responses of ICCA Respondents Serving as Arbitrators, Describing the Frequency of Having at Least One Woman on a Tribunal (Including Women's Self-Reported Appointments)

Answer	Response Percentage	Response Frequency
Never had Tribunal with a Woman	32.2	83
1-5 Tribunals with a Woman	43.4	112
6-10 Tribunals with a Woman	8.9	23
10+ Tribunals with a Woman	15.5	40
Total	100.0	258

Second, using the subset of forty-six female arbitrators, we identified how many times those women sat on tribunals with two or more women. The results suggested that, more often than not, these women were the only women arbitrators on their tribunals. Specifically, 52.2% ($n=24$) indicated they had never sat with another woman; 37% ($n=17$) indicated they had sat with another woman 1-5 times; and 1.5% ($n=4$) indicated they had sat with another woman between 6-10 times. Only one female arbitrator indicated that she had been empaneled with another woman on more than ten occasions. Since most tribunals consist of three members, this suggests it was rare for two women to work together as co-arbitrators.

Turning to nationality and development, we asked respondents whether, in their experience as arbitrators, they had served on a tribunal with an arbitrator from a developing country. We then invited respondents to respond by ticking a box indicating that they had: (1) "never" sat on such a tribunal, (2) sat on such a tribunal 1-5 times, (3) sat on such a tribunal 6-10 times, or (4) sat on a tribunal with a developing-world arbitrator more than ten times.[306] We cross-checked respondents' own development status to ensure that their responses did not ignore their own experience as arbitrators. We classified arbitrators' development status in three ways as a cross-check using OECD, World Bank and HDI status. Results were nearly identical irrespective of how the respondents' development status was coded.[307] Table 17 provides a frequency

---

305. Without adjusting for a woman's own appointments, there was nearly a dead heat between respondents answering they had "never" or only "1-5 times" sat with a woman. Between those two categories alone, this reflected nearly 84% of all responses. Only 7.8% of respondents indicated they had sat with a woman more than ten times.

306. See Annex: Survey Materials, this volume, pp. 121-122.

307. When respondents were analyzed using the World Bank classification of their home state (and classifying non-High Income arbitrators as a "developing-world" arbitrator): (1) 40.2% ($n=102$) had "never" sat with a developing-world arbitrator; (2) 38.6% ($n=98$) had sat with one

distribution of the OECD status results where we ensured that, for nationals of non-OECD states, they did not under-represent their experiences with developing-world arbitrators in their own experience as an arbitrator.

Table 17: Percentages and Frequency of Responses of ICCA Respondents Serving as Arbitrators, Describing the Frequency of Having at Least One Developing-World Arbitrator on a Tribunal (Including Respondents' Self-Reported Appointments Using Their OECD Status)

Answer	Response Percentage	Response Frequency
Never had Tribunal with a Developing-World Arbitrator	40.2	102
1-5 Tribunals with a Developing-World Arbitrator	38.6	98
6-10 Tribunals with a Developing-World Arbitrator	9.8	25
10+ Tribunals with a Developing-World Arbitrator	11.4	29
Total	100.0	254

Much like the results for arbitrators experiencing the presence of a single woman, nearly one-half of arbitrators never experienced having a single developing-world arbitrator on a tribunal. Fourteen respondents indicated that they had sat in 100+ arbitrations, but they worked with developing-world arbitrators in less than ten of their cases. At a time when there is a broad pool of talent in international arbitration, and that talent extends across national borders and gender, the concentration of arbitration appointments suggests that there may be untapped value in diversifying the pool of arbitrators.

---

developing-world arbitrator 1-5 times; (3) 9.8% (*n*=25) had sat with a developing-world arbitrator 6-10 times; and (4) 11.4% (*n*=29) had sat with a developing-world arbitrator 11 or more times. When respondents were analyzed using the HDI ranking of their home state (and classifying arbitrators as "developing" when they were not in the top 30 most developed states under the UNDP's ranking: (1) 39.0% (*n*=99) had never sat with a developing-country arbitrator; (2) 39.4% (*n*=100) had sat with one developing-world arbitrator 1-5 times; (3) 9.8% (*n*=25) had sat with a developing-world arbitrator 6-10 times; and (4) 11.8% (*n*=30) had sat with a developing-world arbitrator 11 or more times.

iii.   Experience of counsel

For those who had acted as counsel, we asked two different questions regarding their experiences. The first question related to how frequently respondents had tribunals with multiple female arbitrators; and the second question related to how frequently respondents had arbitral tribunals with multiple arbitrators from the developing world.

As regards that first question, the mode and median answers were "never", and the vast majority of counsel had "never" argued before a tribunal containing two or three women. Specifically, 74.6% (n=290) of counsel had never had a tribunal with two or more women; 21.3% (n=83) of respondents had only experienced a tribunal with multiple women 1-5 times; 1.8% (n=7) of counsel had experienced tribunals with multiple women 6-10 times; and the remaining 2.3% (n=9) had acted in more than ten cases where there were multiple women. The light gray bar in Figure 6 provides a frequency breakdown demonstrating that, when acting as counsel, the overwhelming majority of respondents had never had more than one woman on a tribunal at a time; and only a sliver (less than 5%) had experienced two or more female arbitrators in more than five cases during the course of their careers. Contrasted with Table 1, where the average counsel worked on 27 cases, the lack of experience with tribunals containing multiple female arbitrators is noteworthy. It also suggests that those perceiving a facial diversity imbalance in international arbitration were justified in their assessment.

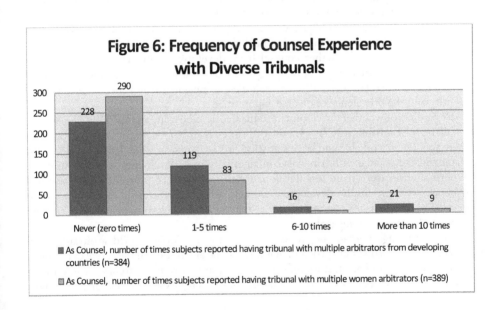

Figure 6: Frequency of Counsel Experience with Diverse Tribunals

- As Counsel, number of times subjects reported having tribunal with multiple arbitrators from developing countries (n=384)
- As Counsel, number of times subjects reported having tribunal with multiple women arbitrators (n=389)

On the theory that female counsel might advise the appointment of female arbitrators – or that clients willing to retain female counsel may be more likely to appoint female arbitrators – we tested whether counsel's gender was reliably linked to the number of tribunals with multiple female arbitrators. Tests were unable to detect a reliable link between those variables.[308] A sample of more than 780 subjects would be required to reliably isolate the presence or absence of an effect as the non-significant latent effect was statistically small.[309]

For the second question of counsel experience with arbitrators' development status, the results were similar but with a small twist. The mode and median answer were also "never" and the majority of counsel had "never" argued before a tribunal with two or three individuals from developing countries. Yet, counsel had somewhat more experience with tribunals containing multiple developing-country arbitrators. Specifically, 59.4% ($n=228$) of counsel had "never" had a tribunal with two or more developing-world arbitrators; 31.0% ($n=119$) of respondents had only experienced a tribunal with multiple developing-country arbitrators 1-5 times; 4.2% ($n=16$) of counsel had experienced tribunals with multiple developing-country arbitrators 6-10 times; and the remaining 5.5% ($n=21$) had acted in more than ten cases where there were multiple arbitrators from the developing world. The dark gray bar in Figure 6 demonstrates that when acting as counsel, the overwhelming majority of respondents had "never" had multiple developing-world arbitrators on a tribunal; but a small number (less than 10%) experienced two or more developing-world arbitrators in more than five cases.

Of note, in response to this question, one respondent offered an unsolicited comment in its response, namely: "when you do Brazil work ... every tribunal is Brazilian".[310] This raised the question of whether counsel from developing states reliably experienced having tribunals with multiple developing-world arbitrators. Unlike the findings related to gender, a correlation coefficient identified a meaningful link between counsel's identity and the prevalence of diverse appointments.

Regardless of whether development status was defined using an OECD ($r(367)=-.44$; $p<.001$), World Bank ($r(367)=.42$; $p<.001$) or HDI ($r(367)=-.42$; $p<.001$) definition, there was *always* a reliable and large statistical link between a respondent's development status and experience with tribunals containing multiple developing-world arbitrators. Where counsel were from less developed states, they were more likely to have had tribunals with multiple developing-country arbitrators; and likewise, the more developed the counsel's country of origin, the less likely they were to have experienced tribunals from developing states.

These findings perhaps begin to explain why developing-world arbitrators also perceived less of a diversity problem in international arbitration. If the actual experience of developing-world arbitrators reflects that they are more likely to have worked with several tribunals composed of primarily developing-world arbitrators, it seems

---

308. A correlation coefficient ($r(389)=-.05$; $p=.34$), a t-test ($t(387)=0.957$; $p=.34$; $r=.05$; $n=389$), and a Pearson's Chi-square Test of Independence were all non-significant ($X2=.275$; $p=.28$).

309. The r-values were less than .10, which means they were less than statistically small. See COHEN, *op. cit.,* fn. 118. A *post-hoc* power analysis indicates that, in order to reliably detect such a miniscule latent effect related to gender, the minimum sample size would need to be 781 to establish .80 power and 1045 to establish .90 power.

310. This comment came from respondent no. 381.

reasonable to infer that respondents would be less likely to readily identify a problem with diversity. By contrast, where developed-world arbitrators were *not* experiencing a caseload with arbitrators from a broad cross-section of arbitrators with various arbitrators from states across a developmental divide, they might rightly identify an imbalance related to nationality or development.

V.   LIMITATIONS

It is necessary to identify research limitations to prevent consumers of research from drawing unwarranted inferences and permitting assessment of the utility of the research. Throughout this Paper, we have included cautions about the limitations of survey questions generally and our questions specifically, limitations of statistical tests, and limitations related to the analyzed sample. For example, we identified concerns related to the representativeness of the sample and the risk of selection bias that derive from the potential over-inclusion of North American respondents, the under-inclusion of other respondents, the use of English language in an international dispute settlement conference, and fiscal cost of attendance. In addition to the traditional caveats that must be appreciated when drawing inferences from scientific research,[311] we also believe it is appropriate to highlight other key issues.

First, there is a risk of external validity. The data from ICCA are now a historical snapshot. It is possible that, as international arbitration continues to expand, several of the findings will change. One might imagine, for instance, certain findings related to diversity changing over time as the group of arbitrators expands; and one day there may be broader variation in age, gender and nationality. Future research should therefore re-assess these aspects periodically – and in different contexts – with more sophisticated measures and models. In this way, we can reconsider what we know now and add to our knowledge over time.[312]

Second, as ICCA respondents had the option both to not attend the initial Plenary and also not complete the survey, there is a risk of a self-selection bias that may limit the inferences. Only 55% of ICCA registrants attended the first Plenary. This means, although the response rate was reasonable, a number of conference participants were not represented in the survey results. Similarly, although distributing surveys at elite conferences may improve response rates, the method also necessarily limits the sample to those arbitration practitioners interested in the conference, willing to attend or able to attend.[313]

Third, for those instances where we conducted tests to look for group differences and obtained non-significant results, it is not possible to claim there is no relationship. As discussed, even with a base sample of over 500 respondents, certain tests were statistically underpowered with an unacceptable risk of a Type II error; and it is possible

---

311. FRANCK, et al., *op. cit.*, fn. 74, pp. 885-899.
312. *Ibid.*, pp. 888-889, 900-902 (discussing external validity issues and opportunities for future research).
313. See CHENG, *op. cit.*, fn. 33, p. 1279 (identifying similar concerns in distributing surveys to judges at judicial conferences).

that a meaningful – but latent – difference is lurking within the data. Future research with an expanded sample size is therefore required before reaching definitive conclusions about the lack of a statistically reliable effect. In any event, for many of the non-significant results, the effect sizes were small or less than small suggesting that any latent differences may not be practically meaningful; and a sample with sufficient power to detect even the small effects will require between 1,200-1,600 subjects. One might therefore hope that a well-attended future ICCA Congress would be an appropriate venue for such an undertaking.

As a result of these cautionary considerations, more research is required to create the sufficient power, stability, statistical control, and enhanced validity necessary to reach more definitive conclusions. Given the practical challenges in obtaining a sufficiently large set of subjects, it may be challenging to recreate this research. Nevertheless, those challenges do not diminish the possibility of future research providing useful replication that confirms – and expands – upon existing research.

VI.   CONCLUSION

The data in this Paper reflect that the modern reality of international arbitration is complex and not subject to an easy unitary narrative. As ICCA may realize this given its willingness to engage in self-reflection, a full appreciation of the complexity offers a powerful opportunity. This data – and other research in the future – will permit the international arbitration community to explore evidence-based solutions to identifiable challenges without reliance on stylized facts or anecdotes. Recognizing that this research is novel in several key aspects, we respect that the initial findings will require re-evaluation. We now explore the complexities of international arbitration by focusing on the most crucial findings related to demographics, issues involving precision and concerns related to justice.

There were both bright spots along with areas for improvement in the basic demographics. The good news reflected that ICCA has moved past historical east/west and market/non-market economy divides. The data demonstrated that arbitrators and counsel reflected a broad spectrum of nationalities, continents and languages. Nevertheless, as old challenges have been conquered, new ones have arisen. The data reflected arguably disproportionate levels of representation by men from states in North America and Europe, which have high levels of economic development. Specifically, only 24% of counsel and 17.6% of arbitrators were women. Meanwhile, 68.6% of counsel and 76% of arbitrators were from Europe and North America; and given those nationalities, it should be unsurprising that 75.2% of counsel and 82.4% of arbitrators were from OECD states, and 76.5% of counsel and 84.8% of arbitrators were from high-income countries. Ultimately, the data supported, rather than disproved, claims that international arbitration is a "white male game".[314]

---

314. Peter F. PHILLIPS, "ADR Continental Drift: It Remains a White, Male Game", National L.J. (27 Nov. 2006); Maria R. VOLPE, et al., "Barriers to Participation: Challenges Faced by Members of Underrepresented Racial and Ethnic Groups in Entering, Remaining, and Advancing in the ADR Field", 35 Ford. Urban L.J. (2008) p. 119.

Precision is key to the legitimacy of rule of law institutions. In this respect, with the limited number of questions we asked, the data revealed precision-related strengths and weaknesses. The core factor supporting a high level of precision involved arbitrator preparation. Despite poignant narratives about well-paid arbitrators who are nevertheless unprepared for hearings, over half of the ICCA respondents revealed that all members of tribunals were fully prepared either "frequently" or "always". High levels of diligence, in turn, stand to generate greater precision and accuracy in the arbitration process. Nevertheless, there were areas requiring attention by the arbitration community or redress by parties. Specifically, there was a disjunction whereby respondents viewed burden of proof as outcome determinative, yet were unable to obtain advance notice of those outcome determinative rules. Likewise, over 66% of arbitrators and counsel said that tribunals either "never" (or only "occasionally") offered advance notice of how tribunals would exercise their costs discretion. As both proof and cost issues exhibited a common/ civil law divide in responses, appropriate remedies in these areas likely require tailoring to reflect jurisdictional differences. Luckily, arbitration offers that flexibility and parties can make targeted adjustments. As a final matter, nearly 75% of arbitrators and counsel identified that parties "sometimes", "frequently" or "always" withheld responsive documents; and less than 2% indicated that such procedural impropriety never occurred in their cases. Given the importance of procedural integrity and generating precise results based upon verifiable facts, document production is an area ripe for targeted reform. Moreover, given that reforms in areas of precision – like burden of proof and document production – relate primarily to procedural matters, generating systemic mechanical reforms will add immediate value for all parties.

Justice – both substantive and procedural – is a core fulcrum of rule of law. Appreciating the preliminary nature of the enquiry, data suggested both positive aspects related to legitimacy and areas in which the arbitration community can make strategic choices about its future. The constructive news was that although respondents viewed arbitration as prestigious (particularly ITA), neither ICA nor ITA arbitrators believed they were motivated by concerns related to reappointment or establishing themselves as collegial players during contemporaneous decisionmaking. For both ICA and ITA, more than 75% of arbitrators indicated that they either disagreed (or simply did not care) about future reappointments. Those findings cut against the theory that arbitrators are self-motivated partisans in adjudication or otherwise actively game adjudication to obtain future appointments. Yet further research is necessary to remove elements of potential self-serving bias that potentially affected the results.

Justice concerns related to fraud and diversity were observable. Respondents identified challenges related to fraud in international arbitration. Nearly 11% of respondents indicated that fraud "frequently" or "always" occurred in arbitration, raising a degree of concern. While others thought fraud was less frequent, over 85% of respondents stated that fraud occurred either "occasionally" or "sometimes". Arbitration insiders should carefully explore how to decrease the incentives to engage in fraud; but particularly as counsel and arbitrators identified lower levels of fraud than other ICCA respondents, education of the public and de-sensitization of the arbitration bar may also be warranted.

Diversity challenges within international arbitration are, however, potentially the most challenging – but also possibly the most rewarding – as they generate a historical

117

opportunity to be a leader within the broader community of international courts and tribunals. At a minimum, there is an important normative question about what is the appropriate baseline against which diversity in international arbitration should be measured. On one hand, one might intuitively look to baselines established by national legislatures and judiciaries. Yet, on the other hand, given the transnational nature of international arbitration, which draws on the "invisible college" of lawyers from many states, perhaps the baseline offered by public international law is the more appropriate baseline. Nonetheless, using either baseline, the small size of the pool of women and developing-world arbitrators was noteworthy.

Perhaps intuitively recognizing demographic imbalance, more than 75% of ICCA respondents identified that they agreed (either somewhat or strongly) with the proposition that international arbitration experiences diversity challenges. Yet, not everyone perceived the same level of challenges. Women and younger respondents were *more* likely to identify diversity challenges than men or older respondents. However, respondents from developing countries (no matter how that term was defined) were *less* likely than their developed-world counterparts to identify diversity challenges. These perceived experiences, however, are juxtaposed with actual experiences related to gender and development status.

Data reflected that entering the "club" of international arbitration was challenging, and the proportion of women arbitrators was only 17.6%. Yet, once women entered the "club" of arbitrators, statistical tests could not identify a meaningful difference in the number of appointments that women had as compared to men. Even counting women's own arbitration appointments, approximately one-third of arbitrators had never sat on a tribunal with a woman. More than 75% of counsel reported they had never had a tribunal with more than two female arbitrators.

Analyzing diversity according to development status was equally challenging with both bright spots and challenges. Recognizing that developing-world arbitrators were *less* likely to identify diversity problems in international arbitration, two aspects are noteworthy. The first was the demographic data reflecting that OECD and/or high-income arbitrators made up more than 75% of the arbitrators in our sample. The second was that, irrespective of how development status was defined, developing-world arbitrators experienced statistically lower numbers of appointments than their developed-world colleagues. Meanwhile, even counting developing-world arbitrators' own appointments, approximately 40% of arbitrators reported never having sat on a tribunal with a developing-world arbitrator; and 59.4% of counsel reported never having worked with a tribunal containing multiple arbitrators from developing countries. Nevertheless, those descriptive findings must be contextualized against tests demonstrating that counsel from developing countries were much more likely to experience high portions of tribunals comprised of developing-world arbitrators. As one respondent volunteered, "when you do Brazil work … every tribunal is Brazilian". While there are other possibilities, localized experiences may account for the divergences of perception and reality for developing-world arbitrators.

Ultimately, diversity challenges in international arbitration are and will continue to generate complex dynamics. As suggested by Sundaresh Menon at the ICCA Congress in Singapore in 2012[315] and Salim Moollan at the ICCA Congress in Miami in 2014,[316] we believe they are a challenge worth undertaking and could serve to enhance arbitration's long-term legitimacy and sustainability. In a time when there is a broad pool of talent in international arbitration, and that talent extends across national borders and encompasses all genders, there is likely untapped value in diversifying the pool of arbitrators.

Considering how best to diversify the "invisible college" of arbitrators may contribute in several ways to the long-term sustainability of international arbitration as a means for solving international disputes. First, as international business activity becomes more complex and international arbitration expands, it is critical to have a pool of arbitrators who are immediately available to resolve disputes and appreciate the unique context from which the dispute arises. This minimizes risk of delay, decreases costs and increases stakeholder satisfaction. Second, as the existing pool of international arbitrators continues to "age up", it is necessary to ensure institutional and historical knowledge is transferred to the next generation. The objective should be to prevent an over-concentration of arbitration experience, so that a broad pool of arbitrators can continue to offer quality adjudicative services in the future. Third, to the extent that conflicts of interests within law firms or subject-matter conflicts of interest limit the services that arbitrators can provide, it is necessary to have both breadth and depth in the pool of potential appointees.

We must also acknowledge, however, that there are inevitable limitations to this research in terms of the population sampled, questions asked, data identified, and derivative inferences. Empirical research, like all quests for human knowledge, can never be perfect. While we were constrained in our capacity to analyze every latent question suggested by the data due to time and space constraints, we hope the initial data and preliminary analyses will offer a useful baseline. We welcome the process of identifying how the results might change over time as international arbitration evolves.

The results provided in this Paper are both designed to elucidate the "invisible college" of international arbitrators and identify the tip of a larger empirical iceberg.[317] We applaud ICCA for taking the first step in generating transparent information about the "invisible college" of international arbitration. In light of the data, we offer two suggestions. First, we encourage ICCA and other researchers to continue exploring how to generate scientifically rigorous data that can inform stakeholders and permit reasoned discussions about how best to improve international arbitration. Second, we encourage ICCA and the international arbitration community to think seriously and strategically

---

315. MENON, *op. cit.*, fn. 133, paras. 74-76 (observing that the international arbitration community should take into account the unique circumstances of developing nations and make an effort to engage developing countries into the development of norms).

316. See MOOLLAN, *op. cit.*, fn. 240 and accompanying text.

317. Further explorations of the implications of research related to diversity is available at FRANCK, et al., fn. 35.

about how to generate areas for improvement, whether structural or incremental.[318] Recognizing that normative debates about the evolution of arbitration matter – but the reality of human behavior is also vital – we hope that evidence-driven approaches will enhance both justice and precision and thereby promote the legitimacy of international arbitration as a strong and viable dispute settlement option.

---

318. That discussion is already beginning. See Lucy REED and James FREDA, "Maxwell Lecture – After ICCA Singapore, After ICCA Miami: The Next Questions", ICSID Rev. (forthcoming 2015).

Annex

Survey Materials

Demographic Questions

1. Your Sex (Male or Female):
2. Your Nationality (or Nationalities):
3. Your Current Age:
4. Your Mother Tongue:
5. Please identify other languages that you speak and/or write proficiently:
6. Please indicate jurisdiction(s) where you received your legal education:
   □ Common Law   □ Civil Law   □ Both

7. Please indicate the number of cases where you have acted as:
   a. *Counsel* in international arbitration:
   b. *Expert* in international arbitration:
   c. *Arbitrator* in an international *commercial arbitration*:
   d. *Arbitrator* in an international *investment treaty arbitration*:
   e. *Adjudicator* in a *public international law dispute* (International Court of Justice, World Trade Organization proceedings, etc.):
   f. *Judge* in a *national court* proceeding:

ICCA Questions

(a) How prestigious is it to have an appointment in international commercial arbitration? [1 (Not Prestigious) to 5 (Very Prestigious)]

(b) How prestigious is it to have an appointment in investment treaty arbitration? [1 (Not Prestigious) to 5 (Very Prestigious)]

(c) In your experience as arbitrator or counsel, how often do tribunals articulate in advance what burden of proof they will require parties to meet? [1 (Never), 2 (Occasionally), 3 (Sometimes), 4 (Frequently), 5 (Always)]

(d) In your experience as arbitrator or counsel, how often has the burden of proof been outcome determinative? [1 (Never), 2 (Occasionally), 3 (Sometimes), 4 (Frequently), 5 (Always)]

(e) In your experience as arbitrator or counsel, how often do tribunals indicate in advance how they will exercise their discretion to shift arbitration costs? [1 (Never), 2 (Occasionally), 3 (Sometimes), 4 (Frequently), 5 (Always)]

(f) In your experience as arbitrator or counsel, how often are all members of the tribunal fully prepared for the hearing? [1 (Never), 2 (Occasionally), 3 (Sometimes), 4 (Frequently), 5 (Always)]

(g) In your experience as arbitrator or counsel, how often have you believed one or both parties have withheld responsive documents? [1 (Never), 2 (Occasionally), 3 (Sometimes), 4 (Frequently), 5 (Always)]

(h) How often do you believe issues of fraud—in the underlying dispute or the arbitration itself—are involved in international arbitration? [1 (Never), 2 (Occasionally), 3 (Sometimes), 4 (Frequently), 5 (Always)]

(i) International arbitration has diversity challenges related to gender, nationality, or age. [1 (Strongly Disagree) to 5 (Strongly Agree)]

(j) When acting as an arbitrator, I consider how I will interact with my co-arbitrators in future cases. [1 (Strongly Disagree) to 5 (Strongly Agree)]

(k) I believe there is value in having default rules permitting institutions to appoint all the arbitrators in a dispute. [1 (Strongly Disagree) to 5 (Strongly Agree)]

(l) When I am sitting as an *international commercial arbitrator*, I consider whether I will be appointed in the future. [1 (Strongly Disagree) to 5 (Strongly Agree)]

(m) When I am sitting as an *investment treaty arbitrator*, I consider whether I will be appointed in the future. [1 (Strongly Disagree) to 5 (Strongly Agree)]

i. In my experience as arbitrator, I have sat with a/another woman: (More than 10 times; 6-10 times; 1-5 times; Never)

ii. In my experience as arbitrator, I have sat with an arbitrator from a developing country: (More than 10 times; 6-10 times; 1-5 times; Never)

iii. In my experience as arbitrator, I have sat with more than one arbitrator from a developing country: (More than 10 times; 6-10 times; 1-5 times; Never)

iv. In my experience as counsel, I have had an arbitral tribunal that has multiple women: (More than 10 times; 6-10 times; 1-5 times; Never)

v. In my experience as counsel, I have had a arbitral tribunal with multiple arbitrators from developing countries: (More than 10 times; 6-10 times; 1-5 times; Never)

A. Precision Stream

A. Precision Stream

1. Proof: A Plea for Precision

The Burden of Proof in International Arbitration

*Anne Véronique Schlaepfer**

I.   GENERAL ACCEPTANCE OF THE PRINCIPLE ITSELF; DIFFERENCES AS REGARDS ITS
     IMPLEMENTATION

1.   The Principle

In international arbitration it is broadly, not to say universally, accepted that each party must prove the facts upon which it relies in support of its case.[1] This principle is explicitly stated in several sets of rules, such as, for instance, in the UNCITRAL Arbitration Rules ("Each party shall have the burden of proving the facts relied on to support his claim or defence")[2] or the Swiss Rules of International Arbitration (Art. 24(1)).

Different views are expressed as to whether the burden of proof is a procedural or substantive issue.[3] Civil law systems tend to consider it to be of substantive nature, whereas common law systems provide that the burden of proof is a matter of procedural law.[4] From a practical point of view, this distinction seems academic. In the end each party has to submit the evidence required to demonstrate the accuracy of the allegations made in the arbitration proceedings. The burden of proof is not only resting on the

---

*   Partner, Schellenberg Wittmer Ltd.
1. R.D. BISHOP, J. CRAWFORD, and W.M. REISMAN, "Chapter 12 – Procedure and Proof: Developing the Case, VII. Burden of Proof" in *Foreign Investment Disputes: Cases, Materials and Commentary* (Kluwer Law International 2005) p. 1445.
2. Art. 24(1) UNCITRAL Arbitration Rules 2010.
3. J. WAINCYMER, "Part II: The Process of an Arbitration, Chapter 10: Approaches to Evidence and Fact Finding" in *Procedure and Evidence in International Arbitration* (Kluwer Law International 2012), p. 762; A. Philip, "Description in the Award of the Standard of Proof Sought and Satisfied" in *The Standards and Burden of Proof in International Arbitration* (1994) p. 362.
4. G. NATER-BASS, Chapter 3, Part II: "Commentary on the Swiss Rules, Article 24", in M. ARROYO, ed., *Arbitration in Switzerland: The Practitioner's Guide* (Kluwer Law International 2013) p. 496.

claimant's shoulders; the respondent also has to prove defenses it has raised against a given claim.

If this principle is broadly acknowledged and, as such, does not give rise to significant controversies, its implementation is much more complex.

2. The Implementation of the Principle

To be in a position to discharge one's burden of proof, one has to know what elements need to be proven or disproven. This implies that the relevant facts are alleged in a manner that permits each party to bring forward the respective means of evidence either proving the accuracy of the allegation or disproving it. There is thus a link between the burden of allegation and the burden of proof. The parties' expectations regarding the burden to allege their respective case vary in view of their legal background and experience in international arbitration. Hence, arbitral tribunals may want to address this point at an early stage of the proceedings in order to determine together with the parties when they are expected to assert the facts underlying their case in a comprehensive manner.

Similarly, the question as to how and when a party must discharge its burden of proof may greatly vary. The following factors, among others, may play a role.

A first factor is the law governing the merits of the case. For instance, the degree and specificity of evidence needed to prove the damage incurred are different depending on whether French law, German law or Swiss law applies.[5]

Similarly, the nature of the fact asserted may influence both the burden and the degree (or standard) of proof. A good example for this is corruption. Since corruption is a particularly serious issue, some scholars consider that arbitral tribunals have to apply a higher standard when determining whether the party alleging corruption has proven it.[6]

Other scholars advocate exactly the opposite view: according to them, corruption is by definition hidden and, therefore, a lower standard of proof shall apply.[7] Another view asserts that the burden of proof shall shift from one party to the other under certain circumstances: according to that latter opinion, once a party has presented sufficient indication for corruption, the burden of proof shifts and it is the opposing party that shall have the duty to disprove these elements.[8] I personally consider that there is no need to shift the burden of proof, or to set any specific standard: arbitral tribunals need to assess evidence submitted to them taking into account the relevant circumstances of the case.

Other factors relate to the personal background of both the parties and the arbitrators.

---

5. C. REYMOND, "The Practical Distinction Between the Burden of Proof and Taking of Evidence — A Further Perspective" in *The Standards and Burden of Proof in International Arbitration* (1994) pp. 23-324.

6. ICC Award No. 8891, published in JDI 2000, 1076.

7. A. MOURRE, "Arbitration and Criminal Law: Reflections on the Duties of the Arbitrator", 22 Arbitration International (2006, no. 1) pp. 102-103 and cited references.

8. C. LAMM, H. PHAM, et al., "Fraud and Corruption in International Arbitration" in *Liber Amicorum Bernardo Cremades* (La Ley 2010) p. 701.

The parties' understanding of how and when during the arbitration they must prove their case may significantly differ. Such understanding and the expectations resulting therefrom are influenced by various elements, such as, for example, the legal and cultural background of the parties (and that of their counsel), the field of activities in which the parties operate, or their experience in international arbitration.

In some jurisdictions witness evidence plays a significant role, while in others it simply does not exist in commercial matters. Although practice and procedural rules before state courts do not apply in international arbitration, they may have an impact on the parties' expectations and on their understanding of the arbitration process, at least for those who are less experienced in international arbitration.

For example, some parties consider that the arbitration itself only commences when the evidentiary hearing starts; they give no consideration at all to the previous written exchanges, which, for them, are part of some sort of limbo phase. For them the hearing is the key moment during which they will both present and prove their case.

For others, the evidentiary hearing is just an unnecessary hurdle, a waste of time and the source of unnecessary costs; it should therefore be as short as possible. In their opinion, their case has been brought during the written phase of the arbitration; they have argued their position and submitted the corresponding documentary evidence. They consider that oral witness testimony belongs to criminal proceedings, and, once an expert has produced his report, it is for the arbitral tribunal to assess its evidentiary weight. Asking oral questions to the expert adds little value. In short, not much, at least nothing good, is to be expected from an evidentiary hearing.

Differences, albeit less striking, may be noted among arbitrators. The confidence placed in certain means of adducing evidence may vary depending on the legal background of the arbitrator[9] and, more importantly in practice, on his or her personality and apprehension of the issues at stake.

Some arbitrators have a(n almost) definitive opinion on a case once they have studied the documentary evidence on record. Others consider that they need first to hear the witnesses to form an opinion on the questions at issue.

Even among arbitrators who consider that witness/expert oral evidence is important, differences are noticeable:

– For some of them, cross-examination is the key feature of this phase. They consider that the cross-examination done by counsel will give them the possibility to determine whether expert or witness evidence may be relied upon.

– For others, cross-examination is not more than a useful tool that must be completed by the arbitral tribunal's own questions. Some arbitrators show a great confidence in their ability (real or supposed) to always ask the right questions in order to shed light on the case.

---

9. I. FADLALLAH, *Arbitration Facing Conflicts of Culture* (2009) pp. 312 et seq.; B. HANOTIAU, "Satisfying the Burden of Proof: The Viewpoint of a 'Civil Law' Lawyer" in *The Standards and Burden of Proof in International Arbitration* (1994) pp. 349-350; R. PIETROWSKI, *Evidence in International Arbitration* (2006) p. 378.

– Finally, there are arbitrators who consider that confronting witnesses and experts is a much more efficient means to discover the "truth" than the classical approach of cross-examining one witness/expert after the other. Whether such practices (viewed by some as innovative and by others as pure heresy) really permit discovery of the "truth" or whether they only advantage those who speak louder and are more self-confident would be a matter for another article.

To conclude, these few examples show that behind the consensus on the principle, significant differences appear in practice. It is certainly a burden resting on the arbitrators' shoulders to make certain that the parties understand what is expected from them and, if possible, accept it. Irrespective of the parties' background and experience, it is most of the time counterproductive for arbitral tribunals to impose self-made rules which have an impact on the parties' duty to prove their case, if the latter are not prepared to accept them. Parties may consider for instance that, by confronting witnesses, arbitral tribunals prevent them from disproving through efficient cross-examination the credibility and accuracy of a testimony. The desire to be innovative or, allegedly, more efficient is not a sufficient justification.

As a general rule, the duty of arbitral tribunals to check that the parties understand how and when they need to prove their case does not go as far as to tell the parties what means of evidence they are expecting, nor what level of evidence they deem appropriate to demonstrate specific allegations. Arbitral tribunals should not either intervene in the course of the proceedings to tell a party that it should bring additional evidence to demonstrate a fact. Some scholars, however, advocate such an approach.[10] I disagree for at least two reasons: the first one is that it is very difficult to do so in practice, especially at an early stage of the proceedings (and once the evidence has been submitted it is unhelpful). The second reason is that it may favor one party over the other, which is by all means a result that arbitral tribunals should try to avoid.

II. THE PARTIES MAY BY CONTRACT AMEND THE GENERAL RULES APPLYING TO THE BURDEN OF PROOF

The parties are free to provide specific rules amending the burden of proof in their contract.[11]

First, parties may contractually alleviate or increase the burden of proof for the party asserting a claim by defining in advance what elements this party will need to prove or the level of evidence that will be required.

The parties can, for example, fix in the contract the amount of damages that may be claimed (liquidated damages; "*dommage forfaitaire*"). Hence, the claiming party has to

---

10. A. REDFERN, "The Practical Distinction Between the Burden of Proof and the Taking of Evidence – An English Perspective" in *The Standards and Burden of Proof in International Arbitration*, 10 Arbitration International (1994, no. 3) p. 324.

11. *Ibid.*, p. 318.

prove the breach, the existence of a damage resulting from the breach, but not the quantum of the damage suffered.

The parties can also contractually limit or exclude liability except for instance in cases of willful misconduct or gross negligence.[12] In such case the claiming party has to prove not only the existence of the breach but also that the opposing party's conduct was grossly negligent or that its behavior amounted to willful misconduct.

Some contractual clauses may also shift the burden of proof. This is the case notably if the parties insert a penalty clause in their contract. The party requesting the payment of the penalty will only have to prove the breach. The existence and the quantum of the damage do not need to be proven.[13] It will be for the opposing party to demonstrate, for instance, that the penalty is excessive and shall therefore be reduced by the arbitral tribunal.[14]

III. IN THE COURSE OF THE ARBITRATION PROCEEDINGS: BURDEN OF PROOF AND DOCUMENT PRODUCTION

Some arbitrators consider that the production of documents should only be ordered after the requesting party has demonstrated that it needs these documents to prove its case. Hence, an order to produce may only be obtained if the requesting party is in a position to identify precisely what allegations it expects to prove with the requested documents.

The purpose of such a rule is clearly to limit the scope of document production and thus to reduce the duration and the costs of this phase of the arbitration proceedings. The goal might be laudable. The means found to achieve it is however questionable, not to say wrong.

Document production does not merely serve the purpose of proving given allegations. First and foremost document production aims at giving access to information. This access is not unlimited in international arbitration, as one knows, and there are several criteria allowing arbitral tribunals to reject a request amounting to a fishing expedition (such as, for example, the lack of relevance of a request or a too broad definition of the documents requested).

However, document production may also legitimately be used for reasons a party is only able to put forward once it has the requested document in hand, such as for example to challenge the credibility of an expert or a witness or to build a defense.

It is thus wrong to establish a link between document production and burden of proof. In doing so one confuses two different issues, namely that of getting the information that may enable a party to build its case and defend itself on one hand, and the submission in the arbitration of evidence that will support the said case and defense on the other hand.

---

12. M. BUOL, *Beschränkung der Verstragshaftung durch Vereinbarung* (Schulthess 1996) pp. 28-29; L. THÉVENOZ in: *Commentaire romand – Code des obligations I* (Helbing Lichtenhahn 2012) ad Art. 100 CO, para. 7, p. 776.

13. M. MOSER in *Commentaire romand – Code des obligations I* (Helbing Lichtenhahn 2012) ad Art. 160 CO, para. 2, pp. 1151-1152.

14. *Ibid.*, ad Art. 163 CO, para. 6, p. 1160.

Documents obtained in the course of the document production phase will often be used as evidence in the arbitration. This shall not, however, become a prerequisite to obtain their production. On a similar note, and as several scholars have noted, the obligation to produce documents ordered by the arbitral tribunal does not shift the burden of proof from one party to the other. It remains for the party bearing the obligation to prove a given fact to determine whether the information received from its opponent is useful for this purpose.[15] Finally, the arbitrators' faculty to draw adverse inferences should a party refuse to abide by an order to produce documents does not affect the burden of proof. Adverse inferences may, in certain circumstances, have an impact on the assessment of the evidence (or lack of evidence) submitted.

IV.   THE IMPACT OF THE BURDEN OF PROOF DURING THE ARBITRAL TRIBUNAL'S DELIBERATIONS

At the end of the process, it is for the arbitral tribunal to decide whether the parties met their obligation to prove their case and experience shows that arbitral tribunals do dismiss claims on the ground that the claiming party has not proven its case.

Some practitioners argue that it would not be appropriate for an arbitral tribunal to dismiss a claim on the sole basis that the party has not proven its case.[16] As we have seen above, some scholars consider that, in order to avoid such a result, the arbitral tribunal should draw the party's attention to the fact that it should submit additional evidence to discharge its burden of proof. The underlying idea is that a party should not lose because it did not realize that the arbitral tribunal was expecting more solid evidence to support its case.

This opinion raises the following comments:

As we have seen, the principle pursuant to which a party must prove the allegations on which it relies is broadly accepted. As a result, it seems incorrect not to apply the consequences of this principle should a party fail to prove its case.

Concretely, it seems particularly difficult, not to say inappropriate, for an arbitral tribunal to draw one party's attention to the fact that the evidence produced is not sufficient or adequate. Let us take the following example. The claimant does not submit any evidence supporting the quantum of its claim with the exception of a spreadsheet established for the purposes of the arbitration. Would it really be correct for an arbitral tribunal to draw this party's attention to the weakness of the evidence produced? Should the arbitral tribunal step in and propose to appoint an expert? We should not forget that by adopting such a proactive attitude the arbitral tribunal may favor a party to the detriment of the other or at least give the impression that it is doing so. For an arbitral tribunal to draw the parties' attention at the outset to the requirement to prove their case is one thing, to intervene in the course of the proceedings to ask for the production of further evidence is quite another.

---

15. B. HANOTIAU, *op. cit.*, fn. 9, pp. 347-348.
16. R.D. BISHOP, J. CRAWFORD, W.M. REISMAN, *op. cit.*, fn. 1, p. 1444.

In fact, the issue is not whether it is appropriate for arbitral tribunals to reject a claim for lack of evidence when evidence is de facto missing or insufficient. It is, however, far more problematic when the underlying ground for dismissing a claim is not the lack of evidence submitted, although the reasoning in the award goes that way, but rather either the lack of motivation of the arbitral tribunal or its incomprehension of the evidence adduced. This may happen for instance when documentary evidence meant to support the calculation of the damage is (too) voluminous and not easy to follow. Instead of reviewing all invoices and checking whether the calculations made by the party are correct, it may be tempting to reject the claim on the ground that it has not been proven. To avoid such an outcome, parties tend to frequently provide expert evidence asserting the correctness of the calculations made. There is however no requirement in international arbitration to produce expert evidence.

Similarly, there may be a temptation to dismiss a claim on the ground that it has not been sufficiently established, when the arbitrators do not understand the explanations given by the party or by its expert.

More generally, arbitrators may be tempted to reject a claim involving complex technical and financial aspects, if there is no expert evidence supporting it.

This statement prompts the following comment: a party's obligation to discharge its burden of proof also implies the submission of evidence that is useful for and may be used by the arbitral tribunal. One cannot expect an arbitral tribunal to reorganize a file or to try to reconcile thousands of invoices to determine whether their total corresponds to the amount claimed. Moreover, the evidence produced should be intelligible so that the arbitral tribunal may understand it and assess its probative value.

A party must prove the allegations supporting its case. This principle is broadly accepted and easy to understand. However, the implementation of such a principle raises numerous questions. Which party has to prove what, when and how are issues that parties, counsel and arbitral tribunals address on a daily basis. As we have seen, there is not one "fit them all" answer to these questions and multiple factors may influence the way one addresses it.

It is certainly true that frequent users of international arbitration tend to develop some common understanding of these issues. For instance parties often involved in international arbitration know that both documentary and oral evidence may be important, irrespective of their own or the arbitrators' legal background. They also tend to organize their files in a similar manner, which corresponds to what arbitrators usually expect to receive. This also implies the production of expert evidence in support of technical, financial or even legal allegations with a given degree of complexity. Arbitral tribunals may, however, by no means take for granted at the outset that the parties will always share their understanding and expectations. As the examples reviewed in the previous sections show, even experienced practitioners do not all share the same views, nor adopt the same approach as regards the implementation in practice of the burden of proof. It is for arbitral tribunals to make sure, at the outset, that there is no major misunderstanding regarding these issues. Such a need exists, to some extent at least, in all cases. It becomes, however, more significant when all parties involved in the proceedings do not share the same level of experience in the field of international arbitration.

The Illusive Standard of Proof in International Commercial Arbitration

Jennifer Smith*and Sara Nadeau-Séguin**

I. INTRODUCTION

It is now well established in international arbitration that each party bears the burden of proving the facts relied on in support of its claims or defenses. There is much less certainty, however, on the standard of proof required to prevail. What degree of conviction must the arbitrators have to be satisfied that the burden has been met?

This subject is rarely addressed in the arbitral process. Arbitrators are often either completely silent on the subject or dodge the question and draft around it. Judge Buergenthal's observation of twenty years ago still holds true today: "What standard of proof to apply in a given case is yet another question that is of importance to international judicial fact-finding. There is nevertheless very little international precedent on the subject."[1] Considering the importance of the issue to both parties and practitioners, this lack of progress is surprising.

This article seeks to provide guidance on this issue. The first part of this article introduces the function of the standard of proof. The second part explores the differences between the standard of proof most often applied in common law jurisdictions, balance of probabilities, and the standard most often applied in civil law jurisdictions, inner conviction of the decision-maker. In the third part of this article we analyze which body of law is applicable to the standard of proof. Regardless of their legal background, where should arbitrators look for the applicable standard of proof? Is the standard of proof a matter of procedural or substantive law? In the fourth and final part, we consider whether difficulties in accessing evidence, heightened ramifications of findings of liability and other circumstances may justify lowering or strengthening the standard of proof.

---

* Partner, Baker Botts LLP, Houston office.
** Associate, Baker Botts LLP, London office.
1. Richard B. LILLICH, ed., *Fact Finding Before International Tribunals* (1992) at p. 271.

II.   WHY IS THE STANDARD OF PROOF IMPORTANT?

For each claim or type of adjudication, the standard of proof instructs the tribunal as to the degree of confidence the tribunal must have in the accuracy of its factual conclusions. In common law jurisdictions, the stand of proof generally indicates the relative importance society attaches to the ultimate decision and it calibrates and allocates the risk of error to be borne by the respective parties.[2]

Achieving the right balance and establishing the correct standard is important in international arbitration as it impacts how parties and users of arbitration judge the fairness of arbitration as an adjudicative process. Once the tribunal has assigned a degree of probability to the evidence, the finding is treated for the purposes of entering an award and spelling out the rights of the parties as if the propositions found were true. The arbitrators' findings are converted into "juridical truth" for the purpose of settling the dispute with finality and permitting the parties to go forward with their affairs.[3]

The fact-finding process is not a mathematical process, but rather is one designed to generate acceptance of the decision as fair and equitable; only an acceptable decision will project the underlying legal rule to the parties (and consumers of arbitration services generally), affirm the rule's behavioral norm and give the process legitimacy.[4] Articulating the standard of proof required for the adjudication can only assist in instilling confidence in the international arbitration system.

Despite its significance, the degree of proof applicable in international arbitration remains a slippery subject – even in jurisdictions where the standards of proof used in court have been set in stone for generations. Where it is discussed at all in the context of international arbitration, confusion and complexity reign. Professor Clermont wrote, "Magisterially, but opaquely, the law tells its fact-finder to apply the standard of proof."[5] Further complicating the issue, agreement as to which law provides the fact-finder with the standard of proof is frequently lacking. As discussed further below, the civil law and the common law traditions have different approaches to the standards of proof.

When addressing this subject at the International Court of Justice (ICJ), the problem has been described as follows:

---

2. See *In re Winship*, 397 U.S. 358 (1970) (Justice Harlan concurring: "the choice of the standard for a particular variety of adjudication ... reflect[s] a very fundamental assessment of the comparative social costs of erroneous factual determinations"); *Conservatorship of Wendland*, 26 Cal. 4th 519, 110 Cal Rptr. 2d 412, 28 P.3d 151 (2001); *Weisman v. Connors*, 76 Md. App. 488, 547 A.2d 636 (1988); *Matter of Simpson*, 126 Misc. 2d 162, 481 N.Y.S.2d 293 (Fam. Ct. 1984); *Kent K. v. Bobby M.*, 210 Ariz. 279, 285, 110 P. 3d 1013, 1019 (2005) (interpreting state statute to require best interests of the child to be proved by preponderance of the evidence in suit involving termination of parental rights).
3. See V.C. BALL, "The Moment of Truth: Probability Theory and Standards of Proof", 14 Vand. L. Rev. (1960) p. 807; Jerome MICHAEL and Mortimer Jerome ADLER, *The Nature of Judicial Proof* (Ad Press 1931) p. 49.
4. Charles NESSON, "The Evidence or the Event? On Judicial Proof and the Acceptability of Verdicts", 98 Harv. L. Rev. (May 1985, no. 7) p. 1357.
5. Kevin M. CLERMONT, "Standards of Proof Revisited", 33 Vt. L. Rev. (2008) p. 469.

"If the matter of the burden of proof seems complicated in the context of the ICJ, the standard of proof is even more so. The difficulties have their root once again, in the contrasts of the common and civil legal traditions. Whilst there is general agreement in both traditions as to the ultimate rule on the burden of proof, and merely an additional stage or element of the common law burden, with regard to the standard of proof the difference is far more pronounced, and this is apparent throughout the jurisprudence of the Court. Naturally, the matter is of much importance to States who litigate before the Court, and certainty, or at least some general indication as to the appropriate standard, would be desirable. It appears however that the court prefers not to provide a definitive standard, most probably because the judges from the different legal traditions cannot agree."[6]

One could easily substitute "international arbitration" for "ICJ" in the above quote, and it would hold equally true. As important as it is for the parties in an international arbitration to understand the degree to which the tribunal must be persuaded of a particular conclusion, the applicable standard of proof is addressed at the outset in only exceptional cases. In the authors' experience, tribunals often do not articulate the standard of proof applied in the award either. While the goal of ascertaining the truth and deciding every international arbitration fairly is laudable, it may prove difficult in practice if the parties and tribunal are unwilling to clearly define the standard of proof applicable to the proceedings.

As international arbitrators have a natural tendency to draw from their own legal culture, the inquisitorial/adversarial divide is surely an important element of the analysis. Similarly, expectations of the parties and counsel as to the degree of proof required may be tempered by virtue of the legal regime from which they hail. There may be genuine differences between arbitrators as to where they set the bar when assessing the evidence put before them. That is, arbitrators may apply the standards familiar to them as a result of their own legal background: "[e]ach tribunal tends to be a law unto itself, the rules adopted and applied for the occasion being to a considerable degree determined by the legal background of the members of the tribunal".[7] Applying the most familiar standard may even occur unconsciously. As Lord Mustill observed: "A working lifetime in one particular system inevitably nourishes the idea, not that it is free from imperfection (for often the fiercest critics come from within the system), but that nevertheless it is in tune with the fundamentals of the administration of justice."[8]

---

6. Anna RIDDELL and Brendan PLANT, *Evidence Before the International Court of Justice* (BIICL 2009) p. 123.
7. Durward V. SANDIFER, *Evidence Before International Tribunals* (Photo reprint 1971) (1939) p. 6.
8. Matthieu de BOISSÉSON, et al., *Taking of Evidence in International Arbitral Proceedings*, Dossiers of the Institute of International Business Law and Practice, No. 440/8, (ICC Pub. 1989), Preface.

III.   A COMPARATIVE LAW PERSPECTIVE

The difficulty in ascertaining the relevant standard of proof in international proceedings is undoubtedly compounded by the different approaches to the standard of proof found in different jurisdictions. Generally speaking, common law jurisdictions apply the "preponderance of the evidence" or "balance of probability" standard in non-criminal cases, whereas in civil law jurisdictions the standard applied in both criminal and civil cases is one of *"intime conviction du juge"*. The latter is frequently equated to the higher "beyond a reasonable doubt" standard applied in criminal cases in common law jurisdictions.[9]

1.   The Standard in Common Law Jurisdictions

The standard of proof, at least in some common law jurisdictions, is driven by the nature of the claim and the policy considerations implicated. What is the nature of the risk of error involved in the decision? What is the gravity of the consequences that result if the tribunal errs? The standard of proof ultimately reflects a fundamental assessment of comparative costs of any error in the determination. In criminal cases, for example, the prosecution typically must prove its case beyond a reasonable doubt. This standard gives meaning to the presumption of innocence and to the larger importance society places on erring on the side of acquitting guilty people rather than incarcerating innocent ones.[10]

In common law jurisdictions, something akin to a "preponderance of the evidence" standard is applied in civil cases. In the United States and England, the preponderance standard generally applies in civil actions, unless especially important individual interests or rights are at stake.[11]

Preponderance of the evidence is understood to be a requirement that something be proved more likely than not. It describes evidence that has more convincing force when compared with the opposing side's evidence.[12] According to a typical pattern jury instruction used in US civil proceedings, it means the following:

> "Establish by a 'preponderance of the evidence' means evidence, which as a whole, shows that the fact sought to be proved is more probable than not. In other words, a preponderance of the evidence means such evidence as, when considered and

---

9. Robert PIETROWSKI, "Evidence in International Arbitration", 22 Arb. Int. (2006, no. 3) p. 373 at p. 379.
10. *Baum v. U.S.*, 541 F.Supp. 1349 (M.D. Pa. 1982); *In re Winship*, 397 U.S. 358 (1970) at p. 372 (noting that "it is a fundamental value determination of our society that it is far worse to convict an innocent man than to let a guilty man go free"); *Speiser v. Randall*, 357 U.S. 513 (1958), 525-526 ("Where one party has at stake an interest of transcending value – as a criminal defendant his liberty – this margin of error is reduced as to him by the process of placing on the other party the burden ... of persuading the factfinder at the conclusion of the trial of his guilt beyond a reasonable doubt.").
11. See, e.g., *Herman & MacLean v. Huddleston*, 459 U.S. 375, 389-390 (1983); *Grogan v. Garner*, 498 U.S. 279 (1991); *Miller v. Minister of Pensions*, [1947] 2 All E.R. 372.
12. Kevin O'MALLEY, et al., *Federal Jury Practice and Instructions*, 6th ed., 3A at para. 154:20.

compared with the evidence opposed to it, has more convincing force, and produces in your minds belief that what is sought to be proved is more likely true than not true. This standard does not require proof to an absolute certainty, since proof to an absolute certainty is seldom possible in any case."[13]

In England, a celebrated definition comes from Lord Denning in *Miller v. Minister of Pensions* where, referring to the degree of cogency required for discharging the burden of proof in a civil case, he wrote:

"That degree is well settled. It must carry a reasonable degree of probability, but not so high as is required in a criminal case. If the evidence is such that the tribunal can say: 'we think it more probable than not', the burden is discharged, but if the probabilities are equal, it is not."[14]

In Canada, the Supreme Court has on various occasions reiterated that the standard of proof applicable in civil cases is proof on a "balance of probabilities". In *F.H. McDougall*, for instance, Justice Rothstein for the Supreme Court explained in unambiguous terms that:

"Like the House of Lords, I think it is time to say, once and for all in Canada, that there is only one civil standard of proof at common law and that is proof on a balance of probabilities. Of course, context is all important and a judge should not be unmindful, where appropriate, of inherent probabilities or improbabilities or the seriousness of the allegations or consequences. However, these considerations do not change the standard of proof."[15]

In Australian civil proceedings, the standard of proof is also "on balance of probabilities", which is often translated as meaning more likely than not.[16]

---

13. E. DEVITT, C. BLACKMAR and M. WOLFF, *Federal Jury Practice and Instructions: Civil Sect. 72.01*, 4th ed. (1987).
14. *Miller v. Minister of Pensions* [1947] 2 All ER 372.
15. *F.H. v. McDougall*, 2008 SCC 53 (holding the standard of proof was one of balance of probabilities in civil suit for sexual assault).
16. Andrew PALMER, *Principles of Evidence* (Cavendish Publishing, Australia 2010) p. 342. Sect. 140 of the Civil Evidence Act 1995 provides that:

"(1) In a civil proceeding, the court must find the case of a party proved if it is satisfied that the case has been proved on the balance of probabilities. (2) Without limiting the matters that the court may take into account in deciding whether it is so satisfied, it is to take into account: (a) the nature of the cause of action or defence, and (b) the nature of the subject-matter of the proceeding, and (c) the gravity of the matters alleged."

These standards apply to facts to be proved by claimants and respondents alike, reflecting the common law system's goal of minimizing the probability of error.[17] In theory, this standard is satisfied by the thinnest conceivable margin. The determination of whether the standard has been met is not an exercise that can be undertaken mathematically. The volume or quantity of evidence presented in favor of a particular point is not the decisive factor; rather it is the quality of the evidence presented that must be judged.

In certain civil actions in the United States, a higher standard such as "clear and convincing evidence", is applied – typically where society has deemed it necessary to protect important rights. In these cases, the fact-finder is charged with applying a standard of proof adjusted to the circumstances of the case and the causes of action to be proved. Typically, the claims or defenses involved are ones involving fundamental rights of the litigants and in which the ramifications of the decision are serious. The courts (or legislature) have deemed an intermediate standard of proof appropriate, higher than the "preponderance of the evidence" standard but lower than the "beyond a reasonable doubt" standard. This heightened standard requires that what must be proved is highly probable or reasonably certain. In other words, it requires a finding based on evidence so clear as to leave no substantial doubt and sufficiently strong to command the unhesitating assent of every reasonable mind.[18] Evidence is "clear" if it "is certain, unambiguous, and plain to the understanding", and it is "convincing" if it is "reasonable and persuasive enough to cause the trier of fact to believe it".[19]

Examples of when a heightened standard is required in US proceedings are termination of parental rights cases, deportation cases, civil commitment proceedings, suits on oral contracts to make a will, claims for specific performance of an oral contract, claims to invalidate a written instrument by forgery, claims to vary or contradict the recitals of a written instrument such as a bill of lading or a lease, or claims to establish

---

17. *U.S. v. Fatico*, 458 F.Supp. 388, 403 (E.D.N.Y. 1978), judgment aff'd 603 F.2d 1053 (2d Cir. 1979).

18. *Conservatorship of Wendland*, 26 Cal. 4th 519, 110 Cal. Rptr. 2d 412, 28 P.3d 151 (2001) (applying clear and convincing standard where conservator was attempting to withhold artificial nutrition and hydration from conscious conservatee).

19. *Foster v. Alliedsignal, Inc.*, 293 F.3d 1187 (10th Cir. 2002).

a fiduciary relationship.[20] Clear and convincing evidence may also be required to prove willful, wrongful, and unlawful acts, fraud or undue influence, or gross negligence.[21] In England, by contrast, instead of "clear and convincing", the courts require that evidence be more "cogent" in the case of some claims, but nonetheless retain the more likely than not standard. Lord Hoffman elucidated the civil standard of proof to measure fraud under English law as follows:

"[t]he civil standard of proof always means more likely than not. The only higher degree of probability required by the law is the criminal standard. But ... some things are inherently more likely than others. It would need more cogent evidence to satisfy one that the creature seen walking in Regent's Park was more likely than not to have been a lioness than to be satisfied to the same standard of probability that it was an Alsatian. On this basis, cogent evidence is generally required to satisfy a civil tribunal that a person has been fraudulent or behaved in some other reprehensible manner. But the question is always whether the tribunal thinks it more probable than not."[22]

In Australia, while the standard of "balance of probabilities" applies even in cases where the action involves an allegation of criminal conduct or fraud on the part of one of the parties, the High Court has recognized that "the strength of the evidence necessary to establish a fact or facts on the balance of probabilities may vary according to the nature of what it is sought to prove" and given the "conventional perception that members of

20. *McCormick on Evidence*, 5th ed. (West Group 1999), Sect. 340. *Kyle v. Kyle*, 18 Tenn. App. 200, 74 S.W.2d 1065 (1934) (holding evidence to prove invalidity of a deed must be full, convincing and conclusive and not merely raise a suspicion or indicate probability); *Taylor v. Merchants Nat. Bank*, 236 Ark. 672, 367 S.W. 2d 747 (1963) (holding evidence must be clear, cogent, and convincing to establish oral contract to devise property); *Whitson v. Aurora Iron & Metal Co.*, 297 F.2d 106 (7th Cir. 1961) (holding that clear and convincing evidence was required to support finding of fraudulent misrepresentation); *Detroit & T.S.L.R. Co. v U.S.*, 105 F.Supp. 182 (N.D. Ohio 1952) (clear and convincing proof was required to show by parole evidence that bill of lading was incorrect); *Miller v. Belknap*, 75 Idaho 46, 266 P.2d 662 (1954) (holding that party asserting parole modification of written lease has burden of clear and convincing proof); *Children's Home of Rockford v. Andress*, 380 Ill. 452, 44 N.E.2d 437 (1942) (holding that to establish a fiduciary relationship by parole evidence the proof must be clear and convincing and so strong, unequivocal and unmistakable as to lead to but one conclusion).
21. *ODECO Oil & Gas Co v. Nunez*, 532 So. 2d 453 (La. App. 1st Cir. 1988), writ denied, 535 So. 2d. 745 (La. 1989) (explaining that the clear and convincing standard of proof is usually applied when there is a special danger of deception, or when a particular type of claim is disfavored on public policy grounds); *Roberts v. Saukville Canning Co.*, 250 Wis. 112, 26 N.W.2d 145 (1947) (holding that alleged conspiracy must be proved by clear and convincing evidence); *Lutz v. Orinick*, 184 W.Va. 531, 401 S.E.2d 464 (1990) (holding that party seeking to prove fraud, mistake or other equally serious fault in connection with the creation of a joint account must do so by clear and convincing evidence); *Kruse v. Horlamus Industries, Inc.*, 130 Wis. 2d 357, 387 N.W.2d 64 (1986) (explaining that presumptions at common law and all statutory presumptions which do not express a question of proof require evidence sufficient to prove that the nonexistence of the presumed fact is more probable than its existence).
22. *Secretary of State for the Home Department v. Rehman*, [2003] 1 A.C. 153, at [55].

our society do not ordinarily engage in fraudulent or criminal conduct, a court should not lightly make a finding that, on the balance of probabilities, a party to civil litigation has been guilty of such conduct".[23]

2. The Standard in Civil Law Jurisdictions

In many if not most civil law countries, standards of proof are not set forth in either statutes or codes. Nor are they discussed and debated as they are in common law jurisdictions. It is frequently only in secondary sources where one can occasionally find a passing reference to how judges evaluate proof. As Bond put it when researching the issue: "When discussing this in Central Europe recently, the lawyers there looked entirely blank. There was no such distinction; the term 'standard of proof' had no resonance."[24]

Where it is discussed by legal scholars, practitioners, or found in codes, the applicable standard is expressed in terms that are higher than preponderance of the evidence.[25] The civil law asks whether the facts are so probable as to create an inner and deep-seated conviction of its truth. The "*intime conviction*" or "*l'intime conviction du juge*" standard has been described as proof which must be very certain before the burdened party's proof can be upheld.[26] The same standard applies to criminal matters. With regard to balancing the risk of error, some commentators have asserted that it is much more likely that a false negative will be accepted than a false positive.[27]

As tempting as it is to generalize the standard across civil law jurisdictions, the reality is that there exist important differences in how the standard is applied within each system. Just as there are differences between American and other common law systems, there are also differences between the Germanic and Latin civil law systems. As Professor Raymond noted in his conclusions to a symposium held by the ICC in 1989, "it is not possible simply to declare that there is a dichotomy between the common law and civil procedural laws".[28]

In France and in Belgium, "to satisfy the burden of proof means to establish the existence of a probability or likelihood which is sufficient to convince the judge and when this result is reached, the judge gives the other party the opportunity to explain himself in order to create eventually in his turn a contrary likelihood.... although this approach

---

23. *Neat Holdings Pty Ltd. v. Karajan Holdings Pty Ltd.* (1992) 110 ALR 449, 450. Andrew PALMER, *op. cit.*, fn. 16, p. 342.

24. Michael J. BOND, "The Standard of Proof In International Commercial Arbitration", 77 Arbitration (2011, no. 3) p. 304 at p. 309.

25. Andreas REINER, "Burden and General Standards of Proof" in *The Standards and Burden of Proof in International Arbitration*, 10 Arb. Int. (1994, no. 3) pp. 317-364 at p. 335 (noting in particular the use in Austrian law of the term "full conviction" ("*volle Uberzeugung*").

26. Kevin M. CLERMONT, *op. cit.*, fn. 5, p. 469.

27. See Kevin CLERMONT and Emily SHERWIN, "A Comparative Puzzle: Standards of Proof" in James A.R. NAFZIGER and Symeon SYMEONIDES, eds., *Law and Justice in a Multistate World: Essays in Honor of Arthur T. von Mehren* (2002) p. 629.

28. Matthieu de BOISSÉSON, et al., *op. cit.*, fn. 8, p. 159.

remains contrary to the rules set up by the *Cour de cassation* [which] requires the one who bears the burden of proof to establish the existence of a certainty".[29]

In Germany, the Code of Civil Procedure provides that: "The court shall decide at its discretion by taking into account the entire substance of the hearings and the result of any evidence taken, whether an allegation regarding the facts should be regarded as true or untrue."[30] The German Supreme Court has stated that the judge may not content herself with a mere assessment of probabilities but rather should rely upon judicial intuition.[31] German practitioners explain that the standards of proof in criminal and civil cases are "pretty much 'beyond reasonable doubt'".[32]

Other civil law countries, such as Spain and Italy, do not expressly articulate a specific standard of proof in civil cases and the judges are, in theory, permitted to apply whatever standard the judge thinks appropriate in the search for "truth" or "moral certainty".[33]

These differences among civil law jurisdictions regarding the standard of proof are particularly important in measuring damages. For example, while French judges have the reputation of taking a pragmatic and realistic approach towards the measure of economic damages in the case of a breach of contract, Austrian and German judges have the reputation of requiring meticulous proof.[34]

3.   *The Common Law Versus Civil Law Standard: Is the Difference Really so Great?*

Whereas American law strives to set objective and rational standards of persuasion, the Continental law notion of *intime conviction* conceives of judicial fact-finding as a considerably more subjective and intuitive process.[35] Professor Engel states, "[T]he heart of the conflict between American and Continental law is therefore their different assessments of cost and benefit. Whereas Continental law is attracted by the benefit, American law is scared of the cost."[36] Others have been more strident, describing the Continental process as lacking sophistication and being "downright bizarre" while calling on practitioners to improve their system in light of the "superior American solution".[37] An Italian commentator, Taruffo, responds that "[Americans] rely on a rather naïve idea

---

29. Bernard HANOTIAU, "Satisfying the Burden of Proof: The Viewpoint of a 'Civil Law' Lawyer" in *The Standards and Burden of Proof in International Arbitration*, 10 Arb. Int. (1994, no. 3) pp. 317-364 at p. 345.

30. *Zivilprozessordnung* 5 Dec 2005, BGBl. I 3202, Sect. 286(l) (F.R.G.) translated in S. RUTZEL, G. WEGEN and S. WILSKE, *Commercial Dispute Resolution in Germany* (2005) p. 224.

31. *Bundesgerichtshof*, 17 Feb 1970, 53 *Entschedidungen des Bundesgerichtshofes in Zivilsachen* 245 (F.R.G).

32. Michael J. BOND, *op. cit.*, fn. 24, at p. 309.

33. Michele TARUFFO, "Rethinking the Standards of Proof", 51 Am. J. Comp. L. (2003) p. 659 at p. 667 (characterizing *intime conviction* as "a sort of black box").

34. See, e.g., Andreas REINER, *op. cit.*, fn. 25, at p. 330.

35. Christoph ENGEL, "Preponderance of the Evidence Versus *Intime Conviction*: A Behavioral Perspective on a Conflict Between American and Continental European Law", 33 Vt. Law Rev. (2009) pp. 435-467.

36. *Ibid.*, p. 438.

37. Kevin CLERMONT and Emily SHERWIN, "A Comparative View of Standards of Proof", 50 Am. J. Comp. L. (2002) p. 243 at pp. 254-259.

of probability, roughly corresponding to the popular concept of statistical or quantitative probability, and upon a naïve and unqualified idea of truth."[38] This has prompted some to conclude that "Continental law is irrational. American law is irresponsible."[39]

It is important to keep the jurisdictional differences in context. The two primary legal systems adopt fundamentally different methods of collecting, marshaling and interpreting evidence. "Not only do the two predominant legal traditions have different rules on the standard of proof, but their entire conceptual basis is different."[40] Under the adversarial system utilized in common law systems, the judge or jury is charged with ascertaining the "actual events" after each party has presented its evidence. The judge or jury is charged with upholding the rules established for the litigation and impartially reaching its conclusion as to which side has been more successful. It is incumbent upon the parties to bring the evidence forward.

In the civil law system, the search for the truth is left, at least partially, in the hands of the judiciary, relying on the judge's expertise in developing the facts, even to the extent of permitting the judge to conduct an independent investigation, obtain her own evidence and question witnesses. The judges are expected to bring their skill and experience to bear before making their decision.

When the function the standard of proof is to serve within its respective legal system is considered, it is fair to ask whether the claimed differences are so great in practice. While the articulated Continental law standard could be interpreted as establishing a higher standard than common law, many believe that in practice the difference is not as great as one would think.[41]

For example, in 2004 the American Law Institute (ALI), in conjunction with the International Institute for the Unification of Private Law (UNIDROIT), adopted the Principles of Transnational Civil Procedure, which attempted to bridge the gap in the common and civil law expressions of a standard of proof. The ALI/UNIDROIT proposed standard was that "Facts are considered proven when the court is reasonably convinced of their truth." The comment suggested that the "standard of 'reasonably convinced' is in substance that applied in most legal systems. The standard in the United States and some other countries is 'preponderance of the evidence' but functionally that is essentially the same."[42]

One commentator has summarized the lack of practical differences as follows:

> "It may be that legal families are speaking at cross purposes or are describing only part of the picture. To speak of the inner conviction of an adjudicator as opposed to the balance of probabilities makes for a difficult comparison as each formulation is incomplete. How is the balance of probabilities to be determined other than by the inner conviction of the adjudicator as to the probability of each view? To a

---

38. Michele TARUFFO, *op. cit.*, fn. 33, p. 669.
39. Kevin CLERMONT and Emily SHERWIN, *op. cit.*, fn. 37, pp. 254-259.
40. Anna RIDDELL and Brendan PLANT, *op. cit.*, fn. 6, p. 125 (internal citations omitted).
41. Andreas REINER, *op. cit.*, fn. 25, p. 335.
42. *ALI/UNIDROIT Principles of Transnational Civil Procedure* (New York, Cambridge University Press 2006).

civilian adjudicator, what is their inner conviction to be about if not that the other side's evidence is more believable or is preponderant to that of the other?... Another reason why there is unlikely to be any significant difference between the articulations in different legal families, is that no system allows a party to succeed if their opponent's contentions are preferred. In any contest, one side's contentions will outweigh the other. If they are equal, all systems would conclude that the party with the burden has failed, as it has failed to prove that its contentions are properly preferred."[43]

Does this analysis really advance the issue? Under both systems the ultimate determination comes down to convincing the fact-finder, which is a matter of belief. Under both systems it is also true that if the opponent's evidence is preferred, the claim or defense will fail. What is left unanswered, however, is the degree of conviction the fact-finder must hold to rule in favor of a claim or defense.

Some researchers have suggested that despite the instruction given with the preponderance of the evidence standard in the common law system, the standard of proof as applied is considerably higher than 50 percent. Through empirical studies, they posit that both plaintiffs and defendants view the status quo prior to the litigation as the natural point of reference. As fact-finders tend to be averse to loss, the researchers suggest that they will err on the side of denying a plaintiff relief to which she or he is legally entitled as it is considered less detrimental to the plaintiff's well-being than is the injury to the defendant's well-being when undeserved relief is erroneously awarded.[44] Other studies support the hypothesis that fact-finders do not mathematically integrate evidence or compare probabilities, but instead make decisions based on their need to make sense of the evidence put before them and to construct a coherent story from the evidence.[45] These researchers suggest that what inevitably happens is that information supporting the favored interpretation is mentally highlighted, whereas the importance and reliability of information contradicting their favored interpretation is reduced.[46]

The United States Supreme Court, at least, has rejected any notion that the difference between the preponderance and reasonable doubt standards, is meaningless, holding the

---

43. Jeff WAINCYMER, *Procedure and Evidence in International Arbitration* (Kluwer Law International 2012) Chapter 10, pp. 743-824 at p. 767; See also, Andreas REINER, *op. cit.*, fn. 25, p. 328; George M. VON MEHREN and Claudia SALOMON, "Submitting Evidence in an International Arbitration: The Common Lawyer's Guide", 20 J. Int'l Arb. (2003, no. 3) pp. 285-294 at pp. 290-291 ("the degree or level of proof that must be achieved in practice in an international arbitration is not capable of precise definition, but it may be safely assumed that it is close to the balance of probabilities".).

44. Eyal ZAMIR and Ilana RITOV, "Loss Aversion, Omission Bias, and the Burden of Proof in Civil Litigation", 41 Journal of Legal Studies (Jan. 2012, no. 1) pp. 165-207 at p. 171.

45. See, e.g., Andreas GLÖCKNER and Christoph ENGEL, "Can We Trust Intuitive Jurors: Standards of Proof and the Probative Value of Evidence In Coherence-Based Reasoning", 10(2) Journal of Empirical Legal Studies, (June 2013, no. 2) pp. 230-252.

46. *Id.* at pp. 231, 245 (manipulating the probative value of the evidence and showing it had no significant effect on the decision-maker's verdict).

suggestion of a "tenuous difference" between the two to be "singularly unpersuasive".[47] In a concurring opinion, Justice Harlan (quoting Professor Wigmore) was compelled to add that "the truth is that no one has yet invested or discovered a mode of measurement for the intensity of human belief. Hence, there can be yet no successful method of communicating intelligibly ... a sound method for self analysis for one's belief."[48] Empirical studies support this finding, concluding that there were considerable differences in conviction rates when study participants were asked to apply different standards of proof.[49]

IV. THE LAW APPLICABLE TO THE STANDARD OF PROOF

1. The Lack of Standardized Rules of Proof

Arbitral statutes, laws and rules rarely articulate the principles of standard of proof. Generally speaking they provide that the parties must be treated fairly and with equality, each being given an opportunity to present its case. As the Eritrea-Ethiopia Claims Commission aptly observed, however, international rules generally "do not articulate the quantum or degree of proof that a party must present to meet [its] burden of proof".[50] If addressed at all, most rules will give the tribunal discretion with regard to the presentation of evidence. Some authors argue that this lacuna is deliberate: international arbitration brings together parties drawn from different legal systems: "It would be too difficult – and too cumbersome – to lay down detailed rules; and it would mitigate against the flexibility of the arbitral process, which is one of its great virtues."[51] While this may be true with regard to establishing rules of evidence, failure to articulate a standard of proof is not a virtue of the arbitral process.

2. The Procedural / Substantive Divide

Considering the silence of arbitration rules, national arbitration laws and international arbitration conventions, it is left to the parties and the arbitral tribunal to articulate the applicable standard. Typically, however, there is little discussion about the standard of proof applied in international commercial arbitration. If anything, tribunals tend to make

---

47. *In re Winship*, 397 U.S. at p. 368.
48. *Id.* at p. 369.
49. See, e.g., Andreas GLÖCKNER and Christoph ENGEL, *op. cit.*, fn. 45, pp. 230-252 (the data reflected that the probability odds for a guilty verdict were almost five times as high under the preponderance of the evidence instruction compared with the beyond reasonable doubt instruction).
50. *Prisoners of War, Ethiopia's Claim 4*, Eritrea-Ethiopia Claims Commission, Partial Award of 1 July 2003, at p. 8.
51. Alan REDFERN, "The Practical Distinction Between The Burden of Proof and The Taking of Evidence – An English Perspective" in *The Standards and Burden of Proof in International Arbitration*, 10 Arb. Int. (1994, no. 3) pp. 317-364 at p. 321.

findings that sufficient evidence has or has not been presented to establish the facts, without mentioning the standard by which the evidence has been judged.[52]

The doctrine is divided as to whether arbitrators should look to the law of the seat or the substantive law governing the merits for the standard of proof. If an arbitrator is applying New York law to a contract dispute seated in Paris, would she need to satisfy herself by the "inner conviction" standard applied by French judges or is it sufficient to apply the American preponderance of the evidence standard? At the heart of this debate lies an issue of characterization. If the standard of proof is considered to be procedural, then it should be governed by the lex fori. If it is considered substantive, then it is it governed by the lex causae.

There is a surprising lack of consensus between national systems on whether the standard of proof is a matter of procedural or substantive law. According to one commentator, common law legal systems treat the standard of proof as procedural, whereas civilian systems treat it as a substantive question.[53] While this may be the case in some countries, this broad generalization oversimplifies the matter. In fact, in the common law world the laws of some jurisdictions like the United States consider the standard of proof to be a matter of substantive law, rather than procedural. As Bond put it: "In the US state and federal practice the standard of proof is not set forth in any civil code or legislation; instead, it is found in case law. And, I daresay, all US trained lawyers who are asked about it would respond that the standard of proof is a matter of substantive law and not mere procedure."[54]

In the United States, the applicable standard of proof is either created by statute for a particular cause of action or, where there is no controlling statute, determined through jurisprudence. It is considered a matter of substantive law, governed by the same law that establishes the claim or defense on the merits.[55] The United States Supreme Court has held that the standard of proof "has constitutional stature".[56]

In England, there is support for the proposition that the standard of proof in international arbitration is a matter to be determined according to the lex arbitri. In *Fiona Trust*, the High Court of Justice stated that: "It is a matter for the lex fori, in this case English law, to determine how the relevant facts are proved and the standard of proof."[57]

---

52. See, e.g., *World Duty Free Company Ltd. v. the Republic of Kenya* (ICSID Case No. ARB/00/7), Award of 4 October 2006, 46 ILM 339 (2007) (finding that fraud and corruption existed without stating the standard of proof applied).
53. Jeff WAINCYMER, *op. cit.*, fn. 43, p. 765.
54. Michael J. BOND, *op. cit.*, fn. 24, p. 316.
55. See, e.g., *Baum v. U.S.*, 541 F.Supp. 1349 (M.D. Pa. 1982) (noting that federal courts look to the substantive state law applicable to the dispute to ascertain standard of proof in a diversity action); *Weisman v. Connors*, 76 Ms. App. 488, 503, 547 A.2d 636, 643 (1988) (applying standards of the intermediate "clear and convincing proof" to an allegation of fraud).
56. *In re Winship*, 397 U.S. 358 (1970) (holding that, where juvenile rights are at stake, even though delinquency is not a crime and the proceedings are not criminal, the courts are constitutionally required to apply the standard of beyond a reasonable doubt to the evidence).
57. *Fiona Trust v Privalov*, [2010] EWHC 3199 (Comm), at para. 138.

146

Some point to Sect. 34 of the English Arbitration Act 1996 in support of this position.[58] Sect. 34 provides that in procedural and evidential matters:

"(1) It shall be for the tribunal to decide all procedural and evidential matters, subject to the right of the parties to agree any matter.
(2) Procedural and evidential matters include ...
(f) whether to apply strict rules of evidence (or any other rules) as to the admissibility, relevance or weight of any material (oral, written or other) sought to be tendered...."

Sect. 34, however, is silent on the applicable standard of proof. One could argue that the Arbitration Act therefore leaves the standard of proof to be governed by the substantive law that governs the dispute. In fact, under English conflict of laws rules much is to be said for the view that the law governing matters of substance must regulate the burden of proof because the outcome of a case can depend on where the burden lies.[59] For the same reason, logic suggests that the law governing matters of substance should also apply to the closely related issue of standard of proof.

In civil law jurisdictions, the characterization of the standard of proof as procedural or substantive is further complicated by the fact that neither judges nor codes in most civil law jurisdictions directly address the standards.[60] In France, for instance, a prototypical civil law country in most respects, there is a paucity of code, case or commentary on the subject. No general statutory provision articulates the civil standard of proof: both the old *Code Civil* and the New Code of Civil Procedure are silent on the subject. As one French practitioner points out, there does not seem to exist an "equivalent to the English law approach to standard of proof under French law".[61] The closest one gets to a discussion of the standard is Art. 9 of the French New Code of Civil Procedure, which regulates the burden of proof.[62] It leaves unanswered the question of whether standard of proof is a matter of procedural law.

In Switzerland, international arbitration practitioners indicate that the standard of proof is a matter for the lex arbitri.[63] In Germany, the principle of free evaluation of proof is found in the German Code of Civil Procedure (Sect. 286, also indicating that the standard of proof is considered a procedural matter). One notable exception would be Quebec, a Canadian province subject to civil law, where the rules on the standard of proof are found in the Civil Code, indicating that it is a matter of substantive law.[64]

---

58. Michael J. BOND, *op. cit.*, fn. 24, p. 308.
59. DICEY, MORRIS and COLLINS, *The Conflict of Laws*, 14th ed., Volume 1 (Thomson & Sweet & Maxwell) at para.7- 027.
60. Kevin CLERMONT and Emily SHERWIN, *op. cit.*, fn. 37, p. 259.
61. Michael J. BOND, *op. cit.*, fn. 24, p. 309 (surveying practitioners from different jurisdictions).
62. Art. 9 of the *Nouveau Code de Procedure Civile* provides: "*Il incombe à chaque partie de prouver conformément à la loi les faits nécessaires au succès de sa prétention.*"
63. Michael J. BOND, *op. cit.*, fn. 24, p. 312 (surveying practitioners from different jurisdictions).
64. Art. 2804 Quebec Civil Code.

In Latin America, the codes are also silent on the question of standard of proof and generally only address the burden of proof, more often than not as a matter of procedure. In Argentina, Brazil, Ecuador and Mexico, for instance, the procedural codes only address the question of burden of proof.[65] In Colombia, one practitioner has remarked that "We do not really have 'standards of proof' in the same sense as described for English law."[66] In Chile, by contrast, the burden of proof is found in the Civil Codes suggesting that the closely related standard of proof may be considered a matter of substantive law. Rather than enunciating a general standard of proof, Chilean civil law provides for specific rules regarding means, admissibility and appraisal of evidence.[67]

At first blush, it may seem attractive to characterize the standard of proof in international commercial arbitration as procedural; after all, the law of evidence is generally procedural. Furthermore, the parties (and the major rules) give much discretion to the tribunal to determine what evidence can be submitted to prove the claims and defenses at issue, and the process by which the evidence may be presented. The tribunal's discretion to receive and evaluate evidence or information that might assist it in determining the merits, however, is not coterminous with the standard or degree of proof that is applied to determine which party prevails.

Regardless of national idiosyncrasies, there are compelling reasons to treat the standard of proof as a substantive matter that should follow the applicable governing law. The standard of proof is closely tied to the substantive claims and defenses asserted. "A distinction must be made between these questions [relating to the production of evidence] because the question of the burden of proof is part of substantive law while the production of evidence is governed by procedural law."[68] The standard of proof can often be outcome-determinative, and represents "such an important consideration in the decision of the case that it has the quality of substance rather than procedure".[69]

Although not directly applicable to arbitration, Art. 14(1) of the Rome Convention supports the proposition that the burden and the standard of proof should be governed

---

65. Brazil: Art. 333 Code of Civil Procedure (*Código de Processo Civil*); Mexico: Arts. 1252 et seq. of the Mexican Code of Civil Procedure (*Código de Procedimientos Civiles del Estado de México*); Argentina: Art. 377 of the Code of Civil and Commercial Procedure (*Código Procesal Civil y Comercial de la Nación*); Ecuador: Arts. 117 and 118 Code of Civil Procedure (*Código de Procedimiento Civil*).

66. Michael J. BOND, *op. cit.*, fn. 24, p. 308.

67. Art. 1698 Chilean Civil Code; See also, Michael J. BOND, *op. cit.*, fn. 24, p. 308.

68. Lambert MATRAY, "*Les Traits Caractéristiques De L'Administration De La Preuve Dans Certaines Procedures De Type Romaniste*" in *Taking of Evidence in International Arbitral Proceedings, op. cit.*, fn. 8, p. 113 at p. 115. See also Peter EIJSVOOGEL, ed., *Evidence in International Arbitration Proceedings* (1994) p. 5 ("In countries where Roman law had an influence, the law of evidence relating to the admissibility and the weight of evidence, as well as the burden of proof is traditionally considered to form part of substantive civil law. The rules relating to the collection and presentation of evidence, however, are considered to constitute procedural law.").

69. Robert VON MEHREN, "Burden of Proof in International Arbitration" in A.J. VAN DEN BERG, ed., *Planning Efficient Arbitration Proceedings: The Law Applicable in International Arbitration*, ICCA Congress Series no. 7 (Kluwer 1994) p. 123 at fn. 3. ("The 'truth' found in both judicial and arbitral proceedings is relative rather than absolute. It is derived from the evidence presented by the parties and is dependent upon the standard of proof applied to the evidence.")

by the law applicable to the substance of the dispute. Art. 14(1) of the Rome Convention provides: "The law governing the contract under this Convention applies to the extent that it contains, in the law of contract, rules which raise presumptions of law or determine the burden of proof."[70]

There are also practical reasons why the standard of proof should be determined according to the applicable substantive law. Parties require certainty. Whether a cause of action exists and can be supported with evidence is typically a matter evaluated before proceedings are initiated. The burden and sufficiency of the evidence will also most often be evaluated by the respective parties before the procedure has been established by the tribunal. The degree of proof required will be factored into a determination of whether a claim or defense should be asserted and may even be relevant to whether an arbitration is initiated at all.

Reiner articulates a number of cogent arguments in favor of tying the required standard of proof to the applicable substantive law:

> "The first, and probably the most important, reason [that the governing law should attract the standard of proof of its jurisdiction] is that the burden of proof, including the standard of proof, determines how easy or how difficult it is for the claimant to enforce a claim. The ... standard(s) of proof consequently affect the value of the claim and actually decide whether a claim exists at all.... A further reason in favour of the substantive law is the greater foresee-ability for the parties, even prior to the commencement of any proceedings."[71]

Von Mehren adds that this approach is the most consistent with party autonomy:

> "The parties have either chosen by agreement the controlling law or the arbitrator, in the absence of a choice by the parties, has selected the controlling law, usually on the basis of the law that has the most contacts or the closest connection in the case. If the governing law attracts the standard of proof, the factual aspect of the determination of the dispute is most closely assimilated to the legal rules which are being applied. This would seem to harmonize with the presumed intent of the parties in choosing the controlling law, or, if the law is to be selected by the arbitrator, to be consistent with the approach of applying the standard of proof which has the closest connection with the case."[72]

In sum, although some jurisdictions view the standard of proof in court proceedings as a matter of procedure, we conclude that there are compelling reasons in international commercial arbitration to characterize it as a matter of substance. As a result, parties and arbitral tribunals should look to the law governing the substance of the dispute for the standard of proof to be applied.

---

70. Convention on the Law Applicable to Contractual Obligations opened for Signature in Rome on 19 June 1980 (80/934/EC). See also Andreas REINER, *op. cit.*, fn. 25, p. 330.
71. Andreas REINER, *op. cit.*, fn. 25, pp. 331-332.
72. Robert VON MEHREN, *op. cit.*, fn. 69, p. 126.

V.   SHOULD TRIBUNALS APPLY HIGHER (OR LOWER) STANDARDS OF PROOF?

Is it open to arbitral tribunals to apply a heightened (or lowered) standard of proof to a particular claim or defense? In practice, arbitral tribunals sometimes take different approaches to questions of standard of proof depending on the issues, legal norms involved, or the nature of the allegation made regardless of the applicable law. The debate is particularly heated when allegations of corruption or fraud are at stake. Paradoxically, the inherent difficulty of proving corruption is at the heart of arguments both in favor of lowering and strengthening the standard of proof. International tribunals have, for example, applied a higher standard when allegations of corruption or fraud are made and a lower standard when damages are concerned. If the standard of proof is considered a matter of the substantive law, attached to the claim or defense itself, there is a strong argument that it should not be open to a tribunal to apply any other standard without the consent of the parties.

We conclude that arbitrators should not depart from the applicable law to hold the parties to a different standard depending on the allegations and facts before them. The principle of predictability militates against it.

1.   A Higher Standard for Corruption / A Lower Standard for Damages

It is often argued in international arbitration that allegations of serious wrongdoing such as corruption require more convincing evidence than that required for other claims. For example, von Mehren and Salomon propose that it is appropriate to apply a higher standard of proof to bribery claims and certain types of fraud in international arbitration.[73]

There is precedent for arbitral tribunals requiring a higher standard of proof when deciding allegations of corruption. For example, in ICC Case No. 6401, the tribunal found that pursuant to the laws of the Philippines and the United States (which were the relevant governing laws), "clear and convincing evidence" of corruption amounting to "more than a mere preponderance" was required.[74] Similarly, in ICC Case No. 5622, the tribunal applying Swiss law required proof "beyond doubt" of corruption.[75] While it must be noted that some have applied a higher standard because the governing law requires it, cases in other tribunals have required a higher standard of proof without a discussion of the requirements of the governing law.

A study conducted by Crivellaro reveals that out of twenty-five arbitrations involving allegations of corruption, in fourteen cases, a "high" standard of proof was applied.[76]

---

73. George M. VON MEHREN and Claudia SALOMON, *op. cit.*, fn. 43, p. 291 (citing examples).

74. *Westinghouse Int'l Projects Co., Westinghouse Elec. S.A. and Barns & Roe Enterprises, Inc. v. Nat'l Power Corp. and The Republic of the Philippines*, ICC Case No. 6401, Preliminary Award of 19 December 1991, paras. 31-35.

75. *Hilmarton Ltd. v. Omnium de Traitement et de Valorisation S.A.*, ICC Case No. 5622 (1988), para. 23.

76. It was found that a low standard of proof was applied in just one out of the twenty-five cases, whereas in fourteen cases, i.e., more than 50 percent of the cases, a "high" standard of proof was applied. Antonio CRIVELLARO, "Arbitration Case Law on Bribery: Issues of Arbitrability, Contract Validity, Merits and Evidence" in Kristine KARSEN and Andrew BERKELEY, eds.,

What is not clear is whether tribunals did so on the basis of a higher standard being required by the law governing the underlying dispute or whether the tribunal did so on its own volition, without regard to the substantive law.

Other tribunals have declined to apply any higher standard to claims of corruption. The partial award rendered in ICC Case No. 12732 is illustrative. The tribunal, seated in London and applying English law to the substance of the dispute was asked to address claims that the contract at issue was part of a corrupt transaction and entailed conduct that was illegal under the applicable law. Noting that the general rule under English law is that in the case of alleged corruption the standard of balance of probability applies, the tribunal went on to explain that:

> "the standard of proof need not be, and should not be, weakened, nor that it need be or should be strengthened. The same standard of proof, namely one based upon the balance of probability, should be applied. That standard does not require 'certainty' or even 'likelihood beyond a reasonable doubt'. Nor does it require conclusive, direct evidence. It requires evidence, to be sure, but such evidence may be indirect or circumstantial, to the extent it is sufficient, in the context of the surrounding circumstances, to tip the balance of probability."[77]

There also may be a trend in arbitral practice to apply a lower standard of proof to the measure of damages, irrespective of the applicable law. It has been suggested that arbitrators frequently ignore the applicable substantive law to apply a lower standard of proof based on equity to the damages finding.[78] For example, in an ICC award concerning a seller's non-performance, the arbitrators concluded that the buyer's loss amounted to a specific sum but nevertheless awarded only 50 percent of this sum, holding that in the absence of "all exactness on these costs, it appears equitable to fix them at about 50% and to reduce the damage claimed under this head by the plaintiff". As another example, in an unpublished award, the tribunal awarded damages at "*rounded*" figures and cut in half actual damages for the sake of equity, without giving reasons.[79]

2. The Merits of Applying a Higher or Lower Standard of Proof

Most would agree that tribunals are bound to apply the substantive law governing the dispute to determine the merits. If the substantive law also dictates a higher or lower standard of proof, it follows that the tribunal should be bound to apply it. If, however, the applicable substantive law does not mandate a standard other than preponderance of the evidence, it should not be open to the tribunal to alter it.

Arbitration – Money Laundering, Corruption and Fraud, Dossier of the ICC Institute of World Business Law (ICC 2003) p. 109 at pp. 115-117.
77. Partial Award in Case No. 12732, 22 ICC International Court of Arbitration Bulletin, (2011, no. 2) p. 76.
78. George M. von MEHREN and Claudia SALOMON, *op. cit.*, fn. 43, p. 291.
79. Andreas REINER, *op. cit.*, fn. 25, p. 336, note 16.

If tribunals are utilizing equitable powers not granted to them, this practice is regrettable. As with arbitrations involving allegations of corruption or other illegal conduct, it should not be open to the tribunal to depart from the standard of proof if a party failed to prove its damages.

First, it is debatable — and debated — whether a higher standard is, as a matter of principle, appropriate in cases involving corruption. The main argument of those in favor of a higher standard is that corruption is, by nature, difficult to prove. For instance, in the *EDF* case, the tribunal explained:

> "In any case, however, corruption must be proven and is notoriously difficult to prove since, typically, there is little or no physical evidence. The seriousness of the accusation of corruption in the present case, considering that it involves officials at the highest level of the Romanian Government at the time, demands clear and convincing evidence."[80]

This reasoning has been under attack as being a "surprising — if not contradictory — juxtaposition of facts". Commenting on the reasoning of the tribunal in the *EDF* case, Partasides notes:

> "The Tribunal is telling us that allegations of this type of illegality are by definition 'notoriously' difficult to prove. Yet, it nevertheless proceeds to impose an enhanced standard of proof on the allegation. Its message is a difficult one to accept: 'Dear investor, you will inevitably find the allegation almost impossible to prove, but we are nonetheless going to raise the evidential hurdle to make it even harder.'"[81]

In fact, some commentators argue that the difficulty of proving corruption is a persuasive reason to lower — rather than heighten — the standard of proof. One international tribunal at least has been receptive to the imposition of a lower standard.[82] Supporters of this school of thought cite the fact that tribunals do not have the same enforcement and subpoena powers as courts to compel the production of evidence.[83] They also refer to the risk that the imposition of a higher standard will play in favor of guilty parties. In the words of Hwang: "… given the difficulty in proving corruption, a criminal standard of proof would be almost impossible to satisfy and plays directly into the hands of unscrupulous parties, who can simply deny wrongdoing and exploit the high

---

80. *EDF (Services) Ltd. v. Romania* (ICSID Case No. ARB/05/13), Award of 8 October 2009.

81. Constantine PARTASIDES, "Proving Corruption in International Arbitration: A Balanced Standard for the Real World", 25 ICSID Rev. (2010, no. 1) p. 47 at p. 56.

82. ICC Case No. 6248 of 1990, ICCA *Yearbook Commercial Arbitration* XIX (1994) p. 124. See also Antonio CRIVELLARO, *op. cit*, fn. 76, p. 109 at pp. 115-117.

83. Matthias SCHERER, "Circumstantial Evidence in Corruption Before International Arbitral Tribunals", 5 Int'l Arb. Law. Rev. (2002) p. 29.

threshold of proof to avoid liability".[84] Finally, they note that arbitral tribunals are dealing with the consequences of corruption as a matter of civil liability: "A tribunal does not impose criminal sanctions, which renders it unnecessary and undesirable for it to proceed with the same degree of caution as a criminal court would apply in ascertaining the facts before it."[85]

Conversely, the application of a lower standard of proof where damages are concerned has been heavily criticized.[86] Waincymer notes that the issue is less about the standard of proof and more about the evidence that the tribunal will require as well as the time and effort it will wish to apply to calculations. If blame is in order, the fault may well lie with counsel if they put more effort into preparing the liability stage than the quantum stage.[87] The lesson to be learned is perhaps that counsel should ensure that their calculations are solid and supported by the best evidence.

More generally, the application of a lower or higher standard of proof can lead to contradictory results. As noted by Sayed:

> "It does appear from the above arbitral cases that the choice of the standard of proof to be applied is often indicative of the attitude that the arbitrator would take on the facts. The setting of a high standard of proof often leads arbitrators to conclude that the facts do not suggest any intent or act of corruption. The low standard of proof, often indicates that arbitrators seek to facilitate the task of concluding that there is indeed an intent or an act of corruption in the facts at their disposal. What remains puzzling is the perspective that the same type of fact can produce contradictory interpretations, depending on the standard of proof taken by the arbitrator."[88]

In sum, the merits of applying a lower or higher standard of proof based on the existence of certain facts rather than the applicable law is dubious. It arguably recalibrates the risk of error in the final determination in a way not intended by the parties. It may also be an exercise of ultra vires power. Ultimately, unless an adjusted standard of proof is justified by the law governing the dispute or agreed by the parties, the practice of adjusting standards at the time of the decision runs the risk of eroding the confidence placed in the international arbitral process.

Finally, given the flexibility in the standard itself there is arguably little reason to adjust it. To return to the example of corruption, this flexibility allows arbitral tribunals to consider circumstantial evidence, as well as draw adverse inferences, in determining

---

84. Michael HWANG S.C. and Kevin LIM, "Corruption in Arbitration – Law and Reality", 8 Asian Int'l Arb. J. (2012, no. 1) pp. 1-119 at p. 19.
85. *Ibid.*
86. Alan REDFERN, et al., *op. cit.*, fn. 8.
87. Jeff WAINCYMER, *op. cit.*, fn. 43, Chapter 10, pp. 743-824 at p. 770.
88. Abdulhay SAYED, *Corruption in International Trade and Commercial Arbitration*, cited in Stephen WILSKE and Todd FOX "Corruption in International Arbitration and Problems with Standard of Proof: Baseless Allegations or Prima Facie Evidence?" in Stefan KRÖLL, et al., eds., *Liber Amicorum Eric Bergsten, International Arbitration and International Commercial Law: Synergy, Convergence and Evolution* (Kluwer Law International 2011) p. 504.

whether the corruption alleged has actually been proved. "The balance of probabilities should be understood and applied in a nuanced fashion, which cannot be divorced from the particular circumstances of each case."[89] As Richards LJ explains:

> "Although there is a single civil *standard* of proof on the balance of probabilities, it is flexible in its application.... [T]he flexibility of the standard lies not in any adjustment to the degree of probability required for an allegation to be proved ... but in the strength or quality of the evidence that will in practice be required for an allegation to be proved on the balance of probabilities."[90]

VI.   CONCLUSION

Despite being crucially important to the success of a case, there is little agreement on or even sometimes thought given the subject of standard of proof in international commercial arbitration. The institutional rules, arbitration laws and statutes provide little guidance on the topic, and some arbitrators (and counsel) tend to avoid the question entirely. While there are two different "models" of the standard of proof: the common law probabilistic "preponderance of the evidence" approach, and the civil law's "inner conviction" of the trier of fact, there may be little practical difference between these two standards. The different legal regimes also appear to diverge on whether the standard of proof is a matter of procedure (governed by the law of the seat) or of substance (governed by the governing law). In our view, there are compelling reasons to treat the standard of proof as substantive, rather than procedural.

While it is important that the tribunal not automatically make the domestic rules or judicial practices of one party prevail over the rules and practices of the other, it is equally important that the degree of proof, particularly to the extent there are circumstances justifying its variance, be clearly articulated. Arbitrators should raise the issue of the applicable standard of proof at the outset of proceedings, along with other substantive and procedural issues that must be addressed. Counsel and arbitrators all too often assume a certain degree of proof will be applied without confirming the assumption during an early stage of the arbitration. If there is disagreement, it should be dealt with early.

Just as it is incumbent upon a party who alleges a fact to introduce evidence to establish it, it is also necessary for that party to establish the law applicable to the dispute and the elements of its claims. The parties must present materials to the tribunal sufficient to establish the content of that law. As it is the parties' responsibilities to provide the tribunal with all facts, relevant laws and regulations, it should also be the parties' responsibility to establish the applicable standard of proof required where there is disagreement. This is particularly so if the claim or defense involved carries a burden higher or lower than the preponderance of the evidence standard.

---

89. Michael HWANG S.C. and Kevin LIM, *op. cit.*, fn. 84, pp. 19-20.
90. *R(N) v. Mental Health Review Tribunal (Northern Region)*, [2005] EWCA Civ. 1605 at para. 62 (italics in original).

Finally, while there are examples in practice of arbitral tribunals departing from the standard found in the governing law in favor of a higher or lower standard when confronted with certain facts or allegations (in particular allegations of corruption or fraud) there are sound reasons for the tribunal not to do so absent consent of the parties.

Practice and Procedure Regarding Proof:
The Need for More Precision

*Richard Kreindler**

I.   INTRODUCTION

To what extent is a plea for precision in the context of the procedure respecting burden of proof and standard of proof justified? Even if it is justified, is such a plea realistic? What are the myths, the realities and the challenges in considering a plea for precision?

In short, the plea is surely at least partially justified and at least partially realistic. It is justified in the sense that "precision" is often nowhere to be found, let alone even pretended to be practiced. It is realistic in the sense that while "precision" is a precise word, and therefore probably too lofty a goal, incrementally at least somewhat more precision can probably be achieved if we define realistic parameters. At the same time, in view of the tools already available to the parties and the tribunal and often regularly exercised in at least some legal cultures, the plea for more precision is surely realistic. However, the current trend does not appear to be in favor of more precision, but in fact less. For that reason alone, the subject is an urgent one especially if one accepts, as is done here, that that trend is a troublesome one.

Whether in litigation or arbitration, there are conceptual difficulties in defining burden and standard of proof generally. These difficulties already discourage and disincentivize the parties, or the arbitral tribunal, from seeking precision on these issues, especially at an early stage of an arbitration. It is worth initially identifying certain of these difficulties.

First, there is no single theory, rule or measure of burden of proof or thresholds of evidence which applies from case to case, let alone cross-border.[1] Multiple theories, postulated rules and advocated measures exist in theory and practice and are defended

---

* Partner, Cleary Gottlieb Steen & Hamilton LLP, Frankfurt, Germany.

1. A. REDFERN, "The Practical Distinction Between the Burden of Proof and the Taking of Evidence – An English Perspective" in A. REDFERN, C. REYMOND, et al., *The Standards and Burden of Proof in International Arbitration*, 10 Arbitration International (1994) pp. 321 et seq.; G.M. von MEHREN and C. SALOMON, "Submitting Evidence in an International Arbitration: The Common Lawyer's Guide", 20 Journal of International Arbitration (2003, no. 3) pp. 290 et seq.

as being most appropriate. Some of these multiple theories are even occasionally simultaneously or alternatively mentioned or applied in one and the same proceeding.

Second, there is not even a unitary approach to the fundamental purpose of evidence: Is it to ascertain the truth or simply to resolve the dispute, or something in between? Does evidence and the burden of adducing it serve to establish what happened, to establish the probability that something happened or to allow the best advocate to prevail?

Third, there is no single approach to allocation of the burden of proof, to reversal or to alleviation of the burden, even if one might identify an international "best practice" for allocating burden of proof.[2] The increasing institutionalization, globalization and transparency of international commercial and investment arbitration have contributed to such a concept of a best practice, but have also equally well allowed competing approaches to continue to flourish.

Fourth, there is no single applicable standard of proof; different legal systems have different approaches running from so-called preponderance of the evidence to clear and convincing evidence to proof beyond a reasonable doubt.[3] These different approaches are influenced by civil law, criminal law and other concepts of taking of evidence which have no real common denominator.

Fifth, both the admissibility of the evidence and the proper weight to be given to admitted evidence are subject to various approaches; different weight may be assigned to different kinds of evidence. In the case of admissibility, the formalism of Anglo-American evidentiary rules has largely been rejected in international arbitration in favor of a more generous and flexible approach. In the case of weight of evidence, the orality of Anglo-American advocacy has to a great extent intruded upon the Continental European emphasis on written evidence and written proceedings.

Sixth, uniformity is lacking as to the proper role of adverse inferences and whether such inferences can or should be drawn by the arbitrator expressly or impliedly.[4] In

---

2. A. REINER, "Burden and General Standards of Proof" in A. REDFERN, C. REYMOND, et al., *The Standards and Burden of Proof in International Arbitration*, 10 Arbitration International (1994) pp. 340 et seq.

3. A. REDFERN, supra fn. 1, pp. 326 et seq.; G. M. VON MEHREN and C. SALOMON, supra fn. 1, p. 291; S. WILSKE and T.J. FOX, "Corruption in International Arbitration and Problems with Standard of Proof: Baseless Allegations or Prima Facie Evidence?" in S. KRÖLL, L. MISTELIS, et al., eds., *International Arbitration and International Commercial Law: Synergy, Convergence and Evolution* (The Hague, Kluwer Law International 2011) pp. 496 et seq.

4. Art. 9 of the 2010 IBA Rules on the Taking of Evidence in International Arbitration attempts to address several of these issues in the context of disclosure or discovery of witnesses and documents:

"1. The Arbitral Tribunal shall determine the admissibility, relevance, materiality and weight of evidence.
2. The Arbitral Tribunal shall ... exclude from evidence or production any Document, statement, oral testimony or inspection for any of the following reasons:
(a) lack of sufficient relevance to the case or materiality to its outcome;
(b) legal impediment or privilege under the legal or ethical rules determined by the Arbitral Tribunal to be applicable;
...
(f) grounds of special political or institutional sensitivity (including evidence that has been classified

modern-day international arbitration, inferences are an unspoken element in the taking of evidence, and so differences in approach to them will lead to differences in the approach to burden and standard of proof.

Against the foregoing background, it is therefore no surprise that there are special challenges and burdens in the case of burden of proof. These challenges and burdens are magnified when one attempts to reconcile similarities and differences between common law and civil law approaches as well as between the commercial and the investment treaty contexts.

Let us look at the myths, the realities and the challenges in the context of the legitimacy of the international arbitral process regarding proof. What should interest us most are the challenges, and thus possible opportunities for the future.

II.   THE MYTHS

Certain myths suggest themselves in the context of precision and proof, and can be addressed roughly chronologically in the life of an international arbitration dispute.

1.   Contract Drafting Stage

At the contract drafting stage, it is a myth that parties routinely consider burden and standard of proof when deciding whether to opt for international commercial arbitration. When opting for arbitration, what the parties essentially have considered is that arbitration is a compromise solution generally, in order to avoid the local courts and procedures especially in the home jurisdiction of the counterparty. It is also a myth that parties regularly consider proof when agreeing on the substantive law, apart from the general maxim of *actori incumbat probatio*, that is, each party has the burden of proving the facts on which it relies.

Moreover, it is a myth that parties generally consider what the relevance of the seat, and the lex arbitri, might be to the question of proof. Furthermore, it is also a myth that parties consider any impact of a given set of institutional or ad hoc arbitration rules on proof. Finally, it is a myth that most parties generally consider aspects of procedure relevant to proof at this early stage, other than the occasional reference to taking of evidence, especially a reference to document production or possibly US-style depositions, in the arbitration clause itself. In treaty-based arbitration, it is a myth to consider any of these to be factors at the forefront, including when parties engage in

---

as secret by a government or a public international institution) that the Arbitral Tribunal determines to be compelling; or

(g) considerations of procedural economy, proportionality, fairness or equality of the Parties that the Arbitral Tribunal determines to be compelling.

(....)

5. If a Party fails without satisfactory explanation to produce any Document ... ordered to be produced by the Arbitral Tribunal, the Arbitral Tribunal may infer that such document would be adverse to the interests of that Party."

treaty shopping, while largely speaking the same general maxim of *actori incumbat probatio* is recognized and applied by international courts and tribunals.[5]

2. Commencement of the Arbitration

At the stage of commencing the arbitration, it is a myth that the claimant has routinely fully analyzed burden of proof and standard of proof when filing its initial statement – what the burden is, what the standard is, which law applies to it, what the likely counterevidence is. This is especially the case in classical bare-bones "notice pleading". In Anglo-American and especially US practice as often experienced in the courts, both the facts and the law may not be particularly detailed, in large part because of the assumption that document and witness disclosure will have a prominent place later on.

The notable contrast to this approach is to be found in certain legal cultures best exemplified by Continental European countries like Germany. Here, often the initial statement of claim and statement of defense are front-loaded. There is an early and detailed recitation of the facts, a description of the law and its relevance to the facts, extensive documentary exhibits, and most notably specific offers of witness and documentary proof, etc. This front-loading is partly predicated on the opposite expectation, namely that document and witness disclosure will have no prominent place later on.

This latter expectation is noteworthy since it is based more in a litigation culture of relatively dirigiste national court judges, who indicate which proof may be required and which not. The expectation is based much less in any specific actual arbitration law or legislation respecting how to deal with proof procedurally. Indeed irrespective of whether based on the UNCITRAL Model Law on International Commercial Arbitration (the UNCITRAL Model Law), arbitration law and legislation in most of the leading arbitral jurisdictions, including Continental European countries such as France, Germany and Switzerland, have in common that they largely stress procedural freedom and discretion, including as to proof.

This procedural freedom is reflected, e.g., in the UNCITRAL Model Law Art. 19. It provides that "[s]ubject to the provisions of this Law, the parties are free to agree on the procedure to be followed by the arbitral tribunal in conducting the proceedings"[6]and that "[f]ailing such agreement, the arbitral tribunal may, subject to the provisions of this Law, conduct the arbitration in such manner as it considers appropriate. The power conferred upon the arbitral tribunal includes the power to determine the admissibility, relevance, materiality and weight of any evidence."[7] And in investment arbitration, procedural freedom is reflected, e.g., in ICSID Arbitration Rules 34(1): "The Tribunal shall be the judge of the admissibility of any evidence adduced and of its probative value,"

---

5. The International Court of Justice as well as arbitral tribunals constituted under the Convention on the Settlement of Disputes between States and Nationals of Other States (ICSID Convention) and under the North American Free Trade Agreement (NAFTA) have characterized this rule as a general principle of law: See, e.g., *Military and Paramilitary Activities in and against Nicaragua*, I.C.J. Reports 1984, p. 437, para. 101.
6. Art. 19 UNCITRAL Model Law.
7. Art. 19 UNCITRAL Model Law.

as also discussed in, e.g., *Tradex v. Albania*, ICSID (1999)[8] and *Asian Agric. v. Sri Lanka*, ICSID (1990).[9]

It is also a myth that those parties who front-load their proof in the belief that they have conclusively addressed procedural aspects of burden and standard of proof are well prepared to parry contrasting approaches of the opposing party or of the arbitral tribunal, once it is constituted. And it is a myth that most parties have any particular sense of how the arbitrators considered and then selected will approach burden and standard of proof, other than expectations based on the legal education and background of the tribunal members and their known prior rulings. However, these carefully considered data points may be of limited utility if there is no connection in the new arbitration between the background of an arbitrator and the law or laws applicable.

In investment treaty-based arbitration without a juridical seat and with no direct link to any national procedural law, these data points will be even more inconclusive as to burden and standard of proof. Interestingly, in terms of the sources of the standard of proof applied by investment tribunals in the absence of a direct reference to a national procedure, three approaches can be identified broadly speaking. *First*, some tribunals have offered no specification of a standard of proof, as opposed to a burden of proof: see, e.g., *World Duty Free v. Kenya*, ICSID (2006);[10] *TSA v. Argentina*, ICSID (2008);[11] *Inceysa v. El Salvador*, ICSID (2006); [12] and *Wena Hotels v. Egypt*, ICSID (2000).[13] *Second*, some tribunals have applied effectively a domestic standard under the host state law: see, e.g., *SGS v. Pakistan*, ICSID (2003);[14] and *Fraport v. Philippines*, ICSID (2007).[15] *Third*, occasionally a generalized standard has been applied in the abstract: see, e.g., *EDF v. Romania*, ICSID (2009).[16] It is submitted that the first approach is clearly the easiest to apply, but also likely the least satisfying to the parties and the least helpful to future

---

8. *Tradex Hellas S.A. v. Republic of Albania* (ICSID Case No. ARB/94/2), Award of 29 April 1999, para. 77 (available at <http://italaw.com/sites/default/files/case-documents/ita0871.pdf>).

9. *AAPL v. Sri Lanka, Asian Agricultural Products Ltd. (AAPL) v. Republic of Sri Lanka* (ICSID Case No. ARB/87/3), Final Award of 27 June 1990, 6 ICSID Review – Foreign Investment Law Journal (1991) pp. 526 et seq., paras. 55 et seq.

10. *World Duty Free Company Limited v. The Republic of Kenya* (ICSID Case No. ARB/00/7), Award of 4 October 2006, para. 166 (available at <http://ita.law.uvic.ca/documents/WDFv.KenyaAward.pdf>).

11. *TSA Spectrum de Argentina, S.A. v. Argentine Republic* (ICSID Case No. ARB/05/5), Award of 19 December 2008, para. 175 (available at <http://italaw.com/documents/TSAAwardEng.pdf>).

12. *Inceysa Vallisoletana S.L. v. Republic of El Salvador* (ICSID Case No. ARB/03/26), Award of 2 August 2006, paras. 245 et seq. (available at <http://ita.law.uvic.ca/documents/Inceysa_Vallisoletana_en_001.pdf>).

13. *Wena Hotels Limited v. Arab Republic of Egypt* (ICSID Case No. ARB/98/4), Decision on Annulment of 5 February 2002, 41 International Legal Materials (2002) p. 943, paras. 59 et seq.

14. *SGS Société Générale de Surveillance S.A. v. Islamic Republic of Pakistan* (ICSID Case No. ARB/01/13), Decision on Objections to Jurisdiction of 6 August 2003 (available at <www.italaw.com/sites/default/files/casedocuments/ita0779.pdf>).

15. *Fraport AG Frankfurt Airport Services Worldwide v. The Republic of the Philippines* (ICSID Case No. ARB/03/25 (L. Yves Fortier, Bernardo M. Cremades, W. Michael Reisman)), Award of 16 August 2007, para. 399 (available at <http://ita.law.uvic.ca/documents/FraportAward.pdf>).

16. *EDF (Services) Limited v. Romania* (ICSID Case No. ARB/05/13), Award of 8 October 2009, para. 221 (available at <www.italaw.com/sites/default/files/case-documents/ita0267.pdf>).

parties. The second approach is probably the most rooted in a specific legal system and the third approach is probably close to the first one but marginally more helpful.

3. Discussion of Procedure with the Arbitral Tribunal

Moving on chronologically, we come to the stage of discussing or even agreeing on procedure with the tribunal. Here, it is a myth that most parties have considered whether or how to procure precision from the tribunal as to how it intends to approach proof in an international arbitration. The exception is when all parties or their counsel are from one of the Continental European jurisdictions which favor the above-referenced front-loading. Even in that case, increasingly agreement on such issues is not present or even possible. There will be various reasons for this, including that the internationality of the procedure, the parties or the tribunal leads opposing counsel from one and the same legal culture to stray somewhat from the local approach to proof known in that culture.

It is also a myth that the tribunal itself in most cases has considered whether or how to approach the burden and standard of proof, separate and apart from any wishes voiced by the parties. Moreover, it is a myth that the tribunal in most cases is willing to raise the issue in any more than general terms and structures. The exception is when the tribunal considers that its knowledge of the case already allows it to do so at such early stage. By contrast, if the early pleadings are more in the nature of notice pleading or for some other reason do not provide sufficient background to the tribunal, the chances of having an early consultation and discussion on these issues are likely to be remote. And finally even once the tribunal is able to enter into a discussion on the first procedural order and timetable with the goal of lending precision to burden and standard of proof, it is a myth that then the parties will be amenable to agreement on anything more than a very superficial basis.[17]

A partial analogy might be made to the debate about how useful "Terms of Reference" are, especially in the International Chamber of Commerce (ICC) scheme. The 2012 revision to the ICC Rules, like the 1998 Rules, maintains the requirement of Terms of Reference as well as the option of a "list of issues to be determined" (Art. 23(1)(d): "... unless the arbitral tribunal considers it inappropriate, a list of issues to be determined"). More often than not, an experienced tribunal will initially forego such a list. Alternatively, it will draft the list in such an anodyne fashion that the content of the list

---

17. See, e.g., *Metal-Tech Ltd. v. The Republic of Uzbekistan* (ICSID Case No. ARB/10/3), Award of 2 October 2013 (available at <http://italaw.com/sites/default/files/case-documents/italaw3012.pdf>):

> "The Parties diverge considerably on burden and standard of proof to sustain an allegation of corruption. Put simply, according to the Claimant, as the allegation of corruption was made by the Respondent, the Respondent bears the burden of proof. Further, given the seriousness of the allegations raised, the appropriate standard of proof is 'clear and convincing evidence or more.' On the contrary, the Respondent submits that the Claimant has the burden of proving the facts necessary to support a finding of jurisdiction and that the standard of proof of serious illegality is that the allegation is 'more likely than not to be true.'"

could easily be applied to any other case interchangeably to the extent it simply has the classical questions of jurisdiction, liability, quantum and interest. One legitimate reason for this anodyne approach is surely to allow for maximum flexibility going forward, especially at an early stage where the tribunal's appreciation of the facts and law is limited.

The same rationale might be applied to justify foregoing a "list" of issues respecting the burden and standard of proof to be determined. In fact not even an anodyne version of such a list finds its way into most disputes at this early stage, e.g., the issue of the law applicable to the burden and standard of proof, the issue of who bears the burden and what the burden is, and the issue of what the standard is. We question whether even a generic list would be better than none at all in many cases. Not least because it would place an onus on both parties to brief these issues in detail and to orient their evidentiary expectations around these issues.

4. The Written Phase of the Arbitration

At the stage of subsequent written submissions, it is a myth that most parties will slavishly heed any prior guidance or order of the tribunal and tailor their future submissions to it, other than in terms of meeting deadlines, complying with length requirements, etc. It is also a myth that most parties will have an agreed understanding of the procedures in terms of precision of written offers of evidence, the utility of fact witness statements, the sensible volume of document demands and document exhibits, and the proper function of expert witness statements in terms of burden and standard of proof.

5. The Oral Hearing and Witness Testimony

At the stage of oral hearings, all of the foregoing myths can conspire to create tension and discord in at least some cases, and not just those where the parties or counsel are from disparate legal cultures. It is a myth that such tension or discord can be eliminated or substantially reduced by the occasionally encountered, highly lengthy and all-encompassing procedural order which attempts to address virtually all procedural eventualities. The reason is that such orders usually do not address burden or standard of proof. Furthermore, it is a myth to assume that at the latest in the oral hearing most arbitral tribunals will clearly guide the parties as to proof, how to approach it, how to meet it, who has the burden, what the burden is. There are exceptions to be sure, but not many.

6. Rendering of the Arbitral Award

Finally, the arbitral award. It is a myth that an arbitral award routinely addresses with anything approaching "precision" the burden of proof and the standard of proof which the tribunal considers applicable, the reasons for applying them, and the sources of such applicability – especially if the parties themselves have not addressed the matter. It is also a myth that the arbitral award will set forth the procedural aspects of the burden of proof and standard of proof other than a generic listing of the procedural milestones and filings

162

in the case, as evidence of upholding the right to be heard and equal treatment. Whether a party has met the applied burden and standard of proof or not, it is also a myth to assume that most awards regularly explain in what way the burden has or has not been met, other than stating that this is the case. And where a party has previously objected to the arbitral procedure in terms of proof, it is a myth that the award will extensively address how and why the procedure was in its view adequate, other than stating that it was adequate.

The foregoing enumeration of myths might sound like a parade of horrors, whereas in fact it is not meant to be. Nor is it meant to be condemnatory or pessimistic. It is simply an attempted snapshot of myths in the context of the standard posited here – "precision" with respect to procedure and proof – and without yet taking a view on whether such precision is desirable or achievable.

III.   THE REALITIES

The foregoing enumeration of myths, in my own personal experience, also contains within itself an enumeration of realities in the context of precision and proof. Namely, certain would-be realities are ephemeral at best. What about the other realities respecting proof and procedure, which will then assist in addressing challenges for the future?

1.   *The Goal to Be Achieved*

The first reality of proof and procedure is that in international arbitration precision as to proof is not necessarily a goal in and of itself. It starts with the question of whether the goal of the arbitration overall is to ascertain the "truth" or simply to resolve the dispute, or both? This can and will have implications for the procedure which the parties desire or which the tribunal applies to burden and standard of proof.

Thus it could make a difference to the procedure whether the standard of proof is, as is often the case, assumed to be the "balance of probabilities" or rather "more likely than not" or instead "preponderance" as opposed to "clear and convincing". And it could make a difference whether and when the tribunal has settled upon such a standard, has communicated it to the parties, has asked them to opine on it and has called on the parties to structure their submissions and evidence accordingly.

2.   *Differing Degrees of Tribunal Activism*

A second reality is that the parties and tribunal may, and often should, openly discuss the interplay of proof and procedure in view of the more limited powers of investigation and compulsion possessed by the arbitrator as compared with a judge. The broadly worded prerogative to investigate essentially "by all appropriate means" is encountered in most leading arbitration laws and rules. Yet the reality is that there is a great diversity in the degree of arbitrator activism and initiative taken in defining the standards for the parties, in instructing or guiding them on how to meet the standards, and in undertaking further investigation as part of the effort. The broad textual empowerment in most rules and legislation often will not translate into broad activism and initiative.

As for the power of compulsion, including subpoena power and the ability to refer evidentiary issues to national courts of appropriate jurisdiction, the reality suggests even less activism and initiative. While each tribunal is different, the reality indicates that neither parties nor tribunals are particularly interested in exploring such areas of compulsion in the name of precision in the burden and standard of proof. In those cases where a party does raise the issue and exhorts the tribunal to wield such powers, the tribunal will often decline to do so. The tribunal will not necessarily consider the impact of that decision on burden of proof and standard of proof. And even if it does, it will often not explain the impact to the parties.

3. *The Already Existing Landscape of Tools: Commercial Arbitration*

A third reality of proof and procedure is that, both conceptually and statutorily, all of the building blocks are already well in place for achieving more precision. These building blocks are sufficient to enable and encourage parties and arbitral tribunals to seek more precision in crafting a procedure around burden and standard of proof in a given case.

The rights and duties of the parties versus the rights and duties of the tribunal to craft such a procedure are in careful balance, but the balance is already recognized. On the one hand is the right of the parties to procedural due process, including the right to agree or to be informed of which standards of proof will be applied, so as better to be able to meet them. This includes an important right not to be surprised by the application of a particular standard which, had the parties been informed of it in a more timely fashion, they could have attempted to meet, or to contest, before its final application in the award. This also may be seen as including a right not to be surprised by a lowering, a heightening or a reversal of a burden or standard of proof without proper advance notice of the possibility and the basis for adopting such an approach.

This right of the parties is a continuous one. It applies most urgently at the early stage of the arbitration in the context of the verification of the tribunal's competence, the arbitrability of the subject matter and any other possible impediments to enforceability at least under the law of the seat. To the extent the tribunal has a duty to verify its competence, then the parties have a right to guidance as to the burden and standard of proof attaching to the verification of its competence, including as part of any decision on bifurcation of the proceedings. It is partly simply a question of communication and notice by the tribunal to the parties.

Indeed the leading arbitration rules and guidelines are wholly consistent with the notion of a duty to communicate and notify the parties of the applicable burden and standard of proof, to the extent they have not already agreed on the issue. And even if the tribunal considers the parties to have agreed to a particular substantive or procedural law which it deems to govern proof issues, the need for communication and notice still applies. The fact that parties frequently disagree on the burden and standard of proof even while agreeing on the choice of substantive law demonstrates that they are still beholden to the tribunal for guidance on this issue.

How do prevailing rules and guidelines address burden and standard of proof in terms of procedure? UNCITRAL Arbitration Rules Art. 27 is generally axiomatic in this context: "(1) Each party shall have the burden of proving the facts relied on to support its claim or defence" and (4) "The arbitral tribunal shall determine the admissibility, relevance, materiality and weight of the evidence offered." This is to be compared with the approach, for example, in the Swiss Civil Code Art. 8, applicable to civil litigation, which provides: "Unless the law provides otherwise, the burden of proving the existence of an alleged fact shall rest on the person who derives rights from that fact." This is generally consistent with the concept of *"Ei qui affirmat non ei qui negat incumbit probatio"* or *"onus probandi actori incumbit."*

Procedural freedom of the parties is also enshrined in UNCITRAL Model Law Art. 19(1) ("Subject to the provisions of this Law, the parties are free to agree on the procedure to be followed by the arbitral tribunal in conducting the proceedings."). Thus the parties have within their grasp the ability to agree procedures for meeting the burdens, and binding the tribunal to them. Likewise, procedural freedom of the tribunal is established in Art. 19(2) ("Failing such agreement, the arbitral tribunal may, subject to the provisions of this Law, conduct the arbitration in such manner as it considers appropriate. The power conferred upon the arbitral tribunal includes the power to determine the admissibility, relevance, materiality and weight of any evidence.").

It would be hard to imagine a broader empowerment than this to guide and instruct the parties as to the burden and standard of proof throughout the proceeding, and not just in the evidentiary hearing itself. Insofar as the burden and standard of proof may be considered to be rooted in or influenced by the substantive law which stipulates the elements of the cause of action, the substantive freedom is also clearly in place in the form of UNCITRAL Model Law Art. 28 (1) ("The arbitral tribunal shall decide the dispute in accordance with such rules of law as are chosen by the parties as applicable to the substance of the dispute. Any designation of the law or legal system of a given State shall be construed, unless otherwise expressed, as directly referring to the substantive law of that State and not to its conflict of laws rules.").

4.   *The Already Existing Landscape of Tools: Investment Treaty Arbitration*

Another reality is that in the investment treaty-based context these tools are just as present. This is so even with the possible absence of a lex arbitri and lack of a unitary national law governing the causes of action. Thus party autonomy in selecting the substantive and procedural framework, and in addressing questions of burden of proof as procedural versus substantive, is evident in their agreement to ICSID Arbitration Rule 34(1), which in turn gives the tribunal the procedural freedom to "be the judge of the admissibility of any evidence adduced and of its probative value". And the substantive freedoms are already reflected in, e.g., ICSID Convention Art. 42(1) ("The Tribunal shall decide a dispute in accordance with such rules of law as may be agreed by the parties. In the absence of such agreement, the Tribunal shall apply the law of the Contracting State party to the dispute (including its rules on the conflict of laws) and such rules of international law as may be applicable.").

Even more so than in commercial arbitration, in treaty-based arbitration an undisputed agreement to the application of a certain bilateral investment treaty and public international law principles does not automatically result in agreement as to the consequences for the burden and standard of proof and the procedure for meeting them. Again, any and all tribunal guidance here can only help.

5.   *"Best Practices" and the Procedure as to Burden and Standard of Proof*

A further reality is that with the increasing globalization and convergence of arbitration practice and procedure in the last twenty-odd years, notions of "best practices" in the taking of evidence have developed which can directly impact on the procedure respecting burden and standard of proof. The parties and tribunal do not have to have agreed to the IBA Rules on the Taking of Evidence in International Arbitration (IBA Rules of Evidence or IBA Rules) to apply the approach behind them, consciously or not, to the procedure of burden and standard of proof. In many international arbitrations, most of the general concepts and mechanisms of procedure for proof embodied in the IBA Rules find their way into the arbitration, regardless of whether a common law or more civil law approach applies. This may sound surprising considering that both supporters and detractors of the IBA Rules and of their attempt at non-binding guidance cannot even agree on whether the IBA Rules are more common law or more civil law in their approach, or somewhere in the middle. The probable reason for their inability to agree on this question is that the IBA Rules, when examined properly and closely, do not favor any particular approach to disclosure.

In any event, the reality is that the IBA Rules concepts are applied by party and tribunal alike in many cases, even without expressly mentioning the Rules themselves. Thus Art. 9(1) states, as indicated above, the cardinal principle that the tribunal "shall determine the admissibility, relevance, materiality and weight of evidence" while Art. 9(2) empowers the tribunal to "exclude from evidence or production any Document, statement, oral testimony or inspection" for specific stipulated reasons, including "lack of sufficient relevance to the case or materiality to its outcome" or "considerations of procedural economy, proportionality, fairness or equality of the Parties that the Arbitral Tribunal determines to be compelling". And Art. 9(5) and (6) codify the concept of "adverse inference" ("5. If a Party fails without satisfactory explanation to produce any Document … ordered to be produced by the Arbitral Tribunal, the Arbitral Tribunal may infer that such document would be adverse to the interests of that Party."). These provisions go to the heart of procedure respecting proof.

6.   *Less Formal Standards and Less Precision*

But the most important reality respecting procedure for the burden and standard of proof is saved for last. Namely, while the parties possess many procedural freedoms, the specification of the burden and standard of proof is still usually in the hands of the tribunal. And the tribunal has considerably more discretion and freedom than the state court judge to address admissibility and weight of evidence. The reality which often results from this is that less formalistic and stringent standards and procedure on admissibility (allowing hearsay, etc.) in fact translate into less precise standards and procedure on weighing of evidence. They can also translate into less specification of the burden or standard of proof and of the law applicable to the burden or standard. They can also translate into a failure to ask the parties to address such issues specifically and

166

into a failure to specify the proper role of adverse inferences, including express inferences, implied inferences and the threat of inferences.

This abdication of precision is all the more surprising since in case law and practice the "requirements" for drawing adverse inferences are to a great extent agreed. And the failure to put the parties on notice before drawing an adverse inference is likewise surprising, since the party against whom the inference might be drawn must or should be put on notice of its opportunity to produce evidence so as to preempt or at least rebut the inference. And in ICSID arbitration, ICSID Rule 34(3) clearly requires the tribunal to "take formal note of the failure of a party to comply with its obligations under this paragraph and of any reasons given for such failure".

IV.   THE CHALLENGES

Having looked into the myths and the realities, what are the challenges in the context of the legitimacy of the international arbitral process regarding proof, and thus the possible future approaches? How should tribunals address issues around burden or standard of proof in terms of procedure?

1.   Contract Drafting Stage

At the contract drafting stage, there would seem to be only a limited benefit to having a specific party agreement on burden of proof and standard of proof as part of the consent to international commercial arbitration. Most parties to international commercial arbitration agreements agree on a specific substantive law, a specific set of arbitral rules and a specific lex arbitri. The combination of these routinely leads to a general concept of burden and standard of proof, but not to further specifics. Even if the parties expressly agree in their arbitration clause to a specific standard, it is not necessarily likely that this agreement alone will result in more precision in the arbitration, and in the procedural conduct of the arbitrator. The precision meant here would still need to await procedural agreements or decisions by the parties and the tribunal once the arbitration is commenced. And again in treaty-based arbitrations the opportunity to enter into such a precise agreement in the submission to arbitration will not present itself.

2.   Commencement of the Arbitration

At the stage of commencing the arbitration, the opportunity for more precision does, however, exist. The question is whether a party is willing or able to rise to the challenge of suggesting more precision. This will depend on the legal culture, the degree of preparedness for the arbitration, and whether suggesting more precision is in the party's strategic interests in the particular case.

Certainly in classical notice pleading of the American variety which presupposes subsequent "discovery", the party and its counsel may have a very precise conception of proof, and in some cases may even plead it in cursory terms. In most cases, however, even if a party does plead it, such pleading will probably be of little use or persuasiveness to the tribunal once in office. Indeed the notice pleading on its own will not normally purport to meet that burden. Exceptions will arise in the case of "summary judgment"-like pleadings which contend that there are no disputes of "material" fact requiring a trial to be resolved and that in applying the law to the undisputed facts the moving party is clearly entitled to judgment. Yet such motions are few and far between in international arbitration. These motions are also little known and less understood by many non-American arbitrators. They do not generally cause the arbitral tribunal to specify the standards of proof in a first stage of proceedings.

What is more likely to encourage the parties and particularly the tribunal to enter into a more precise discussion of proof at an early stage is the opposite of notice pleading, namely the Continental European front-loaded comprehensive statement of claim or defense with facts, law, exhibits, offers of witness and documentary proof, etc., again partly predicated on expecting no subsequent "discovery". The challenge here is for the parties to agree on the burden and standard of proof at an early stage after the exchange of initial pleadings, or for the arbitral tribunal to take a position on the issue where there is no party agreement. In international arbitration involving parties and counsel of different cultures, the chances of achieving such agreement are often remote. Those chances can be improved if there is a meeting of the minds on the issue within the arbitral tribunal. Those chances are rendered less likely if the tribunal members do not share a common view on the issue.

3.   *Discussion of Procedure with the Arbitral Tribunal*

The challenge then is to seize the moment, on a case-by-case basis, at the stage of discussing or even agreeing on procedure with the tribunal. Many if not most parties have not considered the proof issue with any precision, or in any event have not shared those views with the tribunal. Here, an early discussion as to how to approach proof may make sense more than first meets the eye. On the one hand, the more detailed the parties' initial pleadings, the more basis the tribunal has to consult with the parties at a relatively early stage already based on a certain appreciation of the dispute. On the other hand, the less detailed the parties' initial pleadings, the more useful it could be for the tribunal to promote such consultation early on and ensure that the arbitration becomes "grounded" as soon as possible.

Experience suggests that the real challenge here is that the parties will normally not be in agreement as to the issue of proof. The tribunal will not feel sufficiently well informed to voice views on the issue with any precision at an early stage. And even a well-informed tribunal will be loath to launch such a discussion. It may fear that the prematurity of doing so will trigger concerns about due process or equal treatment and will damage the atmosphere from the start. Even in the best of cases, where the parties have comprehensively pled their case early on and generally agree on the proof issues, and where the tribunal shares its view on the issues, it is a bold international tribunal that at the earliest stage offers precise indications on burden and standard of proof and invites the parties to meet them. In the case of an objection to jurisdiction or admissibility which results in bifurcated proceedings, as is often the case in investment treaty cases, such precision will often be lacking. Indeed the tribunal will often provide no texture whatsoever as to the burdens which need to be met to sustain that objection, either in the first round or in a rebuttal round, or then in oral argument.

The question arises of how realistic it is for that texture to be provided at an early stage. While each case will be different, the answer should be that it is far more realistic than one might initially assume. Again, the conceptual and legal framework for such early intervention and precision is already available, both in the revised IBA Rules provisions and in the best practice of Continental European "*Beweisbeschlüsse*" and "*Rechtsgespräche*".

The IBA Rules are meant to apply interchangeably to any and all international arbitrations and to reflect converging best practice. The Preamble already establishes the "principle" that each party shall "be entitled to know, reasonably in advance of any Evidentiary Hearing or any fact or merits determination, the evidence on which the other Parties rely". It thus goes in the direction of front-loading the submission and exchange of evidence. This is certainly a step toward providing more precision with respect to the burden and standard of proof. Until the evidence as well as the pleadings regarding that evidence are on the table, it will be difficult for the tribunal to provide meaningful guidance as to the burden and standard of proof. And if the goal is to have that guidance "reasonably in advance" of any evidentiary hearing, Art. 2(1) makes an even more important contribution, at least on paper: the arbitral tribunal "shall" consult the parties "at the earliest appropriate time" and "invite them to consult with each other with a view to agreeing on an efficient, economical and fair process for the taking of evidence".

Art. 2(1), it is submitted, is a powerful tool for both the parties and the tribunal to address burden and standard of proof as early on as practicable. In both its spirit and its wording, it requires the members of the arbitral tribunal to consult with each other and in turn with the parties as to whether the burden and standard of proof can or should be articulated as part of an efficient, economical and fair process for taking of evidence. If the burden or standard of proof is already agreed or determined to call for a particular process, then the arbitral tribunal can and should address this early on. If the burden or standard is already agreed to call for no particular process, or only a process devoted to a preliminary threshold issue such as jurisdiction, then here too the tribunal can and should address this early on.

Art. 2(3) of the IBA Rules says as much. It "encourages" the tribunal, without requiring it, to identify "as soon as it considers it to be appropriate" any issues "that the Arbitral Tribunal may regard as relevant to the case and material to its outcome; and/or for which a preliminary determination may be appropriate". Art. 2(3) is in fact reminiscent of the German *Beweisbeschluss*, which often plays a role in German litigation and German-influenced arbitration. In such decisions of the court or tribunal, the order contains a designation of the specific disputed facts as to which evidence is to be taken, of the evidence with the fact or expert witnesses indicated by name, and of which party relies on which evidence. And in the case of the *Rechtsgespräch*, which is likewise a mainstay of such proceedings, the judge or arbitral tribunal conducts a generally unscripted discussion with the parties as to the factual and legal issues in dispute. It does so with a view toward narrowing the issues and thereby focusing the kinds of evidence, if any, which might be called for. Such a discussion can take place before or after witness evidence has been adduced: it is likely to serve efficiency more if it occurs beforehand,

and indicates to the parties the legal issues as to which the tribunal considers such witness evidence, if any, to be potentially beneficial.

4. *The Written Phase of the Arbitration*

At the stage of subsequent written submissions, if such consultation or orders have issued, then the challenge will be for the tribunal to obtain the parties' adherence to the prior guidance or order of the tribunal and to tailor their future submissions to it. If the tribunal has provided precision on the burden and standard of proof before the further written submissions including witness statements and expert reports, then the party will have only itself to blame for not tailoring its further presentation. This includes which contemporaneous documents to rely on, how many documents to rely on, how many for each element of the burden and which ones. This also includes whether or not to rely on fact witness statements, how many and from whom, and the issues to address in the statements as compared with the evidence from the contemporaneous documents themselves. This moreover includes whether to rely on experts, for what issues and for what reasons, all in terms of the burden and standard of proof.

If the burden and standard have been substantially agreed or determined to the knowledge of the parties, then often the volume and scope of documents and witness statements should be reduced and narrowed even considerably. The opposite might also be true. But then at least the greater volume would have a reason based on efficiency, and not solely on broad-brush advocacy. The enormous challenge here, in the stage before the oral hearings, is whether and to what extent disclosure or discovery is to take place before further written submissions, afterward, or in between, and whether simultaneously or consecutively.

In international arbitration, with or without analogy to the IBA Rules, every conceivable permutation is possible and has been experienced: document requests taking place immediately after constitution of the tribunal, document requests taking place only after several rounds of written submissions, document requests in between written submissions and witness statements, witness statements taking place before and also taking place after written submissions. There is also the not infrequent phenomenon of document requests being foreseen either at the earliest or the latest stage and all or substantially all such requests being denied for lack of sufficient materiality or relevance or for some other reason, including those encapsulated in Art. 9 of the IBA Rules.

More often than is warranted, these arrangements are agreed by the parties without significant aforethought as to the burden or standard of proof. They are therefore not fully consistent with efficiency or economy. And precisely because many parties wish to keep open the possibility of benefiting from document discovery at a later stage, such arrangements will still occur even after issuance of clear and precise thoughts or determinations as to the burden or standard of proof. The difference however, as experience shows time and again, is that even a party desirous of extensive discovery will whittle down its appetite in the later proceedings when faced with clearer indications as to burden and standard of proof. And indeed if the party does not focus its presentation, especially in a manner consistent with good faith, then the arbitral tribunal can and should take such conduct into consideration, on a case-by-case basis, in its later decision on allocation of costs. Preamble No. 3 of the IBA Rules states that each party "shall act in good faith" and Art. 9(7) empowers the arbitral tribunal to take the failure to do so "into account in its assignment of the costs of the arbitration". In fact, these powers exist with or without the IBA Rules. Yet experience suggests that they are exercised less frequently than they could be. Experience also indicates that they are highlighted in advance to the parties far less frequently than they could be.

The additional challenge here is to provide greater precision at the earliest appropriate stage respecting issues of proof without running afoul of the tribunal's duties to remain impartial, to ensure due process and the opportunity to be heard, and to treat the parties equally. While these three mandates are separate and distinct, they can also be seen as overlapping. Challenges to arbitral awards frequently claim a violation of these duties interchangeably for one and the same fact pattern of alleged arbitral misconduct. While these mandates are sacrosanct, they can normally be upheld when an arbitral tribunal rises to the task and provides the parties with early guidance or determinations respecting burden and standard of proof. Indeed one could reason that these mandates, especially the opportunity to be heard, are actually better met by informing the parties earlier on as to what the tribunal would like to be "heard" and what not. The earlier and the more precise such guidance, the more focused the exercise of the right to be heard can be.

What about the challenge of maintaining impartiality and equal treatment in this process? Does not the arbitrator run the risk of seeming at least to be partial, even prejudiced, in his views, such as to trigger and even justify a challenge to the arbitrator, or to the ultimate award, on that basis? Indeed in those cases where arbitral tribunals provide the parties with provisional non-binding assessments of the case, they invariably do so under the condition that the parties waive their right to challenge the tribunal for lack of impartiality related to the assessment itself. And is not an indication or order in the manner of Art. 2(3) IBA Rules, a *Beweisbeschluss* or a *Rechtsgespräch* precisely also an indication of partiality toward one party to the detriment of the other?

Normally, no. Standards for challenge of an arbitrator or award based on lack of impartiality may differ from one lex arbitri to the other. However, it is submitted that in most cases early guidance on proof is not tantamount to an assessment of the case and is not a vitiation of the tribunal's impartiality. Indications of the burden and standard of proof may be seen as favoring one party over another and of imposing a burden on the one but not the other. Yet this is simply an exercise of the tribunal's right and duty to investigate the case and render a decision, and not a manifestation of partiality or prejudice per se. Nor is it in most cases a circumscription of the right to be heard or of equal treatment. Nonetheless, many tribunals will be loath to provide such guidance either *sua sponte* or even when asked. The reason is likely either a fear of an enforceability risk, a lack of sufficient appreciation of the case or both. While lack of appreciation of the case could be a valid reason, fear of enforceability risks normally should not be.

Arbitral tribunals can skillfully provide guidance as to the proof required, and thereby indirectly at least of the burden and standard of proof, without engaging in a potentially "partial" assessment of the case. A recent and constructive example is the ICSID case of *Metal-Tech Ltd. v. The Republic of Uzbekistan*, in which the claimant's claims were ultimately dismissed. In that case, the arbitral tribunal issued a series of procedural orders requesting and then ordering the parties to produce additional information and documents after new facts came to light at a first evidentiary hearing respecting the reality and legitimacy of services rendered for which the claimant had made payment.

171

As part of a repeated effort to obtain such additional information and documents, the arbitral tribunal stated in one of its orders that it "believes that it would benefit from knowing the amounts paid to (as well as the services rendered by …) each Consultant", that "knowledge of the amounts received by each individual Consultant may aid the Tribunal in coming to a conclusion about the Respondent's corruption defence", and that "the Tribunal believes that it would be prudent to invite the Claimant to substantiate its submission that services were rendered by the Consultants".[18]

In the final Award, the arbitral tribunal summarized its orders as follows:

> "The Claimant was thus *put on notice* that: (i) if substantial payments were made to one Consultant, then the services rendered by that Consultant would deserve greater scrutiny; (ii) *it was expected* that the Claimant should have some record or knowledge of the services rendered by the Consultants and the payments made in consideration for those services; (iii) where different individuals may have been involved at different times in providing different services, *it was expected* that the Claimant, which received these services, would be aware of the individuals who provided them and of the nature of the services; (iv) so far the Claimant had substantiated neither the nature nor the reality of the services; and (v) contemporaneous documents supporting these facts *would assist the Tribunal in reaching a conclusion regarding the Respondent's corruption defense.*"[19] (Emphasis added)

Thus the tribunal clearly took pains, in putting the parties on notice of the respective burdens, to keep an open mind on the ultimate conclusions. It was not for lack of guidance and notice by the tribunal that the claimant failed to comply with the directions to provide additional evidence. Whether the explanations for non-compliance were convincing was a separate matter.

5.   The Oral Hearing and Witness Testimony

The next challenge in terms of procedure and proof is at the stage of oral hearings. As stated, it is a myth that the occasionally encountered very lengthy and all-encompassing procedural order will preempt or resolve issues of proof and it is a myth to assume that at the latest in the oral hearing the arbitral tribunal will invariably clearly guide the parties as to proof. The challenge, therefore, is to consider whether procedures can be improved before and during the oral hearing to focus the witness testimony and pleading on those elements which are necessary in terms of the burden and standard of proof.

At the latest at this stage, any and all written submissions, witness statements, expert reports and taking of evidence will have taken place and, apart from occasional nova, will define the record to be applied to issues of proof. If the arbitral tribunal has given no indications as to the burden of proof, even where the parties have themselves briefed it, then the pleadings and witness statements may well overshoot the mark: some of the

---

18. *Metal-Tech Ltd. v. The Republic of Uzbekistan* (ICSID Case No. ARB/10/3), Award of 2 October 2013, para. 252 (available at <http://italaw.com/sites/default/files/case-documents/italaw3012.pdf>).

19. *Ibid.*, para. 253.

submissions and testimony will be relevant and material, some not, and other evidence which might have been submitted will not be present at all. If the arbitral tribunal has given indications as to the burden of proof, whether the parties requested it or not, then there is a greater likelihood that the prior pleadings and written witness statements will have been framed accordingly, and that the oral pleadings and testimony will be more focused and likely more economical.

The more precise the indications the arbitral tribunal has given leading up to the hearing, the less likely the arbitral tribunal runs the risk of "surprising" any party in the hearing in this regard. Likewise, the less likely the tribunal runs the risk of appearing to "unduly assist" one party to the detriment of the other in the hearing in terms of which live testimony it would like to hear, especially where that evidence was not actually contained in the prior written statement of the witness or expert now sitting before the tribunal. The arbitral tribunal has considerable powers and discretion to ask questions not addressed in the prior statements and/or to decline to hear a witness on issues which were addressed in the prior statements. While such conduct can give rise to enforceability risks, and to general dissatisfaction among the parties, it is far better received, and perceived, if it comes as no real surprise. Thus the more guidance and the more of a road map in advance, the less likely it is that such unforeseen developments will occur in the hearing itself.

More guidance and more of a road map in advance are not inconsistent with the inclination of some tribunals, notably in England, to stress the orality of the proceedings, to allow the parties free reign in bringing any and all witnesses for oral testimony, and to allow considerable or even full direct testimony in embellishment of the prior written witness statements. If desired by the parties or decided by the arbitral tribunal, such an approach can still be applied. Yet it would in fact work even better and more economically if prior guidance on proof were provided.

Experience dictates again and again that the parties will often heed such guidance. They will rein in their insistence on extensive testimony and oral pleadings, and indeed focus more on what the tribunal has asked for. The onus for this to occur, however, is more on the arbitral tribunal than on the parties. The tribunal needs to master the file as early as is feasible, and as early as there is in fact a useful file. It needs to engage the parties in a discussion of proof as early as possible, but only if the file before it is sufficiently informative. At the latest prior to a final structuring of the oral hearing, the tribunal needs to confer with the parties as to how many witnesses will appear, which ones will appear, and indeed why.

6.   *Rendering of the Arbitral Award*

The final challenge as to procedure and proof is the arbitral award. Again, it is a myth that arbitral tribunals routinely address, with anything approaching "precision", the burden of proof and the standard of proof which they consider to apply, the reasons for applying it, and the sources for its application. This is especially the case if the parties themselves have not addressed the issue. More often than not, the arbitral award will not set forth the procedural aspects of the burden of proof and standard of proof. Rather, it will simply make a generic listing of the procedural milestones and filings in the case, as evidence of upholding the right to be heard and equal treatment. Many awards will not expressly address whether and how a party has met the applied burden and standard of proof.

It is submitted that in some cases this could be done differently, better and with more precision. If the arbitral tribunal has not given such guidance prior to issuing the award, then anything it does state in the award runs the risk of being perceived as a "surprise" to one or both sides. If the arbitral tribunal has given such guidance prior to issuing the award, then surely it should apply that guidance already given to its determination in the award. Anything less in terms of precision is likely to leave one or both sides less than entirely satisfied with the decision-making process. Indeed one of the hallmarks of a properly and well-drafted award is that the losing side is at least satisfied to the extent of understanding how and why it lost, even if it disagrees with the how and the why. Lack of transparency as to the how and the why may be almost as bad as the fact of losing itself. This surely applies to the issue of proof.

We question why some, indeed many awards are lacking in this regard. At the latest in the deliberations leading to drafting the award, the arbitral tribunal should have decided on the burden and standard of proof. This should be the case irrespective of how much guidance it gave earlier, how much discovery took place, whether consultations on the issue took place with the parties, and whether the parties themselves argued the issue of proof before the tribunal. We also query whether one of the reasons why many awards lack this component is the concern that more precision and texture on proof would enhance the likelihood of a challenge to the award, whereas more obliqueness makes the award harder to set aside. The truth may be somewhere in the middle, and will obviously differ from tribunal to tribunal and case to case. And in the case of investment treaty-based awards especially under the ICSID Convention, the expectation of a petition to annul the award is probably present in any event, with or without precision on proof.

In any case, such fears of set-aside are both illegitimate and unjustified in most cases: illegitimate in the sense that the arbitral tribunal should be seen as having a duty to craft an award which addresses the *petita* and the issues before it, which certainly includes burden and standard of proof; unjustified in the sense that in most leading arbitral jurisdictions the discretion of the tribunal to investigate the case and to disregard evidence not considered material or relevant is considered to be so broad that the chances of successful challenge of an award on the basis of application of a particular burden or standard of proof are remote at best. Even the more recent trend of asserting the existence of an international or transnational procedural public policy as grounds for challenge is not likely to increase the risk to the tribunal here.

In this regard, reference, for example, to such sources as the UNCITRAL Model Law,[20] the 1958 New York Convention on the Recognition and Enforcement of Foreign Arbitral Awards,[21] the International Law Association Report on Public Policy as Bar to

---

20. Cf., e.g., Art. 34(2)(a)(ii) of the UNCITRAL Model Law and Part B, Sect. 7(b), para. 46 Explanatory Note by the UNCITRAL Secretariat on the Model Law on International Commercial Arbitration: "[Public policy] is to be understood as serious departures from fundamental notions of procedural justice."

21. Cf., e.g., Art. V(1)(b) and (d) New York Convention.

Enforcement of International Arbitral Awards, national arbitration laws,[22] and national case law as well as arbitral awards give ready support to a consensus of three kinds:

First, the right to a reasonable opportunity to be heard and the right to equal treatment are fundamental procedural rights that may not be violated.

Second, however, violation of these rights does not necessarily automatically give rise to grounds for denial of enforceability to the award. In addition, some jurisdictions require the argument (and in some cases evidence) provided for by the petitioner that the violation has had (or could have had) an impact on the outcome of the arbitral award.

Third, even where such a violation does lead to set aside or refusal of enforcement because the violation affected the outcome of the award, the violation does not necessarily trigger the separate ground of contravention of (procedural) public policy. In order to constitute grounds for non-enforcement, the violation of procedural laws or rules must be severe and deprive a party of fundamental rights.[23] In this regard, transnational procedural public policy is arguably more problematic and elusive than transnational substantive public policy.

Thus, there is a ready assumption that opportunity to be heard and equal treatment are universally protected. Yet both statutory and case law approaches show that some jurisdictions will uphold an award where one of these rights was even manifestly violated *unless* the violated party can demonstrate that the violation affected the outcome of the award. Thus some jurisdictions, such as Switzerland by case law and Germany by both case law and statute, require an outcome-determinative test. Not every violation of these

---

22. For example, the English Arbitration Act explicitly provides that an arbitral award may be vacated if "the award *or the way in which it was procured* [is] contrary to public policy". English Arbitration Act, Art. 68(2)(g) (emphasis added). See also, e.g., Art. 1065(1)(e) Netherlands Code of Civil Procedure ("the award, or the manner in which it was made, violates public policy or morals"). For a definition of procedural public policy under Swiss law, see *X Inc. c/ Z. Corp.*, BGer [Swiss Federal Supreme Court], 3 Apr. 2002, 20 ASA Bull. (2002) p. 358 ("*L'ordre public procédural garantit aux parties le droit à un jugement indépendant sur les conclusions et l'état de fait soumis au Tribunal arbitral d'une manière conforme au droit de procédure applicable; il y a violation de l'ordre public procédural lorsque des principes fondamentaux et généralement reconnus ont été violés, ce qui conduit à une contradiction insupportable avec le sentiment de la justice, de telle sorte que la décision apparaît incompatible avec des valeurs reconnues dans un Etat de droit*") ("Procedural public policy guarantees to the parties the right to an independent judgment respecting the conclusions and the nature of the facts submitted to the arbitral tribunal in a manner conforming to the applicable procedural law; public policy is being violated when fundamental and generally recognized principles were violated, leading to an unbearable contradiction to the sense of justice such that the relevant decision appears to be incompatible with the accepted values in a state governed by the rule of law." (Author's translation)). See also Richard H. KREINDLER and Timothy J. KAUTZ, "Agreed Deadlines and the Setting Aside of Arbitral Awards", 15 ASA Bull. (1997) p. 576.

23. Richard H. KREINDLER and Anna TEVINI, "The Impact of Public Policy Considerations" in Thomas D. HALKET, ed., *Arbitration of International Intellectial Property Disputes* (JurisNet, LLC 2012) p. 437 at p. 461; Dirk OTTO and Omaia ELWAN, "Article V(2)" in Herbert KRONKE et al., eds., *Recognition and Enforcement of Foreign Arbitral Awards: a Global Commentary on the New York Convention* (2010) p. 389 (with further references).

rights will be fatal. And not every violation of New York Convention Art. V(1)(*b*) or V(1)(*d*) would also be a violation of Art. V(2)(*b*).[24]

Even where the violation is fatal because the violated party succeeds in showing that the violation affected the outcome, the violation will not necessarily also offend public policy, in this case procedural public policy. Thus not every denial of equal treatment is fatal. And not every fatal denial of equal treatment is also proscribed by procedural public policy. In fact, vacatur or non-enforcement of an arbitral award on grounds of procedural public policy violations is rare.[25] By way of example, in the oft-commented-upon Swiss Federal Tribunal decision in *Egemetal v. Fuchs*[26] a wrong or arbitrary application of the agreed arbitration rules was not egregious enough to constitute a violation of public policy, in this case procedural public policy, under Sect. 190(2) of the Swiss Federal Private International Law Act (PILA).

Further examples of actions in violation of the agreed rules, equal treatment, and/or due process which were held not to be violations of procedural public policy, in recent years, include denial of the right to introduce or comment on certain evidence where the arbitral tribunal did not base its award on such evidence;[27] denial of the right to introduce or comment on certain evidence where the arbitral tribunal based its award on multiple sources of evidence, and not solely on the one source of evidence as to which due process was denied; denial of the right of further argument on points which the arbitral tribunal considered or would have considered to be irrelevant to its award; allowing claimant to modify the legal basis for its claim in its final brief, on the grounds that a new legal clarification to the facts did not constitute *ultra petita*;[28] and refusal of the

---

24. See Art. V(1)(*b*) New York Convention:

    "Recognition and enforcement of the award may be refused, at the request of the party against whom it is invoked, only if that party furnishes to the competent authority where the recognition and enforcement is sought, proof that: ... The party against whom the award is invoked was not given proper notice of the appointment of the arbitrator or of the arbitration proceedings or was otherwise unable to present his case";

    Art. V(1)(*d*) New York Convention:

    "(*d*) The composition of the arbitral authority or the arbitral procedure was not in accordance with the agreement of the parties, or, failing such agreement, was not in accordance with the law of the country where the arbitration took place";

    Art. V(2)(*b*) New York Convention:

    "Recognition and enforcement of an arbitral award may also be refused if the competent authority in the country where recognition and enforcement is sought finds that: ... (*b*) The recognition or enforcement of the award would be contrary to the public policy of that country."

25. Richard H. KREINDLER and Anna TEVINI, supra fn. 23, p. 460; Philippe PINSOLLE and Richard H. KREINDLER, "*Les limites du rôle de la volonté des parties dans la conduite de l'instance arbitrale*", Rev. Arb. (2003) p. 41 at p. 60.
26. BGE 126 III 249.
27. German Supreme Court, BGHZ 31, 43, 48.
28. Swiss Federal Tribunal, BGE 1994.

arbitral tribunal to permit further cross-examination, where no effect on the outcome was shown and the arbitral tribunal was held not to have taken into account the objectionable contents of the prior witness testimony in rendering its award.[29]

Interestingly, the yardstick for the outcome-determinative test here is the perspective of the arbitral tribunal, and not of the reviewing court or of the allegedly aggrieved party. This is potentially problematic, however, since it means that no violation will be found as long as the arbitrators establish the "fact" of there being no effect of their own violation on the outcome of the award. Moreover, the complaint of violation of procedural public policy can be precluded if it is not invoked during the ongoing arbitration procedure itself but only at the post-arbitration stage.[30] On the other hand, the US Federal Arbitration Act annulment grounds respecting procedure[31] are arguably more expansive or in any event more explicit than those in the UNCITRAL Model Law,[32] German law,[33] or Swiss law.[34] They include within "arbitrator misconduct" acts such as "refusal to postpone the hearing, upon sufficient cause shown, refusal to hear evidence pertinent and material to the controversy, or of any other misbehavior by which the rights of any party have been prejudiced".[35] Similarly, the English Arbitration Act 1996 Sect. 68(1) and (2) speak to "serious irregularity," including "the award or the way in which it was procured being contrary to public policy".[36] Here the test is not solely outcome-determinative in contrast to Germany: if the procedure used in order to reach the award was seriously irregular, it may offend public policy irrespective of whether it impacted on the outcome of the award.[37]

We question whether US case law is actually converging more with Continental European concepts of procedural public policy. The ILA Final Report states that "[i]t is widely accepted that procedural public policy should not include manifest disregard of the law or of the facts". Case law in the United States has however allowed for such a set-aside ground, arguably within the context of procedural public policy. However, the relatively recent US Supreme Court decision in *Hall Street Associates, LLC. v. Mattel, Inc.*[38] betokens a possible retreat, and thereby a possible falling in line with transnational procedural public policy. In any event, the overall message here is that the chances of successful challenge of an award on the basis of having (mis)applied a particular burden or standard of proof are remote at best.

---

29. *Generica, Ltd. v. Pharmaceutical Basics*, Inc., 125 F.3d 1123 (7th Cir. 1997).
30. See *Cour d'appel* [CA] [regional court of appeal] Paris, 18 Nov. 2004, 132 J.D.I. 357 (2005) (Fr.).
31. See Sect. 10(a) Federal Arbitration Act (FAA).
32. See Art. 34(2)(b)(ii) UNCITRAL Model Law.
33. See Sect. 1059 ZPO [German Code of Civil Procedure].
34. See Art. 190(2)(e) PILA.
35. FAA Sect. 10(a)(3).
36. See Sect. 68(2)(g) English Arbitration Act.
37. See Sect. 68(1) English Arbitration Act which explicitly provides for the possibility to challenge the arbitral award "on the ground of serious irregularity affecting the tribunal, the proceedings *or* the award" (emphasis added).
38. 128 S.Ct. 1396 (2008).

V.   SPECIFIC RECOMMENDATIONS

At the contract drafting stage, in the highly unlikely event of a specific party agreement on burden and standard of proof the arbitral tribunal should consider itself bound by such agreement, but the precision which is meant here would still depend largely on the procedural agreements or decisions by the parties and the tribunal once the arbitration is commenced.

At the stage of commencing the arbitration, the parties should be more open to the mutual benefit of agreeing on the burden and standard of proof at an early stage after the exchange of initial pleadings, or for the arbitral tribunal to take a position on the issue absent agreement. The less detailed the parties' initial pleadings, the more useful it could be for the tribunal to promote such discussion early on and ensure that the arbitration becomes "grounded". It is far more realistic than one might initially assume to create the conceptual and legal framework for early intervention and precision respecting burden and standard of proof, both in the best practice of Continental European "*Beweisbeschlüsse*" and "*Rechtsgespräche*" and the revised IBA Rules provisions.

Moreover, in view of the quite liberal approach of many international arbitration tribunals to the admissibility of evidence in the written phase, even to the point of accepting late filings and extending deadlines for such purposes, more procedural precision as to proof would be beneficial. It would not undermine the liberality of admissibility standards even assuming that those liberal standards remained. Indeed there is no tension between liberal admissibility standards on the one hand and more precise guidance as to who has the burden of proof, what the burden is and how it can be discharged on the other hand. Unless and until a party is on notice as to the admissibility standards, and is informed that the burden of proof may be on the party who is contesting an inference in favor of admissibility, the burden as to admissibility itself will be less clear than it should be.

Nor is there any tension between liberal admissibility standards on the one hand and precise guidance as to whether the tribunal considers expert testimony to be useful on specific topics, or rather considers that the principle of *jura novit curia* suffices. How often have parties spent considerable time and money on experts of law only to learn that the tribunal did not consider such testimony to be called for or useful? Surely it would make more sense for the arbitral tribunal to address this issue, to the extent possible, in advance. Likewise, it might make sense for the tribunal to address which body of law it considers to govern the questions of burden and standard of proof, so that the parties are on notice that they may wish to submit evidence on this question of applicable law.

Thus, if the parties are in agreement on the law which applies to the question of burden and standard of proof, then expert testimony on that issue will not clearly be needed or helpful. If the arbitral tribunal makes clear that it is not bound by, but may be guided by, general principles of law prevailing in the domestic forum relating to evidence, this guidance may be instrumental for the further pleadings of the parties. Likewise if the arbitral tribunal makes clear that it considers itself bound by certain national procedural rules respecting the burden or standard of proof because it considers them to be part and parcel of the substantive law underlying the cause of action, then guidance on that issue may be critical. This will be the case especially where those national procedural rules which it applies are different than the national procedural rules at the seat of arbitration. Left to their own devices, certain parties would not conclude that because a cause of action is subject to, e.g., German substantive law, therefore the burden or standard of proof, including alleviation of the same, might also be subject to German (procedural) law even if the seat of arbitration is not Germany.

At the stage of subsequent written submissions, if the tribunal has provided precision on the burden and standard of proof before the further written submissions including witness statements and expert reports, then it is the party's own fault if it fails to tailor its further presentation accordingly. There is no inconsistency per se between providing such precision on the one hand and entertaining document discovery subsequently on the other hand. Nor is there any inconsistency between having such precision and maintaining generally liberal standards of admissibility of written evidence. Finally, there is no inconsistency per se between providing such precision at the earliest appropriate stage respecting issues of proof and complying with the duties to remain impartial, to grant a "reasonable" or even "full" opportunity to be heard, and to treat the parties equally.

Later, at the stage of oral hearings, the more precise indications the arbitral tribunal has given leading up to the hearing, the less likely it is that the arbitral tribunal runs the risk of "surprising" any party in the hearing, including in terms of admissibility of hearsay evidence and nova. It is crucial that the arbitral tribunal will not have unwittingly "misled" the parties as to their evidentiary requirements leading up to and in the hearing itself. One approach to avoiding such misleading is simply to leave open entirely the question of burden and standard of proof, but experience suggests that this approach is not satisfactory. With no guidance as to proof, each party will conclude on its own what the proper burden and standard of proof are, without any guarantee that they are in alignment with the conception held by the tribunal. By contrast, with more precise guidance as to proof, each party is on notice as to the respective burdens and standards; it then fails to adhere to them, or fails to try to disprove them, at its own peril.

Of particular relevance here in the hearing and leading up to it is the issue of evidentiary "presumptions" and "inferences". Depending on the legal culture, the parties and the arbitral tribunal members may have different understandings of presumptions and inferences, including "legal" presumptions or inferences with a probative value and "judicial" presumptions or inferences as to facts. Rules establishing presumptions or shifting the burden of proof under certain circumstances, or drawing inferences from a lack of proof, are generally deemed to be part of the *lex causae*. In the case of an investment treaty-based arbitration, the *lex causae* is essentially the treaty itself, which in the case of most bilateral investment treaties invariably provides no rules for shifting the burden of proof or establishing presumptions.[39]

In the category of legal presumptions or inferences, there would not appear to be a consensus in international law or international arbitration as to how and when they should apply. What is clear is that for that reason alone and because presumptions affect the burden of proof, earlier guidance may be called for. Thus applying a presumption in favor of the proponent of the burden should trigger an "alert" to the adversary that he has an opportunity to refute the presumption; if he is not on notice as to the operation of the presumption, he is probably also not on notice as to the need to attempt to refute it.

---

39. See, e.g., *Metal-Tech Ltd. v. The Republic of Uzbekistan*, supra fn. 17, para. 238.

Alerting the opponent to the presumption only on the eve of the hearing or in the hearing may simply be too late, and be seen as an unacceptable surprise. This is all the more the case where the arbitral tribunal concludes that there is an "irrebuttable" presumption.

In the second category are judicial presumptions or inferences as to facts (such as "circumstantial evidence"). While such evidence is normally clearly admissible, again advance guidance to the extent possible would be preferable as to when it will be accepted. In the case of "adverse inferences", parties appear to have invoked this tool and invited the arbitral tribunal to apply it with increasing frequency in recent years. Here too there is no international consensus as to when and how an adverse inference may be drawn. At the same time, the encapsulation in Art. 9(5) and (6) of the IBA Rules may serve as a generally acceptable reflection of best practices.

Yet even this codification begs the question of what in a given case is a failure "without satisfactory explanation" to produce a document or any other relevant evidence including witness testimony. Presumably a "satisfactory explanation" would overlap with the grounds for objecting to production of evidence or refusal to admit evidence summarized in Art. 9(2) of the IBA Rules, but this is by no means exclusive or limitative. And presumably the inference to be drawn must be sufficiently weighty, accurate and concordant with the remaining universe of evidence in the record, as for example set forth in Art. 1353 of the French Civil Code ("The presumptions which are not established by a statute are left to the insight and carefulness of the judges, who shall only admit serious, precise and concurrent presumptions, and in the cases only where statutes admit oral evidence, unless a transaction is attacked for reason of fraud or deception."). Other criteria which have evolved for the drawing of adverse inferences include that the claimant has made a prima facie case[40] and that the requested party has had sufficient time and opportunity to produce the evidence which it fails to produce.[41]

What is occasionally misunderstood in the invocation or threat of adverse inference is that the party to whose benefit the inference would redound must still prove his claim. This too should be clearly and precisely explained to that party. Furthermore, insofar as all inferences are rebuttable by presenting direct evidence or relying on another inference, for this reason alone the arbitral tribunal should provide more precision by putting the parties on notice that it may draw such inference, especially after the tribunal itself has specifically ordered production of evidence which a party still fails to produce. The arbitral tribunal has the power and discretion to infer a different conclusion from that of the party urging the inference or to make reasonable assumptions in the absence of any specific evidence. For these reasons too, more precision is possible and desirable in the form of advance notice by the tribunal. Learning for the first time about the drawing of such an inference in the arbitral award is neither satisfactory nor, arguably,

---

40. Evidence which if "unexplained or uncontradicted, is sufficient to maintain the proposition affirmed": Bin CHENG, *General Principles of Law as Applied by International Courts and Tribunals* (1953) p. 324.

41. See, e.g., *Marvin Feldman v. Mexico* (ICSID Case No. ARB(AF)/99/1), Award of 16 December 2002, para. 178; *Europe Cement Investment & Trade SA v. Turkey* (ICSID Case No. ARB(AF/07/2)), Award of 13 August 2009, para. 152.

fully consistent with the right to be heard of the party against whom the inference was drawn.

Also of particular relevance here in the hearing and leading up to it is the issue of sanctions. Presumptions and inferences, as already discussed, may be seen as a form of sanctions. The connection to precision on proof is that the threat of sanctions is more likely to be heeded if the party against whom it is directed is informed more precisely of the background to the sanction and its consequence in terms of burden of proof. Thus if a sanction, whether in the form of an inference or an adversary allocation of costs, is threatened for unexplained and unjustified failure to produce evidence, the threat is more likely to have impact, and result in production, if it is specifically linked to the tribunal's conception of burden and standard of proof.

Making this link is likely to be more persuasive, and more convincing, than simply ignoring the failure of the party without comment and factoring it into the award without comment. Even at least taking formal note of the failure would be halfway toward putting the party on notice and avoiding complete surprise at the stage of the award. Such formal taking of note is in fact already foreseen in, e.g., Art. 49 of the International Court of Justice Statute ("The Court may, even before the hearing begins, call upon the agents to produce any document or to supply any explanations. Formal note shall be taken of any refusal.") and Art. 34(3) of the ICSID Arbitration Rules ("The parties shall cooperate with the Tribunal in the production of the evidence and in the other measures provided for in paragraph (2). The Tribunal shall take formal note of the failure of a party to comply with its obligations under this paragraph and of any reasons given for such failure."). Indeed in a number of cases international tribunals have expressly stated that they would draw inferences from a failure or refusal of production of evidence.[42]

Finally, at the stage of rendering the arbitral award at the latest, the arbitral tribunal should address whether and how a party has met the applied burden and standard of proof or instead has not met the burden. Fears that doing so in any detail will undermine the enforceability of the award are illegitimate and unjustified in most cases. Many if not most of the above-mentioned opportunities for more precision as to proof leading up to and through the hearing also apply to the drafting of the arbitral award itself. The one difference is that providing such precision does not serve the role of putting the parties on notice in order to address the burden and standard of proof, since it is too late for the parties to react. Rather, precision in the award serves the role of applying the burden and standard deemed to govern and drawing the consequences.

On the one hand, failing to offer more precision on these issues especially where the parties squarely briefed and disputed the issues can be unsatisfying to the parties; it might even be seen as a dereliction or abdication of duty. On the other hand, failing to offer more precision may be considered a logical consequence of the tribunal's determination that precision is not needed to explain and motivate the result, or at best would have the quality of *obiter dictum*. In reverse, taking pains to offer more precision on these issues runs little risk in most cases of undermining the enforceability of the award at the seat

---

42. See, e.g., *Waste Management v. Mexico II* (Additional Facility), Award of 30 April 2004, para. 30; see also *Europe Cement Investment & Trade SA v. Turkey* (ICSID Case No. ARB(AF)/07/2), Award of 13 August 2009, para. 152.

of arbitration or elsewhere; it does, however, provide the parties with an appropriate road map to the outcome of the arbitration.

Nonetheless, the concern that providing such precision would be either gratuitous or even risky will die hard. And it is not apparent what might succeed in mollifying this concern. This does not, however, alter the desirability and urgency of putting this concern in its proper perspective on a case-by-case basis.

In conclusion, the plea for more precision in the context of the practice and procedure respecting proof is to a great extent justified. The procedural deficits respecting precision as to proof are frequently encountered and often bemoaned. The tools to supply this greater precision are already available to the parties and tribunal and are often exercised as a matter of course in certain legal cultures. For these and other reasons, the plea for more procedural precision is also realistic. The challenge of implementing that greater precision in most international arbitrations can be met, but will realistically require considerable further time and effort. The time and effort are clearly worthwhile.

182

A. Precision Stream

2. Early Stages of the Arbitral Process: Interim Measures and Document Production

Report on the Session
Early Stages of the Arbitral Process:
Interim Measures and Document Production

Natalie L. Reid* and John Barkett**

TABLE OF CONTENTS

I.   INTRODUCTION

Session A2 focused on two early stages of arbitration proceedings that can have a critical effect on the overall course of a case—the disclosure of relevant and material documents that are in the possession, custody, or control of a party; and the availability of interim measures of protection to safeguard a party's rights, prevent aggravation of a dispute, and preserve the ability of the arbitral tribunal to award effective relief on the merits.

Much attention has been paid to the formal rules and standards governing these stages. On disclosure, the rules of the major arbitral institutions reaffirm the authority of the tribunal to direct the production of documents, whether explicitly or as part of its general power to issue procedural orders with regard to the conduct of the arbitration.[1] Arts. 3 and 9 of the International Bar Association's Rules on the Taking of Evidence in International Arbitration are regularly adopted by tribunals and parties as the guidelines for document disclosure, while at least one arbitral institution has incorporated an updated version of its previously freestanding guidelines into its rules as part of a recent revision of those provisions.[2] Likewise, a tribunal's authority to order interim measures

---

*   Panel Rapporteur; Partner, Debevoise & Plimpton LLP, based in New York.
** Panel Chair; Partner, Shook, Hardy & Bacon LLP, based in Miami.

1. See International Centre for Dispute Resolution International Arbitration Rules, amended and effective June 2014 (2014 ICDR Rules), Art. 21; International Institute for Conflict Prevention and Resolution Rules for Administered Arbitration of International Disputes, effective 1 December 2014 (2014 CPR Rules), Rule 11; London Court of International Arbitration Rules, effective 1 October 2014 (2014 LCIA Rules), Art. 22(v); Hong Kong International Arbitration Centre Administered Arbitration Rules, effective 1 November 2013 (2013 HKIAC Rules), Art. 22.3; Arbitration Rules of the Singapore International Arbitration Centre, Fifth Edition, effective 1 April 2013 (SIAC Rules), Rule 24.1(g); Rules of Arbitration of the International Chamber of Commerce, effective 1 January 2012 (2012 ICC Rules), Art. 22; Stockholm Chamber of Commerce Arbitration Rules, effective 1 January 2010 (2010 SCC Rules), Art. 26(3); see also UNCITRAL Arbitration Rules, as revised in 2010 (2010 UNCITRAL Rules), Art. 27(3). Note that the versions of the ICDR Rules, CPR Rules, and LCIA Rules in force as of the time of publication all entered into effect after the 2014 ICCA Congress.
2. 2014 ICDR Rules, Art. 21.

is expressly affirmed in the major institutional rules,[3] and international arbitral decisions and practice have developed a common set of factors that tribunals frequently apply in determining whether to grant applications for such measures.[4]

But these are simply the framework within which the parties in any given case operate. They are the rules of road; but what about conduct of the drivers? The actual experience of users, counsel, and arbitrators in proceedings conducted under these rules, guidelines, and standards suggests that, at times, parties have sought improper advantages through these mechanisms, and that tribunals have not necessarily fully exercised their powers to control such conduct – thereby jeopardizing the legitimacy of the arbitral process.

II.   PART I OF THE SESSION

In keeping with the theme of the 2014 Congress, this session sought to test certain key propositions about what actually happens in the course of disclosure and interim measures applications: which are myths, and which are the realities of current arbitral practice?

On disclosure, the session considered whether document production is fairly conducted by the parties and appropriately policed by tribunals. Through papers presented by Stephen Drymer, Murray Smith, and Nicolas Swerdloff, and a lively discussion with the audience, this first part of the session examined five propositions:[5]

(1) *Document production in international arbitration is fair and not rife with gamesmanship to obtain tactical advantage or to avoid production of unfavorable information, in part because the IBA Rules on the Taking of Evidence in International Arbitration have eliminated concerns parties might have with the fairness of document production;*
(2) *Tribunals in international arbitration have the inherent power to sanction a party or a party's legal representative for abuse of the document production process and do so for failure to comply with an order of the tribunal;* and

---

3. See 2014 ICDR Rules, Art. 24; 2014 CPR Rules, Rule 13; 2014 LCIA Rules, Art. 25; 2013 HKIAC Rules, Art. 23; 2013 SIAC Rules, Rule 26; 2012 ICC Rules, Art. 28; 2010 SCC Rules, Art. 32; see also 2010 UNCITRAL Rules, Art. 26.
4. See, e.g., 2006 UNCITRAL Model Law on International Commercial Arbitration, Art. 17A(1)(b); Gary BORN, *International Commercial Arbitration* (2014), at 2467-2468; Julian D. M. LEW, *Commentary on Interim and Conservatory Measures in ICC Arbitration Cases*, 11 ICC Int'l Ct. Arb. Bull. (2000, no. 1) p. 23 at p. 27; *Paushok et al v. Mongolia* (UNCITRAL), Order on Interim Measures of 2 September 2008 para. 45. See also HKIAC Rules, Art. 23.4 (expressly listing these factors for tribunals to take into account when evaluating the circumstances of the case).
5. To better reflect the discussion among the panelists and the audience, the propositions are listed and grouped here in a slightly different order than as presented at the Opening Plenary. Given the large number of propositions discussed in the session, this note includes only succinct summaries of the key points of the discussion. Readers are encouraged to review the detailed papers prepared by the panelists.

(3) Where an attorney acts in bad faith in the document disclosure process, a tribunal has a duty to report the attorney to the attorney's bar association.

Mr. Swerdloff summarized the kinds of disclosure tactics that are often employed by uncooperative parties to gain undue advantage, and noted that arbitrators have both express authority to impose sanctions for such abuses – including through provisions of the applicable law, rules, or guidelines (such as the IBA Rules) – and inherent authority to protect the integrity of the arbitral process. Mr. Swerdloff also noted that, depending on the seat of the arbitration and the applicable rules, arbitrators may be able (and perhaps required) to report counsel to his or her regulatory or professional body for breaches of ethical requirements in the course of disclosure.

Mr. Drymer observed that problems often arise even when parties in international arbitration seek to act in good faith, because they come from different legal traditions with widely varying approaches and understandings with regard to disclosure. Consequently, the solution lies not just in sanctions after the fact, but also in the adoption of common-sense measures at the outset of proceedings (including, but not limited to, the IBA Rules) to bridge the gaps between parties and ensure clarity and fairness in document production.

When polled by moderator John Barkett, very few in the audience disagreed with the proposition that document production is generally fair. Instead, audience members emphasized that counsel and parties are accustomed to the rules and practices in domestic proceedings, so those from jurisdictions where there are no (or few) sanctions for non-disclosure have not internalized the habits encouraged by the threat of such consequences. The evolving practices, amendments to rules, and other possible solutions described by the panelists may be helpful means of addressing this problem. As a practical matter, however, while audience members agreed that tribunals have the inherent authority to impose sanctions on parties,[6] few recalled any instances of counsel being sanctioned or reported to a bar association or other regulatory body, leading some to the conclusion that the prospect of sanctions are a reality for parties, but not (yet) for counsel.

(4) Documents used for impeachment should never be required to be disclosed before being used.

The panelists and most of the audience disagreed with this proposition, at least in the absolute terms in which it was phrased. Both Mr. Smith and Mr. Swerdloff noted that significant prejudice can ensue if parties are allowed to delay disclosure or withhold documents on the ground that the materials will be used for impeachment. Mr. Smith proposed that, as part of a comprehensive approach to document matters at the beginning of a case, the order issued by a tribunal after the first procedural hearing

---

6. But see *Seagate Technology, LLC v. Western Digital Corp.*, 854 N.W.2d 750, 761 (Minn. 2014), in which the Minnesota Supreme Court affirmed a sanction that resulted in a significant award, but rejected the notion of inherent authority in a tribunal: "While courts possess inherent judicial powers that enable them to impose punitive sanctions, arbitrators have no correlating inherent authority and receive their powers from either the arbitration agreement, or the Legislature."

should discourage parties from "lying in the weeds" with clearly relevant evidence, by barring or restricting late disclosure except in defined extraordinary circumstances.

(5) It is unnecessary for a tribunal to address confidentiality of non-public documents produced in international arbitration.

Neither the panelists nor the audience agreed with this proposition, because the need for confidentiality and the challenges it poses in international arbitration are widely discussed in the literature and among practitioners. As requirements can vary across jurisdictions, Mr. Smith recommended that parties conclude an agreement on confidentiality to reduce or avoid conflicts, and eliminate the need for the tribunal to make specific directions as to the confidentiality of individual documents. Noting that there was no need to reinvent the wheel, Mr. Smith suggested that tribunals could offer parties a model of such an agreement that can be adapted for purposes of the case, and cited as an example the language in Debevoise & Plimpton's Annotated Model Arbitration Clause for International Contracts.

III.   PART II OF THE SESSION

The second part of the session explored why parties seek interim measures from arbitral tribunals, whether the right standard is being applied, and whether there is a better way to achieve interim protection during the pendency of the arbitration. Through papers presented by Francisco González de Cossío, Hilary Heilbron QC, and Robert Sills, and continued discussion with the audience, this part of the session examined a further five propositions:

(1) In a majority of cases, interim measures are sought by parties for tactical advantage or unmeritorious reasons.

Neither the panelists nor the audience agreed with the proposition as framed, but most concurred that interim measures are at least sometimes sought for improper reasons – and that at least some improper applications may ultimately be granted. As discussed in detail in her paper, Hilary Heilbron argued that tribunals should apply an analytical framework that minimizes the likelihood of granting an unmeritorious application, while maintaining the balance between strict standards and the flexibility to do justice under the circumstances of the case.

(2) There is no uniform standard in international arbitration when it comes to determining whether interim measures should be granted; and
(3) Assuming a likelihood of success on the merits, "balancing the conveniences" to each party, rather than requiring a finding of irreparable harm, is the appropriate test in evaluating whether to award interim measures.

The panelists and the audience agreed that there is no single uniform standard applied to requests for interim measures in international arbitration. In their respective presentations, Ms. Heilbron and Dr. González de Cossío observed that while there is broad apparent consensus on the factors that tribunals generally consider in determining whether to grant interim relief, there may be potentially significant differences in how those factors are applied by arbitrators in individual cases.

Dr. González de Cossío focused on the factor variously described as the "balance of harms," "balance of conveniences," or "proportionality," where tribunals weigh the harm that the moving party contends will result if interim measures are not granted against the harm that the opposing party argues will occur if the measures are imposed. He proposed that it is this factor, rather than a finding of irreparable harm, that should ultimately determine whether interim measures are granted. Most in the audience, however, favored retaining a distinct requirement that the applicant demonstrate a risk of "irreparable harm" – however that is defined under the applicable standard and determined on the facts – before it can obtain interim relief.

(4) *Interim measures are so rarely granted in international arbitration or fraught with enforcement difficulties that a party should seek an early hearing on the merits rather than spend the resources on seeking interim measures*; and
(5) *If interim measures are truly needed by a party, the solution is the use of an emergency arbitrator.*

The panelists noted some indications that the time and resources parties spend on seeking interim relief may not always be warranted: while acknowledging the limitations of the available information, Ms. Heilbron cited a summary of ICC interim measures awards reporting that applications were granted in fewer than half of the cases, and Mr. Sills observed that tribunals are often unable to grant effective interim relief, either because the measures cannot be granted in time to provide the necessary protection, or because relief is sought against third parties outside the jurisdiction of the arbitral tribunal. Nevertheless, neither the panelists nor the audience believed that parties should ignore the availability of interim relief from the arbitral tribunals; rather, this practical experience should inform decision-making on whether and when to seek such relief.

In particular, Mr. Sills noted that most of the leading institutional rules have recently adopted emergency arbitrator procedures, which provide for the rapid appointment of a single arbitrator to hear and resolve urgent applications on an accelerated timetable, before the constitution of the arbitral tribunal that will hear the merits of the case. While this is a welcome development, and should address concerns about timing, Mr. Sills cautioned that there may still be common circumstances in which a party is better advised to seek relief from competent national courts, especially in the United States, the jurisdiction discussed in his paper. He argued that in contrast to the interim measures available in arbitration even on an emergency basis, US courts can frequently offer quicker interim relief, under standards that are well settled and therefore predictable, through orders that are immediately enforceable. While many on the panel and in the audience were from different jurisdictions, there was broad agreement that emergency arbitrators are not – and may never be – the sole solution for parties that need interim measures.

Reliance Document Management

Murray L. Smith[*]

I.   INTRODUCTION

The reputation of arbitration has suffered as the cost and time to complete complex cases have increased. International commercial arbitration has in many cases become less efficient and less effective. One of the most important tasks in the organization of efficient proceedings is the management of documents. The arbitral tribunal can make a significant contribution to fairness and efficiency by establishing ground rules for the organization of the documentary record.

Stephen Jagusch writes that it is rare for arbitrators to get involved in organizing and presenting documentary evidence, "it being a matter considered the domain of the advocates", but he adds that there is a role for the tribunal in the early stages of document-heavy cases to streamline the presentations of counsel.[1]

Parties come from varying backgrounds and traditions. Misunderstandings and confusion relating to requirements for document productions can impair the efficiency of the proceeding and lead to perceptions of unfairness.

The effective management of documents in arbitration is a key element in minimizing costs and delay. The parties tender the documents that will be relied upon to prove their case. In addition, documents will be produced in response to discovery requests or as exhibits to expert reports. The concern is typically not that a party discloses too few documents but rather that there are too many documents that are tendered in a disorganized fashion.

---

[*] LL.M., Chartered arbitrator; <www.smithbarristers.com>, msmith@smithbarristers.com.
1. Stephen JAGUSCH, "Organization and Presentation of Documents to the Tribunal", Chapter 11 in Doak BISHOP and Edward G. KEHOE, eds., *The Art of Advocacy in International Arbitration*, 2nd edn. (Juris Publishing 2010).

The parties must be treated equally and be given a full opportunity to make their own case and know the case to be met. These objectives can be imperiled where documents are not presented in a concise or coherent fashion or where documents are not tendered in time to allow an adequate opportunity for response.

The arbitral tribunal should issue guidelines at the earliest stage of the proceeding so that the parties will know what is expected in terms of relevance, materiality, timing and organization of document productions. The tribunal can streamline the process by obtaining the agreement of the parties regarding requirements for tendering Reliance Documents, the need for authentication of documents, the process for challenges to disputed documents as well as expectations in respect of confidentiality of productions.

II.   RELIANCE DOCUMENTS

There are four stages in an arbitral proceeding when Reliance Documents might be tendered:

(1) accompanying pleadings;
(2) discovery disclosures;
(3) attachments to witness statements and expert reports; and
(4) documents used for impeachment purposes.

1.   *Documents Filed with Pleadings*

The offset to very limited discovery being available in international commercial arbitration is the early disclosure of all Reliance Documents. Statements of Claim, Defence and Reply are commonly accompanied by Reliance Documents. The Rules of the London Court of International Arbitration (LCIA), for example, provide that pleadings shall be accompanied by copies of all essential documents on which the party relies and which have not been previously submitted by another party.[2]

The Arbitration Rules of the United Nations Commission of International Trade Law (UNCITRAL) provide that pleadings should as far as possible be accompanied by all documents relied upon.[3]

Under the heading "Documents on Which a Party Relies", the Guidelines for Arbitrators Concerning Exchanges of Information published by the International Centre for Dispute Resolution (ICDR) recommend that: "Parties shall exchange, in advance of the hearing, all documents upon which each party intends to rely."

The International Bar Association (IBA) Rules on the Taking of Evidence in International Arbitration provide for each party to submit all documents available to it on which it relies. The IBA Rules contemplate submission of additional documents which have become relevant to the case and material to its outcome as a consequence of issues raised in witness statements, expert reports or submissions of the parties. The IBA Rules further provide that copies of documents shall conform to the originals and be available

---

2. LCIA Arbitration Rules, Rule 15.6.
3. UNCITRAL Arbitration Rules, Art. 20.

for inspection, that documents in electronic form should be produced in a form that is reasonably useable by the recipients and that translations should be submitted.[4]

Even where the rules adopted do not specify that pleadings be accompanied by Reliance Documents or that Reliance Documents be exchanged in advance of the hearing, or where the parties have not agreed to use institutional rules or the IBA Rules, it is more common than not in international cases for the parties to agree that pleadings be accompanied by Reliance Documents.

One of the objectives for the tribunal at the preliminary hearing is to encourage counsel to apply their minds to documents early on. Supplementary lists from both parties will follow in most cases. It is incumbent upon counsel to get a handle on necessary documents at the very earliest stages of the arbitration proceeding.

The arbitral tribunal should be proactive to clarify procedures for the tendering of Reliance Documents and should seek the agreement of the parties regarding the nature, form and timing of document deliveries. The IBA Rules, whether adopted in full by the parties or not, are a good starting point for suggestions to the parties. Discussions among the tribunal and counsel should result in the tribunal issuing directions covering when documents are to be submitted, whether documents may be delivered in electronic form, whether the tribunal members should be provided with hard copies, whether translations will be required, and whether or not originals should be made available for inspection.

At the pleadings stage the parties should be encouraged to restrict productions to those documents that are relevant and material. In this context the requirement for materiality is meant to confine productions to those documents that are necessary or essential for the proof of a party's case or to answer the opposing party's case. The tribunal should gently admonish the parties to avoid excessive productions, discourage the proverbial document dump and direct that document deliveries be in a form reasonably digestible by the tribunal and the other parties. Early directions for documents to be indexed and listed in chronological or other coherent fashion will streamline the process. It is not unheard of for counsel to file lists of documents that are hundreds of pages long referencing thousands and thousands of pages, perhaps out of an abundance of caution to maintain maximum latitude for access to documents that may become relevant as the case unfolds.

A proactive arbitral tribunal will strive to limit productions to avoid unnecessary expense and confusion without impeding the right of a party to make its case. By addressing this subject at the earliest possible stage, the tribunal can encourage counsel to focus on the documents that are necessary. How to concentrate the minds of counsel on the need for limited productions is a matter for the creativity of the tribunal. The first step is simple moral suasion and the final step may be cost consequences for document productions that are excessive. There are few metrics for measuring excessive productions because only the parties know what documents are essential to make their case. One such metric may be whether or not a document is required reading for the tribunal members.

Arbitrators take different approaches to reviewing Reliance Documents. Some arbitrators read all documents that accompany pleadings well in advance of the hearing

---

4. IBA Rules on the Taking of Evidence in International Arbitrations, Art. 3.

date. Others prefer to wait until a common book of documents or core bundle is delivered before the arbitration hearing. The parties should expect that the members of the tribunal may read all of the documents that accompany pleadings, witness statements, expert reports and written briefs unless told to do otherwise. The cost to review unnecessary documents could be substantial. If it is apparent that a party has tendered documents that were not necessary reading or that have increased the time and expense for response or that have extended the time necessary to complete the hearings then cost sanctions may be appropriate. It is imperative that the direction regarding Reliance Documents issued at the preliminary meeting address the potential for cost sanctions so that the parties are forewarned and naturally encouraged to limit document productions to necessary documents.

2. *Discovery Disclosures*

Much has been written about document discovery in arbitration. Such disclosures as are made do not necessarily become Reliance Documents for use in the arbitration. Typically, the party obtaining disclosure will use those documents that are helpful to its case. Such documents may not be listed as Reliance Documents by the producing party. To avoid confusion, a party planning to use documents produced on discovery as Reliance Documents should list those documents as Reliance Documents at some stage of the proceeding. The process for answering discovery demands, the legal test for disclosure, the use of a Redfern Schedule and the question of whether or not, in answering an order made for disclosure, privileged documents must be listed in a manner that asserts the privilege but that does not reveal the contents of the privileged document is a matter for much more detailed consideration and may be too much for the first preliminary meeting and the initial Documents Direction. It may be that simply asserting privilege on a Redfern Schedule will be considered by the parties as sufficient.

The party making discovery disclosures may consider that the documents it has disclosed are available at large for use in cross-examination or in oral submissions at the hearing. The party receiving disclosure may also consider that the documents are generally available for use whether listed as Reliance Documents or not. To avoid confusion this matter should be discussed at a preliminary hearing. Each party should have a Master List of Reliance Documents. This list will be condensed when a Common Book of Documents (to be discussed below) is prepared.

The right of a party to prove its claim and to make full answer and defence cannot be restricted. The fundamental principle is to avoid a situation where a party is caught by surprise by documents produced out of the blue. That concern is lessened where documents that have been disclosed are listed as Reliance Documents because a party intends to rely upon them. The parties may wish to have a direction that any party planning to use documents produced on discovery must provide a supplementary list of such Reliance Documents.

Whether or not a direction is made for the listing of discovery documents as Reliance Documents that will be used in the hearing, there is a minimum role for the tribunal in managing documents disclosed on discovery. Documents disclosed in response to discovery requests or produced on orders for disclosure are equally susceptible of the document dump problem and the tribunal should encourage the parties to exercise reasonable caution in producing documents that are relevant and material and that are organized in a fashion that make them reasonably useable by the other party.

3. Witness Statements

Witness statements and expert reports will often have documents attached as exhibits. In theory the documents attached to witness statements should already have been listed as Reliance Documents. The potential for the other party to be caught by surprise is reduced by the opportunity to provide rebuttal witness statements and to comment in briefs that will follow witness statements.

The circumstance may arise where a party is able to assert unfair prejudice caused by late disclosure. In such a case the tribunal must make a ruling on admissibility or allow an adjournment to permit an opportunity to deal with the late listing of Reliance Documents. The Direction on Documents could address this potential problem by specifying whether or not new Reliance Documents will be permitted as attachments to witness statements and expert reports generally, or only in more limited circumstances such as where a case can be made for late documents being tendered only in unforeseeable circumstances.

The initial Documents Direction might provide that document lists may be supplemented but that a reason must be given for late disclosure and, if prejudice to the other party results, that an adjournment may be required with cost consequences to the party making late disclosures.

4. Documents Used for Impeachment

This is a problematic area. Parties may uncover a topic in the course of cross-examination that calls for impeachment with documents that have not been made part of the record in the proceeding. An objection may be made based on prejudice resulting from late production. The objecting party might argue they have been caught by surprise and were not permitted a reasonable opportunity to respond. The cross-examining party will say that the need for the document was not foreseeable and that it is tendered on cross-examination because it goes to credibility as opposed to the unfolding of the narrative. While a party cannot be restricted from a full opportunity to prove its case or to make full answer or defence, a party should be discouraged from lying in the weeds with clearly relevant evidence. This is a situation which brings into sharp relief the distinction between common law and civil law traditions. In the common law tradition a party would be obliged to disclose all documents in possession or control that were relevant or that could lead to a relevant train of inquiry, while in the civil law tradition a party would only disclose those documents that were necessary for their own case.

There is no one-size-fits-all solution to problems that arise when new documents are used solely for impeachment purposes. The potential for such problems was considered in the Protocol on Disclosure of Documents in Presentation of Witnesses in Commercial Arbitration published by the International Institute for Conflict Prevention and Resolution (CPR). That protocol provides as follows:

"Except for the purpose of impeaching the testimony of witnesses, the tribunal should not permit a party to use in support of its case, at a hearing or otherwise, documents or electronic information unless the party has presented them as part of its case or previously disclosed them. But the tribunal should not permit a party to withhold documents or electronic information otherwise required to be disclosed on the basis that the documents will be used by it for the impeachment of another party's witnesses."[5]

The Documents Direction issued at the preliminary hearing should record the agreement of the parties as to how to deal with documents produced for the first time in the course of the hearing. Such a direction will restrict late productions except in defined extraordinary circumstances that permit sufficient flexibility for the tribunal to do justice to the party seeking to use an undisclosed document because of unforeseeable circumstances, yet protect the other party from prejudice that would result from late disclosure. There are more complicated issues that may arise that may not be suitable for early resolution. An example is the question of whether or not a party may withhold privileged documents for use in cross-examination when the privilege would then be waived. As with the question of whether or not privileged documents must be listed in responding to an order for production of documents on requests for discovery, this may be a matter for much more detailed consideration and may be too much for the first preliminary meeting and the initial Documents Direction.

III.   COMMON BOOK OF DOCUMENTS

While the parties may be inclined to be expansive in listing Reliance Documents as part of the pleading process, the time and cost for the tribunal members to review relevant and material documents will be reduced by the parties preparing a common book of documents or core bundle. Mustill and Boyd, 2nd ed. (1989) at p. 327 describe what has come to be known as the core bundle in English practice:

"Recent experience has shown that the labour of conducting the hearing has been increased, and hence the efficiency of the process has been materially reduced, by the need to man-handle large quantities of copy documents, most of them quite useless, and to keep track of the much smaller number which are really relevant; so much so, that it has now become the practice for each side to isolate a 'working bundle', containing the documents which are likely to be relied upon, and to ignore the 'agreed bundle' altogether."

---

5. Protocol on Disclosure of Documents in Presentation of Witnesses in Commercial Arbitration, International Institute for Conflict Prevention and Resolution, p. 9. The Protocol can be downloaded from <www.cpradr.org/Resources/ALLCPRArticles/tabid/265/ID/614/CPR-Protocol-on-Disclosure-of-Documents-and-Presentation-of-Witnesses-in-Commercial-Arbitration.aspx>.

To the fullest extent possible, the parties should be encouraged to list documents to be relied upon in a common book or core bundle of documents to be delivered shortly in advance of the hearing. If this approach is adopted by the parties, the panel members may not consider it necessary to review every listed Reliance Document in advance of the hearing and will trust that the parties will cull the necessary documents for actual review. A common book of documents will also go some way in minimizing confusion regarding which documents produced on discovery will be relied upon at the hearing. Significant time savings will be realized where everyone at the hearing can quickly turn to the same page of the book to read the same document being referenced by a witness or by counsel.

The College of Commercial Arbitrators Guide to Best Practices in Commercial Arbitration, 3rd ed. (2014) at p. 185 makes the following suggestion:

> "Arbitrators should consider requiring the parties to jointly assemble and submit, as soon after the preliminary conference as feasible, a tabbed and indexed notebook that (depending on the preferences of the arbitrators) can be paper or electronic or both and that contains paginated copies of the key documents in the case (the core exhibits)."

This approach can be improved by starting out with a well-indexed list of Reliance Documents from each side that can be supplemented as the case goes on and that can be reduced shortly in advance of the hearing to a core book of documents that comprises all of the documents that should be reviewed by the tribunal before the hearing starts.

The mechanics of preparing the Common Book of Documents can be fairly straightforward. The claimant will provide a list of core documents. The respondent will add its key documents that have not already been listed. The claimant can add new documents to the list that are necessary to respond to the respondent's key documents. When that process is complete the documents in the book will be assembled, usually in chronological order. Documents listed for the Common Book will have two numbers at the top. The first number will be the order in which the document is listed in the Common Book and the second number will be the number of the same document from the list of Reliance Documents of the party adding the document to the list. Thus the first Tab of the Common Book will have at the top right the number "#1" and beside it the number "Cl. #77", for example. Where the respondent adds a new document to the list or a different version of one listed by the claimant it would be numbered "#122- R. #99", for example, for the 122nd Tab of the Common Book. One of the parties will prepare identical tabbed binders for the tribunal, with another copy to be marked as the formal Exhibit, one for opposing counsel and one copy for use by the witness who is testifying. Everyone will always be looking at the same document that can be easily found and it will not be necessary to mark hundreds of exhibits.

Assembly costs initially would be shared pending final allocation of costs by the tribunal in the final award. At the hearing, the Common Book will be marked as Exhibit A. Other documents that are used at the hearing and that were previously listed as Reliance Documents but not included in the Common Book will be marked as separate exhibits as the case unfolds. Documents attached to expert reports would just be made a part of the expert report that is marked as a separate exhibit.

A party that does not cooperate by either listing too few documents for the Common Book, or by listing too many documents, may attract cost consequences at the end of the day for wasteful or bad faith conduct. The situation of too few documents will become apparent if one party seeks to mark extensive documents as exhibits on the hearing that were not listed by that party for the Common Book. The too many documents situation will become apparent if the Common Book contains excessive documents listed by a party that were not used.

IV.   DOCUMENTS THAT ARE NOT USED

Every experienced arbitrator has come across the situation where a documents record is extensive, often filling many volumes, but many documents were not relied upon. Documents may have been contained in the Common Book but not referenced by any witness. There may be many documents in the binders at the end of the hearings that were never mentioned by counsel. What use is to be made of surplus documents that were tendered and made part of the evidentiary hearing record? Should unused documents be pulled from the binders? Would the tribunal err in law (possibly going to a denial of due process such as to imperil the final award under the New York Convention) if the tribunal were to say in the final award that documents that were not referenced by a witness or in argument were not taken into consideration? Must the tribunal members review all tendered documents to ensure that there is no relevant information missed whether or not they were referenced in the hearings or briefs? There are ways to confront this issue in advance. One way is to have the parties enter into a Documents Agreement that deals with whether or not tendered documents serve as proof of the truth of the contents (as discussed below). A recent court case in British Columbia highlighted the problem of unused documents. In *Kim v. Hong*, [2013] BCSC 587 beginning at para. 449 Griffin J. wrote:

> "I wish to make an observation about the volume of documents filed in this case. The parties filed a large number of binders of documents as exhibits during the trial, by agreement. This is a common practice, meant to speed up the hearing of oral evidence during the trial.
>
> With the expectation that the documents were going to be referred to by a witness, or at a minimum, in submissions where the impact of the evidence was agreed, I allowed these volumes of documents to be marked as exhibits. In hindsight, I now consider this to have been less than helpful.
>
> Unfortunately there were vast volumes of documents filed as exhibits to which there was no reference by any witness and either no reference in final argument or no agreement as to how they could be interpreted. I presume the documents were filed by counsel just in case they needed them during examination of a witness, but it turned out that they did not refer to many of them. Those documents that were referred to were scattered throughout the numerous binders."

It is apparent from the comments of the judge that she either did not consider or did not give any weight to documents that were not used during the hearings. Is this an error of law that would implicate due process? A hypothetical question might arise in such a case as to whether or not the judge was entitled to find as a fact, for example, that there was no evidence of tax consequences to one of the parties when there was extensive reference to the nature and amount of tax consequences in unused documents.

The unused documents issue was considered by the College of Commercial Arbitrators in the *Guide to Best Practices in Commercial Arbitration*, 3rd ed. (2014), a consensus of the views of many arbitrators, at p. 184:

> "More specifically, an early discussion with the parties regarding what will be done with marked but unmentioned exhibits can best insure (1) that the parties are provided an opportunity to resolve the question by agreement; (2) that none of the parties are later surprised by the fact that such exhibits have been excluded from, or included in, the record; (3) that when such exhibits are not to be included in the record, the parties are able to conform their presentations in a manner that guarantees their ability to introduce all material evidence through a live witness, or if permitted, by mention in prehearing briefing or oral argument; and (4) that disputes do not arise regarding whether the parties were unfairly deprived of an opportunity to be heard with respect to exhibits that were marked by their opponent and included in the record even though not mentioned in the hearing."

V.   DOCUMENTS AGREEMENT

The time and cost to prove a document may be minimized by the parties agreeing in advance to a Documents Agreement that confirms the authenticity of documents unless specifically challenged. A typical Documents Agreement will specify that copies may be tendered (with originals available on request) and that the documents were sent and received where indicated and record accurately the information contained therein. Either party is able to challenge any particular document or class of documents that may then require more elaborate proof. With the benefit of a Documents Agreement the parties will be able to avoid unnecessary proofs and the tribunal may take some comfort in relying upon the authenticity of documents that have not been specifically challenged.

The parties might attempt to reach consensus on a Documents Agreement using the following model that could be circulated by the tribunal and amended as the parties see fit:

DOCUMENTS AGREEMENT

1. For the purpose of this arbitration, the parties agree as follows with respect to the documents tendered during the course of the proceedings:

> *a. Copies of documents may be tendered in evidence as representing true copies of the originals;*

b. The original of any copy, if in the possession or control of the party relying upon the document, will be produced for inspection upon request;

c. Unless challenged, it will be presumed that a document was prepared by or on behalf of the author on or about the date indicated on its face, and that the author had knowledge of its contents at the time. If the document indicates that it was delivered to another person, it will be presumed that it was sent to and received by the intended recipient in the ordinary course on or about the date shown;

d. Purported signatures appearing on a document are authentic;

e. If any party wishes to challenge a document for any reason then at least 30 days before hearings begin notice must be given of the reason for challenge so that more formal proof of the document may be made.

2. Nothing in this Agreement shall limit the right of either party to:

a. Lead evidence or prove documents in any manner that might otherwise be permitted if this Agreement had not been made including reliance upon civil rules or legislation in the arbitral forum for the proof of business records;

b. Lead evidence to contradict any document;

c. Object to the admissibility of any document on grounds of privilege or any other ground not in conflict with this Agreement;

d. Argue the weight or relevance that should be attributed to any document;

e. Challenge any document on the basis that it is fraudulent or does not accord with one or more of the matters identified in paragraph 1 of this Agreement;

f. Challenge the truth or authenticity of any document in the course of hearings or the authority of the tribunal to hear such challenge in the absence of advance notice of challenge where the tribunal is satisfied that there is a reasonable explanation for no challenge notice having been given. In that event the party tendering the challenged document will be given a reasonable opportunity to make a more formal proof of the document.

3. This Agreement does not constitute an admission by either party as to the truth of the contents of any document.

4. Nothing in this Agreement will prevent a party from seeking further directions from the tribunal to resolve questions related to proof of documents.

VI.   CONFIDENTIALITY AGREEMENT

There will invariably be concerns regarding the confidentiality of documents disclosed on discovery requests or listed as Reliance Documents. The laws on confidentiality vary from jurisdiction to jurisdiction. The LCIA Rules provide in Art. 30 that the parties, as a general principle, undertake to keep all matters relating to the proceedings confidential. There is an exception for disclosures that are necessary to protect a legal duty or to protect or pursue a legal right. The English Arbitration Act 1996, unlike the arbitration statutes of some countries, does not address confidentiality, so the parties to arbitrations seated in England would be governed by the LCIA rules (or other Rules that may be chosen) and common law principles regarding any duty of confidentiality. Because there are different approaches internationally, the parties should be encouraged to make a Confidentiality Agreement, especially so as to avoid the tribunal having to make specific confidentiality directions in respect of individual documents. The confidentiality conundrum is much discussed in the literature. It is not necessary to re-invent the wheel. The tribunal could offer the parties a precedent. A good precedent is contained in the Debevoise and Plimpton publication "Annotated Model Arbitration Clause for International Contracts", 2011. The Debevoise and Plimpton clause reads as follows:

> "The parties, any arbitrator, and their agents or representatives, shall keep confidential and not disclose to any non-party the existence of the arbitration, non-public materials and information provided in the arbitration by another party, and orders or awards made in the arbitration (together, the "Confidential Information"). If a party or an arbitrator wishes to involve in the arbitration a non-party – including a fact or expert witness, stenographer, translator or any other person – the party or arbitrator shall make reasonable efforts to secure the non-party's advance agreement to preserve the confidentiality of the Confidential Information. Notwithstanding the foregoing, a party may disclose Confidential Information to the extent necessary to: (1) prosecute or defend the arbitration or proceedings related to it (including enforcement or annulment proceedings), or to pursue a legal right; (2) respond to a compulsory order or request for information of a governmental or regulatory body; (3) make disclosure required by law or by the rules of a securities exchange; (4) seek legal, accounting or other professional services, or satisfy information requests of potential acquirers, investors or lenders, provided that in each case of any disclosure allowed under the foregoing circumstances (1) through (4), where possible, the producing party takes reasonable measures to ensure that the recipient preserves the confidentiality of the information provided. The arbitral tribunal may permit further disclosure of Confidential Information where there is a demonstrated need to disclose that outweighs any party's legitimate interest in preserving confidentiality. This confidentiality provision survives termination of the contract and of any arbitration brought pursuant to the contract. This confidentiality provision may be enforced by any arbitral tribunal or any court of competent jurisdiction, and an application to a court to enforce this provision shall not waive or in any way derogate from the agreement to arbitrate."[6]

The Debevoise and Plimpton model clause provides that disputes regarding confidentiality may be enforced by an arbitral tribunal or any court of competent jurisdiction, but this may leave questions as to the best or most appropriate forum. Would the existing arbitral tribunal have jurisdiction to resolve confidentiality complaints, including claims for damages for breach confidentiality in the existing arbitration? Until the existing tribunal is *functus* would disputes arising out of alleged

---

6. Debevoise and Plimpton "Annotated Model Arbitration Clause for International Contracts" (2011) p. 42.

breaches of confidentiality in the existing arbitration be subject to the original arbitration agreement, or would the matter need to go to a court in the arbitral forum? This cause for uncertainty is well described by Simon Crookenden in "Who Should Decide Arbitration Confidentiality Issues?" As he notes at p. 606:

> "In the past, such issues have generally been determined by the court but the view has been expressed in the English Court of Appeal that, at least as long as there is an existing tribunal in a pending arbitration, issues of confidentiality should be determined by the tribunal in the reference in which the documents in issue have been produced or generated."[7]

The Debevoise and Plimpton Model Confidentiality Agreement might be amended to specify which tribunal or court will have jurisdiction to decide confidentiality issues that arise up to the point that the existing tribunal becomes *functus*, and which tribunal or court is agreed for disputes regarding confidentiality that arise thereafter. The Debevoise and Plimpton model agreement might also be amended to address requirements for destruction of documents produced in the arbitration once the proceeding or any appeal or review process is concluded.

VII. WHAT CAN THE TRIBUNAL DO TO LIMIT DOCUMENTS?

As already noted, the tribunal cannot restrict a party from reliance upon any document that might assist its case. But there are techniques to limit the volume of the document record and minimize the amount of reading for the tribunal. One way to limit the size of the core bundle or Common Book is to include only relevant excerpts of long contracts or accounting records. The full document can be made available electronically or otherwise if context is needed but for the most part only the relevant clause need be read in advance of the hearing, will be commented upon by a witness or in argument or need be referenced when writing the final award. It would be of immense value to the tribunal if counsel were to use a core bundle or Common Book that can be referenced in written or oral submissions that would allow the arbitrators to move quickly to the necessary and relevant excerpts and thus allow greater continuity when reading briefs. Much time will be saved.

Another device that may assist in document-heavy cases is the use of a secretary to the tribunal. The extra cost is immediately ameliorated by the time saved by a three member tribunal attempting to coordinate or organize massive volumes. Even with a sole arbitrator, who may not be very expert in managing the flow of electronic filings, there can be significant costs savings by the arbitrator employing a skilled assistant.

Should the tribunal discuss with the parties a need for proportionality in the number of documents to be tendered? For a case in which the amount in issue is not large should there be an admonition to the parties that excessive document production disproportionate to the amount in controversy might attract cost consequences?

---

7. 25 Arbitration International (2009, no. 4) p. 603.

The tribunal has few tools beyond moral suasion to keep the document binders down to a manageable size. The only coercive tool available is to sanction a party in costs where there are excessive unused documents of marginal relevance, where there have been disorganized disclosures or there are examples of bad faith such as deliberate late production or the proverbial document dump to hide a few documents. It is only fair that the innocent party should not have to bear the costs of the other party's sins.

VIII.   COST SANCTIONS

No arbitrator likes to impose cost sanctions. It is a tool to be used sparingly. Nevertheless, and especially where there have been warnings in advance, cost sanctions can be a useful tool to ensure that a case proceeds in a less expensive, fairer and more efficient way. Mustill and Boyd, 2nd ed. (1989) at p. 327 suggest that an arbitrator "make clear his opposition to the deployment of large quantities of waste paper" and in respect of costs sanctions write:

> "In particularly bad cases, the arbitrator would be justified in penalizing in costs a party whose lawyers have copied, not those documents which have in the event not proved to be useful (for this is hard to predict) but those which on any possible turn of events could not have been relevant."

Most institutional Rules of Procedure will confer a general discretion and authority upon the tribunal to impose costs sanctions for wasteful conduct. In addition to the broad discretion given arbitrators under such Rules as Art. 31 of the ICDR Rules which allow an arbitrator to apportion costs, specific Rules may give a more direct authority to impose sanctions. Art. 31(5) of the ICDR Arbitration Rules, for example, provides that:

> "(5) Unless the parties agree otherwise, the parties expressly waive and forego any right to punitive, exemplary or similar damages unless a statute requires that compensatory damages be increased in a specified manner. *This provision shall not apply to any award of arbitration costs to a party to compensate for dilatory or bad faith conduct in the arbitration.*" (Emphasis added)

IX.   MODEL DOCUMENTS DIRECTION

A model direction for the management of documents might be circulated by the arbitral tribunal at, or even before, the first preliminary meeting. The arbitration belongs to the parties who may design the process in any fashion they choose. Some counsel are not familiar with international best practices. By circulating a proposed direction for documents in advance of the preliminary hearing, the parties may consider whether or not to agree to some or all of the proposed directions. Not every issue may be appropriate for the initial direction. Procedures for dealing with discovery requests, the use of a Redfern Schedule and any requirement for listing discovery documents over which the parties intend to claim privilege might be better dealt with in a subsequent direction.

The following is a suggested Documents Direction to cover the basics:

MODEL DOCUMENTS DIRECTION

Pleadings including Statements of Claim, Defence, Counterclaim and Reply shall be accompanied by Reliance Documents. Reliance Documents are those documents upon which a party will rely in making its case or defence. Reliance Documents must be listed in an organized fashion, whether chronologically or otherwise, that allows the other party and the tribunal to easily identify documents and connect the documents to the relevant issues. The manner of organization is left to counsel but Reliance Documents should be indexed in a coherent fashion. The tribunal shall be provided with an electronic copy of the List of Reliance Documents and the documents themselves but need not be provided with hard copies until a Common Book of Documents as described below is agreed. Hard copies of critical documents or excerpts may be filed with pleadings at the discretion of counsel.

Reliance Documents should include only those documents that are necessary to a claim or defence. Counsel are encouraged to be vigilant to ensure that documents listed as Reliance Documents are not excessive and do not include documents of marginal relevance. Wherever possible excerpts of documents should be used with the full document made available upon request.

Documents in languages other than English shall be accompanied by translations.

The parties will attempt to reach an agreement on documents using as a guide the Model Documents Agreement attached to these directions.

The parties will attempt to reach an agreement in respect of confidentiality of documents tendered in the proceeding using as a guide the Model Confidentiality Agreement attached to these directions.

Parties will be permitted to supplement their list of Reliance Documents with documents that were not reasonably foreseen as relevant but are deemed necessary at later stages of the arbitration where new issues are raised in witness statements, expert reports or pre-hearing submissions. Documents may not be used at the evidentiary hearings that were not listed and produced earlier except for impeachment purposes on cross-examination. New documents will not be admissible at the evidentiary hearings except in the most extraordinary of circumstances. Impeachment documents not previously listed must be relevant only to credibility and not consist of documents that should obviously have been listed as Reliance Documents because, for example, they were essential to the natural unfolding of the narrative. Witness statements should not refer to documents that were not listed as Reliance Documents unless a reasonable justification is provided and in the event supplementary listing of new documents necessitates an adjournment to permit the other party an opportunity to respond then cost consequences may follow. A document should not be deliberately withheld where the relevance of the document was clear at an earlier time.

In addition to Lists of Reliance Documents the parties are directed to prepare a Common Book of Documents or core bundle for use at the hearing. The parties will agree that one of the parties will produce hard copies of the Common Book with one copy to be marked as the formal exhibit, one copy for each member of the tribunal, one copy for the other party and one copy for the witness. The costs of preparing the hard copies will be initially shared subject to the final award as to costs. The common book of documents will contain all of the documents or excerpts that each party expects will be referenced in the course of the hearing and that should be reviewed by the arbitral tribunal in advance. The Common Book of Documents should be delivered in hard copy and electronic form to the tribunal 14 days in advance of the first day of hearings. The parties should advise the tribunal as to whether or not the tribunal need not review the documents in the Common Book in advance of the evidentiary hearings. There is no objection to a party using a document at the hearing that is not contained in the Common Book so long as the document was listed as a Reliance Document. Unused documents in the Common Book that are not referenced by a witness or by counsel in argument need not be considered by the tribunal in making the award. Excessive use of unnecessary or marginally relevant documents by a party may attract cost consequences.

Copies of Reliance Documents may be delivered to the other party in electronic form. Originals of documents, where available, must be produced for inspection upon request.

The tribunal may consider costs consequences where it is determined that documents have been delivered or indexed in a manner that is not coherent and does not admit of reasonable review for relevance.

X.   CONCLUSION

It will always be difficult at the preliminary hearing to anticipate every problem that might arise in respect of Reliance Documents. Some cases will have relatively few documents while others will be document heavy. Usually though, there will be a sufficient number of documents to warrant a robust direction by the tribunal so that the parties will have a clear understanding of what is expected.

Most arbitrators will prepare an agenda for the preliminary meeting but do not always circulate a draft Documents Direction in advance of the first meeting. We do not have to re-invent the wheel every time. There is much to recommend a modest yet robust early approach to management of Reliance Documents relying upon a Model Documents Agreement, a Confidentiality Agreement and a Documents Direction. A Common Book of Documents or Core Bundle can be a godsend. The parties will know what is expected, the arbitrators can limit unnecessary reading of documents and the parties will have confidence that they will not be caught by surprise. The haphazard tendering of documents and piecemeal treatment of basic Reliance Document issues as they arise can only extend the time for completion and increase the cost of arbitration.

We have all had the experience of coping with disorganized and late filing of documents. It makes the arbitrator's task that much more difficult. Time and money can be saved by anticipating problems. To quote Benjamin Franklin: "An ounce of prevention is worth a pound of cure." Or in a more modern context: "A good preliminary direction on documents can save a lot of Benjamins."

Document Production in International Arbitration: Communicating Between Ships in the Night

Stephen L. Drymer* and Valérie Gobeil**

TABLE OF CONTENTS	Page

I. INTRODUCTION

International arbitration by its very nature throws together individuals and entities from different jurisdictions. It also involves interaction among multiple jurisdictions and legal systems. This translates into a complex web of interrelationships among disparate laws, procedures, politics and legal cultures.[1]

Acting in good faith, parties and their counsel appearing before international tribunals often replicate practices which, though standard and perhaps even mandatory in their respective state courts or before domestic arbitration tribunals, are irreconcilable in international arbitral proceedings. Document production is a case in point.

In a domestic legal context, document production is an inexact science at best. This is so even though all concerned share a common understanding of the practice and technical rules by which it is governed. The problem is particularly acute in international arbitration, in which it is not typically the case that the parties and their counsel, let alone the arbitrators, all have the same – or similar; or perhaps any – experience in the area. One party's understanding of the obligation to produce documents may mean, for

---

* Partner, Head of International Arbitration and ADR, Woods LLP.

** Associate, Woods LLP

1. Catherine A. ROGERS, "When Bad Guys Are Wearing White Hats", 1 Stanford Journal of Complex Litigation (Spring 2013, no. 2) p. 487 at p. 489. Professor Rogers's article concerns international or transnational (she explains that she uses the terms interchangeably) litigation, in particular international class litigation and what she refers to as the asymmetrical ethical risks in such a practice. However, her comments in this respect are applicable equally to international *arbitration*. Professor Rogers goes on to observe, in terms that are also clearly applicable to the practice of international arbitration, that "[e]ffective representation of clients in transnational litigation therefore requires not only a passport and plane ticket", but a familiarity with various "procedure, institutions and jurisprudential values" (*Id.*). She further notes that "[t]he necessary skills and knowledge for this type of practice were not historically taught in law schools, and are not easy to acquire except through direct experience" (*Id.*).

another party's lawyers, a violation of their professional obligations. In both a literal and a figurative sense, parties and others may simply not speak the same language.

Under most major international arbitration rules parties are required to produce, at an early stage of the proceedings, the documents on which they rely to prove the facts alleged in support of their claims and defenses.[2] As has been observed: "Thus far, the document production story is uncontroversial."[3] The plot thickens, however.

What of documents that a party possesses, on which it does *not* wish to rely yet which may be relevant to one or other of the issues pleaded by another party? Are such documents to be produced as well; and if so, by what process and according to what standard? The problem is unique to international arbitration.

> "In litigation in national courts the applicable civil procedure rules apply and should offer clear solutions to questions relating to production of documents that a party is reluctant to disclose. In domestic (national) arbitrations the document production procedure is usually also clear, either under applicable rules or by custom and practice operated by the local arbitrators and bar. However, international arbitration exists under an entirely different procedural regime...."[4]

There's the rub.

Although foreign to many national legal systems, some form of expanded document production, including document "discovery", has over recent decades become the norm in international arbitration as one element of the taking, or gathering, of evidence. By document discovery we mean, broadly, a defined procedure whereby a party is permitted to request the production of documents in the possession of another party; and the requested party is required to produce the documents requested. Whether or not this development is to be applauded remains a subject of debate whenever arbitration specialists gather in conference or symposium. It is, however, a fact. And this fact gives rise to a number of challenges, certain of which are reflected in the issues to be explored in this session of the 2014 ICCA Congress: Do there exist "consistent standards applicable to the preservation and production of documents"? Can a requesting party ever know if "all relevant sources of documents are in fact searched and produced by an opposing party"? Is "arbitrator discretion preferable to consistent treatment"?

For many, these may seem basic questions that concern equality and fairness. For others, such questions only highlight the vast and fundamental differences in

---

2. See, for example, the Arbitration Rules of institutions such as the International Chamber of Commerce (ICC), the London Court of International Arbitration (LCIA), the International Centre for Dispute Resolution (ICDR), as well as the UNCITRAL Arbitration Rules (as revised in 2010). The International Bar Association's IBA Rules on the Taking of Evidence in International Arbitration (IBA Rules of Evidence or IBA Rules) provide at Art. 3 that "each Party shall submit to the Arbitral Tribunal and to the other Parties all Documents available to it on which it relies" within the time period ordered by the tribunal.
3. Nigel BLACKABY, Constantine PARTASIDES, Alan REDFERN, Martin HUNTER, eds., *Redfern and Hunter on International Arbitration*, 5th ed. (Oxford University Press 2009) para. 6.103 (henceforth REDFERN and HUNTER).
4. *Ibid*, paras 6.104 et seq.

understanding that exist with respect to the nature and aims of arbitration (or litigation and dispute resolution more generally). Whatever one's take on the subject, such questions suggest a very practical problem: *How to deal with the variability – of understanding, attitudes and practice – that exists with respect to document production?*

This modest paper seeks to address this problem by exploring measures that may be adopted to ward off potential collisions. We refer to these as "*ex ante*" mechanisms. Such mechanisms can be contrasted with "*ex post*" measures, which seek to address actual problems that have arisen as a result of document production gone awry. Sect. II provides a brief overview of the common law / civil law divide with respect to document production, and the reasons why problems can arise when these systems meet and occasionally collide. Sect. III offers a high-level survey of some of the efforts by the international arbitration community to articulate rules that bridge this divide. Various attempts to define the obligations of counsel in international arbitration are considered in Sect. IV. We conclude, in Sect. V, by cherry-picking from among a number of ideas to suggest a way forward as regards document production in international arbitration. Nothing revolutionary, but a common-sense approach to the challenge of managing divergent understandings and expectations; a sort of semaphore for communicating across vast distances or choppy seas on a subject in respect of which the players either do not speak the same language or are too far apart to hear each other.[5]

II.   DOCUMENT PRODUCTION UNDER DIFFERENT LEGAL TRADITIONS

It is generally understood that in most common law jurisdictions, "the initiative for the collection and presentation of evidence is almost wholly in the hands of the parties.... By contrast, in the courts of most civil law countries the judge takes a far more active role in the conduct of the proceedings and in the collection of evidence."[6] This contrast stems from divergent perceptions of the nature and objective of the adjudicative process and of the role of evidence and fact-finding in that process.

In the civil law tradition, the essential purpose of evidence is to allow a court to be informed of facts necessary for it to articulate and ultimately determine the legal issues required to resolve the dispute.[7] In a certain sense, by accepting that not every fact need be revealed, disputing parties in civil law systems are content that disputes be decided on the basis of what has been called "relative truth".[8]

---

5. In addition to its meaning and usage in computer science, *semaphore* is "a method of visual signaling, usually with flags or lights". Before radio, semaphore was widely used to send messages between ships. A person would stand with arms extended, moving two flags to specific angles to indicate letters or numbers. Before the invention of the telegraph, semaphore signaling with lights on high towers was used to transmit messages between distant points; messages were read by telescope. <www.merriam-webster.com/dictionary/semaphore> (last accessed 6 March 2014).

6. REDFERN and HUNTER, *op. cit.*, fn. 3., paras. 6.84-6.85.

7. Yves DERAINS, "*La pratique de l'administration de la preuve dans l'arbitrage commercial international*", Rev. Arb. (2004, no. 4) p. 786.

8. Pierre TERCIER and Tetiana BERSHEDA, "Document Production in Arbitration: A Civil Law Viewpoint" in *The Search for "Truth" in Arbitration* – ASA Special Series No. 35, p. 83.

In the common law tradition, evidence is viewed as necessary to allow the parties to take cognizance of all of the facts so as to allow them to frame the legal issues that the judge will determine.[9] Unlike her civil law cousin, the common law judge is traditionally more of a referee in a process led by the parties; she administers rules of evidence and procedure as the parties duke it out, and at the end decides the outcome on the basis of the case presented by each party.

Of course, these are gross generalizations. The truth is more nuanced and complex. Each system has many variations. Rules of procedure and evidence differ significantly between civil law jurisdictions, just as they do between common law jurisdictions. However, for purposes of this paper such descriptions, while simplistic, are useful as a means to highlight the challenges associated with addressing document production in an international arbitral setting.

Under the civil law approach, it is understood that the principle "*onus probandi incumbat alleganti*" excludes or at least vastly restrains the opportunity to obtain evidence in support of one's own allegations from the other side.[10] "Discovery" procedures are viewed with apprehension. By opposition, in common law jurisdictions and in the United States in particular, the discovery process is considered to play a "vital role"[11] in the preparation for trial and is habitually used by parties to obtain evidence that would not otherwise be available to them. Indeed, parties will initiate cases with the intention of refining their allegations and claims once documents have been obtained from the other party.

To borrow an analogy, the civil law lawyer plays the cards that he or she has in hand as well as those that the other party has discarded; the common law lawyer will also ask to pick from among the cards in the other party's hand before playing.[12] Consistent with the idea of "relative truth", civil law lawyers are relatively unconcerned about the possibility that a card held by another party may never be revealed or played, even if that card might prove helpful to one's own case. The idea that a critically important piece of evidence – the fabled "smoking gun", for example – may exist and may be deliberately withheld by the opposing party, resonates far less than in the common law tradition. For a common law lawyer, the possibility that a party may possess evidence and be under no obligation to disclose it – the possibility that there may exist no means even for the parties to discover the evidence in each other's possession – is antithetical to the nature of the litigation process.

Despite such differences, commonalities between legal traditions must be acknowledged. Across different jurisdictions the concept of "due process", which includes procedural fairness, is recognized in legislation pertaining not only to litigation before national courts but also to arbitration. This may be the result of the harmonization

---

9. DERAINS, *op. cit.*, fn. 7, p. 786.
10. Claude REYMOND, "Civil Law and Common Law Procedures: Which Is the More Inquisitorial? A Civil Lawyer's Response", 5 Arbitration International (Kluwer Law International 1989, Issue 4) p. 360.
11. *Hickman v. Taylor*, 329 U.S. 495 (1947).
12. TERCIER and BERSHEDA, *op. cit.*, fn. 8, p. 81.

of arbitration laws around the world.[13] However, even in the case of such widely accepted and apparently uncontroversial principles as fairness, the particular elements of the principle remain influenced by the local legal culture. The risk of clashes across cultures, and their consequences, has fueled various attempts at developing uniform procedural rules.

III.   BRIDGING THE DIVIDE: THE IBA RULES OF EVIDENCE

As much as party autonomy and procedural flexibility are essential features of international arbitration, certainty and predictability also have value. Arguably the most successful initiative to bring a degree of certainty to document production in international arbitration is the International Bar Association's IBA Rules on the Taking of Evidence in International Arbitration.[14]

Designed to provide an efficient, economical and fair process for the taking of evidence in international arbitration, "particularly those between Parties from different legal traditions",[15] the IBA Rules of Evidence are intended to supplement the legal provisions and the institutional, ad hoc or other rules that apply to the conduct of proceedings.[16] Overall, the IBA Rules purport to provide guidance to parties on how to deal with evidentiary issues in international arbitration proceedings without sacrificing core values such as party autonomy, equality and procedural flexibility.[17]

To some observers, the IBA Rules reflect a successful and practicable compromise between differing cultural and legal traditions.[18] To others, they are insufficient in bridging the civil law-common law divide or in providing for the essential aspects of

---

13. Gabrielle KAUFMANN-KOHLER, "Globalization of Arbitral Procedure", Vand. J. Transnat'l L. (2003) pp. 1320-1321.

14. Adopted by resolution of the IBA Council, 29 May 2010, available at <www.ibanet.org/Publications/publications_IBA_guides_and_free_materials.aspx> (last accessed 23 March 2014) (henceforth IBA Rules of Evidence or IBA Rules). As early as 1983, the IBA adopted the IBA Supplementary Rules Governing the Presentation and Reception of Evidence in International Commercial Arbitration. These Rules were replaced in 1999 by the IBA Rules on the Taking of Evidence in International Commercial Arbitration. The current (2010) IBA Rules of Evidence in turn revise, update and replace those earlier Rules.

15. *Ibid.*, Preamble, para. 1.

16. *Ibid.*

17. 1999 IBA Working Party and 2010 IBA Rules of Evidence Review Subcommittee, Commentary on the revised text of the 2010 IBA Rules on the Taking of Evidence in International Arbitration (2010), pp. 1-2 available at <www.ibanet.org/Publications/publications_IBA_guides_and_free_materials.aspx> (last accessed 16 February 2014) (henceforth Commentary on the revised text of the 2010 IBA Rules).

18. KAUFMANN-KOHLER, *op. cit.*, fn. 13, pp. 1324-1325, William W. PARK, "The 2002 Freshfields Lecture – Arbitration's Protean Nature: The Value of Rules and the Risks of Discretion", 19 Arbitration International (Kluwer Law International 2003, Issue 3) p. 290.

evidence-taking in international arbitration.[19] Say what one will, perhaps no other element of the IBA Rules has gained as "wide acceptance within the international arbitral community"[20] as their procedure for document production, the guts of which are contained in Art. 3 (Documents).

It is not the purpose of this paper to describe or analyze in any detail the components of the document production procedure set out in the IBA Rules. It suffices to note that the provisions of Art. 3 of those Rules reflect an important degree of international consensus on the subject and appear to be widely used by parties and tribunals, at least as guidelines to if not as binding rules. They provide modalities for a document production process that, as with all elements of the IBA Rules, deliberately reflect an amalgam of "procedures in use in many different legal systems" that may be used in establishing rules appropriate to the conduct of the particular arbitration in which parties and arbitrators find themselves.[21] The instrumental nature of the IBA Rules – the fact that they are intended to be understood and applied in the particular context of particular cases – is made clear in Art. 1(4): where arbitrators are required to interpret the IBA Rules, they shall do so "in the manner most appropriate for the particular arbitration".

In addition to setting out detailed procedural rules, or guidelines, the IBA Rules of Evidence also highlight two important themes: the *shared responsibility* of parties and arbitrators for the elaboration and conduct of the document production process; and the *intersection between procedural and ethical norms* in the taking of evidence in general and document production specifically.

The IBA Rules provide that the "arbitral tribunal shall consult the Parties at the earliest appropriate time in the proceedings and invite them to consult with each other with a view to agreeing on an efficient, economical and fair process of the taking of evidence".[22] Arbitrators and parties are encouraged to include in this consultation "the requirements, procedure and format applicable to the production of documents". The IBA Rules thus provide a framework for a discussion between and among the arbitrators and the parties on the nature and modalities of the document production process, and their respective roles and obligations in that process. They indicate that such a discussion should occur early on (*ex ante*), before difficulties arise. And they suggest – significantly in our view – that elaborating rules that are understood by and acceptable to all, and ensuring compliance with what will necessarily be a compromise as between disparate national practices, is a responsibility that is shared among parties and arbitrators.[23]

---

19. Detlev KUHNER, "The Revised IBA Rules on the Taking of Evidence in International Arbitration", 27 Journal of International Arbitration (Kluwer Law International 2010, Issue 6) p. 667.
20. IBA Rules of Evidence, *op. cit.*, fn. 14, Foreword.
21. *Ibid.* See also: Preamble, para. 2.
22. *Ibid.*, Art. 2(1).
23. The IBA Rules are not alone in encouraging early and active case management in international arbitration. For example, the 2012 Rules of Arbitration of the International Chamber of Commerce (ICC Rules) require the arbitral tribunal to convene a case management conference to consult the parties on procedural measures for the conduct of the arbitration (Art. 24(1)). Similarly, Art. 14 of the draft 2014 LCIA Arbitration Rules encourages the parties and tribunal to contact each other soon after the tribunal is formed, to discuss the conduct of the proceedings.

Among the new aspects of the most recent (2010) version of the IBA Rules are the repeated references to fairness,[24] and the principle that parties "shall act in good faith"[25] in all matters related to the taking of evidence – including document production. The IBA Rules go further still. They empower arbitrators to take appropriate measures where they determine that a party "has failed to conduct itself in good faith in the taking of evidence".[26] It has been said that this provision illustrates the trend in international arbitration to scrutinize parties' conduct more closely.[27] Yet the provision has also been criticized. According to Martinez-Fraga, for example, it diminishes party autonomy by allowing the arbitral tribunal to evaluate and sanction parties' conduct on largely discretionary grounds.

The introduction of good faith as an integral component of purely procedural rules – especially rules intended to bridge the divide between the common law and civil law traditions – is noteworthy, though not surprising. The process of gathering and presenting evidence in fact depends to a large degree on the parties' lawyers' perception of their professional ethical obligations. This is implicit in the IBA Rules, which acknowledge the importance of the legal or ethical rules to which parties and their counsel may be subject, and the balancing required in order for arbitrators to maintain fairness and equality, in particular as between parties "subject to different legal or ethical rules".[28]

Procedure and ethics are intertwined. The prevalence given to bona fides in the IBA Rules, in addition to the explicit nods to mandatory ethical rules, illustrates an acknowledgment that the taking of evidence is informed among other things by ethical norms.

IV.   ETHICS IN EVIDENCE

Rules of evidence do not exist in a vacuum. They are developed and designed to apply in particular contexts, and they are invariably closely tied to other procedural or substantive rules that apply in those contexts. At the outset of this paper we commented that document production – we may just as well speak of the application of rules of evidence generally – is an inexact science rendered even more nebulous in an international setting. We have also stated that the process of the taking of evidence is informed by ethical norms. The fact is that in international arbitration the elaboration and application of rules of evidence must necessarily be coupled with (at the very least) an appreciation of applicable ethical rules since in many cases those rules, issued by

---

The 2014 LCIA Rules are discussed further below.

24. IBA Rules of Evidence, *op. cit.*, fn. 14, Preamble, para. 1. The Review subcommittee revised this part of the Rules specifically so that the principle of fairness would be included. Fairness is emphasized repeatedly in the IBA Rules: see for example, Arts. 2(1), 9(3).

25. *Ibid.*, Preamble, para. 3.

26. *Ibid.*, Art. 9(7).

27. KUHNER, *op. cit.* fn. 19, p. 670.

28. IBA Rules of Evidence, *op. cit.*, fn. 14, Art. 9(3)(e).

national legislatures, law societies or bar councils, bind the lawyers from various jurisdictions who appear before international tribunals.

The rules of document production, as with any element of the taking of evidence, diverge as between legal traditions and jurisdictions as a result of any number of factors – historical, cultural, juridical. One of those factors is the divergence in ethical standards and obligations. Add to this observation the fact that the withholding of evidence is qualified by some authors as an "ethically borderline guerilla tactic"[29] and that international arbitration itself has been famously likened to an "ethical no-man's land"[30] and it seems sensible at least to attempt to confront the issue of document production in international arbitration from the perspective of legal ethics.

1.   Attempts to Address the Conduct of Lawyers in International Practice

As long ago as 1956, the IBA adopted an International Code of Conduct. The document purported to apply to lawyers practicing their profession generally, and did not address either international arbitration or the taking of evidence with any specificity. Last revised in 1988, the document, which has been described as more "an aspirational statement of professional culture"[31] than a set of rules of conduct, could fairly be said to have languished.

In 1988 the Council of Bars and Law Societies of Europe (CCBE) first adopted its Code of Conduct for European Lawyers (CCBE Code). The CCBE Code has since been amended three times, most recently in 2006. It is a binding text on all Member States of the European Union: all lawyers who are members of the bars of these countries are meant to comply with the CCBE Code in their cross-border activities[32] within the

---

29. Gunther J. HORVATH, "Guerrilla Tactics in Arbitration, an Ethical Battle: Is there Need for a Universal Code of Ethics?" in Christian KLAUSEGGER, Peter KLEIN, et al., eds., *Austrian Yearbook on International Arbitration 2011*, pp. 297-313.

30. Catherine A. ROGERS, "Fit and Function in Legal Ethics: Developing a Code of Conduct for International Arbitration", 23 Mich. J. Int'l L. (2002) p. 341, p. 342 (henceforth ROGERS, "Fit and Function in Legal Ethics"). Professor Rogers's seminal article is lacking in neither foresight nor entertaining prose. In her frequently cited description of the problem, she writes:

"International arbitration dwells in an ethical no-man's land. Often by design, arbitration is set in a jurisdiction where neither party's counsel is licensed. The extraterritorial effect of national ethical codes is usually murky.... There is no supra-national authority to oversee attorney conduct in this setting, and local bar associations rarely if ever extend their reach so far ... specialized ethical norms for attorneys in international arbitration are nowhere recorded. Where ethical regulations should be, there is only an abyss."

See also Catherine A. ROGERS, "Context and Institutional Structure in Attorney Regulation: Constructing an Enforcement Regime for International Arbitration", 39 Stan J. Int'l L. (2003) p. 1 (henceforth ROGERS, "Context and Institutional Structure in Attorney Regulation").

31. ROGERS, "Fit and Function in Legal Ethics", *op. cit.*, fn. 30, p. 396.

32. "Cross-border activities" are defined as: "(a) all professional contacts with lawyers of Member States other than the lawyer's own; (b) the professional activities of the lawyer in a Member State other than his or her own, whether or not the lawyer is physically present in that Member State".

European Union, the European Economic Area and Switzerland as well as within EU associate and observer countries (broadly, Europe).

The CCBE Code provides that its "rules governing a lawyer's relations with the courts apply also to the lawyer's relations with arbitrators",[33] which opens the door to their application at least to European lawyers engaged in international arbitrations with other European lawyers or in European countries other than their own. However, other than a few statements of general principle to the effect that a lawyer must have due regard for the fair conduct of proceedings,[34] maintain due respect and courtesy toward the court or tribunal[35] and never knowingly give false or misleading information to a court or tribunal,[36] there is little in the CCBE Code of special relevance to evidentiary matters and nothing that concerns document production specifically. Moreover, although such provisions could have an incidence on the production of documents, their generality calls into question the extent to which they could actually have any practical normative force or effect.

As applied to international arbitration, it might be said that the CCBE Code also begs the very question that it seeks to address. It provides that a lawyer who takes part in a case before a court or tribunal must comply with the rules of conduct applied before that court or tribunal.[37] But in international arbitration, what rules of conduct apply? It is not clear whether or what combination of the rules of conduct of each party's or lawyer's home jurisdiction, the seat of arbitration or the place where the hearing physically takes place might govern.[38] Further, rules developed for the domestic practice of law, including litigation before state courts, are not necessarily well suited to international arbitration. In the end, the question raised by the CCBE Code – *What are the rules that apply before an international arbitral tribunal?* – takes us back to square one. This is the same question that is asked with respect to rules of evidence, or indeed *any* rules applicable to the conduct of international arbitration where parties, counsel, arbitrators are used to diverse and potentially conflicting practices.

In May 2011, the International Bar Association adopted the IBA International Principles on the Conduct for the Legal Professions (International Principles).[39] Intended to "promote and foster the ideals of the legal profession", the International Principles consist of "ten principles common to the legal profession worldwide" – a sort of lawyer's

---

(CCBE Code, Art. 1(5)).

33. CCBE Code, Art. 4(5).

34. *Ibid.*, Art. 4(2).

35. *Ibid.*, Art. 4(3).

36. *Ibid.*, Art. 4(4).

37. *Ibid.*, Art. 4(1).

38. R. Doak BISHOP, "Advocacy and Ethics in International Arbitration: Ethics in International Arbitration" in Albert Jan VAN DEN BERG, ed., *Arbitration Advocacy in Changing Times*, ICCA Congress Series no. 15, 2010 Rio Volume (Kluwer Law International 2011) (henceforth *ICCA Congress Series no. 15*) p. 385.

39. IBA International Principles on Conduct for the Legal Professions available at <www.ibanet.org/Publications/publications_IBA_guides_and_free_materials.aspx> (last accessed 23 March 2014).

Ten Commandments.[40] They expressly do not cover in any detail many areas of lawyer conduct, for instance in relation to courts or other lawyers, nor are they meant to be used as criteria for imposing sanctions of any kind. As with the CCBE Code, there is little in the International Principles of concrete application to the mechanics of the evidentiary process. That is simply not their objective.

The limitations of these and other international or cross-border rules of conduct lie, among other things, in the imprecise boundaries and co-habitation between them and other, typically national, binding ethical norms. This uncertainty and potential discrepancy have the potential to cause inequality between the parties and breach of due process. Paulsson articulated the problem very presciently many years ago: "[I]n cases where counsel come from two different countries where standards are quite inconsistent on a given point, does the client whose lawyer is subject to the lowest standard have an unfair advantage?"[41]

In order for the solution to conflicting ethical obligations in international arbitration not to be merely a race to the bottom, many authors and practitioners have advocated the development of a sort of universal code of ethics for counsel.[42] Rogers argues for the necessity to develop such a code so as to ensure that parties adhere to the same rules and that the process is fair on procedural grounds.[43] Bishop explains that such a code would accomplish three major goals: "first ... clarify the applicable rules and reduce ambiguity; second, level the playing field so that conflicting obligations do not unduly benefit one party at the expense of the other; and third, provide greater transparency, thus building confidence in the system".[44]

Such goals are not achieved without challenge. On its own a universal code would not resolve the problem of diverse and potentially conflicting rules applicable to the same players, also referred to as "double deontology".[45] And apart altogether from the task of conceiving and drafting a code that might successfully capture and reconcile the differing obligations that apply to lawyers under the rules of different jurisdictions, the challenge of enforcement would remain.[46]

---

40. The International Principles are grouped under the following ten headings: Independence; Honesty, integrity and fairness; Conflicts of interest; Confidentiality/professional secrecy; Clients' interest; Lawyers' undertaking; Clients' freedom; Property of clients and third parties; Competence; Fees.

41. Jan PAULSSON, "Standards of Conduct for Counsel in International Arbitration", 3 Amer. Rev. Int. Arb. (1992) p. 214.

42. William J. ROWLEY, "Guerrilla Tactics and Developing Issues" in Günther J. HORVATH and Stephan WILSKE, eds., *Guerilla Tactics in International Arbitration*, International Arbitration Law Library, Volume 28 (Kluwer Law International 2013) pp. 29-30. See also: PAULSSON, *op. cit.*, fn. 41.

43. ROGERS, "Fit and Function in Legal Ethics", *op. cit.*, fn. 30.

44. BISHOP, *op. cit.*, fn. 38, p. 388.

45. See for example ROGERS, "Context and Institutional Structure in Attorney Regulation", *op. cit.*, fn. 30, pp. 345-346.

46. Many suggestions have been made as to who could be in charge of enforcing professional legal obligations such as local bar associations, the arbitral tribunal, arbitral institutions or even domestic courts. Many authors reject the idea of involving local courts for reasons of added delays and costs.

Our intent here is not to weigh into the ongoing debate regarding the wisdom, usefulness or means of crafting codes of conduct for counsel in international arbitration. Our point is simply to illustrate what we refer to above as the intersection of procedural and ethical norms and the similarity of certain of the questions that arise when one tries to regulate either ethics or procedure in a consistent fashion across the board in international arbitration.

2.   *Once More unto the Breach: The IBA Guidelines on Party Representation*

Any discussion of this "intersection" must include mention of the IBA Guidelines on Party Representation in International Arbitration.[47] Adopted in May 2013 after five years of effort and much passionate debate, the Guidelines take up many of the challenges identified above, including as regards enforcement – which the Guidelines address under the heading "Remedies for [counsel] misconduct".[48] In fact this is as close to an actual code of conduct for lawyers in international arbitration as exists. The Guidelines largely eschew invocation of broad principles and focus instead on concrete rules: specific DOs and DON'Ts for lawyers in many aspects of their work before international arbitral tribunals, from the moment they appear in the case through the process of taking of evidence. An entire section is devoted to document production.[49]

(See for example: BISHOP, *op. cit.*, fn. 38, p. 389; ROWLEY, *op. cit.*, fn. 42, p. 24). As for local bar associations, Rogers has suggested that they be informed by the arbitral tribunal if any misconduct is found and that they be in charge of applying appropriate sanctions. (ROGERS, "Context and Institutional Structure in Attorney Regulation", *op. cit.*, fn. 30, pp. 35-36. To overcome the question of confidentiality of the process, Rogers further suggests that sanction awards should be published as they do not deal with substantive issues related to the parties. This would also allow for the development and refinement of ethical norms.) However, it is uncertain whether they would truly be willing to take measures against counsel acting in a neutral venue and in the context of international arbitration (ROWLEY, *op. cit.*, fn. 42, p. 24). More basically, the confidentiality aspect of the arbitral process may be an obstacle to disclosure of misconduct to local bar associations or law societies. Bishop and Stevens privilege a system where arbitral institutions and tribunals would be in charge of enforcement (R. Doak BISHOP and Margrete STEVENS, "Advocacy and Ethics in International Arbitration: The Compelling Need for a Code of Ethics in International Arbitration: Transparency, Integrity and Legitimacy" in *ICCA Congress Series no. 15*, pp. 406-407). As far as institutions are concerned, they can offer their support by incorporating a code of conduct into their rules. Some authorities and practitioners consider that the arbitral tribunal is likely in the best position to deal with the enforcement of ethical behavior, notwithstanding that its powers are limited to those determined by the parties (See ROWLEY, *op. cit.*, fn. 42, pp. 26-27 discussing decisions by International Centre for Settlement of Investment Disputes (ICSID) tribunals on the subject of arbitrators' powers to address issues of counsel conduct).

47. IBA Guidelines on Party Representation in International Arbitration (2013), available at <www.ibanet.org/Publications/publications_IBA_guides_and_free_materials.aspx> (last accessed 23 March 2014) (IBA Guidelines or Guidelines).

48. *Ibid.*, Guidelines 26-27.

49. The Guidelines are comprised of seven substantive sections: Application; Party Representation; Communications with Arbitrators; Submissions to the Arbitral Tribunal; Information Exchange and Disclosure; Witnesses and Experts; Remedies for Misconduct. Document production is

Again, we do not intend to dissect the IBA Guidelines or to subject either their whole or their component parts to microscopic scrutiny. Rather, two points are noted. First, the international arbitration community has once again seen fit to take up the challenge of developing rules that attempt to bridge the divide between divergent yet overlapping legal traditions, cultures and practices. Second, it is noted that the Guidelines in question deliberately tackle the taking of evidence from the stance of legal professional ethics.

3.   *Where Angels Fear to Tread: The 2014 LCIA Rules*

The nexus between procedure and ethics in international arbitration is nowhere more evident than in the draft of the 2014 Arbitration Rules of the London Court of International Arbitration (LCIA Rules).[50]

Art. 18.5 of the draft requires each party to "ensure that all its legal representatives have agreed to comply with the general guidelines contained in the Annex to the LCIA Rules, as a condition of appearing by name before the Arbitral Tribunal". Art. 18.6 empowers the tribunal, in the event of a complaint by a party or upon the tribunal's own initiative, to determine whether a party's legal representative has "violated the general guidelines" and, if so, impose a range of sanctions against the offending person.[51]

The guidelines themselves, entitled "General Guidelines for the Parties' Legal Representatives" are contained in an annex. They consist of seven paragraphs, of which one (Paragraph 5) deals directly with a matter related to document production: "A legal representative should not knowingly conceal or assist in the concealment of any document (or any part thereof) which is ordered to be produced by the Arbitral Tribunal."

---

addressed in Guidelines 12-17. According to Honlet, Guidelines 12-17 are amongst the most controversial and are likely to be difficult to apply in practice: Jean-Christophe HONLET, "The IBA Guidelines on Party Representation in International Arbitration", 30 Journal of International Arbitration (Kluwer Law International 2013, Issue 6) pp. 702, 707.

50. LCIA Rules, 2014, revised draft dated 18 February 2014 (draft 2014 LCIA Rules), available at <www.lcia.org/Default.aspx> (last consulted 25 May 2014). According to the LCIA's website (as at 25 May 2014), this final draft was to be discussed by the LCIA Court at its meeting at Tylney Hall on Friday 9 May 2014, "with a view to the promulgation of the new rules shortly thereafter".

51. Art. 18.6 reads in full:

"In the event of a complaint to the Arbitral Tribunal by a party against another party's legal representative or by the Arbitral Tribunal upon its own initiative, the Arbitral Tribunal may decide (after consulting the parties and granting that legal representative a reasonable opportunity to answer the complaint) whether or not the legal representative has violated the general guidelines; and, if such violation is found by the Arbitral Tribunal, the Arbitral Tribunal may order any or all of the following sanctions against the legal representative: a written reprimand; a written caution as to future conduct in the arbitration; [a reference to the legal representative's regulatory and or professional body]; and any other measure necessary to maintain the general duties of the Arbitral Tribunal under Article 14.4(i) and (ii)."

V.   TOWARD A COMMON-SENSE APPROACH TO DOCUMENT PRODUCTION

The theme of this year's ICCA Congress is "Legitimacy: Myths, Realities, Challenges". The program posits that two of the pillars of arbitral legitimacy are *justice* ("arbitration must further justice, and be seen to be furthering justice in both procedure and outcome") and *precision* ("the process must have legal precision at every phase"). It is in the context of exploring precision in the arbitral process that the question of document production is posed.

We do not believe that there is or can be any such thing as precision in document production, if precision is understood as the assurance that the same circumstances will always give rise to the same outcome when considered by different tribunals. Nor do we believe that this can be remedied by aspiring to ultra-detailed, universally applicable rules.

Document production is indeed an inexact science. A requesting party can never be absolutely certain that all relevant sources of documents are in fact searched by the opposing party or that all relevant documents are produced. Even where all parties agree on the method and extent of the search required – elements of document production that are subject to a greater degree of precision than others – the meaning of "relevant" is elusive and difficult of precise application. No matter how consistent the treatment, no matter that the formula prescribed by the IBA Rules of Evidence is applied time and again, the determination of whether a particular document is "relevant to the case and material to its outcome" depends on an arbitrator's appreciation of the document and of the circumstances of the case, in addition to an interpretation of the rule itself. It depends, in other words, on the exercise of discretion. Here, as elsewhere, precision is relative. This is not so very different than in a domestic litigation context.

Fortunately, in our view, justice and precision are attainable in international arbitration – to the degree that they are attainable at all – by a variety of means. This is a good thing. A level playing field does not mean a single playing field. International arbitration allows for a multiplicity of fields of play, each suited to the particular players and the particular contest at issue in a given case. We see no reason why document production, a practice that varies widely between jurisdictions, cannot vary just as widely between international arbitral tribunals without compromising in any way the legitimacy of international arbitration. The goals underlying Bishop's and Stevens's call for universal standards in the realm of ethics[52] are certainly attainable as far as document production is concerned, without the need to insist on uniform practices. On the contrary, what is required is clarity and a level playing field, that is, fairness[53] in each case.

1.   Communication

Clarity and fairness are based on communication. Divergent expectations lead to discontent. Parties' and arbitrators' expectations with respect to document production

---

52. BISHOP and STEVENS, *op cit.*, fn. 46.
53. BISHOP, *op. cit.*, fn. 38, p. 388.

deserve to be thoroughly hashed out in the context of what we have referred to as early and active case management.

Where all involved are familiar and comfortable with tools such as the IBA Rules of Evidence, little more may need to be said beyond agreeing that those rules will apply in some manner to guide or determine the resolution of questions that arise. In other instances, particular concerns or approaches may need to be discussed. Is it anticipated that there may be a need for extensive document discovery? Is extensive electronic discovery anticipated? If so, what modalities may need to be agreed? Do all parties understand what is expected of them as far as preservation of documents is concerned? What about privilege or other legal impediment to the disclosure of certain documents? The point is that it should never merely be assumed that all concerned understand what is expected of themselves or others.

Parties should consider what they hope to achieve in the document production process and how they envisage the process unfolding – beyond merely providing for the opportunity to make or object to requests and to submit disputes to the tribunal – and they should make clear their wishes. It is, in the end, their process.

Arbitrators too should make known their wishes and expectations, and engage openly with the parties on the question. Few parties or counsel appreciate sphinx-like tribunals. Inscrutability as arbitrators hear evidence or submissions is one thing. It is another thing entirely, and inappropriate, when what is at issue is the development and adoption of rules for the conduct of the proceedings.

2. Preparation

If parties and arbitrators are to communicate their expectations, they must prepare. There may or may not be peculiarities associated with the case at hand that require particular treatment insofar as document production is concerned. However, that can only be determined if all concerned have a sense of the case and of the potential importance of the document production process.

There is obviously a limit to what can be foreseen in this regard, especially at the outset of an arbitration. Yet parties and their counsel especially should turn their minds to the sort of questions suggested above before the first procedural conference call or case management conference with the tribunal.

3. Check Please!

Benson has proposed the use of a checklist as a tool to address the type of issues described above: a sort of *à la carte* menu allowing parties to identify from among a suite of options the specific areas of conduct to be addressed in the rules adopted in their particular arbitration.[54] He argues that this is an alternative to the attempt to establish a uniform code of conduct, and in many ways more useful, since, even if certain duties may be fairly common across jurisdictions, the practical obligations that stem from them can be

---

54. Cyrus BENSON, "Can Professional Ethics Wait? The Need for Transparency in International Arbitration", 3 Dispute Resolution International (2009, no. 1) pp. 85-94.

contradictory. Although counsel may be required to act with an eye to fairness, for example, they may be prone to practices that are considered entirely fair in their home jurisdictions but which lead to unfairness in international proceedings where not everyone is used to the same standards.[55] Other authors have endorsed Benson's suggestion, emphasizing that a checklist approach has the potential, among other things, to "provide an early indication of potentially sharp conduct by revealing which guerrilla tactics both parties consider permissible...".[56]

There is no reason why a checklist cannot be adapted to deal specifically with the mechanics of document production. Nor can there be any doubt that one benefit of a checklist approach is to force parties to reflect on the options available to them and actively to consider, in discussion with the other parties and arbitrators, which measures they wish to adopt and which they do not. The result cannot but be a clear and fair bespoke procedure – no mere *formule* or *prix-fixe* menu – with the added benefit of being fully transparent. And of course, the parties are free to commit to whatever degree of procedural detail and precision they desire.

4. Shared Responsibility

Finally, as noted above, we consider it important that all concerned – beginning with the parties and the lawyers who advise them – accept that if the goal is to identify and avoid potential problems in the conduct of the arbitration, the responsibility lies with them, in conjunction with tribunals, to take the steps necessary to do so in each and every case. This includes the responsibility to devise and adopt rules for the conduct of document production that are understood and accepted by all.

VI. CONCLUSION

Confidence in international arbitration is built in large part on the perceived neutrality and fairness of its procedures. The best way to ensure that arbitral proceedings are governed by clear and fair rules is to identify and bridge conflicting expectations from an *ex ante* perspective.

As with other aspects of the rules governing the conduct of arbitral proceedings, the earliest possible determination of agreed document production procedures is called for – before recourse to *ex post* powers of control by the arbitrator or the courts[57] becomes necessary. Communication, preparation, an understanding of the alternatives available, an appreciation of the shared nature of the responsibility to develop coherent rules appropriate to the parties and case at hand – these are all keys to success.

---

55. *Ibid.*, pp. 83-84.
56. HORVATH, *op. cit.*, fn. 29, p. 305.
57. A certain number of jurisdictions recognize the possibility to resort to the court system for assistance in forcing production of documents, including the United States, England and Switzerland: see REDFERN and HUNTER, *op. cit.*, fn. 3, pp. 454-456.

No rules can ever be detailed or rigorous enough to prevent misconduct by parties or counsel. The criminal law does not eradicate crime; it merely allows society to define and confront it, while hopefully encouraging and enabling those who would to avoid it. The most precise rules of document production and the most active oversight on the part of the arbitral tribunal cannot guarantee that parties or their counsel will always conduct themselves appropriately or that absolute certainty will prevail in each case. Enforcement (to the extent possible) of the applicable rules may be necessary. However, an *ex ante* approach as we see it, although far from perfect, likely best serves to ensure that all concerned understand each other – certainly the first step in managing expectations, identifying standards to which all accede, leveling the playing field and articulating clear rules.

Arbitrators' Power to Sanction
Non-Compliance in Discovery in International Commercial
Arbitration

Nicolas Swerdloff,* Hagit Elul** and Andreas Baum***

I. INTRODUCTION

With the increasing globalization of the legal business, arbitration has taken on practices from different legal systems and lawyers. One such practice is the abuse of the discovery process for a perceived tactical advantage. There are many ways a party in an international arbitration can attempt to gain an advantage over the opposing party by abusing the discovery process. In general, the tactics employed by uncooperative parties can be divided into three categories: first, a recalcitrant party may simply decide to withhold documents or testimony to prevent the opposing party from obtaining valuable evidence (perhaps even the "smoking gun"); second, it may attempt to delay production with the intent of ambushing the other party with new evidence to bolster its case or with the goal of depriving the other party of the opportunity to incorporate the evidence in its case; finally, it may use various tactics to frustrate and delay the arbitral process.

This article describes these abuses (Sect. II), the arbitrators' authority to address them (Sect. III), procedures employed by arbitrators to sanction discovery abuses (Sect. IV), and potential recourse to court (Sect. V).

II. OVERVIEW OF TYPES OF DISCOVERY ABUSES

One of the greatest challenges in dealing with discovery abuses – whether as an arbitrator sitting on a tribunal or as the innocent party seeking to obtain evidence – lies in identifying them. Where evidence is withheld, an innocent party may have no reason to even suspect that the document exists. And even when the innocent party has reason to

---

*   Managing Partner of the Miami office, Hughes Hubbard & Reed LLP.
**   Partner, Hughes Hubbard & Reed LLP, residing in the firm's New York office.
*** Associate, Hughes Hubbard & Reed LLP, New York office.

believe that the document exists, it may be difficult for it to prove that the other party is willfully concealing the evidence. In some cases, documents that previously existed may have been destroyed, whether intentionally or accidentally. This may be the case, for example, where the dispute arises out of a long-term relationship between the parties, and the evidence sought relates to events that took place years prior to the claim being brought. In particular, in countries where document-retention policies in anticipation of litigation are not as robust as they are in the United States, evidence may be destroyed in the normal course of business.

One potential aid in helping alleviate this issue, at least after a dispute has arisen, is the International Bar Association's Guidelines on Party Representation in Arbitration, published in May 2013 (the IBA Guidelines), which attempt to harmonize the ethical obligations governing the conduct of attorneys from various legal systems. These rules provide ethical guidelines for counsel conduct, which parties may agree to be bound by or a tribunal may decide to adopt. Guidelines 12-17 deal specifically with "Information Exchange and Disclosure". In particular, Guideline 12 provides that a "Party Representative should inform the client of the need to preserve, so far as reasonably possible, Documents, including electronic Documents that would otherwise be deleted in accordance with a Document retention policy or in the ordinary course of business, which are potentially relevant to the arbitration."[1] Guideline 14 requires the attorney to explain to its client "the necessity of producing, and potential consequences of failing to produce" documents that the client has undertaken or been ordered to produce,[2] and Guideline 15 requires the attorney to advise and assist its client in identifying and producing all non-privileged and responsive documents.[3] Guidelines 16 and 17 impose on the legal representatives a continuing obligation to not suppress or conceal any documents that should be produced, even if they become aware of the existence of such documents after they should have been produced.[4]

In addition, the examples identified below provide some guidance in identifying discovery abuses. Because most international commercial arbitrations are confidential, many of these examples are derived from confirmation and setting-aside procedures in US courts.

1.   Withholding of Evidence

It should come as no surprise that a party in possession of incriminating evidence may be reluctant to hand over that evidence when requested by the opposing party or even ordered to do so by the arbitral tribunal. While arbitration has taken on aspects from both the common law and civil law systems, the question of how much discovery is

---

1. IBA Guideline 12.
2. IBA Guideline 14.
3. See IBA Guideline 15.
4. See IBA Guidelines 16-17.

appropriate remains a topic of heated debate.[5] Some tribunals may be reluctant to order any kind of discovery, in particular when both parties are from civil law jurisdictions where parties are often not required to disclose incriminating evidence.

An example of a party withholding evidence is provided by *Superadio Ltd. Partnership v. Winstar Radio Productions, LLC.*[6] In *Superadio*, the plaintiff brought an action to vacate an arbitration award in favor of Winstar's predecessor in interest, Walt "Baby" Love Productions, Inc., in a dispute arising from a radio network agreement.[7] In the arbitration, Baby Love had claimed damages for Superadio's alleged failure to turn over advertising revenues that it had collected on Baby Love's behalf for advertisements that had aired before the agreement terminated.[8] Baby Love sought discovery of documents in Superadio's possession to support its damages. Despite being ordered by the tribunal to produce the documents, which it admitted were in its possession, Superadio refused to produce them.[9] While the tribunal "could not enter an award for contract damages because of Baby Love's inability to prove its damages",[10] it remedied the situation by imposing sanctions against Superadio, as described in greater detail in Sect. IV.3, infra.

2. Ambush

Another common category of discovery abuses in international arbitration includes various tactics to "ambush" the other party, depriving it of the opportunity to respond to new evidence. Many arbitrators reject trial by ambush – even when cross-examining witnesses – requiring instead that each side give prior notice of all documents it intends to rely on. Whereas a litigator in the United States may have the option to rely on a document not previously submitted to impeach a witness during cross-examination,[11] some arbitrators may require such documents to be exchanged by the parties well in advance of hearings. Thus, parties who have failed to obtain evidence in support of their case prior to production deadlines may find themselves unable to rely on evidence obtained late.

a. Evidence introduced through witnesses

Some parties may attempt to circumvent production deadlines by introducing new evidence through witnesses at a hearing. This problem is somewhat mitigated in international arbitration where direct testimony is usually presented in witness

---

5. See, e.g., Kyriaki KARADELIS, "Getting a Grip on Discovery", Global Arbitration Review (31 Jan. 2014) (summarizing deliberations of Oxford Union-style debate about whether disclosure in international arbitration should be limited to the documents each party relied upon), available online at <http://globalarbitrationreview.com/news/article/32356/getting-grip-discovery/> (last visited 25 Mar. 2014).
6. 446 Mass. 330 (Mass. 2006).
7. *Id.* at 331.
8. *Id.* at 332.
9. *Id.* at 332-333.
10. *Id.* at 333.
11. See Fed. R. Evid. 613(b).

statements submitted with a party's memoranda, and any live testimony at the hearing is typically limited to providing a summary of the witness's statement, clarifying testimony from the prior witness statements or addressing new arguments or evidence introduced by the other party since the submission of the witness's statements.

b. Late production

Another ambush tactic consists of delaying production of evidence that the ambushing party has no intention of relying upon but that would bolster the opposing party's case. The party in such a situation may try to avoid production deadlines and produce evidence as late as possible so as to deprive the other party of a meaningful opportunity to review the evidence. The more blatant delays in production (for example, when a party produces key evidence only after the opposing party has completed its written submissions) are likely to raise suspicion and to elicit strict sanctions. As an example, in *In re Interchem Asia 2000 PTE Ltd. v. Oceana Petrochemicals AG*, Oceana withheld several documents that would have been highly relevant at the parties' 24 May 2004 hearing, producing them only a week after the hearing at the arbitrator's request.[12] The arbitrator observed that Oceana's pre-hearing document production was "'peculiarly sparse and unrevealing' and that the production on 1 June 2004 revealed critical documents and evinced 'patently dilatory and evasive document production carried out by [Oceana's counsel] for his client'".[13] This article will discuss in Sect. IV.4.*a*, infra, the sanctions imposed by the tribunal in that case.

Instead of such blatant tactics, a party may attempt to produce evidence *before* the other party's expected submission, but late enough that such other party will have difficulty assessing the evidence and relying on it.

3. Other Delay Tactics

Other discovery abuses may have a lesser impact on a party's ability to present its case, but may still lead to the inefficient administration of the case by causing unnecessary costs and delay. Consider, for example, the arbitration discussed in *Comerica Bank v. Howsam*:[14] in that dispute, the respondent's counsel belatedly notified the claimant that the respondent would refuse to attend his deposition, causing the claimant's counsel to unnecessarily travel to Toronto at the cost of attorney's fees and travel expenses. To make matters worse, the respondent's counsel had misled the claimant's counsel into believing that the respondent would be deposed by disingenuously objecting to the videotaping of the deposition.[15] The arbitrator found that – through these actions – the respondent's counsel had "engaged in abusive discovery practices" and exercised his powers to sanction the respondent and its counsel through an allocation of costs and the imposition of a monetary sanction.[16]

---

12. 373 F.Supp.2d 340, 344 (S.D.N.Y. 2005).
13. *Id.*
14. 208 Cal. App. 4th 790, 815-816 (Cal. Ct. App. 2012).
15. *Id.*
16. *Id.*

III.   THE TRIBUNAL'S AUTHORITY TO IMPOSE SANCTIONS AND THE LIMITS THERETO

In international commercial arbitration the powers of the tribunal are almost always derived from the parties' consent. Thus, a tribunal's authority to impose sanctions will also derive from the parties' agreement: the parties may contract for (or out of) such powers through explicit language in the arbitration agreement, through their choice of arbitral rules and, to some extent, through the choice of the seat of arbitration.

1.   The Arbitration Agreement

While unusual in practice – as parties often use boilerplate arbitration agreements – the parties can confer upon the tribunal powers to impose sanctions for discovery abuses by explicitly granting such powers in the arbitration agreement. For example, in *Metropolitan District Commission v. Connecticut Resources Recovery Authority*, the contract's arbitration provision called for the application of the rules of the American Arbitration Association (AAA Rules) "[e]xcept as modified herein", and explicitly provided that "[t]he arbitrators shall use all reasonable means to expedite discovery and to sanction non-compliance with reasonable discovery requests or any discovery order. The arbitrators shall not consider any evidence or argument not presented during [the discovery] period and shall not extend such period except by the written consent of both parties."[17]

2.   The Arbitral Rules

More often the powers of the tribunal are laid out in the arbitration rules, which the parties select in their arbitration agreement. Some institutional arbitration rules set out the powers that arbitrators have to enforce discovery procedures. For example, the JAMS Comprehensive Arbitration Rules & Procedures, effective 1 October 2010 (the JAMS Rules), provide an exhaustive list of sanctioning powers:

> "*Rule 29. Sanctions.* The Arbitrator may order appropriate sanctions for failure of a Party to comply with its obligations under any of these Rules. These sanctions may include, but are not limited to, assessment of Arbitration fees and Arbitrator compensation and expenses; assessment of any other costs occasioned by the actionable conduct, including reasonable attorneys' fees; exclusion of certain evidence; drawing adverse inferences; or, in extreme cases, determining an issue or issues submitted to Arbitration adversely to the Party that has failed to comply."[18]

The tribunal is endowed with similar powers under the Commercial Arbitration Rules and Mediation Procedures of the American Arbitration Association effective 1 October 2013 (the AAA Rules):

---

17. 130 Conn. App. 132, 141 n. 2 (Conn. App. Ct. 2011).
18. JAMS Rule 29.

"The arbitrator shall have the authority to issue any orders necessary to enforce the provisions of [discovery rules] and to otherwise achieve a fair, efficient and economical resolution of the case, including, *without limitation* ... in the case of willful non-compliance with any order issued by the arbitrator, drawing adverse inferences, excluding evidence and other submissions, and/or making special allocations of costs or an interim award of costs arising from such non-compliance."[19]

Art. 31 of the International Centre for Dispute Resolution's International Dispute Resolution Procedures (Including Mediation and Arbitration Rules), effective 1 June 2009 (the ICDR Rules), allows the tribunal to "apportion [costs of arbitration] among the parties if it determines that such apportionment is reasonable, *taking into account the circumstances of the case*".[20] Moreover, Art. 28 makes it clear that the tribunal can award "arbitration costs to a party *to compensate for dilatory or bad faith conduct* in the arbitration".[21] For example, in the arbitration discussed in *Millmaker v. Bruso*,[22] the arbitrator applied Art. 28 in deciding to award the respondent approximately $129,000 in expenses and attorneys' fees in addition to $126,000 for prevailing on its contract counterclaim, in large part due to the claimant's discovery abuses. The arbitrator strongly criticized the "strategy and tactics employed by [the claimant] in responding, or failing to respond, to properly-propounded discovery requests", and observed that the claimant's CEO "was playing fast-and-loose with the production process, producing documents only when it served his or [claimant's] interest", to the extent that "[i]t seemed as though every witness sparked new revelations of documents that had not been produced...".[23] The District Court for the Southern District of Texas upheld the award of expenses and attorneys' fees, noting that "[i]t is not for this Court to determine a reasonable award of expenses and fees or to opine on whether the arbitrator's award was reasonable, but only to judge whether the arbitrator exceeded his authority or acted in manifest disregard of the law".[24]

In addition to institutional rules, the IBA Rules on the Taking of Evidence in International Arbitration, effective 29 May 2010 (the IBA Rules) – which are frequently deemed applicable in international arbitration – likewise provide an arbitral tribunal with some explicit powers. For example, Art. 9(5) of the IBA Rules allows the tribunal to draw adverse inferences from a party's failure to comply with discovery orders:

"If a Party fails without satisfactory explanation to produce any Document requested in a Request to Produce to which it has not objected in due time or fails to produce any Document ordered to be produced by the Arbitral Tribunal, the

---

19. AAA Rule 23 (emphasis added).
20. ICDR Rules, Art. 31 (emphasis added).
21. ICDR Rules, Art. 28 (emphasis added).
22. No. H-07-3837, 2008 WL 4560624, at *7 (S.D. Tex. 9 Oct. 2008).
23. *Id.* (internal quotations omitted).
24. *Id.*

226

Arbitral Tribunal may infer that such document would be adverse to the interests of that Party."[25]

Art. 9(6) similarly provides for adverse inferences with respect to "other relevant evidence, including testimony".[26] Moreover, under Art. 9(7), the tribunal may take into account a party's "fail[ure] to conduct itself in good faith in the taking of evidence" in "assign[ing] the costs of the arbitration, including costs arising out of or in connection with the taking of evidence".[27]

Where other arbitration rules do not enumerate explicit powers, they nonetheless can be read to authorize the tribunal to impose sanctions through the award of costs. For example, the Arbitration Rules of the London Court of International Arbitration, effective 1 January 1998 (the LCIA Rules) generally require the tribunal to follow the principle that "costs should reflect the parties' relative success and failure in the award or arbitration".[28] However, the tribunal may ignore this principle "in the particular circumstances this general approach is inappropriate".[29] Similarly, the Arbitration Rules of the International Chamber of Commerce, effective 1 January 2012 (the ICC Rules), allow the tribunal to "take into account such circumstances as it considers relevant, including the extent to which each party has conducted the arbitration in an expeditious and cost-effective manner" in allocating the costs of the arbitration between the parties.[30]

More recently, some arbitral rules have extended their reach to regulate not only the parties but also their attorneys. In February 2014, the LCIA unveiled a final draft of its revised arbitration rules (the New LCIA Rules), which include a number of ethical guidelines for counsel.[31] These general guidelines – with which legal representatives must agree to comply as a condition of appearing before the tribunal –[32] prohibit legal representatives from "engag[ing] in activities intended unfairly to obstruct the arbitration or jeopardize the finality of any award" and from "knowingly conceal[ing] or assist[ing] in the concealment of any document (or any part thereof) which is ordered to be produced by the Arbitral Tribunal".[33] Should a tribunal find that a legal representative violated any of the general guidelines, the New LCIA Rules will empower it to issue a written reprimand to the offending counsel and a caution as to their future conduct in the arbitration, as well as to take "any other measure necessary to maintain the general

---

25. IBA Rules, Art. 9(5).
26. IBA Rules, Art. 9(6).
27. IBA Rules, Art. 9(7).
28. LCIA Rules, Art. 28.4.
29. *Id.*
30. ICC Rules, Art. 37(5).
31. See Sebastian PERRY and Richard WOOLLEY, "LCIA Unveils Draft Guidelines for Counsel Conduct", Global Arbitration Review (27 Feb. 2014), available online at <http://globalarbitrationreview.com/news/article/32458/lcia-unveils-draft-guidelines-counsel-conduct/> (last visited 18 Mar. 2014).
32. New LCIA Rules (Draft dated 18 Feb. 2014), Art. 18.5, available online at <www.lcia.org//media/download.aspx?MediaId=336> (last visited 18 Mar. 2014).
33. New LCIA Rules, Annex at paras. 2, 5.

duties of the arbitral tribunal".[34] The February draft of the New LCIA Rules also allowed the tribunal to refer the offending legal representative to the legal representative's regulatory and/or professional body, but this provision was removed as a result of recent deliberations.[35]

3. The Arbitration Law at the Seat of Arbitration

In addition to the arbitration rules, the arbitration law of the seat of the arbitration may have some bearing on the arbitrators' power to impose sanctions for discovery abuses. For example, Sect. 41 of the Arbitration Act 1996 of England, Wales, and Northern Ireland (UK Arbitration Act) provides for broad sanctioning powers unless the parties have agreed otherwise:

> "(7)If a party fails to comply with any other kind of peremptory order, then, without prejudice to section 42 (enforcement by court of tribunal's peremptory orders), the tribunal may do any of the following
> (a) direct that the party in default shall not be entitled to rely upon any allegation or material which was the subject matter of the order;
> (b) draw such adverse inferences from the act of non-compliance as the circumstances justify;
> (c) proceed to an award on the basis of such materials as have been properly provided to it;
> (d) make such order as it thinks fit as to the payment of costs of the arbitration incurred in consequence of the non-compliance."[36]

Similarly, Sect. 53 of the Hong Kong Arbitration Ordinance (Cap. 609) grants the tribunal the power to issue peremptory orders, including orders directing a party to produce evidence. Sub-para. 4 of that article outlines the measures a tribunal may employ should a party fail to comply:

> "(4) If a party fails to comply with a peremptory order ... the arbitral tribunal may—
> (a) direct that the party is not entitled to rely on any allegation or material which was the subject matter of the peremptory order;
> (b) draw any adverse inferences that the circumstances may justify from the non-compliance;
> (c) make an award on the basis of any materials which have been properly provided to the arbitral tribunal; or

---

34. New LCIA Rules, Art. 18.6; see also Richard WOOLLEY, "New LCIA rules nearly ready, says president", Global Arbitration Review (28 May 2014).
35. See Richard WOOLLEY, supra fn. 34.
36. UK Arbitration Act, Sect. 41, available online at <www.legislation.gov.uk/ukpga/1996/23/section/41> (last visited 25 Mar. 2014).

(d) make any order that the arbitral tribunal thinks fit as to the payment of the costs of the arbitration incurred in consequence of the non-compliance."[37]

Under Art. 1467 of the 2011 French Arbitration Law, the tribunal may enjoin a party to produce evidence, determine the manner in which such evidence is to be produced, and impose a procedural penalty (a so-called "astreinte") for the party's failure to comply.[38]

In the United States, the Federal Arbitration Act (FAA), while silent on the types of sanctions that a tribunal may impose on a party who fails to comply with discovery requests or orders by the tribunal, does not expressly prohibit such sanctions. In fact, in *Hamstein Cumberland Music Group v. Williams*, the Fifth Circuit Court of Appeals observed that "arbitrators enjoy inherent authority to police the arbitration process and fashion appropriate remedies to effectuate this authority, including with respect to conducting discovery and sanctioning failure to abide by ordered disclosures".[39] In the arbitration at issue in *Hamstein*, which concerned the payment of royalties pursuant to an agreement, the arbitrator awarded the claimant $500,000 in sanctions against the respondent for repeated failure to respond to multiple written requests for information and documents.[40] Additionally, the arbitrator imposed a deadline for production and warned the respondent that failure to meet that deadline would preclude him from subsequently offering any evidence of royalties owed to the claimant.[41] The arbitrator eventually awarded the claimant $1,149,140.19.[42] The District Court for the Western District of Texas *sua sponte* reduced the award, declining to confirm the sanctions portion of the award on the basis that the arbitrator had exceeded his authority within the meaning of the FAA.[43] The Court of Appeals vacated the district court's judgment and reinstated the entirety of the arbitral award, finding that the arbitrator had not exceeded his authority in any respect.[44]

---

37. Arbitration Ordinance, (2011) Cap. 609, 21 Sect. 53(4) (H.K.) (Hong Kong Arbitration Ordinance), available online at <www.legislation.gov.hk/blis_pdf.nsf/6799165D2FEE3FA948 25755E0033E532/C05151C760F783AD482577D900541075/$FILE/CAP_609_e_b5.pdf> (last visited 25 Mar. 2014).
38. Republic of France Decree No. 2011-48 of 13 January 2011 Reforming the Law Governing Arbitration (French Arbitration Law), Art. 1467, effective 1 May 2011, available online at <www.legifrance.gouv.fr/affichTexte.do?cidTexte=JORFTEXT000023417517&categorieLie n=id> (last visited 25 Mar. 2014) (*"Si une partie détient un élément de preuve, le tribunal arbitral peut lui enjoindre de le produire selon les modalités qu'il détermine et au besoin à peine d'astreinte."*). An unofficial translation is available at <www.parisarbitration.com/French-Law-on-Arbitration.pdf> (last visited 25 Mar. 2014).
39. 532 F. App'x 538, 543 (5th Cir. 2013).
40. *Id*. at 541.
41. *Id*.
42. *Id*.
43. *Id*. at 542.
44. *Id*. at 544.

Under the Florida Arbitration Code, an arbitrator "may ... take action against a noncomplying party to the extent a court could if the controversy were the subject of a civil action in [Florida]".[45]

In contrast, some domestic laws may limit the powers of an arbitrator. For example, under Sect. 25 of the Swedish Arbitration Act – which applies to arbitrations seated in Sweden – "[t]he parties shall supply the evidence", but the arbitrators "may [not] impose conditional fines or otherwise use compulsory measures in order to obtain requested evidence".[46]

IV.   TYPES OF SANCTIONS

As the source of the tribunal's power to impose sanctions depends on the parties' agreement, the applicable rules, and even the applicable arbitration law, it should come as no surprise that the scope of these powers will vary on a case-by-case basis. The type of sanction available will also depend on the type of discovery abuse at issue: compare the case of a party suspected of withholding evidence to that of a party attempting to ambush the other party with evidence introduced at a hearing. In the former, the tribunal may find it appropriate to draw an adverse inference, whereas in the latter, it would be more appropriate to exclude the late-produced evidence. Sect. IV of this article attempts to set out the most common categories of sanctions, drawing on examples where available.

1.   Adverse Inferences

Adverse inferences are one of the most common forms of sanctions used to remedy the improper withholding of evidence. An adverse inference consists of inferring from the party's failure to comply with discovery orders that the documents or testimony withheld would have been adverse to the interests of the withholding party. Much has been written about this remedy, and a tribunal's power to draw adverse inferences is considered widely accepted as a general principle of law.[47]

Many arbitral rules explicitly grant the tribunal the authority to draw adverse inferences. For example, where a party fails to produce a document or other relevant evidence "without satisfactory explanation", Art. 9(5) and (6) of the IBA Rules permit the tribunal to "infer that such evidence would be adverse to the interests of that Party".[48]

---

45. Fla. Stat. Sect. 682.08(4) (2013).

46. *Svensk Författningssamling* 1999:116 (Swedish Arbitration Act), unofficial translation provided by the Arbitration Institute of the Stockholm Chamber of Commerce, available online at <www.sccinstitute.com/?id=23746> (last visited 25 Mar. 2014).

47. Abba KOLO, "Witness Intimidation, Tampering and Other Related Abuses of Process in Investment Arbitration: Possible Remedies Available to the Arbitral Tribunal", 26 Arbitration International (2010, no. 1) p. 43 at p. 75 ("As the ICJ observed in the *Corfu Channel* case: '[t]his indirect evidence is admitted in all systems of law, and its use is recognized by international decisions'." (citing *Corfu Channel (United Kingdom v. Albania)* (Merits) [1949] ICJ Rep. 18)).

48. IBA Rules, Art. 9(5)-(6).

Rule 23 of the AAA Rules allows the tribunal to draw adverse inferences "in the case of willful non-compliance with any order issued by the arbitrator".[49] Rule 29 of the JAMS Rules allows the arbitrator to draw adverse inferences as a sanction for the "failure of a Party to comply with its obligations under any of the [JAMS] Rules".[50]

However, adverse inferences have their limitations. It is generally accepted that several requirements must be met before adverse inferences are imposed:

– the documents must plainly be relevant and material to the proceedings – some commentators put it as high as "essential to the disposition of the case";
– the documents are in the control of the requested party;
– the claim or defense on which the inference might be drawn is established at a prima facie level even in the absence of the requested document;
– no satisfactory explanation is provided; and
– sufficient time and opportunity have been given to produce.[51]

Another commentator summarizes additional requirements distilled from a review of arbitral awards as follows:

(1) the party seeking the adverse inference must produce all available evidence corroborating the inference sought;
(2) the requested evidence must be accessible to the inference opponent;
(3) the inference sought must be reasonable, consistent with facts in the record and logically related to the likely nature of the evidence withheld;
(4) the party seeking the adverse inference must produce prima facie evidence; and
(5) the inference opponent must know, or have reason to know, of its obligation to produce evidence rebutting the adverse inference sought.[52]

Because the party seeking an adverse inference must first produce prima facie evidence, the adverse inference may be insufficient where the party is entirely dependent on documents in the other party's possession.[53] However, if the party is able to produce some prima facie evidence to corroborate the inference drawn, the adverse inference will have the effect of shifting the burden of proof onto the recalcitrant party.[54] A party may be required to exercise some ingenuity to meet the difficult threshold burden of providing prima facie evidence. For example, it may consider hiring an outside

---

49. AAA Rule 23(d).
50. JAMS Rule 29.
51. Peter ASHFORD, "Documentary Discovery and International Commercial Arbitration", 17 Am. Rev. Int'l Arb. (2006) p. 89 at p. 102.
52. Jeremy K. Sharpe, "Drawing Adverse Inferences from the Non-production of Evidence", 22 Arbitration International (2006, no. 4) p. 549 at p. 550.
53. Gabrielle KAUFMANN-KOHLER and Philippe BÄRTSCH, "Discovery in International Arbitration: How Much Is Too Much?", 2004 SchiedsVZ (2004, no. 1) p. 13 at p. 21.
54. A. KOLO, "Witness Intimidation, Tampering and Other Related Abuses of Process in Investment Arbitration: Possible Remedies Available to the Arbitral Tribunal", supra fn. 47, at pp. 75-76.

investigator to conduct fact interviews of former employees of the opposing party and others (provided local laws permit such investigations).

2.   Exclusion of Evidence

A common sanction used by arbitrators faced with ambush tactics – for example, when a party attempts to introduce evidence late in order to deprive the other party of an opportunity to respond – is to exclude the late-produced evidence entirely. Some arbitral rules explicitly permit arbitrators to exclude evidence that was introduced in violation of discovery deadlines: for example, the AAA Rules allow a tribunal to "exclud[e] evidence and other submissions",[55] and the JAMS Rules provide for the "exclusion of certain evidence".[56] But even where rules are silent on the issue of exclusion of evidence, the weight accorded to evidence presented in arbitration is generally left to the discretion of the tribunal. As a result – and so as to avoid giving the losing party grounds to vacate the award – the tribunal may simply decide to give less weight to such late-produced evidence without explicitly stating so in its award.

3.   Monetary Sanctions

An alternative way to sanction a party abusing the discovery process is through the use of monetary sanctions. Monetary sanctions will most frequently take the form of an allocation of costs: some rules explicitly allow the tribunal to shift costs of the arbitration based on a party's failure to comply with discovery orders,[57] or its failure "to conduct itself in good faith in the taking of evidence";[58] others allow the tribunal to shift costs of the arbitration based on the circumstances of the case[59] or based on whether a party has "conducted the arbitration in an expeditious and cost-effective manner".[60] More unusual are the rules that allow for fines separate from an allocation of costs,[61] which may be illegal under certain national arbitration laws.[62] In some cases, it may be possible for the tribunal to impose a "security for costs" measure in order to prevent abuses.

Case law illustrates how arbitrators can use monetary sanctions to enforce procedural orders. For example, in *Superadio*, discussed supra in Sect. II.*1*, Superadio failed to comply with discovery requests made by Baby Love.[63] On 21 August 2000, the tribunal entered an order directing Superadio to satisfy certain discovery requests by 22 September 2000, or to pay Baby Love "$1,000 per day until Superadio is either in

---

55. AAA Rules, Art. 23(d).
56. JAMS Rule 29.
57. See, e.g., JAMS Rule 29; AAA Rules, Art. 23(d); IBA Rules, Art. 9(7); UK Arbitration Act Sect. 41(7).
58. IBA Rules, Art. 9(7).
59. See, e.g., LCIA Rules, Art 28.4.
60. ICC Rules, Art. 37(5).
61. See, e.g., French Arbitration Law, Art. 1467.
62. See, e.g., Swedish Arbitration Act, Sect. 25.
63. *Superadio*, 446 Mass. at 332-333.

compliance or until the date of the [h]earing, whichever shall occur first".[64] Superadio ignored this procedural order, and its failure to produce evidence prevented Baby Love from proving its damages.[65] Rule 45(a) of the AAA Rules in effect at that time provided the tribunal with the authority to "grant any remedy or relief that the arbitrator deems just and equitable", and Rule 23(c) provided that "[t]he arbitrator is authorized to resolve any disputes concerning the exchange of information".[66] Construing these rules together, the tribunal determined that it had the authority to impose the sanction it had outlined in the procedural order. Having found for Baby Love on the issue of liability, the tribunal imposed a sanction against Superadio in the amount of $271,000, corresponding to "an assessment of $1,000 per day from 23 September 2000 (the day following the deadline for discovery compliance), to 20 June 2001 (the day that the arbitration hearing commenced)".[67]

In rejecting Superadio's claim that the arbitration panel exceeded its authority by awarding monetary damages for Superadio's discovery violations, the Supreme Judicial Court of Massachusetts observed that the object of the discovery – namely, the amount of money owed because of Superadio's alleged violation of the agreement between it and Baby Love – related to the core of the agreement.[68] In the absence of fraud, Superadio was bound by the tribunal's interpretation of the arbitration rules,[69] and the arbitration rules applicable to the dispute lacked "any language limiting the means by which an arbitrator or arbitration panel may resolve discovery disputes, or language restricting the application of the broad remedial relief of rule 45(a) to final awards...".[70]

4.   Sanctions Against Counsel

While tribunals routinely take action against parties who fail to comply with discovery orders – whether through the use of adverse inferences, the shifting of costs or the imposition of separate monetary sanctions – taking action against counsel for the delinquent party is a more difficult proposition. However, case law provides examples of situations where tribunals have attempted to do precisely that.

a.   Monetary sanctions

It may be tempting for a tribunal to impose monetary sanctions against the law firm representing a party for systematically failing to comply with the tribunal's orders. However, given that the jurisdiction of an arbitral tribunal is based on the mutual consent of the parties and limited in scope to matters covered by the arbitration agreement, it may prove more challenging to extend this jurisdiction to the actions taken by counsel to the parties.

---

64. *Id.* at 332.
65. *Id.* at 333.
66. *Id.* at 338.
67. *Id.* at 333.
68. *Id.* at 338.
69. *Id.* at 339.
70. *Id.* at 338.

In *In re Interchem*, discussed supra in Sect. II.2.*b*, illustrates this problem.[71] In a dispute under the Commercial Arbitration Rules of the American Arbitration Association, the arbitrator – as a result of dilatory document production tactics – imposed sanctions (in the form of attorney's fees) not only against the party but also against its attorney individually. While the court found that "the awarding of attorney's [fees] was within the [a]rbitrator's authority" as against the party because the rules allowed it to shift fees for bad faith conduct, it held that "the [a]rbitrator did not have the authority to award these fees against [the attorney] personally".[72] The court noted that it could not "identify, nor did the [a]rbitrator provide, any authority that supports an arbitrator's ability to award attorney's fees against an attorney appearing before him".[73]

Polin v. Kellwood Co. offers a counter-example in which the court affirmed the arbitrator's power to impose sanctions against the attorney (albeit not in the context of abusive discovery).[74] The plaintiff Charles Polin had brought claims of discrimination, fraud and tortious interference against its former employer. After "four years of pre-trial litigation and numerous rancorous discovery disputes", the parties agreed to submit their dispute to binding arbitration under the National Rules for the Resolution of Employment Disputes of the American Arbitration Association.[75] During the course of the arbitration, Polin's attorney wrote an unsubstantiated letter to the AAA accusing the chairman of the tribunal of being biased.[76] The tribunal took great offense at the attorney's accusations and presented the attorney with an opportunity to defend his actions,[77] before concluding that the attorney had "committed a contempt of the panel by sending [his] letter to the AAA before the proceedings had terminated...".[78] In addition, the tribunal reported that Polin's attorney:

> "1) falsely accused Kellwood and its counsel of interfering with witnesses testimony, of maintaining false financial documents, and of destroying evidence; 2) improperly transcribed a telephone conference with [the chairman] and Kellwood's counsel without telling either party; 3) unduly prolonged the hearings by a constant repetition of questions, a reiteration of the same areas of inquiry, and by continuously interposing spurious objections; [and] 4) pursued a frivolous age discrimination claim...".[79]

Finding that the attorney's misconduct warranted sanctions, the tribunal unanimously awarded Kellwood one-half of the arbitration costs – amounting to over $150,000 – to

---

71. 373 F.Supp.2d at 355.
72. *Id.*
73. *Id.* at 356.
74. 103 F.Supp.2d 238 (S.D.N.Y. 2000).
75. *Id.* at 241-242.
76. *Id.* at 246.
77. *Id.* at 247.
78. *Id.* at 249.
79. *Id.*

be paid by Polin's attorney *personally*.[80] The tribunal cited the applicable AAA rules, which gave it the power to "grant any remedy or relief that the arbitrator deem[ed] just and equitable, *including any remedy or relief that would have been available to the parties had the matter been heard in court*".[81] Observing that federal courts have equitable power to award sanctions when counsel "has acted in bad faith, vexatiously, wantonly or for oppressive reasons",[82] and have the authority to sanction parties or attorneys for filing and continuing frivolous claims under Rule 11 of the Federal Rules of Civil Procedure, the tribunal concluded that it had authority to impose similar sanctions.[83] Finding the award to be compensatory to Kellwood rather than punitive,[84] and noting that arbitrators have the power to interpret the procedural rules of the proceeding,[85] the District Court confirmed the award. Extremely vexatious behavior in discovery could presumably justify applying a similar reasoning.

b.   Excluding counsel from arbitration

It is conceivable – albeit unlikely – that a tribunal could under exigent circumstances remove counsel for serious procedural misconduct. Commentators have noted that arbitration tribunals have an "inherent authority" to protect the integrity of the arbitral process by enforcing orders and rules.[86] The ICSID tribunal's ruling in *Hrvatska Elektroprivreda d.d. v. Republic of Slovenia* illustrates this authority.[87] In *Hrvatska*, a two-week hearing was scheduled to take place in May 2008, more than two years after the commencement of the arbitration and after both parties had already submitted extensive pleadings.[88] On 25 April 2008, less than two weeks before the hearing, the respondent notified the tribunal that a barrister belonging to the same chambers as the tribunal's president would be present at the hearing, thereby creating the appearance of a conflict. Rather than force the tribunal's president to recuse himself as a result of the conflict, the tribunal determined it had the authority under the ICSID Rules to remove the barrister.[89] The tribunal acknowledged that "[t]he ICSID Convention and Rules do not ... explicitly give the power to tribunals to exclude counsel" and that a party's right to counsel of its

---

80. *Id*. at 247.
81. *Id*. at 242; see also, *Interchem*, 373 F.Supp.2d at 357 (emphasis added).
82. *Id*. at 248 (citing the tribunal's award, in turn citing *First National Supermarkets, Inc. v. Retail, Wholesale and Chain Store Food Employees Union Local 338*, 118 F.3d 892, 898 (2d Cir. 1997)).
83. *Id*.
84. *Id*. at 267-268.
85. *Id*. at 260.
86. Gary V. MCGOWAN, "Sanctions in US and International Arbitrations: Old Law In Modern Context", Kluwer Arbitration Blog (10 Oct. 2013), available online at <http://kluwerarbitrationblog.com/blog/2013/10/10/sanctions-in-us-and-international-arbitrations-old-law-in-modern-context/> (last visited 25 Mar. 2014).
87. ICSID Case No. ARB/05/24, Ruling regarding the participation of David Mildon QC in further stages of the proceedings (6 May 2008), available online at <https://icsid.worldbank.org/ICSID/FrontServlet?requestType=CasesRH&actionVal=show Doc&docId=DC950_En&caseId=C69> (last visited 25 Mar. 2014).
88. *Id*. at paras. 1-3.
89. *Id*. at 15.

choice was a "fundamental principle".[90] Nevertheless, recognizing that the respondent already had other counsel, the tribunal held that it was "compelled ... to preserve the integrity of the proceedings and, ultimately, its Award",[91] and that it had inherent power to take measures to do so under Art. 44 of the ICSID Convention, "which authorizes the [t]ribunal to decide 'any question of procedure' not expressly dealt with in the Convention, the ICSID Arbitration Rules or 'any rule agreed by the parties'".[92]

However, overriding a party's right to counsel of its choice – which the *Hrvatska* tribunal identified as a "fundamental principle" –[93] is a drastic measure that may leave the award vulnerable to challenges in court. The *Hrvatska* tribunal was prepared to make an exception to this principle only because of "the overriding principle ... of the immutability of properly constituted tribunals (Article 56(1) of the ICSID Convention)".[94] As this overriding principle is unlikely to come into play in the case of discovery abuses, a tribunal facing non-compliance with discovery orders would be well advised to avoid disqualifying counsel.

c.   Notifying counsel's bar association

Where an attorney is acting in bad faith in discovery, the tribunal (or even opposing counsel) may be able – or, depending on the jurisdiction, obligated – to report the attorney to his or her bar association:[95] bar associations often impose ethical codes of conduct or guidelines on their members, which may in some cases apply in international arbitration:

> "Domestic regulations governing attorneys' conduct may in some jurisdictions apply in international arbitration; the classic example is found in the United States where attorneys licensed in one of the US states are bound by their applicable bar rules irrespective of whether they appear before a court or arbitral tribunal in the jurisdiction in which they are licensed or elsewhere."[96]

As discussed in Sect. III, the new draft LCIA Rules circulated in February specifically provided that – in the event the attorney violates the general conduct guidelines contained in those rules – the tribunal may make "a reference to the legal

---

90. *Id.* at para. 24.
91. *Id.* at para. 30.
92. *Id.* at para. 33.
93. *Id.* at para. 24.
94. *Id.* at para. 25.
95. Günther J. HORVATH et al., "Countering Guerrilla Tactics at the Outset, Throughout and at the Conclusion of the Arbitral Proceedings" in Günther J. HORVATH and Stephan WILSKE, eds., *Guerrilla Tactics in International Arbitration* (2013) p. 33 at p. 46.
96. *Id.*

representative's regulatory and/or professional body".[97] However, this provision has reportedly been deleted from the most recent draft of the New LCIA Rules.[98]

The ability to report misconduct to an attorney's bar association is more likely to serve as an effective deterrent than it is to act as a remedy in addressing non-compliance with discovery orders. As one commentator and experienced arbitrator observes, "it is unlikely that the relevant bar association(s) will be able to do anything in a timely way to manage any alleged problem. And, after the event, it is questionable whether the affected party will see fit to lodge and prosecute a complaint before a far distant law society or its equivalent."[99]

d.   Notifying arbitral institution to exclude counsel from future arbitrations
In addition to reporting attorney misconduct to the attorney's bar association, the tribunal may have the option of reporting the misconduct to the arbitral institution administering the proceedings. Indeed, even where the arbitral institution does not integrate an enforceable ethical code of conduct into its rules, it is in the institution's interest to police misconduct so as to promote the efficient adjudication of disputes administered by it. Commentators have discussed the sanctions that arbitral institutions could impose, which range from minor reprimands to monetary sanctions, and even exclusion from participation in future arbitrations administered by the institution:

> "One such sanction could be that counsel is barred for a certain period of time from participating in arbitrations administered by this arbitral institution – a sanction which is not unusual for US practitioners.... Counsel would certainly try to avoid a situation in which he or she would be required to tell clients that he/she cannot personally represent them in ICSID or ICC arbitration because of a current ban due to misconduct in previous proceedings."[100]

There appear to be no public reports of any arbitral institution ever barring counsel from participating in proceedings as a result of prior misconduct.

V.   RECOURSE TO LOCAL COURTS

Should the tribunal be unable to enforce its procedural orders, it may in some cases be able to seek the assistance of local courts to deal with a recalcitrant party.

---

97. New LCIA Rules (Draft dated 18 Feb. 2014), Art. 18.6.
98. See Richard WOOLLEY, "New LCIA rules nearly ready, says president", Global Arbitration Review", supra fn. 34.
99. William J. ROWLEY, Q.C., "Guerrilla Tactics and Developing Issues" in Günther J. HORVATH and Stephan WILSKE, eds., *Guerrilla Tactics in International Arbitration* (2013) p. 20 at p. 24.
100. Günther J. HORVATH et al., "Countering Guerrilla Tactics at the Outset, Throughout and at the Conclusion of the Arbitral Proceedings", at p. 47 (see supra fn. 95); see also Hagit ELUL, "Experiences from the Common Law System" in Günther J. HORVATH and Stephan WILSKE, eds., *Guerrilla Tactics in International Arbitration* (2013) p. 118.

1. Enforcement of Procedural Orders

In some jurisdictions, the tribunal can appeal to the courts to enforce its procedural orders. For example, Sect. 41 of the UK Arbitration Act 1996 provides that "[i]f without showing sufficient cause a party fails to comply with any order or directions of the tribunal, the tribunal may make a peremptory order to the same effect, prescribing such time for compliance with it as the tribunal considers appropriate".[101] Should the party fail to comply with a peremptory order issued under Sect. 41, Sect. 42 allows the tribunal to make an application to the courts for an order "requiring a party to comply with a peremptory order made by the tribunal".[102] Similarly, Art. 184 of the Swiss Federal Act on Private International Law provides that "[i]f the assistance of state judiciary authorities is necessary for the taking of evidence, the arbitral tribunal or a party with the consent of the arbitral tribunal may request the assistance of the state judge at the seat of the arbitral tribunal…".[103] Art. 27 of both the 1985 UNCITRAL Model Law on International Commercial Arbitration (the UNCITRAL Model Law) and the UNCITRAL Model Law as amended in 2006 – which form the basis for the domestic arbitration legislation in numerous jurisdictions – provide for court assistance from a competent court in taking evidence.[104] For example, Sect. 55 of the Hong Kong Arbitration Ordinance (Cap. 609) implements Art. 27 of the UNICTRAL Model Law and allows the tribunal or a party with the approval of the arbitral tribunal to request court assistance in taking evidence. Under this section, "[t]he Court may order a person to attend proceedings before an arbitral tribunal to give evidence or to produce documents or other evidence".[105]

Under the Singapore Arbitration Act, "[a]ll orders or directions made or given by an arbitral tribunal in the course of an arbitration shall, *by leave of the Court*, be enforceable in the same manner as if they were orders made by the Court and, where leave is so given, judgment may be entered in terms of the order or direction".[106] However, even where court assistance is available under the domestic arbitration law, the remedy may be of limited use in practice, and is generally "thought to be cumbersome and ineffective compared to the other alternatives".[107]

The FAA in the United States does not directly provide for court enforcement of discovery orders, but such mechanisms may be available under certain state laws. For example, the Florida Arbitration Act – which implements the UNCITRAL Model Law

---

101. UK Arbitration Act Sect. 41(5).
102. *Id.* Sect. 42.
103. Federal Act on Private International Law, 18 Dec. 1987, Art. 184 (Switz.) (the original French statute reads "*Si l'aide des autorités judiciaires de l'Etat est nécessaire à l'administration de la preuve, le tribunal arbitral, ou les parties d'entente avec lui, peuvent requérir le concours du juge du siège du tribunal arbitral; ce juge applique son propre droit.*").
104. UNCITRAL Model Law 1985, Art. 27; UNCITRAL Model Law 2006, Art. 27.
105. Hong Kong Arbitration Ordinance, Sect. 55.
106. Arbitration Act, (2002) Cap. 10, Sect. 28 (Sing.) (emphasis added), available online at <http://statutes.agc.gov.sg/aol/search/display/view.w3p;page=0;query=CompId%3Ad80 6f86c-be56-471b-b418-bdfa342deb3c;rec=0;whole=yes> (last visited 25 Mar. 2014).
107. Gabrielle KAUFMANN-KOHLER and Philippe BÄRTSCH, "Discovery in International Arbitration: How Much is Too Much?", supra fn. 52, at p. 21.

on International Commercial Arbitration – provides that "[a]n interim measure issued by an arbitral tribunal must be recognized as binding and, unless otherwise provided by the arbitral tribunal, enforced upon application to the competent court, irrespective of the country in which it was issued…".[108]

2. Court Assistance in Discovery through 28 U.S.C. Sect. 1782

In the United States, the question of whether an international commercial arbitration tribunal sitting outside the United States or a party to such arbitration can obtain US court assistance in discovery remains unsettled and the subject of a circuit split. The relevant statute – 28 U.S.C. Sect. 1782 – provides:

> "The district court of the district in which a person resides or is found may order him to give his testimony or statement or to produce a document or other thing for use in a proceeding in a foreign or international tribunal…. The order may be made pursuant to a letter rogatory issued, or request made, by a foreign or international tribunal or upon the application of any interested person and may direct that the testimony or statement be given, or the document or other thing be produced, before a person appointed by the court."[109]

One big advantage of Sect. 1782 is that – provided the jurisdiction permits the use of the statute for private commercial arbitration – reliance on the statute is not limited to discovery from parties to the arbitration. A party may use this statute to obtain a document found in the United States even if in the hands of a third party. However, not all jurisdictions will allow applications under Sect. 1782 where the foreign tribunal is a purely commercial arbitration tribunal.

The Courts of Appeals for the Second and Fifth Circuits have held that a private commercial arbitration tribunal is not a "foreign or international tribunal" within the meaning of Sect. 1782.[110] District courts in the Seventh and Ninth Circuits have also interpreted the statute to not extend to private international commercial arbitrations.[111] District courts in the First, Third, and Eighth Circuits have – to the contrary – found that

---

108. Fla. Stat. Sect. 684.0026(1) (2013).

109. 28 U.S.C. Sect. 1782 (2014); see also *Intel Corp. v. Advanced Micro Devices, Inc.*, 542 U.S. 241, 249 (2004) (leading Supreme Court case interpreting Sect. 1782, clarifying that "a proceeding in a foreign or international tribunal" encompasses "administrative and quasi-judicial proceedings" but leaving unresolved the question of whether private arbitrations fall within the scope of the statute).

110. See, e.g., *Nat'l Broad. Co., Inc. v. Bear Stearns & Co., Inc.*, 165 F.3d 184 (2d Cir. 1999) (finding that a commercial arbitration administered by the International Chamber of Commerce (ICC) was not an international tribunal within the meaning of the statute); *Republic of Kazakhstan v. Biedermann Int'l*, 168 F.3d 880 (5th Cir. 1999) (same but arbitration administered by Stockholm Chamber of Commerce).

111. See, e.g., *In re Arbitration in London, England*, 626 F.Supp.2d 882 (N.D. Ill. 2009); *In re Dubey*, 949 F.Supp.2d 990 (C.D. Cal. 2013) ("[B]ecause the proceeding here is a private arbitration contractually agreed upon by the parties, it does not fall within the meaning of Sect. 1782.").

Sect. 1782 does in fact extend to international commercial arbitrations.[112] The Eleventh Circuit Court of Appeals recently declined to resolve the question of whether Sect. 1782 extends to private commercial arbitration,[113] but district courts even within that Circuit are divided on the issue.[114]

VI.   CONCLUSION

In conclusion, depending on the seat of the arbitration and the applicable rules, a tribunal is likely to have at its disposal an arsenal of remedies to combat discovery abuses. The tribunal's authority to impose sanctions will depend on the domestic arbitration law, the rules selected by the parties, and occasionally the explicit terms of the arbitration agreement. In most popular centers of international arbitration, the tribunal's authority to enforce its own procedure is well established, whether it be explicitly articulated in the domestic arbitration law or recognized as an inherent authority.

---

112. See, e.g., *In re Babcock Borsig AG*, 583 F.Supp.2d 233 (D. Mass. 2008) (concerning an arbitration administered by the ICC); *Comision Ejecutiva Hidroelectrica del Rio Lempa v. Nejapa Power Co., LLC*, No. 08-135-GMS, 2008 WL 4809035, at *1 (D. Del. 14 Oct. 2008); *In re Hallmark Capital Corp.*, 534 F.Supp.2d 951, 954-955 (D. Minn. 2007) (concerning private arbitration in Israel).

113. Application of *Consorcio Ecuatoriano de Telecomunicaciones S.A. v. JAS Forwarding (USA), Inc.*, No. 11-12897, 2014 WL 104132, at *5 n. 4 (11th Cir. 10 Jan. 2014).

114. Compare *In re Operadora DB Mexico, SA. de C.V.*, No. 6:09-cv-383-Orl-22(GJK), 2009 WL 2423138, at *12 (M.D. Fla. 4 Aug. 2009) ("[A]fter applying a functional analysis of the ICC Panel, the Court finds that it is not a foreign or international tribunal under Sect. 1782."), with *In re Pinchuk*, No. 13-22857-MC, 2013 WL 5574342, at *2 (S.D. Fla. 20 Sept. 2013) (finding that arbitration tribunal administered by the London Court of International Arbitration constituted a proceeding before a foreign tribunal within the meaning of Sect. 1782, citing *In re Winning (HK) Shipping Co., Ltd.*, No. 09–22659–MC, 2010 WL 1796579, at *6-7 (S.D. Fla. 30 Apr. 2010)), and *In re Roz Trading Ltd.*, 469 F.Supp.2d 1221, 1225-1228 (N.D. Ga. 2006) (concerning arbitration administered by Arbitral Centre of the Austrian Federal Economic Chamber in Vienna).

Interim Measures in International Commercial Arbitration – Useful Weapon or Tactical Missile: By What Standards Should Arbitral Tribunals Fire the Shots?

*Hilary Heilbron QC** *

I.   INTRODUCTION

The proliferation and increased globalization of international arbitration has brought in its wake an increasing use of applications for interim measures before commercial arbitral tribunals. Uncertainties abound as to when such applications are made, why they are made, and the basis upon which tribunals reach their decision. Questions also arise as to the extent to which they are now a regular feature of the arbitral process.

The presumed assumption is that such applications are made for legitimate reasons to protect the requesting party from interference with its rights, including the right to an enforceable award, or from interference with the due process of the arbitration. However, there is a sense that some of these applications are in fact brought to achieve a perceived tactical advantage under the guise of some alleged, but unfounded, need for protection. It is an aspect of interim relief which has not to date really been addressed, contrary to other aspects of the arbitral process, such as tactical challenges to arbitrators. Yet unmeritorious applications can involve considerable costs and delay and illegitimate and increased pressure on the opposing party to settle or adjust the presentation of its case.

For all these reasons, there is therefore an increasing need to ascertain whether there are any norms as to how tribunals approach or should approach such applications or whether the inherent flexibility of the arbitral process means that the imposition of too stringent standards and guidelines is inimical to that process. Much of what is known remains anecdotal, particularly in commercial arbitration. Some guidance can be sought from the published awards of interim relief in investment treaty cases, but there are some significant differences in approach stemming from the fact that such arbitrations

---

*   Barrister and international arbitrator, Brick Court Chambers, London.

involve sovereign states. From the limited evidence available it would seem that the basis upon which arbitral tribunals in commercial cases are willing to grant interim relief has evolved in the last decade to meet changing expectations.

However, before one can make any meaningful evaluation of interim measures granted by arbitral tribunals, one needs to step back and ask first what is their purpose and secondly, what actually are interim measures? It is only then that one can assess whether or not parties are using them for the right, as opposed to the wrong, reasons and whether or not the standards applied measure up so as to ensure that interim measures remain a useful weapon in the arbitral armoury and not just a tactical missile to be used by a recalcitrant party to undermine or derail the process.

II.   THE PURPOSE OF INTERIM MEASURES

The need for tribunals to have the power to grant interim measures, variously described also as provisional measures, interim measures of protection and conservatory measures, is not in dispute, but there remains a potential debate as to their purpose. The traditional prescriptive view is that such measures provide a form of temporary and urgent relief to protect or preserve the status quo, or a party's assets or the evidence, or to avoid irreparable harm or prejudice to the conduct of the arbitration[1] and require the requesting party to establish "irreparable harm".

Art. 17 of the UNCITRAL Model Law 1985[2] confined such relief to measures of protection which the arbitral tribunal considered "necessary in respect of the subject-matter of the dispute". Art. 17(2) of the amended Model Law, introduced in 2006, moved away from the traditional view as to the need to establish "irreparable harm" in favour of a more balanced assessment, but still prescribes the purposes for which a tribunal can grant interim relief, albeit wider than in the earlier version of the Model Law. Art. 17(2) states:

> "(2) An interim measure is any temporary measure, whether in the form of an award or in another form, by which, at any time prior to the issuance of the award by which the dispute is finally decided, the arbitral tribunal orders a party to:
> (a) Maintain or restore the status quo pending determination of the dispute;
> (b) Take action that would prevent, or refrain from taking action that is likely to cause, current or imminent harm or prejudice to the arbitral process itself;
> (c) Provide a means of preserving assets out of which a subsequent award may be satisfied; or
> (d) Preserve evidence that may be relevant and material to the resolution of the dispute."

---

1. N. BLACKABY and C. PARTASIDES with A. REDFERN AND M. HUNTER, *Redfern and Hunter on International Commercial Arbitration*, fifth ed. (Oxford University Press 2009) para. 5.24.
2. UNCITRAL Model Law on International Commercial Arbitration 1985 with amendments adopted in 2006.

Most modern rules, however, which, unlike the Model Law, are directed to the parties rather than to legislatures, provide a less prescriptive power and hence arguably meet a wider purpose. Several institutions delineate the power by reference to interim measures to what the tribunal "deems appropriate";[3] others refer to "whatever measures it [the tribunal] deems necessary";[4] and others hedge their bets by referring to "it deems necessary or appropriate"[5] or "it deems necessary or proper".[6]

Moreover, the revised 2010 UNCITRAL Arbitration Rules (UNCITRAL Rules), which are based on the amended 2006 Model Law, qualify the examples referred to in paragraphs (a)-(d) of Art. 17(2) of the Model Law with the introductory words "for example and without limitation". This less prescriptive form of power arguably meets a need in certain cases to go beyond maintaining the status quo to protect the wider legal rights of a party and extends, inter alia, to the making of provisional orders for payment or provisional awards.

In a recent case in the Privy Council in London in the context of the grant of a court injunction Lord Hoffmann stated:

> "It is often said that the purpose of an interlocutory injunction is to preserve the status quo, but it is of course impossible to stop the world pending trial. The court may order a defendant to do something or not to do something else, but such restrictions on the defendant's freedom of action will have consequences, for him and for others, which a court has to take into account. The purpose of such an injunction is to improve the chances of the court being able to do justice after a determination of the merits at the trial. At the interlocutory stage, the court must therefore assess whether granting or withholding an injunction is more likely to produce a just result."[7]

An improved chance of "being able to do justice after a determination of the merits" must, in the modern global world, also be the broad and ultimate goal and purpose of interim measures in arbitrations and encapsulate under the rubric of doing justice, the enforceability of any award made. In an arbitral context, based on private contract rather than a national judicial system, it is necessary to add an additional limb to this goal, namely the need to ensure and preserve the integrity of the arbitration.

However, it is "not generally the purpose of such measures to improve as opposed to protect the position of one of the parties relative to the other as at the time of the

---

3. E.g. Art. 28(1) International Chamber of Commerce Arbitration and ADR Rules 2012 (ICC Rules); Art. 26.1 Arbitration Rules of the Singapore International Arbitration Centre (5th Edition, 1 April 2013) (SIAC Rules); Art. 32(1) of the Arbitration Rules 2010 of the Arbitration Institute of the Stockholm Chamber of Commerce (SCC Rules).

4. E.g. Art. 21(1) International Dispute Resolution Procedures (Including Mediation and Arbitration Rules) Rules Amended and Effective 1 June 2009 (ICDR Procedures); Rule 37 American Arbitration Association (AAA) Commercial Arbitration Rules 2013.

5. E.g. Art. 26(1) Swiss Chambers' Arbitration Rules 2012 (Swiss Rules).

6. E.g. Art. 21(1) China International Economic Trade and Arbitration Commission Rules of Arbitration (CIETAC Rules).

7. *National Commercial Bank Jamaica Ltd v. Olint Corpn Ltd* [2009] 1 WLR 1405 at 1409 A-B.

application".[8] Nor is its purpose to make orders which amount to "a possible amendment of the parties' agreements".[9]

Thus interim measures are frequently sought to prevent a party taking a tactical and unmerited advantage over its opposing party. Orders preventing dissipation of assets to defeat an award are a prime example, but there are many other variants of such "guerrilla tactics"[10] which interim measures are intended to prevent.

It is certainly not the purpose of interim measures to enable less scrupulous parties to use them for tactical ends by bringing frivolous or unmeritorious or unsubstantiated applications in an attempt to derail the arbitral process or to pressurize the opposite party to settle. As stated above, such applications can not only lead to delay in the progress of the arbitration, but also put the other party to unnecessary expense simultaneously distracting it from the main issues in the arbitration while it gathers evidence to, and concentrates its efforts on, defeating the application. Moreover, such applications have an additional sting if the opposing party is a small enterprise with limited funds and the requesting party a large conglomerate with unlimited funds.

Aside from purely tactical manoeuvres it does not appear that enough consideration is always given to the realistic chances of obtaining such interim relief. This may be partly due to the lack of clear guidelines or standards, but more likely to the lack of appreciation by parties and their legal advisers of the need for sufficient evidence to bolster a party's argument.

It is noteworthy, for instance, that in the recent Bulletin on "Interim, Conservatory and Emergency Measures in ICC Arbitration"[11] of the twenty-five ICC interim awards[12] between 1999 and 2008 referred to, only ten requests were granted. It is, of course, not known whether these statistics are reflective of a wider position in relation to interim measures in commercial arbitration.[13] This is not only because they only provide a snapshot of a selection of such awards from one institution, but also because they appear to exclude interim measures granted by way of order, which means of granting interim relief one suspects represents by far the greater majority of interim measures sought and/or granted.

Unfortunately, there is no real deterrent to such tactical or unmeritorious applications other than a possible immediate costs sanction and the potential, but probably short-lived, wrath of the tribunal, both of which consequences may seem a small price to pay for the perceived tactical advantage. There is no gateway that has to be passed before an application can be made nor prior arbitral costs that have to be incurred. A requesting party is entitled to make such an application as of right subject to the three prior requisites set out in Sect. IV.*1* below.

---

8. ICC Case No. 12361, Interim Award, "Interim, Conservatory and Emergency Measures in ICC Arbitration", 22 ICC Int'l. Ct. Arb. Bull., Special Supplement (2011).

9. ICC Case No 10648 Interim Award. *Op. cit.*, fn. 8.

10. Günter J. HORVATH and Stephan WILSKE *Guerrilla Tactics in International Arbitration* (Kluwer Law International 2013).

11. *Op. cit.*, fn. 8.

12. Including one Interim Measures Agreement.

13. An informal survey of about thirty international arbitral practitioners conducted by the author for her talk at the ICCA Miami Congress, April 2014, found that approximately 50 per cent of applications for interim measures, taking account of all types of measures, were successful.

Given that arbitral tribunals should grant interim relief only for legitimate purposes on genuine grounds, there needs to be an awareness among the international arbitration community of broad, recognized international standards rather than leaving such applications to an open-ended exercise of the arbitral tribunal's discretion. As the international arbitral community expands across continents to meet the increasing workload, it is as important for practitioners as arbitrators to have some basic framework by which to judge applications for interim relief. It enables arbitral tribunals to eliminate the tactical and unmeritorious and to assess on recognized principles the genuine applications. But equally, it may make advisers think twice before bringing unmeritorious or tactical applications, though it is unlikely to eliminate them altogether.

III.   THE NATURE OF INTERIM MEASURES

The potential range of interim measures is infinite, dependent on the facts of the particular case. Their inherent value is that they can be adjusted to meet the facts of a particular case. But what is an interim measure? The Secretary-General in his report at the thirty-third session of UNCITRAL in 2000,[14] at the beginning of the discussions on the revised Model Law in relation to interim measures, described their characteristics as: "[M]easures ... given at the request of one party, made in the form of an order or an award and intended to be temporary, pending a final outcome of the arbitration."

In some cases an interim measure is in reality more procedural than substantive, for example an order preventing a party from disclosing the confidences of the arbitration – is this an interim measure or a measure relating to the conduct of the arbitration? – there are differing views. However, arguably anti-suit orders from tribunals, although likewise relative to the due process of the arbitration, are more in the nature of a substantive order.

Some types of measures straddle both categories and could be termed either procedural or substantive. Such an instance would be the preservation of evidence or the subject matter of the arbitration. The preservation of documents or even samples or an order to permit inspection by experts of a construction site or building might fall into the former category, whilst an order forbidding the sale of shares or equipment would fall into the latter category.

Undoubtedly, the preponderance of applications for interim measures are substantive in nature. They in turn fall broadly into two categories: those which relate to the dispute itself and those which relate to securing the effectiveness of an award. The former, particularly claims which relate to contractual performance in their various guises, include such measures as preventing a call on a guarantee or a letter of credit, or suspending the effect of a company resolution, preventing a party from walking away from a contract or requiring it to desist from doing something in breach of contract.

---

14. United Nations Commission on International Trade Law Working Group on Arbitration. (UNCITRAL Working Group): Thirty-third Session Vienna, 20 November-1 December 2000: Report of the Secretary-General.

The latter are likewise wide-ranging. They include applications for security not only for the legal or other costs of the arbitration,[15] but also for the claim itself. This can be by way of guarantee, attachment of assets, payment into an escrow account or other appropriate means. Additionally, there are applications for provisional orders or awards for actual or allegedly undisputed sums due or unpaid deposits or payment of instalments due under a contract. A few cross the line and payment is ordered as a partial award.

The substantive nature of such measures means that they can have long-term effects on business irrespective of the temporary nature of the order. They can affect cash flow; credit rating; business development; share value and other aspects of normal trading. Such repercussions are potentially even more uncertain when many parties are part of a group structure with inter-company financial and other links often across national borders. Thus, the classic statement that interim measures are, as eponymously described, interim or temporary, may, at least so far as their effects go, no longer be wholly accurate in the world of global business and instant communications.

It is particularly in the context of such substantive provisional measures that tribunals have to be alert to tactical ploys and unmeritorious applications aimed at putting one party at a commercial disadvantage rather than levelling the playing field so that justice prevails. Yet at the same time, in genuine cases, tribunals need to be able to feel that they can act robustly to ensure that neither the process nor the result is jeopardized.

IV.   THE APPROACH

It is against this background of the purpose and nature of interim measures that the approach of tribunals to the granting of interim measures should be analyzed and assessed.

1.   The Three Prerequisites

There are three initial pre-requisites to the grant of any interim measures, to which the rest of the commentary in this Paper is subject, namely:

(i) The absence of anything in the law of the seat, lex arbitri, which precludes or restricts such measures[16] and the desirability of a provision that permits them.[17]
(ii) The agreement of the parties to empower the arbitral tribunal to issue interim measures pursuant either to institutional or similar rules or otherwise and the absence of any limitation or agreement to the contrary in the arbitration agreement or otherwise. Such consent is of course fundamental to the jurisdiction of the tribunal to grant interim measures. It does not, in most jurisdictions, exclude the court's jurisdiction, which is

---

15. The author's informal survey referred to in fn. 13 indicated that a surprisingly large number of applications for security for costs are being made. A contributing factor may be the greater use of third-party funding.
16. E.g. Italy Art. 818 of the Italian Code of Civil Procedure which provides: "The arbitrators may not grant attachment or other interim measures of protection."
17. E.g. Sects. 38 and 39 of the English Arbitration Act 1996.

often invoked before the constitution of the tribunal and/or at other times, depending on the law of the seat. However in investor-state arbitration, ICSID tribunals invariably have exclusive jurisdiction to order provisional relief.[18]

(iii) The tribunal needs to be constituted and have prima facie jurisdiction.[19] The exception to this is the use of an emergency arbitrator which is increasingly being used and appears in many revised institutional rules.[20] A mere challenge to the tribunal's jurisdiction does not prevent the tribunal from ordering interim measures.[21] However, tribunals do not have jurisdiction over third parties and measures which impact on third parties cannot be made.[22]

2.   Various Institutional Rules

The parties' agreement is frequently reflected in the institutional rules used in the particular arbitration, but not always. These rules provide a framework for the application of the tribunal's powers and exercise of discretion, but there is limited uniformity in the guidance they give. Several of these adopt a broad approach leaving the tribunal an unfettered discretion to do what it deems is "appropriate" both as to whether to grant such measures and the terms thereof. A few examples serve to make the point: Art. 28 of the ICC Rules (2012) provides:

> "*Conservatory and Interim Measures*
> 1. … the arbitral tribunal may, at the request of a party, order any interim or conservatory measure *it deems appropriate*. The arbitral tribunal may make the granting of any such measure subject to *appropriate security* being furnished by the requesting party. Any such measure shall take the form of an order, giving reasons, or of an award, as the arbitral tribunal considers appropriate."[23]
> (Emphasis added)

Art. 26.1 of the SIAC Rules (2013) provides:

> "The Tribunal may, at the request of a party, issue an order or an award granting an injunction or any other interim relief *it deems appropriate*. The Tribunal may

---

18. Arts. 26 and 47 of the Convention on the Settlement of Investment Disputes between States and Nationals of Other States (ICSID Convention) and Rule 39 of the International Centre for Settlement of Investment Disputes (ICSID) Arbitration Rules. See also: Yves FORTIER C.C., Q.C.: "Investor-State Arbitration: 'Interim Measures: An Arbitrator's Provisional Views'", Fordham Law School Conference on International Arbitration and Mediation; Dan SAROOSHI, "Provisional Measures and Investment Treaty Arbitration", 29 Arbitration International (2013, no. 3).

19. E.g. *Sergei Paushok, CJSC Golden East Company, CJSC Vostokneftgaz Company v. The Government of Mongolia*: Ad hoc investment arbitration conducted under UNCITRAL Rules (1985 Version).

20. E.g. Art. 29 of the ICC Rules 2012.

21. Gary BORN, *International Commercial Arbitration* (Wolters Kluwer 2009) pp. 1992-1993. ICC Case No. 12351. Interim Award. *Op. cit.*, fn. 8.

22. E.g. ICC Case 10062 Interim Award. *Op. cit.*, fn.8.

23. *Op. cit.*, fn. 3.

order the party requesting interim relief to provide appropriate security in connection with the relief sought."[24] (Emphasis added)

Art. 26 of the Swiss Rules provides:

"Interim Measures of Protection
(1) At the request of a party, the arbitral tribunal may grant any interim measures *it deems necessary or appropriate*. Upon the application of any party or, in exceptional circumstances and with prior notice to the parties, on its own initiative, the arbitral tribunal may also modify, suspend or terminate any interim measures granted.
(2) Interim measures may be granted in the form of an interim award. The arbitral tribunal shall be entitled to order the provision of appropriate security."[25] (Emphasis added)

Art. 32 of the SCC Rules provides:

"(1) The Arbitral Tribunal may, at the request of a party, grant any interim measures *it deems appropriate*.
(2) The Arbitral Tribunal may order the party requesting an interim measure to provide appropriate security in connection with the measure.
(3) An interim measure shall take the form of an order or an award."[26] (Emphasis added)

Art. 25 of the new LCIA Rules 2014, due to come into effect on 1 October 2014, similarly gives the tribunal a wide discretion, but purports to delineate, albeit very widely, categories of interim and conservatory measures, although the use of the phrase "any relief" in Art. 25.1(ii) is a catch-all:

"25.1 The Arbitral Tribunal shall have the power upon the application of any party, after giving all other parties a reasonable opportunity to respond to such application and upon such terms as the Arbitral Tribunal considers appropriate in the circumstances:
i. to order any respondent party to a claim or cross-claim to provide security for all or part of the amount in dispute, by way of deposit or bank guarantee or in any other manner;
ii. to order the preservation, storage, sale or other disposal of any documents, goods, samples, property, site or thing under the control of any party and relating to the subject-matter of the arbitration; and
iii. to order on a provisional basis, subject to a final decision in an award, any relief which the Arbitral Tribunal would have power to grant in an award,

---

24. *Op. cit.*, fn. 3.
25. *Op. cit.*, fn. 5.
26. *Op. cit.*, fn. 3.

including the payment of money or the disposition of property as between any parties.

Such terms may include the provision by the applicant party of a cross-indemnity, secured in such manner as the Arbitral Tribunal considers appropriate, for any costs or losses incurred by the respondent party in complying with the Arbitral Tribunal's order. Any amount payable under such cross-indemnity and any consequential relief may be decided by the Arbitral Tribunal by one or more awards in the arbitration.

25.2 The Arbitral Tribunal shall have the power upon the application of a party, after giving all other parties a reasonable opportunity to respond to such application, to order any claiming or cross-claiming party to provide or procure security for Legal Costs and Arbitration Costs by way of deposit or bank guarantee or in any other manner and upon such terms as the Arbitral Tribunal considers appropriate in the circumstances...."

3.   UNCITRAL Rules

Art. 17 of the 1985 UNCITRAL Rules provided that a tribunal could order interim measures of protection against a party where it considered it "necessary in respect of the subject-matter of the dispute". Art. 26 of the revised 2010 UNCITRAL Rules, based on the new Model Law has moved away from the test of "necessity" and replaced the old rule with a wider, but more prescriptive rule, and provides:

"1. The arbitral tribunal may, at the request of a party, grant interim measures.
2. An interim measure is any temporary measure by which, at any time prior to the issuance of the award by which the dispute is finally decided, the arbitral tribunal orders a party, for example and without limitation, to:
(a) Maintain or restore the status quo pending determination of the dispute;
(b) Take action that would prevent, or refrain from taking action that is likely to cause, (i) current or imminent harm or (ii) prejudice to the arbitral process itself;
(c) Provide a means of preserving assets out of which a subsequent award may be satisfied; or
(d) Preserve evidence that may be relevant and material to the resolution of the dispute.
3. The party requesting an interim measure under paragraphs 2 (a) to (c) shall satisfy the arbitral tribunal that:
(a) Harm not adequately reparable by an award of damages is likely to result if the measure is not ordered, and such harm substantially outweighs the harm that is likely to result to the party against whom the measure is directed if the measure is granted; and
(b) There is a reasonable possibility that the requesting party will succeed on the merits of the claim. The determination on this possibility shall not affect the discretion of the arbitral tribunal in making any subsequent determination.
4. With regard to a request for an interim measure under paragraph 2 (d), the requirements in paragraphs 3 (a) and (b) shall apply only to the extent the arbitral tribunal considers appropriate.

....

> 6. The arbitral tribunal may require the party requesting an interim measure to provide appropriate security in connection with the measure.
>
> ....
>
> 8. The party requesting an interim measure may be liable for any costs and damages caused by the measure to any party if the arbitral tribunal later determines that, in the circumstances then prevailing, the measure should not have been granted. The arbitral tribunal may award such costs and damages at any point during the proceedings...."

Thus with the exception of the UNCITRAL Rules, no real attempt has been made to assist tribunals in determining how to approach the exercise of their discretion. Even these rules are not all-embracing in their guidance. The UNCITRAL Rules were the product of extensive discussion and much deliberation, the Working Group recognizing that the UNCITRAL Rules need to be applicable to all types of arbitration irrespective of the subject matter of the dispute which would have made the remedy "overly-restrictive"[27] and adaptable to a variety of circumstances. The starting point was the Model Law, but the UNCITRAL Rules adapted the Model Law in several respects recognizing that the former were directed to parties and the latter to legislatures.

Aside from the absence of provisions relating to enforcement and ex parte preliminary orders featured in the revised Model Law, three changes are relevant.[28] First, the use of the phrase "for example and without limitation" at the beginning of Art. 26(1) of the UNCITRAL Rules provides for a wider range of circumstances and conditions in which interim measures are allowed than those set out in the Model Law; secondly, the separation in Art. 26(2)(b) of "current or imminent harm" from "prejudice to the arbitral process" enlarges the category of potential matters to be prevented or refrained from; and thirdly, the addition of the words "then prevailing" after "circumstances" in Art. 26(8) meets the concern expressed early on in the UNCITRAL Working Group that the party requesting the measure took the risk of causing damage even if it had made the request in good faith and disclosed all relevant material.

Undoubtedly the UNCITRAL Rules will be widely used, but in the many cases where they are not, the debate will linger as to the need for international norms or standards and whether or not those in the Model Law or the UNCITRAL Rules should act as a guide. On the one hand, it can be argued that the absence of standards or criteria enables a tribunal to tailor the remedy to the facts of the particular arbitration and particular application. On the other hand, the absence of any basic norms can lead to widely differing approaches. This in turn can only encourage ill-advised applications by parties who want to try their luck for tactical reasons and simultaneously discourage

---

27. Report of the Working Group on Arbitration on the work of its forty-fifth session (Vienna, 11-15 September 2006) UNCITRAL 45th Session Working Group Report Forty-fifth session, UN Doc. A/CN.9/614, UNCITRAL, Fortieth session (25 June-12 July 2007) para. 105.

28. Lee Anna TUCKER: "Interim Measures Under Revised UNCITRAL Arbitration Rules; Comparison to Model Law Reflects Greater Flexibility and Remaining Uncertainty", 1 International Commercial Arbitration Brief (2011, no. 1).

parties whose lawyers cannot with any conviction advise their clients as to the likely outcome or the impact on the overall proceedings.

V.   STANDARDS AND NORMS – GENERAL CONSIDERATIONS

1.   Prescription Versus Flexibility

The case for having certain basic universally accepted international norms under whose umbrella tribunals can exercise their discretion to grant interim relief according to the facts of the particular application is compelling. Interim measures granted by tribunals can have a draconian effect and almost invariably cannot be appealed to state courts.

What is much less clear is whether such a set of international standards exists and, if so, what those standards are. As stated earlier, one of the problems is the lack of reliable information as to how commercial arbitrators deal with such applications. Provisional measures in investment treaty cases, which are publicly available, have different considerations to be borne in mind, not least that one party is sovereign, but do offer some guidance. From the limited material available one can deduce that there is a broad consensus that there has to be a balancing of risk, but how that is done and the emphasis given to other aspects, such as urgency, preserving the status quo, can vary.

Moreover, the sea shift in global commerce, the proliferation of electronic and instantaneous communications, the greater number of practitioners in the field of international arbitration, many of whom are relatively inexperienced in international arbitration, the potential for increased use of tactical applications, require that norms which were acceptable even a decade ago, may need to be reassessed or adjusted. The importance in appropriate cases of the ability to grant such interim measures means that international arbitration has to be able to meet the need.

Equally important to the issue of any standards is the balance between the prescriptiveness of those standards and the flexibility they give to the tribunal to meet the justice of the particular case. Too prescriptive and the tribunal loses the ability to tailor the remedy to the case. Too wide and there can be no yardstick by which the various assessments can be made.

2.   What Law Should Be Applied?

There also remains the important question of the law by which any such standards should be applied: Is it the lex arbitri, the law governing the parties' underlying contract or relationship or international standards? Gary Born argues that: "The better view is that international sources [i.e. awards] provide the appropriate standards for granting provisional measures in international arbitration."[29] There is considerable force in this view, but there are only a limited number of such awards publicly available.

The supervisory jurisdiction of the seat empowers tribunals with either expansive or curtailed powers, as the case may be, to exercise procedural and substantive jurisdiction. But within those defined powers the tribunal has a free rein subject to the

---

29. Gary BORN, *op. cit.*, fn. 21, p. 1978.

agreement of the parties. It may, of course, be different in the case of jurisdictional issues, where the law of the seat may be compelling in the absence of another obvious law. The law of the contract or the relationship between the parties may have some bearing on the assessment of the merits of the claim for the purpose of the application, but it is difficult to see, absent anything specific in the contract, how otherwise it can affect the exercise of a jurisdiction which may bear no relation to the law of the contract. Thus, the need for a framework of international understanding as to the process of assessment to be undertaken by tribunals when considering interim measures.

3,   The Evidence

Finally, by way of preliminary comment, in any discussion about interim measures in the context of standards and their application, it is often forgotten that tribunals can only make decisions on the material put before them. However strong one party's argument is, it is of little value without the evidence to support it. Equally parties frequently fail to make clear precisely what order they are seeking and if orders are to be made there needs to be clarity and certainty as to what they order. It is thus incumbent on parties and their lawyers to provide the necessary evidence, and many fall at this hurdle. Thus it is therefore equally important for the parties, as for the tribunal, to know to what factors such evidence should go.

VI.   THE INITIAL GATEWAY

First, the tribunal has to make some sort of assessment of the merits of the case to eliminate frivolous and hopeless cases. However, such assessment cannot amount to anything resembling a pre-judgment of the merits. Various tests have been suggested. Should the test be that "there is a reasonable possibility that the requesting party will succeed on the merits of the claim" as prescribed by the UNCITRAL Rules or a "prima facie case"?

Such phrases raise more questions than they answer. What does "reasonable possibility" or "reasonable chance"[30] actually mean? Does it equate with a success rate of less than 50 per cent; more than 25 per cent; more than just a possibility or a chance, but less than a reasonable probability, or is it simply the antonym to frivolous? Is there any difference if it is a non-counterclaiming respondent making the application? What happens if the view taken is that both parties have a "reasonable possibility of success"? Does the requesting party have to discharge the onus in relation to the chances of it succeeding or is it enough to show that there is "a serious issue" to be tried between the parties? Is it sufficient if the requesting party merely has a good case on that part of its claim to which the application is made?

Then there are the more peripheral questions. Does the nature of the application have an impact? Would a higher threshold be needed for say an order to prevent

---

30. Natalie VOSER: "Interim Relief in International Arbitration: The Tendency Towards a More Business-Oriented Approach", 1 Dispute Resolution International (2007, no. 2).

someone terminating a contract than an order to prevent a party divulging confidential information from the arbitration? Does the time when the application is made affect the position? If made at the outset after the Request for Arbitration has been served, the tribunal may know little of the merits and particularly of the defence.

In looking at this question what law should the tribunal apply if no law is designated in the contract? Does it have to make a provisional determination as to the applicable law? What if one party does not appear — does the tribunal have to be more — or less — convinced as to the prospects of success?

Clearly there has to be some basic threshold over which a requesting party must pass to rule out applications based on purely frivolous or hopeless claims, but it has to be a flexible one for the tribunal to resolve in a particular case. It will be much easier to determine whether a claimant has a reasonable possibility or chance of succeeding in a claim under a guarantee than in a complex multi-party financial fraud and ultimately it will depend on the material before the tribunal at the time.

In *Sergei Paushok, CJSC Golden East Company, CJSC Vostokneftgaz Company v. The Government of Mongolia*, an ad hoc investment arbitration conducted under UNCITRAL Rules (1985 Version), the tribunal stated that:

> "At this stage, the Tribunal need not go beyond whether a reasonable case has been made which, if the facts alleged are proven, might possibly lead the Tribunal to the conclusion that an award could be made in favour of Claimants. Essentially, the Tribunal needs to decide only that the claims made out are not frivolous or obviously outside the competence of the Tribunal. To do otherwise would require the Tribunal to proceed to a determination of the facts and, in practice, to a hearing on the merits of the case, a lengthy and complicated process which would defeat the very purpose of interim measures."

There is much to be said for a test related to the nature of the issue or dispute, i.e. a serious as opposed to a frivolous or hopeless one, but the alternative of equating the test with the requesting party's case seems to be the accepted approach in international arbitration. The obligation to establish a reasonable possibility of success does not impose too onerous a burden on the requesting party nor constrain the tribunal too much in making its initial assessment as to whether the first hurdle is met. It would be a bold tribunal which refused an application on this basis alone unless the chances of success were obviously hopeless or the claim frivolous.

VII. THE FACTORS IN THE BALANCING EXERCISE

The much more difficult question is how a tribunal should approach the exercise of its discretion to grant or refuse an application for interim measures and what factors it should take into account. In other words in what circumstances is it deemed "appropriate" to award interim relief?

1.   The Nature of the Harm or Prejudice to Be Shown by the Requesting Party

The starting point is the obligation, and onus, on the part of the requesting party to show on the evidence a need for the remedy requested. Traditionally this was expressed as the need to show a risk of irreparable harm. However, as Natalie Voser argues in her article written before the revised 2010 UNCITRAL Rules: "[T]he trend in international arbitration today is for a more commercial or economic approach, which equates irreparable harm with substantial prejudice."[31] The ICC approach is that an order should be made to prevent irreparable or substantial harm in sense of "a sufficient degree of harm for it to be categorized as irreparable".[32]

The UNCITRAL Rules, however, retain the reference to "harm" in the context both of some of the matters to be protected (Art. 26(2)(b)(i)) and also in the balancing exercise "harm not adequately reparable by an award of damages" (Art. 26(3)(a)). The Working Group considered this phrase "less rigid" than "irreparable harm". "Prejudice" only appears in the context of the arbitral process so that "it would appear distinct" from "current or imminent harm".[33] The reference to "prejudice" comes from the Model Law, which in 2006 introduced this second limb to give tribunals the power to prevent obstruction or delay of the arbitral process, including by issuing anti-suit injunctions a remedy available in some countries.[34]

However, the difference between "prejudice" and "harm" is largely semantic – they are synonymous, the only difference being that the word "prejudice" seems to slip off legal lips more readily than "harm" and is more frequently used in the context of legal proceedings.

In this context only very limited guidance can be given by investor-state cases. Historically, an approach based both on "necessity" as opposed to appropriateness and "irreparable" harm or prejudice has been regarded as the test, a relatively high threshold adopted from the International Court of Justice (ICJ). The reported cases using UNCITRAL Rules are based on the 1985 version and there is yet to appear a body of law based on the revised 2010 UNCITRAL Rules. In his article, Dan Sarooshi[35] argues that ICSID tribunals should adopt a lower threshold test of a "significant harm or threat" to the parties when deciding whether provisional measures are "necessary", rather than using the ICJ's higher threshold of "irreparable damage".

In fact in *Sergei Paushok & ors v. The Government of Mongolia,* supra, the tribunal considered that "irreparable harm" in international law had a flexible meaning commenting on the absence of any reference to the phrase in the revised Art. 17A of the Model Law.

---

31. *Ibid.*
32. Commentary by Ali YEŞILIRMAK in ICC Bulletin, *op.cit.,* fn. 8.
33. Report of Working Group II (Arbitration and Conciliation) on the work of its fiftieth session (New York, 9-13 February 2009) UNCITRAL, 42nd Sess., UN Doc. A/CN.9/669 (29 June-17 July 2009).
34. Report of the Working Group on Arbitration and Conciliation on the work of its forty-third session (Vienna, 3-7 October 2005) UNCITRAl, 39th Sess., UN Doc. A/CN.9/589 (19 June-7 July 2006).
35. *Op. cit.,* fn. 18.

The UNCITRAL Rules have been changed for a purpose and it is reasonable to assume that broadly they reflect the current approach to interim relief. However whichever of the phrases referred to in the first three paragraphs of this Section (VII.*1*) is used there remain other aspects which require consideration.

First, if the harm is not current and ongoing, what degree of risk of harm is necessary – is it a real risk or a substantial risk, a reasonable risk, a sufficient degree of risk[36] or just more than a minimal or fanciful risk? The UNCITRAL Rules speak to the temporal nature of the harm "current or imminent" rather than the degree of risk, but the risk could be high though not necessarily imminent.

Second, at what time should the risk be assessed? Should it be at the time the contract was entered into or at the time of the application? For example where a party failed to take adequate security and provided for payment by instalments, it was not entitled to seek protection because of a deterioration in the paying party's financial position particularly in the absence of any evidence of an imminent insolvency or the implementation of a scheme to strip the paying party of its assets.[37]

Finally, with what degree of certainty is a tribunal able to determine that the harm cannot be adequately reparable or compensable in damages, and what if the claim is not one for damages in the first place? How can this be assessed going forward when what happens in the future may be unpredictable and/or affected by actions of third parties not before the tribunal or global economic issues.

In some cases, the position will be clear. Damage to someone's reputation or the viability of a business may be classic examples of situations where the damage cannot be adequately repaired at a later date. However, the position becomes more difficult where the harm is potentially reparable by damages, but the financial situation of the party against whom an order is sought is uncertain or not known, for instance where the party against whom an order is sought is a special purpose vehicle or holding company with no independent assets or where the beneficial owners are not known. If the requesting party knowingly entered into a business relationship with such a party is that a relevant fact? Thus a claimant was refused an interim order for payment into an escrow account relating to an alleged breach of a framework agreement on the basis that the opposing party was a holding company and there existed a reasonable risk that inter-company restructuring could lead to an inability to pay.[38]

As can be seen from the above uncertainties, it is not desirable to put the quality of harm that a requesting party has to show into a semantic straightjacket and thereby remove the freedom and flexibility inherent in the arbitral process to assess the initial justification for the remedy. A broad description provides the necessary framework to provide consistency of approach while simultaneously permitting variations of implementation and enabling unmeritorious claims to be weeded out. A composite of the various permutations above is thus suggested (see below, p. 259).

---

36. ICC case No. 9950, Interim Award. *Op. cit.*, fn. 8, where the sufficiency was not further elaborated.
37. ICC Case No. 12361, Interim Award. *Op. cit.*, fn. 8.
38. ICC Case No. 14287, Interim Award. *Op. cit.*, fn. 8.

2. *The Tribunal's Evaluation*

It is of course the harm or prejudice to both parties which has to be balanced – the need for proportionality. Just as the requesting party has to produce evidence to show that prejudice or harm is likely to result which cannot be adequately compensated in damages if the protective measure is not ordered, so the opposing party has to indicate the harm or prejudice such a measure would cause it and/or which likewise cannot be adequately compensated by some form of counter-security from the requesting party. Similar considerations will come into play in assessing the opposing risks as those set out above.

The tribunal's task is thus to evaluate the respective positions of the parties and balance the risks as shown by the evidence. The UNCITRAL Rules state that the harm to the requesting party must "substantially outweigh" that of the opposing party. Other writers suggest that the harm or damage resulting from the imposition of the interim measure should not be disproportionately advantageous to the requesting party compared with any detriment to the opposing party.

However a more nuanced result may be the outcome of this evaluation such that the relative positions of the parties are evenly balanced. In particular the position may be ameliorated by the use of cross-undertakings, the provision of security in the form of bank guarantees or otherwise, or the offer of more limited or different undertakings. Moreover other factors may come into play in determining whether or not in the exercise of its discretion, the order as requested should be made.

3. *Five Other Factors*

The following are five such matters which may or may not be relevant:

(1) The status quo

First, the relevance of the status quo. Maintaining or restoring the status quo has been and remains one of the prime objectives of many orders for interim relief and is reflected in Art. 26(2)(a) of the UNCITRAL Rules. However, it is far from clear at what date the status quo should be judged – the date of the application, the date the relief is granted, the date the dispute arose or the date of the commencement of the arbitration. Huge changes can occur during these time lags, for example alleged breaches of a contract can lead to threats to terminate and then to actual termination of the contract. In an interim award in ICC Case No. 9950 where the tribunal granted an application made by a counter-claiming respondent for security for a subsequent award, it stated that "[t]he status quo should … be judged as at the date the arbitration was initiated".[39]

There are numerous examples of interim orders which maintain the status quo until the Final Award, such as orders to prevent a sale of shares or for the preservation of property, but one can conceive of other situations where the protection of a party's rights might necessitate more radical orders which actually alter the status quo. Sometimes it is in any event too late to restore the status quo. It is suggested that the

---

39. *Op. cit.*, fn. 8.

reference to status quo means no more than seeking to ensure that the ability to make an award at the end of the day and the process by which it is to be achieved is not jeopardized by actions of one of the parties. Maintaining or restoring the status quo is clearly one of the key ways of achieving this goal in relevant circumstances.

(2) The nature and extent of the relief sought
Second, the nature and extent of the relief sought. This is one of the most critical considerations for a tribunal to take into account. There may be little difficulty in ordering a party to desist from placing news of arbitral proceedings in the media, a form of aggravation affecting the due process of the arbitral proceedings, but mandatory orders may be of a different order. They can range from ordering the continued performance of a contract; to enabling a shareholder to retain its voting rights to the ordering of provisional payments. Inevitably in cases where the potential downside for the opposing party is greater, the greater the care that has to be exercised in determining where the balance of convenience lies. Moreover tribunals have to be alert to the impact of any order sought on third parties.[40]

(3) Urgency and delay
Urgency has always historically been a key requirement for an interim order, but it does not appear in any of the modern rules. The UNCITRAL Rules refer to "current or imminent harm". In the context of investor-state arbitrations it has been said that:

> "[t]he concept of urgency appears to have evolved and relaxed somewhat over the years, morphing from a requirement that the harm be immediately likely and imminent to the seemingly more widespread standard today that the harm occur prior to the tribunal's issuance of the final award".[41]

In some cases urgency as understood in common parlance will be self-evident, but in others less so. If the matter is really urgent, then parties may be able to make use of an Emergency Arbitrator. But urgency for these purposes is often in reality no more than that the order cannot await the Final Award. The more critical questions will be the degree of risk and the nature of the harm.

The corollary, however, might be that by knowingly delaying bringing an application without good reason, a party has exacerbated the situation or, more frequently, has undermined its case as to the real need for such an order in the first place.

(4) Alternative protection
Tribunals will always be alert to considering whether or not there is an alternative means of protection which would achieve the same or a similar result with less resultant harm or prejudice. For example where an order is sought to prevent a sale of property, the subject matter of the claim, so that it is available for the hearing, the concern may

---

40. ICC Case No. 10648, Interim Award. *Op. cit.*, fn. 8.
41. Caline MOUAWAD and Elizabeth SILBERT: "A Guide to Interim Measures in Investor-State Arbitration", 29 Arbitration International (2013, no. 3).

be met by ordering an independent expert to inspect and take photographs and provide a report as to condition rather than prevent the sale altogether.

Equally, tribunals frequently order bank guarantees or payments into escrow funds to abide the result rather than order outright payments. Similarly, cross-undertakings and counter-indemnities are a most important consideration when making such orders.

(5) Enforcement

It is not intended in this Paper to deal with the subject of enforcement of awards or orders for interim relief, a topic for a paper in itself, save to note that some institutional rules provide for such relief to be made only by order; others by both orders and awards and others are silent. Issues arise as to the enforceability of such awards under the New York Convention, because ex hypothesi such interim awards are intended to be temporary. Some countries will assist in enforcement if it is the seat of the arbitration[42] and the Model Law has introduced an enforcement regime under Art. 17 H and I.

It is always open to a tribunal to make an order with a more draconian order as a sanction if a party does not comply. In an ICC case in 2013[43] the tribunal ordered the opposing party to produce certain records and to pay over a percentage of certain sales' past and future proceeds. It further ordered that if the opposing party failed to hand over the records within fourteen days it was to pay a lump sum as an interim amount pending the determination of the actual amount of the sale proceeds from the records.

VIII.   CONCLUSION

There is little doubt that interim measures are an extremely useful and increasingly used weapon in an arbitral tribunal's armoury in its ultimate aim to do justice between the parties. It is thus important that this weapon can be readily deployed in the right case and adjusted to the particular facts of the case. In the context of the above analysis this means that any framework of guidance is not too prescriptive.

But what of the tactical missile – or even the Exocet! From the limited evidence available it is likely that approximately 50 per cent or less of applications for interim measures are granted.[44] The majority of applications result in orders rather than awards. Undoubtedly, some applications will be refused simply because the evidence is not good enough; others because the balancing exercise clearly favours the opposing party; and others because the application is perceived to be tactical or unmeritorious. Accordingly, continuing the metaphor from the title of this Paper, when the tribunal pulls the trigger it needs a framework to discourage and, if brought, to minimize the likelihood of such tactical or unmeritorious applications succeeding.

There does seem to be a broad but unwritten overall consensus of approach by arbitral tribunals in international commercial arbitration, but it is sufficiently variable

---

42. Sect. 39 of the English Arbitration Act 1996.

43. *American Energy Group, Ltd v. Hycarbex American Energy Inc & ors.*

44. See fn. 13 and p. 244, fourth paragraph, above. It is a higher figure than which appears from the ICC Bulletin, *op. cit.*, fn. 8.

as to suggest the need for a more recognized framework. Of course UNCITRAL has sought to provide this, but not everyone will agree with the end result as set out in the UNCITRAL Rules. The basis of awarding interim measures has undoubtedly evolved in recent years to cater for the growth in arbitration, the expectations of its users and the greater need for suitable interim remedies in a fast-moving commercial world.

With considerable timidity this Paper concludes by drawing together the various threads set out above and suggesting some deliberately very broad parameters as to how an international commercial tribunal should approach applications for interim relief.

The tribunal needs to be satisfied that:

i. there is a reasonable possibility that the requesting party could succeed on the merits of the dispute;

ii. the evidence establishes a sufficient degree of risk of substantial harm or prejudice to the requesting party from the action or inaction threatened, taken or likely to be taken by the opposing party which cannot adequately be repaired or compensated by damages or otherwise if the order requested is not made; and

iii. the degree of greater harm likely to be suffered by the requesting party is such that when balanced against that likely to be suffered by the opposing party and taking all other relevant considerations into account justifies the granting of the order sought or a similar order so as to ensure both the integrity of the arbitral process and ultimate justice between the parties.

Interim Measures in Arbitration: Towards a Better Injury Standard

Francisco González de Cosío[*]

I.   INTRODUCTION

Interim measures are instruments procuring justice and efficiency. Without them, regrettable outcomes ensue, be they impracticable awards, swollen indemnification orders and unnecessary, less than desirable situations.

A survey of international practice displays a wide consensus on most requirements to be fulfilled to secure interim relief. However, difference exists as to one: the injury standard to satisfy. I wish to focus on this point of contention and advocate in favor of one of the visible standards – which, admittedly, is not the one most often used.

II.   STANDARDS

Diverse standards are observed when assessing the issuance of interim relief: for instance, in "appropriate circumstances"; presence of threat of "not easily reparable prejudice", "serious injury", "grave injury", "substantive prejudice", "irreparable injury". The *precise* difference, however, is not only not easily ascertainable from case law, but often understood differently amongst practitioners and experts using any of them as their analytical frame of reference. One common point of agreement seems to be focusing on whether the injury is of the type which can be remedied with money damages. But apart from this metric, agreement – both conceptual and practical – seems more apparent than real.

Another approach is to perform what some call "balance of interests" or "balance of convenience", which involves the task of not choosing an adjective for the harm complained of, but simply comparing its outcome with what would be required from the interim relief addressee, and then balancing both so as to decide who should prevail: the

* Arbitrator and advocate. González de Cossío Abogados, SC, Mexico City. (<www.gdca.com.mx>).

    I wish to recognize and thank Laura González Luna and Ana Paula Portilla Ariza for their assistance in the elaboration of this work.

moving or the objecting party. In other words, should the costs of the measure be lower than the benefits, it shall be granted. And vice versa.

III.   EMPIRICAL OVERVIEW

The standard of choice tends to vary. To show why, I shall delve into the following four sources of experience: commercial arbitration, investment arbitration, public international law and the works of the United Nations Commission on International Trade Law (UNCITRAL).

1.   Commercial Arbitration

Commercial arbitration is a rich source of authority on the topic. Within this realm, the experience of the International Court of Arbitration of the International Chamber of Commerce (ICC) stands out given the sheer volume of cases and the meticulousness with which they have been analyzed, both in periodic journals[1] and ICC-specialized doctrine.

Review of this corpus of material allows for interesting insights and conclusions. One is that the majority of cases have confined their analysis to "irreparable harm, or serious or actual damage, if the measure requested is not granted".[2]

That this conclusion is warranted may be readily verified in the cases found in the extract section of the cited ICC Bulletin. For instance, "the claimant would not incur any grave and irreparable harm if not granted the sought provisional measure…".[3]

Interestingly, a few years later, Ali Yeşilırmak reexamined the topic and reiterated the conclusion that the most frequently used standard when assessing interim measures is "threat of grave or irreparable damage to the counterparty in the arbitration proceedings".[4]

Albeit that this tendency exists, the cases extracted in Mr. Yeşilırmak's latest piece display examples all across the spectrum – from those requiring "satisfaction of

---

1. Several volumes of the ICC Bulletin have analyzed the topic: the 1993 ICC Bulletin focusing on Conservatory and Provisional Measures in International Arbitration; 10 ICC Bulletin (Spring 1999, no. 1), where an experienced practitioner analyzes the topic (Donald Francis DONOVAN, "Powers of the Arbitrators to Issue Procedural Orders, Including Interim Measures of Protection, and the Obligation of Parties to Abide by Such Orders", p. 65); 11 ICC Bulletin (Spring 2000, no. 1), where Mr. Ali YEŞILIRMAK writes an interesting piece on the matter from the ICC perspective (Ali YEŞILIRMAK, "Interim and Conservatory Measures in ICC Arbitral Practice", p. 31); 22 ICC Bulletin, Special Supplement (2011), dedicated to Interim, Conservatory and Emergency Measures in ICC Arbitration, where Ali YEŞILIRMAK takes another stab at the subject (Ali YEŞILIRMAK, "Interim and Conservatory Measures in ICC Arbitral Practice 1999-2008", pp. 5-11).
2. Ali YEŞILIRMAK, "Interim and Conservatory Measures in ICC Arbitral Practice", 11 ICC Bulletin, (Spring 2000, no. 1) p. 31 at p. 34.
3. ICC case 8113, Partial Award, October 1995, p. 67.
4. Ali YEŞILIRMAK, "Interim and Conservatory Measures in ICC Arbitral Practice 1999-2008", 22 ICC Bulletin, Special Supplement (2011) p. 9.

irreparable harm",[5] "imminent damage",[6] "substantial harm",[7] and cases echoing doctrine requiring "irreparable or otherwise substantial harm".[8] Upon analyzing the cases in the 1999-2008 period, the following conclusions which are relevant to our topic are advanced:[9]

(i) "Substantial" harm is to be understood as "irreparable" harm;
(ii) The better standard is "appropriate circumstances" since it is better suited to the language and spirit of the ICC Rules and the needs of international commerce;
(iii) Arbitrators must endeavor to balance the relative harm to each party that may or may not flow from the granting or denial of the measures requested.

Arnaldez, Derains and Hascher's *Recueil*[10] cites ICC Case 10596 of 2000 echoing the "irreparable harm" standard, understood as "significant harm". As to what this means, the following is articulated:

> "monetary loss is not irreparable harm…. Although, strictly speaking, this view may be correct, the arbitral tribunal considers that it would be unreasonable to refuse the relief sought on those grounds…. it would be foolish for the tribunal to wait for a foreseeable, or at least plausibly foreseeable, loss to occur, to then provide for its compensation in the form of damages (assuming that B is entitled to such damages, which is not the issue here), rather than to prevent the loss from occurring in the first place…."[11]

A good way to summarize the ICC experience is by echoing what an authoritative text explains on the matter:

> "Arbitrators have an obligation to try to find an equitable and commercially practicable procedural solution to prevent irreparable and unnecessary injury to the parties…."[12]

Practice under the London Court of International Arbitration (LCIA) Rules mimics the position. As described by a leading treatise:[13]

---

5. ICC Case 11225, Partial Award of 2001; ICC Case 12361, Interim Award of 2003.
6. ICC Case 12122, Partial Award of 2002.
7. ICC Case 12040, Partial Award of 2002. ICC Case 11740, Partial Award of 2002.
8. ICC Case 12361, Partial Award of 2003.
9. 22 ICC Bulletin, Special Supplement: Interim, Conservatory and Emergency Measures in ICC Arbitration (2011) p. 10.
10. Jean-Jacques ARNALDEZ, Yves DERAINS and Dominique HASCHER, *Collection of Arbitral Awards 2001-2007 / Recueil des sentences arbitrales de la CCI 2001-2007* (Wolters Kluwer 2009).
11. *Ibid.*, p. 321.
12. W. Laurence CRAIG, William W. PARK and Jan PAULSSON, *International Chamber of Commerce Arbitation* (Oceana Publications 2000) p. 462.
13. Peter TURNER and Reza MOHTASHAMI, *A Guide to the LCIA Arbitration Rules* (Oxford University Press 2009) p. 168, paras. 6.121-6.122.

"As to the meaning of the notion of 'harm not adequately reparable by an award of damages',[14] it has been suggested that it should be understood in the economic sense:

'In this respect "irreparable" must be understood in an economic, not a literal, sense. It must take account of the fact that it may not always be possible to compensate for actual losses suffered or sullied business reputation through damages.'[15]

Schwartz, however, states the definition construed by arbitral bodies is even broader, in that although 'Anglo-American lawyers often understand "irreparable" harm as meaning harm that cannot readily be compensated by an award of monetary damages', ICC arbitral tribunals have sometimes also construed risk of financial loss to be included within this definition."[16]

2.   Investment Arbitration

Investment arbitration displays its share of interim measures providing insight into our topic. To address them, I shall touch upon the textual point of departure (Sect. *a*) and the case law stemming therefrom (Sect. *b*), so as to finalize with a conclusion (Sect. *c*).

a.   Textual point of departure

Art. 47 of the ICSID Convention states:

"Except as the parties otherwise agree, the Tribunal may, if it considers that the circumstances so require, recommend any provisional measures which should be taken to preserve the respective rights of either party."[17]

Art. 39(1) of the ICSID Arbitration Rules provides:

"At any time after the institution of the proceeding, a party may request that provisional measures for the preservation of its rights be recommended by the Tribunal. The request shall specify the rights to be preserved, the measures the recommendation of which is requested, and the circumstances that require such measures."[18]

---

14. "UNCITRAL Model Law, Art. 17.A(1)(*a*)." (Citation in original.)
15. "*Lew, Mistelis, Kröll* 604." (Citation in original.)
16. "Eric SCHWARTZ, 'The Practices and Experiences of the ICC Court' in *Conservatory and Provisional Measures in International Arbitration* (ICC Publishing 1993) p. 45." (Citation in original.)
17. Convention on the Settlement of Investment Disputes between States and Nationals of Other States (ICSID Convention), Art. 47, p. 24.
18. The Rules of Procedure for Arbitration Proceedings of ICSID (ICSID Arbitration Rules).

Review of the *travaux préparatoires* of the ICSID Convention does not allow for a conclusion other than that the appropriate standard to satisfy was not solved.[19] Two delegates remarked on the matter, however:

> "There would be very few, if any, cases of irreparable damage, because disputes would concern investments and investments could always be valued in terms of money."[20]

> "[P]rovisional measures ought not be prescribed unless absolutely necessary in the circumstances, and if pecuniary compensation would be adequate in lieu of some preliminary measure, then no preliminary measure ought to be prescribed. On that basis, such measures ought to be included in the enforcement provision. That might also have the effect of discouraging tribunals from prescribing preliminary measures save in the most exceptional cases."[21]

And the following conclusory statement:

> "The provision in the Working Paper defines the measures which a tribunal may prescribe as those which are 'necessary for the protection of the rights of the parties'. Several delegations thought the criterion might be spelled out in more detail (by specifying such matters as avoidance of frustration of an eventual award, irreparable damage and urgent necessity and clarifying the term 'rights of the parties') and indication might be given in general terms of what the provisional measures would be ... the latitude given to arbitral tribunals by the Working Paper ... in accordance with generally accepted custom...."[22]

However, no resolution on the matter exists. The reason, one surmises, is that the different views were catered for by the adopted text, as it allows for such matter to be determined by the tribunal. I would also venture to explain that the focus was on other aspects of the topic deemed more salient, such as jurisdiction and the power of the tribunal to issue interim relief. And doctrine reflects this. For instance, Professor

---

19. *History of the ICSID Convention*, International Centre for Settlement of Investment Disputes, Washington, D.C. (1970). Doc. 25, Vol. II, pp. 268-270, Vol. III, pp. 94 and 96; Doc. 27, Vol. II pp. 337-338 and 347, Vol. IV, pp. 103-105 and 115; Doc. 29, Vol. II, p. 442, Vol. III, p. 198; Doc. 31, Vol. II, pp. 515-516, 518 and 523, Vol. III, pp. 315-318 and 325; Doc. 33, paras.70-72, Vol. II, p. 573, Vol. III, p. 384, Vol. IV, pp. 160-161; Doc. 45, Vol. II, pp. 655, 664 and 668, Vol. III, pp. 459-460, 470 and 474, Vol. IV. pp. 239 and 249; Doc. 84, Vol. II, pp. 812-815, Vol. III, pp. 641-644, Vol. IV, pp. 434-437; Doc. 85, Art. 50, Vol. II, p. 818, Vol. III, p. 647, Vol. IV, p. 441; Doc. 104, Art. 50, Vol. II, p. 864, Vol. III, p. 695, Vol. IV, p. 498; Doc. 113, Vol. II, p. 891, Vol. III, p. 723, Vol. IV, p. 530; Doc. 124, Vol. II, p. 939, Vol. III, p. 775 and Vol. IV, p. 591; Doc. 132, para. 40, Vol. II, p. 987; Doc. 142, Art. 47, Vol. IV, p. 640; Doc. 143, Art. 47, Vol. IV, p. 663.
20. Comment voiced by Mr. Tsai (China), *ibid.*, 1968, Vol. II-1, p. 516.
21. Comment articulated by Mr. O'Donovan (Australia), *ibid.*, p. 523.
22. *History of the ICSID Convention*, Vol. II-1, Washington, D.C. (1968) para. 72, p. 573.

Schreuer analyzes the matter but does not posit a standard; he only expresses what most tribunals have done.[23]

b.   *Interpretation*

i.   Irreparable harm

Most cases have used "irreparable harm" as the analytical lodestar: for instance, *Millicon v. Senegal*,[24] *Occidental v. Ecuador*,[25] *Cemex v. Venezuela*,[26] *Tethyan Copper v. Pakistan*,[27] *Tokios Tokelés v. Ukraine*,[28] *Plama Consortium v. Bulgaria*,[29] *Phoenix v. Czech Republic*.[30] In doing so, however, a definition of the concept is usually not advanced. Exceptions exist, however. In *Plama v. Bulgaria* the tribunal stated that "harm is not irreparable if it can be compensated by damages".[31] Understood thus, other cases exist which use the criteria, but do not voice the term of art "irreparable harm", such as *Tanzania Electrical Supply Company Limited v. Independent Power Tanzania Limited*, which favored *sub silentio* the "monetary compensation" standard when it reasoned:

> "There is no reason to believe that TANESCO would be unable to satisfy any award of damages in respect of this...."[32]

---

23. Christoph H. SCHREUER, *The ICSID Convention, A Commentary*, 2nd edn. (Cambridge University Press 2009) p. 776.

24. *Millicom International Operations B.V. and Sentel GSM SA v. The Republic of Senegal* (ICSID Case No. ARB/08/20), Decision on the Application for Provisional Measures Submitted by the Claimants of 24 August 2009, para. 46.

25. *Occidental Petroleum Corporation and Occidental Exploration and Production Company v. The Republic of Ecuador* (ICSID Case No. ARB/06/11), Decision on Provisional Measures, Order of 17 August 2007, para. 59.

26. Where the standard was described to be "irreparable prejudice" (*Cemex Caracas Investments B.V. and Cemex Caracas II Investments B.V. v. Bolivarian Republic of Venezuela* (ICSID Case No. ARB/08/15), Decision on the Claimant's Request for Provisional Measures, Order of 3 March 2010, para. 41).

27. *Tethyan Copper Company Pty Limited v. The Islamic Republic of Pakistan* (ICSID Case No. ARB/12/1), Decision on Claimant's Request for Provisional Measures, Order of 13 December 2012, para. 138.

28. *Tokios Tokelés v. Uraine* (ICSID Case No. ARB/02/18), Procedural Order No. 3, 18 January 2005, para. 8.

29. *Plama Consortium Ltd. v. Bulgaria* (ICSID Case No. ARB/03/24), Order of 6 September 2005, para. 38.

30. "Irreparable prejudice of rights involved" was the standard employed in *Phoenix Action, Ltd. v. The Czech Republic* (ICSID Case No. ARB/06/5), Decision on Provisional Measures, 6 April 2007, paras. 33 and 47.

31. *Plama Consortium Limited v. Republic of Bulgaria* (ICSID Case No. ARB/03/24), Order of 6 September 2005, para. 46.

32. *Tanzania Electric Supply Company Limited v. Independent Power Tanzania Limited* (ICSID Case No. ARB/98/8), Decision on the Respondent's Request for Arbitration, Order of 22 December 1999, para. 18.

Other examples exist that follow this approach. In *Burlington v. Ecuador* the test was "harm not adequately reparable by the award of damages".[33] In *Perenco v. Ecuador and Petroecuador* it was "irreparable loss" ("*pérdida irreparable*"),[34] understood as injury not monetarily compensable.[35] *Occidental v. Ecuador* elaborated that:[36]

> "An order for provisional measures will only be made where such measures are found to be necessary and urgent in order to avoid imminent and irreparable harm."[37]

> "[P]rovisional measures may not be awarded for the protection of the rights of one party where such provisional measures would cause irreparable harm to the rights of the other party...."[38]

In *Quiborax v. Bolivia* the tribunal was specific as to the notion:

> "The Tribunal considers that an irreparable harm is a harm that cannot be repaired by an award of damages."[39]

ii.   Other criteria

Criteria different from "irreparable harm" have also been used. For instance, in *Victor Pey Casado v. Chile* the assessment of the issuance of the measure followed a comparative analysis and whether the concern evoked was "hypothetical", which would not justify the measure.[40] A somewhat similar approach was followed in *Maffezini v. Spain*[41] where the emphasis was the existence of the rights,[42] that the fear not be deemed "hypothetical",[43] and relation to the subject matter of the dispute.[44]

---

33. *Burlington Resources Inc. and Others v. Republic of Ecuador and Empresa Estatal Petróleos del Ecuador (PetroEcuador)* (ICSID Case No. ARB/08/5), Procedural Order No. 1 on Burlington Oriente's Request for Provisional Measures, 29 June 2009, para. 82.

34. *Perenco Ecuador Ltd. v. Republic of Ecuador and Empresa Estatal Petróleos del Ecuador (Petroecuador)* (ICSID Case No. ARB/08/6), Decision on Provisional Measures, 8 May 2009, para. 43.

35. *Ibid.*

36. *Occidental Petroleum Corporation, Occidental Exploration and Production Company v. Republic of Ecuador* (ICSID Case No. ARB/06/11), Decision on Provisional Measures of 17 August 2007, para. 87.

37. Spanish original: "*Sólo puede dictarse una orden de medidas provisionales cuando se llega a la conclusión de que éstas son necesarias y urgentes para evitar perjuicios inminentes e irreparables....*"

38. *Op. cit.*, fn. 36, para. 93. Spanish original: "*no pueden disponerse medidas provisionales para la protección de los derechos de una parte si ellas han de causar perjuicios irreparables para los derechos de la otra parte*".

39. *Quiborax S.A., Non Metallic Minerals S.A. and Allan Fosk Kaplún v. Plurinational State of Bolivia* (ICSID Case ARB/06/2), Decision on Provisional Measures, 26 February 2010, para. 156.

40. *Victor Pey Casado and President Allende Foundation v. Republic of Chile* (ICSID Case No. ARB/98/2), Decision on Interim Measures of 25 September 2001, paras. 66, 89.

41. *Emilio Agustin Maffezini v. Spain* (ICSID Case No. ARB/97/7), Procedural Order No. 2, 28 October 28 1999.

42. *Ibid.*, para. 13 et seq.

43. *Ibid.*, para. 16 et seq.

44. *Ibid.*, para. 24.

iii.   Balancing, even if by another name

Cases exist performing a balancing of interest analysis – some of them without ostensibly recognizing it. For instance, *Burlington v. Ecuador*, where, after taking note of the irreparable harm test,[45] a balancing of interests and the "degree of harm" was the preferred course of action when the tribunal considered that:

> "The words 'necessity' or 'harm' do not appear in the relevant ICSID provisions. Necessity is nonetheless an indispensable requirement for provisional measures. It is generally assessed by *balancing the degree of harm* the applicant would suffer but for the measure.
>
> (....)
>
> In the circumstances of the present case, this Tribunal finds it appropriate to follow those cases that adopt the standard of 'harm not adequately reparable by an award of damages' to use the words of the UNCITRAL Model Law. It will also *weigh the interests of both sides in assessing necessity*."[46] (Emphasis added)

In *Railroad v. Guatemala* the request involved safeguarding evidence which *could* allegedly be destroyed (no evidence of shredding or imminent danger thereof was advanced). An "analysis of interests in play" was effected as evidenced by the following: "the Request would place an unfair burden on the Government because of its excessive breadth and that no need or urgency has been proven to justify the recommendation".[47]

Another interesting case is *Saipem v. Bangladesh* where, in ruling upon the interim relief sought, the tribunal's reasoning touches upon both irreparable harm and balancing of interests when it said to have:

> "weigh[ed] the *parties' divergent interests* in the light of all the circumstances of the case...".[48] (Emphasis added)

> "[T]he Tribunal considers that there is both necessity and urgency. This finding is reinforced by the facts that, apart from denying that it called the Warranty Bond, Bangladesh does not contest Saipem's contentions and that there is a risk of *irreparable harm* if Saipem has to pay the amount of the Warranty Bond."[49] (Emphasis added)

---

45. *Burlington Resources Inc. and Others v. Republic of Ecuador and Empresa Estatal Petróleos del Ecuador (PetroEcuador)* (ICSID Case No. ARB/08/5), Procedural Order No. 1 on Burlington Oriente's Request for Provisional Measures, 29 June 2009, para. 81.

46. *Ibid.*, paras. 78 and 81.

47. *Railroad Development Corporation v. Republic of Guatemala* (ICSID Case No. ARB/07/23), Decision on Provisional Measures, Order of 15 October 2008, para. 36.

48. *SAIPEM S.p.A. v. The People's Republic of Bangladesh* (ICSID Case No. ARB/05/07), Decision on Jurisdiction and Recommendation on Provisional Measures, Order of 21 March 2007, para. 175.

49. *Ibid.*, para. 182.

and then concluded that the measure (a "recommendation"): "strikes a fair *balance between the parties' interests...*".[50] (Emphasis added)

Something similar occurs in *Biwater Gauff v. Tanzania* where the tribunal reasoned that:

> "The determination of this application for provisional measures entails a *careful balancing between two competing interests*: (i) the need for transparency in treaty proceedings such as these, and (ii) the need to protect the procedural integrity of the arbitration."[51] (Emphasis added)

An interesting approach was followed in *Cemex v. Venezuela*. Although "irreparable damage" was employed,[52] the tribunal made an interesting point by echoing the International Court of Justice (ICJ) distinction between:

> "(a) Actions which should be restrained, because their effects, though capable of financial compensation, are such that compensation cannot fully remedy the damage suffered;
> (b) and actions which may well prove to have infringed a right and caused harm, but in respect to which it will be sufficient to award damages, without taking provisional measures."[53]

After doing so, it reasoned that:

> "ICSID Tribunals, when considering government actions which may well prove to have infringed a right and caused harm, make a distinction between:
> (a) situations where the alleged prejudice can be readily compensated by awarding damages;
> (b) and those where there is a serious risk of destruction of a going concern that constitutes the investment.
> In the first category of cases, provisional measures were denied because of the absence of an *'irreparable harm'*. In the second category of cases they were granted, the tribunals using other standards – although they could have based their decision on the fact that, the destruction of the ongoing concern that constituted the investment, would have created an *'irreparable harm'*."[54] (Emphasis added)

---

50. *Ibid.*, para. 184.

51. *Biwater Gauff (Tanzania) Ltd. v. United Republic of Tanzania* (ICSID Case ARB/05/22), Procedural Order No. 3, Order of 29 September 2006, para. 112, 22 ICSID Review – Foreign Investment Law Journal (Spring 2007, no. 1) p. 204.

52. *Cemex Caracas Investments B.V. and Cemex Caracas II Investments B.V. v. Bolivarian Republic of Venezuela* (ICSID Case No. ARB/08/15), Decision on the Claimant's Request for Provisional Measures, Order of 3 March 2010, para. 46.

53. *Ibid.*, para. 49.

54. *Ibid.*, para. 55.

The outcome of such an analytical route was that the generally accepted standard of "irreparable harm" was not retained.[55]

The tribunal in *Sergei Paushok, CJSC Golden East Company, CJSC Vostokneftegaz Company v. The Government Of Mongolia* did something similar but with nuances when it reasoned that:[56]

> "39. ... interim measures are extraordinary measures not to be granted lightly....
> Even under the discretion granted to the Tribunal under the UNCITRAL Rules, the Tribunal still has to deem those measures urgent and necessary to avoid *'irreparable' harm* and not only convenient or appropriate.
> (....)
> 45. It is internationally recognized that five standards have to be met before a tribunal will issue an order in support of interim measures. They are (1) prima facie jurisdiction, (2) prima facie establishment of the case, (3) urgency, (4) imminent danger of *serious prejudice* (necessity) and (5) proportionality.
> [(Emphasis added)]
> (....)
>
> *4- Imminent danger of serious prejudice (necessity)*
> 68. .... the possibility of monetary compensation does not necessarily eliminate the possible need for interim measures. The Tribunal relies on the opinion of the Iran-U.S. Claims Tribunal in the *Behring* case to the effect that, in international law, the concept of 'irreparable prejudice' does not necessarily require that the injury complained of be not remediable by an award of damages. To quote K.P. Berger who refers specifically to Art. 26 of the UNCITRAL Rules,
>
> > *'To preserve the legitimate rights of the requesting party, the measures must be "necessary". This requirement is satisfied if the delay in the adjudication of the main claim caused by the arbitral proceedings would lead to a* **"substantial" (but not necessarily "irreparable"** *as known in common law doctrine)* **prejudice**[57] *for the requesting party.'*[58]
>
> 69. The Tribunal shares that view and considers that the *'irreparable harm'* in *international law has a flexible meaning*
> (....)
> 77. ... the Tribunal has come to the conclusion that Claimants are facing ... *very substantial prejudice* unless some interim measures are granted."
> (Emphasis added)

---

55. *Ibid.*, para. 46. It is worth noting that the standard was understood to form part of the "necessity" requirement under Art. 47 of the ICSID Convention.
56. Under the Arbitration Rules of the United Nations Commission on International Trade Law, Order On Interim Measures, 2 September 2008, paras. 39, 45, 68, 69, 77.
57. Emphasis in boldface added.
58. "BERGER, K.P., "International Economic Arbitration" in *Studies in Transnational Economic Law*, vol. 9 (Kluwer Law and Taxation Publishers 1993) p. 336." (Citation in original.)

As may be observed, the analysis has a notorious "balancing" flavor. However, it stated that *substantial* – in contrast to *irreparable* – prejudice need be proven, but that it has a "flexible meaning". One surmises from the text and outcome that the level of injury was in fact lowered by the widening of the (*sic*) "flexible" meaning.

c.   *Conclusion*

Most cases that have addressed the matter have used "irreparable harm" as the prism. Exceptions exist which have employed related criteria, and a few others have balanced the interests of parties involved, whether they recognized it or not.

3.   *Public International Law*

Art. 41(1) of the Statute of the International Court of Justice (ICJ) reads:

> "The Court shall have the power to indicate, if it considers that circumstances so require, any provisional measures which ought to be taken to preserve the respective rights of either party."

The *jurisprudence constante* of the ICJ flowing from this proviso is particularly interesting. In order to work with a manageable sample from the corpus of interim measures the ICJ has issued,[59] I have focused on the most recent cases from the last ten years.

In *Construction of a Road in Costa Rica along the San Juan River (Nicaragua v. Costa Rica)* the ICJ echoed *Certain Activities carried out by Nicaragua in the Border Area (Costa Rica v. Nicaragua)*[60] thus:

> "The power of the Court to indicate provisional measures will be exercised only if there is urgency, in the sense that there is a real and imminent risk that *irreparable prejudice* will be caused to the rights in dispute before the Court has given its final decision...."[61] (Emphasis added)

Having found that Nicaragua had not established that the ongoing construction works led to a substantial increase in the sediment load in the river, no real and imminent risk of *irreparable prejudice* to the rights invoked was found to be substantiated, and hence the

---

59. Although the ICJ website displays 315 results, out of the 156 published ICJ cases from 1947 to 2014, 43 cases exist where interim relief was considered or issued. (Date of consultation: February 2014).

60. Provisional Measures Order of 8 March 2011, I.C.J. Reports 2011 (I), pp. 21-22, para. 64.

61. *Construction of a Road in Costa Rica along the San Juan River (Nicaragua v. Costa Rica)*; *Certain Activities carried out by Nicaragua in the Border Area (Costa Rica v. Nicaragua)*. Request Presented by Nicaragua for the Indication of Provisional Measures. Order of 13 December 2013, para. 25.

Court rejected the request for provisional measures.[62] In *Cambodia v. Thailand* the ICJ reasoned that:[63]

> "46. [T]he Court, pursuant to Article 41 of its Statute, has the power to indicate provisional measures when *irreparable prejudice* could be caused to rights which are the subject of the judicial proceedings;[64]
> 47. ... [the] power of the Court to indicate provisional measures will be exercised only if there is urgency, in the sense that there is a real and imminent risk that *irreparable prejudice* may be caused to the rights in dispute before the Court has given its final decision...." (Emphasis added)

> "61. it is for the Court to ensure, in the context of these proceedings, that no *irreparable damage* is caused to persons or property in that area pending the delivery of its Judgment on the request for interpretation....[65] (Emphasis added)

In *Certain Activities carried out by Nicaragua in the Border Area (Costa Rica v. Nicaragua)* the ICJ stated:

> "the Court ... has the power to indicate provisional measures when *irreparable prejudice* could be caused to rights which are the subject of the judicial proceedings...;
> ... the power of the Court to indicate provisional measures will be exercised only if there is urgency, in the sense that there is a real and imminent risk that *irreparable prejudice* may be caused to the rights in dispute before the Court has given its final decision...".[66] (Emphasis added)

Identical rationale was advanced in:

(i) *Questions relating to the obligation to prosecute or extradite (Belgium v. Senegal)*;[67]

---

62. *Ibid.*, paras. 34-36.
63. Request for Interpretation of the Judgment of 15 June 1962 in the *Case Concerning the Temple of Preah Vihear (Cambodia v. Thailand)*. Request for the Indication of Provisional Measures. Order of 18 July 2011, paras. 46-47.
64. "See, for example, Request for Interpretation of the Judgment of 31 March 2004 in the *Case concerning Avena and Other Mexican Nationals (Mexico v. United States of America)*, Provisional Measures, Order of 16 July 2008, I.C.J. Reports 2008, p. 328, para. 65; *Certain Activities carried out by Nicaragua in the Border Area (Costa Rica v. Nicaragua)*, Provisional Measures, Order of 8 March 2011, I.C.J. Reports 2011 (I), p. 21, para. 63." (Citation in original.)
65. Request for Interpretation of the Judgment of 15 June 1962 in the *Case Concerning the Temple of Preah Vihear (Cambodia v. Thailand)*, Request for the Indication of Provisional Measures, Order of 18 July 2011, para. 61.
66. *Certain Activities carried out by Nicaragua in the Border Area (Costa Rica v. Nicaragua)*, Request for the Indication of Provisional Measures. Order of 8 March 2011, paras. 63-64.
67. Request for the Indication of Provisional Measures. Order of 28 May 2009, paras. 62-63, 72.

(ii) *Request for Interpretation of the Judgment of 31 March 2004 in the Case concerning Avena and Other Mexican Nationals (Mexico v. United States of America)*;[68]

(iii) *Case concerning Pulp Mills on the River Uruguay (Argentina v. Uruguay)*;[69]

(iv) *Pulp Mills on the River Uruguay (Argentina v. Uruguay)*,[70] where rejection was premised on absence of "imminent risk of *irreparable prejudice* to the rights of Uruguay in dispute before it";

(v) *Case concerning Application of the International Convention on the Elimination of All Forms of Racial Discrimination (Georgia v. Russian Federation)*,[71] where the following interesting *ratio* was advanced:

> "Whereas the power of the court to indicate provisional measures will be exercised only if there is urgency in the sense that there is a real risk that action *prejudicial to the rights* of either party might be taken before the court has given its final decision...."[72] (Emphasis added)

(vi) *Case Concerning Certain Criminal Proceedings in France (Republic of the Congo v. France)*,[73] where the following was said:[74]

> "Whereas, independently of the requests for the indication of provisional measures submitted by the parties to preserve specific rights, the Court possesses by virtue of Article 41 of the Statute the power to indicate provisional measures with a view to preventing the aggravation or extension of the dispute whenever it considers that *circumstances so require*...."[75] (Emphasis added)

As may be observed, "irreparable prejudice" is the most commonly used standard to assess whether interim relief should be ordered, albeit not the only one. Other standards employed are "prejudice to rights", "preservation of rights" and "if the circumstances so require".

4. UNCITRAL Model Law on International Commercial Arbitration

The UNCITRAL Model Law on International Commercial Arbitration was recently amended precisely on our topic. In the context of conditions for granting interim measures, (revised) Art. 17A(1)(*a*) reads:

---

68. Request for the Indication of Provisional Measures. Order of 16 July 2008, paras. 66, 68 and 73.
69. Request for the Indication of Provisional Measures. Order of 13 July 2006, para. 62.
70. Request for the Indication of Provisional Measures. Order of 23 January 2007, para. 50.
71. Request for the Indication of Provisional Measures. Order of 15 October 2008, paras. 24, 118.
72. *Ibid.*, para. 129.
73. Request for the Indication of a Provisional Measure. Order of 17 June 2003, paras. 22, 29, 36.
74. *Ibid.*, para. 39.
75. "Cf. *Land and Maritime Boundary between Cameroon and Nigeria (Cameroon v. Nigeria)*, Provisional Measures. Order OJ 15 March 1996, I.C.J. Reports 1996 (I), p. 22, para. 41; Frontier Dispute (Burkina Fasol Republic of Mali), Provisional Measures. Order of 10 January 1986, I.C.J. Reports 1986, p. 9, para. 18." (Citation in original.)

"The party requesting an interim measure ... shall satisfy the arbitral tribunal that ... *Harm not adequately reparable by an award of damages* is likely to result if the measure is not ordered, and such *harm substantially outweighs the harm that is likely to result to the party against whom the measure is directed if the measure is granted....*" (Emphasis added)

The import of the change is not addressed by the Explanatory Note, which focuses on other aspects of the innovations of (revised) Art. 17. Nor does it articulate reasons involving the use of the balance of interests language *in lieu* of[76] irreparable harm.[77]

The Digest of UNCITRAL Case Law[78] points to one single case indicating:

"[W]hether the *harm* caused by the defendants is adequately *reparable* by an award of damages ... and whether that harm substantially outweighs the harm that the defendants are likely to suffer if the interim relief is granted, is essentially an assessment of the *balance of convenience*."[79] (Emphasis added)

However, the case is premised on the language of Art. 17 *before revision*. Hence, it is not fruit from the textual seed in comment. Fortunately, the *travaux préparatoires* do shed light on the issue:

"Subparagraph (a) follows the proposal made by the Working Group to replace the words 'irreparable harm' with the words 'harm not adequately reparable by an award of damages'.... [I]rreparable harm might present too high a threshold and would more clearly establish the discretion of the arbitral tribunal in deciding upon the issuance of an interim measure.... [T]he Working Group expressed concerns that that provision could be interpreted in a very restrictive manner, potentially excluding from the field of interim measures any loss that might be cured by an award of damages. The Working Group also noted that, in current practice, *it was not uncommon for an arbitral tribunal to issue an interim measure merely in circumstances where it would be comparatively complicated to compensate the harm with an award of damages....* [T]he paragraph should be interpreted in a flexible manner, keeping in mind *balancing the degree of harm suffered by the applicant* if the interim measure was not granted *against the degree of harm suffered by the party opposing the measure* if that measure was granted."[80] (Emphasis added)

---

76. Or "in addition to"? Admittedly, the text could be read to provide for *additive* – not *alternative* – prongs of analysis.
77. Explanatory Note by the UNCITRAL Secretariat, United Nations documents A/40/17, annex I and A/61/17, annex I, p. 31. UNCITRAL Model Law on International Commercial Arbitration, as amended by the United Nations Commission on International Trade Law on 7 July 2006.
78. UNCITRAL 2012 Digest of Case Law on the Model Law on International Commercial Arbitration, p. 87.
79. "*Safe Kids in Daily Supervision Limited v. McNeill*, High Court, Auckland, New Zealand, 14 April 2010 [2010] NZHC 605." (Citation in original.)
80. A/CN.9/WG.II/WP.1388 August 2005, para. 16.

As may be observed, balancing was underscored as the new trend in interim relief. The development has merited the criticism of a renowned expert.[81]

5.   *Conclusion*

The following conclusions can be drawn from the above survey:

(i) "Irreparable harm" is the most often used standard to assess whether interim relief should be issued;
(ii) "Irreparable harm" is understood as harm not adequately addressed through monetary compensation; and
(iii) An exceptional trend is visible in some cases and rules that tend to lower the standard. Sometimes, the exercise is alluded to as balancing. Sometimes it is not.

IV.   BALANCE OF INTERESTS AS A BETTER STANDARD

Although "irreparable harm" is the most commonly accepted and used standard to assess the issuance of interim measures, I wish to argue in favor of "balance of interests" (or "balance of convenience", as it is sometimes referred to). The reasons are threefold. Namely, it makes for a:

(1) more apposite tool;
(2) more efficient tool; and
(3) more refined concept.

I shall explain each.

1.   *More Apposite Tool*

Interim measures are the response of procedural law to urgency. Should the need surface during proceedings to address circumstances provoking injury that cannot await the final outcome, interim relief will be the means.

The prevalent paradigm has been that not just *any* injury merits immediate attention. Should the injury involved be of the type which may be remedied with money, it is not worth addressing prematurely. After all, the tribunal will in all likelihood not be adequately educated as to the intricacies of the dispute at the time the interim relief is sought. And risk of error militates in favor of avoiding premature decisions.

The paradigm, it is to be admitted, has merit. It recognizes the limits of adjudication and favors prudence. I wish to question it however.

Granted, risk of mistake abounds when taking decisions before the entire picture is presented before the decision maker. However, under the balance-of-convenience test,

---

81. Gary B. BORN, *International Commercial Arbitration*, Vol. II (Kluwer Law International 2009) p. 1979.

the issuance of the measure will turn on whether harm can be avoided with less burden than that placed on the shoulders of the party resisting it. The determination of the issue will therefore need only consider the pros and cons of the measure, including the impact on the parties. And if the requested measure provokes less inconvenience than the injury it avoids, it will be in the best interest of *both parties* to secure it.

Taking a moment to reflect on this last statement is worthwhile. Should an interim-relief-seeking claimant not prevail in the case, it will have to assume the costs it tried to avoid through the interim relief. If the relief was granted, it will ex hypothesi be lower than the counterfactual (i.e., the outcome absent the interim measure). Should the interim-relief-addressee respondent lose the arbitration, it will have been saved the need to indemnify claimant for the injury claimant was trying to avoid through interim relief. In both scenarios, the tab to shoulder will be lower – irrespective of *who* shoulders it. This makes balance of convenience a better tool if the lodestar is reducing unnecessary costs. It is also the better tool if the goal is efficient dispute resolution proceedings, to which I now turn.

2.   More Efficient Tool

Premising interim relief on "irreparable" harm necessarily means that injury of less import that does not satisfy this threshold will be forced upon one of the parties. Doing so is unnecessary. As explained in the preceding section, by using balance of interests the arbitral tribunal will be able to assess to what extent a measure is justified in the goal of avoiding waste. And if it is less wasteful to order that certain conduct take place, the tribunal will do so. In the jargon of law and economics, it will be more *efficient*. An example may illustrate why.

Consider moving party (*A*) which is inconvenienced by a set of circumstances inflicting on it a cost of US$ 100. Avoiding this cost involves requesting that another, respondent (*B*), perform certain conduct costing US$ 30. A cost of US$ 30 is evidently a preferable outcome to a cost of US$ 100. However, *B* will naturally prefer avoiding this conduct (and cost): it only benefits *A*, and the cost is borne by *B*. The canvassed scenario is such that *A* would be willing to pay *B* for its inconvenience. After all, irrespective of who wins, the damage will be lower. Therefore, forcing the outcome through an interim measure makes sense: *B* is the cheaper cost avoider. Absent interim relief, *B* will not act. After all, they are involved in litigation! And under the standard of irreparable harm, it need not do so. As a result, *A* will always have to shoulder US$ 100. And should it prevail over *B* in the arbitration, it is fair to assume that *B* will be forced to pay as damages the US$ 100 *A* wanted to avoid in the first place. As may be observed, such scenario is lose-lose. The only question is *who* loses more.

Balance of convenience avoids such outcome. It allows for harm reduction – irrespective of who suffers the harm. Viewed game-theoretically, it is a win-win outcome: irrespective of who foots it, the bill will be smaller.

Efficiency therefore militates in favor of preferring balance of convenience. And for those with a palate for law and economics, it will be what such theoreticians call "Kaldor Hicks efficiency".[82]

3.   More Refined Instrument, Better Suited to the Needs of Arbitration

Restricting interim relief to irreparable harm scenarios is not only suboptimal, but a more rudimentary use of the instrument: it is unnecessarily restrictive. As a result, it condemns cases displaying otherwise remediable circumstances to costly outcomes – which need not be so, and *should not* be so. One of the reasons parties choose arbitration is the desire for quality of justice. That includes avoiding waste and suboptimal outcomes – such as those fostered by using an unnecessarily high threshold, like irreparable harm.

V.   POST SCRIPTUM

I am delighted to see the (avalanche) in response to my (provocative) proposal. During my speech at the ICCA Congress I sensed a skeptical response from the panel and public. After the Q&A session, our moderator, John Barkett, asked for a vote on my proposal, and a meager four hands were raised in support. I thought to myself: "This is natural. After all, questioning an age-old paradigm always triggers reticence. Not only for status quo bias reasons, but also because of *adaptive preferences*: we tend to prefer that which we know and have become accustomed to."

Interestingly, however, upon walking down the steps of the podium, I was approached by several colleagues who stated that, upon reflection, they *did* agree with my proposal. And during the next day or so, my inbox swelled with emails echoing approval.

Hence, it is fair to say that, whilst many ICCA Congress attendees opposed the proposal, many approved it. It is against this background that I wish to do one thing, and one thing only: comment upon *the* reason evinced by those opposing the idea, so as to allow the reader to come to her own informed conclusion.

1.   Lowering the Standard May Foster Litigiousness

Although there may admittedly be more,[83] the only argument I was made privy to against the proposal was that lowering the standard would have the effect of fostering over-

---

82. "Kaldor Hicks efficiency" is an economic term of art bearing the name of its fathers: Nicholas Kaldor and John Hicks. The gist of the concept is applauding scenarios where a change of circumstances benefits a party more than it hurts another. That this outcome occurs is illustrated by the possibility that the party standing to gain from the change would be willing to pay the party standing to lose from it, even if this does not happen. The reason: the aggregate result is better, more efficient, even if in the process someone stood to lose something.
83. Sharing them will be appreciated at fgcossio@gdca.com.mx.

litigiousness. Relaxing the (currently high) standard ("irreparable harm") would have the effect of throwing oil onto what already is a burning issue.

2.   Response

I avow that the outcome *could* ensue. Albeit it is not self-evident that this will necessarily occur, I query whether it is a sufficiently good reason not to improve.

As explained above,[84] the zeitgeist is that "irreparable harm" need be shown to secure an interim measure. As explained, the consequence of this paradigm is that regrettable situations will ensue which could have been avoided – including costs. Should the articulated concern be deemed sufficient to quash my initiative, ex hypothesi the outcome will be that we accept a suboptimal scenario for fear of abuse.

I submit to the reader that the concern voiced is founded on an unwarranted assumption (Sect. *a*) and overlooks the fact that the fear evinced can be catered for by another procedural device: distribution of costs (Sect. *b*).

a.   Unacceptable assumption

The view contrary to my proposal assumes lack of sophistication. The assumption is unwarranted not only as a matter of fact, but as a basis to construct a legal theory.

Granted, parties *could* be tempted to advance more interim measure requests simply because they are (apparently) easier to obtain. However, under the proposed standard, it would need to be shown that the balance of harm outweighs the balance of inconvenience placed on the shoulders of the interim measure addressee – not an easy task. Hence, albeit the lowering of the standard may appear to some to facilitate the obtention of interim measures, in fact it does not: a balance test is a more difficult intellectual (and factual) exercise.

So, in reality, the better view, the better understanding, of the idea I am advancing is that it *does not involve a lowering of the standard, but replacing it with a better one.* A mechanical rule is substituted by a balancing exercise. In itself, this makes for a better procedural instrument; better law.

b.   Cost allocation

The fear articulated by the skeptical view is catered for by the cost-distribution power of arbitral tribunals: Parties abusing the system will be made to shoulder the costs of the measure. Hence, the danger is self-contained.

In and of itself, this is a sufficiently good counterargument to rebut the concern advanced. Parties abusing the system will be made to shoulder the costs they inflict. This includes cases where interim measures were granted to a party that eventually loses the case: that party would be made to compensate its adversaries who were put to the task of defending against and effecting an interim measure.

These two circumstances have the effect of sending a powerful message to practitioners: *beware of what you wish for, you may get it!*

---

84. Sect. IV of this Paper, pp. 274-276.

The Continuing Role of the Courts in the Era of the Emergency Arbitrator

*Robert Sills**

I. INTRODUCTION

One of the parties to a dispute governed by an arbitration clause often finds itself in need of urgent interim relief. The assets in dispute may be about to leave the jurisdiction, critical evidence may be at risk of being destroyed, or its counterparty may refuse to perform under a critical contract. More dramatically, the counterparty may refuse to arbitrate at all, initiating (or threatening to initiate) litigation in its national courts, in violation of the arbitration agreement. The fundamental choice facing such a party is whether to seek interim relief in the designated arbitral forum or, where available, in the national courts.

Most, if not all, institutional rules provide for the grant of interim relief by the arbitration tribunal, at the same time that they allow for applications to the national courts.[1] At the same time, it is often the case that arbitrators are unable to grant effective

---

* Partner, New York office and head of the international arbitration practice, Orrick. The author would like to thank his colleague Jeffrey Prokop for his assistance in preparing this article.

1. See, e.g., International Chamber of Commerce (ICC) Arbitration Rules Arts. 28(1) (providing that the Tribunal may order "any interim or conservatory measure it deems appropriate"); *Ibid.*, Art. 28(2) (parties may apply for interim or conservatory measures to "any competent judicial authority" at any time "[b]efore the file is transmitted to the arbitral tribunal, and in appropriate circumstances even thereafter".); International Centre for Dispute Resolution (ICDR) Rules Arts. 21(1) and 21(3). Art. 17 of the UNCITRAL Model Law on International Commercial Arbitration (the Model Law) expressly allows for the award of interim relief by an arbitral tribunal, and sets out the standard to be applied in Art. 17A, as follows:

   "(1) The party requesting an interim measure under article 17(2)(a), (b) and (c) shall satisfy the arbitral tribunal that:

278

relief, either because of timing issues or because relief against third parties which are not subject to the jurisdiction of the tenant, such as banks or other financial institutions holding the respondent's assets, is sought. This article briefly surveys the factors that should inform the choice between seeking urgent interim relief from the arbitration institution or tribunal, on the one hand, or the courts, on the other, for arbitrations seated in the United States, and for which the lex arbitri is the Federal Arbitration Act (FAA).[2]

II.   THE ADOPTION OF EMERGENCY ARBITRATOR PROVISIONS

Until recently, a party seeking urgent relief before the formation of the arbitration tribunal had no choice but to resort to the national courts. However, many arbitral institutions have now adopted some version of an emergency arbitrator procedure. As a general matter, such rules provide for the institution to appoint, on very short notice, a single arbitrator from a pre-approved list, who is to hold a hearing within a very short time after his or her appointment. The emergency arbitrator is typically allowed to grant broad equitable relief in an accelerated proceeding. For example, Appendix V of the Arbitration Rules of the International Chamber of Commerce (ICC), which sets out the ICC's Emergency Arbitrator Rules, provides that an emergency arbitrator will ordinarily be appointed within two days of the receipt of the request by the Secretariat.[3] A procedural schedule is to be fixed two days thereafter,[4] and an order deciding the application is to be rendered within fifteen days of the transmission of the file to the emergency arbitrator, subject to extension upon a reasoned request.[5] Other leading arbitral institutions, with the significant exception of the London Court of International Arbitration (LCIA), have adopted roughly similar structures for the appointment of an emergency arbitrator.[6]

(a) Harm not adequately reparable by an award of damages is likely to result if the measure is not ordered, and such harm substantially outweighs the harm that is likely to result to the party against whom the measure is directed if the measure is granted; and

(b) There is a reasonable possibility that the requesting party will succeed on the merits of the claim. The determination on this possibility shall not affect the discretion of the arbitral tribunal in making any subsequent determination."

2. 9 U.S.C. Sect. 1, et seq.
3. ICC Rules, Appendix V, Art. 2(1).
4. ICC Rules, Appendix V, Art. 5(1).
5. ICC Rules, Appendix V, Art. 6(4).
6. See, e.g., Singapore International Arbitration Centre (SIAC) Rules (2010), Rule 26.2 and Schedule 1 (effective 1 July 2010); Arbitration Institute of the Stockholm Chamber of Commerce (SCC) Rules, Appendix II (Effective 1 January 2010); International Centre for Dispute Resolution (ICDR) Rules, Art. 37 (effective 1 May 2006). The London Court of International Arbitration (LCIA) has not, as yet, adopted any emergency arbitrator provisions, opting instead for the "expedited formation" of a tribunal (LCIA Rules, Art. 9), which could then grant interim relief under Art. 25. Surveys of the emergency arbitrator provisions of various institutions are set out in Peter J.W. SHERWIN and Douglas C. RENNIE, "Interim Relief Under International Arbitration Rules and

While the wide adoption of emergency arbitrator provisions is a very welcome development, and can provide full (or at least adequate) interim relief in many cases, they can be of limited utility in certain common circumstances. First, those provisions are generally applicable only to disputes arising under contracts executed after the rules allowing for emergency arbitrators went into effect. Given that the emergency arbitrator rules are all of relatively recent vintage, it will be many years before they can be generally invoked against a recalcitrant party.[7] Of course, for non-administered arbitrations, including those governed by the UNCITRAL Arbitration Rules, there is no arbitral remedy available at all before the formation of a tribunal, and a recalcitrant party can ordinarily frustrate the formation of a tribunal well past the date when interim relief from the arbitrators would be effective.

There is also little guidance at this time regarding the remedies that can be granted by an emergency arbitrator or what standards govern his or her discretion.[8] For example, the ICC Rules provide no guidance at all regarding the standards governing emergency applications, other than simply to provide that emergency relief is available to "[a] party that needs urgent interim or conservatory measures that cannot await the constitution of an arbitral tribunal".[9] Similarly, the Arbiration Rules of the International Centre for Dispute Resolution (ICDR Rules) refer only to "[a] party in need of emergency relief prior to the constitution of the tribunal…".[10] The rules for emergency arbitrators of the Arbitration Institute of the Stockholm Chamber of Commerce (SCC) refer only to its general rule regarding interim measures, Art. 32, which itself sets out no specific standard for granting relief. Given that the ruling of an emergency arbitrator can be the decisive moment in a case, the lack of meaningful guidance will likely give pause to any practitioner weighing the option of proceeding before an emergency arbitrator against an application before the national courts, with their well-known and settled standards for urgent relief.[11]

Guidelines: A Comparative Analysis", 20 Am. Rev. Int'l Arb. (2009) p. 317 and Raja BOSE and Ian MEREDITH, "Emergency Arbitration Procedures: A Comparative Analysis", 5 Int'l Arb. Law Rev. (2012) p. 186.

7. The ICC Rules apply to agreements executed after 1 January 2012; the SIAC rules became effective on 1 July 2010; the SCC Rules took effect on 1 January 2010; and the ICDR Rules on 1 May 2006.

8. One could, and probably should, look to the UNCITRAL Model Law as an expression of accepted best practice in international arbitration, but there is, as yet, no consensus to that effect.

9. ICC Rules, Art. 29(1).

10. ICDR Rules, Art. 37(2).

11. Gary Born has suggested that a single international standard should govern applications for interim relief in international arbitration, noting that most tribunals require a showing of serious or irreparable harm, urgency, and no prejudgment on the merits, and that others add a requirement that the applicant show a prima facie case on the merits. Putting to one side the tension between the notion of "no prejudgment" and the requirements of a prima facie showing of merit, Professor Born acknowledges that "[i]t is also unclear precisely what sort of showing is required for the various elements of a request for provisional measures", and notes "the limited precedent that exists on the topic". Gary BORN, *International Commercial Arbitration* (Kluwer 2009) at pp. 1980, 1978. That uncertainty is far greater in the context of applications to emergency arbitrators than for those presented to fully constituted tribunals.

One would expect that a generally accepted standard for urgent applications will eventually emerge from published awards and academic work. However, at this point, relatively few emergency awards or orders have been published – indeed, many, if not most, are confidential – and those that have been published (many in redacted form or as abstracts) provide relatively little guidance on the standards that were followed in granting or denying relief. However, as emergency arbitration orders, or at least summaries or abstracts of them, become increasingly available, an accepted and predictable standard should emerge.

Some of this information is slowly becoming public. For example, the SCC website links to an article surveying all its emergency arbitrator proceedings, entitled "SCC Practice: Emergency Arbitrator Decisions, 1 January 2010 - 31 December 2013".[12] For each of the nine cases decided during that period, the article summarizes the factual setting, reports on the relief granted or denied, and summarizes the reasoning of the emergency arbitrator. While greater detail would be useful and welcome, this data is invaluable to any practitioner considering an application for urgent relief before the SCC, or for that matter, any other institution.[13] Similarly, a former case manager at the ICDR published an article in 2008 which described and analyzed four decided applications.[14] However, a consistent practice will emerge only if the arbitral institutions that have emergency arbitrator rules routinely publish at least abstracts of their rulings, and preferably the awards themselves, redacted to maintain an appropriate degree of confidentiality.[15]

III.   THE CONTINUING ROLE OF THE COURTS

Even if an emergency arbitrator is available and prepared to grant relief, a significant difficulty in seeking effective relief in connection with an arbitration seated in the United States is that arbitration awards in the United States are not self-executing. That is, the only sanction against a party willing to disobey an arbitral award, including an award of interim relief, is in the arbitration itself. Until the award is enforced as a judgment – that is, "confirmed" in the language of the FAA – it cannot be enforced by an order of

---

12. Johan LUNDSTEDT, "SCC Practice: Emergency Arbitrator Decisions", Arb. Institute of the Stockholm Chamber of Commerce (2010-2013); available at <http://www.sccinstitute.com/ filearchive/4/46698/SCC%20practice%202010%20-%202013%20emergency%20arbitrator_ FINAL.pdf>.

13. The standard that seems to be followed in the SCC cases is that a successful applicant must show both a prima facie case on the merits – that is, a reasonable likelihood of prevailing, and irreparable harm that cannot be remedied through an award of damages. Interestingly, of the nine cases reported, relief was granted in only two of those. In three cases, the arbitrator found that a prima facie case had been made out, but that there had been no showing of irreparable harm.

14. Guillaume LEMENEZ and Paul QUIGLEY, "The ICDR's Emergency Arbitrator Procedure in Action, Part I: A look at the Empirical Data", Int'l Dispute Res. J. (August/October 2008).

15. Another helpful survey of the applicable rules and a small number of case studies under various emergency arbitrator provisions is set out in R. BOSE and I. MEREDITH, "Emergency Arbitrator Procedures: A Comparative Analysis", op. cit., fn. 6.

contempt or the other arsenal of enforcement mechanisms available to a litigant in the United States. While it is almost certainly the case that the majority of parties subject to an emergency arbitrator's ruling will comply rather than risk sanctions later in the proceeding for that disobedience, there are always parties who have no intention of participating in arbitration if they can avoid interim relief at the outset. In such cases, the lack of an enforcement mechanism may prevent a wronged party from obtaining any relief at all, even after obtaining an award of interim relief from an emergency arbitrator. To avoid such harm, the availability of the coercive mechanisms available only in the national courts is particularly important, especially at the inception of a case against a recalcitrant party.[16]

One might think, therefore, that the solution would be to seek prompt confirmation of the emergency arbitrator's award before a court, in order to obtain an enforceable order. However, there is some question whether an arbitrator's grant of interim relief can be confirmed at all. The general rule under the FAA is that, as set out in the Second Circuit's opinion in *Michaels v. Mariforum Shipping, S.A.*, if "arbitrators make an interim ruling that does not purport to resolve finally the issues submitted to them, judicial review is unavailable", and that only final awards can be confirmed.[17] The relatively few US courts confronted with this issue in the context of grants of interim relief by full tribunals have generally held that grants of such relief are reviewable before the federal courts, reasoning that otherwise a grant of interim relief could be rendered an empty formality.[18] However, there is almost no authority on whether that doctrine extends to an award or order made by an emergency arbitrator, other than two district court cases reaching opposite results. In 2011, a district court in the Southern District of California denied a motion to vacate an order made by an ICDR emergency arbitrator, holding that "the interim order ... is not subject to review by this Court".[19] However, late last year, a federal district judge sitting in New York reached the opposite result, and confirmed an emergency arbitrator's order, holding that "if an arbitrable award of equitable relief based upon a finding of irreparable harm is to have any meaning at all, the parties must be capable of enforcing or vacating it at the time it is made".[20] The holding of the *Yahoo!*

---

16. While the large majority of the losing parties in international arbitration comply with adverse awards, there is, nonetheless, a significant number who refuse to comply. See P. SHERWIN and D. RENNIE, *op. cit.*, fn. 6, at 324 nn. 47-49.

17. 624 F.2d 411, 414 (2d Cir. 1980).

18. See *Publicis Commc'n v. True N. Commc'ns Inc.*, 206 F.3d 725, 728 (7th Cir. 2000); *Yasuda Fire & Marine Ins. Co. v. Continental Cas. Co.*, 37 F.3d 345, 347-348 (7th Cir. 1994); *Pac. Reinsurance Mgmt. Corp. v. Ohio Reinsurance Corp.*, 935 F.2d 1019, 1022-1023 (9th Cir. 1991); *Island Creek Coal Sales Co. v. City of Gainesville, Fla.*, 729 F.2d 1046, 1049 (6th Cir. 1984).

19. *Chinmax Med. Sys. Inc. v. Alere San Diego, Inc.*, Case No. 10cv2467 WQH (NLS), 2011 U.S. Dist. LEXIS 57889, at *14 (S.D. Cal. 27 May 2011).

20. *Yahoo! Inc. v. Microsoft Corp.*, 13CV7237 (Part I), 2013 U.S. Dist. LEXIS 151175 at *22 (quoting *Southern Seas Navigation Ltd. v. Petroleos Mexicanos*, 606 F.Supp. 692, 694 (S.D.N.Y. 1985)). Following confirmation, the judgment was stayed by a single judge of the Court of Appeals on 24 October 2013. That stay was then dissolved by a three-judge panel on 7 November 2013, and Yahoo! abandoned its appeal. The author's firm served as counsel to Microsoft, the successful applicant, in that case.

case seems clearly correct, but it remains the only authority for the reviewability of an emergency arbitrator's ruling; one swallow does not a Spring make, and the enforceability of awards by emergency arbitrators remains uncertain.

Interestingly, the UNCITRAL Model Law draws a distinction for purposes of confirmation between what it calls a "preliminary order" in Art. 17C – the rough equivalent of a temporary restraining order in federal practice in the United States, and which would presumably include an emergency arbitrator's order – and an "interim measure" in Art. 17A, the analogue of a preliminary injunction. As set out in Art. 17C(5), "[a] preliminary order shall be binding on the parties but shall not be subject to enforcement by a court". In contrast, Art. 17H(1) provides that an interim measure shall be "enforced upon application to the competent court". The Explanatory Notes of the UNCITRAL Secretariat provides no explanation for that distinction, although the party awarded "preliminary relief" may be the one most in need of judicial enforcement. Nonetheless, even though United States courts are governed by the FAA and not the Model Law, those provisions presumably reflect the views of the drafters that awards of short term urgent relief should not be regarded as awards entitled to enforcement in court.

Even assuming that an interim award is confirmable, however, there are nonetheless numerous situations, familiar to any practitioner, in which seeking a remedy from an emergency arbitrator before proceeding in court by way of an application to confirm would remain inadequate because of timing issues. In the *Yahoo!* case cited above, only twenty-five days elapsed from the appointment of the emergency arbitrator until the court confirmed his order. However, even such a remarkably expedited proceeding might not suffice to protect a party's ability to obtain effective emergency relief.[21] One can easily think of situations in which a recalcitrant party could take advantage of such a timing gap in order to move assets, cease the supply of essential goods, disclose confidential information or otherwise alter the *status quo* in a manner that no subsequent award could fully remedy.[22] Worse yet, litigation commenced by a counterparty in another jurisdiction in violation of the arbitration clause may have proceeded to a point where the arbitration cannot be held at all. Accordingly, the ability to seek urgent relief from a court remains an essential weapon in any practitioner's arsenal. Moreover, even if the applicable emergency arbitrator provisions allow for ex parte relief, and such relief

---

21. One commentator noted that "*Yahoo! v. Microsoft* may be an anomaly in going from start to judicial confirmation in 25 days – a feat that only the most motivated and well-financed parties can match." "Microsoft Case is Great Example of Emergency Arbitration", Law360 (13 Dec. 2013) at <www.law360.com/articles/495144/print?section=commercialcontracts> (last accessed 26 Feb. 2014).

22. Arbitral tribunals lack jurisdiction over third parties, so that remedies such as attachment can be obtained only in court. The ability to freeze assets, such as cash or securities held in a financial institution, can be decisive in a case against a party willing to transfer assets beyond the reach of the tribunal or the courts at the seat of arbitration. While some have suggested a work-around for that lack of authority, such as ordering a recalcitrant party to place assets in the custody of the tribunal, there is no way for a tribunal to compel such a deposit. At the same time, as discussed below, one court, the Third Circuit, holds that attachment (or presumably any other remedy) is unavailable in aid of an international arbitration.

is actually provided, an application to confirm an interim award granted ex parte by the emergency arbitrator will necessarily be on notice, and a recalcitrant party will thereby obtain an opportunity to move assets or otherwise alter the equities before an enforceable order can be entered.[23]

In the United States, the federal district courts have original and removal jurisdiction over cases concerning international arbitration agreements, including applications for interim relief in connection with such disputes.[24] The Federal Rules of Civil Procedure, which apply in all of the nation's federal courts of first instance, the district courts, expressly allow for almost immediate equitable relief in the form of a temporary restraining order, and allow for ex parte applications upon an appropriate showing.

IV.   INTERIM RELIEF IN AID OF ARBITRATION IN THE SECOND CIRCUIT

The Supreme Court has yet to rule on the availability of injunctive relief in aid of arbitration.[25] However, the weight of authority from the Courts of Appeals has endorsed that right. In particular, the Court of Appeals for the Second Circuit, which has jurisdiction over the federal district courts in New York, has a long and consistent line of cases allowing for such relief, beginning with *Roso-Lino Beverage Distributors, Inc. v. Coca-Cola Bottling Co.*, which ordered Coca-Cola to continue a disputed dealership during

---

23. A good example of judicial recognition of such timing issues in arbitration is the Fourth Circuit's decision in *Merrill Lynch, Pierce, Fenner & Smith, Inc. v. Bradley*, a domestic case in which the plaintiff sought and was granted a preliminary injunction to prevent the defendant from using plaintiff's records and from soliciting its clients. 756 F.2d 1048 (4th Cir. 1985). The court upheld the grant of the injunction and noted that:

"We think that our decision will further, not frustrate, the policies underlying the Federal Arbitration Act. In this case preliminary injunctive relief pending arbitration furthers congressional policy by ensuring that the dispute resolution would be a meaningful process because, without such an injunction, Bradley's conduct might irreversibly alter the status quo. When an account executive breaches his employment contract by soliciting his former employer's customers, a nonsolicitation clause requires immediate application to have any effect. An injunction even a few days after solicitation has begun is unsatisfactory because the damage is done. The customers cannot be "unsolicited". It may be impossible for the arbitral award to return the parties substantially to the status quo ante because the prevailing party's damages may be too speculative."

Ibid. at 1054. See also *Aggarao v. MOL Ship Mgmt. Co.*, 675 F.3d 355, 376-377 (4th Cir. 2012) (extending *Merrill Lynch v. Bradley* to claims arising under contracts subject to the 1958 New York Convention).

24. 9 U.S.C. Sects. 203, 205. See *Borden, Inc. v. Meiji Milk Prods. Co.*, 919 F.2d 822, 826 (2d Cir. 1990) (noting that "[e]ntertaining an application for such a [provisional] remedy ... is not precluded by the [New York] Convention, but rather is consistent with its provisions and its spirit".); *Karaha Bodas Co. v. Perusahaan Pertambangan Minyak Dan Gas Bumi Negara*, 335 F.3d 357, 365 (5th Cir. 2003); *Aggarao*, 675 F.3d at 376.

25. See *Merrill Lynch, Pierce, Fenner & Smith, Inc. v. McCollum*, 469 U.S. 1127, 1130 (1985) (White, J., dissenting from denial of writ of certiorari, and noting "[t]he importance of resolving the question of the availability of preliminary injunctive relief in cases subject to arbitration...").

the pendency of the arbitration.[26] Rather remarkably, the arbitrator in *Roso-Lino* had already denied the distributors' application for interim relief before the case was heard in the Court of Appeals. Nonetheless, the Court of Appeals did not even remand the case to the district court for further proceedings, but instead directed the entry of a preliminary injunction, which was to remain in effect "pending completion of the arbitration".[27]

In a subsequent case, the Second Circuit held that "[a]rbitration can become a 'hollow formality' if parties are able to alter irreversibly the status quo before the arbitrators are able to render a decision in the dispute.... A district court must ensure that the parties get what they bargained for – a meaningful arbitration of the dispute."[28] Later cases in that court have uniformly adhered to that view.[29]

In fact, the Second Circuit has expressly rejected the view that the availability of interim relief from an arbitral tribunal is a basis for a court to abstain from ruling on an application for a preliminary injunction. In *American Express Financial Advisors Inc. v. Thorley*,[30] the district court had refrained from ruling on an application for interim relief, reasoning that the applicant "could just as quickly obtain the same temporary equitable relief from the arbitrator as from a court".[31] The Court of Appeals reversed and rejected the notion of deferring to arbitral proceedings in forceful language, holding that "[t]he *Roso-Lino* rule, that courts should consider the merits of a requested preliminary injunction even where the validity of the underlying claims will be determined in arbitration, does not admit of the exception that the district court made in this case".[32] Moreover, the approach taken in *Roso-Lino*, that injunctive relief granted by a court should remain in effect until the arbitration is resolved, and not merely as a "bridge" to the arbitral tribunal's relief, remains the prevailing view in the Second Circuit. One district court recently summarized the jurisprudence of the Court of Appeals on this point as follows, "[i]n the context of preliminary injunctions sought in aid of arbitration,

---

26. 749 F.2d 124 (2d Cir. 1984).

27. *Ibid.* at 127.

28. *Blumenthal v. Merrill Lynch, Pierce, Fenner & Smith, Inc.*, 910 F.2d 1049, 1053 (2d Cir. 1990) (citations omitted). *Blumenthal* and *Roso-Lino* were both domestic cases decided under Chapter 1 of the FAA. However, in the *Borden* case discussed above, the Court made it clear that the fact that a dispute fell within the New York Convention does not oust the Court of jurisdiction to issue an injunction in aid of arbitration. 919 F.2d at 826.

29. Although most litigations in connection with international arbitrations are pursued in federal court, the state courts of New York, which do have coordinate jurisdiction over such matters, are expressly vested by statute with the power to grant injunctive relief, "but only upon the ground that the award to which the applicant may be entitled may be rendered ineffectual without such provisional relief". N.Y. C.P.L.R. Sect. 7502(c). The New York Court of Appeals had previously held that preliminary relief in aid of arbitration could not be granted in a case arising under the New York Convention. *Cooper v. Ateliers de la Motobécane*, 442 N.E.2d 1239, 1243 (N.Y. 1982), superseded by statute, N.Y. C.P.L.R. Sect. 7502(c), as recognized in *Sojitz Corp. v. Prithvi Information Solutions Ltd.*, 921 N.Y.S. 2d 14 (2011). That decision was then legislatively overruled.

30. 147 F.3d 229 (2d Cir. 1998).

31. *Ibid.* at 230-231.

32. *Ibid.* at 231.

[t]he Second Circuit has made it clear in a series of decisions that the Court has both the power and duty to entertain [such a motion] pending the results in [an] arbitration".[33]

The majority of the other Courts of Appeals allow applications for interim relief, although with somewhat different rationales and some limitations on scope, and somewhat less robustly than the Second Circuit. The views of those courts are briefly summarized below.

V.   OTHER CIRCUITS IN WHICH INTERIM RELIEF IN AID OF ARBITRATION IS PERMITTED

1.   The First Circuit

In *Teradyne, Inc. v. Mostek Corp.*,[34] a First Circuit decision involving a dispute between two US parties, the district court had enjoined the defendant from disposing of or encumbering certain of its assets and directed it to set aside a certain amount in an interest bearing account to satisfy any judgment or arbitration award obtained by the plaintiff. The Court of Appeals upheld the grant of relief, extensively surveying the law of other circuits and concluding that "the congressional desire to enforce arbitration agreements would frequently be frustrated if the courts were precluded from issuing preliminary injunctive relief to preserve the *status quo* pending arbitration and, *ipso facto*, the meaningfulness of the arbitration process".[35]

However, in *Next Step Medical Co. v. Johnson & Johnson International*,[36] the court held that, in contrast to the Second Circuit's approach in *Roso-Lino*, interim relief from a court is available only between the time the district court orders arbitration and the time the arbitral tribunal is constituted, and would be able to grant interim relief itself.[37] The court explained that under *Teradyne*, interim relief "assumes a showing of some short-term emergency that demands attention while the arbitration machinery is being set in motion".[38]

---

33. *Solar & Envtl. Techs. Corp. v. Zelinger*, 726 F.Supp.2d 135, 142 (D. Conn. 2009) (citations and internal quotation marks omitted).
34. 797 F.2d 43 (1st Cir. 1986).
35. *Ibid.* at 51 (first emphasis added). In *Danieli & C. Officine Meccaniche S.p.A.*, 19 F.Supp.2d 148, 154 (D. Mass. 2002), a district court extended *Teradyne* to a case falling within the New York Convention.
36. 619 F.3d 67 (1st Cir. 2010).
37. *Ibid.* at 70.
38. *Ibid.* No decision from the First Circuit – or, as far as the author is aware, any other Court of Appeals – has addressed whether the availability of an emergency arbitrator procedure would satisfy the condition set by the First Circuit regarding the availability of relief in an arbitral forum and close the courthouse door to an applicant.

2.   *The Fourth Circuit*

In the *Aggarao* case mentioned above at fn. 23, the Fourth Circuit endorsed the availability of injunctive relief in a case governed by the New York Convention. The Court endorsed the availability of preliminary relief in particularly broad terms:

> "The status quo to be preserved by a preliminary injunction, however, is not the circumstances existing at the moment the lawsuit or injunction request was actually filed, but the 'last uncontested status between the parties which preceded the controversy'…. 'To be sure, it is sometimes necessary to require a party who has recently disturbed the status quo to reverse its actions', but as the Tenth Circuit has explained, '[s]uch an injunction restores, rather than disturbs, the status quo ante'…. Hence, the district court is entitled to apply the hollow-formality test to Aggarao's injunction request and determine whether an arbitral award in his favor in the Philippines might be an empty one, if maintenance and cure is not restored in the interim."[39]

3.   *The Sixth Circuit*

In *Performance Unlimited, Inc. v. Questar Publishers, Inc.*,[40] a domestic case, the Sixth Circuit analyzed whether Sect. 3 of the FAA deprived courts of the power to order preliminary injunctive relief. In that case, a district court denied a motion for preliminary injunction that sought to require the defendant to continue paying royalties during the pendency of the arbitration. The district court had denied the injunction, reasoning that it should not involve itself in the merits of a dispute when the parties have agreed to arbitration. The Sixth Circuit reversed, and held that district courts have jurisdiction to grant preliminary injunctive relief because it furthers the congressional purpose behind the FAA, where the absence of injunctive relief could render the arbitral proceedings a "hollow formality".[41]

4.   *The Seventh Circuit*

In *Sauer-Getriebe KG v. White Hydraulics, Inc.*,[42] plaintiff sought preliminary injunctive relief barring the defendant from transferring any manufacturing rights pending arbitration. The Court of Appeals held that the district court had improperly abstained from ruling on the application for an injunction, and directed that one be granted "until the London arbitration … is completed".[43] Strikingly, the Court of Appeals examined one of the traditional factors supporting the grant of a preliminary injunction in federal

---

39. 675 F.3d at 378 (citations omitted).
40. 52 F.3d 1373 (6th Cir. 1995). In *Nexteer Auto. Corp. v. Korea Delphi Auto. Sys. Corp.*, Case No. 13-CV-15189, 2014 U.S. Dist. LEXIS 18250 (E.D. Mich. 13 Feb. 2014), a district court within the Sixth Circuit applied *Performance Unlimited* in an international case.
41. 52 F.3d at 1380.
42. 715 F.2d 348 (7th Cir. 1983).
43. *Ibid.* at 352.

practice – the likelihood of success on the merits – and based its ruling in part on a finding that Sauer, the applicant, was likely to prevail on the merits of the arbitration itself.[44]

5.   *The Ninth Circuit*

In *Simula, Inc. v. Autoliv, Inc.*, the Ninth Circuit seemed to have held that preliminary relief was not available in aid of arbitration.[45] However, in *Toyo Tire Holdings of Americas Inc. v. Continental Tire North America, Inc.*,[46] the Ninth Circuit explained that the grant of preliminary injunctive relief is not contrary to the federal policy in favor of arbitration and distinguished *Simula* by pointing out that, in the former case, interim relief would have been available from the tribunal, where the application should have been brought.[47] Accordingly, the Ninth Circuit, like the First, appears to limit the ability of district courts to grant injunctive relief to a "grant [of] interim relief to maintain the status quo while the parties are waiting for the arbitration panel to be formed and for the arbitration panel to consider whether to grant interim relief".[48] That is precisely how one district court in the Ninth Circuit recently construed *Toyo*:

> "[W]here an arbitration panel has already been empaneled and that tribunal has the power to grant the injunctive relief sought, a federal court may intervene only in a very narrow circumstance, namely, if a party has already petitioned the arbitrator for injunctive relief and a provisional remedy is necessary to maintain the status quo until the arbitral panel can consider and rule upon [the] application for interim relief."[49]

6.   *The Tenth Circuit*

In *Merrill Lynch, Pierce, Fenner & Smith, Inc. v. Dutton*,[50] the Tenth Circuit held that a preliminary injunction preserving the status quo until the arbitration panel assumed jurisdiction of the dispute did not violate Sect. 3 of the FAA.[51] In that case, the district court had issued what the Tenth Circuit considered to be an "open-ended" preliminary injunction. On remand, the district court was directed to modify the preliminary

---

44. *Ibid.*

45. 175 F.3d 716, 725 (9th Cir. 1999) ("Because the district court correctly concluded that all of Simula's claims were arbitrable and the ICC arbitral tribunal is authorized to grant the equivalent of an injunction *pendente lite*, it would have been inappropriate for the district court to grant preliminary injunctive relief.").

46. 609 F.3d 975 (9th Cir. 2010).

47. 609 F.3d at 979-980.

48. *Ibid.* at 979.

49. *Dealer Computer Servs., Inc. v. Monarch Ford*, 1:12-CV-01970-LJO-SKO, 2013 U.S. Dist. LEXIS 11237, at *10 (E.D. Cal. 25 Jan. 2013) (internal quotation marks and citation omitted).

50. 844 F.2d 726 (10th Cir. 1988).

51. *Ibid.* at 727.

injunction to expire when the matter was presented to and considered by the arbitral panel, following the same rule as in the First and Ninth Circuits.

VI.   THE OUTLIERS – THE THIRD AND EIGHTH CIRCUITS

1.   The Third Circuit

In *Ortho Pharmaceutical Corp. v. Amgen, Inc.*,[52] the Third Circuit addressed the issue of whether the FAA deprives a district court of the power to issue a preliminary injunction in a domestic arbitrable dispute. The plaintiff in that case filed a demand for arbitration with the American Arbitration Association but also filed suit in district court seeking preliminary injunctive relief during the pendency of the arbitral proceedings. The district court ruled that, under the FAA, it had the authority to issue a preliminary injunction to preserve the *status quo* pending arbitration.[53] However, the Third Circuit's prior decision in *McCreary Tire & Rubber Co. v. CEAT S.p.A.* had held that the district court lacked jurisdiction to grant an order of attachment in a case subject to the New York Convention.[54] That decision has been widely criticized, and is arguably distinguishable because the attachment was not sought in aid of arbitration at all, but was granted in a litigation brought in violation of the parties' arbitration agreement.[55] Nonetheless, *McCreary* remains the law in the Third Circuit, and may pose a barrier to any party seeking interim relief in aid of an international arbitration there.

2.   The Eighth Circuit

The Eighth Circuit's decision in *Merrill Lynch, Pierce, Fenner & Smith, Inc. v. Hovey* held that the issuance of injunctive relief in the context of an arbitrable dispute violates the FAA.[56] The court characterized the congressional intent behind the FAA as the facilitation of quick, expeditious arbitration, which, according to the Court, would be obstructed by additional proceedings in the courts.[57] However, the Court did allow for a narrow exception where the contract containing the arbitration clause contains "qualifying contractual language".[58] However, a later decision of that Court clarified that such language is not, as one might think, language authorizing the parties to pursue an application for interim relief, but rather language expressly requiring performance

---

52. 882 F.2d 806 (3d Cir. 1989).
53. *Ibid.* at 812-813.
54. 501 F.2d 1032, 1038 (3d Cir. 1974).
55. See *Borden*, 919 F.2d at 826; *China Nat'l Metal Prods. Import/Export Co. v. Apex Digital, Inc.*, 155 F.Supp.2d 1174, 1178-1180 (C.D. Cal. 2001).
56. 726 F.2d 1286, 1291 (8th Cir. 1984) (citations omitted).
57. *Ibid.* at 1291-1292.
58. *Ibid.* at 1292.

during the pendency of the arbitration.[59] Otherwise, in the Eighth Circuit, the only remedy available is before the arbitrators.

VII. THE UNDECIDED COURTS

In the Fifth, Eleventh and District of Columbia Circuits, the availability of injunctive relief in aid of international arbitration is unresolved. As one district court in the Fifth Circuit observed in 2012, that Court of Appeals allows injunctive relief pending the decision of a motion to compel arbitration, but has not decided whether the FAA "require[s] that a federal court immediately divest itself of any power to act to maintain the status quo *once it decides that the case before it is arbitrable*" (emphasis added).[60] The district court went on to note that most district court decisions within the Fifth Circuit allow for the possibility of injunctive relief, and determined that an injunction would be granted. The district court declined, however, to endorse either the Second Circuit's approach of granting an injunction until the conclusion of the arbitration or the First Circuit's more limited rule. Instead, relying on its interpretation of the contractual language, the Court determined that the parties had expressly contemplated the possibility of an injunction lasting the life of the arbitration, and entered such an order.[61]

Similarly, in the Eleventh Circuit, a district court has held that contractual language stating the claimant was "entitled to an injunction from a court of competent jurisdiction to keep you from violating these restrictions while the arbitration is pending" was sufficient to allow a court to act, and declined to rule on the broader question of the availability of injunctive relief in aid of arbitration absent such language.[62]

In the District of Columbia Circuit, the Court of Appeals has likewise declined to decide whether an injunction in aid of arbitration is generally available. In *National Railroad Passenger Corp. v. Expresstrak, L.L.C.*,[63] a district court noted that the availability

---

59. *Peabody Coalsales Co. v. Tampa Elec. Co.*, 36 F.3d 46, 47-48 (8th Cir. 1994). In *Manion v. Nagin*, the Eighth Circuit held that language in the arbitration agreement that "contemplates the possibility of interim judicial relief in the event of a dispute" is not sufficient, but only language providing "that a party is automatically entitled to injunctive relief". 255 F.3d 535, 539 (8th Cir. 2001).

60. *Amegy Bank National Association v. Monarch Flight II, LLC*, 870 F.Supp.2d 441, 451 (S.D. Tex. 2012).

61. *Ibid.* at 453. Most arbitration rules expressly allow applications to a court for interim relief, at least before formation of the tribunal. See, e.g., ICC Rules Art. 28(2); ICDR Rules, Art. 21(3). In the Second Circuit, a line of cases holds that a provision for arbitration under a particular set of rules incorporates them into the contract. See *Contec Corp. v. Remote Solution Co.*, 398 F.3d 205, 208-209 (2d Cir. 2005). That rule would seem to meet the test of courts that require contractual consent to injunctive relief, but, as noted, it was rejected by the Eighth Circuit.

62. *Am. Express Fin. Advisors, Inc. v. Makarewicz*, 122 F.3d 936, 940-941 (11th Cir. 1997).

63. 233 F.Supp.2d 39, 50 (D.D.C. 2002), rev'd on other grounds by *Nat'l R.R. Passenger Corp. v. ExpressTrak, L.L.C.*, 330 F.3d 523 (D.C. Cir. 2003) (declining to resolve issue of whether preliminary injunction should be issued because "when the Operating Agreement in this case was executed, a form of injunctive relief was clearly contemplated pending the submission of a dispute to the arbitration process".).

of injunctive relief was unsettled in that Circuit, but granted an injunction based on a status quo provision set out in the contract at issue.

VIII. RECENT DEVELOPMENTS IN AVAILABILITY OF ANTI-SUIT INJUNCTIONS: NEW YORK AS A CASE STUDY

It is unfortunately not uncommon for one party to an arbitration agreement to initiate litigation in violation of that agreement. In such circumstances, US courts have generally been more willing than those of other jurisdictions to enjoin such litigation. However, the Supreme Court has yet to speak to this issue, and there is some variance in the doctrinal approach of the various Circuits.[64]

The Second Circuit is the leading exponent of what has been characterized as the "restrictive" approach to issuance of anti-suit injunctions.[65] In *China Trade & Development Corp. v. M.V. Choong Yong*,[66] which involved parallel proceedings in the United States and Korea, the trial court held that it had the power to grant the requested injunction halting the Korean proceedings, stating that "[t]he power of federal courts to enjoin foreign suits by persons subject to their jurisdiction is well-established".[67] In a later case, *Paramedics Electromedicina Comercial, Ltda. v. GE Medical Systems Information Technologies, Inc.*,[68] the Second Circuit set out the test to be applied in determining whether an injunction halting foreign litigation in favor of arbitration would be granted. The Court summarized its test as follows:

> "It is beyond question that a federal court may enjoin a party before it from pursuing litigation in a foreign forum.... But principles of comity counsel that injunctions restraining foreign litigation be 'used sparingly' and 'granted only with care and great restraint'....

---

64. The anti-suit injunction is virtually unknown in civil law jurisdictions. The English Courts pioneered the use of the anti-suit injunction to protect the right to arbitrate, but in the celebrated *West Tankers* decision, the European Court of Justice held that an injunction could not be granted to halt litigation brought in another member state of the European Union in violation of an arbitration agreement.

65. The "restrictive" approach, which is followed in the Second, Third, Sixth, Eighth, and D.C. Circuits, and to some extent in the First and Eleventh, places significant emphasis on comity, whereas the "liberal" approach followed by the Fifth, Seventh and Ninth Circuits, emphasizes more traditional equitable factors. Compare *China Trade*, supra, 837 F.2d at 36 (internal quotations and citations omitted) ("an anti-foreign–suit injunction should be used sparingly ... and should be granted only with care and great restraint") with *E. & J. Gallo Winery v. Andina LaCorila S.A.*, 446 F.3d 984, 991 (9th Cir. 2006) ("[moving party] need only demonstrate that the factors specific to an anti-suit injunction weigh in favor of granting the injunction"). This article focuses on the anti-suit injunction jurisprudence of the Second Circuit, because that is the most common seat for international arbitration in the United States.

66. 837 F.2d 33, 37 (2d Cir. 1987).

67. *Id*. at 35.

68. 369 F.3d 645 (2d Cir. 2004).

An anti-suit injunction against parallel litigation may be imposed only if: (A) the parties are the same in both matters, and (B) resolution of the case before the enjoining court is dispositive of the action to be enjoined.... Once past this threshold, courts are directed to consider a number of additional factors, including whether the foreign action threatens the jurisdiction or the strong public policies of the enjoining forum.... Tecnimed contends that neither threshold requirement has been satisfied, and that comity considerations render the injunction inappropriate."[69]

In practice, the formal test requiring identity of the parties has been somewhat relaxed in the Second Circuit. For example, in *Storm LLC v. Telenor Mobile Communications AS*,[70] a dispute arose between the parties, one Norwegian and one Ukrainian, to a shareholders agreement for the largest mobile telecommunications provider in Ukraine. After an arbitration seated in New York was commenced by the Norwegian party pursuant to the agreement, its Ukrainian counterparty was sued in the Ukrainian courts by its own corporate parent, a Cyprus corporation, which sought a judgment invalidating the shareholders agreement and enjoining the New York arbitration.[71] The Ukrainian courts, proceeding in the absence of the Norwegian party, declared the shareholders agreement invalid and enjoined the arbitration.[72]

On Telenor's application for an anti-suit injunction halting the Ukrainian litigation, the district court was confronted by the fact that the Cypriot parent of the Ukrainian party was a party neither to the arbitration nor the shareholders agreement. In holding that the "same parties" test of *China Trade* was, nonetheless, satisfied, Judge Gerard Lynch, then sitting in the District Court, observed as follows:

> "*Paramedics* itself illustrates that although the threshold requirement is usually formulated as requiring that the parties be 'the same', the rule is not so strict in practice. In *Paramedics*, the Second Circuit held that the fact that a different party was present in the foreign proceedings did not defeat the 'same parties' requirement, because the purportedly distinct party was a close affiliate of one of the parties in the New York action, and was involved only because of its affiliation. Thus, the Court ruled, '[t]he district court did not abuse its discretion in ruling that the parties to the two actions are thus *sufficiently similar* to satisfy the first threshold requirement of *China Trade*'....
>
> [T]he Court agrees that Telenor [the Norwegian party] will likely succeed in establishing that Storm [the Ukrainian party], Alpren and Altimo [Storm's direct

---

69. *Id.* at 652 (internal quotations and citations omitted).
70. 06 Civ. 13157 (GEL), 2006 U.S. Dist. LEXIS 90978 (S.D.N.Y. 18 Dec. 2006). The author was counsel for Telenor in those proceedings.
71. *Ibid.* at *6. The grounds advanced in the Ukrainian case were that the individual who signed the shareholders agreement on behalf of the Ukrainian party – its president – lacked authority to do so, and that the agreement – which was expressly governed by New York law – was not written in Ukrainian, in supposed violation of a requirement of Ukrainian Law. *Ibid.* at *7.
72. *Ibid.*

and indirect parents] are alter egos of one another, at least to the extent necessary to warrant the relief Telenor seeks against them. Even if they are not, however, the parties in the two actions are sufficiently similar to satisfy the threshold requirement for a preliminary anti-suit injunction. The litigation in Ukraine, while nominally between Alpren and Storm, seeks to influence the arbitration proceedings and has resulted in orders that are directed at Telenor. Although Alpren is a participant in the Ukrainian litigation, Alpren is not merely a shareholder of Storm but is part of a family of affiliated corporations that collectively owns the entirety of Storm. The real parties in interest in the Ukrainian lawsuit are essentially the same entities that are involved in the arbitration here."[73]

Having addressed the issue of the identity of the Parties, the threshold issues, the Court went on to grant the requested injunction. The Court summarized the basis for its holding as follows:

"Attempts to interfere with arbitration of international disputes are so powerfully disapproved that the Second Circuit has suggested, albeit not decided, that 'an attempt to sidestep arbitration' might be 'sufficient to support a foreign anti-suit injunction'. Where this factor is present, little else is required to authorize an injunction. But here there is much else. The foreign litigation here has been conducted in the most vexatious way possible."[74]

The injunction was effective in ending the Ukrainian litigation, and the arbitrations proceeded to an award directing specific performance in favor of Telenor. Following confirmation, the award was enforced by two separate contempt orders, which finally obtained compliance. Such robust relief can be obtained only through the national courts. In particular, the need for relief against third parties, as was the case in *Storm*, would preclude relief by an arbitrator, whether an emergency arbitrator or a regularly constituted tribunal, because an arbitrator is without power to enter an award binding on third parties. Moreover, absent the coercive nature of a court order, a recalcitrant party could simply return to the foreign court and obtain injunctive relief against the arbitration or, as sometimes happens, the arbitrators.

In practice, for arbitrations seated in New York, the district courts have followed the approach set out in *Storm* and have been anything but restrictive in their willingness to grant anti-suit relief. In fact, the district courts within the Second Circuit have almost invariably been willing to enjoin foreign litigations brought in violation of an arbitration agreement providing for an arbitration seated in New York. For example, in *Amaprop Ltd. v. Indiabulls Financial Services Ltd.*,[75] the district court granted, in effect, an anti-anti-suit injunction, ordering a halt to proceedings in India that had enjoined an arbitration brought in New York in accordance with the parties' contract, noting that it is "difficult

---

73. *Id.* at *17 (internal citations and quotations omitted).
74. *Id.* at *26 (internal citations and quotations omitted).
75. 10 Civ. 1853 (PGG), 2010 U.S. Dist. LEXIS 27117, at *18-20 (S.D.N.Y. 23 Mar. 2010).

to overstate the strong federal policy in favor of arbitration".[76] Other courts in the Second Circuit have more or less routinely granted anti-suit relief on essentially the same basis and without regard to questions of comity, so long as the arbitration was seated in New York, the contract was governed by New York law, and relief was promptly sought.[77]

On the other hand, for arbitrations seated outside of the United States or governed by foreign law, the courts are far more deferential to foreign proceedings. For example, in *LAIF X. SPRI v. Axtel, S.A. de C.V.*, an injunction was sought to halt Mexican litigation involving some of the same issues as in the arbitration.[78] The Mexican party pursuing the arbitration simultaneously sought declaratory relief in a Mexican court. The Court held that an injunction could not be issued, noting that principles of comity "weigh heavily in the decision", and noted that the Mexican party was participating in the arbitration at the same time it sought "a ruling of Mexican law from a Mexican court".[79]

Accordingly, for arbitrations seated outside of the United States, or governed by foreign law, the district court and the Second Circuit are inclined to emphasize comity, and follow the approach of *LAIF* and exhibit reluctance to enter anti-suit injunctions.[80] For arbitrations seated in New York, and governed by New York laws, they have been far more willing to enjoin foreign proceedings.[81]

---

76. The Indian proceedings were then withdrawn, and the arbitration proceeded, resulting in an award in favor of Amaprop. See *Amaprop Ltd. v. Indiabulls Fin. Servs. Ltd.*, 11 Civ. 2001 (PGG), 2011 U.S. Dist. LEXIS 102419 (S.D.N.Y. 9 Sept. 2011) (confirming award). The author was counsel for Amaprop in that case. Following the award, the plaintiff again sought and obtained further anti-suit relief in New York, this time halting Indian proceedings that sought to enjoin confirmation and enforcement of the award.

77. See, e.g., *T-Jat Systems 2006 Ltd. v. Amdocs Software Sys. Ltd.*, 13 Civ. 5356 (HB), 2013 U.S. Dist. LEXIS 172969, at *4 (S.D.N.Y. 9 Dec. 2013) (enjoining litigation in Israel where "parties are similar enough" to satisfy *China Trade* test); *Alstom Chile S.A. v. Mapfre Compania de Seguros Generales Chile S.A.*, 13 Civ. 2416 (LTS) (DCF), 2013 U.S. Dist. LEXIS 156294, at *10 (S.D.N.Y. Oct. 31, 2013) (enjoining Chilean litigation, noting that anti-suit relief is particularly appropriate to halt "an attempt to sidestep arbitration"); *Travelport Global Distrib. Sys. BV v. Bellview Allinea Ltd.*, 12 Civ. 3483 (DLC), 2012 U.S. Dist. LEXIS 128604, at *21 (S.D.N.Y. 10 Sept. 2012) (enjoining Nigerian arbitration), *Suchodolski Assoc. v. Cardell Fin. Corp.*, 03 Civ. 4148 (WHP), 2006 U.S. Dist. LEXIS 3, at *8-*9 (S.D.N.Y. 3 Jan. 2006) (enjoining Brazilian arbitration); *SG Avipro Fin. Ltd v. Cameroon Airlines*, 05 Civ. 655 (LTS) (DFE), 2005 U.S. Dist. LEXIS 11117, at *5 (S.D.N.Y. 8 June 2005) (enjoining action in Cameroon, noting that the real parties in interest in that case and in the arbitration were the same).

78. 390 F.3d 194 (2d Cir. 2004).

79. *Ibid.* at 200.

80. Those cases granting anti-suit relief in favor of foreign arbitrations have also tended to stress the vexatious nature of the litigation being pursued by the enjoined party. See *Karaha Bodas Co. v. Perusahaan Pertambangan Minyak Dan Gas Bumi Nagara*, 500 F.3d 111 (2d Cir. 2007); *Sonera Holding B.V. v. Çukurova Holding A.S.*, 11 Civ. 8909 (DLC), 2013 U.S. Dist. LEXIS 69560, at *7-8 (S.D.N.Y. 15 May 2013).

81. In *Suchodolski Assoc., Inc. v. Cardell Fin. Corp.*, the Court granted an anti-suit injunction and distinguished *LAIF* because the claims at issue in *LAIF* being pursued in arbitration and those being pursued in court, although related, were distinct, and because "it involved issues of Mexican law". Nos. 03 Civ. 4148 (WHP), 04 Civ. 5732 (WHP), 2006 WL 3327625, at * 2 (S.D.N.Y. 16 Nov.

IX.   CONCLUSION

The widespread adoption of emergency arbitrator provisions will substantially reduce the need to seek interim relief from courts at the outset of litigation. At the same time, there are critical forms of equitable relief that can be obtained only through the courts, such as orders of attachment, or which are likely more effective if obtained through courts, such as anti-suit relief, which will continue to play an essential role in protecting the arbitral process.

2006). An interesting empirical study of anti-suit injunctions in the United States appears at Laura Eddleman HEIM, "Protecting Their Own? Pro-American Bias and the Issuance of Anti-Suit Injunctions", 69 Ohio St. L. J. (2008) p. 701.

A. Precision Stream

3. Matters of
Evidence: Witness and Experts

Report on the Session
Matters of Evidence: Witness and Experts

*Nicholas Lingard**

I.   SUMMARY

With presentations from two counsel and two economic experts, this session explored the utility of – and means to enhance the utility of – various forms of witness and expert evidence.

Larry Shore's provocative paper encouraged reflection on the utility of standard, lawyer-drafted, voluminous fact witness statements. Shore invited consideration of various possible reforms, including:

– a rule – or, at least, a practice – by which witness statements be limited to facts that are not apparent on the face of the documentary evidence on the record;
– the idea that witness statements should include, in granular detail, a description of the process of their preparation, including dates, times and durations of meetings between the witness and counsel; and
– the use of videotaped witness "statements" in large cases, adopting a question-and-answer format, affording the tribunal a more meaningful sense of the witness' demeanour.

Notwithstanding the scope for reform, the paper underscored – and the audience concurred with – the importance of fact witness testimony via written witness statements. In particular, Shore acknowledged (with the consensus of the audience) that there was little or no appetite for a return to full-scale direct, oral examinations.

Judith Levine's paper explored the jurisprudence around the authority of tribunals to require the appearance of witnesses and to "gate" witnesses by excluding irrelevant or cumulative testimony (and to do something about witnesses who do not show up).

Levine's review suggested that, under many rules and many legal systems, arbitrators enjoy the power both to request the appearance of non-witnesses and to exclude witnesses whose testimony is deemed to be cumulative or irrelevant. In practice, however, the use of the available mechanisms is more limited.

Levine urged caution – including close consultation with the parties – before tribunals take steps to invite the appearance of a witness not called by either party. She also

---

* Panel Rapporteur; Senior Associate, Freshfields Bruckhaus Deringer, Tokyo/Singapore.

surveyed the diversity of views on the propriety of "gating" witnesses: some in the community suggest that tribunals should exercise their powers more aggressively, while others caution that the authority (in a tribunal) not to hear a witness must be exercised sparingly. As to no-show witnesses, the picture in jurisprudence and practice is complex: the paper showed that while a variety of options is available to tribunals, few are accompanied by coercive powers.

Turning to expert evidence, Santiago Dellepiane explored issues of over- and under-compensation based on expert economic evidence in commercial arbitration.

Working via hypothetical examples, Dellepiane exposed risks of over-compensation by, among other economic errors, conflating (and allowing recovery for both) sunk costs and going-forward lost profits. He also explained the risks of under-compensation flowing from, among others, over-estimation of discount rates and a failure to compensate for future (but necessary) investments in the business at issue. Dellepiane's deceptively simple examples revealed both the superficial attraction of adopting these approaches, as well as their obvious wrong-headedness.

Notwithstanding the risk of error, Dellepiane was forceful in his view – endorsed by many in the audience – that tribunals tend to get damages, and the underlying economic analysis, at least basically right.

Finally, Howard Rosen addressed directly the question: How useful are party-appointed experts? His answer: potentially very. That view was shared by most in the audience.

Rosen explored a variety of mechanisms to enhance the utility of expert evidence, including witness conferencing (so-called "hot-tubbing"), upfront agreement by the tribunal with a witness' terms of engagement and issues to be canvassed, witness meetings, and joint reports. Rosen suggested the potential for each such mechanism to be used to assist the expert to manage the conflicting forces (client, opposing expert, counsel, tribunal) she confronts, to deliver expert assistance of most utility to the tribunal.

The paper also traversed the rules (and sanctions) applicable to the conduct of experts in international arbitration. The conclusion suggested that there is no shortage of rules – including from the experts' own professional bodies – but in practice a lack of sanctions of noncompliance.

II.   PROPOSITIONS: THE PANEL'S FINDINGS

Proposition	Myth	Reality	Other	Comment
1. Written witness statements are useless because they have been drafted by lawyers.	✓			
2. Cross-examinations are useless for tribunals because the witnesses are too (well) prepared.	✓			
3. It is for the parties alone to decide which witnesses will tell the story.	✓			
4. Tribunals cannot do much about a no-show witness.			✓	Somewhere between myth and reality
5. Arbitral tribunals always get it wrong: they will award too much or too little.	✓			
6. Party-appointed experts are partial and thus useless in determining complex technical or other issues which the arbitral tribunal cannot determine itself.	✓			
7. The conduct of experts is a rule-free and sanction-free zone in arbitration.			✓	(not rule-free, but possibly sanction-free?)

Do Witness Statements Matter –
And If So, How Can They Be Improved?

*Laurence Shore**

I.   INTRODUCTION

Lawyers draft witness statements. Everyone knows this. The statements are often very long and principally offer a tedious chronology of documents. To the limited extent that a witness statement offers first-hand evidence of disputed facts, the evidence is the product of (i) a partisan connection to the party submitting the statement or (ii) the witness's unreliable memory or (iii) both partisanship and unreliability.

As a consequence, even when cross-examination of the witness does not discredit his or her statement, the statement itself is rarely relied on by the arbitral tribunal.[1] We take this situation for granted. But we should not do so if we consider the applicable law of contract interpretation, and if we acknowledge the reality that even though all men and women are fallen, some have fallen farther than others. I will attempt to demonstrate the following five propositions by referring to English and New York law on contract interpretation, some relatively uncontroversial principles of proof, and routine international arbitral practice:

– Fact witness evidence often matters if the arbitral tribunal is to reach a sound result;
– Unless arbitration truly becomes "Americanized", oral examination-in-chief will continue to be a non-feature of the process;
– Witness statements in some form will continue to be part of the process;
– For the continuing vitality of the process, that form needs to change from the current written form; and
– There are some concrete changes of varying appropriateness for varying types of cases that can foster the continuing vitality of the process, without either (a) succumbing to

---

*   Herbert Smith Freehills-New York.
1. Portions of a cross-examination transcript are much more likely to be quoted in an arbitral award than portions of a witness statement.

the free-for-all of witness conferencing or (b) banning the burgeoning practice of "mock" cross-examination preparation.

To support the first point, i.e., fact witness evidence often matters in arbitration cases, I think I could refer to any number of national law systems, civil and common. Perhaps the clearest "transnational" instance where it matters is where there is an absence of documentary evidence relating to an issue that is material to the resolution of the dispute.[2] However, apart from this instance, civil law practitioners often observe with some degree of fervor that witness testimony (written or oral) is rarely submitted in commercial cases in their courts.[3] That is largely because it is deemed inherently unreliable (see the first paragraph of this Paper above), and, concomitantly, because of the belief that "documents speak for themselves" (common law lawyers frequently use this expression as well, though without suggesting the same significant imbalance between witness and documentary evidence).[4] To be sure, there are many cross-currents in civil law systems – for example, the significance of "good faith" in contract performance and interpretation, and, at least in French contract law, the view that the intentions of the parties are "a pure question of subjective fact"[5] – that render a "documents only" characterization far too simplistic.[6] Still, if one keeps the general contentions of civil law practitioners in mind, I have to at least be able to make a case for my five propositions on the basis of English and New York law, or face a quick return to the unhappy situation described in my opening paragraph, in which witness statements are and can only be little more than counsel's pleadings in another format. So, the best I can hope for, because of my common-law blinkers, is a "necessary but not sufficient" result. Still, one could do worse than that.

---

2. See Jennifer KIRBY, "Witness Preparation: Memory and Storytelling", 28 Journal of International Arbitration (2011, no. 4) p. 401, at p. 402.

3. See, e.g., Hans VAN HOUTTE, "Counsel–Witness Relations and Professional Misconduct in Civil Law Systems", 19 Arbitration International (2003, no. 4) p. 457, at pp. 458-459.

4. See, e.g., "Act III: Advocacy with Witness Testimony", 21 Arbitration International (2005, no. 4) p. 583, at pp. 588-589 (the comments of Michael SCHNEIDER and Michael MOSER).

5. See the discussion comparing English and French contract law in *Chartbrook Ltd v. Persimmon Homes Ltd* [2009] 1 A.C. 1101, 1119-20, in which Lord HOFFMANN, relying on an article by Professor Catherine Valcke, comments that because of the French position on subjectivity, "[i]t follows that any evidence of what they [the parties] said or did, whether to each other or to third parties, may be relevant to establishing what their intentions actually were".

6. Moreover, civil law practitioners who believe that documents somehow offer direct access to reality are expressing views that legions of European historians, literary critics, and philosophers have debunked for quite some time, arguing that a document requires a specific interpretive framework. See, e.g., Carlo GINZBURG, "Checking the Evidence: The Judge and the Historian" in *Questions of Evidence: Proof, Practice, and Persuasion Across the Disciplines* (Chicago 1994) p. 290, at pp. 294-295. Lord Hoffmann's approach to contract interpretation, discussed below, is very much like Ginzburg's approach to interpretation of historical documents.

II.   PROPOSITION 1 – ENGLAND (AND WALES) AND NEW YORK LAW

Here are Lord Hoffman's "common sense principles" of interpretation, set out in *Investors Compensation Scheme Ltd. v. West Bromwich Building Society* (ICS),[7] which provide a compelling foundation for the potential importance of witness evidence, at least when English law is the governing law of the contract:

> "(1) Interpretation is the ascertainment of the meaning which the document would convey to a reasonable person having all the background knowledge which would reasonably have been available to the parties in the situation in which they were at the time of the contract.
> (2) The background was famously referred to by Lord Wilberforce as the 'matrix of fact', but this phrase is, if anything, an understated description of what the background may include. Subject to the requirement that it should have been reasonably available to the parties and to the exception to be mentioned next, it includes absolutely anything which would have affected the way in which the language of the document would have been understood by a reasonable man.
> (3) The law excludes from the admissible background the previous negotiations of the parties and their declarations of subjective intent. They are admissible only in an action for rectification. The law makes this distinction for reasons of practical policy and, in this respect only, legal interpretation differs from the way we would interpret utterances in ordinary life. The boundaries of this exception are in some respects unclear. But this is not the occasion on which to explore them.
> (4) The meaning which a document (or any other utterance) would convey to a reasonable man is not the same thing as the meaning of its words. The meaning of words is a matter of dictionaries and grammars; the meaning of the document is what the parties using those words against the relevant background would reasonably have been understood to mean. The background may not merely enable the reasonable man to choose between the possible meanings of words which are ambiguous but even (as occasionally happens in ordinary life) to conclude that the parties must, for whatever reason, have used the wrong words or syntax: [citation omitted].
> (5) The 'rule' that words should be given their 'natural and ordinary meaning' reflects the common sense proposition that we do not easily accept that people have made linguistic mistakes, particularly in formal documents. On the other hand, if one would nevertheless conclude from the background that something must have gone wrong with the language, the law does not require judges to attribute to the parties an intention which they plainly could not have had...."

In a case decided one year before *ICS*, *Mannai Investment Co. Ltd. v. Eagle Star Life Assurance Co. Ltd.*,[8] Lord Hoffman also explained that "background" evidence is not a supplement to assist in interpretation of contracts or other documents, but instead is integral to the

---

7. [1998] 1 W.L.R. 896, 912-913.
8. [1997] A.C. 749, 775.

meaning of the contract or document. (Or as he subsequently put it in *Chartbrook* at 1114, fn. 5 above, since regard to background or context "is part of the single task of interpretation, the background and context must always be taken into consideration".) In *Mannai Investment*, Lord Hoffmann emphasized that it is the

> "background which enables us, not only to choose the intended meaning when a word has more than one dictionary meaning but also, in the ways I have explained, to understand a speaker's meaning, often without ambiguity, when he has used the wrong words. When, therefore, lawyers say that they are concerned, not with subjective meaning but with the meaning of the language which the speaker has used, what they mean is that they are concerned with what he would objectively have been understood to mean. This involves examining not only the words and the grammar but the background as well."

Lord Hoffmann acknowledged that there are some documents, e.g., those required by bankers' commercial credits, "in which the need for certainty is paramount and which admissible background is restricted to avoid the possibility that the same document may have different meanings for different people according to their knowledge of the background".[9] But in

> "the case of commercial contracts, the restriction on the use of background has been quietly dropped. There are certain special kinds of evidence, such as previous negotiations and express declarations of intent, which, for practical reasons which it is unnecessary to analyse, are inadmissible in aid of construction.[10] But apart from these exceptions, commercial contracts are construed in the light of all the background which could reasonably have been expected to have been available to the parties in order to ascertain what would objectively have been understood to be their intention." (Citation omitted)[11]

What does this very brief recapitulation of the sayings of Hoffmann mean for fact witness evidence in arbitration? As one of England's lower court judges explained, *ICS* points both to the need for such evidence and to important limitations on its use. I would submit that the guidance from Mr. Justice Toulson, in *N.V. Sabena S.A. v. European Aviation Ltd* [21 July 2000] QBD (Commercial) No. Folio 949 of 1999 [transcript; approved by the court for handing down], can assist all who participate in the international arbitral process. In striking or disregarding vast portions of the witness

---

9. *Id.* at 776.
10. In *Chartbrook*, 1116-1121, Lord Hoffmann discussed at great length the reasons for excluding pre-contractual negotiations. He did not dispute the propriety of the rule excluding evidence of what was said or done during the course of negotiating a contract for the purpose of "drawing inferences about what the contract meant". However, this rule did not exclude such evidence for other purposes, in particular "to establish that a fact which may be relevant as background was known to the parties". This was not an exception to the rule; rather, it operates outside the rule.
11. *Id.* at 779.

statements in a case concerning the interpretation of an aircraft leasing contract (as well as an expert's report because there was no market practice), Mr. Justice Toulson commented that the

> "proper function of a witness of fact in a case of this kind is to inform the court of facts not evident from the documents, or which can be more conveniently summarized in a witness statement, *that are relevant to a proper understanding of the context in which the parties entered into the agreement which the court is being asked to construe. It is not the function of a witness statement to set out a detailed narrative of the negotiations or make assertions about the intention of the parties in order to press one construction as preferable to another,* because the law excludes evidence of the previous negotiations of the parties and their declarations of subjective intent as material which may be used in construing a contractual document: *Investors Compensation Scheme Ltd v West Bromwich Building Society* [1998] 1 WLR 896, 913." (Emphasis added)

In criticizing the witness statements submitted to him in *N.V. Sabena*, Mr. Justice Toulson stated that

> "far more evidence was assembled than was necessary or appropriate for the purpose of determining what are essentially short issues of construction.... There is a responsibility on the parties and their legal representatives to see that material sought to be placed before the court is limited to that which is properly admissible and reasonably necessary."

There it is, a trial court's summary statement readily transferable to international commercial arbitration: as a matter of law, fact witness evidence may be important, even necessary, if it describes the context in which the parties entered into the agreement that the tribunal is being asked to construe, but to the extent that counsel seek to do more with fact witnesses, it has nothing to do with the law and is a waste of time and money. Stated differently, since contracts and other documents don't speak for themselves, witnesses endow them with the power of speech by describing the context out of which the contract emerged. Of course, witnesses are not counsel, and should not be making arguments to construe the contract. On the other hand, unless counsel are going to take the oath and deliver hearsay evidence of a special heightened quality of unreliability regarding background or context, fact witness evidence remains crucial to the process.

Just as it would be ill-advised to lump all civil law jurisdictions into one undifferentiated category of the approach to contract interpretation, one should recognize differences within the common-law systems. However, for present purposes – the importance of fact witness evidence – a focus on England/New York differences would be to indulge in the Freudian pastime of the "narcissism of small differences". New York law on contract interpretation, like English law, is attentive to the circumstances surrounding the parties' entering into the contract, for which witness evidence is singularly appropriate. And this is not a new development. New York's highest court, the Court of Appeals, has consistently emphasized the importance of context, or the parties' purpose in making the contract in New York law-speak, in conducting the

306

exercise of contractual interpretation. Among the clearest statements are the following: –

– *Aron v. Gillman*, 309 N.Y. 157, 163 (1955):

> "It is well settled that in construing the provisions of a contract we should give due consideration to the circumstances surrounding its execution, to the purpose of the parties in making the contract, and, if possible, we should give to the agreement a fair and reasonable interpretation."

– *Becker v. Patter A. Frasse & Co.*, 255 N.Y. 10, 14 (1930):

> "We think a construction so literal does violence to intention. The rule has often been declared that a contract is to be read in the light of the circumstances existing at its making, and that these may avail to stamp upon a word or phrase a loose or secondary meaning as distinguished from the strict or primary meaning to be gathered from the instrument unenlightened by extrinsic aids."

– *Empire Properties Corporation v. Manufacturers Trust Co.*, 288 N.Y. 242, 248-249 (1942):

> "We have said, 'The intention of the parties must be sought for in the language used. To understand the language we may put ourselves in their place and discern if possible the objects they had in view and the motives which dictated their choice of words. A wider meaning may thereby be disclosed.' (*Halsted v. Globe Indemnity Co.*, 258 N. Y. 176, 180.) The object which the parties had in view is, in this case, clear, and so are the motives which dictated their choice of words. The construction which has been placed upon the words the parties have chosen might defeat the object of the parties. The parties have chosen words which leave room for construction. Even literal construction would leave the meaning of the words open to doubt. The courts should then choose that construction which will carry out the plain purpose and object of the indenture."

– *William C. Atwater & Co. v. Panama R. Co.*, 246 N.Y. 519, 524 (1927) (quoting *Robertson v. Ongley Electric Co.*, 146 N.Y. 20 (1895)):

> "'Contracts are not to be interpreted by giving a strict and rigid meaning to general words or expressions without regard to the surrounding circumstances or the apparent purpose which the parties sought to accomplish.'... The Court should examine the entire contract and consider the relation of the parties and the circumstances under which it was executed. Particular words should be considered, not as if isolated from the context, but in the light of the obligation

as a whole and the intention of the parties as manifested thereby. Form should not prevail over substance and a sensible meaning of words should be sought."[12]

In addition to evidence of context and purpose, New York law's implied covenant of good faith and fair dealing in contract law and, in cases where the Uniform Commercial Code (UCC) applies, an express good faith obligation, carry further potential for the importance of adducing witness evidence (and which bring New York contract law closer to, e.g., Sect. 242 of the German Civil Code; Art. 1143(3) of the French Civil Code; and Italian Code Art. 1366 – which expressly provides that a contract must be interpreted in good faith). The New York courts were the first in the United States to introduce the implied covenant of good faith and fair dealing.[13] In 1962 New York adopted the UCC, in which Sect. 1-203 states that every "contract or duty within this Act imposes an obligation of good faith in its performance or enforcement". The comment to this section notes that it "sets forth a basic principle running throughout this Act. The principle involved is that in commercial transactions good faith is required in the performance and enforcement of all agreements or duties."

New York's good faith contractual obligation is usually thought not to be separable from the obligation to perform one's specified duties under the contract. Rather, the good faith obligation aids in the interpretation and performance of the terms of the contract. A tribunal is directed to interpret the contract within the commercial context in which it is created and performed. The New York good faith jurisprudence underscores the potential significance of fact witness evidence in contract cases where New York law applies to the merits.

If these two common law systems, at least, seemingly have witness evidence embedded in contract interpretation – to borrow a Lord Hoffmann expression, it can be seen as part of the "single task of interpretation" – what about the problems of witnesses' unreliable memory? Here, common law systems are perhaps too confident in the power of cross-examination to provide a check on the numerous and inherent flaws of recollection.[14] However, the concerns about these flaws, though no doubt heightened in recent years by the proliferation of experiments by psychologists showing how skewed the recollections of well-intentioned individuals can be, are not new, and cross-examination has not been regarded as the only tool for addressing the flaws. One of the greatest common-law scholars of evidence in the twentieth century, Professor J.H. Wigmore, spent hundreds of pages of his treatises dealing with the fallibility of witness testimony.

---

12. Under New York law, if the terms of the contract are deemed to be ambiguous, it is a basic rule that evidence extrinsic to the agreement's "four corners" may be considered to ascertain the intent of the parties. See, e.g., *Scholastic, Inc. v. Harris*, 259 F.3d 73, 82 (2d Cir. 2001).
13. See, e.g., *New York Central Iron Works Co. v. US Radiator Co.*, 174 NY 331 (1903).
14. Toby LANDAU QC's 2010 Kaplan Lecture in Hong Kong not only details the problems with witness recollection, but also has much to teach about the current flaws of witness statements in international arbitration and questions the common assumption of common law practitioners that the truth comes out in cross-examination. For a useful summary of Landau QC's Kaplan Lecture, see Alison ROSS, "Kaplan Lecture: Tricks of Memory or Tricks of Cross-Examination", 5 Global Arbitration Review (1 December 2010, no. 6).

One point that Wigmore made in his *Principles of Judicial Proof: As Given by Logic, Psychology, and General Experience, and Illustrated in Judicial Trials*, was that it was strange that we should even expect a witness to have something other than a flawed recollection: "A witness cannot be assumed beforehand by the law to know things; the most it can assume is that he thinks he knows."[15] That is why a tribunal needs to listen to a number of persons, and to assess the witness's memory in a variety of ways by reviewing a variety of sources of information. It is also why the substance of the witness's preparation for her testimony is a proper subject of inquiry. The fallibility of witness testimony is just one of the complex aspects of a case that an experienced and skilled decision maker must deal with. Moreover, part of the complexity in assessing witness testimony is that, as Wigmore's treatises clearly indicate, a witness's entire testimony should not necessarily be disregarded simply because one element is shown to be unsound. Some common law cross-examiners, particularly those who appear before juries, believe in the one-drop presumption: the decision maker will disregard everything a witness testifies to if one drop of it, even on a collateral matter, is shown to be spoiled. But Wigmore believed that judges (and arbitrators) are not like juries in this respect. Inherently flawed recollection as to the background of a contract is not useless evidence.[16]

III.   PROPOSITION 2 – ORAL EXAMINATION-IN-CHIEF A CONTINUING NON-FEATURE OF INTERNATIONAL ARBITRATION

If the above description of English and New York contract law arguably indicates a continuing foundation for the importance of witness evidence, and there is continuing unhappiness about written witness statements failing to serve as the witness's recollection (even if that recollection is flawed), is oral direct examination, perhaps preceded by a list of the topics and documents that the witness will refer to on direct examination, a plausible alternative? I think the uncontroversial answer to this question is no.

---

15. (Little, Brown: 1913) at p. 416.
16. Professor Kim Lane SCHEPPELE, in her article "The Ground-Zero Theory of Evidence", 49 Hastings L.J. (January 1998) p. 321, at pp. 333-334, provides another perspective on why we should not perhaps be so concerned about the vagaries of memory and so determined to try to capture the account that is closest in time to the event. She explains that many common-law practitioners (including the drafters of the Federal Rules of Evidence) take an approach to assessing witness testimony that rests on the shaky conception that "description without reflection is possible, and that one can find a somehow untainted or 'raw' description which becomes tainted or 'cooked' in subsequent retellings". However, as Professor Scheppele observes, "the first version of events also has a perspective embedded in it, like any other version of events". Professor Scheppele cautions that more belief should be placed in the later stories than in the "ground-zero" stories. A "rush to description", as she explains in her article, is not necessarily better than a "rush to judgment". Although her article does not address witness testimony in complex cases of contract interpretation, Professor Scheppele does provide an intriguing perspective that might also make it a bit easier for us to live with the reality that Professor Wigmore acknowledged and analyzed in his treatises.

There may be a few cases in which the parties may seek, and a tribunal may permit, oral direct examination. Gerald Aksen, in an Institute for Transnational Arbitration (ITA) workshop, recounted his experience in a Paris-seated arbitration between Russian and German parties regarding a large project that was built in Russia, and in which

> "the two principal testifiers were the chief executive officers of major corporations. What apparently happened was that they told their lawyers – a very high-quality, high-powered American team of lawyers on one side, and a very high-powered team of British and Russian lawyers on the other – look, we don't care what you learn at this ITA Conference, we want to tell our story, we are not going to put it in writing, and we want to tell it in our own words. And they did. They were both very effective."[17]

But it is doubtful that this situation described by Mr. Aksen has been or will be repeated with any frequency. At a minimum, not many parties are content to have so much of their case depend on the oral testimony of one witness, and in complex cases one witness is usually not sufficient to relate the story of background and performance. Perhaps more importantly, the notion of oral direct examination is, at this stage, largely a United States jury artifact that runs against not only civil law procedural approaches but also other common law approaches to the presentation of cases at evidentiary hearings. In addition, oral direct evidence in US courts is premised on a "discovery" regime, including but not limited to oral discovery depositions and interrogatories, that is designed to prevent against ambushes at trial; this US regime is not going to become part of international commercial arbitration. Moreover, the time and cost imperatives of the international arbitral process dictate against the implementation of oral direct evidence to any significant degree: hearings would undoubtedly become significantly longer if a witness's narrative is only heard at the final hearing, with all the messiness that such oral narratives entail, even when the direct examiner is adept at asking a series of non-leading questions or when the testimony has been rehearsed to death.

Finally, the possible palliative indicated in the first paragraph of this Section (a list of topics and documents that the witness will testify to) is not a satisfactory solution in most cases. This may be a relatively familiar procedure in, for example, Society of Maritime Arbitrators cases, but the opportunity for evidential ambushes remains a significant concern.

IV.   PROPOSITION 3 – WITNESS STATEMENTS IN SOME FORM ARE HERE TO STAY

In short, as a practical matter international commercial arbitration cannot do without witness statements filed in some form before the evidentiary hearing:

---

17. See fn. 4 above, at pp. 588-589.

(a) contract law and/or the absence of critical documents may require witness evidence;
(b) very few cases will be appropriate for the presentation of witness evidence primarily by oral examination-in-chief at the final hearing; and
(c) international arbitral practice – whereby memorials or briefs are the foundation of the presentation of a case before the final hearing, and such written submissions need to refer to the witness evidence, and not simply the documentary evidence, that the parties rely on – mandates the submission of witness statements in some form.

V.   PROPOSITION 4 – HOW CAN WRITTEN WITNESS STATEMENTS BE IMPROVED?

Since witness evidence is here to stay, as a matter of law (reminder: as a matter of the applicable law that I have chosen to discuss here) and arbitral practice, and such evidence needs to be filed in some form in conjunction with the parties' written submissions, what form should that be? In the concluding section below, *Proposition 5*, I am going to suggest that a form other than the usual written statement may be appropriate in some cases. But the written witness statement, written by counsel, is undoubtedly going to continue to be a principal part of the process. Given this reality, what are a few of the things that may nonetheless be done to address the amply justified general unhappiness with written witness statements and preserve the vitality of the arbitral process? The ones that I propose below are not new; they are just rarely implemented. And who needs to be responsible for implementing these (and other) proposals to address the problems with witness statements?

Based on Mr. Justice Toulson's guidance, everyone in the arbitral process – arbitrators, external counsel, and parties themselves – needs to be willing to push for changes, and above all be responsible for submitting "properly admissible and reasonably necessary" witness statements. However, as Mr. Justice Toulson's judgment in *N.V. Sabena* indicates, the arbitral tribunal must set out at the beginning of the case, or at least before witness statements are being prepared, how they should be prepared and, based on the applicable law, what they should and should not contain. Unless the arbitrators conduct the case in that way, it is difficult to see how they will avoid facing precisely what the court in *N.V. Sabena* so unhappily faced: lengthy statements that are effectively counsel's submissions and do not bear on the points at issue on which fact witnesses can actually provide assistance. If the arbitrators are not taking control of this issue, counsel (even if just one side of the table) should at least attempt to push the tribunal to issue the necessary guidance to the parties.

Accordingly, my short, non-exhaustive list of written witness statement improvement points, as issued by the tribunal to counsel, is as follows:

– The beginning of each statement should contain a full description of how the statement was prepared. This description must be detailed – "I met with counsel who then sent me a draft that I reviewed" is insufficient. Dates of meetings, time spent at meetings and in reviewing drafts, and the set of documents shown to the witness – not only the ones referred to in her statement – should be included. (The tribunal should explain that lengthy time spent by the witness on her statement is not considered a sign of improper

311

memory correction, but due care – the tribunal prefers the witness's correction of the narrative drafted by counsel.)

– The witness statement should be limited, per Mr. Justice Toulson, to properly admissible and reasonably necessary evidence from the witness, based on the applicable law. By way of example, then, the witness statement should not contain a chronology of documents, should not detail the history of negotiations, and should not argue the meaning of the terms of the contract. To the extent that the statement does so, it will be disregarded by the tribunal, and opposing counsel will be directed not to spend any time on cross-examination on those portions of the statement.

– The statement should, as much as possible, be a narrative that is the witness's narrative. This does not necessarily mean that the witness's "voice" can somehow be captured. But it means that every sentence in the statement is one that the witness adopts as her own testimony, and the witness must expressly say so when she affirms the truth of her statement.

– Since the statement stands as the witness's examination-in-chief, it must be in the same language as the witness's testimony during cross-examination, accompanied by a translation if it is in a language other than the language of the arbitral proceedings.

– One option that may be considered for some witness statements is to produce, in the actual manner of direct examination, a statement in question-and-answer format. Arbitrators are very familiar with reading transcripts, and the witness's most accurate recollection may be much easier to prompt and to reflect if the statement is in this format. There is still an unfortunate artificiality in conveying the testimony through this written method (see *Proposition 5*, below), but it may be useful, for example, if the witness is discussing technical matters.

– To avoid opposing counsel seeking to diminish the effect of a highly important witness's testimony by not calling the witness for cross-examination, counsel should indicate when the witness statement is submitted that if the witness is not called for cross, the witness should nonetheless be allowed to appear to respond to questions from the tribunal and to give a brief oral summary of her statement, provided that no other witness statement has covered or will cover the same issues to be summarized.

The discipline that the tribunal should seek to impose on counsel is the Toulson-Hoffmann discipline of providing background and context in witness statements, rather than argument, and if New York law is applicable (for example), providing testimony that goes directly to the issue of good faith. Witness statements will inevitably become shorter and more useful if this discipline is imposed. Witness memories will still arguably be slanted by the process of rehashing the past and reviewing the documents with counsel, but as Wigmore would say, that is why tribunals wish to see more than one witness speak to an issue. Witness statements adhering to the Toulson guidance will still carry the disadvantage that, when the witness appears at the hearing, the tribunal will principally see the witness under attack from a cross-examiner, and will not have the benefit of hearing the witness speak her narrative. But a witness who has been properly prepared for cross-examination (see below), and simply recounts what she knows first-hand of the relevant background, should survive the experience reasonably well. In any event, every approach to the submission of witness evidence carries certain disadvantages. The key point is that witness statements are not necessarily useless because drafted by counsel.

VI. PROPOSITION 5 – OTHER FORMS OF WITNESS EVIDENCE SHOULD BE CONSIDERED

Even the best witness statement carries the disadvantages indicated above (and probably more than just those): (a) it is written by counsel who, unless counsel has missed her calling as a brilliant novelist, will not capture the witness's voice; and (b) whether produced in narrative or question-and-answer form, the statement is not spoken by the witness and the tribunal does not hear and see the witness's direct account, but only sees the witness responding to unfriendly questions that pose a counter-narrative or otherwise seek to discredit or limit the effectiveness of the witness and her statement. This is not just a problem for the witness and her counsel: a tribunal that has not carefully read a witness statement immediately prior to the witness's appearance at the hearing may have little appreciation for the cross-examination and whether the cross-examiner has effectively dealt with the witness statement. In short, the tribunal may have no "base line" of demeanor or of substance from which to assess the witness's reasonableness and reliability on cross-examination. And that is unfortunate for counsel and their clients on each side of the room.

Accordingly, in cases of reasonably high value, it may be effective, as some arbitration practitioners have proposed, for the witness statement to be not a written statement (at least not originally), but instead a video. Of course, merely seeing someone read a lengthy (or even a short) statement in narrative form may be unhelpful to the tribunal. It would probably be much more effective if the video were in direct examination format, with questions and answers. The video and a written transcript of the video would then serve as the witness's "statement". It is difficult to see why opposing counsel should consider this problematic. In fact, it may assist cross-examination, because the cross-examiner gets to see and hear the witness before she appears at the hearing.

In view of the available technology and the significant amounts of attorney-time that already go into the drafting of witness statements, there would seem to be every reason for arbitrators and counsel and parties to at least consider witness evidence by video in place of written witness statements. Of course, there will always be the danger of diminished value of the exercise because the witness is either reading from a script or at least has been so heavily prepared from a script that she is simply delivering well-rehearsed lines handed to her by her counsel. The better actor may become the more effective witness. But as Wigmore would say, that is an inherent problem with witness testimony, and we do not discard all such testimony for that reason. One of the qualities that arbitrators presumably have is the ability to assess a witness's evidence on more than just fluency in speaking a role, though "witness preparation services" focus on precisely that type of fluency, and are somehow viewed as less problematic in certain jurisdictions than lawyers who work with witnesses on matters of substance, so that their evidence will be as accurate as possible.

Whether on matters of style or substance, is witness evidence so intrusively rehearsed, including through mock cross-examination exercises, that it has been rendered largely useless in international commercial arbitration? If so, aren't more radical changes called for than the modest ones proposed in this short paper?

I cannot imagine what those radical changes would be, other than (a) to return to a traditional civil law court procedure in which witnesses rarely appear, or (b) to institute much more "witness conferencing"[18] for fact witnesses than currently exists in international arbitration. But even though many witness statements are largely useless, the elimination of witnesses has about as much chance of being implemented as a routine feature of arbitration as US-style discovery depositions. Further, even though the exercise of mock cross-examination and, of much greater concern, improper "coaching" (which mock cross-examination does not necessarily entail) have probably rendered real cross-examination less useful to arbitrators in reaching their decisions, I question whether fact-witness conferencing is a good solution. Everyone has their own experience of this technique, and perhaps an increasing number of common-law trained practitioners are growing fonder of it. For my own part, I fail to see how it helps tribunals understand, better than cross-examination (and presuming that an effective witness statement – or video! – has been submitted before the hearing), which witness's recollection is sounder or which witness acted more reasonably in the face of factual uncertainty at the relevant time. The confrontation that conferencing entails does not necessarily recapture relevant background; instead, it may feature the type of past negotiation evidence that has little bearing on the tribunal's reaching a sound result.

Whatever one's view may be of the effectiveness of witness conferencing, this technique, according to Wolfgang Peter, still requires "from each witness a prior written statement for the preparation of the arbitral tribunal, counsel and the other witnesses and often this includes the filing of counter-witness statements" (see fn. 17). Witness conferencing, he notes, "will somewhat discourage witnesses from submitting witness statements drafted entirely by counsel".[19] Perhaps not entirely drafted by counsel, but still enough, I would say, to raise the same concerns voiced by international arbitration practitioners – and to lend support for the changes tentatively proposed in this Paper.

---

18. See, e.g., Dr. Wolfgang PETER's famous 2002 article, "Witness 'Conferencing'", 18 Arbitration International (2002, no. 1) pp. 47-58.

19. *Id.*

Can Arbitrators Choose Who to Call as Witnesses? (And What Can Be Done If They Don't Show Up?)

*Judith Levine**

I.   INTRODUCTION

In international arbitration, it is normally for the parties to decide how to present their case, including which witnesses to put forth to tell their story. This is consistent with each party having the burden of proving the facts relied on to support its claim or defence,[1] and accords with the notion of party autonomy.[2]

Occasionally, however, international arbitral tribunals might wish to hear from individuals who have not been made available by the parties but who could be of crucial interest to fill evidentiary gaps in the case. As set out in **Sect. II**, there is consensus that, under exceptional circumstances, a tribunal can call for the appearance of a witness at its own initiative. A tribunal's power to do so is consistent with its general authority to

---

*   Senior Legal Counsel, Permanent Court of Arbitration (PCA), The Hague. BA/LLB (UNSW); LLM (NYU); admitted to practice in New South Wales (Australia) and New York; Board Member, Australian Centre for International Commercial Arbitration. The views expressed are personal to the author and in no way attributable to the PCA. The author is grateful for the research assistance of Mariyana Toseva, Assistant Legal Counsel at the PCA in 2013.

1. See UNCITRAL Arbitration Rules (2010), Art. 27(1); ICDR Arbitration Rules (2010), Art. 19.1. See Paul A. GÉLINAS, "Evidence Through Witnesses" in Laurent LÉVY and V.V. VEEDER, eds., *Arbitration and Oral Evidence*, 689 Dossiers of the ICC Institute of World Business Law, p. 29 (henceforth "Gelinas") at p. 34 ("[I]t rests upon [each party] to identify and present the witnesses upon whose evidence he intends to rely. This aspect is inherent to the burden of proof rule.").

2. See Nigel BLACKABY, Constantine PARTASIDES with Alan REDFERN and Martin HUNTER, *Redfern and Hunter on International Arbitration* (OUP 2009) (henceforth "Redfern & Hunter") p. 365 at [6.08] ("Party autonomy is the guiding principle in determining the procedure to be followed in an international arbitration."); Phillip LANDOLT, "Arbitrators' Initiatives to Obtain Factual and Legal Evidence", 28 Arbitration International (2012) at p. 198 (henceforth "Landolt") ("It is unmistakable that arbitration as it is practised today places the primary responsibility for initiatives to obtain both factual and legal evidence upon the parties.... [T]his reality is explained by the importance of party autonomy in international arbitration.").

conduct proceedings and regulate the taking of evidence in an arbitration.[3] The possibility is expressly addressed in the IBA Rules on the Taking of Evidence in International Arbitration (IBA Rules) and provided for in the UNCITRAL Rules of Arbitration, most institutional rules and even some national arbitration laws. Examples, including recent arbitrations administered by the Permanent Court of Arbitration (PCA), illustrate how in practice tribunals have taken the initiative to seek the appearance of a witness.

This paper proceeds on the basis that witness evidence is useful. While contemporaneous documents are often considered the most important kind of evidence, witness evidence is valuable when it can supplement and clarify the documentary evidence, and bring to life what is written.[4]

The corollary to a tribunal's initiative to hear from a particular witness, is a tribunal's initiative when it does *not* wish to hear from a particular witness. **Sect. III** explores the power of arbitrators to exclude the appearance of a witness whose testimony has been offered by the parties, on the basis of it being irrelevant, immaterial, unreasonably burdensome, duplicative or otherwise objectionable. This power, which is covered by the IBA Rules and institutional rules, has the appeal of economy and efficiency. Yet some commentators consider its exercise to be perilous, in that it might encroach upon the parties' rights to be heard and treated equally. Some arbitral awards have been challenged, with mixed success, on the basis of the arbitrators' decision not to hear from witnesses. As with tribunal initiatives to *seek* the appearance of a witness, tribunal initiatives to *limit* the appearance of a witness should be exercised rarely, with caution, and in consultation with the parties.

It is one thing for a tribunal to have the power to *request* the appearance of a witness, but quite another to *compel* the appearance of a witness. **Sect. IV** of the paper considers the options available to a tribunal when the witness chair remains empty. If the tribunal is not content to let it lie, as a first step, the tribunal can ask the parties to use their best efforts to procure the attendance of the witness. Depending on the circumstances

---

3. REDFERN & HUNTER, *op. cit.*, fn. 2, p. 316 at [5.14] (noting that "[i]n general terms, the arbitral tribunal enjoys a very broad power to determine the appropriate procedure"); Gary B. BORN, *International Commercial Arbitration*, Vol. II (Kluwer 2009) pp. 1900-1902 (discussing tribunal's witness powers as "deriv[ing] from the tribunal's general authority to conduct and regulate the taking of evidence in the arbitration").

4. See Larry SHORE's Paper for this Panel, this volume, pp. 302-314. See also Christian OETIKER, "Witnesses Before the International Arbitral Tribunal", 25 ASA Bulletin (2007, no. 2) pp. 253-278. ("Examination of witnesses is widely considered to be a practical and important supplement that offers both parties and the arbitral tribunal the opportunity to clarify uncertainties concerning the relevant facts. Beyond this, testimonies of witnesses make what is written in documents and legal briefs vivid, giving them an additional dimension."); Antonias DIMOLITSA, "Some Reflections on Oral Evidence vs Documentary Evidence and on the Obligations and Rights of the Witnesses" in Laurent LÉVY and V.V. VEEDER, eds., *Arbitration and Oral Evidence*, 689 Dossiers of the ICC Institute of World Business Law, p. 11 (henceforth "Dimolitsa") at pp. 13-14 ("Oral evidence also satisfies [the] need of the arbitral tribunal ... to meet the people involved in the performance of the contractual relationship in order to gain a better understanding, do better in general, and progress more effectively towards forming its conviction."); GÉLINAS, *op. cit.*, fn. 1, at p. 30 (Live testimony "brings about an indispensable contribution to arbitrators in the pursuit of the truth").

(including the reasons for non-appearance and the extent to which the witness is within the control of a party), a tribunal may decide to disregard any witness statement or draw an adverse inference. In a few jurisdictions, arbitrators themselves have subpoena powers. In most jurisdictions, a tribunal and/or the parties may seek assistance from national courts in obtaining the appearance of witnesses present at the seat of the arbitration. The law at the place where the witness is located may also provide for the questioning of a witness through a court-sanctioned or court-operated process. Engaging the courts can be complex, time-consuming, uncertain and costly. Nevertheless, if tribunals and parties are prepared to assume those risks, they may have success in procuring key witness testimony to fill missing links in the evidentiary chain. Indeed, as some of the examples discussed in Sect. IV show, merely mentioning the possibility of resort to available court processes might have the effect of encouraging a reluctant witness to come forward and testify.

II. TRIBUNAL INITIATIVES TO CALL A WITNESS

In international arbitration, primary responsibility for obtaining evidence and selecting witnesses rests upon the parties. It is widely acknowledged, however, that in "more exceptional circumstances" a tribunal might require a particular witness that was not proposed to be called.[5]

In practice "the assessment of a case and of the relevant issues by the arbitral tribunal sometimes diverges form that of all parties involved".[6] In such situations, it is appropriate for the tribunal to take steps to ensure that it is presented with evidence on issues it considers pertinent. The parties for whatever reason may not have presented evidence from an individual that the tribunal believes to have crucial insight into an event or document material to the determination of the case.

A tribunal can ask the parties to use their best efforts to arrange that individual's appearance. An employee, a former employee or someone in a formal business relationship with the party could be expected to be responsive to such efforts. However, the parties' reasonable efforts might be futile if the individual is not within the control of the parties, or if there are factors such as animosity, infirmity, political or commercial sensitivity. In such cases, a request directly from the tribunal to the individual may be more appropriate. The tribunal may wish to hear from a witness whose statement was

---

5. Bernard HANOTIAU, "The Conduct of the Hearings", Chapter 16 in Lawrence W. NEWMAN and Richard D. HILL, *The Leading Arbitrators' Guide to International Arbitration* (Juris 2004) (henceforth "Hanotiau") at p. 382; Jeff WAINCYMER, *Procedure and Evidence in International Arbitration* (Kluwer 2012) (henceforth "Waincymer") p. 888; BORN, *op. cit.*, fn. 3, p. 1843; Peter R. GRIFFIN, "Recent Trends in the Conduct of International Arbitration – Discovery Procedures and Witness Hearings", 2 Journal of International Arbitration (2000) p. 19 (henceforth "Griffin") at p. 25.
6. Tobias ZUBERBÜHLER, Dieter HOFMANN, Christian OETIKER, Thomas ROHNER, *IBA Rules of Evidence: Commentary on the IBA Rules on the Taking of Evidence in International Arbitration* (2012) at pp. 17 and 87 (henceforth "Zuberbühler").

withdrawn by one of the parties, or even a witness whose testimony was not offered at all.

1. A Tribunal's Power to Call a Witness at Its Own Initiative

A tribunal's power to request witness evidence derives from the tribunal's general authority over arbitral proceedings.[7] The power is also provided for, expressly or implicitly, in some arbitration rules and laws, as discussed below. The arbitration agreement in the applicable contract or treaty is unlikely to contain any provisions expressly directed to this scenario.

a. National arbitration laws

Most national arbitration laws, including the UNCITRAL Model Law on International Commercial Arbitration, provide generally for arbitrators to "conduct the arbitration in such manner as it considers appropriate".[8] Some provide expressly for arbitrators to take initiatives in matters of evidence, but without specifically addressing initiatives to call witnesses.

For example, the **English Arbitration Act 1996** provides in Sect. 34 that "It shall be for the tribunal to decide all procedural and evidential matters, subject to the right of the parties to agree any matter" and specifies that "procedural and evidential matters" include "(g) whether and to what extent the tribunal should itself take the initiative in ascertaining the facts and the law".

Art. 184(1) of the **Swiss Private International Law Act** provides that "the arbitral tribunal shall itself conduct the taking of evidence". This is subject to the overriding duty to accord "equal treatment to the parties and their right to be heard in an adversarial proceeding".[9]

Arbitration statutes in some civil law jurisdictions, such as **China, Korea, Japan, Germany** and **Brazil**, expressly confer on tribunals the right to establish the facts of the case by all appropriate means, including the taking of evidence ex officio and by

---

7. Nathan O'MALLEY, *Rules of Evidence in International Arbitration* (Informa, London 2012) (henceforth "O'Malley") at [4.74]; LANDOLT, *op. cit.*, fn. 2, at p. 189 ("... arbitrators most certainly have th[e] power [to take initiatives to obtain evidence] ... this operates so widely in international arbitration that it may be considered a general principle. The simple reason for this is that, as a general rule in arbitration, the arbitrators are masters of the procedure..."); WAINCYMER, *op. cit.*, fn. 5, at p. 888 ("while few arbitral statutes expressly provide a tribunal with a power to summon witnesses, the better view is that general discretionary powers are broad enough to justify this".).

8. UNCITRAL Model Law on International Commercial Arbitration (as amended in 2006), Art. 19(2).

9. Arts. 182(3) and 184 of the Swiss Private International Law Act. See generally Matthias SCHERER and Martin DAWIDOWICZ, Switzerland Arbitration Guide, IBA Arbitration Committee <www.lalive.ch/data/publications/IBA_Arbitration_Guide_(Switzerland).pdf>.

investigating facts on its own initiatives. Usually such a power is accompanied by a duty to submit such facts to the parties.[10]

Commentators in the **Netherlands** have noted with respect to Art. 1039(3) of the Dutch Arbitration Law that "although the law stipulates that witnesses can only be examined at the request of one of the parties, it is generally presumed that an arbitral tribunal may also request the hearing of witnesses".[11]

As discussed below in Sect. IV, international arbitral tribunals sitting in the **United States** may not only request the attendance of witnesses, but also compel their attendance through issuance of subpoenas.

By contrast, the **Swedish Arbitration Act** places more emphasis on the parties having responsibility for matters of evidence. Kaj Hobér states that under the Swedish law "the initiative with respect to evidence is exclusively in the hands of the parties",[12] observing that Sect. 25(1) stipulates that "the parties shall supply the evidence...". This means that "the parties are in charge of the evidence, including witnesses, that they wish to rely on and the way the evidence will be presented to the arbitrators.... Notwithstanding this, parties may benefit from the arbitrators' case management activities in this respect, at least in the sense that the arbitrators may indicate which facts they deem relevant." Overall, he observes, "the principle of party autonomy applies also with respect to evidence, save for some limited powers of the arbitrators to dismiss evidence manifestly irrelevant or untimely presented".[13]

b.   Arbitration rules

The **UNCITRAL Arbitration Rules (UNCITRAL Rules)** provide in Art. 27(3): "At any time during the arbitral proceedings the arbitral tribunal *may require the parties to produce* documents, exhibits or *other evidence* within such a period of time as the arbitral tribunal shall determine."[14] (Emphasis added)

---

10. See Arbitration Law of the People's Republic of China, effective from 1 September 1995, Art. 43 ("Parties shall provide evidence in support of their own arguments. The arbitration tribunal may of its own motion collect such evidence as it considers necessary."); Arbitration Act of Korea Enacted by Law No. 1767, amended by Law No. 6083 of 31 December 1999, Art. 20; German Arbitration Law, Sect. 1042(4) ("The arbitral tribunal is empowered to determine the admissibility of taking evidence, take evidence and assess freely such evidence."); the Brazilian Act, Law No. 9.307 of 23 September 1996, Japanese Arbitration Law No. 138 of 2003, Art. 25(1). As cited by Teresa GIOVANNINI, "Ex Officio Powers to Investigate the Facts: When Do Arbitrators Cross the Line?", oral presentation delivered at IBA Arbitration Day, 4 March 2011.

11. Marieke van HOOIJDONK and Peter EIJSVOOGEL, *Litigation in the Netherlands: Civil Procedure, Arbitration and Administrative Litigation* (Wolters Kluwer 2009) p. 107 [3.2.3.2.] For the Dutch Act, which is soon to be revised, see <www.jus.uio.no/lm/netherlands.arbitration.act.1986/>; in hard copy in Prof. Pieter SANDERS and Dr. Albert Jan van den BERG, *The Netherlands Arbitration Act 1986* (Kluwer 1987).

12. Kaj HOBÉR, *International Commercial Arbitration in Sweden* (OUP 2011) p. 224 at [6.93].

13. *Ibid.*, at [6.97]

14. Available at: <www.uncitral.org/uncitral/en/uncitral_texts/arbitration/2010Arbitration_rules. html> . For equivalent in 1976 version see Art. 24(3).

In his commentary on the UNCITRAL Rules, David Caron confirms that the reference to "other evidence" was intended to encompass evidence by witnesses.[15] Thomas Webster agrees, and notes that initiatives by the tribunal to seek evidence involve a balancing exercise "between the Tribunal's desire to fully understand the facts of the case with the right of the parties to present their cases as they wish".[16]

The UNCITRAL Rules frame the tribunal's initiatives in respect of witnesses as being channelled through requests to the parties. Examples of how tribunals have exercised their initiative to call for additional witness testimony in UNCITRAL cases are discussed in Sect. II.2 below.

A provision identical to Art. 27(3) of the UNCITRAL Rules appears in the **PCA 2012 Arbitration Rules (PCA Rules)**, the **International Centre for Dispute Resolution/American Arbitration Association Arbitration Rules (ICDR/AAA Rules)** and the **Arbitration Rules of the Swiss Chambers' Arbitration Institution (Swiss Rules)**.[17]

Art. 25(3) of the **International Chamber of Commerce Rules of Arbitration (ICC Rules)** allows for the tribunal to "summon any party to provide additional evidence".[18] According to Derains and Schwartz, this provision implicitly authorizes the arbitral tribunal to order the appearance of witnesses.[19]

The **Arbitration Rules of the London Court of International Arbitration (LCIA Rules)** in Art. 22.1(c) provide for arbitral tribunals to "conduct such enquiries as may appear to the Arbitral Tribunal to be necessary or expedient, including whether and to what extent the Arbitral Tribunal should itself take the initiative in identifying the issues and ascertaining the relevant facts and the law(s) or rules of law applicable to the arbitration, the merits of the parties' disputes and the Arbitration Agreement". Some have noted that a tribunal's initiative to call for the appearance of a witness is a step more in the civil law tradition of inquisitorial procedures than in the common law tradition of an adversarial procedure. Bühler and Dorgan suggest that "this may explain why the LCIA Rules do not provide expressly for the arbitral tribunal to order the appearance of a witness" but consider that the arbitral tribunal would "arguably ... have that power under Art. 22.1(c)".[20]

---

15. David D. CARON, Lee M. CAPLAN, Matti PELLONPÄÄ, *The UNCITRAL Arbitration Rules: A Commentary* (OUP 2006) pp. 574-579.
16. Thomas H. WEBSTER, *Handbook of UNCITRAL Arbitration* (Sweet & Maxwell 2010) paras. 27-72 et seq., at [27-106].
17. PCA Rules, Art. 27(3); ICDR Rules, Art. 19(3); Swiss Arbitration Rules 2012, Art. 24(3).
18. Art. 25 of the 2012 ICC Rules ("1. The arbitral tribunal shall proceed within as short a time as possible to establish the facts of the case by all appropriate means.... 3. The arbitral tribunal may decide to hear witnesses, experts appointed by the parties or any other person, in the presence of the parties, or in their absence provided they have been duly summoned.... 5. At any time during the proceedings, the arbitral tribunal may summon any party to provide additional evidence.").
19. Yves DERAINS and Eric A. SCHWARTZ, *A Guide to the New ICC Rules of Arbitration* (Kluwer Law International 1998) pp. 256-257.
20. Michael BÜHLER and Carroll DORGAN, "Witness Testimony Pursuant to the 1999 IBA Rules of Evidence in International Arbitration – Novel or Tested Standards?", 17 Journal of International Arbitration (2000, no. 1) pp. 3, 18 (henceforth "Bühler and Dorgan").

Art. 29(1) of the **Arbitration Rules of the Netherlands Arbitration Institute (NAI Rules)** deals with witness hearings, stating that "the arbitral tribunal shall determine the day, time and place of the examination of witnesses, as well as the manner in which the examination shall proceed unless the parties agreed to a manner of examination...". A commentary to the NAI Rules observes that "[a]lthough the NAI Rules do not include a provision that explicitly allows the arbitral tribunal to examine witnesses at its own initiative, it may be assumed that it follows implicitly from Art. 29(1) that the arbitral tribunal has the authority do to so. This authority may be relevant, for example, if the parties fail to call a key witness that the arbitral tribunal wishes to examine."[21]

The **Arbitration Rules of the China International Economic and Trade Arbitration Commission (CIETAC Rules)**, consistent with the Chinese arbitration law, go further, in providing that "the arbitral tribunal may, on its own initiative, undertake investigations and collect evidence as it considers necessary".[22] The parties need only be notified of such investigating process if the tribunal considers it necessary, although the evidence thus collected shall be transmitted to the parties for them to comment.[23] The rules do not expressly refer to witness evidence.

Art. 24.1 of the 2013 **SIAC Rules** contains a list of a tribunal's "additional powers" that are said to be "not in derogation of the mandatory rules of law applicable to the arbitration". This list includes in para. (d) the power to "conduct such enquiries as may appear to the Tribunal to be necessary or expedient" but does not expressly refer to calling of witnesses on the tribunal's initiatives (whereas it does refer to production of documents, making items available for inspection and directing "any *party* to give evidence by affidavit or in any other form" (emphasis added).

Finally, mention is made of Art. 43 of the **Convention on the Settlement of Investment Disputes between States and Nationals of Other States (ICSID**

---

21. Bommel van der BEND, Marnix LEIJTEN and Marc YNZONIDES, *A Guide to the NAI Arbitration Rules, Including a Commentary on Dutch Arbitration Law* (Kluwer 2009) (henceforth "Van der Bend, et al.") p. 144. The authors warn that based on Dutch case law, "the rules of impartiality and independence dictate that an arbitrator cannot gather evidence himself outside the parties" without the explicit permission of the parties, referring to a Dutch Supreme Court case of 29 June 2007, in NJ 2008, 177. It involved a medically qualified arbitrator who conducted his own medical examination of an employee. The Court ruled that arbitrators should in principle restrict themselves to examination of evidence and may use their specific expertise to resolve the dispute, but if this requires them to conduct their own inquiry, the parties must explicitly permit them to base the judgments on their own findings.

22. Arbitration Law 1994, Sect. 43, which empowers a Chinese arbitral tribunal to undertake its own investigations and collect evidence, although reportedly such power is rarely used. Peter MEGENS, Paul STARR, et al., "Compulsion of Evidence in International Commercial Arbitration: An Asia-Pacific Perspective", 2 Asian International Arbitration Journal (2006, no. 1) at p. 52 (henceforth "Megens").

23. CIETAC Arbitration Rules, Art. 37 ("1. The Arbitral Tribunal may, on its own initiative, undertake investigations and collect evidence as it considers necessary.... 3. The Arbitral Tribunal shall, through the Secretariat of the CIETAC, transmit the evidence collected by itself to the parties and afford them an opportunity to comment.").

Convention), which provides:[24] "Except as the parties otherwise agree, the Tribunal may, if it deems it necessary at any stage of the proceedings, (a) Call upon the parties to produce documents or other evidence...."

According to Christophe Schreuer's commentary on the Convention, the tribunal's power under Art. 43 is "supplementary in the sense that it is designed to close gaps left after the parties have adduced all the material they deem relevant".[25] Schreuer notes that the "initiative to provide relevant evidence will be primarily with the parties... If in the tribunal's view the evidence thus supplied remains incomplete, it may request further information," even after the closure of the proceeding.[26] ICSID tribunals have asked parties to provide answers to specific questions, to produce specific documents and witnesses or have appointed experts on their own motion. Examples of ICSID tribunals asking the parties to produce witness testimony are discussed below in Sect. II.*2.b*.

Schreuer also points out that "the Convention's text provides that the tribunal direct its call for further information to the parties. During the Convention's drafting, there was some discussion of a possible power to compel the appearance of witnesses before the tribunal.... A proposal to give the tribunal the right to call witnesses directly and not through the parties was defeated narrowly." He notes that only parties to ICSID arbitrations may approach courts for assistance and there is no explicit legal basis for a tribunal's request for judicial assistance. He observes that:[27]

> "In the majority of instances, tribunals have directed their calls for evidence to the parties. In this manner, questions were asked and the production of documents was ordered. When witnesses were heard, they were normally brought to the tribunal through the intercession of the parties.... There is nothing that would prevent a tribunal from directly inviting a witness to appear before it and to testify.... But it is clear that a tribunal has no power to compel a witness's appearance."

c.   The IBA Rules on the Taking of Evidence

Most of the laws and rules discussed above are concerned with a tribunal's initiatives with respect to evidence generally or are couched in terms of tribunals requesting the *parties* to arrange witness testimony. The IBA Rules[28] go one step further in articulating

---

24. ICSID Convention, Art. 43(a); see also Art. 38 of the ICSID Rules of Arbitration.
25. Christophe H. SCHREUER with Loretta MALINTOPPI, August REINISCH, Anthony SINCLAIR, *The ICSID Convention: A Commentary*, 2nd ed. (Cambridge University Press 2009) (henceforth "Schreuer") p. 649.
26. *Ibid.*, p. 650.
27. *Ibid.*, p. 654.
28. See IBA Rules on the Taking of Evidence in International Arbitration (henceforth "IBA Rules"), adopted 29 May 2010, available at: <www.ibanet.org/Publications/publications_IBA_guides_and_free_materials.aspx#takingevidence>. The IBA Rules "contain procedures initially developed in civil law systems, in common law systems and even in international arbitration processes themselves. Designed to assist parties in determining what procedures to use in their particular case, they present some (but not all) of the methods for conducting international arbitration proceedings. Parties and arbitral tribunals may adopt the [IBA Rules] in whole or in part – at the

the tribunal's powers with respect to calling witnesses, either via the parties, or on its own. Art. 4.10 provides:

> "At any time before the arbitration is concluded, the Arbitral Tribunal may order any Party to provide for, or to use its best efforts to provide for, the appearance for testimony at an Evidentiary Hearing of any person, *including one whose testimony has not yet been offered.* A Party to whom such a request is addressed may object for any of the reasons set forth in Article 9.2." (Emphasis added)

While Art. 4.10 concerns requests via the parties, Art. 8.5 makes it clear that a tribunal may make such a request directly:

> "Subject to the provisions of Article 9.2, the Arbitral Tribunal may request any person to give oral or written evidence on any issue that the Arbitral Tribunal considers to be relevant to the case and material to its outcome. Any witness called and questioned by the Arbitral Tribunal may also be questioned by the Parties."

Art. 9.2 states that the tribunal "shall, at the request of a Party or on its own motion, exclude from evidence or production any Document, statement, oral testimony or inspection for any of the following reasons" which include "(a) lack of sufficient relevance to the case or materiality to its outcome...; (c) unreasonable burden to produce the requested evidence... ; and (g) considerations of procedural economy, proportionality, fairness or equality of the Parties that the Arbitral Tribunal determines to be compelling".

The Commentary on the IBA Rules acknowledges that

> "Witnesses of fact are the responsibility of the parties. The parties have to select the witnesses they will present and the issues on which they will testify.... [However] Article 8.1 means that the arbitral tribunal may request the appearance of a particular witness even if neither party requests that witness's appearance."[29] In general, as articulated in Art. 4.10, the tribunal "may order any party to provide for, or to use its best efforts to provide for, the appearance for testimony of any person, including one whose testimony has not yet been offered". This is balanced by the fact that "a party also has the right to object to any such request addressed to it for the reasons set forth in Article 9.2".

---

time of drafting the arbitration clause in a contract or once an arbitration commences – or they may use them as guidelines. Parties are free to adapt them to the particular circumstances of each matter." See *Commentary on the revised text of the 2010 IBA Rules on the Taking of Evidence in International Arbitration*" by the 1999 IBA Working Party and 2010 IBA Rules of Evidence Review Subcommittee, available at: <www.ibanet.org/Document/Default.aspx?DocumentUid= DD240932-0E08-40D4-9866-309A635487C0> (henceforth "IBA Commentary").

29. IBA Commentary, p. 24.

With respect to "Tribunal Witnesses", the IBA Commentary explains:

"Inquisitorial powers of the arbitral tribunal follow from the *lex arbitri* of the seat of the arbitration.[30] Inquisitorial powers may also follow from the arbitration rules agreed by the parties.[31] The IBA Rules of Evidence do not provide for similarly sweeping inquisitorial powers of the arbitral tribunal, but *Art. 8.5 covers the main case where inquisitorial powers may be exercised: the hearing of a key witness* who typically had an earlier association with both parties but whom the parties for some reason failed to persuade to appear, perhaps because they no longer have close ties with the witness. Such a tribunal witness will often be questioned in the inquisitorial fashion described above. To proceed in this fashion is *not mandated*, but is contemplated by the second sentence of Art. 8.5." (Emphasis added)

The IBA Rules are regarded as reflecting a consensus view on international best practice but will only be binding if the parties so agree. Parties often agree to them simply having a guiding function.[32] Although the IBA Commentary claims that the Rules do not amount to "sweeping inquisitorial powers", others have noted that the provisions in Arts. 4.10 and 8.5 are "more in the civil law tradition of inquisitorial procedures than in the common law tradition of an adversarial procedure".[33] Zuberbühler considers that Art. 8.5 in particular "grants the arbitral tribunal a wide discretion reminiscent of inquisitorial powers: the arbitral tribunal may request any person to give oral or written evidence on any issue the arbitrators consider to be relevant to the case and material to its outcome".[34]

O'Malley notes that tribunals may act *sua sponte* to order the production of evidence before it, including hearing from individuals who have particular information about the dispute but who have not been formerly tendered as witnesses. He regards Art. 4.10 of the IBA Rules as confirming a tribunal's "inherent authority that it may expect a party to cooperate in producing evidence to it" and as acknowledgement of the arbitrator's "basic authority to request a party to present a witness to be heard that has relevant and material evidence".[35]

The powers in Arts. 4.10 and 8.5 will be particularly fruitful if a party has some control over or influential relationship with the individual. According to Gary Born, the "classic examples of such witnesses are corporate officers, directors, or senior employees

---

30. Citing as examples Art. 34(2) of the English Arbitration Act 1996; and Art. 184 Swiss Private International Law Act.
31. Citing as examples ICC Rules, Art. 20 and LCIA Rules, Art. 22.1(c).
32. Some institutional rules have embraced the IBA Rules as part of their own arbitral rules. For example, see the Australian Centre for International Commercial Arbitration Rules, Art. 27.2, which provides that "the Arbitral Tribunal shall have regard to, but is not bound to apply, the International Bar Association Rules on the Taking of Evidence in International Arbitration in the version current at the commencement of the arbitration".
33. BÜHLER and DORGAN, *op. cit.*, fn. 20, p. 17.
34. ZUBERBÜHLER, *op. cit.,* fn. 6, p. 161.
35. O'MALLEY, *op. cit.*, fn. 7, at [4.74-4.77].

of a party to the arbitration".[36] The kinds of "best efforts" that a party might be expected to use include contacting the individual, making financial and logistical arrangements for their travel to the hearing and otherwise ensuring their presence. A party who does not cooperate with the tribunal's request under Art. 4.10, or has no valid excuse for failing to present the person in response to the tribunal's order may run the risk of an adverse inference being drawn against it.[37]

In instances where the parties have little control or relationship with the individual in question, a tribunal may be more likely to call a witness on its own motion pursuant to Art. 8.5 of the IBA Rules. How the tribunal goes about calling the witness may depend on where it is sitting. It may do so simply by sending a written request, or it might opt for a more formal method such as a tribunal subpoena, or request via the national courts, mechanisms which are discussed in Sect. IV of this paper. As one of the below examples shows, the request of a tribunal will need to be sensitive to the contours of confidentiality of the case. Despite the broad language of "any person" in Art. 8.5 of the IBA Rules, the identity of the individuals sought by the tribunal is unlikely to be a surprise to the Parties. O'Malley notes that "while the text of the article casts the net quite widely, the authority in Art. 8.5 will often be used to summon persons whom the parties have identified in their pleadings as possessing relevant information, but whom, for one reason or another, they have not called as a witness".[38]

Whether a tribunal requests a witness testify using its powers under Art. 4.10 (via the parties) or via Art. 8.5, it should consult with the parties in the process, and provide them with an opportunity to comment on whether any of the considerations in Art. 9.2 should be taken into account. However, "the simple fact that one party does not wish the witness to be present at the hearing does not abrogate a tribunal's authority to act to hear the witness. It may also be that a tribunal will call a witness once tendered by a party, but which it later withdraws."[39] The tribunal should of course give the parties the opportunity to question the witness it calls. Finally it should be observed that Arts. 4.10 and 8.5 in no way *oblige* the tribunal to call a witness to appear. As noted in Sect. IV, it may have other tools at its disposal if it considers calling the witness would not be likely to assist the tribunal or would hamper the fairness or efficiency of proceedings.

The IBA Rules dealing with arbitrator initiatives to call witnesses are not without their critics.[40] Zuberbühler submits that "this inquisitorial power is very far-reaching and should be applied cautiously by the arbitral tribunal".[41] Oetiker also considers that the power in the IBA Rules "to order the hearing of persons who were not named as witnesses by the parties... is too broad":[42]

---

36. BORN, *op. cit.*, fn. 3, pp.1900-1902.
37. See BÜHLER and DORGAN, *op. cit.*, fn. 20, p. 17; O'MALLEY, *op. cit.*, fn. 7, at [4.77-4.78].
38. O'MALLEY, *op. cit.*, fn. 7, at [8.86].
39. *Ibid.*
40. GÉLINAS, *op. cit.*, fn. 1, at p. 36 (noting that when a tribunal wishes to hear a person whose testimony has not yet been offered, early action may be required and "it could raise questions in the parties' mind".).
41. ZUBERBÜHLER, *op. cit.*, fn. 6, at paras. 17 and 87.
42. OETIKER, *op. cit.*, fn. 4, p. 263.

"Certainly it is correct that arbitral tribunals ... should endeavour to effectively resolve the dispute and not merely to settle the proceedings. However, it must be left to the discretion of the parties as to which arguments and evidence they wish to present in support of their position. The only valid exceptions are those in which an arbitral tribunal must consider certain aspects '*ex officio*' and the parties have not, or at least not adequately, commented on these aspects. Even in this area, however, the arbitral tribunal must be cautious, since it runs the risk of exceeding its powers."

One commentator recently stated that it is

"one thing ... to say that arbitrators have inquisitorial powers, another is to say that arbitrators effectively use such powers. And many are the reasons why arbitrators quite often don't use them. On the one hand, an arbitrator of common law tradition may not be keen in using powers far from his background. On the other hand ... the use of inquisitorial powers may be seen as in favor of one party against the other. In other words, there is a great difference between what may be done and what is effectively done."[43]

Having surveyed what *may* be done under various arbitral laws and rules,[44] this paper now turns to the subject of what *is effectively done* in practice, a subject less trodden in the commentaries.

2. Examples of the Power Being Exercised in Practice

a. PCA-administered cases

The PCA has since 1899 facilitated arbitration and other forms of resolution of disputes involving various combinations of states, state entities, intergovernmental organizations and private parties.[45] As at April 2014 it is administering ninety-one cases, comprising fifty investor-state arbitrations, twenty-seven cases arising under contracts between private parties and states or other public entities, ten inter-state disputes and four other

---

43. Edoardo F. RICCI, "Evidence in International Arbitration: a Synthetic Glimpse" in M.Á. FERNÁNDEZ-BALLESTEROS and David ARIAS, eds., *Liber amicorum Bernardo Cremades* (2010) p. 1025 at p. 1028.
44. See also American Arbitration Association, Code of Ethics for Arbitrators in Commercial Disputes, 1 March 2004, Canon IV, Paragraph E, ("When the arbitrator determines that more information than has been presented by the parties is required to decide the case, it is not improper for the arbitrator to ask questions, call witnesses, and request documents or other evidence, including expert testimony.").
45. See <ww.pca-cpa.org>. For description of recent PCA activities see: Yanying LI and Camille M. NG, "The Permanent Court of Arbitration in 2012" in *Hague Yearbook of International Law 2012*, at p. 221; Paul-Jean LE CANNU and Daniel DRABKIN, "Assessing the Role of the Permanent Court of Arbitration in the Peaceful Settlement of International Disputes" in 27 L'observateur des Nations Unies: Revue de l'Association Française pour les Nations Unies, Section Aix-en-Provence (2009, Issue 2) at p. 181.

types of disputes. Most of the cases are conducted under the UNCITRAL Rules, or versions of the PCA's own rules which are modelled on the UNCITRAL Rules.[46] Except for those cases listed on the PCA's website, the cases are confidential. Pursuant to the PCA's headquarters agreement with the Netherlands, privileges and immunities extend to participants (including witnesses) in PCA proceedings held in The Hague and similar conditions are offered where the PCA has a host country agreement.[47] The PCA has experience with facilitating arrangements for witnesses who have concerns about logistics, visas, security or other travel restrictions, by liaising with the host state authorities to procure witness certificates for safe passage, and setting in place arrival and departure procedures.

Tribunals' initiatives to call for additional witness evidence have arisen in several recent PCA-administered cases. In some of these cases, the tribunal-led initiatives resulted in useful additions to the evidentiary record.

The first example is *Guaracachi & Rurelec v. Bolivia*, a bilateral investment treaty (BIT) arbitration concerning the claimants' investments in the electricity sector in Bolivia. The case was conducted under the 2010 UNCITRAL Rules and seated in The Hague. The respondent sought to exclude certain portions of the claimants' expert report on damages, on the basis that the expert had been assisted by consultants in preparing price forecasts and those consultants had not been tendered as witnesses.[48] The claimants resisted the request and accused the other party's expert of similarly relying on consultants who had not been presented for testimony. The tribunal "deem[ed] that it would be useful to have representatives of [both sets of consultants] appear at the hearing" to answer questions. The tribunal ordered the parties to "take the measures necessary to ensure" that representatives who had participated in preparing portions relied on in their respective expert reports appear at the hearing for cross-examination. With respect to one set of consultants, the tribunal acknowledged that they were no longer within the control of the parties, and suggested that the PCA, acting as registry, contact them and arrange their appearance, the costs of which would come out of the parties' deposit. The tribunal further conferred with the parties about the conduct of questioning the additional witnesses. All the requested witnesses appeared and were questioned at the hearing. The data they provided were ultimately relied upon by the parties, and referenced and analyzed by the tribunal in its final Award.[49] The decision by the tribunal to call the consultants avoided an impasse of cross-

---

46. See <www.pca-cpa.org/showpage.asp?pag_id=1188>. Brooks W. DALY, Evgeniya GORIATCHEVA and Hugh A. MEIGHEN, *A Guide to the PCA Arbitration Rules* (OUP 2014) (henceforth "Daly").

47. See <www.pca-cpa.org/showpage.asp?pag_id=1280>. A subsequent exchange of notes with the Netherlands pursuant to the Headquarters Agreement sets out arrangements for safe passage of witnesses. See DALY, *op. cit.*, fn. 46, at [4.78].

48. *Guaracachi America, Inc. & Rurelec PLC v. The Plurinational State of Bolivia* (PCA Case No. 2011-17) (UNCITRAL Rules 2010), Procedural Order No. 16 dated 21 March 2013 available at: <www.pca-cpa.org/showpage.asp?pag_id=1436>. See also Transcript Day 1 at pp. 19-20 for claimants' additional argument that the expert's reliance on the data produced by the consultants was no different in nature than his use of a calculator.

49. *Ibid.*, Award dated 31 January 2014, see paras. 50, 75, 287, 294, 316-324, 330, 485-488 and Annex.

filed applications for exclusion of evidence, and ultimately enriched the evidentiary record available.

The second PCA example is the case of *Eureko v. Slovak Republic*, an arbitration pursuant to the Netherlands-Czech/Slovak BIT which was conducted under the UNCITRAL Rules and seated in Frankfurt. The respondent raised preliminary objections about the validity of the treaty, on the basis that the Slovak Republic's accession to the European Union (EU) in 2004 terminated the treaty or rendered its arbitration clause inapplicable. During the hearing on jurisdiction, the tribunal raised with the parties the "possibility of approaching the European Commission and the Netherlands government to provide comments to the Tribunal".[50] After subsequent consultations with the parties, the tribunal, via the PCA, wrote to those entities seeking comments on specified issues. The parties were given an opportunity to make submissions in response. The tribunal reflected on the comments of those entities in their decision to uphold jurisdiction. While not strictly an example of a tribunal calling a fact witness, the case shows that the tribunal was able, with the consent and involvement of the parties, to take initiatives to obtain what it considered to be important information from the perspectives of relevant players involved in the negotiation of the underlying agreement or the application of European law.

The third PCA example is a case conducted under the 1976 UNCITRAL Rules. In advance of the hearing on the merits, the tribunal issued a Procedural Order, a draft of which had been circulated to the parties, providing:

> "The Tribunal may, after consulting with the Parties at a reasonable time in advance of the hearing, request a Party to make available for testimony at the hearing a witness whose appearance has not been requested by the other Party. The Tribunal may also request the Parties to provide for, or to use their best efforts to provide for, the appearance for testimony of a person for whom no witness statement has been submitted."

After receiving the parties' witness lists, the tribunal informed the parties that in light of its review of the written submissions, the tribunal would benefit from the testimony of two individuals whom the parties had not presented as fact witnesses. The tribunal considered that testimony from those individuals would help shed further light on the facts of the case and the parties' arguments. The individuals had close involvement in events underlying the dispute, but were not related to or within the control of the parties. Invoking the above-mentioned Procedural Order, the tribunal requested the parties "to use their best efforts to provide for the appearance for testimony of these two persons at the hearing". The tribunal asked the parties to agree on who would reach out to the witnesses and to advise the individuals in question that (i) the tribunal would like to have the benefit of their views in the present arbitration and to request their appearance at the hearing, and (ii) no steps toward compelling the appearance of these two individuals through legal proceedings need be undertaken. The tribunal specified the topics on which it would be interested in hearing the individuals' accounts, and set certain limits on access to the record

---

50. *Eureko B.V. v. Slovak Republic* (PCA Case No. 2008-13), Award on Jurisdiction, Arbitrability and Suspension, 26 October 2010, paras. 9, 30-42, 175-196.

in the case. The parties agreed that the costs related to the appearance of these witnesses were part of the costs of arbitration. Both individuals showed up (one came with a lawyer) and answered questions from the tribunal and the parties. The example shows that it can be quite effective for a tribunal to seek witness testimony via the parties, and that requests for voluntary cooperation may enjoy some success.

The above three examples can be contrasted with other PCA-administered cases in which tribunals were aware of the possibility of calling individuals at their own initiative or seeking national court assistance to do so, but ultimately decided not to pursue those options out of concern for costs, timing, party autonomy and/or satisfaction with the record before them. In one case a tribunal indicated to the parties its interest in hearing from certain individuals and expressed disappointment that neither party had produced them. The tribunal decided not to press further but did forewarn the parties that it might draw conclusions from the absence of the individuals in question. This allowed both sides to explain efforts previously undertaken to obtain testimony from the individuals and to make submissions on what, if any, inferences could be drawn from their absence.

Finally, it should be noted that the issue of tribunal initiatives to call witnesses remains a delicate one. Decisions in this respect are not taken lightly, even with respect to witnesses that have provided statements and even when the tribunal's procedural orders make clear that a party may be called upon "by the tribunal or the other party" to produce a witness. In practice some arbitrators will be reluctant to call a witness whom the other side chose not to cross-examine, out of deference to the parties' choices over how to run their case.

b.   ICSID cases

ICSID tribunals have invoked Art. 43 of the ICSID Convention to request new witness evidence, with some success, on a number of occasions.[51]

In *Duke Energy v. Peru* the parties indicated during a pre-hearing call that they were not intending to call any witnesses at the hearing.[52] The tribunal requested each side to call one witness of its choice to address the history of the negotiations in connection with the issues relevant to jurisdiction. The parties complied, the witnesses attended the hearing for questioning, and at least one of the parties relied on their testimony in making submissions on jurisdiction.[53]

In *Champion Trading v. Egypt* the tribunal instructed the respondent "to produce one or several witnesses in regard to questions concerning the Egyptian cotton sector".[54] The parties subsequently agreed on a separate hearing in advance of the merits hearing, exclusively for the purpose of examining the cotton witnesses. The award extensively

---

51. See *Vacuum Salt v. Ghana* (ICSID Case No. ARB/92/1), Award, 16 February 1994, p. 78 (referencing a "witness whose presence was requested by the Tribunal"); *Maffezini v. Spain* (ICSID Case No. ARB 97/7), Award, 13 November 2000, paras. 26-32 (in which witnesses, including the claimant, were requested by the tribunal. Some of the witnesses invited by the tribunal testified. Two of them agreed to depositions.).

52. *Duke Energy v. Peru* (ICSID Case No. ARB/03/28), Decision on Jurisdiction, 1 February 2006, para. 20.

53. *Ibid.*, para. 73.

54. *Champion Trading Company Ameritrade International, Inv. v. Arab Republic of Egypt* (ICSID Case No. ARB/02/9), Award, 27 October 2006, para. 15.

discusses the cotton industry in Egypt. The example is closer in line with the more universally accepted practice of tribunal's calling for experts on their own initiative.

A more recent example of an ICSID tribunal taking initiative with respect to witness testimony is *Metal-Tech Ltd v. Uzbekistan*.[55] During the hearing, new facts came to light about the nature and origins of certain consulting agreements in connection with the claimant's investment in a molybdenum plant in Uzbekistan. The tribunal's curiosity was piqued when it learned of an earlier version of the consulting agreements. It was intrigued about the nature of the "lobbyist activity", the qualifications of the consultants and what they actually did to earn millions of dollars paid into offshore corporate vehicles. At the end of the hearing, the tribunal indicated that it would order the parties to produce "additional information and documents, pursuant to its powers under Article 43 of the ICSID Convention". The tribunal issued procedural orders directing the claimant to submit specific information in the form of a new written statement from the claimant's CEO. Rebuttal witness statements were also invited from the respondent. The tribunal held a further hearing for questioning of witnesses on this new evidence.[56]

The new evidence proved determinative to the outcome of the case. The tribunal found that the claimant's payments to "consultants" (among them the brother of the prime minister of Uzbekistan) breached the requirement in the BIT that investments be made in accordance with Uzbek law. The tribunal dismissed the case on jurisdictional grounds.[57]

It has been noted that the approach taken by the *Metal-Tech* tribunal is a "distinct one" because

> "unlike other tribunals, it did not remain passive arbiter of the contentions of the parties, evaluating ultimately the level of comprehensiveness and persuasion of their arguments and evidence. To the contrary – the Tribunal sought to clarify the factual scenario as much as possible so as to make a well-informed decision regarding the existence of grounds for jurisdiction (or, as in this case, their absence)."[58]

One commentator described the tribunal's initiative as "noteworthy insofar as it speaks to the potential for arbitrators to delve into suspicious transactions on a given claimant's books, and to demand proof that they reflect the outlay of funds for legitimate activity".[59]

---

55. *Metal-Tech Ltd v. Republic of Uzbekistan* (ICSID Case No. ARB/10/3), Award, 4 October 2013. See also Richard KREINDLER, "Practice and Procedure Regarding Proof: The Need for More Precision", this volume, pp. 156-182 and Aloysius LLAMZON and Anthony SINCLAIR, "Investor Wrongdoing in Investment Arbitration: Standards Governing Issues of Corruption, Fraud, Misrepresentation and Other Investor Misconduct", this volume pp. 451-530.

56. *Metal-Tech*, paras. 86-100.

57. *Ibid.*, para. 372.

58. Deyan DRAGUIEV, "Proving Corruption in Arbitration: Lessons to Be Learned from *Metal-Tech v. Republic of Uzbekistan*", at <kluwer.practicesource.com/blog/2014/proving-corruption-in-arbitration-lessons-to-be-learned-from-metal-tech-v-republic-of-uzbekistan/>.

59. Luke E. PETERSON, "Testimony by foreign investor piques tribunal's curiosity as to legitimacy of consulting contracts with local fixers, and leads to unraveling of case vs. Uzbekistan", IA Reporter (5 December 2003).

c.   International commercial arbitrations

Tribunal initiatives with respect to witness testimony are also taken in international commercial arbitrations, though examples are harder to find given confidentiality.

In the case of *Industrial Risk Insurers v. MAN Gutehoffnungshutte* the US Court of Appeals for the 11th Circuit found that an **AAA** tribunal had not acted unfairly, and acted within its power by calling a witness *sua sponte*.[60] The tribunal summoned a witness to testify about his involvement in a redesign of an industrial facility. The individual had been an expert retained by the respondent to review the site, and to analyze the effect of a prior accident and the prospects of a new design. The respondent refused to summon him and objected to claimant's request to do so. The tribunal acted on its own motion and requested his attendance at the hearing. In later challenging the award, the respondent unsuccessfully argued that the tribunal's decision to call the expert violated public policy prohibiting experts from testifying against a party who had previously retained them. According to O'Malley, the decision "affirms the basic authority which a tribunal has to call witnesses to a hearing".[61]

In a 1998 **ICC** arbitration about the sale of allegedly non-conforming goods, the tribunal ordered that a retired quality control specialist be made available to answer questions. The claimant refused to make him available, and the tribunal drew conclusions about the claimant's knowledge of the non-conformity. The claimant justified its refusal by stating that the person in question had retired and furthermore was not an employee of the claimant but of the supplier.[62]

A case between a European company and an African oil authority, conducted at the **Cairo Regional Centre for International Commercial Arbitration**, provides a further example. The tribunal had to consider the quality of goods supplied under an oil purchase agreement.[63] The parties had agreed to submit samples to a testing facility but disagreed over the interpretation and weight to be given to the results. Neither party had tendered employees from the testing facility. The tribunal requested that a representative of the inspection office should be present to give testimony regarding the certificates and the integrity of the seals placed on the samples submitted.

A slightly different scenario arose in a **Geneva Chamber of Commerce** arbitration.[64] A witness tendered by a party was later withdrawn. The tribunal nevertheless remained interested in the witness and found that the withdrawal did not disqualify the witness from being called to give testimony before a tribunal. The tribunal acknowledged that the party was free to name and renounce witnesses as it deemed fit, but later attempted to contact the witness and requested their attendance at a hearing.

---

60. *Industrial Risk Insurers v. MAN Gutehoffnungshütte GmbH*, 141 F.3d 1434 (11th Cir. Fla. 1998) cited by O'MALLEY, *op. cit.*, fn. 7, at [8.86].

61. *Ibid.*, at [8.86].

62. Final Award, ICC Case No. 8547, cited by O'MALLEY, *op. cit.*, fn. 7, at [4.75].

63. Cairo Regional Centre, Final Award, Case No. 102/1997 (1998), pp. 3-10, cited in O'MALLEY, *op. cit.*, fn. 7, at [4.75].

64. Cited in O'MALLEY, *op. cit.*, fn. 7, p. 312, n. 48.

d.   Other international courts and tribunals

Outside the arbitration context, international courts and tribunals have inherent general authority to take fact-finding measures on their own initiative. Dr. Kazazi commented as follows in his 1996 study on evidence before international tribunals:

> "In the field of the international law of evidence, the power of international tribunals to ask for the production of evidence or to investigate the facts at issue *proprio motu* is not disputed. The Statute of the International Court of Justice provides, *inter alia,* that '[t]he Court may, even before the hearing begins, call upon the agents to produce any document or to supply any explanations' [Art. 49] and that 'the Court may, at any time, entrust any individual, body, bureau, commission, or other organization that it may select, with the task of carrying out an enquiry or giving an expert opinion'. [Art. 50]. These rights ... reflect a common feature of the authority of international tribunals which is usually specified in their rules of procedure....
>
> The fact-finding power of international tribunals appears to be inherent and thus even in cases where it is not specifically referred to in their rules of procedure, international tribunals are entitled to require parties to produce evidence and to investigate the disputed facts at their own initiation. Theoretically, the parties always remain empowered to agree to the contrary in order to limit the fact finding power of a tribunal if they so choose."[65]

However, in relation to witnesses, Dr. Kazazi noted that "international tribunals are not principally allowed to call witnesses of their own. Nor do they normally have the power to compel the presence of a witness at the request of parties." He cites two international bodies as exceptions, the European Court of Justice (ECJ) and the International Criminal Tribunal for the former Yugoslavia (ICTY).

The courts in the European Justice system (formerly the ECJ and the Courts of First Instance) had an express rule allowing for the summoning of witnesses proprio motu. Art. 66(1) provided: "The Court may, either of its own motion or at the request of one of the parties, and after hearing the Advocate General, order that certain facts be proved by witnesses."[66] Any witness examination is a rare occurrence in the judicial system of the European Union, which relies primarily on documentation for establishing facts. Summoning of witnesses proprio motu has only happened in a few reported disputes involving employment of the staff of EU institutions determined by courts at first instance.[67]

---

65. Dr. Mojtaba KAZAZI, *Burden of Proof and Related Issues, A Study on Evidence Before International Tribunals* (Kluwer 1996) p. 165.

66. After the entry into force of the Lisbon Treaty, an identical provision still applies for General Courts (the former Courts at First Instance), but for the Court of Justice of the European Union (formerly the ECJ), the Rule is phrased as "The Court may, either on its own motion or at the request of one of the parties, and after hearing the Advocate General, order that certain facts be proved by witnesses." See Rules of Procedure of the Court of Justice of 2012, Art. 66(1), in Official Journal, L 265/21, 29 September 2012.

67. See discussion in L. Neville BROWN and Tom KENNEDY, *The Court of Justice of the European Communities,* p. 200, at p. 278. *Kupka-Floridi v. ECOSOC,* Case T-26/91 [1992] ECR p. 1615, para. 8 (court summoned a witness to testify about a probationary period); *Frederksen v. Parliament,* Case

The types of questions the Court of Justice itself is concerned with (e.g., referrals for preliminary rulings, appeals on points of law and challenges by EU institutions and Member States) do not tend to attract witness testimony, and thus Art. 66(1) has "de facto, become largely inapplicable" in that context.[68]

The ICTY provision for tribunal-summoned witnesses is found in Rule 98: "A Trial Chamber may order either party to produce additional evidence. It may *proprio motu* summon witnesses and order their attendance."[69]

This Rule has been particularly useful in relation to individuals who may wish to avoid the appearance of siding with either prosecution or defence. When relying on Rule 98, ICTY trial chambers have usually consulted with the parties in advance, and occasionally laid out extensive practical guidelines as to specific questions or lists of topics for the witness, logistical support for the witness's travel and preparation, and advance notice of documents to be referred to during the examination.[70] The power has been used for a variety of witnesses, including fact witnesses who were present at specific meetings or crime scenes, handwriting experts, military and political leaders.[71] As compared with an international commercial tribunal, a war crimes tribunal's role may be considered as going beyond the resolution of a dispute between two sides, but entailing the search for truth and the delivery of justice, which would justify the ICTY's express proprio motu powers.

3. Lessons

A number of lessons can be derived from the above survey of rules and practical examples. The first is, that arbitral tribunals undoubtedly have the power to call for witness testimony that is not otherwise put before them by the parties. This can be done, and this has been done.[72]

T-106/92 [1995] ECR p. II-99, para. 16 (court summoned a witness to testify about an applicant's skills).

68. Bertrand WÄGENBAUER, *Court of Justice of the EU, Commentary on Statute and Rules of Procedure* (2013) p. 290.

69. <www.icty.org/x/file/Legal%20Library/Rules_procedure_evidence/IT032Rev48_en.pdf> (amended 25 July 1997).

70. See, for example, "Order on Procedure for the Testimonial Evidence of Witnesses Pursuant to Rule 98" in *Prosecutor v. Stanisic and Zupljanin,* Trial Chamber II, 6 February 2012, available at <www.icty.org>.

71. See further examples in "Order for a Witness to Appear (3)" in *Prosecutor v. Krstic,* Trial Chamber, 15 December 2000; "Order Summoning Miroslav Deronjic to Appear as a Witness of the Trial Chamber Pursuant to Rule 98" in *Prosecutor v. Nikolic,* Trial Chamber I, 10 October 2003; "Amended Further *Proprio Motu* Order to Call a Handwriting Expert", *Prosecutor v. Oric,* Trial Chamber II, 7 February 2006; "Order to Summon Momir Nikolic", in *Prosecutor v. Popovic et el,* Trial Chamber II, 10 March 2009; all available at <www.icty.org>.

72. It has been noted that some situations may be more prone to such tribunal initiatives, including when there are valid interests other than those of the parties; the arbitrator has been appointed for her particular expertise which is the subject of the initiative; if there is a non-appearing party or an inequality of arms with a party that has less wherewithal to provide its own defence; see LANDOLT *op. cit.,* fn. 2, at pp. 215-218.

Second, it is advisable that tribunals consult with the parties before calling for the additional witness evidence, and if possible leave it to the parties to undertake the suggested initiatives. This has the practical benefit of engaging the parties in the process and thus reducing the (small) risk that the award could be challenged on the basis that a tribunal deprived the parties of a right to be heard. Landolt posits that

> "in extreme cases, where the arbitrators have introduced considerations, especially unexpected considerations, without hearing the parties on them, or by their inquisitorial zeal have entirely suffocated the parties' opportunity to test the evidence, there may be a violation of the right to be heard which attracts legal consequences.... Otherwise, arbitrators' discretion is unconfined in taking initiatives to obtain factual and legal evidence."[73]

Giovannini also notes that while clearly a tribunal has the "power to investigate the facts on its own accord" as a general rule it should only use the power after consulting with the parties and any evidence thus ascertained must be submitted to them for comment.[74]

It would be advisable to sound out the parties early how they view arbitrators' initiatives to obtain evidence, for example on a conference call or in draft procedural orders, as was done in some examples discussed in Sect. I.2.[75] The parties may agree on the scope of topic areas on which the witness will be questioned and who will be responsible for contacting and arranging his or her attendance. Landolt also observes that while "the expansion of factual evidence may lead to a more correct outcome", "[a]ny actions by the arbitral tribunal which expand the factual evidence risk expanding the dispute, with the attendant evils of increased uncertainty, time and costs being thereby visited upon the parties".[76] The cases discussed above show that tribunals can make provision for costs and logistics of getting the witness to appear, and can take measures to ensure confidentiality is protected.

III.   TRIBUNAL INITIATIVES NOT TO CALL A WITNESS

Just as a tribunal's power to call a witness at its own initiative derives from the tribunal's general authority over proceedings, there is consensus that, stemming from the same general authority, a tribunal has the power to decide *not* to hear from a witness.[77] The power is expressly provided for in the IBA Rules and LCIA Rules, and case law from various jurisdictions confirms that the power can be exercised without denying a party's

---

73. *Ibid.*, at p. 192, see also p. 219 ("Providing the arbitrators give the parties a sufficient opportunity to comment on the evidence obtained ... the parties' rights to be heard will be fulfilled.").

74. GIOVANNINI, *op. cit.*, fn. 10, at p. 9. See also LANDOLT *op. cit.*, fn. 2, at p. 223.

75. See LANDOLT, *op. cit.*, fn. 2, at p. 202.

76. *Ibid.*, at p. 220.

77. See, for example, J-F. POUDRET and S. BESSON, *Comparative Law of International Arbitration* (Sweet & Maxwell, Thomson 2007) p. 558 ("An arbitral tribunal is not obliged to hear all the witnesses proposed by the parties. It may refuse to hear testimony which it does not deem relevant.... Except in special circumstances, such refusal will not constitute a violation of the right to be heard leading to the award being set aside.").

right to due process. The decision not to hear from witnesses (or "gating") is especially appealing if the testimony of that witness would be irrelevant or duplicative.[78]

Lew, Mistelis and Kröll articulate the advantages as follows:

> "The question arises whether parties are always entitled to call and examine witnesses irrespective of the circumstances and the nature of the dispute. The short answer must be negative; it has been argued that the use of too many and irrelevant witnesses can often undermine the cost-effectiveness of arbitration. This is particularly true where the witness evidence is oral and the parties and their witnesses are based in various jurisdictions, frequently different from the seat of arbitration."[79]

They conclude that "whilst normally it is up to the parties to decide what witnesses they wish to present, arbitration tribunals may refuse to hear some or all witnesses orally" and a refusal to hear the testimony of a witness is unlikely to be the sole ground for the setting aside of the award.

Back in 1989, Arthur Marriott observed that "common law arbitrators are more likely to allow a party to call as many witnesses as he likes and to have them examined, cross-examined and re-examined in the manner followed in the English or American courts, than are civil lawyers".[80] More recent commentaries, such as Lew's, actually show common lawyers among those embracing the practice of "gating" witnesses. By contrast, commentators with a civil law background have been amongst those urging that such power be exercised "sparingly", with "restraint" and "hesitation", and only in "exceptional circumstances".[81] The case law discussed at Sect. III.2.b shows that common law courts have been just as tolerant of arbitrators exercising this power as their civil law counterparts.

Redfern & Hunter consider that the trend in international arbitration "toward shorter hearings with greater reliance upon documentary evidence … is a necessary step in the interests of economy of time and costs". Landolt argues that so long as the parties are consulted, "negative initiatives" of arbitrators to exclude testimony on the basis that it relates to a legally irrelevant issue can be of "unalloyed benefit to the parties … [saving] costs and time while respecting … party autonomy".[82]

Situations in which a tribunal might decide not to hear from a witness include when the tribunal "considers itself to be sufficiently well informed of the facts through the other evidence that has already been admitted into the proceedings"[83] and when the tribunal

---

78. See GÉLINAS, op. cit., fn. 1, at p. 37.

79. J. LEW, L. MISTELIS, S. KROLL, Comparative International Commercial Arbitration (Kluwer 2003) at p. 570 [22.61-22.71] (henceforth "Lew, et al."), citing LEW, "Achieving the Potential of Effective Arbitration", 65 Arbitration (1999) p. 283 at p. 288.

80. Arthur MARRIOTT, "Evidence in International Arbitration", 5 Arbitration International (Kluwer 1989, Issue 3) pp. 280-290 at p. 283.

81. VAN DER BEND, et al., op. cit., fn. 21, at p. 143; M. RUBINO-SAMMARTANO, International Arbitration, Law and Practice, 2nd ed. (Kluwer 2001) pp. 653-656; ZUBERBÜHLER, op. cit., fn. 6, para. 70.

82. LANDOLT, op. cit., fn. 2, p. 178.

83. GRIFFIN, op. cit., fn. 5, at 25.

considers the witness's testimony "is not relevant, or would appear unreasonably burdensome or involving disproportionate cost to be obtained as compared to the likely result".[84]

Most commentators acknowledge that the authority to limit witness testimony "must be tempered by a tribunal's duty to afford the parties a fair opportunity to present their case".[85] Some are more restrictive in their approach than others. For example, Bernard Hanotiau expects that "it would be very unusual for an arbitral tribunal to decide not to hear a witness, notwithstanding the request of a party to present it, unless the testimony of the said witness were deemed to be manifestly irrelevant".[86]

According to Bühler and Dorgan, the requirement to treat the parties equally and allow them a reasonable opportunity to present their case means that, in practice, tribunals "will hear virtually any witnesses whom the parties wish to present, although the arbitrators may actively exercise their power to limit witness testimony and/or to limit the testimony of a witness to a particular subject".[87] The perceived safer option seems to be to wait and see what the witness has to say, and then decide only *after* hearing the witness that the testimony added nothing of value to the record. Rubino-Sammartano disapproves of the practice of limiting the number of witnesses with a view to saving time because, except in special situations, the arbitrator is not in a position to assess, before hearing the witnesses, whether one or more of them will be necessary.[88]

Ultimately there must be a balance. As O'Malley observes, "[a] rule requiring arbitrators to hear all witnesses presented by the parties could possibly be burdensome, and at odds with an arbitrator's duty to provide for procedural efficiency".[89] As seen below, national laws and arbitral rules offer little guidance in finding the right balance, but the IBA Rules do deal directly with the "gating" power.

1. A Tribunal's Power to "Gate" Witnesses

a. National arbitration laws

Most national laws are silent with respect to initiatives to limit the appearance of witnesses. National laws invariably allow tribunals to conduct the proceedings as they consider appropriate subject to treating the parties with equality and affording them a right to be heard. Beyond such generalities, powers with respect to witness gating can only be inferred.

For example, Art. 1039(3) of the **Dutch Arbitration Law** provides that the arbitral tribunal *may* allow parties to examine witnesses. From this, Van der Bend et al. imply that the arbitral tribunal has the authority to reject the hearing of a proposed witness.[90] They

---

84. B. BERGER and F. KELLERHALS, *International and Domestic Arbitration in Switzerland* (Sweet & Maxwell) p. 348.
85. O'MALLEY, *op. cit.*, fn. 7, at [8.20-8.24].
86. HANOTIAU, *op. cit.*, fn. 5, at p. 382.
87. BÜHLER and DORGAN, *op. cit.*, fn. 20, p. 17.
88. M. RUBINO-SAMMARTANO, *op. cit.*, fn. 81, pp. 653-656.
89. O'MALLEY, *op. cit.*, fn. 7, at [8.20-8.24]. See also ZUBERBÜHLER, *op. cit.*, fn. 6, at p. 72.
90. VAN DER BEND, et al., *op. cit.*, fn. 21, p. 143.

caution that this authority should be used with "restraint" lest the refusal to examine a witness might violate principles of due process.

As noted in Sect. II, **Swiss law** provides that "the arbitral tribunal shall itself conduct the taking of evidence".[91] Swiss lawyers seem to agree that, as part of "anticipated assessment" of evidence, a tribunal may refuse to hear a witness if it considers that their testimony is not relevant, or would appear unreasonably burdensome or involve cost disproportionate to the likely result.[92] When preparing for the hearing, the tribunal must decide which of the witnesses called by the parties it actually intends to summon. Oetiker remarks that as a fall-back position, the "parties will tend to call witnesses even on points that are hardly decisive for the outcome of the proceedings, that prove to be not contentious, or that have already been proven by documents. For reasons of procedural economy, it is therefore appropriate that the arbitral tribunal makes a selection of the witnesses to be summoned." He suggests that it is expedient for the tribunal to discuss with the parties the list of witnesses to be heard.[93]

Under **Swedish law**, according to Kaj Hobér, there is an emphasis on party autonomy and the adversarial system, which would mean that "arbitrators sitting in Sweden would *not* exclude evidence on their own motion".[94]

b.   Arbitration rules

Many arbitration rules deal with the decision whether to have a hearing at all, as opposed to deciding the case on the papers alone. Art. 17 of the **UNCITRAL Rules** provides:

> "3. If at an appropriate stage of the proceedings any party so requests, the arbitral tribunal shall hold hearings for the presentation of evidence by witnesses, including expert witnesses, or for oral argument. In the absence of such a request, the arbitral tribunal shall decide whether to hold such hearings or whether the proceedings shall be conducted on the basis of documents and other materials."

The **ICC Rules** do not specify that a hearing includes presenting evidence of witnesses. Art. 25 provides:

> "(2) After studying the written submissions of the parties and all documents relied upon, the arbitral tribunal shall hear the parties together in person if any of them so requests or, failing such a request, it may of its own motion decide to hear them.
> ....
> (6) The arbitral tribunal may decide the case solely on the documents submitted by the parties unless any of the parties requests a hearing."

---

91. Art. 184(3) of the Swiss Private International Law Act.
92. B. BERGER and F. KELLERHALS, *op. cit.*, fn. 84, p. 348. See also Nathalie VOSER, "Right to Be Heard Not Violated by Arbitrator's Refusal to Hear Witness Whose Evidence Anticipated to Be Irrelevant", *PLC Arbitration, Arbitration in Switzerland,* 2 May 2012, available at <http://arbitration.practicallaw.com/8-519-2655>.
93. OETIKER, *op. cit.*, fn. 4, at p. 262.
94. HOBÉR, *op. cit.*, fn. 12, p. 224 at [6.108].

The **LCIA Rules** provide that parties may request to be heard orally on the merits of the dispute:

> "19.1 Any party which expresses a desire to that effect has the right to be heard orally before the Arbitral Tribunal on the merits of the dispute, unless the parties have agreed in writing on documents-only arbitration."

With respect to witness gating, the LCIA Rules stand out from other sets of rules in that they contain a separate provision in Art. 20.2, stating that the arbitral tribunal "has a discretion to allow, refuse, or limit the appearance of witnesses (whether witness of fact or expert witness)".

The **ICDR Arbitration Rules** also relevantly provide in Art. 16(3) that the tribunal "may in its discretion ... exclude cumulative or irrelevant testimony".

c.   IBA Rules on the Taking of Evidence
The IBA Rules deal with the gating of witnesses in Art. 8.2:

> "The Arbitral Tribunal shall at all times have complete control over the Evidentiary Hearing. The Arbitral Tribunal may limit or exclude any question to, answer by or appearance of a witness, if it considers such question, answer or appearance to be irrelevant, immaterial, unreasonably burdensome, duplicative or otherwise covered by a reason for objection set forth in Article 9.2...."

The IBA Commentary explains that "Article 8.2 makes clear that the power to manage the evidentiary hearing rests with the arbitral tribunal, not the parties, an idea which originally came from civil law procedure but which has been widely adopted." The provisions in Art. 8 "are all designed to give the arbitral tribunal the ability to focus the hearing on issues material to the outcome of the case and thereby make hearings more efficient".

O'Malley suggests that it is important for tribunals to specify their motivation for excluding a witness from a hearing in connection with one of the reasons listed in Art. 8.2, so that any subsequent reviewing court might understand that the determination was made based upon due consideration of the proffered testimony and the procedural requirements of the arbitration.[95]

In commenting on the IBA Rules, Bühler and Dorgan suggest that the question whether the arbitral tribunal has the discretion to refuse the hearing of a witness over the objection of a party is one that arises "in commentary probably more often than practice" and predict that it would be a "very unusual case where the arbitral tribunal could properly decide not to hear witnesses, notwithstanding the request of a party to present a witness".[96] While still quite rare, the decisions reviewed in the next section show that the question can indeed arise not just in commentary but also in practice.

---

95. O'MALLEY, *op. cit.*, fn. 7, at [8.23].
96. BÜHLER and DORGAN *op. cit.*, fn. 20, at 16-17.

2. Examples of the Power Being Exercised in Practice

a. Common law jurisdictions

Courts in common law jurisdictions have largely supported decisions of arbitrators against the hearing of witnesses. A classic case cited in commentaries is *Dalmia Dairy Industries Limited (India) v. National Bank of Pakistan*.[97] It involved an ICC arbitration conducted in **England** in which Professor Lalive was the sole arbitrator. He refused to hear any oral evidence on the grounds that he could decide the matter on the documents and on hearing arguments of counsel. Although subject to some criticism amongst English lawyers, the Court of Appeal upheld his award.

The **United States** offers examples of successful and unsuccessful challenges to awards when a tribunal chose not to hear a witness. In *Tempo Shain Corp. et al v. Bertek Inc.*,[98] an award was successfully challenged on grounds of fairness where the tribunal had decided not to hear a witness because it considered the witness's evidence to be cumulative. The reviewing court found there was

> "no reasonable basis for the arbitration panel to determine that [the] omitted testimony would be cumulative with regard to the fraudulent inducement claims. Said differently, the panel excluded evidence plainly 'pertinent and material to the controversy', 9 USC Sect. 10(a)(3). The panel did not indicate in what respects [the] testimony would be cumulative, but stated that there were 'a number of letters in the file' and that [the witness] 'was speaking through the letters [he wrote], and the reports he received.' These letters and reports were not specifically identified by the arbitration panel."

The lesson for arbitrators from this case appears to be that when deciding not to hear from a witness, be specific about the documents relied on which are found to render the testimony unnecessary.

In other cases US courts have approved tribunals' decisions not to have witnesses testify at a hearing.[99] In *Weizmann Institute of Science v. Neschis et al.*, the court declined to vacate the award, observing that "the tribunal's decision to forgo live testimony in favor of affidavits from some witnesses is common practice".

In **Singapore**, the 2010 case of *ALC v. ALF* involved an arbitrator who had denied the defendant's request that an employee of the plaintiff provide sworn testimony about the plaintiff's discovery. The arbitrator did not think it was necessary to have a witness on that point. The defendant tried to bypass the arbitrator's decision by going to the court for a subpoena. The court confirmed the arbitrator's powers, discretion and control over procedural matters, noting that the arbitrator was best apprised to deal with the submissions

---

97. [1978] 2 Lloyd's Rep. 223 at 270. Cited in MARRIOTT, *op. cit.*, fn. 80, at p. 283; GRIFFIN, *op. cit.*, fn. 5, at p. 25; POUDRET and BESSON, *op. cit.*, fn. 77, at p. 558.

98. 120 F.3d 16, p. 20 (2nd Cir. 1997), cited by O'MALLEY, *op. cit.*, fn. 7, p. 237 at [8.19].

99. Intercarbon Bermuda Ltd v. Caltext Trading & Transport Corp 146 FRD 64, pp. 72-74 (SDNY 1993); and also *Weizmann Institute of Science et al. v. Janet Neschis et al*, 421 F.Supp.2d 654, p. 681 (SDNY 2005). Both cited in O'MALLEY, *op. cit.*, fn. 7, at [8.20] at fn. 35.

of parties seeking to adduce evidence. The court considered the defendant's actions in obtaining the court subpoena, without seeking prior direction from the arbitrator, to constitute "a direct circumvention and usurpation of the Arbitrator's control of the procedure.... The Arbitrator's discretion encompassed the ability to determine the relevance, admissibility, materiality of evidence and the appearance of witnesses. The application to issue a subpoena against the witness was, to my mind, premature, and improperly obtained and in my view constituted an abuse of the court's process."[100] The judge set aside the subpoena obtained in the lower courts, noting that the "issue of whether the evidence of Mr. [XY] ought to be adduced should be a matter reserved for the discretion of the arbitral tribunal".

b.   Civil law jurisdictions

The **Swiss Federal Tribunal** confirmed in 2004 that the refusal of a tribunal to hear a witness who had provided a written statement did not constitute a violation of the right to be heard, noting that there was no right to have witnesses heard under the applicable ICC Rules.[101] In 2005 a Swiss court held that the dismissal of document requests and the refusal to hear witnesses did not violate a claimant's right to be heard in circumstances where the tribunal had concluded that the parties had already established all the facts necessary for it to make its decision regarding jurisdiction.[102]

Courts in **France** have also declined to set aside an award solely on the ground that the tribunal refused to hear the testimony of a particular witness.[103]

Some tribunals have adopted a more cautious approach. For example, in **ICC Case** No. 5926,[104] the tribunal agreed to hear certain witnesses, despite its own determination that it was unnecessary to do so. The tribunal explained that in making its decision:

> "the arbitral tribunal which so far does not see the necessity of the appearance of witnesses, thanks to the very thorough and complete briefs and documentation filed by the two parties, has been guided by the essential principle of offering to each party the full opportunity to present its case as it wishes while, at the same time, keeping up with the characteristic of arbitration of avoiding unnecessary delays".

In their guide to the **Dutch Arbitration Law** and NAI Rules, VAN DER BEND, et al., cite two cases in support of their view that "in exceptional circumstances, the arbitral tribunal may refuse to hear one or more witnesses proposed by the parties, if this is justified

---

100. *ALC v. ALF* [2010] SGHC 231 at paras. 49, 56; available at: <www.singaporelaw.sg/sglaw/laws-of-singapore/case-law/free-law/high-court-judgments/14258-alc-v-alf-2010-sghc-231>. Discussed by Michael Hwang and Ziuha Su, in their contribution for the ITA Board of Reporters, Kluwer Law International.

101. OETIKER, *op. cit.*, fn. 4, at p. 259, citing Swiss Federal Tribunal, 4 January 2004, 4P.196/2003, ASA Bull. (2004) p. 592, at p. 600 et seq.

102. Examples cited by O'MALLEY, *op. cit.*, fn. 7, at [8.24], p. 239, fn. 35.

103. *Soubaigne v. Limmareds Skogar*, Cour d'Appel, Paris, 15 March 1984, 1985 Rev.Arb. 285, cited in GRIFFIN, *op. cit.*, fn. 5, at p. 25.

104. As reported by Dominique HASCHER, ed., *Collection of Procedural Decisions in ICC Arbitration 1993-1996*, 2nd ed. (1998) p. 105, cited in O'MALLEY, *op. cit.*, fn. 7, at [8.24].

by the circumstances of the case". One example involved a party attempting to frustrate the proceedings by calling a disproportionate number of witnesses, and in the other example, the proposed witnesses would be heard at a later stage of the proceedings in any event.[105]

c. Examples from investor-state arbitration

The concept in Art. 8.2 of the IBA Rules has been mirrored in procedural orders of investor-state arbitration tribunals. For example, in *GAMI Investments v. Mexico*, the tribunal ordered that it "shall at all times have control over oral proceedings, including the right to limit or deny the right of a Party to examine a witness when it appears to the Arbitral Tribunal that such evidence for examination is not likely to serve any further relevant purpose".[106]

An ICSID *ad hoc* annulment committee was called on to consider the issue in *Duke Energy International v. Peru*.[107] The respondent alleged that the tribunal had committed a procedural error by not calling for the cross-examination of one of its key expert witnesses. It was evident in the final award that the tribunal had a number of reservations concerning the respondent's expert report (and ultimately preferred the evidence of the claimant's expert). The respondent argued that if the tribunal had reservations concerning the report, it should have given the expert an opportunity at the hearing to answer the questions or concerns under cross-examination. The *ad hoc* committee rejected the annulment application, and observed that a tribunal "is not obliged to hear from all witnesses orally. On the contrary, it is empowered under ICSID Arbitration Rule 36 to admit evidence given by a witness or expert in a written deposition. It follows that it may also evaluate the probative value of the evidence given in such a form."

3. Lessons

Under many arbitral rules, a tribunal may only be able to dispense with a hearing altogether if the parties do not object. Even so, as part of its general authority to control the proceedings, a tribunal may be able to limit the appearance of certain witnesses. The best way to do this would be in consultation with the parties (via a written exchange or teleconference) seeking to agree on witness lists.

Absent agreement, the tribunal could indicate to the parties the specific reasons that the tribunal considers it unnecessary to hear from particular witnesses. The list in Art. 8.2 of the IBA Rules is useful in this regard. If the reasons stem from the tribunal appraising the content of the witness statement and determining that the issues on which the witness testified are manifestly irrelevant or already proved beyond question by

---

105. VAN DER BEND, et al., *op. cit.*, fn. 21, at p. 144, citing NAI 6 Apr. 2000 and NAI 1 Aug. 2003, TvA (2004) pp. 20-21, para. 5.3.

106. *GAMI Investments Inc. v. Government of the United Mexican States, NAFTA/UNCITRAL*, Procedural Order No. 1 (2003) para. 8.6, available at: <http://naftaclaims.com/Disputes/Mexico/GAMI/GAMIproceduralOrder1.pdf>.

107. Dietmar W. PRAGER and Rebecca JENKIN, *"Duke Energy International Peru Investments No. 1, Ltd and others v. Republic of Peru*, ICSID Case No. ARB/03/28", A Contribution by the ITA Board of Reporters, para. 258 (2011), cited by O'MALLEY, *op. cit.*, fn. 7, at fn. 33.

contemporaneous documents, then its decision not to hear the witness is less likely to be challenged. If the lines are not so clear, tribunals may wish to be more cautious. What is gained from a face-to-face observation of the witness and listening to their account may be considered more valuable than the cost and efficiency gains of curtailing the hearing.

Bühler and Dorgan caveat against arbitrators turning the hearing into a perfunctory exercise, conducted merely in order to go through the motions of fulfilling the obligation to hear the parties. They advise that "arbitrators should not lightly presume that the parties' written submissions have adequately informed them regarding the relevant factual and legal issues. The arbitrators may conclude that a witness' testimony added nothing of value to the record, but normally they should do so only *after* hearing that witness."[108] If the arbitral tribunal decides not to hear a witness, the written statement will remain in the record, but the arbitral tribunal will likely attribute little weight to such testimony having declined to have the witness examined.

IV. TRIBUNAL'S OPTIONS WHEN THE WITNESS IS A NO-SHOW

This paper has so far surveyed the possibilities for tribunals to take initiatives with respect to witness testimony when it is not totally satisfied with the line-up offered by the parties. We have seen that tribunals have the power to *request* the attendance of a witness. In some examples, the tribunal's requests to the parties to use their best efforts to arrange the voluntary appearance of the witness were effective, and the testimony proved determinative. Indicating the importance of particular evidence and particular issues encouraged the parties to cooperate and satisfy the tribunal's curiosity.

If the parties' best efforts fail, other tools may still be available to a tribunal to deal with the "empty chair". This section does not purport to exhaust all possible avenues, but to flag the tools that a tribunal may have at its disposal when a key witness seems unwilling to show up.

The tribunal's willingness to pursue the different options will depend on a number of factors, including the adequacy of the existing evidentiary record, the importance of the missing witness, the amount or public interest at stake in the dispute as compared to the costs and delays involved in engaging in court procedures; and the views of the parties. The number of options will depend on the applicable arbitral rules, the law of the place of the arbitration and the laws applicable at the location of the witness.

1. Options That Do Not Involve Recourse to the Courts

a. Request and encourage the individual to attend

Sometimes the parties' best efforts to elicit the appearance of a witness would be, or prove to be, futile, in light of prior efforts, animosity or the reluctance of the witness to be seen as taking sides (e.g., if they have ongoing relationships with both parties). In those circumstances it might not hurt for the tribunal simply to "ask nicely" by writing to the potential witness directly. Gélinas notes that "an official invitation letter from the

---

108. BÜHLER and DORGAN, *op. cit.*, fn. 20, p. 18.

arbitral tribunal may suffice".[109] Zuberbühler agrees that "in some occasions, a person will be more willing to appear at an evidentiary hearing if (also) called by the arbitral tribunal and not by a party only".[110] An individual may be more likely to cooperate with a request from a neutral authority than a party. One observes at hearings that witnesses take on a more helpful attitude in answering questions from arbitrators, as compared to the defensive stance taken under cross-examination from a party's counsel. A tribunal would be advised to share a draft of the letter with the parties and solicit their comments before proceeding to make contact with the individual. The tribunal's letter could flag specific questions or topics of evidence in which it is interested.

To maximize the chances of cooperation, the request could also offer to put in place arrangements to overcome any logistical obstacles (such as costs, travel, safe passage, interpretation, access to documents).[111] The tribunal might also indicate that it would be prepared to accept the testimony via video-conference, or via written answers to specific questions. Lucy Reed and Laurent Lévy acknowledge that arbitrators will sometimes organize examination by video-conferencing "to placate a recalcitrant witness".[112] In one PCA-administered arbitration, efforts to have a key witness (who had submitted a statement) attend a hearing in The Hague failed. When he submitted a statement indicating that he was unavailable to testify for medical reasons, the tribunal and parties relocated to the location of the witness in the respondent state in order to question him. In another case at the PCA, a witness who had provided a witness statement declined on medical grounds to appear for examination even via video conference. Despite the tribunal indicating its preparedness to travel to the location of the witness, the party who had proffered his evidence expressed a preference to conclude the hearings and rely instead on the record as it stood.[113]

The tribunal should be conscious of any possible recourse to the courts for assistance (discussed in Sect. IV.2.b below). Even if the tribunal hopes (and expects) not to resort to court, it can be helpful to explain to a potential witness that these possibilities exist. As Megens points out, "[o]ften these options work not because they have to be used, but because a person knows that the possibility exists that the option may be used and co-operation may be less troublesome than actually being forced to comply".[114] This worked as effective leverage in a commercial case conducted in South Africa under the rules of the Arbitration Federation of Southern Africa (AFSA). The South African Arbitration Act and the AFSA rules provided for an "appointment of commissioner procedure" as well

---

109. GÉLINAS, *op. cit.*, fn. 1, p. 36.
110. ZUBERBÜHLER, *op. cit.,* fn. 6, para. 81.
111. See discussion on safe passage in PCA cases in Sect. II.2.a.
112. Laurent LÉVY and Lucy REED, "Managing Fact Evidence in International Arbitration" in A.J. van den BERG, ed., *International Arbitration 2006: Back to Basics?* ICCA Congress Series no. 13 (Kluwer 2007) p. 636.
113. In both cases the other side sought to catch out the witness who had claimed infirmity as an excuse not to attend, by submitting photographs of the witness engaged in activities allegedly inconsistent with the claimed infirmity.
114. MEGENS, *op. cit.*, fn. 22, p. 38.

as summons powers of tribunals and courts.[115] The tribunal's letter indicated it would be willing to use such procedures and this was sufficient to encourage the witness to appear voluntarily.

b.   Give no weight or due weight to any statement submitted

Tribunals are under no obligation to call a witness or seek court assistance to compel a witness's appearance, and a tribunal will not violate the parties' right to be heard if it does not seek the assistance of a state court judge.[116] It has been remarked that "in the practice of international commercial arbitration, arbitrators will very rarely order *sua sponte* the appearance of a witness; absent special circumstances, they rely instead on the parties' burden of proof".[117] Thus tribunals often simply take the non-appearance of the witness into account when appraising the evidence.

The **IBA Rules** contain provisions reflecting best practice on how tribunals should deal with statements of witnesses who do not appear at the hearing. Art. 8.1 provides that "each Party shall inform the Arbitral Tribunal and the other Parties of the witnesses whose appearance it requests". Pursuant to Art. 4.8, if the appearance of the witness is *not* requested, then "none of the other Parties shall be deemed to have agreed to the correctness of the content of the Witness Statement". The Commentary explains that "if the parties and the arbitral tribunal agree that a fact witness need not appear, the progress of the arbitration may be enhanced".[118]

Art. 8.1 of the IBA Rules makes clear (subject to the gating provisions in Art. 8.2) that each witness whose appearance has been requested by any party *or* by the arbitral tribunal shall appear for testimony at the hearing. Under Art. 4.7:

> "If a witness whose appearance has been requested pursuant to Art. 8.1 fails without a valid reason to appear for testimony at an Evidentiary Hearing, the Arbitral Tribunal *shall disregard* any Witness Statement related to that Evidentiary Hearing by that witness unless, in exceptional circumstances, the Arbitral Tribunal decides otherwise." (Emphasis added)

The rule in Art. 4.7 has been decried as "rather strict and inflexible".[119] The **LCIA Rules** take a slightly more liberal approach in Art. 20.4, providing that: "If the Arbitral Tribunal orders that other party to produce the witness and the witness fails to attend the oral hearing without good cause, the Arbitral Tribunal may place such weight on the

---

115. Arbitration Act No. 42 of 1996, Sects. 14(1)(a)(iv) and Sect. 16; AFSA Rules Art. 11.2.12. See below at Sect. IV.*1.d.*
116. Swiss Federal Supreme Court, DFT of 28 January 1997, ASA Bull (1998) cited by ZUBERBÜHLER, *op. cit.,* fn. 6, at para. 84.
117. ZUBERBÜHLER, *op. cit.,* fn. 6, para. 78. See also WAINCYMER, *op. cit.,* fn. 5, p. 888 ("while a tribunal has a power to call for the attendance of a particular witness, it may choose not to do so, relying instead on the application of burden and standards of proof to the material presented".).
118. See Commentary, p. 17.
119. ZUBERBÜHLER, *op. cit.,* fn. 6, para. 68; Oetiker, *op. cit.,* fn. 4, p. 258.

344

written testimony (or exclude the same altogether) as it considers appropriate in the circumstances of the case."

c.   Draw an inference from non-appearance

If a witness fails to appear, another tool available to the tribunal is the drawing of adverse inferences from the party's failure to secure the presence of the witness.[120] Art. 9.6 of the IBA Rules provides for adverse inferences in the context of a no-show witness requested by a party:

> "6. If a Party fails without satisfactory explanation to make available any other relevant evidence, *including testimony*, sought by one Party to which the Party to whom the request was addressed has not objected in due time or fails to make available any evidence, including testimony, ordered by the Arbitral Tribunal to be produced, the Arbitral Tribunal may infer that such evidence would be adverse to the interests of that Party."

Gary Born explains that

> "[i]f a witness whose attendance has been requested refuses to attend the arbitral hearing, the tribunal must consider what evidentiary or other consequences (if any) should be drawn from their refusal. The witness may have satisfactory justifications (such as illness or fear of incrimination), which explain his or her refusal. If not, however, a tribunal must decide whether to draw adverse inferences about the party's case on the basis of the witness's refusal. In many cases, this will be more difficult to justify than in instances where a party refuses to produce documents within its control, because a party may be genuinely unable to procure a witness' attendance."[121]

---

120. REDFERN & HUNTER, *op. cit.*, fn. 2, at [5.19] ("absent any powers to call upon the forces of public order, if such a witness fails to appear, the arbitral tribunal is usually limited to drawing adverse inferences from the party's failure to secure the presence of the witness"); WAINCYMER, *op. cit.*, fn. 5, at 10.4.8.2 ("It is readily accepted that tribunals may draw adverse inferences from a party's failure to provide information and documents where it would be reasonable for them to do so. Adverse inferences can apply to witnesses who could easily be called or who refuse to answer certain questions as well as to documents not produced. Absent a valid excuse, it is logical to presume that withheld information is adverse to the interests of the party controlling it. An appropriately drawn adverse inference is not a violation of a party's right to be heard."); GÉLINAS *op. cit.*, fn. 1, at p. 36 ("There appears to be consensus amongst arbitration experts that tribunals may request the parties to produce witnesses that are within their control. However, tribunals are unlikely to have the power to compel the presence of such witnesses. As a result, adverse inferences are the usual consequence of the absence of a witness. In some circumstances even adverse inferences may not be appropriate if there are good reasons justifying the absence of the witness.").
121. BORN, *op. cit.*, fn. 3, at pp. 1901-1902.

Jeremy Sharpe has formulated a series of general requirements for drawing adverse inferences:[122]

"(1) the party seeking the adverse inference must produce all available evidence corroborating the inference sought;
(2) the requested evidence must be accessible to the inference opponent;
(3) the inference sought must be reasonable, consistent with the facts in the record and logically related to the likely nature of the evidence withheld;
(4) the party seeking the adverse inference must produce prima facie evidence; and
(5) the inference opponent must know, or have reason to know, of its obligation to produce evidence rebutting the adverse inference sought."

Simon Greenberg and Felix Lautenschlager analyzed thirty-three ICC awards rendered between 2004 and 2010 in which a party requested the tribunal to draw an adverse inference.[123] Their survey included the following information about the making of adverse inferences from the non-appearance of witnesses:

"The authors sensed that arbitral tribunals were reluctant to draw adverse inferences. They sometimes skirt around the issue and decide the case by other means, presumably in an effort to avoid creating due process concerns.... In 12 of the 36 instances the arbitral tribunal actually drew an adverse inference.... [I]n two [of those 12] cases the arbitral tribunal expressly reinforced inferences drawn from the non production of documents with the non-presentation of a witness.... In nine instances out of the 36 (25%), the arbitral tribunal was asked to draw adverse inferences because the opposing side either did not call a critical fact witness or did not present a witness for cross-examination. While it was generally acknowledged in these awards that this could be a ground for drawing adverse inferences, no case was based on adverse inferences because of absent witnesses alone....

In three instances the arbitral tribunal refused to draw an inference because the party requesting it had not attempted to call the witness either, let alone subject him or her to a subpoena or deposition. In another instance the arbitral tribunal refused to draw adverse inferences because the witness allegedly could not appear for cross-examination due to ill health, but the arbitral tribunal stated that it would attach very little weight to the written witness statement of that witness.

---

122. Jeremy K. SHARPE, "Drawing Adverse Inferences from the Non-production of Evidence", 22 Arbitration International (Kluwer 2006, Issue 4) pp. 549-571, at p. 551. The criteria, based on the case law of the Iran-US Claims Tribunal, have found support in ZUBERBÜHLER, *op. cit.,* fn. 6, p. 182; O'MALLEY, *op. cit.,* fn. 7, [7.42-7.43]; and Simon GREENBERG and Felix LAUTENSCHLAGER, "Adverse Inferences in International Arbitral Practice" in S. KRÖLL, L.A. MISTELIS, P. PERALES VISCASILLAS, V. ROGERS, eds., *International Arbitration and International Commercial Law: Synergy, Convergence and Evolution. Liber amicorum Eric Bergsten* (2011) (henceforth "Greenberg") pp. 190, 197-202.
123. GREENBERG, *op. cit.,* fn. 122, pp. 190-192.

346

In three instances the arbitral tribunal avoided the issue by noting that whether or not it drew any inference made no difference to its conclusions of the result. In two instances, the arbitral tribunal stated that it would draw adverse inferences based on the absence of a witness, but in both instances the finding was coupled with an inference based on the refusal to produce documents."

d.   Use direct tribunal subpoena powers under (some) national laws
In most cases arbitrators cannot compel a third party to appear and testify.[124] International arbitral tribunals seated in the **United States** are a notable exception. The US Federal Arbitration Act provides in Sect. 7 that arbitrators may "summon in writing any person to attend before them or any of them as a witness…".[125] The summons is to be issued in the name of the arbitrators and served in the same way as court-issued subpoenas. If any person so summoned to testify fails to obey, then upon petition, a US District Court at the place of the arbitration may compel the attendance or punish the person for contempt.[126]

In **South Africa**, under the Arbitration Act No. 42 of 1965,[127] the arbitrator is empowered to regulate the summoning of witnesses. Sect. 16 provides that the issue of a summons to compel any person to attend before an arbitration tribunal to give evidence may be procured by any party in the same manner and subject to the same conditions "as if the reference were in a civil action pending in the court". The effect of Sect. 16 is that "the arbitrator generally has the same authority … as the court".[128] Sect. 16 states that "on the application of any party … the court may order the process of the court to issue to compel the attendance of a witness before the arbitral tribunal". A party may also apply to a tribunal under Sect. 14 to appoint a "commissioner" to take the evidence of any person in South Africa (or even abroad) and to forward such evidence to the tribunal as if it were a court-appointed commissioner proceeding. Art. 21 of the Act also enables the courts to order examination of a witness by a commissioner, but the terms make clear that this provision "shall not be construed so as to derogate from any power which may be vested in an arbitration tribunal".

---

124. DIMOLITSA, *op. cit.*, fn. 4, p. 11.
125. Discussed in BORN, *op. cit.*, fn. 3, pp. 1900-1902; GÉLINAS, *op. cit.*, fn. 1, at p. 36 (noting the Uniform Arbitration Act in various states); Thomas H. WEBSTER, "Obtaining Evidence from Third Parties in International Arbitration", 17 Arbitration International (2001, no. 1) p. 2. For guidance on how this procedure works in practice, see Paul D. FRIEDLAND and Lucy E. MARTINEZ, "Arbitral Subpoenas Under U.S. Law and Practice", 143 American Review of International Arbitration (2003) pp. 197-229.
126. USC 9 FAA, Sect. 7.
127. The current South African Act is modeled on the former English Act of 1950. See discussion in Patrick MM LANE SC and R. Lee HARDING, National Report South Africa in ICCA *International Handbook on Commercial Arbitration* (Supplement 61, Sept 2010). For similar legislation in the region, see Lesotho Arbitration Act 1980; Botswana Arbitration Act Sect. 16; Swaziland Arbitration Act 1904, Sect. 24; Malawi Arbitration Act, Sect. 13(4). South Africa is soon to adopt new arbitration legislation which is expected to adopt the Model Law.
128. South Africa Chapter of the International Comparative Law Guide, 2011, available at <www.werksmans.com/wp-content/uploads/2013/04/2.-ICLG-2011_Arbitration_SA.pdf>.

In **Hong Kong**, arbitral tribunals have the power to make orders "directing the attendance before the tribunal of witnesses in order to give evidence or to produce documents or other material evidence".[129] However, the tribunal can only "direct" the witness to attend; it cannot "compel" a non-party witness to do so, without the additional step being taken of the court giving leave. Under Sect. 2GG of the Ordinance, an order or direction made in relation to arbitration proceedings by an arbitral tribunal "is enforceable in the same way as a judgment, order or direction of the Court that has the same effect, but only with the leave of the Court".[130] This step then enables an arbitrator's order to be enforced against a non-party witness. Sect. 2GG was amended to clarify that it applies to orders and direction made whether in or outside Hong Kong.[131]

As with the second step in the Hong Kong process, most jurisdictions provide for a tribunal (or the parties, with the tribunal's consent) to resort to the national courts for assistance in compelling witness attendance.

2.   *Options That Involve Recourse to the Courts*

If arbitrators "consider it extremely important to hear a person who has refused to appear, they can apply to a national court".[132] The **IBA Rules** acknowledge this possibility in Art. 4.9:

> "If a Party wishes to present evidence from a person who will not appear voluntarily at its request, the Party may, within the time ordered by the Arbitral Tribunal, ask it to take whatever steps are legally available to obtain the testimony of that person, or seek leave from the Arbitral Tribunal to take such steps itself. In the case of a request to the Arbitral Tribunal, the Party shall identify the intended witness, shall describe the subjects on which the witness's testimony is sought and shall state why such subjects are relevant to the case and material to its outcome. The Arbitral Tribunal shall decide on this request and shall take, authorize the requesting Party to take or order any other Party to take, such steps as the Arbitral Tribunal considers appropriate if, in its discretion, it determines that the testimony of that witness would be relevant to the case and material to its outcome."

The **IBA Commentary** to Art. 4.9 recalls that under most arbitration laws, "either the arbitral tribunal or a party with the approval of the arbitral tribunal may ask the State courts to compel the witness to appear or to examine the witness itself" and that, as a general rule "it shall be the State courts at the seat of arbitration which may help the arbitral tribunal to obtain testimony from a recalcitrant witness".[133] Recourse to courts

---

129. Hong Kong Ordinance, Sect. 2GB(5), cited in MEGENS, *op. cit.*, fn. 22, at p. 47.
130. Art. 12 of the Singapore International Arbitration Act contains similar provisions.
131. See discussion in MEGENS, *op. cit.*, fn. 22, at p. 47.
132. DIMOLITSA, *op. cit.*, fn. 4, fn. 21.
133. IBA Commentary, p. 18.

at the seat of arbitration is discussed in Sect. IV.*2.a* below. This will only be of assistance, however, if the witness is at the place of arbitration. As the IBA Commentary acknowledges, in transnational proceedings "witnesses often are not domiciled in the country where the arbitration has its seat. The arbitral tribunal may then have to request help from foreign courts, directly or indirectly." Those options, discussed in Sect. IV.*2.b* below, are slightly more complex, and will depend on where the witness is located. That is why Art. 4.9 of the IBA Rules acknowledges that the power of the tribunal is limited to "whatever steps are legally available".

The two-step process in Art. 4.9 (party to request the tribunal to act, tribunal to act only if satisfied the testimony would be relevant and material) helps avoid "unnecessary efforts" are wasted in ensuring the appearance of an irrelevant witness.[134] The IBA commentary also points out that "the tribunal may elect instead to authorise a party to take such steps and approach the foreign courts itself. Proceeding in this manner might be more practical or efficient if, for instance, the party requesting the evidence was located in that country, spoke the local language or already had local legal counsel."

a.   Court assistance at the place of the arbitration

The **Model Law** sets out the capacity of the tribunal to approach the courts in Art. 27:[135]

> "The arbitral tribunal or a party with the approval of the arbitral tribunal may request from a competent court of this State assistance in taking evidence. The court may execute the request within its competence and according to its rules on taking evidence."

The sanctions for a witness refusing to appear in the face of a national court's order to do so will obviously depend on the common procedural law in that country of the court. Usually the penalty will be a fine.[136]

For illustrative purposes, the relevant provisions of arbitration laws in a few key jurisdictions are highlighted below.

Arbitrations seated in the **United States** are discussed above.

A tribunal seated in **England** does not have the power to compel the attendance of non-party witnesses.[137] Under Sect. 43 of the English Arbitration Act 1996, with permission of the tribunal or agreement of other parties, a party may apply to the court to use the same procedures as are available in relation to court proceedings to secure the attendance before the tribunal of a witness. Such procedures are only available where the

---

134. ZUBERBÜHLER, *op. cit.,* fn. 6, at para. 80.
135. By Art. 1(2) of the Model Law, which provides that the provisions of the Model Law "apply only if the place of arbitration is in the territory of th[e] State [where the Model Law is enacted]".
136. DIMOLITSA, *op. cit.,* fn. 4, p. 11. See also Oliver KNÖFEL, "Judicial Assistance in the Taking of Evidence Abroad in Aid of Arbitration: A German Perspective", Journal of Private International Law (2009) p. 281.
137. See Joseph TIRADO, Sherina PETIT, et al., "Factual Evidence" in Julian D. M. LEW, Harris BOR, et al., eds., *Arbitration in England, with chapters on Scotland and Ireland* (2013) p. 483 (henceforth "Tirado").

witness is in the United Kingdom and the arbitral proceedings are being conducted in England, Wales or Northern Ireland. The court procedures in Sect. 43 are set out in CPR Part 34 and involve the court issuing a witness summons. In *Assimina Maritime Ltd v. Pakistan National Shipping Corporation*,[138] a Sect. 43 order was granted requiring the director of a marine survey organisation to attend a hearing before the tribunal in order to produce a feasibility study. While Sect. 43 is drafted in such a way as to only allow a *party* to apply to a court, Redfern & Hunter point out that a *tribunal* may indirectly achieve the same result, at least if the witness sought is under the control of one of the parties. The tribunal could issue a "peremptory order requiring the presence of a witness in the power of a party which, if disobeyed, may be followed by a court order in support. If the court order is disobeyed, it is a contempt of court which may lead to a criminal prosecution."[139]

For arbitrations seated in **Switzerland,** Sect. 184 of the Swiss Private International Law Act provides that the arbitral tribunal or a party with the consent of the tribunal may request a state judge for assistance for the taking of evidence.[140]

In the **Netherlands**, under Sect. 1041(2) of the Dutch Code of Civil Procedure, if a witness does not attend voluntarily, the arbitral tribunal may allow a party who so requests to petition the President of the District Court to appoint a judge-commissary before whom the examination of the witness shall take place. The examination shall take place in the same manner as in ordinary court proceedings. The arbitrators have the opportunity to attend the examination of the witness, and the court must promptly communicate to the tribunal and the parties a transcript of the examination.[141]

For international arbitrations in **Hong Kong**[142] the Arbitration Ordinance incorporates the UNCITRAL Model Law and, as noted in the above section, empowers the tribunal to make orders directing the attendance before the tribunal of witnesses in order to give evidence. With leave of the court, such an order by the tribunal obtains the force of law such that it can bind third party witnesses.[143] Another power vested in the High Court is Sect. 2GC(3) of the Arbitration Ordinance which provides: "The Court or a judge of the Court may order a person to attend proceedings before an arbitral tribunal to give evidence...." This power implicitly assists parties to obtain orders against non-parties. For court assistance in these matters, applications must be made by summons to the judge-in-charge of the Construction and Arbitration List and sitting in chambers. The evidence sought must be specific. In view of Art. 27 of the Model Law, it would be advisable for a party to seek the tribunal's consent before making a Sect. 2GC(3) application.

---

138. [2005] Lloyd's Rep 525, cited in Kieron O'CALLAGHAN and Jerome FINNIS in Julian LEW, Harris BOR et al., eds., *Arbitration in England, with chapters on Scotland and Ireland* (2013) p. 483.
139. REDFERN & HUNTER, *op. cit.*, fn. 2, at [5.19].
140. Swiss Private International Law Act, Sect. 184(2). See ZUBERBÜHLER, *op. cit.,* fn. 6, para. 81; DIMOLITSA, *op. cit.*, fn. 4, p. 11; MARRIOTT, *op. cit.*, fn. 80, p. 285.
141. VAN DER BEND, et al., *op. cit.*, fn. 21, p. 145.
142. For Mainland China, see MEGENS, *op. cit.*, fn. 22, at p. 50. The Arbitration Law of 1994 does not make provision for the compulsion of evidence from non-parties. The Civil Procedure Law of 1991 is of no assistance in this regard and there are no applicable treaties. Parties are totally dependent on the co-operation of witnesses.
143. Sect. 2GB(5) and 2GG(1). See discussion in MEGENS, *op. cit.*, fn. 22, at pp. 47-49.

Singapore has adopted the Model Law in Sect. 3(1) of its International Arbitration Act and therefore by virtue of Art. 27 of the Model Law, the tribunal, or the parties with the tribunal's consent, can request court assistance. Sect. 13 of the Act contains provisions facilitating the compulsion of witnesses by subpoena to testify in arbitral proceedings, upon application of a party.[144]

Under the **Mauritius** International Arbitration Act of 2008, a tribunal or a party with the approval of the arbitral tribunal may request from the Supreme Court assistance in taking evidence. The Act confirms that this means the Court may "(a) issue a witness summons to compel the attendance of any person before an arbitral tribunal to give evidence or produce documents or other material; or (b) order any witness to submit to examination on oath before the arbitral tribunal, or before an office of the Court, or any person for the use of the arbitral tribunal".

In **Australia**, the International Arbitration Act 1974 imports the Model Law and thus provides by virtue of Art. 27 for the tribunal or a party to access the Australian courts for assistance in taking evidence. Under reforms introduced in 2010, the Act specifies (without limiting Art. 27 of the Model Law) that a party with permission of the tribunal may apply to a court to issue a subpoena requiring a person to attend for examination before the tribunal. Before issuing a subpoena to a non-party, the court must be satisfied that it would be reasonable in all the circumstances. Sect. 23A of the Act contains additional opt-out provisions allowing a party to apply to a court for an order ordering a person who has refused to attend before the arbitral tribunal when required to do so under a Sect. 23 subpoena. Separately, with permission of the tribunal, a party may also apply to a court if a person has refused to comply with a request by the tribunal itself to appear as a witness, in which case the court can order the person to attend the court for questioning. The court will only make such an order in respect of a non-party if that person has been given an opportunity to make representations to the court, and the court is satisfied that it is reasonable in all the circumstances to make the order.[145]

b.   *Court assistance at the place of the witness*
When the witness is located in a country other than the place of the arbitration, the tribunal may need to get more creative if it wishes to compel the appearance of the witness. There is no uniform cross-border process for obtaining witness testimony abroad for use in international arbitration proceedings.

If the relevant countries are parties to the **Hague Convention** on the Taking of Evidence Abroad in Civil or Commercial Matters, that Convention can streamline procedures for obtaining evidence, but requests should come from "judicial

---

144. See discussion in MEGENS, *op. cit.*, fn. 22.
145. See Michael J. MOSER and John CHOONG, *Asia Arbitration Handbook* (OUP 2011) at [23.38]. See also discussion by MEGENS, *op. cit.*, fn. 22, pre-dating the 2010 amendments, noting that international arbitral tribunals holding hearings in Australia may also be subject to the regimes of the state uniform Commercial Arbitration Acts, which offer "relatively cheap, expeditious and effective" procedures that allow "both the arbitral tribunal and, if necessary, the court in aid of the arbitral tribunal, to exercise fairly wide-ranging powers of evidence gathering", even with respect to non-parties.

authorities".[146] Thus a request made from an arbitral tribunal does not fall within the scope of the Hague Convention. The tribunal would need to approach the state court judge at its seat, who in turn would have to prosecute the request through channels of legal assistance for the witness to be heard by the state court at its domicile.[147] Redfern & Hunter note that "nonetheless, many of the signatory States to the Hague Convention lend their judicial assistance to an arbitral tribunal with its judicial seat in another contracting State".[148] Commentators also note the possibility of using "letters rogatory".[149]

In some jurisdictions there may be scope for a direct approach by the parties or the tribunal to the witness's local courts, but these regimes vary greatly from country to country, as demonstrated by the examples below. Accordingly, Nesbitt advises: "if faced with a reluctant witness in a jurisdiction other than that of the seat of the arbitration, parties should seek advice on the options available in the witness's jurisdiction, or risk losing the opportunity to call that evidence".[150]

In the **United States**, one potential mechanism for a tribunal to use for purposes of obtaining non-party witness testimony is Sect. 1782 of Title 28 of the United States Code ("**Sect. 1782**"), which provides:[151]

> "(a) The district court of the district in which a person resides or is found *may order him to give his testimony* or statement or to produce a document or other thing *for use in a proceeding in a foreign or international tribunal*, including criminal investigations conducted before formal accusation. The order may be made pursuant to a letter rogatory issued, or *request made, by a foreign or international tribunal or upon the application of any interested person* and may direct that the testimony or statement be given, or the document or other thing be produced, before a person appointed by the court…. To the extent that the order does not prescribe otherwise, the testimony or statement shall be taken, and the document or other thing produced, in accordance with the Federal Rules of Civil Procedure…." (Emphasis added)

---

146. Simon NESBITT and Saira SINGH, "What to Do with a Reluctant Witness", 24 European Lawyer (2002, no. 3) p. 46 (henceforth "Nesbitt").
147. ZUBERBÜHLER, *op. cit.*, fn. 6, para. 83.
148. REDFERN & HUNTER, 3rd ed. (Sweet & Maxwell 1999).
149. See, e.g., DIMOLITSA, *op. cit.*, fn. 4, referring to Order issued by the tribunal in ICC case No. 6401, 1 Oct 1990, Order issued by Geneva First Instance Court, 31 Jan 1991, addressing rogatory letters to the authorities of Vaduz (Liechtenstein) and Paris (France), ASA Bull. (1994) p. 310. Order issued by the Egerna First Instance Court, 1 Feb 1993 addressing rogatory letters to the competent authorities in France, Germany and United States, ASA Bull. (1994) p. 314.
150. NESBITT, *op. cit.*, fn. 146, at p. 47.
151. See Arthur ROVINE, "Section 1782 and International Arbitral Tribunals Some Key Considerations in Key Cases", 23 The American Review of International Arbitration (2012, no. 4) p. 461 (henceforth "Rovine").

US Courts were not initially receptive to use of Sect. 1782 in support of international arbitration proceedings.[152] However, in the landmark 2004 decision of *Intel v. Advanced Micro Devices, Inc*, the Supreme Court decided that the word "tribunal" as used in Sect. 1782 "'is not confined to proceedings before conventional courts,' but extends also to 'administrative and quasi-judicial proceedings'".[153] The Court set out four factors for district courts to consider when deciding to exercise discretion to grant a Sect. 1782 application: (i) whether the person from whom discovery is sought is a participant in the foreign proceeding; (ii) whether the foreign tribunal is receptive to the application; (iii) whether the discovery sought is an attempt to "circumvent foreign proof-gathering restrictions"; and (iv) whether the discovery sought is "unduly intrusive or burdensome".[154]

There are many examples of **US courts** granting Sect. 1782 discovery in the context of international arbitrations seated abroad, including investor-state arbitrations.[155] Nevertheless, the author is not familiar with a case where it was the *arbitral tribunal* acting on its own initiative, and not a party to the arbitration, who sought assistance from a US Court under Sect. 1782, let alone one where the tribunal sought to question a witness.[156]

---

152. See e.g. *Kazakhstan v. Biederman* 168 F.3d 880 (5th Cir. 1999).

153. 542 US 241, 249 (2004).

154. *Intel* 542 US at 264-265.

155. See *Methanex v. USA* (Final Award on Jurisdiction and Merits, 3 August 2005), Part II, Chapter G, para. 21 (recounting Methanex's later withdrawn application under 28 USC Sect. 1782); See *In the Matter of an Application of Oxus Gold PLC for Assistance before a Foreign Tribunal*, MISC06-82, LEXIS 74118 (D.N.J., 10 October 2006) (henceforth "*Oxus Gold 2006*"). Affirmed on appeal: *In the Matter of an Application of Oxus Gold PLC for Assistance before a Foreign Tribunal*, MISC-06-82-GEB, LEXIS 24061, (D.N.J., 2 April 2007) (in which the court interpreted *Intel* as allowing Sect. 1782 applications in investor-state arbitrations); see, e.g., *In re Chevron Corp.*, 753 F.Supp.2d 536 (D. Md. 2010) and *In re the Application of: The Republic of Ecuador and Dr. Diego Garcia Carrion, Applicants, for the Issuance of a Subpoena Under 28 U.S.C. Sect. 1782 to Dr. Michael A. Kelsh for the Taking of a Deposition and the Production of Documents in a Foreign Proceeding* No. C 11-80171 CRB,C 11-80172, CRB (D.N. Cal., 23 September 2011) (henceforth "*Re Ecuador*"). (*Chevron v. Ecuador* is a PCA-administered BIT arbitration under the UNCITRAL Rules, Both sides have applied under Sect. 1782 to several district courts throughout the United States to compel evidence from third parties in support of arbitration.); *In Re Broadsheet LLC, To Issue Subpoenas For the Production of Documents*, Civil Action No. 11-cv-02436-PAB-KMT, LEXIS 120473 (D.CO., 18 October 2011) (in support of a contract arbitration conducted in London); *In Re Application of Mesa Power Group, LLP Pursuant to 28 U.S.C. § 1782 for Judicial Assistance in Obtaining Evidence from NextEra Energy Resources, LLC, Armando Pimental, Jr., Mitchell F. Davidson, Michael O'Sullivan, Mark Sorenson, T.J. Tuscal, Louis Coakley and Ross Groffman for use in a Foreign and International Proceeding*, Case No. 11-24335-CIV-UNGARO/TORRES, LEXIS 97329 (S.D. Fla., 13 July 2012) (henceforth "*In re Mesa Power*") pp. 11-12.

156. *In Re Application Of Caratube International Oil Company, LLP*, 730 F.Supp.2d 101 (D.D.C., 11 August, 2010) p. 108 (the Court denied Caratube's application due to its having chosen to arbitrate under the ICSID Rules rather than the UNCITRAL Rules, but suggested that Caratube could have applied to the tribunal which in turn could have sought discovery assistance on its own through section 1782. Rovine agrees the better approach to Sect. 1782 is for the request to come from the tribunal or with its consent, and that "the judiciary should utilize its discretion in

Under the **English Arbitration Act 1996**, it is recalled that Sect. 43 provides for a court to assist in securing the attendance of witnesses if the tribunal or parties agree, if the witness is in the United Kingdom, and if the arbitral proceedings are being conducted in England, Wales or Northern Ireland. Sect. 44 of the English act expands the scope of this power to arbitrations that have their legal seat outside of the United Kingdom, only where the court is satisfied that "it is appropriate" by reason of a connection with England and Wales or Northern Ireland.

Thus, an arbitral tribunal seated outside of the United Kingdom could have a one-off witness hearing in England and seek the assistance of the court in compelling the witness to attend. This was confirmed, in theory, in the case of *Commerce and Industry Insurance Co, Canada v. Certain Underwriters of Lloyds of London*.[157] Arbitrators sitting in New York issued a "letter of request" directly to an English court, asking for an order that witnesses resident in England be examined on a number of questions. The court dismissed the application. The court held that it had discretion under Sect. 44 of the Arbitration Act to make an order for the examination of witnesses in support of arbitration proceedings, even though the seat of arbitration was in New York and the curial law was New York law. However, the court declined to exercise that discretion, noting that discovery was not a part of English procedure and that it would not assist in a fishing expedition.

For arbitration proceedings held in **Singapore** the Rules of Court provide an avenue to obtain the evidence of witnesses who reside outside of Singapore. This is by way of obtaining evidence by deposition in foreign jurisdictions, pursuant to Order 39 of the Singapore Rules of Court. Order 69A, rule 8, provides that Order 39 shall apply in relation to the taking of evidence for arbitration proceedings under Art. 27 of the Model Law. Megens also notes that an arbitration proceeding held outside of Singapore may potentially require assistance from witnesses within Singapore, by virtue of Sect. 13 of the International Arbitration Act.[158] Singapore's Evidence (Civil Proceedings in Other Jurisdictions) Act may also be an avenue to obtain evidence from witnesses in Singapore for use in proceedings held outside of Singapore, pursuant to a request issued by a "court or tribunal" exercising jurisdiction in a country or territory outside Singapore.

Finally, it is recalled from the discussion in Sect. IV.*1.d* above, that under Sect. 21(c) of the **South African** arbitration law, a court can request a commissioner to examine a witness abroad, in aid of an international arbitration conducted in South Africa.

---

applying Sect. 1782 in accordance with the preferences of the arbitrators, meaning at the request of the arbitrators, or with their consent, and within the framework and limits the arbitrators have chosen." ROVINE, *op. cit.*, fn. 151, p. 469.

157. High Court of Justice, QBD, 01/849, 1 August 2001, reported by John BEECHEY; see also Hew R. DUNDAS, "English Court Powers in Support of Foreign Arbitral Proceedings: Exercise of Court's Discretion: *Commerce & Industry Insurance Company of Canada v. Certain Undewriters at Lloyds*", 69 Arbitration (2003, no. 1) p. 40.

158. They consider Art. 13 of the Singapore International Arbitration Act to be broad enough to compel persons in Singapore to attend and give evidence in arbitration proceedings outside Singapore, but note that there is some case law in Hong Kong to suggest otherwise. Hong Kong's Evidence Ordinance provides a similar avenue for obtaining evidence from witnesses in Hong Kong for use in proceedings outside Hong Kong.

3.   Lessons

An arbitral tribunal has a menu of tools at its disposal to deal with non-appearance by a witness. The tribunal might accept the situation and simply decide the case on the available evidence, or by drawing appropriate inferences from the non-appearance. If it wants to push further to procure the appearance of the witness, and all attempts to do so via the parties' best efforts have failed, it should not underestimate the potential effectiveness of simply sending a request to the witness to attend. Anticipating arrangements for travel, cost, interpretation, safe passage or being prepared to take the testimony via video or at the witness's own location may help encourage cooperation.

The tribunal should also familiarize itself with more formal options for compelling the witness to attend, whether by summons, letters rogatory or other procedures unique to the arbitral seat or domicile of the witness. Merely raising the prospect of such measures may be sufficient to encourage the witness's voluntary cooperation. If it does not have that effect, the tribunal will need to decide whether in fact to pursue court-assisted processes. In so deciding, the following considerations are mentioned by one commentator:[159]

> "In the normal course, a tribunal will be reluctant to see the arbitral process derailed because of the need to wait for a witness to be compelled to appear by a foreign court. Ultimately, much will turn on the supposed value of the evidence in question. In coming to its decision, the tribunal will be mindful of its general duties to give each party a 'reasonable opportunity' of presenting its case and adopting proportionate procedures."

V.   CONCLUSIONS

Arbitration is traditionally viewed as a private, consensual process between parties to the arbitration agreement. Party autonomy and procedural efficiency are hallmark values. It is therefore understandable to expect that it is for the parties alone to decide which witnesses will tell the story in an international arbitration. This paper has tested that proposition in two respects.

First, it has examined whether tribunals may request testimony on their own initiative, even from an individual who has not been offered by the parties. Second, it has considered whether tribunals can act as gate-keepers in deciding that a witness who provided a statement need not appear at the hearing. Arbitration legislation and rules provide that tribunals have the power to take initiatives in both scenarios. Most commentators advise that tribunals exercise those powers only in exceptional circumstances, and always in consultation with the parties.

When a tribunal faces an evidentiary gap that would best be filled by hearing from a certain individual, it has a number of possible tools at its disposal. The first step is to ask the parties to use their best efforts to arrange that witness's testimony. That can be a

---

159. TIRADO, *op. cit.*, fn. 137, at [23-45].

challenge if the individual is not in the control of the parties. But futile party attempts do not spell the end of the road. A tribunal will weigh up the importance of the potential evidence and the costs and delays associated with pursuing it further. As shown in this paper, depending on where the tribunal is seated and where the elusive key witness is located, the tribunal may well have access to some powerful tools which could ensure that a key individual is available to help fill significant voids in the evidentiary record.

The concrete examples discussed in this paper show that, exercised with caution, the tribunal's powers with respect to seeking witnesses can be effective at completing and improving the accuracy of the evidentiary record and thereby increasing the fairness, justice and legitimacy of the ultimate result.

A Primer on Damages Assessment:
Towards a Framework for Fair Compensation

Santiago Dellepiane, *Lucia Quesada* ** *and Pablo T. Spiller* ***

I.   INTRODUCTION

This paper is aimed at providing a framework to help counsel and arbitrators understand certain basic concepts affecting the computation of damages through the income approach.[1] While arbitration tribunals often worry about over-compensating the damaged party, under-compensation is equally problematic, as systematic under-compensation promotes inefficient breach and opportunistic behavior in contracting. Using a hypothetical joint-venture breach of contract case, and following simple numbers, we begin by exemplifying the workings of a standard, simplified discounted cash flow valuation and use this example to quantify the effects on compensation of mistreating each of the following issues: (a) double-counting sunk costs and lost profits; (b) double-counting by claiming for loss of income and loss of value; (c) the use of inappropriate discount rates; (d) the use of pre-judgment interest rates that are inconsistent with discount rates; and (e) the inclusion or exclusion of investments not yet made.

---

*   Senior Vice President, Compass Lexecon in New York.
**   Senior Economist, Compass Lexecon in Buenos Aires.
*** Distinguished Professor (Emeritus) Professor of Business and Technology, Haas School of Business, and Professor of Graduate Studies, University of California, Berkeley; Senior Consultant (Affiliate), Compass Lexecon, New York.

The authors' views are their own and do not represent the views of other experts at Compass Lexecon or its clients.

1.   In explaining typical reasons for over and under-compensation, we build on the examples examined by Spiller and Dellepiane in Chapter 6 of H. WÖSS, A. SAN ROMÁN RIVERA, P.T. SPILLER, and S. DELLEPIANE, *Damages in International Arbitration under Complex Long-Term Contracts* (Oxford University Press 2014).

II.   A HYPOTHETICAL COMMERCIAL CASE

Consider the following hypothetical case. A project is the result of a Joint Venture Agreement (JVA) between two companies. Company "Tech" commits to provide the appropriate know-how and technical assistance for the venture, while Company "Opco" commits to operating the project, and both companies agree to share the profits of the JV in equal parts. The project requires an initial investment by Opco of $100 that takes place at the venture's kick-off date, or t=0. During the first two years, the project is expected to generate negative cash flows to Opco (and to the overall JV). Starting on the third year of operation, cash flows generated by the project are expected to be positive, and then increase, until they stabilize. The annual (undiscounted) cash flows that the project is expected to generate to Opco are shown in Figure 1 below.[2] The terminal value (TV) summarizes the value, discounted as of year seven (t=7) of the future cash flows that the project is expected to generate from that point onwards, expressed as of that date.

---

2. To simplify the exposition, we only show the value of the project to Opco. Therefore, each time we refer to "the value of the project", this means "the value of the project to Opco".

Figure 1. Annual Cash Flows to OPCO

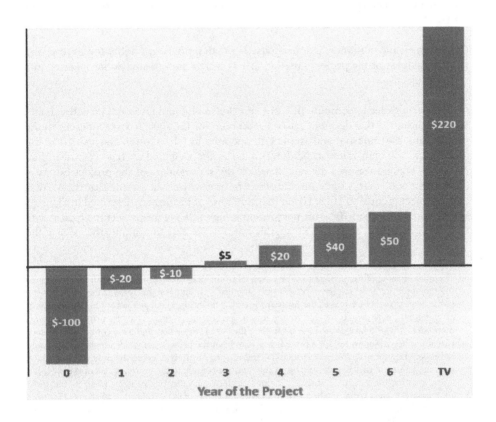

Assuming that Opco can sell its share of the project to another operator, the market value of the project to Opco, measured as of a particular date, is equal to the present value of the cash flows that the project is able to generate multiplied by its percentage share in the project's profits.[3] A present value needs to be computed in order to account for two fundamental issues:[4]

(i) the time value of money: a dollar today is worth more than a dollar tomorrow; and (ii) the riskiness of the project: a safe dollar is worth more than a dollar invested in a riskier project.

Hence, in order to compute the present value, a discount rate must be defined, and to do so properly, that discount rate must account for the specific risks inherent to the project and the industry and market it operates in.[5] It is often the case that the appropriate discount rate can be determined as the weighted average cost of capital (WACC), which measures the rate at which the stakeholders of the project can raise funds (debt and equity).[6] For simplification purposes, we will assume that the WACC of the project is equal to 10%. Given the cash flows of the project described in Figure 1 and the discount rate of 10%, the net present value (NPV) of the project to Opco at date t=0 is approximately equal to $57.[7] In this way, it is possible to compute the value of the

---

3. The market value of the project to Opco is equal to the price at which Opco would be willing to sell its project to a willing buyer, under no compulsion to sell. For this reason, the market value of the project must be equal to the future profits that the project will generate. On the one hand, no potential buyer would be able to pay for the project more than what the project can yield; otherwise, it would be making losses. On the other hand, the seller, under no compulsion to sell, would not be willing to sell for a price lower than what the project can yield; otherwise, it would rather keep the project and collect its expected earnings from it. Hence, the only price at which both the seller and the buyer would be willing to trade is equal to the present value of the project's future profits. To valuate a business, a forward-looking valuation strategy is often the most appropriate because it mirrors how investors assess the value of income-producing assets. The value generated by these assets comes from their anticipated future production, not their past investments. The Discounted Cash Flow (DCF) approach provides the methodological mainstay for forward-looking valuations. See BREALEY and MYERS, *Principles of Corporate Finance*, 7th ed., Chapters 2-3 (2003).
4. In fact, cash flows that are not appropriately discounted to account for the risk and time are not comparable, as they are measured in different units.
5. See BREALEY and MYERS, *op. cit.*, fn. 3, Chapter 2 and Chapter 9, See also E.F. FAMA, "Risk-Adjusted Discount Rates and Capital Budgeting Under Uncertainty", 5 Journal of Financial Economics (1977, no. 1).
6. When the WACC is determined via the capital asset pricing model (CAPM), and when the latter is properly applied, risks are being determined by the interaction of market participants in the relevant industry.
7. Given the expected cash flows of the project to Opco in our example, and the discount rate we have assumed, the NPV can be computed according to the following formula:

$$NPV = -100 - \frac{20}{1+10\%} - \frac{10}{(1+10\%)^2} + \frac{5}{(1+10\%)^3} + \frac{20}{(1+10\%)^4} + \frac{40}{(1+10\%)^5} + \frac{50}{(1+10\%)^6} + \frac{220}{(1+10\%)^7}$$

project or NPV to Opco at any point in time by computing the present value of the future cash flows.[8] In this particular example, we show the value of the project at any possible date between date t=0 and date t=7 in Figure 2.

Figure 2. Value of the Project at Alternative Dates

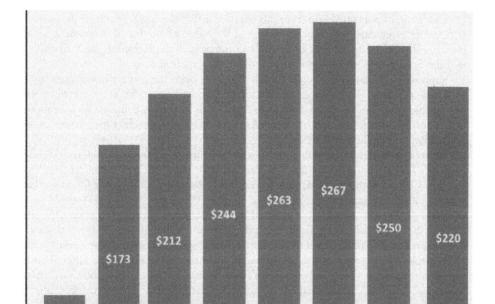

See BREALEY and MYERS, *op. cit.*, fn. 3, Chapter 3. *op. cit.*, fn. 3,
8. For simplicity, we assume that the discount rate (WACC) remains the same at different dates. This is clearly a simplification, as at different dates the perception of risks or the time value of money may be different.

We observe from Figure 2 that, once the initial investment has been made, the value of the project computed as of subsequent dates increases, as the negative cash flows of the first years are left behind. While past investments and other factors (market prices, costs, other) affect the state that a project might be in at a given point in time, its value is independent of the stream of past cash flows. Instead, its value depends on the expected future profits it can generate as of that particular date (e.g., how much it can sell, at what prices it can sell, and the perception of risk in that particular industry at that point in time).[9]

Thus, one important lesson from this exercise is that the market value of the project at any date after date t=0 is independent of the value of the initial investment. This lesson will turn out to be very useful for our purpose of understanding how to ensure that the damages assessment guarantees a fair compensation.

Suppose now that at the beginning of year t=4, once the project has started to be profitable to Opco, Tech decides to unilaterally terminate its technology contributions in breach of the JVA. Without Tech's input, Opco is unable to continue its operations and is forced to liquidate its business. As a result of the breach, Opco commences arbitration proceedings against Tech.

The tribunal in this case will have to determine the compensation that Tech should pay Opco for breaching the contract. Assume, barring legal differences which may affect the standards of compensation, that the tribunal wishes to compensate Opco so that compensation will make it whole. That is, to place Opco in the position it would have been had the breach not taken place. For that, the tribunal determines to grant Opco its share of the *market value of the project* (i.e., the economic value of the cash flows that will not materialize due to the breach). We know from Figure 2 above that the market value of the project to Opco as of the date of the breach (date t=4) is equal to $263. This is also shown in Table 1, where "cash flows" represent revenues net of incremental costs (historical cash flows are shown, but do not affect the calculation of the market value).

---

9. See I. MARBOE, *Calculation of Compensation and Damages in International Investment Law* (2009) p. 71.

Table 1. Market Value as of the Date of the Breach

	0	1	2	3	4	5	6	TV
		Historical Cash Flows				Future Cash Flows		
Cash Flows	-$100	-$20	-$10	-$5	$20	$40	$50	$220
Discount Factor @ 10%					1.00	0.91	0.83	0.75
Cash Flows Discounted to t=4					$20 + $36 + $41 + $165			
Market Value at DoV					$263			

If the tribunal wants to set compensation based on the market value of the project as computed at the date of the breach, it should rule that the compensation owed by Tech to Opco has to be equal to $263.[10] Notice that in this example, assessing market value is equivalent to assessing lost profits (lost revenues minus avoided costs), that is, future expected profits that will not materialize due to the contract breach.

1. Date of Valuation

From the previous example, and in particular from Figure 2, it is clear that the market value of the project depends crucially on the date at which we compute such value, the date of valuation (DoV). Different dates of valuation produce different values, because the stream of expected future cash flows changes over time. Hence, when assessing damages, the definition of a date of valuation is key. In this example, we will consider two alternative dates of valuation:

(i) the date of the breach
(ii) the date of the award, assuming this occurs two years after the breach

The distinction is important for the following reason: when the date of valuation is chosen to be the date of the breach, all the losses that result from the breach should be considered as *going forward* losses. On the other hand, as of the date of the award, total losses should be considered as the sum of (i) historical lost profits (between the date of breach and date of award) *and* (ii) expected future earnings that would not yet have materialized (between the date of the award and the end of the project).

---

10. This assumes that the tribunal agrees that a 10% discount rate appropriately captures project risk.

Suppose that in our previous example the award takes place at date t=6 (two years after the breach). Hence, fair compensation must account for the market value of the project as of date t=6 (going forward losses) *and* lost profits between the date of the breach and the date of the award (historical losses). Table 2 below shows the calculation of fair compensation computed as of the date of the award.[11]

TABLE 2. Going Forward Losses v. Historical Losses

	0	1	2	3	4	5	6	TV
		Historical Cash Flows			Historical Lost Profits		Future Lost Profits	
Cash Flows	-$100	-$20	-$10	-$5	$20	$40	$50	$220
Discount Factor @ 10%					1.21	1.10	1.00	0.91
Cash Flows Discounted to t=6					$24 + $44		$50 + $200	
Historical and Going-Forward Losses					$68		$250	
Fair Compensation at DoV							$318	

As we explained above, when computing compensation as of a date later than the date of the breach, e.g., the date of the award, one part of the compensation must account for historical losses, those corresponding to the period between the date of the breach and the date of valuation. In our example, historical losses amount to $68 corresponding to dates t=4 and t=5. The rest of the compensation accounts for future expected profits from the date of valuation to the end of the project. In our example, going forward losses amount to $250 from t=6 onward.[12]

Notice that we have maintained the same nominal cash flows across both examples, reflecting the fact that as of t=6, expectations have not changed (i.e. the world looks the same in t=4 and t=6). Despite this, compensation at a later date yields a higher value.

---

11. Note that in these scenarios we assume cash flows are but for the breach (in effect, the breach has put the project on hold and thus it is not currently producing cash flows of any kind). Considering *but-for* performance rather than performance as affected by the breach is another crucial part of assessing damages.

12. Note that, according to Figure 2 and Table 2, going forward losses are exactly equal to the market value of the project as of the date of the award. Under this framework, as a general rule, compensation as of any date posterior to the date of the breach is equal to the project's market value at that date *plus* compounded historical losses between the date of the breach and the date of valuation.

This is natural. Since the award occurs at a later date, historical cash flows can be updated to that date using a rate that accounts for the opportunity cost of those lost profits, and expected future profits are discounted by two fewer periods when we stand in t=6. Observe, however, that once corrected for the time and risk value of money, or "in present value terms", the two values are equivalent. That is, $318 at t=6, with a discount rate equal to 10%, is worth exactly $263 at t=4.[13] This confirms that the only source of discrepancy between the two values is the change in the date of valuation. Should the arbitration in fact take two years, following the example, pre-award interest at the cost of capital (i.e., 10% in this example) would reconcile the difference between both assessments.

III.   (UN)FAIR COMPENSATION AND DISCOUNT RATE

Another critical variable in the computation of the market value is the rate that is used to discount future cash flows and compound historical cash flows. The use of an inappropriate discount rate may lead to over- or under-compensation, depending on whether the chosen discount rate is too low or too high.

Therefore, to assess the market value of the project (and, hence, fair compensation), after defining the streams of cash flows that will be projected into the future, one must determine a discount rate applicable to those cash flows. As a general rule, the discount rate should be equal to the cost of raising funds for an investor in a project with similar systematic risks. The discount rate is essentially the investor's minimum required return on investment, as it guarantees that the investment will be recovered, with an additional return that compensates for the time value of money and the riskiness of the project.[14] The cost of raising funds, as we explained in Section II, is often measured by the WACC.

At this point, it is useful to recall that the WACC of a project is different from its internal rate of return (IRR). While the WACC measures the cost of raising funds for the investors (equity and debt holders), the IRR measures the actual return of the project. That is, the WACC indicates the minimum return that the project must generate in order to compensate its stakeholders for sinking their money in the project, whereas the IRR measures the return that the project actually generates. Hence, the IRR is completely independent of the WACC, and could be above or below the WACC.[15]

---

13. $263 = \$318/(1+10\%)^2$.

14. As such, an investor will not invest in a project with an implicit return below the cost of raising funds, as it will be expecting to make losses from its investment.

15. By definition, the IRR is the rate that, if used to discount the cash flows of the project, gives an NPV equal to 0. See BREALEY and MYERS, *op. cit.*, fn. 3, Chapter 5. Hence, if a project has a positive NPV its IRR is necessarily above the WACC. If, on the contrary, the project's NPV is negative, its IRR is lower than the WACC.

It is important to emphasize that IRRs (whether IRR of the project or IRRs of comparable projects) should not be used to discount future cash flows for the purpose of market valuation and damages assessment because they do not measure the cost of raising funds. For the case of projects that have a positive net present value, their IRR will be above their WACC and, hence, using the IRR as a discount rate instead of the WACC would lead to under-compensation (i.e., cash flows would be more heavily discounted than what they should be). Consider the example presented in Section II. Since the project has a positive NPV (see Figure 2), its IRR has to be higher than the WACC. As a matter of fact, it can be shown that the IRR of the project is approximately equal to 14%.[16]
Suppose that we mistakenly compute the project's market value as of the date of the breach using this IRR to discount future cash flows. We show this computation below:

TABLE 3. Wrong Market Value from Incorrect Use of Discount Rate

	0	1	2	3	4	5	6	TV
		Historical Cash Flows			Future Cash Flows			
Cash Flows	-$100	-$20	-$10	-$5	$20	$40	$50	$170
Discount Factor @ 14%					1.00	0.88	0.77	0.67
Cash Flows Discounted to t=4					$20 + $35 + $38 + $114			
Value at DoV					$207			
Value at t=0 @ 14%	$0							

In Table 3, we observe that the present value of the lost profits as of date t=4, when using a discount rate equal to 14%, is $207. This value falls short by $56 from fair compensation as computed in Table 1. Hence, Opco in this case is being under-compensated, as its actual compensation is 79% of the fair value. The difference between

---

16. In this example, the IRR is computed as the rate that solves the following equation:

$$0 = -100 - \frac{20}{1+IRR} - \frac{10}{(1+IRR)^2} + \frac{5}{(1+IRR)^3} + \frac{10}{(1+IRR)^4} + \frac{40}{(1+IRR)^5} + \frac{50}{(1+IRR)^6} + \frac{TV}{(1+IRR)^7}$$

Note that the TV has to be adjusted to the higher discount rate. We assume that the new TV is equal to $170.

366

these two values and the magnitude of under-compensation is shown below in Figure 3. Note that the magnitude of under-compensation would increase if the difference between the IRR and the WACC increased.[17]

Symmetrically, discounting at rates that do not fully capture all known risks of a project will result in awards that overestimate the present value of expected future profits. We show this possibility in Figure 3, assuming that an incorrect discount rate of 8% is used. With such a discount rate, compensation would be estimated at $288, or 110% of the fair value.

FIGURE 3. Using Incorrect Discount Rates Leads to Unfair Compensation

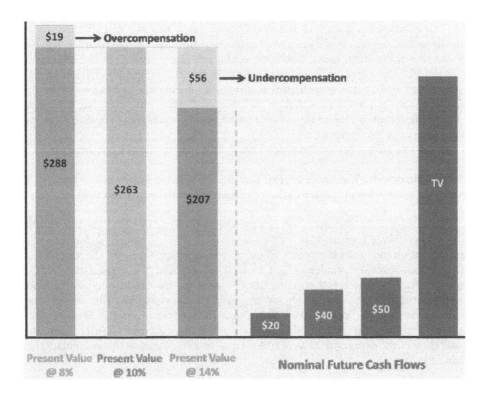

---

17. Experts often use IRRs of comparable projects, or of the industry, as a proxy for the cost of capital of the project. This, as discussed, is conceptually flawed, but may also lead to misinterpretation of facts. Consider, for example, the oil and gas industry, which showed very high IRRs due to the run-up in prices that started in 2002, even though their cost of capital was relatively low.

IV.   POSSIBLE ISSUES LEADING TO OVER-COMPENSATION

1.   *Double-Counting Investments and Lost Profits*

Over-compensation usually arises from double-counting damages under different categories. One common example of such double-counting occurs when the injured party claims damages simultaneously for lost profits *and* for its sunk investments. In this context, double-counting is a direct implication of our previous discussion and the example in Figure 2. As explained above, the market value of a project is unrelated to the investments in the project as long as the investments have already been made. That is, although investments are necessary for the project to generate positive cash flows (i.e., have value greater than zero), once they have been sunk into the project they become irrelevant in the computation of the project's value.

The fundamental reason of this double-counting is that the market value of an investment is not given by the amount of money actually invested (often captured in the book value of the investment), but by the profit-generating capacity of that amount of money. When we compute the value of the profits that the company would not be able to generate due to the breach, this is already capturing the market value of the investment in the project as of the date of valuation.[18] Therefore, including a measure of past investments on top of the value of future profits would lead to double-counting and hence to over-compensation.

In our example, suppose that Opco's claim following the breach consisted of:

(i) compensation for lost future profits; *plus*
(ii) compensation for the present value as of date t=4 of the past investment.

We know that the amount of lost profits as of t=4 is equal to $263. The value of the initial investment, compounded to t=4 is equal to $146.[19] Hence, adding the past investment on top of the lost profits would over compensate Opco by a factor of 55%. The double-counting problem exists even if we account for depreciation of the investments. The reason is that depreciations spread the amount invested over a finite period of time, without accounting for time value of money or risk. Thus, the present value of the depreciations is always lower than the amount invested.[20] To show this, suppose that the depreciation of the initial investment spreads over 10 years. Then, the total value of the depreciations as of t=4 is equal to $90. We show this computation in Table 4 below.

---

18. See S. RIPINSKY, and K. WILLIAMS, *Damages in International Investment Law* (British Institute of International Comparative Law 2008) p. 296. These authors explain that, to avoid double-counting, "… expenditures must be deducted from the amount of cash flows to be generated by an asset…". See also I. MARBOE, *Calculation of Compensation and Damages in International Investment Law* (2009) p. 73.
19. $146=100*(1+10\%)^4$.
20. See S. RIPINSKY, and K. WILLIAMS, *op. cit.*, fn. 18, pp. 296-297.

TABLE 4. Total Depreciations as of Date of Valuation

	1	2	3	4	5	6	7	8	9	10
	Historical Cash Flows			Future Cash Flows						
Depreciations	$10	$10	$10	$10	$10	$10	$10	$10	$10	$10
Discount Factor @ 10%	1.33	1.21	1.10	1.00	0.91	0.83	0.75	0.68	0.62	0.56
Discounted to t=4	$13 +	$12 +	$11	$10+	$9 +	$8 +	$8 +	$7	+ $6	+ $6
		$36					$54			
Depreciations at DoV				$90						

The value of the past investment, net of depreciations, at t=4 is equal to $56. Hence, compensation accounting for lost profits and past investments, even when depreciations are accounted for would be equal to $319, or 20% more than the market value of the project, according to Table 1.

2.   Loss of Income v. Loss of Value

A contract breach may create loss of income as well as loss of value. We refer to income as the net cash flows generated by a project, and value as the price at which an interest in the project can be sold. Both concepts are closely related and tribunals should make sure that they are not awarding damages twice for the same thing. In the case of our hypothetical scenario described in Section II, Opco, the injured party, could make a claim for loss of income, accounting for the profits lost due to the breach. Alternatively, Opco could make a claim for loss of value, given the unilateral termination of the joint venture (assuming it cannot be mitigated) has implied the loss in the value of its investment. However, it cannot ask for compensation on both grounds, since loss of income and loss of value are identical in this example.

Alternatively, one could envision Opco making a claim for loss of income between the time of the breach and the date of the award (i.e. historical lost profits) and loss of value for beyond the date of award, as, in this case, loss of income and loss of value have been defined as such as to avoid double-counting.

In some other cases, a breach may result in loss of value without loss of perceived income.[21] For instance, this would arise if, as a result of a breach, the cost of raising funds (WACC) of the project increases. Then, even if cash flows are unaffected by the breach, they would now be more heavily discounted, reducing the market value of the project, without generating a loss of income (at least in the short run). The use of a market

---

21. See, for example, S. RIPINSKY and K. WILLIAMS, *op. cit.*, fn. 18, p. 263.

discount rate that is generic to the industry but not specific to the company in dispute may address this problem.

In our hypothetical example, suppose that, as a consequence of the termination of the JVA, Opco was unable to comply with its obligations to certain clients related to the operations of this JVA. Suppose also that Opco had other commercial relations with these clients, who now have lost confidence in Opco as a supplier and decide to reduce or terminate their relations with Opco. In this case, Opco could claim both a loss of income for the market value of the JVA project with Tech and a loss of value for the reputational consequences of the breach.[22]

Another example of this, which is unlikely to affect commercial disputes as much as it would affect investment treaty cases, is the imposition of a dividend payment restriction or dividend repatriation restriction: under such type of measure, while the present value of a project may continue to be positive, the market value to a party or to the investor may be affected by their inability to enjoy the benefits of those cash flows.

V.   POSSIBLE ISSUES LEADING TO UNDER-COMPENSATION

1.   Pre-judgment Interest Rate

When compensation is computed as of a date prior to the date of the award (such as the date of the breach), a pre-judgment interest ("PJI") rate needs to be introduced to compensate the injured party for the time between the date of valuation and the date of the award.[23] The longer this period of time is, the more important PJI becomes, as it may account for a large proportion of total damages while the injured party awaits a ruling and is deprived of funds. Thus, in order to guarantee fair compensation it is important to understand how PJI should be computed.

Various theories exist, each suggesting alternative interest rates for PJI. One such theory asserts that PJI should be computed based on the relevant risk-free interest rate.[24] The basis for this theory is that once the tribunal asserts the existence of a breach and assesses damages, the loss becomes certain, and hence the injured party only needs to be compensated for the time value of money. Thus, while a risk-adjusted discount rate must be used to discount cash flows from the date of valuation onwards, a risk-free rate needs to be used to update such cash flows from the date of valuation to the date of the award, which may precede or come after the end of the damage period. There are various problems with this approach. Abdala, López Zadicoff and Spiller explain that such

---

22. See I. MARBOE, *op. cit.*, fn. 9, pp. 306-307.
23. As we saw in Section II.1 above, compensation is naturally lower when computed as of an earlier date.
24. See J.M. PATTEL, R.L. WEIL, and M.A. WOLFSON, "Accumulating Damages in Litigation: The Roles of Uncertainty and Interest Rates", 11 Journal of Legal Studies, (1982, no. 2).

approach leads to what they call an "invalid round trip" ("IRT"),[25] through which compensation for a loss that takes place at a date past the date of the breach may be lower than the loss itself, when valued as of the date of the award.[26] To illustrate the IRT in our hypothetical example, consider the expected cash flow at the date of the award (t=6), equal to $50 according to Figure 1. In Table 1 we see that this is equivalent to $41 as of the date of the breach when we discount at a rate equal to the WACC. If we update this back to the date of the award using a risk-free rate of, say, 2%, we would get a compensation equal to $42,[27] instead of $50, which is the actual expected cash flow at date 6. We show this in Figure 4 below.

FIGURE 4. Invalid Round Trip

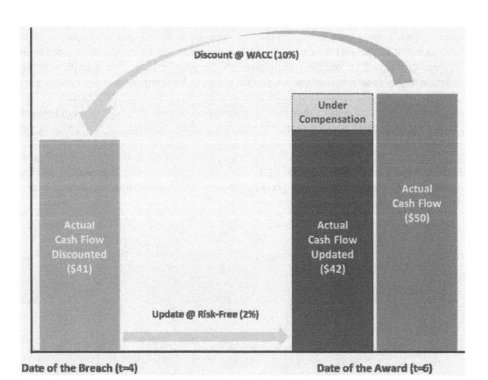

---

25. See M.A. ABDALA, P.D. LÓPEZ ZADICOFF and P.T. SPILLER, "Invalid Round Trips in Setting Pre-Judgment Interest in International Arbitration", 5 World Arbitration and Mediation Review (2011, no. 1) p.1.
26. The magnitude of the problem associated with the IRT is larger, the longer the distance between the date of the valuation and the date of the award.
27. $42 = 41*(1+2\%)^2$.

The problem of the IRT can be avoided by computing PJI from the date of valuation to the date of the breach using the same rate that was used to discount cash flows to the date of valuation. From a theoretical point of view, computing PJI based on the cost of capital makes sense because this rate reflects the cost of raising funds that the company would have faced as of the date of the breach, had it intended to cash out the (expected) award as of the date of the breach.[28]

2. Future Investments – Uncertainty and Loss of Chance

In our example in Section II, we assume that the development of the project entails a unique initial investment that has to be made at the beginning of the project. In some cases, however, it is more efficient to schedule total investment in phases, or to consider an initial commitment and an option to undertake one or more additional rounds of investment. For instance, if demand is expected to grow over time, it may be economically rational not to build the entire capacity at date 0, but to spread the total investment of the project over time. Assuming that the contract breach takes place at an interim date at which only certain phases of the project have been completed, the question arises as to whether the injured party has to be compensated for investments that have not yet taken place, but were already planned, at the date of the breach. Other times, an investment project may carry the prospect, beyond the expected net present value, of incremental business opportunities (i.e., other "chances") to take place in the future.

Consider a modified version of our example, with the cash flows as shown in Figure 5. For convenience, we identify those cash flows that would correspond to the development of phase 1 only (dark gray) and those additional cash flows generated by the development of phase 2 (light gray).

---

28. Although the damaged party was entitled to compensation at the date of the breach, the only way it can cash out at the time of the breach is by raising funds equivalent to the expected award. Since the risk of repaying a loan – or paying dividends to compensate for equity contributions – is given by the risk of the affected company, lenders would not lend at a rate lower than the company's cost of raising funds. Similarly, since equity contributions would be compensated based on the company's overall performance, the relevant cost of raising those funds is the cost of capital of the affected company.

FIGURE 5. Annual Cash Flows by Phases

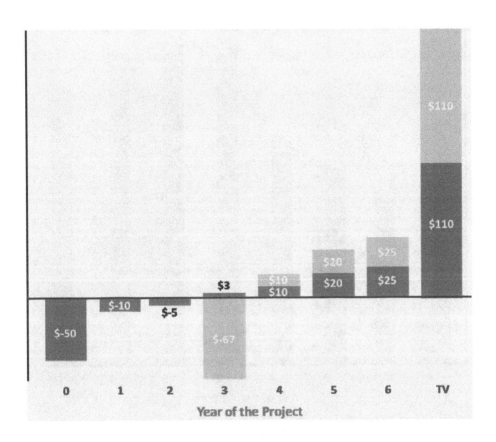

The relevant modification is that investment takes place in two phases, the first one consisting of $50 to be invested at date t=0 and the second one consisting of $67 to be invested at date t=3. As in the original example, it is possible to compute the value of the project (NPV) to Opco at any point in time by computing the present value of the future cash flows.[29] In Figure 6 below, we show the value of the project at any possible date between date 0 and date 7. We also identify the share of the project's value that corresponds to investments from Phase 1 only.

---

29. For simplicity, we maintain the same discount rate (WACC) that we used in the previous example.

373

FIGURE 6. Market Value of the Project to Opco

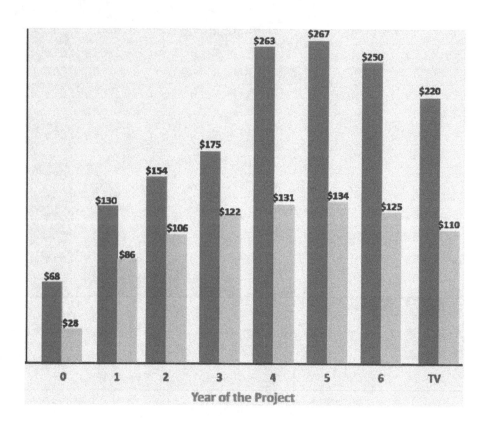

The lesson we learn from Figure 6 is that as long as *investments not yet made generate value to the project* and to the extent that business and market conditions make them likely to have taken place, they should be included in the computation of damages in order to be consistent with the notion that the expert tries to recreate a business scenario but for the breach.[30]

---

30. See I. MARBOE, *op. cit.*, fn. 9, p. 73.

Suppose further that the breach of the contract takes place at the beginning of date 3, that is, right before the investment corresponding to Phase 2. According to Figure 6 above, the market value of the full project as of the date of the breach is $175, while it goes down to $122 if Phase 2 is not taken into account.[31] This is also shown in Table 5.

TABLE 5. Market Value as of Date of the Breach with and without Phase 2

	0	1	2	3	4	5	6	TV
	Historical Cash Flows			Future Cash Flows				
Total Cash Flows	-$50	-$10	-$5	-$64	$20	$40	$50	$220
Cash Flows (Phase 1)	-$50	-$10	-$5	$3	$10	$20	$25	$110
Discount Factor @ 10%				1.00	0.91	0.83	0.75	0.68
Full Project Cash Flows Discounted to t=3				-$64 + $18 + $33 + $38 + $150				
Market Value of Full Project at DoV				$175				
Phase 1 Cash Flows Discounted to t=3				$3 + $9 + $17 + $19 + $75				
Market Value of Phase 1 at DoV				$122				

In Table 5 we present total expected cash flows in each period and those that would arise if only Phase 1 were to be developed. Phase 2 is not developed until t=3, so total cash flows before t=3 are equal to Phase 1 cash flows. From t=3 on, the difference between cash flows of the full project and cash flows of Phase 1 corresponds to the additional cash flows that Phase 2 generates. Then, we compute the market value of the project to Opco as of t=3 assuming (a) that the full project is developed, and (b) that only Phase 1 is developed.

By ignoring Phase 2 in the damages assessment, the expert is valuing a smaller project than the one envisioned by the parties at the outset. The value of the compensation as of the date of the breach computed with this smaller project is equal to $122, which accounts for only 70% of the fair compensation (market value of the full project) computed above. Hence, ignoring future (profitable) investments leads to under-compensation. One way to think about this issue is to interpret fair compensation as coming from two (and possibly three) different sources:

---

31. That is, the $122 is computed assuming that the $67 investment does not take place and neither do the additional cash flows generated from this investment.

(i) Lost profits associated with investments already made (loss of income);

(ii) Lost profits associated with scheduled future investment (other expected value);

(iii) Additional loss of chance/opportunities from investment (i.e., projects that would have likely resulted from rights acquired or from the experiences of completing the original project).

Uncertainty is always an issue in business valuation, but it is even more important when the business in question has not yet started or is at a very early stage of development, such as the example shown above. For a young project, forecasting the cash flows that the business will be able to generate can be especially challenging. This does not mean, however, that reasonable business projections for damages assessment purposes cannot be implemented.

In any case, uncertainty should not be a reason to reject damages for lost opportunities or investments not yet undertaken. All business carries uncertainty. Even acquiring real estate to rent out in a busy city may not result in the rents that one initially expected, but that does not prevent business persons and providers of capital from taking on investment opportunities while understanding the risks and upsides, and developing a base case expectation of what the business is likely to be. Lost opportunities are as just as valid for damages assessment as the more certain, easily projected lost profits from past investments, as long as they are grounded in reliable business and market forecasts. The key to estimate compensation from future investments is to base the business forecast on the use of reasonable assumptions supported by the best available evidence and to use an appropriately risk-adjusted discount rate that effectively accounts for all the relevant risks, including those specific to undeveloped business ideas or early-stage projects.

Consider again the hypothetical example developed in Section II. Suppose that, the damages expert wanted to account for the fact that future cash flows are uncertain due to the early-stage of development of the project. One possible way to do that would be to add an *early-stage risk premium* to the discount rate that accounts for this additional risk (uncertainty). For instance, suppose that the expert estimates an early-stage premium equal to 200 basis points to be added to the (mature project) WACC estimated at 10%. Expected future cash flows would then be discounted at 12%, including the market related risks for mature projects *plus* the early-stage risk premium. In Table 6 below, we show the computation of the market value of the project to Opco using a 12% discount rate.[32]

---

32. Note that, once again, we had to adjust the terminal value to the new discount rate. We assume that with a discount rate of 12% the terminal value is reduced to $195.

376

TABLE 6. Compensation Accounting of Early-Stage Risk Premium

	0	1	2	3	4	5	6	TV
		Historical Cash Flows				Future Cash Flows		
Cash Flows	-$100	-$20	-$10	-$5	$20	$40	$50	$195
Discount Factor @ 12%					1.00	0.89	0.80	0.71
Cash Flows Discounted to t=4					$20 + $36 + $40 + $139			
Market Value at DoV					$234			

We see in our example that accounting for the risk associated with the early stage of the project reduces the market value of the project from $263 according to Table 1 to $234. A rule, however, cannot be established as to what type of risk premium has to be used and when, or if at all. Business projections often account for startup risks in different ways (one common example is by building on contingencies in their capital cost projections). The tribunal, however, needs to understand how experts have considered these types of risks and if not, why.

VI.   SUMMARY AND CONCLUSIONS

We have explained common issues relating to damages assessment that may lead to over- or under-compensation if they are not treated appropriately. Our purpose was to highlight the different issues that frequently arise in arbitrations and often are not clarified until the oral hearing takes place, as well as their potential effect on the computation of damages. To that end, we developed a hypothetical case that allowed us to explain and quantify the potential problems. The lessons we have learned from this exercise illustrate the basic workings of the concept of present value of future cash flows, namely:

(i) Changing the date of valuation may alter the market value of the project and, therefore, the value of compensation.
(ii) The proper discount rate must be applied to *but-for* cash flows, and must account for the time value of money as well as the risks associated with (a) the market in which the project operates (industry and country) and (b) the potential additional risks associated with the maturity of the project. Improper use of the discount rate may lead to both under- or over-compensation.

377

(iii) Once investments are sunk, they do not determine the market value of the project, which is instead determined by the expected stream of cash flows that it will produce. Hence, awarding compensation for lost profits and past investments would lead to double-counting and over-compensation.

(iv) Pre-judgment interest rates should be chosen so as to avoid the invalid-round-trip problem. In this sense, the appropriate PJI rate should match the rate used to discount future cash flows.

(v) Future investments often generate value to the project. As such, they can be included in the market value of the project and, as a result, in the computation of damages. Excluding planned, profitable investments not yet undertaken would lead to under-compensation.

(vi) Uncertainty should not be a reason to exclude cash flows arising from future investments, especially if these would have been likely undertaken by the parties but for the breaches. The additional uncertainty related to young projects can be estimated and included as a premium in the discount rate or may already be incorporated in the expected cash flows that are forecasted.

The lessons we learned from this paper should help tribunals to evaluate the damages claims presented by the parties in arbitration so as to ensure that the injured party is fairly compensated for the contract breach.

How Useful Are Party-Appointed Experts in
International Arbitration?

Howard Rosen*

TABLE OF CONTENTS

I.   INTRODUCTION

The role of the expert witness is a subject that has been often written about, debated, scrutinized and reviewed. Experts, being in the role of "neutrals" with the obligation to assist arbitrators in reaching decisions on issues that require special expertise, have come under suspicion as being advocates in disguise for the party retaining them. As such, their reports and testimony in front of arbitral tribunals are frequently met with skepticism. Further, published decisions from arbitrators have failed to adequately identify those experts, or attributes of expert reports, that they find unhelpful, and thus there is no formal feedback mechanism for the arbitration community to identify those experts, or qualities found in expert reports, which are perceived to be inappropriate.

This paper examines experts (in my case "quantum experts"), their reports, and their role, picking up from the observations of Klaus Sachs from his paper at ICCA 2010 dealing with expert witnesses, continuing with an examination of professional rules that guide or prescribe expert behaviour; rules governing experts in various arbitral fora; the relationship with instructing counsel; the role of tribunals in "gating expert witnesses"; dos and don'ts for experts and expert reports; and procedures that exist for encouraging appropriate behaviour for experts. The paper concludes with recommendations to further encourage experts to act as true neutrals.

The first recommendation is focused at the outset of the expert retainer, and deals with the instructions received by the expert. I believe that expert reports will be more

---

*   Leader of the global arbitration practice for FTI Consulting.
      The author would like to acknowledge the following individuals for their contribution in researching this paper: James Searby, Neal Mizrahi and Ellen Dong.

useful to the parties and arbitral tribunals if the instructions, once received from the parties, are reviewed with the tribunal.

The second recommendation is aimed squarely at the arbitrators. Arbitrators should be required to explicitly report in their awards their views on the roles the experts played in the arbitration, and if their reports, and conduct at the hearing, were helpful to the arbitrators.

The third recommendation is to require a joint expert report in all cases where party appointed experts provide opinions. Attached as Annex IV is a sample joint expert report that I have been using for years, which I feel allows the tribunal an excellent summary document of the important issues that have an effect on the expert's opinion as to quantum of damage.

I also advise the reader that all of the comments and views expressed in this paper are done so from the point of view of a damages or quantum expert, and that the same considerations may not apply equally to other types of technical experts.

II.   PARTY-APPOINTED EXPERTS AND TRIBUNAL-APPOINTED EXPERTS

1.   The Two Traditions

The role of party-appointed experts differs considerably between the common law and civil law traditions. In common law jurisdictions, party-appointed experts are the norm. The common law places much emphasis on the role of cross-examination of witnesses to inform a court or tribunal of the relevant issues and to expose the strength of the evidence supporting each side's case. However, this adversarial system is sometimes criticized for encouraging bias in experts.

Such bias might come about in a variety of ways. First, party-appointed experts are primarily exposed to the evidence and reasoning supporting the case of the party appointing them. In time, they may be inclined to adopt the assumptions and thinking underpinning that case. Second, criticism from an opposing expert and cross-examination by counsel itself may encourage witnesses to defend their point of view more strongly than they would under a more consensual approach, tending to reinforce a party-appointed expert's perceived partisanship. Third, it is possible that parties will seek to appoint only experts whose views are most likely to support their case, a process known as "expert shopping". Aside from opening the door to evidential bias, expert shopping may also increase the likelihood of a court or tribunal being presented with extreme or irreconcilable evidence from opposing experts.

In contrast, civil law systems generally allow a greater role for court- or tribunal-appointed experts. It is usually a requirement that such an expert be independent of the parties. In principle, such independence should remove the bias allegedly inherent in the adversarial system. The appointment of a single expert may also tend to reduce costs, all else equal, compared to a system in which each party appoints its own expert. Civil law systems sometimes explicitly attribute less weight to the evidence of party-appointed experts, whether by raising the court-appointed expert's testimony to the status of "conclusive" evidence (e.g. in France) or by reducing that of the party-appointed expert to mere assertion (e.g. in Germany).

The civil law approach to expert evidence is not without its critics either. Court-appointed experts are often drawn from lists, which might be out-of-date or unrepresentative of the consensus of opinion on a given topic. Equally, judges or arbitrators may not be skilled in the selection of appropriate experts for a given issue. A single expert may also be prone to "own theory" bias, a tendency to promote his or her own published views over consensus opinion in their field of expertise – such unrepresentative views might not be exposed if a consensual process suppresses challenges to expert evidence. Finally, parties may also appoint their own experts to review and challenge the evidence of the court-appointed expert, leading to an increase in cost over a system of party-appointed experts alone.

2. The Best of Both Worlds?

In principle, arbitrators often have the power to appoint their own experts, for instance under Art. 6 of the International Bar Association Rules on the Taking of Evidence in International Arbitration (the IBA Rules) or the UNCITRAL Model Law on International Commercial Arbitration (the UNCITRAL Model Law), Art 29. In practice, however, arbitral tribunals have followed the common law model of party-appointed experts. This state of affairs mirrors that in England, where Part 35.7 of the Civil Procedure Rules (CPR) allows courts to appoint a single expert. According to one source, however, English courts have only infrequently appointed experts because "given the choice, the parties mostly appear to prefer to each have their own expert".[1] It is not known, however, if that is because common law lawyers wish to increase the probability of "favourable" evidence being provided, or because they are unwilling to cede their customary control of proceedings to the court (or both).

The IBA Rules require expert witnesses to state their experience and qualifications, set out the facts on which their opinions are based, describe the method, evidence and information relied upon and (in the past) to affirm the "truth" of their expert report.[2] Like the CPR, the IBA Rules allow a tribunal to order a meeting of experts for the purpose of reaching agreement, where possible, and document areas of agreement and disagreement.[3, 4] The CPR has historically gone further than the IBA Rules to promote independence in party-appointed experts, in two main ways. First, Part 35.3 of the CPR imposes on experts a duty to "help the court on matters within their expertise", which duty "overrides any obligation to the person from whom experts have received instruction or by whom they are paid". Second, Part 35.6 of the CPR allows each party to submit written questions to the other party's expert, who is obliged to respond to those questions. Presumably, the possibility of written questions is intended to restrain

---

1. R. TRITTMANN and B. KASOLOWSKY, "Taking Evidence in Arbitration Proceeding Between Common Law and Civil Law Traditions – The Development of a European Hybrid Standard for Arbitration Proceedings", 31 UNSW Law Journal (no. 1) p. 338 available at <www.austlii.edu.au/au/journals/UNSWLJ/2008/18.pdf> (last accessed 2 March 2014).
2. IBA Rules, Art. 5.2, 1 June 1999.
3. *Ibid.*, Art. 5.3.
4. Civil Procedure Rules (CPR), Part 35 Experts and Assessors, available at <www.justice.gov.uk/courts/procedure-rules/civil/rules/part35> (last accessed 20 February 2014).

experts, whose failure to answer those questions may be taken into account by an English court.

The updated IBA Rules, adopted on 29 May 2010, move closer to the forms contained in the CPR. Experts are now required to describe their instructions and make a statement of their independence from "the Parties, the legal advisors and the Arbitral Tribunal".[5, 6] In place of the affirmation as to the "truth" of their expert report, party-appointed experts must instead affirm that the opinions in his or her expert report are "his or her genuine belief".[7] The IBA Rules and CPR may be seen as an attempt to achieve the benefits of independence promised by the civil law tradition, but in the context of the adversarial model of party-appointed experts followed in the common law tradition. Suspicions linger, however, as to the extent of their success.

3.   Sachs Protocol

a.   Overview

At the 2010 ICCA Conference in Rio de Janeiro, Klaus Sachs proposed a solution to the problem of perceived bias in party-appointed expert evidence in an article entitled "Protocol on Expert Teaming: A New Approach to Expert Evidence". Dr. Sachs' proposal is for each side to identify a number of possible experts it would be prepared to rely on, with the tribunal ultimately selecting one expert from each side's list. The two tribunal-appointed experts would have full duties of independence and be paid by the tribunal out of the common arbitration fund. Their terms of reference would be framed by the tribunal and they would be required to work as a team and produce a single report. The report would be provided to the parties as a preliminary draft, on which the parties will have the opportunity to comment. The experts would testify together at the hearing and be questioned by both parties. Crucially, each expert would not be permitted to communicate separately with the parties, but could seek input and assistance from both parties.

Dr. Sachs' proposal, quickly referred to as "the Sachs Protocol", contains a number of appealing aspects:

---

5. IBA Rules on the Taking of Evidence in International Arbitration, Art. 5.2(c), 29 May 2010, available at <www.ibanet.org/Publications/publications_IBA_guides_and_free_materials.aspx> (last accessed 21 February 2014).

6. M. KANTOR, "A Code of Conduct for Party-Appointed Experts in International Arbitration – Can One Be Found?", 26 Arbitration International (LCIA 2010, no. 3) available at <http://arbitrateatlanta.org/wp-content/uploads/2013/04/Code-of-Conduct-for-Party-Appointed-Experts.pdf> (last accessed 6 February 2014). Mark Kantor notes that the term "independent" (or "impartial" or "neutral") is not unique to the IBA Rules as a characterization of the relationship between an expert and the party appointing him or her, but also appears in Art. 7 of the ICC Rules and elsewhere. Whether one believes the characterization a fair one or not, the drafters of these documents seem to consider, at a minimum, that omission of the term would not be useful.

7. IBA Rules, Taking of Evidence in International Arbitration, Art. 5.2 (g), 29 May 2010, available at <www.ibanet.org/Publications/publications_IBA_guides_and_free_materials.aspx> (last accessed 21 February 2014).

— It may help to increase the perceived independence of expert testimony by breaking the explicit link between the expert and the party paying his or her fees;
— It may, as Dr. Sachs suggests, reduce costs if it is the case that party-appointed experts are at risk of "missing the points which the tribunal and the parties regard as relevant";[8]
— The production of a single report may save time, compared to a system of sequential exchange of reports between party-appointed experts;
— The appointment of two experts would provide peer review that is not available if a single expert were appointed; and,
— It avoids the potential pitfalls of civil law experts, such as arbitrators selecting experts from lists of the "usual suspects", "own theory" bias or the need for parties to employ extra experts to challenge a single tribunal-appointed expert.

It therefore seems that the "Sachs Protocol", in conjunction with the recently adopted revisions to the IBA Rules of Evidence, may form a useful addition to the conduct of expert testimony in international arbitration. For the reasons set out below, however, the Sachs Protocol may not represent a complete solution to party-appointed experts' perceived lack of independence and may also fail in its aim to control the time and cost incurred by party-appointed experts.

I have summarized a comparison of the traditional system against the Sachs Protocol and further identified the benefits and drawbacks in Annex I.

b.   Potential shortcomings
Despite the benefits outlined above, the Sachs Protocol may not achieve all of its aims because of two potential shortcomings.

The first of those relates to the incentives for efficiency, whether in terms of effort, time or money. Dr. Sachs has an expectation that the framing of instructions by the tribunal, in conjunction with the parties, will lead to a situation that is more "successful as regards effectiveness, time and cost" because experts will focus on the issues and materials that the tribunal and parties all consider relevant. I venture to suggest that a system of expert teaming might often do the opposite.

First, Dr. Sachs' proposals require one to confront the practicalities of two experts working together. It is a fact that many experts have quite serious professional disagreements between them. In some cases, experts do not even agree about the fundamental precepts underpinning a particular topic. A failure to agree on the best manner to proceed, the correct assumptions to use or the appropriate interpretation of data could result in duplication of effort and/or an exhaustive thoroughness – the very opposite of the benefits in terms of effectiveness and time sought by Dr. Sachs.

Second, as acknowledged by Dr. Sachs, party-appointed experts play a wider role in the context of litigation or arbitration than the provision of written and/or oral testimony. For instance, at the outset of a proposed arbitration, an expert may be helpful in evaluating the merits of a claim or defence, so avoiding the (potentially costly) pursuit of unfruitful actions or arguments. Experts may also assist their party's legal team to "frame the problem" so that the claim or defence is sound in principle as well as in law.

---

8. K. SACHS, "Protocol on Expert Teaming: A New Approach to Expert Evidence" in *Arbitration Advocacy in Changing Times*, ICCA Congress Series no. 15 (2011) p. 147.

Parties may also benefit from expert input during the process of disclosure and, at a hearing, in formulating cross-examination questions.

Under Dr. Sachs' proposals, those functions cannot be performed by tribunal-appointed experts. Instead, Dr. Sachs envisages that parties might appoint additional experts (or "expert consultants") to supplement those appointed by the tribunal. To the extent that the parties need to appoint additional experts to achieve their objectives from the arbitration, the Sachs Protocol will tend to increase the number of experts. The extra costs so incurred might well exceed any savings generated by "expert teaming". It is inevitable that such "expert consultants" will want to review and, potentially, challenge the findings of the tribunal-appointed experts. Such a process might actually lengthen, rather than shorten, arbitral proceedings.

Third, reduced party oversight might weaken the incentives to control costs that exist under a system of party-appointed experts. Today, parties can, and do, freely negotiate discounts, caps or fixed fees with their experts and can monitor and influence those fees once a case has commenced. It is not clear that tribunals are best placed to negotiate, monitor or control experts' costs, or that the parties would have a strong incentive to do so either. To the extent that costs could be increased, a well-funded party might have every incentive to raise them in the knowledge that the other side would have to share in the burden. If that were so, a developing country government (for instance) might well end up paying more for tribunal-appointed experts than it could negotiate on its own.

Weak incentives might also cause a tendency for fees to rise to the highest common denominator: no teamed expert is going to want to find out that his remuneration is inferior to that of his counterpart. The knowledge that further "expert consultant" positions might be available with the parties might also reduce the extent to which higher-priced experts are willing to offer their services to an expert team at all, let alone at a discount. In short, it is not clear that an expert team would be more effective, faster or cheaper than two party-appointed experts.

The second, and potentially more serious, drawback relates to the quality incentives faced by tribunal-appointed expert teams. The natural tendency within such a team will be to achieve consensus, for both parties to seek to occupy the middle ground of any debate. Indeed, it may be that this is one of the main thrusts of Dr. Sachs' proposals. In those circumstances, however, it would be a brave expert who promoted critical evaluation of the other's work or encouraged debate: it is not clear that a tribunal would regard such an expert as being "helpful". It may be that this situation creates the greatest risk associated with "expert teaming", namely, the emergence of a lazy consensus on any given issue. More generally, experts who are strongly associated with particular ideas may find that they are excluded from the pool of potential experts, narrowing the field of experts from which testimony might be sought.

Those possibilities are potentially dangerous. For all its defects, a system of party-appointed experts encourages competition between experts to win a "battle of ideas". Certainly, that competition can sometimes be unhealthy, leading experts to defend extreme positions or minor points of difference. At its best, however, competition between experts and the process of peer review promotes effort, efficiency, rigour, thoughtfulness and, where appropriate, originality. In contrast, co-operation (or at least a reduction in competition) between experts seems likely to blunt the incentives favouring such virtues. For example, the terms of debate in fields such as competition law and economic regulation in recent years has moved forward precisely because of such rivalry between economists on behalf of their clients. Arbitral tribunals will not be best served by expert teaming if the result is a bland consensus and a stifling of the incentive for experts to stake out new ground.

For the reasons set out above, expert teaming may not improve either the quality of testimony or the efficiency of the process. In this paper, I discuss several measures that may serve to increase the independence of experts' testimony without losing the benefits of their being appointed by the parties.

III.   RULES GOVERNING EXPERT WITNESSES

1.   Jurisdictional Rules

This section will examine the rules from several countries' national courts, and how experts are appointed, influenced and guided. It will be used to both compare and contrast the manner in which experts are treated in international commercial arbitration.

Before an expert testifies in the Canadian courts, a *voir dire* is conducted whereby the qualifications of the expert are presented and verified through cross-examination.[9] The judge then rules on the scope of the expert's qualifications and tests for relevance and necessity.[10] Case law has set the admittance of expert evidence based on the fulfillment of the following four criteria: relevance; necessity in assisting in the trier of fact; the absence of any exclusionary rule; and a properly qualified expert.[11] For purpose of clarity, the expert's duty is defined under the Federal Court Rules under the Code of Conduct for Expert Witnesses:[12]

> "An expert witness named to provide a report for use as evidence, or to testify in a proceeding, has an overriding duty to assist the Court impartially on matters relevant to his or her area of expertise. This duty overrides any duty to a party to the proceeding, including the person retaining the expert witness. An expert is to be independent and objective. An expert is not an advocate for a party."

In addition to the expert qualification process, an expert must also submit form 52.2 accompanying an affidavit or statement to attest to the expert's compliance with the code of conduct under Rule 52 of the Federal Court Rules.

---

9. Igor ELLYN and Evelyn Perez YOUSSOUFIAN, "Using Financial Expert Witnesses in Business Litigation", available at <www.slideshare.net/IgorEllynQCCSFCIArb> (last accessed 20 February 2014).
10. *Ibid.*
11. *R. v. Mohan*, (1994) S.C.R.
12. Canadian Federal Court Rules, Sect. 52 Expert Witnesses, available at <http://laws-lois.justice.gc.ca/eng/regulations/SOR-98-106/> (last accessed 19 February 2014).

Similarly, experts in US courts must meet the applicability threshold established under Rule 702 of the *Federal Rules of Evidence*:[13]

– The expert's scientific, technical or other specialized knowledge will help the trier of fact to understand the evidence or to determine a fact in issue;
– The testimony is based on sufficient facts or data;
– The testimony is the product of reliable principles and methods; and,
– The expert has reliably applied the principles and methods of the facts of the case.

The Federal Rules of Evidence are silent on the duties of independence and impartiality, however, as further discussed below, Rule 702 is supplemented by the criteria established by the judgment on *Daubert v. Merrell*[14] (the "*Daubert* Criteria").

In the 1993 judgment on *Daubert v. Merrell*, the role of the judge as a "gatekeeper" for the qualification of scientific experts was established, and subsequently in 1999, the judgment on *Kumho Tire v. Carmichael* extended the scope of the *Daubert* Criteria for admissibility of scientific experts to include all experts.[15]

A non-exhaustive list of the *Daubert* Criteria requires the consideration for the following:[16]

– Has the technique/theory been tested, or can it be tested;
– Has the technique/theory been subject to peer review and publication;
– What is the potential rate of error;
– Whether there exist standards controlling its operation; and,
– Has the technique/ theory attracted widespread acceptance within the relevant scientific community?

In the United Kingdom, the duties expected of an expert are derived from the iconic decision known as *The Ikarian Reefer*:[17]

– Expert evidence should be, and should be seen to be, the independent product of the expert uninfluenced as to form or content by the exigencies of litigation;
– An expert witness should provide independent assistance to the court by way of objective, unbiased opinion in relation to matters within his expertise and never assume the role of an advocate;

---

13. Federal Rules of Evidence, Rule 702. Testimony by Experts, available at <www.uscourts.gov/uscourts/rulesandpolicies/rules/2010%20rules/evidence.pdf> (last accessed 19 February 2014).
14. *Daubert v. Merrell Dow Pharmaceuticals*, (1993) U.S.
15. "*Daubert* Challenges to Financial Experts: An 11-year study of trends and outcomes", available at <www.pwc.com/us/en/forensic-services/publications/daubert-study-2010.jhtml> (last accessed 20 February 2014).
16. *Daubert v. Merrell Dow Pharmaceuticals*, (1993) U.S.
17. *National Justice Compania Naviera SA v. Prudential Assurance Company Limited* [1993] 2 Lloyd's Rep. 68 at 81-82 (Q.B.D.).

– An expert witness should state the facts or assumptions upon which his opinion is based. He should not omit to consider material facts which could detract from his concluded opinion;

– An expert witness should make it clear when a particular question or issue falls outside his expertise;

– If an expert's opinion is not properly researched because he considers that insufficient data are available, then this must be stated with an indication that the opinion is no more than a provisional one. In cases where an expert witness who has prepared a report could not assert that the report contained the truth, the whole truth and nothing but the truth without some qualification, that qualification should be stated in the report;

– If, after exchange of reports, an expert witness changes his view on a material matter having read the other side's expert's report, or for any other reason, such change of view should be communicated (through legal representatives) to the other side without delay and when appropriate to the court; and

– Where expert evidence refers to photographs, plans, calculations, analyses, measurements, survey reports or other similar documents, these must be provided to the opposite party at the same time as the exchange of reports.

Additionally, Rule 35.3 of the CPR outlines the duty of the expert to "help the court on matters within their expertise" and specifies that this "duty overrides any obligation to the person from whom experts have received instructions or by whom they are paid".[18] Unlike the Canadian and US courts, English case law has a low reliability review of expert evidence in court and relies upon detailed review at the adjudication stage by the trier of fact.[19]

The expert's general duties in the Federal Court of Australia echo those of the UK CPR, as it states the expert: "has an overriding duty to assist the court on matters relevant to the expert's expertise; is not an advocate for a party; and has a paramount duty to the Court and not to the person retaining the expert".[20]

It is clear, based on the above rules that govern experts, that the focus is on accepting properly qualified experts that prepare reports which are relevant, sufficient, and reliable, based on acceptable methodologies. The overriding duty to the court and the necessity of independence and objectivity are explicitly stated in the United Kingdom, Canada, and Australia, but absent from the federal rules governing experts in the United States.

The absence of a specific rule governing independence and objectivity in and of itself is not evidence that experts from the United States are any less prone to adopt these

---

18. CPR, Part 35 Experts and Assessors, available at <www.justice.gov.uk/courts/procedure-rules/civil/rules/part35> (last accessed 20 February 2014).

19. A.W. JURS, "Balancing Legal Process with Scientific Expertise: Expert Witness Methodology in Five Nations and Suggestions for Reform of Post-Daubert U.S. Reliability Determinations", 95 Marquette Law Review (2012, no. 4) pp. 1378-1379, available at <http://scholarship. law. marquette.edu/cgi/viewcontent.cgi?article=5134&context=mulr> (last accessed 19 February 2014).

20. Expert witnesses in proceedings in the Federal Court of Australia, Guideline 1, available at <www.fedcourt.gov.au/law-and-practice/practice-documents/practice-notes/cm7> (last accessed 20 February 2014).

important attributes. Professional guidelines set out by the various professional bodies of which damages experts are generally members, further serve to guide the behaviour of experts. Further, specific cases or case law may also serve to reinforce and modify behaviour and guide expert conduct.

The other significant way in which national courts differ from international arbitration is the practice of "qualifying" an expert. In some jurisdictions, an expert's experience and credentials are examined for the purposes of determining whether the expert being proffered possesses the necessary expertise to assist the court with issues that are beyond its own expertise. Frequently a process of *voir dire* is employed to determine the competency of an expert witness, and what their opinion should be limited to. No such exercise or procedure is used in international arbitration.

2. Rules and Practice in Arbitration

a. Arbitration rules

Party-appointed and tribunal-appointed experts are regulated by a set of rules specific to each arbitral institution. These procedural guidelines often include broad instruction relevant to the use of experts, expert testimony and expert reports. The parties may also choose to adopt standardized rules published by the International Bar Association (IBA) or United Nations Commission on International Trade Law (UNCITRAL) to supplement institutional rules.

Arbitral institutions do not provide uniform guidance on experts to the tribunal or parties; however, several themes are universal. Most of the arbitral institutions explicitly give the tribunal authority to appoint an expert witness. In most instances, the tribunal must consult with the parties before a tribunal-appointed expert can be selected. As an exception, the International Centre for Dispute Resolution (ICDR) and China International Economic and Trade Arbitration Commission (CIETAC) do not give the parties discretion in this process.

The ability of the parties and tribunal to question expert witnesses during a hearing is also pervasive among institutional rules. For each of the arbitral institutions examined, a specific rule requires that experts be available for cross-examination or a similar form of questioning by the tribunal and counsel. Parties do not have discretion in this matter if the institutional rules are applied as written.

Rules published by the IBA, International Centre for Settlement of Investment Disputes (ICSID) and Hong Kong International Arbitration Centre (HKIAC) expressly permit the use of party-appointed experts. Although the ICDR, ICC, and LCIA are silent on this issue, experts are routinely appointed by parties in practice. Furthermore, "Despite the common law roots of this method of appointment, international arbitral tribunals typically adapt this practice to fit the needs of their proceedings, and even arbitrations involving arbitrators, parties and counsel from civil law backgrounds may leave to the parties the responsibility to engage exerts."[21]

The IBA and UNCITRAL Rules are generally more descriptive on the subject of tribunal-appointed expert witness procedure than institutional rules. Akin to institutional

---

21. D. FREYER, "Assessing Expert Evidence" para. 5, available at <www.skadden.com/sites/default/files/publications/Publications1405_0.pdf> (last accessed 27 August 2014).

rules, these rulemaking bodies allow for tribunal-appointed experts and questioning of experts by the tribunal and counsel. Expanding on these rules, both the IBA and UNCITRAL Rules require that experts submit a description of qualifications and statement of independence before accepting appointment. Access to documentation is another point of convergence, as both rulemaking bodies expressly allow the expert access to all relevant documentation and also permit the parties to view all documents that the expert relied upon. As mentioned previously, the IBA Rules explicitly define rules for party-appointed experts, and the UNCITRAL Rules are silent on this issue.

A detailed table comparing the arbitration rules applicable to experts can be located at Annex II.

b.   Expert declaration
Experts commonly provide written declarations to comply with arbitration rules and to establish credibility before tribunals. This practice delineates the expert's ethical and independence obligations, but equally serves to remind the expert of his or her duty to assist the tribunal above all other responsibilities. Guidance for providing oral or written declarations is limited; however, the IBA has set out general requirements that must be adhered to if the arbitration has adopted the IBA Rules.[22] Furthermore, the Chartered Institute of Arbitrators has published a recommended template for experts to follow when drafting a declaration, known as the Protocol for the Use of Party-Appointed Expert Witnesses in International Arbitration (the CIArb Protocol).

Art. 5(2) of the IBA Rules requires party-appointed experts to address certain topics in written expert reports. Two of these requirements are applicable to an expert's declaration, including the obligation to provide "a statement of his or her independence from the Parties, their legal advisors and the Arbitral Tribunal". Additionally, the IBA Rules require that the expert make "an affirmation of his or her genuine belief in the opinions expressed in the Expert Report". These assertions are an important step forward in developing a code of conduct for party-appointed experts, but are not without criticism. For instance, the IBA Rules may "conflate impartiality and objectivity with independence"[23] and do not explain how a party-appointed expert can truly be "independent" from parties that hired the expert and work jointly to develop evidence.[24] Moreover, the IBA Rules do not address an expert's inherent duty to disclose material adverse information and also assess the reasonableness of assumptions provided by counsel.[25]

The CIArb Protocol, Art. 8, offers an idealistic model for party-appointed experts to reference. It covers the expert's primary obligation, which is to assist the tribunal, and the requirement to remain independent from other parties to the arbitration. Additionally, an expert must confirm that matters discussed in the report are complete, accurate, and within his or her area of expertise. Further, the protocol recommends that an expert bring to the attention of the tribunal all matters which may adversely affect his

---

22. IBA Rules, 29 May 2010, Art. 5, available at <www.ibanet.org/Publications/publications_ IBA_guides_and_free_materials.aspx> (last accessed 21 February 2014).
23. M. KANTOR, *op. cit.*, fn. 6.
24. *Ibid.*
25. *Ibid.*

or her professional opinion. Lastly, an expert should be required to notify the parties of the arbitration if their opinion requires correction subsequent to submission of a written expert report. However, the CIArb Protocol has yet to be adopted by the international community, and is often criticized for following the English court system without consideration for more diverse civil and common law jurisdictions.[26]

Experts may also be required to make a verbal declaration prior to giving evidence. For example, experts appearing before ICSID tribunals are required to state, "I solemnly declare upon my honor and conscience that my statement will be in accordance with my sincere belief."[27] The presence or absence of an oath, however, is unlikely to give arbitrators any comfort over ethical parameters to which each expert witness is adhering. This is because perjury prosecutions are rare in arbitrations and the boundary between advocacy and false testimony is often ambiguous.[28]

c.   The tribunal's role as "gatekeepers"

Rather than forcing all international arbitration proceedings to fit the mold of procedural rules on "qualifying" an expert, tribunals are able to customize their procedures.

Under the CIArb Protocol, any term of appointment of an expert and all instructions thereof are not privileged during arbitral proceedings; should the tribunal believe there to be "good cause", it may instruct disclosures relating to or permit the questioning of the expert on such instructions or appointment.[29]

At its discretion, the tribunal may adduce expert evidence by directing the party-appointed experts to discuss, prepare and exchange draft reports, which are privileged from production to the tribunal, for the purposes of discussing the issues identified and where possible reaching an agreement on those issues.[30] Additionally, the manner in which expert testimony is delivered is ultimately directed by the tribunal, such that the tribunal may at any time direct further written reports and hold preliminary meetings with the experts to narrow the issues between the experts and/or to gain further understanding of the expert evidence provided.[31] Further, the tribunal is able to disregard the expert's written opinion or testimony, if for example the expert's written opinion is biased due to the influences of the party who appointed him.[32]

Additionally, the tribunal is capable of appointing its own experts to assist in its understanding of the issues presented by the party-appointed experts or to provide evidence on a particular piece of the dispute.[33] The tribunal-appointed expert will

---

26. *Ibid.*

27. ICSID Convention, Regulation and Rules; Rules of Procedure for Arbitration Proceedings, 10 April 2006, Rule 35, available at <https://icsid.worldbank.org/ICSID/StaticFiles/basicdoc/CRR_English-final.pdf> (last accessed 6 February 2014).

28. M. KANTOR, *op. cit.*, fn. 6.

29. Chartered Institute of Arbitrators, "Protocol for the Use of Party-Appointed Expert Witnesses in International Arbitration", Art. 5 Privilege, at <www.ciarb.org/information-and-resources/The%20use%20of%20party-appointed%20experts.pdf> (last accessed 2 March 2014).

30. *Ibid.*, Art. 6 Expert Evidence.

31. *Ibid.*, Art. 7 Expert Testimony.

32. *Ibid.*, Art. 7 Expert Testimony and Art. 8 – Expert Declaration.

33. R.D. Kent, "Expert Witnesses in Arbitration and Litigation Proceedings" (2007) available at <www.transnational-dispute-management.com> (last accessed 2 February 2014).

provide an "equalization of information disparity"[34] on technical and financial issues and assist as in a quasi-arbitral role by examining the facts, hearing the parties and even issuing an opinion on the evidence presented by the party-appointed experts.[35]

From a practical point of view, tribunals seldom appoint their own expert to assist in the interpretation of the evidence of party-appointed expert witnesses. In fact, if party-appointed expert witnesses haven't made themselves clear in their explanations of their conclusions, they haven't properly discharged their obligation to the tribunal. Further, if party-appointed experts haven't properly considered the positions put forward by the opposing expert, they have also failed in their obligation to assist the tribunal in understanding various possible outcomes, which will likely depend on the tribunal's finding of fact.

The role of the tribunal as "gatekeepers" in these circumstances is to attempt to force the party-appointed experts to properly address these issues and, failing that, to disregard their evidence.

Too often, I have heard tribunals refer to experts as "ships passing in the night". In these circumstances, the experts may have received very different instructions from the counsel retaining them; however, through the exchange of expert reports, the experts do have an opportunity to understand the positions put forward by opposing experts, and properly address these positions.

Proper reply to different approaches should not be restricted to criticisms of opposing experts, but should also include a proper response expressing the expert's view on quantum, assuming similar instructions were received.

To simply ignore the position of opposing experts, and restrict comments to criticism, leaves the tribunal in a difficult position. In many circumstances, the tribunal will not simply choose the position of one expert over the other. In my experience, tribunals will adopt some opinions of each expert, which adoption is substantially driven by the tribunal's finding on factual issues.

In my opinion, tribunals should meet with experts during the proceedings to ensure the experts deal with issues that are of import to the tribunal. If this is not practical because of timing, geography or cost, then tribunals should insist that instructions to each expert include the positions that are pleaded by both parties to ensure the experts address different possible factual findings by the tribunal. Further, tribunals should encourage experts to meet after exchange of their initial reports to ensure there is an opportunity for dialogue between the experts, and opportunity for each expert to properly consider the positions of the other.

The use of joint reports and witness conferencing is referred to elsewhere in this paper, but these are also tools that should be used with increased regularity to ensure tribunals get the most out of the party-appointed experts.

---

34. P.D. GALLOWAY, "Using Experts Effectively and Efficiently in Arbitration" (2012) available at <www.pegasus-global.com/assets/news/Galloway-Using-Experts-2012.pdf> (last accessed 16 February 2014).

35. G.D. BERTI, "Experts and Expert Witnesses in International Arbitration: Adviser, Advocate or Adjudicator", p. 62, available at <www.dejalex.com/pdf/pubb_11_AYIA.pdf> (last accessed 2 March 2014).

3. *Professional Body Rules and Financial Experts*

Financial experts who assist the tribunal in its understanding of valuation and damage issues are typically comprised of professional accountants, business valuators, academics, finance experts and economists. Some of these experts are governed by self-regulated professional bodies, whereas others are not. In this section, I will first outline the ethical standards offered by the various professional bodies pertaining to the financial experts, and contrast that to the rules applying to experts that do not belong to a professional body, but instead rely on the arbitration rules discussed earlier and relevant case law.

A general professional code of conduct has been adopted by the Chartered Professional Accountants Canada (CPA), which outlines professional behaviour, integrity and due care, professional competence, confidentiality, and integrity. Similarly, accountants in the United States and the United Kingdom have also established general practice standards under the American Institute of Certified Public Accountants (AICPA) and the Institute of Chartered Accountants of Scotland (ICAS).

As a part of the AICPA code of conduct, "when providing expert witness services, a member must comply with Rule 102, Integrity and Objectivity, which requires that a member maintain objectivity and integrity and not subordinate his or her judgment to others".[36] The AICPA Practice Aid 10-1 provides specific guidance to members serving as expert witnesses or consultants for litigation services, and this Practice Aid applies specifically to members who possess the credentials of either a Certified in Financial Forensics (CFF) or an Accredited in Business Valuation (ABV). The professional codes of conduct of CPA and ICAS, however, provide no guidance to members acting in the capacity of an expert witness. Similarly, the Certified Financial Analyst (CFA) code of ethics and standards of professional conduct do not provide specific guidance to its members acting as expert witnesses, but does broadly address the issue of independence.[37]

In Canada, specific standards governing the conduct of expert witness services by accountants have been established by the Canadian Institute of Chartered Business Valuators (CICBV) and the Alliance for Excellence in Investigative and Forensic Accounting (IFA). In addition to the code of ethics which echoes that of the CPA, the CICBV provides guidance on the requirements for review, analysis and reporting required in expert reports.[38] IFA practitioners are further provided with practice

---

36. The Canadian Institute of Chartered Accountants, Standard Practices for Investigative and Forensic Accounting Engagements, November 2006, Sect. 700, available at <www.cica.ca/focus-on-practice-areas/forensic-accounting/item61477.pdf> (last accessed 12 February 2014).

37. CFA professional conduct standard I (B). "Members and Candidates must use reasonable care and judgment to achieve and maintain independence and objectivity in their professional activities...." available at <www.cfainstitute.org/ethics/codes/ethics/Pages/index.aspx> (last accessed 12 February 2014).

38. CICBV Practice Standard No. 310 (report disclosure) No. 320 (scope of work), and No. 330 (file documentation), available at <https://cicbv.ca/practice-standards/> (last accessed 12 February 2014).

standards specific to the role of serving as an expert witness,[39] which clearly outline the "duty to provide independent assistance to the tribunal by way of objective unbiased testimony in relation to matters within their expertise". The IFA standards emphasize the importance of "never assuming the role of an advocate" and providing the tribunal with "the information, assumptions on which their testimony is based, and any limitations that impact their testimony".

Other professional bodies such as the Certified Valuation Analyst (CVA) and American Society of Appraisers (ASA) also provide guidance to their members acting as an expert witness that is generally consistent with the guidelines stated above.

Alternatively, academic and economic experts are not governed by a specific professional body, but are instead guided by the standards set by the aforementioned arbitration rules and jurisdictional case law.

It is not being suggested that a lack of a professional body to discipline or govern expert behaviour will lead to experts ignoring their duty to the tribunal, and their roles as neutrals. I merely point out that some professional bodies imbed and reinforce this type of behaviour in the very fibre of professional training, and thus the role of the expert is well established in the training of emerging experts. The existence of oversight and disciplinary procedures in these professions contributes to more consistent behaviour in that regard.

IV.   OPPOSING FORCES ON THE EXPERT

1.   Overview

Notwithstanding the well-known role of the expert, and his or her duty to the trier of fact, experts find themselves pulled in different directions by the various factors that influence their behaviour. As has been noted above, it is a well-understood, overriding principle that experts owe their first priority to the tribunal, to be open, honest, independent and objective.

The criticism frequently levelled at experts is based on the manifestation of factors that can be seen at the bottom and to the right in the chart below. It is generally assumed that party-appointed experts will behave in a manner that ingratiates them to their clients and retaining counsel in order to "plant the seed" for future engagements and financial rewards. In these circumstances, it is assumed that party-appointed experts will act as an advocate to further the position of their client, and not to assist the tribunal in understanding the expert issues. This further manifests itself most blatantly when we see expert reports that are a thin disguise for their client's pleadings.

In fact, the expert should be influenced by a variety of factors, none of which should lead to the inappropriate behaviour that seethes beneath the surface, occasionally boiling over to the advocating expert.

---

39. AICPA, ET Section 101 – Independence, available at <www.aicpa.org/Research/Standards/Code ofConduct/Pages/et_101.aspx#et_101.08> (last accessed 12 February 2014).

The chart below summarizes these various forces:

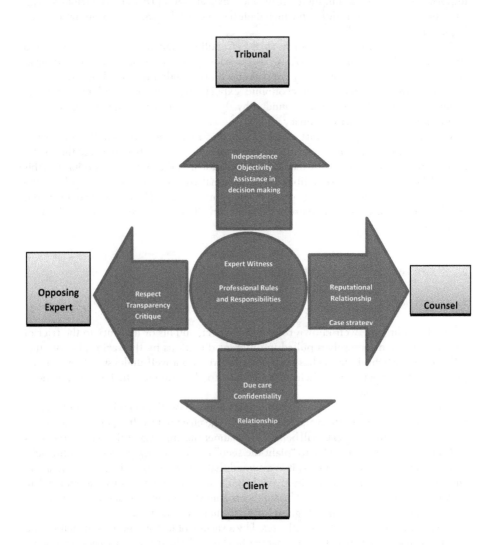

The factors that should and do influence experts (to a lesser or greater degree) are listed below. This is certainly not meant to be an exhaustive list, but representative of the major category of influences.

a. Duty to the tribunal
The prevailing duty of the expert to remain independent "overrides any obligation to the person from whom experts have received instruction or by whom they are paid".[40] This is acknowledged as an aspirational goal, which under ideal circumstances is met.

To be truly impartial from the retaining party, experts must consider a balance of evidence to provide a neutral opinion in their written report and oral testimony, which is to be based on the facts and documents underpinning such opinion.[41] Experts should not simply advance the theories of their client, but rather complete an independent verification of the key issues and assumptions.[42] The expert report "must logically and realistically lead to the conclusions drawn by the expert setting out the assumptions, reasoning, methodology and supporting evidence".[43] Lastly, "he or she should be able to articulate his or her opinions clearly and persuasively, to demonstrate how such opinions were reached and most importantly, not lose sight of what the Tribunal needs to understand".[44]

b. Duty to counsel
At the early onset of a proceeding, the expert may be involved with providing input for the case strategy in terms of managing the client's expectations.[45] The expert report should highlight points that support the retaining party's position, but not advocate it.[46] Additionally, "the expert must possess the mental agility to withstand the challenging test of cross-examination, i.e. be able to react to surprises and defend his or her opinion effectively".[47] It is not uncommon for the involvement of the expert to continue post-hearing, in providing assistance to counsel for the identification of the weaknesses in the opposing expert's testimony for the preparation of post-hearing submissions, if any.[48]

From a lawyer's perspective, an expert is a "hired gun" who must follow the lawyer's instructions and directions.[49] However, "if the judge thinks that you have become the voice of the lawyer, you may lose credibility you need to succeed in your presentation".[50]

---

40. CPR, Part 35.3 – Experts and Assessors, available at <www.justice.gov.uk/courts/procedure-rules/civil/rules/part35> (last accessed 20 February 2014).
41. *Dulong v. Merrill Lynch Canada Inc.*, (2006) ON SC.
42. *Alfano v. Piersanti*, (2012) ONCA.
43. Bernd EHLE, "Practical Aspects of Using Expert Evidence in International Arbitration" in M. ROTH and M. GEISTLINGER, eds., *Yearbook on International Arbitration*, Volume II, p. 81, available at <www.lalive.ch/data/publications/Ehle.pdf> (last accessed 12 February 2014).
44. *Ibid.*, p. 78.
45. *Ibid.*, p. 79.
46. *Ibid.*, p. 81.
47. *Ibid.*, p. 78.
48. *Ibid.*, p. 84.
49. R. MONGEAU, "The Expert Status: From a 'Hired Gun' to an Advisor to the Judge", CICBV Eastern Regional Conference, p. 5.
50. *Ibid.*, p. 6.

Hence, there is a distinct line between independence and assuming the role as the "lawyer's assistant".[51] Some experts have asserted legal arguments within their expert report and have gone as far as filing a Notice of Objection on behalf of their retaining party.[52] Meanwhile, other instances of advocacy include efforts by the defence experts to justify the actions of the defendant by interjecting specific legal arguments, rather than providing their independent opinion. In a recent medical malpractice case, the judge found "the efforts of the defence witnesses to justify Dr. Edington's inclusion of alcohol in his differential diagnosis completely unreasonable". He further found that "the defence experts exhibited partiality and advocacy in their evidence in this regard".[53]

Lastly, the expert should refrain from providing any comments regarding the legal merits of the case; as summarized below:[54]

> "An expert witness is entitled to give his opinion as to whether a judicial decision is inconsistent with binding authority or the general state of the law; however, it will generally be inappropriate for expert witnesses to comment on the likelihood of a decision being upheld or reversed on appeal."

c. Duty to the client

The majority of experts are professionals and as such, the expectation for delivering their services in an expert capacity are no different than what is typically expected of that professional, whereby the exercise of reasonable skill and due care is required. Furthermore, due to the reliance on, and exposure to, confidential client information, the duty to preserve that confidentiality is owed.

Multiple engagements by the same client are common; however, a close personal relationship with the client has been viewed as a potential conflict of interest:[55]

> "Where it is demonstrated that there exists a relationship between the proposed expert and the party calling him which a reasonable observer might think was capable of affecting the views of the expert so as to make them unduly favourable to that party, his evidence should not be admitted however unbiased the conclusions of the expert might probably be."

Nevertheless, disclosure for any conflict of interest is required and "it is for the court and not the parties to decide whether a conflict of interest is material or not".[56]

d. Duty to the opposing expert

It is standard practice for a tribunal to request the experts to meet in advance of the evidentiary hearing in an "attempt to reach an agreement on issues within the scope of

---

51. *Ibid.*
52. *Brampton Vee World Motors Limited v Her Majesty the Queen*, (2006) TCC.
53. *Boyd et al. v. Edington et al.*, (2014) ONSC.
54. *JPMorgan Chase Bank v. Lanner (The)*, (2008) FCA.
55. *Liverpool Roman Catholic Archdiocesan Trust v. David Goldberg QC*, (2001) WLR.
56. *Toth v. Jarman*, (2006) EWCA.

their expert reports".[57] Another avenue to resolve disparate opinions can be achieved through witness conferencing, whereby "the arrangement of testimony by particular issues or in such a manner that witnesses be questioned at the same time and in confrontation with each other."[58] In either instance, the meeting of the experts should be conducted in a manner of mutual respect, while concurrently allowing for the critique on the areas of weakness in the opinion of the opposing expert.

The appearance of impartiality by both experts should allow for the "lack of fear of changing an opinion if presented with new facts of which he or she was not aware at the time of writing the report".[59]

2.   Counsel-Expert Communication

The method that lawyers adopt in the preparation of expert witnesses can be guided by each lawyer's country of origin. Differences in guiding principal can lead to very different expert preparation approaches, which lead to varying results in the performance of experts in cross-examination, and witness conferencing.

For example, professional rules governing lawyers from the United States view the witness preparation process as an essential component of the lawyer's duties. Such preparation is permissible so long as the lawyer does not offer evidence that the lawyer reasonably believes is false[60] and/or results in the lawyer improperly influencing witness testimony.[61] Some rules even go so far as to classify inadequate witness preparation as legal malpractice.[62] Under the Federal Rules of Civil Procedure, attorney-expert communication is protected to allow attorneys to communicate with their retained experts without exposing such communications to discovery.[63]

Commentators describe the approach in the United States as follows: [64]

---

57. B. EHLE, *op. cit.*, fn. 43, p. 82.
58. IBA Rules, Taking of Evidence in International Arbitration, Art. 8.3 (f), 29 May 2010, available at <www.ibanet.org/Publications/publications_IBA_guides_and_free_materials.aspx> (last accessed 21 February 2014).
59. R. MONGEAU, *op. cit.*, fn. 49, p. 6.
60. American Bar Association Model Rules of Professional Conduct, Rule 3.3(a)(3), available at <www.americanbar.org/groups/professional_responsibility/publications/model_rules_of_pr ofessional_conduct/rule_3_3_candor_toward_the_tribunal.html> (last accessed 20 February 2014).
61. *Geders v. United States* (1976) U.S.
62. S.P. ANWAY (Squire Sanders US LLP), "The Ethics of Preparing Witnesses in International Arbitration: Is There an Uneven Playing Field?", ADR Institute of Canada 2013/ ICC Canada 2013 Conference (24 October 2013).
63. Rules 26(b)(3)(A) and (B) of the Federal Rules of Civil Procedure Exceptions to the protection of attorney-expert communication include: compensation for the expert testimony and identification of facts, data, or assumptions the party's attorney provided to the expert and that the expert relied on in forming their opinion.
64. R.K. FLOWERS, "Witness Preparation: Regulating the Profession's 'Dirty Little Secret'", Hastings Constitutional Law Quarterly (2011) p. 1007 available at <http://papers. ssrn.com/sol3/papers.cfm?abstract_id=2039480> (last accessed 2 March, 2014).

"Since the ABA Rules do not speak directly to the permitted or prohibited conduct of the lawyer when preparing a witness, 'there remains a vast realm of conduct that could potentially be characterized as improperly seeking to influence a witness' testimony. Within this, there are very few guideposts to assist the attorney in maximizing his effectiveness as an advocate while still remaining within the recognized limits of professional responsibility.'"

In contrast, the Bar's Code of Conduct of the United Kingdom indicates that "A barrister must not rehearse practice or coach a witness in relation to his evidence."[65] This view adopted in the United Kingdom is meant to eliminate the risk of influencing an expert's witness objectivity and independence. As Lord Chief Justice stated:[66]

"The witness should give his or her own evidence, so far as practicable uninfluenced by what anyone else has said, whether in formal discussions or informal conversations. The rule reduces, indeed hopefully avoids any possibility, that one witness may tailor his evidence in the light of what anyone else said, and equally, avoids any unfounded perception that he may have done so. These risks are inherent in witness training. Even if the training takes place one-to-one with someone completely remote from the facts of the case itself, the witness may come, even unconsciously, to appreciate which aspects of his evidence are perhaps not quite consistent with what others are saying, or indeed not quite what is required of him. An honest witness may alter the emphasis of his evidence to accommodate what he thinks may be a different, more accurate, or simply better remembered perception of events."

In Canada, email exchanges between counsel and its expert have always been heavily scrutinized:[67]

"The emails reveal a pattern of Mr. Anson-Cartwright attempting to craft his report to achieve Mr. Piersanti's objectives in the litigation. Each draft of Mr. Anson-Cartwright's report was delivered to Mr. Piersanti for review, revision and approval."

In the most recent Ontario judgment of *Moore v. Getahun*, the guideline of expert witness preparation has been further clarified:

"The expert's primary duty is to assist the court. In light of this change in the role of the expert witness, I conclude that counsel's prior practice of reviewing draft reports should stop. Discussions or meetings between counsel and an expert to review and shape a draft report expert report are no longer acceptable."[68]

---

65. The Bar Standards Board Handbook (January 2014), Rule C9.4, available at <www.barstandards board.org.uk/media/1553795/bsb_handbook_jan_2014.pdf> (last accessed 20 February 2014).
66. *R. v. Momodou*, (2005) EWCA.
67. *Alfano v. Piersanti*, (2012) ONCA.
68. *Moore v. Getahun*, (2014) ONSC.

International rules generally allow attorney-expert communication in the preparation of witness statements and witness testimony; again emphasis is placed on the encouragement of providing truthful information to the witness.

Under the IBA Guidelines on Party Representation in International Arbitration: "A Party Representative may assist Witnesses in the preparation of Witness Statements and Experts in the preparation of Expert Reports"[69] but "should ensure that a Witness Statement reflects the Witness's own account of relevant facts, events and circumstances".[70]

Lawyers who are members of the bars in Belgium, France, Italy and Switzerland are prohibited from contacting witnesses, however each of these jurisdictions has created an exception when its lawyers are acting as party representatives in international arbitration.

The IBA Guidelines are intended to reflect the best practices with respect to witness preparation but acknowledge the jurisdictional differences in expert preparation: "Disparate practices among jurisdictions may create inequality and threaten the integrity of the arbitral proceedings."[71]

Similarly under the 2010 Hague Principles: "Counsel may engage in pre-testimonial communication with a witness, subject to such rules as the international court or Tribunal may have adopted."[72]

The role of counsel should be to assist witnesses in developing the confidence and clarity of thought required to testify truthfully and effectively based upon their own knowledge or recollection of the facts.[73] The lack of a clear distinguishing factor between what is considered "improper influence" and that of appropriate witness preparation, further complicated by the confidential nature of commercial disputes, generally results in a lack of enforcement or detection.

3. Tribunals Dealing with Conflicting Opinions

The quantification of economic damages often hinges on lost profits, the fair market value of an investment, asset, or business interest, or both. In determining the value of a business interest, the expert must identify and analyze all relevant aspects of the business environment: the economy, industry, and factors specific to the business. On the basis of that analysis, the expert then determines the appropriate valuation methodology. Generally, there are three valuation methodologies typically employed in determining the value of a business that is expected to operate as a going concern:

---

69. IBA Guidelines on Party Representation in International Arbitration 25 May 2013, Guideline 20, available at <http://www.ibanet.org/Publications/publications_IBA_guides_and_free_materials. aspx> (last accessed 21 February 2014).

70. *Ibid.*, Guideline 21.

71. *Ibid.*, Comments to Guidelines 18-25.

72. Hague Principles on Ethical Standards for Counsel Appearing before International Courts and Tribunals, 27 September 2010, Sect. 6.2, available at <www.ucl.ac.uk/laws/cict/docs/ Hague_Sept2010.pdf> (last accessed 21 February 2014).

73. Alan REDFERN, et al., *Law and Practice of International Commercial Arbitration* (Sweet & Maxwell, London 2004) p. 207.

– The income-based approach, based on the present value of future expected cash flows. While other approaches, such as the Capitalized Cash Flow approach, are occasionally employed, the most popular and widely applied income-based approach is the Discounted Cash Flow (DCF) methodology. In applying the DCF, the business' expected future cash flows are forecasted, typically on an annual basis; the present value of which is determined based on a discount rate which reflects the risks associated with the realization of such cash flows. The DCF methodology is the most appropriate in cases where future cash flows can be reasonably estimated, and where a proxy for an appropriate discount rate is available. The strength of this approach lies in its theoretical and practical soundness, in that its basis is the economic theory that the value of an asset is a function of its future economic benefits. Conversely, its weakness is that its forward-looking nature requires assumptions which relate to future revenues and costs, among other things. To the extent that key assumptions are not well reasoned and properly supported, a DCF analysis may result in an unreliable conclusion as to value;

– The market-based approach, where the value conclusion is derived with reference to valuation metrics observed in comparable publicly traded companies and open market transactions. The strengths of this approach are that it is relatively straightforward to apply and understand, and that its conclusions are driven by valuation metrics that are observable in the marketplace. The main downside to this approach is the inherent difficulty in finding a company that is truly "comparable" to the subject company, as no two businesses or projects are identical. Often compounding this is the general lack of sufficient detail regarding transactions to completely analyze and understand the underlying data; and,

– The asset-based approach, where value is determined based on the value of each of the underlying tangible and intangible assets of the business. An example of such an approach is the Adjusted Book Value (ABV) methodology, whereby the book value of equity is taken as a starting point, and is then adjusted to reflect the fair market value of specific assets and liabilities. This approach is useful, as it compartmentalizes value based on each asset and liability. Its main disadvantage stems from the difficulty in its application, as it requires the identification and separate valuation of each asset and liability. Additionally, since the valuation of a business interest using the income or market approach accounts for the value of both tangible and intangible assets and liabilities, the ABV approach may not be necessary in all circumstances. Generally, the asset-based approach is not used as the primary valuation approach for an operating business deemed to be a going concern unless it is commonly used by buyers and sellers in that particular industry.

While the selection of an appropriate valuation approach is important, the fair market value of a business should be the same or similar regardless of the methodology applied. In order to bolster a conclusion of value, it is often useful to apply multiple valuation methodologies. Generally, when sufficiently reliable information is available, the income approach is applied as a primary methodology, with the market approach or asset approach as the secondary methodology.

In this discussion, I focus primarily on the most widely applied valuation methodology, the DCF. However, since a key element of the DCF involves estimating future (and in the context of damages quantification, foregone) cash flows, this discussion also applies to cases that involve damages based on lost cash flows or profits. In both cases, the expert creates an expectation of the profits or cash flows of a business or project in a 'but for' or counter-factual scenario.

Areas of disagreement among experts regarding the appropriate valuation approach arise when the subject of a dispute involves a business or project that is in the early stage of the business life cycle. Early-stage businesses or projects typically lack a track record of positive earnings and require investment prior to progressing from a period of little or no earnings, to a period of growth and maturity. This progression is generally plagued with uncertainty with respect to the quantum and timing of cash flows. Additionally, as is the case with any start-up, there is a risk that the business or project will not progress and will never experience growth and maturity.

In the context of an economic damages analysis, an early-stage business or project makes it difficult to formulate assumptions regarding the counter-factual or 'but for' world. In the valuation of a mature business, the expert will typically look to historical results in order to form a baseline expectation of the business' cash flows. The expert would then take into account future expectations regarding all relevant business, industry and economic factors that prevail as at the effective date of the analysis. Based on this review of historical performance and information regarding the future, the expert is able to formulate an expectation with respect to future cash flows. In the case of a business in its early stage, such an analysis is not fruitful, as historical cash flows are typically nominal and bear little semblance to subsequent cash flows. The difficulty is compounded if the subject business is one that operates in an industry that is in its infancy, as the level of research and analysis of the industry may be sparsely available.

The expert may (and often does) take steps to mitigate the challenges associated with valuing an early-stage business. For example, they may base their analysis (in part or in whole) on business plans or forecasts that were prepared at or around the date of the alleged wrongdoing – assuming that proper diligence was exercised in preparing these contemporaneous documents, they may be viewed as management's best estimate of the future prospects of the business or project. If relying on such documents, the expert should independently evaluate whether the business plans or forecasts were reasonable in light of all relevant factors as at the valuation date.

The quantum expert may base their quantification of economic damages on the analysis of an independent industry expert. Industry expertise tends to enhance the reliability of the damages analysis. Industry experts may be useful in, for example, analyzing relevant industry trends, forecasting drivers of revenues and expenses, providing fair market value of tangible assets and identifying comparable assets in the market. This expertise is particularly useful in specialized industries, such as energy and mining. In these ways, an industry expert may mitigate the uncertainty associated with utilizing a DCF (or lost profits approach) to value an early-stage business.

As a result of the uncertainty in forecasting future cash flows that would have been generated by the early-stage business in the "but for" world, tribunals tend to consider conclusions drawn by the DCF methodology or lost profits approach (normally put forward by the claimant's expert) to be too uncertain to form the basis of an award of economic damages. In these cases, tribunals generally award damages on the basis of sunk costs (or less frequently, market-based approaches). Sunk costs do not take into account the intangible value and goodwill that generally accumulate as a business or project develops and matures over time. Thus, an award based only on sunk costs does not encompass the full extent of the claimant's economic loss. In Annex III, I provide a summary of the various valuation approaches adopted in ICSID cases.

There appears to be a trade-off between certainty and the perceived equity of an award. At one end of the spectrum is an award based on sunk costs – while sunk costs are generally certain, in that they are grounded in historical transactions and can be supported by independent evidence, they generally do not adequately compensate the claimant, for reasons explained previously. At the other end of the spectrum is the award based on a DCF-based valuation or lost profits-based damages quantification – these approaches necessitate assumptions regarding the future and/or the "but for" world and by their very nature, they are less certain than the sunk costs approach. However, if applied properly, a DCF-based valuation (or lost profits-based damages quantification) is equitable to the claimant, as it is a comprehensive measure of the value of a business and, by extension, economic loss. Ultimately, it is the role of the tribunal to weigh certainty and equity in making its decision on damages.

The duty of the expert is first and foremost to be helpful to the tribunal. An ideal expert fulfills this duty by conducting an analysis and providing an opinion that is independent and objective, opining on matters that are within their area(s) of expertise and articulating their opinion clearly. Experts that are truly independent would provide the same opinion irrespective of which party retained them. Unfortunately, this is not what we have observed in practice.

We find that experts, when retained by the claimant, tend to utilize a DCF approach (or other income-based approach) or a lost profits-based calculation to quantify economic damages. Some expert reports are independent and credible, while others are aggressive, using model inputs – relating primarily to cash flows and the discount rate – that are optimistic and thus favourable to the client. When retained by the claimant, most experts will employ the DCF or lost profits approach regardless of whether the business or project was at an early stage or at the maturity stage of its life cycle.

The respondent's expert tends to have a different view of the appropriateness of the DCF and lost profits approach, particularly in the case of a start-up or early-stage business or project. Our observation is that experts that are retained by the respondent almost always refute the use of a DCF, characterizing the approach as speculative. Some expert reports will even cite case law to support their position (a practice that I believe should be reserved for counsel arguing on behalf of the client). These reports generally consist of lengthy critiques of the assumptions employed by the claimant's expert and do not put forward an alternative conclusion. While I understand that certain pressures, particularly from their client and counsel, may affect the expert's approach and assumptions in certain cases, in my view, these expert reports advocate for their client's position and are generally not helpful to the tribunal.

Overall, damages quantification and business valuation are tasks that require judgment in formulating reasonable assumptions based on a thorough analysis of all relevant factors. The task of placing the claimant in the same economic position it would have enjoyed "but for" an alleged act is by definition uncertain or speculative; it requires making assumptions regarding a scenario that has not occurred. The role of the expert – whether retained by claimant or respondent – should be to identify the uncertainties and properly account for the risk inherent in their valuations. While there are cases where the DCF methodology or lost profits approach is not the most appropriate, it should not be for the reason that it is speculative or uncertain.

The tendency for tribunals to award damages in cases that involve early-stage businesses or projects on the basis of sunk costs encourages experts who act on behalf of respondents to refute the use of the DCF or lost profits approach, rather than using their expertise to identify and address the uncertainty inherent in the task of quantifying the fair market value of an investment in a "but for" world.

This practice of awarding damages on the basis of sunk costs may have one more undesirable side effect: it may change the behaviour and decision-making process exercised by respondents. By tribunals awarding damages based on costs, this arguably encourages respondents to act unlawfully prior to the point that the business or project reaches its earnings potential. Consider the following scenario. Claimants will invest capital at the inception of a project, which tends to be its riskiest stage. As the project is developed (with the passage of time and investment of funds by the claimant) some uncertainties are resolved and the overall risk of the project is reduced. If faced with a choice of whether to act unlawfully to achieve economic gain (or for other reasons) at this point, the respondent may act on precedent awards of damages – that if the respondent acts unlawfully, it may lose nothing more than the claimant's investment if the dispute is arbitrated. This may be a less costly alternative than, perhaps, purchasing the claimant's interest in the business or project at that time. In reality, however, the claimant put costly capital at stake in resolving uncertainties associated with the project at the earliest stages of development. Clearly, the above scenario – encouraged by the tribunal's tendency to award damages based on sunk costs – is undesirable.

V.   EXPERT MEETINGS AND JOINT REPORTS

Prior to the hearing, a tribunal may require the experts to meet to attempt to resolve as many issues as possible between them, as well as document areas of agreement and disagreement. The benefits of such a meeting and a joint report are obvious. To the extent any issues as between the experts can be "taken off the table", it serves to shorten and clarify the process of hearing and testing expert evidence.

In order to be meaningful, the expert meeting must be based on a good faith, open and objective meeting of the experts, unhampered by the agenda of the advocates and parties that have retained them. The downside to facilitating a meeting of the experts, free from instructions by retaining counsel and the parties, is that there are issues of fact and law that are not within the expertise of the experts that are meeting, and thus an agreement on certain issues may have an effect on legitimate arguments that counsel wishes to make. In these cases, an agreement by an expert on a certain point, may lead to the inadvertent prejudicing of the point in question. It is therefore extremely important that experts are fully briefed by retaining counsel on what issues are in fact open for the expert to discuss, and importantly, disclose any limitations in their joint report.

I have been part of expert meetings and preparation of joint reports on numerous occasions and find that they are currently requested by tribunals in over two-thirds of the cases I have been involved in.

I have found the best way to approach these joint meetings is to reduce the important issues and opinions of the experts to a spreadsheet (attached as Appendix IV). The experts can add or delete issues as agreed, and are able to clearly establish where there are points of agreement that require no further investigation, and where there are differences between the experts.

It is also helpful to prepare a schedule that informs the tribunal of the approximate impact of the differences between the experts (some points will be interrelated, and therefore it may be impossible to precisely isolate the impact of one issue on its own). In some cases, I have prepared a financial model saved on a CD-Rom disk that identifies the issues between the experts, and allows the tribunal to select either position proposed by the expert, or any position in between. This provides some further latitude to the tribunals as they may not agree with the conclusions of either expert, and wish to find an answer based on other findings.

The work product of such good-faith meetings of the experts, at best resolves a number of issues that allows for a more efficient conduct of the hearing, and at worst (when there is no or little agreement between the experts), is a useful summary of the expert evidence on a spreadsheet.

There is of course the possibility, due to pride of authorship or lack of independence, that experts will come to a joint meeting unwilling to entertain any possible position but their own. In this case, the joint meeting and joint report may still be useful, as it will assist the tribunal in establishing some unwarranted or unreasonable positions of experts that may reveal their bias and thus reduce or impact their overall credibility.

Further, if witness conferencing is employed during the hearing (again, in my experience in over two-thirds of the cases in which I am involved), the joint report presents a useful tool to the tribunal in testing the positions of the experts. Again, this is an opportunity for the experts to explain the basis of their opinions, but equally for the tribunal to determine the objectiveness and open-mindedness of the experts.

VI. MY PERSONAL EXPERIENCE AS A DAMAGES EXPERT

My own personal experiences in national courts and international arbitration hearings have been remarkably similar to other experts that I have canvassed. Although most experts know their role, much of the bias that exists seems to "creep" into some expert reports based on a lack of understanding of the role of experts, or due to the perception of short term commercial benefits (i.e. do what clients/counsel ask). In short, most of the problems that do exist in expert reports stem from a simple lack of professionalism. Although the majority of experts do know how to behave properly, there are a sufficient number of experts that do not, and this has stirred much of the debate regarding experts.

In the long term, this type of behaviour (as noted in a number of cases in Sect. IV above) lessens the impact and usefulness of expert reports, and undermines the very purpose of opinion evidence.

Poorly constructed expert reports characteristically contain some or all of the following attributes (in the context of a quantum report):

– Sections of their client's pleadings;
– Legal argument;
– Aggressive and subjective language;
– Conclusions or opinions that are outside of the expertise of the author;
– Calculations or conclusions that are not transparent;
– They are not responsive to issues raised by the parties; and,
– They are inconsistent with past methodologies for the same or similar circumstances (i.e. a discounted cash flow approach was appropriate when acting for a Claimant, but in like or similar circumstances it is inappropriate when acting for a Respondent).

Poor or biased experts (advocates) in providing oral evidence characteristically display some or all of the following attributes:

– Being evasive or non-responsive in cross-examination;
– Making "speeches", volunteering information, or advocating a position;
– Use of selected information in answering questions in order to "defend" a position;
– Inventing new or novel responses in order to defend a position;
– Wasting counsel's time in cross-examination;
– Displaying lack of respect for counsel, the tribunal, or opposing experts; and,
– Being close-minded to properly constructed cross-examination questions.

Further, some experts will refuse to constructively participate in expert meetings, and in even more extreme cases, boast in marketing material about "winning" cases for clients (forgetting the neutral nature of their role, and frequently citing cases that were determined on jurisdiction or liability, with no consideration of damages). The insidious nature of these practices is to push experts further apart, and further erode the legal community's perception of experts.

Sadly, there will always be examples of experts that offend the principles upon which expert evidence is based. For the most part, I believe experts generally understand their role and are helpful to courts and tribunals. Some modifications to how we produce expert reports and oral evidence, which I summarize below, have been canvassed as a means to encourage more consistent behaviour in experts.

VII.   SUGGESTIONS FOR THE FUTURE

As noted above, the IBA Rules and English CPR seek to mitigate the potential for partisanship and bias inherent in a system of party-appointed experts. It is possible, however, that they do not go far enough towards achieving their goal. For that reason, I suggest below three measures that might help to preserve the best features of party-appointed experts while blunting those experts' incentives to take unreasonable, contradictory or partisan positions.

The first of those measures relate to experts' terms of reference. It is my experience (and that of my colleagues) that the vast majority of the differences between party-appointed experts arise in consequence either of their having received different instructions or their having employed different assumptions. When party-appointed

405

experts reach strong opposing conclusions, it may be difficult for a tribunal to know how much weight to place on either expert's evidence or to identify the instructions or assumptions that polarize the experts' opinions.

The new IBA Rules take a useful step towards transparency by requiring party-appointed experts to describe their instructions. A further step in that direction would be for parties to submit their proposed instructions to the tribunal prior to their delivery to the expert. The tribunal could then review those instructions and agree (or order) changes so that the instructions were clear and fitted the purposes of the tribunal. In the extreme, the tribunal could order that both experts received identical instructions to deprive parties of the opportunity to use instructions to guide their experts' testimony.

In my view, such requirement would be strengthened if experts were obliged to document the assumptions that they have made in drawing their conclusions. Although such clarification may currently emerge from a meeting of experts, those meetings may also produce dozens of pages of disagreement that serve to cloud rather than clarify the issues. The clear documentation of assumptions – highlighting those that are a matter of instruction – will assist tribunals' understanding of the underpinnings of each expert's evidence.[74] It could also allow a tribunal to order both experts to prepare their conclusions on the basis of one or more sets of instructions and assumptions, which I shall refer to as "common-basis conclusions". Such an order seems likely either to close the gap between two experts or, at a minimum, sharply to define the source of any further assumption(s) leading to divergent views.

In principle, an order to reach common-basis conclusions might be more powerful than existing procedures aimed at narrowing differences between experts, such as meetings of experts or witness conferencing. In my experience, those procedures do not result in a substantive narrowing of the gap if the experts' approaches embody incompatible instructions or assumptions or if one of the parties seeks to emphasize sources of disagreement. An order to present one or more sets of common-basis conclusions solves these problems and could be used by a tribunal either before or after a hearing to aid its understanding of the impact of different assumptions or instructions.

The second suggested measure relates to the incentives faced by a party-appointed expert in responding to his or her instructions. It might be thought that party-appointed experts face pressure to adopt assumptions, points of view or approaches that are favourable to the party that instructed them. In my experience, that is generally untrue. The actual incentives faced by experts are more subtle.

Chief among the incentives faced by experts is that their testimony in a current case may have a bearing on their future opportunities to testify. At first glance, therefore, it might be thought that experts would wish to be known for their pliancy and helpfulness to the instructing party. In practice, that is unlikely to be the case, because a pliant expert might well find that tribunals assign a lower weight to his or her testimony. That, in turn, would potentially diminish any future stream of expert instructions. A good

---

74. That is not to say that counsel-directed assumptions are always illegitimate. Occasionally, an expert may reach a "fork in the road" in the course of analysis, each path being open to a reasonable expert. In such cases, the expert must either seek instruction from counsel as to which assumption should be preferred, or present his or her conclusions on the basis of both assumptions. If the expert chooses to take instruction, however, the fact should be clearly documented.

expert therefore has an incentive to know where to draw the line between being helpful and being partisan and to resist unreasonable pressure to cross it.

In national courts, where expert evidence and judges' opinions of it are often made public, the incentive to remain independent is strong: a partisan expert may quickly be "found out". International arbitrations, however, provide much weaker incentives, particularly when the parties have agreed to strong privacy controls: in many arbitrations, the proceedings, expert evidence, awards and tribunals' reasoning remain confidential. In those circumstances, a tribunal's disregard for or criticism of an expert's testimony may be known only to a small circle of insiders. Under a veil of confidentiality, a partisan expert might prosper for a considerable period. The diffuse nature of international arbitration may also mean that word travels only slowly between seats of arbitration or between arbitrators.

The best antidotes to expert partisanship, therefore, are transparency, feedback and peer review. The more that arbitrators comment on the merits of experts' work and the more that those comments are published, the greater will be the incentives for experts to remain independent of the parties appointing them. Those incentives will counteract, and probably outweigh, an expert's desire to please, leading to an increase in actual as well as perceived independence.

The third measure I suggest is for the tribunal to order a joint report of the experts in a summary form (as attached in Annex IV), which isolates the technical points of the experts, where they agree completely, have some agreement, or disagree completely. It would also identify the approximate effect on the quantum of damages of each position. Using this summary report, the tribunal can then decide which issues are best brought up in witness conferencing, and determine based on the quality of the evidence, which expert position they prefer.

Additionally, in complex quantum cases, I suggest the tribunal work with its own expert. The expert could be appointed by the tribunal in an advisory capacity, as tribunals are normally entitled to do, even if they have rarely exercised that power in the past. If tribunals were to appoint their own "expert consultant" (to use Dr. Sachs' term) more often, if only to review the party-appointed experts' reports and offer their findings to the tribunal, they could offer a powerful incentive towards independent testimony by party-appointed experts. That could be achieved at a relatively low cost – no original work being required – but without the duplication of experts implicit in expert teaming supplemented by party-appointed "expert consultants". A refinement of the model might be for the tribunal-appointed expert to adjudicate on the technical matters before the tribunal and issue his or her own ruling on them, in a manner similar to that employed in the process of expert determination.   This paper has outlined the various factors that influence the behaviour of experts and posited that the best way to increase the perceived independence of party-appointed experts is to increase transparency and disclosure, so as to align the interests of experts with those of the tribunal. A requirement for experts to document their assumptions, highlighting those upon which they have received instruction, will serve to highlight the sources of difference between experts. A requirement for experts' instructions to be agreed with the tribunal, or for common instructions to be imposed on experts, may also limit the potential for experts to address or emphasize different issues in their reports. An order for experts to issue common-basis conclusions may assist tribunals' understanding of the impact of different assumptions and help narrow the differences between experts. If tribunals were also encouraged to comment on expert testimony and to publish those comments, experts would receive feedback on their work and be subject to outside scrutiny. That feedback and scrutiny will alter experts' incentives and go some way to resolving party-appointed experts' perceived lack of independence. Finally, tribunals might be bolder in appointing their own experts to review – and possibly rule on – the merits of party-appointed experts' work, a power that is exercised as the exception rather than the rule.

Although I accept that there is currently no requirement for transparency in many arbitrations, I am aware of comments by legal professionals arguing that publication of awards would advance the law upon which arbitration relies. The interests of tribunals, experts and counsel on this point might therefore be aligned, even if parties often prefer confidentiality.

Annex I: Sachs Protocol and Traditional System

Traditional System	Sachs Protocol	Pros of Sachs Protocol	Cons of Sachs Protocol
Lawyers hire/pay the expert.	Each party to identify a list of possible experts it would be prepared to rely on.	Promotes objectivity and independence:	The Tribunal-appointed expert cannot assist in evaluating the merits of the claim:
Parties will seek experts whose views are most likely to support their case.	The Tribunal ultimately selects one expert from each party's list.	The link is broken between the expert and the lawyers.	Potential pursuit of unfruitful actions.
Court appointed experts are drawn from lists that may be out-of-date.		Avoids the selection of the "usual suspects".	Tribunal members may not be skilled in the selection of appropriate experts for a given issue.
Experts are only exposed to evidence and reasoning to support the case of the party who appointed them.	Each expert is permitted to seek assistance from both parties, but is not permitted to communicate separately with the parties.	Experts are made aware of all relevant issues framed by the Tribunal and all parties.	

Traditional System	Sachs Protocol	Pros of Sachs Protocol	Cons of Sachs Protocol
High costs due to a system of sequential exchange of reports and testimonies between party-appointed experts.	The two experts are required to work as a team to produce a single report and testify together.	Cost reduction: Joint-expert report with peer review Testify together and questioned by both parties.	Fundamental difference in views and failure to agree could result in exhaustive thoroughness. Tendency to achieve consensus/ middle-ground of debate
Each party may appoint their own expert to challenge a Tribunal-appointed expert.		Eliminates the appointment of additional experts in challenge of the Tribunal appointed expert.	

Annex II: Arbitration Rules and the Expert Witness

Name of Rules	Clause	Summary of Rules
ICDR International Arbitration Rules (June 1, 2009)	Article 22 (Experts)	**22:1**: The tribunal may appoint one or more independent experts to report to it, in writing, on specific issues designated by the tribunal and communicated to the parties. **22.2**: The parties shall provide such an expert with any relevant information or produce for inspection any relevant documents or goods that the expert may require. **22.3**: Upon receipt of an expert's report, the tribunal shall send a copy of the report to all parties and shall give the parties an opportunity to express, in writing, their opinion on the report. A party may examine any document on which the expert has relied in such a report. **22.4**: At the request of any party, the tribunal shall give the parties an opportunity to question the expert at a hearing. At this hearing, parties may present expert witnesses to testify on the points at issue.
ICC Arbitration Rules (2012)	Article 25 (Establishing the facts of the case)	**25.3**: The tribunal may decide to hear witnesses, experts appointed by the parties, or any other person. Parties have the opportunity to be present. **25.4**: The tribunal, after having consulted the parties, may appoint an expert(s), define their terms of reference, and receive their reports. Parties have the opportunity to question any such expert at a hearing.
LCIA Arbitration Rules (January 1, 1998)	Article 21 (Experts to the Arbitral Tribunal)	**21.1**: Unless otherwise agreed by the parties in writing, the Tribunal may (a) appoint an expert(s) to report on specific issues, and (b) require the parties to give the expert(s) access to relevant documents, goods, samples, property or site for inspection. **21.2**: If, a party requests, or the Tribunal finds it necessary, the expert(s), after delivering the expert report to the Tribunal, shall participate at a hearing(s) where the parties will have opportunity to question the expert and present their expert witnesses to testify on the issues.

Name of Rules	Clause	Summary of Rules
JAMS International Arbitration Rules (August 1, 2011)	Article 24 (Experts and Other Witnesses)	**24.1:** Before any hearing, the Tribunal may require either party to give notice of the identity of the witness it wishes to call, as well as of the subject matter of their testimony and its relevance to the issues. **24.2:** The Tribunal has the power to summon witnesses and to compel the production of relevant documents by subpoena or other compulsory process where authorized to do so by the law of the location where the testimony of the witness is to be heard, or the production of documents is to be made, whether such location is at the place of arbitration or in another location designated by the Tribunal. **24.3:** The Tribunal has discretion, on the grounds of redundancy and irrelevance, to limit or refuse the appearance of any witness, whether witness of fact or expert witness. **24.4:** In the discretion of the Tribunal, evidence of witnesses may also be presented in the form of written statements signed by them. In the discretion of the Tribunal, the presentation of witness testimony in the form of written statements may be made conditional upon the witnesses' appearance for the purpose of cross-examination. **24.5:** Subject to the provisions of any applicable law or ethical rule, it will not be improper for any party or its legal representatives to interview any witness or potential witness for the purpose of presenting his or her testimony in written form or producing him or her as an oral witness. **24.6:** Any person intending to testify to the Tribunal on any issue of fact or expertise will be treated as a witness under these Rules even if that person is a party to the arbitration or was or is an officer, employee or shareholder of any party. **24.7:** The Tribunal, after having consulted the parties, may appoint one or more experts, define the scope of their work and receive their reports. At the request of a party, the parties will be given the opportunity to question at a hearing any such expert appointed by the Tribunal and comment on any reports. **24.8:** The fees and expenses of any expert appointed by the Tribunal under this Article will form part of the costs of the arbitration.
HKIAC Administered Arbitration Rules (2013)	Article 22 (Evidence and Hearings)	**22.5:** Any person may be a witness or an expert. If a witness or expert is to be heard, each party shall communicate to the arbitral tribunal and to the other party the name and address of the witness or expert it intends to present, and the subject upon and the language in which such witness or expert will give his or her testimony.
	Article 25 (Tribunal-Appointed Experts)	**25.1:** The arbitral tribunal, after consulting with the parties, may appoint one or more experts. **25.2:** The parties shall give the expert any relevant information or produce for his or her inspection any relevant documents or goods that he or she may require of them. **25.3:** Upon receipt of the expert's report, the arbitral tribunal shall send a copy of the report to the parties who shall be given the opportunity to express, in writing, their opinions on the report. The parties shall be entitled to examine any document on which the expert has relied in his or her report. **25.4:** At the request of either party the expert, after delivery of the report, shall attend a hearing at which the parties shall have the opportunity to be present and to examine the expert. At this hearing either party may present experts in order to testify on the points at issue.

Name of Rules	Clause	Summary of Rules
DIAC Arbitration Rules (1992)	Article 29 (Witnesses) & Article 30 (Experts Appointed by the Tribunal)	**29.1:** If witnesses are to be heard, at least fifteen days before the hearing each party shall communicate to the Tribunal and to the other party the identities and addresses of the witnesses he intends to call, the subject matter of their testimonies and its relevance to the issues in arbitration, and the languages in which such witnesses will give their testimony. **29.2:** The Tribunal has discretion, on the grounds of avoiding duplication or lack of relevance, to limit the appearance of any witness, whether witness of fact or expert witness. **29(3):** Any witness who gives oral evidence may be questioned, by each of the parties under the control of the Tribunal. The Tribunal may put questions at any stage of the examination of the witnesses. **29.4:** The testimony of witnesses may, either at the choice of a party or as directed by the Tribunal, be submitted in written form, whether by way of signed statements, sworn affidavits or otherwise, in which case the Tribunal may make the admissibility of the testimony conditional upon the witnesses being made available for oral testimony. **29.5:** A party shall be responsible for the practical arrangements, cost and availability of any witness it calls. **29.6:** The Tribunal shall determine whether any witness shall retire during any part of the proceedings, particularly during the testimony of other witnesses. **29.7:** The Tribunal shall require witnesses to swear an oath before the Tribunal before giving evidence in accordance with any mandatory provisions of the applicable procedural law. **30.1:** The Tribunal may, after consultation with the parties, appoint one or more independent experts to report to it on specific issues designated by the Tribunal. A copy of the expert's terms of reference, established by the Tribunal, having regard to any observations of the parties, shall be communicated to the parties. Any such expert shall be required to sign an appropriate confidentiality undertaking. **30.2:** The Tribunal may require a party to give any such expert any relevant information, documents, or provide access to goods, property or site for inspection by the expert. Any dispute between a party and the expert as to the relevance of the requested information or goods shall be referred to the Tribunal for decision. **30.3:** Upon receipt of the expert's report, the Tribunal shall provide a copy of the report to the parties, who shall be given the opportunity to express, in writing, their opinion on the report. A party may examine any document on which the expert has relied in such a report. **30.4:** At the request of a party, the parties shall be given the opportunity to question the expert at a hearing. At this hearing, the parties may present expert witnesses to testify on the points at issue. **30.5:** The opinion of any expert on the issue or issues submitted to the Tribunal expert shall be subject to the Tribunal's power of assessment of those issues in the context of all the circumstances of the case, unless the parties have agreed that the Tribunal Appointed expert's determination shall be conclusive in respect of any specific issue. **30.6:** The fees and expenses of any expert appointed by the Tribunal under this Article shall be paid out by the parties in accordance with the Appendix-Cost of Arbitration.

Name of Rules	Clause	Summary of Rules
CIETAC Arbitration Rules (May 1, 2012)	Article 42 (Expert's Report and Appraiser's Report)	**42.1:** The arbitral tribunal may consult experts or appoint appraisers for clarification on specific issues of the case. Such an expert or appraiser may be a Chinese or foreign institution or natural person. **42.2:** The arbitral tribunal has the power to request the parties, and the parties are also obliged, to deliver or produce to the expert or appraiser any relevant materials, documents, property, or goods for checking, inspection or appraisal by the expert or appraiser. **42.3:** Copies of the expert's report and the appraiser's report shall be communicated to the parties for their comments. At the request of either party and with the approval of the arbitral tribunal, the expert or appraiser shall participate in an oral hearing and give explanations on the report when the arbitral tribunal considers it necessary.
ICSID Convention, Regulations and Rules (April 10, 2006)	Rule 28 (Witnesses and Experts) & Rule 32 (The Oral Procedure) & Rule 35 & Rule 36 (Witnesses and Experts: Special Rules)	**28.1:** Each party may, at any stage of the proceeding, request that the Commission hear the witnesses and experts whose evidence the party considers relevant. The Commission shall fix a time limit within which such hearing shall take place. **28.2:** Witnesses and experts shall, as a rule, be examined before the Commission by the parties under the control of its President. Questions may also be put to them by any member of the Commission. **28.3:** If a witness or expert is unable to appear before it, the Commission, in agreement with the parties, may make appropriate arrangements for the evidence to be given in a written deposition or to be taken by examination elsewhere. The parties may participate in any such examination. **32.1:** The oral procedure shall consist of the hearing by the Tribunal of the parties, their agents, counsel and advocates, and of witnesses and experts. **35.1:** Witnesses and experts shall be examined before the Tribunal by the parties under the control of its President. Questions may also be put to them by any member of the Tribunal. **35.3:** Each expert shall make the following declaration before making his statement: "I solemnly declare upon my honour and conscience that my statement will be in accordance with my sincere belief." Notwithstanding Rule 35 the Tribunal may: **36(a):** admit evidence given by a witness or expert in a written deposition; and **36(b):** with the consent of both parties, arrange for the examination of a witness or expert otherwise than before the Tribunal itself. The Tribunal shall define the subject of the examination, the time limit, the procedure to be followed and other particulars. The parties may participate in the examination.

Name of Rules	Clause	Summary of Rules
IBA Rules on the Taking of Evidence in International Arbitration (May 29, 2010)	Article 5 (Party Appointed Experts) & Article 6 (Tribunal-Appointed Experts)	**5.1:** A party may rely on an expert as a means of evidence on a specific issue. Party must identify any expert it intends to rely on, and the expert must submit a report.
		5.2: Expert report must contain: name/address of expert with statement of any past relation to parties or Tribunal as well as summary of qualifications; description of instructions pursuant to which expert is providing opinions/conclusions; statement of facts upon which expert opinion is based; description of methods, evidence, and information used.
		5.3: If expert reports are submitted, any party may submit revised or additional expert reports, including use of non-previously identified experts so long as response is to matters contained within another party's expert's statements or reports.
		5.4: Tribunal may order any party's experts to meet and confer on the issues, recording in writing areas of agreement and disagreement.
		5.5: If a party-appointed expert fails to appear for the hearing, his or her report shall be disregarded.
		6.1: Tribunal may appoint an expert(s) to report on specific issues; report shall be provided to the parties.
		6.2: Before expert accepts appointment, they will submit description of qualifications and statement of independence to the parties.
		6.3: Parties shall provide to expert(s) access to any relevant documents or property; experts shall make note of any non-compliance.
		6.4: Expert shall provide a report containing: name/address of expert with description of their background/qualifications; statement of facts opinion is based upon; expert's opinion, including providing any document relied upon not previously produced.
		6.5: Tribunal shall provide expert report to the parties, and the parties have opportunity to review any document or property used in report.
		6.6: Tribunal and/or parties may request the expert to appear at a hearing where they can pose questions to the expert.
		6.7: A report by a Tribunal-appointed expert shall be assessed by the Tribunal with due regard to all circumstances of the case.
		6.8: Fees/costs from a Tribunal-appointed expert shall form part of the costs of the arbitration.

Name of Rules	Clause	Summary of Rules
UNICITRAL Arbitration Rules (2010)	Article 28 (Hearings) & Article 29 (Experts appointed by the arbitral tribunal)	**28.2:** Witnesses, including expert witnesses, may be heard under the conditions and examined in the manner set by the arbitral tribunal.
		29.1: Tribunal may appoint an independent expert(s) to offer report on specific issues determined by tribunal. A copy of the expert's terms of reference, established by the arbitral tribunal, shall be communicated to the parties.
		29.2: Expert shall provide a description of qualifications and statement of independence before accepting appointment; parties may object with tribunal deciding whether or not to take action.
		29.3: The parties shall give the expert any relevant information or produce for his or her inspection any relevant documents or goods that he or she may require of them. Any dispute between a party and such expert as to the relevance of the required information or production shall be referred to the arbitral tribunal for decision.
		29.4: Upon receipt of the expert's report, the arbitral tribunal shall communicate a copy of the report to the parties, which shall be given an opportunity to express, in writing, their opinion on the report. A party shall be given the opportunity to examine any document on which the expert has relied in his report.
		29.5: At the request of any party, the expert, after delivery of the report, may be heard at a hearing where the parties shall have the opportunity to be present and to interrogate the expert. At this hearing, any party may present expert witnesses in order to testify on the points at issue.

Annex III: Summary of Valuation Approaches in ICSID Decisions

Name	Region of Dispute	Industry	ICISID number	Outcome of proceeding	Date of Award	Quantification methodology 1 - General	Quantification methodology 2 - Specific	Economic loss as assessed by the Tribunal	Valuation method finally retained
AGIP S.p.A. v. People's Republic of the Congo	Sub-Saharan Africa	Oil & Gas	ARB/77/1	Award	11/30/1979	Income-based approach	DCF	DCF	
Amco Asia Corporation Pan American Development Limited, PT Amco Indonesia v. Republic of Indonesia	Asia	Hotel & Leisure	ARB/81/1	Rejection of both Claimant's and Respondent's Applications for Annulment	6/5/1990	Income-based approach	DCF	Loss of stream of profits generated under the hotel management contract (the business was a going concern)	DCF
Société Ouest Africaine des Bétons Industriels (SOABI) v. Senegal	Sub-Saharan Africa	Cement	ARB/82/1	Award	2/25/1988	Income-based approach	Not based on DCF	1) Loss of the investment 2) Loss of future profits 3) Damages claimed by sub-contractors (architects) Claim for compensation for damages owed to the Chairman of SOABI rejected Claim for 'Moral damages' rejected because such damages are too hypothetical	Out-of-pocket expenses Estimation of future revenues through expected sales Compensatory interest

417

Name	Region of Dispute	Industry	ICISID number	Outcome of proceeding	Date of Award	Quantification methodology 1 - General	Quantification methodology 2 - Specific	Economic loss as assessed by the Tribunal	Valuation method finally retained
Southern Pacific Properties (Middle East) Ltd v. Republic of Egypt	North Africa & the Middle East	Hotel & Leisure	ARB/84/3	Settlement	5/20/1992	1) Income-based approach 2) Cost-based approach	DCF No value determination	Loss of a share in a business	Out-of-pocket expenses
Asian Agricultural Products Ltd v. Republic of Sri Lanka	Asia	Agricultural Products & Equipment	ARB/87/3	Award	6/27/1990	Income-based approach	DCF	Loss of the investment. Claim for loss of 'goodwill' rejected because doubtful. Claim for loss of future profits rejected due to lack of evidence	A reasonable price a willing buyer would pay for the shareholding, determined on the basis of the value of the company's tangible assets less global liabilities
American Manufacturing & Trading Inc v. Republic of Zaire	Sub-Saharan Africa	Manufacturing	ARB/93/1	Settlement	2/21/1997	Not explicitly mentioned		Destruction and damage to the company's property. Closure of the business	FMV of the damaged property assessed on the basis of an expert report. This report is not publicly available
Compañía del Desarollo de Santa Elena SA v. The Republic of Costa Rica	Latin America	Hotel & Leisure	ARB/96/1	Award	2/17/2000	Asset-based approach	FMV of property	Loss of property	FMV of the property
Fedax N.V. v. Republic of Venezuela	Latin America	Banking, Insurance & Finance	ARB/96/3	Award	3/9/1988	Asset-based approach		1) the principal of each of the six promissory notes subject matter of its claim, 2) regular interest on five of such promissory notes, 3) penal interest from the dates of maturity on all six such promissory notes.	Due amount and interest

Name	Region of Dispute	Industry	ICSID number	Outcome of proceeding	Date of Award	Quantification methodology 1 - General	Quantification methodology 2 - Specific	Economic loss as assessed by the Tribunal	Valuation method finally retained
Metalclad Corporation v. The United Mexican States	Latin America	Waste Management	ARB(AF)/97/1	Award	8/30/2000	1) Income-based approach 2) Asset-based approach - investment costs	DCF	Loss of the planned waste landfill business, resulting in a complete loss of investment Claim for lost profits rejected because the landfill had never started its operations Claim for 'negative impact on other business operations' rejected due to lack of evidence	Actual investment method
Compañía de aguas del Aconquija (CAA) SA and Vivendi Universal SA v. Argentine Republic	Latin America	Infrastructure (Water and Sewers)	ARB/97/3	Award	8/15/2007	Income-based approach	DCF	Loss of the concession	Actual investment method
Emilio Agustin Maffezini v. The Kingdom of Spain	Western Europe	Construction	ARB/97/7	Award	11/13/2000	Not explicitly mentioned		Loss of the amount irregularly transferred from the investor's account	Compensation equal to the amount irregularly transferred
Wena Hotels Ltd v. Arab Republic of Egypt	North Africa & the Middle East	Hotel & Leisure	ARB/98/4	Award	12/8/2000	1) Income-based approach 2) Cost-based approach	DCF No value determination	Loss of the investment (invested capital and ability to pursue the hotel business to gain profits)	Actual investment method
Marvin Feldman v. Mexico	Latin America	Agricultural Products & Equipment	ARB(AF)/99/1	Award	12/16/2002	Income-based approach	DCF	Amounts of unpaid tax rebates Claim for lost investment rejected because no finding of expropriation Claim for lost profits rejected because the Tribunal was not convinced that CEMSA's operations would have been profitable	Tax rebates due

Name	Region of Dispute	Industry	ICISID number	Outcome of proceeding	Date of Award	Quantification methodology 1 - General	Quantification methodology 2 - Specific	Economic loss as assessed by the Tribunal	Valuation method finally retained
Middle East Cement Shipping and Handling Co. SA v. Arab Republic of Egypt	North Africa & the Middle East	Cement	ARB/99/6	Award	4/12/2002	Not explicitly mentioned		Loss of future profits / The value of the seized and auctioned ship	Concluded contracts' future revenue / Book value
Autopista Concesionada de Venezuela C.A (Aucoven) v. Bolivarian Republic of Venezuela	Latin America	Infrastructure (Road)	ARB/00/5	Award	9/23/2003	1) Income-based approach 2) Cost-based approach	DCF / No value determination	Out-of-pocket expenses ('sunk' investment) / Claim for lost profits rejected because the Claimant did not prove the amount of its loss to sufficient certainty	Out-of-pocket expenses
Tecnicas Medioambientales Tecmed SA v. The United Mexican States	Latin America	Waste Management	ARB(AF)/00/2	Award	5/29/2003	Income-based approach	DCF	Loss of the investment / Loss of the business ('going concern' with 2 years of operation) / No compensation for moral damage due to lack of evidence	Actual investment method
MTD Equity Sdn. Bhd. And MTD Chile SA v. Republic of Chile	Latin America	Real Estate Development	ARB/01/7	Award	5/25/2004	Cost-based approach	No value determination	Money invested in the project	Out-of-pocket expenses
CMS Gas Transmission Company v. The Argentine Republic	Latin America	Oil & Gas	ARB/01/8	Award	5/12/2005	Income-based approach	DCF	Loss in the value of the shareholding / Loss of revenue due to the abolition of tariff adjustments	DCF

Name	Region of Dispute	Industry	ICISID number	Outcome of proceeding	Date of Award	Quantification methodology 1 - General	Quantification methodology 2 - Specific	Economic loss as assessed by the Tribunal	Valuation method finally retained
Azurix Corp v. The Argentine Republic	Latin America	Infrastructure (Water and Sewers)	ARB/01/12	Award	7/14/2006	1) Asset-based Approach 2) Book value		Loss of business based on the concession contract Compensation for: - loss of investment (price paid for the Concession and additional investments), - arbitral proceedings costs. Claim for unpaid bills rejected because the claimed amount was owed by the Argentinean Province to the Claimant's subsidiary and therefore should not be part of the compensation awarded to the Claimant Claim for the reimbursement of negotiation costs rejected due to lack of evidence	Actual investment method
PSEG Global Inc and Konya Ilgin Elektrik Uretim ve Ticaret Limited Sirketi v. Republic of Turkey	North Africa & the Middle East	Energy & Power (Electric)	ARB/02/5	Award	1/19/2007	1) Asset-based approach 2) Income-based approach; 3) Opportunity costs.	FMV of expropriated property DCF	Investment expenses	Out-of-pocket expenses

Name	Region of Dispute	Industry	ICISID number	Outcome of proceeding	Date of Award	Quantification methodology 1 - General	Quantification methodology 2 - Specific	Economic loss as assessed by the Tribunal	Valuation method finally retained
Siemens A.G. v. The Argentine Republic	Latin America	Government Services	ARB/02/8	Settlement	2/6/2007	1) Asset-based approach; 2) Income-based approach; 3) Post-expropriation costs; 4) Outstanding receivables; 5) Return on the performance bond.	Book value of investment DCF	Total loss of the investment's value. Claim for lost profit rejected due to the uncertainty of the project's profitability	Book value
CDC Group plc v. Republic of Seychelles	Sub-Saharan Africa	Banking, Insurance & Finance	ARB/02/14	Award	12/17/2003	Asset-based approach		Compensation for: - The unpaid principal, - Interest, - Arbitration costs	Due amount and interest
ADC Affiliate Limited and ADC & ADMC Management Limited v. The Republic of Hungary	Latin America	Infrastructure (Airport)	ARB/03/16	Award	10/2/2006	Income-based approach	DCF	Loss of the contract-based business	DCF
OKO Pankki Oyj and others v. Republic of Estonia	Eastern Europe & the CIS	Banking, Insurance & Finance	ARB/04/6	Award	11/19/2007	Asset-based approach	Book value of investment	The total unrecovered investment (the loan) assessed at the time of the Payment Agreement, with interest	Due amount and interest
Gemplus, S.A. and Talsud S.A. v. United Mexican States	Latin America	Government Services	ARB(AF)/04/3	Award	6/16/2010	Income-based approach	DCF	Lost value of the Claimants' shares in the Concessionaire	Hypothetical price agreed by hypothetical buyer and seller
Talsud, S.A. v. United Mexican States	Latin America	Government Services	ARB(AF)/04/4	Award	6/16/2010	Income-based approach	DCF	Lost value of the Claimants' shares in the Concessionaire	

Name	Region of Dispute	Industry	ICISID number	Outcome of proceeding	Date of Award	Quantification methodology 1 - General	Quantification methodology 2 - Specific	Economic loss as assessed by the Tribunal	Valuation method finally retained
Archer Daniels Midland Company and Tate & Lyle Ingredients Americas, Inc. v. United Mexican States	Latin America	Food & Beverage	ARB(AF)/04/5	Award	11/21/2007	Not explicitly mentioned		Assume lost profits was accepted since the Tribunal awarded damages based on Claimant's calculations, however this section of the award has been redacted	
Duke Energy Electroquil Partners and Electroquil S.A. v. Republic of Ecuador	Latin America	Energy & Power (Electric)	ARB/04/19	Award	8/18/2008	Cost-based approach	No value determination	Losses caused to Electroquil due to breaches	Losses due to breaches
Waguih Elie George Siag and Clorinda Vecchi v. Arab Republic of Egypt	North Africa & the Middle East	Hotel & Leisure	ARB/05/15	Award	6/1/2009	1) Market-based approach; 2) Asset-based approach; 3) Income-based approach.	Comparable sales valuation / Residual land valuation / DCF	Claimant was permanently deprived of a valuable investment	The comparables valuation
Cargill, Incorporated v. United Mexican States	Latin America	Agricultural Products & Equipment	ARB(AF)/05/2	Award	9/18/2009	Not explicitly mentioned	DCF	The present value of the net lost cash flows	DCF

Name	Region of Dispute	Industry	ICISID number	Outcome of proceeding	Date of Award	Quantification methodology 1 - General	Quantification methodology 2 - Specific	Economic loss as assessed by the Tribunal	Valuation method finally retained
Desert Line Projects LLC v. Republic of Yemen	North Africa & the Middle East	Infrastructure (Road)	ARB/05/17	Award	2/6/2008	Cost-based approach	No value determination	Claims accepted: **1)** Non-payment of the work actually executed under the Contracts **5)** Moral damages including loss of reputation Claims rejected: **2)** The late release by the Respondent of the Claimant's bank guarantees **3)** The deprivation of the Claimant's rights over the management, use, enjoyment and transfer of its machinery, equipment and vehicles **4)** Loss of business opportunities	Amount outstanding under a previous Award
Ioan Micula, Viorel Micula and others v. Romania	Eastern Europe & the CIS	Food & Beverage	ARB/05/20	Award	12/11/2013	1) Income-based approach 2) Cost-based approach		3-1 Tribunal partly accepted claim for lost profits related to sales of finished goods. 3-2 Tribunal rejected claim for lost profits related to sales of sugar-containing products to industrial users (page 286). This claim was deemed too speculative. 3-3 Tribunal rejected claim for lost profits related to incremental investments	Lost Profits however on the basis only of those with an established track record.
Joseph C. Lemire v. Ukraine	Eastern Europe & the CIS	Telecom & Media	ARB/06/18	Award	3/28/2011	Income-based approach	DCF EBITDA multiple	Violation of the Fair and Equitable Treatment of the BIT	DCF

Name	Region of Dispute	Industry	ICISID number	Outcome of proceeding	Date of Award	Quantification methodology 1 - General	Quantification methodology 2 - Specific	Economic loss as assessed by the Tribunal	Valuation method finally retained
Alpha Projektholding GmbH v. Ukraine	Eastern Europe & the CIS	Hotel & Leisure	ARB/07/16	Award	10/20/2010	1) Income-based approach - DCF 2) Sum of due payments and expected payments 3) Estimation of the expropriated going concern value	DCF	1) 'Historical losses' (the outstanding payments) 2) ' Foregone income' (the total income Claimant would have received under JJAs) 3) 'Terminal value of the joint activity' (the estimate of half of the going concern value)	DCF analysis to calculate the Net Present Value of outstanding and expected payments Sum of due payments and expected payments Estimation of the expropriated going concern value
Burimi SRL and Eagle Games SH.A v. Republic of Albania	Eastern Europe & the CIS	Hotel & Leisure	ARB/11/18	Award	5/29/2013	Not explicitly mentioned		N/A	N/A

Name	Region of Dispute	Industry	ICISID number	Outcome of proceeding	Date of Award	Quantification methodology 1 - General	Quantification methodology 2 - Specific	Economic loss as assessed by the Tribunal	Valuation method finally retained
Mr. Franck Charles Arif v. Republic of Moldova	Eastern Europe & the CIS	Retail	ARB/11/23	Award	4/8/2013	1) Income-based approach - DCF 2) Cost-based approach	DCF Wasted costs - no value determination	MDL 35,136,294	The Tribunal accepts the accuracy of the records on which the claimant calculated his wasted costs figures. The evidence regarding stock in the airport store is not entirely satisfactory as it is clear that some will be sold in future, but not all, so an amount for stock should be included in the wasted cost calculation, but the actual amount remains uncertain. In these circumstances the Tribunal accepts a 20% reduction in the claimant's figure as an acceptable adjustment.
Enron Corporation and Ponderosa Assets L.P. v. The Republic of Argentina	Latin America	Oil & Gas	ARB/01/3	Award annulled, now resubmitted	5/22/2007	Income-based approach	DCF	Loss in the value of the shareholding Loss of revenue due to the abolition of tariff adjustments	DCF

Name	Region of Dispute	Industry	ICISID number	Outcome of proceeding	Date of Award	Quantification methodology 1 - General	Quantification methodology 2 - Specific	Economic loss as assessed by the Tribunal	Valuation method finally retained
LG&E Energy Corp, LG&E Capital Corp, LG&E International Inc v. Argentine Republic	Latin America	Oil & Gas	ARB/02/1	Award, annulment pending	7/25/2007	FMV calculation based on stock prices		Refusal to compensate for future damages because the continuous breach is 'uncertain' Refusal to make an incentive to Argentina because it would result in an undue interference with sovereignty Equitable allocation of the costs of arbitration because not all Claimants' claims are successful and some Respondent's defences prevail Compensation defined as: The dividends that would have been received by the shareholders but for the breaches	"Damages-in-arrears" approach
Sempra Energy International v. Argentine Republic	Latin America	Energy & Power (Electric)	ARB/02/16	Award annulled	9/28/2007	Income-based approach		Decrease in the market value of share as a result of breaches Partial loss of a loan extended to the subsidiaries Unpaid subsidies Damage suffered due to suspension of the PII adjustments	DCF

Name	Region of Dispute	Industry	ICISID number	Outcome of proceeding	Date of Award	Quantification methodology 1 - General	Quantification methodology 2 - Specific	Economic loss as assessed by the Tribunal	Valuation method finally retained
EDF International S.A., SAUR International S.A. and León Participaciones Argentinas S.A. v. Argentine Republic	Latin America	Energy & Power (Electric)	ARB/03/23	Award, annulment pending	6/11/2012	Income-based approach	DCF	The Pre-Emergency Measures affecting the Concession contravened explicit and important rights granted by Respondent to Claimants as an inducement to invest. The Renegotiation Process was conducted in such a way that Claimants were left little alternative but to mitigate their losses by selling their investment to a local buyer. Only after the 2005 sale was the originally-promised economic equilibrium restored, even though during the intervening period the Provincial Emergency Law explicitly obligated EDEMSA to continue complying fully with the Concession Agreement, thus further exacerbating its financial plight and creating a markedly unfair asymmetrical relationship.	DCF
Impregilo S.p.A. v. Argentine Republic	Latin America	Infrastructure (Water and Sewers)	ARB/07/17	Award, annulment pending	6/21/2011	Combination of: 1) Asset-based method assigned a weight of 1/3 to calculate FMV of investment 2) Income-based method assigned a weight of 2/3 to calculate FMV of investment		Loss that may may result from the denial of 'Fair and Equitable treatment' This loss does not correspond to the complete value of the Concession because the failure is partly due to Claimant's risk taking	Capital contribution

Annex IV: Spreadsheet for Joint Expert Meetings

Category	Issue	Claimant Expert	Respondent Expert	Agreement or Disagreement	Reason for Agreement/ Disagreement
Valuation Date	Date of alleged taking or current date of report.	2007 as advised by counsel.	2009 as advised by counsel.	Not Applicable	This is a factual issue that neither the Claimant Expert nor the Respondent Expert offers an opinion on.
Cost Method of Valuation	Applicability	FMV based on the cost approach, based on the assumptions stated in paragraph 101 of the Claimant Expert report.	FMV based on the cost approach, based on the following assumptions: 1) A development license would be granted and that commerciality would be achieved; 2) Expert A's estimates of production would be realized; and, 3) Contract X supply could be used to feed the Plant.	Disagree	Methodological difference.
Market Method of Valuation	Applicability	The Claimant Expert has reviewed comparable companies and transactions to assess the reasonability of the range of values estimated for the Project. The comparable companies approach resulted in an estimated value for the Project of $500 million and the comparable transactions approach resulted in an estimated value for the Project of $600 million.	The Respondent Expert does not comment on the comparable companies and transactions assessed by the Claimant Expert.	Disagree	Methodological difference.
Discounted Cash Flow Method of Valuation	Applicability and sufficiency of information to enable construction of a meaningful future cash flow model.	Claimant Expert has assumed Contract X supply cannot be obtained and a cash flow model is not applicable.	Respondent Expert has assumed Contract X supply will be used to allow for commercial viability of the Project and as such has performed a DCF valuation approach in accordance with paragraph 56 of the Respondent Expert Report.	Disagree	Methodological difference.

429

Category	Issue	Claimant Expert	Respondent Expert	Agreement or Disagreement	Reason for Agreement/ Disagreement
WACC	Relevant discount factor	Real WACC assuming: 1) Capital structure based on historical debt/equity ratios; and, 2) Tax rate of 40%.	Real WACC assuming: 1) Capital structure based on optimal debt/equity ratios; and, 2) Tax rate of 40%.	Disagree	Difference in the assumption of the appropriate capital structure.
Cost of Equity	Relevant discount factor	Cost of Equity is calculated by assuming: 1) Risk free rate of borrowing of 6%; 2) Beta factor assuming the theory that the beta of a company will eventually revert to the beta of the market, which is 1; 3) Equity risk premium based on the arithmetic average of returns between 1926 to 2010; and, 4) A country risk premium of 3%.	Cost of Equity is calculated by assuming: 1) Risk free rate of borrowing of 6%; 2) Beta factor based on comparable companies in the same industry; 3) Equity risk premium based on the geometric average of returns between 1980 to 2010; and, 4) A country risk premium of 6%.	Disagree	Methodological difference.
Pre-Judgement Interest rate	WACC versus cost of debt.	Claimant Expert has assumed the prejudgment interest should be based on WACC, as the cash flow foregone could have been invested into other projects that the Company was pursuing.	Claimant Expert has assumed the prejudgment interest should be based on the cost of debt; absent the incident the Company would have drawn a correspondingly lower amount from its debt facility.	Disagree	Methodological difference.
Cost of Debt	Relevant discount factor	Cost of Debt is calculated in accordance with Debt Contract XY.	Cost of Debt is calculated in accordance with Debt Contract XY.	Agree	
Future Price Curve	Futures price cruve.	2007 futures price for commodity Y.	2009 futures price for commodity Y.	Agree	Same methodology, differences in values are based on differences in valuation date.
Taxation	Applicable tax rate.	Conclusions are presented on an after-tax basis and that an additional gross up of damages may be required if taxes are levied on the damages.	Conclusions are presented on an after-tax basis.	Agree	
Inflation	Applicable inflation factor.	Inflation factor is based on the cumulative monthly inflation adjustment from the month immediately after the date of the valuation.	Inflation factor is based on the cumulative monthly inflation adjustment from the month immediately after the date of the valuation.	Agree	Same methodology, differences in values are based on differences in valuation date.

A. Precision Stream

4. Treaty Arbitration: Pleading and Proof of Fraud and Comparable forms of Abuse

Introduction to the Session
Treaty Arbitration: Pleading and Proof of Fraud and Comparable Forms of Abuse

*Klaus Reichert SC**

This short and decidedly personal introduction was written in rural Bavaria some four months after the conclusion of the ICCA 2014 Congress in Miami and just over two years from a conversation in Dallas with the then-newly-appointed chair of the programme committee, Lucy Reed. That conversation touched upon the issue of precision, particularly when it came to the making of serious allegations in treaty arbitration. What were the myths, legends, and granular realities in treaty arbitration of fraud, misrepresentation, corruption, abuse of rights and so on and so forth; hence the session in Miami on just these issues.

These two rather disparate places, a Tex-Mex restaurant[1] and a rural Bavarian retreat,[2] bookend a particularly privileged time for the author in two respects as regards this topic.

First, there was the privilege of chairing an exceptional panel of speakers, particularly the authors of the major Congress Paper, Louie Llamzon and Anthony Sinclair, combined with the observations of Carolyn Lamm and Utku Coşar. This resulted in a traditional ICCA format which has yielded a set of written papers and research for the ages.

Secondly, in the many months between the Dallas conversation and the Miami Congress, the opportunity arose to gauge views from an exceptionally wide group of practitioners with an eye ahead to the discussions and debate. This was not simply the usual arbitration chit-chat, but a constant engagement with these troublesome issues. It became obvious rather quickly that the overall topic was one which energetically captured practitioners' attention.

Conversation topics included many of the following points. What exactly does fraud mean in a treaty arbitration context? What does "in accordance with the [whatever host state one might care to mention] law" involve? Does corruption abound? Is arbitration soft on corruption? How does one go about proving these matters? Quite apart from these points, there was the debate about jurisdiction, admissibility, merits and so on, and where such arguments might properly fit into the overall context of a case.

Unlike almost any other substantive issue which falls to be resolved by arbitration, investor-state matters engage a granular discussion amongst practitioners with extraordinary energy and remarkable diversity of views. Could one really imagine many

---

* Panel Chair at Precision Panel A4 at the 22nd International Council for Commercial Arbitration (ICCA) Congress in Miami, 6-9 April 2014; Senior Counsel with Brick Court Chambers, London, UK.
1. MiCocina.
2. Schloss Elmau.

thousands of delegates packing a room (or the blogosphere) to discuss a knotty issue of English law on the interpretation of contracts, namely what is the "admissible background common to both parties at the time of the making of the agreement"? Undoubtedly not, even though that precise question is a potentially challenging one for the vast array of cases conducted internationally each year under English law. However, the relatively small number of treaty cases begets a global discussion with each award minutely pored over and parsed for what it might or might not say.

Depending on with whom one was talking, issues like "in accordance with the law" could mean many things. For some, this meant almost any transgression (perhaps, because of a particular philosophical view, or a practice on the defence side); or for others nothing would suffice short the CEO of the investor photographed handing over a large bag with a Dollar symbol on its side to the President-for-Life of the host country on the day of the awarding of the concession – and even then there would have to be compelling proof of the contents of the bag.

Similarly with fair and equitable treatment; for some this means state responsibility for almost anything which displeases the investor, and for others the phrase is simply a nice collection of words designed to make everyone feel better, but with no real teeth.

Ultimately, for the arbitrator and for counsel, these are substantive issues. In fact, if these cases were determined by national courts one might probably see the same issues being debated. However, what is inextricably related to the process of arbitration and one of the most challenging issues to pin down with any degree of certainty, is the applicable standard of proof when such allegations are made.

What constitutes proof, as discussed thoroughly in the "A1" session in Miami (insofar as commercial arbitration was concerned), is a classic instance of a division between the common law and civil law communities. However, that difference or division may be more apparent than real to those who are working on a daily basis in the field. That, though, is of little comfort to a wider and thorough scrutiny of the issue (the old maxim of *I cannot describe an elephant, but I know one when I see one* springs to mind) and also for the purposes of making practice and theory thoroughly accessible and transparent to all.

Immediately prior to writing this introduction, the author had cause to read an English case from an entirely different area of the law. The analysis of standard of proof makes for compelling reading and is now offered up as providing useful and flexible (as we all know, flexibility is (dare one say) akin to a sacred canon which must be adhered to at all times in international arbitration) approach which may well work in the international context. We should not be hesitant to look beyond our world and take note of legal analysis of the first rank in other fields.

The opinion[3] of Lord Carswell (Lords Scott and Bingham concurring – a demonstration of the significant judicial weight behind the opinion) in a House of Lords appeal from the Court of Appeal in Northern Ireland concerned issues as regards whether or not a prisoner would be likely to commit certain particularly serious offences if released early. The analysis in the opinion on the subject of standard of proof is set out below in full as to extrapolate a summary would do a disservice to Lord Carswell, and also to the reader (though for present purposes certain passages have been emphasized):

---

3. *In re CD* [2008] UKHL 33.

"22. I turn then to the main subject of the appeal before the House, the standard of proof applicable in a case such as the present. The Court of Appeal said in terms in the passages which I have quoted from its judgment that the 'flexible approach to the civil standard of proof' required 'more cogent evidence than would be conventionally required' and that 'a more compelling quality of evidence' was needed. It was submitted by Mr Larkin QC on behalf of the appellants that this was a misunderstanding of the principles, which have now been settled if they were at any time in doubt, applying to the standard of proof.

23. Much judicial time has been spent in the last 50 or 60 years in attempts to explain what is required by way of proof of facts for a court or tribunal to reach the proper conclusion. It is indisputable that only two standards are recognised by the common law, proof on the balance of probabilities and proof beyond reasonable doubt. The latter standard is that required by the criminal law and in such areas of dispute as contempt of court or disciplinary proceedings brought against members of a profession. The former is the general standard applicable to all other civil proceedings and means simply, as Lord Nicholls of Birkenhead said in *In re H (Minors) (Sexual Abuse: Standard of Proof)* [1996] AC 563, 586, that

'*a court is satisfied an event occurred if the court considers that, on the evidence, the occurrence of the event was more likely than not.*'

24. Any confusion which has crept into the application of this principle appears to have stemmed from statements made in a number of earlier cases, which may have been misunderstood but certainly have not always been applied correctly. The earliest example appears to be *Bater v. Bater* [1951] P 35, 37, in which Denning LJ referred to the necessity in the proof of fraud or some allegations requiring proof in a divorce case for 'a higher degree of probability', not as high as in a criminal court but a degree of probability which is commensurate with the occasion. It is apparent from what Morris LJ said in *Hornal v. Neuberger Products Ltd* [1957] 1 QB 247, when quoting this statement, that he did not regard it as laying down a more exacting standard than the balance of probabilities. He said at page 266:

'Though no court and no jury would give less careful attention to issues lacking gravity than to those marked by it, the very elements of gravity become a part of the whole range of circumstances which have to be weighed in the scale when deciding as to the balance of probabilities.'

25. The phrase 'degree of probability' was picked up and repeated in a number of subsequent cases - see, for example, *In re Dellow's Will Trusts* [1964] 1 WLR 451, 455, *Blyth v. Blyth* [1966] AC 643, 669 and *R v. Secretary of State for the Home Department, Ex p Khawaja* [1984] AC 74, 113-114 – and may have caused some courts to conclude that a different standard of proof from the balance of probabilities or a higher standard of evidence was required in some cases. In so far as such misunderstanding has occurred, it should have been put to rest by the frequently-cited remarks of Lord Nicholls of Birkenhead in *In re H (Minors)*.

Immediately after the passage which I have quoted from his opinion, he went on at pages 586-587:

'When assessing the probabilities the court will have in mind as a factor, to whatever extent is appropriate in the particular case, that the more serious the allegation the less likely it is that the event occurred and, hence, the stronger should be the evidence before the court concludes that the allegation is established on the balance of probability. Fraud is usually less likely than negligence. Deliberate physical injury is usually less likely than accidental physical injury. A stepfather is usually less likely to have repeatedly raped and had non consensual oral sex with his under age stepdaughter than on some occasion to have lost his temper and slapped her. Built into the preponderance of probability standard is a generous degree of flexibility in respect of the seriousness of the allegation.

Although the result is much the same, this does not mean that where a serious allegation is in issue the standard of proof required is higher. It means only that the inherent probability or improbability of an event is itself a matter to be taken into account when weighing the probabilities and deciding whether, on balance, the event occurred. The more improbable the event, the stronger must be the evidence that it did occur before, on the balance of probability, its occurrence will be established ... No doubt it is this feeling which prompts judicial comment from time to time that grave issues call for proof to a standard higher than the preponderance of probability.'

26. If any further clarification were required, it was provided by Lord Hoffmann in *Secretary of State for the Home Department v. Rehman* [2001] UKHL 47, [2003] 1 AC 153, where the Special Immigration Appeals Commission had held that the Secretary of State had not established to a high degree of probability that the applicant, who was the subject of a deportation order, was likely to be a threat to national security. The House of Lords held that where past acts were relied on they should be proved to the civil standard of proof. Lord Hoffmann said at paragraph 55:

'I turn next to the commission's views on the standard of proof. By way of preliminary I feel bound to say that I think that a 'high civil balance of probabilities' is an unfortunate mixed metaphor. The civil standard of proof always means more likely than not. The only higher degree of probability required by the law is the criminal standard. But, as Lord Nicholls of Birkenhead explained in *In re H (Minors)(Sexual Abuse: Standard of Proof)* [1996] AC 563, 586, some things are inherently more likely than others. It would need more cogent evidence to satisfy one that the creature seen walking in Regent's Park was more likely than not to have been a lioness than to be satisfied to the same standard of probability that it was an Alsatian. On this basis, cogent evidence is generally required to satisfy a civil tribunal that a person has been fraudulent or behaved in some other reprehensible manner. But the question is always whether the tribunal thinks it more probable than not.'

Lord Hoffmann recently returned to the topic in *In re B (Children)* [2008] UKHL 35, where, with support from Baroness Hale of Richmond, he reaffirmed in emphatic terms the views which he expressed in *Rehman*.

27. Richards LJ expressed the proposition neatly in R (N) v Mental Health Review Tribunal (Northern Region) [2005] EWCA Civ 1605, [2006] QB 468, 497-8, para. 62, where he said:

'*Although there is a single civil standard of proof on the balance of probabilities, it is flexible in its application. In particular, the more serious the allegation or the more serious the consequences if the allegation is proved, the stronger must be the evidence before a court will find the allegation proved on the balance of probabilities. Thus the flexibility of the standard lies not in any adjustment to the degree of probability required for an allegation to be proved (such that a more serious allegation has to be proved to a higher degree of probability), but in the strength or quality of the evidence that will in practice be required for an allegation to be proved on the balance of probabilities.*'

In my opinion this paragraph effectively states in concise terms the proper state of the law on this topic. I would add one small qualification, which may be no more than an explanation of what Richards LJ meant about the seriousness of the consequences. That factor is relevant to the likelihood or unlikelihood of the allegation being unfounded, as I explain below.
28. It is recognised by these statements that a possible source of confusion is the failure to bear in mind with sufficient clarity the fact that in some contexts a court or tribunal has to look at the facts more critically or more anxiously than in others before it can be satisfied to the requisite standard. The standard itself is, however, finite and unvarying. Situations which make such heightened examination necessary may be the inherent unlikelihood of the occurrence taking place (Lord Hoffmann's example of the animal seen in Regent's Park), the seriousness of the allegation to be proved or, in some cases, the consequences which could follow from acceptance of proof of the relevant fact. The seriousness of the allegation requires no elaboration: a tribunal of fact will look closely into the facts grounding an allegation of fraud before accepting that it has been established. The seriousness of consequences is another facet of the same proposition: if it is alleged that a bank manager has committed a minor peculation, that could entail very serious consequences for his career, so making it the less likely that he would risk doing such a thing. *These are all matters of ordinary experience, requiring the application of good sense on the part of those who have to decide such issues. They do not require a different standard of proof or a specially cogent standard of evidence, merely appropriately careful consideration by the tribunal before it is satisfied of the matter which has to be established.*"

The discussion of the standard of proof is offered to the reader of this ICCA Congress Book as a thorough, yet accessible description of the evidential hurdle which should be overcome by a party wishing to make serious allegations in a treaty arbitration.

We should be on our guard against either making the proof hurdle too high, or lowering it to the level of an ornamental picket fence.

If the standard of proof is too high then almost no serious allegation will ever pass the test and arbitration will truly become a soft touch for any sort of nefarious conduct. If the standard of proof is too low then the flimsiest allegations thrown onto paper with enough vim, vigour, and flowery language will abound even more than already is the case. In this author's opinion, saying that, for example, corruption is difficult to prove therefore we must lower the applicable standard so that corrupt investments are not tolerated, does a disservice to the integrity of due process and is akin to a plea *ad misericordiam*. International arbitration is a flexible process, but flexibility does not mean gullibility when it comes to the rigours of proof.

Finally, the author wishes to express his particular thanks to Elizabeth Karanja, the Rapporteur for this Session at the ICCA Congress for her tireless work.

Report on the Session
Treaty Arbitration: Pleading and Proof of Fraud and Comparable Forms of Abuse

Elizabeth Karanja[*]

I.   INTRODUCTION

The panel comprised Klaus Reichert SC (Chairman), Aloysius Llamzon and Anthony Sinclair (Main Speakers), Carolyn Lamm and Utku Coşar (Commentators), and Elizabeth Karanja (Rapporteur).

For the Congress, Llamzon and Sinclair prepared an in-depth Paper exploring investor wrongdoing (including fraud and corruption) in investment arbitration, entitled: "Investor Wrongdoing in Investment Arbitration: Standards Governing Issues of Corruption, Fraud, Misrepresentation and Other Investor Misconduct" (this volume, pp. 451-530). The detailed paper is set forth in the next section.

Bearing the Paper in mind, five propositions were presented for discussion during the panel session, aimed at determining whether these are myths or realities. The propositions were as follows:

(1) *All investor wrongdoing is the same and it does not matter when it occurs.*
(2) *This is an appropriate maxim for all respondents: throw mud, it may stick, and if it does not, what matter?*
(3) *No one really agrees as to what fraudulent misrepresentation is.*
(4) *The graver the charge, the more confidence there must be in the evidence relied on.*
(5) *Tribunals and counsel are not properly equipped to address the issue of corruption, both as regards expertise, and the tools at their disposal.*

II.   THE PANEL PRESENTATIONS

Llamzon and Sinclair presented the highlights of their Paper. They focused on (i) proposing a coherent typology of the various forms of investor wrongdoing; (ii) evidentiary issues such as the the proper burden and standard of proof for deciding investor wrongdoing; and (iii) the legal principles applicable to the consequences of

---

[*] Panel Rapporteur; Senior Associate at JMiles & Co., Nairobi, Kenya; Panel Rapporteur.

investor wrongdoing. Their presentation was split into two parts: Llamzon presented on the categories of investor wrongdoing and questions of evidence and proof; and Sinclair presented the legal principles that applied to proven investor wrongdoing and the consequences that accrue.

Coşar and Lamm each provided a critical commentary on the paper and presentations of Llamzon and Sinclair, with Coşar focused on corruption (this volume, pp. 531-556) and Lamm focused on fraud and other investor wrongdoing (this volume, pp. 557-573).

1.   Categories of Investor Wrongdoing

Llamzon began by setting out an emerging truth: *Investment arbitration was thought of by many as a system whose scales tilted too heavily in favor of investors. Recent developments have shown, however, that the system is not so one-sided: increasingly, it is the* investor itself *and the* legality of its conduct *that are the subject of intense scrutiny* before *the investor's allegations are decided.*

He noted that at least six forms of investor wrongdoing have been identified in investment arbitration: (1) lack of good faith, (2) corruption, (3) fraud, (4) deceitful conduct, (5) misuse of the system of investment protection and (6) violation of host State law.[1]

Out of these, three distinct species of investor wrongdoing were distilled, namely: (1) Corruption; (2) fraud (more precisely, fraudulent misrepresentation); and (3) other violations of host State laws.[2] Llamzon set out the following rough schematic to help summarize the decision making process that tribunals undertake when deciding issues of investor wrongdoing:

---

1. As noted in *Gustav F. W. Hamester GmbH & Co KG v. Republic of Ghana* (ICSID ARB/07/24), Award, 18 June 2010.
2. Llamzon posited that lack of good faith is insufficiently precise to merit its own category, as its manifestations usually fall within one of the three identified categories. This is also the case with abuse of process.

Category of Wrongdoing   Legal Princples   Consequences

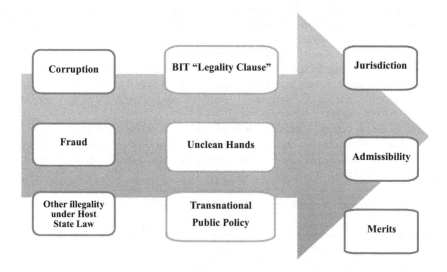

Llamzon differentiated the three types of wrongdoing by focusing on the participants: corruption is bilateral in nature, and requires the free participation of both the investor and public officials of the host State. Fraud occurs unilaterally, as the investor alone makes the misrepresentation with the intent to defraud the State; and for other violations of host State law, even less may be required: for example, misrepresentation alone violates many national procurement laws.

In relation to corruption, Llamzon presented some interesting statistics: the World Bank estimates that US$ 1 Trillion (which equates to 3 per cent of the World's economy) is paid in bribes *annually*. Corruption accounts for up to 10 per cent of the cost of doing business globally and up to 25 per cent of the cost of procurement contracts in developing countries. However, the response in investment arbitration has been anemic. While an allegation or insinuation of corruption was made in about thirty investment cases, there were very few instances where corruption was found. In the only two publicly available cases where positive findings of corruption were made by investment tribunals (*World Duty Free*[3] and *Metal-Tech*[4]), the decisions were arguably made possible only because the investors provided evidence of corruption.

---

3. *World Duty Free Company Limited v. The Republic of Kenya* (ICSID Case No. ARB/00/7), Award, 4 October 2006.
4. *Metal-Tech Ltd. v. Republic of Uzbekistan* (ICSID Case No. ARB/10/3), Award, 4 October 2013.

2.   State Responsibility

According to Llamzon, the bilateral nature of corruption raises the question of whether States should be held responsible under international law for the corrupt conduct of their public officials. There is no easy answer, and although he noted that the issue of State responsibility has not been discussed significantly in ICSID arbitrations, tribunals appear to be uncomfortable to accept a complete lack of State responsibility, and this has principally manifested itself in costs decisions. In *Metal-Tech,* for example, it was decided that because the nature of corruption is that both parties participate, it is fair that the parties share the costs of the arbitration.

The question posed by Llamzon was whether in invoking corruption as a defense, more should be required of States, such as showing that they are prosecuting the errant public official. Should principles of anti-corruption law, estoppel or even elementary fairness demand this?

3.   Proving Investor Wrongdoing – Is It a Mud-Slinging Exercise?

In many instances, claims of corruption may be perceived as a mud-slinging exercise – *throw mud, perhaps it will stick.* Llamzon referred to the case of *Thunderbird,* in which Professor Wälde expressed concerns that insinuations of corruption tend to "colour" the perceptions of arbitrators. Llamzon asked whether insinuations of corruption often affected case outcomes. From his interviews with leading arbitrators, he agreed that insinuations sometimes affect outcomes. That is not to say that arbitrators decide cases on the basis of bare allegations, however. Many corruption allegations appear to have been dealt with by tribunals through their outward manifestations, such as the violation of host State law or abuse of public discretion that was purchased by the bribe, these acts and omissions being easier to prove.

Coşar, in her commentary, noted that corruption is by its very nature difficult to prove, and a respondent's corruption defence may appear as an attempt to throw mud but it may take shape as the case develops. Lamm, in her commentary, noted that claims of fraud must be credible and be supported by evidence.

4.   Proving Investor Wrongdoing – Burden of Proof and Standard of Proof

Corruption is difficult to prove, and other forms of investor wrongdoing less so – many host State laws on investment are violated by mere representations, while fraud requires misrepresentation coupled with an intent to defraud and reliance thereon by the host State. Corruption requires even more, including evidence of a *quid pro quo.* Llamzon likened proving investor wrongdoing to trying to ascend a mountain, except that the mountain is turned upon its head, with the summit at the bottom: decision makers and counsel would see little need to ascend to the "top" (corruption) if proving misrepresentation or fraud leads to the same outcome as a finding of corruption would (i.e., a lack of jurisdiction or inadmissibility of claims). In their study, Llamzon and Sinclair found more instances where fraud and violation of host State law were found, compared to corruption.

In her Commentary, Coşar noted that in investment treaty arbitrations, tribunals generally have wide discretion to determine the applicable burden and standard of proof for corruption. In relation to burden of proof, the generally accepted rule is that each party has the burden of proving the facts on which it relies. There have been suggestions to shift the burden of proof where there is a prima facie indication of corruption, due to the difficulty of uncovering evidence in corruption claims. However, for Coşar this approach is not widely supported.

When it comes to standard of proof in relation to corruption, Llamzon discussed two schools of thought:

(i) One is to adopt a "clear and convincing" evidentiary standard akin to US law, the logic being that serious allegations demand a high standard; and
(ii) The other school adopts the "balance of probabilities" standard, found in civil law tradition as well as English law, with a caveat that because of their improbability, fraud and corruption require a higher degree of confidence or quality in the evidence provided.

Coşar noted that commentators generally support the view that tribunals should adopt the "balance of probabilities" standard in corruption cases. It is only in a few investment cases (such as EDF^5 and $Siag$) where tribunals have adopted the heightened "clear and convincing" standard.

Lamm, in her Commentary relating to fraud, pointed out additional standards of proof, such as: beyond reasonable doubt; preponderance of evidence; and prima facie evidence – direct or circumstantial. While the "balance of probabilities" standard was often used, it was more appropriate for an international tribunal to use a relative standard, as did the tribunal in *Rompetrol v. Romania*.[6]

5. Proving Investor Wrongdoing – Arbitrators' Duty to Investigate Corruption

Llamzon discussed the extent to which arbitrators should pro-actively investigate suspicious facts that suggest corrupt activity, and whether they were sufficiently using the legal tools at their disposal. Some arbitrators have lamented that they have no power of contempt and thus have no ability to subpoena witnesses or documents, unlike in national courts.

Llamzon however noted that arbitrators are not powerless, and tribunals have considerable discretion under the Rules of the International Centre for Settlement of Investment Disputes (ICSID) and the United Nations Commission on International Trade Law (UNCITRAL) to admit and evaluate evidence. Coşar and Lamm agreed with this. Arts. 43-45 of the ICSID Convention and Rule 34 of the ICSID Arbitration Rules allow

---

5. *EDF (Services) v. Romania* (ICSID Case No. ARB/05/13), Award, 8 October 2009.
6. See *Rompetrol v. Romania* (ICSID Case No. ARB/06/3), Award, 6 May 2013, where the tribunal said that, "*[B]y stating the standard of proof as relative, the Tribunal means that whether a proposition has in fact been proved ... depends ... on the overall assessment of the accumulated evidence put forward by one or both parties...*"

tribunals to determine admissibility of evidence, credibility and weight; and produce evidence.

Llamzon pointed out two underutilized tools in cases of wrongdoing: circumstantial evidence and adverse inferences.

a.   Circumstantial evidence

According to Llamzon, this tool involves taking a "connect the dots" approach to the circumstances.[7] NGOs, the World Bank and white collar crime practices often advance "red-flags" of possible corruption. Each individual, proven "red-flag" may be insufficient, but taken together can lead to a fair finding of corruption.

In support of this tool, Coşar noted that due to the nature of corruption, tribunals are often presented only with circumstantial evidence, and a tribunal applying the balance of probabilities standard can fully consider the totality of the evidence and determine whether corruption was *"more likely than not"*. In *Metal-Tech*, the tribunal acknowledged that corruption can be shown through circumstantial evidence.[8]

b.   Adverse inferences

Where one party is in control of documents that can help prove or disprove the allegation, that party can be required to provide such evidence, failing which an adverse inference may be drawn by the Tribunal. On this tool, Coşar pointed out that a tribunal can use its investigatory powers to request additional evidence.

Although the above tools are under-utilized, they were used effectively in the recent *Metal-Tech* case.

6.   The Legal Principles

Sinclair spoke on the legal principles for analyzing investor wrongdoing and sanctioning it where it is found. He noted that although the facts of investor wrongdoing are often murky, the consequences are black and white. In investment arbitration, tribunals have been criticized by some for disproportionately rewarding States in the case of investor wrongdoing. He however warned that equivocation in the face of proven serious investor wrongdoing presented a systemic threat to the future of investment treaty arbitration.

Not all investor wrongdoing is the same, and it matters when it occurs. The question posed by Sinclair was *whether we have the tools by which to test and sanction investor wrongdoing when it is found*. His answer was *yes*, and he identified three legal principles for proving and sanctioning investor wrongdoing: (a) the "in accordance with host State law" clause; (b) the "unclean hands" concept; and (c) transnational public policy.

---

7. This methodology was endorsed in *Methanex v. U.S.* (2005).

8. In *Metal-Tech*, the tribunal demonstrated how circumstantial evidence such as the amount of payments awarded, the qualifications of the alleged consultants, the unsubstantiated nature of services and the consultant's relationship with those in power can be evaluated as a whole.

Coşar noted that where there are allegations of corruption, the tribunal must decide whether it is an issue for jurisdiction, admissibility or merits. The legal consequences could be significant, as issues of merit are in principle not subject to further recourse.[9]

a.   The "in accordance with host State law" clause
Sinclair started with a query as to whether "*in accordance with host state law*" clauses had been misunderstood entirely. Were they more limited in scope as concluded by Professor Douglas in ICSID Review 2014?[10] Douglas, taking inspiration from Cremades' dissenting view in *Fraport AG v. Philipines*,[11] says that such clauses should concern only the conditions upon which a beneficial interest in an asset (i.e. an investment) may be formed or acquired under host State law and that illegality will seldom, if ever, impinge upon the formation of the agreement to arbitrate, which is a matter of separability and competence-competence. Sinclair concluded that these views are not widely accepted. The widely accepted view is that such clauses operate as a limit to a host State's consent to arbitration (hence a jurisdiction issue) and that compliance with host State law is intrinsic to the formation of the arbitration agreement. "In accordance with law" clauses qualify the offer of treaty protection, including the scope of the host State's offer to arbitrate disputes and thereby directly impinge upon the formation of an agreement to arbitrate.

Lamm generally noted that most national legal systems and international investment law condemn the knowing misrepresentation or concealment of a material fact to deceive another to their disadvantage. In *Desert Line v. Yemen*, the tribunal found that "in accordance with law clauses" are intended to insure the legality of the investment by excluding investments in breach of host State law.

Whether a finding of investor wrongdoing is a jurisdictional or admissibility issue will depend on whether the State's consent was in the form of express wording in a treaty or not. Coşar noted that a finding of corruption at the initiation of an investment may be considered as a jurisdictional matter if the underlying treaty contains a host State law clause. So far, denying jurisdiction where an investment was procured by corrupt means has only been based on the explicit provision of a legality clause, as in *Metal-Tech*. She however pointed out that even if a tribunal asserted jurisdiction (where there is no express host State law clause), it may still deny a corrupt investor treaty protections and declare the claim inadmissible based on the principle that "*nobody can benefit from his own wrong*" or on transnational public policy grounds.

---

9. Coşar also pointed out that where corruption is raised as a preliminary objection, or the claims of corruption are distinct from the facts and issues in the merits phase, it is preferable to handle these as preliminary issues for efficiency and judicial economy.
10. See Z. DOUGLAS, *The Plea of Illegality in Investment Treaty Arbitration*, 1 ICSID Review—Foreign Investment Law Journal (2014) p. 5.
11. *Fraport AG v. The Republic of the Philippines* (ICSID Case No. ARB/03/25), Award, 16 August 2007, Dissenting Opinion of Bernardo M. Cremades, paras. 12-14.

In her commentary, Lamm agreed with Coşar insofar as fraud was concerned.[12] According to Lamm, some tribunals conclude that an explicit legality requirement is necessary for legality to be a jurisdictional requirement. However, Art. 31 of the Vienna Convention on the Law of Treaties allows tribunals to conclude that legality is an implicit requirement (express terms are not necessary) and most tribunals have found the legality requirement to be implicit, referring to international public policy.[13]

Sinclair stressed that the timing of the wrongdoing matters and the general view is that "in accordance with host State law" conditions must be satisfied at the initiation of an investment and non-compliance would give rise to jurisdictional issues. Tribunals however do not seem to agree that these clauses also concern the way an investment is carried out (in the duration of the investment).

Sinclair also stressed that the nature of the wrongdoing also matters. The *Quiborax*[14] and *Metal-Tech* tribunals suggest that the "in accordance with law" clause engages laws concerning the admission of foreign investment and extends also to compliance with fundamental principles of host State law concerned with the admission of investments, including fraud. In this regard, Lamm stated that in the wake of BIT withdrawals, one cannot ignore States' significant interest in the legality of investments operated within their territory.

b.   Unclean hands

"*He who comes to equity must come with clean hands.*" Sinclair reckoned that this is a principle that is well established in many national laws, with the effect of barring claims where there has been improper conduct. The wrongful conduct must be willful, involving some element of dishonesty. The concept is less well established in general international law. The International Court of Justice and United Nations Convention on the Law of the Sea (UNCLOS) Annex VII arbitral tribunals have yet to uphold this doctrine. That being said, international investment arbitration seems to be forging its own path and the "unclean hands" concept has been recognized in several cases, including *Inceysa*[15] and *World Duty Free*. In *Plama v. Bulgaria*,[16] the investment was found to have been acquired by deceitful conduct in violation of Bulgarian law, and the tribunal found that to allow it would violate the principle that a claimant should not be able to benefit from its own wrongdoing. Precision is required in defining the necessary connection between the claim, and the investor wrongdoing. There needs to be sufficient proximity.

---

12. In *Anderson v. Costa Rica* the tribunal noted that "*[t]he fact that the Contracting Parties to the Canada-Costa Rica BIT specifically included such a provision [legality with host state law clause] is a clear indication of the importance that they attached to the legality of investments made by investors of the other Party and their intention that their laws with respect to investments be strictly followed*".

13. This was the case in *Plama v. Bulgaria*, *Hamester v. Ghana* and *Phoenix Action v. Czech Republic*.

14. *Quiborax S.A., Non Metallic Minerals S.A. and Allan Fosk Kaplún v. Plurinational State of Bolivia* (ICSID Case No. ARB/06/2), Decision on Jurisdiction, 27 September 2012, para. 266.

15. *Inceysa Vallisoletana v. Republic of El Salvador* (ICSID Case No. ARB/03/26), Award, 2 August 2006.

16. *Plama Consortium Limited v. Bulgaria* (ICSID Case No. ARB/03/24), Award, 27 August 2008.

c. Transnational public policy

Sinclair described "transnational public policy" as referring to fundamental principles of law that are considered to be common among developed legal systems, and to have mandatory application regardless of the chosen applicable law. The notion is recognised in both civil law and common law. Among the categories of investor wrongdoing, the application of transnational public policy for corruption at least is well established.[17]

Sinclair noted that transnational public policy can also stretch to encompass fraud and misrepresentation, as asserted in *Plama*. In agreeing with this, Lamm referred to *Plama* where the tribunal said that "... It would also be contrary to the basic notion of international public policy – that a contract obtained by wrongful means (fraudulent misrepresentation) should not be enforced by a tribunal."

Sinclair concluded by stressing the value of transnational public policy. The principle appears to offer grounds to exclude claims tainted by corruption or fraud notwithstanding provisions under national law limiting consequences to voidability, or even exhibiting tolerance for such practices. It therefore affords a vehicle through which arbitrators can fulfill their perceived wider moral and educative duties.

7.   Sanctions for Investor Wrongdoing

In her commentary, Coşar discussed how an investment tribunal may sanction corruption and other similar investor wrongdoing as follows:

(i) Where there is a finding of corruption or fraud, the tribunal should explicitly condemn such illegality in the award. Although tribunals are not bound by previous decisions, they have significant effect and influence on future cases; and
(ii) Awarding of costs is another important way to sanction wrongdoing. In *Europe Cement*[18] and *Cementownia*[19], the tribunals cited the fraudulent nature of the claims as a basis for awarding full costs. In cases of corruption, which involves representatives of both parties, the award of costs may affect both parties. In *Metal-Tech*, the tribunal held that each party should bear its own costs and share the administrative costs, even though the host State prevailed, based on the fact that the host State participated in creating the situation.

---

17. As applied in cases such as *World Duty Free*.
18. *Europe Cement Investment & Trade S.A. v. Republic of Turkey* (ICSID Case No.ARB(AF)/07/2), Award, 13 August 2009.
19. *Cementownia "NowaHuta" S.A. v. Republic of Turkey* (ICSID Case No. ARB(AF)/06/2), Award, 17 September 2009.

8.   *The Three Canons*

In concluding his discussion on the legal principles to be applied in dealing with investor wrongdoing, Sinclair outlined the paper's proposed three guiding principles (or Canons) to bear in mind in relation to investor wrongdoing in investment arbitration:

Canon 1: The underlying facts matter.
Canon 2: For contract-based investment arbitration, investor wrongdoing is either an admissibility or merits issue.
Canon 3: For treaty-based investment arbitration, investor wrongdoing can be a jurisdiction, admissibility or merits issue.

The audience was encouraged to review the detailed elements of each proposed canon as contained in the paper.

III.   CONCLUSION

The issues discussed in the Panel Session, which are summarized above, are dealt with in more detail in Llamzon's and Sinclair's Paper. Lamm and Coşar have also each prepared more detailed papers on the issues of fraud and corruption respectively, based on their commentaries to the Paper and presentation of Llamzon and Sinclair.

The final part of the Panel Session was interactive and attracted a fair amount of audience reaction. Perhaps the most significant of the audience comments related to Proposition 1: *All Investor wrongdoing is the same and it does not matter when it occurs.* One audience member felt that the distinction between investor wrongdoing at the inception of investment and investor wrongdoing during the course of the investment is an artificial/lawyers' distinction which should not be there. This was an interesting take which was posed to the break-out session for further discussion. Other questions posed related to standard of proof: (i) one audience member queried whether tribunals shouldn't just apply the standard of proof required by the applicable host State law instead of trying to identify their own standard; (b) another question was on the appropriate standard of proof levels that should be applied. It will be interesting to read the report on the proceedings in the Break-out Sessions in relation to these questions (this volume, pp. 901-910).

The conclusions reached by the Panel in the five propositions are as follows:

Proposition	Myth	Reality	Other	Comment
1. All Investor wrongdoing is the same and it does not matter when it occurs.	✓			Investor wrongdoing is not the same. The facts matter enormously, the applicable investment treaty matters (is there a legality clause?), and the timing of wrongdoing matters (if at the outset of an investment, it may be a jurisdictional issue. If in the duration of the investment, it may be an admissibility/merits issue).
2. This is an appropriate maxim for all respondents: throw mud, it may stick, and if it does not, what matter.			✓	Some parties may be guilty of this, but certainly not all. In the case of corruption, even if allegations lack sufficient evidence at the beginning, facts and evidence can emerge as the case develops. A respondent's corruption case may initially appear as an attempt to throw mud but it may develop over the course of the proceedings (e.g. document disclosure). One should consider the difficulty of obtaining evidence of corruption. With regard to fraud, it is generally agreed that the claim must be credible and supported by evidence.
3. No one really agrees as to what fraudulent misrepresentati on is.			✓	There is considerable confusion in the case law equating fraud with misrepresentation. The most cogent decisions are those that inquire beyond "mere" misrepresentation and ask whether the investor knowingly sought to defraud the host State, with the latter acting in reliance on the mispresentation. One must consider the applicable law, be

449

Proposition	Myth	Reality	Other	Comment
				it international law, host state law or other national law.
4. The graver the charge, the more confidence there must be in the evidence relied on.	✓			While many cases endorse a heightened standard (e.g. "clear and convincing" evidence), in corruption and fraud-related claims, the most recent cases suggest greater acceptance of an ordinary standard of proof (i.e., "balance of probabilities").
5. Tribunals and counsel are not properly equipped to address the issue of corruption, both as regards expertise, and the tools at their disposal).	✓			Tribunals have wide discretion and investigatory powers afforded by arbitral procedural rules and have sufficient tools to address the issues of corruption, such as adverse inferences or the use of circumstantial evidence.

Investor Wrongdoing in Investment Arbitration: Standards Governing Issues of Corruption, Fraud, Misrepresentation and Other Investor Misconduct

Aloysius Llamzon* and Anthony Sinclair**

I.   INTRODUCTION AND OVERVIEW

Once thought of as a system whose scales tilted too heavily in favor of investors, the system of international investment arbitration has proven in recent years to be far from one-sided: increasingly, the investor itself, and the legality of its conduct, become the subject of intense scrutiny. It is now common for a tribunal to be faced at the outset with a host State objection that the investor committed bribery or fraud. The impact of proven wrongdoing is often existential to the investor's claim, resulting in a lack of jurisdiction, the inadmissibility of claims, or the avoidance of the investment agreement. For the investor, the practical result is the same: no effective remedy in investment arbitration.

This paper explores and seeks to catalogue the standards that govern the presentation and resolution of serious allegations that may impugn either an investor's claims or the investment itself in investor-state arbitration. How do these issues arise? And how do tribunals address them? Is there a common understanding of the pleading and standards of proof of allegations of corruption, fraud, or the bona fides of an investment? Precise, holistic, and well substantiated answers to these questions are seldom found. The paper seeks to articulate answers to all these questions, based on a review of arbitral practice and commentary to date.

---

*   A.B., J.D. (Ateneo de Manila), LL.M, J.S.D. (Yale); King & Saplding LLP, New York; former Senior Legal Counsel, Permanent Court of Arbitration, The Hague.
** LLB Hons., B.A. (Canterbury, New Zealand), LL.M, Ph.D. (Cambridge); Partner, Quinn Emanuel Urquhart & Sullivan LLP, London.
For their invaluable assistance and insight, the authors would like to thank Jennifer Nettleton, Daniel Litwin, and Philip Devenish, as well as our co-panelists at the 2014 ICCA Congress in Miami: Klaus Reichert SC (Chair), Carolyn Lamm and Utku Cosar (Commentators), and Elizabeth Karanja (Rapporteur).

The paper proceeds as follows. Part II offers a typology of categories of investor wrongdoing, distilling varied concepts into their purest expressions, namely (i) corruption; (ii) fraud and misrepresentation; and (iii) other violations of host State law. Part III seeks to address how investor wrongdoing is proven, focusing specifically on arbitral practice and the doctrine on applicable burdens and standards of proof, the proper use of circumstantial evidence or "red flags", and the deployment of adverse inferences. Part IV is a discussion of the three legal standards, having disregarded other more nebulous concepts, through which allegations of investor wrongdoing must pass: (i) "legality" requirements found in many investment treaties; (ii) the concept of "unclean hands"; and (iii) transnational public policy. Part V concludes by summarizing the sometimes binary outcomes of investor wrongdoing in investment arbitration.

II.   A TYPOLOGY OF INVESTOR WRONGDOING

Acts commonly aggregated under the genus investor "wrongdoing" typically exhibit multiple facets of corruption, fraud, deceit and misrepresentation. Such conduct is more than likely a violation of the host State's laws as well. This section offers a description of the ways in which such wrongdoing manifests in investment treaty cases, as characterized and addressed in the case law. More than this, however, the following discussion calls for greater rigor in the analysis, beginning with closer attention to the proper characterization of closely related species of wrongdoing.

1.   *The Operative Categories of Investor Wrongdoing*

Any serious effort at drawing a typology of investor wrongdoing will involve the elimination of duplicative or insufficiently precise allegations of investor misconduct, allowing focus on the core operative categories of wrongdoing.

Many of the forms mentioned in the case law and commentaries – the "violation of the host State's laws", "deceitful conduct", the "misuse of the system of international investment protection", the violation of "good faith"[1] or "transnational public policy",[2]

---

1. Cases mentioning good faith include: *Inceysa Vallisoletana v. Republic of El Salvador* (ICSID Case No. ARB/03/26), Award, 2 August 2006 ("Good faith is a supreme principle, which governs legal relations in all of their aspects and content"); *Plama Consortium Limited v. Bulgaria* (ICSID Case No. ARB/03/24), Award, 27 August 2008 ("[t]he principle of good faith encompasses, inter alia, the obligation for the investor to provide the host State with relevant and material information concerning the investor and the investment"); *Phoenix Action, Ltd. v. Czech Republic* (ICSID Case No. ARB/06/5), Award, 15 April 2009 ("[t]he purpose of the international mechanism of protection ... cannot be to protect investments ... not made in good faith"); *Gustaf F.W. Hamester GmbH & Co KG v. Republic of Ghana* (ICSID ARB/07/24, Award, 18 June 2010 ("[a]n investment will not be protected if it has been created in violation of national or international principles of good faith"); *Fraport AG v. The Republic of the Philippines* (ICSID Case No. ARB/03/25), Award, 16 August 2007 ("The principle of good faith in international law precedes and transcends Article 26 of the Vienna Convention").

2. "Transnational public policy" or "truly international public policy" has almost always been used as a supra-national source of law to proscribe corruption, particularly in commercial arbitration or contract-based investment arbitration (e.g. *World Duty Free Company Limited v. The Republic of Kenya*

in the making (or sometimes, the carrying out) of an investment[3] – will fall analytically within two principal species of wrongdoing: corruption and fraud.

Corruption is used almost uniformly to describe bribery between an investor's employee or intermediary and a public official of the host State. *Fraud* is often used in a generic sense and can further be subdivided into deceit (i.e., a form of fraud that involves the intent to deceive the host State to the investor's advantage) and to misrepresentation (which need not delve into whether there existed wilful intent to deceive).

The cases also speak of the *lack of good faith* in the making of an investment and two of its manifestations – abuse of process and abuse of rights. International law[4] and various domestic legal systems recognize "good faith", broadly conceived, and to some extent the provenance of these terms can be traced to customary international law and general principles. They possess commonality in that they are "framed in order to avoid misuse of the law".[5] However, the content of the obligation of "good faith" is difficult to pin down, and it is thus difficult to define precisely what constitutes a lack of good faith. As observed by Bin Cheng, "what exactly this principle implies is perhaps difficult to define ... such rudimental terms applicable to human conduct ... elude *a priori* definition".[6]

In order to receive investment treaty protection, it has been asserted in a line of arbitral practice that an investment must have been made or acquired in good faith. In *Hamester v. Ghana*, the tribunal declared that an investment will not be protected if it has been created "in violation of international principles of good faith ... or if its creation itself constitutes a misuse of the system of international investment protection under the

---

(ICSID Case No. ARB/00/7), Award, 4 October 2006). See also, *Inceysa Vallisoletana v. Republic of El Salvador* (ICSID Case No. ARB/03/26, Award, 2 August 2006 ("the inclusion of the clause 'in accordance with law' in various BIT provisions is a clear manifestation of said international public policy"); *Plama Consortium Limited v. Bulgaria* (ICSID Case No. ARB/03/24), Award, 27 August 2008; *Fraport AG v. The Republic of the Philippines* (ICSID Case No. ARB/03/25), Dissenting Opinion of Bernardo M. Cremades ("In some cases, for example, the principles of good faith and public policy may bar a claim"); *Phoenix Action, Ltd. v. Czech Republic* (ICSID Case No. ARB/06/5), Award, 15 April 2009 ("nobody would suggest that ICSID protection should be granted to investments made in violation of the most fundamental rules of protection of human rights").

3. *Gustaf F.W. Hamester GmbH & Co KG v. Republic of Ghana* (ICSID ARB/07/24), Award, 18 June 2010, para. 123 ("An investment will not be protected if it has been created in violation of national or international principles of good faith; by way of corruption, fraud, or deceitful conduct; or if its creation itself constitutes a misuse of the system of international investment protection under the ICSID Convention. It will also not be protected if it is made in violation of the host State's law.")

4. *Nuclear Tests* Case, 1974 I.C.J. 253 (20 December), para. 46; See also M. SHAW, *International Law*, 6th edn., 104 (CUP 2008), ("The principle of good faith is a background principle informing and shaping the observance of existing rules of international law and in addition constraining the manner in which those rules may legitimately be exercised"); Rudolf DOLZER and Christoph SCHREUER, *Principles of International Investment Law* (2012) p. 156, ("[G]ood faith is a broad principle that is one of the foundations of international law in general and of foreign investment law in particular").

5. *Mobil Corporation and others v. Bolivarian Republic of Venezuela* (ICSID Case No. ARB/07/27), Decision on Jurisdiction, 10 June 2010, para. 169 ("The Tribunal first observes that in all systems of law, whether domestic or international, there are concepts framed in order to avoid misuse of the law. Reference may be made in this respect to 'good faith' ('bonne foi'), '*détournement de pouvoir*' (misuse of power) or '*abus de droit*' (abuse of right)").

6. Bin CHENG, *General Principles of Law as Applied by International Courts and Tribunals* (1953) p. 105.

ICSID Convention".[7] Similarly, the tribunal in *Phoenix Action v. Czech Republic* declared that "States cannot be deemed to offer access to the ICSID dispute settlement mechanism to investments not made in good faith",[8] while the *SAUR v. Argentina* tribunal considered that the purpose of the system of investment arbitration is to protect only legitimate and bona fide investments.[9]

As categorical as they are, these sweeping statements in fact offer more questions than answers. What is the legal source from which such norms arise? While the doctrine of good faith has been invoked as a "fundamental principle of all legal systems", as one commentator concludes, the "general normative bases of the abuse of process doctrine ... remain open to question".[10] Tribunals have denied that such requirements can be implied into the term "investment" as it is used in the ICSID Convention. For example, faced with a host State's allegation that the investor's investment violated the principle of good faith since the investment was aimed at artificially transforming a dispute between Turkish nationals and the Turkish State into an international dispute between Turkey and a foreign investor (so-called "treaty shopping"), the *Saba Fakes* tribunal held:

> "The principles of good faith and legality cannot be incorporated into the definition of Article 25(1) of the ICSID Convention without doing violence to the language of the ICSID Convention: an investment might be 'legal' or 'illegal,' made in "good faith" or not, it nonetheless remains an investment. The expressions 'legal investment' or 'investment made in good faith' are not pleonasms, and the expressions 'illegal investment' or 'investment made in bad faith' are not oxymorons. ... While a treaty should be interpreted and applied in good faith, this is a general requirement under treaty law, from which an additional criterion of 'good faith' for the definition of investments, which was not contemplated by the text of the ICSID Convention, cannot be derived."[11]

Indeed, reference to good faith may have been superfluous in certain cases where the tribunal declined jurisdiction on the basis of the investor's alleged lack of good faith in acquiring an investment. In *Inceysa v. El Salvador*, for example, the tribunal found a lack of good faith on the part of the investor because of its deliberate falsification of key facts relating to its bid, which would imply that the investment would not be a covered

---

7. *Gustaf F.W. Hamester GmbH & Co KG v. Republic of Ghana* (ICSID Case No. ARB/07/24), Award, 18 June 2010, para. 123, cited with approval in *Teinver S.A., Transportes de Cercanías S.A. and Autobuses Urbanos del Sur S.A. v. The Argentine Republic* (ICSID Case No. ARB/09/1), Decision on Jurisdiction, 21 December 2012, para. 317.

8. *Phoenix Action, Ltd. v. Czech Republic* (ICSID Case No. ARB/06/5), Award, 15 April 2009, para. 106.

9. *SAUR International S.A. v. Argentine Republic* (ICSID Case No. ARB/04/4), Decision on Jurisdiction and Liability, 6 June 2012, para. 308 (French original: *"Il entend que la finalité du système d'arbitrage d'investissement consiste à protéger uniquement les investissements licites et* bonafide").

10. John P. GAFFNEY, "Abuse of Process in Investment Treaty Arbitration", 11 J. World Investment & Trade (2010) pp. 515-538.

11. *Saba Fakes v. Republic of Turkey* (ICSID Case No. ARB/07/20), Award, 14 July 2010, paras. 112-113.

"investment" within the meaning of the specific bilateral investment treaty (BIT).[12] But the *Inceysa* tribunal also invoked the "in accordance with law" provision contained in Art. 1(2) of the El Salvador-Spain BIT.[13] It is far from certain, therefore, that the decision in *Inceysa* stands for the general proposition that an investor must make or acquire an investment in good faith in order for an investment treaty tribunal to assert jurisdiction, since the case can be confined to the specific application of the El Salvador-Spain BIT, in conjunction with Salvadorean law.

The difficulty in identifying with any precision what a "lack of good faith" might be, independent of fraud (including deceit and misrepresentation) or other specific violations of host State law, places this putative form of investor wrongdoing at an unhelpful degree of abstraction. Clearly "good faith" relates to the notion of the law-abiding investor, who is cognizant and respectful of the host State's laws, makes a genuine "investment" as defined under the relevant BIT, and does not engage in corruption or fraud while doing so. But these are all themselves well-developed categories; "good faith" cannot, by itself, identify how, by what rules, and under what conditions a purported lack of good faith actually occurs.[14]

The doctrine of *abuse of rights* (*abus de droit*) denotes circumstances whereby an actor is prohibited from improperly exercising otherwise legitimate legal rights.[15] In international law, the doctrine may arise where the exercise of a legal right "either ... impedes the enjoyment by other States of their own rights", or where the State purports

---

12. *Inceysa Vallisoletana v. Republic of El Salvador* (ICSID Case No. ARB/03/26), Award, 2 August 2006, paras. 238-239 ("El Salvador gave its consent to jurisdiction of the Centre, presupposing good faith behaviour on the part of future investors ... by falsifying [certain] facts, Inceysa violated the principle of good faith from the time it made its investment and, therefore, did not make it in accordance with Salvadorean law. Faced with this situation, the Tribunal can only declare its incompetence to hear Inceysa's complaint, since its investments cannot benefit from protection of the BIT.") See also *Hulley Enterprises (Cyprus) Limited, Yukos Universal Limited (Isle of Man) and Veteran Petroleum Limited (Cyprus) v. Russian Federation*, PCA Case Nos. AA226-228, Final Awards, 18 July 2014, para. 1352 ("In imposing obligations on States to treat investors in a fair and transparent fashion, investment treaties seek to encourage legal and *bona fide* investments. An investor who has obtained an investment in the host State only by acting in bad faith or in violation of the laws of the host State, has brought itself within the scope of application of the ECT through wrongful acts. Such an investor should not be allowed to benefit from the Treaty.").

13. *Inceysa Vallisoletana v. Republic of El Salvador* (ICSID Case No. ARB/03/26), Award, 2 August 2006, paras. 192-193.

14. In *Klöckner v. Cameroon,* the ad hoc committee did not consider good faith alone, without further reference to "legislative texts, to judgments, or to scholarly opinions" articulating a more precise standard, sufficient: "[i]t is true that the principle of good faith is 'at the basis' of French civil law, as of other legal systems, but this elementary proposition does not by itself answer the question. In Cameroonian or Franco-Cameroonian law does the 'principle' affirmed or postulated by the Award, the 'duty of full disclosure', exist? If it does, no doubt flowing from the general principle of good faith, from the obligation of frankness and loyalty, then *how,* by what *rules* and under what *conditions* is it implemented and within what *limits*?": *Klöckner Industrie-Anlagen GmbH and others v. United Republic of Cameroon and Société Camerounaise des Engrais* (ICSID Case No. ARB/81/2), Decision of the ad hoc Committee, 3 May 1985.

15. Hersch LAUTERPACHT, *The Development of International Law by the International Court* (1958) p. 164 ("There is no legal right, however well established, which could not, in some circumstances, be refused recognition on the ground that it has been abused").

to invoke a right "for an end different from that for which the right was created, to the injury of another State".[16] On one view, the doctrine of abuse of rights is a manifestation of the broader principle of good faith.[17] Others have argued that the doctrine's juridical basis lies either in the general principles of law recognized by civilized nations under Art. 38(1)(c) of the International Court of Justice (ICJ) Statute,[18] or in customary international law.[19] A finding of abuse of rights is highly context-dependent and necessarily requires impugning the motives of an alleged perpetrator.[20]

Abuse of process also derives from the notion of good faith.[21] Arguably, it is a special application of the prohibition against abuse of rights.[22] It provides for the stay or dismissal of proceedings where their continuance would be unjustifiably vexatious or oppressive.[23]

---

16. See Alexandre KISS, "Abuse of Rights" in Rudolf BERNHARDT, ed., *Encyclopedia of Public International Law* (1992) p. 1 at p. 4; Sir Robert JENNINGS and Sir Arthur WATTS, eds., *Oppenheim's International Law*, 9th edn. (1992) p. 407 ("An abuse of rights occurs when a state avails itself of its right in an arbitrary manner in such a way as to inflict upon another state an injury which cannot be justified by a legitimate consideration of its own advantage").

17. Bin CHENG, *op. cit.*, fn. 6, p. 123 ("The principle of good faith requires that every right be exercised honestly and loyally. Any fictitious exercise of a right for the purpose of evading either rule of law or a contractual obligation will not be tolerated. Such an exercise constitutes an abuse of the right, prohibited by law."); Robert D. SLOANE, "Breaking the Genuine Link: The Contemporary Legal Regulation of Nationality", 50 Harvard International Law Journal (2009, no. 1) p. 24 ("The principle of abuse of rights in international law ... may be conceptualized as one concrete manifestation of that abstract international requirement [of good faith]").

18. LAUTERPACHT, *The Function of Law in the International Community* (1933) pp. 286-306; *Nottebohm*, 1955 I.C.J. 4; G.D.S. TAYLOR, "The Content of the Rule Against Abuse of Rights in International Law", 46 Brit. Y. B. Int'l L. (1972-1973) p. 323 at p. 352 ("Upon translation into international adjudication, the jurisprudence [of domestic courts] shows sufficient coherence to posit a general principle prohibiting abuse of right in international law"); Andreas ZIMMERMAN, et al., *The Statute of the International Court of Justice: A Commentary* (2012) p. 304 ("Abuse of rights ... is a general principle of international law").

19. Alexandre KISS, *L'abus de droit en droit international* (1953) pp. 193-196.

20. Hersch LAUTERPACHT, *op. cit.*, fn. 15, p. 162 ("The determination of the point at which the exercise of a legal right has degenerated into an abuse of a right is a question which cannot be decided by an abstract legislative rule, but only by the activity of courts drawing the line in each particular case").

21. Chester BROWN, "The Relevance of the Doctrine of Abuse of Process in International Adjudication", 2 TDM (2011) pp. 6-7; Michael BYERS, "Abuse of Rights: An Old, Principle, A New Age", 47 McGill L. J. (2002) p. 389; Eric DE BRABANDERE, "'Good faith', 'Abuse of Process' and the Initiation of Investment Treaty Claims", 3 Journal of International Dispute Settlement (2012, no. 3) p. 11.

22. Andreas ZIMMERMAN, et al., *op. cit.*, fn. 18, p. 304 ("Abuse of procedure is a special application of the prohibition of abuse of rights, which is a general principle of international law"); Eric DE BRABANDERE, *op. cit.*, fn. 21, p. 11 ("'Abuse of process' is a particular feature of the broader principle of 'abuse of rights', in that the right claimed is a procedural one").

23. Chester BROWN, *op. cit.*, fn. 21, p. 7 ("The essential content of the doctrine seems to be this: that proceedings before a court should be stayed as an abuse of process if, even if their circumstances do not give rise to the plea of res judicata, the continuance of those proceedings would be unjustifiably vexatious and oppressive for the reason that the claimant is trying to relitigate a matter which should already have been disposed of in earlier proceedings"); Vaughan LOWE, "Overlapping Jurisdiction in International Tribunals", 20 AYBIL (1999) p. 202 ("[Abuse

The doctrine is based on notions of public policy,[24] and comprises one of the inherent powers of international courts and tribunals to ensure the integrity of their own proceedings.[25] The scope of application of the doctrine is narrow, however, and claims of abuse of process have usually been rejected when raised before the ICJ[26] and investment treaty tribunals.[27]

Some investment tribunals have attempted to differentiate between abuse of rights and abuse of process through the lens of good faith, by splitting it into sub-categories of "material" and "procedural" good faith (with the former a "misuse of power" considered an issue of either jurisdiction or the merits, and the latter a "misuse of process" considered as either a jurisdiction or admissibility issue).[28] Allegations of "material bad faith" or abuse of right have typically arisen where an investment has been made or structured after a dispute has arisen, in an attempt to gain access to protections available under a given investment treaty.[29] But this is more properly a form of deceit or

of process will apply] in a range of circumstances where the action is rendered vexatious. These include cases where the purpose of the litigation is to harass the defendant, or the claim is frivolous or manifestly groundless").

24. Chester BROWN, *op. cit.*, fn. 21, p. 7 ("The doctrine is not based on the doctrine of res judicata, nor is it based on any strict doctrine of issue estoppel or cause of action estoppel. Rather, it is a rule of public policy").

25. Vaughan LOWE, *op. cit.*, fn. 23, p. 203; See generally Chester BROWN, "The Inherent Powers of International Courts and Tribunals", 76 BYIL (2005) p. 195; ILA Committee on International Commercial Arbitration, Interim Report: *"Res judicata" and Arbitration* (2004), available at <www.ila-hq.org/en/committees/index.cfm/cid/19> ("The doctrine [of abuse of process] rests upon the inherent power of the court to prevent a misuse of its procedures even through a party's conduct may not be inconsistent with the literal application of the procedural rules").

26. See *Certain Phosphate Lands in Nauru* ICJ Rep 240 (1992); *Armed Activities on the Territory of the Congo (New Application: 2002)*, 41 ILM 1175 (2002); *Request for Interpretation of the Judgment of 31 March 2004 in the Case concerning Avena and other Mexican Nationals (Mexico v. United States)*, Judgment of 19 January 2009.

27. See, e.g., *CME Czech Republic BV v. Czech Republic*, Partial Award, 13 September 2001; *Bayindir Insaat Turizm Ticaret Ve Sanayi AS v. Pakistan* (ICSID Case No. ARB/03/29), Decision on Jurisdiction, 14 November 2005.

28. *Mobil Corporation and others v. Bolivarian Republic of Venezuela* (ICSID Case No. ARB/07/27), Decision on Jurisdiction, 10 June 2010, para. 169; *Abaclat and Others (Case formerly known as Giovanna a Beccara and Others) v. Argentine Republic* (ICSID Case No. ARB/07/5), Decision on Jurisdiction and Admissibility, 4 August 2011, paras. 648-650.

29. Tribunals and commentators have taken the view that structuring an investment solely to gain access to treaty protections constitutes an abuse of right if such restructuring occurs when a dispute has already arisen. This position has been adopted by tribunals in *Phoenix Action, Ltd. v. Czech Republic* (ICSID Case No. ARB/06/5), Award, 15 April 2009; *Mobil Corporation and others v. Bolivarian Republic of Venezuela* (ICSID Case No. ARB/07/27), Decision on Jurisdiction, 10 June 2010; *Malicorp Ltd v. Arab Republic of Egypt* (ICSID Case No. ARB/08/18), Award, 7 February 2011 and *Tidewater Inc., Tidewater Investment SRL, Tidewater Caribe, C.A., Twenty Grand Offshore, L.L.C., Point Marine, L.L.C., Twenty Grand Marine Service, L.L.C., Jackson Marine, L.L.C. and Zapata Gulf Marine Operators, L.L.C. v. Bolivarian Republic of Venezuela* (ICSID Case No. ARB/10/5), Decision on Jurisdiction, 8 February 2013. The justification for such a rule was summed up by the tribunal in *Société Générale in respect of DR Energy Holdings Limited and Empresa Distribuidora de Electricidad del Este, S.A. v. The Dominican Republic*, LCIA Case No. UN 7927, Award on Preliminary Objections to Jurisdiction, 19 September 2008, as follows:

misrepresentation characteristic of fraud, or simpler still a proven example of lack of jurisdiction for not being at the relevant times a covered "investor" with a covered "investment" as contemplated under the relevant investment treaty.[30] It may be better to employ those concrete norms rather than more abstract, untethered principles. Indeed, the cases reveal that concepts such as lack of good faith, abuse of right and abuse of process, have frequently been used to chastise investor conduct in circumstances in which jurisdiction is already objectively lacking, or where such conduct actually amounts to fraud or corruption.[31] Investment treaty arbitration is familiar with a multitude of

---

"One such limit [to application of investment protection treaties] is that the transaction in question must be a bona fide transaction and not devised to allow a national of a State not qualifying for protection to obtain an inappropriate jurisdictional advantage otherwise unavailable by transferring its rights after-the-fact to a qualifying national."

30. In *Société Générale,* for example, the claimant's attempt to structure an investment so as to benefit from treaty protection "after the event" was held to have not been a bona fide transaction. In making such a determination, the tribunal necessarily impugned the claimant's motivation in restructuring its investments. However, in such circumstances, a claimant's investment will not have been a covered investment at the time of the events giving rise to the dispute and would not therefore support jurisdiction or any treaty claims. Further findings as to an investor's "good faith" seem gratuitous. *Société Générale in respect of DR Energy Holdings Limited and Empresa Distribuidora de Electricidad del Este, S.A. v. The Dominican Republic,* LCIA Case No. UN 7927, Award on Preliminary Objections to Jurisdiction, 19 September 2008.

Similarly, in *Europe Cement Investment & Trade S.A. v. Republic of Turkey* (ICSID Case No. ARB(AF)/07/2), Award, 13 August 2009, para. 175, the tribunal stated as follows:

"The Claimant asserted jurisdiction on the basis of a claim to ownership of shares, which the uncontradicted evidence before the Tribunal suggests was false. Such a claim cannot be said to have been made in good faith. If, as in *Phoenix*, a claim that is based on the purchase of an investment solely for the purpose of commencing litigation is an abuse of process, then surely a claim based on the false assertion of ownership of an investment is equally an abuse of process."

The claim in *Europe Cement* was dismissed for lack of jurisdiction. The tribunal's decision was not, however, based on the alleged investment having been made in bad faith or as an abuse of process. Rather, the tribunal declined jurisdiction since no investment existed at all, the claimant having brought its claim on the basis of purported ownership of shares, which the tribunal found to be false (and which the claimant did not contest).

31. The *Phoenix* tribunal took a more explicitly broad approach as to the basis on which it declined jurisdiction over an investment made in bad faith, stating:

"In the instant case, no question of violation of a national principle of good faith or of international public policy related with corruption or deceitful conduct is at stake. The Tribunal is concerned here with *the international principle of good faith as applied to the international arbitration mechanism of ICSID.* The Tribunal has to prevent an abuse of the system of international investment protection under the ICSID Convention, in ensuring that only investments that are made in compliance with the international principle of good faith and do not attempt to misuse the system are protected."

Phoenix Action, Ltd. v. Czech Republic (ICSID Case No. ARB/06/5), Award, 15 April 2009, para. 113 (emphasis in original). The claimant had acquired certain Czech companies. At the time of this acquisition, those companies had been engaged in no economic activity for more than a year. The only activity in which they were engaged at the time of the alleged investment was the litigation

procedural transgressions of lesser degrees of seriousness, however, which might be termed "abuse of process". Depending on the circumstances, such conduct might be more appropriately punished by means, for instance, of an adverse costs order.[32]

Investors are often accused of *violations of the laws of the host State*, whether at the inception of an investment or during its operation. Theoretically, these violations may take as many different forms as there are national laws. Yet violations of national law very often cluster around a relatively narrow band of fact patterns that constitute violations of national and international laws relating to corruption, fraud or misrepresentation in the making or performance of the investment, subversion of laws limiting the types of assets or sectors in which investors may invest, or in the identity or capabilities of the investor. Illegality may take the form of a transgression of host State laws concerning the admission of foreign investment, including a limit or an outright prohibition against foreign investors acquiring a particular category of investments (such as public utilities), carrying out certain business activities, or prescribing the manner in which foreign investors may hold such investments. Alternatively, investments which are otherwise lawful, such as shareholdings, may have been acquired by illegal means. Although such conduct is often analyzed in terms of compliance with host State law, and a distinct body of decisions has emerged on the application of treaty provisions which

---

that formed the basis for the ICSID arbitration. [para. 129] According to the tribunal, this alone would not be enough to disqualify the operation as an investment, provided that the claimant "really had the intention to engage in economic activities". [para. 133] On the facts, the tribunal found that there were "strong indicia that no economic activity in the market place was either performed or even intended by Phoenix". [para. 140] In the tribunal's ultimate analysis, it declined jurisdiction since the claimant's "initiation and pursuit of this arbitration [was] an abuse of the system of international ICSID investment arbitration ... the ICSID mechanism does not protect investments that it was not designed to protect, because they are in essence domestic investments disguised as international investments for the sole purpose of access to this mechanism". [para. 144] Thus, an abuse of process, framed in terms of the claimant's subjective motives, was arguably of dispositive significance.

32. See, e.g., *Cementownia "NowaHuta" S.A. v. Republic of Turkey* (ICSID Case No. ARB(AF)/06/2), Award, 17 September 2009, paras. 158-159 ("With respect to the sanction in case of an abuse of rights, ICSID tribunals can award costs against parties as a sanction against what they see as dilatory or otherwise improper conduct in the proceedings"), citing *Benvenuti & Bonfant v. People's Republic of Congo* (ICSID Case No. ARB/77/2), Award, 15 August 1980, 1 ICSID Reports 365; *MINE v. Guinea* (ICSID Case No. ARB/84/4), Award, 6 January 1988, 4 ICSID Reports 78; *American Manufacturing Trading v. Zaire* (ICSID Case No. ARB/93/1), Award, 21 February 1997, 36 ILM 1531; *Liberian Eastern Timber Corporation v. Republic of Liberia* (ICSID Case No. Case No. ARB/83/2), Award, 31 March 1986, 2 ICSID Reports 370.

expressly state that investments must be made "in accordance with host State law";[33] these issues are very frequently co-mingled with principles of fraud or corruption.

From the foregoing it is suggested that it is not necessary to parse out some of the more abstract or parasitic concepts that arise in the reasoning of some cases; instead, it is proposed that there are three operative categories of investor wrongdoing in the vast majority of treaty cases: (i) corruption; (ii) fraud, deceit and misrepresentation; and (iii) other breaches of host State law. These categories are now considered in turn.

2.   Corruption

a.   The concept and bilateral nature of corruption

"Corruption" is a polyvalent word that defies easy definition but communicates, at its essence, an abuse of a duty owed to the public or third person.[34] As a term of art in the area of foreign investment, corruption has many modalities and its operational codes have changed over time. But its essential elements are the relationship between the foreign capital-provider and the public official of the host State who is the repository of public trust, and the undisclosed payment made by the investor to that official in expectation of a favorable public decision.[35]

---

33. See M. SORNARAJAH, *The International Law on Foreign Investment* (Cambridge University Press 2004) p. 106; C. KNAHR, "Investments in Accordance with Host State Law", 4 Transnational Dispute Management (2007) p. 5; Z. DOUGLAS, *The International Law of Investment Claims* (Cambridge University Press 2009) p. 53 et seq.; G. BOTTINI, "Legality of Investments under ICSID Jurisprudence" in M. WAIBEL, A. KAUSHAL, K-H. Liz CHUNG and C. BALCHIN, *The Backlash Against Investment Arbitration* (Wolters Kluwer 2010) p. 297; U. KRIEBAUM, "Illegal Investments" in *Austrian Yearbook on International Law* (2010) p. 307; R. MOLOO and A. KHACHATURIAN, "The Compliance with the Law Requirement in International Investment Law", 34 Fordham Int'l L.J. (2011) p. 1473; S. SCHILL, "Illegal Investments in International Arbitration" (4 January 2012) available at SSRN: <http://ssrn.com/abstract=1979734>; A. NEWCOMBE, "Investor Misconduct: Jurisdiction, Admissibility or Merits" in C. BROWN and K. MILES, *Evolution in Investment Treaty Law and Arbitration* (Cambridge University Press 2012) p. 187; Z. DOUGLAS, "The Plea of Illegality in Investment Treaty Arbitration", 29 ICSID Review—Foreign Investment Law Journal (2014, issue 1) (henceforth "Plea of Illegality").

34. The United Nations' Office on Drugs and Crime has resisted attempts to lay out a precise definition, maintaining that there is "no single, comprehensive, universally accepted definition of corruption", and that "[a]ttempts to develop such a definition invariably encounter legal, criminological and, in many countries, political problems". Instead, the UN prefers to identify its particular forms, including "corruption, bribery, embezzlement, theft and fraud, extortion, abuse of discretion, favoritism, nepotism and clientelism, conduct creating or exploiting conflicting interests, and improper political contributions." *United Nations Office on Drugs and Crime, The Global Programme against Corruption: UN Anti-Corruption Toolkit*, 3rd edn. (2004) Ch. 1.

35. See OECD Anti-Bribery Convention, Art. 1(1), which does not contain a definition of corruption at all, but instead identifies these operative elements. However, the Convention's terminology also imports a degree of uncertainty since it uses terms such as "improper" or "undue" advantages and "abuse" of power, which necessitate the exercise of judgment on the part of the observer. It is also evident from this terminology that corruption in its broad sense does not refer merely to illegal acts done by public officials by nature of their powers and duties; they are meant to include discretionary acts or omissions that are *per se* legal, but are motivated by private gain considerations.

The inherently *bilateral* nature of corruption is unique among the species of investor wrongdoing, unlike fraud, misrepresentation or other forms of wrongdoing that are essentially *unilateral* acts perpetrated by an investor against the host State. Often but not always in violation of the host State's national legislation, corruption is only consummated when there is a meeting of offer and acceptance between the investor and public officials of the host State (often via intermediaries). The corrupt transaction is frequently simplified, sometimes inaccurately so, into the "active" or "supply", and "passive" or "demand" sides of corruption. The impression derived from most anti-corruption instruments is of inflexible roles; there is the active bribe initiator, the investor, and the public official taking the bribe acting in a more passive role. However, the reciprocity of transnational corruption makes it sometimes confusing, even counterproductive, to label the sides of the transaction in this way, as each seek and receive reciprocal benefits in return for providing scarce resources. As a practical matter it will often be difficult to separate solicitation and *extortion*[36] from mere receipt of a bribe. Most incidences of corruption will lie somewhere within a spectrum animated on one side by the unscrupulous investor seeking to maximize economic gains by obtaining contracts yielding above-market returns; and the (sometimes-kleptocratic) host State government run by public officials who require all foreign investors to pay bribes, not just for so-called "facilitation payments",[37] but as a precondition to being allowed to invest or to maintain an investment, or both.

One perspective from which extortion extracted by host State public officials can be distinguished from opportunistic bribery is to inquire into the nature of the public decision-making sought to be purchased by the investor. Corruption is often used as a risk-mitigating tool by investors coming into unfamiliar markets, and an investor seeking to minimize risk might engage in corrupt activity for two purposes: first, there is the *economic* reason. Bribery of public officials will make a risky investment worth the risk by ensuring that the profit potential exceeds those found in "safer" markets. This can often be distinguished from a second reason: to secure leave from what the investor deems to be unfair or oppressive regulation perpetrated by public officials; in other

---

36. "Extortion" (one common form of which is "blackmail") is another important type of corruption. One can distinguish extortion from bribery by looking into whether the payer receives "better than fair treatment" or must pay to be treated fairly. Put another way, "[t]he term *extortion* may be reserved for those situations in which the capacity of the official to withhold a service or benefit otherwise required by law exceeds the capacity of the private party to sustain the loss of that service or benefit". W. Michael REISMAN, *Folded Lies: Bribery, Crusades, and Reforms* (1979) p. 38.

37. Low-level extortion is often linked with the concept of "facilitation payments", where money is used to induce functionaries (usually low-ranking government workers and officials) to perform their duties efficiently. It is a response to "extortion" considered largely acceptable because the degree of deviance from the law the payment seeks to obtain is small at best – the official is usually paid just to "do their job". As clarified in the commentary to the OECD Anti-Bribery Convention, "small 'facilitation' payments do not constitute payments made 'to obtain or retain business or other improper advantage' within the meaning of paragraph 1 and, accordingly, are also not an offence". "Commentaries on the Convention on Combating Bribery of Foreign Public Officials in International Business Transactions", adopted by the Negotiating Conference on 21 November 1997.

words, to protect the potential or already existing investment from political risk.[38] An analysis of corruption-related issues from the perspective of risk would ask: precisely what form of government action or inaction did the bribe purchase – *protection from commercial risks, or from political risk*? Not coincidentally, political risk insulation is more typical of public official-led extortion, while economic risk minimization is more akin to investor-led bribery. Pressure to make corrupt payments to insulate an investment from *political* uncertainty bears some consistency with precisely the same forms of political and non-commercial risks that investment treaties themselves were designed to protect foreign investors against, such as fair and equitable treatment, or freedom from arbitrary and discriminatory treatment. Nonetheless, such activities are all illegal, as a general matter, and open the investor to sanction.

While corruption is universally proscribed in national law, arbitrators and commentators have increasingly classified it also as a violation of transnational (or "truly international") public policy,[39] as well as a violation of public international law.[40]

Initial national anti-corruption legislation (such as the US Foreign Corrupt Practices Act (FCPA)) and international conventions (such as the OECD Anti-Bribery Convention) centered on the "supply" side, i.e., the conduct of the foreign investor. Gradually, however, focus on the "demand" side – that of public officials of host States – has begun

---

38. Indeed, the Multilateral Investment Guarantee Agency (MIGA), which like the ICSID is another member of the World Bank Group, was created precisely to address the reality that political risks were hampering global economic development, particularly in developing countries. MIGA was designed to encourage the flow of foreign investment in poorer countries by "alleviating concerns related to non-commercial risks". See Convention Establishing the Multilateral Investment Guarantee Agency [MIGA Convention], Second Preambular Clause ("*Recognizing* that the flow of foreign investment to developing countries would be facilitated and further encouraged by alleviating concerns related to non-commercial risks").

39. See Pierre LALIVE, "Transnational (or Truly International) Public Policy and International Arbitration" in *Comparative Arbitration Practice and Public Policy in Arbitration*, ICCA Congress Series no. 3 (1987) (henceforth *ICCA Congress Series no. 3*); *World Duty Free Company Limited v. The Republic of Kenya* (ICSID Case No. ARB/00/7), Award, 4 October 2006; *Metal-Tech Ltd. v. Republic of Uzbekistan* (ICSID Case No. ARB/10/3), Award, 4 October 2013.

40. See The Inter-American Convention Against Corruption (Adopted: 29 March 1996; Entry into force: 3 June 1997); OECD Convention on Bribery of Foreign Public Officials in International Business Transactions (Adopted: 21 November 1997; Entry into force: 15 February 1999); Council of Europe Criminal Law Convention on Corruption (Adopted: 4 November 1998; Entry into force: 1 July 2002); United Nations Convention against Transnational Organized Crime (Adopted: 15 November 2000; Entry into force: 29 September 2003); Council of Europe Civil Law Convention (Adopted: 4 November 1999; Entry into force: 1 November 2003); Southern African Development Community Protocol Against Corruption (Adopted: 14 August 2001; Entry into force: 6 July 2005); United Nations Convention Against Corruption (Adopted: 31 October 2003; Entry into force: 14 December 2005); The African Union Convention on Preventing and Combating Corruption (Adopted: 11 July 2003; Entry into force: 5 August 2006). These treaties have placed beyond any real doubt the authoritative status of the proscription against corruption, and transnational bribery in particular, as a matter of public international law. The instruments' strong condemnation of corruption has resulted in consensus that individual States must investigate, prosecute, and punish corruption as a matter of criminal law, and that failure to legislate or set in place effective enforcement mechanisms amount to a violation of international treaty and customary obligations.

to take hold. The UN Convention Against Corruption, the most universally subscribed of the multi-lateral anti-corruption instruments, requires Contracting States to criminalize in their national legislation not only the "promise, offering or giving, to a public official, directly or indirectly", but also "the solicitation and acceptance by a public official, directly or indirectly, of an undue advantage".[41]

As to the civil consequences of such corruption, however, there is little consensus. The UN Convention is typical in this regard, allowing parties significant leeway in ascertaining the proper sanction to be given to particular corrupt acts.[42]

b.   Corruption as an investor claim

Because of corruption's inherently bilateral nature, the issue can be employed both by investors and host States as a *shield* as well as a *sword*. Corruption is primarily raised by host States as a putative complete defense against all claims made by the claimant – a study of the significant corruption-related decisions in international investment arbitration has found that corruption has been raised or insinuated to a significant degree about three times as often by host States as by investors.[43] As a sword, the form of corruption typically invoked by investors are bribe solicitations or extortion within the

---

41. UN Convention Against Corruption, Art. 15 ("Bribery of National Public Officials").

42. The consequences of corruption for vital matters such as contract validity and damages were left to contracting States, who determine for themselves the "effective remedies" to take against corruption as well as the "rights of third parties acquired in good faith" deserving of protection. See Council of Europe, Resolution (97)24 on the Twenty Guiding Principles for the Fight Against Corruption, adopted by the Committee of Ministers on 6 November 1997. Principle 17 of the Guiding Principles asks governments "to ensure that civil law takes into account the need to fight corruption and in particular provides for effective remedies for those whose rights and interests are affected by corruption".

   The UN Convention Against Corruption, for example, speaks only of employing corruption as a "relevant factor" when States determine "in legal proceedings [whether] to annul or rescind a contract, withdraw a concession or other similar instrument or take any other remedial action". (see Art. 34).

   The one treaty designed to deal with the civil aspects of corruption – the Civil Law Convention on Corruption of the Council of Europe – does progress the matter somewhat, providing for limited guidelines on contract validity that give definite sanctions for "easy" cases while maintaining indeterminacy in "hard" cases: (i) the treaty requests that each member state "provide in its internal law for any contract or clause *providing for* corruption to be null and void"; and (b) "[e]ach party shall provide in its internal law for the *possibility* for all parties to a contract whose consent has been undermined by an act of corruption to be able to apply to the court for the contract to be declared void, notwithstanding their right to claim for damages" (emphasis added). Civil Law Convention on Corruption, Art. 8(1).

43. See Aloysius LLAMZON, *Corruption in International Investment Arbitration* (OUP 2014). Of the twenty or so cases in investment arbitration where corruption issues were raised or insinuated to a notable degree, only five instances of investor-alleged corruption occurred. These are: *Methanex Corporation v. United States of America,* NAFTA/UNCITRAL, Final Award on Jurisdiction and Merits, 3 August 2005; *F-W Oil Interests, Inc. v. Republic of Trinidad & Tobago* (ICSID Case No. ARB/01/14), Award, 3 March 2006; *Rumeli Telekom AS and Telsim Mobil Telekomunikasyon Hizmetleri AS v. Republic of Kazakhstan* (ICSID Case No. ARB/05/16), Award, 29 July 2008; *EDF (Services) v. Romania* (ICSID Case No. ARB/05/13), Award, 8 October 2009; and *RSM Production Corporation v. Grenada* (ICSID Case No. ARB/05/14), Award, 13 March 2009.

context of fair and equitable treatment or minimum standards violations,[44] where investors allege that they have been made to pay to be spared arbitrary or unjust treatment from the host State. As a form of investor claim, these allegations are thus treated by tribunals as issues to be decided on the merits, instead of peremptory issues (i.e., ones of jurisdiction or admissibility) whenever raised by host States.

That investors have raised corruption issues far less frequently than host States is perhaps understandable, since the circumstances in which an investor can raise a plausible issue of corruption without indicting itself is presumably limited to attempts at corruption (i.e., bribe solicitations or extortion by public officials). Once the public official's attempt to extract payment is reciprocated, that act arguably becomes one of *consummated* corruption and may implicate the investor. While tribunals seem not to take issue with the possibility that host States can be held internationally responsible for the extortion or corrupt solicitations of their public officials,[45] in reality, such allegations have never directly been sustained. No investor in investment arbitration has, in the publicly available cases to date, successfully invoked a host State's corruption as the basis for compensation. In *EDF (Services) v. Romania*,[46] for example, it was alleged that the then-Prime Minister of Romania had sought a US$ 2.5 million bribe before agreeing to extend the investor's lease. Despite evidence including a purported audio tape of the extortion attempt, the tribunal ultimately ruled that the investor had failed to meet the "clear and convincing" evidentiary standard to demonstrate that a bribe was demanded, a result that is mirrored in other cases where the investor alleged corruption. Also, unproven investor-raised allegations of corruption do not appear to affect outcomes in favor of the investor by "coloring" the behavior of the host States; there is little evidence to suggest that pleas of extortion or corrupt solicitation have even an indirect effect on arbitral outcomes.[47]

c.   Corruption as a host State defense

Unlike investor-alleged corruption, the fact patterns involved when corruption is raised by the host State almost always concern consummated corruption, where the offer of the bribe was met with acceptance. The bilateral nature of consummated corruption has not

---

44. See *Rumeli Telekom AS and Telsim Mobil Telekomunikasyon Hizmetleri AS v. Republic of Kazakhstan* (ICSID Case No. ARB/05/16), Award, 29 July 2008; *RSM Production Corporation v. Grenada* (ICSID Case No. ARB/05/14), Award, 13 March 2009.

45. In the *EDF* tribunal's analysis, the corrupt solicitation of a bribe by "a State agency" would be a "violation of the fair and equitable treatment obligation owed to the Claimant pursuant to the BIT as well as a violation of international public policy". See *id.* paras. 187 et seq. The tribunal also agreed with the Claimant's submission that when the host State's discretion was exercised on the basis of corruption, a "fundamental breach of transparency and legitimate expectations" occurs. *Id.* para. 221.

46. *EDF (Services) v. Romania* (ICSID Case No. ARB/05/13), Award, 8 October 2009.

47. Of the five cases surveyed where investors invoked corruption as a claim against the host State, four cases were dismissed without the investor having obtained any relief from the arbitral tribunal. See *Methanex Corporation v. United States of America*, NAFTA/UNCITRAL, Final Award on Jurisdiction and Merits, 3 August 2005; *F-W Oil Interests, Inc. v. Republic of Trinidad & Tobago* (ICSID Case No. ARB/01/14), Award, 3 March 2006; *EDF (Services) v. Romania* (ICSID Case No. ARB/05/13), Award, 8 October 2009 and *RSM Production Corporation v. Grenada* (ICSID Case No. ARB/05/14), Award, 13 March 2009.

prevented host States from invoking corruption as a defense, however; if anything, host States have been raising corruption issues increasingly over the last few years.[48] When so raised, corruption allegations may serve to defend against even unrelated claims by the investor. As *Metal-Tech v. Uzbekistan* demonstrates, once a finding of corruption has been made, tribunals may dismiss the case for lack of jurisdiction as a form of illegality that strikes at the very consent of the host State to investment arbitration by virtue of the investment treaty's "legality clause", where one is present and possibly even when not.[49] The implications are thus existential for the claim: no matter how egregious the host State's conduct might have been, if the investor was complicit in corruption at the inception of the investment, no relief at all can be obtained.

Of the many instances where corruption was insinuated or overtly alleged, the only investment cases in which a finding of corruption was actually made came in 2006, in *World Duty Free v. Kenya*[50] and, more recently, in 2013, in *Metal-Tech v. Uzbekistan*. In *World Duty Free*, the tribunal considered that the payment of US$ 2 million (including US$ 500,000 directly to Kenya's Head of State, President Daniel Arap Moi) to set up duty-free airport concessions was a bribe, invalidated the investment contract and denied the claimant any form of monetary or non-monetary relief. In *Metal-Tech*, the tribunal found itself without jurisdiction, as corruption (the payment of over US$ 4 million in "consultancy" fees to a group that included the brother of Uzbekistan's Prime Minister for services that could not be substantiated and were not within their expertise) placed the investment outside the protection of the BIT, the host State not having consented to the arbitration of such illegal investments.[51] These are the only publicly known investment cases where corruption explicitly determined the outcome of the case. In

---

48. Of the twenty significant corruption-related cases surveyed spanning the last two decades, beginning with the 1992 award in *SPP v. Egypt*, over half of these cases arose after the leading case of *World Duty Free* was decided in 2006.

49. *Metal-Tech Ltd. v. Republic of Uzbekistan* (ICSID Case No. ARB/10/3), Award, 4 October 2013. In *Metal-Tech,* the applicable investment treaty was the Israel-Uzbekistan BIT, Art. 1(1) of which stated that "[t]he term 'investments' shall comprise any kind of assets, *implemented in accordance with the laws and regulations of the Contracting Party in whose territory the investment is made,* including, but not limited to: ..." (emphasis added).

   The tribunal concluded that corruption existed "to the extent sufficient to violate Uzbekistan law in connection with the establishment of the Claimant's investment in Uzbekistan". [para. 372] As such, the Claimant was not compliant with Art. 1(1) of the BIT and its investment did not fall within Art. 8(1). The tribunal thus found that Uzbekistan's consent did not extend to this dispute, and "this Tribunal lacks jurisdiction over this dispute". [para. 373]

   In *Hulley Enterprises (Cyprus) Limited, Yukos Universal Limited (Isle of Man) and Veteran Petroleum Limited (Cyprus) v. Russian Federation*, PCA Case Nos. AA226-228, Final Awards, 18 July 2014, para. 1352, the tribunal expressed its agreement, without having to decide the issue, with the proposition that investments covered by the Energy Charter Treaty (ECT) do not include those made "only by acting in bad faith or in violation of the laws of the host State", and that "[s]uch an investor should not be allowed to benefit from the Treaty".)

50. *World Duty Free Company Limited v. The Republic of Kenya* (ICSID Case No. ARB/00/7), Award, 4 October 2006.

51. For a critical analysis of *Metal-Tech,* see Cecily ROSE, "Circumstantial Evidence, Adverse Inferences, and Findings of Corruption: *Metal-Tech v. The Republic of Uzbekistan*", 15 J. World Investment & Trade (2014) pp. 747-756.

both of these cases, the tribunal's conclusion that corruption had occurred arose from admissions made by the principal witnesses of the claimant during the course of the proceedings; there appears to be no publicly available investment arbitration decision thus far where corruption was found absent such factual admissions. More will be said about proving corruption and other forms of investor wrongdoing – including issues of burdens and standards of proof – in Part III below.

d.   State responsibility for corruption
The symbiosis between investor employee (or other agent or intermediary) and public official of host State also engenders important questions about the role, if any, the international law on State responsibility should play when corruption issues are decided upon by investment tribunals. [52]

Despite its bilateral nature, host States that invoke corruption contend, often implicitly, that they have also been the victim of unscrupulous public officials who were never authorized to receive bribes or act pursuant to such payments. In principle, the law on State responsibility would not permit such arguments to succeed:

> "a State will be responsible even for *ultra vires* acts of its servants, that is to say, even when they acted beyond their powers. Indeed, one can go further and say that, if an organ of State, or public servants of States, acted in a way expressly forbidden by the State and which violated international law, the State would still be responsible for that wrongful conduct." [53]

By that standard, the *World Duty Free* holding that a head of State's corruption is not attributable because that act was in violation of Kenyan law [54] would not have been sustained in international law, had the law on State responsibility been applied. (*World Duty Free,* unlike most investment law cases, did not derive its consent to arbitration from a bilateral or multilateral investment treaty where public international law would naturally apply). [55]

---

52. For a detailed discussion, see LLAMZON, "State Responsibility for Corruption: The Attribution Asymmetry in International Investment Arbitration", 3 Transn'l Disp. Mgt. (2013).

53. R. HIGGINS, *Problems and Process: International Law and How We Use It* (1994) p. 150, citing Theodore MERON, "International Responsibility of States for Unauthorized Acts of Their Officials, 23 British Y.B. Int'l. L. (1957) p. 85.

54. *World Duty Free Company Limited v. The Republic of Kenya* (ICSID Case No. ARB/00/7), Award, 4 October 2006, para. 185 ("Moreover, there can be no affirmation or waiver in this case based on the knowledge of the Kenyan President attributable to Kenya. *The President was here acting corruptly, to the detriment of Kenya and in violation of Kenyan law (including the 1956 Act).* There is no warrant at English or Kenyan law for attributing knowledge to the state (as the otherwise innocent principal) of a state officer engaged as its agent in bribery"). (Emphasis supplied)

55. For Professor Kreindler, *World Duty Free's* attribution findings may have been in serious error: "in the case of *World Duty Free,* it strains credulity to conclude after the admission of the bribery and the underlying circumstances that the Kenyan head of State was not acting in his official capacity. It seems curious to conclude that he was not acting with apparent authority. And it seems strained to decide that he was not acting manifestly, and not just by 'happenstance', as an organ or agent of the State. Indeed he was the State." Richard KREINDLER, "Competence-Competence in the Face of Illegality in Contracts and Arbitration Agreements", 361 Recueil des Cours (2013)

Nonetheless, the contemporary jurisprudence in investment arbitration casts some doubt on whether corruption can engage State responsibility. From the case law, the following principles may be derived:

(i) Depending on the circumstances, corruption involving public officials of a host State can engage the international responsibility of that State.

(ii) Responsibility for corruption is an issue separate from that of contractual or conventional liability for the agreement procured through corruption; such investment agreements would likely be voidable or unenforceable under the applicable national contract law.

(iii) If a public official bribes another party, the international responsibility of the State of that corrupting official is engaged.

(iv) Similarly, if public officials of a host State solicit or extort bribes from investors, and the other party does *not* freely pay the bribe, the international responsibility of the host State is engaged.

(v) But if the public official accepts a bribe, the State of that corrupted official is *arguably* not responsible towards the party that paid the bribe because such corruption amounted to purely private conduct *and* was known to be so by the investor, and thus cannot be attributed to the host State.[56]

(vi) The host State may nonetheless be responsible towards third parties who did not know of or participate in the corrupt acts at issue.

(vii) In any case, when a host State invokes corruption as a defense against investor claims, both the principles of acquiescence under international law (including the law on State responsibility) and the duty to prosecute corruption (under national and international anti-corruption law) should oblige the State to demonstrate that it has or is actively investigating and prosecuting those public officials who allegedly received bribes.

An asymmetry thus seems to exist: when it is the investor that is the victim of bribe solicitations and extortions, the case law seems to have no doubt that international responsibility for the public official's conduct can attach. It is less certain that State

---

pp. 292-293.

56. Art. 7 of the UN International Law Commission's Articles on International Responsibility of States for Internationally Wrongful Acts embodies the concept of attribution of acts in excess of authority or in contravention of instructions:

"*Excess of authority or contravention of instructions.* The conduct of an organ of a State or of a person or entity empowered to exercise elements of the governmental authority shall be considered an act of the State under international law if the organ, person or entity acts in that capacity, even if it exceeds its authority or contravenes instructions."

Arguably, the qualification "if the organ, person or entity *acts in that capacity*" obviates State responsibility for consummated corruption, as the public official is clearly acting in excess of his authority *and* the other party, knowing that the public official is acting for private gain, freely participated in the corrupt act. In other words, the investor knew the public official was engaged in an act manifestly not "in th[e] capacity" of a State organ, person, or entity.

responsibility can apply to attribute corrupt acts by public officials to the host State when it is the investor that is defending itself against corruption allegations, even if corruption in that case has been consummated. Tribunals acknowledge this asymmetry in various ways and are clearly uncomfortable with its implications.[57] Further discussion on the consequences of investor wrongdoing, including corruption, is found in Part V below.

e. Allegations of corruption and arbitral reasoning

Over the twenty-year span of investment arbitration cases concerning corruption, arbitrators have mostly exhibited reluctance to deal with the issue directly. In some ways, this is understandable, as parties themselves – even those who insinuated or even explicitly invoked corruption at the initial stages of the proceedings – have often stopped short of formally alleging or offering evidence of corruption. Instead, initial insinuations or allegations of corruption have often given way to defenses based on some of its more visible manifestations, such as fraud or any other serious illegality.[58]

The trend towards insinuating but not fully articulating corruption suspicions has not gone unnoticed, including by arbitrators themselves. In *Thunderbird v. Mexico*, Professor Wälde cautioned against what he considered a dangerous trend – the tendency of insinuations of corruption to subtly steer the tribunal into deciding against investors without giving them the ability to defend themselves against such allegations.[59] Instead, to achieve the same end as a positive finding of corruption would have, a *modus vivendi* seems to have developed where arbitrators deal with corruption through other means, such as the so-called "legality clause" present in many investment treaties, which can

---

57. See, e.g., *Metal-Tech Ltd. v. Republic of Uzbekistan* (ICSID Case No. ARB/10/3), Award, 4 October 2013, para. 422 ("The law is clear – and rightly so – that in such a situation [of an investment tainted by corruption] the investor is deprived of protection and, consequently, the host State avoids any potential liability. That does not mean, however, that the State has not participated in creating the situation that leads to the dismissal of the claims. Because of this participation, which is implicit in the very nature of corruption, it appears fair that the Parties share in the costs.").

58. See, e.g., *Inceysa Vallisoletana v. Republic of El Salvador* (ICSID Case No. ARB/03/26), Award, 2 August 2006; *Industria Nacional de Alimentos, S.A. and Indalsa Perú, S.A. (formerly Empresas Lucchetti, S.A. and Lucchetti Perú, S.A.) v. Republic of Peru* (ICSID Case No. ARB/03/4), Award, 7 February 2005, and *Fraport AG v. The Republic of the Philippines* (ICSID Case No. ARB/03/25), Award, 16 August 2007.

59. *International Thunderbird Gaming Corporation v. The United Mexican States*, NAFTA/UNCITRAL, Award, 26 January 2006, Separate Opinion of Professor Thomas Wälde, para. 20.

"[Corruption] insinuations are now frequently employed by both claimant investors and respondent governments. They should be disregarded – explicitly and implicitly, except if properly and explicitly submitted to the tribunal, substantiated with a specific allegation of corruption and subject to proper legal and factual debate for the tribunal. That is simply the implication of the 'fair hearing' principle.... It is therefore particularly important for a tribunal not to get influenced, directly or indirectly, by 'insinuations' meant to colour and influence the arbitrators' perception and activate a conscious or subconscious bias, but to make the decision purely on grounds that have been subject to a full and fair hearing by both parties. Cards should be placed, 'face up', on the table rather than be waved around, with hints and suggestions. If the Mexican government had wanted to prove bribery it had the opportunity both to raise it and to try to prove it by providing its officials involved in the transaction for cross-examination; but it chose not to produce them."

penalize corruption indirectly by pointing to overt (and therefore easier to prove) violations of host State law permitted or otherwise acquiesced to by public officials through corruption. In the very rare instances where there have been findings of corruption by another authoritative body (invariably a national court or prosecutorial agency, as was the case in *Siemens v. Argentina* and *Niko Resources v. Bangladesh*), or when facts were admitted by a party within the arbitral proceedings that allowed for a straightforward corruption finding (as was the case in *World Duty Free* and *Metal-Tech*), corruption will be made the explicit basis for the judgment. Short of that, however, corruption will be a consideration borne in the minds of arbitrators, but the import and effect given to those allegations will remain largely unarticulated in the final award or decision.

3. Fraud and Misrepresentation

a. The concept and unilateral nature of fraud
Fraud has been defined as a "knowing misrepresentation of the truth or concealment of a material fact to induce another to act to his or her detriment".[60] In general terms, and as contained in the civil and criminal statutes of many countries,[61] a statement or omission is legally considered to constitute fraud when the following elements are present: (i) the *knowing* misrepresentation or concealment; (ii) of a *material* fact, (iii) with a view to *deceiving* another; (iv) to that other's *disadvantage*.[62] Commentators in international investment law have endorsed virtually identical definitions of fraud in the context of foreign investment disputes.[63]

In investment arbitration, however, "fraud" is frequently not alleged in this legal sense, and decisions rarely break fraud down to its constituent elements for detailed

---

60. *Black's Law Dictionary* (9th edn. 2009) p. 731.
61. See C.B. LAMM, H.T. PHAM and R. MOLOO, "Fraud and Corruption in International Arbitration" in FERNANDEZ-BALLESTEROS and ARIAS, eds., *Liber Amicorum Bernardo Cremades* (Wolters Kluwer 2010) p. 716.
62. National laws often have a further requirement concerning the other party's *reliance* upon the fact misrepresented or concealed. This element has hardly ever been identified as a separate element in investment arbitration case law, although the same can often be said of the other elements of fraud. Some exceptions are *Robert Azinian et al v. The United Mexican States* (ICSID Case No. ARB(AF)/97/2), Award, 1 November 1999; *Gustaf F.W. Hamester GmbH & Co KG v. Republic of Ghana* (ICSID Case No. ARB/07/24), Award, 18 June 2010, and *Jan de Nul N.V. & Dredging International N.V. v. Egypt* (ICSID Case No. ARB/04/13), Award, 6 November 2008. In *Azinian,* the NAFTA tribunal emphasized the reliance Mexico had placed on certain representations made by the investor within its analysis on fraud (see para. 113), thus impliedly including reliance as an element of fraud. In *Hamester,* the tribunal stressed that even if Ghana had been able to adduce sufficient evidence of the claimant's alleged fraudulent actions, Ghana would still have been unsuccessful as it had not proven "that the alleged fraud was decisive in securing the [joint venture agreement]" (see paras. 135, 137). In *Jan de Nul,* the tribunal stated that "there is no fraud when the alleged victim could have known about the relevant facts by another means", therefore implicitly requiring genuine reliance by the alleged victim (see para. 208).
63. See C. LAMM, et al., *op. cit.*, fn. 61, at p. 699 (defining fraud as "a knowing misrepresentation of the truth of a material fact to induce another to act in a manner that is detrimental to their interests").

analysis. Instead, the term is sometimes used loosely to describe all manner of undesirable behavior (including violations of the host State's laws, corruption and a lack of good faith). This unfortunately has led to the conflation of two distinct forms of misrepresentation found in the laws of numerous jurisdictions: that which is truly fraudulent (with its emphasis on the intent to deceive, or recklessness as to the true position), and that which is merely negligent (where deceit need not be proven). English contract and tort law, for example, recognize that a party who induces another to enter into a contract entirely or partly by a false statement of fact (i.e., by misrepresentation)[64] may have done so fraudulently, negligently, or non-negligently (innocently). *Fraudulent* misrepresentation occurs when a party makes a representation which is false, with the knowledge that it is false or with recklessness as to its truth.[65] *Negligent* misrepresentation occurs when a party carelessly makes a representation whilst having no reasonable basis to believe it to be true.[66] *Innocent* misrepresentation occurs when the representor has reasonable grounds for believing that his or her false statement is true.[67] The better practice, it is submitted, would be for tribunals to reserve the term "fraud" for the more serious form of misrepresentation that combines the false statement with the intent to deceive. The distinction is important, not only because the elements constituting fraudulent misrepresentation (such as intent to deceive) are different, but also because fraud has traditionally been considered a very serious allegation subjected to a higher standard of proof (discussed in Part III *infra*). Misrepresentation without deception would more properly be considered a possible violation of host State law, as that form of conduct is proscribed in most national jurisdictions.

Another characteristic that distinguishes fraud from some other forms of investor wrongdoing is its unilateral nature. Unlike corruption, the acts or omissions of only one party are necessary for fraud to occur. The other party to an arbitration need not have participated; indeed, the other party's explicit or tacit participation would call into question whether that party was truly defrauded. Fraud has accordingly been invoked in

---

64. Note that whilst there is no single meaning of "misrepresentation" for the purpose of all English law remedies, it has been generally assumed in the cases that a "misrepresentation" bears the core meaning common to most remedies: a false statement, by words or conduct (but not silence), of fact which is sufficiently certain to be relied upon by the representee excluding, therefore, statements of opinion and intention, and "sales talk" or "mere puffs". See J. CARTWRIGHT, *Misrepresentation, Mistake and Non-Disclosure* (Sweet & Maxwell 2007) p. 240.

65. The case most commonly cited as the origin of the tort in the modern English law is *Pasley v. Freeman* (1978) 3 T.R. 51; 100 E.R. 450 (fraudulent misrepresentation of a third party's creditworthiness, which caused the representee to extend credit and suffer losses); see *Derry v. Peek* (1889) LR 14 App. Cas. 337.

66. This form of misrepresentation is relatively new and was introduced to allow damages in situations where the negligence is based on the party's failure to take reasonable care, rather than intentional wrongdoing. It was first identified in the case of *Hedley Byrne v. Heller* [1964] A.C. 465, where the court found that a statement made negligently that was relied upon can be actionable in court.

67. Prior to *Hedley Byrne*, all misrepresentations that were non-fraudulent were considered to be innocent.

investment arbitration case law almost uniformly by host States as a defense against investor claims,[68] and continues to be used as a *shield* by host States.

When considering fraud as a shield in investment arbitration, national anti-fraud statutes are relevant. Because of the "legality clauses" found in many bilateral investment treaties, host States have referred to such legislation by *renvoi* to demonstrate that an investment has not been made or performed in compliance with national law, and are thus not covered "investments" to which the host State has offered the protection of any investment treaty. Even where there is no legality clause contained in the relevant investment treaty, acts of fraud are still relevant, as they may violate international public policy, usually within the ambit of concepts such as *nemo auditur propriam turpitudinem allegans*.[69] Further analysis of legality clauses, unclean hands, and international (or transnational) public policy as legal principles applicable to fraud is found in Part III infra.

Tribunals have also maintained a strict temporal differentiation in the treatment of fraud cases based on when in the life of an investment they occurred. In *Hamester*, referencing the Germany-Ghana BIT, the tribunal stated that "the legality of the creation of the investment is a jurisdictional issue," and "the legality of the investor's conduct during the life of the investment is a merits issue".[70] This temporal distinction has limited practical relevance, however: virtually all of the relevant cases surveyed involve instances of fraud that allegedly occurred at the inception of the investment. The remaining cases related not to fraud occurring during the life of the investment, but fraud in the transfer of shareholdings or claims in order to attract protection of the applicable investment treaty.

---

68. One notable exception to this is *Jan de Nul N.V. & Dredging International N.V. v. Egypt* (ICSID Case No. ARB/04/13), Award, 6 November 2008. Uniquely, that case saw the *investor* allege fraudulent misrepresentation by the host State at the inception of the investment, i.e., "at the tender stage about the scope and nature of the contract works [that induced] the Claimants to a loss-making investment", (para. 112) including the alleged "willful withholding of vital information" in that the host State entity failed to disclose pre-dredging activities already conducted, and did not provide correct geological information (para. 210).

    Egypt's anti-fraud statutes played a prominent role in the tribunal's analysis of whether a denial of substantive justice by an Egyptian court occurred, even when the parties did not themselves discuss applicable standards governing the fraud allegations. *Id.* para. 208 ("The Parties did not discuss the standards on which the alleged fraud must be measured. They have argued their case on the basis of the facts."). Finding that intent is a necessary element under Egyptian law and that "there is no fraud when the alleged victim could have known about the relevant facts by other means", the tribunal proceeded to assess the facts to review whether material information had indeed been intentionally withheld leading the claimants to enter into the contract "on wrong premises". *Id.* The tribunal analyzed each alleged fraudulent misrepresentation in detail, see paras. 230-237, 249, and concluded that the evidence did not establish fraud, and thus no issue of substantial denial of justice could be maintained.

69. E.g., *Inceysa Vallisoletana v. Republic of El Salvador* (ICSID Case No. ARB/03/26), Award, 2 August 2006, paras. 230-239 and *Plama Consortium Limited v. Bulgaria* (ICSID Case No. ARB/03/24), Award, 27 August 2008, paras. 138-146.

70. *Gustaf F.W. Hamester GmbH & Co KG v. Republic of Ghana* (ICSID Case No. ARB/07/24), Award, 18 June 2010, para. 127.

b.   The treatment of the elements of fraud in the investment case law

There is a growing body of jurisprudence on fraud in investment arbitration. This type of investor wrongdoing is frequently alleged or insinuated, with the elements of fraud having been analyzed in some depth in at least fifteen cases.[71] Some of these decisions mention both fraud *and* corruption,[72] or couple fraud with issues of good faith and clean hands.[73] As discussed earlier, the unilateral nature of fraud may have caused some tribunals to rely solely on fraud-related issues in order to avoid difficult questions of equity and State responsibility, or to make it easier to make an affirmative finding of investor wrongdoing.

Of these fifteen cases, the majority resulted in a positive finding of fraud leading to a decision that the tribunal had no jurisdiction over the case,[74] whether for violation of

---

71. *Robert Azinian et al v. The United Mexican States* (ICSID Case No. ARB(AF)/97/2), Award, 1 November 1999; *Inceysa Vallisoletana v. Republic of El Salvador* (ICSID Case No. ARB/03/26), Award, 2 August 2006; *Plama Consortium Limited v. Bulgaria* (ICSID Case No. ARB/03/24), Award, 27 August 2008; *Cementownia "NowaHuta" S.A. v. Republic of Turkey* (ICSID Case No. ARB(AF)/06/2), Award, 17 September 2009; *Europe Cement Investment & Trade S.A. v. Republic of Turkey* (ICSID Case No.ARB(AF)/07/2), Award, 13 August 2009; *Libananco Holdings Co. Limited v. Republic of Turkey* (ICSID Case No. ARB/06/8), Award, 2 September 2011; *Fraport AG v. The Republic of the Philippines* (ICSID Case No. ARB/03/25), Award, 16 August 2007; *Waguih Elie George Siag and Clorinda Vecchi v. The Arab Republic of Egypt* (ICSID Case No. ARB/05/15), Award, 1 June 2009; *Jan de Nul N.V. & Dredging International N.V. v. Egypt* (ICSID Case No. ARB/04/13), Award, 6 November 2008; *Gustaf F.W. Hamester GmbH & Co KG v. Republic of Ghana* (ICSID Case No. ARB/07/24), Award, 18 June 2010; *Quiborax S.A., Non Metallic Minerals S.A. and Allan Fosk Kaplún v. Plurinational State of Bolivia* (ICSID Case No. ARB/06/2), Decision on Jurisdiction, 27 September 2012; *Teinver S.A., Transportes de Cercanías S.A. and Autobuses Urbanos del Sur S.A. v. The Argentine Republic* (ICSID Case No. ARB/09/1), Decision on Jurisdiction, 21 December 2012; *Hulley Enterprises (Cyprus) Limited, Yukos Universal Limited (Isle of Man) and Veteran Petroleum Limited (Cyprus) v. Russian Federation*, PCA Case Nos. AA226-28, Final Awards, 18 July 2014.

72. *Inceysa Vallisoletana v. Republic of El Salvador* (ICSID Case No. ARB/03/26), Award, 2 August 2006; *Fraport AG v. The Republic of the Philippines* (ICSID Case No. ARB/03/25), Award, 16 August 2007; *Waguih Elie George Siag and Clorinda Vecchi v. The Arab Republic of Egypt* (ICSID Case No. ARB/05/15), Award, 1 June 2009. Conversely, in *Metal-Tech Ltd. v. Republic of Uzbekistan* (ICSID Case No. ARB/10/3), Award, 4 October 2013, the host State made specific allegations of fraud (see para. 110: "In particular, the Claimant engaged in corruption and made fraudulent and material representations to gain approval for the investment."), but the tribunal considered that it could dispense with an analysis of these allegations, having already made a finding that the admissions made by the claimant's principal witness was sufficient for a finding of corruption, resulting in the tribunal's dismissal of the case for lack of jurisdiction.

73. E.g., *Plama Consortium Limited v. Bulgaria* (ICSID Case No. ARB/03/24), Award, 27 August 2008; *Inceysa Vallisoletana v. Republic of El Salvador* (ICSID Case No. ARB/03/26), Award, 2 August 2006.

74. One contrary example is *Siag v. Egypt,* where the majority of the tribunal found a lack of evidence based on the failure to meet the high standard of proof found applicable to fraud allegations (see *Waguih Elie George Siag and Clorinda Vecchi v. The Arab Republic of Egypt* (ICSID Case No. ARB/05/15), Award, 1 June 2009, paras. 325-326); the dissenting arbitrator, Prof. Francisco Orrego Vicuña, advocated a less restrictive standard and did find evidence of fraud and corruption. See also *Gustaf F.W. Hamester GmbH & Co KG v. Republic of Ghana* (ICSID Case No. ARB/07/24), Award, 18 June 2010 (jurisdictional objection dismissed for lack of proof of an "overall scheme of deceit" and that the State would not have entered into the agreement had it known of the

the "legality clause" in an investment treaty,[75] on the basis of failure to prove that the claimant is a covered "investor",[76] or because fraudulent conduct as a violation of national law and "international public policy" should result in a denial of jurisdiction.[77] In other cases concerning investment treaties without explicit "legality clauses", fraud findings resulted in tribunals determining that the investor's claims are inadmissible,[78] or must be denied on the merits due to the invalidity of the underlying investment contract.[79]

While the outcomes of fraud have displayed some consistency, the discussion of what conduct must be present to lead to a conclusion of fraud has been less so. Identification and analysis of the constitutive elements of fraudulent misrepresentation were rare, and no attempt was made to distinguish between fraud and the more "simple" forms of negligent or innocent misrepresentation, whether under national law or some principle of international public policy. Nonetheless, in most of the cases where fraud plays an outcome-determinative role, deliberate intent to deceive concerning a material fact which worked to the detriment of the host State was found by the tribunal (albeit implicitly): notable examples of these include *Plama v. Bulgaria, Inceysa v. El Salvador, Azinian v. Mexico,* and *Hamester v. Ghana.*

In *Plama,*[80] the host State argued that the tribunal did not have jurisdiction as the claimant's investment was void ab initio under Bulgarian law due to misrepresentations made in the process of procuring the investment.[81] The tribunal found that the claimant had indeed engaged in fraud, having "represented to the Bulgarian Government that the investor was a consortium – which was true during the early stages of negotiations" but then "failed deliberately to inform [the] Respondent of the change in circumstances"

---

deceit); *Teinver S.A., Transportes de Cercanías S.A. and Autobuses Urbanos del Sur S.A. v. The Argentine Republic* (ICSID Case No. ARB/09/1), Decision on Jurisdiction, 21 December 2012 (host State failed to demonstrate that investor committed illegalities in the process of acquiring its investment); *Jan de Nul N.V. & Dredging International N.V. v. Egypt* (ICSID Case No. ARB/04/13), Award, 6 November 2008 (evidence did not establish that the host State entity committed fraud upon the investor); *Quiborax S.A., Non Metallic Minerals S.A. and Allan Fosk Kaplún v. Plurinational State of Bolivia* (ICSID Case No. ARB/06/2), Decision on Jurisdiction, 27 September 2012 (allegations of fraudulent fabrication of evidence of investor's shareholdings not substantiated by host State).

75. *Fraport AG v. The Republic of the Philippines* (ICSID Case No. ARB/03/25), Award, 16 August 2007.

76. *Cementownia "NowaHuta" S.A. v. Republic of Turkey* (ICSID Case No. ARB(AF)/06/2), Award, 17 September 2009; *Europe Cement Investment & Trade S.A. v. Republic of Turkey* (ICSID Case No.ARB(AF)/07/2), Award, 13 August 2009; *Libananco Holdings Co. Limited v. Republic of Turkey* (ICSID Case No. ARB/06/8), Award, 2 September 2011.

77. *Inceysa Vallisoletana v. Republic of El Salvador* (ICSID Case No. ARB/03/26), Award, 2 August 2006.

78. In *Plama v. Bulgaria,* the applicable investment treaties (the Energy Charter Treaty and the Cyprus-Bulgaria BIT) did not contain legality clauses; the tribunal nonetheless found the claims inadmissible for violating Bulgarian and international anti-fraud principles: *Plama Consortium Limited v. Bulgaria* (ICSID Case No. ARB/03/24), Award, 27 August 2008.

79. *Robert Azinian et al v. The United Mexican States* (ICSID Case No. ARB(AF)/97/2), Award, 1 November 1999.

80. *Plama Consortium Limited v. Bulgaria* (ICSID Case No. ARB/03/24), Award, 27 August 2008.

81. Under Art. 5(1) of the Bulgarian Privatization Act, the obtaining of Bulgaria's consent to an investment by misrepresentation vitiated consent.

when the investor became an individual acting alone, without significant financial resources.[82] The Tribunal found that even though Bulgaria did not ask for the withheld information, the claimant was aware of new facts about which it was obliged to inform State officials.[83] As such, the tribunal found that the investor had engaged in "deliberate concealment amounting to fraud, calculated to induce the Bulgarian authorities to authorize the transfer of shares to an entity that did not have the financial and managerial capabilities required…".[84] The tribunal also found that the investor engaged in "deceitful conduct that is in violation of Bulgarian law", and that granting the Energy Charter Treaty's protections "to the claimant's investment would be contrary to the basic notion of international public policy – that a contract obtained by wrongful means (fraudulent misrepresentation) should not be enforced by a tribunal",[85] invoking the principle *nemo auditur propriam turpitudinem allegans*.[86]

In *Azinian*, Mexico objected to the tribunal's jurisdiction on the basis of alleged misrepresentations made by the claimants in relation to a waste collection and disposal concession, both as to their financial capabilities and experience, as well as to the continued interest of a partner company having the necessary expertise.[87] While the tribunal did not discuss each element of fraud schematically, its analysis implicitly did so, focusing on whether there had been a knowing misrepresentation[88] of a material fact,[89] with an intent to deceive[90] and on which government authorities had relied.[91] The tribunal found that the city government "was led to sign the Concession Contract on false pretences" and denied the claimant any redress on the merits: "the claim has failed in its entirety".[92]

---

82. *Plama Consortium Limited v. Bulgaria* (ICSID Case No. ARB/03/24), Award, 27 August 2008, paras. 133-134.

83. *Id.* at para. 134.

84. *Id.* at para. 135.

85. *Id.* at para. 143.

86. *Id.* at paras. 136-138. It bears noting that while the ECT does not contain an "in accordance with law" clause, the tribunal held nonetheless that among the treaty's aims was the strengthening of the rule of law on energy issues. As such, the tribunal held that the ECT should "be interpreted in a manner consistent with the aim of encouraging respect for the rule of law .... which means that it cannot apply to investments made contrary to law". See *id.*, paras. 138-140.

87. *Robert Azinian et al v. The United Mexican States* (ICSID Case No. ARB(AF)/97/2), Award, 1 November 1999. *Azinian* is the first NAFTA case where a decision on the merits was rendered. *Id.* at para. 79.

88. *Id.* at para. 33 ("The evidence compels the conclusion that the Claimants entered into the Concession Contract on false pretences, and lacked the capacity to perform it.").

89. *Id.* at para. 109 ("an absolutely fundamental fact had changed: the Claimants had fallen out with Sunlaw Energy, who had disappeared from the project" before the signing of the Concession Contract).

90. This may be implied by the tribunal's finding that, "[f]or the Claimants to have gone ahead without alerting the Ayutamiento to this [Sunlaw's non-involvement] was unconscionable". *Id.* at para. 110.

91. *Id.* at para. 104 ("Ayutamiento was misled as to DESONA's capacity to perform the concession") and para. 113 ("the contemporaneous written evidence relating to the period prior to signature shows reliance on the representations of the Claimant as to their own capabilities".).

92. *Id.* at paras. 121, 125.

In *Inceysa*, the tribunal found that the claimant had made fraudulent misrepresentations and non-disclosures during a public bid for a concession to mechanical inspection services for vehicles in El Salvador.[93] The tribunal discussed in detail various misrepresentations made by the claimant in its bid,[94] and considered whether the false information provided (or withheld) concerned a "central aspect of the bid", thus addressing materiality.[95] The tribunal made findings on the deceitful intent of the investor: for example, it found that Inceysa had falsely and "deliberately" made the host State believe that its strategic partner was a large public entity with relevant experience.[96] The tribunal also identified aspects of deceit in the claimant's conduct misrepresenting its compliance with bid requirements, and inferred that such misrepresentations would have led El Salvador to award the bid to the Claimant.[97] But *Inceysa* did not stop at fraud: for the tribunal, fraud was also considered indicative of a lack of good faith, with good faith "a generally accepted rule or standard".[98] Because the claimant had "falsified the facts", a lack of good faith ensued from the inception of the investment in violation of Salvadoran law, which for the tribunal meant that it "can only declare its incompetence to hear *Inceysa's* complaint, since its investment cannot benefit from the protection of the BIT".[99] *Inceysa* then linked fraud to the Latin maxim *nemo auditur propriam turpitudinem allegans* (as well as six related Latin maxims).[100] Identifying *ex dolo malo non oritur actio* ("an action does not arise from fraud") as applicable, the tribunal

> "affirm[ed] that the foreign investor cannot seek to benefit from an investment effectuated by means of one or several illegal acts and, consequently, enjoy the protection granted by the host State, such as access to international arbitration to

---

93. *Inceysa Vallisoletana v. Republic of El Salvador* (ICSID Case No. ARB/03/26), Award, 2 August 2006, para. 236.
94. The tribunal identified five instances of misrepresentation: (i) submitting false and incorrect financial statements (paras. 103-110), (ii) submitting false information on the identity of the claimant's strategic partner, as well as the capacity and experience of the claimant and its partner (paras. 111-118), (iii) submitting false documents regarding the experience of the claimant's sole administrator (paras. 119-122), (iv) omitting information about the connection between the claimant and another bid participant (paras. 123-127), and (v) submitting false documents allegedly signed with municipalities in the Philippines and Panama (para. 128).
95. The tribunal considered that each instance of misrepresentation was fundamental to the bid, and in one case, was "a deceit of one of the central aspects of the bid".
96. *Inceysa Vallisoletana v. Republic of El Salvador* (ICSID Case No. ARB/03/26), Award, 2 August 2006, para. 112.
97. *Id.* at paras. 118, 123.
98. It is unclear whether this was meant to be a general principle of law within the meaning of Art. 38(1)(c) of the ICJ Statute. See *Inceysa Vallisoletana v. Republic of El Salvador* (ICSID Case No. ARB/03/26), Award, 2 August 2006, paras. 231 et seq. ("absence of deceit and artifice during the negotiations and execution of instruments that gave rise to the investment").
99. *Inceysa Vallisoletana v. Republic of El Salvador* (ICSID Case No. ARB/03/26), Award, 2 August 2006, para. 239.
100. *Id.* at para. 240.

resolve disputes, because it is evident that its act had a fraudulent origin and, as provided by the legal maxim, 'nobody can benefit from his own fraud'."[101]

This "kitchen sink" approach saw fraud as leading to a lack of jurisdiction (the El Salvador-Spain-BIT having been found to limit its protection to investments made in accordance with the laws of the host State)[102] as well as inadmissibility for lack of good faith, unclean hands, and a violation of international public policy.

Unlike the foregoing cases, in *Hamester v. Ghana* the host State's jurisdictional objections that the claimant's investment (a joint venture cocoa production operation) was tainted with fraud were not sustained. Ghana had made multiple allegations of fraud against the investor, allegedly occurring both at the inception of the investment[103] and while it was operating in Ghana.[104] However, the Tribunal considered that only instances of fraud at the initiation of the investment were relevant at the jurisdictional phase: "the only question here is whether Hamester perpetrated a fraud, and thereby procured the signing of the [joint venture agreement]".[105] The tribunal sought proof of knowingly perpetrated fraud (an "overall scheme of deceit orchestrated by the claimant");[106] it also emphasized the element of materiality that fraud needed to play for the procurement of the investment, and found no proof "that the alleged fraud was decisive in securing the JVA".[107] The tribunal ultimately held that there was no conclusive evidence of "an overall scheme of deceit" at the initiation of the investment.[108]

Many of the other cases raise a different form of fraud that resides in the arbitral process itself rather than the investment in question. In the trio of separate but related cases involving the concession agreements with the Turkish Government – *Cementownia,*

---

101. *Id.* at para. 242.
102. *Id.* at para. 207.
103. Although not entirely clear, Ghana's fraud allegations in this regard appear to relate to the falsification of certain invoices: "[t]he documents in this arbitration confirm that Hamester presented false invoices to the GCB [Respondent] and to Wamco and that Hamester did indeed obtain loan repayments from Wamco to which it was not entitled. Messrs Opferkuch and Erhardt and Hamester thereby committed the felony of obtaining property by false presences, in contravention of section 131 of Ghana's Criminal Code of 1960. They also breached Ghana's common law rules against fraud and the statutory fiduciary duties under the Companies Code 1963.": *Gustaf F.W. Hamester GmbH & Co KG v. Republic of Ghana* (ICSID Case No. ARB/07/24), Award, 18 June 2010, para. 130.
104. See *Gustaf F.W. Hamester GmbH & Co KG v. Republic of Ghana* (ICSID Case No. ARB/07/24), Award, 18 June 2010, paras. 97-122. These alleged acts of fraud involved various means for extracting profit, such as price manipulation.
105. *Id.* at para. 129.
106. *Id.* at para. 136.
107. *Id.* at para. 135. While there was evidence of some invoices for the modernization of the factory being inflated (failing to record discounts received) without the respondent's knowledge (para. 132), the tribunal held that this inflation went back to a time before the JV, when the rehabilitation of the factory was being done on a Loan Agreement (para. 132). However, the Tribunal held that the evidence submitted did not prove that all the invoices were so inflated (para. 134). In addition, the tribunal found that there was also no proof that the invoices induced the respondent to sign the JV agreement (paras. 135-138).
108. *Id.* at paras. 132-137.

Europe Cement, and *Libananco* – the tribunal found that the claims themselves were fatally tainted by fraud because shares in the claimant company were transferred from Turkish companies to companies with other (Polish and Cypriot) nationalities *post factum* in order to appear as if the investments were eligible for protection and arbitration under the relevant investment treaties.[109] These, along with *Quiborax v. Bolivia*,[110] are more properly characterized as abuse of process cases.

Finally, there are cases that straddle both fraud and other violations of host State law. In *Fraport v. Philippines*, for example, both corruption and fraud allegations had initially been made by the host State, which then stated that these would be redressed in other venues.[111] The case could thus be classified as primarily a case concerning other forms of illegality, as the primary national criminal statute under consideration, the Philippine Anti-Dummy Law, regulated a form of conduct that would not be considered *mala in se* but merely *malum prohibitum*; the law prohibited the exercise of foreign managerial control over certain designated areas of the economy, including public utilities such as airport terminals (the investment project in question). Still, the case is notable from the perspective of investor fraud because it is another instance in which a tribunal looked seriously into the elements of fraud, particularly whether the investor had *knowingly* engaged in misrepresentation against the host State. The tribunal learned over the course of the hearing that a secret shareholders' agreement had been entered into between the investor and its local partner that gave the investor managerial control over the joint

---

109. See *Cementownia "NowaHuta" S.A. v. Republic of Turkey* (ICSID Case No. ARB(AF)/06/2), Award, 17 September 2009, paras. 158 ("Cementownia and Kemal Uzan invented *post factum* the transaction and transfer of the shares"), 172 ("the Claimant has filed a fraudulent claim against the Republic of Turkey"); *Europe Cement Investment & Trade S.A. v. Republic of Turkey* (ICSID Case No. ARB(AF)/07/2), Award, 13 August 2009, para. 167 ("All of the evidence ... is that the share transfer agreements are not what they claim to be and that no transfer of CEAS and Kepez shares to Europe Cement took place at least before 12 June 2003. Indeed, the evidence points to the conclusion that the claim to ownership of the shares at a time that would establish jurisdiction was made fraudulently.").

In a similar vein, in *Libananco v. Turkey*, although the host State had requested that the tribunal declare that the claimant had asserted its claims in bad faith and on the basis of fraudulent documents, the tribunal did not delve into the allegations of fraud, finding a lack of jurisdiction on the basis that the claimant had not proven that it owned the relevant shares at the time of the alleged expropriation. *Libananco Holdings Co. Limited v. Republic of Turkey* (ICSID Case No. ARB/06/8), Award, 2 September 2011.

110. In *Quiborax S.A., Non Metallic Minerals S.A. and Allan Fosk Kaplún v. Plurinational State of Bolivia* (ICSID Case No. ARB/06/2), Decision on Jurisdiction, 27 September 2012, Bolivia raised as a jurisdictional objection the alleged "fabricated evidence purporting to show" that the claimants were shareholders of the Bolivian company NMM "solely to gain access to ICSID arbitration under the Chile-Bolivia BIT". The tribunal found that the allegations of fraudulent fabrication of evidence (i.e., certain share transfer documents) were not substantiated by Bolivia. It ruled that the claimants' account of the facts was "consistent and well-documented" and that while there were some "documentary discrepancies ... these do not provoke fraud or suffice to overcome the plentiful evidence in support of the Claimants' case". *Id.* at para. 192.

111. *Fraport AG v. The Republic of the Philippines* (ICSID Case No. ARB/03/25), Award, 16 August 2007, para. 5. The Philippines stated that evidence for fraud and corruption was being provided in a related ICC arbitration with the investor and that investigations were underway in various countries.

venture company which held a concession to build and operate the new terminal at the international airport in Manila. The claimant had thus "knowingly and intentionally circumvented the [Anti-Dummy Law] by means of secret shareholder agreements".[112] The investor did this despite having been advised by national lawyers that such an arrangement would violate Philippine law.[113] The element of reliance by the host State on the misrepresentation was arguably also considered through the tribunal's discussion on estoppel.[114] *Fraport* is discussed further in the next category of investor wrongdoing – the breach of host State law.

4. Breach of Host State Law

The "in accordance with host State law" condition found in many investment treaties would almost certainly cover corruption and fraud, since this conduct will in all likelihood amount to a violation of the laws of any host State. At first glance, these clauses might introduce much broader restrictions besides these on access to investment treaty arbitration. Indeed, some States argue that any breach of host State law should be grounds to exclude treaty protection.

In fact, the publicly available cases reveal a growing consensus that such clauses only cover the investor's illegal conduct at the inception of an investment, and relate to host State laws on the admission of foreign investment, or possibly other fundamental principles of host State law. In *Quiborax*, the tribunal stated that the "subject-matter scope of the legality requirement" is limited to the following categories:

(i) non-trivial violations of the host State's legal order (*TokiosTokelés*, *LESI* and *Desert Line*),
(ii) violations of the host State's foreign investment regime (*Saba Fakes*), and
(iii) fraud – for instance, to secure the investment (*Inceysa*, *Plama*, *Hamester*) or profits (*Fraport*).[115]

---

112. *Id.* at para. 401.
113. *Id.* at para. 323 ("Despite having been advised and plainly understanding [that Fraport's controlling and managing the investment was illegal under Philippine law], Fraport secretly designed its investment in the project so as to have that prohibited management and control...").
114. The *Fraport AG* tribunal considered in what situations, due to the complicity of public officials, an estoppel might arise. While maintaining that "principles of fairness should require a tribunal to hold a government estopped from raising violations of its own law as a jurisdictional defense when it knowingly overlooked them and endorsed an investment which was not in compliance with its law", the claimant's "covert" arrangement was, by its nature, unknown to public officials and thus the tribunal held that this "cannot be any basis for estoppel": *Fraport AG v. The Republic of the Philippines* (ICSID Case No. ARB/03/25), Award, 16 August 2007, paras. 346-347, 387.
115. *Quiborax S.A., Non Metallic Minerals S.A. and Allan Fosk Kaplún v. Plurinational State of Bolivia* (ICSID Case No. ARB/06/2), Decision on Jurisdiction, 27 September 2012, para. 266. Similarly, in *Metal-Tech Ltd. v. Republic of Uzbekistan* (ICSID Case No. ARB/10/3), Award, 4 October 2013, a case concerning corruption, the tribunal explained the subject-matter scope of the applicable treaty's legality requirement as follows:

"In general, on the basis of existing case law, it considers that the subject-matter scope of the legality requirement covers: (i) non-trivial violations of the host State's legal order (*Tokios Tokeles*

Instances of violation of host State law tend to concern investor fraud, deceit, or misrepresentation at the inception of an investment. Typically such conduct takes the form of a transgression of laws concerning the admission of foreign investment, including limits or an outright prohibition against foreign investors acquiring a particular category of investments, such as interests in public utilities, carrying out a certain business activity, or prescribing the manner in which foreign investors may hold such investments. Alternatively, investments which are otherwise lawful, such as shareholdings, may have been acquired by illegal means, fraud, or otherwise breach other fundamental principles of host State law. Arbitral practice concerning such conduct, in the light of the "in accordance with host State law" provision, is discussed in Part IV below.

III. PROVING INVESTOR WRONGDOING

Arbitrators faced with allegations of investor wrongdoing are no longer concerned with questions of first principle – there is wide consensus that transnational corruption and fraud, as seen in investment arbitration cases, are unlawful as well as immoral, and should be sanctioned. Investments that were either obtained or performed under a cloud of illegality under other national laws are treated in much the same way by international tribunals. But this unity in proscription has not translated into similar procedural rules and methodologies in proving corruption. Although the rules are outwardly the same – similar standards of proof apply to corruption and fraud, for example – the results have been very different.

Corruption. The primary difficulty that most tribunals profess to encounter when faced with corruption allegations is how they are to be tested or proven. The most common modality of corruption in transnational investment, bribery, is perpetrated by parties who have power and resources, and collude precisely to avoid any trace of corrupt conduct.[116] This raises questions about the proper evidentiary standard that must be

---

v. Ukraine (ICSID Case No. ARB/02/18), Decision on Jurisdiction, 29 April 2004; *LESI SpA and Astaldi SpA v. People's Democratic Republic of Algeria* (ICSID Case No. ARB/05/03), Decision on Jurisdiction, 12 July 2006 and *Desert Line Projects LLC v. Republic of Yemen* (ICSID Case No. ARB/05/17), Award, 6 February 2008), (ii) violations of the host State's foreign investment regime (*Saba Fakes v. Republic of Turkey* (ICSID Case No. ARB/07/20), Award, 14 July 2010), and (iii) fraud – for instance, to secure the investment (*Inceysa Vallisoletana v. Republic of El Salvador* (ICSID Case No. ARB/03/26), Award, 2 August 2006; *Plama Consortium Limited v. Bulgaria* (ICSID Case No. ARB/03/24), Award, 27 August 2008; *Gustaf F.W. Hamester GmbH & Co KG v. Republic of Ghana* (ICSID Case No. ARB/07/24), Award, 18 June 2010) or to secure profits."

Metal-Tech Ltd v. The Republic of Uzbekistan (ICSID Case No. ARB/10/3), Award, 4 October 2013, para. 165 (footnotes omitted).

116. In a similar fashion, a commentator has noted that "like most crimes and intentional misconduct, and perhaps more so, acts of corruption and collusion are specifically designed not to be able to be identified or detected". Karen MILLS, "Corruption and Other Illegality in the Formation and Performance of Contracts and in the Conduct of Arbitrations Relating Thereto" in *International Commercial Arbitration: Important Contemporary Questions*, ICCA Congress Series no. 11 (2003)

applied; how parties are charged with burdens of proving corruption allegations; and under what circumstances, if any, such burdens of proof should shift. These evidentiary issues also lead to broader questions about the identity and role of arbitral tribunals as decision-makers of fact: should arbitrators be pro-active in trying to ferret out corruption? And if allegations are made, what are the evidentiary rules, and do these rules implicitly aid or actually deter arbitrators from undertaking this sensitive task?

There are rare cases such as *World Duty Free*, *Azpetrol*, and *Metal-Tech* where the investor openly admitted, in varying degrees, to the facts that established corruption during the proceedings. It is also likely that in the future, situations where investor corruption is admitted before national prosecutors and courts in their home States, such as in *Siemens* and *Niko*, will continue to grow, as capital-exporting States continue to take steps to police transnational corruption effectively. Those cases point to the impact national prosecutorial agencies may have in affecting arbitral outcomes where corruption is at issue by aiding in the establishment of the underlying facts, a development that is to be encouraged, although not unqualifiedly.[117] Ultimately, international tribunals must make independent assessments of key facts irrespective of the findings of national authorities.[118]

In the majority of cases where corruption may attend the investment, however, arbitrators will be faced with the question of how to ascertain whether corruption did occur on the basis of imperfect, episodic, and often contradictory evidence, with little aid from national authorities. The absence of an unbroken chain of facts leading to a morally certain conclusion that corruption did occur necessitates reliance on longstanding legal tools familiar to national and international courts and tribunals concerning rules of evidence on standards and burdens of proof, presumptions, and

---

(henceforth *ICCA Congress Series no. 11*) p. 295.

117. In *Niko Resources v. Bangladesh*, the tribunal acknowledged that national authorities were better placed to gather evidence and establish the necessary proof of corruption. See *Niko Resources (Bangladesh) Ltd. v. Bangladesh & Ors* (ICSID Case No. ARB/10/11 and ARB/10/18), Decision on Jurisdiction, 19 August 2013, para. 425 ("In the present case, the acts of corruption of which the Claimant was convicted were committed in Bangladesh. If there were any other such acts committed they must have concerned persons making decisions in Bangladesh. Therefore, the authorities of Bangladesh were best placed to investigate and collect proof of corruption relevant for the present case.").

There is always a risk, however, that domestic investigations are used either for political ends or even tactically to buttress the strength of a host State's position in arbitration. In *EDF (Services) v. Romania* (ICSID Case No. ARB/05/13), Award, 8 October 2009, the investor criticized the domestic investigation and exoneration of public officials; this stands in contrast to *Fraport AG v. The Republic of the Philippines* (ICSID Case No. ARB/03/25), Award, 16 August 2007, where national prosecutorial authorities' findings were that there was no violation of national "anti-dummy law" legislation, which ran against the host State's position in the arbitration.

118. In *Inceysa*, the tribunal held that State parties' determinations as to the legality or illegality of investment are not determinative of the issue for the purposes for the purposes of establishing the Tribunal's jurisdiction under a BIT (see *Inceysa Vallisoletana v. Republic of El Salvador* (ICSID Case No. ARB/03/26), Award, 2 August 2006, paras. 209-213). It is thus for the tribunal to determine if actions are fraudulent and domestic court findings regarding such actions are not res judicata for the purposes of determining jurisdiction under a BIT.

inferences that lead to a proper "connecting of the dots".[119] Rather than leaving parties to guess at the appropriate standard and burden of proof to apply in cases of corruption and beyond, if there is doubt, one suggestion is that arbitrators "should give the parties some guidance, preferably prior to the taking of evidence, as to the burden of proof and the standard of proof, so that the parties can adapt themselves to those requirements and standards",[120] thereby strengthening due process in arbitration.

Fraud and misrepresentation. Accusations of fraud and misrepresentation appear to be treated with relative ease, indeed perhaps with too much ease, by investment tribunals. Commentators have observed the straightforward manner in which accusations of fraud and misrepresentation were proven in *Plama*.[121] The host State had alleged that the investor had made misrepresentations in procuring its investment, particularly with respect to the identity of its own investors, and "simply had to submit to the tribunal the correspondence received from the claimant describing its company, and evidence confirming the true ownership of the company".[122]

Similarly, in *Inceysa*, El Salvador alleged fraud on the part of the investor during the public bidding process. The tribunal concluded that fraudulent misrepresentations had occurred in respect of the investor's financial information after a comparison of the investor's financial statements submitted pursuant to the bid against those filed for the same fiscal years with the Spanish Commercial Registry.[123]

Thus, while arbitrators tasked with deciding fraud and corruption allegations are in theory faced with similar evidentiary burdens, allegations of fraud and misrepresentation have in reality been easier to prove. The bilateral nature of corruption vis-à-vis other (unilateral) forms of investor wrongdoing certainly plays a role here: for corruption, *both* parties have taken care to conceal their actions, and the case law has accordingly shown that corruption has never been affirmatively proven, absent admissions of fact made by the investor. But perhaps the more compelling explanation is that tribunals appear to

---

119. See *International Thunderbird Gaming Corporation v. The United Mexican States*, NAFTA/UNCITRAL, Separate Opinion of Thomas Wälde, para. 3 (citations omitted):

"Since the arbitration has, as often or always, not elucidated all relevant facts, one needs to rely on standard practice of rules of evidence, burden of proof and presumptions to determine when the claimant and when the respondent has to bear the respective burden. In addition, as recently explained again by the *Methanex v. US* award, what is unknown but relevant has to be dealt with by inference, *i.e.* by taking the 'dots' that are available, drawing explanatory lines between them and then determine what explanation can be inferred by relying on burden of proof allocation, prima facie evidence and arbitral determination of the evidence. They need to be assessed not only from the lofty spheres of commercial arbitration law, but also with a real-life understanding of the 'coal-face' of foreign investment practices." (footnote omitted)

120. José ROSSELL and Harvey PRAGER, "Illicit Commissions and International Arbitration: The Question of Proof", 15 Arb. Int'l. (1999) p. 329 at p. 348.

121. C. LAMM, et al., *op. cit.*, fn. 61, citing *Plama Consortium Limited v. Bulgaria* (ICSID Case No. ARB/03/24), Award, 27 August 2008, para. 128.

122. See C. LAMM, et al., *op. cit.*, fn. 61, citing *Plama Consortium Limited v. Bulgaria* (ICSID Case No. ARB/03/24), Award, 27 August 2008, para. 128.

123. *Inceysa Vallisoletana v. Republic of El Salvador* (ICSID Case No. ARB/03/26), Award, 2 August 2006, para. 105.

have been ready to make affirmative findings of fraud by focusing only on the *objective* fact that an investor's statement or representation was false, without going further to the *subjective* element of the investor's intent to deceive. As discussed in Part II, the intent to deceive has certainly been found to be present in a number of fraud cases but these have mostly been stated as a conclusion, with little reasoning to demonstrate how that conclusion was reached. To this extent, the present state of investment jurisprudence on fraud is unsatisfactory.

Breach of host State law. Finally, as to investor wrongdoing arising from breaches of host State law, each of these violations of civil and criminal statutes would of course have specific rules on proof found within those domestic systems. Arbitrators would thus have ready rules from which they may make determinations on the appropriate standards and burdens of proof. That said, the fact-finding process in international arbitration is not bound to national standards, a fortiori in ICSID arbitration, in which Art. 34 of the Convention confirms that tribunals are not bound by domestic rules of evidence. Yet in applying domestic law, international tribunals are obliged "to strive to apply the law as interpreted by the State's highest court, and in harmony with its interpretative... authorities".[124]

1. *Tribunals as Inquisitors? The Scope of an Arbitrator's Duty to Seek Out Evidence of Investor Wrongdoing*

Summarizing the obligations of arbitrators faced with resolving issues concerning corruption, fraud and related forms of wrongdoing, Cremades stated:

> "[t]he position today is that the international arbitrator has a clear duty to address issues of bribery, money laundering or serious fraud whenever they arise in the arbitration and whatever the wishes of the parties and to record its legal and factual conclusions in its award. This is the only course available to protect the enforceability of the award and the integrity of the institution of international commercial arbitration.[125]

---

124. *Soufraki v. United Arab Emirates*), Decision on Annulment, 5 June 2007, para. 97; and see Case concerning the Payment in Gold of Brazilian Federal Loans Contracted in France, Permanent Court of International Justice, 12 July 1929, PCIJ Reports, Ser. A, No. 21, 1929, pp. 27-28 ("Once the Court has arrived at the conclusion that it is to apply the municipal law of a particular country, there seems no doubt that it must seek to apply it as it would be applied in that country. It would not be applying the municipal law of a country if it were to apply it in a manner different from that in which that law would be applied in the country in which it is in force. It follows that the Court must pay the utmost regard to the decisions of the municipal courts of a country, for it is with the aid of their jurisprudence that it will be enabled to decide what are the rules which, in actual fact, are applied in the country the law of which is recognized as applicable in a given case.").

125. B. CREMADES and D.J.A. CAIRNS, "Transnational Public Policy" in Kristine KARSTEN, Andrew BERKELEY, eds., *Arbitration: Money, Laundering, Corruption and Fraud* (2003) p. 65 at p. 85.

While there has been some doubt about the precise scope and content of the duties of arbitral tribunals towards national authorities when dealing with illegality,[126] there is no doubt that tribunals are obliged *to the parties* to address issues of wrongdoing that are directly raised before them as part of their decision-making duty, particularly when corruption can potentially affect the outcome of the case. But if tribunals are faced with only insinuations of corruption, or certain facts arise that lead to no more than a suspicion of corruption, or tribunals suspect that a party is not forthcoming with all evidence that can be given to prove corruption or other wrongdoing, would tribunals nonetheless be under a duty to pursue and investigate?

For a number of reasons, it seems that tribunals are so obliged. As discussed previously, investment arbitrators bear obligations not only to the immediate parties to a dispute, but to the public of the host State and indeed the international community as a whole;[127] it is no coincidence that public international law and transnational public policy form part of the law that must be applied in investment arbitration. Thus, to the extent that the substantive law requires actors to pursue wrongdoing (for example, the application of contemporary anti-corruption law in good faith requires enforcement), tribunals should deal with the issue *propio motu* as soon as certain facts emerge that raise concerns as to whether corruption attended the investment at some stage. Indeed, even apart from international anti-corruption norms *per se*, some commentators have argued that arbitral tribunals have a duty to investigate a potential issue of corruption *sua sponte*, not least to ensure the enforceability of its award.[128]

The practice of tribunals has been inconsistent, with some tribunals preferring to allow the adversarial process to take its course without intervening directly absent compelling indications.[129] But other cases exhibit more inquisitorial leanings. In *Metal-*

---

126. As recently as 2003, there seemed to be little by way of mandatory requirements of disclosure to national authorities. B. Cremades and D.J.A. Cairns were "aware of no express legislation requiring a tribunal to disclose to regulatory authorities that criminal activity might have occurred in connection with a transaction before it". B. CREMADES and D.J.A. CAIRNS, "Corruption, International Public Policy and the Duties of Arbitrators", 58 Dispute Resolution Journal (2003) p. 83. Acknowledging that the law may be changing, more recently, the rules of some arbitration institutions now specifically allow disclosure made in accordance with national law requirements. See M. HWANG and K. LIM, "Corruption in Arbitration – Law and Reality", 8 Asian Int'l. Arb. J (2012) p. 48 (referring to the 2010 Rules of the Singapore International Arbitration Centre (SIAC) which provide that parties or arbitrators may disclose matters relating to an arbitration "in compliance with the provisions of the laws of any State which are binding on the party making the disclosure".).

127. The contrast with commercial arbitration, with its emphasis on party autonomy, in the treatment of corruption bears mention; see Abdulhay SAYED, *Corruption in International Trade and Commercial Arbitration* (2004) p. 8, citing, inter alia, Yves DEZALAY and Bryant GARTH, *Dealing in Virtue* (1996) pp. 245-246.

128. See M. HWANG and K. LIM, *op. cit.*, fn. 126, pp. 14-22.

129. For example, in *Micula v. Romania* (ICSID Case No. ARB/05/20), Decision on Jurisdiction and Admissibility, 24 September 2008, a tribunal faced an allegation that Mr. Viorel Micula had obtained his Swedish nationality by fraud or material mistake. The tribunal noted that:

"Respondent has presented only limited evidence, none of which is sufficient to make the necessary showing"; it is also observed "The record does not include any elements which should

Tech v. Uzbekistan, for example, the testimony of the claimant's principal witness lead to the admission of facts concerning the nature of the relationship between the investor and its contracted consultants (including the fact that the services provided were "lobbyist activity" and not assistance with the operation, production, and delivery of the joint venture's products as originally stated, and that US$ 4 million was paid).[130] From these facts, the tribunal pro-actively employed its ex officio powers under Art. 43 of the ICSID Convention, and by a series of procedural orders propio motu requested the parties to adduce additional information.[131] The tribunal was in this way able to obtain sufficient information to satisfy itself of the existence of corruption in that case.[132]

There are practical limits of course to any tribunal's power to investigate wrongdoing – forcing discovery or testimony by compelling witnesses is difficult, as acknowledged by tribunals and scholars alike.[133] But *Metal-Tech* demonstrates that arbitral tribunals determined to establish the facts are not without tools to pursue their suspicions.

2. Burdens of Proof, Presumptions, Inferences

The question of which party bears the burden of proving wrongdoing has been relatively straightforward, despite some theoretical uncertainty as to the conflict of laws rules that might apply.[134] Following the maxim *onus probandi incumbit actori,* the prevailing principle

---

lead the Tribunal to investigate facts that are not before it. Nor do Respondent's allegations of facts lead to the need for opening a fact-finding procedure. Given the factual evidence presented by Respondent, the Tribunal, in its letter of 11 July 2008, directed Respondent how to proceed in the event that Respondent believed that it needed additional supplemental documentary production – an option that Respondent chose not to pursue" (see para. 95).

130. *Metal-Tech Ltd. v. Republic of Uzbekistan* (ICSID Case No. ARB/10/3), Award, 4 October 2013, paras. 86, 274.
131. *Id.* at paras. 247-256.
132. *Id.* at para. 256. ("[T]he Tribunal made a considerable effort to ensure that it had all the relevant evidence that it needed to decide on the corruption allegations.").
133. Commenting on its treatment of the evidence on corruption provided, the *F-W Oil v. Trinidad and Tobago* tribunal recounted how F-W withdrew its corruption allegations at the very end of the hearing "under pointed questioning from the Tribunal itself as to whether there was any real evidence to sustain allegations of that breadth and gravity". The Tribunal was "naturally much concerned from the outset" about the corruption allegations, not only because of their serious nature, but also "because it was faced with the problems inherent in investment arbitrations (by contrast with proceedings in a court of law): no evidence on oath, and no compellability of witnesses", *F-W Oil Interests, Inc. v. Republic of Trinidad & Tobago* (ICSID Case No. ARB/01/14), Award, 3 March 2006, para. 211. See also M. SCHERER, "Circumstantial Evidence in Corruption Cases Before International Arbitral Tribunals", 2 Int'l. Arb. L. Rev. (2002) p. 29 ("[e]veryone familiar with international commercial arbitration concedes that the tools available for pre-hearing discovery are sharply limited".).
134. See Gary BORN, *International Commercial Arbitration* (2009) p. 1858 ("Allocating the burden of proof arguably presents choice-of-law questions. In particular, tribunals must decide whether to apply the law of the arbitral seat (on the theory that the burden of proof is 'procedural'), the law governing the underlying substantive issues, or some international standard.... The better view is that the tribunals should allocate the burden of proof in light of its assessment of the applicable

is that each party has the burden of proving the facts on which it relies.[135] When investor wrongdoing is pled as a defense, the burden would fall on the host State; for investors seeking to prove host State wrongdoing (e.g., fraud by public officials against a bidding investor, or corrupt solicitation or extortion by the host State's public officials), the investor would bear the burden. The procedural rules applied by international courts and tribunals recognize this rule widely,[136] and tribunals consistently confirm this in the case law, including in cases of investor wrongdoing.[137] On occasion, allegations of investor fraud in relation to a tribunal's jurisdiction ratione personae raise interesting questions on who bears the burden of proof. In *Quiborax v. Bolivia,* for example, the host State argued that although it was the one raising the allegations of fraud against the claimants, it did "not consider that it must prove its allegation of fraud" and that "it is enough if those allegations 'raise... a doubt'".[138] The host State based its argument on the fact that the claimants bore the burden of proof that they had genuinely acquired the shares in question (a condition precedent to their being an "investor" under the BIT), and therefore "when there is room for doubt, the burden is not discharged".[139] The tribunal, for its part, held that:

> "[i]t will first examine whether the Claimants have discharged their burden of proving that they are 'investors'. Assuming the answer is positive, it will then review whether the Respondent has disproven or raised sufficient doubts on the Claimants' allegations that they are investors. Finally, on the basis of this overall analysis, it will conclude whether or not the Claimants are 'investors'."[140]

---

substantive law and procedures adopted in the arbitration. In so doing, the tribunal need not apply the burden of proof rules of any specific jurisdiction, but can instead fashion specialized rules in light of the particular substantive issues and procedures at issue in a specific instance."). An investment tribunal's freedom to adopt evidentiary rules it deems more appropriate is greater given its international law remit.

135. D.V. SANDIFER, *Evidence before International Tribunals* (1975) p. 127 ("[t]he burden of proof rests upon him who asserts the affirmative of a proposition that if not substantiated will result in a decision adverse to his contention").

136. See, e.g., Art. 27(1), UNCITRAL Arbitration Rules; *Case Concerning Military and Paramilitary Activities in and Against Nicaragua* [1984] ICJ Rep. 392, 437 ("it is the litigant seeking to establish a fact who bears the burden of proving it").

137. For corruption, see *Metal-Tech Ltd. v. Republic of Uzbekistan* (ICSID Case No. ARB/10/3), Award, 4 October 2013, para. 237 ("The principle that each party has the burden of proving the facts on which it relies is widely recognised and applied by international courts and tribunals."). For fraud, see *Teinver S.A., Transportes de Cercanías S.A. and Autobuses Urbanos del Sur S.A. v. The Argentine Republic* (ICSID Case No. ARB/09/1), Decision on Jurisdiction, 21 December 2012, para. 324, citing *Rompetrol v. Romania* (ICSID Case No. ARB/06/3), Award, 6 May 2013, para. 75; *Desert Line Projects LLC v. Republic of Yemen* (ICSID Case No. ARB/05/17), Award, 6 February 2008, para. 105; and *Gustaf F.W. Hamester GmbH & Co KG v. Republic of Ghana* (ICSID Case No. ARB/07/24), Award, 18 June 2010, para. 132 (all confirming that the party alleging fraud bears the burden of proof).

138. *Quiborax S.A., Non Metallic Minerals S.A. and Allan Fosk Kaplún v. Plurinational State of Bolivia* (ICSID Case No. ARB/06/2), Decision on Jurisdiction, 27 September 2012, para. 112.

139. *Id.*

140. *Id.* at para. 114.

Rather than engaging in each party's factual evidence sequentially, the tribunal appeared to weigh the evidence of both parties concerning the alleged share transfer together. It concluded that while there were documentary discrepancies, "these do not prove fraud nor suffice to overcome the plentiful evidence in support of the Claimants' case".[141] Thus, while not specifically addressing the host State's argument that it need only "raise a doubt",[142] the tribunal evidently conducted a thorough analysis of both parties' factual submissions and decided on the balance of evidence before it.

For the most part, *onus probandi incumbit actori* applies without significant complexity. The more controversial question lies in what instances it would be appropriate, if any, to shift the burden of proof from the party asserting corruption to the party acting in defense. Partasides has noted in the context of corruption issues that "a simple shifting of the burden of proof, all in one go, is rightly difficult for any lawyer to accept".[143] There are few endorsements by tribunals of direct burden-shifting for corruption allegations in international arbitration[144] and none in international investment arbitration.[145] Burden shifting appears to be more widely used in WTO adjudication, which allows for the burden of proof to be shifted once a *prima facie* violation has been

---

141. *Id.* at para. 192.
142. On this point, the case of *Micula et al v. Romania* is relevant. There, the host State alleged that Mr. Viorel Micula acquired his Swedish nationality either fraudulently or as a result of a material error. The tribunal made it clear that it was the host State's burden to produce evidence of this allegation, and that "[f]or this purpose, casting doubt is not sufficient". *Ioan Micula, Viorel Micula and others v. Romania* (ICSID Case No. ARB/05/20), Decision on Jurisdiction and Admissibility, 24 September 2008, para. 94.
143. PARTASIDES, "Proving Corruption in International Arbitration: A Balanced Standard for the Real World", 25 ICSID Review (2010, no. 1) p. 53.
144. In international commercial arbitration, ICC Case No. 6497 is one of the few examples where burden shifting was endorsed by a tribunal. Even here, however, the tribunal cautioned that "such change to the burden of proof is only to be made in special circumstances and for very good reasons".
145. Suggestions that the standard of proof should be reversed have generally been rejected as inconsistent with due process: see, e.g., M. HWANG and K. LIM, *op. cit.*, fn. 126, p. 14; A. MOURRE, "Arbitration and Criminal Law: Reflections on the Duties of the Arbitrator", 22 Arbitration International (2006, no. 1) p. 95 at p. 102 (arguing that a reversal of the burden of proof "does not seem to be acceptable or compatible with the right to a fair trial"). However, some commentators have advocated shifting the burden of proof to the allegedly corrupt party upon a prima facie showing of corruption: see K. MILLS, *op. cit.*, fn. 116, at p. 295 ("Because of the near impossibility to 'prove' corruption, where there is a reasonable indication of corruption, an appropriate way to make a determination may be to shift the burden of proof to the allegedly corrupt party to establish that the legal and good faith requirements were in fact duly met."); C. LAMM, et al., *op. cit.*, fn. 61, (citing Mills, supra, with tacit approval, and stating: "Another argument in favour of burden shifting is that the party accused of corruption is typically easily capable, if it is actually innocent of the allegations, of producing countervailing evidence").

established.[146] But the WTO's practice is generally not found in other international courts and tribunals.[147]

Is there something specific about the nature of particular forms of investor wrongdoing that justifies a re-allocation of the burden of proof? In the case of fraud, the many instances in which tribunals have made findings of fraud or misrepresentation demonstrate that host States have not considered bearing the burden of proving fraud particularly onerous. In the case of corruption, however, scholars, particularly those focused on improving the effectiveness of arbitration in combating corruption, have argued the necessity of burden-shifting.[148] Institutions such as the World Bank employ burden shifting as well in their fraud and corruption investigations, partly in appreciation of the fact that (as with arbitral tribunals) they have no subpoena or contempt powers.[149] The argument made is that after a prima facie showing of certain indicia of corruption, the burden should be placed on the party that, by virtue of its control over the evidence, has the ability to rebut those initial indicators of corruption. As discussed below, *Metal-Tech* can be viewed as supportive of this idea of burden shifting, at least through the use of adverse inferences.

The absence of significant investment jurisprudence where corruption was found to have existed (except for those few instances where admissions of the underlying facts supporting corruption were made by the investor's primary witnesses) certainly buttresses the idea that the status quo is ineffective, and that the clandestine and highly complex nature of transnational corruption requires a candid admission that unless the evidentiary principles applied by tribunals are equal to the ingenuity of those who are engaged in corruption, it will be difficult to find corruption in most cases.[150] Indeed, there is some national legislation that shifts the burden on a party to explain why a finding of corruption should not be made, once certain facts have been established; these

---

146. In *EC—Hormones*, for example, the WTO Appellate Body explained that "the initial burden lies on the complaining party, which must establish a prima facie case of inconsistency with a particular provision of the SPS Agreement on the part of the defending party, or more precisely, of its SPS measure or measures complained about. When that prima facie case is made, the burden of proof moves to the defending party, which must in turn counter or refute the claimed inconsistency".

147. The prima facie rule has been applied consistently by WTO panels and the Appellate Body but is "at variance with the manner in which most other international courts [and tribunals] deal with the allocation of the burden of proof". Chester BROWN, *A Common Law of International Adjudication* (2007) p. 93.

148. See, e.g., Cecily ROSE, "Questioning the Role of International Arbitration in the Fight Against Corruption", 31 J. Int'l. Arb. (2014) p. 183 (advocating the greater utilization of a number of solutions to perennial evidentiary problems in corruption; in addition to identifying appropriate instances where the burden of proof should be shifted, the drawing adverse inferences, placing greater reliance on circumstantial evidence, lowering the standard of proof, and drawing on factual findings in domestic proceedings are also suggested).

149. See World Bank, Guidelines on Preventing and Combating Fraud and Corruption in Projects Financed by IBRD Loans and IDA Credits and Grants, 15 October 2006, <http://siteresources.worldbank.org/INTOFFEVASUS/Resources/WB_Anti_Corruption_Guidelines_10_2006.pdf>.

150. See M. SCHERER, *op. cit.*, fn. 133, p. 29 at p. 31 ("it is very rare that direct proof of corruption is available ... [m]ost arbitral tribunals have to content themselves with circumstantial evidence").

methods may have begun to take hold in the jurisprudence. In *Metal-Tech,* for example, the tribunal recognized the international community's establishment of lists of indicators of corruption (often called "red flag" principles), and considered the red flag principles drafted by a former Chief Justice of England and Wales, including an advisor's lack of experience in the sector involved and any close personal relationship the advisor may have with the government that could improperly influence the latter's decision.[151]

These "red flags" and similar indicia of corruption can be conceived as potential forms of circumstantial evidence that, once established, can lead to a shifting of the burden of proof, requiring the rebuttal of allegations by evidence to the contrary, failing which certain inferences and conclusions might be drawn. Indeed, circumstantial evidence, particularly when direct evidence of corruption is unavailable, is increasingly, albeit cautiously, accepted as a tool to evaluate allegations of corruption by arbitral tribunals.[152] *Methanex v. United States* is instructive in this regard, as its endorsement of the "connect the dots" methodology to reach a conclusion based on proven facts provides a detailed discussion of the applicability of circumstantial evidence in investment arbitration case law.[153]

As for the use of adverse inferences, as early as 1939 Sandifer already noted that "the most effective sanction [international tribunals] have to impose upon parties negligent

---

151. *Metal-Tech Ltd. v. Republic of Uzbekistan* (ICSID Case No. ARB/10/3), Award, 4 October 2013, para. 293, citing Woolf Committee Report, Business Ethics, Global Companies and the Defence Industry: Ethical Business Conduct in BAE Systems Plc 25-26 (2008); and fn. 340 ("... the red flag lists merely assemble a number of factors which any adjudicator with good common sense would consider when assessing facts in relation with a corruption issue..."). While *Metal-Tech* ultimately made no findings on burdens and standards of proof, the acknowledgment of "red flags" is significant and opens the possibility of future tribunals adopting these principles when clear admissions from witnesses are not available to the tribunal.

152. See ICC Case No. 4145 (a fact can be proven by circumstantial evidence if its leads to "very high probability"); ICC Case No. 8891 ("indices must be serious").

153. In a detailed analysis of the investor's corruption-related allegations (See *Methanex Corporation v. United States of America,* NAFTA/UNCITRAL, Final Award on Jurisdiction and Merits, 3 August 2005, Part III, Ch. B), the tribunal's approach towards evaluating the evidence of corruption was particularly noteworthy. It adopted a "connect the dots" methodology (*Methanex,* Part III, Ch. B, para. 2. ("while individual pieces of evidence when viewed in isolation may appear to have no significance, when seen together, they provide the most compelling of possible explanations of events...")), with the caveat that each "dot" (i.e., key event) be examined in its own context as well as within the overall pattern, and that the tribunal must ultimately determine what the "dots" are from the evidence presented by both parties:

"Connecting the dots is hardly a unique methodology; but when it is applied, it is critical, first, that *all* the relevant dots be assembled; and, second, that each be examined, in its own context, for its own significance, before a possible pattern is essayed. Plainly, a self-serving selection of events and a self-serving interpretation of each of those selected, may produce an account approximating verisimilitude, but it will not reflect what actually happened. Accordingly, the Tribunal will consider the various 'dots' which Methanex has adduced – one-by-one and then together with certain key events (essentially additional, noteworthy dots) which Methanex does not adduce – in order to reach a conclusion about the factual assertions which Methanex has made."

or recalcitrant in the production of evidence is the threat to draw an adverse inference against the party in the event of the continued refusal to bring forward the needed documents".[154] Similarly, the International Bar Association's *Rules on the Taking of Evidence in International Arbitration* provides that "[i]f a Party fails without satisfactory explanation to produce any Document ... ordered to be produced by the Arbitral Tribunal, the Arbitral Tribunal may infer that such document would be adverse to the interests of that Party".[155]

While cases like *Hamester v. Ghana* emphasized that a tribunal would "only decide on substantiated facts, and cannot base itself on inferences",[156] more investment arbitration decisions concerning investor wrongdoing seem to draw conclusions on the basis of inference, either because a party did not produce evidence when asked to do so by the tribunal or because that party should have had within its possession exonerative evidence but did not produce it. In *Europe Cement v. Turkey,* the host State alleged that the share purchase agreements relied upon by the claimant had been backdated in order to confer temporal jurisdiction over the claimant's investment. The tribunal observed that the claimant could have rebutted the host State's evidence suggesting back-dating by producing originals of the documents in question, and yet failed to do so.[157] The claimant's failure to produce the original share purchase agreements, in the tribunal's view, "contribute[d] to the inference that the originals of the documents copied in its Memorial and on which its claim was based either were never in the Claimant's possession or would not stand forensic analysis". For the tribunal, the necessary inference was that the claimant's jurisdiction ratione temporis claim was fraudulent.

More to point, the *Metal-Tech* tribunal considered that adverse inferences can indeed be drawn in appropriate instances to prove corruption: "the Tribunal may draw appropriate inferences from a party's non-production of evidence ordered to be provided. In a number of cases, tribunals have indeed stated that they would draw inferences from non-production."[158] *Metal-Tech* is a particularly instructive precedent for future tribunals, as the utilization of procedural orders to seek further information, coupled with the reminder that failure to cooperate fully in satisfying the tribunal that all available evidence and testimony has been provided on a given corruption allegation may lead to adverse inferences, is not only sanctioned by international procedure (in this case, the ICSID Convention and Rules),[159] but can in the hands of a tribunal committed

---

154. SANDIFER, *op. cit.*, fn. 135, p. 101.

155. IBA Rule 9(5)-(6).

156. *Gustaf F.W. Hamester GmbH & Co KG v. Republic of Ghana* (ICSID Case No. ARB/07/24), Award, 18 June 2010, para. 134, cited in *Niko Resources (Bangladesh) Ltd. v. Bangladesh & Ors* (ICSID Case No. ARB/10/11 and ARB/10/18), Decision on Jurisdiction, 19 August 2013, para. 424.

157. *Europe Cement Investment and Trade S.A. v. Republic of Turkey* (ICSID Case No. ARB(AF)/07/2), Award, 13 August 2009, para. 164.

158. *Metal-Tech Ltd. v. Republic of Uzbekistan* (ICSID Case No. ARB/10/3), Award, 4 October 2013, at para. 245. See also: in commercial arbitration, ICC Case No. 5622 ("It is true that it is possible to prove something through indirect evidence and that Art. 8 of the Swiss CC does not exclude indirect evidence." (footnote omitted)); in inter-State adjudication, the ICJ in the Corfu Channel Case (*UK v. Albania*), Merits, Judgment of 9 April 1949, 1949 ICJ Rep. 4, 18 (States "should be allowed a more liberal recourse to inferences of fact and circumstantial evidence".).

159. See Arts. 43-45, ICSID Convention; Rule 34, ICSID Arbitration Rules.

to unearthing the truth lead to strong findings of fact, no matter what standard of proof is advanced as relevant.[160]

Although presumptions and inferences can aid in establishing sufficient direct or circumstantial evidence that can discharge a party's burden of proving its case or a particular defense asserted, questions on burdens of proof should not be confused with the establishment of *sufficient* proof. These are related but different questions, and in the area of investor wrongdoing, it is not so much the burden of proof as the *standard* of proof where much uncertainty remains.

3.   Standards of Proof

The burden of proof identifies which party bears the obligation to prove a given allegation. The *standard of proof* defines the threshold of evidence necessary to establish either an individual fact or contention or the party's case as a whole. This distinction makes apparent, as well-expressed by the *Rompetrol* tribunal:

> "that the burden of proof is absolute, whereas the standard of proof is relative. [I]f, according to basic principle, it is for the one party, or for the other, to establish a particular factual assertion, that will remain the position throughout the forensic process, starting from when the assertion is first put forward and all the way through to the end."[161]

Standards of proof are "relative" in the sense that "[w]hether a proposition has in fact been proved by the party which bears the burden of proving it depends not just on its own evidence but on the overall assessment of the accumulated evidence put forward by one or both parties, for the proposition or against it".[162] In essence, the burden of proof refers to who must prove a particular assertion, while the standard of proof refers to whether sufficient evidence has been provided to prove that assertion. In national law, the applicable standard of proof varies between systems of common law and civil law. Broadly speaking, the general standard of proof for civil actions in common law is the "balance of probabilities", while in civil law systems it is typically the "inner conviction"

---

160. See also *Rompetrol v. Romania* (ICSID Case No. ARB/06/3), Award, 6 May 2013, para. 181 ("an ICSID tribunal is endowed with the independent power to determine, within the context provided by the circumstances of the dispute before it, whether particular evidence or kinds of evidence should be admitted or excluded, what weight (if any) should be given to particular items of evidence so admitted, whether it would like to see further evidence of any particular kind on any issue arising in the case, and so on and so forth. The tribunal is entitled to the cooperation of the parties in that regard, and is likewise entitled to take account of the quality of their cooperation. When paragraph (2) of Rule 34 lays down that '[t]he tribunal shall take formal note of the failure of a party to comply with its obligations under [that] paragraph and of any reasons given for such failure,' it no doubt intends, among other things, that a given tribunal is specifically authorized to draw whatever inferences it deems appropriate from the failure of either party to produce evidence which that party might otherwise have been expected to produce.").

161. *Rompetrol v. Romania* (ICSID Case No. ARB/06/3), Award, 6 May 2013, para. 178.

162. *Rompetrol v. Romania* (ICSID Case No. ARB/06/3), Award, 6 May 2013.

of the adjudicator.[163] International arbitration has often adopted the "balance of probabilities" approach when setting a standard by which facts can be deemed proven.[164] When serious allegations of wrongdoing are involved in civil proceedings, however, both systems generally demand a heightened standard of proof;[165] the "clear and convincing" proof standard, derived from US law, is often employed.[166] More recent cases in English law have cast doubt on whether it is proper to link the gravity of the misconduct alleged with the standard of proof that should apply; in *Re B (Children)*, the House of Lords came to the conclusion that "the time has come to say, once and for all, that there is only one civil standard of proof and that is proof that the fact in issue more probably occurred than not".[167] Both the heightened standard and the ordinary standard have found their way into investment arbitration case law on investor wrongdoing,[168] a

---

163. See REINER, "Burden and General Standards of Proof", 10 Arbitration International (1994) p. 335. It might be assumed that it was to this "inner conviction" standard referred to in a number of ICC arbitrations concerning corruption. See ICC Case No. 7047 (a Tribunal "must be convinced that there is indeed a case of bribery"); ICC Case No. 4145 ("the Defendant's accusation is not supported by direct evidence or even circumstantial evidence to be retained as convincing").

164. Alan REDFERN and J. Martin HUNTER, *Redfern and Hunter on International Arbitration*, (2009) p. 387 ("[t]he degree of proof that must be achieved in practice before an international arbitral tribunal is not capable of precise definition, but it may be safely assumed that it is close to the 'balance of probability'"). The balance of probabilities standard is "a reasonable degree of probability, but not so high as is required in a criminal case. If the evidence is such that the tribunal can say: 'We think it more probable than not,' the burden is discharged but, if the probabilities are equal, it is not." *Id.,* citing *Miller v. Minister of Pensions*, 2 All ER 372 (1947) (Denning, J).

165. REINER, *op. cit.*, fn. 163, at p. 336 ("the Anglo-Saxon and the continental systems require higher standards of proof for particularly important or delicate questions such as bribery or other types of fraud").

166. Professor Wigmore provides the classic statement of the standard: "[i]n several civil actions a different phrase has been adopted to signify a stronger persuasion ... the phrase, viz., 'clear and convincing proof' ... [s]uch a test is in many or most Sates used for an issue involving fraud". *Wigmore on Evidence* 446 (1935).

167. In *Re B (Children)(FC)*, UKHL 35 (2008), para. 13. That said, "[t]here are some proceedings, though civil in form, whose nature is such that it is appropriate to apply the criminal standard of proof", such as when the consequences of a finding are penal in nature. See para. 69. The need for a higher degree of *probability* that serious allegations are indeed true may yet be valid: as earlier stated by Lord Denning, "in civil cases the case must be proved by a preponderance of probability, but there may be degrees of probability within that standard. The degree depends on the subject-matter. A civil court, when considering a charge of fraud, will naturally require for itself a higher degree of probability than that which it would require when asking if negligence is established": *Bater v. Bater* (1951) (Denning LJ).

168. Compare *Waguih Elie George Siag and Clorinda Vecchi v. The Arab Republic of Egypt* (ICSID Case No. ARB/05/15), Award, 1 June 2009, paras. 325-326 ("It is common in most legal systems for serious allegations such as fraud to be held to a high standard of proof. The same can be said in international proceedings.... The Tribunal accepts that the applicable standard of proof is greater than the balance of probabilities but less than beyond reasonable doubt. The term favoured by the Claimants is 'clear and convincing evidence.' The Tribunal agrees with that test.") *with Rompetrol v. Romania* (ICSID Case No. ARB/06/3), Award, 6 May 2013, paras. 180-183 (applying the "normal rule of 'balance of probabilities' as the standard appropriate to the generality of the

reflection of the different legal traditions that inform arbitrators of varied backgrounds to issues of proof.

International commercial arbitration tribunals have, by and large, adopted high standards of proof. In one of the rare publicly known ICC arbitrations that dealt with corruption issues concerning the validity of the main agreement, *Westinghouse v. National Power Corporation, Republic of the Philippines*,[169] the tribunal viewed bribery as a species of fraud in civil cases, thus demanding "clear and convincing evidence" under the applicable US and Philippine law:[170]

> "Fraud in civil cases must be proved to exist by clear and convincing evidence amounting to more than mere preponderance, and cannot be justified by a mere speculation. This is because fraud is never lightly to be presumed..."[171]

Other international commercial arbitration decisions have adopted the same "clear and convincing" standard of proof or equivalent high standards.[172]

Similarly, investment tribunals which are not similarly constrained by national standards of proof have largely adopted high standards of proof. In *EDF v. Romania*, for example, the tribunal placed, without any real attempt at harmonization, the fact that corruption is "notoriously difficult to prove" against the "demand" for clear and convincing evidence:

> "corruption must be proven and is notoriously difficult to prove since, typically, there is little or no physical evidence. The seriousness of the accusation of

---

factual issues before it", while also "where necessary adopt[ing] a more nuanced approach" when deciding "whether an allegation of seriously wrongful conduct ... has been proved on the basis of the entire body of direct and indirect evidence before it".).

169. *Westinghouse Projects Company, et al. v. National Power Corporation, The Republic of the Philippines*, Preliminary Award, 10 December 1991, reprinted in 7 Mealey's Int'l Arb. Rep., No. 1, Sect. B (Jan. 1992).

170. The tribunal determined the standard of proof by electing to apply the standards found in both US and Philippine law; these national laws were found to be applicable because of the identities of the Parties and the link between the facts to be determined and the rules being applied. *Westinghouse Projects Company, et al. v. National Power Corporation, The Republic of the Philippines*, Preliminary Award, 10 December 1991, reprinted in 7 Mealey's Int'l Arb. Rep., No. 1, Sect. B (Jan. 1992), at 31.

171. *Westinghouse Projects Company, et al. v. National Power Corporation, The Republic of the Philippines*, Preliminary Award, 10 December 1991, reprinted in 7 Mealey's Int'l Arb. Rep., No. 1, Sect. B (Jan. 1992) at p. 34.

172. As with *Westinghouse*, the *Himpurna* tribunal set the standard of proof at "clear and convincing proof". See *Himpurna California Energy Ltd. v. PT. (Persero) Perusahaan Listruik Negara*, Final Award of 4 May 1999, in *ICCA Yearbook Commercial Arbitration* XXV (2000) (henceforth *Yearbook*) p. 11 at p. 43. Similarly, in ICC Case No. 6401, the tribunal stated: "bribery, a form of fraud, must be proved by 'clear and convincing evidence'. ICC Case No. 5622 went even closer to an overtly criminal standard of proof: "bribery has not been proved beyond doubt". Indeed, some cases seem to adopt even stricter standards, employing language more commonly associated with criminal proceedings – see ICC Case No. 5622 (*Hilmarton*) ("In the present case, bribery has not been proved beyond doubt").

corruption in the present case, considering that it involves officials at the highest level of the Romanian Government at the time, demands clear and convincing evidence. There is general consensus among international tribunals and commentators regarding the need for a high standard of proof of corruption."[173]

This is not to say, however, that arbitrators have never considered less rigid evidentiary methodologies that better comport with the clandestine nature of transnational corruption. *Siag v. Egypt* bears discussion in this regard, as it places in clear relief how the choice of the applicable standard of proof directly affects whether a set of facts is considered to have crystallized into fraud or corruption. In that case, a divided tribunal equated the corrupt act complained of by Egypt to fraud, which it considered could only be proven through the "heavy" standard of "clear and convincing evidence", located somewhere between the "preponderance of evidence"/"balance of probabilities" standard for civil cases and the "beyond reasonable doubt" standard in criminal cases under US law.[174] But the dissenting arbitrator, Orrego Vicuña, believed that there was sufficient evidence to establish that corruption did occur in the procurement of the investor's Lebanese citizenship, which would bear the legal repercussion that the investor was in actuality an Egyptian citizen and thus not permitted ratione personae to bring a BIT claim against Egypt. Orrego Vicuña began his analysis by emphasizing that his divergence from the majority did not in any way mean that the majority was condoning corruption.[175] It was not the principles involved that were the source of difference; rather, it was a "different assessment of the evidence and whether it is sufficient to establish such impropriety".[176] The standard of proof the majority chose – that of clear and convincing evidence – was for the dissenting arbitrator not appropriate:

> "It is my view that arbitration tribunals, particularly those deciding under international law, are free to choose the most relevant rules in accordance with the circumstances of the case and the nature of the facts involved, as it has been increasingly recognized."[177]

In this case, the facts could be best judged under a standard of proof allowing the tribunal "discretion in inferring from a collection of concordant circumstantial evidence (*faisce au d'indices*) the facts at which the various indices are directed".[178]

Professor Orrego Vicuña's view that arbitrators "are free to choose the most relevant rules" based on the "circumstances of the case and the nature of the facts involved" has

---

173. *EDF (Services) v. Romania* (ICSID Case No. ARB/05/13), Award, 8 October 2009, para. 221.

174. *Waguih Elie George Siag and Clorinda Vecchi v. The Arab Republic of Egypt* (ICSID Case No. ARB/05/15), Award, 1 June 2009, para. 325.

175. *Waguih Elie George Siag and Clorinda Vecchi v. The Arab Republic of Egypt* (ICSID Case No. ARB/05/15), Dissenting Opinion of Professor Francisco Orrego Vicuña, p. 1 (the difference in views "in no way reflects adversely on any of the distinguished counsel that have represented the Claimants in these proceedings, nor on my colleagues in the Tribunal, as none would be willing to condone [fraud or corruption]").

176. *Id.*

177. *Id.*, at p. 4, *citing* Abdulhay SAYED, *op. cit.*, fn. 127, pp. 89-92.

178. *Id.*

been affirmed by the most recent cases in investment arbitration dealing with corruption and other forms of fraud and illegality. *Metal-Tech* is the most recent statement that evidentiary questions on corruption, including standards of proof, are based on international law due to the BIT being the *lex causae* and are therefore open questions, for the reason that such tribunals have "relative freedom in determining the standard necessary to sustain a determination of corruption."[179] This is so because investment treaty arbitration, and indeed the broader system of international dispute settlement, is characterized largely by principle rather than procedural formality, and the rules of evidence are neither rigid nor technical.[180]

Notwithstanding this freedom of action, however, the cases still yield useful doctrine. The guidance drawn by the *Rompetrol* tribunal from arbitral practice is highly instructive. The tribunal considered:

> "that there may well be situations in which, given the nature of an allegation of wrongful (in the widest sense) conduct, and in the light of the position of the person concerned, an adjudicator would be reluctant to find the allegation proved in the absence of a sufficient weight of positive evidence – as opposed to pure probabilities or circumstantial inferences. But the particular circumstances would be determinative, and in the Tribunal's view defy codification."

The *Rompetrol* tribunal then referred to *Libananco v. Turkey,* a case where the host State alleged investor fraud:

> "In relation to the Claimant's contention that there should be a heightened standard of proof for allegations of 'fraud or other serious wrongdoing,' the Tribunal accepts that fraud is a serious allegation, but it does not consider that this (without more) requires it to apply a heightened standard of proof. While agreeing with the general proposition that – the graver the charge, the more confidence there must be in the evidence relied on …, this does not necessarily entail a higher standard of proof. It may simply require more persuasive evidence, in the case of a fact that is inherently improbable, in order for the Tribunal to be satisfied that the burden of proof has been discharged."

---

179. *Metal-Tech Ltd. v. Republic of Uzbekistan* (ICSID Case No. ARB/10/3), Award, 4 October 2013, para. 238. In a mild conflation of different evidentiary concepts, the tribunal stated:

> "Here, the question is whether for allegations of corruption, the burden should be shifted to the Claimant to establish that there was no corruption. Rules establishing presumptions or shifting the burden of proof under certain circumstances, or drawing inferences from a lack of proof are generally deemed to be part of the *lex causae*. In the present case, the *lex causae* is essentially the BIT, which provides no rules for shifting the burden of proof or establishing presumptions. Therefore, the Tribunal has relative freedom in determining the standard necessary to sustain a determination of corruption."

180. See *Rompetrol v. Romania* (ICSID Case No. ARB/06/3), Award, 6 May 2013, paras. 178, 181.

While it would apply the "normal" balance of probabilities standard to the factual issues before it, the *Rompetrol* tribunal held that it:

> "will where necessary adopt a more nuanced approach and will decide in each discrete instance whether an allegation of seriously wrongful conduct by a [host] state official at either the administrative or policymaking level has been proved on the basis of the entire body of direct and indirect evidence before it."[181]

Several other tribunals have endorsed a flexible approach towards matters of evidence in cases where evidence is difficult to obtain, finding that indirect or circumstantial evidence may be sufficient for a party to discharge the applicable standard of proof. As one commentator has explained, "[i]nternational tribunals have, where a party has genuinely encountered problems beyond its control in securing evidence, more frequently than not recognized its hardship".[182] In the Iran-US Claims Tribunal case of *Rockwell*, for instance, the tribunal found that "[p]rima facie evidence must be recognized as a satisfactory basis to grant a claim where proof of the facts underlying the claim presents extreme difficulty and an inference from the evidence can reasonably be drawn".[183] Similarly, the tribunal in *AAPL v. Sri Lanka* endorsed the "established international law rule" that "[i]n cases where proof of a fact presents extreme difficulty, a tribunal may thus be satisfied with less conclusive proof, i.e. *prima facie* evidence".[184] One commentator has concluded, based on a survey of twenty-five arbitral awards involving bribery and corruption charges, that arbitrators frequently rely on indirect evidence of corruption in those cases where credible allegations of corruption have been made.[185]

Thus, the current state of evidentiary principles on investor wrongdoing seems to be at the beginning of a move away from the uniformity and rigidity of high standards of proof, with tribunals refusing to be pinned down *a priori* either by particular standards or by formal rules on burden-shifting or presumptions. Given the inability of the prevailing doctrine to generate positive findings of corruption, despite its anecdotal frequency and repeated invocation, this is surely a positive development. Without such room for the exercise of discretion, investor wrongdoing would likely continue to reside in the margins of arbitral decision-making, and would have no practical impact on the outcomes of a vast majority of cases. That unsatisfactory *status quo* – where to date not a single investment arbitration case has resulted in a finding of corruption on the basis of

---

181. *Id.* at paras. 182-183.

182. C. AMERASINGHE, *Evidence in International Arbitration* (2005) p. 138.

183. *Rockwell International Systems, Inc. v. Iran*, Award No. 438-430-1, 5 September 1989, reprinted in 23 *Iran-US Cl. Trib. Rep.*, p. 150 at p. 158 (in which case the claimant was unable to obtain better quality evidence because the Iranian government was not willing to grant the claimant access to the relevant documents it had taken possession of).

184. *Asian Agricultural Products Ltd. (AAPL) v. Sri Lanka* (ICSID Case No. ARB/87/3), Award, 27 June 1990, para. 56.

185. C. LAMM ET AL., *op. cit.*, fn. 61, p. 699 at p. 703 (citing A. CRIVELLARO, "Arbitration Case Law on Bribery: Issues of Arbitrability, Contract Validity, Merits and Evidence" in K. KARSTEN and A. BERKELEY, eds., *Arbitration: Money Laundering, Corruption and Fraud* (ICC 2003) p. 109).

contested evidence – would expose international arbitration to further criticism for being a "soft touch" on corruption.[186]

Why arbitrators have hesitated for so long to adopt more flexible evidentiary processes that are "equal to the ingenuity of those that conceal corruption"[187] is open to debate. The reason for choosing a high standard of proof seems to make good sense: higher standards of proof have been subscribed to by tribunals because of the serious legal consequences of a finding of corruption.[188] Reading the cases closely, it seems that adopting a high standard of proof was motivated in part by the need to ensure that the serious consequences most commonly associated with corruption in international arbitration – contract invalidation, the unenforceability of the contract, the lack of jurisdiction, the inadmissibility of claims (all acting to preclude any assessment of host State wrongdoing) – would apply sparingly. And indeed, adopting a high standard of proof has the practical value of helping to flush out the increasingly tactical or cynical use of corruption to derail the arbitral process.

Thus, it would be too reductive to view the frequent employment of the "clear and convincing proof" standard as done only because formal law demands that outcome. Rather than simply identifying a standard they are pre-ordained to take, arbitrators are in reality choosing one standard over another in a situation where either (or all) standards proffered are squarely within that arbitrator's scope of choice. In so doing, evidentiary principles, particularly the applicable standard of proof, are used as valves from which the pressure of applying the full consequences of norms on investor wrongdoing can be regulated. Arbitrators choose higher or lower standards of proof based at least in part on their appreciation of the equities of the case and the role they believe corruption should play in the ultimate outcome of the arbitration.

---

186. See Former Kenyan Attorney-General Amos Wako, quoted in Alison ROSS, "The Man Behind Kenyan Arbitration", Global Arbitration Review (20 January 2012) ("Unfortunately, in the case of international contracts it can be hard to prove corruption and to point the finger at a particular player. We must ensure that international arbitration tribunals do not develop an unacceptable reputation for being 'a soft touch' on corruption and other forms of illegality. Arbitrators need to emerge from their ivory towers, recognise how difficult an allegation of corruption can be to substantiate and show procedural flexibility to take these difficulties in proving corruption into account.").

187. See Constantine PARTASIDES, "Proving Corruption in International Arbitration: A Balanced Standard for the Real World", *Presentation to the British Institute of International and Comparative Law*, 18 January 2011, available at: <www.biicl.org/files/5683_partasides_19-01-11_biicl.pdf>. ("How can our process ensure that it is equal to the ingenuity of those that conceal corruption?" To which he answers: "Our process will not ensure that it is equal to the ingenuity of corruptors, and/or those that they corrupt, if arbitrators simply fail to take account of that ingenuity, and where necessary adapt for it, in the conduct of their proceedings.").

188. Indeed, a number of tribunals in fraud and corruption have adopted Judge Higgins' view of there seeming to be "general agreement" that "the graver the charge the more confidence there must be in the evidence relied on". Oil Platforms (*Islamic Republic of Iran v. United States of America*) 42 ILM 1334, 1384-1386 (2003) (Higgins, J., sep. op.), cited with approval in *Rompetrol v. Romania* (ICSID Case No. ARB/06/3), Award, 6 May 2013 at para. 182, *Libananco Holdings Co. Limited v. Republic of Turkey* (ICSID Case No. ARB/06/8), Award, 2 September 2011 and *Metal-Tech Ltd. v. Republic of Uzbekistan* (ICSID Case No. ARB/10/3), Award, 4 October 2013.

With a nod to this reality, the less formalistic sensibility of *Rompetrol* and *Metal-Tech* towards the evidentiary rules to be applied to corruption issues is helpful. Because corruption is a serious charge with serious consequences attached, the degree of confidence a tribunal should have in the evidence of that corruption must be high. But this does not mean that the standard of proof itself should necessarily be higher, or that circumstantial evidence, inferences, or presumptions and indicators of possible corruption (such as "red flags") cannot come to the aid of the fact-finder. Tribunals are given the freedom and burden of choice, which they should not abdicate by rote reference to an abstract "heightened" standard of proof.

IV.   APPLICABLE LEGAL PRINCIPLES

Once proven, investor wrongdoing is then analyzed by investment tribunals typically through one or more of three key legal principles, depending on the circumstances: (i) investment treaty provisions which provide that investments must comply with the national laws of the host State; (ii) "clean hands" and cognate legal doctrines; and (iii) transnational public policy.

Other arguments are frequently advanced in the cases, including that investments must be "made in good faith", or that "abusive" claims may be excluded, but it is suggested that reference to these concepts is typically for reasons of reinforcement and elaboration and, on a close reading of the cases, the decisions can actually be explained by application of one or more of the three identified operative principles.

Application of these legal principles to investor wrongdoing is dependent on certain conditions and yields distinct consequences (see Part V), so an understanding of the scope and content of each principle is important.

1.   *Treaty Provisions Requiring that Investments Comply with the Laws of the Host State*

The prism through which investor wrongdoing is typically addressed is the clause of many investment treaties, albeit found in more than one principal form, according to which it is asserted that covered investments are only those made "in accordance with" the laws of the host State.[189]

Eloquent arguments exist that such clauses have been misunderstood and misapplied. In *Fraport*, Cremades dissented from the majority stating that such clauses only concern whether "assets", which would otherwise qualify as investments", could in the context of that case be owned by foreigners.[190] Douglas endorses Cremades' dissent and adds that such clauses should concern only the conditions upon which a beneficial interest in an

---

189. S. SCHILL, *op. cit.*, fn. 33, pp. 281-323. (Differentiates between (i) the "in accordance with host State law" sub-clause found in many treaty definitions of investment; (ii) clauses governing the admission of new investments; and (iii) clauses defining temporal scope of application, which confirm that a treaty applies inter alia to investments lawfully made prior to its entry into force.).

190. *Fraport AG v. The Republic of the Philippines* (ICSID Case No. ARB/03/25), Dissenting Opinion of Bernardo M. Cremades, paras. 12-14.

asset (i.e., an investment) may be formally acquired under host State law.[191] He adds that illegality will seldom, if ever, impinge upon the formation of the agreement to arbitrate disputes. These views, whilst worthy of further consideration, are not widely accepted.

Rather, the preponderance of arbitrators and commentators confirm that such terms precisely operate as a limit on a host State's consent to refer disputes to arbitration (and thus, the formation of the agreement to arbitrate), and thereby operate as a condition for jurisdiction.[192] These treaty provisions refer to "the validity of the investment and not its definition".[193]

Denial of jurisdiction by application of an "in accordance with law" clause does not inevitably imply that the circumstances surrounding the acquisition of an investment will not be fully tested, as some critics forewarn; tribunals routinely make final determinations of jurisdictional facts (including matters of alleged investor wrongdoing) in the course of ruling on their jurisdiction.[194]

The approach is different, however, in the absence of express wording qualifying the scope of the host State's consent. As discussed further below, some tribunals have concluded that a legality requirement can be found by inference, whether in the ICSID Convention or in an investment treaty.[195] Most tribunals, however, have rejected any reading of the ICSID Convention, at least, that would import a sweeping jurisdictional requirement of lawfulness by implication, but admit that States may expressly condition

---

191. See Z. DOUGLAS, "Plea of Illegality", *op. cit.*, fn. 33, p. 5. Douglas' thesis begins from the premise that treaty protection will arise merely upon the acquisition of an asset falling within the scope of the definition of "investment" in an applicable treaty. From this, he concludes that a breach of host State law will only exceptionally vitiate the agreement to arbitrate disputes, which commercial arbitral tribunals, by analogy, widely consider to be "separable" from the "main" contract in which they are embedded. Douglas does not address, however, the weight of arbitral practice holding that "in accordance with law" clauses qualify the scope of the host State's offer to arbitrate disputes (and, logically, also make contingent the offer of substantive treaty protection too) and thereby directly impinge upon the formation of an agreement to arbitrate.

192. See M. SORNARAJAH, *op. cit.*, fn. 33, p. 106; C. KNAHR, op. cit., fn. 33, p. 5; G. BOTTINI, *op. cit.*, fn. 33, p. 297; U. KRIEBAUM, *op. cit.*, fn. 33, p. 307; R. MOLOO and A. KHACHATURIAN, *op. cit.*, fn. 33, p. 1473; S. SCHILL, *op. cit.*, fn. 33, available at SSRN: <http://ssrn.com/abstract=1979734>; A. NEWCOMBE, *op. cit.*, fn. 33, p. 187; C.A. MILES, "Corruption, Jurisdiction and Admissibility in International Investment Claims", 3 Journal of International Dispute Settlement (2012, no. 2) p. 329 at p. 347.

193. *Salini Costruttori S.p.A. and Italstrade S.p.A. v. Morocco* (ICSID Case No. ARB/00/4), Decision on Jurisdiction, 23 July 2001, para. 46; *Tokios Tokeles v. Ukraine* (ICSID Case No. ARB/02/18), Decision on Jurisdiction, 29 April 2004, para. 84; *Railroad Development Corporation v. Republic of Guatemala* (ICSID Case No. ARB/07/23), Second Decision on Objections to Jurisdiction, 18 May 2004, para. 140; *Ioannis Kardassopoulos v. Georgia* (ICSID Case No. ARB/05/18), Decision on Jurisdiction, 6 July 2007, para. 182.

194. Cf. Z. DOUGLAS, pp. 1, 8-9, 19 and *Malicorp Ltd v. Arab Republic of Egypt* (ICSID Case No. ARB/08/18), Award, 7 February 2011, para. 119.

195. *Phoenix Action, Ltd. v. Czech Republic* (ICSID Case No. ARB/06/5), Award, 15 April 2009, paras. 136-143. The *Phoenix Action* tribunal arguably over-extended the principle that treaties must be interpreted in "good faith" (Vienna Convention, Art. 31) by transforming it into an implicit substantive component of the term "investment". See further, C.A. MILES, *op. cit.*, fn. 192, p. 1 at p. 35 ("*Phoenix Action* is best explained as juridical overreach").

access to treaty protection in this manner. In *Saba Fakes*, for example, the tribunal explained:

> "As far as the legality of investments is concerned, this question does not relate to the definition of 'investment' provided in Article 25(1) of the ICSID Convention and in Article 1(b) of the BIT. In the Tribunal's opinion, while the ICSID Convention remains neutral on this issue, bilateral investment treaties are at liberty to condition their application and the whole protection they afford, including consent to arbitration, to a legality requirement of one form or another."[196]

In similar terms, the tribunal in *Metal-Tech* ruled that:

> "... the Contracting Parties to an investment treaty may limit the protections of the treaty to investments made in accordance with the laws and regulations of the host State. Depending on the wording of the investment treaty, this limitation may be a bar to jurisdiction, i.e. to the procedural protections under the BIT, or a defense on the merits, i.e. to the application of the substantive treaty guarantees. Similarly, a breach of the general prohibition of abuse of right, which is a manifestation of the principle of good faith, may give rise to an objection to jurisdiction or to a defense on the merits."[197]

The prevailing view is that absent express wording in the applicable investment treaty, breach of host State law whether at the inception of an investment or subsequently is not a jurisdictional matter. Rather, it is a matter which may, depending on the circumstances, lead to claims being excluded on grounds of inadmissibility, or present the host State with a possible defence to allegations of treaty breach.

The precise effect of an express treaty condition, where present, will obviously depend on the wording in question. However, subject to that important caveat, some generalizations are tolerable given the similarity of treaty language under consideration.

a.   Legality as a condition of access to treaty protection
One test, articulated in *Inmaris v. Ukraine*, is that the breach of host State law must mean the investment is "illegal as such", not merely susceptible of sanction or penalty under host State law.[198] Precisely what this means is unclear. Certainly it should not mean that the result that would flow from application of host State law must be the loss of the investment if an investor is to be denied access to investment treaty arbitration.[199] State sovereignty dictates that the grant of rights to investment treaty arbitration may be conditioned upon *mere* lawfulness, unrelated to the consequences of any breach under

---

196. *Saba Fakes v. Republic of Turkey* (ICSID Case No. ARB/07/20), Award, 14 July 2010, para. 114.
197. *Metal-Tech Ltd. v. Republic of Uzbekistan* (ICSID Case No. ARB/10/3), Award, 4 October 2013, para. 127.
198. *Inmaris Perestroika Sailing Maritime Services GmbH and others v. Ukraine* (ICSID Case No. ARB/08/8), Decision on Jurisdiction, 8 March 2010, para. 145.
199. Cf. Z. DOUGLAS, "Plea of Illegality", *op. cit.*, fn. 33, p. 3.

domestic law. There is no *a priori* category of assets which *must* attract treaty protection. Put differently, States may legitimately withhold access to treaty arbitration where the consequences under their own law may be, for instance, only that a contract is voidable at the option of the injured party.[200]

b.   *The timing of wrongdoing*

Tribunals have considered whether it makes a material difference if an investor's wrongdoing occurs in the context of the admission or establishment of an investment, or if it occurs later. Host States have frequently argued that the legality requirement, interpreted in the light of the object and purpose of investment treaties in fostering cross-border investment flows, should not concern solely whether investments were made in accordance with the law of the host State, but whether they were also lawfully carried out. However, tribunals have not tended to support that position. Rather, the weight of arbitral practice supports the conclusion that, absent express words to the contrary, the legality requirement of treaties is concerned with wrongdoing solely at the date of admission or establishment of an investment. A consistent line of decisions can be traced to *Inceysa,* where the tribunal found that:

> "[a] foreign investor cannot seek to benefit from an investment *effectuated* by means of one or several illegal acts and, consequently, enjoy the protection granted by the host state, such as access to international arbitration to resolve disputes, because *its act had a fraudulent origin*".[201]

In the recent *Yukos* arbitrations, the tribunal rejected the contention that the right to invoke the Energy Charter Treaty must be denied to an investor not only in the case of illegality in the making of the investment but also in its performance. The tribunal explained that:

> "[i]f the investor acts illegally, the host state can request it to correct its behavior and impose upon it sanctions available under domestic law, as the Russian Federation indeed purports to have done by reassessing taxes and imposing fines. However, if the investor believes these sanctions to be unjustified (as Claimants do in the present case), it must have the possibility of challenging their validity in accordance with the applicable investment treaty. It would undermine the purpose and object of the ECT to deny the investor the right to make its case before an

---

200. See *World Duty Free Company Limited v. The Republic of Kenya* (ICSID Case No. ARB/00/7), Award, 4 October 2006, para. 164, discussing the opinion of Lord Mustill and the policy reasons why English law affords the bribed party a right of election to affirm a tainted contract. See also *Niko Resources (Bangladesh) Ltd. v. Bangladesh & Ors* (ICSID Case No. ARB/10/11 and ARB/10/18), Decision on Jurisdiction, 19 August 2013, para. 451.

201. *Inceysa Vallisoletana v. Republic of El Salvador* (ICSID Case No. ARB/03/26), Award, 2 August 2006, para. 242 (emphasis added).

arbitral tribunal based on the same alleged violations the existence of which the investor seeks to dispute on the merits."[202]

Other tribunals have reached the same conclusion, applying treaty language which referred to investments "made",[203] "acquired or effected",[204] "accepted"[205] or "implemented",[206] in accordance with the laws of the host State. Tribunals have concluded from the plain meaning of such terms and the past tense in which they are cast that the intention behind such treaty provisions is that the legality of the creation of the investment should be a jurisdictional issue, but subsequent illegality is not.[207] It is now widely accepted, although not without criticism,[208] that the legality requirement found in many investment treaties thus "concerns the question of the compliance with the host State's domestic laws governing the admission of investments in the host State".[209]

The corollary is that subsequent wrongdoing, after the initiation of an investment, may not have jurisdictional consequences. This too has been widely upheld.[210] The *Fraport* tribunal rejected the argument that a legality requirement applied beyond the acquisition of the investment. Subsequent illegality "might be a defense to claimed substantive violations of the BIT, but could not deprive a tribunal acting under the authority of the BIT of its jurisdiction".[211] In *Metal-Tech*, the tribunal elaborated that the legality requirement, in that treaty at least, "simply does not address whether or not the

---

202. *Hulley Enterprises (Cyprus) Limited, Yukos Universal Limited (Isle of Man) and Veteran Petroleum Limited (Cyprus) v. Russian Federation*, PCA Case Nos. AA226-228, Final Awards, 18 July 2014, para. 1355.

203. *Quiborax S.A., Non Metallic Minerals S.A. and Allan Fosk Kaplún v. Plurinational State of Bolivia* (ICSID Case No. ARB/06/2), Decision on Jurisdiction, 27 September 2012, para. 266.

204. *Teinver S.A., Transportes de Cercanías S.A. and Autobuses Urbanos del Sur S.A. v. The Argentine Republic* (ICSID Case No. ARB/09/1), Decision on Jurisdiction, 21 December 2012, para. 318.

205. *Fraport AG v. The Republic of the Philippines* (ICSID Case No. ARB/03/25), Award, 16 August 2007, paras. 401-404.

206. *Metal-Tech Ltd. v. Republic of Uzbekistan* (ICSID Case No. ARB/10/3), Award, 4 October 2013, para. 193.

207. *Gustaf F.W. Hamester GmbH & Co KG v. Republic of Ghana* (ICSID Case No. ARB/07/24), Award, 18 June 2010, para. 127; *Quiborax S.A., Non Metallic Minerals S.A. and Allan Fosk Kaplún v. Plurinational State of Bolivia* (ICSID Case No. ARB/06/2), Decision on Jurisdiction, 27 September 2012, para. 266; *Teinver S.A., Transportes de Cercanías S.A. and Autobuses Urbanos del Sur S.A. v. The Argentine Republic* (ICSID Case No. ARB/09/1), Decision on Jurisdiction, 21 December 2012, para. 318.

208. See Z. DOUGLAS, "Plea of Illegality", *op. cit.*, fn. 33, p. 21.

209. *Saba Fakes v. Republic of Turkey* (ICSID Case No. ARB/07/20), Award, 14 July 2010, para. 119.

210. *Gustaf F.W. Hamester GmbH & Co KG v. Republic of Ghana*, (ICSID Case No. ARB/07/24), Award, 18 June 2010, para. 127; *Quiborax S.A., Non Metallic Minerals S.A. and Allan Fosk Kaplún v. Plurinational State of Bolivia* (ICSID Case No. ARB/06/2), Decision on Jurisdiction, 27 September 2012, para. 266; *Teinver S.A., Transportes de Cercanías S.A. and Autobuses Urbanos del Sur S.A. v. The Argentine Republic* (ICSID Case No. ARB/09/1), Decision on Jurisdiction, 21 December 2012, para. 328.

211. *Fraport AG v. The Republic of the Philippines* (ICSID Case No. ARB/03/25), Award, 16 August 2007, para. 345.

investment must be operated lawfully after it is in place".[212] Similarly, the tribunal in *Vannessa Ventures v. Venezuela* found that "the jurisdictional significance of the 'legality requirement' in the definition of an investment ... is exhausted once the investment has been made".[213]

This consistent arbitral practice has the attraction of simplicity, but does present complications. In situations where multifaceted investments are made in phases or tranches over a period of time, how is a tribunal to define the moment in which an investment is made or acquired? How should tribunals consider investments implemented in stages or subsequently expanded beyond their initial scope? One suggested approach is that breach of host State law may be raised only in relation to the inception of an investment but "not with regard to the subsequent conduct of the claimant in the host state, even in relation to the expansion or development of the original investment".[214] If so, it will be a factual matter for each tribunal to determine whether subsequent illegality concerns the inception of a fresh investment, in which case there may be an obstacle to jurisdiction, or the expansion of an existing investment in respect of which jurisdiction cannot be impeached. Such a distinction has some rationale, as the tribunal in *Arif v. Moldova* explained, since "the passage of time and the actions of the parties on the mutual assumption of legality cannot be ignored in the determination of jurisdiction".[215] In the circumstances, the tribunal confirmed that subsequent illegality should "be treated as an issue of liability and not jurisdiction".[216] In the *Yukos* cases, the tribunal added that what is called for, when an investment comprises a series of acts over time, is not merely an examination of whether the last in a series of transactions comprising the investment was in conformity with the law. The tribunal clearly stated: "[t]he making of the investment will often consist of several consecutive acts and all of these must be legal and *bona fide*".[217] Overall, arbitral practice recognizes temporal limitations on a jurisdictional argument based on the illegality of an investment, where

---

212. *Metal-Tech Ltd. v. Republic of Uzbekistan* (ICSID Case No. ARB/10/3), Award, 4 October 2013, para. 193.

213. *Vannessa Ventures Ltd v. The Bolivarian Republic of Venezuela* (ICSID Case No. ARB(AF)/04/6), Award, 16 January 2013, para. 167.

214. Z. DOUGLAS, *The International Law of Investment Claims, op. cit.*, fn. 33, p. 53, paras. 106-108.

215. *Arif v. Republic of Moldova* (ICSID Case No. ARB/11/23), Award, 8 April 2013, para. 376. See also *Railroad Development Corporation v. Republic of Guatemala* (ICSID Case No. ARB/07/23), Second Decision on Objections to Jurisdiction, 18 May 2004, paras. 140-147, in which the host State was precluded from advancing an objection to jurisdiction due to its awareness of the alleged illegality on the part of the claimant.

216. *Arif v. Republic of Moldova* (ICSID Case No. ARB/11/23), Award, 8 April 2013, para. 376.

217. *Hulley Enterprises (Cyprus) Limited, Yukos Universal Limited (Isle of Man) and Veteran Petroleum Limited (Cyprus) v. Russian Federation*, PCA Case Nos. AA226-228, Final Awards, 18 July 2014, para. 1369.

the legality of the investment has been accepted and acted upon in good faith by both parties over a period of time.

c.   The type of wrongdoing

The case law places importance on the type of wrongdoing in question. Arbitral practice, as summarised by the *Quiborax* and *Metal-Tech* tribunals, collectively suggests that the "in accordance with law" clause engages laws concerning (i) the admission of foreign investment, and extends also to (ii) compliance with fundamental principles of host State law concerned with the admission of investments, and (iii) fraud.[218]

i.   Laws on the admission of foreign investment

Many if not most States have laws concerning the admission of foreign capital or other investment in domestic projects, property or entities. Some laws include specific conditions for the admission of investment, whether substantive or procedural. Some States require foreign investments to be registered or specifically approved. Whatever the rigour or detail of such requirements, the cases are clear that breach of such conditions in the host State law on the admission of foreign investment would violate the "in accordance with host State law" requirement of many investment treaties. Thus, in *Saba Fakes* the Tribunal expressed the view that such clauses concern "the question of the compliance with the host State's domestic laws governing the admission of investments in the host State".[219] That passage was approved by both the *Quiborax* and *Metal-Tech* tribunals.[220]

ii.   Fundamental principles of host State law

As for the breach of "fundamental principles" of the host State's laws, several tribunals have asserted that such a breach, not directly related to the admission of foreign investment, may have jurisdictional or substantive consequences, provided the breach is significant. In *LESI SpA and Astaldi SpA v. People's Democratic Republic of Algeria*, the Tribunal ruled that the legality clause required *"l'exclusion de la protection pour tous les investissements qui auraient été effectués en violation des principes fondamentaux en vigueur"*.[221] In *Rumeli v. Kazakhstan*, the tribunal reinforced this conclusion, stating: "as was determined by the arbitral tribunal in the *Lesi* case, investments in the host State will only be excluded from the protection of the treaty if they have been made in breach of fundamental legal principles of the host country".[222] The *Desert Line* tribunal clarified that

---

218. *Quiborax S.A., Non Metallic Minerals S.A. and Allan Fosk Kaplún v. Plurinational State of Bolivia* (ICSID Case No. ARB/06/2), Decision on Jurisdiction, 27 September 2012, para. 266; *Metal-Tech Ltd v. The Republic of Uzbekistan* (ICSID Case No. ARB/10/3), Award, 4 October 2013, para. 165 (footnotes omitted).

219. *Saba Fakes v. Republic of Turkey* (ICSID Case No. ARB/07/20), Award, 14 July 2010, para. 119.

220. *Quiborax S.A., Non Metallic Minerals S.A. and Allan Fosk Kaplún v. Plurinational State of Bolivia* (ICSID Case No. ARB/06/2), Decision on Jurisdiction, 27 September 2012, para. 266; *Metal-Tech Ltd v. The Republic of Uzbekistan* (ICSID Case No. ARB/10/3), Award, 4 October 2013, para. 165.

221. *LESI SpA and Astaldi SpA v. People's Democratic Republic of Algeria* (ICSID Case No. ARB/05/03), Decision on Jurisdiction, 12 July 2006, para. 83(iii).

222. *Rumeli Telekom AS and Telsim Mobil Telekomunikasyon Hizmetleri AS v. Republic of Kazakhstan* (ICSID Case No. ARB/05/16), Award, 29 July 2008, para. 319.

in accordance with law clauses "are intended to ensure the legality of the investment by excluding investments made in breach of fundamental principles of the host State's law, e.g. by fraudulent misrepresentations or the dissimulation of true ownership".[223] Implicit in this articulation of the standard is causality between the illegality and the acquisition or inception of the investment.[224]

An example of the application of the "in accordance with law" clause in this context is *Fraport AG v. The Republic of the Philippines*. In that case the investor was found to have circumvented a domestic law restricting foreign investors to not more than a 40 percent interest in the shares of a local company that holds a concession in the public utilities sector, and crucially, prohibiting the foreign investor from managerial control over that company. By a majority, the tribunal found that a violation of that law meant that the investor had not made an investment "accepted in accordance with the respective laws and regulations" of the Philippines, as required under the applicable investment treaty.[225] The majority, finding the breach to be fundamental, concluded that it did not have jurisdiction, due to a lack of consent to arbitrate disputes concerning such investments.[226]

iii.   Other breaches of host State law

At the same time, tribunals insist that violations of host State law not directly concerned with "the admission of investments" or "investment regulation" should not serve as a bar to jurisdiction. In *Saba Fakes v. Turkey*, the tribunal explained the limits of the clause as follows:

> "The Tribunal is not convinced by the Respondent's position that any violation of any of the host State's laws would result in the illegality of the investment within the meaning of the BIT and preclude such investment from benefiting from the substantive protection offered by the BIT. As to the nature of the rules contemplated in Article 2(2) of the Netherlands-Turkey BIT, it is the Tribunal's view that the legality requirement contained therein concerns the question of the compliance with the host State's domestic laws governing the admission of investments in the host State. This is made clear by the plain language of the BIT, which applies to "investments ... established in accordance with the laws and regulations ...". The Tribunal also considers that it would run counter to the object and purpose of investment protection treaties to deny substantive protection to those investments that would violate domestic laws that are

---

223. *Desert Line Projects LLC v. Republic of Yemen* (ICSID Case No. ARB/05/17), Award, 6 February 2008, para. 104.

224. See *Gustaf F.W. Hamester GmbH & Co KG v. Republic of Ghana* (ICSID Case No. ARB/07/24), Award, 18 June 2010, para. 129.

225. *Fraport AG v. The Republic of the Philippines* (ICSID Case No. ARB/03/25), Award, 16 August 2007, para. 401. As already noted, the dissenting arbitrator, Cremades, took another view, finding that the assets comprising the investment were not themselves unlawful in the hands of a foreign investor, and stating that the question of the investor's compliance with the local law on the restriction on foreign control was a matter for the merits: *ibid.*, Dissenting Opinion of Bernardo M. Cremades, para. 38.

226. *Fraport AG v. The Republic of the Philippines* (ICSID Case No. ARB/03/25), Award, 16 August 2007, paras. 391, 401-402. The decision was later annulled on unrelated grounds.

unrelated to the very nature of investment regulation. In the event that an investor breaches a requirement of domestic law, a host State can take appropriate action against such investor within the framework of its domestic legislation. However, unless specifically stated in the investment treaty under consideration, a host State should not be in a position to rely on its domestic legislation beyond the sphere of investment regime to escape its international undertakings vis-à-vis investments made in its territory."[227]

Thus, tribunals have rejected the suggestion advanced in some cases that *any* breach of host State law could have jurisdictional consequences.[228] The *Quiborax* tribunal stated that an expansive construction, which encompasses any breach of the host State legal order irrespective of seriousness or timing, would create "deleterious incentives, as host States would be in a position to strip investors of treaty protection by finding any minor breach at any time".[229] In *Saba Fakes*, the tribunal explained that breaches of host State law unrelated to the regulation of foreign investment may attract domestic legal consequences "within the framework of its domestic legislation", but unless expressly stated, these should not impinge upon investment treaty protection.[230] A breach of host State law unrelated to the admission of investment should therefore have no bearing on jurisdictional cover. Other violations of host State law pertain mostly to the domestic order, and may have domestic law consequences, but will not typically impact upon the jurisdiction of an investment treaty tribunal. This conclusion does not preclude the possibility, of course, that the investor's conduct may bear upon the question of whether there has been a breach of substantive treaty standards.

---

227. *Saba Fakes v. Republic of Turkey* (ICSID Case No. ARB/07/20), Award, 14 July 2010, para. 119.
228. *Cf. Gustaf F.W. Hamester GmbH & Co KG v. Republic of Ghana* (ICSID Case No. ARB/07/24), Award, 18 June 2010, para. 123; *Teinver S.A., Transportes de Cercanías S.A. and Autobuses Urbanos del Sur S.A. v. The Argentine Republic* (ICSID Case No. ARB/09/1), Decision on Jurisdiction, 21 December 2012, para. 317. In *Rumeli v. Kazakhstan,* while the tribunal first noted that "in order to receive the protection of a bilateral investment treaty, the disputed investments have to be in conformity with the host State laws and regulations", the allegations of illegality were on the facts of that case not sufficiently connected with the investments in question in the territory of the host State to present an obstacle to jurisdiction: *Rumeli Telekom AS and Telsim Mobil Telekomunikasyon Hizmetleri AS v. Republic of Kazakhstan* (ICSID Case No. ARB/05/16), Award, 29 July 2008, para. 319.
229. *Quiborax S.A., Non Metallic Minerals S.A. and Allan Fosk Kaplún v. Plurinational State of Bolivia* (ICSID Case No. ARB/06/2), Decision on Jurisdiction, 27 September 2012, para. 263.
230. *Saba Fakes v. Republic of Turkey* (ICSID Case No. ARB/07/20), Award, 14 July 2010, para. 119.

d.   De minimis threshold

Authority exists to suggest that inadvertent breaches of host State law may fall foul of the in accordance with host State law clause. The Tribunal in *Alasdair Ross Anderson et al. v. Costa Rica* suggested that such an approach would be supported by public policy, including a country's "fundamental interest in securing respect for its laws" and the need to encourage investors to "exercise due diligence before committing funds to any particular investment proposal".[231]

Tribunals have, however, refused to apply the legality clause as a jurisdictional bar for mere *de minimis* violations of host State law. Thus, in *Tokios Tokelés v. Ukraine*, the tribunal disregarded alleged violations of Ukrainian administrative laws in respect of an investment that was not illegal *per se*:

> "The Respondent now alleges that some of the documents underlying these registered investments contain defects of various types, some of which relate to matters of Ukrainian law. Even if we were able to confirm the Respondent's allegations, which would require a searching examination of minute details of administrative procedures in Ukrainian law, to exclude an investment on the basis of such minor errors would be inconsistent with the object and purpose of the Treaty. In our view, the Respondent's registration of each of the Claimant's investments indicates that the 'investment' in question was made in accordance with the laws and regulations of Ukraine."[232]

In *Alphaprojektholding v. Ukraine*, the tribunal explained that an "investment is not excluded from the Tribunal's jurisdiction by virtue of alleged defects in Claimant's

---

231. *Alasdair Ross Anderson et al. v. Cost Rica* (ICSID Case No. ARB(AF)/07/13), Award, 19 May 2010, para. 53. In declining jurisdiction, in this case, to unwitting investors in a Ponzi scheme, effected through unregulated brokers, the tribunal may have over-extended the scope of the "in accordance with law" clause to include the illegal conduct of the entity into which the claimants invested, as opposed to the conduct of the claimants themselves. The tribunal in *Hulley Enterprises (Cyprus) Limited, Yukos Universal Limited (Isle of Man) and Veteran Petroleum Limited (Cyprus) v. Russian Federation*, PCA Case Nos. AA226-228, Final Awards, 18 July 2014, para. 1372 explained this decision by the fact that although the claimants in *Anderson* were no to be blamed for the illegality that tainted their investment, "nevertheless it is the very transaction by which their respective investments were obtained that was considered illegal by the tribunal, and led it to decline jurisdiction". In *Fraport*, the tribunal left open the possibility that its result would have been different if the investor had violated host State law unintentionally, perhaps if the law was unclear or if it had received mistaken local law advice: *Fraport AG v. The Republic of the Philippines* (ICSID Case No. ARB/03/25), Award, 16 August 2007, paras. 396-397.

232. *Tokios Tokeles v. Ukraine* (ICSID Case No. ARB/02/18), Decision on Jurisdiction, 29 April 2004, para. 86.

registration paperwork".[233] Other tribunals have concurred that only significant contraventions of host State law should lead to a denial of treaty protection.[234]

e.   In the absence of an express "legality" clause
Several tribunals have inferred a jurisdictional requirement similar to an express "in accordance with host state law" clause, even in the absence of specific treaty language. In *Yaung Chi Oo Trading v. Myanmar*, the tribunal found that there exists a "general rule that for a foreign investment to enjoy treaty protection it must be lawful under the law of the host State".[235] Subsequently, the *Phoenix Action* tribunal stated that "conformity of the establishment of the investment with the national laws... is implicit even when not expressly stated in the relevant BIT".[236] Likewise, for the *Hamester* tribunal,

> "[an investment] will also not be protected if it is made in violation of the host State's law (as elaborated, e.g. by the tribunal in Phoenix).
> These are general principles that exist independently of specific language to this effect in the Treaty."[237]

Finding such an implicit requirement as well in a multilateral treaty (in this case the Energy Charter Treaty), the *Plama* tribunal also stated:

> "[u]nlike a number of Bilateral Investment Treaties, the ECT does not contain a provision requiring the conformity of the Investment with a particular law. This does not mean, however, that the protections provided for by the ECT cover all kinds of investments, including those contrary to domestic or international law."[238]

The consequences of breach of host State law in the *Plama* case were different, however, from the outcome where the applicable treaty contains an express legality clause. In the presence of such a clause, the consequences of breach tend to be jurisdictional. In *Plama*, the tribunal found that the claimant's misrepresentation did not vitiate consent to

---

233. *Alpha Projekt Holding v. Ukraine* (ICSID Case No. ARB/07/16), Award, 8 November 2010, para. 297.

234. *Inceysa Vallisoletana v. Republic of El Salvador* (ICSID Case No. ARB/03/26), Award, 2 August 2006 and *Rumeli Telekom AS and Telsim Mobil Telekomunikasyon Hizmetleri AS v. Republic of Kazakhstan* (ICSID Case No. ARB/05/16), Award, 29 July 2008; *Mytilineos Holdings SA v. Serbia and Montenegro*, UNCITRAL, Partial Award on Jurisdiction, 8 September 2006, para. 151.

235. *Yaung Chi Oo Trading Trading Pte.Ltd v. Government of the Union of Myanmar*, ASEAN Case No. ARB/01/01, Award, 31 March 2003, para. 58.

236. *Phoenix Action, Ltd. v. Czech Republic* (ICSID Case No. ARB/06/5), Award, 15 April 2009, para. 101.

237. *Gustaf F.W. Hamester GmbH & Co KG v. Republic of Ghana* (ICSID Case No. ARB/07/24), Award, 18 June 2010, paras. 123-124.

238. *Plama Consortium Limited v. Bulgaria* (ICSID Case No. ARB/03/24), Award, 27 August 2008, para. 138.

arbitration but supplied grounds to exclude the claims on grounds of inadmissibility.[239] The *Phoenix Action* tribunal's decision to deny jurisdiction (as opposed to admissibility or ruling on the merits of the claims) does not point strongly to a different conclusion, since the precise formulation of the consequences was self-avowedly motivated less by principle and more by "judicial economy".[240]

The preferred view is that in the absence of express treaty wording, illegality affecting an investment is not a jurisdictional precondition for a treaty claim but rather, may be a basis to exclude the claims on grounds of inadmissibility, or may point to a defense to the merits.

2. Unclean Hands

The maxim, "He who comes into equity must come with clean hands", together with its many equivalent variants (usually couched in Latin),[241] is a well-established principle of equity jurisprudence found in many municipal systems of law,[242] the effect of which is to bar a claimant's claims due to its illegal or improper conduct in relation to those claims.[243] Claims tainted by wrongdoing therefore will not succeed, and the loss will lie where it falls. The principles that underpin the clean hands doctrine are judicial integrity, justice, and the public interest.[244] The doctrine is frequently phrased, "He who has done iniquity shall not have equity",[245] or, "He who desires relief in equity must himself be free

---

239. *Id.* at paras. 135, 138-140, 146. Although the tribunal did not expressly cast its decision in terms of inadmissibility, it may be properly understood as such: see C.A. MILES, *op. cit.*, fn. 192 at p. 30.

240. *Phoenix Action, Ltd. v. Czech Republic* (ICSID Case No. ARB/06/5), Award, 15 April 2009, para. 104.

241. The "clean hands" doctrine is sometimes termed the "unclean hands" or "dirty hands" doctrine. The clean hands doctrine is also closely related to several other Latin maxims, such as *ex delicto non orituractio* ("an unlawful act cannot serve as the basis of an action at law", *nemo ex suo delicto meliorem suam conditionem facit* ("no one can put himself in a better legal position by means of a delict"), *ex turpicausa non oritur* ("an action cannot arise from a dishonourable cause"), *inadimplenti non est adimplendum* ("one has no need to respect his obligation if the counter-party has not respected its own"), and *nullus commodum capere potest de in juria sua propria* ("no one can be allowed to take advantage of his own wrong").

242. The doctrine was originally developed in England in the late eighteenth century, but today can be found in the laws of many civil and common law jurisdictions. See J. POMEROY, *Equity Jurisprudence,* 5th edn. (1941) Sects. 397-404 (referring to the clean hands doctrine as "a universal rule guiding and regulating the action of equity courts in the interposition on behalf of suitors for any and every purpose and in their administration of any and every species of relief").

243. See E. MARTIN, ed., *A Dictionary of Law,* 3rd edn. (1994) (describing the clean hands doctrine as follows: "a person who makes a claim in equity must be free from any taint of fraud with respect to that claim. For example, a person seeking to enforce an agreement must not himself be in breach of it"); *International News Service v. The Associated Press,* 248 U.S. 215 (US Supreme Court 1918) (stating that the court would "refuse to aid a complainant in protecting any right acquired or retained by inequitable conduct".).

244. *Precision Instrument Mfg. Co. v. Automotive Maintenance Mach. Co.,* 324 U.S. at 815.

245. See, e.g., *Reynolds v. Boland,* 202 Pa. 642, 52 Atl. 19 (1902).

from fault".[246] But whatever the manner of expression, the doctrine demands that a claimant seeking equitable relief come into court having acted equitably in that matter for which he seeks a remedy.

The inequitable conduct which causes the clean hands doctrine to be invoked typically must be willful, and the claimant's alleged misconduct must have reference to the matters in controversy. The doctrine is invoked and applied to deny relief in three general circumstances, that is, where transactions are (i) fraudulent; (ii) illegal; or (iii) unconscionable. The misconduct need not of necessity be such as to be punishable as a crime under the law of the State in question, or actually be fraudulent, provided it is connected with the instant litigation and of such a nature as to affect the clean hands of the applicant.[247] It has been said that "[t]here must be some element of dishonesty or sharp practice in the matter relied upon for saying that he does not come with clean hands".[248] Examples of domestic law cases falling under this maxim involve individuals not being allowed to assert title to property where they have dealt with the property solely in order to defeat creditors[249] or to evade taxes.[250]

The clean hands doctrine as found in domestic law has been discussed and applied by ICSID tribunals in contractual arbitrations where the investments in question were tainted by corruption. The ICSID tribunal in *World Duty Free v. Kenya* reached a unanimous decision that an investor that has engaged in bribery comes to arbitration with unclean hands in relation to its investment and should therefore not be entitled to pursue a claim to protect that investment, regardless of whether the host State has facilitated or participated in the wrongdoing.[251] In finding thus, the tribunal reviewed principles of English law, which was the governing law of the underlying contract. The tribunal invoked the views of Lord Mansfield of the UK House of Lords, who in 1775 had stated:

> "The principle of public policy is this: *ex dolo malo non oritur actio*. No court will lend its aid to a man who founds his cause of action upon an immoral or illegal act. If, from the plaintiff's own stating or otherwise, the cause of action appears to arise *ex turpi causa*, or the transgression of a positive law of this country, there the court says he has no right to be assisted."[252]

The tribunal also invoked the decision of Kerr LJ, more than two centuries later, in the *Euro-Diam* case, who found that the "*ex turpi causa* defence":

> "rests on a principle of public policy that the courts will not assist a plaintiff who has been guilty of illegal (or immoral) conduct of which the courts should take

---

246. See, e.g., *Harms v. Stern*, 231 Fed. 645 (C.C.A. 2d, 1916).
247. See J. PAYNE, "'Clean Hands' in Derivative Actions", 61 Cambridge Law Journal (2002, no. 1) p. 76.
248. *Loosley v. National Union of Teachers* [1988] I.R.L.R. 157, 162 *per* Sir Denys Buckley.
249. See, e.g., *Gascoigne v. Gascoigne* [1918] 1 K.B. 223.
250. See, e.g., *Re Emery's Investment Trusts* [1959] Ch. 410.
251. *World Duty Free Company Limited v. The Republic of Kenya* (ICSID Case No. ARB/00/7), Award, 4 October 2006, paras. 180-181.
252. *Id.* at paras. 161, 181 (citing *Holman v. Johnson* (1775) 1 Cowp. 341, 343, *per* Mansfield J).

notice. It applies if in all the circumstances it would be an affront to public conscience to grant the plaintiff the relief which he seeks because the court would thereby appear to assist or encourage the plaintiff in his illegal conduct or to encourage others in similar acts."[253]

Further, the tribunal endorsed the statement of Lord Browne-Wilkinson that "[a] party to an illegality can recover by virtue of a legal or equitable property interest if, but only if, he can establish his title without relying on his own illegality".[254]

Applying these principles of law to the facts of the case, the Tribunal found that the claimant's pleaded claims were inadmissible because its investment had been tainted by bribery:

> "In conclusion, as regards public policy both under English law and Kenyan law (being materially identical) and on the specific facts of this case, the Tribunal concludes that the Claimant is not legally entitled to maintain any of its pleaded claims in these proceedings on the ground of *ex turpi causa non oritur actio.*"[255]

By upholding Kenya's *ex turpi causa* defence in this manner, the tribunal appears to have applied the clean hands doctrine as found to exist in municipal law as a stand-alone basis for dismissing claims. The status of the doctrine in international law is discussed next.

a.   *The unsettled status of the clean hands doctrine in international law*

As investment treaty arbitration is created and sustained by international law, which therefore forms part of the applicable law in investment treaty arbitrations,[256] it has been asserted that the clean hands doctrine can be applied by investment tribunals even in the absence of support from applicable national law. But the status of that doctrine in international law is far from settled.

On the one hand, international courts and tribunals have historically considered and applied concepts of equity found in municipal law.[257] This practice is derived from Art.

---

253. *Id*. at para. 161 (*citing Euro-Diam Ltd v. Bathurst* (1990) QB 1, *per* Kerr LJ).

254. *Id*. at para. 162 (citing *Tinsley v. Milligan* [1994] 1 A.C. 340, 385).

255. *Id*. at para. 179. See R. KREINDLER, "Corruption in International Investment Arbitration: Jurisdiction and the Unclean Hands Doctrine" in K. HOBER, et al., *Between East and West: Essays in Honour of Ulf Franke* (2010) p. 309 at p. 319 ("Reliance on the maxim *ex turpi causa non oritur action* can and should be considered as another application of the Unclean Hands Doctrine.").

256. See, e.g., ICSID Convention, Art. 42(1) ("The Tribunal shall decide a dispute in accordance with such rules of law as may be agreed by the parties. In the absence of such agreement, the Tribunal shall apply the law of the Contracting State party to the dispute (including its rules on the conflict of laws) *and such rules of international law as may be applicable*") (emphasis added).

257. See, e.g., *North Sea Continental Shelf (Federal Republic of Germany/Denmark; Federal Republic of Germany/Netherlands)* ICJ Reports 3, 53 (1969) (directing a final delimitation between the parties "in accordance with equitable principles"); *Continental Shelf (Tunisia/Libya)* ICJ Reports 18, 60 (1982) (finding that "the legal concept of equity is a general principle directly applicable as law"); I. BROWNLIE, *Principles of Public International Law*, 7th edn. (2008) p. 25 ("'Equity' is used here in the sense of considerations of fairness, reasonableness, and policy often necessary for the sensible application of the more settled rules of law. Strictly, it cannot be a source of law, and yet it may be an important factor in the process of decision. Equity may play a dramatic role in

38(1)(c) of the Statute of the International Court of Justice, which lists as a source of international law "the general principles of law recognised by civilised nations", and may thus include legal principles that are common to a large number of municipal legal systems.[258] The doctrine of "clean hands", having been adopted in the domestic legal orders of many States, is frequently asserted to qualify as a "general principle of law" pursuant to Art. 38(1)(c) of the ICJ Statute.[259] Some tribunals have applied principles that may arguably be considered part of the clean hands doctrine in the nineteenth[260] and twentieth[261] centuries, finding claims inadmissible where claimants had engaged in wrongful conduct in relation to their claims. A number of individual opinions by judges of the Permanent Court of International Justice[262] and the ICJ[263] also identify clean hands

---

supplementing the law or appear unobtrusively as a part of judicial reasoning").

258. Given the limits of treaties and custom as sources of international law, Art. 38(1)(c) of the ICJ Statute is generally viewed as a directive to the ICJ to fill any gaps in the law and prevent a *non liquet* by reference to general principles. See I. BROWNLIE, *op. cit.*, fn. 257, pp. 16-17.

259. The application of the clean hands doctrine in international law also finds support in the writings of commentators, another source of international law pursuant to Art. 38(1)(d). See, e.g., G. FITZMAURICE, "The General Principles of International Law Considered from the Standpoint of the Rule of Law", 92 Revue Canadienne de Droit International (1957) p. 1 at p. 119 ("'He who comes to equity for relief must come with clean hands'. Thus a State which is guilty of illegal conduct may be deprived of the necessary *locus standi in judicio* for complaining of corresponding illegalities on the part of other States, especially if these were consequential on or were embarked upon in order to counter its own illegality – in short were provoked by it").

260. In the *Medea* and *Good Return* cases, the Ecuador-United States Claims Commission found that the claimant had "committed depredations" against two nations, which disqualified him as a legitimate claimant on the basis that "[a] party who asks for redress must present himself with clean hands". *Medea and The Good Return cases*, Ecuadorian-United States Commission, 8 August 1865, in J. MOORE, *History and Digest of the International Arbitrations to which the United States Has Been a Party* (1995) p. 2739.

261. *Diversion of Water from the Meuse (Netherlands v. Belgium)*, Ser. E, (No. 14) (PCIJ, 1937). The case concerned the interpretation of a treaty between Holland and Belgium regarding the regime of diversions of water from the River Meuse. Holland sought to prevent Belgium from making use of waters from the Meuse which it considered contrary to the applicable treaty, but Holland itself was making use of the waters in a similar manner. The PCIJ rejected Holland's claim, and in so doing applied the clean hands doctrine, as follows: "the Court finds it difficult to admit that the Netherlands are now warranted in complaining of the construction and operation of a lock of which they themselves set an example in the past": *ibid.* 25. See also *Factory at Chorzow (Germany v. Poland) (Merits)*, Ser. A, (No. 9) (PCIJ, 1927) 31 ("one party cannot avail himself of the fact that the other has not fulfilled some obligation ... if the former party has, by some illegal act, prevented the latter from fulfilling the obligation in question or from having recourse to the tribunal which would have been open to him".).

262. In *Diversion of Water from the Meuse*, Judge Hudson noted that "[w]hat are widely known as principles of equity have long been considered to constitute part of international law, and as such they have often been applied by international tribunals". With reference to English law, Judge Hudson proceeded to apply the doctrine "He who seeks equity must do equity", concluding:

"It would seem to be an important principle of equity that where two parties have assumed an identical or reciprocal obligation, one party which is engaged in a continuing non-performance of that obligation should not be permitted to take advantage of a similar non-performance of that obligation by the other party ... a tribunal bound by international law ought not to shrink from

511

as a principle of international law. The clean hands doctrine has also been invoked by States in other ICJ proceedings, namely, by the United States in *Oil Platforms*,[264] *La Grand*,[265] and *Avena*,[266] by the NATO respondents in the *Legality of Use of Force* cases,[267] and by Israel in the advisory proceedings on *Legal Consequences of the Construction of a Wall in the Occupied Palestinian Territory*.[268]

Despite the above-mentioned practice, there remains serious debate as to the scope of application of the clean hands doctrine in international law. This is due partly to the fact that the ICJ has yet to uphold the clean hands doctrine in a majority opinion, despite having had the aforementioned opportunities to do so. A recent inter-State arbitral tribunal has been similarly hesitant to recognize the doctrine.[269] Indeed, even the utilization of unclean hands in most of the early claims commission cases resulted from violations of laws on slavery and neutrality, and also arose within the context of diplomatic protection. According to Crawford,

> "it appears that these cases are all characterized by the fact that the breach of international law by the victim was the sole cause of the damage claimed, [and]

---

applying a principle of such obvious fairness."

Diversion of Water from the Meuse (Netherlands v. Belgium), Ser. E, (No. 14) (PCIJ, 1937), Individual Opinion of Judge Hudson, 77. In similar terms in that case, Judge Anzilotti in his Dissenting Opinion held:

"I am convinced that the principle underlying this submission (*inadimplenti non est adimplendum*) is so just, so equitable, so universally recognised, that it must be applied in international relations also. In any case, it is one of these 'general principles of law recognised by civilised nations' which the Court applies in virtue of Article 38 of its Statute."

Id., 50. Judge Anzilotti reached a similar conclusion in his Dissenting Opinion in *Legal Status of Eastern Greenland*, where he held that "[t]his claim should, in my view, be rejected, for an unlawful act cannot serve as the basis of an action at law": *Denmark v. Norway*, Ser. A/B, (No. 53) (PCIJ, 1933), Dissenting Opinion of Judge Anzilotti, 95.

263. See *Military and Paramilitary Activities in and against Nicaragua (Nicaragua v. United States)*, Merits, ICJ Reports 14 (1986), Dissenting Opinion of Judge Schwebel. Nicaragua had brought claims against the United States for various alleged military and paramilitary acts conducted in and against Nicaragua. The ICJ, both at the provisional measures and merits stages, gave no weight to considerations of clean hands, for the reason that it (controversially) found the hands of Nicaragua to be clean. Judge Schwebel disagreed with the majority decision, finding that the United States' acts were in response to what was tantamount to an armed attack by Nicaragua against El Salvador.

264. *Oil Platforms (Iran v. United States)*, Merits, ICJ Reports 161, 176-178 (2003).

265. *LaGrand (Germany v. United States)*, Merits, ICJ Reports 466, 488-489 (2001).

266. *Avena (Mexico v. United States)*, Merits, ICJ Reports 12, 38 (2004).

267. See S. SCHWEBEL, *Clean Hands in the Court*, 31 Stud. Transnat'l Legal Pol'y (1999) p. 74.

268. See J. DUGARD, "Sixth Report on Diplomatic Protection" (57th Session, 2005), A/CN.4/546, para. 5.

269. See *Guyana v. Suriname* (UNCLOS Annex VII Tribunal), Award, PCA Awards Series (2007), para. 418 ("use of the clean hands doctrine has been sparse, and its application in the instances in which it has been invoked have been inconsistent").

that the cause-and-effect relationship between the damage and the victim's conduct was pure, involving no wrongful act by the respondent State. When, on the contrary, the latter has in turn violated international law in taking repressive action against the applicant, the arbitrators have never declared the claim inadmissible."[270]

Crawford concluded in his report as Special Rapporteur on State Responsibility to the UN International Law Commission that: "it is not possible to consider the 'clean hands' theory as an institution of general customary law".[271] Similarly, ILC Special Rapporteur on diplomatic protection John Dugard stated that:

"evidence in favour of the clean hands doctrine is inconclusive. ... In these circumstances the Special Rapporteur sees no reason to include a provision in the draft articles dealing with the clean hands doctrine. Such a provision would clearly not be an exercise in codification and is unwarranted as an exercise in progressive development in the light of the uncertainty relating to the very existence of the doctrine and its applicability to diplomatic protection."[272]

The position in general international law is therefore unsettled, at best. Arbitral practice in investment treaty arbitration is also mixed, with some tribunals determined to forge their own path but others firmly unpersuaded of the existence of the principle.

b.   *The clean hands doctrine in investment arbitration*
Notwithstanding the unsettled status of the clean hands doctrine as a principle of public international law, the doctrine has been repeatedly argued in respect of claims made by investors against States in investment treaty arbitration.[273]

As a threshold point, tribunals and commentators have argued that the clean hands doctrine informs and helps explain the "in accordance with host State law" treaty provision.[274] The view that only investors with clean hands are entitled to protection

---

270. ILC Second Report on State Responsibility by James Crawford, Special Rapporteur (3 May-23 July 1999), UN Doc A/CN.4/498/Add.2, citing Jean J.A. SALMON, *"Des 'Mains Propres' Comme Condition de Recevabilite des Reclamations Internationales"*, 10 Annuaire Français de Droit International (1964) p. 224 at p. 259.

271. J. CRAWFORD, "Second Report on State Responsibility" in *Yearbook of the International Law Commission* (vol. II, part 1) (1999), A/CN.4/SER.A/1999/Add.1 (part 1) para. 336, citing ROSSEAU, *Droit international public*, p. 177, para. 170.

272. J. DUGARD, *op. cit.*, fn. 268, para. 18, fn. 1772.

273. See R. KREINDLER, *op. cit.*, fn. 255, p. 309; C. LAMM, et al., *op. cit.*, fn. 61, p. 699, at pp. 723-726; R. MOLOO, "A Comment on the Clean Hands Doctrine in International Law", 8 Transnational Dispute Management (2011, no. 1); R. MOLOO and A. KHACHATURIAN, *op. cit.*, fn. 33, p. 1473 at pp. 1485-1486 ; P. DUMBERRY and G. DUMAS-AUBIN, "The Doctrine of 'Clean Hands' and the Inadmissibility of Claims by Investors Breaching International Human Rights Law", 10 Transnational Dispute Management (2013, no. 1).

274. See, e.g., Germany-Philippines BIT, Art. 1(1) ("the term 'investment' shall mean any kind of asset accepted in accordance with the respective laws and regulations of either Contracting State"); and see R. MOLOO, *op. cit.*, fn. 273.

under such treaties was confirmed in *Inceysa v. El Salvador*, a case which concerned the interpretation and application of such a clause.[275] As discussed above, the investor in that case procured a concession contract for vehicle inspection services in El Salvador through fraud in the public bidding process. The tribunal found that the claimant's investment did not meet the applicable treaty's requirements of legality,[276] and declined jurisdiction on grounds that the investment fell outside the scope of conditional consent expressed by the Contracting Parties to the treaty.[277] The tribunal reached its decision also by analyzing the claimant's investment in light of the general principles of law, which it found formed "part of Salvadoran law".[278] These included the maxim *nemo auditur propriam turpitudinem allegans* ("no one is heard when alleging one's own wrong"),[279] said to be a manifestation of the "clean hands" doctrine, which the tribunal understood as prohibiting an investor from "benefit[ting] from an investment effectuated by means of one or several illegal acts".[280] The tribunal found that the claimant's violation of this principle meant that the investment was not within the scope of the offer to arbitrate disputes and for that reason denied jurisdiction.[281]

But what of those situations where an investment treaty does not contain an express provision stating that protected investments are only those made "in accordance with the law"? A good illustration is *Plama v. Bulgaria*. As discussed above, the claimant in that case obtained its investment by fraudulently concealing certain facts regarding its financial and managerial capacities required to operate an oil refinery in Bulgaria.[282] The tribunal's investment was thus deemed to have been made in violation of Bulgarian law.[283] In assessing the consequences of this misconduct, the tribunal stated that the lack of a specific provision requiring the conformity of the investment with national law "does not

---

275. *Inceysa Vallisoletana v. Republic of El Salvador* (ICSID Case No. ARB/03/26), Award, 2 August 2006.

276. *Id.* at paras. 248-252. The applicable BIT in that case stated that "[e]ach Contracting Party shall protect in its territory the investments made, *in accordance with its legislation*", by investors from the other Contracting Party: Spain-El Salvador BIT, Art. III (emphasis added).

277. *Inceysa Vallisoletana v. Republic of El Salvador* (ICSID Case No. ARB/03/26), Award, 2 August 2006, para. 257 ("because Inceysa's investment was made in a manner that was clearly illegal, it is not included within the scope of consent expressed by Spain and the Republic of El Salvador in the BIT and, consequently, the disputes arising from it are not subject to the jurisdiction of the Centre").

278. See *Inceysa Vallisoletana v. Republic of El Salvador* (ICSID Case No. ARB/03/26), Award, 2 August 2006, at para. 243.

279. See *Inceysa Vallisoletana v. Republic of El Salvador* (ICSID Case No. ARB/03/26), Award, 2 August 2006, Part VI(A)(viii)(b).

280. *Inceysa Vallisoletana v. Republic of El Salvador* (ICSID Case No. ARB/03/26), Award, 2 August 2006, paras. 240-242.

281. *Id.* at para. 243 ("Inceysa acted improperly in order to be awarded the bid that made its investment possible and, therefore, it cannot be given the protection granted by the BIT. Sustaining the contrary would be to violate the aforementioned general principles of law which, as indicated, are part of Salvadoran law").

282. *Plama Consortium Limited v. Bulgaria* (ICSID Case No. ARB/03/24), Award, 27 August 2008, Part IV(B)(3).

283. *Plama Consortium Limited v. Bulgaria* (ICSID Case No. ARB/03/24), Award, 27 August 2008, Part IV(B)(4).

mean ... that the protections provided for by the ECT cover all kinds of investments, including those contrary to domestic or international law".[284] The tribunal proceeded to cite with approval the *Inceysa* tribunal's observations that the claimant's improper conduct in that case violated certain general principles of law, including the principle of *nemo auditur propriam turpitudinem allegans*.[285] Applying that principle to the facts at hand, the *Plama* tribunal concluded as follows:

> "Claimant, in the present case, is requesting the Tribunal to grant its investment in Bulgaria the protections provided by the ECT. However, the Tribunal has decided that the investment was obtained by deceitful conduct that is in violation of Bulgarian law. The Tribunal is of the view that granting the ECT's protections to Claimant's investment would be contrary to the principle *nemo auditur propriam turpitudinem allegans* invoked above."[286]

On the basis of this finding, which the tribunal termed the "*ex turpi causa* defence", the claimant's pleaded claims were deemed inadmissible under international law.[287] Thus, although the words "unclean" or "clean hands" were never explicitly stated in its award, the *Plama* tribunal found that the investor's unclean hands constituted an independent basis for dismissing the claim.[288] The source of this norm was said to derive from principles of good faith found in both Bulgarian law and general international law,[289] and it is not entirely clear whether the tribunal considered clean hands a stand-alone general principle of international law (in the sense of Art. 38(1)(c) of the ICJ Statute), or a principle of transnational public policy, or both.

In another contract-based ICSID arbitration, *Niko Resources v. Bangladesh*, the tribunal found that "[t]he question whether the principle forms part of international law remains

---

284. *Plama Consortium Limited v. Bulgaria* (ICSID Case No. ARB/03/24), Award, 27 August 2008, para. 138.

285. *Id.* at para. 141 (citing *Inceysa Vallisoletana v. Republic of El Salvador* (ICSID Case No. ARB/03/26), Award, 2 August 2006, paras. 240-242).

286. *Plama Consortium Limited v. Bulgaria* (ICSID Case No. ARB/03/24), Award, 27 August 2008, para. 143.

287. *Id.* at para. 146 ("In consideration of the above and in light of the *ex turpi causa* defence, this Tribunal cannot lend its support to Claimant's request and cannot, therefore, grant the substantive protections of the ECT.").

288. It bears noting that in *Plama,* there was no jurisdictional requirement in the ECT that an investment must be made in accordance with the law; thus, whilst the tribunal had jurisdiction to hear the dispute, the illegality of the investment rendered the claimant's claim inadmissible. By contrast, in the *Inceysa* decision, where the applicable treaty contained an express "in accordance with the law" clause, breach of which was found to absolve the tribunal of jurisdiction. It therefore appears, based on the limited available jurisprudence, that where an obligation to comply with the law is implicit rather than explicit, non-compliance with the law cannot be deemed a condition for host State consent to arbitration, and will be dealt with as a matter of admissibility rather than jurisdiction. See R. MOLOO and A. KHACHATURIAN, *op. cit.*, fn. 33, pp. 1475, 1486.

289. *Plama Consortium Limited v. Bulgaria* (ICSID Case No. ARB/03/24), Award, 27 August 2008, para. 144.

controversial and its precise content is ill defined".[290] Adopting a narrow view of the doctrine, the tribunal set a legal test for the application of the clean hands doctrine composed of three elements: (i) the claimant's conduct said to give rise to "unclean hands" must amount to a continuing violation, (ii) the remedy sought by the claimant in the proceedings must be "protection against continuance of that violation in the future", not damages for past violations, and (iii) there must be a relationship of reciprocity between the obligations considered.[291] In other words, investor misconduct unrelated to the claims before the arbitral tribunal ought not, on a strict application of the principle, trigger the doctrine of unclean hands. On the facts of the case, in fact, the tribunal found that the respondent's objection in respect of the investor's alleged "unclean hands" did not meet the articulated criteria for the application of the clean hands doctrine in international law.[292] As to the third criterion, for example, the tribunal found that in a situation where corruption occurred after the joint venture agreement which was the subject of the investment had already been concluded, "there is no relation of reciprocity between the relief which the Claimant now seeks in this arbitration and the acts in the past which the Respondents characterise as involving unclean hands".[293]

Perhaps the most considered expression of the status of the clean hands doctrine in investment arbitration case law is found in the *Yukos* arbitrations. Following a detailed review of the authorities, the tribunal concluded that:

> "[t]he Tribunal is not persuaded that there exists a 'general principle of law recognized by civilized nations' within the meaning of Article 38(1)(c) of the ICJ Statute that would bar an investor from making a claim before an arbitral tribunal under an investment treaty because it has so-called 'unclean hands.' General principles of law require a certain level of recognition and consensus. However, on the basis of the cases cited by the Parties, the Tribunal has formed the view that there is a significant amount of controversy as to the existence of an 'unclean hands' principle in international law."[294]

In sum, there is significant doubt as to the status of the clean hands doctrine as a general principle of international law. Indeed, the *Yukos* cases are emphatic in closing the door

---

290. *Niko Resources (Bangladesh) Ltd. v. Bangladesh & Ors* (ICSID Case No. ARB/10/11 and ARB/10/18), Decision on Jurisdiction, 19 August 2013, para. 477.

291. *Id.* at para. 481 (applying the three criteria identified by the UNCLOS arbitral tribunal in *Guyana v. Suriname*, Award, 17 September 2007, paras. 420-421).

292. *Niko Resources (Bangladesh) Ltd. v. Bangladesh & Ors* (ICSID Case No. ARB/10/11 and ARB/10/18), Decision on Jurisdiction, 19 August 2013, paras. 483-485.

293. *Id.* at para. 484. Relatedly, scholarly commentators have mentioned that the *ex turpi causa* principle "insofar as the claim itself is based on an unlawful act. It does not apply to cases where, although the claimant may be guilty of an unlawful act, such act is judicially extraneous to the cause of action." B. CHENG, *op. cit.*, fn. 6, pp. 157-158.

294. *Hulley Enterprises (Cyprus) Limited, Yukos Universal Limited (Isle of Man) and Veteran Petroleum Limited (Cyprus) v. Russian Federation*, PCA Case Nos. AA226-228, Final Awards, 18 July 2014, paras. 1358-1359.

on the application of this principle,[295] at least in the context of the Energy Charter Treaty. It remains possible that the clean hands doctrine may apply whenever the parties agree to be bound by a particular national law that contains the principle (such as in *World Duty Free*). *Niko Resources*, again an ICSID arbitration but not a treaty case, also points to a continued, albeit limited, application of the clean hands doctrine as a universal principle affecting the administration of equitable rights and remedies in ICSID proceedings. Where the doctrine has been invoked and applied in the investment treaty context, those cases might be better explained by reference to the applicable investment treaty's legality clause.

As discussed further in Part V *infra*, the consequences of a finding that a claimant has unclean hands are likely to concern the merits or admissibility of claims.

3.   Transnational Public Policy

The most serious forms of investor wrongdoing often trigger an analysis in terms of "transnational public policy" or "truly international public policy", usually in conjunction with one or both of the preceding legal principles.[296] The English House of Lords defined the term "public policy" as early as 1853 as meaning "that principle of law which holds that no subject can lawfully do that which has a tendency to be injurious to the public, or against public good".[297] Modern "transnational public policy" tends to be traced back to the late *doyen* of international arbitration, Pierre Lalive, who spoke in 1986 of a "transnational (or truly international) public policy"[298] that could potentially "trump" applicable national law.

Arbitrators in international arbitration (both in a purely commercial and in an investment context) avow that they are, or are often said to be, bound to respect an overarching set of principles of "transnational public policy", independent of specific national rules or interests. Whereas national public policy is used to refer to fundamental principles of one particular State (such as, for example, prohibitions against gambling), transnational public policy is a term:

---

295. *Id.* at para. 1363: ("The Tribunal therefore concludes that 'unclean hands' does not exist as a general principle of international law which would bar a claim by an investor, such as the Claimants in this case.").

296. Although often used interchangeably in the cases, some scholars would define "international public policy" as a forum state's public policies applicable in an international context, while "transnational public policy" points to an autonomous and generally applicable group of international policies derived from international sources and national practices. See Gary BORN, *op. cit.*, fn. 134, pp. 2621-2623; P. LALIVE, *op. cit.*, fn. 39, pp. 257-318.

297. *Egerton v. Earl Brownlow*, IV HLC 1, 196 (1853).

298. P. LALIVE, "*Ordre Public Transnational (ou réellement international) et Arbitrage International*", Revue de l'Arbitrage (1986) p. 329.

"usually employed to refer to certain fundamental principles of law that are considered to be common among developed legal systems, and to have mandatory application, regardless of what the parties have agreed".[299]

Such principles are said to reflect the values and fundamental interests of the international community. Kessedjian has described transnational public policy in these terms:

"[T]ransnational public policy is composed of mandatory norms which may be imposed on actors in the market either because they have been created by those actors themselves or by civil society at large, or because they have been widely accepted by different societies around the world. These norms aim at being universal. They are the sign of the maturity of the international communities (that of merchants and that of the civil societies) who know very well that there are limits to their activities."[300]

Indeed, adherents to this approach urge arbitrators to extend their role – beyond fulfilling the mission conferred by the parties – to education and to moralization in this respect. The notion of "transnational public policy" has been recognized by courts of several jurisdictions, both civil and common law based, as well as in arbitral practice. This practice led commentators to announce already some time ago the end of any debate as to the existence of transnational public policy:

"Although it may not be part of the substantive law of every sovereign state, genuinely international public policy is nevertheless a reality, and it is perfectly able to operate so as to override the law which would otherwise apply, just as the local conception of international public policy would operate in a national court."[301]

It is also recognized that the concept and content of public policy, by its very nature, is not capable of any precise definition, but is flexible and variable, both in space and in time.[302] Nevertheless, some objectivity is essential; otherwise the impression would be that arbitrators are free to decide based on personal predispositions. They are not. Indeed, it has long been understood that the role of investment tribunals when finding appropriate systems of law governing the dispute

---

299. G. BORN, *op. cit.*, fn. 134, pp. 2194-2195 (citing prohibitions against agreements to perform criminal acts, slavery and similar abuses, supplying arms to terrorist groups, and comparable acts within the concept of international public policy).

300. C. KESSEDJIAN, "Transnational Public Policy" in *International Arbitration 2006: Back to Basics?*, ICCA Congress Series no. 13 (2007) (henceforth *ICCA Congress Series no. 13*) p. 857, at pp. 861-862 (citations omitted).

301. GAILLARD, SAVAGE, eds., *Fouchard Gaillard Goldmann on International Commercial Arbitration* (Kluwer 1999) p. 864.

302. P. LALIVE, *op. cit.*, fn. 39, p. 257 at p. 293.

"is not one of unbridled freedom, as is sometimes popularly assumed. The categories of materials to be considered have been more or less determined by a long development of international jurisprudence, and standards are available for appraising their value."[303]

In determining the existence and content of a certain transnational public policy, it therefore must be shown that there is consensus on the issue. According to Sayed,

"when one talks of transnational public policy or universal values, one is at some point bound to refer to values, which are perceived as (1) essential; (2) supported by a large adherence or what in a usual language is called a large consensus, let alone a universal one; and (3) therefore requiring immediate application, regardless of any contrary agreement".[304]

The categories of investor misconduct which are most likely to impinge upon transnational public policy are bribery or other forms of corruption, but also possibly fraud,[305] to which transnational public policy appears to emerge as a supranational source of law to exclude treaty claims or eliminate jurisdiction. The bribing of public officials to achieve a particular end has been specifically singled-out by international conventions, in arbitral practice and by scholarly commentators as being contrary to universally accepted principles of transnational public policy. Even three decades prior to the first major multilateral instruments regulating corruption, Judge Lagergren as sole arbitrator in ICC Case No. 1110 declared:

"Whether one is taking the point of view of good government or that of commercial ethics it is impossible to close one's eyes to the probable destination of amounts of this magnitude, and to the destructive effect thereof on the business pattern with the consequent impairment of industrial progress. Such corruption is an international evil; it is contrary to good morals and to international public policy common to the community of nations."[306]

Corruption of state officials is generally considered as incompatible with fundamental moral and social values and thus constitutes both a clear violation of "international public policy" or "transnational public policy" and also of the national public policy of most States. This has been recognized by a large number of judicial decisions and by

---

303. M. HUDSON, *International Tribunals: Past and Future* (1944) p. 107.
304. Abdulhay SAYED, *op. cit.*, fn. 127, pp. 287-288.
305. *Plama Consortium Limited v. Bulgaria* (ICSID Case No. ARB/03/24), Award, 27 August 2008, para. 143 ("The Tribunal is of the view that granting the ECT's protections to Claimant's investment would be contrary to the principle *nemo auditur propriam turpitudinem allegans* invoked above. It would be contrary to the basic notion of international public policy – that a contract obtained by wrongful means ... should not be enforced by a tribunal.").
306. ICC Case No. 1110, 10 Arb. Int'l (1994, no. 3) at p. 294.

international arbitrators alike in commercial arbitrations, applying numerous different national laws.[307]

More recent commentary confirms that bribery and corruption of foreign public officials "can no longer be considered as simply as reprehensible business practices, or unavoidable evils of doing business in difficult parts of the world".[308] Multilateral instruments on the subject, notably the OECD Convention, point to a "consensus ... within and outside the international arbitration community"[309] condemning such practices, and have arguably "contributed to, or confirmed, the development of certain national and transnational concepts of public policy in abhorrence of illegality of contracts".[310]

A transnational public policy condemning corruption has been confirmed to exist and found application in certain commercial and primarily contract-based investment arbitrations, most notably *World Duty Free v. Kenya*. In that case, the tribunal was faced with a question of whether a transnational public policy against bribery existed and how this principle should affect the proceedings. The tribunal used the term "international public policy" to signify "an international consensus as to universal standards and accepted norms of conduct that must be applied in all fora"; i.e., what is more frequently referred to as *transnational* public policy.[311] It noted the wide acceptance of anti-bribery and anti-corruption policies in the national law of many countries,[312] the significant number of international conventions addressing corruption and bribery,[313] and a line of arbitral decisions holding that proof of corruption mandated a tribunal to refrain from applying the contract on transnational public policy grounds.[314] The tribunal concluded "that bribery [was] contrary to international public policy of most, if not all, States or,

---

307. See, e.g, ICC Case No. 1110, 10 Arb.Int'l (1994, no. 3) at p. 294; *Westacre Investments. Inc. v. Jugoimport SDPR Holding*, English Court of Appeal (Civil Division), 12 May 1999, *Yearbook* XXIV(1999) pp. 753-776; *Omnium de Traitement et de Valorisation S.A. v. Hilmarton*, English High Court, Queen's bench Division, 14 Mealey's Int. Arb. Rep. (1999, No. 6) A1-A5; *European Gas Turbines v. Westman*, Paris Court of Appeals, 30 September 1993, Revue de l'arbitrage 359 (1994); *National Power Corp. v. Westinghouse*, Swiss Federal Tribunal, Decision of 2 September 1993, ASA Bulletin 244, 247 (1994); ICC Case No. 3913 of 1981, cited in Y. DERAINS, Journal du droit international, (Clunet) 985, 989 (1985); *Frontier AG & Brunner Sociedade v. Thomson CSF*, ICC Case No. 7664, Award of 31 July 1996, cited in Abdulhay SAYED, *op. cit.*, fn. 127, pp. 306-307; ICC Case No. 8891 of 1998, Journal du droit international (Clunet) 1080 (2000).

308. B.M. CREMADES and D.J.A. CAIRNS, *op. cit.*, fn. 125, p. 65 at p. 77.

309. K.D. BEALE and P. ESPOSITO, "Emergent International Attitudes Towards Bribery, Corruption and Money Laundering", 75 Arbitration (2009) p. 360 at p. 369.

310. R. KREINDLER, *op. cit.*, fn. 116, at p. 211 ("[O]ver the last several years a number of states have acceded to multilateral conventions condemning illegal contracts, corruption, bribery of public officials, etc. These accessions have arguably contributed to, or confirmed, the development of certain national and transnational concepts of public policy in abhorrence of illegality of contracts.").

311. *World Duty Free Company Limited v. The Republic of Kenya* (ICSID Case No. ARB/00/7), Award, 4 October 2006, para. 139.

312. *Id.* at para. 142.

313. *Id.* at paras. 143-144.

314. *Id.* at paras. 148 et seq.

to use another formula, to transnational public policy".[315] As a consequence, the *World Duty Free* Tribunal held that "the claims based on contracts of corruption or contracts obtained by corruption cannot be upheld by this Arbitral Tribunal".[316]

There are also references to *international ordre public* in *Société d'Investigation de Recherche et d'Exploitation Minière v. Burkina Faso*. In that case, a tribunal considered whether the fact that a contract was concluded further to actions constituting corruption might justify its invalidation, not only by virtue of contract law principles with respect to fraud, but also by the invocation of public order, in either the municipal or international context. The tribunal did decline to allow the claimant to rely on the legal rights contained in the contract due to its "breach of public order".[317]

There are other references in investment treaty cases to a transnational public policy sanctioning investor wrongdoing. In *Inceysa Vallisoletana v. El Salvador*, the tribunal found that recognition of rights arising from illegal acts would violate "the respect for law", which it said is a principle of international public policy.[318] It added that "the inclusion of the clause 'in accordance with law' in various BIT provisions is a clear manifestation of said international public policy".[319] *Plama v. Bulgaria* considered the claims to be "contrary to the basic notion of international public policy – that a contract obtained by wrongful means (fraudulent misrepresentation) should not be enforced by a tribunal".[320] In *Fraport v. Philippines*, Cremades, dissenting, opined that "in some cases, for example, the principles of good faith and public policy may bar a claim".[321] And in *Phoenix Action v. Czech Republic*, the tribunal said "nobody would suggest that ICSID protection should be granted to investments made in violation of the most fundamental rules of protection of human rights".[322] In that case the tribunal took notice of the order in which the *Word Duty Free* Tribunal discussed the sources of law proscribing corruption. The *Phoenix Action* tribunal observed that in *World Duty Free* the tribunal "insisted on the international aspect of the principle, dealt with in priority before examining English and Kenyan law. The tribunal concluded that corruption is contrary to 'an international public policy common to the community of nations'."[323]

---

315. *Id*. at para. 157.

316. *Id*. at para. 157.

317. *Société d'Investigation de Recherche et d'Exploitation Minière v. Burkina Faso* (ICSID Case No. ARB/97/1), Award, 19 January 2000, excerpts available at <www.investmentclaims.com>.

318. *Inceysa Vallisoletana v. Republic of El Salvador* (ICSID Case No. ARB/03/26), Award, 2 August 2006, para. 249 ("It is not possible to recognize the existence of rights arising from illegal acts, because it would violate the respect for the law which ... is a principle of international public policy").

319. *Id*.

320. *Plama Consortium Limited v. Bulgaria* (ICSID Case No. ARB/03/24), Award, 27 August 2008, paras. 143-144.

321. *Fraport AG v. The Republic of the Philippines* (ICSID Case No. ARB/03/25), Award, 16 August 2007, para. 40.

322. *Phoenix Action, Ltd. v. Czech Republic* (ICSID Case No. ARB/06/5), Award, 15 April 2009, para. 78.

323. *Id*. at para. 112, n. 82, citing *World Duty Free Company Limited v. The Republic of Kenya* (ICSID Case No. ARB/00/7), Award, 4 October 2006, paras. 148, 157.

From the foregoing doctrine and arbitral practice, there appears to be sufficient authority to conclude that a transnational public policy exists proscribing bribery and corruption, at least, in the context of an investment treaty dispute. Authority also exists, albeit that it is thin, on fraudulent misrepresentation and other investor misconduct. Can it be said that a misrepresentation by an investor, whether fraudulent or negligently made, is wrongdoing of a kind that it can be said to be amongst the most reprehensible forms of human conduct? This may be possible, depending on the facts of the particular case, at least where wrongdoing is intentional. *Plama*, at least, stands for the proposition that an investor should not be entitled to benefit from its own intentional wrongdoing.

The question then arises whether there is any need for tribunals to invoke any "transnational public policy"? Generally tribunals are obligated and limited by their own mandate to references to the applicable law and "transnational public policy", however conceived, should never be the first port of call. States invariably prohibit corruption, and international law contains similar proscriptions. Thus, there may not be a strict need, in many cases, to invoke a transnational principle.[324]

Commentators question the propriety of applying a superseding "policy" over the parties' own free choice of the applicable law or the otherwise applicable law of the host State. Critics speak of transnational public policy's relative imprecision and subjectivity as a wider threat to the stability of contracts, as it implicitly allows arbitrators to supplant the parties' chosen law by other principles deemed by the decision-maker to be of "higher" importance.[325] Others add that to do so only adds an element of uncertainty and potential arbitrariness to an arbitral tribunal's decision-making process.[326] Many if not all of the principles identified as part of transnational public policy merely mirror the national laws that already exist within virtually all States. Thus, in most instances in which transnational public policy might be invoked to sanction investor wrongdoing, that conduct will also violate an "in accordance with host State law" clause, if present in the applicable treaty. Moreover, it is hardly necessary to resort to transnational public policy in situations where the applicable law points to the use of international law,[327] and the public policies sought to be invoked are actually part of international law. Indeed, some expressly maintain that transnational public policy against corruption forms *part* of international law, relying on the strong conventional and customary international law status among the vast majority of States that receive investments. At best, transnational public policy produces no better guidance for arbitral decision-makers than the OECD

---

324. See D. DONOVAN, "The Relevance (or Lack Thereof) of the Notion of 'Mandatory Laws'", 18 Am. Rev. Int'l. Arb. (2007) p. 205 at p. 215; *Richardson v. Mellish*, 2 Bing 229, 303 (1824) cited in W.M. REISMAN, "Law, International Public Policy (So-called) and Arbitral Choice in International Commercial Arbitration" in *ICCA Congress Series no. 13, op. cit.*, fn. 300, p. 849 ("Public Policy – it is an unruly horse, and when once you get astride it, you never know where it will carry you. It may lead you from the sound law. It is never argued at all but when other points fail").

325. See W.M. REISMAN, *op. cit.*, fn. 324, p. 849.

326. See, e.g., W.M. REISMAN, *ibid.*, p. 849; A. REDFERN, "Comments on Commercial Arbitration and Transnational Public Policy in *ICCA Congress Series no. 13, op. cit.*, fn. 300, p. 871 at p. 874.

327. C. LAMM, et al., *op. cit.*, fn. 61.

Convention or other very general statements of policy, and is certainly much less specific than national law.[328]

Nonetheless, for adherents, reference to transnational public policy in cases of corruption "is not entirely obsolete", since the multilateral conventions that do exist, whilst emphatic in the criminalization of such conduct, do not address the civil consequences of corruption in such prescriptive terms.[329] Recent investment cases invoking transnational public policy in an outcome-determinative manner have found that inadmissibility is the consequence of a violation of its principles; writ large, this would perhaps justify an investment tribunal's finding that an investment tainted by corruption or fraud is inadmissible, notwithstanding any provision under national law limiting consequences to voidability.

Transnational public policy can also conceivably play a role in the absence of an "in accordance with host State law" provision, or when arbitral decision-makers deal with corruption in situations in which a particular State's formal law demonstrates tolerance or even condones such practices.[330] And even if the principle does no more than offer one additional legal tool to the international arbitrator, asserting that the condemnation of investments procured or maintained by corruption is an international or transnational "public policy" does not detract either from the evident universality of opinion on the matter.

V.   THE CONSEQUENCES OF INVESTOR WRONGDOING

1.   *Bifurcation and Binary Outcomes*

Testing the legality of a host State's actions in respect of an investment is the essence of investment treaty arbitration, a system that was conceived to de-politicize and de-nationalize disputes in order to better protect foreign investment from host State misconduct. Recent years have demonstrated, however, that the system is by no means one-sided: investors have increasingly been subjected to intense scrutiny for any wrongdoing that they might have done at the inception of the investment, during its life, or indeed in accessing the system of investment arbitration itself. Host States have been successful in raising claims of corruption, fraud, and other forms of illegality under the host State's national law. The range of consequences can tend towards the "draconian",[331] at least from the investor's perspective: investor wrongdoing has often been asserted and accepted as a complete defense by the host State (i) contesting the jurisdiction of the

---

328. See A. REDFERN, *op. cit.*, fn. 326, p. 871 at p. 874.

329. See C. KESSEDJIAN, *op. cit.*, fn. 300, p. 857 at p. 861.

330. The latter scenario may be more theoretical than real. It is clear that many States operate with various levels of tolerance for the operational codes that comprise "accepted" business practices; but such practices will invariably violate the laws of that State.

331. See Z. DOUGLAS, "Plea of Illegality", *op. cit.*, fn. 33, p. 22 ("It would appear that the category of violations that do not provoke a jurisdictional infirmity is expanding in the jurisprudence to avoid the draconian effects of the approach to the plea of illegality under consideration.") and p. 27 ("Tribunals must exercise care in their recognition of grounds of international public policy given the draconian consequences that follow the application of this doctrine.").

investment tribunal in its entirety;[332] or (ii) disputing the admissibility of the claims raised;[333] or (iii) seeking annulment of the underlying investment agreement, or other substantive defenses (i.e., a defense on the merits).

In this context, *jurisdiction* is a "plea that the tribunal itself is incompetent to give any ruling at all whether as to the merits or as to the admissibility of the claim," while *admissibility* is "a plea that the tribunal should rule the claim to be inadmissible on some ground other than its ultimate merits".[334] While jurisdiction and admissibility have different legal effects, particularly as to the res judicata effect of the decision rendered by the investment tribunal,[335] the immediate effect is the same, for practical purposes.[336] Investor wrongdoing acts as a complete defense, a "trump" with preclusive effect vis-à-vis any investor claim for expropriation, etc.[337] From the perspective of the host State, no liability attaches; for the investor, no relief is possible in investment arbitration (and often, in any fora at all).

As for the third consequence, contract invalidity, fraud and corruption would under the laws of most States result in a voidable contract. In *World Duty Free*, for example, the tribunal's primary finding, employing English and Kenyan law, was to confirm the host State's avoidance of the investment agreement for corruption, dismissing the case on the merits; it also arguably considered the claims inadmissible.[338] In so doing, the investor's

---

332. See, e.g., *Metal-Tech Ltd. v. Republic of Uzbekistan* (ICSID Case No. ARB/10/3), Award, 4 October 2013; *Fraport AG v. The Republic of the Philippines* (ICSID Case No. ARB/03/25), Award, 16 August 2007; *Inceysa Vallisoletana v. Republic of El Salvador* (ICSID Case No. ARB/03/26), Award, 2 August 2006; *TSA Spectrum v. Argentina.*

333. See *Plama Consortium Limited v. Bulgaria* (ICSID Case No. ARB/03/24), Award, 27 August 2008; *World Duty Free Company Limited v. The Republic of Kenya* (ICSID Case No. ARB/00/7), Award, 4 October 2006.

334. G. FITZMAURICE, *The Law and Procedure of the International Courts of Justice* (1986) pp. 438-439.

335. See J. PAULSSON, "Jurisdiction and Admissibility" in Gerald ASKEN ET AL., eds., *Global Reflections on International Law, Commerce and Dispute Resolution: Liber Amicorum in Honour of Robert Briner* (2005) p. 601 (observing that whereas decisions that do not respect jurisdictional limits may be overturned, determinations as to admissibility are final).

336. The tribunal in the *Pac Rim* case held that "the Respondent's jurisdictional objection based on abuse of process by the Claimant does not, in legal theory, operate as a bar to the existence of the Tribunal's jurisdiction; but, rather, as a bar to the exercise of that jurisdiction, necessarily assuming jurisdiction to exist". On the particular facts of that case, the *Pac Rim* tribunal determined that it was nevertheless a "distinction without a difference". *Pac Rim Cayman LLC. v. Republic of El Salvador* (ICSID Case No. ARB/09/12), Decision on Jurisdictional Objections, 1 June 2012, para. 2.10.

337. For R. Kreindler, the wrongdoing raised need not be connected in any direct way with the investor's cause of action; and the treaty need not even have an explicit legality clause: "Illegal investments are not protected by the ECT. Therefore, even if an arbitral tribunal were to find that a respondent committed an expropriation, such expropriation might not constitute an actionable breach of Article 13 ECT. The illegality attributable to the claimant and its investment could render a claim for ECT protection inadmissible. When the respondent failed to provide for fair and equitable treatment in breach of Article 10 ECT, the same consequences should follow." R. KREINDLER, *op. cit.*, fn. 255, p. 326.

338. See *World Duty Free Company Limited v. The Republic of Kenya* (ICSID Case No. ARB/00/7), Award, 4 October 2006, para. 188: "The Claimant is not legally entitled to maintain any of its pleaded claims in these proceedings as a matter of *ordre public international* and public policy under the

claims of contractual breach and allegations of expropriation were not discussed at all. Conversely, in *Niko Resources v. Bangladesh*, the tribunal refused to uphold the host State's submission that the tribunal was without jurisdiction, whilst also noting that the State-owned enterprises that entered into the contract did not seek to avoid the contract in question.

Binary outcome. While investor wrongdoing in contract-based investment arbitration tends towards admissibility or merits, in investment *treaty* arbitration, accusations of wrongdoing have led increasingly to a binary set of results: if unproven, no results attach. But if proven, tribunals can find a lack of jurisdiction or exclude the claims on grounds of inadmissibility. In *Metal-Tech*, a treaty arbitration where the underlying BIT contained a legality clause, the tribunal's conclusion that corruption had indeed occurred was considered to have impacted upon the tribunal's very jurisdiction due to an interpretation that there was a lack of consent to arbitrate disputes tainted by investor illegality. Issues of fraud and other illegalities have, as noted above, resulted in positive findings of investor wrongdoing in a significant number of cases, the majority of which concluded that the tribunal had no jurisdiction, whether for violation of the legality clause in an investment treaty,[339] on the basis of failure to prove that the claimant is a covered "investor",[340] or broader still, because fraudulent conduct as a violation of "transnational public policy" should result in a denial of jurisdiction.[341] While a number of commentators and jurists have criticized the treatment of investor wrongdoing as a jurisdictional issue,[342] arbitral practice has, if anything, only further coalesced around the principle that investor wrongdoing can affect the host State's *consent* to investment arbitration, thereby affecting a tribunal's very power to adjudicate.

Bifurcation. The question of consequences should not be conflated with whether investor wrongdoing should be separated from the merits of the judgment and heard only at a separate jurisdictional phase. While it is true that under the UNCITRAL Rules, "[i]n general, an arbitral tribunal should rule on a plea concerning its jurisdiction as a preliminary question",[343] and this idea is found in the "preliminary objection" provisions

---

contract's applicable laws." Interpreting the phrase "not legally entitled to maintain", A. Newcombe states "the claim was inadmissible because of a breach of international public policy".: A. NEWCOMBE, *op. cit.*, fn. 33, p. 187 at p. 197.

339. See, e.g., *Fraport AG v. The Republic of the Philippines* (ICSID Case No. ARB/03/25), Award, 16 August 2007.

340. See, e.g., *Cementownia "NowaHuta" S.A. v. Republic of Turkey* (ICSID Case No. ARB(AF)/06/2), Award, 17 September 2009; *Europe Cement Investment & Trade S.A. v. Republic of Turkey* (ICSID Case No. ARB(AF)/07/2), Award, 13 August 2009; *Libananco Holdings Co. Limited v. Republic of Turkey* (ICSID Case No. ARB/06/8), Award, 2 September 2011.

341. See, e.g., *Inceysa Vallisoletana v. Republic of El Salvador* (ICSID Case No. ARB/03/26), Award, 2 August 2006.

342. In *Fraport*, the dissenting arbitrator Cremades observed that: "[i]f the legality of the Claimant's conduct is a jurisdictional issue, and the legality of the Respondent's conduct is a merits issue, then the Respondent Host State is placed in a powerful position. In the Biblical phrase, the Tribunal must first examine the speck in the eye of the investor and defer, and maybe never address, a beam in the eye of the Host State." Bernardo CREMADES, Dissenting Opinion, *Fraport v. Philippines* (ICSID Case No. ARB/03/25, 19 July 2007, para. 37. See Z. DOUGLAS, "Plea of Illegality", *op. cit.*, fn. 33; A. NEWCOMBE, *op. cit.*, fn. 33, p. 187.

343. UNCITRAL Arbitration Rules 1976, Art. 21(4).

prevalent in inter-State adjudication and arbitration,[344] a full ventilation of the issues at the merits phase does not stop a tribunal from determining that it has no jurisdiction or that the claims are inadmissible.[345]

In *Glamis Gold v. USA*, the tribunal determined that a jurisdictional objection should be decided as a preliminary matter if the following conditions for granting bifurcation are satisfied: (1) the objection is substantial rather than frivolous; (2) resolving the objection as a preliminary matter will result in a material reduction of proceedings at the next phase; and (3) the facts and issues to be addressed in the jurisdictional phase are so distinct from the facts and issues of the merits phase that having a single proceeding would not result in savings of cost and time. The first two conditions can be assumed with every invocation of substantial investor wrongdoing, but the third is a source of genuine contention. Bifurcation would be appropriate when, for example, the jurisdictional objection concerns a distinct condition precedent to arbitration not related to the merits or its underlying facts, such as the requirement under some investment treaties that an investor wait six months after the events giving rise to its claim prior to initiation of the arbitration.[346] There would be little dispute over the critical facts relevant to this jurisdictional issue; a matter unlike investor wrongdoing. If efficient management of the arbitral process is a primary consideration when deciding upon bifurcation, then isolating investor wrongdoing in a bifurcated proceeding would often not yield such efficiencies, highly contested facts will often need to be considered at key moments at the inception or through the life of an investment. Indeed, in *Metal-Tech* jurisdiction and merits were not bifurcated,[347] even when the tribunal ultimately found that it had no jurisdiction due to corruption.

2. Conclusion: Outline of Consequences

Existing commentaries and cases often tend to speak of "corruption", "fraud", and "illegality" as if these are monolithic concepts. They are not. While many of the issues concerning wrongdoing are still in flux, the beginnings of a *jurisprudence constante* is emerging, from which certain guiding "canons" can be identified. Although not

---

344. See ICJ Rules of Court, Rule 79; Rules of Procedure in the Arctic Sunrise Arbitration (*Netherlands v. Russia*; UNCLOS Annex VII PCA-administered Arbitration), Art. 20(3), which both similarly state that the Court/Tribunal shall rule on any plea concerning its jurisdiction as a preliminary question, unless the objection "does not possess an exclusively preliminary character".

345. See *Waste Management, Inc. v. United Mexican States* (ICSID Case No. ARB(AF)/98/2, dissenting opinion of Keith Highet, para. 58 ("A claim of lack of jurisdiction ought normally be decided without trenching upon the merits of the case at all; in some instances, however, this will not be possible. Likewise, a tribunal may be able to determine a challenge to the admissibility of a claim without invading the merits of the case, but it is more likely that such an examination will have to be postponed and joined to the merits").

346. See, e.g., *Murphy v. Ecuador* (ICSID Case No. ARB/08/4), Award on Jurisdiction, 15 December 2010; *Burlington v. Ecuador* (ICSID Case No. ARB/08/5), Award on Jurisdiction, 2 June 2010 (US-Ecuador BIT).

347. *Metal-Tech Ltd. v. Republic of Uzbekistan* (ICSID Case No. ARB/10/3), Award, 4 October 2013, para. 421 (jurisdiction was not bifurcated from merits "because the Respondent's objections addressed facts that related to both jurisdiction and merits".).

exhaustive, the following factors should be considered in any investigation into investor wrongdoing.

Canon 1: The underlying facts matter.

A.   Corruption
(i) The decision-maker must ascertain whether the corrupt act alleged is a facilitation payment or a variance bribe (i.e., payment made in order to violate the host State's law or influence the public official's exercise in a non-routine matter): if facilitation payment, depending on circumstances and the applicable law, it may not be a jurisdiction/admissibility issue, but still one of merits.
(ii) Next, the tribunal needs to consider whether the corrupt act was meant to alter the economic bargain to the investor's benefit. If what is "purchased" is protection against political risk instead of commercial risk, the tribunal needs to consider the possibility that extortion or coercion akin to extortion has occurred.
(iii) The decision-maker must also inquire as to whether the host State has taken effective steps to prosecute corrupt public officials whose conduct is being impugned as part of its defense – otherwise, the question of State Responsibility and/or estoppel, and acquiescence may have to be taken into account.[348]

B.   Fraud
(i) The key elements of fraud must be present: misrepresentation of a material fact, the intent to deceive or reckless disregard of the truth, and the host State's implicit or explicit reliance upon that fact (e.g. as a precondition to admitting the investment).
(ii) If jurisdictional questions are to be engaged, the fraud perpetrated must go to the nature of the "investment" or its inception, or to the qualifications of the "investor", otherwise the issues are more likely to be matters of inadmissibility or merits.

C.   Other Illegality under the Host State's Law
(i) For other illegal conduct not falling under the ambit of fraud, there must be a violation of the host State law concerning the admission of investment or some other fundamental national law that relates to the "investment" or the "investor".[349]
(ii) Depending on the national law in question, it may not be necessary to prove intent to deceive and reliance.

---

348. *Cf. World Duty Free Company Limited v. The Republic of Kenya* (ICSID Case No. ARB/00/7), Award, 4 October 2006.
349. *Saluka Investments B.V. v. Czech Republic*, PCA Case, Partial Award, 17 March 2006: violation of law must be serious, see also *Tokios Tokeles v. Ukraine* (ICSID Case No. ARB/02/18), Decision on Jurisdiction, 29 April 2004; *Phoenix Action, Ltd. v. Czech Republic* (ICSID Case No. ARB/06/5), Award, 15 April 2009: obiter, consequences of serious illegality would be no jurisdiction.

D. Costs

(i) Costs are often liberally assessed based on the underlying equities. Taking account of corruption's bilateral nature, costs have been shared even in the cases where a positive finding of corruption had been made.[350]

(ii) Given its unilateral nature, fraud and other illegality has often resulted in a finding that the investor must bear most or all of the host State's costs in defending itself.[351]

Canon 2: For contract-based investment arbitration, investor wrongdoing is either an admissibility or merits issue.

A. Admissibility

Based on applicable national law, investor wrongdoing may be an *admissibility* issue. Unclean hands may play a role.[352] Transnational public policy (particularly as to corruption) may also lead to an inadmissibility result.[353]

---

350. See *World Duty Free Company Limited v. The Republic of Kenya* (ICSID Case No. ARB/00/7), Award, 4 October 2006 and *Metal-Tech Ltd. v. Republic of Uzbekistan* (ICSID Case No. ARB/10/3), Award, 4 October 2013, in which the tribunals refused to allocate the costs of proceedings entirely to the investor notwithstanding the finding of investor corruption. In *Metal-Tech,* for example, the tribunal stated at para. 422:

> "The Tribunal found that the rights of the investor against the host State, including the right of access to arbitration, could not be protected because the investment was tainted by illegal activities, specifically corruption. The law is clear – and rightly so – that in such a situation the investor is deprived of protection and, consequently, the host State avoids any potential liability. That does not mean, however, that the State has not participated in creating the situation that leads to the dismissal of the claims. Because of this participation, which is implicit in the very nature of corruption, it appears fair that the Parties share in the costs."

351. See *Plama Consortium Limited v. Bulgaria* (ICSID Case No. ARB/03/24), Award, 27 August 2008, at paras. 321-322, where the claimant was made to bear the costs of the proceedings, including those of the host State; *Cementownia "NowaHuta" S.A. v. Republic of Turkey* (ICSID Case No. ARB(AF)/06/2), Award, 17 September 2009 ("While many ICSID tribunals have ruled that each party should bear its own costs, some have applied the principle that 'costs follow the event', making the losing party bear all or part of the costs of the proceeding and attorney fees.... The Claimant has filed a fraudulent claim.... The Claimant has delayed the present arbitration proceeding and therefore raised its costs ... using its discretionary power, the Arbitral Tribunal concludes that the Claimant is to bear all ICSID costs.").

352. See *World Duty Free Company Limited v. The Republic of Kenya* (ICSID Case No. ARB/00/7), Award, 4 October 2006.

353. *World Duty Free* can also be argued to have dismissed the case on grounds of inadmissibility: "the Claimant is not legally entitled to maintain any of its pleaded claims in these proceedings as a matter of *ordre public international* and public policy under the contract's application laws". One interpretation: tribunal considered the claim inadmissible due to a breach of *ordre public international*. *World Duty Free Company Limited v. The Republic of Kenya* (ICSID Case No. ARB/00/7), Award, 4 October 2006.

B. Merits

Corruption, fraud, and other illegality may also be a merits issue, resulting in a voidable contract depending on the circumstances. The host State may avoid the contract but normally must explicitly do so under national law.[354]

Canon 3: For treaty-based investment arbitration, wrongdoing can be a jurisdiction, admissibility, or merits issue.

A. Jurisdiction

(i) If the wrongdoing points to the claimant not having a covered "investment" or not being a qualifying "investor", the tribunal cannot exercise jurisdiction.

(ii) If a "legality clause" is found in the applicable investment treaty, bearing Canon 1 in mind, investor wrongdoing may be jurisdictional: either not a covered "investment" (ratione materiae),[355] or, more often, no consent to submit to arbitration (ratione voluntatis).[356]

B. Admissibility

If there is no legality clause, bearing Canon 1 in mind, investor wrongdoing may be an admissibility matter,[357] whether based on transnational public policy or, in certain instances, the unclean hands and cognate doctrines.

C. Merits

(i) Tribunals should reserve to the merits an *investor's allegation* that the host State engaged in wrongdoing by either: (a) extortion/solicitation of corrupt payments (corruption); (b) host State misrepresentation of investment terms or conditions

---

354. As hinted in *World Duty Free*, even as the contract is considered void, non-contractual restitution to prevent unjust enrichment may be possible in exceptional circumstances. See *World Duty Free*, para. 186 (The tribunal left open the possibility of "legal consequences following the avoidance of the Agreement", implying that some form of restitution is possible — although this was qualified by stating that "*restitutio in integrum* cannot include the return of the bribe to the Claimant". But because such "legal consequences" were not pleaded by the claimant, "they do not form part of this Award".). But this is beyond the scope of this paper. *World Duty Free Company Limited v. The Republic of Kenya* (ICSID Case No. ARB/00/7), Award, 4 October 2006.

355. See, e.g., *Fraport AG v. The Republic of the Philippines* (ICSID Case No. ARB/03/25), Award, 16 August 2007.

356. See, e.g., *Inceysa Vallisoletana v. Republic of El Salvador* (ICSID Case No. ARB/03/26), Award, 2 August 2006.

357. *Plama Consortium Limited v. Bulgaria* (ICSID Case No. ARB/03/24), Award, 27 August 2008, para. 143:

"The Tribunal is of the view that granting the ECT's protections to Claimant's investment would be contrary to the principle *nemo auditur propriam turpitudinem allegans* invoked above. It would be contrary to the basic notion of international public policy — that a contract obtained by wrongful means ... should not be enforced by a tribunal."

It can be argued, therefore, that the tribunal considered investor claim inadmissible (or unenforceable) for violation of *nemo auditur* principle.

(fraud/breach of legitimate expectations); and (c) other illegal conduct by host State (i.e. the "traditional" investor claim).

(ii) All other possibilities not covered in Canons 2 and 3 above might be considered issues for the merits.[358] Most common among these is investor wrongdoing alleged by the host State to have occurred over the life of an investment (as opposed to its inception), which can be a defense on the merits (e.g. justification for what would otherwise have been host State conduct in violation of investor protections).[359] Modifications of host State law *after* the establishment of an investment is also properly considered a matter for the merits, not jurisdiction.[360] Finally, investor wrongdoing may still factor into treaty decision-making when there may have been an element of (partial) estoppel or acquiescence involved.[361]

---

358. Some early tribunals have also invalidated the underlying investment contract on the merits due to fraud. See *Robert Azinian et al v. The United Mexican States* (ICSID Case No. ARB(AF)/97/2), Award, 1 November 1999, the first NAFTA case award on the merits. Subsequent developments in the law, not least on the "legality clause", may arguably have superseded this finding.

Other cases where investor wrongdoing was weighed on the merits against host State misconduct include *International Thunderbird Gaming Corporation v. The United Mexican States*, NAFTA/UNCITRAL, Award, 26 January 2006 (expropriation, but Thunderbird did not disclose key information about gaming machines comprising part of its investment) and *Alex Genin and others v. Republic of Estonia* (ICSID Case No. ARB/99/2), Award, 25 June 2001 (revocation of banking license justified by serious violation of Estonian Banking Code).

359. *Fraport AG v. The Republic of the Philippines* (ICSID Case No. ARB/03/25), Award, 16 August 2007, para. 343 ("allegations by the host state of violations of its law in the course of the investment … might be a defense to claimed substantive violations of the BIT, but could not deprive a tribunal acting under the authority of the BIT of its jurisdiction"); *Gustaf F. W. Hamester GmbH & Co KG v. Republic of Ghana* (ICSID Case No. ARB/07/24), Award, 18 June 2010, para. 127 ("the legality of the creation of the investment is a jurisdictional issue" and "the legality of the investor's conduct during the life of the investment is a merits issue".).

360. See, e.g., *Phoenix Action, Ltd. v. Czech Republic* (ICSID Case No. ARB/06/5), Award, 15 April 2009.

361. See *Fraport AG v. The Republic of the Philippines* (ICSID Case No. ARB/03/25), Award, 16 August 2007, para. 346 ("principles of fairness should require a tribunal to hold a government estopped from raising violations of its own law as a jurisdictional defense when it knowingly overlooked them and endorsed an investment which was not in compliance with its law".); *Desert Line Projects LLC v. Republic of Yemen* (ICSID Case No. ARB/05/17), Award, 6 February 2008 (endorsement at the highest level of the State, respondent "is estopped from relying on it to defeat jurisdiction"); *Wena Hotels Limited v. Arab Republic of Egypt* (ICSID Case No. ARB/98/4), Award, 8 December 2000, para. 116 ("given the fact that the Egyptian government was made aware of this agreement … but decided (for whatever reasons) not to prosecute Mr. Kandil, the Tribunal is reluctant to immunize Egypt from liability in this arbitration because it now alleges that the agreement with Mr. Kandil was illegal under Egyptian law"); *Técnicas Medioambientales Tecmed, S.A. v. The United Mexican States* (ICSID Case No. ARB (AF)/00/2), Award, 29 May 2003 (authorities could not have been unaware of irregularities, they did not act or inform the investor); *Ioannis Kardassopoulos v. Georgia* (ICSID Case No. ARB/05/18), Decision on Jurisdiction, 6 July 2007 (content of the agreements approved by Georgian Government officials for many years without objections).

Claims of Corruption in Investment Treaty Arbitration: Proof, Legal Consequences and Sanctions

*Utku Coşar**

I.   INTRODUCTION

As the anti-corruption movement has gained global prominence, so too has there been greater consideration of the role of international tribunals in combating corruption.[1] Investment arbitration, in particular, with its adjudication of disputes between State parties and foreign investors, is an arena where claims of corruption will inevitably surface and, consequently, where corruption must be condemned. In this paper, I will examine three facets of investment arbitration that are particularly significant for claims of corruption: proof, legal consequences and sanctions. The examination below will illustrate the ways in which investment tribunals may approach corruption claims and their attendant difficulties. At the same time, however, the small number of corruption cases strikes a cautionary note as to the uncertainty of such approaches, especially in regard to legal consequences.

---

*   Partner, Coşar Avukatlik Burosu. This article is an extension of the author's presentation at the 22nd International Council for Commercial Arbitration (ICCA) Congress in Miami, 6-9 April 2014. The original presentation was a comment on the paper presented by Dr. Aloysius Llamzon and Dr. Anthony Sinclair titled, "Investor Wrongdoing in Investment Arbitration: Standards Governing Issues of Corruption, Fraud, Misrepresentation and Other Investor Misconduct in Investment Treaty Arbitration", this volume, pp. 451-530.

1.   Arts. 15, 16, 18 and 21 of the United Nations Convention against Corruption (UNCAC) form a widely accepted definition of corruption. These articles contemplate the bribery of national public officials (Art. 15), the bribery of foreign public officials and officials of public international organizations (Art. 16), trading in influence (Art. 18) and bribery in the private sector (Art. 21). For the purposes of investment arbitration, where corruption generally manifests in the bribing of public officials or intermediaries, Arts. 15, 16 and 18 are most pertinent.

II.   PROOF OF CORRUPTION AND OTHER SERIOUS ILLEGALITY

International arbitration tribunals "are not bound to adhere to strict judicial rules of evidence".[2] Furthermore, as investment treaties generally do not contain definitive procedural rules, investment treaty tribunals are relatively free to determine the burden and standard of proof to apply.[3]

The applicable procedural rules provide very little guidance regarding burden of proof in investment arbitration. The Arbitration Rules of the International Centre for Settlement of Investment Disputes (ICSID) are silent on the matter. The United Nations Commission on International Trade Law (UNCITRAL) Arbitration Rules confirm the general rule accepted by commentators[4] and tribunals[5] in international arbitration: "[e]ach party shall have the burden of proving the facts relied on to support its claim or defence".[6] Due to the difficulty of procuring direct evidence of corruption, some have suggested amending the general rule and shifting the burden of proof once prima facie evidence of the alleged corruption is shown.[7] This approach is not widely supported,

---

2. *AAPL v. Sri Lanka* (ICSID Case No. ARB/87/03), Award, 27 June 1990, para. 56. See also Alan REDFERN, "The Practical Distinction Between the Burden of Proof and the Taking of Evidence – An English Perspective", 10 Arb. Int'l (1994) p. 317 at p. 321. Lucy REED, Jan PAULSSON and Nigel BLACKABY, *Guide to ICSID Arbitration*, 2nd edn. (Kluwer Law International 2011) p. 142. Matthias SCHERER, "Circumstantial Evidence in Corruption Cases Before International Arbitral Tribunals", 5 Int'l Arb. L. Rev. (2002) p. 29 at p. 31.

3. *Metal-Tech Ltd. v. The Republic of Uzbekistan* (ICSID Case No. ARB/10/3), Award, 4 October 2013, para. 238 ("In the present case, the *lex causae* is essentially the BIT, which provides no rules for shifting the burden of proof or establishing presumptions. Therefore, the Tribunal has relative freedom in determining the standard necessary to sustain a determination of corruption."). See also *Oostergetel v. The Slovak Republic*, UNCITRAL, Final Award, 23 April 2012, para. 147.

4. Gary BORN, *International Commercial Arbitration*, 2nd edn. (Kluwer Law International 2014) p. 2313 ("This is consistent with commentary, which cites the general rule of *actori incumbit probatio*: each party bears the burden of proving the facts relied on in support of its case.").

5. See *Metal-Tech, op. cit.*, fn. 3, para. 237 ("The principle that each party has the burden of proving the facts on which it relies is widely recognised and applied by international courts and tribunals. The International Court of Justice as well as arbitral tribunals constituted under the ICSID Convention and under the NAFTA have characterized this rule as a general principle of law. Consequently, as reflected in the maxim *actori incumbat probatio*, each party has the burden of proving the facts on which it relies."). *The Rompetrol Group N.V. v. Romania* (ICSID Case No. ARB/06/3), 6 May 2013, para. 179. *Oostergetel, op. cit.*, fn. 3, paras. 146-147.

6. UNCITRAL Arbitration Rules (2010), Art. 27(1), available at <www.uncitral.org/pdf/english/texts/arbitration/arb-rules-revised/arb-rules-revised-2010-e.pdf> (last accessed 14 August 2014).

7. See, e.g., *AAPL, op. cit.*, fn. 2, para. 56 ("In case a party 'adduces some evidence which *prima facie* supports his allegation, the burden of proof shifts to his opponent'."). Karen MILLS, "Corruption and Other Illegality in the Formation and Performance of Contracts and in the Conduct of Arbitration Relating Thereto" in *International Commercial Arbitration: Important Contemporary Questions*, ICCA Congress Series no. 11 (2003) p. 294 ("Because of the near impossibility to 'prove' corruption, where there is a reasonable indication of corruption, an appropriate way to make a determination may be to shift the burden of proof to the allegedly corrupt party to establish that the legal and good faith requirements were in fact duly met."). Cecily ROSE, "Questioning the Role of International Arbitration in the Fight against Corruption", 31 J. Int'l Arb. (2014) p. 183 at pp. 216-219.

however, and instead it has become more prevalent to focus on the standard of proof and the powers of the tribunal when it comes to matters of evidence in corruption and fraud claims.[8] The reasoning behind this emphasis on the standard over the burden of proof becomes clear when considering the distinction between the two made by the *Rompetrol* tribunal: the burden of proof is absolute, whereas the standard of proof is relative.[9]

The standard of proof applicable to corruption and fraud claims in investment treaty cases has been contested, with some arguing for tribunals to apply the general principle of balance of probabilities and others supporting the implementation of a higher standard. Despite a number of International Chamber of Commerce (ICC) awards calling for a standard of proof higher than the balance of probabilities,[10] there have been relatively few investment cases where the tribunal employed a heightened standard.[11] Commentators generally support the view that tribunals should employ the balance of probabilities standard in cases where there are claims of illegality, particularly corruption.[12]

---

8. See, e.g., Michael HWANG and Kevin LIM, "Corruption in Arbitration – Law and Reality", 8 Asian Int'l Arb. J. (2012) p. 1 at p. 28. Constantine PARTASIDES, "Proving Corruption in International Arbitration: A Balanced Standard for the Real World", 25 ICSID Review—Foreign Investment Law Journal (2010) p. 47 at p. 53. *Rompetrol, op. cit.*, fn. 5, para. 178. *Waguih Elie George Siag and Clorinda Vecchi v. The Arab Republic of Egypt* (ICSID Case No. ARB/05/15), Award, 1 June 2009, para. 317.

9. Rompetrol, *op. cit.*, fn. 5, para. 178.

10. Antonio CRIVELLARO, "Arbitration Case Law on Bribery: Issues of Arbitrability, Contract Validity, Merits and Evidence" in Kristine KARSTEN and Andrew BERKELEY, eds., *Arbitration – Money Laundering, Corruption and Fraud* (ICC Publications 2003) p. 109 at p. 115 ("There were fourteen cases in which a 'high' standard of proof was applied, i.e., more than 50% of cases."). See, e.g., ICC Case No. 6401 (*Westinghouse*) (1991): (The tribunal held a higher standard of "clear and convincing evidence" was required for assessing allegations of corruption.); ICC Case No. 5622 (*Hilmarton*) (1988) (The tribunal found that bribery was not "proved beyond doubt"); ICC Case No. 6497 (1994) (The tribunal found that the respondent had not "conclusively" proved bribery and more generally held that if a party alleging corruption does not provide a convincing demonstration, "the tribunal should reject its argument, even if the tribunal has some doubts about the possible bribery nature of the agreements".); ICC Case No. 4145 (The tribunal rejected the defendant's accusation of bribery because it was "not supported by direct evidence or even circumstantial evidence to be retained as convincing".). See also BORN, *op. cit.*, fn. 4, p. 2315 (In regard to applying a higher standard of proof to allegations of serious wrongdoing such as fraud and corruption: "This approach is sensible, both in evidentiary terms and in discouraging baseless allegations of misconduct.").

11. See, e.g., *Himpurna California Energy (Bermuda) v. PT Persero (Indonesia)*, UNCITRAL, Award, 4 May 1999, paras. 116, 118. *EDF (Services) Limited v. Romania* (ICSID Case No. ARB/05/13), Award, 8 October 2009, para. 221. *Liman Caspian Oil BV and NCL Dutch Investment BV v. Republic of Kazakhstan* (ICSID Case No. ARB/07/14), Excerpts of Award, 22 June 2010, paras. 422-423. *Siag, op. cit.*, fn. 8, paras. 325-326. One major difficulty in assessing how tribunals have approached evidence in cases of corruption is that there are so few cases to examine. For this reason, investment cases featuring fraud and other serious illegal conduct will also be examined, although the focus of this paper is ostensibly corruption.

12. See PARTASIDES, *op. cit.*, fn. 8, p. 57. HWANG, *op. cit.*, fn. 8, p. 19. *Siag, op. cit.*, fn. 8, Dissenting Opinion of Professor Francisco Orrego Vicuña, 11 May 2009, p. 4 (Prof. Vicuña disagreed with the tribunal's application of the US standard of clear and convincing evidence).

Tribunals seem to sidestep formal discussions of the applicable standard of proof and instead concentrate on the evidence at hand and the probative value of such evidence in accordance with the flexibility and authority afforded to them.[13] Although not explicitly categorized as such, one can consider this approach as an application of the balance of probabilities. By applying this standard, a tribunal may consider all relevant factors to determine whether there is sufficient evidence of corruption, namely whether it is "more likely than not". In this way a tribunal may still adhere to the adage that "the graver the charge, the more confidence there must be in the evidence relied on", without necessarily applying a higher standard of proof.[14]

This flexibility to consider all relevant aspects stems from the wide discretionary power tribunals are granted on matters of evidence. A tribunal is "free to determine the weight and credibility to be accorded to the evidence presented".[15] Furthermore, this flexibility has been confirmed by awards; tribunals have generally found that claims of corruption may be proven solely by circumstantial evidence.[16] This is especially significant when considering that direct evidence of corruption, such as the admission of bribery in *World Duty Free v. Kenya*,[17] can be difficult to procure.

Carolyn LAMM, Hansel PHAM and Rahim MOLOO, "Fraud and Corruption in International Arbitration" in Miguel Angel FERNANDEZ-BALLESTEROS and David ARIAS, eds., *Liber Amicorum Bernardo Cremades* (La Ley 2010) p. 699 at pp. 700-701.

13. *Libananco Holdings Co. Limited v. The Republic of Turkey* (ICSID Case No. ARB/06/8), Award, 2 September 2011, para. 126 ("In any event, the question of the applicable standard of proof for allegations of 'fraud or other serious wrongdoing' and the other disputed issues set out in paragraph 116 above (as to which party should bear the burden of proof in relation to the second, third and fourth preliminary jurisdictional objections) are of academic interest only..."). *Metal-Tech, op. cit.*, fn. 3, para. 239 ("While the debate about standards of proof and presumptions is an interesting one, the Tribunal finds that it does not require the application of the rules on burden of proof or presumptions to resolve the present dispute."). See also Florian HAUGENEDER and Christoph LIEBSCHER, "Chapter V: Investment Arbitration – Corruption and Investment Arbitration: Substantive Standards and Proof" in Christian KLAUSEGGER, Peter KLEIN, et al., eds., *Austrian Arbitration Yearbook 2009* (C.H. Beck, Stämpfli & Manz 2009) p. 539 at p. 546.

14. *Ibid.*, para. 125 ("While agreeing with the general proposition that 'the graver the charge, the more confidence there must be in the evidence relied on' ..., this does not necessarily entail a higher standard of proof. It may simply require more persuasive evidence, in the case of a fact that is inherently improbable, in order for the Tribunal to be satisfied that the burden of proof has been discharged.").

15. LAMM et. al., *op. cit.*, fn. 12, p. 701. See also *Rompetrol, op. cit.*, fn. 5, para. 181 ("The overall effect of these provisions is that an ICSID tribunal is endowed with the independent power to determine, within the context provided by the circumstances of the dispute before it, whether particular evidence or kinds of evidence should be admitted or excluded, what weight (if any) should be given to particular items of evidence so admitted, whether it would like to see further evidence of any particular kind on any issue arising in the case, and so on and so forth.").

16. See, e.g., *Metal-Tech, op. cit.*, fn. 3, para. 243. *Oostergetel, op. cit.*, fn. 3, para. 303. *Rumeli Telekom A.S. v. Republic of Kazakhstan* (ICSID Case No. ARB/05/16), Award, 29 July 2008, para. 709 (The tribunal asserts that it is possible for an allegation of conspiracy to be supported only by circumstantial evidence, although it must lead "clearly and convincingly to the inference that a conspiracy has occurred".).

17. *World Duty Free Company Limited v. The Republic of Kenya* (ICSID Case No. ARB/00/7), Award, 4

When an investment tribunal applies the balance of probabilities standard to allegations of corruption, the question becomes how the tribunal weighs the evidence provided by both parties.[18] As the *Rompetrol* tribunal posited: "[W]hether a proposition has in fact been proved by the party which bears the burden of proving it depends not just on its own evidence but on the overall assessment of the accumulated evidence put forward by one or both parties, for the proposition or against it."[19] In *Metal-Tech v. Uzbekistan*, the tribunal demonstrated how various forms of circumstantial evidence, such as the amount of payments awarded, the qualifications of the alleged consultants, the (lack of) documentary evidence of services rendered and the consultants' relationships with those in power, can and should be contemplated as a whole.[20] Thus, although the tribunal did not address the burden or standard of proof, it did acknowledge that corruption can be shown through circumstantial evidence and then proceeded to determine whether corruption was established "with reasonable certainty".[21]

When a tribunal is faced with allegations of corruption and no direct evidence, there are a number of actions it may take. First, a tribunal is not solely restricted to evidence presented by the parties and has the authority to request additional evidence. As provided for in ICSID Convention Art. 43, ICSID Arbitration Rule 34(2) and UNCITRAL Arbitration Rules Art. 27(3), and confirmed by various tribunals[22] and commentators,[23] a tribunal may request the production of documents, witnesses and experts,[24] and more generally has investigatory powers.[25] If necessary, it could also

---

October 2006, paras. 130-136.

18. It is both provided in the ICSID Arbitration Rules and accepted by tribunals that the arbitral tribunal shall freely judge the probative value of evidence. See ICSID Arbitration Rules, Rule 34(1), available at <https://icsid.worldbank.org/ICSID/StaticFiles/basicdoc/CRR_English-final.pdf> (last accessed 14 August 2014). See also *AAPL*, *op. cit.*, fn. 2, para. 56.

19. *Rompetrol*, *op. cit.*, fn. 5, para. 178; paras. 182-183 ("[the Tribunal] will where necessary adopt a more nuanced approach and will decide in each discrete instance whether an allegation of serious wrongful conduct ... has been proved on the basis of the entire body of direct and indirect evidence before it".). See also *Libananco*, *op. cit.*, fn. 13, para. 536 ("For all the foregoing reasons, the Tribunal considers that the Claimant has failed to meet its burden of proof when all the evidence is viewed as a whole.").

20. *Metal-Tech*, *op. cit.*, fn. 3, para. 351 (These indicia of corruption are sometimes called "red flags", which the tribunal addresses in para. 293). See also *Europe Cement Investment & Trade S.A. v. Republic of Turkey* (ICSID Case No. ARB(AF)/07/2), Award, 13 August 2009, para. 167.

21. *Metal-Tech*, *op. cit.*, fn. 3, para. 243 (The tribunal later states that "corruption is established to an extent sufficient", para. 372). See also *Cementownia "Nowa Huta" S.A. v. Republic of Turkey* (ICSID Case No. ARB(AF)/06/2), Award, 17 September 2009, para. 149.

22. See, e.g., *Metal-Tech*, *op. cit.*, fn. 3, para. 241. *Rompetrol*, *op. cit.*, fn. 5, paras. 181-182. *World Duty Free*, *op. cit.*, fn. 17, para. 52.

23. See, e.g., Christoph SCHREUER, et al., *The ICSID Convention: A Commentary*, 2nd edn. (Cambridge University Press 2009) p. 651. REED, et al., *op. cit.*, fn. 2, p. 142.

24. The powers in relation to evidence afforded by the ICSID Convention and ICSID Arbitration Rules are echoed in the 2010 IBA Rules on the Taking of Evidence in International Arbitration (Arts. 3.10 and 4.10), available at <www.ibanet.org/Publications/publications_IBA_guides_and_free_materials.aspx#takingevidenc> (last accessed 14 August 2014).

25. See, e.g., *Metal-Tech*, *op. cit.*, fn. 3, para. 239. See also Hilmar RAESCHKE-KESSLER, "Corrupt

consider modifying its previous orders, holding hearings and issuing a fresh procedural timetable after fully reviewing the parties' submissions on the applications before it.[26] When there are serious allegations of corruption, a tribunal should make use of these broad powers to deal with the issue of corruption swiftly and to procure evidence from reluctant parties.

The party alleging corruption or other forms of illegality can also take advantage of the various mechanisms at its disposal to substantiate corruption allegations and overcome evidentiary obstacles. When faced with the difficulties of providing direct evidence of corruption and/or an opposing party that is reluctant to produce evidence, a party may submit requests for production of documents[27] and inspection of originals,[28] requests for examination of witnesses[29] and, in some exceptional cases, requests for provisional measures.[30] If these requests go unheeded, a party may also request the tribunal to draw adverse inferences.[31]

Taking advantage of investment arbitration's procedural flexibility, a tribunal may also rely on the drawing of adverse inferences when evaluating evidence in disputes where corruption is alleged.[32] More specifically, a tribunal can and should require "an adequate

---

Practices in the Foreign Investment Context: Contractual and Procedural Aspects" in Norbert HORN and Stefan Michael KRÖLL, eds., *Arbitrating Foreign Investment Disputes: Procedural and Substantive Legal Aspects* (Kluwer Law International 2004) p. 471 at pp. 494-495 ("The reason for the arbitrator's own duty to investigate is based on the principle that an arbitral tribunal has to make its best efforts to render an award, which is enforceable and may not be set aside according to Art. V(2) lit. b of the New York Convention." As for treaty-based awards under ICSID, which are not subject to annulment or enforcement proceedings before national courts, this "lack of control by state courts does not mitigate the duty of an ICSID arbitral tribunal to investigate on its own" so that it does not become "involved in a breach of international public policy".). HWANG, *op. cit.*, fn. 8, p. 18. However, Hwang then goes on to suggest that "[t]ribunals should only pursue the issue of corruption where there is some *prima facie* evidence of wrongdoing, and not 'every suspicious element in the execution or performance of the contract should set the tribunal off on an inquisitorial exercise of its own irrespective of the wishes of the parties'. A *laissez-faire* attitude that closes its eyes to all evidence of corruption is as undesirable as an over-zealous approach to detecting corruption." (p. 25).

26. *Libananco, op. cit.*, fn. 13, paras. 38, 49, 530-536.
27. Provided for in ICSID Arbitration Rules, Rules 33 and 34(2); ICSID Convention, Art. 43; and UNCITRAL Arbitration Rules, Art. 27(3). See, e.g., *Libananco Holdings Co. Limited v. Republic of Turkey* (ICSID Case No. ARB/06/8), Decision on Preliminary Issues, 23 June 2008, paras. 68 and 71. *Europe Cement, op. cit.*, fn. 20, para. 15. *Cementownia, op. cit.*, fn. 21, para. 34.
28. *Ibid.* for legal basis. See, e.g., *Europe Cement, op. cit.*, fn. 20, paras. 28, 99. *Cementownia, op. cit.*, fn. 21, para. 119. *Libananco, op. cit.*, fn. 13, para. 30.
29. *Ibid.* for legal basis. See, e.g., *Rumeli, op. cit.*, fn. 16, para. 65. *CME Czech Republic B.V. (The Netherlands) v. The Czech Republic*, UNCITRAL, Final Award, 14 March 2003, para. 72.
30. Provided for in ICSID Arbitration Rules, Rule 39(1); ICSID Additional Facility Rules, Rule 46; REED, et al., *op. cit.*, fn. 2, p. 146.
31. UNCITRAL Arbitration Rules, Art. 30(3) and ICSID Arbitration Rules, Rule 34(3). See, e.g., *Europe Cement, op. cit.*, fn. 20, para. 99.
32. See, e.g., *Rompetrol, op. cit.*, fn. 5, para. 184 ("This issue [adverse inferences] ... may condition the circumstances under which a Tribunal may take particular factual allegations as 'proved' for the purpose of the arbitration.").

evidentiary showing by the party denying the allegation" when a party alleging corruption has provided plausible evidence.[33] Thus, when documents or evidence that a tribunal could reasonably expect to be produced, such as documentary evidence of services rendered by a consultant, are ultimately not provided, the tribunal may draw an adverse inference.[34] In fact, a number of arbitral tribunals have employed this measure.[35] Even if the opposing party is not able to produce the requested documents, it may provide adequate reasoning as to why it cannot comply with the request.[36] As the tribunal in *Cementownia v. Turkey* found, it is "entirely fair for a tribunal, after giving a disputing party more than adequate extensions of time and notice, to decide that it should consider the other party's application to dismiss the claim in light of such evidence as has been adduced".[37] Even more so in cases of corruption, which by nature involve the deliberate concealment of an illegality, a tribunal should be prepared to draw an adverse inference[38] where it is a "reasonable conclusion to draw from the known or assumed facts".[39]

---

33. PARTASIDES, *op. cit.*, fn. 8, p. 60.
34. The UNCITRAL Arbitration Rules and ICSID Arbitration Rules stop just short of granting a tribunal the authority to draw adverse inferences. Yet, the *Rompetrol* tribunal found that Rule 34, "no doubt intends, among other things, that a given tribunal is specifically authorized to draw whatever inferences it deems appropriate from the failure of either party to produce evidence which that party might otherwise have been expected to produce" (*op. cit.*, fn. 5, para. 181). The IBA Guidelines on the Taking of Evidence confers this authority (Art. 9, nos. 5 and 6) and commentators have also generally recognized this authority. See, e.g., Andreas REINER, "Burden and General Standards of Proof", 10 Arb. Int'l (1994) p. 317 at p. 337. REED, et al., *op. cit.*, fn. 2, p. 142.
35. See, e.g., *Metal-Tech, op. cit.*, fn. 3, paras. 246, 256 and 265. *Europe Cement, op. cit.*, fn. 20, paras. 152, 158, 160 and 163. *Marvin Feldman v. Mexico* (ICSID Case No. ARB(AF)/99/1), Award, 16 December 2002, para. 178.
36. See, e.g., *Europe Cement, op. cit.*, fn. 20, para. 164 ("The Claimant could have rebutted this inference. It could have produced the originals of the share agreements. It could have produced the share certificates that it claimed it owned. Indeed, its response to Procedural Order No. 3 indicated that it had no objection to the production of certain documents and at that stage the Tribunal had no reason to believe it would not do so. But, it never produced any documents. This contributes to the inference that the originals of the documents copied in its Memorial and on which its claim was based either were never in the Claimant's possession or would not stand forensic analysis, in which case the claim that Europe Cement had shares in CEAS and Kepez at the relevant time was fraudulent."). *Rompetrol, op. cit.*, fn. 5, para. 185 (The tribunal asserts that certain failures to produce requested evidence may be excused or mitigated in particular circumstances.) *Marvin, op. cit.*, fn. 35, para. 178.
37. *Cementownia, op. cit.*, fn. 21, para. 121.
38. The tribunal's recourse to adverse inferences is different in form than shifting the burden of proof, an action that many commentators take issue with. The drawing of adverse inferences should not be understood as the allegedly corrupt party taking on the burden of disproving the corruption allegations. Rather, it should be considered as an additional inferred fact that may assist the party making these allegations to discharge its burden of proof. Yet, it should be noted that the reasoning provided in Karen Mills's article for reversing the burden of proof appears similar to the rationale for drawing adverse inferences. Mills proposes that the allegedly corrupt party must provide the requisite evidence when there is a "reasonable indication of corruption" (*op. cit.*, fn. 7, p. 294).
39. PARTASIDES, *op. cit.*, fn. 8, pp. 60-61.

In addition to drawing adverse inferences, a tribunal could consider a number of factors when examining the evidence before it. These issues may include the seriousness of the allegations and, if proven, their legal consequences, the inherent likelihood (or not) of corruption in the circumstances and the difficulty of proving corruption, all of which depend on the specific facts of the case.[40] Where a fact is inherently improbable, the tribunal may "simply require more persuasive evidence".[41] Finally, when assessing evidence of corruption, a tribunal may also contemplate the link between the advantage bestowed and the improper advantage allegedly obtained.[42]

In developing an approach to corruption claims, there should not be a deviation from the general standard of proof, the principle of the balance of probabilities. With the flexibility and powers provided by procedural rules, such as the ability to draw adverse inferences and investigative powers, a tribunal could evaluate the available evidence and relevant factors in a nuanced way so as to determine whether corruption took place. While burden and standard of proof are important legal principles, the main factor in deciding on corruption allegations in investment arbitration is the specific evidence adduced in each individual case and how it is ultimately assessed as a whole by the tribunal.

III.   LEGAL CONSEQUENCES: JURISDICTION AND ADMISSIBILITY

Following a finding of serious illegality, and corruption in particular, a tribunal must determine the appropriate legal consequences. Where allegations of host State corruption form the basis of an investor's claim and in case corruption is found, a tribunal will determine whether the host State's wrongdoing constitutes a breach of the substantive protections provided to the investor under the relevant treaty; consequently, this issue will be dealt with at the merits phase.[43]

Yet when an investor is found to have engaged in corruption, the legal consequences do not seem to be as straightforward. The tribunal must determine whether corruption on the part of the investor is an issue for jurisdiction, admissibility or merits.[44] One legal effect to consider is that an investment tribunal's award on jurisdiction, regardless of whether corruption is a factor, may be subject to further review, as opposed to a decision on admissibility, which is unlikely to be subjected to further recourse.[45] Moreover, there

---

40. HWANG, *op. cit.*, fn. 8, p. 29.
41. *Libananco*, *op. cit.*, fn. 13, para. 125.
42. *Sistem Mühendislik İnşaat Sanayi A.Ş. v. Kyrgyz Republic* (ICSID Case No. ARB(AF)/06/1), Award, 9 September 2009, para. 43.
43. Andrea J. MENAKER, "The Determinative Impact of Fraud and Corruption on Investment Arbitrations", 25 ICSID Review (2010) p. 67. See, e.g., *EDF v. Romania* (*op. cit.*, fn. 11).
44. This paper is mainly concerned with investor corruption at the initiation of the investment as opposed to corruption during the course of the investment. Furthermore, as previously mentioned, due to the dearth of investment awards ruling on corruption, it is necessary to expand the examination of awards to include those featuring serious illegality, a term used here to cover misconduct such as corruption and fraud more generally.
45. Jan PAULSSON, "Jurisdiction and Admissibility" in Gerald AKSEN, et al., eds., *Reflections on*

is debate as to whether treating the legality of the claimant's conduct as a jurisdictional issue and the legality of the respondent's conduct as a merits issue is in line with the "fundamental principles of procedure".[46]

When considering serious illegality as a whole, there is a basic outline of how a tribunal could approach the matter of legal consequences. Although it may be tempting to consider this as an established method for the sake of consistency, it is important to bear in mind that the various approaches described below, especially in regard to admissibility, have not been widely implemented. This is particularly true when looking solely at corruption, of which there are very few proven cases. Moreover, attitudes towards corruption and how to combat it are constantly evolving. For these reasons, it is important to maintain flexibility when determining the legal consequences of corruption.

1. Serious Illegality as a Jurisdictional Issue

A number of arbitral awards have demonstrated how an investment tribunal may treat illegal conduct on the part of an investor in procuring its investment as a jurisdictional impediment, contingent upon treaty specifications. For a tribunal to decline jurisdiction, it must conclude that the claim "could not be brought to the particular forum seized", with the result that the tribunal does not have the power to hear the case.[47]

International Law, Commerce and Dispute Resolution: Liber amicorum in honour of Robert Briner (International Chamber of Commerce 2005) p. 601. Andrew NEWCOMBE, "Investor Misconduct: Jurisdiction, Admissibility or Merits?" in Chester BROWN and Kate MILES, eds., Evolution in Investment Treaty Law and Arbitration (Cambridge University Press 2011) p. 187 at p. 199. Eric DE BRABANDERE, "Good Faith, Abuse of Process and the Initiation of Investment Treaty Claims", 3 J. Int'l Disp. Settlement (2012) p. 609 at pp. 617-618. See also Malicorp Limited v. The Arab Republic of Egypt (ICSID Case No. ARB/08/18), Award, 7 February 2011, para. 118. Abaclat and Others v. The Argentine Republic (ICSID Case No. ARB/07/5), Decision on Jurisdiction and Admissibility, 4 August 2011, para. 247 ("(ii) Whereby a decision refusing a case based on a lack of arbitral jurisdiction is usually subject to review by another body, a decision refusing a case based on a lack of admissibility can usually not be subject to review by another body."). Conversely, a tribunal's decision to assert jurisdiction yet dismiss a claim as inadmissible may also be subject to annulment for an excess of powers. See Rudolf DOLZER and Christoph SCHREUER eds., Principles of International Investment Law, 2nd edn. (Oxford University Press 2012) p. 304 ("Absence of valid consent to arbitration would also mean that there is no jurisdiction and an award on the merits would be an excess of powers.... In Mitchell v. Congo the request for annulment argued that the Tribunal had committed a manifest excess of powers by assuming jurisdiction although the dispute had not arisen from an investment.").

46. Fraport AG Frankfurt Airport Services Worldwide v. The Republic of the Philippines (ICSID Case No. ARB/03/25), Dissenting Opinion of Bernardo Cremades, 19 July 2007, para. 37.

47. PAULSSON, op. cit., fn. 45, p. 617 ("If the reason for such an outcome would be that the claim could not be brought to the particular forum seized, the issue is ordinarily one of jurisdiction and subject to further recourse. If the reason would be that the claim should not be heard at all (or at least not yet), the issue is ordinarily one of admissibility and the tribunal's decision is final."). See also Waste Management, Inc. v. United Mexican States (ICSID Case No. ARB(AF)/98/2), Dissenting Opinion of Keith Highet, 8 May 2000, para. 58 ("Jurisdiction is the power of the tribunal to hear the case; admissibility is whether the case itself is defective – whether it is appropriate for the

In order for treaty-based claims to be entitled to the procedural and substantive protections of the applicable treaty, there must be a qualifying investment. Although not defined under Art. 25 of the ICSID Convention,[48] the notion of "investment" is delineated by most investment treaties, albeit in broad terms. One criterion imposed by a number of treaties is what has been termed a "host State law" or "legality requirement".[49]

Although the exact wording of the legality requirement differs across treaties, this condition in broad terms requires an investment to be made in accordance with host State law.[50] While there has been debate on how to analyze and implement this condition,[51] tribunals have generally interpreted it as a jurisdictional impediment.[52]

---

tribunal to hear it."). Gerald FITZMAURICE, *The Law and Procedure of the International Court of Justice* (Grotius Publications Limited 1986) pp. 438-439.

48. Art. 25(1) of the ICSID Convention reads: "The jurisdiction of the Centre shall extend to any legal dispute arising directly out of an investment, between a Contracting State (or any constituent subdivision or agency of a Contracting State designated to the Centre by that State) and a national of another Contracting State, which the parties to the dispute consent in writing to submit to the Centre. When the parties have given their consent, no party may withdraw its consent unilaterally." DOLZER, et al., *op. cit.*, fn. 45, p. 65 (The editors utilize the *travaux preparatoires* of the ICSID Convention to examine the meaning of the term "investment". "[T]he Report of the Executive Directors, which is frequently cited on this point by arbitral tribunals, summarized the negotiations by way of concluding that the negotiating parties deliberately refrained from adopting any (legal or economic) definition so as to leave room for an understanding by the parties.").

49. SCHREUER, *op. cit.*, fn. 23, p. 140.

50. Some examples of the legality clause from disputes involving claims of serious illegality: Uzbekistan-Israel BIT (examined in *Metal-Tech, op. cit.*, fn. 3): "implemented in accordance with the laws and regulations of the Contracting Party"; Bolivia-Chile BIT (examined in *Quiborax S.A., Non Metallic Minerals S.A. and Allan Fosk Kaplun v. Plurinational State of Bolivia* (ICSID Case No. ARB/06/2), Decision on Jurisdiction, 27 September 2012): "The term 'investment' means any kind of assets or rights related to an investment as long as this has been made in accordance with the laws and regulations of the Contracting Party in whose territory the investment was made"; Spain-Argentina BIT (examined in *Teinver S.A., Transportes de Cercanías S.A. and Autobuses Urbanos del Sur S.A. v. The Argentine Republic* (ICSID Case No. ARB/09/1), Decision on Jurisdiction, 21 December 2012): "'investments' shall mean any kind of assets, such as property and rights of every kind, acquired or effected in accordance with the legislation of the country receiving the investment"; Germany-Ghana BIT (examined in *Gustav F W Hamester GmbH & Co KG v. Republic of Ghana* (ICSID Case No. ARB/07/24), Award, 18 June 2010): "This Treaty shall also apply to investments made prior to its entry into force by nationals or companies of either Contracting Party in the territory of the other Contracting Party consistent with the latter's legislation." It has been found by a number of tribunals that this requirement usually only covers illegality at the initiation of the investment and does not extend to illegalities that may occur during the course of the investment, subject to the text of the treaty (*Teinver*, para. 318; *Hamester*, para. 127; *Fraport AG Frankfurt Airport Services Worldwide v. Republic of the Philippines* (ICSID Case No. ARB/03/25), Award, 16 August 2007, para. 345).

51. Gary BORN, *International Arbitration: Law and Practice* (Kluwer Law International 2012) p. 426 ("BITs frequently require that investments have been made 'in accordance with' the host State's law. There is divergent authority as to whether failure to do so gives rise to jurisdictional issues under a BIT or whether such requirements are instead relevant only to the substance of the parties' claims and defences."). Bernardo Cremades, in his Dissenting Opinion to the *Fraport* award, argued

When faced with jurisdictional arguments that an investor engaged in fraudulent or corrupt measures in procuring its investment, tribunals have generally undertaken an examination of the treaty and relevant host State legislation to determine whether it contains an "in accordance with law" clause and, if so, the parameters of this requirement and whether it was breached.[53] The majority opinion in *Fraport* found the investment to be in breach of this condition, and held that "because there is no 'investment in accordance with law', the tribunal lacks jurisdiction *ratione materiae*".[54]

---

that "the inquiry at the jurisdictional phase required by the phrase 'in accordance with the laws and regulations of the Host State' is limited to determining whether the type of asset is legal in domestic law" and considered, as a matter of principle, the legality of an investor's conduct to be an issue for merits. (Dissenting Opinion of B. CREMADES (*Fraport*), *op. cit.*, fn. 46, paras. 37-38). See also Zachary DOUGLAS, "Plea of Illegality in Investment Treaty Arbitration", 29 ICSID Review (2014) p. 1 at p. 19 (According to Douglas, the interpretation of an "in accordance with" clause as providing for jurisdictional challenges on the basis of illegality has serious ramifications, namely there would be "nothing preventing the claimant from commencing fresh proceedings against the host State if jurisdiction has been previously declined". Such an outcome is "hardly consistent with the effective administration of justice".)

52. *Hamester, op. cit.*, fn. 50, para. 127 (In accordance with the wording of the Germany-Ghana BIT, "the legality of the creation of the investment is a jurisdictional issue"). The tribunals in *Metal-Tech, Fraport, Desert Line Projects LLC v. The Republic of Yemen* (ICSID Case No. ARB/05/17, Award, 6 February 2008) and *Alasdair Ross Anderson et al v. Republic of Costa Rica* (ICSID Case No. ARB(AF)/07/3, Award, 19 May 2010) have all interpreted the legality clause as an impediment to jurisdiction. A legality clause has been construed as such even if it is not contained in the treaty's definition of investment. See *Inceysa Vallisoletana, S.L. v. Republic of El Salvador* (ICSID Case No. ARB/03/26), Award, 2 August 2006, para. 188 ("Consequently, the limitation of consent based on the 'accordance with law clause' may be contained not only in the definition of investment, but also in the precepts related to 'Protection' or even in the chapter related to 'Promotion and Admission'.").

53. This approach was most notably taken by the tribunals in *Fraport, Inceysa* and *Metal-Tech*. Assuming that this legality requirement gives rise to jurisdictional issues, tribunals have had to determine "what violations of the legality requirement exclude the investment from the scope of the Treaty and the jurisdiction of the Tribunal" (*Quiborax, op. cit.*, fn. 50, para. 265). On this matter, the tribunal in *Quiborax* introduced the following parameters: "The subject-matter scope of the legality requirement is limited to (i) non-trivial violations of the host State's legal order (*Tokios Tokelés, LESI* and *Desert Line*), (ii) violations of the host State's foreign investment regime (*Saba Fakes*), and (iii) fraud – for instance, to secure the investment (*Inceysa, Plama, Hamester*) or profits (*Fraport*). Additionally, under this BIT, the temporal scope of the legality requirement is limited to the establishment of the investment; it does not extend to the subsequent performance. Indeed, the Treaty refers to the legality requirement in the past tense by using the words investments 'made' in accordance with the laws and regulations of the host State and, in Spanish, 'haya efectuado' (*Fraport, Hamester, Saba Fakes*)." (internal citations omitted, *op. cit.*, fn. 50, para. 266). See also DOLZER, et al., *op. cit.*, fn. 45, p. 93.

54. *Fraport, op. cit.*, fn. 50, para. 334. It should be noted that the *Fraport* award was annulled for unrelated procedural matters. See also NEWCOMBE, *op. cit.*, fn. 45, p. 198, fn. 49 ("If there is illegal conduct in the acquisition of an investment, there might have been no property rights acquired under host state law in the first place. In this case there might be no investment for the purposes of the investment treaty. In such a case, a tribunal would lack jurisdiction *ratione materiae*.").

In applying the legality requirement, certain tribunals have emphasized that "the State against which proceedings are brought must have validly given its consent".[55] For a host State to have given consent, the party bringing the claim must have "made an investment that meets the requirements the State may have laid down, as well as the general conditions of validity".[56]

The tribunal in *Metal-Tech v. Uzbekistan* decided that it lacked jurisdiction as the investment was procured by corruption; therefore, there was no investment in accordance with the law as required by the underlying treaty and no consent according to the treaty and the ICSID Convention.[57] The tribunal determined that Uzbekistan's consent to arbitrate covers only disputes concerning those investments "implemented in compliance with local law".[58] Consequently, as the investment was in breach of the anti-corruption provisions of Uzbek law and hence, the legality requirement, "the Respondent has not consented to submit the present dispute to ICSID arbitration and the *ratione voluntatis* condition required by Article 25(1) of the ICSID Convention is not satisfied".[59]

Similar reasoning was previously applied by the *Inceysa* tribunal, which found, in addition to other grounds, that "El Salvador gave its consent to the jurisdiction of the Centre, presupposing good faith behaviour on the part of the future investors".[60] The tribunal ruled that the investment was not made in accordance with host State and international law, a condition of the BIT. As a result, it found that "because Inceysa's investment was made in a manner that was clearly illegal, it is not included within the scope of consent expressed by Spain and the Republic of El Salvador in the BIT".[61]

The application of a legality requirement in interpreting the term "investment" and deciding on jurisdiction in relation to corruption claims has, so far, been on the basis of the explicit provision of such a clause.[62] This raises the question of what course of action a tribunal could take when the applicable treaty does not contain a legality requirement – if a tribunal finds corruption in the procurement of the investment, would it assert jurisdiction in such a scenario?

---

55. *Malicorp*, op. cit., fn. 45, para. 117. See also *Phillipe Gruslin v. Malaysia* (ICSID Case No. ARB/99/3), Award, 27 November 2000, para. 26.1 (In this dispute, the tribunal found that Malaysia had not provided consent as the project was not an approved project as required by the Intergovernmental Agreement (the IGA) between Malaysia and the Belgo-Luxemburg Economic Union.).

56. *Ibid.*

57. *Metal-Tech*, op. cit., fn. 3, paras. 372-373.

58. *Ibid.*, paras. 129-130.

59. *Ibid.*, para. 129.

60. *Inceysa*, op. cit, fn. 52, para. 238.

61. *Ibid.*, para. 257.

62. In *Plama Consortium Limited v. Republic of Bulgaria* (ICSID Case No. ARB/03/24, Award, 27 August 2008), the tribunal ruled that although the Energy Charter Treaty (ECT) did not contain a legality clause, such a requirement of legality was implicit and, thus, an investment made contrary to law was not entitled to the substantive protections of the treaty (paras. 138-139). Consequently, the tribunal found the investor's claim to be inadmissible.

Even where there is no explicit legality clause in the underlying investment treaty, it has been debated whether all treaties contain an implicit legality condition that could serve as a bar to jurisdiction, whereby investors are required to comply with the basic rules of transnational public policy or the notion of "investment" under the ICSID Convention, or the applicable treaty is interpreted as covering only those investments made in good faith and in accordance with host State law.[63] The tribunal in *Phoenix Action*, although faced with treaty abuse as opposed to a claim of corruption, notably took this approach when it found that an investment may only qualify for protection under ICSID if it was made in accordance with host State laws and in good faith.[64] However, because it dealt with an abusive claim attempting to exploit the international arbitration mechanism of ICSID, the tribunal declined jurisdiction on the basis that "States cannot be deemed to offer access to the ICSID dispute settlement mechanism to investments not made in good faith," rather than on grounds of illegality.[65] Certain tribunals[66] and

---

63. The tribunal in *Phoenix Action, Ltd. v. The Czech Republic* (ICSID Case No. ARB/06/5, Award, 15 April 2009) considered a valid investment to include not just a requirement that assets were invested in accordance with the laws of the host State, but also that said assets were invested bona fide; the tribunal ultimately denied jurisdiction on the basis of the latter condition (paras. 114, 143). See also *Liman Caspian Oil, op. cit.*, fn. 11, paras. 193-194 ("The Tribunal agrees with the authorities cited by the Parties that it does not have jurisdiction over investments made in violation of international public policy"). Yet ultimately the *Liman* tribunal ruled that the respondent did not satisfy its burden of proof and thus did not adequately show a breach of international public policy. For further discussion on treating corruption as a matter for jurisdiction, see Richard KREINDLER, "Corruption in International Investment Arbitration" in Kaj HOBER, Annette MAGNUSSON, and Marie OHSTROM, eds., *Between East and West: Essays in Honour of Ulf Franke* (Juris 2010) p. 309 at pp. 314-317. LAMM, et al., *op. cit.*, fn. 12, pp. 719-720. Bernardo CREMADES, "Corruption and Investment Arbitration" in Gerald AKSEN, et al., eds., *Global Reflections on International Law, Commerce and Dispute Resolution* (ICC Publications 2005) p. 203 at p. 215.

64. DOLZER, et al., *op. cit.*, fn. 45, p. 72 ("The high-water mark for the autonomous approach, with a requirement of six criteria, came with *Phoenix v. Czech Republic....* [I]n the Tribunal's view, for an investment to benefit from ICSID, it must also be made in accordance with the laws of the host state and, finally, the assets had to be invested bona fide."). See also *Europe Cement, op. cit.*, fn. 20, para. 174 ("[I]n *Phoenix* the tribunal concluded that the purchase of the investment was not a bona fide transaction and thus the investment was not one that could be protected under the ICSID system.").

65. *Phoenix, op. cit.*, fn. 63, para. 106. It should also be noted that the underlying Israel-Czech Republic BIT contains a legality requirement in its definition of "investment", which the tribunal also could have relied upon in case the investment was found to be illegal (para. 98). For more on good faith in investment arbitration, see also *Europe Cement, op. cit.*, fn. 20, para. 171 ("It is well accepted in investment arbitrations that the principle of good faith is a principle of international law applicable to the interpretation and application of obligations under international investment agreements."). *Abaclat, op. cit.*, fn. 45, para. 648 ("With regard to breaches of material good faith, different tribunals have followed two different approaches. Either they have dealt with the question of material good faith within the context of the examination of the Tribunal's jurisdiction or within the context of the examination of the legality of the investment: (i) It can be seen as an issue of consent and thus of jurisdiction, where the consent of the Host State cannot be considered to extend to investments done under circumstances breaching the principle of good faith [*Mobil* and *Phoenix*]; (ii) It can be seen as an issue relating to the merits, where the key question is whether

commentators[67] have taken issue with the tribunal's view that "compliance with the laws of the host State and respect of good faith are elements of the objective definition of investment under Article 25(1) of the ICSID Convention".[68]

In relation to the legal consequences for such a finding of illegality, the *Phoenix* tribunal held that when an investment is manifestly in violation of the laws of the host State, it cannot be granted international protection through ICSID arbitration, and such illegality will "allow the tribunal to deny its jurisdiction".[69] Although a requirement of conformity with law is "important in respect of the access to the substantive provisions on the protection of the investor under the BIT" and this access may consequently be denied by a decision on merits, in a case where it is "manifest that the investment has been performed in violation of the law, it is in line with judicial economy not to assert jurisdiction".[70] It follows that the *Phoenix* tribunal did not consider the question of an

---

the circumstances in which the relevant investment was made are meant to be protected by the relevant BIT [*Rompetrol*].").

66. *Metal-Tech*, op. cit., fn. 3, para. 127. *Saba Fakes v. Republic of Turkey* (ICSID Case No. ARB/07/20), Award, 14 July 2010, paras. 112-113.

67. Rahim MOLOO and Alex KHACHATURIAN, "The Compliance with the Law Requirement in International Investment Law", 34 Fordham Int'l L.J. (2010-2011) p. 1473 at p. 1490 ("As such, the finding made by the *Phoenix Action* tribunal that any investments performed in 'manifest' violation of the law should fail at the jurisdictional stage is questionable."). Andrew NEWCOMBE, "Fakes vs. Phoenix" Kluwer Arbitration Blog (3 August 2010), available at <http://kluwerarbitrationblog.com/blog/2010/08/03/fakes-vs-phoenix/> (last accessed 14 August 2014). See more generally DOUGLAS, op. cit., fn. 51, and the Dissenting Opinion of B. Cremades (*Fraport*), op. cit., fn. 46, both of which argue that questions of illegality should not be a matter for jurisdiction.

68. *Metal-Tech*, op. cit., fn. 3, para. 127. However, there has been some debate over whether the *Phoenix* tribunal was referring to the definition of "investment" in the ICSID Convention and/or the applicable treaty. The tribunal considered the condition that an investment be established in accordance with national laws as "implicit even when not expressly stated in the relevant BIT" (para. 101), yet goes on to state that "international protection through ICSID arbitration cannot be granted to investments that are made contrary to law" (op. cit., fn. 63, para. 102). As a result, MOLOO and KHACHATURIAN interpret this to mean that the *Phoenix* tribunal "did not suggest that an investment must accord with the host-state law as part of the assessment as to whether it satisfied the test under Article 25 of the ICSID Convention" (op. cit., fn. 67, p. 1492).

69. *Phoenix*, op. cit., fn. 63, para. 102; It should be noted, however, that the *Phoenix* tribunal was not dealing with a matter of corruption but an abuse of process, and ultimately ruled that the investment did not pass the "bona fide" test (para. 143). Moreover, the discussion on an implicit legality condition was obiter dictum as the underlying treaty contained an express legality clause.

70. Ibid., para. 104. See also *Swisslion DOO Skopje v. The Former Yugoslav Republic of Macedonia* (ICSID Case No. ARB/09/16), Award, 6 July 2012, para. 125 ("The Tribunal observes that, in most cases, ICSID tribunals have examined arguments that investments were made illegally or in bad faith only at the merits stage. It is only in exceptional circumstances that, for reason of judicial economy, ICSID tribunals have considered the question in a decision on jurisdiction."). For an opposing viewpoint, see Stephan SCHILL, "Illegal Investments in International Arbitration", 11 Law and Practice of International Courts and Tribunals (2012) p. 281 at p. 317 ("Interestingly, for the Tribunal in *Phoenix* it was a matter of 'judicial economy' to decline jurisdiction in case of a manifest breach of domestic law, thus indicating that at the heart of declining jurisdiction was really the lack of a cause of action, rather than non-compliance with a jurisdictional requirement.

illegal investment as being a matter solely for jurisdiction, but rather held the view that it could be considered as either a jurisdictional or merits issue, subject to the specific circumstances of the case.[71]

2. Serious Illegality as a Decision on Admissibility

Even if a tribunal asserts jurisdiction, it may still deny a claimant who has engaged in corruption in relation to its investment the protection of the substantive legal rights contained in the treaty[72] by dismissing the claim as inadmissible.[73]

Some investment treaties, such as the Energy Charter Treaty (ECT), do not contain an "in accordance with law" clause. Yet the lack of such a provision does not permit investments involving corruption to benefit from the substantive rights of the investment treaty.[74] Cases and commentary demonstrate that the tribunal may bar the claimant from such protection and dismiss its claim as inadmissible on the basis of the equitable principle of "nobody can benefit from his own wrong" and transnational public policy.[75]

Ultimately, this renders the limitation of the notion of investment under Article 25(1) of the ICSID Convention to legal investments doubtful, even under the *Phoenix* Tribunal's own reasoning.").

71. SCHILL, *ibid.*, pp. 316-317 ("[T]he Tribunal in *Phoenix* read, contrary to what the Tribunal in *Saba Fakes v. Turkey* held, compliance of the investment with domestic law into Article 25(1) of the ICSID Convention as an additional jurisdictional requirement. Somewhat inconsistently, however, the Tribunal in *Phoenix* did not view domestic legality as a strict jurisdictional requirement. Only in case the violation of the laws of the host State was 'manifest,' would it allow a tribunal to deny jurisdiction; non-manifest disregard of the domestic law, by contrast, would only deprive an investment of the substantive protection of an investment treaty to be assessed during the merits stage of an arbitration.").

72. See, e.g., LAMM, et al., *op. cit.*, fn. 12, p. 722. MENAKER, *op. cit.*, fn. 43, p. 70. Richard KREINDLER, "Legal Consequences of Corruption in International Investment Arbitration – An Old Challenge with New Answers" in Laurent LEVY and Yves DERAINS, eds., *Liber Amicorum en l'honneur de Serge Lazareff* (ICC Publications 2011) p. 383 at p. 387. DOUGLAS, *op. cit.*, fn. 51, p. 26. Kevin LIM, "Upholding Corrupt Investors' Claims Against Complicit or Compliant Host States – Where Angels Should Not Fear to Tread" in Karl SAUVANT, ed., *Yearbook on International Investment Law & Policy 2011-2012* (Oxford University Press 2013) p. 601 at para. 15.

73. See, e.g., NEWCOMBE, *op. cit.*, fn. 45, p. 189, 194. PAULSSON, *op. cit.*, fn. 45, p. 617. Dissenting Opinion of K. Highet (*Waste Management*), *op. cit.*, fn. 47, para. 58.

74. *Plama, op. cit.*, fn. 62, para. 143 ("Claimant, in the present case, is requesting the Tribunal to grant its investment in Bulgaria the protections provided by the ECT. However, the Tribunal has decided that the investment was obtained by deceitful conduct that is in violation of Bulgarian law. The Tribunal is of the view that granting the ECT's protections to Claimant's investment would be contrary to the principle *nemo auditor propriam turpitudinem allegans* invoked above. It would also be contrary to the basic notion of international public policy – that a contract obtained by wrongful means (fraudulent misrepresentation) should not be enforced by a tribunal."). See also Rahim MOLOO, "A Comment on the Clean Hands Doctrine in International Law", 8 Transnational Dispute Management (2011) p. 10. LAMM, et al., *op. cit.*, fn. 12, fn. 2159.

75. LAMM, et al., *op. cit.*, fn. 12, p. 731 ("If a tribunal finds that it has jurisdiction, the claimant's claims will likely be deemed in admissible, whether as a result of the clean hands doctrine or transnational public policy."). See, e.g., *Plama, op. cit.*, fn. 62, paras. 143, 146. *World Duty Free, op. cit.*, fn. 17, para. 157.

a. Unclean hands

A claim involving corruption may be found inadmissible on the basis of the claimant having unclean hands.[76] The "clean hands" doctrine is considered to be a general principle of law[77] and is based on the maxim "he who comes into equity must come with clean hands".[78] Although there is some debate on the scope of its application in international law,[79] the clean hands doctrine seems to have stronger roots in most national law systems, as applied by the tribunal in *World Duty Free*.[80] According to certain tribunals and commentators, this principle applies to investment arbitration in that it precludes an investor who effectuated an investment "by means of one or several illegal acts" from enjoying "the protection granted by the host State, such as access to international arbitration to resolve disputes".[81]

An application of the clean hands doctrine, absent an explicit legality clause in the ECT, can be found in *Plama v. Bulgaria*. The tribunal was faced with an instance of fraud wherein the claimant had misrepresented itself when obtaining the required approvals

---

76. KREINDLER, *op. cit.*, fn. 63, p. 324, 328. MENAKER, *op. cit.*, fn. 43, p. 70. NEWCOMBE, *op. cit.*, fn. 45, p. 197. LAMM, et al., *op. cit.*, fn. 12, pp. 722-725.

77. Bin CHENG, *General Principles of Law as Applied by International Courts and Tribunals* (Cambridge University Press 1953) p. 155-158. See also KREINDLER, *op. cit.*, fn. 63, pp. 317-319, 321. LAMM, et al., op cit., fn. 12, p. 724. CREMADES, *op. cit.*, fn. 63, p. 214. *Inceysa*, *op. cit.*, fn. 52, paras. 240-244, which refer to the maxim *nemo auditur suam turpitudinem allegans* (no one alleging his own wrongdoing is to be heard) and its various permutations as general principles of law that are based on justice.

78. As referenced by the *Inceysa* tribunal, there are a number of Latin maxims associated with the clean hands doctrine, which is also referred to as the "unclean hands" doctrine (*op. cit.*, fn. 52, para. 240).

79. See, e.g., MENAKER, *op. cit.*, fn. 43, pp. 70-71. Ian BROWNLIE, *Principles of Public International Law*, 7th edn. (Oxford University Press 2008) p. 503. John DUGARD, "Sixth Report of the International Law Commission on Diplomatic Protection", U.N. Int'l L. Comm'n, 57th Sess., UN Doc. A/CN.4/546 (Geneva, 2 May-2 June and 4 July-5 August 2005) pp. 8-9 ("Arguments premised on the [clean hands] doctrine are regularly raised in direct inter-State cases before the International Court of Justice, but they have yet to be upheld."). *Yukos Universal Limited (Isle of Man) v. The Russian Federation*, PCA Case No. AA 227, Final Award, 18 July 2014 paras. 1357-1363 ("The Tribunal therefore concludes that 'unclean hands' does not exist as a general principle of international law which would bar a claim by an investor, such as Claimants in this case.")

80. The tribunal in *World Duty Free* applied English and Kenyan law, as prescribed in the contract, in addition to international law. With regard to public policy both under English law and Kenyan law and on the specific facts of the case, the tribunal concluded that "the Claimant is not legally entitled to maintain any of its pleaded claims in these proceedings on the ground of *ex turpi causa non oritur action*". (*op. cit.*, fn. 17, para. 179).

81. *Inceysa*, *op. cit.*, fn. 52, para. 242 (The tribunal in *Inceysa* based its denial of jurisdiction on a multitude of factors, including breach of the "in accordance with law" clause in the treaty. However, the tribunal did not just consider domestic law but also the "generally recognized rules and principles of International Law" (para. 222), of which it included the principle "*nemo auditor propriam turpitudinem allegans*" (para. 240)). The tribunal in *World Duty Free* also included the investor's unclean hands as part of the legal reasoning on which it based its decision, however the claim was contract-based and English law was the applicable law (*op. cit.*, fn. 17). See also LAMM, et al., *op. cit.*, fn. 12, p. 723 ("recent ICSID decisions have made clear that there is an implicit obligation in all investment treaties that a covered investment must accord with the law").

from the local privatization authority. The tribunal decided: "the ECT should be interpreted in a manner consistent with the aim of encouraging respect for the rule of law".[82] Based on this interpretation of the ECT, the tribunal concluded that "the substantive protections of the ECT cannot apply to investments that are made contrary to law".[83] Moreover, the *Plama* tribunal took the position that, due to the investor's deceitful conduct in violation of host State law, "granting the ECT's protections to Claimant's investment would be contrary to the principle *nemo auditor propriam turpitudinem allegans*".[84] The tribunal went on to state that "[i]t would also be contrary to the basic notion of international public policy – ... a contract obtained by wrongful means (fraudulent misrepresentation) should not be enforced by a tribunal".[85] The *Plama* decision suggests that "the unclean hands of the claimant (whether a State before the ICJ or an investor before an arbitral tribunal) may indeed result in the inadmissibility of its claims".[86]

In *Niko Resources v. Bangladesh*, a contract-based ICSID arbitration, the tribunal expressed uncertainty as to whether the clean hands principle forms part of international law, for the principle's "precise content is ill-defined".[87] Consequently, when assessing the State's admissibility argument based on unclean hands, the tribunal applied three criteria identified by a UNCLOS arbitral tribunal as the proper application of the doctrine in international law.[88] As it failed to meet these criteria, the tribunal found that the respondent's objection based on the clean hands doctrine must be dismissed.

---

82. *Plama*, *op. cit.*, fn. 62, para. 139. See also para. 138 ("Unlike a number of Bilateral Investment Treaties, the ECT does not contain a provision requiring the conformity of the Investment with a particular law. This does not mean, however, that the protections provided for by the ECT cover all kinds of investments, including those contrary to domestic or international law.").

83. *Ibid*. The *Yukos* tribunal (*op. cit.*, fn. 79, para. 1352) agreed with this conclusion, namely that "[a]n investor who has obtained an investment in the host State only by acting in bad faith or in violation of the laws of the host state, has brought itself within the scope of application of the ECT through wrongful acts" and, as a result, "should not be allowed to benefit from the Treaty".

84. *Ibid.*, para. 143.

85. *Ibid.*

86. MOLOO, *op. cit.*, fn. 74, p. 10.

87. *Niko Resources (Bangladesh) Ltd. v. People's Republic of Bangladesh & Others* (ICSID Case Nos. ARB/10/11 and ARB/10/18), Decision on Jurisdiction, 19 August 2013, para. 477.

88. *Ibid.*, para. 481 ("When considering the defendant State's admissibility argument based on clean hands, the UNCLOS Arbitral Tribunal, dealing with this doctrine 'to the extent that such a doctrine may exist in international law', referred to three criteria which it had extracted from those cases in which reference to the doctrine had been made, in particular the developments in the opinion of Judge Hudson: (i) the breach must concern a continuing violation, (ii) the remedy sought must be 'protection against continuance of that violation in the future', not damages for past violations and (iii) there must be a relationship of reciprocity between the obligations considered.").

b.   Transnational public policy

Certain arbitral decisions[89] and commentary[90] suggest that a claim arising from an investment tainted by illegality may be declared inadmissible on the basis of transnational public policy. The tribunal in *Plama* not only relied on the clean hands doctrine in its decision to dismiss the investor's claim as inadmissible, but it also found that enforcing a contract obtained by wrongful means would be "contrary to the basic notion of international public policy".[91] Moreover, with specific regard to corruption, the ubiquity of anti-corruption legislation, and the consensus that bribery is "contrary to the international public policy of most, if not all, States or, to use another formula, to transnational public policy", suggest that the fight against corruption is a universal one.[92]

It follows that, even though one of the most comprehensive examinations of corruption as it relates to transnational public policy was undertaken by a tribunal in a contract-based claim, tribunals in treaty-based claims may deny an investor who made or implemented its investment through corruption access to the substantive rights provided in the treaty, and consequently declare its claims inadmissible on that basis.[93]

---

89. See, e.g., *Plama, op. cit.*, fn. 62, para. 143. *Société d'Investigation de Recherche et d'Exploitation Minière (SIREXM) v. Burkina Faso* (ICSID Case No. ARB/97/1), Decision (Excerpts), 19 January 2000, para. 5.41 (the tribunal found the claimant's investment agreement to be void, based on both the applicable substantive law and a "breach of the public order", as a result of its finding that the claimant had engaged in corrupt and fraudulent behavior in relation to that agreement). See also the reasoning on international public policy in *Inceysa*, although the tribunal is formulating this argument within the context of determining whether the investment was made in breach of international law as part of a larger investigation into the "in accordance with law" clause (*op. cit.*, fn. 52, para. 249).

90. DOUGLAS, *op. cit.*, fn. 51, p. 26 ("The concept of international public policy vests a tribunal with a particular responsibility to condemn any violation regardless of the law applicable to the particular issues in dispute and regardless of whether it is specifically raised by one of the parties."). Transnational public policy, or truly international public policy, in international arbitration was conceptualized by Pierre LALIVE, "Transnational (or Truly International) Public Policy and International Arbitration" in *Comparative Arbitration Practice and Public Policy in Arbitration*, ICCA Congress Series no. 3 (1986).

91. *Plama, op. cit.*, fn. 62, para. 143. See also SCHREUER, *op. cit.*, fn. 23, p. 566 ("Provisions that would otherwise be applicable, whether contained in an investment agreement or adopted by reference, which violate these basic principles [of international public policy], would have to be disregarded by an ICSID tribunal." However, it should be noted that Schreuer does not explicitly name prevention of corruption as one of these principles.)

92. *World Duty Free, op. cit.*, fn. 17, para. 157 ("In light of domestic laws and international conventions relating to corruption, and in light of the decisions taken in this matter by courts and arbitral tribunals, this Tribunal is convinced that bribery is contrary to the international public policy of most, if not all, States or, to use another formula, to transnational public policy. Thus, claims based on contracts of corruption or on contracts obtained by corruption cannot be upheld by this Arbitral Tribunal."). See also Abdulhay SAYED, *Corruption in International Trade and Commercial Arbitration* (Kluwer Law International 2004) pp. 287-288 ("[W]hen one talks of transnational public policy or universal values, one is at some point bound to refer to values, which are perceived as (1) essential; (2) supported by a large adherence or what in a usual language is called a large consensus, let alone a universal one; and (3) therefore requiring immediate application, regardless of any contrary agreement.").

93. LAMM et. al., *op. cit.*, fn. 12, p. 726. DOUGLAS, *op. cit.*, fn. 51, p. 26-27 ("[I]f a plea of

Although there could be debate on the scope of transnational public policy, the consensus seems to be that prevention of corruption is one of the fundamental principles of international public order, as evidenced by the fact that most national laws[94] and numerous international conventions[95] condemn bribery.[96]

3. Jurisdiction, Admissibility and Merits: A Clear Divide?

One of the conclusions to be drawn from this examination of various legal consequences resulting from claims of investor wrongdoing is that a tribunal's course of action depends in large part on the particular facts and circumstances of the case and the underlying treaty.

While consistency is an important aspect of investment arbitration, and crucial for maintaining investors and host States as stakeholders in the investment arbitration system, it is important to consider that a number of factors could alter this approach. First, in broad terms, when a tribunal finds that a claimant has procured its investment through illegal means and the investment treaty contains an "in accordance with law" clause, commentators and tribunals alike consider this an issue of jurisdiction. When an investment treaty does not contain a legality requirement, the tribunal may consider corruption at the initiation of the investment as an issue of admissibility.

The stage of the proceedings at which allegations of corruption are made or evidence of corruption emerges will impact how a tribunal handles the matter. A host State could raise corruption as a preliminary objection, or indicia of corruption could arise during the proceedings. If claims of corruption are distinct from the facts and issues of the merits phase, it is preferable for a tribunal to handle these as a preliminary issue for

---

illegality to the effect that the investor has violated a ground of international public policy is successful, then it should result in the rejection of the claims as inadmissible." Douglas then identifies the corruption of public officials as an international norm that is widely endorsed even if it does not have the status of *jus cogens*.).

94. The United Nations Convention Against Corruption (2003) requires signatories to criminalize a wide range of manifestations of international corruption. As of 12 November 2014, there are 140 signatories. The text of the Convention is available at <www.unodc.org/unodc/en/treaties/CAC/signatories.html> (last accessed 5 January 2015).

95. There are a number of global and regional anti-corruption conventions and instruments. Some notable examples include the US Foreign Corrupt Practices Act (1977), Organisation for Economic Co-operation and Development Convention on the Bribery of Foreign Public Officials in International Business Transactions (OECD Convention) (1999), United Nations Convention Against Corruption (2003), and UK Bribery Act (2010). Full texts of these conventions and more are available at < http://archive.transparency.org/global_priorities/international_conventions> (last accessed 14 August 2014).

96. In international commercial arbitration, it has been acknowledged that even though corruption remains a reality in many countries, it is "universally outlawed" and, consequently, "[t]he annulment of an agency agreement that provides for the payment of bribes is the solution under most laws" (SCHERER, *op. cit.*, fn. 2, p. 36). See also SAYED, *op. cit.*, fn. 92. BORN, *op. cit.*, fn. 4, p. 2717 ("There is also broad support for an international public policy – paralleling that in many national systems – against bribery of public officials, recognized in both national case law and commentary."). RAESCHKE-KESSLER, *op. cit.*, fn. 25, pp. 494-496.

efficiency and judicial economy, unless there are circumstances that require joining corruption-related issues to the merits. The decision to bifurcate is especially important in regard to corruption at the initiation of an investment, where a tribunal might be dealing with two different sets of facts and applicable law if jurisdiction is joined to the merits.

Another significant factor is timing and, more specifically, the approach to claims of corruption that pre-date or post-date the initiation of the investment. A number of tribunals have found that investor wrongdoing during the course of the investment does not fall within the scope of the legality requirement and, thus, will be an issue for admissibility or the merits irrespective of the existence of an "in accordance with law" clause.[97] There is also the issue of how relevant corruption is to the investment, and whether illicit payments were made to obtain and/or retain business or an improper advantage; in other words, the degree to which the bribe caused the investment.[98] It may also be the case that bribes were paid to induce officials to perform their normal duties, a practice described as "facilitation payments", which are generally considered as less severe than bribes to obtain an investment or improper advantage.[99] If the corrupt acts are found to be irrelevant to the dispute, the tribunal will have to determine the weight, if any, to give such a finding.[100] For instance, the tribunal in *Niko* accepted jurisdiction despite a finding of corruption on the part of the investor, on the basis that the host State was aware of this bribery when signing the agreements, it did not seek to avoid the agreements, and continued to benefit from them.[101]

The *Niko* arbitration brings to the forefront the question of a host State's complicity. More specifically, there have been calls for tribunals to take the actions of both parties into consideration when there is a claim of corruption.[102] If a host State has alleged

---

97. *Hamester*, *op. cit.*, fn. 50, para. 129 ("In order to ascertain jurisdiction, the only question here is whether Hamester perpetrated a fraud, and thereby procured the signing of the JVA (as was the case, for example, in *Inceysa v. El Salvador*, where the contract was procured through fraudulent misrepresentation). If the JVA was obtained on the basis of fraud, it is an illegal investment that does not benefit from the protection of the ICSID/BIT mechanism. However, the question whether fraudulent behaviour has been committed during the performance of the joint-venture is a different issue that has to be taken into account when judging the merits of the dispute.").

98. *Sistem Muhendislik*, *op. cit.*, fn. 42.

99. HWANG, *op. cit.*, fn. 8, p. 3.

100. See, e.g., *Rumeli*, *op. cit.*, fn. 16, para. 320 ("The allegations of fraud perpetrated by the Uzan Family in Turkey and the judgment rendered on July 13, 2003, in the United States against the Uzans in relation to Motorola loans, are not evidence that the investment made by Claimants in Kazakhstan were themselves fraudulent or illegal [sic].").

101. *Niko*, *op. cit.*, fn. 87, paras. 475, 484.

102. Doak BISHOP, "Toward a More Flexible Approach to the International Legal Consequences of Corruption", 25 ICSID Review (2010) p. 63 at pp. 64-65. Bishop suggests that when corruption occurs between a private party and the government, there are many issues at play. Rather than discuss the specific legal consequences, such as questions of jurisdiction, admissibility and merits, he makes broader statements that corruption occurs within a variety of contexts and that the issues that come up "need to be looked at carefully, and perhaps treated differently". He then poses a number of questions that should be considered when determining how the act in question should be treated in international arbitration. See also LIM, *op. cit.*, fn. 72.

corruption on the part of the investor, the host State's actions in regard to this investment, such as whether the agreements have been voided, whether the parties have been prosecuted, and whether the State is still benefitting from these investments, may be considered.[103] More generally, the issue of State responsibility, or whether individual actions may be attributable to the State, has also been raised in cases of corruption and other investor wrongdoing.[104] The tribunal in *Fraport*, which was deciding on allegations of fraud, found: "principles of fairness should require a tribunal to hold a government estopped from raising violations of its own law as a jurisdictional defense when it knowingly overlooked them and endorsed an investment which was not in compliance with its law".[105] It has even been asserted that jurisdictional decisions are "a very imperfect tool" when there is serious misconduct on both sides, which suggests that a decision on admissibility or merits could provide the tribunal the chance to examine the misconduct of both parties.[106] Pending further development of the law, it appears that drawing a line between treaties that contain a legality requirement and those that do not, and then determining the legal consequences accordingly, has the potential to result in a host State's actions and liability being overlooked in some situations and addressed in others.

In cases of investor wrongdoing, the legal consequences are dependent on the specifics of a case and, consequently, it is difficult to propose formulaic approaches to the legal consequences of illegality as a whole. When an investor has procured an investment by fraud, it is generally assumed that the host State was unaware of or, at the very least, not complicit in the fraud itself. As for bribery, it is a thornier question to determine whether the host State was aware of or involved in such corruption and, if so, to what extent. This raises a number of questions regarding corruption that are as yet unanswered, and suggests that it will be important to maintain flexibility as the study of corruption develops. Thus, the desire to foster consistency must be balanced with the recognition that it may be limiting to contemplate a strict formula, especially when there are so few investment cases on matters of corruption.

---

103. Mohamed Abdel RAOUF, "How Should International Arbitrators Tackle Corruption Issues?", 24 ICSID Review (2009) p. 116 at p. 135 ("A state that has accepted and benefited from a bribe should be precluded from complaining. The requirement of 'clean hands' should be mandated from both parties in order to be a sustainable principle."). Similarly, the *Niko* tribunal (*op. cit.*, fn. 87) asserted jurisdiction despite the respondent's preliminary objections in large part because the host State was aware of the corruption and did not avoid the contract.

104. The topic of State responsibility requires further research and warrants a separate discussion; this paper will only attempt to raise issues and questions that may be of importance in such a study.

105. *Fraport, op. cit.*, fn. 50, para. 346.

106. NEWCOMBE, *op. cit.*, fn. 45, p. 199 ("Jurisdictional decisions are a very imperfect tool where there is misconduct of various shades on both sides."). This, however, raises issues such as whether corruption should be a case for merits and, in case both parties are found to be involved in the alleged corruption, how the tribunal should respond and/or whether there is any way to sanction either party beyond costs.

IV.   SANCTIONS

When there is a finding of corruption or fraud, the question for a tribunal becomes how to sanction such activity. Although there are limited sanctions available in investment arbitration, a tribunal should carefully consider implementing all means at its disposal, depending on the specific facts of the case. Firstly, a tribunal should explicitly condemn the illegality, whether corruption or fraud.[107] Such condemnation is especially necessary when an investor could attempt to abuse the system multiple times and through a variety of avenues.[108] Similarly, the reasoning of an award can play a significant role in denouncing the party tainted by corruption or fraud,[109] providing satisfaction to the wronged party (subject to the specific form of illegality),[110] and contributing to the development of a sound investment treaty system. Although tribunals are not bound by previous decisions, they significantly affect and influence future cases, and an award's reasoning can clearly communicate that such misconduct will not be tolerated.

The other means available for sanctions in investment arbitration is costs. An investment tribunal has wide discretion, as provided in both the ICSID and UNCITAL Arbitration Rules, in awarding the costs of the proceedings.[111] If a tribunal decides to award costs, there are a number of approaches it could take[112] and a multitude of factors it could consider, such as the complexity of the case and the questions raised, the number of procedural phases, the length of the proceedings and the experts involved, among others.[113]

---

107. See, e.g., *Europe Cement*, *op. cit.*, fn. 20, para. 180. LAMM, et al., *op. cit.*, fn. 12, p. 730. NEWCOMBE, *op. cit.*, fn. 45, p. 199 (However, Newcombe goes a step further and posits that finding a claim inadmissible is one of the best ways to handle "egregious cases where the misconduct at issue should be explicitly denounced".).

108. *Cementownia*, *op. cit.*, fn. 21, para. 162 ("By agreeing to dismiss the present claim on the basis of lack of jurisdiction, but only without prejudice to its rights, the risk is considerable that the Claimant will file other similar or identical requests before other international jurisdictions or even before ICSID. The Arbitral Tribunal condemns such conduct, which constitutes a manifest abuse of the international institutional arbitration system. A formal declaration in the present Award would therefore constitute a fully justified remedy in order to prevent the Claimant from filing this baseless claim before other international jurisdictions or even before ICSID again.").

109. *Ibid.*

110. *Europe Cement*, *op. cit.*, fn. 20, para. 181.

111. ICSID Convention, Art. 61(2); ICSID Arbitration Rules, Rule 28(1); UNCITRAL Arbitration Rules, Art. 42; See also *Kılıç İnşaat Ithalat Ihracat Sanayi ve Ticaret A.Ş. v. Turkmenistan* (ICSID Case No. ARB/10/1), Award, 2 July 2013, para. 9.2.5. *Rompetrol*, *op. cit.*, fn. 5, para. 298. *RSM Production Corporation v. Grenada* (ICSID Case No. ARB/05/14), Award, 11 March 2009, para. 494.

112. *RSM*, *ibid.*, paras. 491-493.

113. Although many tribunals have followed the practice of splitting the costs evenly between the parties, (*EDF*, *op. cit.*, fn. 11, para. 322, DOLZER, et al., *op. cit.*, fn. 45, p. 299), this is not a universal approach. Recent years have seen the increasing application in investment arbitration of the principle that "costs follow the event" (*Plama*, *op. cit.*, fn. 62, para. 307, *EDF*, *op. cit.*, fn. 11, para. 327, *Cementownia*, *op. cit.*, fn. 21, para. 176, DOLZER, et al., *op. cit.*, fn. 45, p. 299).

The presence of serious wrongdoing like corruption or fraud in a dispute will almost certainly influence the tribunal in its determination of costs.[114] In such an instance, a tribunal may evaluate a number of additional facts, such as the conduct of the parties during the proceedings, whether a claim has been brought in good faith, and the type of illegality in question.

In disputes where the losing party has committed fraud either in obtaining an investment or bringing a claim, tribunals are likely to award costs as a form of sanctions.[115] When an investment was obtained through fraudulent means, a tribunal may consider that the host State was most likely unaware of the transgression. In such an instance, where an investor brought a claim despite knowing that it had obtained the investment in an improper manner, the duration and cost of the proceedings may be an important factor in allocating costs.[116]

The tribunal may also consider whether a claim was brought in good faith.[117] In *Phoenix*, the tribunal ruled that it was applying the principle that "costs follow the event" not only because the investor's claim failed for lack of jurisdiction, but also because "the initiation and pursuit of this arbitration is an abuse of the international investment protection regime under the BIT and, consequently, of the ICSID Convention".[118] Similar reasoning can be found in *Europe Cement*[119] and *Cementownia*,[120] where the tribunals cited the fraudulent nature of the claims as a basis for awarding full costs. The tribunal in *Europe Cement* further reasoned that an award of full costs serves as a deterrent to

---

114. *Phoenix, op. cit.*, fn. 63, para. 151; *Cementownia, op. cit.*, fn. 21, paras. 176-177; REED, et al., *op. cit.*, fn. 2, p. 156 ("Tribunals are especially likely to award costs to the prevailing party in the face of misconduct, fraudulent activity or abuse of process by the losing party.").

115. *Ibid.* See also DOLZER, *op. cit.*, fn. 45, p. 299 ("In some cases the tribunals awarded costs as a sanction for the improper conduct of one of the parties. This has been the case where the tribunal found that the claim had been frivolous or fraudulent or that there had been dilatory or otherwise improper conduct."). *Plama, op. cit.*, fn. 62, paras. 321-322.

116. *Inceysa, op. cit.*, fn. 52, para. 338 ("Knowing that it had behaved improperly in the bidding process, it initiated this arbitration, in which, again, it hid facts of enormous importance for the resolution of this matter. It was necessary for its counterpart to make a great and costly effort to prove Inceysa's incorrect acts. Therefore, this Tribunal considers that it must bear all of the fees and expenses of the arbitrators and the administrative fees for the use of the Centre.").

117. When assessing costs, the tribunal in *EDF* considered good faith in bringing a claim (*op. cit.*, fn. 11, para. 327).

118. *Phoenix, op. cit.*, fn. 63, para. 151.

119. *Europe Cement, op. cit.*, fn. 20, para. 185 ("In the circumstances of this case, where the Tribunal has reached the conclusion that the claim to jurisdiction is based on an assertion of ownership which the evidence suggests was fraudulent, an award to the Respondent of full costs will go some way towards compensating the Respondent for having to defend a claim that had no jurisdictional basis and discourage others from pursuing such unmeritorious claims.").

120. *Cementownia, op. cit.*, fn. 21, para. 177 ("[T]he Arbitral Tribunal intends to employ this principle [costs follow the event] for the following reasons: The Claimant has filed a fraudulent claim; The Claimant has failed on all its requests for relief; The Claimant has delayed the present arbitration proceeding and therefore raised its costs;... The Claimant used the pendency of the arbitration to dispossess itself of its Polish assets in an attempt to make it 'award-proof'.").

"discourage others from pursuing such unmeritorious claims".[121] When a respondent credibly contends that a claim is abusive and has been brought in bad faith, the tribunal may even consider awarding security for costs so as to ensure that the investor does not dispossess itself of assets in order to become "award-proof".[122] Thus, if security for costs is requested, a tribunal should not hesitate to consider the possibility that costs might never be recouped.

The factors to be considered in cases of corruption may differ, for corruption is unique in that it is an illicit transaction involving representatives of both parties. This is not to say that the actions of the host State will never influence the determination of costs in arbitrations where fraud is a prominent feature.[123] However, the actions of a host State in cases of corruption may be more closely examined by a tribunal due to the bilateral nature of the illegality in question. In *Metal-Tech*, the tribunal held that each party should bear its own costs and share administrative costs even though the host State prevailed.[124] The tribunal found that although the investor was deprived of protection due to the fact that its investment was tainted by corruption, this "does not mean ... that the State has not participated in creating the situation that le[d] to the dismissal of the claims".[125] It was because of "this participation, which is implicit in the very nature of corruption" that the tribunal deemed it fair to have the parties share the costs.[126] Consequently, in cases where there is a finding of investor corruption, a tribunal may consider whether it is fair for costs to follow the event or whether it is more appropriate for the parties to share financial responsibility for the arbitration proceedings.

One final consideration in awarding costs is the often exponential increase of respondent costs in cases involving corruption or fraud. Normally in investment arbitration, a party expects to plead the applicable law and related facts. Yet when an investment is tainted by fraud or corruption, which often only comes to light over the course of the proceedings, the respondent will necessarily have to undertake an examination into new facts and applicable law that are not directly relevant to the initial claim. As a result, the arbitration case essentially involves two subcases – the original

---

121. *Europe Cement*, *op. cit.*, fn. 20, para. 185.
122. *Cementownia*, *op. cit.*, fn. 21, para. 158 ("Meanwhile, Cementownia has sold virtually all of its operating assets and has gone out of business.... The Arbitral Tribunal therefore agrees with the Respondent that Cementownia is now an empty shell the purpose of which was to pursue this arbitral proceeding without any exposure to an award of costs.").
123. *Inceysa*, *op. cit.*, fn. 52, para. 338 ("In spite of the foregoing, the Tribunal considers that the circumstances surrounding the negotiation that gave rise to this dispute, and another undertaken by ANDA at the same time; the naïve handling of bid number 05/2000 by MARN officials and, in general, the way in which they and other public officials of El Salvador reacted to the actions of Inceysa, mean that the conduct of El Salvador cannot be considered beyond reproach. For this reason, the Respondent, like Inceysa, must pay the fees of the counsel contracted by each of them to advise them.").
124. *Metal-Tech*, *op. cit.*, fn. 3, para. 420.
125. *Ibid.*, para. 422.
126. *Ibid.*

claim and the claim regarding corruption or fraud. It follows, then, that the time spent, and thus legal fees and expenses, reflect this reality.[127]

When considering how to award costs in cases of corruption and fraud, the tribunal could consider the time spent on arguing such cases, in addition to issues of good faith, conduct during the proceedings and the type of illegality at hand. Since costs serve as one of the few sanctions provided for in investment arbitration, it stands to reason that tribunals should assess all relevant factors in order to determine the result.

V.   CONCLUSION

It has been questioned whether investment tribunals and counsel are properly equipped to address the issue of corruption, both in regard to expertise and the tools at their disposal. In regard to proof, tribunals have many tools at their disposal; they are afforded wide discretion and investigative powers by the procedural rules, as shown in *Metal-Tech*, and may draw adverse inferences if requested documents are not submitted, nor is a valid explanation provided for not furnishing these documents. Counsel may be more limited in the tools at their disposal, but they are still able to request documents and, in case such documents are not provided, they may request the tribunal to draw adverse inferences; *Cementownia* and *Europe Cement* serve as good examples of this approach.

In case of a finding of corruption, tribunals must then determine the legal consequences to apply. Such a decision depends in large part on whether the claimant or respondent is making the claim of corruption, the nature of the corruption, namely when it took place and its connection to the investment, and the treaty text. Thus, the legal consequences are ultimately dependent on the specifics of a case, and it is difficult to derive a formula for whether corruption should be a matter for jurisdiction, admissibility or the merits. For corruption in particular, there are a number of unanswered questions regarding the role and responsibility of the State, which makes it even more important for tribunals to maintain flexibility in their approach.

Tribunals must also consider how to sanction corruption and other instances of investor wrongdoing. First, a tribunal should consider ordering security for costs when there are serious indications that a claim has been brought in bad faith and condemning any proven investor wrongdoing. In addition, it is likely that a finding of corruption or fraud will affect the tribunal's awarding of costs. When determining how to award costs, a tribunal may consider the type of illegality at hand, the parties' conduct during the proceedings and the time spent on arguing such cases, which may differ significantly from the facts and applicable law of the original claim, among other relevant factors. For findings of corruption, the tribunal may also consider the host State's level of participation, as demonstrated in *Metal-Tech*.

The finding of corruption made by the *Metal-Tech* tribunal, the first of its kind in a treaty-based investment arbitration, demonstrates one way a tribunal may approach

---

127. This factor has been recognized in a number of tribunals: *Phoenix, op. cit.*, fn. 63, para. 152 ("The Tribunal further finds that the Respondent's legal fees and expenses are not unreasonable having regard to the course of these proceedings..."). See also *Europe Cement, op. cit.*, fn. 20, para. 178.

corruption in regard to evidence, legal consequences and sanctions. However, many of the legal issues related to corruption, such as jurisdiction versus admissibility, the applicability of the clean hands doctrine and the scope of transnational public policy, require further investigation and development. Furthermore, these issues are not specific to corruption claims; rather, they reflect fundamental questions that have broad application in investment arbitration. As these matters continue to develop, tribunals must remain flexible in their approach to corruption, while also utilizing the tools and experience they already have to ensure that corruption is not tolerated.

Pleading and Proof of Fraud and Comparable Forms of Abuse in Treaty Arbitration

Carolyn B. Lamm, *Eckhard R. Hellbeck** and *M. Imad Khan****

I.   INTRODUCTION

The paper presented by Aloysius Llamzon and Anthony Sinclair (henceforth the Paper) discusses various categories of investor wrongdoing, such as corruption, fraud, misrepresentation and other violations of host State law; the legal principles that apply to these categories; the burden and standard of proof necessary to establish investor wrongdoing; and its legal consequences. While Utku Coşar has commented on the Paper focusing on corruption,[1] this commentary focuses on fraud and other forms of investor wrongdoing, and comments specifically on the Paper. It addresses in particular the following topics:

— What constitutes fraudulent misrepresentation, as a category of investor wrongdoing, and whether national law or international law should apply to define this concept;
— The standard and burden of proof applicable to establish fraud in the context of investment illegality;
— Whether investment protection treaties generally contain an implicit legality requirement, i.e., a requirement that investors make investments "in accordance with [the host State's] law", or whether such a requirement exists only if it is expressly stated in the applicable treaty; and
— Whether an investment's illegality affects the jurisdiction of the tribunal or the admissibility of the claimant's claims.

---

*   Partner, White & Case LLP, Washington, DC.
**   Counsel, White & Case LLP, Washington, DC.
*** Associate, White & Case LLP, Washington, DC.
1.   Utku COŞAR, "Claims of Corruption in Investment Treaty Arbitration: Proof, Legal Consequences and Sanctions", this volume, pp. 531-556. See also Elizabeth KARANJA, "Report on the Session Treaty Arbitration: Pleading and Proof of Fraud and Comparable Forms of Abuse", this volume, pp. 439-450 (summarizing the discussion).

We conclude with a brief comment on five propositions put before the panel in keeping with the theme of this year's ICCA Congress: "Legitimacy: Myths, Realities, Challenges".

II.   FRAUDULENT MISREPRESENTATION: DEFINITION AND APPLICABLE LAW

1.   Definition

As the Paper states, most national legal systems and international investment law condemn "the *knowing* misrepresentation or concealment of a *material* fact with a view to *deceiving* another to that other's *disadvantage*".[2] In the investment arbitration context, the ICSID tribunal in *Plama v. Bulgaria* similarly defined fraud as the "deliberate concealment" of a material fact.[3] There, the tribunal referred to both Bulgarian and international law to determine that the claimant committed fraud by concealing from the State a change in the claimant's circumstances that were material to Bulgaria's decision to accept the claimant's investment.[4] The tribunal also found that the claimant's deliberate concealment was "calculated to induce the Bulgarian authorities to authorize the transfer of shares to an entity that did not have the financial and managerial capacities required to resume operation of the Refinery".[5] The tribunal, furthermore, emphasized that in this case it was not the State's obligation to ascertain the changed circumstances; rather, it was the claimant's duty to inform the State of the changed circumstances.[6] Discussing the nature of fraudulent misrepresentation, the Paper observes correctly that, unlike corruption, fraudulent misrepresentation is a unilateral act; that is, the acts or omissions of one party are sufficient to establish fraud for purposes of determining whether the tribunal has jurisdiction over the case or whether claimant's claims are admissible.[7] As such, fraud has lent itself to being invoked as a shield by respondents in defending against investor claims. A notable exception, however, to the use of fraud as

---

2. Paper, p. 469 (emphases original; punctuation omitted); see also Carolyn B. LAMM, Hansel T. PHAM and Rahim MOLOO, "Fraud and Corruption in International Arbitration" in Miguel Ángel FERNANDEZ-BALLESTEROS and David ARIAS, eds., *Liber Amicorum Bernardo Cremades* (La Ley 2010) p. 699 (defining fraud as "a knowing misrepresentation of the truth of a material fact to induce another to act in a manner that is detrimental to their interests"); *ibid.*, at p. 716 (noting that most jurisdictions not only treat "fraud as being illegal" but also "refuse to recognize or enforce arbitral awards obtained or affected by fraud").
3. *Plama Consortium Ltd v. Republic of Bulgaria* (ICSID Case No. ARB/03/24), Award, 27 August 2008, (henceforth *Plama* Award), paras. 134-135.
4. *Plama* Award, paras. 134-135.
5. *Plama* Award, para. 135.
6. *Plama* Award, para. 134 ("On the basis of the evidence in the record, Bulgaria had no reason to suspect that the original composition of the consortium, consisting of two major experienced companies, had changed to an individual investor acting in the guise of that 'consortium', and no duty to ask. It was Claimant, knowing the facts, which had an obligation to inform Respondent.").
7. Paper, pp. 470-471.

a shield was the *Jan de Nul v. Egypt* case, in which the claimants raised fraud as a sword against the State.

Jan de Nul v. Egypt involved a dispute about dredging works in the Suez Canal. The claimants alleged, among other things, that during the tender process the State had withheld information about certain geological conditions and about pre-dredging work that was essential to the claimant's bid. According to the claimants, the State's withholding of this information amounted to "fraudulent misrepresentations at the tender stage about the scope and nature of the contract works, thereby inducing the Claimants to a loss-making investment".[8] Although the tribunal ultimately found that the evidence before it did not establish fraud, the tribunal did not reject the applicability of the claimants' theory against the State.[9]

The Paper makes the interesting point that investment treaty tribunals have not always distinguished clearly between "truly fraudulent" misrepresentation, which requires an intent to deceive or at least recklessness as to the truth, and negligent misrepresentation, which does not involve deceit.[10] While, as the Paper analyzes in greater detail, findings of fraud often include a finding of deceit, this often turns on the elements required by the applicable law.[11] We do agree with Canon 1 of the Paper that proof of deception and reliance generally is not mandated.[12] Indeed, as the tribunal in *Anderson v. Costa Rica* reasoned, a claimant must meet the legality requirement "regardless of his or her knowledge of the law or his or her intention to follow the law".[13]

With respect to violations of host State law, we do agree with the *Quiborax* tribunal's formulation of categories, quoted in the Paper,[14] analyzing the decisions of various tribunals; however, we disagree entirely with a cutoff point, i.e., that the illegality must have occurred in the making of an investment. Illegality in performance or implementation cannot be ignored. It is an affront to the host State's sovereignty to ignore illegality, as noted in the Paper.[15] States have a significant interest in legality of investments operated in their territory. A balanced legal regime that addresses the needs of the State must take account of this important sensitivity. An investor can hardly be heard to complain that it has some right to operate its investment in violation of host State law or premised on misrepresentation, and seek the assistance of an international tribunal.

---

8. *Jan de Nul N.V. et al. v. Arab Republic of Egypt* (ICSID Case No. ARB/04/13), Award, 6 November 2008, paras. 75, 76, 112.

9. *Ibid.*, para. 254.

10. Paper, pp. 469-470.

11. Paper, pp. 473-478 (discussing *Plama v. Bulgaria*, *Inceysa v. El Salvador*, *Azinian v. Mexico*, *Hamester v. Ghana*, *Fraport v. Philippines*, and other cases).

12. Paper, p. 527 (Canon 1).

13. *Alasdair Ross Anderson et al. v. Republic of Costa Rica* (ICSID Case No. ARB(AF)/07/3), Award, 19 May 2010, (henceforth *Anderson*), para. 52.

14. Paper, p. 478 (quoting *Quiborax S.A., Non Metallic Minerals SA and Allan Fosk Kaplún v. Plurinational State of Bolivia* (ICSID Case No. ARB/06/2), Decision on Jurisdiction, 27 September 2012, para. 266).

15. Paper, para. 499.

2. Applicable Law

If the applicable investment treaty contains an explicit legality requirement, this is a clear indication that the investor must strictly comply with host State law with respect to its investment.[16] Several tribunals have found legality requirements to be implicitly referring to general principles of international law and international public policy.[17] Even an interpretation of the investment treaty under Arts. 31(1) and 31(3)(c) of the Vienna Convention on the Law of Treaties should lead tribunals to conclude there is an explicit legality requirement.

In *Plama v. Bulgaria*, the tribunal found that the claimant's conduct was "contrary to … Bulgarian law and to international law".[18] The applicable investment treaty in that case was the Energy Charter Treaty (ECT), which did not contain an explicit "in accordance with law" provision.[19] Nonetheless, finding that a "fundamental aim of the Energy Charter Treaty is to strengthen the rule of law on energy issues", the tribunal "conclude[d] that the substantive protections of the ECT cannot apply to investments that are made contrary to law".[20] In the absence of a reference to a particular law, the tribunal looked both to Bulgarian law on fraud and the obligation to negotiate contracts in good faith, and to "applicable rules and principles of international law", including the principles of good faith, *nemo auditur propriam turbitudinem allegans*, and *ex turpi causa non oritur actio*.[21]

In *Desert Line v. Yemen*, where the applicable Oman-Yemen Bilateral Investment Treaty (BIT) did contain an "in accordance with law" provision, the ICSID tribunal found that such provisions "are intended to ensure the legality of the investment by excluding investments made in breach of *fundamental principles of the host State's law*, e.g., by fraudulent misrepresentations or the dissimulation of true ownership".[22] Similarly, noting that the applicable BIT contained an "in accordance with law" provision, the ICSID tribunal in *Phoenix Action v. Czech Republic* recognized that the investment must conform to the laws of the host State. The tribunal stated that "the analysis of the conformity of the investment with the host State's laws has to be performed taking into account the laws in force at the moment of the establishment of the investment".[23] The tribunal then

---

16. *Anderson*, para. 53.
17. *Plama* Award, para. 143; *Gustav FW Hamester GmbH & Co KG v. Republic of Ghana* (ICSID Case No. ARB/07/24), Award, 18 June 2010, (henceforth *Hamester*), paras. 123-124; *Phoenix Action, Ltd v. Czech Republic* (ICSID Case No. ARB/06/5), Award, 15 April 2009 (henceforth *Phoenix Action*), paras. 106, 113; *Inceysa Vallisoletana, S.L. v. Republic of El Salvador* (ICSID Case No. ARB/03/26), Award, 2 August 2006 (henceforth *Inceysa*), para. 249.
18. *Plama* Award, para. 135.
19. *Plama* Award, para. 138.
20. *Plama* Award, para. 139 (quoting Energy Charter Secretariat, *The Energy Charter Treaty and Related Documents: A Legal Framework for International Energy Cooperation, An Introduction to the Energy Charter Treaty*, p. 14).
21. *Plama* Award, paras. 138, 140-145.
22. *Desert Line Projects LLC v. Republic of Yemen* (ICSID Case No. ARB/05/17), Award, 6 February 2008 (henceforth *Desert Line*), para. 104 (emphasis added).
23. *Phoenix Action*, para. 103.

analyzed Czech law to determine whether the investment conformed with the legal order of the Czech Republic.[24] The Paper thus properly characterizes the reference to the host State's law in an "in accordance with law" clause as a *renvoi* to national law relating to investor wrongdoing, such as fraud.[25]

Ultimately, it seems logical that a tribunal would determine the applicable law question differently at the jurisdiction and admissibility stages of its inquiry. When examining its jurisdiction, a treaty-based tribunal should begin its analysis under international law because that is the law applicable to the treaty on which the tribunal's jurisdiction is based.[26] That is essentially what the ICSID tribunal in *Inceysa v. El Salvador* did when it analyzed the legality of the claimant's investment by reference to "general principles of law" within the meaning of Art. 38(1) of the Statute of the International Court of Justice.[27] Where the investment treaty contains a *renvoi* to national law, national law also may become applicable, as discussed above. When analyzing the legality of the investment as an issue of admissibility, a treaty-based tribunal may resort to international law but generally will also apply national law on the basis of any applicable law rules contained in the dispute resolution provisions of investment treaties and/or Art. 42(1) of the ICSID Convention in the case of ICSID arbitration.[28] This was the approach taken in *Plama*.

As noted in the Paper[29] and by several of the tribunals that considered the applicable law issue, international public policy, unclean hands, and good faith all must be considered as part of the analysis.[30]

---

24. *Phoenix Action*, para. 134.

25. Paper, p. 471.

26. See *Siemens AG v. Argentine Republic* (ICSID Case No. ARB/02/8), Decision on Jurisdiction, 3 August 2004, para. 31 ("This being an ICSID Tribunal, its jurisdiction is governed by Article 25 of the ICSID Convention and the terms of the instrument expressing the parties' consent to ICSID arbitration, namely, Article 10 of the [Germany-Argentina BIT]."); *Československa obchodní banka, a.s. v. Slovak Republic* (ICSID Case No. ARB/97/4), Decision on Jurisdiction, 24 May 1999, para. 35 ("The question of whether the parties have effectively expressed their consent to ICSID jurisdiction is not to be answered by reference to national law. It is governed by international law as set out in Article 25(1) of the ICSID Convention.").

27. *Inceysa*, para. 225.

28. See Convention on the Settlement of Investment Disputes Between States and Nationals of Other States (18 March 1965) (henceforth ICSID Convention), Art. 42(1) ("The Tribunal shall decide a dispute in accordance with such rules of law as may be agreed by the parties. In the absence of such agreement, the Tribunal shall apply the law of the Contracting State party to the dispute (including its rules on the conflict of laws) and such rules of international law as may be applicable.").

29. Paper, p. 483.

30. *Plama* Award, para. 143; *Inceysa*, para. 249; *Fraport AG Frankfurt Airport Services Worldwide v. Republic of the Philippines* (ICSID Case No. ARB/03/25), Dissenting Opinion of Mr. Bernardo Cremades, 16 August 2007, paras. 28-29, 40; *Phoenix Action*, paras. 106, 113.

III.   STANDARD AND BURDEN OF PROOF FOR ALLEGATIONS OF FRAUD AND OTHER
       ILLEGALITY

As stated in the Paper, the standard of proof "defines the threshold of evidence necessary to establish either an individual fact or contention or the party's case as a whole".[31] In other words, as the ICSID tribunal in *Rompetrol v. Romania* explained, "the standard of proof defines how much evidence is needed to establish either an individual issue or the party's case as a whole".[32] By contrast, the "burden of proof defines which party has to prove what, in order for its case to prevail".[33]

1.   *Standard of Proof*

Certain national legal systems provide for several different standards of proof, such as: beyond a reasonable doubt, clear and convincing evidence, preponderance of the evidence, balance of probabilities, and prima facie evidence. However, as the Paper notes, in finding the facts, international arbitral tribunals are not bound by national standards.[34] Indeed, international arbitration rules generally do not mandate any particular standard of proof but rather accord tribunals discretion in this respect.[35] In practice, we agree with the Paper that international arbitral tribunals often use the "balance of probabilities" ("more likely than not") standard, which, similar to the preponderance of the evidence standard, requires a showing that an allegation is more likely than not to be true.[36]

---

31. Paper, p. 490.
32. *The Rompetrol Group, N.V. v. Romania* (ICSID Case No. ARB/06/3), Award, 6 May 2013 (henceforth *Rompetrol*), para. 178.
33. *Rompetrol*, para. 178.
34. Paper, pp. 482, 492-493.
35. See ICSID Arbitration Rules, Rule 34(1) ("The Tribunal shall be the judge of the admissibility of any evidence adduced and of its probative value."); UNCITRAL Arbitration Rules, Art. 27(4) ("The arbitral tribunal shall determine the admissibility, relevance, materiality and weight of the evidence offered."); International Centre for Dispute Resolution (ICDR) International Arbitration Rules, Art. 20(6) ("The tribunal shall determine the admissibility, relevance, materiality and weight of the evidence offered by any party."); Arbitration Rules of the Arbitration Institute of the Stockholm Chamber of Commerce, Art. 26(1) ("The admissibility, relevance, materiality and weight of evidence shall be for the Arbitral Tribunal to determine."); London Court of International Arbitration (LCIA) Arbitration Rules, Art. 22.1 (f) ("Unless the parties at any time agree otherwise in writing, the Arbitral Tribunal shall have the power, on the application of any party or of its own motion, but in either case only after giving the parties a reasonable opportunity to state their views ... to decide whether or not to apply any strict rules of evidence (or any other rules) as to the admissibility, relevance or weight of any material tendered by a party on any matter of fact or expert opinion"); International Bar Association (IBA) Rules on the Taking of Evidence in International Arbitration, Art. 9(1) ("The Arbitral Tribunal shall determine the admissibility, relevance, materiality and weight of the evidence.").
36. Paper, pp. 490-491; see also *Tokios Tokelės v. Ukraine* (ICSID Case No. ARB/02/18), Award, 26 July 2007, para. 124 (referring to "the usual standard, which requires the party making an assertion to persuade the decision-maker that it is more likely than not to be true"); *Rompetrol*,

562

Given the absence of express rules on the standard of proof, the *Rompetrol* tribunal observed that "in international arbitration – including investment arbitration – the rules of evidence are neither rigid nor technical" and found that the ICSID Convention and Arbitration Rules grant tribunals "a large measure of discretion over how the relevant facts are to be found and to be proved".[37] Thus, Art. 43 of the ICSID Convention and ICSID Arbitration Rule 34 give ICSID tribunals general discretion to call upon parties to produce documents, witnesses, and experts, and to judge the admissibility and probative value of any evidence adduced.[38] In this context, the *Rompetrol* tribunal specifically referred to ICSID Arbitration Rule 34(3), which provides, inter alia, that "[t]he Tribunal shall take formal note of the failure of a party to comply with its obligations [under Rule 34] and of any reasons given for such failure".[39] The tribunal found that this provision "no doubt intends, among other things, that a given tribunal is specifically authorized to draw whatever inferences it deems appropriate from the failure of either party to produce evidence which that party might otherwise have been expected to produce".[40] The *Rompetrol* tribunal articulated that "the standard of proof is *relative*" meaning that "whether a proposition has in fact been proved by the party which bears the burden of proving it depends not just on its own evidence *but on the overall assessment of the accumulated evidence put forward by one or both parties…*".[41] The *Rompetrol* tribunal thus suggested that tribunals should assess all evidence in context to determine whether a fact is more likely than not to be true.

This relative standard of proof based on a balancing of the evidence is most suitable for establishing fraud. Indeed, as the Paper notes with reference to *Plama* and *Inceysa*, investment tribunals dealing with cases of misrepresentation have relied on an overall assessment and weighing of contemporaneous objective evidence, rather than on a particular standard of proof.[42] The Paper concludes correctly: "The underlying facts matter."[43]

The Paper also accurately notes that where evidence is difficult to obtain, tribunals have adopted a flexible approach by allowing indirect or circumstantial evidence to suffice to satisfy the standard of proof.[44] Conversely, there is generally no basis in the applicable rules for an investment tribunal to adopt a high standard of proof, such as clear and convincing evidence or beyond a reasonable doubt. To adopt such a high standard of proof would disregard the tribunal's and the parties' lack of compulsory power to gather evidence from third parties or to obtain it from a recalcitrant party.[45] It also

---

para. 183 (referring to "the normal rule of the 'balance of probabilities'").

37. *Rompetrol*, para. 181.

38. ICSID Convention, Art. 43; ICSID Arbitration Rules, Rule 34.

39. ICSID Arbitration Rules, Rule 34(3).

40. *Rompetrol*, para. 181.

41. *Rompetrol*, para. 178 (emphases added).

42. Paper, pp. 481-482, 495.

43. Paper, p. 527 (Canon 1).

44. Paper, pp. 495-496.

45. See Paper, p. 484 (acknowledging that "forcing discovery or testimony by compelling witnesses is difficult").

would undermine the discretion specifically granted tribunals under international arbitration rules to assess the evidence. As observed by Professor Orrego Vicuña in his dissent in *Siag v. Egypt*, which the Paper summarizes,[46] "arbitration tribunals, particularly those deciding under international law, are free to choose the most relevant rules in accordance with the circumstances of the case and the nature of the facts involved".[47]

2. Burden of Proof

As a general rule, each party bears the burden of proving the facts it alleges, and the Paper correctly bases its analysis on this starting point.[48]

Where investor fraud or other illegality is raised as a question of jurisdiction or admissibility, however, tribunals enjoy a broad scope of discretion in allocating the burden of proof. Thus, as the Paper states quoting Cremades, when faced with allegations of fraud and other illegality, tribunals must address and carefully assess the related assertions and evidence put before them, including by use of their ex officio powers.[49]

The *Desert Line v. Yemen* tribunal – adopting the test articulated in the separate opinion of Judge Higgins in the *Oil Platforms* case – explained that, with respect to jurisdictional objections, "in the absence of any test set forth in the applicable international instrument or in the rules governing the Court itself, the Court was 'at liberty to adopt the principle which it considers best calculated to ensure the administration of justice, most suited to procedure before an international tribunal and most in conformity with the fundamental principles of international law'".[50] Thus, in the absence of an applicable rule in the BIT or other instrument conferring jurisdiction, tribunals are generally free under arbitration rules to exercise their broad discretion in allocating the burden of proof.

Nevertheless, the rule under international law as to which party bears the burden of proof is quite clear: "[a] number of tribunals have held that a respondent bears the burden of proof with respect to the facts alleged in its jurisdictional objections".[51] Thus, the tribunal in *Desert Line v. Yemen* imposed upon the State the burden to prove the alleged illegality of the investment. The tribunal found that "the Respondent has not come close to satisfying the Arbitral Tribunal that the Claimant made an investment which was either inconsistent with Yemeni laws or regulations or failed to achieve acceptance by the Respondent".[52] The tribunal in *Hamester v. Ghana* also found that the State bore the

---

46. Paper, pp. 493-494.
47. *Waguih Elie George Siag and Clorinda Vecchi v. Arab Republic of Egypt* (ICSID Case No. ARB/05/15), Dissenting Opinion of Professor Francisco Orrego Vicuña, 11 May 2009, at p. 4.
48. Paper, pp. 484-485. Accord, Durward V. SANDIFER, *Evidence Before International Tribunals*, p. 127 (rev. ed. Virginia 1975); Bin Cheng, *General Principles of Law as Applied by International Courts and Tribunals* (Grotius reprint 1987) p. 334.
49. Paper, pp. 482-484.
50. *Desert Line*, para. 129.
51. *Teinver SA et al. v. Argentine Republic* (ICSID Case No. ARB/09/1), Decision on Jurisdiction, 21 December 2012, n. 467.
52. *Desert Line*, para. 105.

burden of proof with respect to its allegation of illegality in the inception of the investment.[53]

Imposing the burden of proof on the investor to establish that there was no investment illegality would generally be inappropriate. As the tribunal in *Quiborax v. Bolivia* found, it would be unrealistic for the investor "to somehow prove that it has complied with the myriad of laws and regulations of the host State".[54]

Nonetheless, in the absence of an applicable rule in the BIT or other instrument conferring jurisdiction, and in exercising their discretion, tribunals have the authority to shift the burden of proof under the ICSID Arbitration Rules. Albeit in the context of corruption, the *Metal-Tech v. Uzbekistan* tribunal thus found that

> "[r]ules establishing presumptions or shifting the burden of proof under certain circumstances, or drawing inferences from a lack of proof are generally deemed to be part of the *lex causae*. In the present case, the *lex causae* is essentially the BIT, which provides no rules for shifting the burden of proof or establishing presumptions. Therefore, the Tribunal has relative freedom in determining the standard necessary to sustain a determination of corruption."[55]

Ultimately, however, the tribunal found that it need not apply the rules on burden of proof or presumptions but achieved the same result by using its ex officio power to require explanations, and applying adverse inferences.[56]

As the Paper explains, investment tribunals increasingly resort to the use of adverse inferences as an effective means of finding the truth where a party does not produce evidence that it should have in its possession or that the tribunal has asked it to produce.[57] Thus, as the Paper points out,[58] the tribunal in *Methanex v. United States* endorsed a "connect the dots" methodology to look at the evidence presented by both parties as a whole, including circumstantial evidence.[59] This is similar to the *Rompetrol* tribunal's "totality of the evidence" approach discussed above that also was applied in *Metal-Tech*.[60] Essentially, therefore, it is for each party to persuade the tribunal of its position, without regard to any strict rules on the burden of proof.

---

53. *Hamester*, para. 132.
54. *Quiborax S.A. et al. v. Plurinational State of Bolivia* (ICSID Case No. ARB/06/2), Decision on Jurisdiction, 27 September 2012, para. 259.
55. *Metal-Tech Ltd v. Republic of Uzbekistan* (ICSID Case No. ARB/10/3), Award, 4 October 2013 (henceforth *Metal-Tech*), para. 238.
56. *Metal-Tech*, paras. 239-243.
57. Paper, pp. 489-490.
58. Paper, p. 488.
59. *Methanex Corporation v. United States of America*, NAFTA Ch. 11/UNCITRAL Arbitration, Award, 3 August 2005, Part III, Ch. B, paras. 2-3.
60. *Rompetrol*, paras. 178-179, 181; *Metal-Tech*, paras. 239, 243, 245.

IV.   EXPLICIT AND IMPLICIT LEGALITY REQUIREMENTS

Many investment protection treaties contain provisions expressly requiring that covered investments be made in "in accordance with" the host State's law.[61] Such requirements may be contained in the treaty's definition of "investment"[62] and/or in other provisions of the treaty.[63] It is widely accepted, as the Paper states, that "[t]hese treaty provisions refer to 'the validity of the investment and not its definition'".[64]

Interpreting the "in accordance with law" provision in the Lithuania-Ukraine BIT, the tribunal in *Tokios Tokelés v. Ukraine* explained that the "purpose of such provisions ... is 'to prevent the Bilateral Treaty from protecting investments that should not be protected, particularly because they would be illegal'".[65] Likewise, the tribunal in *Desert Line v. Yemen* – interpreting the preamble of the Oman-Yemen BIT which references the host State's laws and regulations – stated that such references in investment treaties "are intended to ensure the legality of the investment by excluding investments made in breach of fundamental principles of the host State's law, e.g. by fraudulent misrepresentations or the dissimulation of true ownership".[66]

Not all investment treaties, however, contain express "in accordance with law" provisions. This raises the issue of whether an express "in accordance with law" provision is necessary for the treaty to impose a legality requirement as a limitation or condition of the treaty's protections. One arbitral decision appears to indicate that an express "in accordance with law provision" is necessary for an investment legality requirement to exist under the treaty. In *Anderson v. Costa Rica*, the tribunal attached particular

---

61. The first bilateral investment treaty to have been concluded contained such a reference to the host State's law in its Art. 1: "Each contracting State hereafter called in this Treaty a Party will endeavor to admit in its territory, in accordance with its legislation and rules and regulations framed thereunder the investing of capital by nationals or companies of the other Party ...." Treaty between the Federal Republic of Germany and Pakistan for the Promotion and Protection of Investments (25 November 1959), 457 UNTS 23, Art. 1.

62. See, e.g., *Tokios Tokelés v. Ukraine* (ICSID Case No. ARB/02/18), Decision on Jurisdiction, 29 April 2004, para. 84 ("The requirement in Article 1(1) of the Ukraine-Lithuania BIT that investments be made in compliance with the laws and regulations of the host state is a common requirement in modern BITs."); *ibid.*, para. 74 ("Article 1(1) of the BIT defines 'investment' as 'every kind of asset invested by an investor of one Contracting Party in the territory of the other Contracting Party in accordance with the laws and regulations of the latter...'.").

63. See, e.g., *Fraport AG Frankfurt Airport Services Worldwide v. Republic of the Philippines* (ICSID Case No. ARB/03/25), Award, paras. 334-343 (interpreting various provisions of the Germany-Philippines BIT containing references to the host State's law together) (annulled on other grounds); see also *Inceysa*, para. 188 ("the limitation of consent based on the 'accordance with law clause' may be contained not only in the definition of investment, but also in the precepts related to 'Protection' or even in the chapter related to 'Promotion and Admission'").

64. Paper, p. 498 (quoting *Salini Costruttori SpA and Italstrade SpA v. Morocco* (ICSID Case No. ARB/00/4), Decision on Jurisdiction, 23 July 2001, para. 46).

65. *Tokios Tokelés v. Ukraine* (ICSID Case No. ARB/02/18), Decision on Jurisdiction (29 April 2004), para. 84 (quoting *Salini Costruttori SpA and Italstrade SpA v. Morocco* (ICSID Case No. ARB/00/4), Decision on Jurisdiction, 23 July 2001, para. 46).

66. *Desert Line*, para. 104.

importance to this explicit requirement in the underlying investment treaty when it observed:

> "Not all BITs contain a requirement that investments subject to treaty protection be 'made' or 'owned' in accordance with the law of the host country. The fact that the Contracting Parties to the Canada-Costa Rica BIT specifically included such a provision is a clear indication of the importance that they attached to the legality of investments made by investors of the other Party and their intention that their laws with respect to investments be strictly followed."[67]

The tribunal's finding in *Anderson v. Costa Rica* might suggest that an investment made in violation of host State law is outside the scope of an investment treaty's protections only if the treaty contains an express "in accordance with law" clause.

As the Paper points out, however, other tribunals have found that investment treaties may contain an inferred or implicit legality requirement.[68] While some of these tribunals' decisions do not elucidate the legal basis for this finding,[69] a closer look at the *Plama* Award's reasoning suggests an uncontroversial application of the rules of treaty interpretation reflected in Art. 31(1) of the Vienna Convention on the Law of Treaties (VCLT).

In *Plama v. Bulgaria*, the applicable investment treaty was the ECT, which, as the tribunal noted, does not contain an "in accordance with law" clause.[70] Nevertheless, the tribunal found that "this does not mean ... that the protections provided by the ECT cover all kinds of investments, including those contrary to domestic or international law".[71] The tribunal found that, as stated in the introductory note to the ECT, "[t]he *fundamental aim of the Energy Charter Treaty is to strengthen the rule of law* on energy

---

67. *Anderson*, para. 53.
68. Paper, pp. 498, 507-508.
69. See *Yaung Chi Oo Trading Pte Ltd v. Government of the Union of Myanmar*, ASEAN I.D. Case No. ARB/01/1, Award, 31 March 2003, para. 58 ("the general rule that for a foreign investment to enjoy treaty protection it must be lawful under the law of the host State"); *Phoenix Action*, para. 101 ("this condition – the conformity of the establishment of the investment with the national laws – is implicit [in the ICSID/BIT system] even when not expressly stated in the relevant BIT"); *Hamester*, paras. 123-124 ("An investment will not be protected if it has been created in violation of national or international principles of good faith; by way of corruption, fraud, or deceitful conduct; or if its creation itself constitutes a misuse of the system of international investment protection under the ICSID Convention. It will also not be protected if it is made in violation of the host State's law (as elaborated, e.g., by the tribunal in *Phoenix*). These are general principles that exist independently of specific language to this effect in the Treaty."); *SAUR International S.A. v. Argentine Republic* (ICSID Case No. ARB/04/4), Decision on Jurisdiction and Liability, 6 June 2012, para. 308 (noting that the requirement of not having committed a serious violation of the host State legal regime is a tacit condition, inherent in every BIT, because it cannot be understood under any circumstances that a State is offering the benefit of protection through investment arbitration when the investor, to obtain that protection, has acted unlawfully.).
70. *Plama* Award, para. 138 ("Unlike a number of Bilateral Investment Treaties, the ECT does not contain a provision requiring the conformity of the Investment with a particular law.").
71. *Plama* Award, para. 138.

567

issues...".[72] The tribunal apparently viewed this aim as the ECT's "object and purpose" in accordance with VCLT Art. 31(1) when it concluded that "the ECT should be interpreted in a manner consistent with the aim of encouraging respect for the rule of law".[73] Accordingly, even absent an express "in accordance with law" provision "the substantive protections of the [Energy Charter Treaty] cannot apply to investments that are made contrary to law".[74]

Similarly, the tribunal in *Hamester v. Ghana* found that there are "general principles that exist independently of specific language to this effect in the Treaty", whereby "[a]n investment will not be protected if it has been created in violation of national or international principles of good faith, by way of corruption, fraud or deceitful conduct; ... It will also not be protected if it is made in violation of the host State's law....".[75] The *Hamester* tribunal's analysis clearly applies the rule of interpretation reflected in VCLT Art. 31(3)(c) whereby "any relevant rules of international law applicable in the relations between the parties" must be taken into account in interpreting a treaty, as part of its context.[76]

Most recently, the tribunal in the three *Yukos* arbitrations, whose jurisdiction was based on the ECT, agreed with this approach:

> "In imposing obligations on States to treat investors in a fair and transparent fashion, investment treaties seek to encourage legal and bona fide investments. An investor who has obtained an investment in the host State only by acting in bad faith or in violation of the laws of the host state, has brought itself within the scope of application of the ECT through wrongful acts. Such an investor should not be allowed to benefit from the Treaty."[77]

---

72. *Plama* Award, para. 139 (emphasis added).
73. *Plama* Award, para. 139.
74. *Plama* Award, para. 139.
75. *Hamester*, paras. 123-124.
76. Under Art. 38(1)(c) of the Statute of the International Court of Justice, "the general principles of law" are a source of international law.
77. *Hulley Enterprises (Cyprus) Limited v. Russian Federation*, PCA Case No. AA 226, Final Award, 18 July 2014, para. 1352; *Yukos Universal Limited (Isle of Man) v. Russian Federation*, PCA Case No. AA 227, Final Award, 18 July 2014, para. 1352; *Veteran Petroleum Limited (Cyprus) v. Russian Federation*, PCA Case No. AA 228, Final Award, 18 July 2014, para. 1352. In the parallel proceedings before the European Court of Human Rights, Judges Bushev and Hajiyev similarly concluded that the European Convention on Human Rights "was not designed to protect property rights and interests which were acquired illegally, irrespective of whether they were later breached by the State's unlawful actions". *OAO Neftyanaya Kompaniya Yukos v. Russia*, ECHR, Application No. 14902/04, Judgment (Just Satisfaction), 31 July 2014, p. 27 (Partly Dissenting Opinion of Judge Bushev, Joined in Part by Judge Hajiyev).

The tribunal, however, expressly refrained from deciding "whether the legality requirement it reads in the ECT operates as a bar to jurisdiction or, as suggested in *Plama*, to deprive claimants of the substantive protections of the ECT".[78]

V. THE CONSEQUENCE OF INVESTMENT ILLEGALITY: ISSUE OF JURISDICTION OR ADMISSIBILITY?

The Paper correctly points out the three potential consequences of a finding of investor wrongdoing: lack of jurisdiction, inadmissibility, or defense on the merits.[79] While questions of jurisdiction and admissibility are similar insofar as both usually are treated as preliminary questions and thus may preclude a tribunal from reaching a merits determination, there exists a fine distinction between the two concepts. Jurisdiction refers to the power of the tribunal to hear the case; if a tribunal lacks jurisdiction, the tribunal cannot act.[80] By contrast, admissibility of the claims relates to whether it is appropriate for the tribunal to hear the case. If the claim is inadmissible, "the tribunal has jurisdiction to hear it, but should decline it on grounds relating to the case itself".[81] Distinguishing between these concepts for purposes of determining whether investment illegality is an issue of jurisdiction or admissibility is important because potentially significant consequences may attach. First, an award declining jurisdiction on the basis of investment illegality may be subject to greater review, on the additional ground that the tribunal exceeded its powers, than an award rejecting a claim as inadmissible.[82] Second, if an investment treaty tribunal dismisses a case for lack of jurisdiction on the basis of investment illegality, it will not have jurisdiction either over any counterclaims raised by the State, while it could retain such jurisdiction if it treated the investment illegality as an issue of admissibility.[83]

---

78. *Hulley Enterprises (Cyprus) Limited v. Russian Federation*, PCA Case No. AA 226, Final Award, 18 July 2014, para. 1353; *Yukos Universal Limited (Isle of Man) v. Russian Federation*, PCA Case No. AA 227, Final Award, 18 July 2014, para. 1353; *Veteran Petroleum Limited (Cyprus) v. Russian Federation*, PCA Case No. AA 228, Final Award, 18 July 2014, para. 1353.

79. Paper, pp. 523-524.

80. *Waste Mgmt Inc. v. United Mexican States* (ICSID Case No. ARB(AF)/00/3), Dissenting Opinion of Keith Highet, 8 May 2000, paras. 57-58.

81. *Ibid.*, n. 45.

82. See ICSID Secretariat, "Background Paper on Annulment for the Administrative Council of ICSID", 27 ICSID Rev—Foreign Inv. L.J. (10 August 2012) p. 443 at p. 486, para. 88 ("*Ad hoc* Committees have held that there may be an excess of powers if a Tribunal incorrectly concludes that it has jurisdiction when in fact jurisdiction is lacking, or when the Tribunal exceeds the scope of its jurisdiction. It has been recognized, in the inverse case, that a Tribunal's rejection of jurisdiction when jurisdiction exists also amounts to an excess of powers.").

83. See *Metal-Tech*, para. 413 ("As a consequence of its having no jurisdiction over the claims, this Tribunal has no jurisdiction over the counterclaims."); *Spyridon Roussalis v. Romania* (ICSID Case No. ARB/06/1), Award, 7 December 2011, para. 866 ("The investor's consent to the BIT's arbitration clause can only exist in relation to counterclaims if such counterclaims come within the consent of the host State as expressed in the BIT.").

Tribunals have treated the issue of investment illegality as either a jurisdictional issue or an issue of admissibility of the claimant's claims, as the Paper explains.[84] In *Inceysa v. El Salvador*, for example, the tribunal found that the claimant had "acted improperly in order to be awarded the bid that made its investment possible", in violation of Salvadoran law.[85] The tribunal, therefore, concluded that "because Inceysa's investment was made in a manner that was clearly illegal, it is not included within the scope of consent expressed by the … BIT and, consequently, the disputes arising from it are not subject to the jurisdiction of the Centre".[86] The tribunal in *Plama v. Bulgaria*, on the other hand, declined to treat as jurisdictional the respondent-State's allegation that the claimant had acquired its investment through fraudulent misrepresentation.[87] Instead, the *Plama* tribunal addressed this issue during the merits phase as one of admissibility of the claimant's claims. On the merits, the tribunal found that the claimant's "investment was obtained by deceitful conduct that is in violation of Bulgarian law" and, for this reason, the tribunal "cannot lend its support to claimant's request and cannot, therefore, grant the substantive protections of the ECT".[88]

In light of these differing treatments of investment illegality, the Paper suggests that tribunals attach jurisdictional consequences to investment illegality only where the following three factors are present. First, the applicable investment treaty must contain an express legality requirement. In the absence of such an express requirement, investment illegality may serve only as a basis for inadmissibility or a defense on the merits.[89] Second, the alleged wrongdoing must have occurred at the time of the establishment of the investment.[90] And third, the illegality must result from a breach of host State laws or fundamental principles of host State law that are related to the admission of the investment.[91]

These three requirements go too far and find limited justification in the evolving law or policy. The explicit legality requirement is not well established in the law; indeed, tribunals have dismissed claims on the basis of illegality even in the absence of an explicit legality requirement. The requirement that the illegality occur at the time of establishment of an investment overlooks the serious implications of illegality that develops after the establishment in the implementation and/or operation of the investment. This must be assessed in the context of the circumstances of each case. The suggested requirement that the breach of law be related to the establishment of an investment is similarly misplaced. Such a rigid categorization to establish illegality carries with it the risk that it may replace or get in the way of a proper interpretation of the applicable investment treaty provisions using the rule of interpretation reflected in VCLT

---

84. Paper, pp. 523, 525.

85. *Inceysa*, para. 243.

86. *Inceysa*, para. 257.

87. *Plama* Award, para. 97; *Plama Consortium Limited v. Republic of Bulgaria* (ICSID Case No. ARB/03/24), Decision on Jurisdiction, 8 February 2005, paras. 126-130, 228-230.

88. *Plama* Award, paras. 143, 146.

89. Paper, p. 508.

90. Paper, p. 502.

91. Paper, pp. 501-504.

Art. 31. As the Paper notes, most investment treaties contain broadly similar provisions,[92] but there are subtle differences in their wording. Moreover, each treaty may have its own distinct context and object and purpose, which is equally relevant to a proper interpretation under VCLT Art. 31.[93] Additionally, as the *Hamester v. Ghana* tribunal suggested, the "relevant rules of international law applicable in the relations between the parties' that must be taken into account in interpreting a treaty under VCLT Art. 31(3)(c) may include a legality requirement.[94] Such rules, however, may differ as between different States. Ignoring these differences in the wording, context, and object and purpose of the applicable treaty may expose the resulting award to annulment or set-aside, or render it unenforceable.

For example, as noted above, the *Plama* tribunal found the ECT to contain an implicit legality requirement based on an interpretation that took into account the ECT's object and purpose. Additionally, the absence in the ECT of an express legality requirement was not the reason for which the *Plama* tribunal declined to treat the claimant's misrepresentation in making its alleged investment as a jurisdictional issue. Rather, as stated in the Decision on Jurisdiction, the *Plama* tribunal joined the misrepresentation issue to the merits given the seriousness of the allegations.[95] The tribunal thus allowed the parties to more fully develop the factual record, including through further document exchanges, and then revisited the issue at the merits stage.[96]

Finally, in the wake of various States withdrawing from investment treaties or expressing reluctance to agree to investor-State arbitration, it should be recognized that States have a significant and legitimate interest in the legality of investments made and

---

92. Paper, p. 499.

93. As explained by the International Law Commission in its commentary on the draft article that later became Art. 31 of the VCLT, "application of the means of interpretation in the article would be a single combined operation. All the various elements, as they were present in any given case, would be thrown into the crucible, and their interaction would give the legally relevant interpretation." Reports of the International Law Commission on the second part of its 17th session and on its 18th session, 2 Y.B. Int'l L. Comm'n (1966) p. 169, at pp. 219-220, para. 8, UN Doc A/CN.4/SER.A/1966/Add.1; see also *Aguas del Tunari, SA v. Republic of Bolivia* (ICSID Case No. ARB/02/03), Decision on Jurisdiction, 21 October 2005, para. 91 ("Interpretation under Article 31 of the Vienna Convention is a process of progressive encirclement where the interpreter starts under the general rules with (1) the ordinary meaning of the terms of the treaty, (2) in their context and (3) in light of the treaty's object and purpose, and by cycling through this three step inquiry iteratively closes in upon the proper interpretation. In approaching this task, it is critical to observe two things about the general rule of interpretation found in the Vienna Convention. First, the Vienna Convention does not privilege any one of these three aspects of the interpretation method. The meaning of a word or phrase is not solely a matter of dictionaries and linguistics. As Schwarzenberger observed, the word 'meaning' itself has at least sixteen dictionary meanings. Rather, the interpretation of a word or phrase involves a complex task of considering the ordinary meaning of a word or phrase in the context in which that word or phrase is found and in light of the object and purpose of the document.").

94. *Hamester*, paras. 123-124.

95. *Plama* Award, para. 97; *Plama Consortium Limited v. Republic of Bulgaria* (ICSID Case No. ARB/03/24), Decision on Jurisdiction, 8 February 2005, paras. 229-230.

96. For the sake of full disclosure, Carolyn Lamm and Eckhard Hellbeck served as counsel to the respondent in the *Plama v. Bulgaria* ICSID arbitration.

operated in their territory. That interest exists regardless of whether a legality requirement is expressly stated in a treaty or implied, and it extends to both the making of the investment and its performance or implementation. In this regard, tribunals have the tools they need to protect the rule of law, by finding that an unlawful investment results in either a lack of jurisdiction over a related claim or its inadmissibility, or in treating the illegality as a defense on the merits.

VI.   CONCLUSION: MYTHS OR REALITY?

The jurisprudence of investment treaty tribunals evidences many variations in the approach, manner, and circumstances in which the issue of investment illegality is framed. Tribunals have looked to international public policy, transnational public policy, host State law, the ICSID Convention, investment treaties, and other rules of international law to reject claims relating to investments borne of – or implemented by – fraudulent or otherwise unlawful acts. As the Paper notes, where there is sufficient proof that investors have engaged in such unlawful acts, the consequences can be severe: tribunals may dismiss their claims for lack of jurisdiction, as inadmissible, or on the merits.[97] Yet, there remains some debate about the manner in which fraud is pled and established. In this regard, the ICCA panel discussed whether the following five propositions were myths or realities of pleading and establishing fraud (or other comparable forms of investor abuse) in investor-State arbitration. As the discussion revealed, none of these propositions seems to describe accurately the reality of investment treaty arbitration.[98]

1.   First Proposition: All Investor Wrongdoing Is Not the Same, or Is It?

While it is clear that all forms of investor wrongdoing are not the same, the effects of such wrongdoing are similar. Excluding *de minimis* misrepresentations (e.g., typographical errors in documents submitted by the investor and other innocent mistakes), all forms of misrepresentation by investors have the *same effect* on the host State by depriving it of anticipated investments and imposing the burdens of illegality on the public.

2.   Second Proposition: Maxim for All Respondents: Throw Mud Because It May Stick, and if It Does Not, What Does It Matter?

This too is a myth and not a maxim to be followed. Any claim of investment illegality must be credible and supported by evidence. A party that merely "throws mud" without establishing the credibility of its assertions may lose more than it gains.

---

97. Paper, pp. 523-524.
98. See Elizabeth KARANJA, "Panel Session Summary: Precision Stream A4: Proof of Fraud and Corruption in Treaty Arbitration", this volume, pp. 439-450 (providing a more detailed summary of the panel discussion).

3.   Third Proposition: Does Anyone Really Agree on What Fraudulent Misrepresentation Means?

Tribunals do agree that fraudulent misrepresentation is defined by referencing either international law or the law of the host State, depending on whether an investment treaty contains an "in accordance with law" provision.[99] The definition of fraudulent misrepresentation thus depends on the applicable law in each specific case. Furthermore – and as indicated in the Paper – both national legal systems and international law define the term similarly: knowing misrepresentation or concealment of a material fact with a view to deceiving another to the other's disadvantage.[100] Considering the agreement regarding the approach to defining fraudulent misrepresentation and its generally accepted definition, it cannot be argued that there is no agreement regarding the definition of fraudulent misrepresentation.

4.   Fourth Proposition: Graver Charges of Investment Illegality Require Greater Confidence in the Underlying Evidence

This is a myth. Strict notions of standards and burden of proof are not relevant in treaty-based arbitration, unless required by a lex specialis. Imposing a higher standard or burden of proof would not only undermine the tribunal's discretion to assess evidence, but also disregard the realities of evidence-gathering to establish fraudulent misrepresentation.

5.   Fifth Proposition: Tribunals and Counsel Are Not Properly Equipped to Address the Issue of Corruption, Both as Regards Expertise and the Tools at Their Disposal

This also is a myth. Several investor-State decisions prove otherwise. The tribunals in *Metal-Tech v. Uzbekistan* and *Cementownia v. Turkey*, for example, demonstrated that they had, and knew to use effectively, the authority to call on the parties to produce additional evidence that was needed to establish the relevant facts.[101]

---

99. See, e.g., *Plama* Award, paras. 135, 138-145; *Desert Line*, para. 104; *Phoenix Action*, paras. 103, 134.

100. Paper, p. 469.

101. See *Metal-Tech*, paras. 240-266; *Cementownia "Nowa Huta" S.A. v. Republic of Turkey* (ICSID Case No. ARB(AF)/06/2), Award, 17 September 2009, paras. 118-149.

B. Justice Stream

B. Justice Stream

1. Who Are the Arbitrators?

"To Diversify or Not to Diversify"?
Report on the Session Who Are the Arbitrators?

*Ricardo Dalmaso Marques**

I.   INTRODUCTION

Is it accurate that international arbitrators are mostly male, senior, Western, and drawn from a limited pool of practitioners? If so, are there legitimate reasons for this non-inclusive selection of international arbitrators? Or is this lack of diversity rather a "syndrome" that needs to be cured to ensure the legitimacy of international arbitration? Further, should we just "sit and wait" for diversity to improve, for instance in respect of nationality/region, gender and age of the arbitrators?

These are some of the intriguing questions that were brought up during the "Justice Stream B-1 Session: Who Are the Arbitrators?" at the 2014 ICCA Congress in Miami. The panel – composed of a particularly diverse and provocative group of international arbitration practitioners – was decisive and explicit in questioning the way in which most arbitrators, arbitral institutions, counsel and parties view the selection of the "best" arbitrator, particularly as to nationality/region, gender and age. Notably, the roles to be played (if any) by each of these actors in promoting diversity in international arbitration were called into question and were the subject of some heated debates.

Remarkably, the four propositions of the panel – transcribed and briefly commented on below – were precise in their reflection of the main concerns and uncertainties the panelists and the audience seemed to sustain on this delicate subject. None of the conclusions and prospective initiatives arising from the propositions, however, found unanimous support. As concisely outlined below, although the benefits of a diverse tribunal seem uncontroversial, the following steps to be adopted towards achieving diversity in international arbitration may still need further debate.

---

*   Panel Rapporteur; Associate at Pinheiro Neto Advogados (São Paulo, Brazil); International Visiting Associate at Skadden Arps Slate Meagher & Flom (New York, United States).

II.   PROPOSITION 1: "THERE IS A LIMITED POOL OF ARBITRATORS WHO SHARE A COMMON PROFILE."

As a starting point, this "restrictive" scenario seems to have been acknowledged by the panelists and the audience as an incontestable reality: women,[1] young practitioners,[2] and some nationalities and regions[3] are underrepresented in the international arbitrators' spectrum. This is the premise that guided all the following discussions and propositions. As the leading speaker, Professor Christophe Seraglini, asserted, "[T]his first 'myth' related to the 'arbitrator's common profile' seems factually and historically accurate, even if in a slowly changing process."[4]

On the one hand, it is virtually undisputed that the selection of arbitrators mostly results in the appointment of a limited group of individuals sharing the same characteristics as to nationality/region, gender and age.[5] Numbers, such as (i) the 65.70% of European arbitrators appointed in International Chamber of Commerce (ICC) arbitrations in 2012 (as opposed to 19.60% from the Americas; 12.80% from the Asia/Pacific region; and 1.90% from Africa);[6] (ii) the 47% of Western European

---

1. See, for instance, Annalise NELSON, "The Representation of Women in Arbitration – One Problem, Two Issues", Kluwer Arb. Blog (2 Nov. 2012); Irene TEN CATE, "Binders Full of Women ... Arbitrators?", INTLAWGRRLS (2 Nov. 2011, 4:30AM); Michael D. GOLDHABER, "Madame La Presidente – A Woman Who Sits as President of a Major Arbitral Tribunal Is a Rare Creature. Why?" Transnational Dispute Management (July 2004) at p. 1, available at <www.arbitralwomen.org/files/publication/00072217081344.pdf>. In fact, one of the members of the audience emphasized that similar gender questions have been raised in other fora, for instance concerning the involvement of women as practitioners and academics in international law in general, and as officers and directors of listed companies. The pertinent question, apparently, would be whether women are being denied access to these areas and the legal or managerial professions in general.
2. Panelist Jacomijn van Haersolte-van Hof indicated that age is rarely a subject of statistics, but it is also a factor that must be taken into consideration when diversity is the goal. Jacomijn VAN HAERSOLTE-VAN HOF, "Diversity in Diversity", Sect. III, "Why is Diversity (Potentially) Relevant?" this volume, pp. 641-643. Also, the leading speaker of the panel, Professor Christophe Seraglini, made reference to scholarly writings that confirm that "[r]egularly appointed arbitrators are most of the time above fifty". Christophe SERAGLINI, "Who Are the Arbitrators? Myths, Reality and Challenges", this volume, p. 591.
3. See fns. 6-8 infra.
4. Christophe SERAGLINI, supra fn. 2, this volume, p. 593.
5. As described by Jacomijn van Haersolte-van Hof, diversity is characterized by the composition of differing and varying elements, particularly ethnicity, gender, age, sexual orientation, religion and disability; but perhaps the first three are the key diversity elements in the context of international arbitration. Dr. van Haersolte-van Hof emphasized, notwithstanding, that there is no such thing as an exhaustive list of diversity factors, and that diverse legal systems, legal traditions, languages, professions (lawyers and non-lawyers), and "functions" (academics, practitioners, ex-judges, etc.) are elements that also have a strong influence in the international arbitration system. Jacomijn VAN HAERSOLTE-VAN HOF, supra fn. 2: Sect. II, "What Is Diversity – What Kind of Diversity Matters?" this volume, pp. 639-641.
6. "2012 ICC Statistical Report", ICC Int'l Court of Arb. Bulletin (2013) at p. 24 (report providing a statistical overview of ICC arbitration and ADR in 2012), available at <www.iccwbo.org/Products-and-Services/Arbitration-and-ADR/Articles/2013/New-release-from-the-ICC-International-Court-of-Arbitration-Bulletin/>. The percentage in 2011 was a little

arbitrators historically appointed in International Centre for Settlement of Investment Disputes (ICSID) arbitrations (as opposed to 21% from North America, 11% from South America, and 6% from Africa);[7] and (iii) the 9.60% of female arbitrators appointed in London Court of International Arbitration (LCIA) proceedings in 2012,[8] denote that this first proposition is indeed a reality. The numbers and comparisons depicted by the panelists, both orally and in their papers, are absolute in confirming this fact.[9] Furthermore, prominent researchers have regularly provided data that demonstrate that "diversity" – although improving – most likely can't be considered as a reality in the context of international arbitral tribunals nowadays.[10]

III. PROPOSITION 2: "THIS LIMITED POOL OF ARBITRATORS MIGHT JEOPARDIZE LEGITIMACY OF INTERNATIONAL ARBITRATION."

The second question that arose was whether this lack of diversity would impact or jeopardize the legitimacy of international arbitration, and, if so, whether a pro-inclusiveness attitude should be adopted by the arbitration community. Doubts as to the impartiality, independence and availability of the recurrent arbitrators were of particular interest when the legitimacy of international arbitration was the discussed point of balance.[11] As the question was posed by Professor Seraglini, "Does a typical profile of the arbitrators who belong to an elite serve and preserve international justice?"[12]

higher, 66%. See "2011 ICC Statistical Report", ICC Int'l Court of Arb. Bulletin (2012) at p. 23 (report providing detailed statistics on aspects of ICC dispute resolution proceedings in 2011), available at <www.iccwbo.org/Products-and-Services/Arbitration-and-ADR/Articles/2012/New-release-from-the-ICC-International-Court-of-Arbitration-Bulletin/>.

7. "The ICSID Caseload – Statistics", (Issue 2013-2), ICSID – International Centre for Settlement of Investment Disputes, 2013, available at <https://icsid.worldbank.org/ICSID/FrontServlet?requestType=ICSIDDocRH&actionVal=CaseLoadStatistics> (updating the profile of the ICSID caseload, historically and for the Centre's fiscal year of 2013; based on cases registered or administered by ICSID as of 30 June 2013) (last visited on 13 May 2014).

8. Sarah LANCASTER, LCIA Registrar, LCIA Registrar's Report 2012, available at <www.lcia.org//LCIA/Casework_Report.aspx> (reporting the LCIA casework in 2012, often in comparison with 2011) (last visited on 13 May 2014).

9. Jacomijn van Haersolte-van Hof contended, however, that absolute data is almost impossible to find – with exception made to the numbers disclosed by the arbitral institutions – and to interpret, particularly as to the age and gender of the arbitrators. Jacomijn VAN HAERSOLTE-VAN HOF, supra fn. 2, Sect. IV.1: "The Status Quo", this volume, pp. 643.

10. See, e.g., Susan D. FRANCK, "Empirically Evaluating Claims About Investment Treaty Arbitration", 86 N.C. L. Rev. (2007) at p. 1 (reporting that, before 2007, 75% of the arbitrators sitting in investment cases came from OECD member countries, even though approximately 70% of the disputes were against non-OECD governments). See also Lucy GREENWOOD, "Unblocking the Pipeline: Achieving Greater Gender Diversity on International Arbitration Tribunals", in International Law News (Spring 2013) at p. 42 (mentioning sources that indicate that only 6% of appointments to international arbitration tribunals are female arbitrators).

11. See Darius J. KHAMBATA, "Tensions Between Party Autonomy and Diversity", Sect. X, this volume, pp. 627-632.

12. Christophe SERAGLINI, Sect. II, pp. 592-593.

Professor Seraglini himself pointed out that experience is and should remain a crucial element of the threshold in the selection of arbitrators. An experienced and knowledgeable arbitrator would most likely be better prepared to conduct the proceedings appropriately and to render a satisfactory arbitral award (as to its enforceability and qualitative content).[13] Excellence is and should remain the goal, both in terms of arbitrators' experience and skills, with the aim of guaranteeing a high quality of justice. However, a number of flaws may arise from a common and recurrent profile, such as an alleged uniformity – perhaps unwanted by the parties – in how to conduct the proceedings or even in how to interpret the merits of the case.[14]

As a criticism on how the lack of diversity could impact the acceptability of international arbitration, panelist Jacomijn van Haersolte-van Hof emphatically questioned the delegates as to whether the "insurance policy" desired by most parties when appointing a male, senior and Western arbitrator would indeed be effective as expected. Dr. van Haersolte-van Hof challenged the delegates to consider whether the parties would truly be "playing on the safe side" by relying on a single arbitrator's pattern of decision-making. Lack of availability of the most trustworthy arbitrators, non-suitability of some famous arbitrators for some disputes and increasing cases of conflicted arbitrators were some of the situations mentioned that could reveal that not always focusing on the "arbitrators' common profile" would be the answer to ensure the quality of the arbitration.[15] Under this perspective, legitimacy could be impaired with regard to the excellence and precision of the arbitral proceedings and the award. The discussions lead to the apparent conclusion that it may be understandable that parties may give preference to Western males as arbitrators, but that this solution may do no good for international arbitration, and could even be proven ineffective in practice.[16]

From another angle, a consensus seems to have been reached that diversity is desirable also to enhance the quality of the arbitrators' deliberations. A diverse tribunal is more likely to lead to adequately conducted and satisfactorily decided arbitration proceedings in comparison to a tribunal that is limited to a few nationalities, individualities and qualities. The benefits of a diverse tribunal were emphasized and recognized by

---

13. Christophe SERAGLINI, supra fn. 2, Sect. II.2.a-b, this volume, pp. 593-595.

14. As highlighted by Professor Seraglini, "some have argued that the decisions in arbitral awards are likely to reflect [a] business-oriented profile". Christophe SERAGLINI, supra fn. 2, Sect. III.1.b, this volume, pp. 595-597. An interesting concern expressed by the audience in this regard consisted of the fact that although diversity is apparently improving with regard to different nationalities and cultures of the arbitrators, Western firms are still responsible for the legal education of the most incoming lawyers. Notwithstanding, irrespectively of where the arbitrator was educated and where they practiced, it has been expressed by most panelists that it is still diversity if the arbitrator comes from a diverse country or region.

15. Jacomijn VAN HAERSOLTE-VAN HOF, supra fn. 2: Sect. III, "Why is Diversity (Potentially) Relevant?". Jacomijn van Haersolte-van Hof questioned "who actually does the work in an arbitration" when a recurrent practitioner sits as arbitrator: "the chair, the wing-woman, the staff of the particular institution, the (visible) tribunal secretary, and/or the chair's associate working behind the scene"? Ibid. p. 642.

16. In this same sense, Professor Christophe Seraglini mentioned biased arbitrators, a potential "split the baby" attitude, and a "copy-pasted and inefficient justice" as some of the unfavorable consequences of the existence of an elite group of arbitrators. Christophe SERAGLINI, supra fn. 2, Sect. III.2.a.i-ii, this volume, pp. 598-599.

practically all panelists and by the interveners in the audience, particularly standing out in panelist Darius J. Khambata's quotes from Benjamin Franklin: "If everyone is thinking alike, then no one is thinking,"[17] and Justice Benjamin N. Cardozo: "The eccentricities of judges balance one another."[18] From this viewpoint, the alleged harm to legitimacy would be a result of the limitation of international arbitration to tribunals whose legal education, experience and thus prospective reasoning, would be restricted to one or two cultures or traditions.[19] The main legitimacy-oriented questions that arose in this regard were whether a non-diverse tribunal, limited to a small group of "birds of a feather", would truly be "international",[20] and even neutral or impartial.[21]

Moreover, V.V. Veeder recalled in his paper, making reference to the European legal framework and the noteworthy case *Jivraj v. Hashwani*[22] before the UK courts and the European Commission, that party autonomy in the appointment of arbitrators is not unlimited and, therefore, is not a reasonable answer for the current lack of diversity.[23] Diversity in the selection of arbitrators, he contended, is an issue that triggers limitations concerning discrimination not only on grounds of religion but also of nationality.[24] Accordingly, all arbitration practitioners must consider and address this peculiarity when deciding whom to select or appoint.[25]

IV.   PROPOSITION 3: "THERE IS A NEED FOR GREATER DIVERSITY."

On the other side of the coin, although recognized by most as a desirable objective in the legal profession as a whole, diversity appeared not to be unanimously accepted as a priority for the upcoming years. Darius J. Khambata questioned – and later answered affirmatively – "Has the time come for importing diversity into the appointment of

---

17. *Ibid.*, p. 622.
18. *Ibid.*, p. 598.
19. Darius J. Khambata mentioned during his presentation, for instance, that parties to an international arbitration have the "right to a plurality of ideas among the arbitrators".
20. Darius J. Khambata made the point that "[t]he real elephant in the room" is not neutrality of nationality but rather "the repeated appointment by arbitral institutions of arbitrators of particular nationalities or shared cultural backgrounds". *Ibid.*, p. 624.
21. Professor Christophe Seraglini contended that the non-inclusiveness in international arbitration "can cast a shadow on [the] arbitrators' impartial state of mind" and that repeated appointments may lead an arbitrator "to preconceive the decision to adopt and naturally tend to issue similar decisions in similar cases". *Ibid.*, Sect. III.3.b, pp. 603-605. Nevertheless, he made the disclaimer that some good can also come from this "lack of diversity", such as the need of the most recurrent arbitrators to keep up the quality of the work in their aim to be reappointed. Accordingly, Professor Seraglini recalled, "the fact that the typical arbitrator is selected from a limited pool is an incentive for this arbitrator to act professionally, diligently, independently and impartially, since it is essential for becoming and remaining member of this limited pool". *Ibid.*, p. 601.
22. *Jivraj v. Hashwani* [2011] UKSC 40.
23. V.V. VEEDER, Justice Stream: "Who Are the Arbitrators?", Sect. III, "*Jivraj v. Hashwani*", this volume, pp. 656-660.
24. *Ibid.*
25. *Ibid.*

arbitrators as one of the objectives of selection?"[26] Although the panelists voted for a sound "yes", the audience did not seem as enthusiastic.

While most of the panelists seemed to foster a proactive attitude towards diversity, the reaction of the audience indicated that, for some, a "sit and wait" approach still could be the best answer, either because (i) the need for diversity cannot override party autonomy, (ii) diversity would be a value that would come with time (which is an argument usually based on the understanding that diversity is improving steadily and satisfactorily), or (iii) there would be a good reason for the parties to rely on a particular arbitrator's standard.[27]

If we only look at numbers, it may be true that diversity has been improving in regard to nationality. The ICC, for instance, revealed that, in 2012, increases of 19% and 37.5% were registered in the number of confirmations and appointments of arbitrators from Latin America and South/East Asia, respectively.[28] Apparently, nevertheless, the same cannot be said with regard to gender, if we consider that the reality described by Michael D. Goldhaber approximately ten years ago does not seem to have been altered substantially.[29] A percentage of 6%-10% is not exceeded in any recent research conducted on the representation of women in the position of arbitrator.[30] This does not seem to be a reasonable achievement, mainly if compared to the current numbers of

---

26. Darius J. Khambata, supra fn. 11, this volume, p. 613.

27. Conclusions based on the reactions from the audience to the ideas expressed by the panelists.

28. "2012 ICC Statistical Report", supra fn. 6 (the same report indicated, on the other hand, that as in previous years, British, French, German, Swiss and US arbitrators remained the most frequently chosen worldwide, accounting for 48% of all confirmations and appointments).

29. See Michael D. GOLDHABER, supra fn. 1 (reporting that "[a]s both advocates and arbitrators, women are vastly underrepresented by every measure in this decentralized world. Consider the field's most prestigious advisory boards, appointment panels, and Who's Who guides: Women comprise 11 percent of the International Chamber of Commerce International Court of Arbitration, 5 percent of the International Council of Commercial Arbitration, 5 percent of the ICSID Panel of Conciliators and Arbitrators, 0 percent of the London Maritime Arbitrators Association, and 4 percent of those listed in the Guide to the World's Leading Experts in Commercial Arbitration").

30. Among many others, see Annalise NELSON, supra fn. 1; Irene TEN CATE, supra fn. 1; Lucy GREENWOOD and MARK BAKER, "Getting a Better Balance on International Arbitration Tribunals", Arbitration International – The Journal of the London Court of International Arbitration (2012) at p. 28, available at <www.cpradr.org/Resources/ALLCPRArticles/tabid/ 265/ID/772/Getting-a-Better-Balance-on-International-Arbitration-Tribunals-Jrnl-of-London-Ct-of-Intl-Arb.aspx>; Craig TEVENDALE, et al., "*Jivraj* – It's Back and This Time It's at the European Commission", Kluwer Arb. Blog (28 Sept. 2012), available at <http://kluwer arbitrationblog.com/blog/2012/09/28/jivraj-%E2%80%93-its-back-and-this-time-its-at-the-european-commission/>; Gus VAN HARTEN, "The (Lack of) Women Arbitrators in Investment Treaty Arbitration", Columbia FDI Perspectives, Perspectives on Topical Foreign Direct Investment Issues, Vale Columbia Center on Sustainable International Investment, No. 59 (6 Feb. 2012); Lisa Bench NIEUWVELD, "Women in Arbitration: Lots of Talk, Any Changes?" Kluwer Arb. Blog (22 Nov. 2011), available at <www.vcc.columbia.edu/content/lack-women-arbitrators-investment-treaty-arbitration>; and Susan D. FRANCK, supra fn. 10.

female law students;[31] new, incoming lawyers; and even judges.[32] According to V.V. Veeder, a true waste of the "enormous human resources available to arbitration" is occurring.[33]

The former International Court of Justice Judge Stephen M. Schwebel and the Singaporean Chief-Justice Sundaresh Menon, at ICCA's opening and closing keynotes, respectively, acknowledged that "while many arbitrators are from the West, there is a 'distinct and welcome trend towards diversity'",[34] and that there now would be a "swelling number of international arbitration practitioners from all over the world".[35] It is true that more people have been "joining the game", but is it enough? As a matter of fact, as pointed out by the Session Chair, Adriana Braghetta, it is very rare to see Asian, African or Latin American chairs in cases that do not involve parties from their respective regions.

Besides, as Jacomijn van Haersolte-van Hof stressed, "Diverse diversity is a win-win model; diversity is not only desirable as a (moral) goal per se, but results in better results: doing well by doing good!"[36] Darius J. Khambata was precise when stating that a lack of diversity must be viewed as a "largely unconscious prejudice based on stereotyped and misconceived notions of … incapability…"; it is greatly misconceived to think that proficiency has a regional background, for instance.[37] On the contrary, "[t]he perspective of a diversified tribunal is likely to be more nuanced and fairer", he contended.[38] This was also the opinion of V.V. Veeder in his paper, for whom international commercial arbitration "does not reflect the broad diversity readily available to the arbitral community" and "the collective attention of many in that community has still not succeeded in removing the unfairness, and sheer waste of discrimination".[39]

In any case, if the benefits of a diverse arbitral tribunal were obvious and practically unanimously accepted among the panel and the audience, the steps through which the arbitral community would get there were apparently not the object of a similar agreement.

---

31. See Jacomijn VAN HAERSOLTE-VAN HOF, supra fn. 2, Sect. IV.3, "Where Does This Take Us?", this volume, pp. 647-649.

32. See *ibid.*, Sect. IV.2, "Diversity and the Judiciary", this volume, pp. 646-647.

33. *Ibid.*, "Conclusion", this volume, pp. 649-651.

34. See Kyriaki KARADELIS, "Schwebel Opens ICCA Miami with Defence of BITs", Global Arb. Review (7 April 2014) available at <http://globalarbitrationreview.com/news/article/32554/schwebel-opens-icca-miami-defence-bits/> (last visited on 13 May 2014).

35. See Kyriaki KARADELIS, "Arbitration Gets Its Report Card", Global Arbitration Review (8 April 2014), available at <http://globalarbitrationreview.com/news/article/32630/arbitration-gets-its-report-card/>.

36. Jacomijn VAN HAERSOLTE-VAN HOF, supra fn. 2, Sect. IV.3, "Where Does This Take Us?", this volume, p. 649.

37. Darius J. KHAMBATA, supra fn. 11, this volume, p. 632-633.

38. *Ibid.*, p. 615.

39. V.V. VEEDER, "Who Are the Arbitrators?", this volume, p. 653.

V.   PROPOSITION 4: "A PLEDGE SHOULD BE TAKEN BY RESPONSIBLE USERS."

During probably the hottest topic of the panel, panelists and the audience debated whether arbitral institutions, arbitrators and arbitration practitioners in general should take a stand and promote diversity through concrete initiatives. Panelists focused on the measures that could be taken by all arbitration players, such as clients, law firms, institutions and even conference organizers and prospective panelists at specialized events.[40]

Transparency, awareness and inclusiveness seemed to be the key recommended foundations for the next steps to be taken. Accordingly, most "hands-on" suggestions seemed to be for: (i) the parties and their counsel to stop relying solely on arbitrators that are members of the limited pool, and to accept and analyze thoroughly the appointment of less frequently used arbitrators; (ii) the institutions, when responsible for the appointment, to aim for diversity, and to publish awards and data to demonstrate that this initiative has been observed; (iii) the arbitrators to refuse to accept too many cases, especially when doubts as to their impartiality or independence arise or when the quality of work may decline; and (iv) the arbitration community to consider the publication of guidelines concerning the selection of arbitrators and to take a harsh stance to assure that all players have diversity as a priority.[41]

Some attendees, however, seemed to disagree with the panelists' ideas that proactive measures should be taken by arbitration practitioners. One of the particular criticisms made by a few members of the audience was that a "conspiracy" or a "mafia" within the pool of arbitrators to willfully obstruct diversity does not exist. On the contrary, according to them, diversity should be treated as matter of evolution and should be encouraged, as long as excellence is considered the key point. "Reappointment occurs because the arbitrators are good", highlighted Adriana Braghetta during the heated debates that took place. "Impatience could not be a reason for potential changes" and "we should not fool ourselves", affirmed a member of the audience,[42] who also emphasized that any pledge would be likely to fail due to the counsel's and parties' comprehensible intention to always name the "best arbitrators", notwithstanding their nationality, gender or age.

The main question that arose, therefore, was whether there is anything the arbitral institutions, arbitrators, counsel and arbitration practitioners should do – or should have already been doing – to improve diversity in international arbitration. Should we just accept that diversity is improving steadily and that it will come with time? Darius J. Khambata recurrently reminded us that any and all initiatives should not come at the point of "stretching party autonomy to [the] breaking point".[43]

---

40. See Jacomijn VAN HAERSOLTE-VAN HOF, supra fn. 2, Sect. IV.4: "Conclusion: A Pledge?!", this volume, pp. 649-651 (among others, recommending that conference organizers insist on inclusive panels, and that male speakers refuse to participate in conferences where there is a low female representation).
41. See Christophe SERAGLINI, supra fn. 2, pp. 605-609, and Jacomijn VAN HAERSOLTE-VAN HOF, supra fn. 2, Sect. IV.4: "Conclusion: A Pledge?!", this volume, pp. 649-651.
42. Conclusions based on the reactions from the audience to the ideas expressed by the panelists.
43. Darius J. KHAMBATA, supra fn. 11, this volume, p. 622.

In the end, a true and voluntary pledge among the arbitration practitioners was proposed by Adriana Braghetta and by some of the panelists,[44] but apparently it did not achieve the expected consensus. Positively, however, some fundamental conclusions of the panelists and most of the attendees can perhaps be interpreted as the key findings and contribution of the panel:

(i) arbitral institutions can certainly play an important role in promoting diversity as a long-term objective, by balancing diversity with experience and proficiency in the selection of arbitrators;[45]
(ii) parties also have a role to play and are already requesting from their counsel new alternatives to the well-known – but excessively busy – arbitrators; however, one should not expect a bold pro-diversity attitude from the parties, as they are merely interested in their specific case (i.e., they have a short-term objective in mind);
(iii) more experienced arbitrators can and should share their knowledge with the younger generations to make sure "the ball is kept rolling" properly;
(iv) the adoption of compulsory measures to promote diversity is both unviable and unrealistic, considering that the balance with party autonomy is of the essence;[46] nevertheless, conducting profound studies and audits and collecting periodical data, as well as undertakings[47] and guidelines on diversity in international arbitration, are feasible and desirable propositions; and
(v) diversity consists of an issue, a concept and a concern that must be recurrently discussed in the most diverse fora in the forthcoming years, irrespective of how unpleasant this subject may be for some.

As Professor Seraglini pointed out, most criticisms are indeed unjust; however, because they exist, being right or wrong, the only admissible reaction to their existence is to do something about them. "Appearance and trust matter in our field," he affirmed.[48]

---

44. See Jacomijn VAN HAERSOLTE-VAN HOF, supra fn. 2, Sect. IV.4: "Conclusion: A Pledge?!" this volume, pp. 649-651 (proposing a call to action similar to the 2004 "Call to Action – Diversity in the Legal Profession", put into action by Sara Lee General Counsel Roderick Palmore and signed by a large number of chief legal officers to evidence the commitment of the signatory corporations to diversity in the legal profession).

45. As pointed out by Jacomijn van Haersolte-van Hof, the arbitral institutions are in a better position to provide transparency, and they are the ones adequately informed of the availability and performance of arbitrators. *Ibid.*, Sect. IV.3: "Where Does This Take Us?", pp. 647-649.

46. See Darius J. KHAMBATA, supra, fn. 11, this volume, p. 636 (describing as "bad diversity" the act of an institution to disregard the preferences of the parties and imposing "'diverse' arbitrators only to meet some statistical goal. It is then that party autonomy suffers").

47. Darius J. Khambata pointed out – and criticized – the fact that most of the time arbitral institutions, when acting as appointing authorities, relied on members of the limited pool by preferring predictability and consistency over diversity. According to Dr. Khambata, diversity should also be a key objective, particularly for the institutions, which are the most appropriately suited player to balance party autonomy with diversity aspirations. *Ibid.*, pp. 621-622.

48. Statement made orally by Professor Christophe Seraglini during his presentation.

And if diversity is a desirable goal and this is a change that would strengthen the legitimacy and acceptability of international arbitration, Darius J. Khambata's quoting of Mahatma Gandhi appears to be the most appealing and the best conclusion to be reached from our panel's discussions: "You must be the change you wish to see in the world!"[49]

---

49. Darius J. KHAMBATA, this volume, p. 637.

Who Are the Arbitrators?
Myths, Reality and Challenges

*Christophe Seraglini**

I.   INTRODUCTION

Who are the arbitrators? In a sense, there should be no issue on that topic: they are those chosen by the parties. Indeed, arbitration offers the parties the possibility to appoint the judge who will decide their dispute. Therefore and at least in theory, arbitration allows the parties to designate "the perfect judge", the one most tailored to and adequate for their cause, i.e., a judge with specific skills, notably with specific academic and professional qualifications, dedicated to the parties' cause and who will make his or her best effort to resolve the dispute quickly and efficiently.

This being said, this "perfect judge" could represent a first myth: the myth of an elite arbitrator of a typical profile who serves and preserves international justice (II). But that myth has to be confronted with the current reality and that confrontation highlights some drawbacks of the elitist arbitrator's profile. Indeed, some criticisms or, at least, some suspicions have been formulated against the current common arbitrator's profile. They have to be addressed, again to distinguish myth from reality regarding the relevance of these criticisms and suspicions (III). Moreover, because these criticisms and suspicions, well-grounded or not, do exist, solutions have to be found in order to fight against and lessen them, and to further enhance the legitimacy of international arbitration; in this context, diversity should play a role (IV). In other words, today myths have to be confronted with reality in order to determine if, to what extent and how the system for selection of arbitrators should be reformed or improved to actually serve and preserve international justice.

---

* Professor of Law, France; Founding Partner, Betto Seraglini.

II.   THE MYTH: AN ARBITRAL ELITE WHICH SERVES JUSTICE AND ENHANCES THE
       LEGITIMACY OF ARBITRATION

It is often said that there is a "typical arbitrator's profile". One can wonder to what
extent this is a true statement and how things are evolving in this regard (*1*). It has also
been said that this elite arbitrator's profile better serves an efficient and fair justice in an
international context. This belief also has to be examined (*2*).

1.   *The Current "Arbitrator's Common Profile": A (Too) Slow Evolution*

Recent sociological studies have taken arbitrators as their subject and built a first belief:
all or most of the appointed arbitrators are deemed to have the same very specific
profile. Such profile could be summarized as follows: the typical arbitrator is a white and
mature male, coming from Western Europe or North America and selected from a
limited pool, an "arbitral elite".

Are all these assertions true? The answer is probably positive. The "myth" regarding
the "typical arbitrator's profile" could be regarded as being accurate, even if these
assertions are in a (too) slowly evolving process.

a.   The typical arbitrator is a male
This statement seems hardly debatable. It is well known within the arbitration
community and the few statistics available speak for themselves. As for commercial
arbitration, in 2012, the International Chamber of Commerce (ICC) revealed that more
than 500 men were appointed and confirmed, while 76 women were appointed, and
only 47 were confirmed,[1] and the London Court of International Arbitration (LCIA)
declared that 311 men and 33 women were appointed as arbitrators.[2] The numbers are
equivalent for investment arbitration. The International Centre for Settlement of
Investment Disputes (ICSID) announced that in 2012 106 men and 11 women were
appointed as arbitrators.[3]

However, even if these numbers for women are low, they are better than in previous
years, and one can notice a slow emergence of female determinative figures in the
international arbitration field, establishing that once a female has proven to be a
competent arbitrator, re-appointment multiplies as with males.[4] More generally, things
are improving ... but slowly.

---

1. Benjamin G. DAVIS, "American Diversity in International Arbitration 2003-2013", 13 December
   2013 at <http://papers.ssrn.com/sol3/papers.cfm?abstract_id=2364967> (last accessed 19 May
   2014) p. 7.
2. Sarah LANCASTER, "LCIA Registrar's Report 2012", at <www.lcia.org//LCIA/casework_
   Report.aspx> (last accessed 19 May 2014) p. 4.
3. Benjamin G. DAVIS, *op. cit.*, fn. 1, p. 7.
4. Gus VAN HARTEN, "The (Lack Of) Women Arbitrators in Investment Treaty Arbitration",
   Columbia FDI Perspectives (6 February 2012, no. 59); Lucy GREENWOOD and C. Mark
   BAKER, "Getting a Better Balance on International Arbitration Tribunals", 28 Arbitration
   International (Kluwer Law International 2012, no. 4) p. 653 at pp. 653-667.

b.   The typical arbitrator is senior
It is commonly said that the more an arbitrator has *"gray in the hair"*, the more he gets appointed.[5] Again, it is probably true … and understandable. Having experienced arbitrators might be reassuring for the parties, and maybe for their counsel. Therefore, arbitrators are indeed mostly senior.[6] Most regularly appointed arbitrators are above fifty.[7]

There has been a first generation of arbitrators, composed of the so-called *"grand old men"*[8] who tended to develop their skills and reputation outside of the arbitration field as lawyers or academics and, thanks to their experience or connections, eventually shifted to arbitration after reaching a certain age. These *"pioneers of arbitration"*[9] have been replaced, around the 1980s, by a younger generation. This younger, at least at the time, generation was also mainly composed of prominent academics or lawyers, but who have from the beginning concentrated most of their training and activities in the field of international law and arbitration. Therefore, these "arbitration experts" had the opportunity to integrate into the circle of arbitrators much earlier, "at an age when most of the members of the older generation … had hardly even turned to [arbitration]".[10] Several of today's best arbitration specialists already benefited from a strong reputation as arbitrators in their mid-forties. But that "second generation" which is today in place has become older … and another new generation is emerging, but slowly.…

c.   The typical arbitrator mostly comes from Western Europe or North America
Arbitrators are said to mostly come from Western Europe and North America. Again, the few statistics available seem to speak for themselves. In 2012, the ICC registered 76 different nationalities of confirmed or appointed arbitrators, with the United Kingdom, Switzerland, France and the United States in the top 5, representing 48% of all confirmations and appointments.[11] As for the ICSID, in 2013, 47% of appointed arbitrators came from Western Europe, while 21% came from North America.[12]

These figures could be considered as striking given the fact that parties involved in international arbitration obviously come from more diverse countries. In 2012, the LCIA indeed only registered 16% of British parties, 4.5% of Swiss parties, 2.25% of French parties and 8% of US parties, while it also registered among others 4.25% of Indian parties, 2.25% of Chinese parties, 3.25% of Russian parties, 2.75% of Kazakhstani

---

5. Yves DEZALAY and Bryant G. GARTH, *Dealing in Virtue – International Commercial Arbitration and the Construction of a Transnational Legal Order* (University of Chicago Press 1996) pp. 23 and 60.
6. Thomas CLAY, *"Qui sont les arbitres internationaux? Approche sociologique"* in *Les arbitres internationaux* (Editions de la société de législation comparée 2005) p. 13 at p. 25, para. 25; Yves DEZALAY and Bryant G. GARTH, *op. cit.*, fn. 5, p. 23.
7. Thomas CLAY, *op. cit.*, fn. 6, p. 28, para. 32.
8. Yves DEZALAY and Bryant G. GARTH, *op. cit.*, fn. 5, p. 10.
9. *Ibid.*, p. 34.
10. *Ibid.*
11. "2011 Statistical Report", 23 ICC International Court of Arbitration Bulletin (2012, no. 1).
12. "The ICSID Caseload – Statistics", ICSID (2013, no. 2) p. 18, available at <https://icsid.worldbank.org/ICSID/FrontServlet?requestType=ICSIDDocRH&actionVal=CaseLoadStatistics>.

parties, 2% of Turkish parties, 3.75% coming from the Middle East, 5.5% coming from Africa and 6.5% coming from Asia-Pacific.[13]

However, these figures must be put in perspective. First, almost half of the arbitrators appointed or confirmed do not come from Western Europe or North America and many nationalities are represented in the institutions' numbers. Second, the numbers are improving, even if slowly: in 2012, the ICC registered an increase of 37.5% of confirmations and appointments of arbitrators from South and East Asia, and 19% for those from Latin America.[14] It seems that a new generation of arbitrators, coming from the United States and Europe but also from developing countries, is coming of age.[15]

d.   *The typical arbitrator is a counsel and/or an academic*

Most arbitrators are lawyers, even if the word "lawyer" can cover several realities: counsel and academics constitute a majority of the arbitrators, and most of the time they combine both hats; former professional judges constitute another type of lawyer-arbitrator:[16]

> "[Elite arbitrators'] typical professional profile includes a combination of private practice and academic positions. Some elite arbitrators are highly respected practitioners or academics, others combine academic positions and private practice, and some are retired judges with academic credentials."[17]

e.   *The typical arbitrator is selected from a limited pool, an arbitral elite*

As for the limited pool, a recent and debatable study concerning investment arbitration maintained that "Just 15 arbitrators, nearly all from Europe, the US or Canada, have decided 55% of all known investment-treaty disputes."[18]

It is true that there exist major individual figures in the arbitration field who are appointed very frequently. However, with the recent expansion of international arbitration (both commercial and investment-related), more and more actors (lawyers, academics, former state judges, employees of international companies) are involved in the arbitration field, with different country backgrounds and legal traditions. They want to be "part of the game": they write about arbitration, work in specialized departments of law firms or in specialized law firms. Therefore, the limited pool from which arbitrators are currently selected is expanding and will probably expand in the future, as predicted by scholars: "Arbitration is no longer the closed club of a limited number

---

13. Sarah LANCASTER, *op. cit.*, fn. 2, p. 4.

14. "2011 Statistical Report", ICC International Court of Arbitration Bulletin, *op. cit.*, fn. 11.

15. Catherine A. ROGERS, "The Vocation of the International Arbitrator", 20 American University International Law Review (2005, no. 5) p. 957 at pp. 965-966.

16. Thomas CLAY, *op. cit.*, fn. 6, pp. 30-31, paras. 35-39.

17. Daphna KAPELIUK, "The Repeat Appointment Factor: Exploring Decision Patterns of Elite Investment Arbitrators", 96 Cornell Law Review (2010) p. 47 at p. 79.

18. Pia EBERHARDT and Cecilia OLIVET, "Profiting from Injustice, How Law Firms, Arbitrators and Financiers Are Fuelling an Investment Arbitration Boom", Corporate Europe Observatory and the Transnational Institute (November 2012) p. 8, para. 3.

of international jurists, if it ever was. New faces are emerging with different country backgrounds, perspectives on issues in dispute, and legal traditions."[19]

"The lucrative arbitrators' market attracts many newcomers who wish to have a share of the arbitration pie."[20]

Therefore, the "pool" should be less limited in the near future; but this prediction should also be tempered. It is a fact that arbitration has recently involved more players. However, it does not mean that these players count in the arbitration landscape, and more specifically that they will all become arbitrators.

To conclude on this first myth related to the arbitrators' common profile, one could say that it seems factually and historically accurate, even if in a slowly changing process. Let's turn to the second belief, i.e., that such a profile better serves an efficient and fair justice in the international context.

2. Justification for Elitism: It Serves an Efficient and Fair Justice

What is the function of international arbitration? To resolve disputes in the most satisfactory way, i.e., to render high-quality decisions with independence, efficiency, proficiency, fairness and discretion. Does the "typical profile" influence this and in which way?

The selection of arbitrators is determinative of the quality of the decision considering that "an arbitration is only as good as its arbitrators".[21]

Therefore, the fact that there is a common/elite profile of arbitrators is not a coincidence. Indeed, some aspects of this profile should guarantee a high quality of justice. A limited/elite pool favors repeated appointments. And repeated appointments give experience: the more appointed an arbitrator is, the more experience he acquires. And the more experience an arbitrator has, the more appointed he should be in the future, since he will be familiar with matters at stake in international disputes and the appropriate way to deal with them. There should be a "virtuous circle" there.

Experience indeed has an important role to play in ensuring a high quality of justice regarding the conduct of the proceedings as well as the merits of a case. An experienced arbitrator: (a) knows how to efficiently conduct arbitral proceedings; and (b) has the proper skills to adequately resolve the matter in dispute.

a. An experienced/elite arbitrator knows how to efficiently conduct arbitral proceedings
An experienced arbitrator facing a problem (for example, a procedural problem such as non-cooperative parties) should implement a reasonable solution, based on his past

---

19. Doak BISHOP and Margrete STEVENS, "The Compelling Need for a Code of Ethics in International Arbitration: Transparency, Integrity and Legitimacy" in A.J. VAN DEN BERG, ed., Arbitration Advocacy in Changing Times, ICCA Congress Series no. 15 (Kluwer 2011) p. 391 at p. 394.

20. Daphna KAPELIUK, op. cit., fn. 17, p. 79.

21. Yu JIN TAY, "Reflections on the Selection of Arbitrators in International Arbitration" in Albert Jan VAN DEN BERG, ed., International Arbitration: The Coming of a New Age?, ICCA Congress Series no. 17 (Kluwer Law International 2013) p. 123.

practice (by evicting past solutions that turned out to be deficient and by improving others) and should be more equipped to face new problems.

Having experienced arbitrators should also equate to having diligent arbitrators. Celerity of the procedure is supposed to be one of the advantages of arbitration in comparison to state justice.[22] For example, under the ICC Arbitration Rules, arbitrators have limited opportunities to delay signing the terms of reference[23] or drawing up the award.[24] Diligence is necessary and diligence is a quality that arbitrators should acquire from their experience, as they get used to the various procedural steps. Indeed, if a comparison is drawn between the French Code of Civil Procedure and the ICC Arbitration Rules, for example, the difference between these instruments (the number of rules governing the procedure and the detail with which the procedure is described) is significant and an experienced arbitrator should know how to conduct an arbitration properly and efficiently.

In addition, an experienced arbitrator, familiar with litigants' strategies and procedural tactics, should be less naïve as to what the parties are trying to plead and should adopt a more realistic view of the case.

b.   *An experienced/elite arbitrator has the proper skills to adequately resolve the matter in dispute*

The elite arbitrators usually combine (or have combined) different hats, sometimes acting as counsel, sometimes as arbitrator, sometimes as recognized authors expressing their opinions through articles, conferences, etc., or sometimes as influential lobbyists or consultants to reform arbitration rules or laws. In these different roles, they are constantly in contact with the legal practice and should better realize the expectations of the parties in arbitration. Accordingly, they should be better aware of the business realities and should issue decisions in better adequacy thereof. More occasional arbitrators do not have this insider's advantage.

Moreover, experienced arbitrators would have developed particular skills in arbitration law and on very specific topics as to the merits (construction law, energy law, etc.). It is evident that there is a need for skilled arbitrators. Arbitration cases can sometimes be very specific and technical. For instance, sitting as an arbitrator in a construction case undoubtedly requires certain skills in construction law. A decision of the Italian Supreme Court illustrates that skills are determinative for justice. The dispute at stake concerned construction work, but none of the arbitrators was legally trained. As they were unable to draw up the award, they had to delegate it to an expert. Eventually, the Italian court annulled the award on the ground that arbitrators cannot delegate their decision-making power.[25]

---

22. Gary B. BORN, *International Commercial Arbitration* (Kluwer Law International 2009) pp. 83-85.

23. See Art. 23 of the ICC Rules of Arbitration (2012).

24. See Art. 27 of the ICC Rules of Arbitration (2012); see also Art. 26 of the LCIA Rules of Arbitration (1998).

25. *Corte di cassazione*, 7 June 1989, *Sacheri v. Robotto*, ICCA *Yearbook Commercial Arbitration* XVI (1991) pp. 156-158; Julian D.M. LEW, Loukas MISTELIS and Stefan KRÖLL, *Comparative International Commercial Arbitration* (Kluwer Law International 2003) p. 235, paras. 10-40.

Hence the fact that typical arbitrators are not only prominent academics but also experienced lawyers and practitioners, with good knowledge of the industry sector or the particular type of dispute in question, should ensure that complex arbitration cases receive an adequate solution, suitable to the expectations of the parties as well as legally sound.[26]

III.   THE REALITY: THE DRAWBACKS OF THE CURRENT ELITISM IN ARBITRATION —
        SUSPICION ... OR THE "NEW MYTHS"?

Despite its merits, the current "arbitrators' common profile" has suffered criticisms, or at least suspicions, in recent years. It has been argued that the selection of arbitrators from a limited and elitist pool might also affect the quality of arbitral justice or at least might lead people to perceive that it is affected. In this regard, several criticisms of this common profile have been formulated. This trend could affect the legitimacy of arbitration. But one may wonder whether these criticisms and suspicions are not new forms of a myth.

Obviously, there is at least one criticism that is hardly debatable: the pool lacks women. The less legitimate image of the typical arbitrator is that he is more likely to be male. Who today could seriously argue that men render better justice than women? It is certain that a "woman's touch" in the arbitrators' pool would be a benefit. However, and as observed, this image is currently changing as more and more women are involved in international arbitration and more and more are appointed as arbitrators. Things are evolving, but probably too slowly. In this regard, it should be noted that women do not seem to be excluded mainly because of their gender. As explained by scholars:

> "Diversity is 'the last feature on anyone's mind'. Counsel is likely to be far more pre-occupied with researching the potential arbitrator's track record, his or her writings in the field, his or her language capabilities and in reviewing any previous decisions, rather than noting the potential arbitrator's gender."[27]

Women rather seem to be the victims of a vicious circle: parties like to appoint experienced arbitrators, but women lack experience and this strengthens their exclusion from the circle. They suffer from the fact that since they were not appointed as arbitrators during the past decades, they do not benefit from solid experience assuring reappointment (indeed "[p]revious service as an arbitrator is considered to be the 'pre-eminent qualification for an arbitrator-candidate'").[28]

In this matter, people could say that international arbitration does not stand as an exception, and that, as is the case in other areas, the appearance of female figures will

---

26. Julian D.M. LEW, Loukas MISTELIS and Stefan KRÖLL, *op. cit.*, fn. 25, p. 235, paras. 10-41;
    Jan PAULSSON, "Moral Hazard in International Dispute Resolution", 8 TDM (2011, no. 2) p. 10;
    Yu JIN TAY, *op. cit.*, fn. 21, p. 126.
27. Lucy GREENWOOD and C. Mark BAKER, *op. cit.*, fn. 4, p. 662.
28. *Ibid.*, p. 658.

take some time.[29] But for a true evolution to happen, initiatives probably have to be taken. Some argue that "[u]nconscious gender bias" must be identified and fought appropriately.[30]

I would have more reservations about criticizing the fact that arbitrators are mainly lawyers since I am not sure that this should change.

Other criticisms and suspicions have to be evaluated since some of them can also be close to myths. Three of them should be addressed: (*1*) the fact that the arbitrators' elite is suspected to favor western or private companies in proceedings and awards; (*2*) the fact that the elite arbitrator's personal interests are suspected to influence the content of the award; (*3*) the fact that the arbitrators' elite creates a risk of less independent and impartial arbitrators, i.e., the "inner-mafia" suspicion.

1.   *An Arbitrators' Elite Suspected to Favor Western or Private Companies in Proceedings and Awards*

It has been argued that a link could be established between, on the one hand, the arbitrators' selection and, on the other hand, the procedure followed (*a*) and the decision reached in the award (*b*).

a.   *The typical arbitrator applies a typical procedure*

There is a preconceived idea according to which the profile of the arbitrators determines the "style of arbitration". For instance, a civil law or a common law style in the conduct of the proceedings would depend on the cultural background of the arbitrators.[31] However, the reality might be different. As scholars pointed out, international arbitrators adopt "a relatively uniform approach to arbitral procedure which borrows both from civil law and the common law: from the civil law, the exchange of two consecutive sets of memorials accompanied by documents; from the common law, the submission of witness statements, expert reports, and requests for production of documents, and the conduct of the hearing focused on the examination of witnesses and experts rather than on oral pleadings".[32] A common, typical and unique arbitral procedure has arisen.

At first sight, this typical procedure, tailored after years of experience by a limited pool, should ensure efficiency of the proceedings, as explained above. However, there are also some drawbacks in this standardization.

Parties to arbitration chose this dispute resolution process in order to escape from established national procedures and to enjoy a tailor-made procedure, adapted to the specifics of their dispute. The existence of a unique procedure, applied in any dispute,

---

29. This reflects the lack of women in the upper echelons of the legal profession, see Lucy GREENWOOD and C. Mark BAKER, *op. cit.*, fn. 4, pp. 654, 656 and 661.

30. *Ibid.*, p. 660.

31. Yu JIN TAY, *op. cit.*, fn. 21, pp. 112-132.

32. Bernard HANOTIAU, "International Arbitration in a Global Economy: The Challenges of the Future", 28 Journal of International Arbitration (Kluwer Law International 2011, no. 2) pp. 89-103 at p. 99; Yves DEZALAY and Bryant G. GARTH, *op. cit.*, fn. 5, p. 111.

by the same limited pool of arbitrators, could therefore limit or negate the advantage of arbitration by leading to too much uniformity.

It is true that uniformity currently seems to be a popular trend in international arbitration but one can wonder if it is always for the better. A bit of diversity in the way to conduct arbitral proceedings, brought by arbitrators with different cultural and legal backgrounds, would probably be a good thing since it could bring new procedural perspectives in arbitration.

b. The typical arbitrator suspected to issue business-oriented decisions
It has been argued that the current "common profile" of arbitrators can also influence the outcome of the case. Indeed, the content of an arbitral award may depend on the personal preferences of the arbitrator.[33] As stated by some commentators: "Arbitrators have to make choices to resolve the disputes, which are of course informed by their political standpoint."[34]

It has been noticed that the typical arbitrator often has close links to the corporate world[35] and a "strong market orientation".[36] Therefore some have argued that the decisions reached in arbitral awards are likely to reflect this business-oriented profile.

This would be accentuated by the fact that the typical arbitrator comes from Western Europe or North America, and should therefore likely be sensitive to capitalist issues. This has been especially widely argued in investment arbitration, in which some arbitrators, mostly nationals from developed countries, are said to support investors' rights, to be "investor friendly".[37]

This statement is not perfectly correct. The influence of the geographical origin of the "typical arbitrator" on the content of the award is probably overestimated. But it remains true that a similar cultural background can lead to a similar application of the rule of law in disputes that might involve parties coming from diverse parts of the world with diverse cultural and legal modes of reasoning. Introducing more cultural diversity in arbitrators' panels could help arbitrators to better understand different non-western countries' cultures and needs, and especially to become more sensitive to state regulations aiming at specific non-western public interests. Therefore a balance should be found in this respect.

2.   *The Elite Arbitrator's Personal Interests Suspected to Influence the Content of the Award*

It has been argued that, contrary to the myth of an arbitrator who purely serves justice, arbitrators are also rational "economic actors" preoccupied by their wish to be paid for their services, to make a career and to be re-appointed in future cases.[38]

---

33. Sophie HARNAY, "*Réputation de l'arbitre et décision arbitrale : Quelques éléments d'analyse économique*", Revue de l'arbitrage (2012) p. 761.
34. Alison ROSS, "Brigitte in Brazil", 5 GAR (22 June 2010, Issue 3).
35. Pia EBERHARDT and Cecilia OLIVET, *op. cit.*, fn. 18, p. 36.
36. Yves DEZALAY and Bryant G. GARTH, *op. cit.*, fn. 5, p. 195.
37. See for a critical point of view: Pia EBERHARDT and Cecilia OLIVET, *op. cit.*, fn. 18, pp. 38-39.
38. Sophie HARNAY, *op. cit.*, fn. 33.

It has been stated that arbitrators "to a far greater degree than judges, have a financial and professional stake in the system" since they aim at building a career in this field.[39] Some authorities indeed argue that the arbitrators' incentives correspond to "their self-interest in trying to secure and expand prospects for future arbitral appointments" and that "an arbitrator may perceive that his award is likely to have an impact on his own acceptability, that is, on the probability of his being appointed again".[40] In this respect, an award could be seen as a strategic instrument to serve the private interests of the arbitrator.

Yet, it could be said that the elite arbitrators are not, at least, only motivated by their career. They do have moral and ethical values.

Moreover, the patterns and behaviors caused by the arbitrators' private interests have to be determined and evaluated. Here, there are cons and pros to the influence of the arbitrator's personal interests on the resolution of the case.

a.   Cons of the influence of the arbitrator's personal interest on the decision reached

i.   Biased arbitrators?

Some argue that the arbitrator's personal interests favor biased arbitrators. The supposed link between the personal interest of the arbitrator and the decision reached has been particularly emphasized in the field of investment arbitration. Since the Convention on the Settlement of Investment Disputes between States and Nationals of Other States (the ICSID Convention) offers an asymmetric system, in which only investors can initiate arbitration proceedings against states, it has been argued that the personal interest of arbitrators can lead them to rule in favor of investors, in order to convince the latter to bring new future claims and to re-appoint them as arbitrators.[41] One author argued, after a recent statistical study (based on 140 investment cases), that "arbitrators would tend to adopt an expansive (claimant-friendly) approach to the resolution of the coded issue", i.e., on issues such as definition of "investment" and "fair and equitable treatment".[42] The same author stated that "[t]his result supported the hypothesis that tested expectations that arbitrators would interpret the law in ways that encourage claims and support the economic position of the arbitration industry".[43]

The consequences of a system that would be at least perceived as in favor of investors could be very detrimental to international arbitration, since a supposed "biased" typical arbitrator could undermine if not suppress the legitimacy of arbitration, especially in the field of investment. And one knows that, in 2011, the Australian government announced

---

39. Pia EBERHARDT and Cecilia OLIVET, *op. cit.*, fn. 18, p. 35.
40. Alan S. RAU, "On Integrity of Private Judging", 14 Arb. Int. (Kluwer Law International 1998, no. 2) pp. 139-140.
41. Gus VAN HARTEN, "Arbitrator Behaviour in Asymmetrical Adjudication: An Empirical Study of Investment Treaty Arbitration", 50 Osgoode Hall Law Journal (2012) (henceforth "Arbitrator Behaviour") p. 219.
42. Gus VAN HARTEN, "Pro-Investor or Pro-State Bias in Investment-Treaty Arbitration? Forthcoming study gives cause for concern", Investment Treaty News (IISD) (13 April 2012); Gus VAN HARTEN, "Arbitrator Behaviour", *op. cit.*, fn. 41, p. 238.
43. Gus VAN HARTEN, "Arbitrator Behaviour", *op. cit.*, fn. 41, p. 238.

that it would no longer include investor-state dispute settlement provisions in trade agreements and that Bolivia, Ecuador and Venezuela have already withdrawn from the ICSID.[44] More diversity in the arbitrators' panel might help to lessen this belief.

ii.   A "split the baby" and lukewarm doctrine?

It has also been argued that arbitrators' personal interests favor a "split the baby" and lukewarm doctrine of the arbitrators. In a survey that focused on the patterns of arbitral awards rendered by repeatedly appointed arbitrators, the author saw arbitral awards as decisions trying to keep both parties satisfied, in order to secure the arbitrators' chances to be reappointed in future cases (the so-called "split the baby" practice).[45]

However, the strategy of arbitrators, should it exist, is probably harder to perceive. Arbitrators are likely to display different behaviors sitting as a chair or as a party-appointed arbitrator.[46]

It has also been argued that market pressure might impact the arbitrators' behavior. Integrating into the elitist pool of arbitrators can be a real challenge for newcomers,[47] and first-time appointed arbitrators might not be willing to adopt different or isolated positions from the pool, since it could prevent their re-appointment:[48] "Breaking with the tight-knit community could entail no further appointments as an arbitrator, no promotion in the law firm, isolation in the academic community, and a drop in invitations to investment treaty conferences."[49]

If one follows this idea, arbitrators could be suspected of being willing to render more acceptable decisions for the parties and the arbitrators' community, to the detriment of their personal convictions, in order to preserve their reputation and their ability to serve again later as arbitrators.[50]

This belief is rather debatable. Nevertheless, it is true that the arbitrators' personal interests could lead them to write lukewarm doctrine on international arbitration in order not to prevent future appointments by adopting firm doctrinal positions on disputed issues.

iii.   Copy-pasted and inefficient justice?

A typical arbitrator selected from a limited pool and regularly appointed will be requested to act in multiple cases and, as an economic actor, could accept multiple appointments to increase his revenue. In this context, it has been argued that the repeated appointments of the same people sometimes leads to a copy-pasted justice, due to their workload. Arbitrators might be tempted to apply a decision reached in similar cases without considering the specific characteristics of the merits of each case.

---

44. Pia EBERHARDT and Cecilia OLIVET, *op. cit.*, fn. 18, p. 9, para. 11.
45. Daphna KAPELIUK, *op. cit.*, fn. 17, p. 61; Gus VAN HARTEN, "Arbitrator Behaviour", *op. cit.*, fn. 41, p. 217.
46. Daphna KAPELIUK, *op. cit.*, fn. 17, p. 83.
47. Yu JIN TAY, *op. cit.*, fn. 21, p. 125.
48. Yves DEZALAY and Bryant G. GARTH, *op. cit.*, fn. 5, p. 23.
49. Pia EBERHARDT and Cecilia OLIVET, *op. cit.*, fn. 18, p. 37.
50. Sophie HARNAY, *op. cit.*, fn. 33, p. 763.

In addition, it has been argued that the repeated appointment of the same people also leads to an inefficient justice, since arbitrators appointed in multiple cases are not able to issue a decision within a reasonable time.[51] The excessive work load of arbitrators is a trend against which the arbitral institutions, for example the ICC, have taken initiatives.

Finally, one could consider that the typical arbitrator, belonging to a limited pool and enjoying a comfortable position, might end up rendering a remiss, lazy and easy justice, as his position is not likely to be challenged.

b.   Pros of the influence of arbitrator's personal interest on the decision reached
All of the surveys and the inferences drawn from their results described above have been widely contested and criticized by other studies.[52]

Some scholars have strongly defended the vision of disinterested arbitrators and the absence of any selfish consideration to guide their decision.[53] And it is obviously true that arbitrators are not mainly selfish animals motivated by personal interests. Most arbitrators have moral and ethical values.

Moreover, as some scholars submit, the arbitrators' best (if not only) personal interest is to preserve their reputation within the arbitration world and therefore not to be labeled as biased:

> "Of course, individuals who supplement their incomes as arbitrators are not immune from temptations to greed and bias to which humanity has always been heir. Each arbitrator should be conscious of the risk that he or she may fall prey to astigmatic perspectives. The beginning of wisdom often lies in a healthy fear of latent bias.
>
> Nevertheless, no evidence supports the proposition that the arbitral system as it now exists provides incentives to produce inaccurate decisions that favor either claimants or respondents or even that such incentives actually exist. *Common sense tells us that the big losers would be none other than professional arbitrators themselves if the process did not inspire general confidence.*"[54] (Emphasis added)

---

51. Bernard HANOTIAU, *op. cit.*, fn. 32, p. 100.
52. Stephanie E. KERR, Richard W. NAIMARK, "Arbitrators Do Not 'Split the Baby' – Empirical Evidence from International Business Arbitrations", 18 Journal of International Arbitration (Kluwer Law International 2001, no. 5) pp. 573-578; Daphna KAPELIUK, *op. cit.*, fn. 17, p. 81; see also Stavros BREKOULAKIS, "Systemic Bias and the Institution of International Arbitration: A New Approach to Arbitral Decision-Making", 4 Journal of International Dispute Settlement (2012, no. 3) p. 553 at pp. 568-570.
53. Pierre MAYER, "*La liberté de l'arbitre*", Revue de l'arbitrage (2013), pp. 347-348; Pierre LALIVE, "*Du courage dans l'arbitrage international*" in *Mélanges en l'honneur de François Knoepfler* (Helbing & Lichtenhahn 2005) p. 159.
54. William W. PARK, "Part III Chapter 9: Arbitrator Integrity" in Michael WAIBEL, Asha KAUSHAL, Liz KYO-HWA CHUNG, Claire BALCHIN, eds., *The Backlash Against Investment Arbitration* (Kluwer Law International 2010) p. 207.

"Rumors of prejudice and partiality do little to enhance the credibility of professional decision-makers, who normally benefit from reputations for reliability and accuracy. Bad arbitrators exist, but their lack of integrity does them no favors."[55]

A good reputation amongst practitioners of the arbitration field could be the best insurance of reappointment, since former co-arbitrators will name each other in subsequent cases when acting as counsel based on positive past experience while sitting on the same panel and, in parallel, counsel with a good impression and a good experience with an arbitrator, even appointed by the opponent, might re-appoint this arbitrator in subsequent cases:

"[A]n even stronger incentive exists to safeguard professional status, particularly with peers. Individuals who serve as arbitrators care deeply about the respect of their colleagues, for reasons both personal and professional. Doing a good job builds a positive reputation. Few enticements to good behavior are stronger for those who sit regularly as arbitrators than a colleague's appreciation of one's ability and integrity."[56]

"[A]rbitrators sitting on three-member tribunals have far more to gain from demonstrating intellectual integrity to each other (thus enhancing positive references for future cases) than in urging disregard of the right result."[57]

"[I]n the international arbitration market place, parties appoint arbitrators because of their professional credibility, standing, and reputation.... According to this line of thought, the arbitrators' professional reputation could provide a key incentive for them to remain as impartial and fair as possible.... This observation is especially true for arbitrators who are repeat players in the arbitration market and for those arbitrators whose reputation as credible and independent decision makers is a key characteristic for their selection."[58]

For this part of the doctrine, the fact that the typical arbitrator is selected from a limited pool is an incentive for this arbitrator to act professionally, diligently, independently and impartially, since it is essential for becoming and remaining a member of this limited pool. It therefore constitutes a virtuous circle rather than a vicious circle.

Indeed, one can express some doubts as to whether a split-the-baby practice would be the best guarantee of being reappointed. That is not what the parties are looking for. They are rather looking for a just and accurate decision and an efficient and fair judicial process. More generally, one could add that it is in the arbitrators' best interest to carry out their mission in the best possible way.

---

55. *Ibid.*, p. 214.
56. *Ibid.*, p. 209.
57. *Ibid.*, p. 241.
58. Daphna KAPELIUK, *op. cit.*, fn. 17, pp. 65-66.

3.   *A Risk of Less Independent and Impartial Arbitrators? The Inner-Mafia Suspicion*

Independence and impartiality are essential qualities required to serve as an arbitrator. Indeed and as repeated by French case law, these qualities are linked to the jurisdictional function exercised by arbitrators, who, as any other judge, must not be dependent on the parties or have any prejudgment about the case presented to them.[59] As explained by scholars, "principles of fairness and independence are integral to the legitimizing role of international arbitration".[60]

In this regard, could repeated appointment of arbitrators from the same limited pool give rise to questions regarding their independence and impartiality? As explained by scholars:

> "[P]arties to a large international arbitration may well be alarmed to enter the room and find that everybody (including their own lawyers) knows one another except them. The people they see might be current or former partners of the same law firm, members of the same chambers, panelists at the same arbitral institution, sworn enemies or dear friends. It comes as no surprise, therefore, to see that by far the most common ground for bias challenge is the professional relationship between the arbitrator and a party or his or her counsel."[61]

This inner-mafia suspicion exists. But again, its merits have to be evaluated.

a.   Repeated appointments and supposed lack of independence
Independence depends on the connections between an arbitrator, the parties and their counsel. Repeated appointments of an arbitrator foster regular contacts among arbitration specialists and strengthen the connections within the community. Moreover, arbitration specialists often alternatively serve as arbitrator or as counsel. These repeatedly appointed arbitrators might sit on the same or similar arbitration panels or might be regularly appointed by the same law firms. They even call each other as witnesses in arbitration cases. Even if, as explained, it is understandable that arbitrators will tend to appoint the peers with whom they have worked and who appeared to act professionally and efficiently, this behavior may keep strengthening the appearance of a "*mafia*": "[t]his cycle of mutual recognition ensures that the circle of appointees in the largest or most sensitive cases remains small".[62]

---

59. CA Paris, 28 November 2002, Revue de l'arbitrage (2003) p. 445; CA Paris, 12 February 2009, Revue de l'arbitrage (2009) p. 186.
60. Gus VAN HARTEN, "Pro-Investor or Pro-State Bias in Investment-Treaty Arbitration? Forthcoming study gives cause for concern", *op. cit.*, fn. 42.
61. Sam LUTTRELL, *Bias Challenges in International Commercial Arbitration: The Need for a "Real Danger" Test* (Kluwer Law International 2009) p. 6.
62. Yu JIN TAY, *op. cit.*, fn. 21, p. 125.

This has been described by scholars as the "*inner mafia*" criticism.[63] The smaller the arbitrators' panel, the stronger this feeling might be.

Even if the arbitrator is not repeatedly appointed by the same party (a known situation for which clear rules have been enacted), eventually, the exclusivity of the group of arbitrators increasingly raises conflicts of interests, and arbitrators are sometimes suspected to be less independent, an opinion that could affect the legitimacy of arbitral justice.[64] These criticisms are emphasized in investment arbitration where this problem has been especially raised in multiple and recent arbitration cases. Various decisions have been reached (dismiss the arbitrator; keep the arbitrator; offer the arbitrator a choice between pursuing his arbitrator role or his counsel role, etc.),[65] but these recent cases and their various outcomes have not yet permitted the establishment of clear rules on such topic:

> "[A]lthough certain decisions have, in fact, recognized that the dual arbitrator/counsel role is problematic and can warrant a successful challenge, the rules regarding disclosure and disqualification nevertheless remain unclear. Exacerbating the resulting uncertainty and further threatening the proceedings' legitimacy, many of the decisions are either kept secret or issued without supporting reasons."[66]

b. Repeated appointments and supposed lack of impartiality

The fact that arbitrators are selected from a limited pool with a very specific profile can cast a shadow on these arbitrators' impartial state of mind. Indeed, arbitrators with the same professional and cultural backgrounds might have the same preconceived ideas and stereotypes about various subjects. In a caricatural and, fortunately, old example, regarding a maritime accident off the coast of France between a Portuguese and a Norwegian vessel, submitted to arbitration in London, the arbitrator responded as follows when one of the counsel mentioned an Italian case during the hearings: "Italians are all liars in these cases and will say anything to suit their book. The same thing applied

---

63. Yu JIN TAY, *op. cit.*, fn. 21, p. 125; Daphna KAPELIUK, *op. cit.*, fn. 17, p. 77; Philippe LEBOULANGER, "*Bibliographie* – Dealing in Virtue, International Commercial Arbitration and the Construction of a Transnational Legal Order", Revue de l'arbitrage (1997) p. 319; Yves DEZALAY and Bryant G. GARTH, *op. cit.*, fn. 5, pp. 18-20.

64. Daphna KAPELIUK, *op. cit.*, fn. 17, p. 65.

65. See Nathalie BERNASCONI-OSTERWALDER, Lise JOHNSON and Fiona MARSHALL, "Arbitrator Independence and Impartiality: Examining the Dual Role of Arbitrator and Counsel", IV Annual Forum for Developing Country Investment Negotiators, Background Papers, New Delhi, 27-29 October 2010, pp. 17-27; see also CA Paris, 28 May 2013, no. 11/17672, in which a party challenged the chairman's impartiality and independence on the basis that he participated in a conference and especially in a panel presided by the legal counsel of the mother company of one of the parties.

66. Nathalie BERNASCONI-OSTERWALDER, Lise JOHNSON and Fiona MARSHALL, *op. cit.*, fn. 65, p. 27.

to the Portuguese. But the other side are Norwegians and in my experience the Norwegians generally are a truthful people."[67]

Fortunately, the arbitrator was removed.

Some scholars argued that the arbitrators' common profile may also affect their impartiality in decisions regarding conflict of laws:

> "[A]rbitrators are sometimes tempted to take short cuts or a pragmatic approach and apply laws that are, for instance, more familiar to the arbitrator or more consistent with what the arbitrator believes to be better policy or a better ground for giving parties a 'just' opportunity or result."[68]

Similarly, the repeated appointment of an arbitrator is sometimes said to impair the arbitrator's impartiality. Impartiality is an independent state of mind that precludes an arbitrator from prejudging a certain case.[69] When an arbitrator is repeatedly appointed by different parties but on the same subject matter, he or she will indeed accumulate experience but may also logically tend to preconceive the decision to adopt and naturally tend to issue similar decisions in similar cases.

Impartiality is sometimes also seen to be impaired when arbitrators act as counsel. Indeed, an arbitrator might have argued a legal issue as counsel in one case that it has to decide in another case. The arbitrator therefore does not approach the case with an open mind but is potentially already biased about the legal issue at stake. This may affect the integrity of the arbitral process.[70] There can be a conflict between the role of *"rule-maker"* and the role of *"rule-user"*.[71] However, this argument should not be given too much weight, since a lawyer can argue one case one day and its opposite the next day, without personally adopting a clear position on the matter. A counsel can (and should) "adapt" his views to the case at stake and to the client's interest and needs.

The criticisms regarding the lack of independence and impartiality of arbitrators have been emphasized in investment arbitration. Since, contrary to commercial arbitration, investment cases always raise questions of interpretation of the same (or almost the same) provisions (of BITs or of the ICSID Convention), some authors have feared that an arbitrator might reach a decision with already biased opinions on specific issues (it already decided or pleaded), and possibly in order to be able to invoke this decision in other cases in which it acts as counsel.[72]

---

67. *In re The Owners of the Steamship Catalina & The Owners of the Motor Vessel Norma*, 61 Lloyds L Rep. 360 (1938) cited in William W. PARK, *op. cit.*, fn. 54, pp. 194-195.

68. Kevin K. KIM, "Chapter 4: Arbitrators and Choice-of-Law Decisions" in *Is Arbitration only as Good as the Arbitrator? Status, Powers and Role of the Arbitrator,* Dossiers ICC Institute of World Business Law (2011) p. 65 at p. 65.

69. Julian D.M. LEW, Loukas MISTELIS and Stefan KRÖLL, *op. cit.*, fn. 25, p. 258, para. 11-11.

70. William. W. PARK, *op. cit.*, fn. 54, p. 205.

71. Sam LUTTRELL, *op. cit.*, fn. 61, p. 241.

72. Nathalie BERNASCONI-OSTERWALDER, Lise JOHNSON and Fiona MARSHALL, *op. cit.*, fn. 65, p. 4; William W. Park, *op. cit.*, fn. 54, p. 205.

These criticisms are probably exaggerated and often unjust. But appearance matters since trust in the arbitral process matters. Therefore a challenge exists: the necessary improvement of the arbitrators' nomination process.

IV.   THE CHALLENGE: IS THERE A NEED TO IMPROVE – AND HOW TO IMPROVE – THE
       ARBITRATORS' PANEL AND FURTHER PROMOTE THE LEGITIMACY OF ARBITRATION?

The quality of arbitration depends to a large extent on the arbitrators and it has been said that "an arbitration is only as good as its arbitrators".[73] As explained above, the merits of the current "typical profile" arbitrators have been called into question and perceived as questionable by some of the users and external observers of arbitration. Because these criticisms and suspicions, justified or not, exist and because trust matters, something should be done. It is important not only that justice is done, but also that justice seems to be done in arbitration. More diversity in the arbitrators' panel could play a role in this regard.

Taking into account these criticisms, the arbitral system would benefit from bringing diversity to and modifying the arbitrator's "profile" in order to reinforce the legitimacy of international justice.

In addition, a more diverse panel of arbitrators could develop and improve arbitral proceedings with inputs coming from uncommon legal backgrounds, and could further introduce in arbitration new ways of applying the rule of law.

Arbitrators, arbitral institutions, but also parties and counsel involved in international arbitration will have a key role to play in improving the legitimacy of arbitration and *in fine* increasing the quality of arbitral justice:

> "[Arbitration] can only proceed with the same success in the future if it meets the challenges with which it is confronted today. One thing is certain: this will not be possible without a reconsideration by all participants in the process of their role and duties and an acceptance of some changes in their mode of functioning."[74]

However, there are some "governing rules" to follow when seeking to improve the process of nominating arbitrators.

1.   *A Necessary Balance Between Experience and Proficiency on the One Hand and Diversity in the Selection of Arbitrators on the Other Hand*

The "typical arbitrator profile" is currently raising and will continue to raise difficulties and criticisms. Adding diversity to the selection of arbitrators by enlarging the circle to new arbitrators appears to be a logical and necessary solution to address these concerns.

In addition, diversity in nationalities, gender and age might bring new ways of approaching and deciding legal matters, applying the rule of law, directing arbitral

---

73. Yu JIN TAY, *op. cit.*, fn. 21, p. 123.
74. Bernard HANOTIAU, *op. cit.*, fn. 32, p. 103.

proceedings based on different legal, cultural and even personal backgrounds.[75] It might also lessen the fears related to a too limited pool of arbitrators. It might even develop international arbitration demands: "One way to respond to new demands or to find ways to anticipate them is for institutions to put forward particular individuals – and therefore competences – that can stimulate and serve new demands."[76]

However, diversity should not mean lower quality. Arbitrators must remain high-profile judges. Arbitration has the objective of being a very high-profile justice settling very sensitive cases while taking into account the commercial interests of the parties. In order to keep the system attractive, the prospective arbitrators must then fulfill a high standard of skills.

There should also be a balance between diversity and the parties' wishes and autonomy. Diversity cannot really be imposed on the parties by their counsel. It is rather a question of recommendation to the parties, of educating them to the merits of new practices. More generally, there is a need to remain realistic with respect to the solutions proposed.

With these requirements in mind, several proposals could be submitted to introduce more diversity in the selection of arbitrators.

2.   *Proposals to Introduce More Diversity in the Selection of Arbitrators*

The present contribution will be limited to general considerations regarding such proposals.

Strict and mandatory national legislation regarding gender, origin and even age of potential arbitrators that parties can appoint should be avoided. For example, introducing quotas would simply restrain parties from choosing arbitration, as an essential principle of arbitration (i.e., the right to choose the judge) will be affected. Self-regulation would certainly constitute a better option.

In this regard, arbitral institutions, arbitrators, parties to arbitration and more generally the arbitration community have an important role to play in trying to achieve diversity without jeopardizing quality in arbitration panels.

a.   *Role of the parties to arbitration*
The first actors who can change the current situation are the parties to arbitration, who have the power of appointment. In this regard, parties to arbitration should change their habits and accept appointment of less frequently used arbitrators, convinced that this different appointment could better serve their interests.

The position of the parties is not always easy to ascertain. Parties often blame themselves for what they do. And their expectations might be diverse. This being said, they should be educated by counsel as to the merits of more diversity in the arbitrators' panel.

---

75. Yves DEZALAY and Bryant G. GARTH, *op. cit.*, fn. 5, p. 47.
76. *Ibid.*, p. 294.

b.   Role of the institutions

i.   Role in the appointment of arbitrators

Some authors have suggested the possibility that all arbitrators should be appointed by a neutral body, such as the institutions, instead of by the parties.[77]

It is true that such appointment by a neutral body has some advantages. It could accelerate the process of achieving some diversity in arbitration panels, since the arbitral institutions could open their lists of potential arbitrators to more diverse profiles, with the help of various associations trying to achieve such diversity:

> "Advice on suitable candidates could be sought from organizations such as the International Association of Women Jurists, the International Federation of Women Lawyers or Arbitral Women. Besides tapping the knowledge and networks of the organizations, involving them directly would help loosen the hold of the boys' club."[78]

In addition, such appointment could prevent risks of biased decisions.[79] Indeed, as explained above, parties can potentially put pressure on the appointed arbitrators who want to maximize their chances of future appointments. If arbitrators were to be appointed by a neutral authority, they would be free from any outside pressure, and their decision would be only guided by an ideal of good and fair justice:

> "[A] direct and practical solution is to adopt a mandatory roster system. This would permit a publicly accountable and deliberative process of appointments, free from the strategic pressures that arise after a dispute has been registered.... Likewise, a roster system would improve quality, if based on an open and merit-based process...."[80]

However, such propositions also have their drawbacks and, therefore, should be considered with caution and balanced with the primary interests of international arbitration.

Arbitration is by nature a private and contractual method of dispute resolution. Removing the parties from the process of appointment would alter the very nature of arbitration. The right of the parties to appoint their arbitrator has even been argued to be a *"fundamental right"*:[81]

---

77. Jan PAULSSON, *op. cit.*, fn. 26, p. 6; see also Alan S. RAU, *op. cit.*, fn. 40, p. 144.
78. Gus VAN HARTEN, "The (Lack of) Women Arbitrators in Investment Treaty Arbitration", *op. cit.*, fn. 4.
79. Jan PAULSSON, *op. cit.*, fn. 26, p. 8.
80. Gus VAN HARTEN, "The (Lack of) Women Arbitrators in Investment Treaty Arbitration", *op. cit.*, fn. 4.
81. Jan PAULSSON, *op. cit.*, fn. 26, p. 8.

"It would seem difficult to overcome a widely-shared – and in this setting, somewhat ironic – conviction that the ability to participate in the selection of arbitrators is critical to fairness in dispute resolution."[82]

Furthermore, if arbitrators were indeed to be appointed by a neutral body, it is not certain whether institutions are the best authority to do so. Arbitral institutions are currently facing criticism regarding their policy of appointment of arbitrators. This criticism is directed to most of the institutions, even the most active ones such as the ICC or the LCIA:[83]

"If the only reason to tolerate the unprincipled tradition of unilateral appointment of arbitrators is that there is no better alternative, the organizations that call themselves arbitral institutions need to look at themselves and ask why it is that they are so exposed to suspicions of poor selection of arbitrators, and maybe even worse: cronyism and other forms of corruption."[84]

Before considering giving more responsibilities to arbitral institutions for the selection of arbitrators, priority should be given to preventing the criticism mentioned and regaining trust in their system.

Again, it is necessary to remain realistic in the proposals made. A practical and reasonable proposal to improve the system, without impairing it, would be to already open the lists of potential arbitrators to more diverse profiles. An example in doing so is the Finland Chamber of Commerce, which opened the path to a change. In 2011, 27% of the arbitrators appointed by this institution were women, while "very few" of the party-appointed arbitrators were women.[85]

Publishing arbitral awards, or at least offering to publish awards with the approval of the parties, maybe with disclosure of the arbitrators taking the decision while ensuring the confidentiality of the dispute, could also be a solution as it would grant broader and direct information to the members of the arbitration community,[86] and enhance greater transparency.[87] Indeed, the publication of awards will enable arbitrators who are not part of the small circle of repeatedly appointed arbitrators to achieve some visibility. Newcomers will have more chances to integrate into the club by proving their value.[88] For newcomers, the reinforcement of training programs set up by the institutions would also be welcome.

To answer the criticism sometimes addressed to the supposed lack of independence and impartiality of todays' arbitrators, some scholars have proposed a ban on the

---

82. Alan S. RAU, *op. cit.*, fn. 40, p. 144.
83. William W. PARK, *op. cit.*, fn. 54, p. 202.
84. Jan PAULSSON, *op. cit.*, fn. 26, p. 13.
85. Benjamin G. DAVIS, *op. cit.*, fn. 1, p. 8, fn. 9.
86. Sophie HARNAY, *op. cit.*, fn. 33, p. 766.
87. Michael WAIBEL, Asha KAUSHAL, Liz KYO-HWA CHUNG and Claire BALCHIN, *op. cit.*, fn. 54, p. xli.
88. Catherine A. ROGERS, *op. cit.*, fn. 15, p. 968.

arbitrator-counsel practice. However, such proposition appears to be too extreme, since, as explained above, practicing arbitration both as arbitrator and counsel can offer significant advantages. Indeed a counsel acting as arbitrator can improve his or her procedural methods for handling a case (such as learning to submit reasonable written submissions, or to facilitate and maintain good relations with the other party), while an arbitrator acting as counsel can better understand the strategic choices that parties must take in the course of arbitration.

In any case, no unrealistic solution should be adopted to fight against certain people's belief concerning arbitrators' lack of independence and impartiality, since it would have the adverse effect of worsening the arbitration system by permitting the parties to engage in dilatory tactics or to seek the setting aside of unfavorable awards on the basis of alleged dependence or partiality of the arbitrator. Arbitrators do not have the ambition to become professional judges. Quite the opposite, they are practitioners, who are most of the time involved in other activities such as acting as counsel, academics or experts, and they are chosen for these multiple hats:[89]

> "An alternate route to shipwreck, also reducing confidence in the integrity of the arbitral process, would establish unrealistic ethical standards that render the arbitrator's position precarious and susceptible to destabilization by litigants engaged in dilatory tactics or seeking to annul unfavorable awards."[90]

However, clear rules defining the required qualifications of arbitrators, the potential situations of conflicts of interests, the limits of the duty of disclosure, and the appointment procedure might be helpful,[91] where, currently, most arbitration rules are written in broad and quite vague terms.

ii.   Ensure the seriousness and quality of the work done by arbitrators
To ensure quality along with diversity, arbitral institutions should work to ensure the seriousness and quality of the work done by arbitrators.

Some arbitration rules already provide for some control on the award. For instance, in the ICC system, the award must be approved by the ICC Court, through a scrutiny procedure, before it is formally rendered.[92] However, the ICC Court can in no way whatsoever modify the decision of the arbitrators. It is a good solution but it could be interesting, though, to extend the control to the motivation of the decision for limited purposes, for instance in order to verify if it is a copy-paste of previous decisions.

In this regard, if awards were published, parties and potential *"consumers"* of international arbitration could themselves assess the reputation of arbitrators, their procedural efficiency and whether they render strongly motivated decisions, or appear to decide specific legal issues always in the same way.

---

89. Yves DEZALAY and Bryant G. GARTH, *op. cit.*, fn. 5, p. 34.
90. William W. PARK, *op. cit.*, fn. 54, p. 193.
91. Catherine A. ROGERS, *op. cit.*, fn. 15, p. 1011.
92. Art. 33 ICC Rules of Arbitration (2012).

c.   Role of the arbitrators

An arbitrator should not accept too many cases and should refuse a case if he or she is not well suited to deal with the merits, in order to be able to render a quality job: "Good arbitrators must work and have time to work. Arbitration files are becoming more and more complex, often involving thousands of pages of documents. A good arbitrator must cope with them."[93]

Refusing some appointments would favor diversity since it opens the field to other people.

Moreover, to avoid any criticism as to a supposed lack of independence or impartiality, the behavior of arbitrators shall be guided at all times by high standards of morals and ethics, and these standards shall cause the arbitrator to reassess if his or her situation as a whole could potentially be a threat for arbitral justice, and not only regarding the existing instruments. To put it in a nutshell, arbitrators should bear in mind the myths they are supposed to uphold: "[T]he modern international arbitrator is not simply an instrumentality of the parties' collective will expressed through the arbitration agreement, but instead an integral part of a larger system that depends, in part, on them performing their role as responsible custodians of that system."[94]

d.   Role of the arbitration community

i.   Create/update guidelines

The arbitration community as a whole also has a role to play in the improvement of arbitrators' selection. International organizations, such as the International Bar Association (IBA), have initiated efforts in order to provide standards on required qualifications of arbitrators. The IBA Guidelines on Conflict of Interests in International Arbitration are a significant example. The text adopted in 2004, although not binding, has been widely accepted, used as a reference and applied in many arbitration procedures. These lists could be updated and completed, especially for the situation where an arbitrator has acted as counsel in previous similar cases.

Moreover, such initiatives should spread among the community and go further in the delimitation of the qualities expected of an arbitrator. In this context, the arbitration community could propose some guidelines for designating arbitrators that promote diversity.

---

93. Yves DERAINS and Laurent LEVY, "Introduction" in *Is Arbitration Only as Good as the Arbitrator? Status, Powers and Role of the Arbitrator*, Dossiers ICC Institute of World Business Law (2011) p. 7 at p. 8.
94. Catherine A. ROGERS, *op. cit.*, fn. 15, p. 963.

ii.   Encourage discussions and exchanges among the practitioners to spot any
        substantial downward spiral

As mentioned above, criticism and questioning among the community generate a
dynamic of reassessment that is beneficial for the system.[95] Hence it is important to
encourage initiatives to gather arbitration practitioners to discuss and debate the image
and the role of arbitrators. In this regard, the ICCA Congress is typically the kind of
event that generates positive interactions among the community.

---

95. Michael WAIBEL, Asha KAUSHAL, Liz KYO-HWA CHUNG and Claire BALCHIN, eds., *op. cit.*,
    fn. 54, p. xlii.

Tensions Between Party Autonomy and Diversity

Darius J. Khambata*

I. INTRODUCTION

Party autonomy is the one feature that defines arbitration more than any other. The essence of arbitration is a contract between two or more parties to have a private tribunal conclusively adjudicate their disputes and differences. Classically defined, arbitration is "a private procedure established by agreement…".[1] The freedom to stipulate the dispute resolution procedure can be near absolute "short of authorizing trial by battle or ordeal or, more doubtfully, by a panel of three monkeys".[2]

Autonomy is no doubt the most cherished principle of arbitration. Indeed it encapsulates the very idea of arbitration itself. But with it comes the inevitable consequence of party-*desired* arbitrators who may not necessarily be *desirable* arbitrators.

Of the nine Judges on the US Supreme Court (including the Chief Justice), there are three women, six Roman Catholics, three Jews, one African American, two Italian Americans and one Latina. All Ivy Leaguers and no "WASP" (White Anglo-Saxon Protestant) on the Supreme Court!

The question is whether the composition of the Supreme Court is a beckoning goal or a bridge too far for international commercial arbitration.

---

* Senior Advocate, LLM (Harvard); Advocate General of Maharashtra; former Additional Solicitor General of India; Vice-President, London Court of International Arbitration (LCIA).

The author is grateful to Mr. Ricardo Dalmaso Marques, Advocate, Mrs. Naira Jejeebhoy, Advocate, LLM (Columbia) and interns Mr. Pheroze Mehta and Ms. Nikita Nadkarni for their valuable research.

1. Lord FRAZER in *Amalgamated Metal Corp. v. Khoon Seng Co.* (1977) 2 Lloyds Reports, pp. 310, 317.
2. *Ahmad Baravati v. Josephthal, Lyon & Ross Inc.,* 28 F.3d pp. 704, 709 (7th Circuit 1994).

That great Judge Benjamin Cardozo famously said that "the eccentricities of Judges balance one another".[3] Leave aside their eccentricities, judges from diverse backgrounds bring to the table their accumulated knowledge and different sets of experiences. Most countries acknowledge diversity as a silent but very assertive factor in judicial selection.

Can this work for international arbitration? Diversity, a principle readily accepted in judicial selection, has yet to be fully embraced in arbitral appointments. How far can or should an arbitral institution or laws of a country go in imposing desirability over desire? Has the time come for importing diversity into the appointment of arbitrators as one of the objectives of selection?

II.   PARTY AUTONOMY

1.   The Model Law

The "three monkeys" approach to autonomy is adopted by the laws of most countries but it is subject to certain standard exceptions which are contained in most of these laws and which are, in the main, adopted by the UNCITRAL Model Law on International Commercial Arbitration (the Model Law). The working group that drafted the Model Law observed that "probably the most important principle on which the Model Law should be based is the freedom of the parties in order to facilitate the proper functioning of international commercial arbitrations according to their expectations".[4] The Model Law enunciates the concept of party autonomy in the negative. Art. 5 excludes judicial intervention[5] and Art. 19(1) gives the parties the freedom to agree on the procedure to be followed by the tribunal in the conduct of the proceedings.

Most countries have incorporated Art. 5 into their domestic law. Some have gone further. This includes India. Sect. 5 of the Indian Arbitration and Conciliation Act 1996 (the IACA 1996),[6] which makes one of its rare departures from the strict terms of Art. 5 of the Model Law in providing that: "Notwithstanding anything contained in any other law for the time being in force, in matters governed by this Part, no judicial authority shall intervene except where so provided in this Part." What is immediately apparent is the strengthening of Art. 5 by:

(a)   the insertion of a strong non obstante clause covering all other law in India;[7]

---

3. Benjamin CARDOZO, *The Nature of the Judicial Process* (1921) p. 177.
4. UN Doc. A/CN.9/207, para. 17.
5. Art. 5: "In matters governed by this Law, no Court shall intervene except where so provided in this Law."
6. An Act that is almost entirely a reproduction of the Model Law.
7. The Indian Supreme Court has set aside orders passed by the High Court of Karnataka in a Petition filed by one of the parties under Art. 226 of the Constitution of India, a provision recognizing and conferring upon High Courts plenary jurisdiction to issue writs to any "person or authority". The Supreme Court held that even such constitutionally empowered orders violated the mandate of Sect. 5 of the IACA 1996 since they interfered with pending arbitration proceedings. *CDC Financial Services (Mauritius) Ltd. v. BPL Communications Ltd.* (2003) 12 SCC 140.

(b) the widening of the embargo against intervention by including all judicial authorities, which need not be courts but could also be quasi-judicial tribunals, and regulatory authorities; an important extension where specialized and regulatory tribunals are increasingly replacing courts in important areas of judicial function.

2. The New York Convention

Party autonomy is fully recognized by Art. II and particularly by Art. V(1)(d) of the Convention on the Recognition and Enforcement of Foreign Arbitral Awards 1958 (the New York Convention).[8]

3. Institutional Rules

All leading arbitral institutions emphasize party autonomy in their rules.[9] Most institutions and courts respect party autonomy from the very inception of the arbitration. In the question of appointment of arbitrators specific procedural agreements or qualifications agreed to by the parties concerning the composition of the arbitral tribunal are respected even if they are inconsistent with the arbitration rules chosen to govern the arbitration or those of the arbitral institution concerned.[10]

4. Party-Agreed Qualifications of Arbitrators

A court normally ought to respect party autonomy by exercising such discretion in favour of constituting the agreed tribunal unless it is satisfied that the arbitral process would not lead to a just resolution of the dispute.[11]

---

8. Art. V(1)(d):

> "the composition of the arbitral authority or the arbitral procedure was not in accordance with *the agreement of the parties*, or, *failing such agreement*, was not in accordance with the law of the country where the arbitration took place". (Emphasis added)

9. See for example International Chamber of Commerce (ICC) Arbitration Rules 2012, Art. 19; London Court of International Arbitration (LCIA) Arbitration Rules, Art. 14.1; International Centre for Settlement of Investment Disputes (ICSID) Arbitration Rules, Rule 20; SIAC Singapore International Arbitration Centre (SIAC) Arbitration Rules (2013 edition), Rule 16.1 – all of which provide that the conduct of arbitral proceedings as provided by the rules themselves or as determined by the tribunal is usually subject to the agreement of the parties.

10. Jean-Francois POUDRET and Sebastien BESSON, *Comparative Law of International Arbitration*, 2nd ed. (2007) at p. 334 (para. 395); Swedish, Italian and Swiss law require the Court to grant the request to appoint an arbitrator unless the arbitration agreement is manifestly invalid (POUDRET and BESSON, p. 341 para. 408).

11. *Atlanska Plovidba v. Consignaciones Asturianas SA* (2004) 2 Lloyds Reports 109: (2004) 2 C.L.C. 886 para. 24; *The Iron and Steel Company Ltd. v. Tiwari Road Lines* AIR 2007 SC 2064: The Indian Supreme Court has held

III.   THE IMPORTANCE OF DIVERSITY

Such respect for party autonomy often results in constitution of tribunals that are party preferred. Appointments of arbitrators have tended to reflect the views and personalities of the parties concerned. Parties tend to appoint arbitrators of similar nationality, race or persuasion.

Statistics considered later indicate the serious imbalance that exists in the constitution of arbitral tribunals. Party autonomy does not produce diversity in the appointment of arbitrators. As purely private forums such an imbalance can be justified as a contractual choice. However with the subtle but steady transformation of the arbitral tribunal from an exclusively private forum into one that has public law elements, the question of diversity in tribunals assumes increasing criticality.

The importance of diversity in arbitral tribunals should not be undervalued. Diversity matters for several reasons:

(a)   The parties are entitled to the most meritorious or skilled arbitrators – parties are often ignorant of these qualities or give them a priority lower than factors such as familiarity or the expectation that a particular arbitrator will decide in their favour. In the extreme, unlimited party autonomy can, on occasion, even produce party-oriented arbitrators who, whilst they may not attract the disqualification of impartiality, would certainly not be desirable arbitrators in a public law sense.

(b)   Diversity counters the inherent and often silent prejudice and discrimination in the appointment of arbitrators, particularly by arbitral institutions.

(c)   "The business" of international commercial arbitration is increasingly in competition with other similar service providers that include the various arbitral institutions, national courts and now even an international financial court. The institution that takes diversity into consideration whilst appointing arbitrators will gain a competitive edge.

(d)   Most important of all, pluralism in the constitution of a tribunal is important for the perspective and balance that it brings to the tribunal. The perspective of a diversified tribunal is likely to be nuanced and fairer.[12] How true this would be in purely commercial disputes is debatable but cultural perspectives are also often relevant in determining how parties construe or intend contractual clauses and might also have a bearing when diverse international trade practices are at issue.

"In the matter of settlement of dispute by arbitration, the agreement executed by the parties has to be given great importance and an agreed procedure for appointing the arbitrators has been placed on high pedestal and has to be given preference to any other mode for securing appointment of an arbitrator. It is for this reason that in Clause (a) of Sub-section (8) of Section 11 of the Act it is specifically provided that the Chief Justice or the person or institution designated by him, in appointing an arbitrator, shall have due regard to any qualifications required of the arbitrator by the agreement of the parties."

12. See some interesting comments by Judge Timothy K. LEWIS reported in "Striving for Diversity in ADR", 63 American Arbitration Association Dispute Resolution Journal (February 2008, no. 1) p. 20.

Professor Michael Sandel, in the context of school admissions, argues that "The diversity rationale is an argument in the name of the common good – the common good of the school itself and also of the wider society…. Just as a student body drawn from one part of the country would limit the range of intellectual and cultural perspectives, so would one that reflected homogeneity of race, ethnicity and class." [13]

Perspective is a critical, if often underrated factor that operates as an aspect of the proficiency of arbitrators. It can impact both procedure as well as substance and almost always influences the result.

Several years ago the US Supreme Court struck down the conviction of a white criminal defendant because African Americans had been excluded from the jury venire. It held that removing any identifiable segment of the country from jury service "removes from the jury rooms the qualities of human nature and varieties of human experience, the range of which is unknown and perhaps unknowable". [14]

In other words diversity spawns perspective and the lack of diversity itself was a denial of the benefit of plurality of perspective.

This echoed the earlier similar view of the US Supreme Court, based on exclusion of women from juries. [15]

IV.   IS ARBITRATION A PURELY PRIVATE MATTER?

The concept of arbitration has steadily moved from a purely private creation of contract into a dispute resolution mechanism with public law elements. National laws and the rules and regulations of arbitral institutions rightly bear a pro-arbitration bias precisely because arbitration is seen as the much needed alternative to courts. Arbitration has for decades ceased to rely on contract enforcement law or mechanisms to facilitate the arbitral process and to enforce awards. The common law concept of enforcement of an award is a cause of action in contract, [16] although it invariably yields to the easier and comprehensive mechanisms for facilitation of arbitration and enforcement of awards provided by national statutes.

Most national statutes and the Model Law provide for the assistance of courts and the state machinery in at least the following areas:

---

13. Michael J. SANDEL (Anne T. and Robert M. Bass Professor of Government, Harvard University), *Justice. What is the Right Thing to Do?* (2009) pp. 169, 171.
14. Justice Thurgood MARSHALL speaking for the majority in *Peters v. Kiff*, 407 U.S. 493, 503 (1972); *Rose v. Mitchell*, 443 U.S. 545; *Batson v. Kentucky*, 476 U.S. 709.
15. *Ballard et al v. United States*, 329 U.S. 187 the US Supreme Court held that "the systematic and intentional exclusion of women, like the exclusion of a racial group, or an economic or social class, deprives the jury system of the broad base it was designed by Congress to have in our democratic society".
16. This remains an available but rarely used option. See the judgment of the Indian Supreme Court in *Badat & Co., Bombay v. East India Trading Co.* AIR 1964 SC 538, a judgment recognizing the continued existence of the common law remedy; DICEY and MORRIS, *The Conflict of Laws*, 13th ed., Vol. I, pp. 619-622 (paras. 16-062 to 16-069).

(a) conservatory and protective orders pending arbitration (Art. 9);
(b) appointment of arbitrators where the appointment procedure has failed or a party refuses to appoint (Art. 11);
(c) court assistance in taking evidence (Art. 27);
(d) setting aside an award based on a public policy requirement (Art. 34);
(e) provisions for recognition and enforcement of awards (Arts. 35 and 36).

The New York Convention provides a framework for the recognition and enforcement of foreign awards.

If arbitration was a purely private matter based on a private contract between parties, there could be no justification for the legal matrix of assistance and enforcement that the Model Law, the New York Convention and most national laws provide. Awards would have to be enforced purely as a matter of specific performance of the contract to arbitrate.

V. THE ARBITRAL LEGAL ORDER

1. Public Law Elements

The public character of international arbitration cannot be ignored.[17] Catherine Rogers speaks of an "unmistakable vibrant 'public realm'" of international arbitration. She gives several examples of the public facets of international arbitration including claims based on public and mandatory laws such as antitrust, securities fraud and intellectual property, the increasing precedentiary value of arbitral tribunal decisions, and the development of a professionally skilled and sophisticated network of arbitrators governed by rules and regulations of institutions. All this according to her creates "public goods" apart from public law issues that could have to be decided in arbitration. She argues, convincingly, that the greatest public good created by individual international arbitrations is with regard to the integrity and legitimacy of the international arbitration system.[18]

2. Investment Treaty Arbitrations

Investment treaty arbitrations certainly partake of state and hence public character since they concern the state's sovereign relations with investors.[19] It has been said that although investment treaty arbitrations are best understood in a public law, rather than private law context, in practice they continue to operate as though they were purely in

---

17. Catherine A. ROGERS, "The Vocation of the International Arbitrator", 20 Am. U. Int'l L. Rev. (2005, no. 5) p. 957; There is an excellent discussion of the juridical nature of arbitration by Julian D.M. LEW, Loukas A. MISTELIS and Stefan M. KRÖLL, *Comparative International Commercial Arbitration*, at pp. 71-82 (paras. 5-2 to 5-33).
18. ROGERS, *op. cit.*, fn. 17, p. 993.
19. VAN HARTEN, "The Public-Private Distinction in the International Arbitration of Individual Claims Against the State", 56 ICLQ (2007) pp. 371-394 at p. 372.

the realm of private law.[20] Burke-White and Von Staden classify those arbitrations as falling within the public law sphere as "those in which the outcome-determinative issue in the arbitration requires a determination of the State's power and legal authority to undertake regulation in the public interest".[21]

3. Does International Commercial Arbitration Have a Public Character?

The arbitral legal order transcends the character of the dispute. International awards carry the advantage of easier enforceability than national judgments primarily in view of the substantial success of the New York Convention. The standard of judicial review of international awards has always been a public law standard viz. "public policy". Is there room for treating even private international commercial arbitration as having some public law overtones? It is to the good that the matrix of the arbitral legal order promotes not only the quality control, transparency, ethical conduct, self-regulation that Catherine Rogers writes of[22] but also a more diverse selection of arbitrators.

International commercial arbitrators have been described as "international judges".[23] Emmanuel Gaillard argues that international arbitration is structured as a regime possessing all the attributes of a true legal order. It is not anchored in any one system of municipal or national laws.[24]

If this is so then arbitration can no longer remain a purely private matter, governed exclusively by private contract, to be undertaken behind closed doors and divorced from the public law matrix. Why should the judicial model of diversity not be heartily embraced? Should the international arbitrator not truly evolve into the "quasi-judicial adjudicator", an appellation conferred by the English Courts?[25]

20. William W. BURKE-WHITE and Andreas VON STADEN "Private Litigation in a Public Law Sphere: The Standard of Review in Investor-State Arbitrations", 35 Yale Journal of International Law (2010, Issue 2) pp. 282, 288.
21. *Ibid.*, p. 288.
22. ROGERS, *op. cit.*, fn. 17, p. 1008.
23. Emmanuel GAILLARD, *Legal Theory of International Arbitration* (2010) p. 59 (para. 62); In *P.V. Putrabali Adyamulia v. Rena Holding and Mnogutia Est Epices* the *Cour de Cassation* 1st civ. held that "an international award, which is not anchored in any national legal order, is a decision of international justice...". Rev. arb. (2007) p. 507 (dated 29 June 2007) – referred to in Emmanuel GAILLARD, *op. cit.*
24. GAILLARD, *op. cit.*, fn. 23, pp. 40-45 (paras. 46-49), pp. 56-66 (paras. 62-67); *Putrabali (Cour de cassation) op. cit.*, fn. 23.
25. *K/S Norjarl A/S v. Hyundai Heavy Industries Co. Ltd.* (1992) 1 QB 863, 885.

VI.   IDENTITY OF THE ARBITRATOR: PARTY AUTONOMY NOT ABSOLUTE

1.   *The Model Law Restrictions*

Cherished as it is as an underlying principle of arbitration, particularly international commercial arbitration, party autonomy in arbitration has never been absolute.[26] The Model Law itself recognizes several areas of restriction of party autonomy in the form of non-derogable provisions which the parties are not free to contract out of. Examples of these are Art. 18 (Equal treatment of parties), Art. 27 (Court assistance in taking evidence), Art. 31 (Form and contents of an award) and Art. 34 (Setting aside an award). There are thus several intrusions upon party autonomy which have come to be regarded as a normal part of arbitration life. Diversity is not yet one of these although it may well already be a silent guest at the table of some arbitral institutions.

Redfern and Hunter list four categories of restrictions on party autonomy: Equality, public policy, arbitration rules and the power to hear or involve third parties in the arbitral proceedings.[27] Expanding on these it is easy enough to see several areas in which party autonomy has been limited either by national law or by the rules of arbitral institutions. These areas include:

(a)   the requirement of impartiality and independence of arbitrators. The Model Law (Art. 12) imports both requirements;[28]

(b)   one-sided arbitrator selection clauses;[29]

---

26. "In principle, party autonomy does not mean a complete freedom to exclude a system of law, or particular elements of a system of law, from the relationship between the parties ... if the statute on its proper construction and with regard to the legislative power of the legislature applies to the parties and their conduct of the arbitration and expressly or by (necessary) implication cannot be excluded by agreement, the agreement of the parties to exclude it will count for nothing" [*America Diagnostica Inc. (U.S.) v. Gradipore Ltd. (Australia)* ICCA *Yearbook Commercial Arbitration* (henceforth *Yearbook*) XXIV (1999) p. 574 at p. 585].

27. Alan REDFERN and Martin HUNTER, *Law and Practice of International Commercial Arbitration*, 4th ed. (2004) pp. 267-268 (paras. 6-05 to 6-09).

28. The two requirements are not the same: REDFERN and HUNTER, *ibid.*, pp. 200-201 (paras. 4-54 and 4-55); POUDRET and BESSON, *op. cit.*, fn. 10, pp. 346-347 (paras. 415-417): the English Arbitration Act 1996 requires only impartiality (which could be such lack of independence as to constitute partiality).

29. The Indian Supreme Court has upheld the right of one of the parties to appoint the arbitrator and for such arbitrator to be an employee of such party provided the employee is not associated with the transaction concerned. This is restricted to government undertakings [*Indian Oil Corporation Ltd. v. Raja Transport Private Ltd.* (2009) 8 SCC 520, 532; *International Airports Authority of India v. K.D. Bali* (1988) 2 SCC 360]. However an employee arbitrator is disqualified if he had earlier expressed a view or taken a decision on the matter that suggested that he lacked an impartial mindset [*Bharat Sanchar Nigam Ltd. v. Motorola (India) Private Ltd.* (2009) 2 SCC 337, 348]. The position of the employee of a private corporation is differently treated and it may be reasonable to apprehend bias in view of his interest in the corporation [*Indian Oil Corporation (op. cit.,* fn. 29) 533]. The Supreme Court has now observed that government authorities and corporations should phase out appointments of employee arbitrators given the requirement of "independence" in the IACA 1996 [*Indian Oil Corporation (op. cit.,* fn. 29) 534; *Union of India v. Singh Builders Syndicate*

(c)   the appointment of the presiding or third arbitrator could be left to the two arbitrators nominated or to the governing institution.

The Model Law also provides for several areas in which the intervention of the court is mandated and these areas include Art. 11 (appointment of arbitrators), Art. 13 (challenge procedure) and Art. 34 (setting aside of an award).

It is clear from these provisions that the identity and qualification of an arbitrator is, at the best of times, not left entirely to the discretion of the parties. Even agreements in which the arbitrator is pre-named, are subject to the overriding principles of independence and impartiality that are mandated by Art. 12 of the Model Law.

2.   *The Role of Arbitral Institutions: Appropriating the Power to Appoint and the Imposition of Additional Qualifications*

The interposition of arbitral institutions itself reduces party autonomy particularly in cases where the presiding or third arbitrator is required to be appointed by the institution or where there is a failure to appoint arbitrators and this is to be done by the institution. It is at this stage that considerations of diversity can have a role to play. The role of an institution in reducing party autonomy also arises since most institutions permit appointment even of party-nominated arbitrators only from approved lists of arbitrators.[30]

The rules of institutions also require their confirmation of or concurrence with the appointment of party-nominated arbitrators. These rules often impose additional considerations as a means of ensuring impartiality and independence:

(a)   Art. 13(1) of the ICC Rules 2012 requires the ICC Court to consider the prospective arbitrator's nationality, residence and other relationships with the countries of which the parties or the other arbitrators are nationals and the prospective arbitrator's availability and ability to conduct the arbitration in accordance with the ICC Rules.

(b)   Rule 5.5 of the LCIA Rules provides that the LCIA Court alone is empowered to appoint arbitrators and that, though it will have due regard for any particular method or criteria of selection agreed in writing by the parties, consideration will be given to "the nature of the transaction, the nature and circumstances of the

---

(2009) 4 SCC 523, 528]. Asymmetrical arbitration clauses are usually, however, not enforced [Gary BORN, *International Arbitration – Cases and Materials* (2010) pp. 357-358]. Courts have on the other hand upheld clauses that confer upon one party alone, the right to appoint all members of the tribunal [*Sumukan Ltd. v. Commonwealth Secretariat* (2007) EWCA Civ 1148 (CA)] and have strictly enforced time limits agreed to by permitting one party to appoint both members of the tribunal [*Certain Underwriters at Lloyds London v. Argonaut Insurance Co.*, 500 F.3d 571 (7th Circuit 2007)].

30. This is a species of the principle of equality. However, it may happen that arbitration under the rules of a professional association may contain a list of only the members of that association and this may work unfairly if one of the parties to the dispute is a non-member. POUDRET and BESSON, *op. cit.*, fn. 10, pp. 339-340 (para. 404).

dispute, the nationality, location and languages of the parties and (if more than two) the number of parties".

Rule 11.1 of the LCIA Rules further provides:

"In the event that the LCIA Court determines that any nominee is not suitable or independent or impartial or if an appointed arbitrator is to be replaced for any reason, the LCIA Court shall have a complete discretion to decide whether or not to follow the original nominating process."

(c)   Art. 6(4) of the UNCITRAL Arbitration Rules provides for the appointing authority to have regard to such considerations as are likely to secure the appointment of an independent and impartial arbitrator before making an appointment based on the request of a party.

Such rules operate as a restriction of complete party autonomy in the matter of appointment.

On the other hand some institutions give greater weight to the nominations by parties. Rule 10.2 of the SIAC Rules requires the President (who is the appointing authority) to give credence to the qualifications required of the arbitrator by the arbitration agreement.[31]

VII.   THE CLONE APPOINTMENTS: LOST OPPORTUNITIES AND SILENT BIASES

The interposition of arbitral institutions could secure the consideration of objective factors in the appointment of arbitrators rather than party preferences. The parties' choice may be guided by any consideration which could range from a candidate's actual qualifications, experience or standing to a tactical or speculative analysis of a candidate's likely response to a particular issue or his or her potential influence on other members of the tribunal.[32] On the other hand the institutional choice should, at least theoretically, be objective and offer perspective on the issues involved.

Arbitral institutions however give primacy to predictability and consistency over diversity. Statistics and experience show that arbitral institutions have tended to perpetuate stereotype appointments of arbitrators and have not done enough to promote more balanced tribunals. Internationally the majority of arbitrators appear to be from a select gene pool of western professional males and retired judges. There may be no objection to any of these appointments in principle but the result of their selection is that tribunals run the risk of looking, thinking and acting in the same manner.

---

31. "10.2 In making an appointment under these Rules, the President shall have due regard to any qualifications required of the arbitrator by the agreement of the parties and to such considerations as are likely to secure the appointment of an independent and impartial arbitrator", 5th Edition, 1 April 2013.
32. Toby LANDAU, "Composition and Establishment of the Tribunal: Articles 14 to 36", 9 Am. Rev. Int'l Arb (1998) p. 45.

That typical selection means a typical perspective. When that manner reflects only one perspective there is a real danger that a silent bias creeps into the arbitral process particularly when the case or the parties do not reflect a typical western dispute. A typical tribunal will tend to act in a predictable manner which is good, but it could, albeit rarely, also act in a routine manner. As Benjamin Franklin said, "If everyone is thinking alike, then no one is thinking."

The game changers or the speed breakers in the diversity debate (depending on which way you look at it) must be the arbitral institutions. Arbitral institutions have produced the white western male tribunal (the infamous "pale, male and stale"). One who misses any one of these attributes is apt to feel like the proverbial Martian, who lands in the midst of an international commercial arbitration and feels like someone from outer space in the presence of the typical tribunal.[33]

Predictability and consistency are in themselves worthy objectives, but they are not and should not be the only objectives in constituting a tribunal. It is impartiality, independence and neutrality that are the prized objectives, the leitmotif, as it were, of arbitral appointments.

VIII.   THE PALPABLE TENSION

How much more can and should arbitral institutions do to impose a diverse arbitral tribunal upon parties who may be uncomfortable with such appointments and who in fact may desire a more typical panel of arbitrators? Diversity itself cannot be carried too far. It is not akin to affirmative action and there is no question of applying "quotas". The challenge is to strike a balance between diversity in appointment imposed by an institution without stretching party autonomy to breaking point.

The tensions between party autonomy and the institutional right of appointment of diverse arbitrators are apparent along the following fault lines:

(a)   nationality, race and culture;
(b)   party-issue-arbitrator relationships;
(c)   gender.

IX.   NATIONALITY, RACE AND CULTURE

1.   Neutral Nationality

In international arbitration it is a common tendency for a party to nominate arbitrators of its nationality or race. This usually stems from the perception that an arbitrator of the same nationality or culture will share a common perspective on issues with the appointer. Another motivator is that the arbitrator will be familiar with the current

---

33. My attention was drawn to the Martian by references in V.V. VEEDER, QC, "Who Are the Arbitrators?", this volume, pp. 652-660.

affairs and law of the country of the appointer. Theoretically the country in which the arbitrator was born or the passport carried should be irrelevant.[34] The ground reality is that, although the qualifications, experience and integrity of the arbitrator are factors which should and do count, inexorably, nationality is also a factor that influences the equation.

Neutrality of nationality is a factor that the laws of several countries and the rules of several institutions countenance. Art. 11(1) of the Model Law does not preclude a person from being appointed an arbitrator by reasons of nationality (unless otherwise agreed upon by the parties). Art. 11(5) however does provide that when a court or other party appoints a sole or third arbitrator it shall take into account "the advisability of appointing an arbitrator of a nationality other than those of the parties". Rule 6(4) of the UNCITRAL Arbitration Rules also so provides.

2. Institutional Restrictions

Several institutions forbid appointment of arbitrators sharing a common nationality with the parties. Art. 13(1) of the 2012 ICC Rules requires the ICC Court "to consider the prospective arbitrator's nationality, residence and other relationships with the countries of which the parties or the other arbitrators are nationals" when confirming or appointing arbitrators. Art. 13(5) requires that a sole arbitrator or the President of the arbitral tribunal "shall be of a nationality other than those of the parties". However the same article also provides that in suitable circumstances and provided none of the parties object, such appointment can be of a person from a country of which any of the parties is a national. Art. 6 of the LCIA Arbitration Rules mandates that a sole arbitrator or chairman of the tribunal "shall not have the same nationality as any party unless the parties who are not of the same nationality as the proposed appointee all agree in writing otherwise". Art. 6(4) of the American Arbitration Association International Arbitration Rules makes nationality a disqualification and provides that the administrator "may appoint nationals of a country other than that of any of the parties". On the other hand the SIAC Rules (5th edition, 1 April 2013) do not make nationality a criteria at all and do not consider commonality of nationality to affect the independence and impartiality of the arbitrator.

3. Is "Neutral Nationality" More Important than Expertise?

Often neutral nationality requirements militate against expertise. One who is skilled and experienced in the proper law is the more appropriate arbitrator. That he might happen to share a nationality with one of the parties ought not to be a disqualification. Or is nationality so strong a disqualification that it overrides even merit? Most countries and laws proceed on the basis that neutrality, independence and impartiality are more important than nationality and that the proposed arbitrator is not necessarily disqualified because he is of the same nationality as one of the parties.

---

34. REDFERN and HUNTER, *op. cit.*, fn. 27, p. 202 (paras. 4-58).

The Indian Supreme Court noticed that it was not impermissible under the UNCITRAL model to appoint an arbitrator of a nationality of one of the parties to the arbitration. It cited the example given in Redfern and Hunter[35] of an arbitration in Switzerland between a Swiss and a French company where the proper law was the law of Switzerland and their comment that it appeared sensible that the sole or presiding arbitrator should be a Swiss lawyer who in fact would be disqualified if neutrality of nationality was required.[36] Courts do respect party autonomy and appoint arbitrators in accordance with the nationality requirements or disqualifications provided by the arbitration agreement.[37]

In *Andersen Consulting v. Arthur Andersen and Andersen Worldwide*,[38] both parties had establishments and operations all over the world. The ICC International Court of Arbitration accepted the parties' refusal to waive the requirement of Art. 9(5) (requiring the appointment, as a sole arbitrator, of a person of a nationality different from either of the parties), and proceeded to undertake the arduous task of finding and appointing an arbitrator not belonging to any of the vast majority of countries of the world in which the parties had their operations. Despite the difficulty and impracticality of the request and the task, the ICC Court acknowledged party autonomy and proceeded to appoint an arbitrator from Colombia (one of the few countries with which the parties had no affiliations). The benefit of a sole arbitrator who was not party appointed was that he was not beholden to any of the parties.[39]

4. Neutrality of Cultural Affinity Rather than of Nationality

There is another silent and self-perpetuating prejudice. That is the myth of "neutrality" of nationality. The real elephant in the room is the repeated appointment by arbitral institutions of arbitrators of particular nationalities or shared cultural backgrounds. Neutrality of nationality is not as critical a factor as cultural affinity or sometimes even allegiance of the members of tribunals to each other and to one of the parties.

---

35. *Ibid.*

36. *Malaysian Airlines Systems BHD (II) v. M/s. Stic Travels Private Ltd.* (2001) 1 SCC 509; In a subsequent decision in *Delta Mechcons (India) Ltd. v. Marubeni Corporation* (2007) 7 SCR 281, the Supreme Court appointed as Chairman of the tribunal a person of a nationality different from that of the contracting parties in view of the requirement of the arbitration agreement in that case. However absent a requirement in the arbitration agreement the Supreme Court adopts the view taken by it in *Malaysian Airlines Systems: MSA Nederland B.V. v. Larsen & Toubro Ltd.* (2005) 13 SCC 719.

37. *Delta Mechcons, op. cit.*, fn. 36 (Indian Supreme Court); *Billerbeck Cie v. Bergbau-Handel GmbH*, Judgment of 3 May 1967, *Bundesgerichtshof*, *Yearbook* I (1976) p. 200 (West German Supreme Court) upholding an arbitration clause requiring arbitrators to be chosen from a list comprised exclusively of East German nationals holding that what really mattered was whether the tribunal would be impartial or not.

38. ICC International Court of Arbitration Case No. 9797 (2000).

39. "The *Andersen* Arbitration", 10 Am. Rev. Int'l Arb. (1999) p. 437.

5.   *Statistics*

The statistics make stark reading:

a.   ICC International Court of Arbitration[40]
At the ICC International Court of Arbitration nationals of the United Kingdom, United States, Switzerland, France and Germany were the most frequently chosen. These top 5 nationalities, out of the total of over 70 nationalities, made up 50% of the appointments/confirmations in 2011 and 48% of the appointments/confirmations in 2012. While arbitrators from Europe were appointed 66% of the time in 2011 and 2012, African nationals were appointed only 2.5% of the time in 2011 and 1.9% in 2012. Arbitrators from the Asia/Pacific region and the Americas jointly constituted around 30% of the appointments in 2011 and 2012.

b.   International Centre for Settlement of Investment Disputes (ICSID)[41]
Historically, Western Europeans make up 47% of the total appointments, while North and South Americans account for 32% of the selections. Arbitrators from the Middle East, Africa, Eastern Europe and Central Asia altogether have only been appointed 8% of the time. This historical disparity has continued into 2013: Western Europeans accounted for 48% of the appointments, whereas the Middle East, Africa, Eastern Europe and Central Asia were represented only 3% of the time.

c.   London Court of International Arbitration (LCIA)[42]
In 2012 other than the UK, the nationalities of arbitrators appointed included Australian; Austrian; Bahraini; Bangladeshi; Belgian; Brazilian; Canadian; Colombian; Czech; Dutch; Egyptian; French; German; Greek; Indian; Irish; Lebanese; Maltese; New Zealand; Nigerian; Peruvian; Portuguese; Russian; Singaporean; South African; Swedish; Swiss; and US. However, UK nationals made up over 50% of total appointments.

d.   WTO Trade Disputes
The Panel is the "first instance" court at the WTO, composed of three arbitrators ("judges"). Practice suggests that it is the nationality of the panelist that holds the key to most nominations. Data has been compiled on selection of panelists.[43] Horn et al. divide the origins of panelists into five categories: G2 (EU, US); IND (industrialized countries, members of the OECD, Organization for Economic Cooperation and Development); BIC (Brazil, India, China); DEV (developing countries); and LDCs (least developed

40. "2011 Statistical Report", 23 ICC International Court of Arbitration Bulletin (2012, no. 1); "2012 Statistical Report", 24 ICC International Court of Arbitration Bulletin (2013, no. 1).
41. "The ICSID Caseload – Statistics (2013, no. 2)", ICSID – International Centre for Settlement of Investment Disputes, 2013, available at: <https://icsid.worldbank.org/ICSID/FrontServlet? requestType=ICSIDDoc RH&actionVal=CaseLoadStatistics>.
42. Sarah LANCASTER, "LCIA Registrar's Report 2012", available at: <www.lcia.org/LCIA/Casework_Report.aspx>.
43. Henrik HORN, Louise JOHANNESSON and Petros C. MAVROIDIS, "The WTO Dispute Settlement System: 1995-2010, Some Descriptive Statistics", 45 J. World Trade (2011) p. 1107.

countries). Individuals originating in IND and DEV have appeared as panelists 489/597 times (almost 82%); 54% of panelists are from IND and 10% from G2. Fifty-one different nationalities have been represented, which means that more than two-thirds of all WTO Members have never had a panelist. [44]

6.   Ostensible Neutrality Is Not the Solution

The choice of an arbitrator is perhaps the single most significant step in the arbitral process. Is the search for "neutral" arbitrators a genuine one? If it is, then appointing an arbitrator from a "neutral" European country to arbitrate in a dispute between two Europeans, or appointing arbitrators from developed common law countries such as the United Kingdom, United States, Australia or Canada in a dispute involving a party from one of them and a country from the emerging markets or the developing world might achieve an ostensible neutrality but in substance it could end up perpetuating the same point of view familiar to one of the parties and not to the other. That is a fake neutrality under the cloak of a different passport.

That said, a challenge to the composition of an arbitral tribunal on the ground of the lack of an arbitrator from a developing country would probably fail. [45]

7.   A Clash of Cultures?

The failure to promote diversity in appointments has left the pool of arbitrators limited to the select club of white western males. Arbitral tribunals are not as cosmopolitan as the social orders of several developed countries. The particular problems faced by African Americans have been dealt with in an excellent article by Benjamin G. Davis. [46] It is said that there is a preconceived notion that to bring people of colour into the arbitral process is to sacrifice quality. [47] Race is not limited to colour and perhaps the issue of nationality is in essence an issue of culture even more than it is of citizenship.

Consider an arbitration between an Asian party and an American company. Appointment of an English presiding arbitrator might be viewed by the arbitral institution as being a perfectly legitimate and balanced choice of a "neutral" arbitrator, but it may not be viewed the same way by the Asian party. The Asian might well view the English arbitrator as being in essence from the same cultural stock as the American company. That suspicion might dissolve if the Asian was from a common law country

---

44. See the analysis of this data in Petros C. MAVROIDIS, "Emerging Issues in International Arbitration: Arbitrating Trade Disputes (Who's the Boss?)", 23 Am. Rev. Int'l Arb. (2012) pp. 481 at p. 485.
45. Doak BISHOP and Lucy REED, "Practical Guidelines for Interviewing, Selecting and Challenging Party-Appointed Arbitrators in International Commercial Arbitration", 14 Arb. Int'l (1998, no. 4) p. 395, fn. 37, refer to an ICC case where the Court of Justice at Geneva rejected such a challenge on the ground that two of the arbitrators were from neutral countries viz. Sweden and Switzerland (Egyptian Arab Republic v. Westland Helicopters Ltd., 26 November 1982).
46. Benjamin G. DAVIS, "The Color Line in International Commercial Arbitration: An American Perspective", 14 Am. Rev. Int'l Arb (2003) p. 461.
47. LEWIS, op. cit., fn. 12.

with a British colonial past (such as India or Singapore). Notwithstanding racial differences, an English arbitrator would then be "familiar" and easier to accept.

Thus a range of factors operate. Toby Landau has referred to the kinds of identification that may exist ranging from an easy linguistic understanding, to shared legal cultures, perspectives or even loyalties.[48] The same factors could also operate as factors of alienation. A greater degree of confidence is inspired if neither party is left with the feeling that it will get a worse hearing only because of the lack of a cultural, racial or historical identification between it and the arbitral tribunal.

There is an even more demanding hurdle to be crossed, but one that is inevitable: Will parties from Europe and North America accept arbitrators, presiding or otherwise, from emerging markets? South Africa and India have strong common law traditions and Brazil and South Korea are experienced civil law countries. These countries have an abundance of legal talent. Will arbitral institutions appoint say a South Korean sole or presiding arbitrator in a dispute between a European and an American company? Will the parties readily accept such appointments?

8.   *Jivraj v. Hashwani*

The UK Supreme Court has recently upheld an arbitration agreement providing for arbitration by a panel of three arbitrators each of whom was required to be a respected member of the Ismaili community to which both parties, Mr. Jivraj and Mr. Hashwani, belonged.[49] In allowing the appeal and in upholding the arbitration agreement, Lord Mance relied on Gary B. Born's *International Commercial Arbitration*[50] in which he describes the arbitrator as a service provider but concludes that "arbitrators do not merely provide the parties with a service, but also serve a public adjudicatory function that cannot be entirely equated with the provision of service in a commercial relationship". Indeed the basis of the UK Supreme Court decision in *Jivraj* is that the functions and duties of an arbitrator require him to rise above the partisan and particular interests of the parties and that he is in effect a "quasi-judicial adjudicator".[51]

X.   PARTY-ISSUE-ARBITRATOR RELATIONSHIPS

1.   *Disqualifying Factors*

The independence and impartiality of an arbitrator has several facets. There are clear areas that disqualify an arbitrator and I can do no better than to refer to the excellent

---

48. LANDAU, *op. cit.,* fn. 32, p. 73.
49. *Jivraj v. Hashwani* (2011) UKSC 40; V.V. VEEDER, *op. cit.*, fn. 33, this volume, pp. 656-660, cautions that the issues created by this matter may be far from over and points to the December 2013 order of the European Commission directed at the United Kingdom.
50. Vol. I (2009) pp. 1607-1609 at para. 77 of *Jivraj, ibid.*
51. *Jivraj, op. cit.,* fn. 49, para. 41 relying on *K/S Norjarl A/S v. Hyundai Heavy Industries Co. Ltd.* (1992) QB 863, 885.

work of Doak Bishop and Lucy Reed.[52] Bishop and Reed list six factors that are so indicative of partiality that they are generally disqualifying.[53] These are: a significant financial interest in the relevant project or dispute, or in a party or its Counsel; a close family relationship with a party or its Counsel; non-financial involvement in the relevant project, dispute or its subject matter; a public position taken on the specific matter in dispute; involvement in settlement discussions; and an adversary relationship with the party.

Bishop and Reed refer to other factors that, after full disclosure, generally should not disqualify the arbitrator including professional writings and lectures, membership in professional associations, position in the same industry or similarly situated Government and relationship with the arbitral institutions.[54] Finally Bishop and Reed list six factors which merit close scrutiny but do not necessarily weigh conclusively against selection. These are: past business relationship with the party or its counsel, attenuated family relationship with the party or its counsel, friendship with a party or its counsel, affiliation between law firms, office sharing among unaffiliated lawyers and service in other arbitrations.[55]

I propose to focus on three areas that affect the qualification of arbitrators: the chambers tenancy problem, the repeated appointment problem and the legal repeat problem.

2. The Chambers Tenancy Problem

This is a problem that arises in several common law jurisdictions including the United Kingdom, Australia, South Africa and India which follow the English system and in which, to use Bishop and Reed's expression, "office sharing among unaffiliated lawyers" is common. The sharing of chambers and office expenses may not create a financial relationship between an arbitrator and a lawyer but it could raise issues as to social contact and relationship between two individuals, confidentiality and the use of common infrastructure and services, including of individuals.

Part of the problem is one of perspective. Those who are familiar with the chambers system will immediately appreciate the absolute Chinese walls of confidentiality that exist between barristers, and even between barristers and their juniors, who may be briefed on opposite sides in court. These walls will apply when a member of chambers is appointed an arbitrator. All members of the bar operate independently and do not enjoy a profit-sharing partnership with each other. The system is longstanding and with fairly well-defined conventions and practices.

Consequently English courts have repeatedly rejected challenges to arbitrators on the ground of conflicts of interest arising from the appearance of a colleague of chambers

---

52. *Op. cit.*, fn. 45.
53. *Ibid.*
54. *Ibid.*
55. *Ibid.*

before them.[56] So has a French Court.[57] Both the ICC and the LCIA have rejected similar challenges.[58] The report of the Departmental Advisory Committee on Arbitration Law on the Arbitration Bill 1996 chaired by Lord Justice Saville observed (at paras. 101-102) that the appearance of a barrister as Counsel before an arbitrator from the same chambers did not amount to a lack of independence that gave rise to justifiable doubts about the impartiality of the arbitrator.

However the same perspective may not be shared by those who are not familiar with the English system. One set of commentators have referred to this practice as "*a borderline case*".[59] The IBA Guidelines on Conflicts of Interest 2004 place such a circumstance on the Orange List (Item 3.3.2) thus requiring disclosure. Even an English court has adopted a different standard when deciding whether a barrister called as an expert on behalf of another barrister from the same chambers (who was the litigant and a very good friend of the expert) had the required degree of independence. It did find the existence of a relationship which a reasonable observer might think was capable of affecting the independent views of the expert.[60]

A recent ICSID tribunal ruling (the Slovenia Case) that restrained the participation of Queen's Counsel before the tribunal based on his common membership of chambers with the President of the tribunal considers the matter from the perspective of a reasonable independent observer unfamiliar with the English chambers system.[61] In the Slovenia Case the ICSID tribunal largely based its decision on the fact that the Republic of Slovenia briefed the concerned QC during the course of the arbitration but disclosed his involvement only at an extremely late stage leaving the other party with an apprehension which was important to dispel. The ICSID tribunal expressly clarified that it did not believe that there was a hard and fast rule to the effect that precluded barristers from the same chambers from being involved as counsel and arbitrator in the same case. It however recognized that a party unfamiliar with the practices of English chambers ("a reasonable independent observer") might have a justifiable doubt in the circumstances of Slovenia's decision not to disclose to either the claimant or to the tribunal the involvement of the QC in the arbitration, till very late. The Slovenia Case can probably be explained on the basis of a lack of proper and timely disclosure.

The problem has arisen in India as well. The Bombay High Court heard a challenge which went even further in that it alleged bias based on the fact that the Counsel appearing for one of the parties had been a junior in the chambers of the arbitrator at a time several years prior to the arbitration although he was not when the arbitration took

---

56. *Nye Saunders and Partners v. Allen E. Bristow* (1987) 37 BLR 92 (CA); *Laker Airways Inc. v. FLS Aerospace Ltd.* (1999) 2 Lloyds Reports 45.

57. *KFTCIC v. Icori Estero SpA* (1993) 2 ADRLJ 167, a decision of the Court of Appeal, Paris.

58. See the references to these in a comprehensive article on this vexed issue by Michael HWANG, Senior Counsel and Arbitrator, Singapore, "Arbitrators and Barristers in the Same Chambers – An Unsuccessful Challenge", 6 Bus L.Int'l (2005) p. 235.

59. Julian LEW, et al, *op. cit.*, fn. 17, p. 263 (paras. 11-24 and 11-25).

60. *Liverpool Roman Catholic Archdiocesan Trust v. Goldberg* (2001) 4 All ER 950.

61. *Hrvatska Elektroprivreda, d.d. (Claimant) v. The Republic of Slovenia (Respondent)* (ICSID Case No. ARB/05/24) – Tribunal's ruling regarding the introduction of a QC at an advanced stage of the proceedings, 6 May 2008.

place. In rejecting that challenge, the High Court held that "the high traditions of the bar must not be ignored".[62]

What should an arbitral institution do in such a case? Should it refuse to confirm the party appointment of a chamber counsel? Should it insist on a more diverse choice of legal representation from outside the arbitrator's chamber? Can it so impinge upon party autonomy? Certainly as far as the presiding or sole arbitrator is concerned the institution should attempt to avoid appointment of an arbitrator who will be from the same chambers as the legal representative disclosed to the parties. This obviously cannot take into account the circumstance of a Counsel who may be briefed only during the course of the arbitration. It is a vexed issue but one to which diversity could offer a solution.

3. Repeat Arbitrators

The repeated appointment of an individual as an arbitrator by the same party might cast doubts on his independence. Here too disclosure of such past appointments could go a long way in dispelling any misapprehension that might arise. Disclosure would also expose a pattern of appointment that might lead to the inference of a connection or financial arrangement.

Bishop and Reed[63] list "service in other arbitrations" as a factor that merits closer scrutiny. They raise their basic concerns which are:

(a)   Did the prior arbitral decision pre-judge the liability in the current arbitration?
(b)   Has the arbitrator become aware of any material evidence in the previous proceedings that is unknown to the other arbitrators and to the other party?
(c)   Is the arbitrator dependent upon the fees earned by reason of repeated appointments?

Bishop and Reed find that any of the above three will effectively disqualify the arbitrator but that the mere fact of repeated appointment does not lead to the inference that one of these three disqualifying factors is attracted. Repeated appointments could be attributable also to the expertise and merit of the arbitrator or indeed his familiarity with an area of law or fact that makes it attractive to a party to re-nominate him in a subsequent arbitration.

The real question is whether the repeat appointment affects the independence and impartiality of the arbitrator in the circumstances of the case. Often the challenge has failed if it is based merely on the repetitious appointment or where the allegation of close personal ties has not been substantiated by objective evidence.[64] The real question is

---

62. *ONGC v. Offshore Enterprises Inc.* (1994) 4 Bom. C.R. 538 (DB), p. 565 (para. 46).

63. *Op. cit.*, fn. 45.

64. *Universal Compression International Holdings SA v. The Bolivarian Republic of Venezuela* (ICSID Case No. ARB/10/9) para. 71 – the tribunal held that "A manifest lack of the required qualities must be proved by objective evidence. A simple belief that an arbitrator lacks independence or impartiality is not sufficient to disqualify an arbitrator."; *Nandyal Co-operative Spinning Mills Ltd. v. K.V. Mohan Rao* (1993) 2 SCC 654 – The Indian Supreme Court found that no actual bias was

whether the repeat appointment is symptomatic of a relationship that affects the impartiality or independence of the arbitrator. As Jan Paulsson observes, "Whatever their motivation, arbitrators tend to want to be reappointed."[65]

Disclosure however should in most cases afford sufficient protection.[66] The disclosure requirements under the Model Law and under national laws that follow the Model Law should address this situation. The US Supreme Court reversed the Court of Appeals (First Circuit) and vacated an award purely on the ground that a close business connection between the arbitrator (an engineering consultant whose services were used repeatedly by one of the parties resulting in fees of about $12,000 over a period of four to five years including in respect of the very projects involved in the dispute) had not been disclosed and that this might have created an impression of possible bias.[67]

An institution should perhaps not insist on a diversity of appointment merely by reason of repeated appointment of the same arbitrator. In the case of institutional appointees however repeat arbitrators may even be a useful departure from diversity in that being familiar with the facts in a similar set of circumstances or the legal issues will quicken and focus their decision making.

4.   Legal Repeat Arbitrators

Of a different nature is the issue that arises when an arbitrator has already taken a strong position on a particular issue in a previous arbitration suggesting that he is predetermined on that matter. This might, from the perspective of the appointing party, either make him attractive or disqualify him. It is clear that there might be some inherent bias when an arbitrator has to decide an identical question of fact or law as arose before him in a previous matter.[68] On the other hand however it has been held in cases that the fact that an arbitrator made a finding of fact or a legal determination in one case does not preclude that arbitrator from deciding the law and the facts impartially in another case. It was held that to disqualify an arbitrator merely because he or she had decided a similar matter previously "would have serious negative consequences for any adjudicatory system".[69]

---

proved by reason of repeated appointment; *Karam Chand Thapar & Bros. v. National Hydroelectric Power Corporation*, Delhi High Court 13 October 2009 in C.S. (O.S.) 2143/2002 and OMP 21/2004 – mere reappointment did not qualify. There had to be some other evidence of bias; in *Korsnas Aktiebolag v. A.B.Fortum Varme* (T 156-09) Supreme Court of Sweden – it was held that the number of reappointments were not high enough to merit setting aside the award.

65. Jan PAULSSON, "Ethics, Elitism, Eligibility", 14 Journal International Arbitration (1997) at pp. 13-22.

66. Julian LEW, et al., *op. cit.*, fn. 17, p. 264 (para. 11-27).

67. *Commonwealth Coatings Corporation v. Continental Casualty Company*, 393 U.S. 145 (1968); *Fremarc v. ITM Enterprises* is a similar decision by the *Cour de cassation* 6 Dec 2001, 4 Rev. arb. (2003) pp. 1231-1233.

68. Natalia GIRALDO-CARRILLO, "The 'Repeat Arbitrators' Issue: A Subjective Concept", 19 International Law, Revista Colombiana de Derecho Internacional (2011) pp. 75-106 at p. 97.

69. *Suez Sociedad General de Aguas de Barcelona S.A. et al., and Inter Aguas Servicios Integrales del Agua S.A. v. The Argentine Republic, Suez, Sociedad General de Aguas de Barcelona S.A.* (ICSID Case No. ARB/03/17) and *Vivendi Universal S.A. v. The Argentine Republic* (ICSID Case No. ARB/03/18) (the

French courts have held that there is "neither bias nor partiality" in cases of legal repeat arbitrators.[70]

A strongly worded dissenting or concurring opinion rendered in a previous or preliminary award by itself does not lead to sufficient doubts as to the impartiality of an arbitrator.[71] A dissenting opinion cannot be considered to be a sign of partiality, even if it reveals details of the tribunal's deliberations.[72]

XI.   GENDER

1.   *The Clear Prejudice*

The big issue in the diversity debate must still remain gender. Although it is true that in the last few years the involvement and participation of women has been steadily increasing, the hard statistics disclose that appointment of women arbitrators remains far below optimum levels. In the year 2012, appointments by the following leading arbitral institutions disclose that only a small percentage of such appointments of arbitrators were of women:

(a)   *ICC*: Whereas a total of 555 men were appointed as arbitrators only 79 women were appointed. Similarly, whereas the appointments of male arbitrators were confirmed by the Secretary General of the ICC Court in 614 cases, the corresponding figure for women was only 53.[73]

(b)   *Hong Kong International Arbitration Centre*: one woman arbitrator was appointed/confirmed as opposed to four men.[74]

(c)   *ICSID*: 117 male arbitrators and only 11 female arbitrators were appointed.[75]

(d)   *LCIA*: 311 male arbitrators were appointed as against only 33 female.[76]

---

challenge was made on the ground that the arbitrator had arbitrated earlier on a similar dispute that concerned waste water management and was party to an award against Argentina that was alleged to be flawed).

70. *Ben Nassar et autre v. BNP et Credit Lyonnais, Cour d'appeal de Paris*, Rev. arb (1994) p. 380; POUDRET and BESSON, *op. cit.*, fn. 10, p. 353 (para. 421).

71. Julian LEW, et al., *op. cit.,* fn. 17, pp. 260-261 (paras. 11-17).

72. *Ibid.*

73. Benjamin G. DAVIS, Associate Professor of Law, University of Toledo College of Law, "American Diversity in International Arbitration", 2003-2013,13 December 2013 at <http://papers.ssrn.com/sol3/papers.cfm?abstract_id=2364967> p. 7.

74. *Ibid.*

75. *Ibid.*

76. LANCASTER, "LCIA Registrar's Report 2012", *op. cit.*, fn. 42.

Gus Van Harten estimates that until May 2010, of the 631 appointments in 249 known investment treaty cases just 41 (6.5%) were women. Of the 247 individuals appointed as arbitrators across all cases only 10 were women (4%).[77]

Other commentators have also analyzed this problem. Lucy Greenwood and C. Mark Baker have found that the best estimate of the percentage of women appointed to international commercial arbitration tribunals is around 6%.[78] Greenwood and Baker referred to research by Professor Susan Franck that found in a survey of 145 investment treaty arbitrators that there were only 5 women (3%).[79] Other surveys paint an equally dismal picture.[80]

The percentage of women arbitrators is low even when compared to the percentage of women partners in the international arbitration practices of leading law firms (which is around 10-15%) as opposed to the percentage of women on international arbitration tribunals (around 5-6%). This led Lucy Greenwood to conclude that similar biases were at play.[81] The low percentage of women on the courts or boards of leading arbitral institutions reflects this bias. In 2004 women comprised only 11% of the ICC International Court of Arbitration, 5% of the International Council for Commercial Arbitration, 5% of the ICSID Panel of Conciliators and Arbitrators, 0% of the London Maritime Arbitrators Association and 4% of those listed in the *Guide to the World's Leading Experts in Commercial Arbitration*.[82]

2.   Stereotypes

Several reasons have been offered to explain this imbalance such as an arbitrator selection process that relies on users to select arbitrators and a failure by arbitral organizations to reach out to diverse candidates.[83] Since arbitration is often a private and confidential matter the appointing parties and institutions are not pressured to adopt a politically correct approach. Perhaps the primary reason remains a largely unconscious prejudice

---

77. Gus VAN HARTEN, "The (Lack Of) Women Arbitrators in Investment Treaty Arbitration", Columbia FDI Perspectives (6 February 2012, no. 59) .

78. Lucy GREENWOOD and C. Mark BAKER, "Getting a Better Balance on International Arbitration Tribunals", 28 Arbitration International – the Journal of the London Court of International Arbitration (2012, no. 4).

79. *Ibid.*

80. "HONG KONG: New Women's Network Launched", Global Arbitration Review (31 October 2013); "DUBLIN: Arbitrators Celebrate International Women's Day", Global Arbitration Review (15 March 2013); Irene TEN CATE, "Binders Full of Women ... Arbitrators?" IntLawGrrls (2 November 2013); Lisa Bench NIEUWVELD, "Women in Arbitration: Lots of Talk. Any Changes?" Kluwer Arbitration Blog (22 November 2011).

81. Lucy GREENWOOD, "Unblocking the Pipeline: Achieving Greater Gender Diversity on International Arbitration Tribunals", 42 International Law News (Spring 2013, no. 2).

82. Michael D. GOLDHABER, "Madame La Presidente – A woman who sits as president of a major arbitral tribunal is a rare creature. Why?", 1 Transnational Dispute Management (2004, Issue 3).

83. Sasha A. CARBONE and Jeffrey T. ZAINO, "Increasing Diversity Among Arbitrators – A Guideline to What the New Arbitrator and ADR Community Should Be Doing to Achieve this Goal", NYSBA Journal (January 2012) p. 33.

based on stereotyped and misconceived notions of the incapability of women to discharge roles of "responsibility". This is a self-perpetuating prejudice because the fewer the female appointees, the less their exposure and the scarcer the opportunities for dispelling that prejudice.

3. Fear of the Unknown?

Van Harten also refers to the fact that between them two particular women were appointed 75% of the time.[84] This amazing statistic is a tribute to the acknowledged merit and stature of these two women. It also carries the significant connotation that it is perhaps a fear of the unknown that has resulted in inadequate appointments of women arbitrators. Where arbitrators have been tested and have excelled, as in these two cases, parties and institutions are more than happy to appoint and reappoint them.

4. Cultural and Religious Barriers

There will of course be issues where gender diversity could clash with cultural or religious attitudes. For example, under traditional Islamic law it may be difficult, if at all permissible, to have a woman serve as an arbitrator[85] and an award rendered by a female either solely or as part of a tribunal, might not be enforceable in certain Islamic countries. Further, under traditional Islamic law, a dispute involving a muslim cannot be resolved by an arbitral tribunal that includes a non-muslim arbitrator.[86] Saudi Arabia has specific Shari'a requirements affecting the appointment of arbitrators who sit within it. Such requirements may not affect arbitrations outside Saudi Arabia, unless the parties have agreed that Saudi procedural rules would govern the arbitration even if it is seated outside that country.[87]

5. Is the Tide Turning?

As the experience with the two women arbitrators shows, it is really a matter of taking several first steps and giving opportunities to women to act on arbitral tribunals so that their expertise and merit can be availed of. This is an area where affirmative action and diversity can certainly play a stellar role. It is an extremely heartening fact that leading arbitral institutions and other dispute resolution centres are appointing women to their highest offices.[88] Times are changing. The tribunal in a recent LCIA arbitration seated

---

84. VAN HARTEN, *op. cit.*, fn. 77.
85. Thomas E. CARBONNEAU, *Cases and Materials on the Law and Practice of Arbitration*, 3rd ed. (JurisNet, LLC, 2002) p. 1199.
86. Thomas E. CARBONNEAU, "Symposium: International Commercial Arbitration: The Exercise of Contract Freedom in the Making of Arbitration Agreements", 36 Vand. J. Transnat'l L., p. 1189.
87. Stephen R. BOND, "The International Arbitrator: From the Perspective of the ICC International Court of Arbitration", 12 NW. J. INT'L L. & BUS. 1 (1991-1992, no. 1) pp. 6-7.
88. DAVIS, *op. cit.*, fn. 73.

in India was comprised of two women and a sole male![89] This is some progress from 2004 when the Secretary General of a leading arbitral institution stated that it had no official position on gender diversity.[90] The journey is a slow one but I believe it is inevitable that the "old boys' club" will have to open its doors to women arbitrators.

6.   *The Way Forward*

Dr. Jacomijn J. van Haersolte-van Hof makes several very useful recommendations to encourage diversity including a pledge by male participants to refuse to participate at conferences if there is not an adequate level of participation by females.[91] Additionally the following measures have also been suggested:

(a)   giving women a policy making role in the organization and in ADR in general;
(b)   appointing women with the required experience and background to the panel of the organization; and
(c)   training women as arbitrators and thus encouraging parties to appoint them.[92]

XII.   CONCLUSION: A BRAVE NEW WORLD

1.   *Economic Considerations*

If we aspire to the creation of an international arbitral legal order, then arbitral institutions need to take a serious look at their qualifications and standards for appointment of arbitrators. Party autonomy in the selection process remains of critical importance and party-nominated arbitrators will remain those whose attitudes and attributes will most closely reflect those of the parties. The opportunity lies in the appointment of presiding arbitrators or sole arbitrators by institutions. It is an opportunity that arbitral institutions will let pass at their own peril. Institutions cannot ignore the legitimate demand for greater representation from BRIC countries or from developing countries. Or else economic considerations will ultimately drive arbitral appointments.

2.   *"Good" and "Bad" Diversity*

That diversity is a worthy objective is no longer a matter of doubt. That party nominated arbitrators will not be diverse is equally true. If however we aspire to create an arbitral

---

89. The Hon'ble Justice A.P. Shah (retired Chief Justice of the Delhi High Court and of the Madras High Court), Lucy Reed and Cherie Booth Blair, QC.
90. GOLDHABER, *op. cit.*, fn. 82.
91. Dr. Jacomijn J. VAN HAERSOLTE-VAN HOF, "Diversity in Diversity", this volume, pp. 638-651.
92. "Women and Diversity in ADR: A Roundtable", 51 Dispute Resolution Journal (April 1996, Issue 2/3) p. 64.

legal order, it is inevitable that arbitrators, like judges, are independent of the interests of the parties and reflect social and economic factors. Diversification in terms of gender, race and issue is but a facet of the objective of the truly independent and neutral arbitrator – independent of gender, race and issue bias and neutral to party.

Diversity does not always militate against party autonomy. Cases of national, racial or cultural affinities being taken into consideration whilst confirming or making appointments are indeed cases where the perceptions and desire of parties are given weight. This is, in a sense, party-centric. Where parties desire certain arbitrators as repeat or legal repeat arbitrators, some limit to party autonomy may be in order. Gender issues are usually party and nationality neutral. Thus in most areas party autonomy can be married with diversity without substantial, if any, conflict at all. Such actions in diversity are pro-party and good for the institution of arbitration in the long run. They are examples of "good" diversity.

"Bad" diversity arises when an institution has no real regard for party preferences and affinities and imposes "diverse" arbitrators only to meet some statistical goal. It is then that party autonomy suffers. That is not acceptable for it will test the very limits of what arbitration is.

3. Merit and Diversity Can Co-exist

Merit and expertise should, of course, never be sacrificed. As Professor Seraglini writes, in order to keep the system of arbitration attractive, prospective arbitrators must fulfil high standards of skill.[93] Professor Seraglini offers some counterpoint when he argues that the constant participant in arbitration – whether as arbitrator, author or counsel – gathers experience and an insider's advantage of "the reality of the market". There can of course be no compromise with the integrity, merit or proficiency of the arbitrator. But it is misconceived to assume merit has a racial or geographical bias. "Diversity" arbitrators can and must try harder to bridge the perceived proficiency deficit!

4. Diversity Spawns Perspective

Diversity spawns perspective and a diversified tribunal offers balanced justice. When the expertise of competing candidates is more or less equal, diversity can and must be considered. Thus diversity can be introduced into the equation as an additional, if not a determinative, factor in appointment. Diversity must then be seen as an aspect not only of impartiality but also of merit.

There will be the Cassandras who warn us of the grave error of our ways. They might even quote that great mathematician, philosopher and songwriter, not to say pianist, Tom Lehrer. Speaking of the Army carrying the American ideal to its logical conclusion

---

93. Christophe SERAGLINI, "Who Are the Arbitrators? Myths, Reality and Challenges", this volume, pp. 593-594, 605.

636

he said, "Not only do they prohibit discrimination on grounds of race, creed and colour, but also on ability."[94]

5. The Strategic Role for Institutions

Although not easy, a balance must be struck and well it should be between diversity and party autonomy. This can be done by institutions in several ways:

(a)   Determine the diversified qualities required for arbitrators such as gender, age, cultural background, race and geography;
(b)   Conduct a "diversity audit" of their existing appointments of arbitrators;
(c)   Balance factors of expertise and proven track record with the diversity factors determined to choose a panel of talented and diversified arbitrators. No quotas, nor statistical goals, only acknowledgement of diversity as a factor;
(d)   Put diversity on the table each time an appointment is to be made or confirmed – be bolder in making diversified appointments;
(e)   Publish the diversity factors and the results of the diversity audit;
(f)   Advertise diversity as a positive selling point and persuade users of the benefits of diversity.

The arbitral institution occupies a position of great strategic importance. Whether arbitration moves from the strict domain of private contract to become a truly alternative dispute resolution mechanism will to a large extent depend on the evolution of the arbitrator into a "quasi-judicial adjudicator". Institutions must strike out into this brave new world and utilize their powers of appointment to make wise and diversified choices and to install systems that encourage such choices.

The dream of the truly independent and impartial arbitrator may be Utopian. Nevertheless the imperative to diversify is critical to the future of international arbitration. I call then for more determined steps into this brave new world. None of us can be silent bystanders in the pursuit of diversity. As Mahatma Gandhi said, "You must be the change you wish to see in the world."

---

94. "It Makes a Fellow Proud to Be a Soldier", An Evening (Wasted) with Tom Lehrer (1959). I was reminded of Tom Lehrer by the reference to him in J.VAN HAERSOLTE-VAN HOF, "Diversity in Diversity", *op. cit.*, fn. 91, this volume, pp. 638-651.

Diversity in Diversity

Jacomijn J. van Haersolte-van Hof[*]

I.   INTRODUCTION: WHO ARE THE ARBITRATORS, WHO SHOULD BE THE ARBITRATORS,
      AND WHAT CAN WE DO TO IMPROVE THE LACK OF DIVERSITY?

This paper seeks to comment on the main paper presented by Christophe Seraglini (and the other papers presented by the debaters) and to discuss the propositions presented by this panel. The focus of this paper is "Diversity in Diversity": in describing facts, developments and goals, it is important to keep in mind that diversity is a multi-faceted concept. And although the notion that diversity is desirable may on an abstract and perhaps superficial level find wide support and acceptance, consensus on concrete action points may be more limited. Still, by being explicit and transparent, and perhaps realistic, it should be possible at least to achieve some tangible proposals and results.

The theme of this panel is "Who Are the Arbitrators; Myths, Reality and Challenges". In brief, conscious of the disregard of nuance, Christophe Seraglini's paper describes the myth that forms the starting point for the discussion as follows: arbitrators are old, white men, and that's a good thing, or at least, an understandable fact. He then clarifies that yes, they are, kind of, and yes, there are some justifications for this situation. He describes that changes need to be made, but overall things are moving in the right direction. In his view, having the institutions take over the appointment process is not (necessarily) the way forward. Proposals for the future include "opening the list of potential arbitrators to more diverse profiles".[1] He advocates greater transparency, including by means of publishing awards.

Against this background, this panel is to comment on a number of myths/realities propositions, namely:

---

*   Director General, London Court of International Arbitration (LCIA).
    The author thanks Ricardo Dalmaso Marques for his helpful and cheerful assistance in preparing
    this paper.
1. This volume, p. 606. Specifically, Christophe Seraglini refers to Van Harten's suggestion to engage
    a number of organizations, such as the International Association of Women Jurists, the International
    Federation of Women Lawyers or Arbitral Women. G. VAN HARTEN, "The (Lack Of) Women
    Arbitrators in Investment Treaty Arbitration", Columbia FDI Perspectives (6 February 2012,
    no. 59).

(1)   Is there a pool of arbitrators and/or common profile in international arbitration? Is it a myth or a reality?
(2)   Is the existence of this pool of arbitrators jeopardizing the legitimacy of international arbitration?
(3)   Is there a need for more diversity in international arbitration? Is it a priority for the forthcoming years?

What should be added to this list is what concrete proposals are necessary and feasible to change the status quo. In order to answer these issues and propositions, this paper will first address the definition of diversity and why diversity is relevant and important. This leads to the question whether diversity is developing quickly enough in international arbitration. If not, what can be done to change that and how can (deliberate) inclusion be enhanced? This paper will conclude as follows:

(1)   There is too small a pool of arbitrators dominating the field; in particular age and gender are issues that need to be addressed.
(2)   This dominance jeopardizes the legitimacy of international arbitration and constitutes a risk to the well functioning of arbitration as a method of dispute resolution.
(3)   Diversity and inclusion in international arbitration are a priority for the coming years in order to ensure dispute resolution of an adequate quality and quantity.
(4)   The tools to achieve this are transparency, awareness and concrete changes in behaviour. To this effect, users, including the institutions, can and should take on some commitments which are to be discussed below.

II.   WHAT IS DIVERSITY – WHAT KIND OF DIVERSITY MATTERS?[2]

The Webster dictionary defines diversity as: "the condition of having or being composed of differing elements: variety; especially: the inclusion of different types of people (as people of different races or cultures) in a group or organization".[3]
     The American Bar Association (ABA) identifies race and ethnicity, gender, sexual orientation and disabilities as the main categories of diversity.[4] While these are obviously critical, this cannot be seen as an exhaustive list. For instance, what is absent from this overview is age. Age discrimination in a non-arbitration context often relates to the right of senior people not to be discriminated against. In the diversity debate in arbitration,

---

2. Unless stated otherwise, comments in this paper relate to diversity both in general and specifically in relation to international arbitration. The arbitration process may pose certain specific challenges and opportunities for diversity, such as in relation to nationality requirements, but otherwise, there is no reason to treat international arbitration differently.
3. <www.merriam-webster.com/dictionary/diversity> (accessed 27 October 2014).
4. "ABA Report and Recommendations, Race and Ethnicity, Gender, Sexual Orientation, Disabilities", ABA Presidential Initiative, Commission on Diversity (2009-2010) (henceforth "ABA Report", p. 3, see URL <www.americanbar.org/content/dam/aba/administrative/diversity/next_steps_2011.authcheckdam.pdf> (accessed 27 October 2014).

age can also be seen as a factor that hinders diversity. Other papers (and literature) have referred to the preponderance of senior arbitrators (generally, in the context of the triptych senior, white male).[5]

In addition, a mere list is not necessarily helpful in identifying priorities. Selecting priorities is not an easy matter, anyhow. Diversity issues, as will be discussed later, are diverse, and not necessarily identical everywhere and at every time. Gender is an obvious candidate for a universal list as the entire population is approximately 50% male and female. As Darius Khambata states: "The big issue in the diversity debate must still remain gender."[6] On the other hand, in a population where there is no religious diversity, religion is unlikely to be a factor attracting much interest – though as a matter of principle it may still be equally important. At the same time, as will also be discussed further, different issues will have developed differently in different countries. For example, whereas the United States may be seen as a country at the forefront of the diversity discussion, it is interesting to see that in a country such as the Netherlands the judiciary is predominantly female, whereas the United States lags behind.

The ABA Report and other publications on American diversity list, in addition to gender, persons of minorities, persons with disabilities and LGBT (lesbian, gay, bisexual and transgender) as the target population in enhancing diversity. As will be addressed further below, minorities in international arbitration is a slightly complicated consideration, because diversity of race can be seen as both a consideration within a national population (persons of one nationality can be of different race), but one may also seek diversity of nationality (and race) independently as a potential target in its own right in an international setting.

Not spelled out in this ABA Report, but conceivably included by implication, is religious diversity. In international arbitration, this may have a positive and a negative perspective, in the sense that, while discrimination on the basis of religion is not permissible, parties may choose a particular form of dispute resolution based on their – joint – religious beliefs.

The list does not end here – although some factors may be perceived to be less fundamental than others. In addition to factors which are also morally relevant, certain factors are important to ensure the quality of the decision-making process. This kind of diversity includes considerations such as expertise. Expertise may be thought of in terms of legal expertise, but is in fact a more general consideration. Well known in certain types of arbitration, but arguably more relevant generally, is the inclusion of non-lawyers with particular expertise, such as architects, engineers, surveyors, accountants and economists. Legal expertise is a complex factor and again somewhat of a double-edged sword. Whereas arbitrators with particular legal experience may be considered particularly suitable, certainly in certain types of arbitration, such as investment arbitration, there is somewhat of a contrary trend.

---

5. See, for example, Lucy GREENWOOD and C. Mark BAKER, "Getting a Better Balance on International Arbitration Tribunals", 28 Arbitration International (2012, no. 4) p. 653 (quoting the description of the majority of international arbitrators as "pale, male and stale").

6. P. 632.

In investment arbitration in particular the issue of repeat appointments by a party or law firm, repeat appointments by either investors or states, and the concept of issue conflict with the arbitrator's wearing of "multiple hats", namely as both counsel and arbitrator in distinct cases involving similar legal issues, have increasingly attracted attention and concern.[7]

Finally, and without attempting to provide an exhaustive list, other relevant factors for diversity in international arbitration include legal system, legal tradition, language, as well as diversity of "function", such as academics, practitioners and retired judges.

As will be further addressed below, within this long list of factors, it is necessary to select and prioritize. Priorities are not immutable and will vary from time to time and place to place.

III.   WHY IS DIVERSITY (POTENTIALLY) RELEVANT?

Diversity matters. Diversity in international arbitration is necessary to ensure that arbitration does not go out of synch with the rest of the (legal) world; and it is necessary to guarantee quality of the process.

Diversity and non-discrimination are important for many reasons, largely for two kinds. It cannot hurt to spell out both: discrimination and lack of diversity are undesirable and wrong *per se* because they are morally wrong. Whereas, diversity and inclusion are commendable because they ensure a better product, in this case a better arbitration process resulting in better arbitration awards. An inclusive panel ensures the optimal use of resources, of potential arbitrators, and guarantees that relevant and complementing considerations are brought to the table resulting in unbiased decision-making.[8]

---

7. The fact that these issues are far from simple and may lead to different results is well illustrated by the two decisions involving Emmanuel Gaillard's challenge on the basis of issue conflict by presidents of the The Hague District Court. Without suggesting that either or both decisions are decisive or even persuasive, it is the different approach in these two decisions that makes them an interesting read, a factor perhaps not sufficiently brought out by later comments on these. In brief, in the first decision, the (then sitting) president essentially held that, if the arbitrator stepped down as counsel in his other case (where he was acting as counsel), he could continue as arbitrator in the case formally before the court in which the challenge was brought. This decision implied the notion that simultaneously acting as arbitrator and counsel in cases involving similar legal issues was not permissible, even though the actual challenge failed. The party that had brought the challenge therefore brought a second challenge immediately thereafter, arguing that while for the future the conflict had been cleared, there had been a period of overlap. In the second decision, another judge acted as president, and while he stated that he agreed with his colleague, he effectively ruled the opposite, by considering that the "wearing of different hats" was a fact of life in international arbitration, and on that basis rejected the challenge. Decisions of 18 October and 5 November 2004, reported at *TMB v. Ghana*, 23 ASA Bulletin (2005, no. 1) p. 186.
8. Diversity matters both for international and domestic arbitration, although the considerations will not be identical. Diverse input in terms of legal system and tradition are unlikely to be a relevant input; diversity of gender, but also of – technical – expertise will be equally relevant.

"The overarching message is that a diverse legal profession is more just, productive and intelligent because diversity, both cognitive and cultural, often leads to better questions, analyses, solutions, and processes."[9]

Transposed to tangible examples from the arbitration world, think of the following: appointing an arbitrator from a well-known, small pool or clique may create a sense of comfort, which may or may not be justified. Effectively, the arbitrator here acts as an insurance policy: the client, often the legal department, will want to justify the decision to nominate an arbitration "dinosaur" to its stakeholders and the board, and wants to be able to say that they did everything they could. If the result then disappoints, no one can blame the choice of arbitrator.

This approach may appear understandable, but needs to be questioned. First, the company may do itself disservice by appointing someone based on an abstract notion of "long experience". It may be that the dispute is actually quite technical, and fact intensive. Perhaps the famous professor of law is not actually the best qualified for this particular case. The discrepancy between arbitrator appointments and expectations is striking in this respect. Often, expertise, by which clients do not typically mean knowledge of the law of procedure – or even the law of contracts of a particular country –, is said to be a unique selling point of arbitration. But do arbitrators, the usual suspects, have all that expertise? Who is best qualified to assess the lack of competition on a particular market in a gas price dispute, a lawyer or an economist?

In addition, who actually does the work in an arbitration? Is it the tribunal as a whole, the chair, the wing-woman, the staff of the particular institution, the (visible) tribunal secretary and/or the chair's associate working behind the scene? Often this information is not at all transparent, certainly not at the nomination stage but even thereafter. A party and their counsel will often have no idea how much of the arbitrator's work is going to be delegated, and if so, to whom. Arguably, work well delegated is work well done, but not knowing that there will be – sometimes extensive – delegation complicates the process. It makes planning and anticipating someone's performance more complicated, as it precludes proper due diligence (including with a view to possible challenges) and input in the selection. Especially those who favor maximum party autonomy in the arbitrator-selection process should not act like the proverbial ostrich here, and should take this reality on board in considering the optimal tribunal.

Another factor to consider is the appointment of the arbitrator from a familiar background, such as someone with the same nationality. Nationality is a complex issue that will also be discussed below in the context of obtaining actual data. Two general comments first. On nationality, the notion that someone of one's own nationality is likely to produce a favourable outcome is shortsighted. In commercial cases, the notion that a party is likely to obtain preferential treatment simply because of its nationality is

---

9. "ABA Report", fn. 4 above, p. 3. The Report identifies four main arguments: (i) the Democracy Argument; (ii) the Business Argument; (iii) the Leadership Argument; and (iv) the Demographic Argument. As components thereof, the ABA stresses that a diverse bar and bench create greater trust in the mechanisms of government and the rule of law; as well as the fact that clients expect and sometimes demand lawyers who are culturally and linguistically proficient.

simplistic. There may be improper reasons why an arbitrator favours one party, but nationality as such is hardly likely to do the trick. Then again, there may be perfectly understandable reasons why someone is more comfortable with someone of his or her own nationality, but then the basis for such sense of comfort is likely to be more nuanced. The real reason may be the (expected) familiarity with a particular language, law or legal tradition.

As Darius Khambata discusses, a complication with nationality is also that simply looking at someone's passport is not sufficient. Someone may not only be a dual national, but may also be from a country with particular historical and/or colonial ties or background.[10] Someone who "on paper" is of a neutral nationality may in fact be someone from a legal or cultural mold that is not so neutral after all. And diversity of nationality may (potentially) enhance diversity, but will not guarantee it: one may still end up with three senior, white men.[11]

Finally, lack of diversity does not only lead to lack of quality but there is also the quantitative angle to consider. To ensure an effective decision-making process, one simply needs an adequate supply of (potential) arbitrators. Not only is it unhelpful to have a lack of diversity on a particular panel, it is also unhelpful to have the same small group of people all decide all cases. This will not work properly, and will lead to even more (invisible) delegation as the small group finds itself overly burdened with cases; it will compromise the quality of the work. This is illustrated by the increasing practice of requesting potential arbitrators not only to disclose potential conflicts, but also to commit to availability. Finally, competition and fresh blood are important to ensure that in the years to come, there will be an adequate and well-trained arbitral talent pool.

IV.   WHERE ARE WE NOW AND WHAT MORE CAN BE DONE?

1.   *The Status Quo*

This leads to the question, where are we now, is an alarmingly small pool of arbitrators dominating the field and if so, is this jeopardizing the legitimacy and the efficacy of arbitration? To begin with the conclusion: yes, and yes.

To get to the conclusion, the first step must therefore be an analysis of the facts, which should obviously include a review of the relevant statistics. This is complicated for several reasons. First, actual, absolute data is difficult if not impossible to get hold of. The exception are the reports issued by various arbitration institutions, which do provide at least some numbers. The International Chamber of Commerce (ICC), International Centre for Settlement of Investment Disputes (ICSID) and London Court of International Arbitration (LCIA), for example, provide information about arbitrators'

---

10. P. 627.
11. On nationality and diversity, see Johnny VEEDER's report, this volume, pp. 652-660, which discusses the far-reaching implications of the UK Supreme Court's decision *Jivraj v. Hashwani* [2011] UKSC 40.

nationalities and geographical base,[12] while the LCIA additionally provides information on gender.[13] In addition to these official reports, the only way to obtain information is through publications, which in turn rely on (private) interviews and direct questions addressed to institutions and other players. Although some of these publications have been able to obtain more varied information, most tend to focus on gender.[14]

Both Christophe Seraglini's (pp. 591-592) and Darius Khambata's (p. 621) papers discuss some of these numbers and the preponderance of Western Europeans or Americans as actors in arbitration, certainly as arbitrator. As to gender, men outnumber women by a wide margin (a percentage between 6-11% is found in several sources).[15] The factual picture of a small pool of arbitrators, or at least a pool of not-diverse players, is confirmed by the work performed by Ben Davis, who, in addition to the participation of American women, researched that of American minorities, Americans with disabilities and American LGBTQ. As far as women are concerned, and while he favourably compares the situation from 2004 to the present, he states that "[f]or Americans in international arbitration to reflect the American population, far more women need to be named [as arbitrators]"; for the other categories he simply concludes "the situation is probably even worse – though again, better than it was in international arbitration in the 1980s and 1990s".[16]

Second, interpreting these numbers is not a straightforward exercise. This is due, in part, to the difficulty of assessing the relevant benchmark. Is arbitration to be compared with other forms of judicial decision-making, with Alternative Dispute Resolution

---

12. See, for 2012, the 2012 Statistical Report, in 24 ICC International Court of Arbitration Bulletin (2013, no. 1) p. 8; the LCIA Registrar's Report 2012 (henceforth LCIA Registrar's Report 2012) available at <www.lcia.org/LCIA/Casework_Report.aspx>; and, for 2013, *ICSID Case Load Statistics*, available at <https://icsid.worldbank.org/ICSID/FrontServlet?requestType=ICSID DocRH&actionVal=ShowDocument&CaseLoadStatistics=True&language=English41>.

13. *LCIA Registrar's Report*, fn. 12 above.

14. See, for example, a number of excellent publications by Lucy GREENWOOD, including "Unblocking the Pipeline: Achieving Greater Gender Diversity on International Tribunals", 42 International Law News (Spring 2013, no. 2). An outstanding exception is the work by Ben DAVIS, whose groundbreaking 2004 publications were the first to address American minorities in arbitration, see for example, "The Color Line in International Commercial Arbitration: An American Perspective", 14 American Rev. of Int'l Arb. (2003, no. 4) p. 461; and his very recent and insightful report providing a wide range and a wealth of numbers, see "Diversity in International Arbitration", 20 ABA Dispute Resolution Magazine (2014, no. 2) p. 13. Although the focus of his paper is American Diversity in International Arbitration, his survey contains many categories of diversity and relevant figures, available at <http://www.americanbar.org/content/dam/aba/publications/dispute_resolution_magazine/Winter_2014_final_unified.aut hcheckdam.pdf> (henceforth *"Davis 2014"*). Quoted in these publications are several other publications, which are mainly concerned with investment arbitration. Although it is tempting to use these data, because they are (more) public than for commercial arbitration, the propriety of extrapolating these data is questionable because of the specific "niche" nature of investment arbitration.

15. Greenwood refers to 6%; the *LCIA Registrar's Report*, fn. 12 above, shows a higher number for the LCIA (9.6%); information provided on/by the ICC suggests that the rate is around 10-11%, *Davis 2014*.

16. *Davis 2014*, fn. 14 above, p. 8.

(ADR); is national data relevant, or not at all; and/or should the benchmark be proportional to representation as part of the population? And if so, how should the population be defined, by looking at the global population in absolute terms (i.e., approximately 50% of the population is female);[17] or should one aim for a more relative approach and consider the "relevant" population (i.e., in this segment of industry, all participants are of a certain religious persuasion)?

Here, it is also important to consider the special role and function of nationality in arbitration, and the way in which this factor is regulated in international arbitration. Darius Khambata discusses some of the differences in the various rules. While most laws and rules provide in general terms that arbitrators should be impartial and/or independent, the range of provisions on nationality is broad. Compare, on the one hand, the provision in the UNCITRAL Model Law on International Commercial Arbitration 1985 (as amended in 2006) that (unless otherwise agreed) "[n]o person shall be precluded by reason of his nationality from acting as an arbitrator" (Art. 11(1)), and the various arbitration rules that refer to nationality as a factor to be taken into account in appointment and nomination of arbitrators.[18] By and large, party-appointed arbitrators are likely to have the nationality of the party appointing them.[19] The balance between the parties is effected by the fact that each side appoints someone, and potentially a national, while only the sole or presiding arbitrator may be of a third nationality. This system is quite different from the ICSID system. While also under the ICSID system parties may agree otherwise, the default procedure effectively results in non-nationals of the parties for all three arbitrator slots.[20]

---

17. Ben Davis appears to consider the (American) population the relevant benchmark for women, *Davis 2014*, p. 8.
18. Darius J. KHAMBATA, "Tensions Between Party Autonomy and Diversity", this volume, pp. 620-621.
19. This is a generalization; parties may be more nuanced in their choice, and consider the applicable law, the seat or other rational factors as drivers for their choice. Sometimes these considerations support the choice for a national; at other times nationality and other considerations will point in different directions.
20. While not automatically ensuring the appointment of arbitrators from *regions* that are neutral, or perceived to be neutral, Art. 7 ICSID Rules significantly impacts and restricts the possibility to appoint nationals of the parties:

   "(1) The majority of the arbitrators shall be nationals of States other than the State party to the dispute and of the State whose national is a party to the dispute, unless the sole arbitrator or each individual member of the Tribunal is appointed by agreement of the parties. Where the Tribunal is to consist of three members, a national of either of these States may not be appointed as an arbitrator by a party without the agreement of the other party to the dispute. Where the Tribunal is to consist of five or more members, nationals of either of these States may not be appointed as arbitrators by a party if appointment by the other party of the same number of arbitrators of either of these nationalities would result in a majority of arbitrators of these nationalities.
   (2) Arbitrators appointed by the Chairman shall not be nationals of the State party to the dispute or of the State whose national is a party to the dispute."

The factual situation, based on this limited insight, and with the caveat that the exact comparator is not self-evident and not uniform (see also below), is that at present diversity is poor. The gender numbers provide the most straightforward basis for this conclusion. While for nationality, the ideal standard may be a complex matter, and while not trying to elude this discussion altogether (see below), a (maximum) rate of 10% of women arbitrators is a dismal rate. Before addressing how this and other disparities can be improved, it is useful to make a small sidestep to the judiciary.

2.   Diversity and the Judiciary

Discussing arbitrator diversity benefits from a comparison with diversity and the judiciary. This is not to suggest that the two can be equated, but there are obvious parallels. While arbitration may not be fully public, and not a public function, it does serve to be an alternative to the provision of judicial services.[21] Also, as indicated in some of the other papers, judges or retired judges are a significant source for potential arbitrators.

Rather than presenting a range of data, and pretending to be exhaustive, the point of these data is slightly more nuanced. Data on diversity of the judiciary are interesting because they tell us something about the actual diversity, but by comparing data for different countries they also demonstrate differences in diversity – not merely in quantitative terms, but also in qualitative terms. The following comparison is obviously for illustration purposes only as it only relates to two countries, the Netherlands, and the US federal judiciary.

The first example is the Netherlands. In the overviews presented by the Council for the Judiciary, a basic distinction is made between "regular", district court, judges and appellate judges. The latter group consists of both Supreme Court and Courts of Appeal judges. Fifty-four percent of the district court judges are women. For appellate judges the number is slightly lower, 44%. Striking is the fact that despite these overall numbers, the percentage of presidents of courts is minimal.

But, perhaps even more striking is the age spread of the sitting judiciary: the youngest tier, up to 35 years, is predominantly female (75%); the division for the 50-60 years is about 50%; and only in the over-60s, men are the majority.[22]

These data can be contrasted to data that can be found on the website of the equivalent US organization, the website of the US Courts, containing a section entitled "Diversity on the Bench". More than the numbers themselves, the different nature of the data presented stands out. Whereas the Dutch courts' organization only provides information about gender and age (and shows a high percentage of women and young judges), the US

---

21. See also Darius KHAMBATA, this volume, p. 617 and the sources he quotes. It is interesting to note that Darius Khambata considers that investment arbitration may have the most public nature of all forms of arbitration and is thus most comparable with the judicial system, but as noted above, the comparison of extrapolation of investment arbitration data is fraught with danger because it is (also) a unique and even less diverse subset of arbitration when compared to commercial arbitration.

22. <www.rechtspraak.nl/Organisatie/Publicaties-En-brochures/Documents/Jaarverslagen/Jaarverslag-2012.pdf>.

data are more diverse. The website lists the absolute number of judges of several categories: African American, American Indian, Asian American, Hispanic, Pacific Islander, and women judges.[23]

A report by the National Women's Law Center is helpful in digesting some of these numbers also in an attempt to make them comparable to the Dutch data, and shows that approximately a third of all Supreme Court and active Court of Appeals judges are women.[24] The percentage is similar for district (or trial) court judges. What the US overview then also shows is that for women of colour the numbers are even smaller.[25] The report further describes that there are significant regional differences within the United States, and that President Obama's nominations have had a lot of effect in changing the numbers, quite recently therefore. The overall number for women judges is significantly lower than for the Netherlands.

A second factual input that allows us to interpret these data is the number of women studying law. Again, the only countries compared here are the Netherlands and the United States For the Netherlands, the percentage of women students is 60%.[26] For the United States it approaches 50%.[27]

3.   *Where Does This Take Us?*

(1)   The conclusion of the above is that there is a lack of diversity in international arbitration. Clear data supports this fact for gender. Minorities and other categories are less well documented but paint an even gloomier picture. Age is not even the subject of statistics, but documented by plenty of anecdotal evidence. The same is true for the additional factor that there is not only a lack of diversity in the categories of people serving as arbitrators, but also, it appears that a very small group of individuals performs a large percentage of the cases out there. This is certainly the case for investment arbitration, where data is more public even though arguably this is a niche area of arbitration. It is posited, however, that there is greater variety on the counsel side than on the arbitrator side of the process.

---

23. <www.uscourts.gov/JudgesAndJudgeships/BiographicalDirectoryOfJudges.aspx>.

24. <www.nwlc.org/resource/women-federal-judiciary-still-long-way-go-1>.

25. There are 71 women of color serving as active federal judges across the country (out of 162 active judges), including 36 African-American women, 24 Hispanic women, 9 Asian-American women, 1 woman of Hispanic and Asian descent, and 1 women of Hispanic and African-American descent. There are no Native American women among the over 770 active federal judges across the country. There are only eleven women of color on the US courts of appeals. *Ibid.*

26. For 2012 (this percentage relates to the number of students, not graduates), <www.stichtingdebeauvoir.nl/wp-content/uploads/wetenschap-t1.jpg>.

27. First Year and Total J.D. Enrollment by Gender, 1947-2010, Section of Legal Education and Admissions to the Bar, American Bar Association, available at <www.americanbar.org/content/dam/aba/administrative/legal_education_and_admissions_ to_the_bar/statistics/jd_enrollment_1yr_total_gender.authcheckdam.pdf> (last visited 21 March 2014). A similar disparity between arbitrators and lawyers active in the legal profession more generally is noted by L. BAKER and C.M. GREENWOOD, quoting a rate of 65% for UK trainees, fn. 5 above, p. 656.

The fact that a small group is overloaded with cases is further illustrated by the increasing need for declarations by potential arbitrators that they are not only conflict-free, but have sufficient availability (ICC; LCIA). Lack of availability may also be caused by other commitments, but multiple, simultaneous appointments certainly appears to be a factor.

(2) Facts are the basis for any solution. Facts are too hard to access in this area.[28] While several institutions give information about the nationality/regional background of arbitrators, even information about the basic fact of the arbitrators' gender is not presented transparently (with the notable exception of the LCIA). Information about the arbitrators' age is completely missing. Greater transparency must be part of any plan and solution.

(3) The corollary of transparency is awareness. Awareness requires knowledge of facts, and facts will bring awareness.

(4) The lack of diversity and the existence of a small pool of repeat players is not sustainable. There is a need for constant inflow of new players in order to ensure the functioning of arbitration as a competitive system of dispute resolution in the future. The numbers relating to law school graduates are significant. The countries relied on above for illustrative purposes (the Netherlands and the United States) show that women are equaling men or outnumbering them in the legal profession. Failing to use these lawyers is inefficient, if nothing. In addition, the (legal) profession in general is becoming less male dominated and this further shapes expectations: it is not unusual for the team of lawyers (in house and external) to consist mainly of women.[29] And what is more, the CFO or the CEO of the client may well be a woman. In court, in what would be the alternative forum for resolution of the dispute, and conceivably the setting for subsequent control of the arbitral process, parties and their lawyers could expect a greater diversity than behind the arbitrators' table.

(5) There is a need to focus. A focus on one or more initial priorities does not mean that the other goals are inferior. But in order to change, it is important to start and to be effective. Gender seems an obvious starting point, where some headway has been made, and there is a reasonably filled "pipeline".

(6) In ensuring that a sustainable situation is created, there is a need to distinguish between long-term and short-term goals. While on a macro level much sympathy will exist for the need to educate and train, this may be different on an individual level. Simply put, a party nominating its nominee, or co-arbitrators selecting a chair, will be primarily focused on their one case. Institutions, however, will also have an interest in a more long-term sustainable outcome. The actual case is important, but also the reputation of the institutions over all, and over a longer period of time.

---

28. See, for example, *Davis 2014*, p. 7 (reporting that he was told in a telephone call by the ICC that "the ICC confirmed that it did not maintain information on diversity".)

29. See also L. GREENWOOD and C.M. BAKER who conclude that women are underrepresented, even in comparison with the senior role in law firms, fn. 5 above, p. 654.

(7)   Here, it is important to recognize that the diversity of age, but also the other
        varieties of diversity, all enhance the quality of the process. Is a case really going
        to benefit from a three-lawyer tribunal? Do you really want three Europeans? Do
        you really want three senior arbitrators? Different perspectives bring different
        ideas to the decision-making table. Diverse diversity is a win-win model; diversity
        is not only desirable as a (moral) goal per se, but results in better results: doing
        well by doing good![30]

(8)   All users of arbitration have a role to play in achieving diversity, but in some ways
        institutions may be best placed to take the lead. They are in a position to provide
        transparency (see under (1)), but they are also more likely to have up-to-date
        insight than individual users when it comes to availability and performance of
        arbitrators, whether stars or rising stars.

4.   Conclusion: A Pledge?!

This list of considerations takes us to the concrete action that is required. It is suggested
that the concrete steps that should and can be taken are multi-faceted, but are actually
quite simple. We all need to do something, not only talk about it. What we each can and
should do may differ, but the goal is the same. So do we need more rules, more
guidelines for this? Perhaps not, it is suggested that a straightforward action plan, a
pledge, should do the trick.

The above quoted ABA Report contains recommendations for increasing diversity in
the different sectors of the legal profession, namely law firms and corporations, the
judiciary and government, law schools and the academy, and bar associations. Although
the recommendations are useful and laudable, there are many, and some are very much
long-term and to some extent preliminary to actual action (such as the recommendation
to draft, publicize and implement an updated diversity and general recommendations on
"rethinking diversity").

These recommendations include the need to collect facts and to create transparency,
while setting measurable goals. In addition, what is important about these
recommendations is that they are drafted in a broad way, addressing multiple players in
the legal profession. That is something to consider when taking matters further in the
specific context of arbitration. We all have a role, as party, counsel, institution and an
interest, derived from that role. We all have an obligation, based on that particular role.
And what we should recognize is how each of us in our particular role has the ability to
make changes. Because changes are not happening magically, and certainly not fast
enough.

At this stage, we should recall the 2004 paper *"Call to Action – Diversity in the Legal
Profession"*. Following an earlier Statement signed by chief legal officers to evidence the
commitment of the signatory corporations to diversity in the legal profession, a large
number of companies committed to the following:

---

30. Per Tom LEHRER, "The Old Dope Peddler", Songs by Tom Lehrer (1953).

"As Chief Legal Officers, we hereby reaffirm our commitment to diversity in the legal profession. Our action is based on the need to enhance opportunity in the legal profession and our recognition that the legal and business interests of our clients require legal representation that reflects the diversity of our employees, customers and the communities where we do business. In furtherance of this renewed commitment, this is intended to be a Call to Action for the profession generally and in particular for our law departments and for the law firms with which our companies do business.

In an effort to realize a truly diverse profession and to promote diversity in law firms, we commit to taking action consistent with the referenced Statement. To that end, in addition to our abiding commitment to diversity in our own departments, we pledge that we will make decisions regarding which law firms represent our companies based in significant part on the diversity performance of the firms. We intend to look for opportunities for firms we regularly use which positively distinguish themselves in this area. We further intend to end or limit our relationships with firms whose performance consistently evidences a lack of meaningful interest in being diverse."[31]

As Sara Lee General Counsel, Roderick Palmore, at the time stated, the purpose of the Call to Action was to take the general principle of interest in diversity a step further and translate it into action. Specifically, it connected the general principle to a tangible pledge about retaining law firms based in part on the diversity performance of these firms. And in creating the document, Palmore's goal was brevity. The focus was on three elements: (i) expressing the principle interest in diversity, (ii) the law firms' diversity performance and (iii) the commitment to limit or eliminate law firms not interested in diversity.

Of course, as Chief Legal Officers, the signatories of this Call to Action were in a position in which they could effectively sanction the Call to Action. The pool of players in arbitration is a much wider, more diverse, group.

Nevertheless, the basic point about recognizing the significance and expressing commitment makes perfect sense for all players in arbitration. What can each of us do to enhance diversity and inclusion?[32]

Taking transparency, awareness and inclusiveness as the elements, the concrete actions points follow:

---

31. <www.acc.com/vl/public/Article/loader.cfm?csModule=security/getfile&pageid=16074>.
32. T. Hudson JORDAN, "Moving From Diversity to Inclusion" ("As a start, a common definition of 'diversity' and 'inclusion' is needed. Diversity means all the ways we differ. Some of these differences we are born with and cannot change. Anything that makes us unique is part of this definition of diversity. Inclusion involves bringing together and harnessing these diverse forces and resources, in a way that is beneficial. Inclusion puts the concept and practice of diversity into action by creating an environment of involvement, respect, and connection – where the richness of ideas, backgrounds, and perspectives are harnessed to create business value. Organizations need both diversity and inclusion to be successful.") <www.diversityjournal.com/1471-moving-from-diversity-to-inclusion/>.

- Clients should insist on inclusive lists when law firms present lists of potential nominees. Practically speaking, no list is complete without at least one women and one younger nominee. For signatories of the Call to Action this requirement should be seen as an expression of the general thought contained in that pledge; for non-signatories signing up now would be a clear and constructive signal to the arbitration community;
- As a corollary, law firms should pro-actively staff their own teams on an inclusive basis, and present and defend inclusive lists of arbitrators;
- Institutions should collect and present data on diversity; and "mix and match" insofar as they influence appointments. In this context, because of the greater ability in certain cases to oversee the entire playing field and not merely influence a single arbitrator, they should also consider special expertise to enhance inclusiveness;
- Conference organizers should insist on inclusive panels; and
- Last but not least, perhaps we should all consider a recent and increasingly successful Scandinavian initiative entitled "Thanks, but no thanks". This is a campaign which has led to male speakers refusing to participate in conferences and panel discussions without female representation. Perhaps this is the ultimate pledge that we should all consider: when approached to speak at a conference, to act as counsel, to instruct lawyers, to act as expert or as arbitrator and when confronted with too little diversity, we should ask ourselves "Should I say 'yes', or 'thanks, but under these conditions, no thanks'?"[33]

---

33. #tackanej (Sweden); #TakkNei (Norway), <http://tackanej.se/men-say-no-thanks/> "Scandinavian Men Say No, Thanks to All-Male Panels".

Who Are the Arbitrators?

*V. V. Veeder QC**

I.   INTRODUCTION

If the proverbial green creature from Mars arrived on this planet to study diversity in the practice of international arbitration, it would find a complicated situation where not all is what it seems. No arbitrator is green; and neither Kermit nor Ms. Piggy has ever been appointed an arbitrator. Despite eccentric exceptions in ancient times, the world's modern arbitrators are limited to the human species, discriminating against all other forms of intelligent life.

As the creature learnt English, it would soon find discrimination in the language of arbitration between human left-handers and right-handers. Thus, a good arbitrator is "adroit" and "dexterous", but a bad arbitrator is "maladroit", "gauche", "cack-handed" and even "sinister". Yet this Martian creature would soon learn that linguistic discrimination against lefties amongst the human species (50 percent of the world's population and comprising, so it is said, the best of the world's arbitrators) counts for nothing within the arbitration community, no more than the absence of green and porcine animals.[1] Yet, our Martian friend would eventually discover other forms of discrimination as regards gender and race, which, in his view, threatened to tarnish the legitimacy of international arbitration.

As regards gender, the creature would find in four different continents Meg Kinnear at the International Centre for Settlement of Investment Disputes (ICSID) in Washington DC, Teresa Cheng at the Hong Kong International Arbitration Centre in China, Annette Magnusson at the Stockholm Chamber of Commerce and Bernadette Uwicyeza at the Kigali International Arbitration Centre in Rwanda. Had the creature arrived a decade ago, it would have found Anne Marie Whitesell and earlier still Tila Maria de Hancock at the ICC International Court of Arbitration in Paris; and also Rosalyn Higgins at The Hague as the President of the International Court of Justice, only temporarily interrupting her even more illustrious career as an international arbitrator. If it delayed its arrival for only a few months hence, it would find Jackie van Hof at the LCIA in

---

*   Essex Court Chambers, London; Governing Board Member of ICCA.

1. It should be disclosed that this author is left-handed, as also Leonardo da Vinci, Joan of Arc, Napoleon Bonaparte, Julius Caesar, Greta Garbo, King George VI, Jimmy Connors, John McEnroe, Shirley MacLaine, Harpo Marx, Marilyn Monroe and Pablo Picasso.

London. This Martian creature might therefore at first conclude that gender discrimination by users of arbitration and arbitral institutions plays no significant role in the appointment of arbitrators, just as with left-handers and right-handers.

However, having studied Latin on Mars, the creature would be troubled at the masculine form of "arbitrator", for which there seems to be no feminine equivalent. Next, it would study the available statistics. Women make up half (if not more than half) of the entrants to the legal profession in developed economies; but after entry, something happens. In the field of international commercial and investment arbitration, one commentator has calculated that of the top ten international teams listed by Global Arbitration Review, only 11% of their members are women and that of all arbitrators appointed in, respectively, ICSID arbitrations and commercial arbitrations, only 5% and 6% are women.[2] Many ICCA members have recently completed a questionnaire for the European Commission for arbitration users, practitioners and arbitrators in Europe: only 11.6% of such responses came from women; and only 0.5% were from Afro-Caribbean men and women.[3] These figures cannot of course be precise; but to the discerning Martian, these statistics would suffice to show that something is wrong with diversity in the practice of arbitration as regards both gender and race.

The situation for international arbitration is of course complicated, given its global reach amongst different participants from disparate cultures and jurisdictions. Here, as in many respects, arbitration is not always for the best, but also not always for the worst. Yet, it is surprising that the practice of arbitration does not reflect the broad diversity available to the arbitral community; and that the collective attention of many in that community has still not succeeded in removing the unfairness and sheer waste of discrimination based on grounds of gender and race. It is equally surprising how little reliable research has been done, outside the United States.

This is not an indictment. Few in the arbitral community actually intend to practice discrimination on grounds of gender and race. It is more a matter of habit and unconscious or institutionalized discrimination. Moreover, in a relatively short time, diversity in arbitration has already come a long away. In England, women lawyers and judges are relatively new. In the United Kingdom's archives, there is an extraordinary exchange in 1922 between the Czechoslovak *Chargé d'Affaires* in London (the Czech Republic then being a newly independent state establishing its own legal system) and the British Government:[4]

> "The Czechoslovak Chargé d' Affaires would esteem it a favour if his Lordship [Lord Curzon of the British Foreign Office] could cause him to be informed about the following questions: (1) Are women permitted to act as professional judges, and are they admitted to the preparatory practice necessary for an appointment as judge to the same extent as men?; (2) If so, have they the same rights and duties as men? Also as regards salary and pension?; (3) Are women judges allowed to

---

2. C. TEVENDALE, Kluwer Arbitration Blog of 28 September 2012.
3. This survey was being conducted by Brunel University (London) on the Law and Practice of Arbitration in the European Union.
4. PRO Archives, Kew (London): LCO2/604 XC 25358; L 560/560/405.

marry unconditionally, or does their marriage affect their service relation and their claims and duties?; (4) If so, what are the consequences of pregnancy and childbirth upon their official positions, and in particular, what amount of leave is granted them in this case?; and (5) Has the employment of women judges proved satisfactory in general?"

The Lord Chancellor replied as follows:

"As regards Question 1: "Judges in England, of whatever status, are appointed only from amongst members of the Bar ('*avocats*'). The statutes regulating the qualifications which must be possessed by persons appointed to these offices require in each case that a specified period of time should have elapsed since entry into the profession before a barrister can be appointed to a judicial office. Until the 23rd December, 1919, when the Sex Disqualification (Removal) Act, 1919 (9 and 10, Geo. V, c. 71), passed into law, women could not be admitted to the English Bar. In order to be admitted to the English Bar it is necessary that a candidate for admission should have passed a certain defined period as a student and have passed certain specified examinations. As until 1919 women could not be called to the Bar, it followed that women were not admitted as students. As a consequence, although some women have lately passed through the period of studentship and been admitted to the Bar, no woman has yet fulfilled the conditions relating to length of service which are requisite to qualify the candidate for appointment to any judicial position. No legal decision has as yet been given upon the interpretation of the Act of 1919 so far as it concerns the holding by a woman of a judicial office. It is, however, apprehended that, since the passing of that Act, any woman who fulfils the other statutory condition would be eligible for appointment to a judgeship."

As regards Questions 2 to 5:

"No occasion has arisen for considering the questions asked in paragraphs 2, 3, 4 and 5 in the memorandum from the Czechoslovak Legation. It is, however, apprehended that if and when any woman becomes in fact eligible for appointment as a judge, and if the appointing authority should then see fit to appoint her, she would hold office upon the same conditions as would a man. So far as question 4 is concerned [i.e. maternity leave], judges in England are seldom appointed until they have reached an age which renders the conditions described in the question unlikely to arise."

This was written in 1922. Yet, the first woman High Court Judge was only appointed in 1974, more than fifty years later: Mrs. Justice Heilbron who was born in 1919, called to the English Bar in 1939 and appointed one of Her Majesty's Counsel in 1949, at the young age of thirty-four.[5] In England, woman lawyers began to appear as arbitrators in the 1970s, but not in significant numbers.[6]

II.   GENDER, RACE AND NATIONALITY

In South Africa, notwithstanding its extraordinary first President, Nelson Mandela, race still plays, so it is said, a significant part in the practice of domestic arbitration, with the business community (predominantly white), preferring white arbitrators to black judges and arbitrators. There are, however, no reliable statistics. In the United States, Professor Benjamin Davis has conducted two most interesting studies. The figures are striking; and it is probable that the figures would be similar in England.

In his survey of 2013,[7] Professor Davis, a former officer of the ICC Court for many years, examined US diversity in international arbitration across a target population comprising minorities, women, those with disabilities and LGBTQ (Lesbian, Gay, Bisexual, Transgender, Queer or Questioning) lawyers. (These four groups are the target population described in the American Bar Association's Goal III: Eliminate Bias and Enhance Diversity). In addition to sending a survey to 413 international arbitration practitioners, he approached a diverse group of international arbitral institutions around the world. He concluded:

"It appears safe to conclude that as of today there are a significant number of American women (most likely white) in international arbitration in all phases of being counsel but not so many as arbitrators. To a much lesser extent than American women, while recognizing there may be double-counting, it appears safe to conclude that as of today there are a few American minorities active in international arbitration but even less as arbitrators. To a much lesser extent than American women and minorities (and given the paucity double-counting here is unlikely), there are an infinitesimal number of American LGBTQ lawyers in international arbitration. For me, the bright aspect in this picture as compared to

---

5. See H. HEILBRON, *Rose Heilbron* (2012). This wonderful biography is written by the subject's daughter, herself a Queen's Counsel and arbitrator. In 1949, Rose Heilbron had taken silk with Helena Normanton (of 4 Essex Court) as the first women to be granted silk in English legal history. (In England and most common law countries, senior judges are appointed from senior trial lawyers of a mature age — hence it is pointless to compare judicial statistics under civilian and socialist systems with career-judges appointed at an early age).
6. Margaret Rutherford QC was one the first women arbitrators in England, a remarkable lawyer who proudly confessed that her favourite bedtime reading included the English Arbitration Act 1996. Elsewhere, others included Professor Bastid, Mme Simone Rozés and Judge Birgitta Blom.
7. Benjamin G. Davis, "American Diversity in International Arbitration 2003-2013", available at <http://papers.ssrn.com/sol3/papers.cfm?abstract_id=2364967>. (This survey updates Professor Davis' earlier work: "The Color Line in International Commercial Arbitration: An American Perspective", 14 American Review of International Arbitration (2004) p. 461; "International Commercial Online and Offline Dispute Resolution: Addressing Primacism and Universalism", 4 Journal of American Arbitration (2005) p. 79 and 20 ABA Dispute Resolution Magazine (2014, no. 1).

when I worked in the field in the 1980s and 1990s is best captured in the paraphrase of an old Negro spiritual: there are not as many as there ought to be, but it is slightly better than it was."[8]

It is indeed better; but it is most certainly not for the best. What can be done? We must begin necessarily with party autonomy and legal restrictions on such autonomy. In no legal system worthy of the name can a party appoint a corrupt or partial arbitrator. Equally, parties cannot jointly agree under most arbitration rules the appointment of unsuitable arbitrators, with non-waivable impediments as regards independence, conflicts of interest and availability.

Such limitations on party autonomy were raised in a London ad hoc arbitration in a case under English law and the laws of the European Union. Under EU law, there are several legislative texts intended to promote diversity in many forms, proscribing discrimination on grounds of gender and race. In the Charter of Fundamental Rights of the European Union (2000), Art. 21 prohibits discrimination based on the ground of gender, race, colour, ethnic or social origin, genetic features, language, religion or belief, political or any other opinion, membership of a national minority, property, birth, disability, age or sexual orientation. The EU's Race Directive 2000/43/EC also provides that the principle of equal treatment means that there shall be no direct or indirect discrimination based on racial or ethnic origin. The Race Directive excludes nationality discrimination from its scope (Art. 3(2)); but that is prohibited generally under Art. 12 of the EC Treaty. Art. 10 of the Treaty on the Functioning of the European Union (TFEU) provides that, in defining and implementing its policies and activities, the European Union shall aim to combat discrimination based on sex, racial or ethnic origin, religion or belief, disability, age or sexual orientation.[9]

The EU Directive 2000/78/CE of 27 November 2000 also provides a general framework under EU law for combating discrimination on the grounds of religion or belief, disability, age or sexual orientation as regards "employment and occupation". For religion and belief, this 2000 Directive was first enacted in the United Kingdom by the Employment Equality (Religion or Belief) Regulations 2003 (now superseded, in like terms, by the United Kingdom's Equality Act 2010 and its Regulations). These texts gave rise in the curious case of *Jivraj v. Hashwani,* raising a legal issue regarding discrimination in appointing an arbitrator based on religious grounds, with many considering that similar issues (requiring similar answers) would arise from discrimination based on nationality and, possibly, gender and race.

III.   *JIVRAJ V. HASHWANI*

This case arose under the 2003 Regulations and the 2000 Directive. It illustrates the tension between party autonomy and legal rules precluding discrimination. The case has special facts, but the decision of the UK Supreme Court (2011) has been understood to

---

8. *Ibid.*, p. 10.
9. Arts. 18 and 19 TFEU [Art 23 with Art 6 of EC Treaty].

establish that parties and arbitral institutions can lawfully discriminate against the appointment of an arbitrator on the grounds of religion and nationality, under English and EU law.

Under the 2003 Regulations, the UK Supreme Court decided, in robust terms, that an arbitrator was not an "employee"; that accordingly discrimination in the appointment of an arbitrator on religious grounds was not impermissible under the parties' arbitration agreement; and that, even if prima facie impermissible, it was nonetheless made permissible under a legislative exception for "genuine occupational requirement" (also known as "GOR"). The UK Supreme Court thereby reversed the decision of the Court of Appeal (2010), which had unanimously reversed the decision of the Commercial Court (2009),[10] to widespread acclamation from many users of arbitration in the European Union (including the ICC and the LCIA which had intervened in the appeal as amici curiae). The unusual facts of the case are not directly material to this paper and can, for present purposes, be left aside.[11]

Unfortunately, even with the final decision of the UK Supreme Court, the controversy remains far from over. Implicitly, the effects of the decision are not limited to discrimination in the appointment of arbitrators by users and arbitral institutions on grounds of religion, but extend to other forms of discrimination, particularly those based on nationality (the latter being expressed, albeit in different terms, in almost all rules of international arbitration institutions).[12]

After the UK Supreme Court's decision, Mr. Hashwani complained to the European Commission that the Supreme Court had improperly failed to apply EU law (in the form of the 2000 Directive) and had also declined wrongly, with its Nelsonian view of "acte clair", to refer the case to the Court of Justice of the European Union (CJEU) in Luxembourg under Art. 267 TFEU, as formally requested by Mr. Hashwani. Far from dismissing this complaint summarily, the European Commission recorded the complaint under Art. 258 TFEU and, in December 2013, ordered the United Kingdom to respond in writing to Mr. Hashwani's complaint. There has been, as yet, no such response. Depending on such response and the Commission's resulting opinion, the European Commission may bring infraction proceedings against the United Kingdom (being responsible for the UK Supreme Court) under Art. 260 TFEU; and, if so, the CJEU may

---

10. *Jivraj v. Hashwani* [2011] UKSC 40; [2011] 1 WLR 1872, also reported in ICCA *Yearbook Commercial Arbitration* XXXVI (2011) p. 611; and Revue de l'arbitrage (2011) p. 1007. For the decision of the Court of Appeal, see [2010] EWCA Civ 712; [2010] ICR 1435; and for that of the Commercial Court (Steel J), see EWHC 1364.

11. For those interested, see the author's article on the decision of the Court of Appeal: "Arbitral Discrimination Under English and EU Law" in Yves Derains and Laurent Levy, eds., *Is Arbitration Only as Good as the Arbitrator? Status, Powers and Role of the Arbitrator*, Dossier VIII, ICC Institute of World Busines Law (2011) p. 91.

12. This paper does not address nationality discrimination under international law in state-state or investor-state arbitrations. Given the terms of so many bilateral investment treaties and the ICSID Convention, discrimination on the ground of nationality is there firmly entrenched as the universal badge of neutrality recognized by states. That need not be so as regards international commercial arbitration; nor is it in the European Court of Justice.

direct the United Kingdom to take necessary measures, i.e. for the UK Supreme Court to reconsider its decision leading to a different result.

It is therefore necessary to see what that result might be, starting with the decision of the Court of Appeal which was reversed by the UK Supreme Court. The Court of Appeal decided that this non-discrimination provision encompassed an arbitrator under a contract personally to do any work, being a form of words long used by the UK Parliament to cover those working under both a contract of service (i.e. an employee) and a contract for services (i.e. not an employee):[13]

> "The paradigm case of appointing an arbitrator involves obtaining the services of a particular person to determine a dispute in accordance with the agreement of the parties and the rules of law, including those to be found in the legislation governing arbitration. In that respect it is no different from instructing a solicitor to deal with a particular piece of legal business, such as drafting a will, consulting a doctor about a particular ailment or an accountant about a tax return. Since an arbitrator (or any professional person) contracts to do work personally, the provision of his [sic] services falls within the definition of 'employment', and it follows that his appointor must be an 'employer' within the meaning of Regulation 6(1) [of the 2003 Regulations]" (para. 16).

As Professor Racine rightly notes in his case-note, apart from its special technical meaning under the 2003 Regulations (with the Directive), the Court of Appeal did not decide that an arbitrator was in fact an employee of the disputing parties, it therefore being necessary to dismiss such simplistic criticism as a "caricature".[14]

The UK Supreme Court, in reversing the decision of the Court of Appeal, decided that the distinctive feature was an "employment" relationship, whether in form the person was employed or self-employed and that a difference should be drawn (as also reflected in EU law) between a person who was, in substance, "employed" and a person who was an independent provider of services not in a relationship of subordination with the person(s) receiving those services. Accordingly, so the Supreme Court decided, the role of an arbitrator "is not one of employment under a contract personally to do work" (para. 40), despite the receipt of contractual fees from and the provision of non-delegable services to the disputing parties.[15] As already indicated above, the UK Supreme

---

13. It appears to have been first used in the UK's Equal Pay Act 1970; and it now forms part of the Equality Act 2010 (Sect. 83). At least two decisions of the House of Lords supported a broad interpretation of this wording: *Kelly v. NIHE* [1999] 1 AC 428 and *Percy v. Church of Scotland* [2006] 2 AC 28 (now, *sed quaere*).
14. Jean-Baptiste RACINE, "Much Ado About Nothing", Revue de l'arbitrage (2011) p. 1026 at p. 1031.
15. For commentaries on the decision of the UK Supreme Court, see (inter alia) *ibid.*: where the second footnote lists the significant number of commentaries already then in existence, in the blogosphere and elsewhere; see now also C. STYLE and P. CLEOBURY, *"Jivraj v. Hashwani: Public Interest and Party Autonomy"*, Arb Int (2011) p. 563; C. MCCRUDDEN, "Two Views of Subordination: The Personal Scope of Employment Discrimination Law in '*Jivraj v. Hashwani*'", 41 Industrial Law Journal (2013) p. 30; A.K. HOFFMANN, "Selection and Appointment of

Court also recognized and applied an exception for "genuine occupational requirement". This exception had been applied by the Commercial Court (Mr. Justice Steel); but not by the Court of Appeal, which interpreted this exception more restrictively. Even broadly interpreted, it can only apply in a rational and proportionate manner. It cannot therefore apply by way of general application to all cases.

Even after the Supreme Court's decision, it would be incorrect to assume that party autonomy is unlimited. Under English and EU laws, It would not be permissible for parties to agree always that only men (or only women) could be appointed as arbitrators; or that only WASPs but no Afro-Caribbeans were ever qualified as arbitrators; but it would be permissible for parties to stipulate that only persons religiously qualified or qualified by nationality could be appointed if religious or nationality factors were sufficiently relevant so as to justify such appointments in particular cases, such as (as regards religion) the *Beth Din* or certain Shari'a tribunals (including Ismaili tribunals), applying Jewish law and the Shari'a respectively. It is difficult to imagine any factors which could rationally justify discrimination based on gender and race. As Professor Racine points out, party autonomy regarding arbitration is circumscribed by the European Convention on Human Rights (Art. 14 and Protocol 12, ECHR) and rules of both national and international public policy, of which the French *Dutco* decision (1992) is only one example.[16]

Regrettably, Art. 11(1) of the 1985 UNCITRAL Model Law on International Commercial Arbitration does not restrict party autonomy in regard to discrimination based on gender and race. In regard to nationality, it provides: "No person shall be precluded by reason of his nationality from acting as an arbitrator, unless otherwise agreed by the parties." This provision, expressly respecting the principle of party autonomy, was intended only to remove restrictions in national laws preventing the appointment of foreigners as arbitrators.[17] The UNCITRAL Analytical Note A/CN/.9/264 (25 March 1985) records that there was no intention to preclude parties, arbitral institutions and trade associations "from specifying that nationals of certain States may, or may not, be appointed as arbitrators". This reference to national laws has its roots, amongst others, in the infamous amendment to Art. 1032(2) of Germany's ZPO of 7 April 1933, disqualifying all "non-Aryan" persons from appointment as arbitrators in arbitrations and, as originally intended, invoked against non-German arbitrators.

Accordingly, however uncertain in scope, there are clearly legal limits to party autonomy in the selection and appointment of arbitrators, whether directly by each party or indirectly on their behalf by an arbitral institution. The *Jivraj* case, albeit still

Arbitrators" (Chapter 13) in M. ARROYO, ed., *Arbitration In Switzerland: The Practitioner's Guide* (2013); U.A. OSENI and H.A. KADOUF, "The Discrimination Conundrum in the Appointment of Arbitrators in International Arbitration", 29 Journal of Int Arb (2012, no. 5) pp. 519-544; For an unusual and critical commentary, see Sir Richard BUXTON, "Discrimination in Employment: The Supreme Court Draws a Line", LQR (2012) p. 128. (This author was a member of the Court of Appeal in *Jivraj v. Hashwani*.)

16. J.-B. RACINE, *op. cit.*, fn. 14, "*la discrimination serait tout aussi automatique et évidente .... que le critère soit tiré de la race ou de l'ethnie, du handicap, de l'orientation sexuelle, de l'âge, etc*", p. 1037.

17. See H.M. HOLTZMANN and J.E. NEUHAUS, *A Guide to the UNCITRAL Model Law* (1989) at pp. 359 and 381.

unfinished business, demonstrates that international arbitration is not independent from national and international rules of law, but that it is part of the main, within England and Wales, the European Union and elsewhere.

IV.   CONCLUSION

What can de done? The answer lies primarily with major users and arbitral institutions. It does not lie in more laws, legal rules and regulations. The objective is indisputable: inadvertent discrimination based on gender and race damages arbitration, because it assumes, unthinkingly, that a class of persons have always the relevant qualities and that another class always do not, thereby wasting the human resources available to arbitration. Such discrimination is also grossly irrational in a process otherwise founded upon rationality: the choice of an arbitrator should not be exercised arbitrarily; and if a distinction is to be drawn between arbitral candidates, it should have a rational basis related to the particular requirements of the parties for their arbitration. Lastly, but not least, such discrimination is wrong; and, if allowed to continue, it will bring arbitration into disrepute. Hence, let us support the idea of a voluntary "pledge" by parties, appointing authorities and arbitral institutions, consciously, before appointing an arbitrator, to consider the broadest spectrum of suitable candidates, without unconscious discrimination based on gender and race. It could work, as have like pledges in favour of ADR (before litigation) promoted by the International Institute for Conflict Prevention and Resolution (CPR) for almost thirty years.[18] It would also have the advantage of being the right thing to do. And it might even work on Mars.

---

18. More than 4,000 companies and 1,500 law firms have signed the CPR Pledge, committing the signatory to consider, before litigation, ADR in the form of appropriate negotiation, mediation and other ADR processes (see <www.cpradr.org>; last visited 20 May 2014).

B. Justice Stream

2. Premise:
Arbitral Institutions Can Do More
to Further Legitimacy.
True or False?

Introduction to the Session
Arbitral Institutions Can Do More to Foster Legitimacy.
True or False?

*Belinda McRae**

On Monday 7 April 2014, Panel Chair Salim Moollan challenged nine representatives of international arbitral institutions to evaluate the contribution of those institutions to the system of international arbitration and the scope of their role in fostering its legitimacy.

The insights offered by the panel were grounded in quantitative data. Each panellist submitted independent and in-depth responses to a detailed questionnaire on the subject of arbitral legitimacy, a collation of which is included at the conclusion of this Report. These responses record the panellists' personal views on systemic issues that are popularly cited as undermining arbitration as an acceptable form of dispute resolution and as underlying its perceived legitimacy problem. These issues ranged from developing-world bias to the alleged opaqueness of arbitral institutions. The panellists were also required to provide concrete examples of their institutional practice, as well as precise views on the proper functions of their institutions.

After the responses of each panellist were submitted and reviewed, the panel collectively decided to concentrate on three areas of convergence among their responses. These three areas – pro-developed world bias, the so-called arbitration "mafia", and the proper role of arbitral institutions – gave rise to the three related propositions that the panel debated in three separate sub-panels in Miami.

The first of these propositions – that there is a pro-developed world bias to which arbitral institutions contribute – was addressed by Brooks Daly, Deputy Secretary-General of the Permanent Court of Arbitration; John Beechey, President of the International Court of Arbitration of the International Chamber of Commerce; and Nassib Ziadé, Chief Executive Officer of the Bahrain Centre for Dispute Resolution.

Brooks Daly analyzed the extent to which the present concentration of arbitrators and arbitration practitioners in the developed world threatens the legitimacy of the system. In his view, this prominence results from the expertise of that community, rather than any untoward design, and causes only an appearance of bias, rather than actual bias. That this bias is only perceived makes it no less of a threat to legitimacy, however. Institutions must take steps to invest in the infrastructure necessary to remedy any misperceptions. Mr. Daly also made specific reference to Mr. Ziadé's statement (in the survey) that developed-world arbitrators are dominating the development of international law jurisprudence in the context of investor-State arbitration. Mr. Daly was especially troubled by the proposition that the nature of international law jurisprudence could be purely a function of the geographic origin of arbitrators; this would raise legitimacy concerns not just for investor-State arbitration but for international law generally. Observing that this remark pertained most particularly to investor-State arbitration,

---

* Panel Rapporteur; Pupil barrister, 20 Essex Street Chambers, London.

Mr. Daly considered it to be especially troubling in the light of its potential ramifications beyond the realm of arbitration. In his view, if not addressed, this could raise questions as to the legitimacy of the investor-State dispute resolution system.

From Mr. Beechey's perspective, the very question under debate presupposed the need to widen the pool of arbitrators. Each of the arbitral institutions represented on the panel unequivocally recognized that diversity is an issue of concern. Their power to act, however, is curtailed by the pre-dominant system of party appointment, which operates in approximately 70 per cent of ICC cases. Restrictions are also regularly imposed by the parties themselves, many of whom emanate from countries that offer the most vociferous complainants about the diversity of the system. Despite these realities, Mr. Beechey believes that the institutions should certainly provide leadership on this issue by appointing alternative candidates wherever possible and by offering rigorous training for emerging arbitrators.

Mr. Ziadé concluded the first sub-panel by discussing the role of regional arbitral institutions. He explained that regional arbitration centres were established to counter the perceived lack of transparency of their developed-world predecessors and the desire to have disputes decided in the region in which they arise. Despite this disenchantment with their Western counterparts, regional arbitration centres have not yet proven to be "flying stably at a high altitude".

In order to become truly credible alternatives, these centres must address legitimacy concerns by implementing structural changes. In particular, they should adopt modern rules and codes of conduct, recruit a varied and specialized team of staff, offer a diverse pool of arbitrators, be governed by an international board, operate in an environment favourable to arbitration and maintain a robust governing structure.

Following Mr. Ziadé's reference to the effective use of partnership agreements by several global institutions, Mr. Moollan raised the possibility of traditional arbitration centres transitioning into multi-regional organizations, citing the example of the newly-established Jerusalem Arbitration Centre, which cooperates extensively with the ICC. Mr. Beechey explained the uniqueness of that particular arrangement, which was founded by way of a joint venture agreement between ICC Palestine and ICC Israel, and allows the centre to operate with its own court and secretariat. He observed that as private commercial courts, there are limits as to the institutions' capacity to effect this kind of broader change.

A second sub-panel comprising Mohamed Abdel Raouf, Director of the Cairo Regional Centre for International Commercial Arbitration; Meg Kinnear, Secretary-General of the International Centre for Settlement of Investment Disputes; and Richard Naimark, Senior Vice President of the American Arbitration Association, engaged with the second proposition, which concerned the relationship between the allegedly opaque workings of arbitral institutions and the creation of a "mafia" of arbitrators who rely on repeat appointments and are indifferent to delays and costs.

Mr. Abdel Raouf highlighted the repeated references to the rising costs of international arbitration and to the delays in the arbitral process. The panellists reached broad consensus that the parties' legal counsel are largely responsible for both issues. The parties' legal counsel not only contribute disproportionately to the costs of an arbitration, but often cause delays in arbitral procedure. As a result, the institutions' capacity to reduce costs is limited. Many institutions have nonetheless taken steps to publish cost-controlling guidelines and to revise institutional rules that enable delay in the arbitral process, whether caused by the parties, their counsel, the arbitrators or the institutions themselves. Mr. Abdel Raouf characterized the existence of an arbitration "mafia" as a myth, as the participation of new entrants is actively encouraged by established institutions and arbitration associations. Instead, he described the pool of arbitrators as an "exclusive club" to which membership is open.

Ms. Kinnear echoed Mr. Beechey's remarks as to the parties' responsibility for ensuring diversity in arbitrator appointments. Ms. Kinnear added that while there was broad agreement on the desirability of diversity in institutional appointments, there was little consensus on how to attain it. She also remarked that institutions largely do not view the "two-hat" issue (i.e. the fact of an individual acting alternately as arbitrator or counsel in cases) as inherently problematic, but must assess its impact in the circumstances of an individual case to determine if a conflict arises. Ms. Kinnear also considered the extent to which institutional appointments should be transparent to ensure the legitimacy of the process. In her view, the process itself should be clearly articulated, but granular reasons for the appointment of a particular candidate should not be published. The panellists made a plea for common sense to govern arbitrator disclosure, expressing a certain wariness of a culture of over-disclosure.

Mr. Naimark scrutinized the rationale for transparency in arbitral institutions in order to evaluate institutional policies. Transparency, in his view, seeks to enable greater predictability in arbitral decision-making and to maintain the market's confidence in the integrity of institutional processes. There is, however, a limit to the predictability of the decision-making process. All arbitral institutions seek to balance the desirability of publishing appropriate information with the undesirability of creating a crippling bureaucracy. This balance is achieved by publishing general principles, but not reasoned decisions. In Mr. Naimark's view, transparency is also served by introducing formal policies regulating conduct in the event of conflicts of interest between institutional staff, arbitrators and/or counsel.

The third sub-panel considered the proper function of arbitral institutions. Adrian Winstanley, Director General of the London Court of International Arbitration (1997-2014); Sundra Rajoo, Director of the Kuala Lumpur Regional Centre for Arbitration; and Frederico José Straube, President of the Centre for Arbitration and Mediation of the Chamber of Commerce of Brazil-Canada, debated the third proposition devised by the panellists, considering whether "arbitral institutions unduly focus on profit-making and gaining market share".

Mr. Winstanley explained that the mission statements of each of the nine institutions represented on the panel all confirm their commitment to fostering legitimacy. Each of them operates on a non-for-profit basis. This does not, however, preclude them from engaging in healthy competition. Each institution is dependent on the funds derived from a strong market position to fulfil their mandates. Equally, arbitral institutions have a collective interest in working collaboratively to ensure that they remain an efficient and cost-effective alternative to litigation in domestic fora.

Mr. Rajoo also took the view that arbitral institutions may collaborate and compete simultaneously. While arbitral institutions are certainly vying for the same market, the competition between them results in innovation and the promotion of best practices, which enhances the legitimacy of the entire process. In his opinion, legitimacy is achieved through multiple facets.

Mr. Straube considered that institutional practice contradicts the third proposition. As each arbitral institution recognize s, fostering legitimacy is inherent in their essential function. Collaboration between arbitral institutions, rather than competition, is necessary to protect the legitimacy of the system as a whole. Such collaboration is crucial to the development of regional arbitral institutions in particular, through the provision of training and assistance in the implementation of best practices. Nevertheless, burgeoning arbitral institutions should not lose sight of the need to generate sufficient resources in order to maintain their independence from government and from the private sector.

The panel concluded by debating Mr. Moollan's proposition that arbitral institutions, as not-for-profit entities with an avowed interest in the legitimacy of the system of international arbitration, should seek to combine their efforts and resources to train new arbitrators in a joint project overseen by the United Nations. The proposal was met with scepticism from the panel. While Mr. Abdel Raouf observed that arbitral institutions adopt diverse and perhaps incompatible approaches, Mr. Daly noted that individual institutions generally seek to instruct arbitrators only in their own practices and procedures and would not be qualified to instruct on those of other institutions. Mr. Winstanley remarked that while the idea was attractive in principle, the capacity of institutions to engage in such a large-scale project would be by no means assured.

In the closing ceremony, Mr. Moollan scrutinized the reason for which the collective concern as to the existence of a pro-developed-world bias did not translate into the endorsement of broader collaboration between the represented arbitral institutions, querying whether the real explanation could be that the institutions' training programmes are in fact largely marketing exercises, rather than true capacity-building endeavours.

Survey

Arbitral Institutions Can Do More to Foster Legitimacy.
True or False?*

There is much talk of problems of "legitimacy" of international arbitration as system of dispute resolution. By this, and for the purposes of this questionnaire, we mean systemic issues which are said to undermine the acceptability of this form of dispute resolution as a whole and/or which may lead to its rejection by particular groups, be they countries as a whole or particular categories of users. The purpose of this questionnaire is to collate your views as to whether there are in fact any such problems, and what arbitral institutions can do – if anything – to alleviate them.

A.   GENERAL

A first alleged problem area is legitimacy from the point of view of new entrants in the developing world. This has for instance been put as follows:

"There exists a hiatus today between a formal discourse which emphasizes the 'inclusiveness' of international arbitration and a perception of this field in the developing world as being heavily weighed towards the developed world, with most of the leading arbitration law firms and nearly all of the leading arbitrators based in the developed world. With developing countries being consistently – and rightly – encouraged to accept the process of international arbitration as an effective means of dispute resolution, be it as part of their commercial deals or as a necessary corollary of investment flowing into their

---

*   The Survey Respondents are:

Mohamed Abdel Raouf, Director, Cairo Regional Centre for International Commercial Arbitration (CRCICA);

John Beechey, President, International Court of Arbitration of the International Chamber of Commerce (ICC);

Brooks Daly, Deputy Secretary-General, Permanent Court of Arbitration (PCA);

Meg Kinnear, Secretary-General, International Centre for Settlement of Investment Disputes (ICSID);

Richard W. Naimark, Senior Vice President, American Arbitration Association (AAA), in charge of the International Centre for Dispute Resolution (ICDR);

Sundra Rajoo, Director, Kuala Lumpur Regional Centre for Arbitration (KLRCA);

Frederico José Straube, President, CAM-CCBC (Centre for Arbitration and Mediation of the Chamber of Commerce of Brazil-Canada);

Adrian Winstanley, Director General, London Court of International Arbitration (LCIA) (1997-2014);

Nassib G. Ziadé, Chief Executive Officer, Bahrain Centre for Dispute Resolution.

countries from developed countries, there is a growing risk of arbitration being perceived as a 'foreign' process imposed from abroad."

Question 1
Do you agree that this is a valid concern? If not, why not?

Bahrain Centre for Dispute Resolution – BCDR (Nassib Ziadé)
"I agree that these are valid concerns.

Following an initial phase of rejection of international arbitration by developing countries which stressed its European origin and the lack of sensitivity of certain awards toward non-Western legal regimes, many developing countries have come to accept international arbitration as an objective necessity. These countries nonetheless today express strong reservations, based on first-hand experience, regarding exploding costs, long delays, and the over-commitment of experienced arbitrators. These countries point out that arbitration practitioners wear several hats and that they take the lead in regulating their own activities, while the arbitration institutions often refrain from even enacting basic guidelines for conduct. Other concerns expressed by these countries relate to the lack of transparency in the work of arbitration institutions. This last point will be addressed in my answers to the questions below.

As one way to address these valid concerns, a focused effort should be undertaken by arbitration institutions to diversify the pool of arbitrators through the identification of new, talented, independent and available persons. Arbitration institutions located in Western countries would also be well advised to increase the number of arbitrators originating from developing countries.

Though the situation on this front has been gradually improving in many Western arbitration institutions over the last few decades, there remains substantial room for improvement. For example, the statistics recently published by ICSID reveal that in 2013, 17% of the cases registered at ICSID involved a Western European or North American State, while 68% involved a State from Eastern Europe, Central Asia, the Middle East, North Africa or Sub-Saharan Africa. Meanwhile, 70% of the arbitrators originated from Western Europe or North America, and a grand total of 4% came from Eastern Europe, Central Asia, the Middle East, North Africa and Sub-Saharan Africa. There thus seems to be a neat division of labor, at least at ICSID. Cases are brought against Arab, African, Central Asian and Eastern European States, and Western Europeans and North Americans get to judge them and determine the jurisprudence. In saying all this, I do commend ICSID for publishing its statistics. I would hope, however, that the next step taken would be to address the problems that those numbers so glaringly reveal.

It bears noting that the same individuals tend to be appointed repeatedly, and they even regularly appoint each other. The community of arbitrators is thus often viewed as an exclusive club of notables, access to which is hindered for newcomers. While this club very largely comprises respected arbitration professionals, there is clearly an insufficient representation of women and of individuals from emerging economies.

Arbitration institutions are not solely responsible for these shortcomings in the system. When called upon to make arbitral appointments, parties and their counsel very often prefer to minimize risks by selecting arbitrators with whom they are already familiar, if not necessarily comfortable.

None of the aforementioned difficulties should deter the institutions from making every effort to expand the pool of qualified arbitrators. It behooves the institutions to take the lead in this mission in order to maintain the trust of their users and, more broadly, the

668

legitimacy of the system. The widening of the pool of arbitrators will create a system that will be more inclusive and representative of the international community. It will also reduce the number of challenges based on repeat appointments of arbitrators and other perceived conflicts of interest, the number of such challenges having risen exponentially in recent years.

Those averse to changes in the appointment process will likely point to the risks of occasional problematic appointments of newcomers. While there is some validity to this concern, the risks do not warrant abandoning efforts to diversify, or leaving the arbitration field in a sclerotic, if not decadent, state."

Cairo Regional Centre for International Commercial Arbitration – CRCICA (Mohamed Abdel Raouf)

"As far as Egypt, the country hosting CRCICA's headquarters, is concerned, arbitration is no longer regarded as a 'foreign' process 'imposed from abroad'.

Egypt has hosted a regional arbitral institution since 1979 and enacted a modern law on arbitration in 1994, based on the UNCITRAL Model Law. It has ratified both the 1958 New York and the Washington Conventions in addition to other multilateral regional conventions regarding the recognition and enforcement of non-Egyptian arbitral awards.

According to the available statistics, arbitration is increasingly becoming the normal means of settlement of commercial and investment disputes from simple lease agreements to complex oil and gas concessions, construction contracts and transfer of technology. Recently, disputes arising out of media and entertainment and sports-related contracts are also being referred to arbitration not only in relation to international contracts, but also in relation to domestic ones, which clearly demonstrates that arbitration is very well perceived in this jurisdiction.

That said, in other jurisdictions where arbitration is not very well developed, regardless of whether the jurisdiction itself belongs to the developed or developing world, arbitration may still be perceived as a foreign process. For instance, a country like Libya, which has a great potential, is hostile to international arbitration, which is still perceived as a Western product run by a small club of Western experts. The role of international arbitral institutions is to include Libya and similar countries in the region (Iraq, for instance) in the process. The objective should not be to have a stake in the Libyan pie, but rather to contribute to the development of the arbitration infrastructure of this country. This approach would help to eliminate any concerns about the legitimacy of international arbitration in this part of the world.

While law firms are client-oriented, which is normal, global and regional arbitral institutions should focus on other goals in addition to increasing their caseload."

Centre for Arbitration and Mediation of the Chamber of Commerce of Brazil-Canada – CAM-CCBC (Frederico José Straube)

"The matter regarding the 'apparent inclusion of developing countries' is not a polemic question limited to international arbitration. The debates on their legitimacy involve international law as a whole. In the same way that, in international trade, the WTO is often accused of protecting the interests of developed countries and that the protection of human rights has been approached, by some schools, as if it was a tool of domination used by culturally predominant countries (in other words, a mechanism for imposing occidental culture worldwide), studies have questioned the legitimacy of international arbitration.

Such criticism, however, is rooted in a lack of understanding of the foundation of arbitration, which is a dispute settlement mechanism. Furthermore, it is important to remember that arbitration, in its most primitive version, predates the judiciary. The search for dispute settlement mechanisms is part of the concept of civilization in the same way that disputes, on their part, are inherent to human nature.

It is therefore possible to state that such concerns are the effect of a criticism directed towards international law and are based on a superficial analysis that does not take into consideration the grounds of the institution of arbitration."

International Centre for Dispute Resolution – ICDR (Richard Naimark)

"Yes, it is a valid concern, though it is questionable whether it is a growing concern. The reality is that most countries and regions realize that arbitration based on recognized international standards is a key piece of the puzzle in boosting cross-border trade and investment. No one wants to go to anyone else's court system for fear of unequal treatment.

In Asia and Latin America there is notable growth in regional arbitration expertise and what we see is there are some modest changes to the flavour of arbitration, which reflect regional inclinations. So it is fair to say that international arbitration is already being adapted from any apparently rigid Western-based models.

There may still be some justifiable concerns in Africa and the Middle East."

International Centre for Settlement of Investment Disputes – ICSID (Meg Kinnear)

"If international arbitration is to have credibility and legitimacy, it must reflect the diversity of all participants in the system. In fact, the international arbitration system is becoming more diverse and more inclusive, but it takes time to develop expertise in a specialized field.

ICSID is mandated by its constituent instruments to consider and reflect the diverse nature of parties to international investment disputes.[1] In addition, ICSID reflects the diversity of its member States in its staff, who come from over twenty-five States and collectively speak more than twenty-nine languages."

International Chamber of Commerce – ICC (John Beechey)

"The statement above and the sentiments expressed are a reflection of a longstanding perception, which remains strong despite all evidence to the contrary, rather than the reality.

It is true that a party from a developed country may seek to impose arbitration as a condition for executing the contract. It is true, too, that most law firms specialized in the field are currently based in developed countries. But the former is often a manifestation of nothing more or less than an attempt to ensure a fair hearing in a neutral jurisdiction and the latter becomes less valid an objection as sophisticated practitioners, often educated both locally and abroad, emerge in developing jurisdictions.

If one considers the ratio origin of parties : places of arbitration in 2003 and compares it with ICC figures for 2012, there is clear evidence of an increase in the percentage of places of arbitration located in developing countries. Indeed, whereas the percentage of parties from Africa, Latin America, Central and East Europe and South East Asia increased from 38.3% to 46.9% between 2003 and 2012 (i.e., a 22% increase), the percentage of places of arbitration located in those regions within the same period increased from 15.6% to 25.3% (i.e., a 62% increase).

---

1. See, for example, ICSID Convention Art. 14(2); Report of Executive Directors on the ICSID Convention, para. 11.

It bears repeating that, increasingly, Latin American, Central European or Asian parties are represented by local counsel (occasionally supported by international co-counsel). The sophistication and expertise of counsel located in developing countries have increased significantly in recent years, most probably as a result of an increase in the number of cases directly handled by counsel from those regions and by the exposure of such counsel to international arbitration practice and procedure."

Kuala Lumpur Regional Centre for Arbitration – KLRCA (Sundra Rajoo)

"The concerns emanating from the developing world are valid for a number of reasons. The gap in training, education and exposure to international commercial law and arbitration specifically, means that many developing jurisdictions lack the ability to extract the full benefits of commercial arbitration. This is not limited to decreased trade and foreign investment, but can also directly affect Governments through a similar impact on investor-State arbitration. A country that lacks the expertise and knowledge is likely to be vulnerable to investor claims through arbitration.

These concerns are not insurmountable, however. There are many routes that developing countries can take to promote arbitration and improve the level of domestic arbitration with the attending benefits. The experience of Malaysia together with the Asian-African Legal Consultative Organization (AALCO) is a prime example.

Malaysia is unique in its position as a developing country. Although classified as a developing country by the World Bank,[2] Malaysia enjoys many of the benefits common to developed jurisdictions concerning commercial arbitration. To a large extent this is parallel to the experience of AALCO in the region, and how the practice of arbitration has flourished in this region. AALCO was constituted on 15 November 1956. It is considered to be a tangible outcome of the historic Bandung Conference, held in Indonesia in April 1955. Seven Asian States, namely Burma (now Myanmar), Ceylon (now Sri Lanka), India, Indonesia, Iraq, Japan, and the United Arab Republic (now Arab Republic of Egypt and Syrian Arab Republic) are the original Member States. AALCO was established as an advisory board to Member States on matters of international law; Regional Centres were set up to provide expertise and assistance to Member States in conducting arbitration proceedings.

One of the major achievements of AALCO in its programme in the economic field was the launching of its Integrated Scheme for Settlement of Disputes in Economic and Commercial Transactions in 1978. Pursuant to that Scheme, AALCO decided to establish Regional Arbitration Centres under its auspices, which would function as international institutions with the objectives of promoting international commercial arbitration in the Asian-African regions and providing for conducting international arbitrations under these Centres.[3] This was the time when KLRCA was established. From this, arbitration has long been established in Malaysia. This early establishment of AALCO in Malaysia can be seen as a method used to assimilate the Euro-centric approach to arbitration within the cultural settings of the region.

This assimilation is further aligned with globalization of economies and a desire for uniformity in commercial dispute resolution. It can be said that the globalization of economies relies heavily on arbitration. It is no longer an alternative. However, for it to work in a developing country, real concerns regarding its legitimacy must be addressed in

---

2. Per the World Bank website, <http://data.worldbank.org/country/malaysia>.

3. Sundra RAJOO, Lecture "Role and functions of AALCO's Regional Arbitration Centres", Asian-African Legal Consultative Organisation Fiftieth Annual Session (Colombo, Sri Lanka).

relation to legal infrastructure, maturity of judiciary and also economy. Largely in this sense, developing countries must adapt to developed countries' approach to arbitration.

Of course that is not to say that developing countries cannot contribute their own ideas to the development of commercial arbitration. One example of a jurisdiction not entirely acceding to the international practice of international arbitration, in respect of ad hoc arbitration especially, is China. Notably, only arbitration commissions may hear arbitrations and ad hoc awards will not be confirmed by courts. This, however, can be considered an anomaly. However, diverging from their domestic approach and following an international standard, and in compliance with the New York Convention, ad hoc arbitrations that are seated and confirmed in a foreign jurisdiction, are enforceable under the New York Convention in China.

As for appointing a 'mafia' of arbitrators coming from the developed world, this is not a concern, as regional centres frequently appoint domestic arbitrators or others from the region. The key is education and training over a sustained period to ensure a constant supply of domestic and regional arbitrators. A monopoly of arbitrators from certain regions and countries is perhaps more of a concern for multinational arbitration centres."

London Court of International Arbitration – LCIA (Adrian Winstanley)
"The growing frequency and urgency with which this concern is expressed is, in itself, a cause for concern, and it bears considering whether the aspirations of the founding fathers of the LCIA hold good for commercial arbitration today.

Thus, the principles at the heart of the establishment of the LCIA's forebear at the end of the nineteenth century were reported in the *Quarterly Law Review* as follows:

> 'This Chamber is to have all the virtues which the law lacks. It is to be expeditious where the law is slow, cheap where the law is costly, simple where the law is technical, a peacemaker instead of a stirrer-up of strife.'

'Expeditious where the law is slow'
The *'law'* in this case refers to the English Courts, with whose ponderous and expensive proceedings the business community centred on the City of London was becoming increasingly dissatisfied.

The LCIA's archives suggest that the *'London Chamber of Arbitration'* did, indeed, frequently administer efficient and expeditious proceedings. Arbitration today, on the other hand, can become as bogged down and protracted as litigation through State Courts, and at a time when the Courts of many jurisdictions have made strides to improve efficiency of case management. (There are, of course, some jurisdictions in which disputant parties can still spend half a lifetime in the State Courts on a single dispute.)

And though speed for its own sake has no place in arbitration, if arbitration becomes unduly protracted, then the cost of arbitration inevitably and inexorably rises, to the disadvantage, in particular, of parties who, even if of considerable financial standing in their own jurisdictions, may be relatively under-resourced in the international arena.

'Cheap where the law is costly'
Nobody today would refer to arbitration as *'cheap'*, but it aspires to be less expensive than litigation through the Courts, including the available levels of appeal.

We hear it argued often enough that the cost of arbitration; specifically the cost of legal representation in arbitration, though sometimes very high in absolute terms, is generally proportionate relative to the sums in issue.

But even if this is the case, many parties from the developing world may simply be denied *'access to justice'* through arbitration by no more than the threat or the prospect of having to pay advances on costs that would bankrupt them before they got anywhere near the award that they believe will vindicate their claim.

There may be some role in addressing this concern to be played by the burgeoning third-party-funding industry, but that is a topic for another day.

'Simple where the law is technical'
However simple the LCIA's founding fathers thought that arbitration might be in nineteenth century London, global business and global business disputes are now frequently highly technical, not only as to the subject matter of the contracts in dispute, or as to the terms of those contracts, but also as to the laws, rules and regulations, and the conflicting precedents often brought into play across jurisdictions, notwithstanding the location of the arbitration.

Even acknowledging the sophistication and expertise of a putative Claimant from a developing economy in the specifics of its own contractual relationships, the need to muster the broader expertise to fight its cause and to answer that of a wealthier and better equipped opponent can properly lead to a sense of inevitable defeat.

'A peacemaker instead of a stirrer-up of strife'
It is often said, though I have seen no empirical evidence of this, that arbitration, conducted in privacy and subject to confidentiality, is a forum more conducive to the restoration of commercial relationships once the proceedings are concluded than the spot-lit and public proceedings of State courts. But I am doubtful that long term commercial relations can be sustained if a putative claimant cannot get into arbitration at all for any of the reasons above, or if an actual respondent emerges battered and bruised from a contest with a claimant who knows how to *'play the game'* and who has the nouse and financial means to overwhelm a less prepared or less well-represented opponent.

For all of this, and acknowledging the truth of the observation cited at the opening of this section that most of the leading arbitration law firms and leading arbitrators are based in the developed world, there must be a question mark over the legitimacy of cross-border arbitration from the point of view of new entrants from the developing world."

Permanent Court of Arbitration – PCA (Brooks Daly)
"Arbitration work is commonly referred to Europe, North America, Hong Kong, and Singapore in view of the expertise concentrated there. In principle, there is nothing wrong with choosing the most skilled candidates for the roles of counsel and arbitrator, but in practice, this is a real concern to the extent that the near-exclusive use of lawyers in these jurisdictions may indeed make arbitration appear to be a 'foreign' system imposed from abroad.

As an intergovernmental organization, the PCA will from time to time hear its Member States from outside the above-mentioned regions and countries express concerns about being drawn into arbitral proceedings. The continued faith of these governments and other potential users in international arbitration depends in no small part on their perception of the system as a global one that serves the interests of all regions of the world."

Question 2
A second alleged problem area is the alleged existence of a so-called "mafia". Beyond the developing world perspective, there has been criticism of the internal workings of arbitral institutions, which are said to be too opaque, with the same arbitrators being appointed repeatedly, and a

complacent attitude (despite some posturing at conferences) to issues of increasing delays and increasing costs.
Do you agree that this is a valid concern? If not, why not?

BCDR (Nassib Ziadé)
"Combined answer to Questions 1 and 2 provided under Question 1 above."

CRCICA (Mohamed Abdel Raouf)
"This is indeed a valid concern of some users from our region, especially those who are not assisted by local lawyers with sufficient experience in arbitration.

I have to admit that some regional arbitration centres have contributed to the existence of such concerns, which arise mainly out of the opaqueness of the internal workings of such arbitral institutions, the repeated appointments of the same arbitrators, the possibility for the person(s) running such centres to sit as arbitrators under their auspices, and even to make self-appointments, as well as the lack of predictability in the determination of the arbitrators' fees (one centre used to leave this matter for the arbitrators to freely negotiate with the parties without any guidelines, while in another centre the exceptional increase in the arbitrators' fees became the rule).

It is clear that such practices are currently utterly unacceptable. There is in fact an effort exerted by most regional arbitral institutions to increase transparency and predictability as well as to encourage the appointment of new and young faces from different jurisdictions.

I entirely understand the risk run by some institutions in trying to diversify their appointments, but trust that when such institutions have sufficient experience and are sincerely keen to conduct the necessary reforms, the risk, if it exists, is at least a calculated one.

One area that needs to be reviewed is the procedure of appointment followed under the auspices of certain institutions based on panels of arbitrators to be provided by the states or national committees. While this system efficiently works in most jurisdictions, it constitutes a major barrier for talented individuals in other jurisdictions where the criteria for nomination by national committees or similar entities are far from being transparent if not driven by favouritism."

CAM-CCBC (Frederico José Straube)
"This is, indeed, a very common critical commentary addressed to arbitration. In Brazil, specifically, arbitration had its validity recognized very recently and, as a result, the number of experts in arbitration is still relatively small. On the other hand, its success has stimulated much interest on the topic, mainly among younger legal professionals.

I believe that the lack of a Roster of Arbitrators in some entities and the absence of objective and transparent criteria for the appointment or refusal of arbitrators can lead many to the impression that there is a 'mafia'.

In the pursuit of avoiding such bad impression, besides allowing the parties to choose their co-arbitrators according to their preferences and providing them with the certainty that they will only be refused in cases of clear disrepute, offering mechanisms for the parties to challenge the arbitrator appointed by the other side and offering an objective list of criteria for the Appointing Authority to select an arbitrator were solutions found by some arbitral institutions.

According to my experience in CAM-CCBC, one important element for demystifying this impression is the percentage of cases in which the parties appoint arbitrators whose names do not appear on our list for the position of co-arbitrator. It has increased, but such

674

phenomenon is not related to the quality of our arbitrators, which is of the highest level. I can say, furthermore, that our Roster of Arbitrators is one of our greatest patrimonies and the competition to become a part of it is very intense. Considering that the reason for the parties to appoint arbitrators outside of our list is not its quality, I was led to conclude that such increase is due to a wider opening in the Brazilian arbitral market that managed to grant a certain visibility to less renowned professionals. Also, this data reveals greater understanding regarding the nature of arbitration, due to the fact that one of the main foundations of the legitimacy of the arbitrator is the will of the parties, which is strongly related to the trust that the parties have in them."

ICDR (Richard Naimark)

"This is really three questions: the existence of a 'mafia', opacity of institutions and complacence on issues of delay and cost.

As to the 'mafia', of course there is a traditional practice derived primarily from northern Europe and North America in which there has been an oft-utilized small group of arbitrators and practitioners. The dominance of that small 'mafia' is rapidly dwindling, as demonstrated by the International Bar Association (IBA) Arbitration Section becoming the largest section in the IBA. Droves of highly able younger practitioners are flooding into the field. More women are becoming prominent. Every region has people of fine expertise and growing acceptability in the field.

Institutions are increasingly responding to the opacity concerns. The key concept here is 'responding'. Yes some institutional practices have been and continue to be somewhat opaque, particularly to those recently exposed to the field. In response, institutions are publishing more and more information and decisions; are explaining more in their rules and procedures; and are speaking more clearly about the specifics of their practices.

Complacence on issues of delay and cost is likely less a factor than is the absence of obvious solutions for those issues. The arbitration process is a complex fabric of inputs and outputs, motivations and goals of the various participants. Therefore any solutions are difficult to engineer. Some institutions have put considerable resources into discussing and dealing with these issues, though the effort seems to be somewhat variable."

ICSID (Meg Kinnear)

"I do not believe that these criticisms can fairly be made of the internal workings of ICSID.

Concerns about repeat appointments should be put in context: parties appoint arbitrators in whom they have confidence and often this confidence is based on an arbitrator's established record of cases and awards. Roughly seventy-five percent of all ICSID arbitrators are named by the parties, and ICSID does not interfere with party selection. While a number of party-appointed arbitrators have repeat appointments, we see an increasing number of 'first-time' appointments by parties and increasing diversity in their appointees.

At the same time, a number of arbitral institutions have taken steps to ensure that both 'emerging' and 'established' arbitrators are available to the parties. ICSID has been proactive in this respect and has taken numerous steps to ensure that parties are aware of, and may select, emerging arbitrators. These include:

– In appointments in ICSID Convention cases, ICSID proposes a ballot with at least five candidates. The ballot proposes both emerging and established arbitrators, and aims to include candidates from varied regions. In addition, to the extent possible, each ballot contains the name of at least one female arbitrator.

– Similarly, ICSID has appointed arbitrators using a 'list' procedure (with the consent of the parties). It has proposed a diverse group of arbitrators for party consideration in these lists.
– ICSID is transparent about who is appointed as an arbitrator in ICSID cases. It publishes statistics every six months showing the nationalities of arbitrators at the Centre and the regional origin of arbitrators appointed by parties and those appointed by the Centre.[4] It also lists the names of the arbitrators in every case and denotes who appointed each arbitrator.
– ICSID has written to all member States explaining the necessary qualifications for arbitrators on the ICSID Panel of Arbitrators and has encouraged them to fill vacant and expired positions with qualified persons of any nationality.[5]
– ICSID encourages emerging arbitrators to publish in the ICSID Review and to participate in conferences so that parties will become familiar with, and gain confidence in, these persons.

With respect to delay, this is a difficult challenge for arbitral institutions. However, it is not just an issue for institutions; to be successful, both parties and all three arbitrators must be accountable for the timing of an arbitration. Tribunal Presidents have a particular responsibility for timing in an arbitration and should be sensitive to the need for an expeditious resolution.

ICSID has had certain success in addressing delay. For example, ICSID adopted internal service standards that govern the time taken by the institution. As a result, it has reduced the average time to register a case to twenty-four days, and the time to appoint an arbitrator to an average of six weeks from the date ICSID received the request to appoint until the date of constitution of the tribunal. ICSID Tribunal Secretaries work closely with tribunals and if an award is outstanding for too long, the Secretary and the Secretary-General follow up with the President of the Tribunal. That said, ICSID continues to try to find ways to make proceedings more efficient.

With respect to increasing costs, the administrative fees of the institution are a fraction of the total costs. ICSID monitors arbitration costs carefully and vets each invoice before it is paid. It has also developed a real-time financial reporting system to provide parties with a detailed statement of the costs at any point in an arbitration. Knowing how advances have been disbursed should help discipline the use of funds in a case. However, the largest portion of the cost of an arbitration is for party representation and experts. Institutions have little or no control over those types of costs, and it is for parties to address such costs with their counsel."

---

4. See statistics on the ICSID website, <https://icsid.worldbank.org/ICSID/FrontServlet? requestType=ICSIDDocRH&actionVal=CaseLoadStatistics>, in particular, Chart 12: Arbitrators, Conciliators and *ad hoc* Committee Members Appointed in Cases Registered under the ICSID Convention and Additional Facility Rules – Distribution of Appointments by Geographic Region; Chart 13: Arbitrators, Conciliators and ad hoc Committee Members Appointed in Cases Registered under the ICSID Convention and Additional Facility Rules – Distribution of Appointments by ICSID and by the Parties (or Party-appointed Arbitrators) by Geographic Region; and Chart 14: State of Nationality of Arbitrators, Conciliators and ad hoc Committee Members Appointed in Cases Registered under the ICSID Convention and Additional Facility Rules.
5. On the Panel of Arbitrators, see ICSID Convention, Arts. 12-16, 38, 52.

ICC (John Beechey)

"In the view of the ICC International Court of Arbitration this is not a valid concern, for the following reasons:

– A review of the ICC statistics leaves no room to doubt that the pool of arbitrators in ICC arbitration continues to grow. In 2002, there were 660 individuals from 62 countries fulfilling arbitral appointments in ICC arbitration, whereas in 2012 the numbers increased to 847 individuals from 72 countries (including Ethiopia, Togo and Brunei, among many others).
– The 2012 ICC Rules have specifically addressed the issues of delays and increasing costs by inter alia (i) imposing on parties and arbitrators an obligation to make every effort to conduct the arbitration in a cost-effective manner, having regard to the complexity and value of the dispute, (ii) requiring prospective arbitrators to sign a statement of availability, (iii) requiring the tribunal to convene a case management conference, (iv) encouraging the use of case management techniques for controlling time and costs, and (v) assessing the diligence and efficiency of the arbitrators when setting their fees. In addition, the ICC Court has strictly applied these provisions by increasing the pressure on the timing for the delivery of draft awards (in respect of which arbitrators must provide the ICC Court and the parties with an estimated submission date of the draft), in appropriate cases reducing the fees of an arbitrator at the end of the case or even replacing an arbitrator in extreme circumstances."

KLRCA (Sundra Rajoo)

"This is a valid concern, especially considering many users look to arbitration for reasons of cost and time efficiency as well as party control. At the same time, however, there are always responsibilities that the institution must consider in their internal procedures and policy decisions. Many institutions, for example, have taken initiatives to give opportunities to arbitrators who are more junior: (1) in less complex cases and (2) as a co-arbitrator where there are already two very experienced arbitrators appointed. In other cases, other issues will be relevant in selecting an arbitrator, including subjective factors depending on the characteristics of the case, such as technical expertise or language considerations.

One of the main reasons for utilizing our discretion and expertise to make appointments of arbitrators is to counter delays and increased costs. We include an open panel, listed in a transparent way on our website for parties to be able to see the details of arbitrators that are available or being appointed. In this way, users are able to exercise initial control over the arbitrator that will determine their dispute. When we are requested to make an appointment, however, there will necessarily be a limit to the transparency of the process. Apart from cost and time considerations, as an appointing authority, users are relying on the KLRCA for our expertise and ability to appoint a suitable arbitrator for the dispute in question. The request is made to the institution specifically because the parties are unable to come to agreement and opening the process to the users will necessarily undermine the confidence placed in the institution to make the appointment.

Notwithstanding, the 'how' of the appointment procedure must be transparent. The factors that we take into account are publicly known. Examples of how the KLRCA positively deals with the issue of internal workings on appointments include the issuance of codes of ethics, a clear appointment process, involvement in challenge of arbitrators (to reduce delay in proceedings) and also providing scale fees to ensure costs are reasonable.

Anecdotally, the 'mafia' should not only be perceived as an institutional issue. Often, arbitrators who are 'known' are party-appointed arbitrators. For large cases, parties want the best arbitrators and oftentimes these 'best arbitrators' are members of the 'mafia'. Often appointing these arbitrators leads to unnecessary delays because these arbitrators are simply too busy. This is a further benefit of requesting an institution to appoint an arbitrator on a party's behalf, as it surely will not appoint an arbitrator who is too busy to hear a case. Ironically, it is also the institutions that may offer the most effective route to training new arbitrators."

LCIA (Adrian Winstanley)

"Although the allegation that there exists a 'mafia' that is self-perpetuating and is aided and abetted by institutions is repeated at arbitration conferences, down corridors and in bars, it is not supported by the experience of the LCIA.

In 2013, the LCIA made a total of 367 appointments of a total of 208 different arbitrators, with the majority of those arbitrators who were appointed more than once either being selected by the parties or being appointed for sound reasons in closely-related arbitrations.

I do acknowledge, however, that the internal workings of the LCIA are, to some degree, opaque as regards the selection and appointment of arbitrators. Not as far as the mechanics are concerned – these are well enough documented in the LCIA's published materials – but in the nuance of the debate between Secretariat and Court by which those arbitrators selected by the Court come to be appointed.

But I believe that a degree of opacity is inevitable and necessary as regards, in particular, the exchange between Secretariat and LCIA Court on a selection process informed by confidential information submitted by the parties. And, even though this information would undoubtedly be of public interest, data-protection considerations alone would prevent any institution from naming all the individuals it appoints and stating how often and why.

If a finger of blame for the 'mafia' myth may be pointed in any direction, I submit that it should be pointed in the direction of nominating parties; more specifically, the attorneys of those parties, who may have a propensity to gravitate towards the most high profile arbitrators, described, in good humour by a former colleague on the LCIA Court as the *'800 lb. gorillas'*, leading to the perceived imperative on the part of the opposing party to appoint its own 800 lb. gorilla.

The parties obviously want to succeed in their claim, defence or counterclaim, and may reasonably be expected to nominate arbitrators who they consider likely to be sympathetic to their position (a view simply-enough informed by research).

If the combination of a desire to appoint one of the biggest names, and, further, one with perceived favourable propensities fuels the 'mafia' myth, then it is as well to consider the objective of an institution in selecting an arbitrator.

The institution ultimately wants the *arbitration* to succeed – that is, to reach a just and binding conclusion – and the institution favours arbitrators with no preconceived views on the merits, but with all the required attributes and expertise.

The institution also strives always to ensure that the arbitrators it appoints are able to devote the necessary time to conduct the arbitration expeditiously.

And in this, the institutions can call upon an ever-expanding pool of talented arbitrators, without any need to call only on the *'greatest-and-goodest'*."

PCA (Brooks Daly)

"The majority of arbitral appointments are made by the parties themselves. They tend to choose established and experienced arbitrators in view of the significant stakes that may be involved in international arbitration: the continued existence of a corporation, the financial health of an individual, or the economy of a country. Parties' conservative nature in choosing arbitrators is thus understandable and appropriate in light of their interest in eliminating unpredictability from arbitral decisions.

678

In this context, arbitral institutions must meet parties' expectations when appointing arbitrators. For example, the appointment of a presiding arbitrator with drastically less experience in international arbitration than the party-appointed arbitrators on the same tribunal would shock most parties and subject the institution to severe criticism. Nevertheless, institutions do have opportunities to 'break in' new arbitrators in appropriate cases: when there are small quantified claims, when the parties have themselves chosen to appoint less experienced arbitrators, and when the parties put a premium on potentially lower cost and greater availability of less experienced practitioners.

With respect to delays and rising costs, there may be some blame-shifting away from parties and counsel on these issues. They are certainly problematic, but remain best addressed by parties because they are the primary decision-makers with respect to duration and cost variables. Delays are largely driven by the demands which counsel impose on procedural calendars. For example, parties may agree to long pleading schedules which tribunals may feel compelled to accept. The costs of legal representations constitute by far the highest percentage of total arbitral costs, and third-party funding in this context may be seen as raising its own legitimacy concerns. There is little that arbitral institutions can do to control counsel fees other than to publish examples of cost-controlling methods (which a number of institutions have already done)."[6]

Question 3

Are there any other problem areas which you feel pose threats to the legitimacy of international arbitration as a system of dispute resolution? If so which?

BCDR (Nassib Ziadé)

"The international arbitration system today faces serious problems when it comes to the issue of conflicts of interest. I am aware that in the eyes of many arbitration practitioners, particularly those who are able to obtain lucrative assignments, the system works just fine. This view is not shared, however, by other arbitration practitioners, or by many outside observers, academics and judges deciding on challenges to arbitrators.

Times are changing quickly. Practices that were considered unobjectionable twenty-five years ago are in many cases deemed problematic today. Some relationships may appear to be too close for comfort. Public scrutiny has greatly increased, and demands for transparency have become ever more stringent.

Recognizing and avoiding conflicts of interest lie at the very heart of the arbitration system's credibility and legitimacy. The arbitration institutions' focus should therefore be on building users' trust rather than on making things convenient for arbitration practitioners.

The international arbitration system needs more than cosmetic changes when it comes to conflicts of interest. It requires substantial revamping. Arbitration institutions will sooner or later have to shoulder their responsibilities by first enacting internal codes of conduct applicable to their staffs and practices, and then by enacting external codes applicable to arbitrators and counsel appearing before them. In doing this, arbitration institutions will fulfill their missions more adequately and thereby strengthen their legitimacy.

---

6. See ICC Techniques for Controlling Time and Costs in Arbitration (2007); CIArb Rules of Controlled-Cost Arbitration (2007).

Though this process of reform will likely be resisted by individuals entrenched in the arbitration profession who may wish to preserve the advantages of their incumbency, it should be swiftly implemented in the long-term interests of the institutions and their users."

CRCICA (Mohamed Abdel Raouf)

"From a regional perspective, the main problem that poses a threat to the legitimacy of international arbitration as a system of dispute resolution is the mushrooming of new local arbitral centres established within law firms, training centres and most recently universities.

Unfortunately, not all jurisdictions have the necessary tools to combat such random centres, which lack credibility and therefore tarnish the reputation of arbitration in addition to threatening the legitimacy of the system.

The challenge here is to strike a perfect balance between the need to regulate the creation of new arbitration centres and the concern of avoiding superfluous restrictions.

Another problem is the role of State courts in enforcing arbitral awards. Judges in some jurisdictions are doing an excellent job in applying and interpreting the already liberal provisions of applicable national arbitration laws in an arbitration-friendly fashion. However, in other jurisdictions, the enforcement of arbitral awards is becoming a frustrating marathon.

One should salute here the excellent work done in various jurisdictions and in different languages by certain international organizations like ICCA in raising awareness among national judges with respect to the enforcement of foreign arbitral awards under the New York Convention. However, the enforcement of domestic awards is still encountering some problems in certain jurisdictions, particularly before administrative courts, which seem to be hostile to arbitration. More work on the ground is to be done in this respect, especially by regional arbitral institutions."

CAM-CCBC (Frederico José Straube)

"In Brazil, the major concern, which is ungrounded as I must highlight, is related to the impartiality of the arbitrator. According to some jurists, the judge who has his jurisdiction under the law would tend to be more neutral, since he would not have any previous information regarding the matter or the parties. This situation, however, is not possible in arbitration since, in this latter mechanism, the parties are in charge of choosing the arbitrator.

Also, some researchers state that appointment by the parties would prevent the person in charge of deciding the case from keeping a 'safe distance' from the parties. According to them, this does not happen in state courts, whose jurisdiction is established by legal criteria.

However, none of these concerns, as I have already mentioned, makes sense. The fact is that although the appointment of the arbitrator is made by the parties, the selection of the President of the tribunal requires consensus, which would not be possible if he tended to be partial. The possibility for the parties to challenge the arbitrators appointed by the other side is another element that offers greater legitimacy to the arbitral tribunal. Furthermore, there are situations in which the choice of submitting the matter to an arbitral tribunal can grant some neutrality. This is what happens, for instance, in disputes involving foreign investors and the public administration."

ICDR (Richard Naimark)

"Court enforcement and support continues to be somewhat unpredictable and inconsistent around the world, though the work of UNCITRAL has advanced the practice immeasurably.

Added to the list would be obstructive/destructive party behaviour in proceedings and inadequate case management by some arbitrators."

ICSID (Meg Kinnear)

There are a number of areas where arbitration needs to evolve, and is evolving, but these do not constitute threats to the legitimacy of international arbitration as a system of dispute resolution. These evolving areas include the need to better use consultation periods, to ensure expeditious document disclosure, and to use mediation and other ADR tools more effectively."

ICC (John Beechey)

"Some areas that inexperienced users may consider as undermining the legitimacy of arbitration include:

– *Payment of fees by the parties*: the fact that the parties pay the fees of the arbitrators, who will decide their case is sometimes a cause for concern. One of the advantages of institutional arbitration is that it is for the institution, and not the arbitrators, to deal with and collect the fees from the parties. In this respect, there is an express provision under the ICC Rules that forbids direct payment arrangements between arbitrators and parties.

– *Exchange of favours among arbitrators and counsel*: some practitioners may fear that an arbitrator may be tempted to decide the case in favour of a counsel's client in order to get future nominations from the same counsel. Likewise, there may be a concern that X advises his/her client to nominate Y in a case, with the (implicit) expectation that X will then be nominated by Y in another case. When it comes to ICC arbitration, the Court and the Secretariat will normally be aware of these situations and will seek to avoid them. In any event, the prospective arbitrator will be required to make a disclosure before appointing or confirming him/her. A similarly robust requirement of disclosure is a feature of most leading institutional rules and, indeed, of the UNCITRAL 'ad hoc' Rules.

– *Lack of knowledge as to the operation of the institution*: Institutions are sometimes criticized for not being transparent as to how they work, for instance, when it comes to the appointment of an arbitrator or the decision upon a challenge. The ICC Rules provide a clear indication of how the system works and numerous publications shed light on the Court's practice."

KLRCA (Sundra Rajoo)

"There are several additional areas that pose threats to the legitimacy of the system of international arbitration. One key area is the different ethical codes of conduct regulating lawyers from different jurisdictions, for example, ethical guidelines that conflict depending on the home jurisdiction of a lawyer, involving the coaching of witnesses. Despite the fact that arbitration rules adopt universal or 'international arbitration ethical guidelines', if an individual does something which is against the ethical rules of the regulating body in their home jurisdiction, they will face disciplinary action by that body. The fact that the conduct engaged in was during an international arbitration will not be a valid defence. Despite the need for and development of an international code of conduct, just how this can legitimately guide and regulate lawyers from a multitude of jurisdictions must be called into question.

Additionally, in some instances proceedings become too formal, largely as a result of counsel or arbitrators who are accustomed to court proceedings and inexperienced in the field of arbitration. Further, the conduct of court proceedings differs depending on jurisdiction and when international parties conduct their arbitration proceedings in a formal matter according to their own jurisdictions, there can be cultural conflict in addition to the excessive formality of such arbitral proceedings. When there is cultural conflict between formalistic lawyers, this can become particularly problematic as a result of rigid systems and procedures adopted in various jurisdictions.[7] The solution to this is training arbitrators to be cross-culturally competent to deal with this conflict in addition to the dispute in the arbitration."

LCIA (Adrian Winstanley)

"Following naturally from the observations made above, there is a need for rules and costs structures that are geared to deal efficiently and cost effectively with lower-value claims.

There is also undoubtedly a need to enfranchise more lawyers practicing in the developing world in order to foster and encourage in these individuals the development of best practices in arbitration, whether as attorney or as arbitrator, and to provide a more relevant and familiar framework of arbitration within these jurisdictions."

PCA (Brooks Daly)

"Rising arbitral costs may also entail an issue of access to justice. This may arise when individual consumers are not able to afford to bring their claims within the terms of contractual arbitration clauses, when small corporate investors who have been fully expropriated are left with limited resources to finance claims, and when developing States are significantly outmatched by claimants in their ability to finance robust representation for the duration of arbitral proceedings. In the context of international arbitration's role as an alternative to domestic judicial proceedings, it is noteworthy that pro bono or indigent legal services are more widely available in the latter system."[8]

Question 4
Do you feel that it is part of an arbitral institution's role to foster legitimacy? If not, why not?

BCDR (Nassib Ziadé)

"An arbitral institution fosters its own legitimacy by providing efficient and fair due process so one could say that such a 'role' is actually inescapable for any serious institution. When legitimacy is lacking, there is moral hazard and a real prospect of abandonment by parties, arbitrators, staff and interested members of the public. Addressing threats to legitimacy is therefore the biggest challenge that an arbitral institution can face.

There are specific areas in which the legitimacy of an arbitration institution can be tested in a particularly hard manner. These areas include conflicts of interest, the selection of arbitrators, and the handling of arbitrator challenges. In all of these areas, transparency

---

7. Rizwan HUSSAIN, "International Arbitration – Culture and Practices", 9 Asian International Arbitration Journal (2013, no. 1) at p. 1.
8. See S. MELIKIAN, "Access to Justice in Dispute Resolution: Financial Assistance in International Arbitration" in K.B. Nadakavukaren SCHEFER, *Poverty and the International Economic Legal System: Duties to the World's Poor* (Cambridge Univ. Press 2013).

and consistency are the critical factors in determining whether an arbitral institution has responded successfully."

CRCICA *(Mohamed Abdel Raouf)*

"It is indeed one of the roles of an arbitral institution to foster legitimacy of institutional arbitration. Arbitral institutions are offering a service in an open market and they have an important role to play to protect their reputation as well as the legitimacy of international arbitration in general."

CAM-CCBC *(Frederico José Straube)*

"The arbitral institutions can, indeed, grant greater neutrality to the procedure. Whenever they accept the charge of intermediating all communications between the parties and the arbitrators, or of creating a questionnaire capable of identifying possible bias of a candidate for arbitrator towards one of the parties, or of establishing a transparent procedure that allows the parties to challenge the arbitrator appointed by the other side, the institutions offer more security regarding the impartiality of the tribunal.

However, neutrality is maintained not only through securing mechanisms during the formation of the arbitral tribunal, but also through the isonomic treatment offered to the parties and through the confidentiality regarding the communications and the development of the procedure.

On the other side, the legitimacy of the arbitral tribunal is based on the trust the parties have in the arbitrator. Therefore, when it ensures the neutrality of the tribunal, the arbitral institution protects its legitimacy."

ICDR *(Richard Naimark)*

"Yes it is part of an institution's role, but it is not exclusive to institutions. We need to avoid 'buck passing' and recognize that no sector has exclusive control or responsibility for legitimacy. That said, institutions are in a unique position to educate, advocate and inform both as to issues of importance and the appropriate roles and behaviours of the various players. Institutions are a collection point for experience and perspective."

ICSID *(Meg Kinnear)*

"The role of the arbitral institution is to be an effective service provider, which in turn fosters legitimacy. This is achieved, in part, by supporting the parties and tribunals in individual cases and by offering an effective procedural framework for dispute settlement. ICSID also fosters legitimacy by sharing knowledge through publications and seminars on international investment law and procedure."

ICC *(John Beechey)*

"I agree."

KLRCA *(Sundra Rajoo)*

"Certainly, since an arbitral institution often has the platform and exposure to add value to the arbitral process and develop legitimacy that other groups may not. Notably, an institution should not take a very interventionist role, as doing so takes away the independence of arbitrators. It must be balanced. That is the reason the KLRCA takes a hands-off approach in administering arbitration. In addition to the structural tools of the KLRCA, it is important for an institution to engage in various other activities in the arbitral community. One particular focus of the KLRCA is the education and training of arbitrators. This is done through talks and seminars as well as programs run in conjunction with the Chartered Institute of Arbitrators (CIArb). This in particular helps foster

683

institutional legitimacy by ensuring that the arbitrators the institution appoints are highly skilled and can meet the demands of international commercial arbitration.

From a regional institution's perspective it is of utmost importance to foster legitimacy, not only in the arbitration industry generally but also in the sense of self-legitimacy. This is because international companies coming to the region may not have any experience dealing with a particular centre. That party's experience in the arbitration will largely shape their particular perception of how arbitration is conducted in that region. If new users have a bad experience, they are unlikely to come to that centre again. This is quite important, especially taking into account widely read surveys such as the White & Case International Arbitration Survey.

In addition to fostering the legitimacy of an institution itself, it is an arbitration centre's role to foster the legitimacy of the seat of arbitration where that regional centre is based. This is because a regional arbitration centre is a major stakeholder in a positive perception of the laws of the seat. Additionally, much of the expertise in arbitration and international commercial law generally will often be centred in the institution itself. If a seat is perceived as risky or a jurisdiction that is not friendly to arbitration, despite having a stellar institution, parties will be hesitant in using that centre."

LCIA (Adrian Winstanley)

"It is, in my view, certainly part of an arbitral institution's role to foster legitimacy, as to which I refer again to the aspirations of the founding fathers of the LCIA.

All of the leading institutions strive to support cross-border trade and commerce within the burgeoning global economy, including myriad emerging markets.

It is no part of any institution's role to confine its services to elite business or legal communities."

PCA (Brooks Daly)

"Yes. Arbitral institutions are focal points for the world's perception of international arbitration, so they are uniquely positioned to foster legitimacy and have an obvious interest in doing so."

Question 5
If your answer to Question 4 above is Yes, what do you feel your institution is doing to foster legitimacy?

CRCICA (Mohamed Abdel Raouf)

"As a regional institution, CRCICA has tried to foster the legitimacy of institutional arbitration by doing the following:

– Maintaining its full independence vis-à-vis the country hosting its headquarters;
– Adopting modern arbitration rules based on the UNCITRAL Arbitration Rules (as revised in 2010);
– Offering other rules on mediation;
– Emulating best practice in the administration of arbitration cases;
– Stipulating in the statutes of its Advisory Committee (AC) that its members shall not be appointed by the Centre as arbitrators in its cases unless by way of list procedure from which the selection is made by the parties (Art. 7). The statutes also clearly provide that, for the purpose of the selection of the members of the tripartite committees, composed by

the Centre from among the AC members to decide challenges and requests to remove arbitrators, members having a recognizable conflict of interest shall be avoided (Art. 8);
– Training young practitioners;
– Integrating young talents of different genders and from different jurisdictions;
– Introducing international arbitration in Arabic, the language widely used in the Middle East and North Africa, to the region; and
– Being easily accessible to the users, counsel and arbitrators."

CAM-CCBC (Frederico José Straube)
"Generally speaking, it is possible to state that CAM-CCBC commits itself to the protection of confidentiality and to the isonomic treatment of the parties, as well as helping the arbitral tribunal to take the proper measures to safeguard principles such as due legal process and legal defense.

At this point, I must explain that CAM-CCBC monitors the arbitral procedure from the moment when one of the parties requires our institution to initiate a procedure until its end, when the arbitral award is issued. Each procedure is closely supported by a case manager, who is supposed to intermediate all communication among the parties and the tribunal. Therefore, no exchanges of documents or procedural communication are made directly between the parties involved in the process. Such simple precautions grant isonomic treatment to the parties. In fact, the case manager becomes the guardian of the balance among them.

The CAM-CCBC does not limit itself to monitoring the dispute until the signature of the Arbitration Agreement. It aims to offer the greatest degree of neutrality to the procedure and is continuously willing to assume the role of protector of the legitimacy of the arbitration."

ICDR (Richard Naimark)
"ICDR / AAA publishes redacted awards of interest, revises Rules and practices to adapt to developing trends and encourages party autonomy with its list method for arbitrator selection, administrative conference calls and preliminary hearings with arbitrators. Our website is well populated with information and is being enriched all the time. We also have a track record of defending in court arbitrators who have been sued by vindictive parties. We also participate in UNCITRAL Group II proceedings and numerous educational activities around the world."

ICSID (Meg Kinnear)
"ICSID consistently reviews its practices in order to implement better ways to approach its caseload. For example, ICSID adopted enhanced transparency measures and dismissal for want of legal merit in its 2006 rule amendments. In the last three years ICSID has thoroughly reviewed internal practices, and so, for instance, developed a ballot process (see above) to increase the pool of arbitrators considered in ICSID cases and developed internal 'best practices' for case administration to ensure it is acting consistently and efficiently.

Another aspect of fostering legitimacy is the continuous effort to help facility users and the public to better understand the ICSID system. In this respect, ICSID began publishing detailed caseload statistics profiling its international investment cases and developed an introductory course explaining ICSID arbitration (which it has presented in every region of the world). Staff members of the Centre make numerous presentations to delegations about ICSID, and are always available to answer questions."

ICC (John Beechey)

"– The ICC Court organizes training programmes with users (clients, counsel and arbitrators) and its representatives participate in conferences all over the world, some of the most prominent of which are ICC events.

– The ICC Court sets up meetings with judges and justices, who are invited to attend the Court's sessions, and it also organizes judicial training programmes upon request.

– The ICC Court has been astute to increase the pool of arbitrators appointed by the Court.

– Within the Secretariat, case management teams are composed of lawyers from all parts of the world, which enables parties and arbitrators to discuss any issue with lawyers of their same cultural background and who are responsible for administering cases on a region by region basis."

KLRCA (Sundra Rajoo)

"The KLRCA is continually taking steps to ensure that it is offering services that are considered at the top of international standards. The KLRCA maintains an open list of arbitrators as well as an empanelment term of three years to allow a review of an arbitrator's ethics and work during their tenure. The KLRCA list is comprised of many experienced and prominent arbitrators, both regionally and internationally. If any ethical concerns exist, arbitrators may be removed. Specific measures taken include the constant review of the KLRCA Code of Conduct, which is available on our website and provided to all our appointed arbitrators, as well as the signing of the Corporate Integrity Pledge together with the Malaysian Anti-Corruption Commission. Additionally, the Centre has a very current and up-to-date set of rules; this is to ensure that they are at an international standard relative to the current practice of other leading arbitration institutions. This is not only for the purpose of innovation, as updating our rules allows us to combat oppressive tactics by fine tuning our administrative procedures. The most recent examples are our strengthened confidentiality provisions and the ability to apportion fee deposits between the parties. Lastly, the Centre is moving to new state-of-the-art premises later in 2014. This will ensure that users of the Centre have the best facilities available to them for their hearings at a cost unmatched elsewhere in the region. The inclusion of an auditorium will allow us to provide knowledge and training to the arbitration community with greater effect and frequency.

The abovementioned approaches and efforts made by the Centre in turn translate to positive perception by users of the Centre. If users of the Centre have any comments or suggestions, these are recorded and taken into consideration so that services can always be improved."

LCIA (Adrian Winstanley)

"Legitimacy is at the very heart of the LCIA.

The LCIA operates under a three-tier structure, comprising the Company, the Arbitration Court and the Secretariat.

The LCIA is a not-for-profit company limited by guarantee, whose Board, by design, does not have an active role in case administration.

The LCIA Court is made up of up to thirty-five members, selected to provide and maintain a balance of leading practitioners in commercial arbitration from all corners of the world, and of whom no more than six may be of UK nationality.

As the LCIA's immediate past President, Jan Paulsson, put it: 'the primary concern of the Court is to act as the guardian of the LCIA's ethical and professional standards in an international arena'. And it is the LCIA Court that is the final authority for the proper application of the LCIA rules and for the moderation of the costs of arbitration; both of these in the interests of all of its users from developed and developing economies.

In the past four years, spurred by a concern to remain relevant to the widest user base, the LCIA has spread its wings from its historical London roots.

In 2008, we entered into a joint venture with the Dubai International Financial Centre; in 2009, we opened our first independent overseas office, in New Delhi; and in 2011, we entered into a joint venture with the Government of Mauritius to establish what we believe to be the first credible international commercial arbitration centre in Africa.

In 2013, we opened a liaison office in Seoul, at the new Seoul International Dispute Resolution Centre.

However, typically 85% of LCIA cases involve no English party at all, and the LCIA's operation out of London has a truly international reach. So why the expansion overseas?

Precisely to recognize the growth, and growing sophistication, in arbitration in other jurisdictions; to service regional needs and expectations; and in the interests of greater convenience and cost-saving for the parties.

The LCIA was also the first of the major institutions to establish a young arbitrators' group, YIAG (Young International Arbitration Group), for which membership is free of charge, and which now has more than 6,000 members from 134 different countries.

Under a co-chairmanship of three young practitioners, YIAG puts on seminars and symposia around the world, and publishes an e-newsletter, with the support of Regional Representatives from Africa; Asia Pacific and Australasia; the Middle-East and North Africa; Russia and the CIS Sates; North America; and Central and South America.

These are some of the ways in which the LCIA fosters legitimacy."

PCA (Brooks Daly)

"Twenty years ago, the PCA established its Financial Assistance Fund with the aim of helping developing countries to meet the costs involved in international arbitration or other means of dispute settlement. The Fund remains available to States which are listed on the 'Development Assistance Committee (DAC) List of Aid Recipients' of the OECD. The PCA believes that this improves the legitimacy of the international arbitration system in the eyes of States that would otherwise consider it to be prohibitively expensive.

Encouraged by its Member States, the PCA also seeks to foster legitimacy by establishing a global presence beyond its headquarters in The Hague. This diverse group of States – currently including Argentina, Chile, Costa Rica, India, Singapore and South Africa – has offered to the PCA those privileges and immunities which it has long enjoyed in the Netherlands. Moreover, the PCA has begun to expand its global presence by establishing a permanent PCA office in Mauritius and exploring expansion elsewhere. From its Mauritius platform, the PCA has not only actively assisted the local community in developing its arbitral infrastructure, but also engaged the regional arbitration community by providing educational outreach and training programs throughout sub-Saharan Africa.

Arbitral institutions can also improve perceptions of systemic legitimacy in their role as appointing authorities. Beyond the general need to meet parties' preferences for the most experienced arbitrators available, the PCA also looks very carefully for opportunities to appoint– in appropriate cases – arbitrators with limited experience in international arbitration and those from jurisdictions less frequently represented in arbitral tribunals. With respect to future arbitrators, the PCA's Educational Assistance Fund also aids the PCA's efforts to expand arbitration expertise beyond its current geographic concentrations. This Fund allows the PCA to recruit Fellows from jurisdictions where access to such expertise is not typically available, thereby diversifying the ranks of lawyers who will be competent to work as arbitration practitioners and arbitrators in the future."

Question 6
Do you see your institution's role as being predominantly that of a commercial profit-making service provider, or that of a provider of public services in the field of dispute resolution?

BCDR *(Nassib Ziadé)*
"While the BCDR-AAA is a provider of a public service, it also generates revenues from certain activities.

In order to best fulfill their missions of providing dispute-resolution services and disseminating knowledge, arbitration institutions must cover their costs while also investing in technology and innovative service-delivery techniques. An obvious source of funding for an arbitration institution would be the government of the State in which it is located or the international institution or chamber of commerce which hosts the arbitration institution. This method of funding has its limitations, however, particularly with regard to the ability to maintain autonomy and independence from the funding government, institution or chamber.

To maintain as much independence as possible from political influence, while remaining economically viable, an arbitration institution has no alternative but to charge its users for at least some of the costs of providing its services. This financial reality does not mean that arbitration institutions should shift their focus to seeking ever-greater profits. Institutional arbitration was originally designed as a public service to foster international commerce, investment and development, and to promote the rule of law. While international arbitration has today become a big business for lawyers (and alas sometimes also for arbitrators), institutions should not be so tempted by lucre that they come to betray their core values.

In order to fulfill an important part of their missions, arbitration institutions should devote substantial resources to activities which are not lucrative but nonetheless core functions, such as knowledge-dissemination; training of arbitrators, practitioners and young talents; outreach scholarly publications; and efforts to identify new generations of arbitrators originating from emerging economies and other under-represented regions."

CRCICA *(Mohamed Abdel Raouf)*
"According to the Headquarters Agreement that established CRCICA, it is an independent non-profit international organization. I therefore see CRCICA as a private non-profit service provider. While CRCICA's main objective is not to generate profits, it is expected to, at least, cover its expenses. Any surplus generated from its activities is used in subsidizing courses, training programs and conferences for young practitioners from the region who cannot afford the relevant fees and expenses, as well as in training its staff and renovating its hearing and conference rooms as well as its infrastructure."

CAM-CCBC *(Frederico José Straube)*
"First, it is important to note that CAM-CCBC is a non-profit entity. Its main goal is to manage arbitrations, looking forward to assure a satisfactory settlement of disputes, safeguarding the quality of the decisions rendered, the comfort of the parties and the dynamism of the procedure, among others.

All of its income is therefore used to improve the services provided and not only to support its daily activities. Such means allow us to invest in infrastructure to make available adequate locations for carrying out procedural acts, namely the hearings. Further, such sums are also directed to offer better comfort to the parties, arbitrators and staff. Finally,

688

a relevant amount of the resources is dedicated to the fostering of ADRs in Brazil and worldwide."

ICDR (Richard Naimark)

"If we drop the word 'predominantly' then it is fair to say that both are important, with services being of first importance. But there is a saying that in order to do good one has to do well. Arbitral institutions are extremely difficult to develop into self-supporting entities. Therefore there has to be some considerable effort toward paying attention to efficiencies and covering expenses. Those institutions which are self-supporting, without government assistance, are few in number. On the other hand, institutions that are primarily driven by profit – as opposed to outstanding, principled public service – are not likely to prosper or even last on the international stage over time because profit as a primary motivator is an assault on perceptions of legitimacy and participants in the process will understand this over time."

ICSID (Meg Kinnear)

"ICSID is a non-profit service provider. It was created with a defined public service mandate: to facilitate international investment dispute settlement and thereby promote mutual confidence and increased investment between foreign investors and host States."

ICC (John Beechey)

"The ICC is a non-profit organization. The Jerusalem Arbitration Centre is an example of the ICC's contribution to the development of dispute resolution as an element in peace-keeping."

KLRCA (Sundra Rajoo)

"The KLRCA can be considered as falling under both categories. The KLRCA is an initiative of AALCO and from this perspective can be considered a regional centre with a mission, at the same time as it is part of a larger international network of centres. In this sense the KLRCA is a major player in terms of dispute resolution service providers in the region. The KLCRA administers large commercial matters, and as such in this sphere the KLRCA is commercial.

From an alternative perspective, the KLRCA is a regional centre, focused on a business community outreach approach. For example the KLRCA has a Memorandum of Understanding with The Associated Chinese Chambers of Commerce and Industry of Malaysia (ACCCIM), which has 30,000 members, to conduct a nationwide training roadshow on ADR for their members. Furthermore, as touched on above, one major focus of KLRCA is training, not only of arbitrators, but also of the business and legal community as a whole. The KLRCA organizes talks on a bimonthly or more frequent basis on various topical issues in the area of arbitration.

Finally, the KLRCA also ties into the Malaysian community, with two prime examples being its cooperation with the maritime industry and its involvement in the Islamic finance industry, which is a huge growth project for the country of Malaysia.

From the above, the KLRCA is uniquely placed as a regional centre while also coming under the broader international perspective brought by being a member of AALCO."

LCIA (Adrian Winstanley)

"As above, the LCIA is a not-for-profit company. By definition, therefore, it is not a commercial profit-making service provider at all."

PCA (Brooks Daly)

"The PCA is an intergovernmental organization and, as such, is a public entity designed to render public services. Originally founded '[w]ith the object of facilitating an immediate recourse to arbitration for international differences, which it has not been possible to settle by diplomacy',[9] the PCA has long interpreted its mandate as extending to dispute settlement proceedings involving not only States, but also private entities.[10] In the PCA's experience, public and private users share common interests in the institutional facilitation of international arbitration."

Question 7
"Should the interaction between arbitral institutions be a competitive one aimed at gaining the widest share of relevant markets, or should it be a cooperative one aimed at developing and fostering the best conditions for international arbitration to thrive as a legitimate form of dispute resolution, or both?"

BCDR (Nassib Ziadé)

"If there is to be competition among arbitration institutions, it should have the single goal of improving each institution's services with a view to better catering to its users. It should not be aimed at pushing its sister institutions out of the market. This being said, it is obvious that parties will tend to flock to institutions that offer the best service, all other things being equal.

Success is entirely possible to achieve without strife because there is plenty of business for everyone. Since there is no need to fight over the same pool of users, arbitration institutions can lend each other resources and expertise without harming themselves. In this spirit of harmony, there are various cooperation agreements among arbitration institutions, and it is not uncommon for the hearings in a particular arbitration proceeding to take place in the facilities of a sister institution. More broadly, arbitral institutions can and should cooperate in fostering academic study of the field, and in evaluating and cultivating arbitrators, particularly rising stars from emerging and frontier economies."

CRCICA (Mohamed Abdel Raouf)

Competition is very healthy, especially between credible arbitral institutions. It is in the interest of the users to be able to select from among different arbitration rules, seats and languages. That said, global and regional arbitral institutions should cooperate in order to develop and foster best conditions for international institutional arbitration to thrive as a legitimate means of dispute settlement.

The International Federation of Commercial Arbitration Institutions (IFCAI) offers an ideal forum for interaction between arbitral institutions where they can exchange views and experiences, discuss common problems and seek reliable solutions.

CAM-CCBC (Frederico José Straube)

"The interaction between arbitral institutions should focus mainly on the development of arbitration as an institute, but it is natural that they compete for market share.

---

9. Hague Convention for the Pacific Settlement of International Disputes (1899), Art. 20.
10. See, e.g., *Radio Corporation of America v. China* (1935).

It would be naive to state that all arbitral institutions should work together for the benefit of arbitration and not look at each other as competitors. However, there is still room for fostering domestic and international arbitration. Indeed, the increasing appeal of ADR is deeply connected to the new international society and to the transnational flows. In this context, the reasons why arbitral institutions must create a cooperative environment are clear.

In addition, in the context of regional arbitral institutions, this approach becomes more important due to the fact that, as mentioned, the international arbitration market is very closed. Therefore, an important path to their internationalization depends on international partnership and on a cooperative approach towards the development and diffusion of arbitration.

To briefly mention the experience of CAM-CCBC, the adoption of an internationalization policy includes the signature of several cooperation agreements with other arbitral institutions worldwide and development projects seeking to promote ADRs.

It is therefore possible to state that cooperation is a key element for institutions that are 'new' in the global market to be able to compete."

ICDR (Richard Naimark)

"Competition does spur improvement, but there is a limit … hostility and bad-mouthing damages the reputation of all involved and the totality of the field as well. Arbitral institutions must conduct themselves with dignity if they are to be viewed with credibility as purveyors of justice. Competition should be measured, thoughtful, collegial and even friendly. In a sense, institutions should model responsible behaviour while still spurring each other to improve and adapt appropriately. Joint conferences and cooperative projects greatly benefit our field and mutual credibility."

ICSID (Meg Kinnear)

"The interaction between arbitral institutions is a cooperative one. This cooperation is developed through formal organizations, such as IFCAI, and through informal exchange of views."

ICC (John Beechey)

"Both."

KLRCA (Sundra Rajoo)

"Interaction should be both competitive and cooperative. In terms of competition, it will ensure advancement in arbitration with the best set of rules and processes. Various institutions have initiated various creative processes and have then been emulated by other institutions setting standards in international arbitration. Some of these initiatives include emergency arbitration, expedited proceedings, joinder and consolidation. To take the example of emergency arbitration, its use can be seen as a development over time, the beginning of which was ICC pre-arbitral Referee Procedure and that, after being transformed into the Emergency Arbitration Rules at the Stockholm Chamber of Commerce (SCC), has now been adopted in some form in the rules of most arbitration institutions.

As for an institution aiming to gain the widest market share, it seems that it is an inevitable consequence of international arbitration that a regional centre will aim for a wide share of the market as parties seeking to arbitrate in a regional centre will come from a diversified range of regional jurisdictions. This is notably the case when international parties are dealing with a local company or vice versa, or where two regional parties are looking for a neutral seat for their dispute.

In terms of cooperation, each institution provides for different focus areas and expertise and enhances legitimacy. Fostering cooperation between institutions allows for development of initiatives that one centre could not undertake on its own. One example of this is the development of Asian Domain Name Dispute Resolution that is a joint effort between the KLRCA, CIETAC, HKIAC and KCAB. On a smaller scale, cooperation facilitates the promotion of arbitration generally through the organization of conferences and other events."

LCIA *(Adrian Winstanley)*
"The LCIA has never regarded itself as being *'in competition'* with its sister institutions in any commercial sense. The practical reality, however, is that all of the institutions seek to promote their services and their rules in the same global market, and the business and legal communities to whom these services are promoted will inevitably be making a choice between one institution and another. In that sense, therefore, the institutions necessarily compete.

It bears saying, however, that a common cause of all institutions is to attract more users of arbitration away from the *ad hoc* option towards the administered, institutional option, for the many advantages of institutional arbitration that can be readily demonstrated.

All this said, it is the experience of the LCIA over many years that the leading arbitral institutions do cooperate in many areas aimed at developing and fostering the best conditions for international arbitration as a legitimate form of dispute resolution, as to which ICCA and IFCAI have important roles to play."

PCA *(Brooks Daly)*
"These two forms of interaction are not mutually exclusive, and both should be embraced by arbitral institutions. With respect to competition between institutions, this is a healthy means of assuring that these institutions provide a high level of service and stay abreast of the international community's developing dispute resolution needs. With respect to cooperative efforts, this panel itself reflects the possibility and necessity of achieving consensus among institutions on critical issues. A united approach – i.e., one based on the common views articulated by different participating institutions – allows all institutions to be more effective in establishing the legitimacy of international arbitration.

Of course, no institution is all things to all people. There may be linguistic differences or regional subtleties that make one institution more appropriate for a particular dispute than others. These variations in the needs of users and the roles of particular institutions leave ample room for close cooperation. For example, the PCA has a longstanding cooperation agreement with ICSID,[11] and the PCA's headquarters at the Peace Palace is referenced in the ICSID Convention as a potential venue for ICSID hearings.[12] The PCA also cooperates actively with other institutions with which it has signed joint institutional agreements.[13] Moreover, in a number of jurisdictions seeking to develop a local arbitral

---

11. ICSID, Second Annual Report (1968), Annex VII, pp. 19-20.
12. ICSID Convention (1965), Art. 63(1)(a).
13. These include agreements with ICCA (1989), Multilateral Investment Guarantee Agency (1990), American Arbitration Association (2002), Arbitration Foundation of Southern Africa (2003), Singapore International Arbitration Centre (2008), Australian Centre for International Commercial Arbitration (2010), Association for the Promotion of Arbitration in Africa (2010), China International Economic and Trade Arbitration Commission (2010), Hong Kong International Arbitration Centre (2010) and Dubai International Arbitration Centre (2013).

institution, the PCA seeks to foster systemic legitimacy through advice to governments and other interested parties on aspects of institutional management."

Question 8
"What change(s) to your institution's arbitration rules – if any – do you consider could assist in fostering the legitimacy of the international arbitrations it administers?"

CRCICA (Mohamed Abdel Raouf)
"CRCICA Arbitration Rules are based on the UNCITRAL Rules and were amended in 2011 to reflect the 2010 version of the UNCITRAL Rules with minor modifications emanating mainly from CRCICA's role as an arbitral institution and an appointing authority. The new CRCICA Arbitration Rules give expression to the Centre's long-standing commitment to offer users an arbitral procedure substantially modelled on the UNCITRAL Arbitration Rules and aim at serving four basic purposes that contribute to fostering the legitimacy of international institutional arbitration. First, they guarantee collegial decision-making with respect to several vital procedural matters, including the rejection of appointment, as well as the removal and the challenge of arbitrators. Second, they seek to modernize the legal framework and to promote greater efficiency in arbitral proceedings. Third, they fill in a few holes that have become apparent over the years. Finally, they adjust the original tables of costs to ensure more transparency and predictability in the determination of the arbitrators' fees.

In June 2014, for the first time since its inception in 1979, CRCICA issued eight Practice Notes determining the discretion and role of the Centre as well as its policies regarding certain decisions under CRCICA's Arbitration Rules in force since 1 March 2011. These include the Centre's decision not to proceed with arbitral proceedings and the default appointment of arbitrators in multiparty arbitrations.

The Centre is currently working on the publication of certain policies adopted by its Advisory Committee in 2013 with respect to the decisions made by the Centre pursuant to its rules. The Centre also intends to publish its practice with respect to the decisions on challenges to arbitrators and is inspired by the excellent work done by other arbitral institutions including the SCC.

That said, some other changes could also be introduced to the Centre's arbitration rules in order to foster the legitimacy of arbitrations administered under its auspices, as follows:

– Specifying in full transparency the cases in which members of CRCICA's Advisory Committee do not take part in decision-making due to the existence of a recognizable conflict of interest;
– Considering the possibility of giving reasons for the decisions on removal of and challenges to arbitrators; and
– Considering the possibility of introducing a new provision on the consolidation of cases."

CAM-CCBC (Frederico José Straube)
"In fact, we bore such matters in mind while elaborating our new rules in 2012. There were three different approaches selected in such changing of rules.

The first one concerns institutional aspects. As a matter of fact, in order to provide greater legitimacy to the institution, a Council has been created, which is a new decision-making body composed of former Presidents, who are in charge of verifying modifications and protecting our institutional memory, and of five arbitrators who belong to our Roster, who are supposed to improve our procedural guidelines and expand the reach of our institutional matters. Also, there has been an increase in the number of vice-presidents and CAM-CCBC is now allowed to elect up to two foreign vice-presidents. At the moment, we count on five vice-presidents among whom two are internationally renowned experts in arbitration.

The second is related to the consolidation of the highest level international, domestic and foreign doctrine and jurisprudence, which fosters the legitimacy of the institution through conformity with the most contemporary ideas.

The third one conerns our Roster of Arbitrators, which has considerably increased in number, from 30 to 100. It has also become possible for foreign experts to become members of our Roster."

ICDR (Richard Naimark)

"Additional attention to codes of conduct appears to be necessary given the large number of newcomers in the field. Creative use of other dispute resolution methodology such as mediation and dispute review boards will lead to greater satisfaction for some parties and will thus improve perceptions of legitimacy."

ICSID (Meg Kinnear)

"Certainly ICSID has made, and in the future will make, rule changes to ensure its procedures reflect modern best practice and the needs of facility users. This will be done after broad consultation with user communities, including States, counsel and the public. The consultation process is probably the best guarantee of continuing legitimacy."

ICC (John Beechey)

"Following a wide and wide-ranging consultation process, the ICC Court has already implemented many changes in its 2012 Rules. For example:

– Transparent rules on complex procedural issues such as multiparty arbitrations, arbitrations involving multiple contracts, joinder and consolidation.
– Direct appointments in cases in which a State or State Entity is involved, or when it is appropriate under the circumstances of the case.
– Case Management Conference: the arbitral tribunal is encouraged to invite the parties to attend, which may enhance the confidence of the parties in the system in that they are in a position to participate directly in drawing up the procedural timetable and they can see the tribunal 'in action'.
– Specific time limits for the rendering of the award are fixed by the Court, having regard to the provisional timetable agreed by the parties.
– The way the parties run the case is taken into account by the arbitrators when deciding on the allocation of costs.
– The arbitrators' diligence in the conduct of the proceedings is taken into account by the Court when fixing their fees.
– Examples of case management techniques for controlling time and costs."

KLRCA (Sundra Rajoo)

"The KLRCA's approach to its arbitration rules has always been to apply internationally recognized best practices with minimal interference. This is reflected in our adoption of the 1976 UNCITRAL Arbitration Rules followed by the immediate implementation of the 2010 UNCITRAL Arbitration Rules upon their release.

The 2010 UNCITRAL Arbitration Rules, together with a set of institution-specific rules, make up the KLRCA Arbitration Rules. The institution-specific modifying rules deal with procedural matters such as commencement of proceedings, appointment procedure, fee structure and collection of deposits.

The inclusion of institution-specific rules recognizes that, at their base, the UNCITRAL Arbitration Rules are designed for ad hoc arbitrations. The involvement of an administering institution provides certain benefits, namely procedural certainty and a centralized authority for appointments, challenges, deposit collection and payment of fees. The presence of an institution reduces risk in proceedings and adds value to the process. The KLRCA Arbitration Rules as structured allows users to take advantage of those benefits.

In the Rules, this is manifested by several features. For example, the KLRCA's challenge procedure is different from most in that the Director of the KLRCA will decide on any challenge to an arbitrator. This enhances the legitimacy of the decision on the challenge that is ultimately made, since it is made by an independent person. Another feature is the ability to apportion fee deposits. This gives the Centre the flexibility to deal with oppressive tactics such as artificially inflated claims or counterclaims.

In addition to the overarching approach described above, there are additional specific measures that we use. In 2013, KLRCA commissioned the translation of its full set of products into six languages – Bahasa Malaysia, Bahasa Indonesia, Chinese, Korean, Arabic and Spanish.

In relation to our niche areas, there have also been steps. We have made certain revisions to our i-Arbitration Rules. We have removed any references to a specific jurisdiction (previously Malaysia's Central Bank Shariah Advisory Council was the default Shariah authority) in order to make the Rules more accessible and useful for international users. This is in addition to other steps we are taking to promote the use of the i-Arbitration Rules for all commercial arbitrations involving Shariah law, whether they are seated in Malaysia or not."

LCIA (Adrian Winstanley)

"I write this on the eve of the publication of the LCIA's first new arbitration rules since 1998, and at a time when some of the detail of the new rules has not yet been settled. I am, therefore, constrained to some extent in what I am able to reveal about the changes that will shortly be introduced.

Suffice to say, for the moment, that many of the changes are aimed at ensuring the continuing relevance of the rules in a changing economic and legal environment, as regards, for example, secure online filing; joinder and consolidation for the benefit of the growing number of multi-party disputes; and guidelines for the proper conduct of party representatives in arbitration."

PCA (Brooks Daly)

"The PCA revised its Arbitration Rules in 2012, increasing control over arbitral costs (i.e., tribunal fees) and thus altering the role of institutional oversight. For parties concerned about rising costs in international arbitration, this change helps to increase the institutional legitimacy of the PCA."

B. LEGITIMACY FROM A DEVELOPING WORLD PERSPECTIVE

Question 9
What, in your view, is your institution doing:
(a) To develop a broader base of arbitrators, in particular from the developing world;

(b) To ensure that arbitrators are nominated, and seen to be nominated, from that broader base; and

(c) To ensure that this does not impact on the quality of awards.

BCDR *(Nassib Ziadé)*

"(a)-(c) In each of the three arbitration institutions which I have led in the last years, I have considered it to be one of my primary missions to identify for arbitrator appointments hidden talents in the developing world as well as members of the young generation from both the developing and the developed world, to vet their credentials carefully, and to give them a chance when the right opportunity arises to prove themselves. Typical first appointments of newcomers would arise as sole arbitrators in small and rather uncomplicated cases or as co-arbitrators alongside very experienced arbitrators in big cases. In all of these situations, the secretariat of the arbitral institution would have to be even more supportive and attentive to the need of the new appointees. These experiences have been on the whole very successful and have resulted in the appointment process being more inclusive and representative of the international community. It is a pleasure to report that some of the initially inexperienced appointees have become today among the most sought-after arbitrators."

CRCICA *(Mohamed Abdel Raouf)*

"(a)-(c) CRCICA is headquartered in Egypt, which is a developing country. According to its arbitration rules, co-arbitrators are appointed by the parties and chairpersons are appointed by the co-arbitrators without any confirmation from the Centre, which is the default appointing authority.

In making the appointment of arbitrators in lieu of the parties or the co-arbitrators, the Centre is under an obligation to have regard to such considerations as are likely to secure the appointment of an independent and impartial arbitrator and shall take into account the advisability of appointing an arbitrator of a nationality other than the nationalities of the parties if they are not of a common nationality (Art. 8/4 of the Rules).

Within the above context, CRCICA is duty-bound to develop a broader base of arbitrators from which the parties and the co-arbitrators may make their selections.

CRCICA's panel of arbitrators currently includes around 800 international arbitrators and experts from 68 jurisdictions. While the parties and the co-arbitrators are not obliged to appoint the arbitrators from this panel, the Centre is bound to appoint from among its members when acting as appointing authority.

According to the statistics, out of the seventy-two cases registered under the auspices of the Centre in 2013, the Centre exercised its role as appointing authority in less than ten cases, which clearly demonstrates the fact that the appointments are normally made by the parties and the co-arbitrators with a very little role for the Centre to play in this respect.

In the few cases where the Centre acted as appointing authority, new faces were appointed and were duly assisted by the Centre's case managers during the proceedings in order to ensure the quality of the awards.

The Centre also trains young arbitrators from all over the region and has already managed to have some of them attend real arbitration hearings as observers after obtaining the necessary approvals from the parties and the arbitrators."

CAM-CCBC *(Frederico José Straube)*

"(a) The CAM-CCBC went through major changes of its rules in 2012, when the number of arbitrators of our Roster increased from 30 to 100. It is now also possible for us to include foreign arbitrators in our list and, usually, we invite arbitrators from the institutions with which we have developed some kind of partnership. Considering that we maintain cooperation agreements with institutions in developing countries as well – despite the fact that we are from Brazil, which is an emergent country – this modification is helping to develop a broader base of arbitrators. It is also worth mentioning that the idea of increasing so significantly the number of names in our list was driven by the desire to include experts of the most diversified origins as possible. As a result, there are sufficient vacancies on our Roster for arbitrators from developing countries."

(b) For an arbitrator to be part of an arbitral tribunal managed by CAM-CCBC it is not necessary for him to belong to our Roster of Arbitrators. In fact, only the President of the tribunal must belong to our Roster. It is therefore possible for the parties to choose other arbitrators and, through such nominations, the Centre is able to evaluate the work of other arbitrators who do not appear on its list.

(c) Despite the fact that the parties can choose co-arbitrators who do not belong to the Roster of Arbitrators of CAM-CCBC, in such cases the arbitrators must address to the President of CAM-CCBC their CVs, which must be approved before their nomination. This is not a barrier to arbitrators whose names are not in our list. In fact, I can say that, as the President of CAM-CCBC, I have never refused an arbitrator chosen by the parties. However, it allows us to maintain the high quality of the awards.

Also, the President of the arbitral tribunal must belong to our Roster, composed only by individuals of renown in the legal field."

ICDR (Richard Naimark)

"(a) ICDR/AAA is continually, though carefully, recruiting arbitrators from all regions of the world with the help of local and regional advisors. We have long had an emphasis on recruiting woman and working to enhance their credibility and acceptability to parties to disputes. Recruited arbitrators are required to participate in at least one symposium, training programs conducted in a round-table format. This enables the arbitrators to demonstrate their thinking and problem-solving case management approach and allows us to observe them in action, providing a kind of quality control.

(b) ICDR promotes the 'list method' and utilizes this method as the default nomination process if the parties do not specify a different process. Lists are used in two situations: where the parties, or party-appointed arbitrators are jointly selecting arbitrators, an identical list of nominees is sent to both with instruction to strike those not desired as arbitrators and to number the others in order of preference. Those most mutually acceptable are asked to serve. Also we offer lists of potential arbitrators for those selecting their party-appointed arbitrator.

(c) Typically the Chair will be the most experienced arbitrator, but frankly this question seems infused with a touch of the chauvinism of the 'mafia' mentality. There are plenty of younger, newer arbitrators who render excellent and thoughtful awards."

ICSID (Meg Kinnear)

"See response to Question 1 above, explaining ICSID's approach to arbitrator selection. The assumption behind Question 9(c) that a more diverse pool of arbitrators will be a less qualified one or will produce awards of lesser quality is absolutely not borne out by the facts. Diversity does not come at the expense of quality."

ICC (John Beechey)

"(a) First and foremost, by identifying and appointing arbitrators from those countries. Additionally, by organizing conferences and training programmes in those regions and working closely with the ICC National Committees concerned.

(b) The Secretariat discusses proposals with National Committees beforehand in cases in which a National Committee is called upon to make a proposal; in appropriate cases, the Court makes direct appointments to promote practitioners with no previous experience as arbitrators and encourages National Committees to do the same.

(c) The Secretariat works closely with arbitrators (especially newcomers) throughout the proceedings. The scrutiny of awards by the Court improves their quality, although the ultimate responsibility for the drafting and content of the award remains with the arbitrator."

KLRCA (Sundra Rajoo)

"(a) The KLRCA is spearheading a number of initiatives to train arbitrators and broaden its panel. At the forefront of this training initiative is the Diploma Programme in International Commercial Arbitration in Kuala Lumpur which allows for a fast track for fellowship with the CIArb. The cost of this programme is more affordable not only on a worldwide scale but also relative to comparable programmes in Asia. The programme used to be offered in Oxford only. The KLRCA is now working together with CIArb Australia to offer the same programme through the University of New South Wales and hold the course in Kuala Lumpur. Offering this course has resulted not only in better trained arbitrators but additionally in an increase in the numbers of young arbitrators in the region.

The KLRCA actively encourages individuals across the world to apply to be on our panel. The minimum requirements to apply are fellowship in the CIArb, tertiary qualifications and sufficient experience in arbitration.

It should be noted that in addition to broadening and developing the regional base of arbitrators, the KLRCA includes in our panel a range of eminent arbitrators from across the globe. This panel currently numbers over 700, with arbitrators, mediators and domain name dispute panelists from across the globe. While there are minimum standards for empanelment such as CIArb fellowship, we do recognize that arbitration experience from other areas will likely yield different qualifications, and take that into account.

(b) Our institution provides a list of arbitrators that is available on our portal, which is open to the public, with information relating to their contact details, experience and qualifications. Also, efforts are made in building up young arbitrators. The institution does not impose any limits on this list on which arbitrators may be appointed and allows the appointment of arbitrators who do not appear on the list. The selection process of appointing an arbitrator includes the KLRCA's case counsel putting forward to the Director a number of names of potential arbitrators who would be suited for the arbitration. These nominees are suggested from the list; there are various considerations in suggesting an arbitrator, including the type of dispute matched with an arbitrator's expertise, the arbitrator's availability, whether there are already experienced arbitrators on a panel and making room for a more junior arbitrator. Additionally there are efforts made to propose arbitrators that come from a range of countries.

In putting forward names of prospective arbitrators, there is no systematic ranking or preferred subset of arbitrators; names are provided on a case by case basis.

(c) The Centre imposes high standards on all arbitrators that are included on our panel. The minimum requirement to be a panellist under the KLRCA is 'fellowship with the CIArb UK' and the route to fellowship is a tough one. Additionally, those panellists must be experienced in international arbitration. We are assured of quality as all arbitrators are trained and have the highest qualifications. When there is a tribunal of three arbitrators, generally the chairperson of the tribunal is a more senior arbitrator. Following this, it is the chair who in almost all instances is charged with the submission of the final award. From this, the KLRCA is confident that the senior arbitrators on its panel are very well equipped to render an award of the highest quality."

LCIA (Adrian Winstanley)

"(a) As above, the LCIA is actively engaged, through YIAG, with the *'new blood'* of the arbitration world, across a very large number of jurisdictions. It is, to a considerable degree, the membership of YIAG that constantly rejuvenates and expands the base of arbitrators upon which the LCIA and other institutions can draw.

(b) The LCIA does not have a closed panel or list of arbitrators from which the parties must nominate. This being the case, the LCIA cannot *'ensure'* that the arbitrators appointed by the LCIA Court are nominated from any particular base. However, by actively promoting and supporting an exchange among rising practitioners from all jurisdictions, the profile of these arbitrators is raised, providing disputant parties with that broader base from which they may make their nominations.

(c) Under the LCIA rules, the LCIA Court has an absolute discretion to decline to appoint a nominee who is *'not suitable'*. Although, in my long experience, there have been but one or two occasions on which the LCIA Court has deemed it necessary to decline to appoint a party nominee on the basis that it is plain that that nominee is not equipped to sit as an arbitrator, let alone produce an award of high quality, this power is there if needed.

Of course, where the LCIA Court itself selects the arbitrator, it will carefully review the bona fides of any candidate before appointment."

PCA (Brooks Daly)

"(a) In its search for a broader arbitrator base, the PCA has noted that access to education and training in international arbitration remains unavailable in many regions of the world. This fact makes it very difficult for lawyers outside of the major arbitral jurisdictions to develop the requisite experience to be able to perform competently as an arbitrator.

The PCA has therefore sought to involve promising young lawyers in its Fellowship program through an Educational Assistance Fund (discussed in response to Question 5). This allows lawyers from a far more diverse group of States outside of the major arbitral jurisdictions to gain first-hand exposure and training in international arbitration, starting them on the path to becoming arbitrators.

(b) In every case in which the Secretary-General of the PCA is called upon to appoint an arbitrator, the PCA actively seeks to appoint arbitrators of diverse national backgrounds. One limitation on this effort arises when the seat of arbitration is in a major arbitral jurisdiction, the amount in dispute is small, and the parties have a heightened sensitivity to costs. In such situations, the selection of an arbitrator based at the seat of arbitration is preferred in order to control costs, which may limit the diversity of national backgrounds available for appointment.

With respect to arbitrators' being 'seen to be nominated', further limitations on the public perception of diversity in international arbitration arise from the confidential nature of most PCA proceedings. However, awareness of the availability of arbitrators from a broad base of regional and national backgrounds is assisted through the PCA's publication of its list of Members of the Court. Through this mechanism, PCA Member States (of which there are now 115) may nominate potential arbitrators of 'known competency in questions of international law, of the highest moral reputation and disposed to accept the duties of arbitrators'.[14] While neither parties nor the PCA are bound to appoint from this list, it nevertheless serves as a resource assisting in the identification of a diverse group of potential arbitrators.

---

14. Hague Convention for the Pacific Settlement of International Disputes (1899), Art. 23.

(c) All arbitrators appointed by the PCA meet the highest standards of competence, so there is no impact on the quality of awards."

Question 10
The past few years have seen an increase in regional centres.
(a) In your view, what role, if any, do these play in fostering legitimacy?

BCDR (Nassib Ziadé)
"Regional arbitration centers are designed primarily to offer conveniently located seats for the arbitration of conflicts arising from contracts to be executed, or projects to be implemented, within the region in which the centers are established. Inasmuch as they break the monopoly of traditional arbitration centers located in the West, they give arbitration users in a particular region a sense of ownership over the dispute-resolution system and thereby bolster the acceptability of arbitration.

Regional arbitration centers are definitely more adept than traditional Western arbitration centers at handling purely domestic disputes, and they provide a viable alternative to litigation. Should they conform to best practices (and some of them still have a long way to go), they could become the preferred venue for disputes involving parties from the region. In addition, regional arbitration centers are well-placed to play a pivotal educational and training role for arbitration practitioners, judges and parties from the region."

CRCICA (Mohamed Abdel Raouf)
"(a)-(d) CRCICA was established in 1979 under the auspices of the Asian African Legal Consultative Organization (AALCO) in pursuance to the latter's decision taken at the Doha session in 1978 to establish regional centres for international commercial arbitration in Asia and Africa.

According to the Headquarters Agreement concluded in 1987 between AALCO and the Egyptian Government, CRCICA is established in order to offer to the countries in Africa and west Asia '*an efficient, expeditious and affordable system for the settlement of commercial and investment disputes based on the UNCITRAL Rules*'. Given the fact that the Centre is one of the oldest arbitral institutions in the region, its role was to introduce modern arbitration and ADR in this part of the world and to offer the users a more affordable and accessible venue for the settlement of their disputes. In my view, the mere existence of a credible and successful regional arbitral institution fosters the legitimacy of international arbitration. This could be equally fulfilled by global institutions acting through national committees, branches or otherwise, provided that they integrate regional talents instead of focusing on international experts.

Fear of nepotism and government interference is not justified in the case of genuine regional centres, which have had to learn to walk before they could run. Such centres have had to establish a caseload, trust and experience, and to emulate best practice.

In order for a regional centre to conform with best practice and to deliver services at an internationally acceptable level, it should think small and start by handling domestic cases and offering its administrative services to ad hoc arbitrations before trying to be international in its membership and outlook. It should also have the resources and the leadership and be prepared for change to be slow."

CAM-CCBC *(Frederico José Straube)*
"Considering that the criticisms addressed to the legitimacy of international arbitration are based on the monopoly of traditional arbitral institutions which belong to developed countries and which need to protect their own interests, the emergence of local centres can be identified as a relevant element in the breaking down of such dominance. Moreover, in a context where traditional arbitral institutions are forced to compete with regional centres, there is a natural trend towards respecting local differences. Consequently, this phenomenon has a direct impact on the legitimacy of international arbitration."

ICDR *(Richard Naimark)*
"Regional centres can play an important role in education within the region and in boosting the general comfort level of lawyers, the judiciary and the business community as to the viability and reliability of the process ... if they conduct themselves to the highest standard."

ICSID *(Meg Kinnear)*
"As an international public institution with a specifically defined mandate, ICSID does not take a view on regional centres. ICSID operates globally and its independence is respected by all 150 Member States. World Bank offices in more than 100 countries are available to support ICSID services, including holding hearings and videoconferencing. ICSID also has a number of facility cooperation arrangements with institutions in every region that have been to the mutual benefit of ICSID, the regional organizations, and facility users."

ICC *(John Beechey)*
"The ICC Court welcomes competition, provided it is fair and open competition. Regional centres occasionally face issues in seeking to maintain the required balance and neutrality vis-à-vis users from other regions."

KLRCA *(Sundra Rajoo)*
"(a) Regional centres give parties more choice in how they will resolve their disputes as opposed to institutions that have been historically prominent in the area of international arbitration. They also give those with domestic disputes an alternative to going to court. This ultimately fosters competition between centres and forces centres to offer better services.

An emerging regional centre encourages and fosters the implementation of best law and practice in a region to ensure that law and practice are of international standards. Good domestic arbitration legislation that is of an international standard is a necessary tool to foster legitimacy in a jurisdiction where a regional centre is located. Equally important as good arbitration legislation is that courts in a jurisdiction are seen as arbitration friendly, as otherwise foreign companies will not want to come to that jurisdiction.

Additionally, the centres set the standards of the processes and procedures in arbitration proceedings, implementing creative methods of dealing with commercial needs. Examples mentioned above are the emergency arbitrator rules and also the rules which allow for the consolidation of arbitration or joinder of parties. To some extent, the centres are influencing the evolution of the jurisprudential view of certain practices in international arbitration. This then has an impact on changes made to arbitral laws, whether directly or through consultation.

When a centre can increase its caseload based on the abovementioned factors, it can be said that a regional centre has fostered legitimacy in arbitration."

LCIA *(Adrian Winstanley)*
"I refer to the answer that I have given to Question 5 above."

PCA (Brooks Daly)
"(a) Regional centres play an important role in fostering legitimacy. They improve access to dispute resolution services for residents in the relevant region and may be attractive thanks to cultural affinity with parties in the region, knowledge of legal systems in the region, and the ability to operate in local languages. Access to qualified local practitioners may also be facilitated by an institution's regional presence outside of the major arbitral jurisdictions. Also, regional centres may in some instances operate in lower cost jurisdictions than traditional centres, providing cost savings to users of their services."

(b) Can that role be equally well fulfilled by global institutions acting through national committees, branches or otherwise?

BCDR (Nassib Ziadé)
"Arbitration centers located in the West cannot claim the same level of legitimacy as regional centers even when Western centers act in the region through national committees or branches. The only effective way for a Western arbitration institution to have a presence in the region would be through a partnership with a credible regional arbitration center. A regional branch of a Western arbitration institution cannot earn full legitimacy in the eyes of regional users as long as key decisions are taken in the headquarters by the usual traditional players."

CAM-CCBC (Frederico José Straube)
"Despite the fact that national committees and branches are composed of local staff and arbitrators, decisions are still made by a head office located in and managed by traditional players. As a result, it is possible to state that they do allow global institutions to approximate to local specialities, but that they do not perform the same role of legitimizing arbitration that local centers do."

ICDR (Richard Naimark)
"Yes to the extent they are locally supported and involve the local communities. However, for purely domestic matters, regional centres may be more acceptable."

KLRCA (Sundra Rajoo)
"(b) In terms of domestic and regional arbitration, it is questionable whether a global institution fosters the same degree of legitimacy as does a regional centre. It may not be as successful, influential or effective as an institution working within the jurisdiction. Additionally, it could be perceived that resolution of a dispute through a global institution could add unneeded complexity, and suffer from a lack of local knowhow or experience to handle domestic and regional disputes. Furthermore, one can make the argument that an organization with a local centralized decision making body can be much more efficient than a system that relies on the meeting and decision making of various national committees.

Often a regional centre will be involved in domestic services that a global branch cannot participate in. For us in Malaysia, this includes involvement in the introduction of statutory adjudication to the construction industry, the promotion of maritime dispute resolution and the development of a sports arbitration framework.

From this it can be seen that there are great benefits to operating under a regional centre where, despite the KLRCA dealing with quite a number of international parties, the organization is regionally grounded. From this point of view it appears to be the case that

702

regional companies are more interested in a more locally based regional centre, in contrast to one where the key functions and decisions are performed abroad."

LCIA (Adrian Winstanley)
"There are many options for *'regionalizing'* the services of international institutions, but the LCIA's position thus far has been that *'regionalization'*, in the sense of providing relevant and accessible services for the specific benefit of the region to be served, is best achieved in cooperation with local institutions, governmental or otherwise, or, as in the case of LCIA India, in establishing an independent local subsidiary."

PCA (Brooks Daly)
"Yes. The PCA's experience with its office in Mauritius – including outreach efforts throughout Africa from that platform – gives us confidence that this role can also be fulfilled through global institutions."

(c) One concern regularly levelled at regional or less established centres is a fear (i) of nepotism and/or (ii) of Government interference. Are these justified fears in your view? If so, how can they be countered?

BCDR (Nassib Ziadé)
"As with Western traditional arbitration centers, the risk of nepotism exists in regional arbitration centers. It can be countered by having clear internal policies and guidelines for appointment and removal of arbitrators, which should be based on best international standards, and by having an international board of trustees which oversees the work of the regional arbitration center.

As to government interference in the work of a regional arbitration center, it can also be countered by an international board of trustees which plays a supervisory role over the regional center's operations. It may be noted that when a regional arbitration center attains financial independence and self-sufficiency, it is more likely that it will free itself significantly from any external influences or interferences."

CAM-CCBC (Frederico José Straube)
"I would say that these fears depend strictly on the context in which such regional centre is established. The opportunities for the government to interfere with the arbitral tribunal is smaller when the centre is in a democratic country. Nonetheless, it is clear that an arbitral tribunal tends to be more neutral when compared to the national courts; it also tends to accept less negative influences over the procedure. And, in the end, when inserted in a democratic scenario, the seriousness of the institution is a key element to define whether there are risks of nepotism or government interference or not.

Another detail concerning specifically the Brazilian arbitration market is that most of the several attempts to create smaller arbitral institutions that conform less with international standards, do not last long.

Finally, in Brazil there is a national entity composed of representatives of all the institutions that manage arbitration in the country, which is in charge of controlling the independence and fairness of arbitral institutions."

ICDR (Richard Naimark)
"This is a justified fear because many, if not most cannot survive on their own financially and may need local government support, thus the danger of government interference. This

may also be an issue with exclusive support from local business or legal groups. Even without financial support, local or regional centres may be subject to subtle local influence or politics. This may be a factor even if no overt attempts are made to influence matters. Having arbitrators serve who are from a non-involved country can be effective. There is a certain irony here in that presumably the local centre intends to be of service to local entities yet they may be more susceptible to local pressure, overt or subtle."

ICC (John Beechey)

"They are not without substance. It could be countered by ensuring that all centres are, and are seen to be, autonomous and independent from public or private sponsors."

KLRCA (Sundra Rajoo)

"As explored earlier, the KLRCA was set up pursuant to a Host Country Agreement between AALCO and the Malaysian Government. The Government is given the privilege of hosting the Centre in exchange for certain concessions, most notably immunities and privileges. Those immunities are enshrined in statute and allow the Centre and its Director to carry out their respective roles without interference and free of intervention. This is particularly necessary given that the Government may itself be involved as a user of the Centre.

It is suggested that in developing countries, nepotism can be addressed by having consistent internal practices in place that ensure that there is a rotation of who is appointed and not a regular club of arbitrators. This can be relatively straightforward to achieve, by keeping track of appointments made by an institution and ensuring that they are diversified. By ensuring international best practices are adhered to and through proper training, nepotism can be prevented.

Ultimately, undue influence whether through the Government or internal is not beneficial for a centre in attracting users nor promoting legitimacy. When governments influence arbitration centres and this is known in the arbitration community, caseloads will drop. A safeguard that exists to prevent abuse and bias of arbitrators in this sense is a strong and impartial judiciary. Despite this being an arm of Government, if there was an issue with an arbitration, the judiciary is the appropriate forum to act as a check."

LCIA (Adrian Winstanley)

"These fears are not, in the LCIA's experience, justified, but there can be no complacency in this regard. In the LCIA's case, the supervisory role of the fiercely independent LCIA Court would, we believe, be an effective guardian against favouritism or interference, though it must be said that there has been no hint of either of these in our existing relationships."

PCA (Brooks Daly)

"All institutions must guard against nepotism and government interference. These can be countered in a number of ways, including transparency in the governing structure of the arbitral institution and adoption of best practices in the administration of arbitrations. Such practices can be observed within the largest and best-known arbitral institutions. The PCA is regularly asked to advise less established centres in adopting best practices and aspects of institutional organization that may, inter alia, assist them in addressing these concerns."

(d) More generally, how can one ensure that a regional centre conforms with best practice and delivers services at an internationally acceptable level?

BCDR (Nassib Ziadé)

"There are a number of conditions which ought to be met for a regional arbitration institution to be declared as operating in accordance with acceptable international standards.

The arbitration center should first adopt a set of modern arbitration rules which it should revise from time to time to take account of new trends and developments in the practice of international arbitration.

The arbitration rules should be complemented by a liberal arbitration legislation enacted by the country in which the arbitration center is located. The arbitration legislation and arbitration rules should both be construed by a judiciary which is arbitration-friendly at all times.

Arbitration centers within one region should remain limited in number so as to avoid being viewed as merely local centers. They should furthermore cooperate with each other, rather than fiercely compete, in order to foster the rule of law in the region in which they operate.

With respect to the human infrastructure, regional arbitration centers should recruit a diverse and specialized staff instead of relying exclusively on local staff who work on a part-time basis. Regional centers should have a diversified pool of arbitrators from which they select for tribunals, and the internal work of those centers should be overseen by international boards.

Last but not least, the structure within which the regional center operates should allow the center to enjoy at least a minimum level of administrative and financial autonomy.

If regional arbitration centers were to lack some of these features, their legitimacy would be put into question. Indeed, a regional arbitration institution will not score high grades in the test for legitimacy if it is denied basic administrative and financial autonomy by the hosting chamber of commerce, is deprived of the required number of staff to be able to operate under normal conditions, operates within a country that lacks a modern arbitration legislation, and is subjected to an environment in which its arbitrators are sued as a matter of routine before local courts. In such cases, the sweetest dreams may turn into horror stories."

CAM-CCBC (Frederico José Straube)

"The conformity of a regional centre with best practice can be verified through different elements: the first of them is the existence of a clear and serious set of rules. Also, the respectability of the members of its Roster of Arbitrators is a good sign that it may or may not be in conformity with the international standard. In fact, in situations when many of the arbitrators belonging to the Roster of Arbitrators of an institution also arbitrate in international arbitral institutions, it is certain that such institution will deliver internationally acceptable services. Another important detail that one must observe is the quality of its staff (considering its academic background, education and observance of protocols, among other characteristics) and the structure offered by the institution. Finally, it is important to find out who are members of the board of such institution and their seriousness."

ICDR (Richard Naimark)

"Partnering with an established, credible centre."

ICC (John Beechey)
"N/A: not a matter for ICC comment."

KLRCA (Sundra Rajoo)
"The centre has to adopt a good set of rules which is current and internationally acceptable. This is essential to ensure administrative efficacy with good control over costs and timing. Keeping institutional rules up to date with international standards as well as the implementation of new and innovative tools, such as emergency arbitrator provisions and the i-Arbitration Rules, are very important to maintain best practice and the highest standards.

Once a regional centre has current rules in place, it is essential that these rules are supported by legislation to implement these rules. For example, if there are provisions that provide for interim measures and the jurisdiction is based on the Model Law, that jurisdiction should ensure that it adopts the entirety of Sect. 17 of the Model Law (with or without variation, for example Hong Kong) to ensure that the courts have the tools to enforce the interim measures that are included in an institution's set of rules.

The final ingredient is an institution's staff and internal procedures. Proper training and procedures ensure that an institution's best practices are adhered to and administered in a way that ensures efficiency for the user.

If a regional centre does not conform to best practice and does not meet international standards, that centre will not continue to receive cases. These cases will either go to other institutions internationally or parties will have their domestic disputes resolved by courts."

LCIA (Adrian Winstanley)
"It is always going to be difficult for a new regional centre to achieve a status of demonstrable independence and administrative efficiency. And there is an element of *Catch 22* in this, in that it is only when the business and legal communities have such confidence in a new centre that they will adopt the rules of that centre, but a new centre can only inspire that confidence and demonstrate its independence and efficiency through the administration of arbitrations pursuant to its rules.

I am bound to say, of course, that one way to ensure the regional centres conform to best practice and deliver services at an internationally acceptable level is for such centres to affiliate themselves in some way with an existing global institution."

PCA (Brooks Daly)
"An arbitration user who has doubts concerning a regional centre should confer with the head of the institution and consult the procedural rules of the institution (and, where appropriate, the national courts of its seat), relevant publications as well as lawyers and arbitrators who have served in cases administered by that centre.

With respect to the role of arbitral institutions, direct cooperation among the most established global institutions and regional centres assists newly established regional centres in conforming to internationally acceptable practices. Participation in fora such as the International Federation of Commercial Arbitration Institutions also allows institutions to share and discuss best practices. Institutions' publication of arbitration guides and the dissemination of their own arbitration rules may also encourage their newly established counterparts."

C.   ARBITRATOR APPOINTMENT

Question 11
In the context of arbitrator appointment:

(a) When your institution is requested to appoint an arbitrator, who selects the candidate, on what criteria, and in accordance with what procedure?

BCDR (Nassib Ziadé)
"The procedure which an arbitral institution follows in making arbitration appointments should be transparent and made known to the parties in advance. An arbitral institution which is requested to make an arbitrator appointment takes into account a wide range of relevant circumstances. These include, inter alia, the amount in dispute, the complexity and nature of the case, the technical expertise and legal training required, the procedural language(s), the seat of the arbitration and the law applicable to the dispute, the nationalities of the parties and of the other arbitrators, the arbitrator's availability, and the absence of conflicts of interest with the parties, their counsel and the other arbitrators in the case."

CRCICA (Mohamed Abdel Raouf)
"When required to exercise its role as appointing authority, it is the Director of the Centre who selects the candidate. In making the appointment of arbitrators in lieu of the parties or the co-arbitrators, the Centre is under an obligation to have regard to such considerations as are likely to secure the appointment of an independent and impartial arbitrator and shall take into account the advisability of appointing an arbitrator of a nationality other than the nationalities of the parties if they are not of a common nationality (Art. 8(4) of the Rules).

The Centre is bound to appoint from among its panel of arbitrators, which includes around 800 international arbitrators and experts from 68 jurisdictions.

Pursuant to Arts. 8 and 9 of its arbitration rules, the Centre shall appoint the sole arbitrators and chairpersons as promptly as possible. In making the appointment, the Centre shall use the following procedure, unless the parties agree that such procedure should not be used or unless the Centre determines in its discretion that the use of such procedure is not appropriate for the case:

(a) The Centre shall communicate to each of the parties an identical list containing at least three names;
(b) Within fifteen days after the receipt of this list, each party shall return the list to the Centre after having deleted the name or names to which it objects and numbered the remaining names on the list in the order of its preference;
(c) After the expiration of the above period of time, the Centre shall appoint the arbitrator from among the names approved on the lists returned to it and in accordance with the order of preference indicated by the parties; and
(d) If for any reason the appointment cannot be made according to this procedure, the Centre may exercise its discretion in appointing the arbitrator."

CAM-CCBC (Frederico José Straube)
"The are three hypothetical situations in which CAM-CCBC is requested to appoint an arbitrator. The first occurs when one of the parties does not appoint an arbitrator. The second happens when the two arbitrators of an arbitral tribunal composed of three

members, who are supposed to appoint the third one, do not chose a name. The third is the case in which the parties do not reach an agreement concerning the sole arbitrator (when the tribunal is composed of one single arbitrator). In these situations, the President is in charge of appointing an arbitrator who belongs to our Roster of Arbitrators."

ICDR (Richard Naimark)
"After consultation with the parties, ICDR/AAA uses the list method described above by default; otherwise, the method listed in the parties' arbitration clause."

ICSID (Meg Kinnear)
"With respect to Questions 11(a)-(i), when ICSID selects an arbitrator it follows the applicable rules and any agreement of the parties with respect to the method of appointment. ICSID also applies the requirements imposed by the ICSID Convention and the relevant instrument providing consent, including rules on arbitrator nationality.

Usually when ICSID is asked to appoint, the parties have been unable to agree on a presiding arbitrator. In that case, ICSID will propose a ballot of not less than five candidates to the parties. The ICSID Secretariat compiles a list of potential ballot candidates based on considerations such as experience, expertise, language capacity, gender, regional diversity, ability to preside over a complex arbitration in a timely and fair manner, absence of conflict, and the like. Before proposing the ballot, each of the candidates selected for the ballot is conflict-checked by the Centre and it ensures each candidate is willing to act if selected by the parties. ICSID specifically inquires whether they can act in an expeditious manner if appointed.

The ballot itself is accompanied by the arbitrators' CVs and any disclosure the proposed nominees wish to make. Parties vote 'yes' or 'no' to the ballot nominees and return the ballot to the Centre. They need not share their selection with the opposing party. If a candidate is selected by both parties, that candidate is appointed.

If there is no consensus on the ballot, the Chairman of the ICSID Administrative Council selects an arbitrator from the ICSID Panel of Arbitrators. The Chairman's selection takes into account requirements under the Convention, as well as considerations such as experience, expertise, language capacity, gender, regional diversity, ability to preside over a complex arbitration in a timely and fair manner, absence of conflict, and the like.

This process is explained to the parties in a detailed cover letter, and is explained on the ICSID website. The lists of candidates proposed for each case are not made public, as this would demonstrate who was rejected by the parties.

ICSID makes extensive information about arbitrators available to parties. As noted above, every nomination is accompanied by a full CV and any declaration as to potential conflict of interest. All information provided by ICSID about nominees is provided to both parties simultaneously.

The ICSID website lists every arbitral appointment by case and parties can easily search criteria such as the number of cases of each arbitrator, the awards rendered by them, the time taken by an arbitrator to render a decision, and the like. The website also has a full list of persons named to the Panels of Arbitrators and Conciliators by States and by the Chairman of the Administrative Council. ICSID is currently developing a standard form CV for arbitrators that will be hyperlinked to every reference to the arbitrator on the ICSID website and will provide substantial information about arbitrators in ICSID cases.

With respect to re-visiting party appointment (Question 11(e)), this is an issue for States to address in their investment treaties if they wish to adopt a different method of appointment.

With respect to links between counsel and arbitrators (Question 11(i)), these should be disclosed if they raise concerns about whether an arbitrator can approach a case with an open mind and exercise independent judgment."

ICC (John Beechey)

"First, it is to be emphasized that in more than 60 percent of cases, the ICC Court is required merely to confirm nominations made by the parties. Of the rest, most of the appointments made by the Court are made upon proposal by a National Committee or Group, previously selected by the Court.

However, the Court can also proceed on the basis of a direct appointment in cases where (i) the Court does not accept the proposal made by the National Committee or Group, or the National Committee or Group fails to make a proposal, (ii) at least one of the parties is, or claims to be, a State party, (iii) the Court considers that it would be appropriate to appoint an arbitrator from a country where there is no National Committee or Group, or (iv) the President certifies to the Court that circumstances exist that make a direct appointment necessary and appropriate.

When appointing an arbitrator, the Court will take into account all relevant circumstances, including the nationality of the parties and other arbitrators, applicable law, place of arbitration, language of the arbitration, amount in dispute and the complexity and nature of the dispute."

KLRCA (Sundra Rajoo)

"(a) When a request to appoint an arbitrator is received, the first point of consideration at the KLRCA is the case counsel. Case counsel at the KLRCA will look at a wide range of factors, including: the nature of the dispute, its complexity, the nationalities of parties, the amount in dispute, and any other specific characteristics such as technical expertise or language requirements. They will then sieve through the list of arbitrators that is maintained by the Centre to find the right match with experience and expertise, and also availability. This list will then be forwarded to the Director for selection of the arbitrator. The Director will discuss with the management team and appoint the suitable candidate for the matter. Finally, a conflict check will be conducted before the formal appointment is made."

LCIA (Adrian Winstanley)

"In all cases, whether or not the arbitrators are nominated by the parties, the basic LCIA procedure is as follows, save that steps 4, 5 and 7 are omitted in the case of party nomination:

(1) The LCIA Secretariat reviews the Request for Arbitration and accompanying contractual documents, and the Response (if any).
(2) A résumé of the case is prepared for the LCIA Court.
(3) Key criteria for the qualifications of the arbitrator(s) are established.
(4) The criteria are entered into the LCIA's database of arbitrators, from which an initial list is drawn.
(5) If necessary, other sources are consulted for further recommendations.
(6) The résumé, the relevant documentation, and the names and CVs of the potential arbitrators are forwarded to the LCIA Court.
(7) The LCIA Court advises which arbitrator(s) the Secretariat should contact (who need not be, but usually will be, from among those put forward by the Secretariat) to ascertain their availability and willingness to accept appointment.

(8) In the case of a party nomination, the LCIA Court advises whether it considers the nominee suitable, subject to conflicts checks.

(9) The Secretariat sends the candidate(s) an outline of the dispute.

(10) When the candidate(s) confirm their availability, independence and impartiality, and agree to fee rates in accordance with the LCIA schedule of costs, the form of appointment is drafted.

(11) The LCIA Court formally appoints the tribunal and the parties are notified.

Given the Secretariat's considerable experience in selecting arbitrators, and personal knowledge of many candidates, there are some cases in which a suitable selection of candidate arbitrators may be put forward to the Court by the Secretariat, without the need to interrogate the database. (See step 4, above.)

Whilst the LCIA is, of course, concerned that each arbitrator should be appropriately qualified as to experience, expertise, language and legal training, it is also mindful of any other criteria specified by the parties in their agreement and/or in the Request and Response.

The LCIA is also concerned to ensure the right balance of experience, qualifications and seniority on a three-member tribunal; in particular, what qualities the Chair should have to complement those of his co-arbitrators. The LCIA is mindful also of any particular national and/or cultural characteristics of the parties to which it should be sensitive, so as to minimize conflict. Similarly, it addresses such issues as whether the arbitrator(s) should have a light touch or a firm touch, bearing in mind, for example, the degree of professionalism it expects of the parties given whom they have chosen to represent them.

The LCIA also considers the nature of the case (sum in issue, declaratory, technically complex, legally complex, etc.), the identity and known characteristics of the parties' lawyers and, indeed, whether the parties are represented at all.

The LCIA is equally concerned to ensure that arbitrators are not only suitably qualified and without conflict, but are also available to deal with the case as expeditiously as may be required.

The LCIA is amenable to a joint request by the parties to provide a list of candidate arbitrators, from which they may endeavour to select the tribunal, whether in straightforward negotiation, or by adopting an UNCITRAL-style list procedure. In such cases, the selection process described above is carried out in respect of all candidates to be included on the list, so that any candidate(s) selected by the parties have already confirmed their willingness and ability to accept appointment and have been approved for appointment by the LCIA Court.

Thus, the process of selecting arbitrators is by no means mechanical; it is a considered combination of science and art, as to which the LCIA, both in its Secretariat and in its Court, is well qualified."

PCA (Brooks Daly)

"The Secretary-General of the PCA appoints the arbitrator in accordance with procedures foreseen in either the PCA Arbitration Rules or, frequently, the UNCITRAL Arbitration Rules, under which he is often asked to act as an appointing authority. In addition to impartiality and independence, which are required for every arbitrator, in the circumstances of a specific case any of the following factors may be relevant: nationality, language abilities, relevant experience, knowledge of applicable law, availability, cost (i.e., hourly rate), and any comments which the parties may provide concerning the qualifications of the arbitrator to be appointed."[15]

(b) To what extent should this process be publicized, including the details of any lists of candidates from which you make your selection?

BCDR *(Nassib Ziadé)*
"The institution's procedure for making arbitrator appointments should be included in the institution's rules and other materials which are made available in both print and electronic formats. The short lists of candidates being considered internally for appointment, however, should not be disclosed (except in cases where the parties are invited to choose an arbitrator from such a list of candidates), as an arbitral institution does not have the duty to uncover its own internal deliberative processes."

CRCICA *(Mohamed Abdel Raouf)*
"The process is very transparent as it is provided for in the rules. The details of the list procedure from which the selection is made are explained within the answer to the above question."

CAM-CCBC *(Frederico José Straube)*
"The arbitrator, as mentioned, is chosen among the names on the Roster of Arbitrators, which is public. The criteria are mostly technical: the language of the procedure, the area of expertise of the arbitrator appointed, the availability of the arbitrator to accept the case."

ICDR *(Richard Naimark)*
"The only thing relevant to the parties in the case is listing of the particular arbitrator candidates for the case. The pool from which candidates are drawn can be quite large and have many names that are completely irrelevant to the dispute at hand, in terms of expertise. ICDR has about 700 names and AAA has thousands."

ICC *(John Beechey)*
"The process should be as transparent as possible. The ICC Rules as well as the ICC training programmes, conferences and publications clearly explain how the ICC system works. A benefit of ICC arbitration is that the selection of arbitrators is not restricted to a fixed list."

KLRCA *(Sundra Rajoo)*
"The process of appointing an arbitrator may itself be published; however, it may not be appropriate to publicize the details of the lists of candidates. Often a request to appoint is made at a point where parties are unable to agree on a choice of nominated arbitrator. Accordingly, the parties are relying on the Centre's expertise and also finality in making a decision. Giving the parties access to the list of possible selections may undermine the confidence placed in the Centre to finally decide on the arbitrator, given that there is ordinarily no recourse for the parties if they disagree with the appointment. It is to avoid undue delay by the non-participating party that publicizing the details of the lists of candidates may not be appropriate. Despite not publishing the details of lists for

---

15. See further, B. DALY, E. GORIATCHEVA, H. MEIGHEN, *A Guide to the PCA Arbitration Rules* (Oxford University Press 2014).

arbitrations, there is a predefined procedure in place in the selection of an arbitrator that is applied consistently when the KLRCA appoints arbitrators."

LCIA (Adrian Winstanley)

"This process is publicized in the LCIA's generally available materials, printed and online.

As stated above, the LCIA has no closed list of candidates from which the Court will make its selection."

PCA (Brooks Daly)

"The PCA is not bound by any list of candidates and selects the best candidate for each appointment from the entire world of available arbitrators. The PCA's relevant procedures are widely circulated and explained in multiple publications."[16]

(c) Should arbitral institutions consider factors such as gender, race, ethnic background and nationality in making an arbitrator selection? If so, to what extent?

BCDR (Nassib Ziadé)

"It would be disingenuous to claim that arbitration institutions do not consider factors such as gender and nationality in making arbitration selections.

With respect to nationality, the statutes of many arbitration institutions provide that, absent an agreement to the contrary by the parties, the chair or the sole arbitrator should not have the same nationality of either party. In addition to these statutory requirements, the practice of many arbitration institutions seeks to expand the geographical representation of the pool of appointed arbitrators so it becomes more reflective of human diversity. In addition to bringing inclusiveness, the appointment of arbitrators originating from diverse cultural and legal backgrounds enriches the debate within arbitral tribunals and provides added assurance to the parties that all of the nuances in the case will be grasped.

Similarly, with respect to gender, concerted efforts are being made by many arbitration institutions to identify and promote qualified women arbitrators, who have been historically underrepresented on tribunals.

In all cases, efforts to diversify the pools of arbitrators should be undertaken while simultaneously ensuring that only available, experienced and highly competent individuals are considered."

CRCICA (Mohamed Abdel Raouf)

"Yes, to the extent that this does not negatively impact the quality of the awards."

CAM-CCBC (Frederico José Straube)

"An arbitral institution should not, in most cases, consider such factors in making an arbitrator selection. The only exception to this statement, observed in the rules of CAM-CCBC, arises when the parties have different nationalities. In this case, it is fair that the parties request that the third arbitrator belong to a different State that is neutral regarding the dispute."

---

16. See, e.g., *ibid.*, 3.48-3.51, 4.05-4.38. See also "Arbitration Services" section of PCA website: <www.pca- cpa.org/ showpage.asp?pag_id=1048>.

ICDR (Richard Naimark)

"Yes, part of the institutional purview is to enlarge the pool of acceptable arbitrators and to expand the profile of the pool itself to be more reflective of the various parties' nationalities, gender and cultures."

ICC (John Beechey)

"Nationality (particularly of a sole arbitrator / presiding arbitrator) is a particular factor highlighted in the ICC Rules.

The ICC Court is astute to avoid discrimination on whatever grounds including gender, race or ethnicity. It is a fact of life, however, that in certain very specific circumstances (e.g., appointments to be made in the Islamic world), the Court has to have regard to particular selection criteria."

KLRCA (Sundra Rajoo)

"Yes, to the extent that it is necessary to ensure fairness and neutrality. As mentioned above, the nationality of the parties is a factor that is taken into consideration, in relation to the nationality of the arbitrator that will be appointed. Gender, race and ethnic background should only be considered to the extent that it is necessary to properly determine the dispute, though such an instance is not likely to occur."

LCIA (Adrian Winstanley)

"The LCIA rules specifically provide that a sole arbitrator or the chairman of a tribunal shall not be of the same nationality as any of the parties, unless the parties who are not of the same nationality as the proposed appointee all agree in writing otherwise.

In my view, an institution should be gender, race and ethnicity blind. That said, I refer again to the LCIA's concern to ensure qualities in a tribunal that have regard to any particular national and/or cultural characteristics of the parties to which it should be sensitive."

PCA (Brooks Daly)

"Nationality is a recognized factor in determining the neutrality of presiding arbitrators and sole arbitrators. Arbitral institutions should therefore certainly consider this factor. Some procedural rules may require a presiding arbitrator to be of neutral nationality vis-à-vis the parties, while others may refer to it as a factor to be considered in assuring neutrality.

With respect to gender, race and ethnic background, these should never be considered as limiting factors in the selection of an arbitrator. Where two equally qualified candidates are available for a particular appointment, a candidate from a group that is less often represented in arbitral tribunals may be preferred."

(d) What responsibility do arbitral institutions have for ensuring that the pool of arbitrator candidates is widened and that appointments are made from that widened pool? Does this include a responsibility to provide arbitrator training?

BCDR (Nassib Ziadé)

"As already mentioned, women and individuals from developing countries remain insufficiently represented in the arbitration community. Arbitral institutions have the primary responsibility to identify new generations of rising stars from underrepresented regions and populations, and to provide them with adequate training so that they may be considered for future appointments. Arbitration institutions from the Western world have to a certain extent traditionally played the role of identifying new arbitrators from emerging economies. It is incumbent today on regional arbitration institutions to assume leadership in this area as well as in the area of training arbitration practitioners, judges and parties located in the regions in which they operate."

CRCICA *(Mohamed Abdel Raouf)*
"The best way to widen the pool of arbitrator candidates is to have more than one person within the institution proposing potential names and to have a collegial decision in this respect. Arbitral institutions should naturally provide arbitrator training in order to ensure that appointments are made from a widened pool."

CAM-CCBC *(Frederico José Straube)*
"An arbitral institution must follow the trends of arbitration in general. It is therefore important to participate actively on international forums and to meet experts from diverse origins. From such exposition, it is possible to find names to be part of the pool of arbitrators. It is also important to provide training, not only to arbitrators, but also to researchers, young professionals and counsel, to develop arbitration and to assure its better performance and legitimacy."

ICDR *(Richard Naimark)*
"Yes and Yes as answered above."

ICC *(John Beechey)*
"The first part of this question has been addressed at Questions 2 and 9(a) above.

It is in the best interest of the institutions and all users that the pool of arbitrators is widened, and the achievement of a broader arbitration base is a shared responsibility between institutions and users. This is a matter to which the ICC Court has always given priority.

The ICC regularly organizes training programmes for arbitrators, both experienced and newcomers (e.g., advanced   Programme of the Institute for the Development of its Activities (PIDA), Masterclass)."

KLRCA *(Sundra Rajoo)*
"Institutions have a great responsibility to ensure that the pool of arbitrators is wide and capable of handling disputes. Doing so ensures that a centre has arbitrators with a plethora of expertise, who are able to handle the most complex and unique disputes. One school of thought is that an arbitration institution should bear the responsibility of appointing an arbitrator as opposed to a party. This is a noteworthy debate with regard to this question.

Jan Paulsson, a vigorous supporter of the institutional appointment of arbitrators, states, 'The sole defence of unilateral appointments to which I have no answer is that it is a pragmatic response to an inability to trust the arbitral institution to appoint good arbitrators.'[17] Paulsson's statement highlights the necessity of maintaining a large and well-trained pool of arbitrators.

---

17. Jan PAULSSON, Lecture "Moral Hazard in International Dispute Resolution", University of Miami School of Law (29 April 2010) accessed at: <www.arbitration-icca.org/media/0/1277374 9999020/paulsson_moral_hazard.pdf> at p. 13.

In addition to a great deal of depth in an institution's panel, there does exist a responsibility to provide training to arbitrators. One initiative that has been taken by the KLRCA is to provide a diploma course in international arbitration which is a fast-track approach to becoming a fellow of the CIArb. Additionally the KLRCA provides numerous evening talks and workshops every month.

As a repository of arbitration expertise in Malaysia and the region, it is incumbent on the KLRCA to promote arbitration by providing training services."

LCIA (Adrian Winstanley)
"I refer to the responses that I have given to previous questions.

The LCIA does not undertake any formal arbitrator training, though it does run a full programme of conferences and seminars, including those conducted by and for YIAG."

PCA (Brooks Daly)
"Arbitral institutions typically administer a greater number of proceedings than any individual lawyer in private practice is involved in. As such, they have the opportunity to observe lawyers new to the field (serving either as arbitrators or counsel) who may be gaining requisite experience for future appointments. This opportunity to 'spot talent' from the world of practitioners is unique, and institutions should thus bear the responsibility to act on this access to information for the purposes of appointing arbitrators in future proceedings.

It should be noted that party-appointed arbitrators account for the majority of appointments, and that counsel are often under significant pressure to select the best-known arbitrators for appointment. This may appeal more to their clients, despite the fact that lesser-known arbitrators may be just as competent. Because institutions may be able to identify arbitrators with competence equivalent to those best-known individuals, they are well-positioned to act upon this knowledge. Ultimately, institutions should be primarily concerned with the competence of the arbitrator, and the arbitrator's relative fame in the arbitral marketplace is not necessarily linked to his or her competence. Institutions can act more freely than counsel in this regard because they need not appeal to such external factors. As such, institutions should take responsibility for widening the pool of arbitrator candidates when appropriate candidates present themselves.

Institutions should also have a role in arbitrator training. This may be done in an ad hoc manner, by answering the questions of less-experienced arbitrators in pending proceedings, organizing conferences and producing publications. This may also extend to formal courses; however, administering institutions should be wary of training courses offering institutional certification, as this may risk creating a subset of arbitrators who are perceived as qualified to act within such institutions and may prove counterproductive in efforts to widen the pool of potential arbitrators."

(e) What effect does the predominant system of party appointments have on the legitimacy of international arbitration? Can you imagine that system being revisited by your institution in the future?

BCDR (Nassib Ziadé)
"There are two approaches to the system of party-appointed arbitrators. The predominant and traditional approach emphasizes that the legitimacy of international arbitration rests in large part on the confidence of the parties and their intimate involvement in the

appointment of the arbitrators. According to this view, the system of party appointments is a mere reflection of party autonomy, which remains a pillar of international arbitration.

Leading specialists, on the other hand, have recently called for arbitration institutions to assume greater responsibilities in the selection of arbitrators. These calls are mostly in response to a growing skepticism about what is perceived as a lack of true independence and impartiality on the part of party-appointed arbitrators. Jan Paulsson, a proponent of this second approach, stated that '[t]he practice of unilateral appointments ... implicitly militates in favor of compromise [and] militates against coherently and sincerely motivated awards'.[18]

This second approach is certainly attractive. There is, however, little indication that the current system of party-appointed arbitrators will undergo significant transformations in the near future, as many parties to arbitration – let alone the entrenched forces that continue to oppose calls for systemic reform – are not yet prepared to relinquish what they consider a fundamental right.[19]

Irrespective of the outcome of this debate, which remains largely academic at this juncture, arbitration institutions ought to examine their existing internal processes and working methods in order to determine whether they are well-equipped to even take on these added responsibilities. These institutions must look cautiously at the suggested remedy to ensure that it actually helps to alleviate, rather than worsen, the problem.

Until the time is ripe for a major overhaul, arbitration institutions would do well to adopt codes of ethics for arbitration practitioners appearing before them, strengthen the disclosure requirements imposed on arbitrators at the outset of a case and throughout the arbitration proceedings, and increase transparency in their own appointments of arbitrators and in their challenge decisions."

CRCICA *(Mohamed Abdel Raouf)*

"The predominant system of party appointments is an integral part of the system and contributes to the legitimacy of international arbitration. Whether such appointment is recklessly or incompetently made does not necessarily mean that this system should be revised. It simply means that parties should learn that their approach to appointment could be counterproductive.

I do not think that the system will be changed by CRCICA in the future, unless the parties are willing to waive their fundamental right of selecting their judges.

I would add that the institution is not necessarily better placed than the parties in selecting their arbitrators. The list process and the common practice of co-arbitrators consulting the parties while selecting the chairperson confirm that the party appointment system is here to stay."

CAM-CCBC *(Frederico José Straube)*

"In fact, I believe that the question confuses the concept of legitimacy. The basis of legitimacy in State jurisdiction is not the same as that relied on to ground the legitimacy of

---

18. "Moral Hazard in International Dispute Resolution", 25 ICSID Rev. – FILJ (2010) p. 339, at p. 353.
19. See e.g., Charles N. BROWER and Charles B. ROSENBERG, "The Death of the Two-Headed Nightingale: Why the Paulsson-van den Berg Presumption that Party-Appointed Arbitrators Are Untrustworthy Is Wrongheaded", 29 Arb. Int'l (2013) p. 7 at p. 24 (noting that "it is highly to be doubted that any institution can ever achieve a level of user confidence that even approaches that of selections made by sophisticated parties and counsel".).

an arbitration. The entire basis of arbitration is the trust that the parties have in an expert and this is the reason why they appoint him as an arbitrator. The legitimacy is lost when the reason for appointing an arbitrator is something other than trust or when a party was led to make a mistake in trusting such expert.

In international arbitration, some elements make such legitimacy more difficult. For instance, in a case in which the parties are of different nationalities, one of the parties will tend to be suspicious of the arbitrator appointed by the other party if they are of the same origin. Depending on the case, considering that eventually countries maintain commercial alliances to protect their interests, stipulating a rule forbidding the parties to appoint arbitrators of their own nationality would not be enough. Sometimes, an arbitrator from a different country can be as suspicious as a national of the same country, when they are from a country that shares strategic interests with the other party's home State. This can effectively damage the legitimacy of the arbitral tribunal.

However, it is important to bear in mind that the confidence of the parties, expressed by their appointments, is the base for the legitimacy and, therefore, the solution is not modifying the method for appointing arbitrators. In fact, other means can be more effective to protect legitimacy, namely trying to set rules to prevent the parties choosing an arbitrator who is sympathetic to their cause, including, for instance, the adoption of the duty of the arbitrator to provide a wide disclosure to the parties in order to offer evidence enabling the parties to find possible conflicts. Another idea is to establish transparent rules to set a procedure for the parties to challenge the arbitrator appointed by the other party."

ICDR (Richard Naimark)

"Ultimately the method of arbitrator selection is driven by the contract and party choice. This is fundamental to party autonomy. However, at times the party appointed system is not the best system because there may be a lingering expectation or suspicion that a party-appointed arbitrator may favour the appointing party. Codes of Ethics and Conduct can be helpful here. ICDR promotes the list selection method as it seems to enhance balance and perceptions of impartiality."

ICC (John Beechey)

"Party appointments are of the utmost importance, as they enhance the confidence of the parties in the system. It is particularly important for States or State entities.

There are no plans to move from this model, so far as the ICC Court is concerned."

KLRCA (Sundra Rajoo)

"The predominant system of party-appointed arbitrators is underpinned and legitimized by party autonomy in international arbitration. The system works well by allowing party autonomy and then a default mechanism to deal with situations when such agreement may not be reached. In such an instance the institution plays a best neutral appointer role.

Once again, Jan Paulsson's argument that an institution is best placed to appoint an arbitrator over a party appointment is one that should be given due consideration. The rationale, according to Paulsson, is that a party-appointed arbitrator is 'a species of advocate' for the party nominating them.[20] He rightly goes on to state that the best way to avoid appointments that result in appointments that are not entirely impartial is to heavily

---

20. Jan PAULSSON, Lecture "Moral Hazard in International Dispute Resolution" University of Miami. *op. cit.*, fn. 17.

police or entirely do away with unilateral appointments of arbitrators.[21] With the impartiality of decision-makers being a pillar of arbitration, the institutional appointment of arbitrators would certainly further legitimize international arbitration. If it was the case that the majority of appointments were done by centres, this would have numerous additional benefits such as a likely reduction of the number of challenges to arbitrators resulting in greater efficiency.

Notwithstanding the above, party autonomy and flexibility are fundamental pillars of commercial arbitration and crucial to its continued development. Placing the choice of arbitrators solely with the institution may have benefits in the short term but will stifle the attractiveness of arbitration to users in the long term, who will opt for either ad hoc arbitration or litigation.

The KLRCA has taken small steps, with the Director retaining the discretion to confirm parties' nominations pursuant to the Rules. This at the least provides a level of checks and balances."

LCIA (Adrian Winstanley)

"In 2013, 156 (42.5 per cent) of the 367 appointments made by the LCIA Court were of arbitrators also selected by the Court; 162 (44 per cent) were of arbitrators nominated by the parties; 49 (13.5 per cent) were of arbitrators nominated by the parties' nominees.

On these statistics, party-nomination does not predominate at the LCIA, but there are currently no plans to restrict in any way a party's right to nominate, provided this right is expressly stated in an applicable arbitration agreement."

PCA (Brooks Daly)

"In a three-member tribunal, the parties' appointment of the first and second arbitrators is a standard practice. The PCA considers that parties' participation in the constitution of arbitral tribunals is one of the most attractive features of international arbitration, and it does not imagine revisiting this system in the future. However, while it is not a default procedure under the PCA Arbitration Rules, it is not excluded that parties may agree to the PCA Secretary-General's appointment of all tribunal members in a given case."

(f) What kind of information should routinely be made available to the appointing institution about arbitrator candidates before selection (e.g. profile, availability, links with parties and their counsel, list of past and present cases, data as to average award-rendering time, etc.)?

BCDR (Nassib Ziadé)

"Before selecting an arbitrator, the arbitral institution should be in possession of a detailed CV of the prospective arbitrator (which outlines, among others, the arbitrator's areas of expertise and his or her linguistic abilities) and the arbitrator's statements of availability and independence. Any present or past links between the arbitrator and his or her law firm with the parties and their counsel and with the other arbitrators should be disclosed."

CRCICA (Mohamed Abdel Raouf)

"In addition to the above information, when requested to appoint a chairperson due to the failure by the co-arbitrators to select one, it is advisable for the arbitral institution to

---

21. *Ibid.*, p. 8.

request that the co-arbitrators make available the names that have been discussed and rejected, especially when the parties are consulted by the co-arbitrators. In such cases, it would be grossly unfair for the parties to have as arbitrator someone who was previously rejected by the co-arbitrators simply because this information was not brought to the attention of the institution."

CAM-CCBC (Frederico José Straube)

"The first important piece of information concerns their expertise, in order to ensure the quality of the award. Also, any information regarding the independence of the arbitrator is essential. For instance, someone who was appointed to be an arbitrator must disclose any case in which he has acted as a counsel, advisor or expert for any of the parties. Moreover, he must inform the institution if he has performed the role of arbitrator in any previous case concerning one of the parties. He must disclose any existing link between the parties and people who are close to him, such as a member of his family. Another important piece of information is the availability of the candidate, in order to ensure that the award will be rendered on time and that he will commit to the case."

ICDR (Richard Naimark)

"(f)-(g) All arbitrators should provide full disclosure so that any appearance of conflict can be dealt with at the outset of the case."

ICC (John Beechey)

"All arbitrators acting in ICC cases are requested to sign a statement of independence, impartiality and availability and to provide an updated CV.

The Court and the Secretariat will normally be aware of the other elements mentioned in the question."

KLRCA (Sundra Rajoo)

"The KLRCA, as with other arbitral institutions in Asia, maintains its own panel of arbitrators. All arbitrators appointed by the KLRCA in its capacity as appointing authority, whether under an iteration of the KLRCA Arbitration Rules or under the Arbitration Act 2005, are appointed from that panel. The panel consists of over 700 arbitrators of various nationalities and backgrounds.

In this respect, the information that should be made available to an appointing institution consists of both that to be considered when joining the panel as well as that to be considered when making an appointment. When joining the panel, this includes a candidate's profile – their qualifications and experience, specifically pertaining to arbitration. When making an appointment, this refers to more specific information, including any potential conflicts, availability and suitability for miscellaneous requirements such as language and location.

Certain information, such as average award-rendering time, is not necessarily relevant for an administered arbitration. Under the KLRCA Rules, for example, arbitral tribunals are required to render an award within three months of close of submissions."

LCIA (Adrian Winstanley)

"All candidate arbitrators must provide the LCIA with a full CV, to establish their suitability for appointment. Though not an express requirement of the current rules, the LCIA Secretariat always enquires of an arbitrator as to his or her availability, and this is to be codified in the new LCIA rules.

The LCIA's standard statement of independence requires the disclosure of relationships among arbitrator, parties and counsel.

Past and present cases should not be relevant unless they impact upon independence and impartiality, in which case they must be disclosed.

Although there is much said and written about the time taken to issue awards, there is, I think, no *'average award-rendering time'* that would be relevant."

PCA (Brooks Daly)

"Data that should routinely be made available to the institution include any information which may influence the appearance of arbitrators' impartiality or independence, any links with parties or counsel in a given case, the candidate's availability, and the remainder of relevant information found in his or her CV."

(g) Which of the qualitative/quantitative information referred to in Question 11(f) above, if any, should be shared with the parties before selection to avoid any asymmetry of information between them?

BCDR (Nassib Ziadé)

"An arbitral institution should share with both parties to the arbitration the CVs of the arbitrators appointed, the arbitrators' statements of availability and independence, and any matters that the arbitrators disclose in the context of the arbitration proceedings. The parties will have to do their own due diligence. Any remaining concerns that the parties might have should be addressed to the tribunal or to the arbitral institution."

CRCICA (Mohamed Abdel Raouf)

"Arbitral institutions are required to make appointments as promptly as possible. The appointment process should take into account the qualitative/quantitative information referred to in Question 11(f) above without necessarily sharing such information with the parties before selection."

CAM-CCBC (Frederico José Straube)

"All the information disclosed must be shared with all parties to avoid any asymmetry of information between them."

ICC (John Beechey)

"This is a delicate issue: an institution will try not to interfere in the parties' exercise of free choice in selecting an arbitrator. It is for the parties to make an informed decision, rather than for an institution to risk giving an appearance of failing to treat the parties with equality by exposing itself to a complaint that it is compensating for a lack of knowledge on the part of one or more of the parties."

KLRCA (Sundra Rajoo)

"Much of the information referred to above is publicly available through the KLRCA's website. Any extra information should only be provided where it has been provided to or by one of the parties."

LCIA (Adrian Winstanley)

"The parties should, of course, be provided with a CV and any additional information that may emerge in the context of the statement of independence."

PCA (Brooks Daly)
"All of the information mentioned in the response to the immediately preceding question should be shared with the parties."

(h) What safeguards should arbitral institutions implement, if any, to protect against cronyism?

BCDR (Nassib Ziadé)
"Arbitral institutions must put in place fully transparent and merit-based criteria for the selection of arbitrators and must follow them scrupulously and consistently. The procedure for selection within the institution should be one which has checks and balances rather than lies in the hands of an individual. Any person within the institution who has a close relationship with the substance of the dispute, the counsel or the arbitrators should not be involved in the selection of arbitrators or in the administration of the case.

When the rules of an arbitration institution provide that the parties nominate the arbitrators but the arbitration institution makes the actual appointments, the institution has the power, if not the duty, to question the parties' choices or to request additional disclosures on the part of the nominated arbitrators if it has reason to suspect the existence of cronyism in the nomination process."

CRCICA (Mohamed Abdel Raouf)
"Resorting to the list procedure in appointing arbitrators appears to be the best safeguard to protect against cronyism."

CAM-CCBC (Frederico José Straube)
"Arbitral institutions face different situations which expose them to cronyism. The first of them takes place when the parties choose an arbitral institution. Sometimes, the choice is made in order to keep a good relationship with a specific arbitration centre. A good solution for this is stimulating the parties to decide on the basis of the tradition and the renown of the institution. Another exposure is in the invitation of experts to become part of the Roster of Arbitrators. It is therefore important to create a strict and transparent set of rules for the nomination of experts to the list. Finally, in the situations in which the President appoints the arbitrator, it is important that he follows clear criteria when he makes such decision."

ICC (John Beechey)
"The Court and the Secretariat have an institutional memory, built on the experience of their members in the administration of cases, which allows them to identify any improper situation. In such cases, the Secretariat would ask the individual concerned to make the relevant disclosure if necessary."

KLRCA (Sundra Rajoo)
"In an arbitral institution the power to make appointments is centralized, making it easier to monitor and concurrently take measures to eradicate cronyism. Cronyism generally prevails in an institution where decisions are made according to an individual's choice rather than according to an implemented system of procedures and processes. Accordingly, the solution to preventing cronyism is to implement and maintain a system of best practices that distributes appointments in an appropriate way.

There are specific measures, such as keeping a database of appointments, which can assist such a system to run smoothly. Certain requirements must be observed while in other cases opportunities for diversification may present themselves. If a complex case exists, then a more experienced arbitrator should be appointed. If a smaller, less complex case exists, this is a chance to appoint a more junior arbitrator. Additionally, as outlined above, it is not difficult for institutions to track who has been appointed in prior arbitrations."

LCIA (Adrian Winstanley)

"Whilst there is little doubt that arbitrators who know each other well may be inclined to put forward one another's names as co-arbitrators when charged with selecting the presiding arbitrator, this need not necessarily constitute cronyism. In many cases, it is a matter of confidence in a fellow arbitrator borne of long experience.

The institution must have no truck with cronyism, as to which I refer again to the makeup and independence of the LCIA Court, and to the statistics given in my answer to Question 11(e). And I would add that 20 per cent of the arbitrators appointed by the LCIA Court in 2012 had not previously been appointed in an LCIA arbitration."

PCA (Brooks Daly)

"With respect to parties' appointments, institutions can do little other than to ensure impartiality and independence. As concerns cronyism in institutional appointments, the market for arbitration services is to some extent self-regulating in this context, because arbitration users will not return to institutions when they perceive that institutional appointments are being made on the basis of friendship and without regard to the qualifications of the appointees. The ability of the marketplace to identify cronyism and avoid institutions that indulge in it would be facilitated by transparency concerning individuals appointed by arbitral institutions."

(i) Some have argued that there ought to be very wide ranging disclosure of any links between counsel and arbitrators and of arbitrators relationships *inter se* to counter the fear of cronyism. Do you agree?

BCDR (Nassib Ziadé)

"As discussed earlier, there exists today a relatively small community of arbitration experts who are repeatedly appointed as counsel or arbitrators in arbitration cases. Inevitable links, both professional and personal, will be formed over the years among these different actors in the field of international arbitration. It is therefore crucial that arbitrators, at the time of their appointments and throughout the arbitration proceedings, make full disclosures about their relationships with each other as well as with counsel for the parties, and that they err on the side of caution and transparency in matters of disclosure. The question of whether disclosed matters constitute circumstances giving rise to justifiable doubts as to an arbitrator's impartiality or independence should be left to the parties and, when the parties cannot agree, to a decision by the arbitral institution."

CRCICA (Mohamed Abdel Raouf)

"I think that arbitrators should always have the discretion to disclose any information or circumstances likely to give rise to their impartiality or independence. However, any doubts as to their duty to disclose a fact, circumstance or a relationship should be interpreted in favour of disclosure."

CAM-CCBC (Frederico José Straube)
"Considering that, in fact, the appointment of an arbitrator is made by counsel, it is important to take any necessary measure for avoiding cronyism. The same happens between arbitrators in tribunals on which the President is appointed by the co-arbitrators. In this context, it is clear that a wide-ranging disclosure of any links between counsel and arbitrator or among arbitrators is one of the possible measures that must be taken."

ICDR (Richard Naimark)
"Arbitrators should err on the side of disclosure and disclose, disclose, disclose and then leave it to the parties and the institution to decide if a disclosure constitutes a material conflict. Arbitrators should never 'hang on' to cases by non-disclosure."

ICC (John Beechey)
"The ICC favours disclosures, when they are relevant and appropriate. In case of doubt, we recommend the prospective arbitrator to disclose.

It should be noted that culture has a strong impact on this issue as arbitrators from different regions follow different approaches towards disclosure. In this respect, American arbitrators are known for applying higher standards of disclosures than arbitrators from other regions. For example, in 2012, an American arbitrator disclosed having undertaken an internship at the firm representing one of the parties between June and September ... 1959."

KLRCA (Sundra Rajoo)
"The IBA guidelines on conflicts of interest can be considered the standard in this respect. These guidelines are used as a point of reference in determining the disclosure requirement and whether an arbitrator is conflicted according to the KLRCA Code of Conduct for Arbitrators. These guidelines strike the appropriate balance of what should and should not be disclosed. Of course, party autonomy will also allow a tribunal to adopt the IBA guidelines as they see fit.

Realistically, as the stakes in commercial arbitrations rise, so too do the instances of arbitrator challenges. In the current climate it is advisable that arbitrators err on the side of caution when it comes to disclosures, and many arbitrators do tend towards that attitude. In this respect the IBA guidelines have become a sort of minimum standard.

Notwithstanding the above, the field of international arbitration regionally and internationally is a small one, and an unintended consequence of this is that arbitrators are frequently familiar with other arbitrators or counsel. Advocates and arbitrators conduct themselves professionally and despite personal links between practitioners there should not be a default fear of cronyism between arbitrators and counsel. Accordingly a balance does need to be struck when considering the likelihood of cronyism or other irregularities."

LCIA (Adrian Winstanley)
"There has to be a degree of common sense applied in considering what 'links' between counsel and arbitrators and among arbitrators are properly disclosable in the context of a statement of independence. But I do not propose to give examples, when there are more than enough guidelines available for those arbitrators who need guidance on such matters.

The guiding principle, as expressly stated in the LCIA's statement of independence and in similar terms in the statements of other institutions, is that any doubt about a conflict must be resolved in favour of disclosure."

PCA *(Brooks Daly)*

"Links between counsel and arbitrators or relationships between arbitrators should be subject to disclosure by arbitrators to the extent that they raise justifiable doubts concerning the independence or impartiality of arbitrators."

Question 12

Is it legitimate for the same individual to appear as Counsel in some cases and as arbitrator in other cases? If not, why not? What can or should arbitral institutions do about it in the context of arbitrator appointment?

BCDR *(Nassib Ziadé)*

"To maintain their legitimacy, arbitral institutions will have to confront sooner rather than later the need to avoid blurring the line between advocacy and decision-making. Institutions need to take the initiative in developing codes of conduct and ethics that will impose necessary order on the system and bolster trust in the due process offered.

In the field of commercial arbitration, the appearance of the same individual as counsel in one case and as arbitrator in an unrelated case could be problematic in some situations. For instance, can a person appearing as counsel before an arbitrator in one case sit simultaneously in another case as a co-arbitrator with the arbitrator from the first case?

This is not merely a question of appearances. It is also a matter of substance. The counsel and the co-arbitrator will be deliberating and discussing law together. The counsel could thereby glean from the co-arbitrator insights which the counsel could then use to his or her client's benefit, thereby creating an unfair and prejudicial advantage.

To deal with such a problematic relationship, it is critical that both the counsel and the arbitrator disclose to the parties in the first case their potential work together as co-arbitrators in the second case. Failing to make such disclosures, or proceeding with the second case despite the objection of the other party in the first case, would be an example *par excellence* of engaging in unauthorized *ex parte* communications.

There are reasons to be even more rigorous in the field of investment arbitration, as there is a far greater chance of encountering overlapping issues and fact patterns in such a narrow field. Investment arbitrations frequently turn on the interpretation of investment treaties which contain similar provisions and therefore engender a small set of similar, oft-recurring legal issues. The possibility of overlap between the same issues, if not between the same State Parties, is evident.

There can be little doubt that issue conflicts can serve to disqualify practitioners who choose to serve *simultaneously* as counsel and arbitrators. Investment arbitration specialists have thus in recent years engaged in an animated debate over how to resolve this problem. Some believe that there should be a sharp divide between arbitrators on the one hand, and counsel on the other. Others believe that there is no need to require arbitrators to choose between continuing such functions and performing work as counsel.

Specialists who advocate a separation of roles in investment arbitration argue that arbitrators should not be put into a position where they are tempted, either consciously or subconsciously, to take procedural decisions or to draft awards in such a way as to advance their clients' position in a simultaneous case in which they are acting as counsel.

Others, who oppose a separation of roles, contend that conscientious arbitrators will decide their cases strictly on the basis of the facts and law before them, and will not be unduly influenced by factors extraneous to the merits of that particular case. They observe that a separation of roles would deprive the international arbitration community of some

724

of its best talents who, when forced to choose, might well opt for the more lucrative role of counsel.

Some institutions have addressed such concerns by prohibiting altogether the 'double hat' system. For example, the International Court of Justice (which is admittedly not an arbitral institution) issued in 2002 a Practice Direction asking that States, when choosing a judge *ad hoc*, refrain from nominating a person acting at the same time as an agent, counsel or advocate in another case before the Court, or any person who has acted in that capacity in the three years preceding the date of the nomination.

More recently and relevantly to the arbitration field, the Court of Arbitration for Sport amended its Statute in 2010 to provide that arbitrators and mediators appearing before the Court may not also act as counsel for a party before the Court.

Short of adopting a radical solution completely segregating the roles of counsel and arbitrator in investment arbitrations, one alternative would be to allow the same individual to undertake both roles, subject to a requirement that the proposed arrangement be disclosed to the parties and be accepted by both parties.

Under this arrangement, each time an arbitrator is appointed to an investment treaty arbitration when he or she is also serving as counsel in another investment treaty arbitration, the newly appointed arbitrator must disclose at the outset of the arbitration the simple fact that he or she is serving as counsel in a concurrent investment treaty arbitration. Such a disclosure would take place irrespective of the legal issues raised in the two cases. If one or both parties were for any reason to object to the arbitrator's role as counsel, that arbitrator would have to choose between the arbitrator and counsel appointments.

Similarly, if an arbitrator in the middle of an investment arbitration would like to undertake a counsel role in another investment arbitration, he or she will have to disclose this desire immediately to the parties in the first arbitration. If there is an objection, the arbitrator will have to choose between the two roles.

These proposed practices do not impose an unreasonable burden. If anything, they minimize the risk of challenges to arbitrators while enhancing transparency and trust.

Proper disclosure certainly could be the solution in many situations. There are other situations, however, where disclosure alone cannot be counted on to resolve the issue fairly for both parties. For example, if a party is represented by inexperienced counsel, there is no guarantee that disclosure will trigger proper scrutiny of a potentially conflicted arbitrator. Rules and guidelines should therefore be established to avoid dependence on the parties and their counsel to weed out conflicts.

It is therefore incumbent on investment arbitration institutions (such as ICSID) to take the lead in developing codes of conduct aimed at avoiding conflicts of interest. At a time when challenges to arbitrators are becoming a common feature in investment arbitration, a code of conduct would provide clear guidelines to parties and arbitrators alike. It would bring predictability and consistency to the conduct of arbitration proceedings, and it would help to maintain trust.

Such a code should address questions as diverse as a person serving simultaneously as counsel and as arbitrator in two different cases yet dealing with the same legal issues; a person serving as a member of an ICSID annulment committee while being simultaneously an arbitrator or a counsel in an ICSID arbitration; and more generally issues of problematic relationships between arbitrators and counsel.

It bears noting that the ICSID system provides that in the case of a three-member arbitration tribunal, the two unchallenged arbitrators will normally decide on a challenge brought against the third arbitrator. The deciding arbitrators should have the benefit of detailed guidelines contained in a code of conduct so that they do not instead draw mainly on their own subjective views and personal experiences. Such unguided efforts may, when repeated using different decision-makers, produce an incoherent jurisprudence concerning challenges, or perhaps still worse, one that does not show sufficient respect for fairness and due process."

CRCICA (Mohamed Abdel Raouf)

"It is indeed legitimate for the same individual to appear as counsel in some cases and as arbitrator in other cases. Acquiring experience as counsel in arbitrations is actually the normal path leading to appointments as arbitrator. Arbitral institutions should avoid appointing an arbitrator whose role as arbitrator is likely to serve his or her role as counsel, in particular, when the potential award to be rendered by the arbitrator would serve as a precedent for the case in which he or she acts as counsel."

CAM-CCBC (Frederico José Straube)

"In the Brazilian reality it is not socially acceptable for an arbitrator to work only as an arbitrator and, for him to be nominated, he needs to achieve success as an expert. It is therefore legitimate for him to work as counsel in other cases as well.

Also, considering that arbitrators are appointed in view of their expertise, they must express their positions, not only as counsel, but also as legal experts or professors who offer their opinion, for instance. In fact, if they are not allowed to take positions, they would not inspire the confidence the parties need to appoint an arbitrator.

Actually, the basis of the legitimacy of arbitration is the confidence that the parties have in the expertise of a professional that they will appoint to issue a decision to settle their dispute. It is different from the legitimacy offered by State jurisdiction, where judges are not necessarily experts in a specific area. In view of this observation, it is possible to state that the possibility for an individual to act as an arbitrator and as a counsel does not risk the legitimacy of the cases they decide."

ICDR (Richard Naimark)

"Assuming the question is concerned with related cases or so-called repeat players, this may be problematic for recent cases. Again, disclosure is the antidote."

ICSID (Meg Kinnear)

"The mere fact that an individual acts as counsel in some cases and as arbitrator in other cases does not affect legitimacy in and of itself. The question is whether the overlap in question would lead a reasonable observer, knowing the relevant circumstances, to conclude that the arbitrator/counsel is unable to approach the case with an open mind and unable to exercise independent judgment. If such a concern arises with an institutional appointment, the institution should appoint another candidate. If the concern arises out of a party appointment, the opposing party will have to assess whether a proposal to disqualify would be well-founded."

ICC (John Beechey)

"The question seems to be geared more towards the issues peculiar to investment arbitration, but to the extent that the situation arises in commercial cases, the Court applies its standard disclosure requirements and deals with each matter on a case by case basis."

KLRCA (Sundra Rajoo)

"It is legitimate for an individual to appear as counsel in some cases and as an arbitrator in others. Party autonomy to determine who represents them must prevail, so long as there are no conflicts of interest and those individuals remain impartial. Parties want the best advocates to represent them and institutions want the best arbitrators to preside over their arbitrations. Invariably, these are in many cases the same people. By maintaining a strong

Code of Conduct and ensuring that conflict checks are conducted, independence and impartiality can be protected and the drawbacks of the above situation prevented."

LCIA (Adrian Winstanley)
"There is nothing, in my view, inherently problematic about arbitration practitioners who act sometimes as attorney or advocate and sometimes as arbitrator.

Problems only arise when there are connections that throw up conflicts between the cases in which an individual is appearing in one capacity in one or more of the cases, and in another capacity in others. This, again, is a matter for proper transparency and full disclosure."

PCA (Brooks Daly)
"Subject to requirements of arbitrator independence and impartiality, it is perfectly legitimate for the same individual to act as an arbitrator in some cases and counsel in others."

D. ALLEGED OPAQUENESS

Question 13
To what extent should institutional policy, procedures and policy-making processes be made publicly available?

BCDR (Nassib Ziadé)
"To be perceived as legitimate, procedurally fair and trustworthy, arbitration institutions must exhibit the maximum level of transparency allowed under their rules. The institution's processes must be, and be perceived to be, disciplined and rule-based, and reflecting an ethos of independence, accountability and professionalism.

When called upon to make arbitrator appointments, institutions must have strict, published procedures as well as easily identifiable, merit-based criteria for selection. It will also be helpful, if not necessary, to have access to a large, worldwide pool of talented, independent and available persons from which to draw.

When institutions are called upon to decide on challenges to arbitrators, their decisions ought to be reasoned and made public. Reasoned decisions will enhance public understanding of the process and foster a public expectation of consistent good practices.

As emphasized in the answers to other questions, arbitration institutions should codify and publish their internal procedures as well as their guidelines for their staffs and for the practitioners appearing before them."

CRCICA (Mohamed Abdel Raouf)
"It is extremely important for an arbitral institution to make available to its users its institutional policy, procedures and policy-making processes. This should be done to the extent of ensuring the transparency of the decision-making process without causing unnecessary rigidity. This is particularly relevant when the rules of the institution have not been the subject of an independent commentary."

CAM-CCBC (Frederico José Straube)
"In arbitral institutions, it is possible to observe the same model that is found in most organizations: there is a separation between the institutional matters and the procedures. It is important to keep all the questions related to the procedures, namely, the rules and

criteria, transparent in order to protect legitimacy. However, there are also institutional matters, such as management decisions or long term policies, which do not need to be publicly available."

ICDR (Richard Naimark)

"Generally these things should be available. The problem is that when institutions make decisions on individual matters, advocates sometimes demand to know the policy behind what is essentially a granular, situational decision. And experience has shown that if there is too much specific detail about policy, which generally deals with general contours, difficult parties will try to distort the policy in order to attack or stall the proceedings. So there needs to be a balance between making policy transparent and avoiding creating vulnerabilities in the process."

ICSID (Meg Kinnear)

"Such processes should be made available to the fullest extent necessary to inform and assist the facility user community."

ICC (John Beechey)

"To the extent necessary for the parties fully to understand how the Rules and the institution operate. The 2012 Rules shed light on many procedural aspects that were not fully appreciated by all users previously. Training programmes, conferences and publications serve that purpose as well."

KLRCA (Sundra Rajoo)

"Institutional policy, procedures and policy-making processes ought to be transparent to the point that users can understand the end result and how it was arrived at. Concerning the appointment of arbitrators, for example, it is important for users to know the end decision of the appointing authority and the considerations that went into the making of that decision. At the KLRCA, those considerations include the type and quantum of the claim, the nature of the law involved, the complexity of the matter, and other miscellaneous requirements such as location and language. These considerations are all publicly known. In addition, the full KLRCA Panel of Arbitrators is listed on the KLRCA website, along with the details of each panellist.

Notwithstanding the above, there must be a certain level of privilege maintained concerning the internal workings of the institution. Continuing the above example, it would be counterproductive to make publicly available the list of arbitrators who were considered and why they were or were not selected. The existence of an appointing authority is designed, among other things, to overcome the problem of disagreement between the parties; parties defer to the institution to make decisions on their behalf. Empowering the institution to make those decisions requires confidence in how they carry out their policy, procedures and policy-making processes.

There are additional practical considerations in making institutional procedural processes transparent; efficiency – of both time and cost – being the main one. One of the advantages of arbitrating with the KLRCA is its speed; appointments are usually made in a matter of days. Implementing greater transparency invariably brings with it extra cost and delay, in the way of increased administrative burden. In many instances this does not accord with what the end user wants."

728

LCIA (Adrian Winstanley)

"The LCIA's procedures are publicly available through its rules, schedules of costs, fundholding terms, Court Constitution and the like, which appear on its website and in printed materials.

I do not think matters of policy and policy-making (as I would understand these terms) undertaken by the Boards and Courts of institutions need to or should be made publicly available.

On the other hand, policies such as giving reasoned challenge decisions, or intervening as *amicus* in appropriate cases, or encouraging the new generation of arbitrators through such means as YIAG, should certainly be made publicly available, and they are."

PCA (Brooks Daly)

"To the extent that there is a valid public interest, arbitral institutions should consider making such matters publicly available."

Question 14

Should arbitral institutions have internal protocols governing the way in which their staff deal with confidential information, counsel and arbitrators? Or does this give rise to excessive bureaucracy and create its own difficulties? If so, which?

BCDR (Nassib Ziadé)

"Arbitration institutions need to develop and publish internal codes of conduct applicable to their staffs and organizational practices. It is no substitute to have unwritten rules and policies within the institution, not to mention so-called 'Chinese Walls' that are erected and demolished without anyone in the institution ever hearing a sound. Having institutions develop internal codes is necessary to establish credibility before institutions can credibly enact codes of conduct for users."

CRCICA (Mohamed Abdel Raouf)

"It would be amply sufficient to insert a general provision on confidentiality in the institution's arbitration rules whereby it undertakes to keep confidential all awards and decisions as well as all materials submitted by the parties in the arbitral proceedings not otherwise in the public domain, save and to the extent that disclosure may be required of a party according to a legal duty, to protect or pursue a legal right or to enforce or challenge an award in legal proceedings before a judicial authority.

Introducing internal protocols governing the way in which the staff of arbitral institutions deal with counsel and arbitrators would give rise to excessive bureaucracy and create its own difficulties."

CAM-CCBC (Frederico José Straube)

"I believe that such protocols are extremely important, in order to preserve neutrality and confidentiality. By such statement, I mean that it is necessary not only to keep strict protocols, but, at the same time, that the staff must be continuously trained to deal with confidentiality and not to leak any sort of information from one party to another, to protect neutrality. Another possible practice, which we carry out in CAM-CCBC, is sending satisfaction surveys to the parties to obtain feedback on the quality of the arbitration centre."

ICDR *(Richard Naimark)*
"Absolutely, in contractual arbitration the parties own the process. Arbitral institutions must protect the privacy of the parties in terms of the institution's conduct."

ICSID *(Meg Kinnear)*
"Arbitral institutions should have well-understood policies within the organization so that staff will deal with confidential information, counsel and arbitrators in a consistent and appropriate manner. The ICSID Rules impose an obligation on staff of the Centre to maintain the confidentiality of non-public information, and this is well understood."

ICC *(John Beechey)*
"As a matter of fact, every ICC staff member is bound by a contractual obligation of confidentiality."

KLRCA *(Sundra Rajoo)*
"Confidentiality is treated differently in different jurisdictions. At the KLRCA we endeavour to protect confidentiality in the strongest terms possible, since that is what users in this region desire.

Accordingly, it is of vital importance that all cogs in the arbitration machinery are equipped to handle sensitive information. This includes staff – case counsel and administrative staff dealing with sensitive information, counsel and arbitrators.

Nonetheless, this can be achieved through training and internal procedures rather than excessive bureaucracy. A strong culture and effective training processes ensure that everyone is cognizant of their responsibilities and obligations."

LCIA *(Adrian Winstanley)*
"Arbitral institutions should have such internal protocols, and the LCIA does have such internal protocols. These are not heavily bureaucratic, and parties and their legal representatives, and arbitrators, are entitled to expect such protocols."

PCA *(Brooks Daly)*
"Internal protocols are useful in promoting consistent staff conduct in dealing with these matters."

Question 15
How should arbitral institutions monitor and regulate conflicts of interests between counsel and arbitrators on the one hand and their institutional staff on the other hand?

BCDR *(Nassib Ziadé)*
"Both professional and personal links will inevitably be formed over the years between the different actors in the small field of international arbitration. These links should not prejudice the principles of integrity and impartiality, however, or affect how counsel in arbitration institutions treat parties or their counsel.

Arbitration institutions should regulate potential conflicts of interest arising out of the common situation where a lawyer successively works at an arbitration institution and then an arbitration law firm, or vice versa. The guidelines would regulate staff arrivals from, and departures to, any jobs or other roles that could raise issues of apparent conflicts of interest. They would help to preclude even the appearance of unfair advantage-seeking by

730

staff or other interested parties with whom the staff has close ties. The guidelines would prohibit ex parte communications relating to arbitration cases between staff of the arbitration institutions and parties' counsel, including former colleagues. It is a basic feature of due process that former staff of an arbitration institution who become counsel in law firms should not be allowed to exploit their especially close contacts with the institution and its staff to benefit their clients prejudicially or surreptitiously."

CRCICA *(Mohamed Abdel Raouf)*

"Arbitral institutions are normally capable of monitoring and regulating conflicts of interests between counsel and arbitrators. In addition to general provisions on disclosures and conflicts of interests, institutions would have enough information to make further investigations when necessary, especially with respect to past and present affiliation between the potential arbitrator and the firm representing one of the parties. Raising awareness among new players is also an important means of reducing the number of challenges.

Employment contracts concluded between the arbitral institution and its staff should clearly provide for undertakings on the part of the staff to avoid conflicts of interests in their relationship with counsel and arbitrators not only during the term of such contracts, but also within a reasonable period after the expiry of such term."

CAM-CCBC *(Frederico José Straube)*

"There may be occasional conflicts, but it is difficult to establish, in advance, mechanisms in accordance with every situation. Therefore, the solutions must be reached in concrete situations, finding the best settlement of the problem and at the same time protecting the legitimacy and the efficacy of the procedures."

ICDR *(Richard Naimark)*

"ICDR has a 'no gifts' policy, which extends to meals. If a case manager had a prior personal or working relationship with counsel, party or arbitrator on a case they are removed from any contact with the case."

ICSID *(Meg Kinnear)*

"Arbitral institutions should take appropriate steps to avoid such conflicts. As part of the World Bank Group, ICSID has conflict of interest guidelines and post-employment guidelines."

ICC *(John Beechey)*

"Art. 2 of Appendix II to the ICC Rules contains a number of provisions intended to preclude the participation of any member of the Court or the Secretariat in a case in which he or she may have a conflict of interest with a counsel, an arbitrator or a party itself."

KLRCA *(Sundra Rajoo)*

"Again, this is a matter of internal procedures and training. It is inescapable that staff will have gained experience in firms and worked closely with arbitrators and counsel in other ways. This can give rise to at least the perception of conflicts of interest, with its attached notions of favouritism. This sphere of conflict, however, is not regulated in the same way that conflict between arbitrators and counsel or parties is. Accordingly, it is up to the institution, its management and the staff operating the institution to monitor and implement the proper standards. It is common for institutions to have their own procedures in place for this form of conflict, but since they only apply to administered arbitrations they may never become standardized."

LCIA (Adrian Winstanley)

"As regards conflicts of interest between counsel and arbitrators, I refer to my responses to Questions 11(f) and 11(i).

I cannot immediately recall any occasion on which such conflicts have come into play as between a member of the LCIA's Secretariat and either counsel or arbitrator, so I do not feel qualified to comment on that aspect.

If, however, one were to stretch 'staff' to include members of the LCIA Board and Court, then the following is relevant.

Per my answer to Question 5, the LCIA Board has no active role in the administration of arbitrations, save for those directors who also serve on the Court, of whom there are currently three; one being the Chairman of the Board and another the Director General, both of whom are appointed to the Court *ex officio*. All directors, other than the Director General, are eligible for appointment in LCIA arbitrations on the nomination either of a party or of the Court. The Director General of the LCIA is not permitted to take arbitral appointments, LCIA or others.

Members of the LCIA Court are also eligible for appointment in LCIA arbitrations, but the President is eligible only if jointly nominated by all parties to act either as sole arbitrator or as the presiding arbitrator on a panel of three; a restriction which will extend to the Chairman of the Board under the new rules. Vice Presidents can only be appointed if nominated by a party or the parties. The President or any Vice President nominated as above is precluded from taking any part in the appointment of the tribunal to which (s)he has been nominated and from any other function of the Court relating to the arbitration."

PCA (Brooks Daly)

"The use of appropriate disclosure and ethical walls should be sufficient to regulate any such conflicts."

E.   TRANSPARENCY AND CONFIDENTIALITY OF ARBITRAL PROCEEDINGS

Question 16
Does the confidentiality of arbitral proceedings undermine the legitimacy of international arbitration and the rule of law more broadly?

BCDR (Nassib Ziadé)

"The confidentiality and the secrecy of arbitral proceedings undermine the legitimacy of the system of international arbitration, at least in the eyes of the public and, perhaps more pressingly, those parties and lawyers who do not belong to the exclusive club of arbitration practitioners. Commercial arbitration remains shrouded in mystery and confidentiality extends not only to awards and decisions but also to the mere existence of the cases, the names of the arbitrators, the names of the parties and of the law firms representing them. This is paradoxical when one considers the reporting capabilities of the Internet. And still confidentiality remains an important factor for some parties when opting for commercial arbitration as opposed to resorting to a court system."

CRCICA (Mohamed Abdel Raouf)

"I do not believe that the confidentiality of arbitral proceedings undermines the legitimacy of international arbitration or the rule of law more broadly. It is still regarded as one of the salient features of international commercial arbitration."

CAM-CCBC *(Frederico José Straube)*
"The matters submitted to international arbitration are special cases. The general rule of publicity does not necessarily apply to them. Depending on the matter, confidentiality is necessary to protect the parties or to preserve the neutrality of the tribunal. Also, the purpose of publicity is to avoid opaque judgements and represents the protection of an individual against the State. In international arbitration cases, the entire situation is different: the parties cannot be regarded as disadvantaged and the tribunal is not a sovereign figure capable of oppressing them. Therefore, in most cases, there is not a relationship between confidentiality and lack of legitimacy or violations of the legal order.

Moreover, in many cases submitted to international arbitration, confidentiality is an important element to protect the parties and to avoid undue press exploration, which can cause serious damage to the parties.

However, up to this point, all the ideas expressed concerned international arbitrations among private parties, meaning cases in which there is no relevant public interest involved. In some cases, the State is one of the parties. Therefore the entire syllogism I have been developing cannot be applied, because the matters involving the interest of a State must be made public to the entire society. Therefore, in this specific situation, transparency overlaps the importance of the confidentiality."

ICDR *(Richard Naimark)*
"For contractual arbitration, confidentiality can be an essential attribute of the process. As arbitrators apply applicable law, the rule of law is maintained."

ICSID *(Meg Kinnear)*
Questions 16-18
"With respect to Questions 16-18, ICSID's only mandate is international investment dispute settlement. As a result, ICSID does not have a view on transparency in arbitration other than international investment disputes. As regards international investment arbitration, there is a particular context that warrants enhanced transparency: the disputes involve a government body; they implicate government conduct; they may deal with matters of public interest; and government funds are used to pay litigation expenses and satisfy awards. That context justifies a greater degree of transparency than in a case between two private parties litigating private law issues. ICSID supported enhanced transparency in its 2006 amendments to the ICSID Rules which addressed public hearings, publication of awards, and non-disputing party participation. In addition, ICSID maintains registers detailing each procedural step in a case and these have always been open to the public. It also makes this case-specific information available to the public through its website."

ICC *(John Beechey)*
"It should be noted that, unless otherwise provided under the applicable law or agreed between the parties, ICC arbitration is not confidential per se.

When the arbitration involves private parties, they often agree to keep the proceedings confidential. It is often maintained that confidentiality is an advantage of international arbitration.

In cases involving States, the situation may be different. However, some States have also shown a preference for the proceedings to be confidential."

KLRCA *(Sundra Rajoo)*
"No, the degree of confidentiality in arbitral proceedings is a matter of party autonomy in the selection of the law governing the arbitration agreement. There is a wide range of

degrees of confidentiality exercised according to different jurisdictions. In Sweden, for example, parties must expressly state that an arbitration is to be confidential. Conversely under Malaysian law, arbitrations are prima facie considered confidential. This, if anything, exemplifies that parties have control in determining the degree of confidentiality based on the law governing the arbitration agreement. It is possible that in certain instances confidentiality in proceedings could violate public policy or particular domestic laws such as those relating to security disclosures, but this is rare.

Choosing a governing arbitration law under which arbitration is confidential does not undermine legitimacy for a number of reasons, namely, that this choice is based on party autonomy, which is arguably achieved by the parties carefully selecting a governing law where a salient feature is confidentiality. If anything, this legitimizes arbitration as confidentiality is based on party autonomy.

Confidentiality in relation to rule of law can, in one way, be seen as relevant only to the judiciary, since it plays a role in the development of law. For that reason, case precedents are important. In relation to arbitration, however, the rule of law is more concerned with procedural fairness and natural justice than confidentiality. Arbitration in many ways was developed as a commercially minded tool for the efficient resolution of independent disputes, and in that respect confidentiality is of utmost importance."

LCIA (Adrian Winstanley)

"The LCIA rules provide expressly for the confidentiality of awards and materials in the proceedings created for the purpose of the arbitration, and of all other documents produced by another party in the proceedings not otherwise in the public domain (with certain riders as to disclosure in the case of a legal duty or a legal right).

They also provide that all awards shall be confidential.

However, these provisions are subject to the express contrary written agreement of the parties, and it is difficult to see how confidentiality, thus circumscribed, might undermine the legitimacy of international arbitration, or the rule of law more broadly."

PCA (Brooks Daly)

"No. For some users, confidentiality is an underpinning of the legitimacy of international arbitration, while for others it may reduce legitimacy. These views must be balanced. While the arbitration community is witnessing continually increasing transparency and access to information concerning arbitral proceedings, there are valid reasons for preserving parties' autonomy to choose confidential proceedings without undermining the legitimacy of international arbitration or the rule of law."

Question 17

What, if any, are the justifications for the different approaches of international investment and commercial arbitral institutions to confidentiality?

BCDR (Nassib Ziadé)

"In commercial arbitrations, arbitrators generally interpret private contracts concluded between private parties, consider sets of specific facts, and issue awards of little interest to third parties. Arbitral awards rendered in commercial arbitrations thus remain confidential or are anonymous if published.

Investment arbitration, by contrast, routinely raises fundamental issues of public interest, and the awards rendered may have a serious impact on the State's national budget and the welfare of its citizens. The public thus has a legitimate interest in investment arbitration, and transparency is consequently becoming the norm in investment arbitration.

Investment arbitration, unlike commercial arbitration, frequently turns on the interpretation of investment treaties which contain similar provisions that give rise to a narrow range of recurring legal issues. Although there is no *stare decisis* doctrine in the field of investment arbitration, the publication of investment arbitration awards would address public concerns while also promoting consistency and predictability in the jurisprudence."

CRCICA *(Mohamed Abdel Raouf)*

"Investment arbitrations involve States or State entities, which is not usually the case in normal commercial arbitrations. This would justify the different approaches of international investment and commercial arbitral institutions to confidentiality."

CAM-CCBC *(Frederico José Straube)*

"In fact, in investment arbitrations there are, generally, public interests involved. The same does not apply to international commercial arbitration. If one of the parties is a State, it is important to protect the transparency. Therefore, the approaches concerning confidentiality are not the same for the two cases."

ICDR *(Richard Naimark)*

"Entirely different party context and impacts."

ICC *(John Beechey)*

"In investment arbitration, the outcome of the dispute concerns the people (and, specifically, the taxpayers) of a State, who have the right to be informed of the actions taken by the latter.

In commercial arbitration, there is rarely any public interest at stake, as the case only concerns the parties involved."

KLRCA *(Sundra Rajoo)*

"The justification can be explained due to the differing nature of the disputes. Commercial arbitration is a private dispute between two contracting parties where the stakeholders are generally private parties. Conversely, the stakeholders in treaty arbitration can be seen as including States and the public in general that funds investment arbitrations through taxes. Therefore the parties in whose interest it is to have access to information is much wider.

Additionally, in investment arbitration where disputes are based on treaties, often issues of public policy, legislative regimes, State regulatory measures, as well as the behaviour of public servants and national courts are involved.[22] These issues in treaty arbitration are of economic relations that are in the public sphere as opposed to private. The results of treaty arbitration can directly affect the individuals in a country so these proceedings ought not to be kept confidential. This can be taken even further with regard

---

22. Hans van HOUTTE and Maurizio BRUNETTI, "Investment Arbitration Ten Areas of Caution for Commercial Arbitrators", 29 Arbitration International (LCIA 2013, Issue 4) p. 553 at p. 559 Citing, A COHEN SMUTNY, "Investment Treaty Arbitration and Commercial Arbitration: Are They Different Ball Games? The Actual Conduct' in A. J. VAN DEN BERG, ed., *50 Years of the New York Convention*, ICCA Congress Series no. 14 (Wolters Kluwer 2009) p. 168.

not only to the awards but also to hearings. Canada, the US and Mexico, for example, have stated that they will consent to public hearings in NAFTA cases."[23]

LCIA (Adrian Winstanley)

"The justification for the LCIA's approach to confidentiality in the terms to which I have referred is that the LCIA subscribes to the view of confidentiality as one of the underpinnings of commercial arbitration, but recognizes that the parties may elect for non-confidential arbitration, should they so choose. This, in the LCIA's view provides the appropriate default position of confidentiality, but with scope for the parties to agree otherwise.

I shall leave it to colleagues engaged in investment arbitration to provide such justification as may be required for their approach to confidentiality."

PCA (Brooks Daly)

"Two related justifications for fashioning a distinct approach to international investment arbitration are the involvement of a sovereign State and the magnitude of the stakes typically arbitrated in these disputes. In investor-State arbitration, States may be faced with claims for significant amounts that, if awarded, would have a substantial effect on the finances of the government concerned. As such, these cases engage the public interest to a far greater extent than typical international commercial arbitration proceedings between purely private parties."

Question 18

In what circumstances (if any) should arbitrations other than treaty-based investment arbitration be made public, by default?

BCDR (Nassib Ziadé)

"In some types of arbitration, such as sports arbitration, a coherent corpus of law is being created through arbitral awards. As with investment arbitration, in which legal issues commonly recur, this repetition militates strongly in favor of publication of awards to disseminate useful, if non-binding, precedents.

Some voices have called in recent years for extending to commercial arbitration the regime of investment arbitration, which is to say, the abolition of confidentiality. Of course, nothing prevents parties in commercial arbitration cases from agreeing at the outset that the arbitration awards rendered in their cases will be made public. At a time when confidentiality remains a widely appreciated feature of commercial arbitration, however, it is still premature to posit that the publication of commercial awards should become the default rule.

This does not necessarily mean that the commercial arbitration regime should remain unchanged. It should instead be immediately altered in one respect. In each case, the names of the arbitrators and of the parties' representatives, and, save in the most compelling circumstances, the names of the parties should be made public. The relationships among parties, law firms and arbitrators cannot continue to escape even the minimal control under

---

23. *Id.* p. 561, citing M. KINNEAR, "Transparency and Third Party Participation in Investor-State Dispute Settlement" (ICSID-OECD-UNCTAD Symposium "Making the Most of International Investment Agreements: A Common Agenda", Paris, 12 December 2005 <www.oecd.org/ investment/internationalinvestmentagreements/36979626.pdf>.

the subterfuge that commercial arbitration is confidential. The plea for confidentiality is further weakened by the fact that all details of an arbitration are in any event disclosed when one party tries to enforce or to annul an arbitration award before national courts."

CRCICA (Mohamed Abdel Raouf)
"Arbitrations other than treaty-based investment arbitration should not be made public save and to the extent that disclosure may be required of a party according to a legal duty, to protect or pursue a legal right or to enforce or challenge an award in legal proceedings before a judicial authority."

CAM-CCBC (Frederico José Straube)
"If there is a State or an important governmental entity that is involved in an arbitration to which there is not an applicable international treaty, the rule of the predominance of transparency must be applied by default, due to the grounds on which treaty-based investment arbitrations are made public."

ICDR (Richard Naimark)
"Perhaps some matters where governments are parties. But it is not for institutions to determine."

ICC (John Beechey)
"If the parties agree that the case be made public, they are free to do so. However, the ICC Court can envisage no basis upon which it would propose that arbitrations be made public by default."

KLRCA (Sundra Rajoo)
"The only time that an arbitration should be made public is when the law governing the arbitration stipulates in what if any instances an arbitration is to be made public; this includes considerations of mandatory law or public policy. The KLRCA Arbitration Rules describe these circumstances as instances where disclosure is necessary for purposes of implementation and enforcement or to the extent that disclosure may be required of a party by legal duty, to protect or pursue a legal right or to challenge an award in bona fide legal proceedings before a State court or other judicial authority. There should be no generally applicable exceptions in the commercial context. However, there can be some scenarios in which a confidentiality agreement will be invalid such as under US securities laws reporting obligations.

Ultimately, as mentioned above, the degree of confidentiality varies between jurisdictions, and choosing a seat where arbitration is confidential is a bargained-for consideration. If a party chooses a governing law that does not provide for confidentiality, for example Swedish law, and parties do not agree on confidentiality, then publication is acceptable because of party autonomy to select this governing law."

LCIA (Adrian Winstanley)
"I refer to the responses that I have given to Questions 16 and 17."

PCA (Brooks Daly)
"PCA inter-State arbitrations involving matters such as land or maritime boundaries, natural resources, and the nationality of populations are often considered to involve broad interests justifying public awareness. As such, PCA inter-State arbitrations are generally made public."

F. THE PROPER ROLE OF THE INSTITUTION AND ARBITRATOR DECISION-MAKING

Question 19
"What should be the limits of the role of an arbitral institution? In particular, should it make prima facie assessments of jurisdiction and scrutinize arbitral awards?"

BCDR *(Nassib Ziadé)*
"An arbitral institution should never substitute its own judgment for that of the arbitral tribunal. Nor should the secretariat consider itself to be an additional member of the tribunal. The rules of most arbitration institutions do, however, allow them to perform a screening function at the time at which the arbitration request is received. This is to prevent claims which manifestly lack jurisdiction from wrongly burdening the respondent party.

As to scrutinizing arbitral awards before sending them to the parties, this power is explicitly provided to some arbitration institutions by their rules. Other arbitration institutions wisely perform this role, even in the absence of an explicit rule. In any event, the last word in the drafting of an award belongs to the tribunal which is solely responsible for the award rendered."

CRCICA *(Mohamed Abdel Raouf)*
"In institutional arbitrations, arbitral institutions are expected to make prima facie assessments of jurisdiction. I am not sure whether it would foster the legitimacy of the process if arbitral institutions were to declare their policies in this respect, by indicating for instance that the mere likelihood of an entity being a party to the arbitration agreement, would entail referring the matter to the arbitrators.

As for the scrutiny of arbitral awards, it is very particular to the ICC system and should not be recommended for any other institution not enjoying the same experience and similar resources."

CAM-CCBC *(Frederico José Straube)*
"Considering the costs involved in an arbitration, it is important that the arbitral institution performs a minimal verification before setting an arbitral tribunal. Such verification, however, must adhere strictly to the existence of the conditions for carrying out an arbitration, namely, the presence of an arbitral clause or the agreement of the parties to submit their case to an arbitral tribunal.

Regarding the scrutiny of arbitral awards, I must say that I think it is a practice that subordinates the arbitral tribunal to the institution when, in arbitration, the tribunal must be completely independent. I believe that caring for the quality of the tribunal or Panel, instead of scrutinizing its award, is a more interesting idea to avoid mistakes or errors made by the arbitrators."

ICDR *(Richard Naimark)*
"This question is too broad. Prima facie assessments on the arguable jurisdiction of the institution to proceed are appropriate. ICDR scrutinizes awards for grammar and computational errors and completeness (i.e., all the issues are dealt with). That is the full extent of its scrutiny."

738

ICSID *(Meg Kinnear)*

"Art. 36 of the ICSID Convention requires the Secretary-General to register a request for arbitration unless it is manifestly outside the jurisdiction of the Centre. Once the case is registered, any question of jurisdiction is to be dealt with by the tribunal constituted for the case. This strikes a good balance that allows parties the benefit of tribunal assessment unless the matter is manifestly outside jurisdiction.

With respect to scrutiny of awards, institutions play a very important role in helping the tribunal produce an effective, clear and enforceable award. There is no formal process for scrutiny of the award in the ICSID Convention. However, in practice, the ICSID tribunal Secretary will have attended the hearings and read the documents, and raises with the tribunal any errors or omissions he or she identifies. At the same time, the tribunal has the final word in every award, and the role of the institution is to catch errors or inconsistencies; ICSID does not have a role in determining what is the correct outcome of the case."

ICC *(John Beechey)*

"The prima facie decisions on jurisdiction and the scrutiny of awards are distinguishing features of ICC arbitration.

With regard to the prima facie assessment of jurisdiction, it is the practice of the Court that, save for the most obvious examples of absence of an arbitration agreement, the matter will proceed and any question of jurisdiction will be left for the arbitral tribunal to decide.

With regard to the scrutiny of awards, a unique feature of ICC arbitration that no other institution comes close to emulating, the Court may lay down modifications as to the form of the award and draw the arbitral tribunal's attention to points of substance, without affecting the arbitrators' liberty of decision. The scrutiny exercise involves a full and careful review of every award rendered under the ICC Rules (nearly 500 in 2013)."

KLRCA *(Sundra Rajoo)*

"It is the proper role of the tribunal to determine whether it has prima facie jurisdiction. This determination should be entirely devolved from the institution. If an arbitration is filed with an institution where it is questionable whether jurisdiction exists, that determination is for the arbitrator(s) to make, not for an institution. The agreement of the parties generally is to confer power upon a tribunal as the decision making body and an institutions for its services. This line between provision of services and decision-making should not be blurred by an institution.

Nonetheless, there should be some procedural oversight exercised by the institution to ensure that the correct forum is being used and the correct procedures being employed. This is particularly important concerning multi-tiered clauses. Ensuring that the correct institution has been approached, and that the necessary steps have been taken can avoid wasted time and costs down the line. Of course, it is never for the institution to delve into or determine evidentiary matters; it is sufficient for the institution to obtain a confirmation from the parties. In the case of disagreement the decision-making ought to be left to the tribunal.

As for scrutiny, when parties choose institutional arbitration, they impliedly agree to the services provided to them by these institutions. Prima facie, an institution itself does not itself have a duty to have its arbitrators render an enforceable award. Parties agree to the rules and services of an institution, and scrutiny of an award is one of salient features in some institutions that is bargained for when parties agree on the drafting of an arbitration clause. If parties choose an arbitration institution that offers this scrutiny, then it is that institution's role to scrutinize."

LCIA (Adrian Winstanley)

"The limits of the role of an arbitral institution are those set out in its rules and Constitution, which may be publicly scrutinized.

Whether or not provided for expressly in the rules, an institution (in the LCIA's case, in the person of the LCIA Court) is bound to make a prima facie assessment as to whether, in cases of a lack of clarity, the arbitration agreement invoked by a Claimant gives it jurisdiction over the dispute. This is, however, always subject to the power of the tribunal to determine its own jurisdiction, which cannot be second-guessed or overridden by the institution.

The LCIA is one of the many institutions that does not formally scrutinize arbitral awards. Like many other institutions, however, the LCIA does, at the request of a tribunal, review an award for typographical errors and the like, but never commenting on any point of substance."

PCA (Brooks Daly)

"Prima facie assessment of jurisdiction is an appropriate tool for arbitral institutions. Arbitral jurisdiction is based on consent, and where there is no prima facie evidence of parties' consent to arbitration, constituting a tribunal to examine the case is a waste of resources. With respect to scrutiny of awards, flexibility is a hallmark of arbitral proceedings. The ability to choose procedural options providing for award scrutiny is thus a matter best determined through party autonomy."

Question 20
What role should an arbitral institution have in ensuring that arbitrators produce satisfactory and prompt awards? Should arbitrators be held accountable by the institution for their failure to do so? If so, how?

BCDR (Nassib Ziadé)

"Arbitration institutions need to ensure that the awards rendered by arbitrators contain adequate and coherent reasoning, whatever the nature of the views expressed.

Arbitration institutions must take an even more active role in ensuring that arbitral awards are produced promptly in conformity with due process. When appointing arbitrators, arbitration institutions should avoid turning to arbitrators, no matter how experienced they may be, if the institutions have substantial reason to believe that the arbitration proceeding may be delayed due to the arbitrators' unavailability or apparent over-commitment. Likewise, during the proceeding, the arbitration institution must call to the arbitrators' attention any unacceptable delays in producing work or moving the case forward. Unjustified delays should lead to an avoidance of the offending arbitrator in future appointment processes, and arguably to a notice of the negative experience to sister institutions."

CRCICA (Mohamed Abdel Raouf)

"The strict application of the institutional rules and providing the arbitrators with checklists covering the matters that should be included in the arbitral award would contribute to satisfactory and prompt awards.

One would wonder whether arbitral institutions should have any role in drafting arbitral awards, by summarizing the procedural background, determining the disputed issues and/or providing the arbitrators with relevant precedents.

Arbitrators should be held accountable only to the parties for their failure."

CAM-CCBC (Frederico José Straube)

"An arbitral institution must commit to the quality of the awards and respect the duration of the procedure. If there is in the structure of the arbitral institution a General Secretariat, this organ can exercise oversight of the procedures in order to avoid unjustified delays of the arbitrators and counsels. Another possible solution is to establish a chronology of payment of arbitral fees according to the accomplishment of the main events of the procedure, saving the most substantial part for after the issuance of the award. An extreme penalty for arbitrators is exclusion from the Roster of Arbitrators, if it exists. However, this last mechanism to which I have referred must be provided for in the rules of the institution."

ICDR (Richard Naimark)

"Ensuring timeliness is an important role for the institution. Failure to provide timely awards is reason for removal from the roster of arbitrators."

ICSID (Meg Kinnear)

"As noted above, arbitral institutions play a useful role in helping to ensure an enforceable award is rendered. They can also play an important role in trying to ensure an award is rendered promptly. ICSID has been very conscientious in tracking the time for each step in a case and encouraging arbitrators to make timely decisions.

Institutions consider an arbitrator's availability and record of timeliness when appointing and this builds in accountability. Parties should do likewise when making appointments. Finally, arbitrators must consider timeliness when accepting appointments."

ICC (John Beechey)

"The Court and the Secretariat take an active role in this area. They monitor closely the case, providing assistance and guidance to the arbitrators when requested to do so, and encouraging the arbitrators to comply with the given time limits. For instance, arbitrators must inform the ICC Court and the parties when the draft award is likely to be submitted (the 'rule of thumb' being three months from the last submission).

The conduct of the case by the arbitrators and the quality of the awards rendered are taken into account by the Court when fixing fees and when considering an arbitrator for future appointment."

KLRCA (Sundra Rajoo)

"An institution's formal role regarding satisfactory and prompt awards is defined by that institution's rules. Institutions should use a guiding hand with an arbitrator to ensure that awards are rendered within the time frame set out in the institution's rules; under the KLRCA Rules this is three months from the close of submissions.[24] Extensions for arbitrators should be given sparingly; under the KLRCA Rules, the parties must consent to any extension in consultation with the Director of the KLRCA.[25]

It is important to distinguish between administering the procedure of an arbitration and affecting the decision-making process. The KLRCA, in doing so, provides arbitrators at the outset of proceedings with a guidance note specifying the expectations of the arbitrator in relation to the drafting of the award. We will not, however, interfere with the actual drafting of the award itself.

---

24. Rule 11.1.
25. Rule 11.2.

If an arbitrator does not comply with the rules on timelines or the standards expected in drafting an award, this will affect their standing as an arbitrator. This will inevitably affect their ability to obtain future appointments, and in some cases will result in their removal or non-renewal as a KLRCA panellist. The KLRCA maintains its panel according to a three-year term, allowing review of arbitrators over that period.

Despite the fact that the KLRCA Rules do not impose a direct duty on an arbitrator to render an award that is enforceable, no institution would appoint an arbitrator who has a poor track record in rendering enforceable awards. The reputation of the centre is on the line as well as that of the arbitrator."

LCIA (Adrian Winstanley)

"Arbitral institutions have an important role in ensuring that tribunals appointed by them produce prompt awards.

As to whether these awards may be said to be *'satisfactory'* is another matter, and may depend upon the parties' view of the outcome. That said, the LCIA rules provide expressly that the LCIA Court, the tribunal and the parties shall make every reasonable effort to ensure that an award is legally enforceable.

In the event that an arbitrator fails to produce an award in timely fashion, despite the routine prompting of the parties and of the Secretariat, the LCIA Court may, *in extremis*, deem that arbitrator unfit and remove him or her, with the option of applying a sanction in respect of fees and expenses due."

PCA (Brooks Daly)

"Institutions should monitor the timing of awards. When they are so charged, they must also check awards for completeness before the notification of awards to parties. Arbitrators should be held accountable for failure to produce prompt awards; in this regard, institutions may take into account the arbitrator's performance when considering the level of arbitrator fees to be paid in a specific case and the possibility of future appointments."

G.   COSTS

Question 21
To what extent should arbitral institutions review the fees and costs of arbitrators?

BCDR (Nassib Ziadé)

"The fees and expenses of arbitrators generally far surpass those of arbitration institutions, and make up a significant portion of the total cost of the case (though they remain generally much lower than the fees and expenses of counsel). Arbitration institutions therefore clearly have a duty towards the parties to carefully review the arbitrators' fees and expenses.

Each arbitration institution should maintain and regularly review and update financial regulations governing arbitrators' expenses. Only reasonable and directly relevant expenses should be reimbursed, while exorbitant or undocumented expenses should generally be refused even if this discomfits the refusing institution.

With respect to reviewing fees, there is a distinction to be made between institutions which calculate arbitrators' fees according to the amount in dispute, and those which reimburse arbitrators depending on the number of days or hours worked on the case.

In the former case, an institution can do little except in the case of a settlement, at which point the arbitrators' fees must be determined based on all the circumstances of the case. In the latter case which focuses on time spent, the institution has a duty to review still more thoroughly the fees submitted by the arbitrators and to root out apparent errors or inflated fees."

CRCICA *(Mohamed Abdel Raouf)*

"Arbitral institutions should maintain the general rule according to which the arbitrators' fees shall be paid upon delivery of the award. Partial payment of the fees should be justified and based on real progress of the proceedings. No increase in the fees should be allowed except in very exceptional circumstances.

If an order is issued by the arbitral tribunal, before the final award is made, to terminate the proceedings, the institution should finally determine the costs of the arbitration having regard to when the arbitral tribunal terminated the proceedings, the work performed by the arbitral tribunal and other relevant circumstances.

The institution, in consultation with the remaining arbitrators, should determine the fees of the arbitrator who dies after accepting his or her appointment and before rendering the award, having regard to the work he or she has performed and all other relevant circumstances.

The arbitrator who is removed or successfully challenged should not be entitled to any fees.

Arbitral institutions should also review the arbitrators' expenses to the fullest extent possible. Transparent notes on the reimbursement of such expenses would be extremely helpful."

CAM-CCBC *(Frederico José Straube)*

"Considering that an arbitral institution must offer some certainty and predictability, it must satisfy standards of quality and make it possible for the parties to know how much they will spend during an arbitral procedure. Therefore, the fees and costs of arbitrators must be the same for every arbitrator, related to the number of hours spent and to the value in dispute."

ICDR *(Richard Naimark)*

"We require itemization of charges and will have a discussion with an arbitrator who appears to have presented a bill that is far outside the norm. We also require that arbitrators charge only for items/categories listed on their résumé from which the parties make arbitrator selections. Surprise or unlisted charges are challenged."

ICSID *(Meg Kinnear)*

"Arbitral institutions should review the fees and costs of arbitrators to ensure the invoices submitted are consistent with the fee and cost framework agreed to by the parties and that they reflect a reasonable number of hours given the demands of the case."

ICC *(John Beechey)*

"The Court does not formally 'review' arbitrators' fees. In fixing arbitrators' fees, the Court considers carefully whether the case was conducted efficiently or otherwise and whether the expenses charged are reasonable."

KLRCA *(Sundra Rajoo)*

"The KLRCA Rules provide a Schedule of Fees with a lump sum scale based on the amount in dispute, and specific guidelines regarding costs and expenses of the arbitral tribunal.

Usually the scale fees are used, however under the Rules the tribunal is also free to agree on a separate arrangement with the parties.[26]

Given that set-up, it is only through proactive agreement that fees outside of the scale will be incurred. Accordingly, it is only in exceptional circumstances that the institution should be allowed to review.

The situation in relation to costs and disbursements is quite different. Given the lack of control or certainty over expenses such as accommodation and air transfers, guidelines must be followed and a strict review process put in place. This is achieved through set per diem amounts and calling for receipts. In this way fairness to the user can be ensured while protecting the arbitrator."

LCIA *(Adrian Winstanley)*

"It is an important function of an arbitral institution to seek to moderate the costs of arbitration. The LCIA, being an institution operating by time-based charges, is particularly concerned to ensure that these are reasonable.

Parties may call for financial summaries at any time, to keep track of costs. Every payment on account of arbitrators' fees will be notified in advance and accounted for on disbursement.

It is the LCIA Court which, under the rules, must determine the costs of each arbitration, according to the following procedure.

The Secretariat provides the Court with a financial dossier, which includes a complete financial summary of sums lodged by the parties, sums paid to the arbitrators, outstanding fees and expenses and interest accrued. The dossier also includes a copy of the original confirmation to the parties of the arbitrator's fee rate, a copy of the arbitrator's accounts, a copy of the LCIA's own time and disbursements ledger, a copy of directions for deposits and a copy of all notices given to the parties of payments made from deposits.

The Court reviews the dossier and, if necessary, calls for any further information, or initiates any investigation it may require to satisfy itself that the costs are reasonable and are in accordance with the LCIA schedule of costs, before notifying the Secretariat of the amount to be notified to the tribunal for inclusion in the award.

Any dispute regarding administrative charges or the fees and expenses of the tribunal is determined by the LCIA Court."

PCA *(Brooks Daly)*

"Arbitral institutions should review and make determinations concerning the reasonableness of arbitrator fees and other costs. This adds legitimacy to the arbitral process. Because parties awaiting a tribunal's decision are not in an appropriate position to dispute these fees and costs, this role is most appropriately fulfilled by the institution."

Question 22
Would a default position as to the allocation of costs be appropriate, in your view, to provide predictability for the users of the system?

BCDR *(Nassib Ziadé)*

"Allocating costs under a default rule may provide predictability. If it is too rigid, however, it may prevent the arbitrators from properly taking into account the conduct of the parties

---

26. Rule 12.4.

and their counsel throughout the arbitration proceedings when allocating costs. A default rule for allocation would be appropriate only if it allowed enough flexibility for the arbitrators to sanction poor conduct by the parties or their counsel."

CRCICA (Mohamed Abdel Raouf)

"A default position as to the allocation of costs would be appropriate and would contribute to more predictability for the users of the system.

The institutions' rules could, for instance, state that the costs of the arbitration shall in principle be borne by the unsuccessful party and that the arbitral tribunal may, however, apportion the costs between the parties if it determines that apportionment is reasonable, taking into account the circumstances of the case."

CAM-CCBC (Frederico José Straube)

"A default position as to the allocation of costs allows the parties to decide the main lines for an arbitral tribunal that best fits their case: for instance, the decision between a tribunal composed of a single arbitrator or of three arbitrators. The parties need to know the costs of each possibility before committing to an arbitral clause. The same applies to the costs associated with the structure and fees, among many other examples. Otherwise, the parties risk establishing an arbitral clause in which settling the dispute becomes more expensive than the values in dispute. Such a situation is bad for arbitration as an institution, since the parties will consider it too expensive and probably criticize it."

ICDR (Richard Naimark)

"Probably not, but there does seem to be some reticence by some arbitrators to make an allocation. This seems to be heavily influenced by the original legal tradition of the arbitrator."

ICSID (Meg Kinnear)

"While a default costs mechanism might provide predictability, it detracts from flexibility to exercise discretion based on the particular circumstances of the case. Both positions have advantages and disadvantages."

ICC (John Beechey)

"The ability of ICC arbitrators to exercise their discretion in allocating costs at the end of the proceedings, taking into account the way in which the parties have conducted the case, is a necessary tool to prevent abuses of the arbitral system."

KLRCA (Sundra Rajoo)

"A default position works perfectly well in capping or providing an indication of the costs and also in setting the standards/trend of what are reasonable fees or costs. The KLRCA goes so far as to provide a fee calculator on its website to promote predictability in relation to costs of the arbitration.

There do exist, however, situations in which the default position is not appropriate. In the event of a grossly inflated claim or counterclaim, the default position of sharing costs equally may not yield a just outcome. It may, on the contrary, represent oppressive conduct. This has been overcome in the Rules by providing the Director with the discretion to apportion costs according to the claim and/or counterclaim.

Maintaining a default position ultimately does ensure consistency and predictability, and is the most appropriate commercial approach."

LCIA (Adrian Winstanley)
"The allocation of costs among the members of a tribunal is not applicable in the case of the time-based charges operated by the LCIA."

PCA (Brooks Daly)
"A default position on this point is appropriate as long as discretion remains with the tribunal. There is such diversity of circumstances in international arbitration that tribunals need this discretion in the allocation of costs. The PCA considers that an appropriate default position allocates the costs of arbitration to the unsuccessful party or parties, while preserving the tribunal's general discretion."[27]

H.   INSTITUTIONAL RULES AND REGULATION

Question 23
How should institutions participate, if at all, in the ethical regulation of arbitrators' and counsel's conduct, including in the imposition of sanctions for breach of duties?

BCDR (Nassib Ziadé)
"There exist today a number of instruments, such as the IBA Guidelines on Conflicts of Interest in International Arbitration and the IBA Guidelines on Party Representation in International Arbitration, which provide directions for the regulation of arbitrators' and counsel's conduct. The IBA Guidelines are helpful, but it is widely known that the vast majority of the subcommittee members who drafted the Guidelines are themselves none other than arbitration practitioners who are to be regulated. In other words, the IBA Guidelines represent best practices as these are perceived from the established practitioners' point of view, so they are more enabling than restricting.

It is therefore incumbent on arbitration institutions to adopt codes of conduct (or 'Practice Directions' to use the formulation of the International Court of Justice) which will apply to arbitrators and counsel, and which will impose necessary discipline on the larger system. Before arbitration institutions adopt such codes or practice directions either individually or jointly, however, they would do well to consult with a variety of stakeholders and experts, including arbitration practitioners.

If heads of arbitration institutions do not feel that it is within their duties to regulate the conduct of arbitration professionals working through their institutions, one may wonder what their true function is. It may be glamorous to tour the world attending arbitration conferences and discussing ethics in the abstract, but is this what the users or the public expect?"

CRCICA (Mohamed Abdel Raouf)
"This should be done under the umbrella of IFCAI. Arbitral institutions ought to consult other stakeholders including arbitrators, counsel and users before introducing any provisions/sanctions in this respect. Arbitral institutions, whether individually or through the IFCAI, should try to liaise with other entities like the IBA while preparing ethical regulations of arbitrators' and counsel's conduct."

---

27. See PCA Arbitration Rules (2012), Art. 42.

CAM-CCBC *(Frederico José Straube)*

"It is important for arbitral institutions to preserve strict ethical regulations and also to enact a code of ethics composed of the main rules of conduct for all the people involved in the arbitration, meaning not only arbitrators and staff, but also parties and counsel, in order to preserve not only their reputation, but the legitimacy of institutional arbitration as a concept. One of the advantages for the parties of choosing an institutional arbitration, instead of carrying out an "ad hoc" proceeding, is the security that an institution will provide. Institutions must therefore be concerned with every detail regarding the quality of the award, the delay for the arbitrators to issue a decision and its legitimacy."

ICDR *(Richard Naimark)*

"Sanctions are not viable vis à vis counsel on a case. Arbitrator misconduct risks removal from a roster. Codes of Ethics and Conduct are important."

ICSID *(Meg Kinnear)*

"Realistically, institutions do not have jurisdiction to regulate professional conduct of counsel or arbitrators. This is a matter for domestic Bar rules. However, institutions may take steps if there is an ethical breach, for example by disclosing the relevant facts to the parties and the tribunal."

ICC *(John Beechey)*

"The role of institutions should be limited to the administration of cases. It is not for the institutions to exercise a disciplinary function in respect of an arbitrator's (much less counsel's) ethical conduct.

That said, unethical conduct by an arbitrator will be taken into account by the Court when fixing fees, and it could even trigger replacement proceedings or the non-appointment of the individual concerned in future cases."

KLRCA *(Sundra Rajoo)*

"This can be a particularly problematic issue as ethical guidelines from various legal backgrounds clash, resulting in no universal ethical code. One approach to take to this issue is to regulate lawyers by the ethical regulations of their home jurisdiction.[28] This has a serious drawback, namely that lawyers may not be able to undertake the same activities as their opponents, putting them at a disadvantage. For example, English solicitors may not coach witnesses. Overall, as an international arbitration tribunal may have little connection to the seat itself, it is not ideal to apply local professional conduct rules.[29] The approach to regulate conduct is to adopt an international standard. Doing so would ensure everyone is on the same playing field."[30]

An arbitration institution could participate in ethical regulation by encouraging parties to adopt guidelines. As for sanctions, this is much simpler regarding parties, as sanctions can be imposed by a tribunal through procedural orders in cases of gross misconduct. As for guidelines and the imposition of sanctions on arbitrators, all arbitrators must sign a statement of independence, which is considered a statutory declaration, under which legal sanctions are imposed on those arbitrators who are in breach. From an institutional

---

28. GARY BORN, *International Commercial Arbitration* (2009) at pp. 2316-2317.
29. *Ibid.*, at p. 2317 Citing ABA Model Rules of Professional Conduct, Rule 8.5.
30. *Ibid.*, at p. 2318.

standpoint, one of the best methods to take is to implement codes of conduct and remove the arbitrator from the panel in the event such codes are not observed.

LCIA (Adrian Winstanley)

"The draft of the new LCIA rules, due to be published later in 2014, but as yet not signed off by the LCIA Court, currently includes express references to the conduct of parties' legal representatives.

I must leave it until a time when the new rules become public to comment further."

PCA (Brooks Daly)

"This subject has been a matter of some debate in the international arbitration community in recent years. Should an arbitral institution become aware of unethical conduct on the part of any lawyer, it should of course affect that lawyer's chances of receiving an arbitral appointment by that institution. To the extent that any unethical behavior may also affect an arbitrator's appearance of impartiality or independence, it may provide grounds for the institution to accept a challenge to that arbitrator.

While administering institutions may consider further regulation or sanctions, for the time being, greater guidance is being provided by organizations such as the CIArb,[31] the IBA[32] and ICCA,[33] the last of which has been instrumental in fostering conversation on this subject."

I.   EVALUATION

Question 24
How should arbitral institutions measure their own performance and contribution to the legitimacy of the system? What measure or mechanism does your institution use to measure its legitimacy, if any?

BCDR (Nassib Ziadé)

"Arbitral institutions can and do measure their own performance with respect to administrative timeliness, cost effectiveness and neutrality. To do this, they use statistics, user surveys and informal meetings and dialogue sessions with their users. These measurements should be used as a means to improve service delivery and to enhance the acceptability and legitimacy of the system.

Although it is difficult if not impossible to measure scientifically an institution's contribution to the legitimacy of the arbitration system as a whole, particularly as the notion of legitimacy is itself an abstract and subjective concept, institutions can develop and implement best practices under the guidance of their governing boards."

CRCICA (Mohamed Abdel Raouf)

"Conducting surveys to assess the quality of their services is the normal means of measuring the arbitral institutions' performance and would contribute to the legitimacy of the system.

---

31. See CIArb Code of Professional and Ethical Conduct for Members (2009).
32. See IBA Principles on Conduct for the Legal Profession (2011).
33. See D. BISHOP, "Advocacy and Ethics in International Arbitration", Keynote Address, ICCA 20th Congress, Rio de Janeiro, 23-26 May 2010 in *Arbitration Advocacy in Changing Times*, ICCA Congress Series no. 15 (2011) pp. 383-421.

Publishing and analyzing statistics covering their caseload, types of disputes, nationalities of the parties, arbitrators and counsel as well as the sums in dispute would also help to measure the legitimacy of arbitral institutions.

In spite of the inherent difficulties, arbitral institutions should also exert additional efforts in monitoring the enforcement and the setting aside of awards rendered under their auspices."

CAM-CCBC (Frederico José Straube)

"It is difficult to establish a method for measuring performance. At the CAM-CCBC we have adopted the rules of ISO 9001, which is a well-known international certification, in order to have a guideline. In this scenario, conformity with a serious list of protocols and the satisfaction of the parties are important tools for constantly checking our work. On the other hand, it is more difficult to verify our contribution to the legitimacy of the system. Considering that we are pioneers as an arbitral institution in Brazil, we have, since our formation in 1979, started to promote arbitration as an adequate institution to settle disputes and to develop the culture of this institution in our country. More recently, as a national centre which seeks to be known and recognized abroad, we decided to include arbitrators from different nationalities in our Roster. In view of these reasons, it is possible to state that CAM-CCBC has contributed to legitimate arbitration in Brazil and in Latin America."

ICDR (Richard Naimark)

"Constant feedback, paying attention to complaints, keeping current on the 'issue du jour' at conferences, monitoring arbitrators and staff, heavy input from legal department, statistical performance including time to award and settlement through mediation."

ICSID (Meg Kinnear)

"Arbitral institutions have a variety of mechanisms to measure the extent to which their service meets the demands of facility users and thus contributes to the legitimacy of the system. There are formal tracking measures such as timeliness, consistency, and the like. In addition, institutions obtain much valuable informal feedback from parties, counsel and arbitrators. ICSID relies both on formal tracking under its case management systems and on informal feedback."

ICC (John Beechey)

"The best way to ensure legitimacy is to remain an autonomous and financially independent institution, with no links with any government or private sponsors."

KLRCA (Sundra Rajoo)

"Related to the answers given in Question 10 above, one indicator is that parties use a centre and continue to use that centre. This of course goes beyond the marketing of the use of a model arbitration clause. This should include users of all services provided by a centre, particularly as the KLRCA provides a wide range of dispute resolution services in addition to the administration of arbitrations. For example, the KLRCA is heavily involved in the promotion and administration of mediation and statutory adjudication.

Centres can also measure their own performance by what they add to the general sphere of international arbitration and dispute resolution services, for example, creation of emergency arbitration provisions, the i-Arbitration Rules or participating in other initiatives such as the Asian Domain Name Dispute Resolution Centre and other regional initiatives. All of these are contributions a centre can make to international arbitration generally."

LCIA (Adrian Winstanley)

"I suspect that the best measure of an institution's performance and contribution to the legitimacy of the system is by reference to the confidence placed in the institution as demonstrated by a steady or increasing caseload.

As to measures and mechanisms, I refer to my previous responses."

PCA (Brooks Daly)

"An arbitral institution should engage to the greatest extent possible with arbitration users and potential users in order to understand their perception of the institution's working methods. Highlighting the important role of direct communication with these users, the PCA staff is in constant contact with arbitrators and counsel regarding their satisfaction with PCA services. The PCA considers and, where appropriate, implements their suggestions concerning the improvement of these services."

Question 25

To what extent do you engage with the users of your arbitral institution to ensure that your processes are adapted towards their needs and expectations?

BCDR (Nassib Ziadé)

"I have been at the helm of three international arbitration institutions over the last seven years. Engaging with the users of these institutions, including arbitrators, parties and counsel, has been an integral part of my job at each institution. This engagement is constant and multifaceted, both in respect of specific cases and more general and systemic issues.

The head of an arbitration institution should be easily reachable by users should complications arise in the course of cases. The head of the institution should be able to distinguish immediately between legitimate complaints requiring an immediate response, such as an alleged lack of neutrality on the part of a case manager, or unresponsiveness on the part of an arbitration tribunal, and frivolous claims. In addition, before an arbitral award is rendered, an arbitration institution would do well to circulate to the parties and their representatives a detailed questionnaire on the performance of both the arbitration institution and the arbitral tribunal throughout the proceedings.

With respect to systemic issues, the head of an arbitration institution needs to communicate with users of the system in order to seek their feedback and suggestions for improvement. If an arbitration institution is considering revising its own rules and processes, categories of users should be involved either actively as part of the reviewing committee or indirectly through feedback and comments."

CRCICA (Mohamed Abdel Raouf)

"Users of CRCICA are directly involved and frequently consulted in order to assess their needs and expectations. Regular meetings and roundtables are conducted with the users, who are also represented on the Centre's Board of Trustees and Advisory Committee.

Drafts of any new rules or amendments are communicated to the users for their comments in addition to being made available on the Centre's website.

The Centre regrets, however, that to date it has not managed to fulfil a long-time goal of appointing a corporate counsel to its Board of Trustees and hopes to be able to do this soon."

CAM-CCBC *(Frederico José Straube)*

"As previously mentioned, the CAM-CCBC sends satisfaction surveys to the parties to verify whether our processes and structure are adapted to their needs. Another mechanism developed by CAM-CCBC is the creation of Commissions in specific subject areas. The Commissions are an environment where experts of specific area can debate the flaws of arbitration from the perspective of a third party and the discussions can help us to adapt continuously in order to provide better services."

ICDR *(Richard Naimark)*

"A great deal, including with companies, attorneys, arbitrators and mediators, from many countries around the world. We constantly seek feedback from parties, counsel, arbitrators, governments and advisory groups assembled for this purpose. This is how institutions improve and evolve and how the arbitration process will continue to advance."

ICSID *(Meg Kinnear)*

"We constantly engage with facility users to ensure the process meets their needs and expectations. This includes meeting with tribunals during hearings, speaking with counsel after cases are decided, making public presentations and the like. We have an open door policy asking for feedback, and we receive a lot of very useful commentary."

ICC *(John Beechey)*

"The process adopted for the revision of the 2012 Rules is a clear example of the ICC Court's commitment to its users and it demonstrated how seriously the ICC Court took into account their needs (composition of drafting Sub-Committee, ICC Commission, consultation of National Committees)."

KLRCA *(Sundra Rajoo)*

"The KLRCA records enquiries, input and suggestions received from the industry and users during talks, conferences and seminars. Our staff are also trained to receive enquiries in person or by electronic or other means, and to generally be able to disseminate knowledge and expertise regarding arbitration and arbitration practice. In these ways we ensure broad exposure to our end users, making ourselves as approachable and useful as possible. As a regional centre, our responsibilities are not only commercial: we provide services to the AALCO constituency and to the Asian community generally. We then assimilate that exposure and information to ensure that we implement best practices within our rules and products."

LCIA *(Adrian Winstanley)*

"The LCIA has six long-established Users' Councils, being the African Council; the Arab Council; the Asia Pacific Council; the European Council; the Latin American and Caribbean Council; and the North American Council.

The Constitution of the LCIA Users' Councils, which is available online and in our printed materials, includes the following aims and objectives.

'To establish, foster and maintain links between the LCIA and users, and prospective users, of its services, to enable the LCIA to ensure that the arbitration and ADR services it provides to its users worldwide are relevant, cost effective, efficient and consistent with current best practice.

Through conferences, meetings, publications and personal contacts, to instil in members of the Users' Councils, and others, confidence in the LCIA's arbitration

751

and ADR services, such that, whenever appropriate, they adopt, or recommend the adoption of, LCIA dispute resolution clauses.'

The Users' Councils, then, are one important means by which the LCIA engages with its users and potential users. Other important means include the LCIA's worldwide programme of conferences, and the seminars undertaken by YIAG, to which I have referred previously."

PCA (Brooks Daly)

"As discussed in response to the immediately preceding question, this is a primary means through which the PCA measures its legitimacy, and through which it assures that its processes are adapted to arbitration users' needs and expectations."

B. Justice Stream

3. Treaty Arbitration: Is the Playing Field Level and Who Decides Whether It Is Anyway?

Treaty Arbitration: Is the Playing Field Level and Who Decides Whether It Is Anyway?

*Catherine M. Amirfar**

I. INTRODUCTION

From the standpoint of sheer use, the success of the system of investment protection is unquestionable. In the last quarter-century we have seen a remarkable explosion in the number of bilateral investment treaties (BITs) and other regional treaties containing investment protection clauses. At the end of 2012, UNCTAD reports, there were 2,857 BITs in existence,[1] up from 385 at the end of 1989.[2] Some states, including Germany and China, are parties to a phenomenal number of BITs – over 100 each.[3]

BITs often contain a dispute settlement mechanism,[4] in case a foreign investor and a state have a dispute with respect to whether the protection standards have been met in a particular case. The system of investor-state dispute settlement (ISDS) allows a foreign investor and a state to resort to international arbitration to resolve their dispute. To date,

---

* Currently serving as the Counselor on International Law to the Legal Adviser in the US State Department; former Partner, International Disputes Resolution Group, Debevoise & Plimpton LLP.

    The author would like to thank Terra Gearhart-Serna and Berglind Halldorsdottir Birkland, attorneys in Debevoise & Plimpton LLP's international dispute resolution group, for their invaluable assistance with this article.

1. UNCTAD, *World Investment Report 2013*, at p. xix. Although the rate at which new BITs are being signed is down (20 new BITs were signed in 2012, compared to an annual rate of 200 in the mid-1990s), this appears to be due, at least in part, to a shift in favor of regional agreements. Eight new regional investment agreements were concluded in 2012 and at least 110 countries were involved in negotiations for 22 additional regional agreements in 2013. *Id.* at pp. 101-103.

2. UNCTAD, *Bilateral Investment Treaties 1959-1999*, at p. 1, Figure 1 (2000).

3. UNCTAD reports that, at the end of 2012, Germany and China were party to 136 and 128 BITs respectively. UNCTAD, *World Investment Report 2013*, Annex Table III.2. Egypt, France, Switzerland and the United Kingdom also belong to the 100+ club. *Id.*

4. OECD, *Dispute Settlement Provisions in International Investment Agreements: A Large Sample Survey* (2012), at p. 5, available at <www.oecd.org/daf/inv/internationalinvestmentagreements/50291678.pdf> (analyzing a sample of 1,660 BITs and other investment agreements and finding that ninety-three percent of the instruments surveyed provided for international arbitration).

over 500 international investment arbitrations have been initiated under investment treaties,[5] 58 of them in 2012 alone.[6] Fifty of these cases were registered at the International Centre for Settlement of Investment Disputes (ICSID), bringing the total number of ICSID cases to 419.[7]

This boom has been accompanied by equally remarkable growth in foreign direct investment (FDI), which has seen a steep upward trend since the late 1980s.[8] Global FDI inflows rose by 11% in 2013, to an estimated US$ 1.46 trillion – a level comparable to the pre-crisis average,[9] and more than six times what it was in 1990.[10] FDI flows to developed countries remained at a historically low share of global total FDI flows (39%) for the second consecutive year.[11] FDI flows to developing economies reached a new high of US$ 759 billion, accounting for 52% of global FDI inflows in 2013.[12]

It is in the context of these trends that we must consider the dissenting voices decrying the fairness of ISDS. This paper will address from the investor's perspective the current criticisms of the system, particularly from states who characterize it as unjust. This paper will examine the primary perceptions (and misperceptions) of the treaty system and their legitimacy based on the existing empirical evidence.

II.   TWO STRUCTURAL CRITICISMS OF INVESTMENT TREATY ARBITRATION

In this section, I will consider two broad categories of criticism, both alleging that the playing field favors investors. The first centers on what I will refer to as the question of the "unfair bargain", and argues that the current unfairness of the system is linked to its *origins*, namely because the system was imposed on developing states by developed states. The second focuses on how ISDS functions *in practice*, arguing that the dispute resolution process itself is biased in favor of investors.

For the reasons I discuss below, both criticisms appear misplaced.

---

5. The total number of known treaty-based cases is 514. UNCTAD, "IIA Issues Note: Recent Developments in Investor-State Dispute Settlement (ISDS)" (May 2013, no.1) at p. 3. Because of the number of unreported cases, the actual number is likely much higher.

6. *Id.* at p. 2; UNCTAD, *World Investment Report 2013*, at p. xxi.

7. ICSID, *The ICSID Caseload – Statistics* (Issue 2013-1) at p. 7. An additional forty cases were registered at ICSID in 2013. ICSID, *The ICSID Caseload – Statistics* (Issue 2014-1).

8. UNCTAD, OECD and the World Bank each track FDI data and make it available online at <unctadstat.unctad.org>, <stats.oecd.org> and <data.worldbank.org>.

9. UNCTAD, Global Investment Trend Monitor (28 January 2014, Issue No. 15).

10. According to figures available at <unctadstat.unctad.org>.

11. UNCTAD, supra fn. 9. FDI flows to developed countries increased by 12% to US$ 576 billion, but only to 44% of their peak value in 2007. FDI to the European Union (EU) increased, while flows to the United States continued their decline. *Id.*

12. *Id.* At the regional level, flows to Latin America and the Caribbean and Africa were up and developing Asia remained the largest host region in the world. *Id.*

1.   An Unfair Bargain?

The complaint that ISDS is a device imposed by powerful states on weaker states is not new. Examples persist of representatives of developing states taking the position that the state was misled into signing BITs. On one occasion, a state representative commented that the state signed its BITs "without any knowledge of their implications", thinking they were only "photo-op agreements" and only "realiz[ing] what these words mean[t]" after being "hit by the first investor-state arbitration".[13]

As an initial matter, this argument gives developing countries too little credit. Prof. Orrego Vicuña said it best:

> "The argument is based on the false assumption that developing countries were ignorant of what they were actually signing, and that the BITs were not to their advantage. Thank you for that paternalistic thought, but with respect, I must say that lawyers from developing countries are not dummies. BITs are signed because they offer guarantees and safeguards needed for the investments to come. On occasion, the same guarantees are embodied in national legislation."[14]

Quite apart from the "paternalism" that Prof. Orrego Vicuña notes is inherent in such an argument, this argument also mischaracterizes the nature of the BIT system by suggesting that BITs were designed to benefit developed states at the expense of developing states. But the reality is far different. In the words of the founding father of the ICSID Convention, Aron Broches:

> "The Convention has sometimes been regarded as an instrument for the protection of private foreign investment. This characterization is one-sided and too narrow. The purpose of the Convention is to promote private foreign investment by improving the investment climate for investors and host States alike. The drafters have taken great care to make it a balanced instrument serving the interests of host States as well as investors."[15]

The terms of the overwhelming majority of investment agreements themselves demonstrate such a "balanced" approach. As a recent briefing paper from the International Chamber of Commerce in the United Kingdom notes, most investment

13. Luke Eric PETERSON, "Pakistan Attorney General advises states to scrutinize investment treaties carefully", Investment Treaty News (1 December 2006), available at <www.iisd.org/investment/itn> (summarizing comments made by Mr. Makhdoom Ali Khan at an ICSID colloquium).
14. Francisco ORREGO VICUÑA, "Carlos Calvo, Honorary NAFTA Citizen", 11 NYU Envtl. L. J. (2002, no. 1) p. 19 at p. 30.
15. Aron BROCHES, "The Convention on the Settlement of Investment Disputes between States and Nationals of Other States", 136 Recueil des Cours (1972) p. 331 at p. 348.

agreements have carefully defined investment protection standards to which state parties agree to adhere.[16]

The prevailing practice with respect to BITs is also indicative of their attempt to balance the objectives of both states and investors. Properly conceived, both the large number and diversity of BITs in existence – representing the treaty practice of over 180 states – suggest that BITs are deemed beneficial by states in a large number of bilateral and regional circumstances. Indeed, it is difficult to believe that all of these developing states were ignorant of the BITs' terms – including dispute settlement terms – when they signed them. The reality is that both sides have much to gain from the bargain. In signing BITs, developing states promise to provide certain guarantees in the expectation that, among other benefits, they will receive greater amounts of foreign investment in return.[17] In other words, they choose to exercise their sovereign power to bind themselves.

So where does the benefit of that bargain stand from a state's perspective? Scholars have sought an answer by trying to determine, as an empirical matter, whether there is a causal relationship between the proliferation of investment treaties and the growth of foreign investment. Over the last fifteen years, there have been at least ten major empirical studies attempting to answer that difficult question.[18] Their methodologies differ significantly, reflecting, in part, that trying to define precisely the nature of the BIT-FDI relationship is a messy exercise. The difficulty is exacerbated by the fact that the legal community has yet to adopt the more rigorous standards that have long been the norm in the sciences regarding peer review and actual replication of data to inform conclusions about BIT practice.[19]

While the difficulties in such empirical studies are serious and suggest caution in coming to conclusions about the causal relationship between BITs and FDI, that is not to say, as some have, that there is no evidence to support a connection. For example, the effect of signing a BIT with the United States appears to be particularly significant.[20]

---

16. ICC UK Briefing Paper (2014), "A 'BIT' of a Problem? Briefing on Investment Protection and Investor-State Dispute Settlement Mechanisms in International Agreements", available at <www.international-chamber.co.uk/components/com_wordpress/wp/wp-content/uploads/2014/03/ICC-UK-briefing-on-investment-protection.pdf>.

17. See, e.g., Tim BÜTHE and Helen V. MILNER, "Bilateral Investment Treaties and Foreign Direct Investment: A Political Analysis" in K.P. SAUVANT and L. SACHS, eds., *The Effect of Treaties on Foreign Direct Investment: Bilateral Investment Treaties, Double Taxation Treaties, and Investment Flows* (Oxford University Press 2009) p. 171 at p. 212 (citing anecdotal evidence that developing country governments "have understood BITs as broad commitments to economically liberal policies" and that they enter into them with the goal of encouraging investment).

18. The major empirical studies reviewed are listed in an Annex to this article (pp. 774-775).

19. See Catherine M. AMIRFAR, "Dispute Settlement Clauses in Investor-State Arbitration: An Informed Approach to Empirical Studies About Law", 12 Santa Clara J. Int'l L. (2014, no. 1) p. 303 (discussing difficulties in comparing the results of empirical studies related to BITs where there is no true replication of data).

20. One study found that countries with US BITs experienced a major increase in US FDI outflows – to the tune of $1 billion a year – as compared to countries without a US BIT. Jeswald W. SALACUSE and Nicholas P. SULLIVAN, "Do BITs Really Work?: An Evaluation of Bilateral Investment Treaties and Their Grand Bargain", 46 Harv. Int'l L. J. (2005) p. 67 at p. 109. See also

Another striking observation emerging from the empirical literature is that a BIT's effect extends beyond the particular bilateral relationship. While the results of early studies – which looked exclusively at *bilateral* FDI flows – were underwhelming,[21] later research – which looks at *aggregate* FDI flows – shows a statistically significant correlation.[22] To be clear, "correlation" is not causation, and the studies do not stand for the proposition that BITs lead to increased FDI. What the data does suggest, however, is that there is strong evidence that the existence of BITs is accompanied by increased investment from investors regardless of whether they are protected by the agreement in question.[23] In other words, the positive relationship of a BIT to FDI may lie less in the specific remedies

---

Deborah L. SWENSON, "Why Do Developing Countries Sign BITs?" 12 U.C. Davis J. Int'l L. & Pol'y (2005) p. 131 at p. 152 (finding that "countries who signed a BIT with the U.S. received a boost to foreign investment that was seven and a half times as large as the boost experienced when the average BIT was signed with other countries").

21. See, e.g., UNCTAD, *BITs in the Mid-1990s*, UNCTAD/ITE/IIT/7, Sales No. E.98.II.D.8 (1998) (concluding that BITs play a "minor and secondary role in influencing FDI flows"); Mary HALLWARD-DRIEMEIER, "Do Bilateral Investment Treaties Attract FDI? Only a bit... and they could bite", World Bank Policy Research Working Paper (2003), available at <http://elibrary.worldbank.org/doi/pdf/10.1596/1813-9450-3121> (analyzing twenty years of bilateral FDI flows from OECD countries to developing countries and finding "little evidence that BITs have stimulated additional investment").

22. See, e.g., BÜTHE and MILNER, supra fn. 17, at p. 199 (finding that "BITs are positively and statistically significantly correlated with subsequent inward FDI into developing countries"); SALACUSE and SULLIVAN, supra fn. 20, at p. 120 (finding that "the presence of a U.S. BIT has a large, positive, and significant impact on a country's overall FDI inflows" and that BITs from other OECD countries had "a positive correlation, but without statistical significance"); Andrew KERNER, "Why Should I Believe You? The Costs and Consequences of Bilateral Investment Treaties", 53 Int'l Stud. Q. (2009) p. 72 at p. 97 (finding "consistent evidence that BITs do attract FDI, and that they attract it through direct and indirect channels").

23. See BÜTHE and MILNER, supra fn. 17, at p. 184 and pp. 188-189 (suggesting various reasons why a BIT might boost inflows from capital-rich states who are not parties to the treaty, including because BITs "increase[] the costs of [states'] reneging"); SALACUSE and SULLIVAN, supra fn. 20, at pp. 106-107 (same with regard to effect of US BITs on FDI inflows from other OECD countries); KERNER, supra fn. 22, at pp. 79, 82 (2009) (hypothesizing that since "ratifying a BIT credibly signals that a state is predisposed against expropriating from foreign investors", BITs encourage investments regardless of whether or not the investors are protected by the treaty); Jennifer L. TOBIN and Susan ROSE-ACKERMAN, "When BITs Have Some Bite: The Political-Economic Environment for Bilateral Investment Treaties", 6 Rev. Int'l Org. (2011, no. 1) p. 1 at p. 2 (arguing that "BITs signal a commitment to investor-friendly domestic institutions [and] once signed ... provide an incentive to states to enact and maintain a favorable institutional environment"); Eric NEUMAYER and Laura SPESS, "Do Bilateral Investment Treaties Increase Foreign Direct Investment to Developing Countries?" LSE Research Online (2005) at p. 12, available at <http://eprints.lse.ac.uk/archive/00000627> ("[T]he signing of BITs sends out a signal to potential investors that the developing country is generally serious about the protection of foreign investment.").

it provides than in the signal it sends to potential investors of the state's commitment to facilitating and protecting investment.[24]

Another notable point is that, quite independent of the question of the actual causal relationship between BITs and FDI, increasingly sophisticated investors perceive that the existence of bilateral investment treaties, including the dispute resolution mechanisms they provide, is a factor (if only one of many) in investment decisions.[25] Governments also recognize the need for investors to be comfortable that their investments will be protected and that there will be an effective dispute resolution system.[26] Indeed, there appears to be strong competitive pressure for developing states to enter into BITs on that basis.[27] To the extent such considerations are driving the immense popularity and staying power of BITs, they only vindicate a system that is premised on promoting the rule of law.[28]

In sum, the notion that ISDS is the result of unfair bargaining power is belied not only by the origins of a system premised on balancing the interests of investors and states, but also by the empirical data showing that states have good reason to believe that there is a positive correlation between BITs and the benefit of their bargain, increased FDI.

2. A Biased System?

A second category of critique alleges that, in practice, ISDS favors capital-exporting states and the interests of their investors. In investment arbitration, the argument goes, "the host State never wins" because "host States have no rights; they only have

---

24. Of course, examples exist of significant foreign investment independent of BITs. Brazil is perhaps the most notable in this regard: Despite the fact that the government has failed to ratify a single BIT – or the ICSID Convention – it is the fourth-largest recipient of FDI in the world. UNCTAD, *World Investment Report 2013*, at xiv. But such counter-examples do not, by themselves, rebut the empirical data suggesting a correlation.

25. Susan D. FRANCK, "Foreign Direct Investment, Investment Treaty Arbitration, and the Rule of Law", 19 Pacific McGeorge Global Bus. & Dev. L.J. (2007) p. 337 at p. 340. ("[W]hile investment treaty arbitration may not directly trigger investment," its availability "is a factor in an overall decisional matrix" and plays "a role in promoting development and the rule of law."); BÜTHE and MILNER, supra fn. 17, at p. 210 (reporting that the authors' interviews with senior executives of multinational companies and foreign investment advisors revealed that "they look for information about BITs and a country's record of disputes under their BITs as one of the pieces of information that is easy and quick to obtain but also (in their assessment) genuinely informative").

26. See generally Zachary ELKINS, Andrew T. GUZMAN and Beth A. SIMMONS, "Competing for Capital: The Diffusion of Bilateral Investment Treaties, 1960-2000", 60 Int'l Orgs. (2006) pp. 811-846, available at <http://nrs.harvard.edu/urn-3:HUL.InstRepos:3017499>; Andrew T. GUZMAN, "Why LDCs Sign Treaties That Hurt Them: Explaining the Popularity of Bilateral Investment Treaties", 38 Va. J. Int'l L. (1997) p. 639.

27. *Id.*

28. David RIVKIN, "The Impact of International Arbitration on the Rule of Law", 2012 Clayton Utz International Arbitration Lecture, available at <www.claytonutz.com/ialecture/2012/>.

obligations".[29] Since investors are the only ones with the ability to initiate arbitration (and the lucrative arbitral appointments they entail), arbitrators are biased in their favor.[30] This bias, critics allege, threatens public norms, impinges on public funds and constrains the actions of governments in carrying out the mandate they have received from the populations they serve.[31]

This argument posits that states are frequent losers incurring huge debts under the current system and, conversely, that investors can simply walk into a country, make an investment and essentially have an insurance policy if things go awry: they can go to arbitration, make a claim, and be fairly certain of collecting a hefty award.

If this premise were true, one would expect to see (i) a record of awards demonstrating bias in favor of investors; (ii) high rates of non-compliance by states; and (iii) a mass exodus from the system. None of these has occurred.

First, the perception that arbitrators are biased in favor of investors is unsupported by the numbers. According to UNCTAD, 42% of known investor-state cases have been decided in favor of the state, 31% in favor of the investor and 27% settled.[32] ICSID reports that, cumulatively as of 2013, 54% of the disputes decided under the ICSID Rules were dismissed either on the merits or on jurisdiction.[33] And even when investors do prevail, it is rarely a complete victory.[34] The average amount awarded (approx. US$ 10 million) is a fraction of what investors typically request (approx. US$ 343 million).[35]

---

29. Nathalie BERNASCONI-OSTERWALDER, "Who Wins and Who Loses in Investment Arbitration? Are Investors and Host States on a Level Playing Field? The Lauder/Czech Republic Legacy", 6 J. World Investment & Trade (2005) p. 69 at p. 69.

30. See, e.g., M. SORNARAJAH, "Power and Justice: Third World Resistance in International Law", 10 Singapore Y.B. Int'l L. (2006) p. 19 at pp. 33-34 ("Though neutrality is the ideal subscribed to in international arbitration, the pattern of appointing arbitrators favourable to the articulation of norms that protect the interests of international business has existed for a long time.... Arbitrators must subscribe to the tenets of the powerful if they are to remain in business."). See also Gus VAN HARTEN, "Arbitrator Behaviour in Asymmetrical Adjudication: An Empirical Study of Investment Treaty Arbitration", 50 Osgoode Hall L. J. (2012) p. 211 (finding that investment arbitrators are biased in favor of expansive approaches to issues of jurisdiction and admissibility).

31. See, e.g., Olivia CHUNG, "The Lopsided International Investment Law Regime and Its Effect on the Future of Investor-State Arbitration", 47 Va. J. Int'l L. (2007) p. 953.

32. UNCTAD, "IIA Issues Note", supra fn. 5, at p. 5.

33. ICSID, *The ICSID Caseload – Statistics* (Issue 2014-1) at p. 14.

34. See, e.g., Susan D. FRANCK, "Empirically Evaluating Claims About Investment Treaty Arbitration", 86 N.C. L. Rev.1, (2007) pp. 49-53 (finding, in a data set of merits awards, that although investors were awarded damages in 38.5% of cases, they only prevailed on all their claims in 12.2% of cases); Daphna KAPELIUK, "The Repeat Appointment Factor: Exploring Decision Patterns of Elite Investment Arbitrators", 96 Cornell L. Rev. (2010) p. 47 at p. 81 (finding, in a dataset of awards involving "elite arbitrators", that claimants lost on all their claims in 60.5% of cases and received an award of less than 40% of the amount claimed in more than 80% of cases).

35. FRANCK, supra fn. 34, at pp. 57-66. But see Kevin P. GALLAGHER and Elen SHRESTHA, *Investment Treaty Arbitration and Developing Countries: A Re-Appraisal*, Global Development and Environment Institute, Working Paper No. 11-01 (2011) at p. 9 (arguing that Franck's analysis understates how developing countries are affected by arbitration losses because it does not account for the amount awarded relative to the size of the respondent state's economy).

To be clear, these statistics need to be treated with great caution, and both pro-state and pro-investor advocates have not demonstrated sufficient rigor in drawing conclusions from them. A balanced investor/state win-loss record does not, by itself, demonstrate a level playing field. Rather, each case would need to be compared to a "control" case to show expected outcome based on strength of the case to provide a basis for comparison and, consequently, to determine whether bias can be ruled out. To be sure, this is an exceedingly difficult analysis, making it hard to come to any conclusions. Nevertheless, to the extent that the overall record of outcomes does provide any guidance, it would seem to suggest at least the converse; that is, that while the numbers may not provide affirmative evidence of a level playing field, they do not support the notion that bias exists in favor of investors.

Nor do we see third-party funding leading to a tidal wave of new investor claims to the detriment of states, as feared.[36] Empirical analysis of the impact of third-party funding is made near impossible by the fact that claimants often do not reveal the existence of outside funding in matters, making identification of relevant data difficult. But as a conceptual matter, it is not surprising that the system does not seem to have seen a significant rise in claims since outside funding became popular. To the contrary, such funders tend to approach their participation in international proceedings with the same scrutiny merited by any other decision to invest. In other words, since they are interested in maximizing the odds of victory, third-party funders typically carry out thorough due diligence and only pursue meritorious claims.[37] And investors are not the only ones reaping the benefits of third-party funding: Uruguay's defense against claims brought by Philip Morris is being funded by an American advocacy group backed by the Bloomberg Foundation.[38]

Second, the rate of voluntary compliance with awards provides equally compelling evidence that the deck is not stacked against states. One regularly cited article (albeit now seventeen years old) noted that the rate of successful enforcement of arbitration awards was around 98%, counting both voluntary compliance and recourse to domestic courts for enforcement.[39] More recently, a 2008 study conducted by PricewaterhouseCoopers and Queen Mary University of London's School of International Arbitration found that "84% of the participating corporate counsel indicated that, in more than 76% of their arbitration proceedings, the non-prevailing

---

36. See generally Lisa BENCH NIEUWVELD and Victoria SHANNON, eds., *Third-Party Funding in International Arbitration* (Kluwer Law International 2012).
37. Eric DE BRABANDERE and Julia LEPELTAK, "Third-Party Funding in International Investment Arbitration", 27 ICSID Review (2012) p. 1 at p. 6.
38. Luke Eric PETERSON, "Uruguay hires law firm and secures outside funding to defend against Philip Morris claim; not the first time an NGO offers financial support for arbitration costs", Investment Arbitration Reporter (20 October 2010), available at <www.iareporter.com/articles/20101023_4>.
39. Sir Michael KERR, "Concord and Conflict in International Arbitration", 13 Arb. Int'l (1997) p. 121 at p. 127.

party voluntarily complies with the arbitral award; in most cases, according to the interviews, compliance reaches 90%."[40]

Of course, these studies do not differentiate between commercial disputes between private parties and investor-state disputes; however, in the realm of investor-state dispute resolution, voluntary compliance rates are encouraging. One study in 2007 used publicly available information to determine that in "almost all" of the twenty-three then-existing final ICSID awards upholding claims, "the respondents ultimately discharged their payment obligations, either in accordance with the terms of the awards or in accordance with post-award settlement agreements of the parties."[41] Examples of prompt and voluntary payment are both consistent and relatively easy to come by:

"[N]ot all states hesitate to pay treaty arbitration awards. In the case of Hungary, the government promptly paid a $76.2 Million (US) award rendered at ICSID in 2006. Likewise, the Czech Republic famously paid a hefty award in 2003 – amounting to a third of a Billion Dollars with interest – even though the obligation swelled the country's public sector deficit. Other countries such as Ecuador, Canada, Chile, South Africa, Lebanon[,] Latvia, Mexico, and Poland have also paid awards or reached a settlement thereof."[42]

Though there are a handful of states at any given time that resist payment of a particular award,[43] thus far only Argentina has refused to pay *any* awards as a matter of

---

40. PricewaterhouseCoopers and Queen Mary School of International Arbitration, *International Arbitration Corporate Attitudes and Practices 2008* (2008), at p. 2, available at <www.pwc.co.uk/pdf/PwC_International_Arbitration_2008.pdf>.
   Although Queen Mary University also conducted international arbitration studies in 2010 and 2012, the questions are altered in each survey and neither of these later studies included questions relating to enforcement.
41. Antonio R. PARRA, "The Enforcement of ICSID Arbitral Awards, 24th Joint Colloquium on International Arbitration", 16 November 2007, at p. 10, available at <www.arbitration-icca.org/media/0/12144885278400/enforcement_of_icsid_awards.pdf> (noting that although "[i]nformation regarding payment of the awards is somewhat sketchy [because] settlements [are] often … confidential … successful claimants, if not paid promptly, seldom hesitate to make that fact known").
42. Luke Eric PETERSON, "How many states are not paying awards under investment treaties?", Int'l Arb. Reporter (7 May 2010) available at <www.iareporter.com/articles/20100507_3>. See also Leo SZOLNOKI, "Guatemala satisfies DR-CAFTA award", Global Arb. Rev. (5 December 2013) available at <http://globalarbitrationreview.com/news/article/32104/guatemala-satisfies-dr-cafta-award/>; Matthew POUNTNEY, "Venezuela pays Exxon award", Global Arb. Rev. (16 February 2012) available at <http://globalarbitrationreview.com/news/article/30175/venezuela-pays-exxon-award/>.
43. Leaving aside Argentina's famously recalcitrant position, a 2012 article named five other states who had refused to pay particular awards voluntarily (enforcement proceedings were then pending for the awards): Mexico, Russia, Zimbabwe, Thailand and potentially Kyrgyzstan. An earlier version of the list had included an award against Kazakhstan (which was then settled) and did not include any award against Mexico. See Luke Eric PETERSON, "Cargill says Mexico is latest member of non-payer's club"; "IAReporter review found half-dozen states not paying BIT awards", Int'l Arb. Reporter (14 November 2012) available at <www.iareporter.com/articles/

policy. Yet even that policy has not been steadfast: Argentina recently agreed to settle five of its outstanding arbitral awards.[44]

Third, we have not seen sovereigns "vote with their feet" and exit the treaty arbitration system *en masse*. So far, three states have denounced the ICSID Convention: Bolivia in 2007, Ecuador in 2009 and Venezuela in 2012.[45] Despite these high-profile denunciations, membership in ICSID continues to grow: in the seven years that have passed since Bolivia's denunciation, nine new states have ratified the Convention, including Canada, which should be viewed as a major vindication of the system.[46]

In sum, while the perception persists in some circles that the investment treaty system is biased towards investors as a matter of both origin and practice, the available data showing comparable victory rates as between investors and states, high voluntary compliance by states, and growing participation in the ICSID system are to the contrary. Indeed, there is strong support for the position that treaty arbitration is actually a well-functioning system; claimants do *not* have an edge in terms of success and they have an incentive to go to arbitration only when the stakes are high and they perceive few alternatives.

III.   THE COMPETENCE CONUNDRUM V. THE REALITY OF THE PLAYING FIELD

In addition to the structural criticisms of ISDS discussed above, there exist misperceptions with respect to the arbitration process itself. One of those misperceptions has to do with a dynamic that I will refer to as a "competence conundrum". As the argument goes, ISDS is inherently problematic because tribunals consist of private individuals called upon to sit in judgment of a state's actions, including, in some instances, their policy choices. In other words, there is a fundamental

---

20121114_1>; PETERSON, supra fn. 42.

44. Douglas THOMSON, "Argentina agrees to settle treaty awards", Global Arb. Rev. (11 October 2013) available at <http://globalarbitrationreview.com/news/article/31961/argentina-agrees-settle-treaty-awards/>.

45. There is some doubt about how effective such withdrawal is in freeing these States from their obligations to past and current investors. See, e.g., Barrie SANDER, "Venezuela: The consequences of ICSID denunciation", Global Arb. Rev. (14 February 2012) available at <http://globalarbitrationreview.com/journal/article/30164/venezuela-consequences-icsid-denunciation/>. While Pan American Energy's pending claim against Bolivia has been called a "test case" on these issues, the panel has issued only one non-public decision on preliminary objections, and the proceedings are currently suspended. Sebastian PERRY, "Bolivia test case resumes at ICSID", Global Arb. Rev. (14 September 2012) available at <http://globalarbitration review.com/news/article/30818/bolivia-test-case-resumes-icsid/>; ICSID Case Details for *Pan American Energy LLC v. Plurinational State of Bolivia* (ICSID Case No. ARB/10/8), available at <http://icsid.worldbank.org>. For further discussion of the effect of ICSID denunciation, see Christoph SCHREUER, "Denunciation of the ICSID Convention and Consent to Arbitration", in Michael WAIBEL, et al., eds., *The Backlash Against Investment Arbitration* (Kluwer Law International 2010) p. 353.

46. Other new members include Haiti, Cape Verde and Qatar. A current list of Contracting States is available at <https://icsid.worldbank.org/ICSID>.

competence conundrum: private decision-makers are judging the state, whose actions are (often) subject to a public mandate. In addition, the final award stands as a bill to the taxpayers of a state, and the state's ensuing obligation to pay damages will have an impact on its and other states' future policy choices.

As an initial matter, I agree that investment arbitration awards impact state policy, sometimes profoundly. The areas of policy involved in investment arbitration are quite broad, as evidenced by one report that catalogued the issues in dispute in a number of arbitrations over the past few years: drinking water supply systems in Cochabamba, Bolivia and in Tanzania; Mexico's refusal to grant a permit for a hazardous waste site; the judicial system in Mississippi, USA; California's ban on a polluting gasoline additive; Argentina's response to its fiscal crisis; a Mexican tax on high fructose corn syrup; Chile's system of allocating fishing permits; and many more.[47]

In addition, the implications of this exercise of private decision-making power can also be profound: Prof. Gabrielle Kaufmann-Kohler has applied Lon Fuller's concept of the inner morality of the law to reason that, in the international investment law context, where few rules are explicitly stated and fully developed in the treaties themselves, decision-makers actually *create* law through dispute resolution, even in the absence of a formal system of binding legal precedent.[48] As Jan Paulsson has said, "[i]t is pointless to resist the observation that precedents generate norms of international law. It is a fact of life before international courts and tribunals."[49] In other words, no matter how much anyone may wish to rely on (formally correct) assurances that arbitration is party-specific and tribunals are not "bound" by prior decisions, each new arbitral award is undoubtedly capable of impacting the development of states' laws and policies.

But I do not agree that these points lead to a competence conundrum. In this Section, I will address: *first*, the nature of the tribunals' competence and why it is in line with the bargain struck by states in BITs and other regional investment protection treaties; and *second*, why the current system is generally fair and effective, and certainly more so than the proposed alternatives.

1.   Private Individuals Meet Public Conduct

The apparent surprise (and ensuing criticism) expressed by some that ISDS allows private individuals to sit in judgment of state conduct is largely misplaced. The competence of tribunals to evaluate the legality of state conduct – including regulatory acts – as a result of dispute resolution provisions is the entire point of those provisions. So the question of the resulting impact on policy goes back to the very premise of the BIT bargain: the

---

47. Center for International Environmental Law and International Institute for Sustainable Development, "Revising the UNCITRAL Arbitration Rules to Address State Arbitrations" (February 2007) pp. 3-4 at <www.iisd.org/pdf/2007/investment_revising_uncitral_arbitration.pdf>.

48. Gabrielle KAUFMANN-KOHLER, "Arbitral Precedent: Dream, Necessity or Excuse?", 23 Arbitration International (2007) p. 357 at p. 374.

49. Jan PAULSSON, "International Arbitration and the Generation of Legal Norms: Treaty Arbitration and International Law" in *International Arbitration 2006: Back to Basics?* ICCA Congress Series no. 13 (2007) (henceforth *ICCA Congress Series no. 13*) p. 879 at p. 881.

scope of state consent. Viewed in that light, the result is straightforward: when states signed these BITs, they consented to submit their sovereignty to the decisions of tribunal members. So the competence "conundrum" is no conundrum at all. The prospect of private individuals reviewing state conduct (and all of the concomitant policy implications of that exercise) is the natural result of the bargain struck.

A recent exchange in the US Supreme Court touched on this point and highlighted both the superficial appeal of this argument and the straightforward nature of the answer. The recently decided *BG Group v. Argentina* case involved a claimant's attempt to enforce an arbitral award against Argentina and addressed the question of the competence of arbitrators versus courts to address threshold questions of jurisdiction.[50] The case marks the first time that the US Supreme Court has considered an issue with respect to treaty arbitration. In the oral argument for that case, when the issue of what Argentina understood when it signed the relevant BIT came up, Chief Justice Roberts queried, "I don't know that a sovereign would be anxious to submit its sovereignty to three international law experts."[51] The response from BG Group's counsel was exactly on point:

> "And surely they wouldn't, Mr. Chief Justice, but that's the point of the treaty. Remember, my friend said, look, if it weren't for this treaty, we could never sue them. That's the reason there's the treaty because, if there wasn't the treaty and we couldn't get relief from them, we would have never invested.
>
> And so the whole point of this treaty is to put these disputes into arbitration. There [are] no special substantive rights in this treaty. They are all customary international law. The thing that matters in this treaty – the thing that matters in all the treaties is I don't have to have my case decided by an Argentine court."[52]

It is not just the terms of the BIT, but the practice of tribunals that bolster the fairness of the bargain. While it is the case that tribunals are often faced with issues of great public importance, tribunals are very sensitive to overreaching on policy matters. Indeed, the deliberative exercise of tribunals is infused with the sense that a state's interest and authority in regulating matters of public interest is a very significant consideration that must be given weight. Tribunals tend to be explicit in this regard, and awards are replete with examples of tribunals giving great weight to a state's right to regulate matters of public interest.

For example, tribunals are express in holding that their mandate does not involve substituting their own judgment for that of the state; the inquiry is only whether the state's conduct triggers liability and an obligation to pay fair compensation under the relevant treaty.

---

50. *BG Group plc v. Republic of Argentina*, 572 U.S. ___ (decided 5 March 2014), available at <www.supremecourt.gov/opinions/13pdf/12-138_97be.pdf>.

51. *BG Group plc v. Republic of Argentina*, U.S. Supreme Court Case No. 12-138, Tr. of Oral Arg., 2 December 2013, at p. 61, available at <www.supremecourt.gov/oral_arguments/argument_transcripts/12-138_cb8e.pdf>.

52. *Id.*

To take an extreme example, in the *Paushok v. Mongolia* arbitration, the tribunal was faced with determining whether a "windfall profits tax" on gold production following a surge in world gold prices constituted a breach.[53] In an opinion declining to hold that the tax breached the BIT, the tribunal noted:

> "[T]he fact that a democratically elected legislature has passed legislation that may be considered as ill-conceived, counter-productive and excessively burdensome does not automatically allow to conclude that a breach of an investment treaty has occurred. If such were the case, the number of investment treaty claims would increase by a very large number. Legislative assemblies around the world spend a good part of their time amending substantive portions of existing laws in order to adjust them to changing times or to correct serious mistakes that were made at the time of their adoption. A claim for a breach under an investment treaty has to be proven by claimants under the specific rules established in that treaty."[54]

The tribunal then reasoned that "[i]t is not the role of the Tribunal to weigh the wisdom of legislation, but merely to assess whether such legislation breaches the Treaty. Claimants have not succeeded in demonstrating that [the tax legislation at issue] was an abusive or irrational decision and that it constituted discriminatory treatment."[55]

Equally, decisions in favor of investors have been careful to reflect the onus on investors to demonstrate that a state has acted outside its own regulatory authority in violation of a BIT. For example, in *Saluka v. Czech Republic*, the tribunal was tasked with deciding whether the state had breached its treaty obligations to the claimant during the Czech banking crisis when the government failed to give the same assistance to IPB, the bank in which the claimants had invested, that it had afforded to other banks.[56] The state's failure to provide assistance to IPB "created an environment impossible for the survival of IPB",[57] and the bank failed. The claimants argued that this differential treatment was discriminatory and breached the treaty's fair and equitable treatment guarantee,[58] while the state responded that its choices in dealing with the banks were "closely linked" to government policy on privatization.[59] In deciding the claim, the tribunal first noted that "[i]t is clearly not for this Tribunal to second-guess the Czech Government's privatisation policies", and also that the state's actions with respect to the

---

53. *Sergei Paushok, CJSC Golden East Company and CJSC Vostokneftegaz Company v. The Government of Mongolia*, UNCITRAL, Award on Jurisdiction and Liability (28 April 2011). The legislation approved by the Mongolian legislature established that "any gold sales at prices in excess of USD 500 per ounce were subject to a tax at the rate of 68% on the amount exceeding a base price of USD 500 per ounce.... The base price was set as a fixed amount, without reference to any production cost index." *Id.* at para. 104.
54. *Id.* at para. 299.
55. *Id.* at para. 316.
56. *Saluka Investments B.V. v. The Czech Republic*, UNCITRAL, Award (17 March 2006) para. 310(a).
57. *Id.* at para. 347.
58. *Id.* at para. 310(a).
59. *Id.* at para. 336.

other banks were "perfectly legitimate".[60] The tribunal went on to state that "[t]his, however, did not at the same time relieve the Czech Government from complying with its obligation of non-discriminatory treatment of IPB. The Czech Republic, once it had decided to bind itself by the Treaty to accord 'fair and equitable treatment' to investors of the other Contracting Party, was bound to implement its policies, including its privatisation strategies, in a way that did not lead to unjustified differential treatment unlawful under the Treaty."[61]

In sum, tribunals respect states' legitimate powers to regulate in the public interest and are generally careful to curb state actions only when they impose such a disproportionately heavy and unfair burden on investors as to clearly meet the elements of a treaty violation.

Furthermore, the achievement of an appropriate balance between public and private interests is not illusory, nor is the question left only to tribunals' reasoning in awards. For example, in 2012, the US government issued a new model BIT aimed at maintaining the 2004 model BIT's "carefully calibrated balance between providing strong investor protections and preserving the government's ability to regulate in the public interest."[62] The 2012 model BIT includes several provisions that are deferential to the state receiving the investment. For instance, with respect to the environment, the new model BIT states in Art. 12(3) that "[t]he Parties recognize that each Party retains the right to exercise discretion with respect to regulatory, compliance, investigatory, and prosecutorial matters, and to make decisions regarding the allocation of resources to enforcement".[63] It also maintains the 2004 model BIT's provisions limiting the definition of indirect expropriation, excluding taxation measures as sources of liability for anything other than expropriation (with procedural safeguards even in those cases), an expansive "essential security" clause giving the United States significant leeway in security matters, and more.[64] As explained by two attorneys at the US Department of State,

> "[T]he substantive provisions [of recent U.S. BITs] often are defined with far greater precision and clarity [than their shorter, more vague counterparts from the 1990s], along with various qualifications. For example, the article addressing expropriation not only sets out the well-established standard for expropriation – that it be nondiscriminatory, for a public purpose, in accordance with due process, and accompanied by prompt, adequate, and effective compensation – but also spells out in greater detail what constitutes 'prompt, adequate, and effective.' Additionally, a separate annex sets out the two categories of expropriation –

---

60. *Id.* at para. 337.

61. *Id.*

62. US Dep't of State, Model Bilateral Investment Treaty: Fact Sheet, available at <www.state.gov/r/pa/prs/ps/2012/04/188199.htm>.

63. 2012 US Model Bilateral Investment Treaty, available at <www.state.gov/documents/organization/188371.pdf>.

64. See José E. ÁLVAREZ, "The Evolving BIT", Transnat'l Disp. Mgmt. (2010) at pp. 10-11, available at <www.transnational-dispute-management.com/article.asp?key=1542>.

direct and indirect – and elaborates on factors that are relevant to determining when an indirect expropriation through regulatory conduct may occur."[65]

2.   The Wisdom of Proposed Alternatives

If ISDS were really as "rigged" as some misperceptions imply, one would expect to see states not only vociferously protesting the awards made against them but regularly refusing to comply with those awards and exiting the system in droves. Yet, as discussed above in Sect. II, state compliance with awards is actually the norm and most states remain willing participants in international investment arbitration. There have nevertheless been a number of proposals aimed at overhauling the system as a whole, none of which, as discussed below, actually appear to be improvements over the current system.

The first proposal is extreme and involves essentially scrapping the current system and leaving investors to seek recourse under the framework that prevailed before the advent of international arbitration: diplomatic protection or, in the alternative, suits in domestic courts. Australia appeared to espouse this "total disavowal" approach when it announced in April 2011 that it would not agree to international arbitration provisions in any of its future investment treaties with developing countries.[66] However, the decision has largely failed to survive a change in the state's government: Australia acquiesced to the inclusion of an arbitration provision in the Korea-Australia Free Trade Agreement (KAFTA), whose negotiation closed in December 2013.[67] More recently, there has been speculation that investor-state provisions might be included in the Trans-Pacific Partnership Agreement (TPPA), which Australia is negotiating together with nations such as the United States, Canada, Japan and Malaysia.[68]

Korea's refusal to dispense with international arbitration in the KAFTA and state interest in including arbitration in the TPPA is understandable: the modern ISDS system functions far better than the old mechanism of diplomatic protection ever did. That process was highly politicized, uneven and inconsistent. It provided no certainty or

---

65. Karin L. KIZER and Jeremy K. SHARPE, "Reform of Investor-State Dispute Settlement: The U.S. Experience", 11 Transnat'l Disp. Mgmt. (January 2014) at p. 5.
66. Sebastian PERRY, "Australia to scrap investor-state provisions", Global Arb. Rev. (18 April 2011) available at <http://globalarbitrationreview.com/news/article/29405/australia-scrap-investor-state-provisions/>.
67. Douglas THOMSON, "Australia agrees to investor-state provisions in Korea FTA", Global Arb. Rev., (9 December 2013) available at <http://globalarbitrationreview.com/news/article/32110/australia-agrees-investor-state-provisions-korea-fta/>.
68. See Beth CUBITT, "Potential Investor-State Dispute Settlement Provisions in Trans-Pacific Partnership Agreement – A Change in Policy for Australia?", Kluwer Arbitration Blog, 14 February 2014, available at <http://kluwerarbitrationblog.com/blog/2014/02/14/potential-investor-state-dispute-settlement-provisions-in-trans-pacific-partnership-agreement-a-change-in-policy-for-australia/>.

predictability to investors *or* to states.[69] This is precisely why the BIT system was created. It was designed to give investors and states a more reliable and consistent method of settling disputes instead of turning them, quite literally, into "international incidents." The ICSID Convention specifically provides, in Art. 27, that it is meant to replace the traditional system of diplomatic protection, and – in the words of ICSID's former Secretary General Ibrahim Shihata – it has helped "depoliticize" the settlement of investment disputes.[70]

The other alternative available to investors, if we were to abandon the current system of investment arbitration, would be recourse to domestic courts – assuming that the state in question has waived sovereign immunity and can indeed be sued in those courts. But domestic proceedings initiated by foreign investors are notoriously problematic and unlikely to be more neutral or "fair" than arbitration.[71] Furthermore, foreign judgments, even when favorable, are far less valuable than arbitral awards because a convention on the enforcement of foreign judgments comparable to the New York Convention, which governs the enforcement of arbitration awards, has yet to be concluded, despite many attempts to do so.

In short, throwing out the current system entirely and reverting to diplomatic protection and recourse to domestic courts would be a drastic and unfortunate step backwards in terms of fairness and investor confidence. Fortunately, the overall consensus at present seems opposed to such a radical move.

Another proposal recommends shifting away from ICSID and other global dispute resolution bodies in favor of regional institutions. For example, several Latin American states have proposed the creation of a regional arbitration center under the auspices of the Union of South American Nations (UNASUR). However, the proposal, at least at this stage, appears to inject a regional or even state-centric bias into arbitration (a circumstance unlikely to instill confidence in investors from outside the region).[72] The

---

69. See Christoph SCHREUER, "Do We Need Investment Arbitration?", 11 Transnat'l Dispute Mgmt. (January 2014) at pp. 3-5; Rudolf DOLZER, "Comments on Treaty Arbitration and International Law" in *ICCA Congress Series no. 13*, supra fn. 49, at p. 894 and p. 896 (abandoning the current system "would mean a return to the process of diplomatic protection, to the political process of negotiation with all of its vagaries, to the role of power as is inherent in bilateral negotiations, sometimes of raw power, to the open-endedness of such a process, to sanctions on the bilateral level and to schemes of the unilateral determination of a dispute"); see also Stephan W. SCHILL, "Private Enforcement of International Investment Law: Why We Need Investor Standing in BIT Dispute Settlement" in *The Backlash Against Investment Arbitration*, supra fn. 45, at p. 29 and pp. 39-41 (noting the inadequacies of diplomatic protection from the investor's point of view).

70. Ibrahim F.I. SHIHATA, "Towards a Greater Depoliticization of Investment Disputes: The Roles of ICSID and MIGA", 1 ICSID Rev. (1986) p. 1 at p. 5.

71. See SCHILL, supra fn. 69, at pp. 33-36.

72. See Andrés MEZGRAVIS and Carolina GONZÁLEZ, "UNASUR: A South American ICSID?", Global Arb. Rev. (18 August 2011) available at <http://globalarbitrationreview.com/journal/article/29751/unasur-south-american-icsid/> (describing a number of problems with the UNASUR proposal, including a requirement of exhaustion of local remedies; a potentially imbalanced method of selecting arbitrators; a restrictive scope that excludes disputes relating to energy, tax matters, healthcare, education and the

UNASUR proposal enjoys strong support only from Ecuador, Bolivia and Venezuela – the only three states in the world to have withdrawn from ICSID.[73]

If implemented, the UNASUR plan is likely to have one of two outcomes. If its arbitrators and procedures manage to remain relatively unbiased,[74] it would amount to little more than a slightly altered re-creation of the ICSID system – in which case it would be a waste of resources spent reinventing the wheel.

If, on the other hand, it were intentionally (and successfully) executed in such a way as to introduce "hometown bias" in favor of respondent states, it would suffer from the same difficulty as litigation in domestic courts, resulting in a potentially serious reversal in investor confidence.

If the strongest motivation for creating the new institution is a desire for greater protection of state and regional interests, then the system may lead to serious *state* dissatisfaction as soon as it makes its first finding of state liability. For example, the dispute resolution body of the Southern African Development Community was effectively shut down by its member states after it found Zimbabwe liable to investors for actions taken as part of Zimbabwe's land seizure and redistribution program.[75]

Finally, there has been some discussion of a push to make ISDS more "balanced" by including not only state obligations toward investors but also *investor* obligations – for example, for compliance with environmental, human rights and other standards – capable of enforcement via arbitration.[76] However, as the International Chamber of Commerce's UK branch cogently noted in a recent briefing paper,

> "International investors, like local investors and citizens, are bound by the law and regulations of their host country and potential violations can lead to local civil,

---

environment; and roadblocks to eventual enforcement of an award in domestic courts).

73. Sebastian PERRY, "Is Argentina about to leave ICSID?", Global Arb. Rev. (25 January 2013) available at <http://globalarbitrationreview.com/news/article/31121/is-argentina-leave-icsid/> ("The UNASUR centre, which would also hear state-to-state disputes, was first proposed by Ecuador in 2009 and has the support of Bolivia and Venezuela. However, Colombia, Peru, Chile and Brazil are reportedly opposed to the plan – while Uruguay is said to be concerned that it could scare off foreign investors.").

74. One empirical study has found that, in the current treaty arbitration system, presiding arbitrators from developing states are generally *not* biased in favor of developing-state respondents' interests, although they are somewhat more likely to give smaller awards against *developed* states in some circumstances. Susan D. FRANCK, "Development and Outcomes of International Treaty Arbitration", 50 Harv. Int'l L.J. (2009) p. 435 at p. 435 ("[A]t the macro level, development status [of the arbitrator's home country] does not have a statistically significant relationship with outcome [of a case]. This suggests that the investment treaty arbitration system, as a whole, functions fairly and that the eradication or radical overhaul of the arbitration process is unnecessary.").

75. Luke Eric PETERSON, "Southern African governments move to rein in international tribunal; passing judgment on Zimbabwe has led to political backlash against SADC tribunal", Inv. Arb. Rep. (22 May 2011) available at <www.iareporter.com/articles/20110522>.

76. See, e.g., Patrick DUMBERRY and Gabrielle DUMAS-AUBIN, "A Few Pragmatic Observations on How BITs Should Be Modified to Incorporate Human Rights Obligations", 11 Transnat'l Disp. Mgmt. (January 2014, no. 1).

penal or administrative penalties. In addition, non-legally binding standards of behavior embodied in sectoral, local or international standards and guidelines – such as the widely used OECD Guidelines for Multinational Enterprises – apply to international investors. These guidelines, as well as the "court of public opinion", may provide for alternate means for holding investors to account for their business practices – such as in relation to their social and environmental performance."[77]

In other words, mechanisms already exist that are aimed specifically at corporate social responsibility and compliance. Introducing this issue into ISDS risks drawing out a process that aspires to be efficient and speedy, and in any case would not address the alleged "competence conundrum" that underlies state critiques of the current system.

IV.   CONCLUSION: THE EFFECTS OF MISPERCEPTIONS

The puzzling question here is: If the popular perceptions of huge state losses and rampant state noncompliance with awards are wrong, why do they persist? The answer may lie in an oversized focus on instances of state losses and ensuing noncompliance, which, while few in absolute number, have received sizable media attention. In essence, a small number of states have loudly and persistently emphasized the perceived unfairness of the outcomes in particular cases, and in so doing have captured the debate.

The unfortunate *effect* of this misperception of state disadvantages and losses (as in the "we never agreed to this" argument discussed above) is to make the system seem unfair and thus bolster domestic opposition to arbitration and the individual investors who bring claims. In addition, the perception that the arbitration will not go its way may make a state fight harder to avoid arbitration altogether or prolong the time to an award as much as possible, which only exacerbates disputes and makes the system that much more costly and inefficient for both sides. And yet, as noted above, it seems clear that ISDS is significantly fairer than these common (mis)perceptions would indicate, and produces more reliable and consistent results than some proposed alternatives.

To be sure, there is room for improving the current system. But there appears to be strong support for true reform of the existing system, not abandoning it for ineffective historical practice or replacing it with regional mechanisms likely to introduce bias. The most promising steps towards reform are in the attempts to reshape the bargain itself. For example, the United States has taken steps in its model BIT to curb problems that are the frequent subject of state complaints, by inclusion of "denial of benefits" clauses applicable to claimants without true ties to their state of nationality (thus discouraging forum shopping), elimination of the amorphous "umbrella clause" provisions that have led to such controversial and wide-ranging interpretations in the case law, and so on.[78] Such steps to address perceived problems through revised treaty language get to the heart

---

77. ICC UK, "A 'BIT' of a Problem?", supra fn. 16, at p. 2.
78. KIZER and SHARPE, supra fn. 65, at pp. 9-10.

of the essential point of consent: if sovereigns are dissatisfied with the substantive content of their agreement, they can agree to alterations, just as they agreed to the initial bargain.

Further, the general question of the *legitimacy* of private decision-makers reviewing public policy has also given rise to efforts to improve the system. In this regard, the European Commission "has sought to address concerns about investor-state arbitration provisions in future EU treaties by outlining its priorities for improving the system – including more transparency, provisions to discourage frivolous claims and a binding code of conduct for arbitrators".[79] The Commission's proposals include "explicitly defining indirect expropriation to exclude 'public interest measures' where it cannot be shown that the state has acted in a discriminatory fashion".[80] In this sense, the proposals of the European Commission mirror those of the United States in attempting to provide additional checks and balances for how state conduct is evaluated.

A similar rationale can be found in the significant recent push toward greater transparency in arbitration. By providing a window into the parties' arguments and the tribunal's functioning, transparency reforms aim to promote legitimacy and confidence in tribunals' work. Though the NAFTA parties have been at the forefront of the effort to promote transparency (by making documents in NAFTA arbitrations public to the greatest extent possible),[81] perhaps the most significant move toward greater transparency has come in the form of UNCITRAL's transparency rules, which will go into effect on 1 April 2014.[82]

In sum, the empirical evidence suggests that ISDS is working in providing a neutral forum for investors and states alike to resolve disputes without having to resort to potentially coercive political means. It is our duty as practitioners to promote frank debate about its shortcomings and propose real solutions based on the reality of the playing field, not the misperceptions trumpeted by a vocal few.

---

79. Douglas THOMSON, "EU promises reforms to investment protection", Global Arb. Rev. (2 December 2013) available at <http://globalarbitrationreview.com/news/article/32095/eu-promises-reforms-investment-protection/>.

80. *Id.*

81. NAFTA Free Trade Commission, Notes of Interpretation of Certain Chapter Eleven Provisions, 31 July 2001, Sect. A.2.b, available at <www.sice.oas.org/tpd/nafta/Commission/CH11 understanding_e.asp> ("Each Party agrees to make available to the public in a timely manner all documents submitted to, or issued by, a Chapter Eleven tribunal, subject to redaction of: (i) confidential business information; (ii) information which is privileged or otherwise protected from disclosure under the Party's domestic law; and (iii) information which the Party must withhold pursuant to the relevant arbitral rules, as applied.").

82. UNCITRAL Rules on Transparency in Treaty-based Investor-State Arbitration (2014), available at <www.uncitral.org/pdf/english/texts/arbitration/rules-on-transparency/Rules-on-Transparency-E.pdf>.

Annex

Bibliography of Empirical Studies Regarding BITs and FDI

Tim BÜTHE and Helen V. MILNER, "Bilateral Investment Treaties and Foreign Direct Investment: A Political Analysis" in K.P. SAUVANT and L. SACHS, eds., *The Effect of Treaties on Foreign Direct Investment: Bilateral Investment Treaties, Double Taxation Treaties, and Investment Flows* (Oxford University Press 2009) p. 171 (finding correlation between aggregate FDI inflows and number of BITs signed).

Peter EGGER and Michael PFAFFERMAYR, "The Impact of Bilateral Investment Treaties on Foreign Direct Investment", 32 J. Comp. Econ. (2004) p. 788 (finding that investment treaties exert a significant positive effect on outward FDI).

Mary HALLWARD-DRIEMEIER, "Do Bilateral Investment Treaties Attract FDI? Only a bit… and they could bite", World Bank Policy Research Working Paper (2003), available at <http://elibrary.worldbank.org/doi/pdf/10.1596/1813-9450-3121> (analyzing twenty years of bilateral FDI flows from OECD countries to developing countries and finding "little evidence that BITs have stimulated additional investment").

Andrew KERNER, "Why Should I Believe You? The Costs and Consequences of Bilateral Investment Treaties", 53 Int'l Stud. Q. (2009) p. 73 (finding "consistent evidence that BITs do attract FDI, and that they attract it through direct and indirect channels" benefitting all investors, not only nationals of the signatory states).

Eric NEUMAYER and Laura SPESS, "Do Bilateral Investment Treaties Increase Foreign Direct Investment to Developing Countries?" LSE Research Online (2005), available at <http://eprints.lse.ac.uk/archive/00000627> (finding robust evidence that a higher number of BITs raises FDI inflows).

Jeswald W. SALACUSE and Nicholas P. SULLIVAN, "Do BITs Really Work?: An Evaluation of Bilateral Investment Treaties and Their Grand Bargain", 46 Harv. Int'l L. J. (2005) p. 67 (finding that a US BIT is correlated with a major increase in US FDI outflows to a given country).

Deborah L. SWENSON, "Why Do Developing Countries Sign BITs?" 12 U.C. Davis J. Int'l L. & Pol'y (2005) p. 131 (reporting mixed results suggesting that while "new BIT signing in the early 1990's was not correlated with increased levels of investment … BIT signing in the late 1990's was").

Jennifer TOBIN and Susan ROSE-ACKERMAN, "Foreign Direct Investment and the Business Environment in Developing Countries: The Impact of Bilateral Investment Treaties", William Davidson Institute Working Paper No. 587 (June 2003) (finding that "the number of BITs signed appears to have little impact on a country's ability to attract

FDI [except for c]ountries that are relatively risky [which] seem to be able to attract somewhat more FDI by signing BITs".).

Jennifer TOBIN and Susan ROSE-ACKERMAN, "When BITs Have Some Bite: The Political-Economic Environment for Bilateral Investment Treaties", 6 Rev. Int'l Org. (2011, no. 1) p. 1 (finding that BITs attract FDI to developing countries but only when combined with a favorable domestic investment environment).

UNCTAD, *BITs in the Mid-1990s*, UNCTAD/ITE/IIT/7, Sales No. E.98.II.D.8 (1998) (concluding that BITs play a "minor and secondary role in influencing FDI flows").

Investment Disputes and the Public Interest

*David D. Caron**

I.   INTRODUCTION

This panel asks whether the playing field of treaty arbitration is level and who should decide that question. In other words, it asks how serious are the challenges raised concerning investment treaty arbitration, an assessment that is made difficult by the fact that some, but certainly not all, of the concerns are expressed by actors involved in particular disputes. More broadly, the focus of the panel asks where we can expect treaty arbitration to go. In this vein, I recall the Danish physicist Niels Bohr, who reportedly once said: "Prediction is a difficult thing, especially if it is about the future."

The contributions to this Congress have addressed a variety of particular questions about treaty arbitration's legitimacy. This panel has presented two presentations that review the empirical studies of treaty arbitration and the recent practice and experience of some states. In being given the opportunity to reflect broadly on the question, the following comment offers three particular points: (1) it need be emphasized that the legitimacy concerns regarding treaty arbitration also are a manifestation of broader concerns, (2) it need be considered how the circumstances underlying the international regime for investment are shifting and what that shift suggests about the future of treaty arbitration, and (3) a proposal as to how we should approach assessing the most fundamental challenge to treaty arbitration, namely the call that national courts be used instead.

II.   THE LEGITIMACY CONCERNS OVER TREATY ARBITRATION MANIFEST ALSO BROADER CONCERNS

You may recall the protests that accompanied the World Trade Organization (WTO) Ministerial Conference in Seattle in 1999. Some analysts at the time focused on how to improve decision-making and transparency within the WTO; others were perplexed at the focus on the WTO. In a debate on these questions, Professor Georges Abi Saab rose and said that it should not be surprising that the WTO was the object of such protests.

---

*   Dean and Professor of Law, The Dickson Poon School of Law, King's College London.

He observed that the forces of globalization were diffuse, that there is not a clear agent of globalization and that in such a situation protests often center on particular symbols of the more general phenomenon of concern.

I would suggest to you that the focus on treaty arbitration is somewhat similar. Concern about foreign investment is in part directly a concern about the fairness and legitimacy of that process. It is also, however, a manifestation of concerns about globalization, about economic dislocation and other social interests, about jobs and livelihoods. The proposed Transatlantic Trade and Investment Partnership, for example, involves a very substantial negotiation and would result in a document with numerous chapters. Many parts of that document will have far greater social impact than the arbitration scheme or the worst possible single arbitration one can imagine. But the particular reference of investment disputes to arbitration, like the WTO Ministerial Meeting, is something that provides a relatively clear focus for these more general concerns.

Let me emphasize that this does not mean in my view that reform of treaty arbitration is not needed – to the contrary and far from it, my point is that it should be expected that treaty arbitration will be held to the highest standard of legitimacy. I suggest that this standard is appropriate and that it is a standard that need be met.

To summarize, the concerns addressed by this panel are in part direct concerns with treaty arbitration, but they also manifest concerns that are deeper and broader than the legitimacy of International Centre for Settlement of Investment Disputes (ICSID) or treaty arbitration.

III.   THE CHANGING CIRCUMSTANCES AND SHAPE OF THE FOREIGN INVESTMENT REGIME

Often, to go forward, it is necessary to look back. Judge Schwebel in his opening address to this conference provides a partial trace of the history of foreign investment. But as my co-panelist, Alvaro Galindo, observes that history is sensitive and subject to different interpretations. I return to that history from a slightly different angle – what circumstances shaped the international regime for investment over the last century, how are they changing and what does that tell us about its future.

One study of the history of investment and the international regime for its protection that is for the most part excellent is *Standing Guard* by Charles Lipson.[1] He elegantly and carefully traces the British interest and practice in supporting a rule under public international law of full compensation for expropriation of foreign capital before World War 1, and the challenge to that rule posed by the Soviet revolution and other general questions raised in the interwar period. He then traces how the United States after the Second World War took up the hegemonic position of the United Kingdom in supporting what Lipson terms "international property rights". As Lipson follows events after the Second World War, he eventually turns his attention to the diplomatic efforts of the then so-called Third World to construct a new international economic order in

---

1. Charles LIPSON, *Standing Guard: Protecting Foreign Capital in the Nineteenth and Twentieth Centuries* (University of California Press 1985).

the 1960s and the 1970s, and tells the story of various UN General Assembly resolutions at that time.

Interestingly, Lipson gets into trouble in terms of prediction, however, as he approaches the time of his writing (the book was published in 1985). In broad terms, Lipson's model of the international regime for foreign investment turned on two things. First, the concentration and coherency of interstate restraints that he views as particularly strong when there is a dominant power (a hegemon) supporting the international property rules. Britain played this role in his view prior to World War I and the United States took the UK's place for several decades after World War II. Second, the administrative complexity and the presence of state-driven economic development within various host states which he concludes from the 1960s onwards was increasing, diversifying and making more complex the landscape of international investment.

Lipson's perspective is helpful in several ways but it led Lipson in the early 1980s to come to exactly the wrong conclusion – namely he concludes that the absence of a clear hegemonic power to maintain the content of international property rules and the increasing capacities and diversity of host states meant that the international regime for the protection of investment faced fragmentation, degradation and continued difficult times. In other words, he missed almost everything that has happened over the past three decades. Indeed, he misses entirely what Judge Schwebel described as the two most important developments: Lipson devotes only one paragraph to ICSID and misses bilateral investment treaties (BITs) entirely. I tell this story because it leads us to consider several changing circumstances both that he identified and that he missed.

First, it is instructive to note that Lipson's emphasis on the presence of a dominant power to maintain international property rights is not as necessary as he assumed. Certainly, the concerns he had about waning US influence in this regard in 1980 has not changed. But why has it not mattered? Has it mattered in some ways? Why is it that we see BITs around the world, not only North-South, but also between developing states? I would suggest to you that for much of the time period reviewed by Lipson, state interests as regards international property rules were not symmetric: some states' interests were formed by the fact that they were essentially capital exporting while for others their interest followed that of an entity essentially capital importing. In such an asymmetric situation one should not expect a customary rule to emerge unless there is a strong actor present. That is essentially Lipson's view and his reasoning that the hegemon was necessary follows from that factual assumption. Today, however, state interests have converged – somewhat – in that the majority of states (not the least developed states) are both capital exporting and capital importing. Thus in one sense, the convergence means that hegemon is not necessary for the emergence of some consensus. Simultaneously, the lack of hegemon suggests that we should see some variation among the BITs, that we should see diversity within convergence. In this sense, we should not be surprised if some states withdraw from or renegotiate some BITs. Conversely, we should not expect a model BIT for the world. Nor should we expect that if a multilateral agreement on investment were revived that it would it provide other than a minimum shared baseline of protection while allowing BITs with more specific provisions to remain in place.

Second, as far as Lipson's concern with the increasing role of state-driven development in the 1970's, Lipson can not be faulted for failing to foresee the collapse of the Soviet Union and the shift, with a few notable exceptions, from planned economies. Obviously, that transformation had tremendous political and economic global consequences we are still seeking to understand. One implication I would suggest was the surge throughout the 1990s in ratifications of ICSID, the 1958 New York Convention and other economic agreements. Although there is argument as to the degree to which BITs and other instruments create new investment; it is generally accepted that they have a channeling influence on where existing investment will flow. However, and importantly, an impulse to enter into BITs in order to channel investment only means that the protections offered need be roughly equivalent to the other likely destinations. And in this sense there is a space for what has been termed the return of the state. The convergence that on the one hand leads to a shared view on the protection of investment may also include a convergence on the other hand that there should be defined limited exceptions to such protections.

Thus we should not be surprised to see a measure of continued diversity even as interests converge, but it may also be that states seeing themselves as respondents will come to agree or seek some change in the substantive law and thereby provide some protection to themselves.

I mentioned that Lipson missed the significance of ICSID and BITs. On the one hand, many of us did not appreciate those developments at the time. But, the absence also reflects Lipson's focus on states and not on investors.[2] Lipson observed that corporations were attempting to structure their affairs in the early 1980s seeking political risk insurance for example, but he underestimated the transnational potential of national courts to support a treaty arbitration system. Simultaneously, it must be said there appears to an increasing awareness of the limits of the transnational potential of national courts to support the enforcement of the treaty arbitration system.

But by not focusing on the investors, Lipson did not adequately consider the tendency for significant investment disputes to go somewhere. In the late 1800's, these disputes were transformed via diplomatic protection into disputes between two states. ICSID, in Ibrahim Shihata's words, provided a mechanism to depoliticize disputes at least in the sense of their presentation.[3] The phrasing of the question before this panel assumes that the legitimacy question is one for states. It need be recalled that it also can be viewed as one for investors. Procedurally, their question is usually phrased as one between ICSID and some other arbitration institution. Substantively, the question becomes whether a greater reliance on concession drafting will become apparent.

---

2. To his credit, Lipson does discuss the influence of investors on US policy such as policies leading to denial of aid to expropriating countries.
3. Ibrahim F.I. SHIHATA, "Towards a Greater Depoliticization of Investment Disputes: The Roles of ICSID and MIGA", 1 ICSID REV. (1986) p. 1.

IV.   NATIONAL COURTS AS AN ALTERNATIVE TO TREATY ARBITRATION

The most fundamental consequence of the illegitimacy critique is that the mechanism of treaty arbitration will be replaced with something else. Reform in a sense is a constant replacement or renewal of a mechanism. But, the most fundamental critique is an alternative, namely that the appropriate forum for investment disputes is that of the national courts of the host state. This has been proposed in the statements of various nongovernmental organizations. It has been at times the view of the Australian government. It was quite recently voiced by the German government as a condition of its agreement in the TPIP negotiations. At base, it is undeniable in my view that, as one statement provides, all states "should strengthen their domestic justice system for the benefit for all citizens and communities, including investors".[4] But, how might we test whether national courts at present are an alternative to treaty arbitration.

The World Justice Project has issued for several years its Rule of Law Index reporting on ninety-nine countries. Rule of law is assessed with reference to forty-seven indicators organized around eight themes, several of those themes (particularly civil justice and criminal justice) involve an assessment of domestic courts. Using the Index's methodology, might it be possible to assess the adequacy of the international commercial arbitration system and the treaty arbitration system? What might we expect?

I would suggest the arbitration system would, in many respects, rank rather high in a list of national judiciaries. In that image, one also can imagine pairings of countries with national judiciaries both ranked higher than treaty arbitration, and in that instance, in a manner analogous to the Australian example, it could be argued that mutual recourse to national courts for investment disputes is appropriate.

But there are differences that complicate matters in such an evaluation. First, the Rule of Law Index "civil justice" theme (which evaluates civil matters before domestic courts) can be seen as somewhat comparable to international commercial arbitration between private parties. However, it must be borne in mind that the Rule of Law Index surveys nationals, not foreigners, about the national court system. More significantly, treaty arbitration involves the state itself and in this sense is more comparable to the criminal justice theme or might require a new theme looking at judicial redress against the state. To take it a step further, the comparison would look to redress in national courts for claims against the state by foreigners. In addition, since a public interest is involved in many treaty arbitrations, an aspect of this theme would be to evaluate the transparency, both for nationals and for foreigners, of national judicial redress of claims against the state by foreigners. In my opinion, among the empirical questions not addressed by the literature, a ranking such as this – significant as the effort might be – would be helpful in making clear the alternatives available.

In closing, as we approach the 800th anniversary of the Magna Carta and the significance we attach to that document for development of the rule of law, I believe no greater effort exists before us than the evolution of a greater rule of law on the ground in all countries of the world. It likely is the case that such courts are not alternatives at present to treaty arbitration, but if such arbitration is to be trusted and accepted, I close

---

4. Public Statement on the International Investment Regime, 31 August 2010.

by emphasizing as I did at the outset that it should be expected that treaty arbitration will be held to the highest standard of legitimacy. I suggest that that demand is appropriate; it is a standard that need be met.

B. Justice Stream

4. Universal Arbitration:
An Aspiration Within Reach or a Sisyphean Goal?

Report on the Session Universal Arbitration: An Aspiration Within Reach or a Sisyphean Goal?

*Kathleen Claussen**

I.   INTRODUCTION

Session B4 was devoted to "Universal Arbitration: An Aspiration Within Reach or a Sisyphean Goal?," a topic of considerable relevance given the growth in the practice of arbitration throughout the world. Since Jan Paulsson delivered his 2012 Alexander Lecture on "Universal Arbitration: What We Gain, What We Lose" the concept of "universal arbitration" has been the subject of further reflection by scholars and practitioners active in international arbitrations.

The Chair, Dushyant Dave, opened the conversation by introducing the principal themes and the session propositions for consideration. He invited the participants and the panelists to consider the truth or falsity of the following four propositions:

(1) Arbitration is already universal.
(2) The users of the system have no interest in whether it enhances constitutional morality.
(3) Universality will improve the effectiveness and enforceability of arbitral awards
(4) Greater universality must be driven by arbitral institutions.

The object of the session was to explore these propositions and the presumptions or premises underlying them. The Chair began by noting how if we are to achieve universal arbitration, the goal must be to strengthen ways to bridge the cultural, legal and economic divide. From the Chair's perspective, if arbitration is to become truly universal, justice must both appear to be done and be done. The practice, the elements, and the final vision of justice may vary, but the appearance and the ultimate aim must be to seek to provide and to appear to provide justice. In the Chair's words: universal arbitration must foresee its unity in diversity rather than diversity in unity. Moreover, to accommodate diversity, new entrants require a fair opportunity to enter and participate, taking what is now international and making it truly universal.

---

*   Panel Rapporteur; Assistant General Counsel at the Office of the US Trade Representative; former Legal Counsel, Permanent Court of Arbitration; former Visiting Assistant Professor at the Indiana University Maurer School of Law.

The authors presenting their papers at Session B4 each took up a scholarly perspective on the topic. Diane Desierto addressed principles of Rawlsian fairness underlying an aspirational universal arbitration, while Stephan Schill considered the legitimacy of such a construction.

There were more questions than could be taken up during the short session, leading the Chair to conclude that the conversation should continue as this important topic continues to be advanced by practitioners and scholars in the field.

II.   THE PAPERS

Diane Desierto, our first presenter, approached universality through a Rawlsian vision, asking what "fairness in arbitration" means. She posited: How does Rawls' vision of fairness inform our understanding of fairness in arbitration and the potential for universal arbitration beyond the worldwide nature of the concept. Desierto's paper set out to examine ways to frame our understanding of legitimacy about whether certain aspects of arbitration are fair.

Describing Rawls' principal point of *A Theory of Justice*,[1] that inequality that ensues from bargaining must be directed away from the least advantaged, Desierto elaborated on what structures may be required in arbitration to achieve the same. Evaluating investment arbitration separately from commercial arbitration, Desierto concluded that some features of the current system(s) would remain, while others would not withstand the Rawlsian test. That is, to abide by Rawls' call for justice, reforms to the system would be required. Desierto suggested the following: first, a judicial evidentiary system allowing the parties to fully present their respective cases; second, increased transparency to enhance access for all; third, some capacity for review to avoid unfair outcomes; and fourth, the system would benefit from revising the standard profile of those who maintain it: the arbitral elite. A 2012 report, "Profiting from Injustice", showed that many arbitrators are driven by economic gain and nothing else.[2]

In conclusion, Desierto argued that it may be the case that the current design of international arbitration yields unfairness with respect to certain issues. To move toward universal arbitration, Desierto asserted that what is crucial is to invite a debate on conceptions of fairness. In Desierto's view, applying the Rawlsian theory of justice, international arbitration can be shaped under justice as fairness.

Stephan Schill's remarks addressed legitimacy and universality. He argued that if universality is the future of arbitration, legitimacy of the regime must be conceived in universal terms. Thus, before the regime is reformed to accommodate unity in diversity, a dialogue should be had to explore those changes. In Schill's view, challenges to universal arbitration include those that stem from consumer & labor arbitration (constitutional rights & access to courts). A central question to be studied is whether the

---

1. John RAWLS, *A Theory of Justice* (Bellknap Press 1971).
2. Pia EBERHARDT, Cecilia OLIVET, Tyler AMOS and Nick BUXTON, "Profiting from Injustice: How Law Firms, Arbitrators, and Financiers are Fuelling an Investment Arbitration Boom" (Corporate Europe Observatory and Transnational Institute 2012).

regime is representative of all users (democratic representativeness). Schill described the friction of certain aspects of international arbitration with democratic values.

The language of the criticism of international arbitration often reflects democracy, human rights, and rule of law, in Schill's view. A shift in thinking of arbitration as a recurrent phenomenon to thinking of it as a stable and permanent institution that contributes to ordering social relations has brought these questions into sharper focus. With this shift, arbitration may be seen by some as an exercise of authority in relation to users, parties, host States, and global society.

Schill then outlined responses to these criticisms and concerns. First, he addressed the inadequacy of responses that are limited to understanding arbitration as dispute settlement between two parties. Such approach equates legitimacy with party autonomy and does not take up community legitimacy. Schill suggested a more comprehensive response according to which practitioners and scholars focus on the standards of democracy, rule of law and human rights. This effort can be undertaken, according to Schill, through comparative constitutional law. In sum, Schill sees the task of the arbitral community as engagement with these three standards to show how arbitration can contribute to decisionmaking, furthering the idea of rule of law. These reforms should in turn lead to decisions inclusive to all interests and open to consequences of all affected.

III.   DISCUSSION AND COMMENTS ON THE PAPERS

Each paper discussion was followed by the contributions of a commentator and questions from the audience.

Veijo Heiskanen presented comments on Diane Desierto's paper. He began by noting that it is in many ways counterintuitive to think of the international arbitration "system" as a "system" at all. He disagreed with Desierto's application of the idea of a community of users and the idea of universal arbitration already. Heiskanen argued that to suggest that arbitration is universal by examining the membership of the 1958 New York Convention is a limited Westphalian view. He advocated differentiating between and among different users and groups to customize arbitral services that would better serve each group. The paradox of the premise of the panel, according to Heiskanen, is that to make arbitration more universal, it must be made more customized; in this sense, arbitration is not diverse in the way it is conducted but in terms of the users it serves.

In responding to Stephan Schill, Fei Ning noted that the process of the universalization of arbitration comes to light in a study of China's history. He commented that, although arbitration is a practice found throughout the history of China, commercial arbitration is not. In the last quarter century, commercial arbitration has emerged and evolved in China. In the 1980s, China's legal system changed with the adoption of bilateral investment treaties and China's accession to the New York Convention, among other changes, changing the nature of the arbitration landscape in the country from one that had not been willing to be a part of the universalization of arbitration to one at the forefront of arbitral trends. Reforms to arbitration laws such as those prohibiting State entities from attaining an advantageous position and limitations on judicial review have created this change. Put simply, in Fei Ning's view, universal arbitration has "happened" in China.

A commenter in the audience touched off the discussion with a fundamental question underlying the central premise of the panel: confidentiality. Noting arbitration's historical commitment to confidentiality, the questioner asked whether such a principle puts a limit on universality. In her words, "is not confidentiality the original sin that will prevent universality?" On this point, Desierto noted the Rawlsian view that confidentiality could be an accepted principle within the universal construct if it were part of the "original bargain." Schill acknowledged that confidentiality was the "original sin" in the investment arbitration system, the system on which he focused his attention, and that is a root problem in achieving universality. The Chair drew attention to freedom of information acts in national legislations asking for additional thoughts on how to reconcile these demands on the State with the confidentiality clauses to which States have committed.

A second questioner sharpened the discussion with a query into the definition of "universality" asserting that universal arbitration may never been achieved so long as there are different rules for each type of arbitration, including by way of varying national legislation, and a wide array of enforcement laws despite the broad adoption of the New York Convention. On this point, the panel emphasized the idea of unity in diversity, and posited that universality in arbitration may not require that the same rules be used but that there be common principles that are universal. The fact that most jurisdictions provide for arbitration and accommodate it among dispute resolution mechanisms is a step in that direction. It was a common view among the members of the panel and those involved in the discussion from the floor that it is difficult to conclude that arbitration is indeed universal unless one means to say that it is a global phenomenon. Some suggested that harmonization and uniformity of certain principles of arbitration is a more reasonable goal. In this way, arbitration can be universal but national systems of courts will remain different processes. Other discussants pushed back on the idea of reliance on constitutional principles which they saw as Western ideals.

IV.   CONCLUSION

The quality of the contributions to the discussion in Session B4 showed that the topic of universal arbitration remains aspirational, but an aspiration to which the community seeks to commit resources and thought to evaluate fairness and legitimacy of arbitration in an effort to achieve universality. At the same time, practitioners and scholars need to better understand the justification for the universality. Is it enforcement? Is it only enforcement? While arbitration may have reached "global" status in terms of its reach and effects, the importance of achieving universal arbitration as a means to securing the system's legitimacy is the responsibility of all who practice and study in the field.

Developing a Framework for the Legitimacy of International Arbitration

*Stephan W. Schill**

I.   INTRODUCTION

The issue of legitimacy of international arbitration and its conditions is receiving increasing attention, not only outside the arbitration community, but also within. Questions of legitimacy animate the more abstract debates about the theory, philosophy, and idea of arbitration,[1] just as they serve as the backdrop to more practical controversies, for example about party appointments v. institutional appointments of arbitrators, about the value of dissenting opinions,[2] or about the regulation of questions

---

* Senior Research Fellow, Max Planck Institute for Comparative Public Law and International Law, Heidelberg; Rechtsanwalt; Attorney-at-Law (New York); LL.M. (Augsburg, 2002); LL.M. International Legal Studies (New York University, 2006); Dr. iur. (Frankfurt am Main, 2008); Member of the ICSID List of Conciliators. This paper was written with the support of a European Research Council Starting Grant on "Transnational Private-Public Arbitration as Global Regulatory Governance: Charting and Codifying the Lex Mercatoria Publica" (LexMercPub, Grant agreement no.: 313355). I would like to thank Carlino Antpöhler, Daniela Arrese, Armin von Bogdandy, Matthias Goldmann, Simon Hentrei, Michael Ioannidis, Christoph Krenn, Daniel Litwin and Ximena Soley for comments on earlier versions of this paper and Daniel Litwin and Nadine Berger for their valuable research assistance in the preparation of this paper.

1. See, for example, Emmanuel GAILLARD, *Aspects philosophiques du droit de l'arbitrage international* (Martinus Nijhoff 2008); Emmanuel GAILLARD, *Legal Theory of International Arbitration* (Martinus Nijhoff 2010); Pierre TERCIER, "*La légitimité de l'arbitrage*", Revue de l'arbitrage (2011) p. 653; Jan PAULSSON, *The Idea of Arbitration* (OUP 2013); Pierre-Marie DUPUY, "*Des arbitres sans contrôle? De la légitimité des tribunaux arbitraux dans la domaine des investissements*" in Charles LEBEN, ed., *La procedure arbitrale relative aux investissements internationaux* (Anthemis 2010) p. 316. Earlier discussions include, inter alia, Bruno OPPETIT, *Théorie de l'arbitrage* (PUF 1998); Samantha BESSON, "*La légitimité de l'arbitrage international d'investissement*", Jusletter (25 July 2005).

2.   On the "Paulson-van den Berg-Brower" controversy on these issues see Jan PAULSSON, "Moral Hazard in International Dispute Resolution", 25 ICSID Rev.–FILJ (2010) p. 339; Albert Jan VAN DEN BERG "Dissenting Opinions by Party-Appointed Arbitrators in Investment Arbitration" in M. H. ARSANJANI, J. COGAN, R. SLOANE and S. WIESSNER, eds., *Looking to the Future: Essays on International Law in Honor of W. Michael Reisman* (Martinus Nijhoff 2011) p. 821; Charles N.

of professional ethics in international arbitration.[3] Indeed, the very theme of this conference – "Legitimacy: Myths, Realities, Challenges" of international arbitration[4]– attests to the growing importance of thinking about legitimacy in the field.

The very use of the concept of "legitimacy" in the analysis of international arbitration indicates an emerging awareness for the exercise of power in and through international arbitration.[5] The link between power and legitimacy is drawn by David Beetham, an English political scientist, in *The Legitimation of Power* as follows:

> "Power ... is a highly problematical, as well as recurrent feature of human societies. And because it is so problematical, societies will seek to subject it to justifiable rules, and the powerful themselves will seek to secure consent to their power from at least the most important among their subordinates. Where power is acquired and exercised according to justifiable rules, and with evidence of consent, we call it rightful or legitimate."[6]

BROWER and Charles B. ROSENBERG, "The Death of the Two-headed Nightingale: Why the Paulsson-van den Berg Presumption that Party-Appointed Arbitrators are Untrustworthy is Wrongheaded", 23 Arb. Int'l (2013) p. 7; Charles N. BROWER, Michael PULOS and Charles B. ROSENBERG, "So Is There Anything *Really* Wrong with International Arbitration As We Know It?" in A. ROVINE, ed., *Contemporary Issues in International Arbitration and Mediation: The Fordham Papers* (2012) p. 3.

3. See, for example, Sundaresh MENON, "International Arbitration: The Coming of a New Age for Asia", Keynote address delivered at the 21st ICCA Congress in Singapore in 2012 <www.arbitration-icca.org/media/0/13398435632250/ags_opening_speech_icca_congress_2012.pdf> (last accessed 28 March 2014) paras. 43-46; see generally Catherine Rogers, *Ethics in International Arbitration* (OUP 2014).

4. See <www.iccamiami2014.com/> (last accessed 28 March 2014).

5. I use the word "power" here, instead of "authority", because the latter is often understood as a legal term of art that refers to the capacity to unilaterally reduce somebody's freedom of action based on a legal norm. Cf. Armin VON BOGDANDY, Philipp DANN and Matthias GOLDMANN, "Developing the Publicness of Public International Law: Towards a Legal Framework for Global Governance Activities" in A. VON BOGDANDY, et al., eds., *The Exercise of Public Authority by International Institutions* (Springer 2010) p. 3 at p. 11 ("the legal capacity to *determine* others and to reduce their freedom, i.e. to unilaterally shape their legal or factual situation" (emphasis in original)). What is more, "authority" is also often used to indicate that the exercise of power is legitimate. See Ingo VENZKE, "Between Power and Persuasion: On International Institutions' Authority in Making Law", 4 Transnat'l Legal Theory (2013) p. 354 at p. 357 ("The distinctive element of authority in contrast to coercion by force is typically that it claims to be *legitimate*. It does so above all by claiming to rest on consent or, in other words, a minimal degree of voluntary recognition that leads an actor to *want* to act as the authority indicates. This element also characteristically separates authority from power where power is understood as an actor's ability to impose its will within a social relationship also *against resistance*." (Emphases in original)). In the present context, by contrast, I want to point to the purely social dimensions of power in a Weberian sense without making any statement as to the basis of this power in law. See Max WEBER, *Economy and Society* (University of California Press 1978) p. 53 ("'Power' (*Macht*) is the probability that one actor within a social relationship be in a position to carry out his own will despite resistance, regardless of the basis on which this probability rests.").

6. David BEETHAM, *The Legitimation of Power* (Macmillan 1991) p. 3.

The understanding of the concept of "legitimacy", in turn, will vary widely depending on who uses it in which context. Lawyers will tend to resolve questions of legitimacy in terms of legality. When power, including in the context of international arbitration, is acquired in line with legal rules and exercised accordingly, lawyers will tend to view the institution and its manifestations as legitimate: For lawyers, "legitimacy is equivalent to *legal validity*."[7] Legality turns power into authority.[8] This, however, leaves open the question whether the rules themselves are legitimate, to which lawyers equally answer by turning to other rules, such as rules on competence, statutes governing the parties' mutual rights and obligations, and ultimately constitutional law that determines how and by whom rules can be made and what procedural and substantive guarantees they have to comply with. For moral and political philosophy and political science, by contrast, the question of legitimacy starts where lawyers' expertise ends: Moral and philosophical philosophers will look towards "rationally defensible normative principles";[9] social scientists will look towards the empirical acceptance of actors that are subordinate to power and the reasons for doing so.[10]

The different approaches to legitimacy also entail different methodologies. Asking for the lawyer's "legitimacy" of international arbitration would call for engaging in a quest for the ultimate legal source of an arbitral tribunal's authority, coupled with developing procedural, institutional, and substantive safeguards for the exercise of that authority. Asking for the (legal) philosopher's "legitimacy" will entail developing a framework based on first principles, which are independent from positive law and globally shared by all those engaged in, or affected by, international arbitration. Diane Desierto's analysis of international arbitration is such an approach, given that she applies the Rawlsian framework of normative reasoning to international arbitration.[11] Finally, asking for the social scientist's "legitimacy" would entail an empirical analysis, through the use of qualitative and quantitative methods, of why actors engage in arbitration, how they assess their participation, the arbitral process and outcome, and whether society at large views arbitration, including the respective legislation and the activities of controlling courts, as following acceptable and accepted policies.[12]

---

7. *Ibid.*, p. 4 (emphasis in original).
8. See VENZKE, supra fn. 5, p. 357.
9. BEETHAM, supra fn. 6, p. 5.
10. *Ibid.*
11. See Diane DESIERTO, "Rawlsian Fairness and International Arbitration", U. Penn. J. Int'l Law (forthcoming).
12. For such approaches see, for example, Yves DEZALAY and Bryant G. GARTH, *Dealing in Virtue: International Commercial Arbitration and the Construction of a Transnational Legal Order* (Univ. Chicago Press 1996); Christopher DRAHOZAL and Richard NAIMARK, eds., *Towards a Science of International Arbitration: Collected Empirical Research* (Kluwer 2005); Loukas MISTELIS and Crina BALTAG, "Recognition and Enforcement of Arbitral Awards and Settlement in International Arbitration: Corporate Attitudes and Practices", 19 Am. Rev. Int'l Arb. (2008) p. 319; Susan D. FRANCK, "Development and Outcomes of Investment Treaty Arbitration", 50 Harvard International Law Journal (2009) p. 435; Gus VAN HARTEN, *Sovereign Choices and Sovereign Constraints — Judicial Restraint in Investment Treaty Arbitration* (OUP 2013); Thomas SCHULTZ and Cedric G. DUPONT, "Investment Arbitration: Promoting the Rule of Law or Over-Empowering

In the present chapter, I will focus on the concept of "legitimacy" as part of the legal framework that structures how actors, institutions, norms and processes interact in the system of international arbitration. Yet, in adopting a lawyer's understanding of legitimacy as legality, I will not argue that there is a single source of law, either in contract or statute, in national or international law, that authoritatively determines the criteria under which international arbitration is legal, and hence legitimate. This seems impossible given that international arbitration derives its authority from a variety of sources of national and international, public and private law, that together constitute and stabilize international arbitration as an independent system of law and governance.[13] Instead, I will analyze the legal discourse and argumentative practices relating to the legitimacy of international arbitration both within and outside the international arbitration community and try to carve out common argumentative structures about legitimacy in international arbitration that exist independently of the traditional sources of law. In this context, this chapter will contrast how the international arbitration system justifies its own exercise of authority in legal terms with how and according to which legal standards that authority is analyzed from outside the system.

As I argue in this chapter, the discourse on legitimacy within international arbitration is too focused on the function of arbitration as a mechanism to settle individual disputes, disregarding the increasing importance of international arbitration as an institution of transnational governance. Moreover, the discourse on legitimacy inside international arbitration is too isolated from other discourses dealing with the legitimacy of international dispute settlement and global governance. It reflects what Stavros Brekoulakis has aptly described as a more general problem with the theory of international arbitration: that it "was largely developed under the 'delusion of self-sufficiency as a science of law'".[14] This is particularly problematic in relation to the concept of legitimacy, which cannot, as I argue in this chapter, be limited to a limited system-internal perspective.

The discourse on legitimacy within the international arbitration community needs reorientation and an opening up vis-à-vis other discourses on legitimacy. One source of inspiration for the discourse on legitimacy in international arbitration are the scholarship

---

Investors? A Quantitative Empirical Study", King's College London Dickson Poon School of Law Legal Studies Research Paper No. 2014-16, <ssrn.com/abstract=2399179> (last accessed 7 November 2014); Thomas J. STIPANOWICH, "Reflections on the State and Future of Commercial Arbitration: Challenges, Opportunities, Proposals", Pepperdine University Legal Studies Research Paper No. 2014/29, <ssrn.com/abstract=2519084> (last accessed 13 November 2014); Thomas J. STIPANOWICH and Zachary P. ULRICH, "Arbitration in Evolution: Current Practices and Perspectives of Experienced Commercial Arbitrators", Pepperdine University Legal Studies Research Paper No. 2014/30, <ssrn.com/abstract=2519196> (last accessed 13 November 2014).

13. On the difficulties of scholarship to develop arbitration as an autonomous legal discipline in light of the firm grip different domestic legal orders still exercise in relation to arbitration see Stavros L. BREKOULAKIS, "International Arbitration Scholarship and the Concept of Arbitration Law", 36 Fordham Int'l L. J. (2013) p. 745, at pp. 763-777.

14. *Ibid.*, p. 749 (quoting Roger COTTERRELL, "Ehrlich at the Edge of Empire: Centres and Peripheries in Legal Studies" in M. HERTOGH, ed., *Living Law: Reconsidering Eugen Ehrlich* (2009) p. 75).

on public international law and global governance theory and the debate on the legitimacy of international courts and tribunals that has emerged in this context.[15] Another source of inspiration are the inquiries in private international law on the legitimacy of transnational law and transnational legal processes, and the role dispute settlement, including arbitration, plays in this process.[16] While both of these discourses have much potential for an analysis of international arbitration, the source of inspiration that I am exploring in the present chapter for enhancing the legitimacy discourse in international arbitration and for developing an overarching framework for thinking about the legitimacy of international arbitration comes from yet another framework, namely constitutional legal argument.

In my view, constitutional analysis and constitutional principles should not only serve as an outside check on how arbitration statutes are crafted or how domestic courts control arbitral tribunals; instead, constitutional law thinking should be integrated into the system-internal debates about the legitimacy of international arbitration. This requires a mental leap within the arbitration community given that, from an arbitration-internal perspective, constitutional law and arbitration "appear to be strange bedfellows",[17] as Bo Rutledge has aptly put it. Yet, constitutional law and arbitration are increasingly moving closer together. This is true above all in relation to arbitrations involving states or state entities who operate under a public law framework and have to obey their respective constitutional constraints.[18] But it also holds true in more general terms if we consider that international arbitration functions as a system of transnational governance that has an impact on society at large and that has to conform to generally

---

15. Such a reorientation is advocated by BREKOULAKIS, supra fn. 13, pp. 777 et seq. For some of the literature on the legitimacy of international courts and tribunals, see the contributions by Andreas FOLLESDAL, Armin VON BOGDANDY, Ingo VENZKE, Erik VOETEN, Yonatan LUPU, Shai DOTHAN, Laurence HELFER and Karen J. ALTER, and Clifford CARRUBBA and Matthew J. GABEL as part of a symposium on "International Courts and the Quest for Legitimacy" in 14 Theoretical Inquiries in Law (2013) pp. 339-541; Armin VON BOGDANDY and Ingo VENZKE, In Whose Name? A Public Law Theory of International Adjudication (OUP 2014); Armin VON BOGDANDY and Ingo VENZKE, eds., International Judicial Lawmaking (Springer 2012); Nienke GROSSMANN, "The Normative Legitimacy of International Courts", 86 Temple L. Rev. (2013) p. 61; Nienke Grossmann, "Legitimacy and International Adjudicative Bodies", 41 G. W. Int'l L. Rev. (2009) p. 107; Karen J. ALTER, The New Terrain of International Law: Courts, Politics, Rights (Princeton Univ. Press 2014).

16. Gralf-Peter CALLIES and Peer ZUMBANSEN, Rough Consensus and Running Code: A Theory of Transnational Private Law (Hart 2010) pp. 27 et seq.; Moritz RENNER, Zwingendes transnationales Recht (Nomos 2011); Thomas SCHULTZ, Transnational Legality — Stateless Law and International Arbitration (OUP 2014).

17. Peter B. RUTLEDGE, Arbitration and the Constitution (CUP 2013) p. 1. The unease of combining arbitration and constitutional law arguably stems from the fact that, depending on the respective national epistemic communities, arbitration is treated as part of civil procedure, as is the case in Germany, Austria, Italy, and Greece, as part of private international law or conflicts of law, as in France or Switzerland, or as part of ordinary contract law, as in the common law tradition, but hardly ever as a subject of constitutional law analysis. See BREKOULAKIS, supra fn. 13, pp. 763-764.

18. See Laurence BOISSON DE CHAZOURNES and Brian MCGARRY, "What Roles Can Constitutional Law Play in Investment Arbitration?", 15 J. World Inv. & Trade (2014) p. 862.

accepted standards for governance, such as democracy, the rule of law, and human rights. Constitutional law assumes specific importance in this context because it constitutes the most important source of legality for the exercise of authority and is able to infuse an entire system of law with legitimacy. The fact that it is increasingly constitutional language that is used to criticize international arbitration attests to the importance of constitutional principles for the debate on the legitimacy of international arbitration.

In order to develop a more complete framework for thinking about the legitimacy of international arbitration that draws on constitutional analysis, this chapter first focuses on the reasons why the legitimacy discourse has emerged and why criticism of international arbitration has turned to constitutional language. It argues that this has to do with the transformation of international arbitration from a dispute settlement mechanism into a mechanism of transnational governance (Part II). Next, the chapter zooms in on the concept of legitimacy that is used in international arbitration and exposes its deficits in light of arbitration's functioning as a governance structure. Although theoretical accounts of international arbitration increasingly stress arbitration's systemic nature, they often fail to translate effects of arbitration beyond the disputing parties into a multidimensional concept of legitimacy that encompasses not only "party legitimacy" but also what I call "community legitimacy", "national legitimacy" and "global legitimacy" (Part III). Finally, the chapter introduces comparative constitutional analysis as a conceptual framework to enrich the legitimacy debate in international arbitration. It encompasses, but goes beyond, party autonomy and party consent as sources of legitimacy, and suggests to develop legitimating reasons for the authority of international arbitration on the basis of the commonly accepted constitutional principles of democracy, the rule of law, and human rights (Part IV).

II. THE EMERGING LEGITIMACY DISCOURSE IN INTERNATIONAL ARBITRATION

For most of its existence, international arbitration has been treated primarily as a technical subject, mostly by practicing lawyers, with books and law journal articles focusing chiefly on doctrinal questions, such as the analysis of domestic statutes, international treaties, and case law by domestic courts relating to arbitration, as well as decisions by arbitral tribunals.[19] Questions of legitimacy, by contrast, have hardly played a role in the analysis of the field until recently. In the meantime, the indifference towards questions of legitimacy has given way to a vivid debate on that very topic in international arbitration circles and beyond. One of the challenges, in this context, is to determine what the concept of legitimacy exactly means for different participants in the debate and to develop a common framework of understanding it as a legal concept. In order to develop that framework, it is crucial to reflect on the reasons and context for the emerging legitimacy discourse and the language it uses.

As I argue in this section, the deeper reason for the emerging legitimacy discourse is the metamorphosis international arbitration has undergone from a dyadic dispute

---

19. See BREKOULAKIS, supra fn. 13, pp. 763-770.

settlement mechanism into a stable institution of transnational governance *(1)*. International arbitration today constitutes an institution that contributes to stabilizing and generating normative expectations in transborder social relations and hence has to be analyzed as exercising a form of transnational authority *(2)*. Its normative effects go beyond the realm of the disputing parties and have important repercussions on recalibrating social relations, and the rights connected to them, both private and public. This has implications for constitutional arrangements and the relationship between private rights and public interests and gives rise to constitutional language being used to criticize arbitration and question its legitimacy *(3)*.

1.   International Arbitration as Governance

During the past two decades international arbitration has seen a transformation from a recurrent phenomenon of transborder commercial and inter-state relations with little social significance, whose function was the *ex post* settlement of individual disputes and no more, into a stable and permanent institution with universal aspirations that contributes significantly to ordering social relations *ex ante* between the disputing parties but also beyond. It has broader implications for how the normative foundations of society develop today, at the domestic as well as the global level. This is particularly obvious in the context of investor-state arbitration where tribunals are crafting global rules for the relations between states and foreign investor.[20] But it is also the case when considering how arbitral tribunals contribute to the making of transnational rules for conducting international business generally *(lex mercatoria)*,[21] and more specifically in maritime affairs *(lex maritima)*,[22] or with respect to international sports *(lex sportiva)*.[23] It is this broader social impact that has brought to the fore challenges to international arbitration and has given rise to the question of international arbitration's legitimacy.

While the rise of international arbitration is closely tied to the need for effective and neutral institutions for the settlement of individual transborder disputes, which cannot be fulfilled easily by domestic or international courts, international arbitration has

---

20. See Stephan W. SCHILL, *The Multilateralization of International Investment Law* (CUP 2009); Benedict KINGSBURY and Stephan W. SCHILL, "Investor-State Arbitration as Governance: Fair and Equitable Treatment, Proportionality, and the Emerging Global Administrative Law" in A.J. VAN DEN BERG, ed., *50 Years of the New York Convention*, ICCA Congress Series no. 14 (2009) p. 5.
21. See SCHULTZ, supra fn. 16, pp. 105-118; Stephan W. SCHILL, "Lex Mercatoria" in R. WOLFRUM, ed., *Max Planck Encyclopedia of Public International Law* (OUP 2012), Vol. VI, p. 823 (with references to the increasing literature), available also at <www.mpepil.com> (last accessed 28 March 2014).
22. William TETLEY, "The General Maritime Law – The Lex Maritima", 20 Syracuse J. Int'l L. & Comm. (1994) p. 105; Andrea Maurer, *Lex Maritima: Grundzüge eines transnationalen Seehandelsrechts* (Mohr Siebeck 2012).
23. See, for example, Franck LATTY, *La Lex Sportiva – Recherche sur le droit transnational* (Martinus Nijhoff 2007); Lorenzo CASINI, *Il diritto globale dello sport* (Giuffrè 2010); Lorenzo CASINI, "The Making of a Lex Sportiva by the Court of Arbitration for Sport", 12 German L. J. (2011) p. 1317.

assumed, both institutionally and in substance, large-scale social significance. The central factors for this development are the following:

– *first*, the reorientation from *ad hoc* to institutional arbitration, which led both to a standardization and consolidation of the arbitral procedure applicable in institutional arbitrations and to the creation – through arbitrator and counsel trainings, seminars, and conferences – of a specific professional community with a common professional ethos and mindset, as well as the further promotion of arbitration, for example through the development of model arbitration clauses and agreements by arbitration institutions;[24]
– *second*, the broadening of the subject-matter of disputes that are resolved through arbitration, and the shrinking of areas of non-arbitrability, from initially only business-to-business disputes primarily in regard of international sales contracts and maritime commerce, to a whole variety of areas including corporate disputes, real estate, infrastructure, telecommunications, utilities, banking and financial markets or insurance, between commercial actors, but also between commercial actors and governments in areas of foreign investment, and in some cases even employment, consumer, or family matters, thus extending the social reach of arbitration into virtually any area of social relations;[25]
– *third*, the territorial expansion, and by now global reach, of arbitration, with arbitration no longer only taking place with the involvement of commercial actors from industrialized countries under institutional rules of arbitration institutions located there, such as the Paris-based International Chamber of Commerce, the Arbitration Institute of the Stockholm Chamber of Commerce, or the American Arbitration Association, but also being used to resolve disputes between actors from transitioning and developing countries and with arbitration institutions having emerged in places like Beijing, Cairo, Dubai, Hong Kong, Jerusalem, Kuala Lumpur, Qatar, São Paulo, Shanghai or Singapore;[26]
– *fourth*, aided by specialized law firms and business actors who are repeat players in arbitration, the entrenchment of arbitration as the default mechanism to settle disputes under transborder contracts in the model contracts of industry associations, arbitration

---

24. See generally Walter MATTLI, "Private Justice in a Global Economy: From Litigation to Arbitration", 55 International Organization (2001) p. 919; Alec Stone SWEET, "The New Lex Mercatoria and Transnational Governance", 13 J. Eur. Public Policy (2006) p. 627; A. Claire CUTLER, *Private Power and Global Authority: Transnational Law Merchant in the Global Political Economy* (CUP 2003); Christopher A. WHYTOCK, "Private-Public Interaction in Global Governance: The Case of Transnational Arbitration", 12 Business and Politics (2010, no. 3) Art. 10; DEZALAY and GARTH, supra fn. 12.
25. Loukas A. MISTELIS and Stavros L. BREKOULAKIS, eds., *Arbitrability: International and Comparative Perspectives* (Wolters Kluwer 2009). Particularly graphic, Karim YOUSSEF, "The Death of Inarbitrability" in Loukas A. MISTELIS and Stavros L. BREKOULAKIS, eds., *Arbitrability: International and Comparative Perspectives* (Wolters Kluwer 2009) p. 47 ("In recent years, the scope of rights amenable to arbitration has grown to such an extent that, the concept of arbitrability (or its mirror image, inarbitrability) as central as it may be to arbitration theory, has virtually died in real arbitral life.").
26. See in particular DEZALAY and GARTH, supra fn. 12, pp. 281 et seq.

institutions, and companies, the inclusion of arbitration clauses in international treaties, including in international investment treaties that permit direct treaty-based investor-state arbitration, and the support of arbitration by states through arbitration-friendly legislation and the conclusion of international agreements that allow arbitration to work as a global dispute settlement system, such as the New York or Washington Conventions;

– and *finally*, a convergence of how arbitration is practiced worldwide, which is referred to by Jan Paulsson as "universal arbitration", meaning "the convergence of the way disputes are resolved, so that disputants and advocates and arbitrators of any nationality can be found everywhere, doing the same thing in the same way – with an ever-decreasing number of linguistic barriers".[27]

All of these developments have had the effect that arbitration is not limited to a method for settling individual disputes, even though this remains its principal objective, but performs a host of other functions that are largely similar to those performed by permanent dispute settlement institutions, be they domestic or international courts.[28]

Arbitrators, to start with, also have the (objective) function of asserting and applying the law governing the disputing parties' relations. They are not only agents of the disputing parties tasked to resolve the dispute on the basis of commercial considerations; instead, they are impartial and independent organs of adjudication that, similar to courts, are tasked to apply legal rules to resolving the parties' dispute.[29] Furthermore, arbitrators today also have the function of further developing the law applicable to disputing parties more generally, in particular in cases where arbitral awards become public. This is the case in many investment disputes, but also, albeit to a lesser extent, in purely commercial cases. Reasoning in terms of precedent, where available, is one form through which arbitrators develop global norms that are increasingly independent of applicable national or international legal rules. But also where precedent is not available, the converging practices and culture of international arbitration are likely

---

27. Jan PAULSSON, "Universal Arbitration – What We Gain, What We Lose", Alexander Lecture delivered on 29 November 2012 <www.globalarbitrationreview.com/cdn/files/gar/articles/jan_Paulsson_Universal_Arbitration_-_what_we_gain_what_we_lose.pdf> (last accessed 28 March 2014).

28. On the functions of domestic courts, see Martin SHAPIRO, *Courts: A Comparative and Political Analysis* (Chicago Univ. Press 1981) pp. 1-64; Herbert JACOB, *Courts, Law, and Politics in Comparative Perspective* (Yale Univ. Press 1996) pp. 11-4; Lawrence M. FRIEDMAN, "Trial Courts and Their Work in the Modern World" in L.M. FRIEDMAN and M. REHBINDER, eds., *Zur Soziologie des Gerichtsverfahrens* (Westdeutscher Verlag 1976) p. 25 at pp. 27-30; Roger COTTERRELL, *The Sociology of Law* (OUP 1984) pp. 216-258; Rolf BENDER, "*Funktionswandel der Gerichte*", 7 Zeitschrift für Rechtspolitik (1974) p. 235. See further also Niklas LUHMANN, *Das Recht der Gesellschaft* (Suhrkamp 1993) pp. 124-164. On the functions of international courts, see Armin VON BOGDANDY and Ingo VENZKE, "On the Functions of International Courts: An Appraisal in Light of Their Burgeoning Public Authority", 26 Leiden J. Int'l L. (2013) p. 49 at pp. 52-59.

29. See Jan PAULSSON, "International Arbitration Is Not Arbitration", Stockholm Int'l Arb. Rev. (2008, no. 2) p. 1 at p. 14; see further Susan D. FRANCK, "The Role of International Arbitrators", 12 ILSA J. Int'l & Comp. L. (2006) p. 499 at pp. 504-513 (discussing the different views on the functions and roles of arbitrators).

leading to the development of global law spoken and produced by arbitrators.[30] In applying and developing the law applicable to and in arbitration,[31] international arbitrators uphold and further develop the normative foundations upon which the system of international arbitration is built. This constitutes international arbitration as a system of global governance that goes beyond the settlement of individual disputes.

Similarly, arbitration institutions, which make up an important component of arbitration as an institution, perform many functions that are unrelated to settling individual disputes. Above all, arbitration institutions develop the rules governing the procedural rules arbitrators have to apply. In addition, arbitration institutions can have an important function in building the arbitration community, forging its professional ethos and ensuring the convergence of social practice that is necessary for arbitral procedure and the settlement of disputes to be implemented in a manner that is both predictable and accepted by the parties.[32] Arbitration institutions do so through conferences, publications, including specialized arbitration journals, and educational efforts for counsel and arbitrators and young professionals. In addition to this community-building function, they promote arbitration and their own institution as a preferred and beneficial mode to settle transborder disputes, through outreach programs, marketing, the proposal of model arbitration agreements, and lobbying with industry actors and governments for support of arbitration.

All of these developments reflect the functioning of international arbitration as a system of governance rather than only a dispute settlement mechanism. International arbitrators and arbitration institutions contribute to the creation of expectations of potential users about the functioning and benefits of arbitration, both in respect of the law applicable to arbitration and in arbitration. They are part of the processes of convergence that Jan Paulsson calls "universal arbitration" and that result in international arbitration functioning as a global system of governance.

2.   *International Arbitration and the Exercise of Transnational Authority*

The development of international arbitration into a system of governance not only has upsides; it also brings problems and raises questions of legitimacy, in particular regarding the functions that surpass the settlement of individual disputes, such as law-making by arbitral tribunals, but also the manifold activities of arbitration institutions that impact social expectations and the behavior of disputants and governments. These aspects can usefully be analyzed as instances of transnational authority, as tribunals and arbitration

---

30. See generally Joshua KARTON, *The Culture of International Arbitration and the Evolution of Contract Law* (OUP 2013).
31. On the distinction between law applicable to arbitration and law applicable in arbitration, see PAULSSON, supra fn. 1, p. 29 ("The latter provides norms to guide arbitrators' decisions. The former refers to the source of their authority and the status of their decision: the legal order that governs arbitration.").
32. This is not necessarily the case with all arbitration institutions. Some of them may also be subservient/deferential to the dominant actors of the system they regularly interact with. In such cases, arbitral institutions rather provide an appearance of legitimacy to the institution of arbitration, without legitimizing it in fact.

institutions through their activities that go beyond settling individual disputes reduce the freedom of action of future parties to arbitrations or even entirely third parties based on a combination of national and international laws applying to arbitration.[33] It constitutes authority in the sense that it has effects beyond the disputing parties who have specifically consented to the authority of arbitrators and an arbitration institution; and it is transnational, because international arbitration is supported by domestic laws and international legal instruments and affects both public and private actors.[34]

The exercise of transnational authority raises questions of legitimacy because arbitration affects, and constrains future actions, and hence the liberty, of non-parties.[35] It does so most clearly when considering the effect that arbitrations involving governments can have on the respective populations, either because certain government policies are declared illegal or because governments are ordered to pay damages or compensations and hence must use their taxpayers' money. This raises salient questions: What justification is there for arbitrators to make such decisions? How can one justify the powers of arbitral tribunals to make decisions that affect people's liberty? And how do we legitimize the interpretative powers tribunals possess, which allow them to develop the law governing investor-state relations rather independently from the applicable sources? In particular in investment treaty arbitration, the ability of arbitral tribunals to make law with system-wide implications and with increasingly deep impact on domestic law- and policy-making has been noted and discussed.[36]

---

33. The notion of "authority" is therefore the same as that used by A. VON BOGDANDY, et al., supra fn. 5, p. 11.

34. The notion of transnational law used in this context draws on Philip JESSUP, *Transnational Law* (Yale University Press 1956) p. 2 ("Nevertheless I shall use, instead of 'international law', the term 'transnational law' to include all law which regulates actions or events that transcend national frontiers. Both public and private international law are included, as are other rules which do not wholly fit into such standard categories."). Under this perspective, Jessup invited a perspective on all laws, whether public or private, national or international, that concern the regulation of matters transcending national frontiers.

35. For a parallel view on the legitimacy problems of international courts see Armin VON BOGDANDY and Ingo VENZKE, "In Whose Name? An Investigation of International Courts' Public Authority and Its Democratic Justification", 23 Eur. J. Int'l L. (2013) p. 7 at pp. 17-18.

36. See Ari AFILALO, "Meaning, Ambiguity and Legitimacy: Judicial (Re-)Construction of NAFTA Chapter 11", 25 Nw. J. Int'l L. & Bus. (2005) p. 279; Ari AFILALO, "Towards a Common Law of International Investment: How NAFTA Chapter 11 Panels Should Solve Their Legitimacy Crisis", 17 Geo. Int'l Envtl. L. Rev. (2004) p. 51; Charles H. BROWER, "Structure, Legitimacy, and NAFTA's Investment Chapter", 36 Vand. J. Transnat'l L. (2003) p. 37; Charles N. BROWER, "A Crisis of Legitimacy", Nat'l L.J. (7 Oct. 2002) B9; Charles N. BROWER, Charles H. BROWER and Jeremy K. SHARPE, "The Coming Crisis in the Global Adjudication System", 19 Arb. Int'l (2003) p. 415; Susan D. FRANCK, "The Legitimacy Crisis in Investment Treaty Arbitration: Privatizing Public International Law Through Inconsistent Decisions", 73 Fordham L. Rev. (2005) p. 1521; M. SORNARAJAH, "A Coming Crisis: Expansionary Trends in Investment Treaty Arbitration" in Karl P. SAUVANT, ed., *Appeals Mechanism in International Investment Disputes* (OUP 2008) p. 39; see also Charles N. BROWER and Stephan W. SCHILL, "Is Arbitration a Threat or a Boon to the Legitimacy of International Investment Law?", 9 Chi. J. Int'l L. (2009) p. 471. See also the *Public Statement on the International Investment Regime*, 31 August 2010, 8 Transnational Dispute Management (2011, no. 1).

Yet, the legitimacy of international arbitration may also be influenced negatively by criticism of purely domestic uses of arbitration, in particular under consumer and labor contracts in the United States and their potential to circumvent public policy and substantive and procedural rights that are granted under domestic statutes and the Constitution and are enforced by domestic courts.[37] These debates focus not so much on the power of arbitral tribunals, but on the power of the stronger contracting (and later disputing) party, that may become entrenched through arbitration and exempted from safeguards that are usually in place to control social power in domestic dispute settlement systems. While involving domestic arbitrations, which are generally viewed by arbitration practitioners as belonging to a legal and epistemic context that is separate from international arbitration,[38] the legitimacy critique of some forms of domestic arbitration may have spillover effects on international arbitration because the general public does not necessarily draw a distinction between the universes of domestic and international arbitration. While it is problematic to conflate all systems of arbitration, as it overrides crucial differences between different arbitral systems, the perception of the legitimacy of arbitration in a strictly domestic sense may affect the perception of the legitimacy of international arbitration generally.

But arbitration also raises questions of legitimacy even when only focusing on users of arbitration. They may question the development of law by arbitral tribunals and the various activities of arbitration institutions as having undesired impacts on their contractual right to arbitrate and to have disputes decided by arbitrators that are independent and impartial in deciding disputes based on a neutral analysis of facts and law. Questions may also be raised about the "Northern" and "Western" origin of arbitrators, as well as many powerful arbitration institutions, and the legal-cultural mindset that is behind the substantive and procedural rules developed for and in arbitration.[39] Moreover, the legitimacy of arbitration may be questioned by disputing parties, in light of increasing costs and length of arbitration proceedings, as regards the efficiency and expediency of the process; the legitimacy of arbitration is affected in this context as arbitration institutions and arbitrators may be seen by some as having a financial interest in the number and duration of arbitrations.[40]

All of these concerns ultimately involve the question whether international arbitration as an institution exercises its transnational authority in a way that can deliver fairness and justice for all stakeholders involved, and hence is in line with the fundamental social values, not only of disputing parties or of the community of users of arbitration, but of

---

37. I am thinking here primarily of the recent proceedings before the US Supreme Court involving, inter alia, the circumvention of class actions by means of arbitration agreements in consumer contracts and the extent of the unconscionability doctrine in employment arbitration. See *Stolt-Nielsen S.A. v. AnimalFeeds International*, 130 S.Ct. 1758 (2010); *AT&T Mobility v. Concepcion*, 563 U.S. 321 (2011); *Rent-A-Center, West v. Jackson*, 130 S.Ct. 2772 (2010). See further Thomas J. STIPANOWICH, "The Third Arbitration Trilogy: *Stolt-Nielsen, Rent-A-Center, Concepcion* and the Future of American Arbitration", 22 Am. Rev. Int'l Arb. (2011) p. 323.
38. See PAULSSON, supra fn. 28.
39. Cf. Gus VAN HARTEN, "TWAIL and the Dabhol Arbitration", 3 Trade, Law & Development (2011) p. 131.
40. See Gus VAN HARTEN, *Investment Treaty Arbitration as Public Law* (OUP 2007) pp. 167 et seq.

800

society as a whole, both on the domestic and the international level. It raises questions that go to the constitutional implications of international arbitration, as discussed in the next section.

3. Constitutional Law Challenges

The main catalysts for the current debate about the legitimacy of international arbitration have been three broader challenges to arbitration that invoke constitutional values, including the principle of democracy, the concept of the rule of law and human rights, but also fairness in international relations. Although every single challenge is not necessarily targeted to all forms of arbitration, all challenges taken together do affect the perceptions of the legitimacy of international arbitration more generally because there are likely spill-over effects in the discourses about the legitimacy of different systems or forms of arbitration. Although criticism of arbitration is not new,[41] its constitutional implications are only now emerging.

The first constitutional challenge for arbitration relates to its use in consumer and labor contracts, which is particularly widespread in the United States. It has led to a vivid debate about the constitutional rights to access to courts, due process, and the separation of power.[42] The second challenge relates to the question whether arbitration is able to deliver fairness to all participants and is representative of the interests of all participants, or is a dispute settlement system that is dominated by Northern and Western actors and ideology that disregards interests and values of developing and transitioning countries.[43] This challenge can be understood as questioning the democratic representation and equality on a system-internal level. And finally, the challenge that is most responsible for bringing about the present interest in the legitimacy of international arbitration is the debate about the "legitimacy crisis" in investment treaty arbitration,[44] which has repercussions on international arbitration more generally, despite the significant differences between contract-based commercial and treaty-based investment arbitration.[45]

---

41. Consider, for example, the fervent criticism of arbitration by Heinrich KRONSTEIN, "Business Arbitration – Instrument of Private Government", 54 Yale L. J. (1944) p. 36; Heinrich KRONSTEIN, "Arbitration is Power", 38 NYU L. Rev. (1963) p. 661.

42. See for further detail the discussion and references in RUTLEDGE, supra fn. 17, pp. 127 et seq; Jean R. STERNLIGHT, "Creeping Mandatory Arbitration: Is It Just?", 57 Stan. L. Rev. (2005) p. 1631 at pp. 1642-1646; Richard M. ALDERMAN, "Why We Really Need the Arbitration Fairness Act: It's All About Separation of Powers", 12 J. Consumer & Com. Law (2009) p. 151.

43. Cf. Joseph T. MCLAUGHLIN, "Arbitration and Developing Countries", 13 International Lawyer (1979) p. 211; see more generally also A.A. FATOUROS, "International Law and the Third World", 50 Virg. L. Rev. (1964) p. 783; Muthucumaraswamy SORNARAJAH, "Toward Normlessness: The Ravage and Retreat of Neo-Liberalism in International Investment Law", 2 Yearbook of International Investment Law & Policy (2010) p. 595.

44. See the works cited supra fn. 36.

45. On these differences see Stephan W. SCHILL, "Enhancing International Investment Law's Legitimacy: Conceptual and Methodological Foundations of a New Public Law Approach", 52 Va. J. Int'l L. (2011) p. 57 at p. 75-77.

The criticism of investment treaty arbitration builds on the observation that one-off appointed arbitrators, instead of standing courts, review government acts and reach far into the sphere of domestic public law by crafting and refining the standards governing investor-state relations. Arbitrations against Uruguay and Australia concerning cigarette packaging,[46] or the claim concerning Germany's nuclear power phase-out,[47] are the most recent examples of genuinely constitutional law disputes settled in arbitration. The disputes about Argentina's emergency legislation[48] and Canada's ban on pesticides[49] are others. These arbitrations create friction with domestic constitutional law as arbitrators, who have little democratic legitimacy, often operate in non-transparent proceedings and produce increasing amounts of incoherent decisions. Accordingly, many domestic public lawyers, and also some international lawyers, view investment treaty arbitration as a threat to constitutional law values, such as democracy and the rule of law.[50] In addition, investment treaty arbitration is criticized for not sufficiently taking into account the human rights of non-parties, including the population's right to health, access to water, a clean environment, or the rights of indigenous people.[51] This puts the constitutional law implications of international arbitration center stage and reflects the transformation that international arbitration has undergone from a method to settle individual disputes to an institution of global governance that is engaged in balancing competing rights and interests of the disputing parties as well as non-parties.[52]

Even though consumer and labor arbitration, investment treaty arbitration, and the issue of whether the international arbitration system is sufficiently representative of the interests of the users of arbitration, concern seemingly unrelated questions and systems of arbitration which, from an arbitration-internal perspective, are generally considered to belong to different universes, all of these frameworks of arbitration are connected to each other through a common argumentative structure and because external observers,

---

46. See *Philip Morris Brand Sàrl (Switzerland), Philip Morris Products S.A. (Switzerland) and Abal Hermanos S.A. (Uruguay) v. Oriental Republic of Uruguay* (ICSID Case No. ARB/10/7), registered 19 February 2010; *Philip Morris Asia Limited (Hong Kong) v. The Commonwealth of Australia*, UNCITRAL, PCA Case No. 2012-12, registered 21 November 2011.

47. *Vattenfall AB and others v. Federal Republic of Germany* (ICSID Case No. ARB/12/12), registered 31 May 2012.

48. There are more than forty investment treaty-based arbitrations concerning the lawfulness of Argentina's legislative response to its economic and financial crisis in 2001/2002. On these cases see Paola DI ROSA, "The Recent Wave of Arbitrations Against Argentina Under Bilateral Investment Treaties: Background and Principal Legal Issues", 36 U. Miami Intern-Am. L. Rev. (2004) p. 41.

49. See *Chemtura Corporation (formerly Crompton Corporation) v. Government of Canada*, UNCITRAL (NAFTA) Award, 2 August 2010.

50. Gus VAN HARTEN, supra fn. 40; David SCHNEIDERMAN, *Constitutionalizing Economic Globalization: Investment Rules and Democracy's Promise* (CUP 2008).

51. See Pierre-Marie DUPUY, Francesco FRANCIONI and Ernst-Ulrich PETERSMANN, eds., *Human Rights in International Investment Law and Arbitration* (OUP 2009); Bruno Simma, "Foreign Investment Arbitration: A Place for Human Rights?", 60 Intl. & Comp. L.Q. (2011) p. 573 at p. 576.

52. See generally on how the decisions of international tribunals entail questions of the redistribution of power, Armin VON BOGDANDY and Ingo VENZKE, supra fn. 35, p. 25.

including the general public, do not always distinguish between different systems of arbitration; instead, they draw on an overarching framework to criticize arbitration, whether domestic or international, involving private or public actors. What is more, in all three instances, the criticism of international arbitration invokes constitutional arguments to question the legitimacy of arbitration as a governance mechanism. This common framework demands an analysis of international arbitration in a constitutional perspective.

Yet, the system-internal discourse, to which the next section turns, is not cast in a way to match the structure of constitutional arguments. This leads to a dissonance between internal and external analysis of the legitimacy of international arbitration. Such a dissonance is problematic not least because answers to constitutional challenges must be formulated in constitutional language, unless the international arbitration system intends to risk losing the trust vested in it not only by disputing parties and potential users of arbitration, but also by governments and their voters the world over.

III.   CONCEPTUALIZING LEGITIMACY WITHIN INTERNATIONAL ARBITRATION

The discourse on legitimacy within the international arbitration community only tentatively reflects the constitutional dimensions and the governance functions international arbitration exercises. Certainly, the theory of international arbitration increasingly looks at international arbitration as a system that requires justification and legitimation as a system (1). Yet, the mainstream conceptualization of legitimacy in international arbitration remains in a dispute settlement paradigm that is limited to justifying international arbitration as an instance of settling an individual dispute. It understands legitimacy mainly as "party legitimacy", while disregarding other aspects, such as "community legitimacy", "national legitimacy" and "global legitimacy" (2). In consequence, in order to provide a comprehensive account of the legitimacy of international arbitration as a system of governance, one must recognize that legitimacy cannot only be understood in relation to the disputing parties but constitutes a multidimensional concept that plays different roles in relation to different actors and social constituencies in a transnational legal space (3).

1.   *International Arbitration as an Autonomous System*

In the emerging, albeit still limited number of theoretical accounts of the field, international arbitration is increasingly analyzed as a jurisprudential system that builds on, but operates beyond, individual arbitration proceedings. International arbitration is more than the actual settlement of individual disputes; it is a global, quasi-judicial system that provides the legal infrastructure (norms, actors, and processes) for the consent-based settlement of disputes.

The nature of that system, however, is contested among the main theoretical approaches. These are first the theory that international arbitration is the expression of an entirely private normative order that does not find its legal roots in a national or international legal system (see *a*); second, that international arbitration finds its legal basis in, and is a prolongation of, a specific national legal system; in this view, the system of international arbitration is rooted in a plurality of domestic laws (see *b*); and third, that international arbitration constitutes a transnational legal system whose autonomy is supported by a combination of national laws, international legal instruments and the autonomy of the parties, and hence bridges the national-international, as well as the public-private divide (see *c*).

The way these different theories conceptualize the nature of international arbitration also has repercussion on how the system's legitimacy is construed. This section will discuss these three macro-level accounts of international arbitration and of its legitimacy in turn.

a. *International arbitration as a private normative order*

As a prolongation of the view that individual arbitration proceedings are justified by the disputing parties' consent, one approach to qualify the system of international arbitration is to understand it as part of a private normative order that comes into existence because it is acknowledged by those who use it as creating normative expectations concerning their mutual rights and obligations. Relying on the sociological approach to the concept of law of Santi Romano, Jan Paulsson is probably the most vocal proponent of this view. For him "arbitration may be effective under *arrangements that do not depend on national law or judges at all*".[53] Furthermore, "[a]s the foundation of arbitration, or more precisely a sufficient foundation for some arbitrations, this ... conception does not depend directly either on law or judges. It therefore does not seek to attach itself ... to the somewhat dreamy and self-contradictory premise of an 'autonomous' order recognised by the very state orders from which is [sic] purports to be free."[54] In this view, international arbitration represents a normative system that is implemented independently of state institutions and independently of domestic laws; it is solely based on the participation and consent of current or future disputing parties.

This vision of international arbitration, in turn, derives its legitimacy from the disputing parties and from the acceptance by the community of (past, present, and future) participants in arbitral proceedings for whom arbitration is a means to order private relations independently of the help of states and their institutions. Outsiders to the system, that is, actors who do not use arbitration as a means to settle disputes, play no role in contributing to the legitimacy of arbitration under this view.

This vision has the advantage of widening the focus for grounding the legitimacy of international arbitration beyond national and international law; it rightly appreciates that normative expectations are not only generated by state laws or international treaties, but that a social system itself can generate such expectations and enforce them through the

---

53. Jan PAULSSON, supra fn. 1, p. 30 (emphasis in original); William PARK, "The Lex Loci Arbitri and International Commercial Arbitration", 32 Int'l & Comp. L. Q. (1983) p. 21; William PARK and Jan PAULSSON, "The Binding Force of International Arbitral Awards", 23 Va. J. Int'l L. (1983) p. 253; Jan PAULSSON, "Arbitration Unbound: Award Detached from the Law of its Country of Origin", 30 Int'l & Comp. L. Q. (1981) p. 358; Jan PAULSSON, "Delocalisation of International Commercial Arbitration: When and Why It Matters", 32 Int'l & Comp. L. Q. (1983) p. 53.
54. Jan PAULSSON, "Arbitration in Three Dimensions", 7(1) Transnational Dispute Management (2010) p. 16.

institutional infrastructure of international arbitration. It acknowledges that international arbitration generates normativity and functions as a system of governance; it justifies the effects of international arbitration on actual or potential parties through their consent.

Paulsson's vision does have difficulties, however, with conceptualizing the legitimacy of effects of international arbitration on non-users, for example, the host state's population in investment arbitrations. In fact, effects on non-parties outside the international arbitration community find no place in this theory. Furthermore, law-making by arbitral tribunals that goes beyond the sphere of users of arbitration is difficult to capture by this vision. Similarly, law-making in cases without a real alternative to international arbitration, for example, in sports arbitration, is difficult to legitimize on the basis of Paulsson's purely consent-based model, as it is questionable whether the consent given by at least one class of arbitrants, in this case athletes, was a sufficiently autonomous decision that can infuse the system of arbitration with legitimacy through party autonomy.

While Paulsson rightly points out that the power of arbitration in most cases relies on the agreement of the disputing parties, not on the acceptance of arbitration agreements by national judges, his account, as a theory of legitimacy, disregards that the possibility of state institutions to intervene in arbitration, by regulating questions of arbitrability, but also through set-aside or non-recognition decisions of domestic courts, may be needed to imbue the system with acceptance by outsiders. In fact, the intervention of states – through domestic courts but also as makers of the law applicable to and in international arbitration – is important for legitimacy, because these interventions allow the safeguarding of public interests and the control of spill-over effects that international arbitration may have on non-parties. This is particularly important when international arbitrations involve public entities or make law that affects the general public, which therefore requires justification in relation to social spheres beyond the international arbitration community. But it is equally important to the extent purely commercial cases have implications for society as a whole.

b.   International arbitration's recognition by national law(s)
The directly opposite approach to Paulsson's account are theories that ground arbitration and its legitimacy in national law. Indeed, national law is a necessary component in virtually all international arbitrations.[55] It plays a key role in three contexts: first, as the

---

55. The only exception are ICSID arbitrations which are delocalized to a relatively large extent. They are based only on an international treaty, the Washington Convention, that defines the jurisdictional limits, the applicable substantive and procedural law, and provides rules for the recognition and enforcement of ICSID awards. Yet, even in the context of ICSID arbitrations, national law plays a considerable role. This is the case, first, as regards the applicable substantive law, and second, concerning immunity of enforcement. Thus, Art. 42(1) ICSID Convention provides a place for application of domestic law by stating: "(1) The Tribunal shall decide a dispute in accordance with such rules of law as may be agreed by the parties. In the absence of such agreement, the Tribunal shall apply the law of the Contracting State party to the dispute (including its rules on the conflict of laws) and such rules of international law as may be applicable." Art. 55 ICSID Convention, in turn, leaves domestic law regarding enforcement immunity untouched, by providing: "Nothing in Article 54 [i.e., the provisions regarding the recognition of ICSID awards

law applicable to arbitration, that is, the law governing the validity of arbitration agreements and their interpretation, arbitral procedure and the standard of review exercised by the court at the seat of arbitration; second, as the law applicable at the place of enforcing arbitration awards; and third, as the law applicable in arbitration, that is, the substantive law governing the relations between the parties. This broad presence of national law in international arbitration, in turn, supports the view that international arbitration is essentially a prolongation of, and subject to, the normative structure of national law. In that view, the legitimacy of international arbitration, both in relation to disputing and non-disputing parties, derives from the conformity of international arbitration's functioning with the governing national law or laws.

Such a view, however, faces difficulties because it tends to underestimate the extent to which arbitrators are more than simple *bouches de la loi* that merely apply national law but instead actively develop normative expectations of disputing parties themselves. It disregards that the law applicable to and in arbitration is not so much a restriction on international arbitration, but empowers arbitrators by creating a normative space, within which international arbitrations takes place rather autonomously.

This empowerment derives from several doctrines that ensure that arbitral tribunals can exercise authority in relation to disputing parties without being strictly bound by domestic law.[56] First, the doctrine of separability, widely accepted as a principle of international arbitration in virtually all domestic legal systems, ensures that the jurisdictional powers of arbitral tribunals are independent from the underlying contractual relations and of the substantive domestic law applicable to the contract in question. Second, national laws empower arbitral tribunals in relation to state institutions, in particular state courts. This is done through the principle of Kompetenz-Kompetenz, the support of arbitral tribunals by state courts in conducting arbitrations, for example in helping to collect evidence, the limited scrutiny by state courts of arbitral awards in substance, in particular as regards the correct application of the governing law, and the wide-ranging recognition and enforcement of arbitral awards across jurisdictions.

One consequence of the normative space thus granted to arbitrators by national laws is that it is difficult to see international arbitration as rooted in the national law at the seat of arbitration or the substantive law governing the relations between the parties. The way arbitral tribunals interpret the governing national law will likely not be the same as the interpretation given to it by a domestic court, because arbitrators, in particular when coming from foreign jurisdictions, will not have the same interpretative horizon as domestic court judges: they operate in a different cultural and epistemic context.[57]

---

and the enforcement of pecuniary obligations in all member states as if the awards were final judgments of the member state's highest court] shall be construed as derogating from the law in force in any Contracting State relating to immunity of that State or of any foreign State from execution."

56. See on this and the following Kaj HOBÉR, "Res Judicata and Lis Pendens in International Arbitration", 366 *Recueil des Cours* (2013) p. 99 at pp. 191-211.

57. See KARTON, supra fn. 30, p. 23 ("In many ways, international arbitrators have more in common than the body of legal practitioners within any one country ... [t]herefore, it actually makes more sense to speak of an ICA [i.e., international commercial arbitration] community than to speak of a legal community within a country."

Moreover, it is likely that arbitrators, when interpreting the governing law, will not view this law solely in its domestic context, but bring their own international experiences to bear. This may lead to an interpretative convergence of national laws inside international arbitration. In addition, the domestic law applicable to arbitration is itself often the outcome of international processes that aim at cross-border convergence and harmonization. The UNCITRAL Model Law on International Commercial Arbitration,[58] for example, has heavily influenced the laws on commercial arbitration in numerous countries and brought about a significant amount of covergence. This illustrates that a pure domestic vision of international arbitration is difficult to sustain, because there are processes of norm diffusion through which the international level influences the national legal frameworks and may weaken domestic law as a source of legitimacy.

Finally, national law and national control of tribunal decision-making are limited in view of the possible transborder enforcement of arbitral decisions. In this regard, it is possible that decisions by arbitral tribunals can be enforced in one jurisdiction, even though the decision itself has been set aside by the domestic courts at the seat of the arbitration.[59] The reason for this is that courts in several countries, when asked to recognize and enforce a foreign arbitral award, do not treat awards that have been set aside as a nullity, but determine whether the set-aside decision by the foreign court itself should be recognized or instead be disregarded, for example because of breach of a fundamental rule of procedure or standards of fair administration of justice by that foreign court. As a consequence, only a perspective that encompasses the possibility that international arbitration is rooted in a plurality of domestic legal orders is plausible.

c.   International arbitration as part of a transnational legal order
Finally, a number of scholars qualify international arbitration as part of a transnational legal order. They reject the view that international arbitration can be understood as rooted in a specific legal order, be it domestic or international.[60] Instead, reminiscent of

---

58. Adopted in 1985 and amended in 2006; see <www.uncitral.org/pdf/english/texts/arbitration/ml-arb/07-86998_Ebook.pdf> (last accessed 28 March 2014). On the harmonizing and internationalizing impact of model laws see José Angelo Estrella FARIA, "Legal Harmonization Through Model Laws: The Experience of the United Nations Commission on International Trade Law (UNCITRAL)", available at <www.justice.gov.za/alraesa/conferences/2005sa/papers/s5_faria2.pdf> (last accessed 2 July 2014); José Angelo Estrella FARIA, "Future Directions of Legal Harmonisation and Law Reform: Stormy Seas or Prosperous Voyage?", 14 Unif. L. Rev. (2009) p. 5.

59. *PT Putrabali Adyamulia v. Rena Holding et Societe Mnogitua*, Rev. arb. (2007) p. 507 (*Cour de Cassation*); *Societe Hilmarton v. Societe OTV*, Rev. Arb. (1994) p. 327 (*Cour de Cassation*); *Chromalloy Aeroservs. v. Arab Republic of Egypt*, 939 F.Supp. 907 (D.D.C. 1996); *Radenska v. Kajo*, Supreme Court of Austria (*Oberster Gerichtshof*), 20 October 1993, 49 *Österreichische Juristen-Zeitung* (1994) p. 513. See further GAILLARD, *Legal Theory*, supra fn. 1, pp. 136 et seq.; Philippe FOUCHARD, "*La portée internationale de l'annulation de la sentence arbitrale dans son pays d'origine*", Rev. arb. (1997) p. 329; Jan PAULSSON, "The Case for Disregarding LSAs (Local Standard Annulments) Under the New York Convention", 7 Am. Rev. Int'l Arb. (1996) p. 99.

60. GAILLARD, *Legal Theory*, supra fn. 1, pp. 35 et seq.; Julian D.M. LEW, "Achieving the Dream: Autonomous Arbitration", 22 Arb. Int'l (2006) p. 179 ; Jean-Baptiste RACINE, "*Réflexions sur l'autonomie de l'arbitrage commercial international*", Rev. arb. (2005) p. 305; Jean-Pierre ANCEL,

Philip Jessup's category of "transnational law",[61] they consider international arbitration as having transnational legal foundations that are composed of national and international law, of statutes and private contracts, which together create the infrastructure for international arbitration to function as a system of dispute settlement and governance.

Emmanuel Gaillard is the most explicit proponent of this perspective.[62] In addition to recognizing, like Paulsson, that arbitral tribunals generate law and normative expectations through their dispute settlement activities, Gaillard emphasizes, unlike Paulsson's account of international arbitration as a private normative order, the system-external legal and social constraints that both enable international arbitration to function but also restrict it and hold it in place, such as domestic arbitration laws and international conventions relating to arbitration. At the same time, Gaillard does not understand arbitral tribunals as the prolongation of a specific legal order of which they are agents, but understands them as the central actors of an autonomous, transnational legal regime, in which normative expectations are created by the totality of domestic laws and international conventions concerning arbitration, as well as the dispute settlement and governance activities of arbitral tribunals and arbitration institutions.

The great advantage of conceptualizing international arbitration in this way is that it places arbitral tribunals at the center of analysis of the system, not the national and international legal sources that support international arbitration. Although tribunals are subject to domestic courts' scrutiny, they have the primary authority in interpreting the legal sources applicable to the disputing parties. This view of arbitration does not deny that national and international law influence the outcome of actual disputes because these legal sources are applied and interpreted by arbitral tribunals, but it denies that these sources are per se determinative of the outcome. Legal sources influence governance through arbitration and the actors acting as governors (i.e., primarily tribunals but also arbitration institutions), but do not govern themselves. At the same time, without the domestic and international legal infrastructure, the importance of which risks being denied by Paulsson's view of international arbitration as a private normative order, the communicative practice of international arbitration could not develop.

Domestic and international law are therefore part of the infrastructure that is necessary for a social and communicative practice to function, but they are separate from the content and meaning of the social practice that develops on its basis. National and international law governing international arbitration are like the hardware component of computer networks (i.e., computers, cables, switches, etc.); the software, by contrast, is the practice of arbitration itself. It is this practice that establishes social meaning and, conversely, influences the normative expectations of public and private actors submitting to arbitration in a way that is operationally autonomous from both national and international law. International arbitration uses its own code to function and only reacts to how outside actors interact and influence the system through their own involvement, that is, for example a domestic court that sets aside or recognizes a decision

---

"*L'arbitrage: une juridiction internationale autonome*", Revue de jurisprudence de droit des affaires (2007) p. 883.

61. JESSUP, supra, fn. 34.

62. GAILLARD, *Legal Theory*, supra fn. 1.

by an arbitral tribunal, or the legislator who passes a domestic statute "governing" international arbitration.

The account of international arbitration as constituting a transnational legal order is therefore well-suited to describe the overarching and hybrid nature of international arbitration as national and international law, as based on private contracts and public statutes. Likewise, it provides an apt description of the system as operating in a transnational space in which multiple actors, both private and public, (that is, arbitral tribunals, arbitration institutions, domestic courts, international treaty makers) interact through a variety of instruments (contracts, national laws, international treaties) and in a variety of fora. The description of the underlying argumentative structure of international arbitration as a transnational legal order also provides a solid basis for analyzing the interaction between constitutional arguments and international arbitration.

Legitimacy in a conceptualization of international arbitration as a transnational legal order also has to be conceived differently from the other two approaches discussed before. Unlike the approach that links international arbitration to its recognition by national legal orders, legitimacy in a transnational legal perspective takes into account the plurality of visions of international arbitration by different actors, different domestic legal systems, and the international legal infrastructure supporting international arbitration. Moreover, unlike Paulsson's account of international arbitration as a private normative order, the legitimacy of a transnational arbitral legal order does not content itself with focusing only on the consent of the users of arbitration, but also encompasses the legitimacy visions of different domestic legal orders.

Galliard's approach accounts for a plurality of domestic perspectives on legitimacy, but also privileges those views on legitimacy that remain within some form of consistent transnational practice at the expense of views that are (relative to others) singular or idiosyncratic. It privileges transnationally accepted standards of legitimacy, i.e., transnational rules that are developed through a comparative method,[63] such as transnational public policy, over standards that are specific to more limited social groups and domestic legal orders. At the same time, standards of transnational law, such as transnational public policy, are sufficiently open-textured to allow constitutional arguments and constitutional analysis to inform the functioning of international arbitration, both from the point of view of arbitral tribunals and domestic courts. Notwithstanding this openness, the notion of legitimacy of international arbitration understood as a transnational legal order is not cast expressly in constitutional language and therefore also faces difficulties to engage directly with the various legitimacy critiques voiced against international arbitration addressed earlier.

2.   *Unravelling the Different Dimensions of Legitimacy*

Although the theory of international arbitration, as just discussed, analyzes international arbitration as a system, the system-internal conceptualization of the function of arbitration remains tied to the idea of settling individual transborder disputes effectively

---

63. *Ibid.*, pp. 45 et seq.

in the absence of readily available and neutral alternatives. As explained, for example, by Gary Born:

> "businesses perceive international arbitration as providing a neutral, speedy and expert dispute resolution process, largely subject to the parties' control, in a single, centralized forum, with internationally enforceable dispute resolution agreements and decisions. While far from perfect, international arbitration is, rightly, regarded as generally suffering fewer ills than litigation of international disputes in national courts and as offering more workable opportunities for remedying or avoiding those ills which do exist."[64]

In line with this view, legitimacy is commonly conceived of in terms of benefits international arbitration brings to the disputing parties only. Party autonomy is attributed a central role in this context. While discussing domestic US arbitration, Edward Brunet makes this point very succinctly:

> "In a democratic society, party autonomy should be the fundamental value that shapes arbitration. The personal autonomy inherent in arbitration constitutes a dominant policy in all areas of a democracy. The freedom to select arbitration procedure is a choice that one anticipates should exist in a state that values personal autonomy. Arbitration liberty is achieved by making party autonomy the highest priority in the pantheon of arbitration values.
>
> Viewed in this light, the important value of party autonomy is directly related to the freedom essential in a democratic state. A strong version of arbitration party autonomy exemplifies the significance of freedom of contract. In a state such as ours characterized by the respect for individual liberty, courts should enforce customized agreements to arbitrate and the legislature should regulate minimally. In a society governed by rules of the free market, contract norms that guide exchanges are necessarily based on autonomous action of individual economic actors."[65]

Party consent and neutrality of dispute resolution are therefore widely seen as the legitimating factors for international arbitration. This view is perfectly fine when the dispute settlement function of international arbitration is concerned. Yet, it is insufficient to legitimize international arbitration as a system of governance because it does not take into account the functions of arbitration beyond dispute settlement.

While international arbitration's dispute settlement function can be legitimized by recourse to the disputing parties' consent, and hence party autonomy, the impact of arbitration on social spheres beyond the parties requires a more complex framework. While the theory of international arbitration increasingly reflects on the concept of

---

64. Gary BORN, *International Commercial Arbitration*, 2nd ed. (WoltersKluwer 2009) Vol. I, p. 70.
65. Edward BRUNET, "The Core Values of Arbitration" in E. BRUNET, R.E. SPEIDEL, J.E. STERNLIGHT and S.H. WARE, eds., *Arbitration Law in America – A Critical Assessment* (CUP 2006) p. 3 at pp. 4-5.

legitimacy, it remains in a dispute settlement paradigm that claims the greatest extent of autonomy for arbitration from control through domestic law and institutions, but largely disregards the impact of arbitration on social spheres beyond the parties. While it takes into account social impacts under concepts of (transnational) public policy, that international arbitration must conform to, such social impact is conceptually peripheral; it is generally viewed as an exception from the normal functioning of international arbitration, not as part of the center of the system of international arbitration. What is more, the prevailing discourse in international arbitration makes use of a mono-dimensional concept of legitimacy that does not sufficiently recognize that actors, processes, and norms that are independent from disputing parties and arbitrators have an important role to play in contributing to the overall legitimacy of international arbitration.

In contrast to this system-internal perspective on legitimacy, the following section suggests that there are different dimensions of legitimacy that should be distinguished, namely "party legitimacy", "community legitimacy", "national legitimacy", and "global legitimacy". Recognizing the multidimensionality of the concept of legitimacy is the first step in developing a more comprehensive framework of legitimacy of international arbitration.

a. Party legitimacy

Party legitimacy designates the conditions under which arbitration is seen as legitimate from the perspective of the disputing parties. It corresponds to the function of arbitration to settle the individual dispute in question and refers to the autonomous acceptance of the process by the disputing parties. To be perceived as legitimate by them, the resolution of the dispute has to be performed by an independent tribunal that treats the parties equally and, despite the significant power it has over the parties in rendering a final and binding decision that is reviewable only under limited standards, justifies its decision on the basis of pre-determined legal standards.[66] This heteronomy of the applicable standards of decision-making excludes the arbitrary, and hence illegitimate, exercise of authority by arbitral tribunals. The parties are also protected against tribunal inactivity by the need for tribunals to decide the case; a denial of justice, in other words, is excluded. From the parties' perspective, the legitimacy of arbitration depends on the extent to which the tribunal is independent from the parties and decides on the basis of heteronomous rules and principles. Party autonomy, in other words, is the main source of party legitimacy.

Yet, party autonomy is not equivalent to independence from domestic law and institutions. On the contrary, party legitimacy also depends of the state's recognition and support of arbitration, because the latter has the monopoly of force, which may be necessary (even if only as a credible threat) for enforcement of the parties' arbitration agreement and/or the tribunal's decision. Furthermore, domestic law and domestic institutions can play an important role in safeguarding that party autonomy truly remains the basis of international arbitration by setting limits to arbitrability and ensuring that

---

66. See Christoph MÖLLERS, "*Individuelle Legitimation: Wie rechtfertigen sich Gerichte?*" in A. GEIS, F. NULLMEIER, C. DAASE, eds., *Der Aufstieg der Legitimitätspolitik* (Nomos 2012) p. 398.

arbitration proceedings are conducted in line with the procedural principles deriving from party legitimacy, such as the equality of the parties and due process. Domestic law and the infrastructure provided for by that law (in the form of court support and recognition and enforcement of arbitral awards) are therefore also a source of legitimacy for the efficient functioning of arbitration and the implementation of the parties' agreement to arbitrate. Party legitimacy, in turn, cannot be seen entirely independently from public laws and institutions, as the view of international arbitration as a private normative order would seem to suggest.

At the same time, there are various mechanisms that prevent domestic law and domestic courts from interfering with the disputing parties' idea of arbitration or party legitimacy. First, international law constrains domestic policy on international arbitration as well as the action by domestic courts. This is particularly the case with the New York Convention, which in principle requires the recognition and enforcement of arbitration agreements and arbitral awards in non-domestic arbitrations and only allows a limited number of grounds on which recognition and enforcement can be denied.[67]

Second, there is a dynamic between the acceptance of arbitration by the parties and domestic regulation of arbitration that not only constrains arbitral tribunals, but also limits domestic regulation of international arbitration so as to meet the expectations of actual or potential disputing parties. This mechanism has to do with the choice of disputing parties of the place of arbitration and the applicable procedural law. If domestic law and domestic courts overreach into how parties perceive the legitimacy of international arbitration, they can agree to conduct arbitrations in a different forum and under different rules. Domestic law and policy on international arbitration is therefore constrained to a considerable extent by the forces of the market for arbitration services. The (on a global scale) heterarchical structure of state authority, and the competition between different jurisdictions that develops on its basis, allows parties to choose the domestic control they wish to subject the resolution of their dispute to. This ensures that party legitimacy is protected in two directions: in relation to arbitral tribunals because domestic courts can control them, and in relation to domestic courts, because parties have a choice in opting for the arbitral framework and supervisory institutions they desire.

b. Community legitimacy

Yet, party legitimacy is not the only consideration that is relevant for the comprehensive acceptance of international arbitration; it also needs to be accepted by the users of arbitration as a group. Community legitimacy therefore designates the conditions under which arbitration is seen as legitimate from the perspective of all users of arbitration. It largely coincides with what parties to individual arbitrations expect in order for the mechanism to be legitimate, in particular concerning the safeguard of party autonomy as the hallmark of the international arbitration system. Community legitimacy also includes questions of arbitrator independence and party equality, questions of fairness in arbitral procedure, and reasoning of arbitral awards that is adequate in order for the

---

67. Convention on the Recognition and Enforcement of Foreign Arbitral Awards (the "New York Convention"), signed 10 June 1958, entered into force 7 June 1959, 330 UNTS 38.

users of arbitration to build up normative expectations about the functioning of international arbitration.

Unlike party legitimacy, community legitimacy is, however, less concerned with party-specific questions and individual outcomes of arbitrations. It is rather focused on, and can lend support to, the entrenched practices in international arbitration that are accepted by the user community. Its primary focus is on the law applicable to arbitration, in particular the standards of domestic court review, recognition and enforcement of arbitration agreements and arbitral awards, rather than the law applicable in arbitration.[68] Community legitimacy is both a yardstick for the legitimacy of decision-making of arbitral tribunals and the decisions of national courts regarding matters of international arbitrations, for example when rendering decisions on arbitrator challenges, reviewing arbitral awards, or taking decisions on the recognition and enforcement of arbitral decisions. A decision by a domestic court enforcing an arbitral award that has been set aside at the seat on entirely arbitrary grounds could be supported not only from the perspective of party legitimacy, but also of community legitimacy. By contrast, a domestic decision expanding the review of arbitral decisions to the detriment of arbitral tribunals, denying the separability of arbitration agreements, or the principle of Kompetenz-Kompetenz, would likely find little support in terms of community legitimacy, prompting reactions from the user community, for example by promoting alternative venues for international arbitration.

Finally, community legitimacy is an important yardstick to measure the legitimacy of arbitration institutions, for example institutional practices on appointing or challenging arbitrators, scrutinizing arbitral awards, formulating soft law instruments, or training counsel and arbitrators. Similar to party legitimacy, community legitimacy will be concerned with how well these activities respect party autonomy and party consent, but it will also encompass other considerations. Above all, the community of users of arbitration will also be concerned with how well arbitration institutions represent the interests of all users of arbitration, not only of specific regional or professional sub-groups. These aspects of community legitimacy may impact an arbitration institution's policies on arbitrator appointment and militate for gender and geographical diversity, the recruitment policies of arbitration institutions of staff members and listed arbitrators, the financing of arbitration institutions, and the methods through which they develop soft law standards. In addition to safeguarding party autonomy and party consent, representativeness and participation of users of arbitration will be relevant considerations affecting the legitimacy of international arbitration from the perspective of community legitimacy.

c.   National legitimacy

In addition to party legitimacy and community legitimacy, a third aspect of legitimacy is national legitimacy. It designates the conditions under which arbitration is seen as legitimate from the perspective of a specific country and its society. This aspect of legitimacy is generally expressed in the state's laws regarding arbitration and in the

---

68. Interest in the latter may, however, play a role regarding the arbitration community's interest in the development of globally applicable and uniform non-national law, such as the lex mercatoria.

relevant practice of its supervising courts. Most countries today follow a liberal policy regarding arbitration and recognize the parties' autonomy to have disputes resolved through arbitration with respect to a broad set of disputes, in particular when transborder relations are concerned.

The pro-arbitration policy of many countries finds its expression in the widely recognized doctrines of separability, Kompetenz-Kompetenz, and the limited review of arbitral awards by domestic courts in set-aside, recognition, and enforcement proceedings. National legitimacy therefore largely coincides with party legitimacy and even encompasses providing mechanisms, inter alia through the supervisory jurisdiction of domestic courts, to safeguard that arbitration is not conducted contrary to the hallmarks of party legitimacy, i.e. party autonomy and party consent. This is particularly the case in arbitrations between private businesses, where repercussions on society as a whole are negligible. In fact, most systems of national law even accept that arbitrators misconstrue and misapply domestic law and do not sanction such practice through court-supervision;[69] similarly law-making by arbitral tribunals in the private law context is little controlled. Instead, to the extent arbitration is viewed as an emanation of party autonomy, arbitration is protected as part of the individual's freedom and hence legitimate from the perspective of national legitimacy.

Certain limitations to arbitration do, however, come into play at the national level in order to protect parties from entering into arbitration agreements inadvertently and to protect specific public policies against the danger of being undermined through the use of arbitration. Accordingly, national legitimacy finds its expression in rules on arbitrability, requirements as to the form of arbitration agreements,[70] the review of arbitral awards for breach of *ordre public* and mandatory local laws,[71] or the refusal to recognize and enforce awards that are contrary to public policy.[72]

What is more, in arbitrations involving public bodies, where proceedings not only concern private rights and obligations, principles of constitutional law – above all democracy and the rule of law – may be affected, when the control of government acts and the delineation of private rights and public interests is undertaken by party-appointed, one-off arbitral tribunals. In such cases, compliance of arbitration proceedings with standards of national constitutional law will become an important component of national legitimacy because the legality of government conduct, the government's accountability, and the use of public funds are at issue.[73] Similarly, in private-public

---

69. See Jean Francois POUDRET and Sebastien BESSON, *Comparative Law of International Arbitration* (Sweet & Maxwell 2007) pp. 757-769; BORN, supra fn. 64, Vol. II, pp. 2551-2700.

70. This would include, for example, prohibitions to include agreements to arbitrate in standard terms of consumer contracts; see Annex, clause q), European Council Directive 93/13/EEC of 5 April 1993 on unfair terms in consumer contracts, OJ L 95, pp. 29 et seq.

71. BORN, supra fn. 64, Vol. II, pp. 2620-2631.

72. *Ibid.*, pp. 2827-2863.

73. For illustrations of the type of disputes settled by private-public arbitration se the references supra fns. 46-69. Further examples are arbitrations involving water concessions in Bolivia, Argentina, and Tanzania (see, e.g., *Biwater Gauff (Tanzania) Ltd. v. United Republic of Tanzania* (ICSID Case No. ARB/05/22), Award, 24 July 2004; *Aguas del Tunari S.A. v. Republic of Bolivia* (ICSID Case No. ARB/02/3), Decision on Respondent's Objections to Jurisdiction, 21 October 2005; *Suez,*

arbitrations, national legitimacy reflects, in my view, in a greater emphasis on correctness of decision-making by arbitral tribunals and a greater concern for arbitral law-making as compared to private-private arbitrations; this can be explained in light of the principle of legality and accountability governing the conduct of public bodies.

d.   Global legitimacy
Finally, legitimacy of international arbitration also has a global dimension. Global legitimacy designates the conditions under which arbitration is seen as legitimate from the perspective of global society and global interests. This concept is broader than community legitimacy because it refers to all actors worldwide, whether users of arbitration or not, that are affected by international arbitration. Unlike national legitimacy, it is not concerned with the way international arbitration is perceived, or which effects it may have, at the national level, but rather with its global implications as a system of governance that affects not only how private parties interact amongst each other and have disputes decided, but also how private rights and public interests more generally are (re-)balanced in international arbitration.

Similar to the national level, global legitimacy endorses party autonomy as a value of the international arbitration system and protects it against certain interferences by states. The primary instrument for this is the New York Convention with its rules on the recognition of arbitration agreements and enforcement of arbitral awards by domestic courts. Global legitimacy therefore largely coincides with party legitimacy. At the same time, global legitimacy encompasses the recognition of legitimate national interests as grounds to deny recognition and enforcement of arbitration agreements and awards, for example in the form of the *ordre public* exception in Art. V of the New York Convention. Recognition of such national interests at the global level is important because global legitimacy requires not only the protection of users of arbitration, but also appropriate safeguards for the interests of states (those involved in arbitrations as parties and as regulators of society).

Yet, there are also concerns that are specifically relevant for global legitimacy as compared to other dimensions of legitimacy. Global legitimacy will be particularly concerned with effects of arbitral proceedings and activities of arbitration institutions,

---

Sociedad General de Aguas de Barcelona SA, and Vivendi Universal SA v. Argentine Republic (ICSID Case No ARB/03/19) and *AWG Group v. Argentine Republic*, Decision on Liability (UNCITRAL), 30 July 2010); an arbitration challenging an affirmative action program that aimed at remedying injustices of apartheid in South Africa (see *Piero Foresti, Laura de Carli and others v. Republic of South Africa* (ICSID Case No. ARB(AF)/07/1), Award, 4 August 2010); arbitrations challenging the ban of harmful substances in the United States and Canada (see, e.g., *Methanex Corporation v. United States*, UNCITRAL (NAFTA), Final Award of the Tribunal on Jurisdiction and Merits, 3 August 2005; *Ethyl Corporation v. Government of Canada*, UNCITRAL (NAFTA), Award on Jurisdiction, 24 June 1998); arbitrations challenging measures for the protection of the environment in Germany, Mexico or Canada (*Vattenfall AB, Vattenfall Europe AG, Vattenfall Europe Generation AG & Co. KG v. Federal Republic of Germany* (ICSID Case No. ARB/09/6), Request for Arbitration, 30 March 2009; *Metalclad Corporation v. The United Mexican States* (ICSID Case No. ARB(AF)/97/1 (NAFTA)), Award, 30 August 2000; *S.D. Myers, Inc. v. Canada*, UNCITRAL (NAFTA), Partial Award, 13 November 2000).

or other professional bodies active in the international arbitration system, that have global impact and that affect not only the relations among private economic actors, but also between private and public actors at a global scale. Global legitimacy will, for example, become a yardstick for global law-making by arbitral tribunals, for example in investment treaty arbitration, where tribunals develop a treaty-overarching system of precedent, rebalance private rights and public interests, and thereby craft the substantive law governing investor-state relations at a global level.[74]

Likewise, the activities of arbitration institutions when fashioning standards for how international arbitration proceedings should be conducted, through the formulation of rules and principles of arbitral procedure, but also by issuing practice directions, making arbitrator appointments, or deciding on challenges, contribute to the making of the global system of arbitration and to shaping the expectations not only of users of arbitration, but of everybody (even indirectly) affected by international arbitration. Arbitration institutions themselves influence the balance between private rights and public interests on a global scale, even if they pretend to only have impact on disputing parties and on users of arbitration. An example where questions of global legitimacy are at stake because arbitral procedures directly impact how social relations are conducted is the introduction by various arbitration institutions of emergency arbitration procedures under which parties can ask for the issuance of interim measures for the protection of private rights.[75]

Similarly, global legitimacy is implicated when professional associations develop soft law instruments that (re-)shape arbitral proceedings and thereby have an impact on how international arbitration functions as a system of governance and how it (re-)structures social relations globally. The International Bar Association (IBA) Rules on the Taking of Evidence in International Commercial Arbitration,[76] the IBA Guidelines on Conflicts of Interests in International Arbitration,[77] or the IBA Guidelines on Party Representation in International Arbitration,[78] are just some examples of how professional associations reshape the contours of expectations and global effects of international arbitration. Their

---

74. See SCHILL, supra fn. 20, pp. 321 et seq.
75. See Mark KANTOR, "Arbitration Rules Update: Expedited Emergency Relief under the AAA/ICDR, ICC and LCIA Rules", 21 Mealey's Int'l Arb. Rep. (2006, no. 8) p. 11; Charles N. BROWER, Ariel MEYERSTEIN and Stephan W. SCHILL, "The Power and Effectiveness of Pre-Arbitral Provisional Relief: The SCC Emergency Arbitrator in Investor-State Disputes" in Kaj HOBÉR, Annette MAGNUSSON and Marie ÖHRSTRÖM, eds., *Between East and West: Essays in Honour of Ulf Franke* (Juris Publishing 2010) p. 61.
76. IBA Rules on the Taking of Evidence in International Arbitration, adopted by a resolution of the IBA Council on 29 May 2010, available at <www.ibanet.org/Publications/publications_IBA_guides_and_free_materials.aspx>.
77. IBA Guidelines on Conflicts of Interest in International Arbitration, approved by the Council of the International Bar Association on 22 May 2004, available at <www.ibanet.org/Publications/publications_IBA_guides_and_free_materials.aspx>.
78. IBA Guidelines on Party Representation in International Arbitration, adopted by a resolution of the IBA Council on 25 May 2013, available at <www.ibanet.org/Document/Default.aspx?DocumentUid=6F0C57D7-E7A0-43AF-B76E-714D9FE74D7F> (accessed 25 June 2014).

activities touch upon questions of global legitimacy that go beyond the ambit of party, community, and national legitimacy.

3. The Multidimensionality of Legitimacy in International Arbitration

Unlike the more limited and mono-dimensional focus on the legitimacy of international arbitration in the current system-internal discourse, a broader concept of legitimacy encompasses at least four perspectives that reflect different societal spheres that have an interest in, and may be affected by, the system of international arbitration and its actors, i.e. arbitral tribunals, arbitration institutions, professional bodies, controlling courts, domestic legislators, and international treaty makers. Legitimacy, therefore, should be understood as a multidimensional concept, whose different dimensions have to be taken into account when asking under which conditions international arbitration is legitimate and in relation to whom.

At all four levels of legitimacy discussed above, party autonomy plays an important role. Yet, party autonomy is not the only criterion for the legitimacy of international arbitration because arbitral proceedings, as well as the activity of arbitration institutions, may have repercussion beyond the disputing parties. Instead, community, national and global interests may be implicated and hence demand justification – each in relation to its own underlying values and logic. Above all, party consent is insufficient as the sole source of legitimacy because it cannot legitimize effects of international arbitration other than on the parties to an individual proceeding. It cannot justify international arbitration as a system of governance. At the same time, the legitimacy of international arbitration cannot be explained solely on the basis of shared interests and acceptance by the collectivity of users of arbitration, because this would equally disregard effects of international arbitration in shaping social relation of actors that are not users of arbitration. Both party and community legitimacy as "private" aspects of legitimacy, in other words, can only provide a partial, even if important, account of the legitimacy of international arbitration.

What is equally important is a consideration of "public" legitimacy aspects. These are principally enshrined in domestic laws and domestic court practices and in international treaties relating to arbitration. Yet, national legitimacy, and even more so a specific national legitimacy, of international arbitration cannot be the only source of legitimacy of international arbitration either. Rather, international arbitration must be rooted in a multitude of national legal orders, both in respect of the seat of arbitration, as well as the legal orders of enforcement. While national legitimacy will be important to determine the conditions upon which a specific country participates in the system of international arbitration, national legitimacy will only have a systemic effect to the extent its content is shared among a significant number of states. Finally, global legitimacy will operate at a very general level and reflect minimum requirements for the legitimacy of international arbitration that are globally shared; it will not, however, be able to determine the conditions under which every individual state views international arbitration as legitimate.

A comprehensive framework to think about the legitimacy of international arbitration has to take account of the different dimensions of legitimacy and translate them into norms and processes that structure the interactions of the different actors in international

817

arbitration, in particular arbitral tribunals, arbitration institutions, and controlling courts, and their respective outlook and concerns in relation to legitimacy. The different levels of legitimacy and the varying perspectives of different actors also indicate that no single dimension of legitimacy can determine the legitimacy of the entire system of international arbitration. Instead, what is required is a nuanced analysis of which activities implicate which social sphere and which dimension of legitimacy.

Accordingly, no dimension can demand primacy over other dimensions, but needs to compromise and accommodate other competing private and public interests. Party legitimacy or community legitimacy, in other words, cannot constitute the overall yardstick for the legitimacy of international arbitration, nor can national or global legitimacy. A comprehensive framework of legitimacy will therefore need to reflect a balance between party autonomy and social control, on the one hand, and global convergence and local diversity, on the other. Such a framework can be based, as will be argued in the next section, on a broad comparative constitutional approach to international arbitration. This perspective could help the system-internal discourse on the legitimacy of international arbitration to become more nuanced and forceful in responding to legitimacy-centered criticism of international arbitration.

IV.   TOWARDS A COMPARATIVE CONSTITUTIONAL LAW PERSPECTIVE ON INTERNATIONAL
      ARBITRATION

In developing the elements of legitimacy of international arbitration, the functional justification that arbitration provides a single and neutral forum to settle transborder international disputes and to provide for efficient enforcement mechanisms is of specific importance. It justifies arbitration as a mechanism of dispute settlement. But it cannot in and of itself justify functions of international arbitration that go beyond individual dispute settlement, such as developing the law applicable to and in arbitration, generating and enforcing normative expectations of users of arbitration and third parties, and thereby contributing to building a global regime that impacts the governance of social relations worldwide.

Instead, the concept of legitimacy to be used to analyze international arbitration should be multidimensional, and, what is more, entrusted to a variety of actors who interact in the transnational legal space in which international arbitration operates. In consequence, it is not the arbitration system alone and the parties opting for arbitration that can be a source of legitimacy. Only arbitrators, arbitration institutions, national courts, domestic legislators, and international treaty-makers together are able to sustain international arbitration as a legitimate system of governance. In such a transnational governance system of international arbitration recourse to legal principles that are common to different national laws and international law and that govern the exercise of arbitral authority and its relation to different social values will be crucial.

The most suitable source for developing such common principles upon which the legitimacy of international arbitration as a system of governance can be based, in my view, is comparative constitutional analysis. This could enable the system-internal discourse on legitimacy to develop a vocabulary as well as widely shared principles that directly respond to the current criticism of the functioning of international arbitration as a mechanism of governance in the very terms that criticism of the system employs. This broader perspective would not replace more limited concepts of legitimacy, such as "party legitimacy" or "community legitimacy", but complement them, by illustrating the constitutional dimensions of legitimacy.[79] Comparative constitutional analysis also corresponds to the now widely accepted approach to subject any institution of global governance and the way it exercises governance authority to public law standards, which include basic principles governing public-private relations, such as the principle of legality, due process, reason-giving, access to justice, or reasonableness and proportionality.[80]

Yet, when developing constitutional responses to the legitimacy problems of international arbitration as governance, solutions tied to singular constitutional legal orders are not convincing. Instead, the analysis must be cast in more general terms and consider how international arbitration is looked at from the constitutional perspective of different legal system. In this context, what the principles of democracy, the rule of law, and protection of human rights mean for international arbitration will be of particular interest, as these principles form the core of any constitutional system.[81] These principles may have an impact on the scope of arbitrability, the standards of review of

---

79. Party legitimacy and community legitimacy can be connected to constitutional analysis through the constitutional protection of individual freedom and party autonomy. As a consequence, constitutional analysis would argumentatively strengthen rather than undermine more specific dimensions of legitimacy, such as party or community legitimacy.

80. In fact, a conceptualization of global governance in a public law mindset is common to various strands in international legal scholarship, in particular the growing body of literature on Global Administrative Law (see Benedict KINGSBURY, Nico KRISCH and Richard B. STEWART, "The Emergence of Global Administrative Law", 16 Law & Contemporary Problems (2005) p. 15), constitutional approaches to international law (see Jan KLABBERS, Anne PETERS and Geir ULFSTEIN, *The Constitutionalization of International Law* (OUP 2009); Thomas KLEINLEIN, *Konstitutionalisierung im Völkerrecht* (Springer 2012); Matthias KUMM, "The Cosmopolitan Turn in Constitutionalism: On the Relationship between Constitutionalism in and Beyond the State" in Jeffrey DUNOFF and Joel TRACHTMAN, eds., *Ruling the World? Constitutionalism, International Law and Global Governance* (CUP 2009) p. 258), and the project on International Public Authority (see VON BOGDANDY, *Exercise of Public Authority*, supra fn. 5). All of these projects react to the phenomenon that there are more and more international institutions whose activities, in terms of their effect on private citizens, resemble that of domestic public authorities. Yet, instead of making use of classical public international law concepts and methods, they draw on comparative (domestic) public (administrative and constitutional) law in order to analyze the activity of institutions of global governance and their impact on social relations and to develop standards for the legitimacy of the institutions' exercise of public authority. The same approach, in my view, can be drawn on when analysing international arbitration as a system of governance.

81. Highlighting these principles as the core of the legitimacy of international institutions, Armin VON BOGDANDY, "*Grundprinzipien von Staat, supranationalen und internationalen Organisationen*" in Paul KIRCHHOF and Josef ISENSEE, eds., *Handbuch des Staatsrechts*, 3rd ed.,(C.F. Müller 2013) Vol. 11 p. 275; cf. also Armin VON BOGDANDY, "Common Principles for a Plurality of Orders: A Study on Public Authority in the European Legal Area", Jean Monnet Working Paper 16/14, <www.jeanmonnetprogram.org/papers/14/documents/JMWP16Bogdandy.pdf> (last accessed 14 November 2014).

international arbitration by domestic courts, and the activities by arbitration institutions, among others.

A detailed picture of how comparative constitutional analysis can inform the theory and practice of international arbitration will require a broad and comprehensive analysis of how constitutional law and arbitration interact in various legal systems. Such a study is beyond the scope of the present chapter. Likewise, in the following, I will not engage in a comparative constitutional analysis of a specific topic relating to international arbitration, but limit myself to the more conceptual questions that arise when arbitration is analyzed through a comparative constitutional lens. I will reflect first on the implications the institutional structure of arbitration as one-off dispute settlement has on questions of control mechanisms (*1*). Subsequently, I will discuss the methodological potential of comparative constitutional analysis as a strategy that arbitral tribunals and domestic courts can pursue in order to increase the overall legitimacy of international arbitration (*2*), and finally reflect on how comparatively developed constitutional principles relating to international arbitration can play out (*3*).

1.   *International Arbitration and Checks and Balances*

The structure of international arbitration as a governance mechanism that independently creates and stabilizes normative expectations presents specific challenges if compared to permanent courts. While it is well established that many dispute resolution institutions, including domestic courts, perform functions that go beyond dispute settlement, such as further developing the law and contributing to governing social relations, domestic courts, unlike international arbitral tribunals, are embedded in an institutional context in which the other branches of government can control how courts interpret and further develop the applicable law. Legislators can pass new laws, or amend existing ones, if they do not agree with how courts interpret the existing legal framework. Similarly, administrations in certain circumstances have the possibility of reacting to interpretations of courts through their law-making powers. This institutional setting provides a check on the authority of courts and prevents them from extending their reach too much into the domains of other branches of government. The exercise of authority by courts is therefore, as any form of government under constitutional law, constrained by legal rules and counteracting institutions. In turn, being bound by those constraints and being subject to a system of checks and balances can legitimize activities of courts that are unrelated to dispute settlement and that cannot be grounded in the disputing parties' consent.

In international arbitration, by contrast, control mechanisms are much more reduced. In particular, there is no centralized institutionalized framework that could control the international arbitration system in the same way as domestic legislators control courts. While domestic courts may be able to control arbitral tribunals with respect to the resolution of an individual dispute, there is no overarching institution that could prevent the arbitral system as a whole from developing in directions that are not perceived as legitimate anymore from a national or global perspective. While within the international arbitration community there are mechanisms, through the control by peers and arbitration institutions, that ensure that the functioning of international arbitration as a system of governance is perceived as legitimate by the arbitration community, effects on the national public(s) more generally or even global implications, such as global law-making by arbitral tribunals, can hardly be legitimized through community control mechanisms. They are simply not representative of society as a whole, but at the most represent the constituency of users of arbitration.

As a result, there is a misalignment between the global effects of international arbitration as a system of governance and control mechanisms that can check that arbitration remains legitimate at a global level. Yet, does this mean that international arbitration must be embedded in an institutional framework that is comparable to a constitutional system of checks and balances in order to be considered as legitimate from the perspective of global legitimacy? Do we need a global legislator to counterbalance global law-making by arbitral tribunals? Or are there other ways to square arbitration as a system of global governance with constitutional values and global legitimacy?

Postulating the need for a global legislator to regulate international arbitration would not only be unrealistic, it is also not necessary, in my view, to embed international arbitration into a framework that equals the structure of checks and balances that hold permanent (domestic) courts in place and imbue them with legitimacy. After all, the one-off nature of arbitral tribunals significantly reduces the weight of every single arbitral decision, because later tribunals are not bound by, and hence are free to diverge from, earlier decisions and their interpretation of the applicable law in light of the circumstances of each individual case. Unlike in the context of a hierarchical multi-tiered system of courts, later tribunals are free to adopt not only a different assessment of the facts, or distinguish their case on the basis of different factual circumstances; they are also free to diverge in respect of the interpretation and understanding of the governing law by prior arbitral decisions, even though, in particular in the investment treaty context, a tendency of arbitral tribunals to build a system of de facto precedent exists.[82]

The more limited systemic impact of individual decisions, in my view, alleviates the legitimacy demands on international arbitration significantly, even if it does not eliminate them. While arbitral tribunals do not pool the same amount of authority as national supreme or constitutional courts, their decision-making nevertheless has systemic effects that go beyond the parties to individual disputes in creating normative expectations that demand answers as to their legitimacy that are independent of party consent. Absent the creation of a global law-making institution that can counteract global effects of international arbitration, what then are realistic options to respond to the global legitimacy demands of international arbitration as a system of governance? Above all, how can the international arbitration system itself contribute to alleviating legitimacy concerns stemming from its effects as global governance institutions?

2. Exploring Comparative Constitutional Analysis of International Arbitration

In my view, there is a great and unused potential for the practice of international arbitration itself to develop and implement strategies that can alleviate legitimacy concerns relating to the exercise of transnational authority in international arbitration. Being aware of the effect of international arbitration on non-parties and aiming at

---

82. SCHILL, supra fn. 20, pp. 321 et seq.

limiting these effects, for example by exercising deference towards democratic decision-making processes that reflect concerns about the impact of international arbitration on non-parties, is a start; so is realizing the limitations in the concept of legitimacy as used in mainstream arbitration discourse and aiming for a broader conceptual approach. However, what is needed beyond these basic insights, is an argumentative integration, within the system-internal discourse, of legitimacy concerns stemming from the outside of international arbitration.

This means developing answers to legitimacy concerns in the vocabulary and argumentative frame used by critics rather than in the vocabulary used by those that are part of the system of international arbitration. It means taking up the constitutional challenges to international arbitration and developing solutions to them on the basis of the vocabulary of constitutional law. For this purpose, arbitral tribunals should have regard to comparative legal analysis of how the interaction between international arbitration and issues of constitutional law and constitutional values is viewed in different domestic legal systems.[83] A comparative law approach can also engage in cross-regime comparison with other international regimes. A particularly promising field for such an approach is the comparative evaluation of the jurisprudence developed by international courts and tribunals regarding, for example, questions of procedural fairness or strategies for paying respect to public interests. All of this could lead to the development of globally recognized principles that balance the autonomy of international arbitration with competing public and private interests. It could help in particular in legitimizing global law-making activities of arbitral tribunals by aligning them with how the underlying social relations, between private parties as well as between private and public actors, are structured by other governance institutions at the domestic and international level.

Comparative constitutional analysis should thus involve an assessment of how questions that arise in international arbitration and that have an impact beyond the disputing parties are dealt with and addressed in a variety of domestic and international legal regimes. This can serve several purposes: (1) to concretize and clarify the meaning of applicable cross-cutting standards in international arbitration, concerning for example standards of independence and impartiality of arbitrators, questions of evidence, or decisions on the set-aside or non-recognition of arbitral awards; (2) to help balance the autonomy of both the parties and the arbitration system to concerns of non-parties; (3) to ensure consistency in the interpretation of applicable standards and avoid incoherence across the system of international arbitration; (4) to ensure cross-regime consistency between international arbitration and other systems of governance, whether domestic or international, such as the protection of human rights; and (5) to suggest changes to arbitral practice in order to ensure its acceptance by non-users, in particular under the concept of global legitimacy.

---

83. Cf. MÖLLERS, supra fn. 66, pp. 411 et seq., who in discussing the legitimacy problems of international courts calls these strategies (1) "internalization", i. e., the integration of mechanisms in the system that reduce the intrusion of international courts into democratic decision-making processes, for example through limited standards of review; (2) "moralization", i.e., developing globally acceptable standards for the resolution of disputes; and (3) "individualization", i.e., reducing the impact of individual decisions on the international system.

A comparative constitutional approach to international arbitration not only has different purposes, but can also have varying impact on the activity of various actors:[84] (1) it can have a political function in suggesting changes to the current practice of both arbitral tribunals and supervising courts; (2) it can help arbitrators to become more aware of possible, and possibly better, solutions than those currently applied; (3) it can have direct effect on the interpretation of applicable substantive standards and procedural rules, for example when used to ascertain the ordinary meaning of recurring standards or provisions in international treaties such as *ordre public*; and (4) it can be used to develop general principles of law that need to be applied as default rules by arbitral tribunals and controlling courts in interpreting international and national laws applicable to and in arbitrations.

Depending on the purpose of comparative analysis, the choice of legal orders to be taken into account will vary. In order to suggest legal reform, for example, a single legal order may suffice. When suggesting, however, that certain principles constitute general principles of law, a more exacting methodology must be followed. General principles can be developed by qualified methods of comparative law, taking into account both domestic law and other international legal regimes.[85] In fact, general principles, while often perceived as a subsidiary source of international law, have been used frequently by international courts and tribunals in different contexts: to develop the procedural law of international adjudication; as a source of substantive rights and obligations; to fill lacunae in the governing law; and to aid interpretation and the further development of national and international law.[86]

The comparative method should be explored further also in order to develop standards that arbitral tribunals, domestic and international institutions can apply to their involvement in international arbitration. Comparative law can impact the resolution of questions relevant to the interaction between international arbitration and concerns and interests of non-parties through various channels and in various aspects, both concerning questions of arbitral procedure and substantive law. This requires a rigorous methodology to avoid the criticism that comparative legal analysis is "manipulable

---

84. Cf. Stephan W. SCHILL, "International Investment Law and Comparative Public Law: An Introduction" in Stephan W. SCHILL, ed., *International Investment Law and Comparative Public Law* (OUP 2010) p. 3 at pp. 25 et seq.

85. On the use of a proper comparative methodology see Stephan W. SCHILL, "General Principles of Law in International Investment Law" in Tarcisio GAZZINI and Eric DE BRABANDERE, eds., *International Investment Law − The Sources of Rights and Obligations* (Martinus Nijhoff 2012) p. 133 at pp. 145-154.

86. Numerous dispute settlement bodies have had recourse to such principles, including but not limited to the Permanent Court of International Justice and the International Court of Justice, the World Trade Organization Appellate Body, the various international criminal tribunals, the Court of Justice of the European Union, and the European Court of Human Rights. Likewise, in the context of foreign investment disputes, both under investment treaties and under investor-State contracts, arbitral tribunals frequently draw on general principles of law for a variety of purposes, in particular to fill gaps in the governing law and as an aid to treaty interpretation. Similarly, in international commercial arbitration general principles of law play an important role; see GAILLARD, *Legal Theory*, supra fn. 1, pp. 48, 54-56.

according to subjective preferences".[87] Attention needs to be paid in particular to the choice of comparative legal orders so as to avoid the charges of selectiveness and Euro-centricism.[88]

To be sure, much work still lies ahead for comparative law scholarship to provide a sophisticated method and in-depth comparative analyses of the various issues touched upon in international arbitration. Yet, there are no principled objections why sophisticated comparative law analysis and reasoning should not help to align the practice and outcomes of international arbitrations with standards concerning the law applicable to and in arbitration that are widely accepted also from the perspective of constitutional law. A comparative constitutional analysis, in my view, can help to respond to legitimacy concerns voiced in constitutional language.

3.   *Developing Comparative Constitutional Principles*

Ultimately, comparative constitutional analysis of international arbitration will have the goal of developing globally acceptable principles that the various actors involved in international arbitration, i.e. arbitral tribunals, controlling courts, and arbitration institutions, should apply in order for international arbitration to function as a legitimate institution of global governance. These principles will have to reflect the different dimensions of legitimacy, namely "party legitimacy", "community legitimacy", "national legitimacy", and "global legitimacy".[89]

Principles of comparative constitutional law can operate on several levels. The first set of principles will encompass constitutional principles of international arbitration that concern the institutional structure and founding principles of international arbitration as a dispute settlement mechanism. These include party autonomy, party equality, and arbitrator independence. Furthermore, first-level principles will address a number of procedural concerns that are closely connected to understanding international arbitration as a procedure to administer justice, which is a function international arbitration fulfills in the absence of alternatively available adjudicatory mechanisms; these principles include the right to be heard, the right to a fair hearing, the right to be able to present evidence, and the right to receive a reasoned award. All of them cannot only be grounded in party consent, but are also protected at the level of constitutional law in many legal systems.

---

87. M. SORNARAJAH, *The International Law on Foreign Investment* (3rd edn., CUP 2010) p. 418.

88. See José E. ALVAREZ, "Beware: Boundary Crossings", NYU School of Law, Public Law Research Paper No. 14-51, <ssrn.com/abstract=2498182> (last accessed 14 November 2014).

89. In addition, techniques are necessary for dealing with conflicts between different commands relating to different concepts of legitimacy; these techniques can also draw on how conflicts between different constitutional standards and different constitutional mechanisms of adjudication are dealt with, that is, through mutual cooperation and respect among different actors and methods of reasoning that aim at balancing and optimizing competing interests. For the conceptualization and application of techniques in determining the concept of national identity in the relationship between domestic constitutional courts of EU Member States and the Court of Justice of the European Union see Armin VON BOGDANDY and Stephan W. SCHILL, "Overcoming Absolute Primacy: Respect for National Identity Under the Lisbon Treaty", 48 Comm. Mark. L. Rev. (2011) p. 1417 at pp. 1440-1452.

The second set of principles relates to how international arbitration is controlled in view of effects on non-parties. In this context, the foundational constitutional principles that structure the exercise of any significant public power will also demand application vis-à-vis the international arbitration system. In the domestic context, these are the constitutional principles of democracy, the rule of law, and human rights.

Democracy will in particular come into play as a principle to control the law-making activity of arbitral tribunals. Democracy is behind demands for increased transparency, in particular in the investor-state arbitration context;[90] it also calls for participation of non-parties in arbitrations that may be affected by the proceedings, for example through *amicus curiae* submissions. Similarly, global public interest organizations that support specific global interests affected by arbitrations could rely on the principle of democratic participation to justify their role as advocates for global interests provided these interests find no adequate representation if only the disputing parties are heard by an arbitral tribunal. Finally, the principle of democracy may also become a basis for scrutinizing the representativeness of arbitration institutions in relation to the stakeholders they serve.

Similarly, the protection of human rights as a globally shared concern may increasingly be applied not only as a yardstick to measure the activity of states, but also the conduct of actors in the international arbitration system. To some extent, for example, as regards human rights concerns about proper procedures and fair trial principles, the content of human rights already finds expression in procedural principles applied in international arbitration. After all, arbitration is one form for states to fulfil their obligation to grant access to justice.[91] In other contexts, however, human rights are largely considered to be irrelevant for international arbitration when looking at disputing parties only. Yet, if international arbitrations have repercussions on non-parties and restrict their freedom to act, human rights are directly implicated and have to be brought to bear as structuring international arbitration. In this context, human rights are, for example, a basis for domestic courts to develop and concretize the standards used to control international arbitrators and hold them accountable, whether in the context of challenges of arbitrators or decisions for setting aside, recognizing, or enforcing arbitral awards.

Finally, respect for the rule of law as a globally recognized constitutional law standard could be used as a yardstick for both arbitral tribunals and controlling courts to structure their interaction. The rule of law will militate not only for coherence and predictability and the application of procedures that include the right to be heard or the duty to give reasons, but it can provide guidance for developing appropriate standards for review of both international arbitration and controlling courts that implement the vision of the rule of law

---

90. Julie MAUPIN, "Transparency in International Investment Law: The Good, the Bad and the Murky" in Andrea BIANCHI and Anne PETERS, eds., *Transparency in International Law* (CUP 2013) p. 142; Alessandra ASTERITI and Christian J. TAMS, "Transparency and Representation of the Public Interest in Investment Treaty Arbitration" in Stephan W. SCHILL, ed., *International Investment Law and Comparative Public Law* (CUP 2010) p. 787; UNCTAD, "Transparency", UNCTAD Series on Issues in International Investment Agreements II (United Nations 2012).

91. *Lithgow and Others v. United Kingdom*, Judgment, 8 July 1986, ECHR Series A No. 102, para. 201.

"as a principle of governance in which all persons, institutions and entities, public and private, including the State itself, are accountable to laws that are publicly promulgated, equally enforced and independently adjudicated, and which are consistent with international human rights norms and standards. It requires, as well, measures to ensure adherence to the principles of supremacy of law, equality before the law, accountability to the law, fairness in the application of the law, separation of powers, participation in decisionmaking, legal certainty, avoidance of arbitrariness and procedural and legal transparency."[92]

Again, the idea presented here that national courts, but also arbitral tribunals (acting together and by applying a common framework of reference and mindset), need to develop common and widely accepted standards for mutual control and loyal cooperation in balancing party autonomy and arbitration's independence in order to live up to the concerns of global legitimacy is but a first step towards a more comprehensive engagement with how comparative constitutional thinking can guide arbitral tribunals, arbitration institutions, and controlling courts in balancing the interests of parties to international arbitration and competing public interests that are, albeit indirectly, affected by international arbitration proceedings.

Comparative constitutional analysis is a methodology that allows the development of concrete answers to problems arising out of international arbitration's exercise of transnational authority, that can serve as a basis for making international arbitration function as a legitimate institution of global governance, and that can inform the discourse in and practice of the international arbitration community in a way to respond to the criticism of governance through international arbitration. While much work still needs to be done in order to put flesh to the bones of comparative constitutional analysis of international arbitration, an important first step for now would be the adoption, by all actors involved in international arbitration, of a constitutional legal mindset in thinking about the functioning and legitimacy of international arbitration. This can arguably contribute to enhancing the legitimacy of international arbitration and defending it, on constitutional grounds, against criticism that makes use of constitutional language.

V.   CONCLUSION

Any significant exercise of power raises demands as to its legitimacy. This applies not only to what individual tribunals and arbitrators do or do not do in relation to the disputing parties. It applies all the more to the transnational authority exercised by arbitral tribunals that go beyond settling individual disputes and that affect social relations of both users of arbitration and affected third-parties. To legitimize international arbitration in this broader perspective, recourse to the consent of disputing

---

92. United Nations, "Delivering Justice: Programme of Action to Strengthen the Rule of Law at the National and International Levels, Report of the Secretary General" (UN GAOR, 66th Session, Agenda Item 83, UN Doc A/66/749, 16 March 2012) para. 2.

parties and the argument that arbitrators are merely giving effect to pre-agreed instruments and the law governing the parties' relations is insufficient. To legitimize international arbitration as a system of global governance, a broader concept of legitimacy and a more sophisticated methodological framework to concretize the meaning of legitimacy is required. After all, governance, system-building and law-making by arbitral tribunals constitute a challenge for global democracy, the rule of law, and human rights.

This challenge to international arbitration does not render arbitration unsuitable or illegitimate as a global governance mechanism. But it requires the international arbitration system to open up towards outside perceptions and develop itself a more sophisticated framework for thinking about legitimacy. Opening up should start with realizing that legitimacy is not a mono-dimensional concept that can be defined in relation to disputing parties ("party legitimacy") or the group of users of international arbitration ("community legitimacy") only, but needs to take into account the interests of national societies ("national legitimacy") and global society as a whole ("global legitimacy"). A multidimensional concept of legitimacy, in turn, is the basis for thinking about the interaction between different interests and actors that represent different legitimacy dimensions, i.e., parties, arbitral tribunals, arbitration institutions, domestic courts, national legislators, international treaty-makers, and international institutions.

The legitimacy debate in international arbitration should, however, not stop with a realization of the multidimensionality of the concept of legitimacy. The international arbitration discourse should also engage with the substance of criticism in the critics' own frame of reference and defend its own practice in the context of that framework. The frame of reference, as I have argued in this chapter, is that of constitutional law and constitutional language. While constitutional law will directly interact with "national legitimacy" in relation to international arbitration, it also influences the dimension of global legitimacy, albeit mediated through a comparative constitutional law lens. After all, no specific constitutional system can demand authority over a global system of governance. In response to current criticism, the international arbitration system should integrate constitutional analysis and reasoning in its discourse on legitimacy. This will strengthen, not weaken, international arbitration and allow it to understand itself as a system of governance that respects and contributes to the constitutional principles of democracy, the rule of law, and human rights. Putting international arbitration into this broader context is crucial because compliance with these constitutional principles will ultimately determine the continued survival of international arbitration, not only as a system of global governance, but likely also a mechanism to settle individual private-private and private-public disputes.

Plenary Session:

Spotlight on International Arbitration in Miami and the United States

Introduction to the Session
Spotlight on International Arbitration in Miami and the United States

*Frank Cruz-Alvarez**

I.   PART ONE – *BG GROUP PLC V. REPUBLIC OF ARGENTINA:* A SIMULATED ORAL ARGUMENT
BEFORE THE UNITED STATES SUPREME COURT

This Session, "Spotlight on International Arbitration in Miami and the United States", is divided into two primary sections.

The first part of the Session was a simulated oral argument before the United States Supreme Court in the case of *BG Group PLC v. Republic of Argentina.*[1] The Republic of Argentina was represented by Matthew Slater of Clearly Gottlieb's Washington, DC office, and BG Group PLC was represented by Nigel Blackaby of Freshfields Bruckhaus Deringer's Washington, DC office. The "simulated" Supreme Court consisted of Judge Kathleen M. Williams, of the United States District Court for the Southern District of Florida, Judge Vance E. Salter of Florida's Third District Court of Appeal, and Judge Rosemary Barkett, a former judge with the United States Court of Appeals for the Eleventh Circuit and now Judge on the Iran-United States Claims Tribunal.

The facts of the cases are as follows. In the early 1990s, BG Group PLC, a British firm, made an investment to take a majority interest in a privatized Argentine natural gas utility. At the time that BG Group made the investment Argentine law called for gas tariffs to be linked to the US dollar, and those "tariffs would be set at levels sufficient to assure gas distribution firms ... a reasonable return".[2] In 2001 and 2002, Argentina, facing an economic crisis, enacted new laws that "changed the basis for calculating gas tariffs from dollars to pesos".[3] As a result, BG Group's investment became unprofitable. In 2003, BG Group sought arbitration pursuant to the 1990 bilateral investment treaty between the United Kingdom and Argentina. In 2007, following an arbitration, which was conducted in Washington, DC, the arbitrators concluded that Argentina had not accorded BG Group "fair and equitable treatment" as required by Art. 2(2) of the

---

*   Panel Rapporteur; Partner in the International Arbitration Practice Group of Shook, Hardy & Bacon L.L.P.'s Miami office.

1. 134 S.Ct. 1198 (2014).
2. *Id.* at 1204.
3. *Id.*

investment treaty.[4] Accordingly, the arbitrators awarded BG Group $185 million in damages.

In March 2008, both BG Group and Argentina filed petitions for review in the District Court for the District of Columbia. BG Group sought confirmation of the award under the 1958 New York Convention and Argentina sough an order vacating the award. The principal basis that Argentina asserted for vacating the award was that the arbitrators did not have jurisdiction. The district court confirmed the arbitral award, and Argentina appealed to the Circuit Court for the District of Columbia, which subsequently reversed the district court. The focus of the court of appeals' analysis was Art. 8 of the investment treaty, which contains the dispute resolution provision. Art. 8 essentially stated that when there is a dispute arising under the treaty either party (investor or nation) shall submit its claim "to the decision of the competent tribunal of the Contracting Party in whose territory the investment was made", what the parties called the "local litigation requirement".[5] Art. 8 went on to state that arbitration may then occur,

> "(i) where, after a period of eighteen months has elapsed from the moment when the dispute was submitted to the competent tribunal ... the said tribunal has not given its final decision; [or]
> (ii) where the final decision of the aforementioned tribunal has been made but the Parties are still in dispute".[6]

Art. 8(2)(a). BG Group never litigated its claim in the local Argentine courts. Thus, in the arbitration proceedings, Argentina argued that a condition precedent to arbitration had not occurred, and the arbitrators were without jurisdiction. The arbitrators ultimately concluded that the local litigation requirement was "absurd and unreasonable" under the facts of the case because in addition to the new tariff laws enacted by Argentina, Argentina had passed additional laws which restricted litigation in its courts.[7] In reaching its decision to confirm the arbitral award the district court had deferred to the decision of the arbitrators as it related to the local litigation requirement. The court of appeals disagreed. It reviewed the issue de novo and concluded that BG Group had failed to satisfy the local litigation requirement, which stripped the arbitrators of jurisdiction. The circuit court vacated the arbitral award, and BG Group's petition for review was accepted by the Supreme Court.

The question before the Court in *BG Group PLC v. Republic of Argentina* was whether a court of the United States, in reviewing an arbitration award made under the bilateral investment treaty in issue, should interpret and apply a local litigation requirement found in the treaty de novo, or with the deference that courts ordinarily owe arbitration

---

4. *Id.*
5. *Id.* at 1203.
6. *Id.*
7. *Id.* at 1205.

decisions.[8] In other words, "who – court or arbitrator – bears primary responsibility for interpreting" the treaty provision?[9]

Justice Breyer authored the majority opinion that approached the issue in a two-step process: "initially treat[ing] the document … as if it were an ordinary contract between private parties", and then examining "whether the fact that the document in question is a treaty makes a critical difference".[10] Citing prior decisions of the Court, Justice Breyer explained that in cases involving ordinary contracts between private parties the presumption is that "courts, not arbitrators" will decide any dispute regarding arbitrability and that arbitrators will decide disputes about the "meaning and application of particular procedural preconditions for the use of arbitration".[11] After setting the stage, the Court found that "the text and structure of the [local litigation] provision make clear that it operates as a procedural condition precedent to arbitration".[12] "It determines when the contractual duty to arbitrate arises, not whether there is a contractual duty to arbitrate at all."[13] Thus, the Court concluded that "the litigation provision is consequently a purely procedural requirement", the application and meaning of which is to be determined by the arbitrator (not the court) under normal contract interpretation rules.[14]

The Court then looked to see whether its conclusion should be different here because the contract in question is a treaty between nations and not a contract between the parties to the dispute. In the end, the Court rejected the view expressed by Argentina – and the United States in its amicus brief – that the local litigation requirement was not a procedural condition precedent to arbitration, but rather "a condition on the State's consent" meriting de novo scrutiny.[15] The Court, instead, applied "a [h]ighly [d]eferential" standard of review to the decision of the arbitrators and, then in analyzing the award, concluded that the arbitrators did not "stra[y] from interpretation and application of the agreement" when they disregarded the validity of the local litigation requirement under the circumstances presented in this case.[16]

Chief Justice Roberts, joined by Justice Kennedy dissented. The Chief Justice was troubled by the majority's use of ordinary private contract interpretation tools to interpret a document that is "a treaty between two sovereign nations" to which "[n]o investor is a party".[17] Treaties, including bilateral investment treaties are normally interpreted on the basis of principles of interpretation set forth in Arts. 31 and 32 of the Vienna Convention on the Law of Treaties. Chief Justice Roberts felt that because the

---

8. *Id.* at 1206.
9. *Id.*
10. *Id.*
11. *Id.* at 1206 and 1207.
12. *Id.* at 1207.
13. *Id.*
14. *Id.*
15. *Id.* at 1208.
16. *Id.* at 1212 and 1213.
17. *Id.* at 1215.

majority "start[s] down the wrong road", it "ends up at the wrong place".[18] According to the Chief Justice, Art. 8(2)(a) is a substantive rather than a procedural requirement: it "constitutes only a unilateral offer" by Argentina with respect to investors – an offer that must be accepted by submitting a dispute to a local court before Argentina may be held to have consented to arbitration.[19]

Because the Supreme Court issued its decision on 5 March 2014, the participants in the simulated oral argument were instructed to assume that the Supreme Court's decision was in fact the decision of the lower appellate court. As such, counsel for the Republic of Argentina argued to overturn the decision, and counsel for BG Group PLC argued in favor of affirming the decision.

Counsel for Argentina (Mr. Slater) made several arguments in asking the court to overturn the lower court decision:

– The lower court mistakenly assumed that the investment treaty at issue contained an agreement to arbitrate.
– He argued that the proper interpretation of the treaty is that the dispute resolution clause contained an "offer" to arbitrate that an investor could accept "if" the investor first sought relief in the local courts of Argentina. Until that condition was satisfied, Argentina could not be deemed to "consent" to arbitration.
– In short, his argument was that the issue before the court was whether there was an agreement to arbitrate, and that such a question is typically decided by courts and not arbitrators under US precedent.

Counsel for BG Group PLC (Mr. Blackaby) asked the court to affirm the lower court's decision arguing that:

–There was an agreement to arbitrate because the local litigation clause was a "condition precedent" and not a condition of consent. Indeed, counsel argued that a reading of the dispute resolution clause of the treaty supports this interpretation because despite the local litigation requirement either party is always free to institute arbitration if either is unhappy with the result in the local court, or if after eighteen months there is no resolution in the local court. As such, all avenues lead to arbitration which supports the existence of an agreement to arbitrate.
– Furthermore, counsel argued that because the issue is one of whether a condition precedent to arbitration was fulfilled and that issue is generally resolved by the arbitrators, the court should affirm the lower court enforcing the award and affirming the arbitrators' interpretation and application of the local litigation clause.

After a lively discussion between the panelists and the audience, it is safe to conclude that the takeaway from the Supreme Court's decision in *BG Group*, is that if a nation wants to ensure that courts rather than arbitrators decide whether it has consented to

---

18. *Id.*
19. *Id.* at 1216.

arbitration, the nation would be wise to have that language expressly stated in any investment treaty that may result with enforcement proceedings in the United States.

II.   PART TWO – INTERNATIONAL ARBITRATION IN MIAMI AND THE UNITED STATES

In the second section, an esteemed panel of arbitration practitioners from Miami and across the United States made presentations on the following topics related to international arbitration in Miami and the United States.

The first contribution is from Eduardo Palmer, of Eduardo Palmer PA in Miami, which discusses the recent and ongoing developments in the Miami legal community making Miami an attractive choice for hosting arbitration proceedings. Mr. Palmer highlights the reasons why Miami has increasingly become the seat of international arbitrations, especially for Latin American-centered disputes. For example, he discusses the logistical benefits that Miami has to offer, including flights to and from many Latin American cities, facilities for conducting arbitration proceedings, and the large population of Spanish-speaking professionals in South Florida. In addition, Mr. Palmer addressed the Florida legislature's adoption of the UNCITRAL Model Law on International Commercial Arbitration and the Florida Bar rules that allow foreign lawyers to participate in international arbitrations in Florida, without the need for a license to practice law in the jurisdiction.

The second contribution is from Rachel D. Kent, Vice Chair of Wilmer Hale's International Arbitration Group, who discusses class action arbitrations in the United States after briefly discussing other arbitration centers in the United States. Ms. Kent provides the Congress with some key takeaways including the fact that class action arbitrations are primarily sought in consumer arbitration, where agreements with consumers generally prohibit class action arbitrations or are silent on the topic. She, however, cautions as to the future of the procedural device in the US arbitrations because the US Supreme Court has not yet provided sufficient guidance on the parameters and acceptability of this form of arbitration in a broad context.

The third contribution is from Jack J. Coe, Jr., Professor of Law at Pepperdine University School of Law, which provides a progress report on the American Law Institute's Restatement of the Law (Third) on the U.S. Law of International Commercial Arbitration. In his report to the Congress, Professor Coe explains that the final Restatement will consist of five chapters. To date, two chapters have been completed and released. He explains some of the key propositions contained in the Restatement, one of which is a rejection of the use of forum non conveniens as a basis to reject enforcement of arbitral awards – indeed a rejection of a principal that has popped up in recent case law in the United States.

And the last contribution is from Daniel González, co-leader of Hogan Lovells' International Arbitration Practice, which discusses the enforcement of arbitral awards in the United States and the need for consistency in the law across the various states and the federal courts. The focus of Mr. González's presentation is the need for consistency in certain key areas including the rules governing service of process in the United States because currently there are varied methods for securing service under the rules of the individual states and pursuant to the Federal Rules of Civil Procedure. Moreover,

Mr. González emphasizes the need for judicial consistency when it comes to issues of the defenses available to a party opposing the enforcement of an arbitral award in the United States, and the rules governing personal jurisdiction. And lastly, he called attention to the need for consistency in the application of US law on the enforceability of annulled awards.

Miami's Favorable International Arbitration Climate

*Eduardo Palmer**

I. INTRODUCTION

Miami is a unique and special place. In the United States, Miami has long been referred to as "the Magic City" because of its exotic nature, subtropical locale and climate, and sense of excitement. It is a beautiful cosmopolitan city on the water that serves as the gateway to Latin America for North American, European, and Asian companies doing business in the Americas. Due to its geographic location, Miami has more non-stop daily flights from cities in Latin America than any other location in the region. Miami is also blessed with human capital. It has benefitted from the immigration of many professionals from throughout Latin America, Europe, and elsewhere. As a result, Miami is a truly world-class international city with a formidable bilingual and multilingual professional workforce ideally suited for international arbitration work.

In addition, a survey of over 200 corporate counsel indicated that in terms of the general infrastructure of the seat, the issue of costs (42 percent), was one of the most important factors in choosing a seat.[1] When it comes to costs, Miami fares well in comparison to traditional arbitral venues. A survey found that the cost for arbitration-related services, including court reporters and interpreters, is significantly lower in Miami than in other arbitral venues, such as New York, London, or Paris.[2]

---

* P.A., Miami Florida.
1. Queen Mary University of London and White & Case, "2010 International Arbitration Survey: Choices in International Arbitration", at: <http://www.whitecase.com/files/upload/file Repository/2010-International-Arbitration-Survey-Choices-International-Arbitration.PDF>.
2. "Cost Survey Conducted by Gateway Florida, Inc.", at: <https://www.MiamiInternational Arbitration.com/us/Arbitration/AbitrationinMiami/Convenience&Affordability>.

All of these factors provide Miami with innate competitive advantages vis-à-vis other potential arbitral venues in the Americas. What's more, local practitioners have worked together over the last ten to twenty years to build on these favorable organic elements in order to strategically craft the legal infrastructure necessary to propel Miami as a leading center for international arbitration in the Americas. As described in more detail below, this infrastructure was thoughtfully pieced together by surveying other jurisdictions and consulting with the world's leading international arbitration practitioners in an effort to adopt and implement the best practices in the field.

There is tangible evidence that Miami has arrived as a leading arbitral venue. The International Centre for Dispute Resolution (ICDR) reports that international filings for Miami increased 161 percent from 2010-2013. This led the ICDR to establish a case manager position in its Miami office, which is the first time the ICDR has administered international cases outside of New York. In addition, it was recently announced that the arbitration for the largest infrastructure project in the Americas, the US$1.6 billion Panama Canal dispute, will be seated in Miami.

II.   FREEDOM OF CHOICE OF COUNSEL – FLORIDA BAR RULE 1-3.11

An important factor that is often overlooked in selecting the seat of an international arbitration proceeding is whether the local laws regulating the practice of law in a given jurisdiction make clear that parties are free to select counsel of their choice to represent them in such proceedings, regardless of whether their counsel of choice is admitted to practice in that jurisdiction. This is often a grey area of the law that is fraught with many potential hazards. Only a few jurisdictions throughout the world, especially in the Americas, have laws that clearly provide that an attorney need not be admitted to practice in the location where the arbitration is taking place in order to participate in an international arbitration proceeding occurring in that location. The laws of most jurisdictions either prohibit or place severe restrictions on such a practice, or, at best, are unclear. Although local practitioners in such jurisdictions may attempt to downplay this important hazard by offering assurances that these laws are seldom enforced, the fact remains that this situation presents a substantial and unpredictable risk.

Accordingly, the International Law Section of the Florida Bar worked together with many international arbitration practitioners in Florida in 2003 in order to promote the promulgation of Florida Bar Rule 1-3.11 by the Supreme Court of Florida. That rule contains an express carve out which provides that non-Florida lawyers (domestic or foreign) who engage in international arbitration proceedings in Florida are not subject to the Rules Regulating the Florida Bar, including the potentially applicable rules pertaining to the unlicensed or unauthorized practice of law. Thus, the rule allows parties to select counsel of their choice to represent them in international arbitration proceedings conducted in Florida, regardless of whether their counsel of choice is admitted to practice in Florida.

This rule provides parties a vital right to use their counsel of choice when conducting an international arbitration proceeding in Florida. Usually parties to an agreement choose neutral territory as the location of the arbitration to avoid giving either party an advantage, and the choice of law is typically different from that of the forum. Thus, if parties are prohibited from using their own counsel who is familiar with the transaction and the operation of the parties' businesses, together with the chosen law, many of the benefits of international arbitration are lost.

III.   ADOPTION OF UNCITRAL MODEL LAW ON INTERNATIONAL COMMERCIAL ARBITRATION (THE MODEL LAW)

Recognizing the importance of international trade and commerce to Florida's economy, Florida began to pass legislation in the mid-1970s intended to facilitate Florida's development as the center for commercial activities in the Americas. In fact, in 1986 Florida became the first state in the United States to pass an international arbitration statute, the Florida International Arbitration Act,[3] influenced by the newly minted Model Law. In 2010, Florida again demonstrated its leadership in the field of international arbitration in the United States when it became the first state to enact the Model Law with the 2006 Amendments as the Florida International Commercial Arbitration Act (FICAA).[4]

The FICAA replaced the prior international arbitration statute in its entirety. Unlike many jurisdictions that claim to have passed the Model Law, Florida did not alter any of the provisions of the orthodox text of the amended version of the Model Law. The thinking in Florida was that the most important element of enacting a statute based on the Model Law is that international arbitration practitioners from around the world know and understand the Model Law and are comfortable operating within such a universally known construct. In addition, the body of case law developed around the world interpreting the Model Law provides greater guidance to courts, arbitrators, and practitioners when the version of the Model Law at issue is the same as the original text. Many of these benefits are lost or significantly diluted when jurisdictions enact legislation that is marketed as based on the Model Law but in reality has so many variations from the Model Law that the text is barely recognizable as legislation patterned after the Model Law.

Although Florida did not vary any of the provisions of the amended version of the Model Law, it did add two provisions that fill what were seen as critical voids in the Model Law. The first deals with immunity for arbitrators. Surprisingly, the Model Law does not contain an express provision conferring immunity on arbitrators. While the drafters of the Model Law may have reasoned that the concept of arbitrator immunity is sufficiently enshrined in customary international law so as not to require insertion of a specific provision to that effect, Florida thought it was best to avoid any doubt on the matter by expressly noting the existence of arbitrator immunity in the FICAA. Thus, Sect. 684.0045 of the FICAA provides that "[a]n arbitrator serving under this chapter shall have judicial immunity in the same manner and to the same extent as a judge".[5]

---

3. Sects. 684.01 et seq., Fla. Stat. (1986).
4. Sects. 684.01 et seq., Fla. Stat. (2013).
5. Sect. 684.0045, Fla. Stat. (2013).

The second provision involves the issue of personal jurisdiction. The Model Law does not contain any provision establishing that the courts of the territory in question can exercise personal jurisdiction over the parties involved in an international arbitration matter tied to that venue. The absence of such a provision unnecessarily complicates the ability of the parties involved in an international arbitration matter to seek redress in a state court in connection with said arbitration. In order to avoid such uncertainty and eliminate the need to litigate this issue, Florida recently added a consent to jurisdiction provision to the FICAA. That provision, Sect. 684.0049, provides as follows:

> "The initiation of arbitration in this state, or the making of a written contract, agreement, or undertaking to arbitrate which provides for arbitration in this state, constitutes a consent to exercise in personam jurisdiction by the courts of this state in any action arising out of or in connection with the arbitration and any resulting order or award."[6]

Not only was Florida the first state in the United States to enact the recently amended version of the Model Law, it is currently the only state that has enacted the Model Law and stayed true to the language of the existing text as noted above. Some practitioners in the international arbitration community erroneously believe that the enactment of state international arbitration statutes in the United States is of little consequence because the entire area of arbitration in the United States is preempted by the Federal Arbitration Act (FAA).[7] That is simply not the case.

The doctrine of federal preemption in the United States is based on Art. VI of the United States Constitution which specifies that all laws enacted under the Constitution are the "supreme law of the land" and enjoy legal supremacy over any conflicting provision found in a state constitution or law.[8] The key language here of course is "over any conflicting provision". Thus, as long as state law or statute does not stand "as an obstacle to the accomplishment and execution of the full purpose and objectives of Congress" in enacting the FAA, it can function in harmony alongside the FAA.[9] The essence of the FAA is to promote the strong public policy in the United States in favor of arbitration by ensuring the enforceability of arbitration agreements. Therefore, the main focal point for courts evaluating a state law or statute in order to determine whether it is preempted by the FAA involves determining if the state law or statute in question "requires a judicial forum for the resolution of claims which the contracting parties agreed to resolve by arbitration".[10]

That will rarely if ever be the case with the Model Law. Instead, the Model Law can and does serve as a gap-filler and safety net in connection with the FAA. A simple example illustrates the point. There is conflicting case law in the United States on whether an arbitral tribunal has the authority to issue pre-hearing subpoenas under

---

6. Sect. 684.0049, Fla. Stat. (2013).
7. 9 U.S.C. Sects. 1 et seq.
8. U.S. Const. Art. VI.
9. *Hines v. Davidowitz*, 312 U.S. 52, 67 (1941).
10. *Southland Corp. v. Keating*, 465 U.S. 1, 10 (1984).

Sect. 7 of the FAA. The plain language of Sect. 684.0038 of the FICAA, however, which follows Art. 27 of the Model Law, provides such authority to tribunals. Therefore, where the arbitration proceedings are governed by Florida law, and the FICAA allows a tribunal to seek assistance or to allow the parties to seek assistance from a competent court to obtain evidence, the FAA does not preempt the operation of Sect. 684.0038 of the FICAA.[11]

Accordingly, Florida's enactment of the FICAA, which is true to the text of the most recent version of the Model Law, constitutes a vital piece of the legal infrastructure created to support international arbitration in Miami and sets Miami apart from other competing venues in the United States and the Americas.

IV.   STRONG JUDICIAL SYSTEM AND CREATION OF SPECIALIZED INTERNATIONAL ARBITRATION COURT

One of the most critical components necessary to establish a suitable venue for hosting international arbitration disputes is the existence of an independent and transparent judicial system that has a legal culture which favors arbitration. While the passage of legislation favoring international arbitration and similar measures designed to enhance the arbitration climate in a given jurisdiction are important and necessary, the international business community will not feel confident in selecting a particular location as the seat of an arbitral dispute unless it believes in the integrity of the relevant local and national court systems. Courts are critical to the arbitration process, because they are often called upon to conduct legal proceedings that are ancillary to, or otherwise in aid of, ongoing arbitrations. Such proceedings include efforts to compel or stay arbitrations, requests for interim relief in the form of injunctions, selection and appointment of the tribunal, enforcement of subpoenas issued by tribunals, and various other proceedings, including efforts to either confirm and enforce or vacate arbitral awards.

The United States is fortunate to have a strong and independent judiciary, and its local and national court systems enjoy a well-deserved reputation for honesty, efficiency and transparency. The US government and the State of Florida expend considerable resources in order to build, maintain and operate a first rate judicial system and to pay and train qualified jurists. In addition to the experience, training and integrity of its judiciary, the legal culture in the United States has strongly favored the use of arbitration for over half a century. Moreover, because of Miami's position as the commercial gateway to Latin America, state and federal courts in Miami have vast experience in dealing with complex commercial disputes of an international nature. The immense volume of such international legal disputes litigated in Florida has augmented and refined Florida's body of international commercial law. Thus, whether called upon to provide interpreters in various foreign languages or to apply foreign laws, courts in Miami have the resources and experience necessary to properly adjudicate legal issues related to

---

11. *See Volt Info. Sciences, Inc. v. Bd. Of Trustees of Leland Stanford Junior Univ.*, 489 U.S. 468, 479 (1989) ("Where, as here, the parties have agreed to abide by state rules of arbitration, enforcing those rules according to the terms of the agreement is fully consistent with the goals of the FAA...").

international arbitration proceedings and can be counted on to do so in an efficient, fair and transparent fashion.

In addition, last year Miami established a specialized court within its state court system to hear all matters related to international arbitration proceedings. The creation of specialized courts or judges to handle international arbitration proceedings is widely viewed as an important factor by the international community in determining the most suitable venues to conduct such proceedings. Assigning these cases to a particular court or judge helps to develop greater judicial expertise in this unique area of the law. This system also leads to more uniformity in such rulings, which helps to establish a consistent body of case law.

The mere existence of a specialized court for international arbitration sends an important signal to the international business community that the jurisdiction in question has a sophisticated infrastructure for handling these proceedings, which enhances the jurisdiction's stature and attractiveness as an international arbitration venue. Countries that have historically been leaders in the area of international arbitration, such as England, France, and Switzerland, have all established such courts or procedures.[12] Other countries seeking to enhance their infrastructure for handling international arbitration disputes, including Australia, China, India and Sweden, have followed suit and created similar regimes.[13]

The court for international arbitration matters in Miami is the International Commercial Arbitration Subsection (ICA Subsection) within the current Complex Business Litigation Section, in Miami-Dade County Circuit Court. The ICA Subsection, is only the second such court in the United States and has two judges. All matters relating to international commercial arbitration disputes that arise either under the FICAA or the FAA, will be assigned to the ICA Subsection. Such matters may include requests to appoint an arbitrator, order interim measures, or to recognize and enforce an arbitral award, as well as other requests for relief under these statutes. Thus, parties who select Miami as a venue for their international arbitration proceedings can be confident that in the event either party commences court proceedings related to the arbitration, those matters will be handled by judges who have experience and specialized training in this area.

V.   AREA UNIVERSITIES AND PROFESSIONAL ORGANIZATIONS ARE AN INTEGRAL PART OF MIAMI'S INTERNATIONAL ARBITRATION COMMUNITY

A key component of the mosaic carefully pieced together to build Miami's international arbitration infrastructure is the involvement and support of area universities and professional organizations. Miami has taken a holistic and multifaceted approach to developing itself as an arbitral venue. While its innate competitive advantages and purposefully created legal infrastructure are important, the community spirit for this

---

12. See Barry LEON, "To Specialize or Not: How Should National Courts Handle International Commercial Arbitration Cases?", Kluwer Arbitration Blog, 2 September 2010.

13. *Id.*

endeavor is nourished and developed through the participation of academic institutions and professional organizations.

Miami's outstanding universities provide a strong academic foundation to foster the continued study and development of international arbitration practices. The University of Miami School of Law has a rich tradition in the area of international law, particularly with respect to Latin America, and has a variety of legal programs and academic journals that focus on this area. These programs include various courses in international litigation and arbitration, which are taught by world-renowned scholars and are attended by students from throughout the Americas and Europe. As a further indication of its commitment in this area, the University of Miami has established the International Arbitration Institute. This institute is headed by one of the leading figures in international arbitration, Jan Paulsson, and offers courses in international arbitration, promotes academic research and writing in this area, and provides practical training to international arbitration practitioners. Graduates obtain an LL.M. degree from the University of Miami School of Law specializing in international arbitration, one of the few such programs in the world.

A prime example of how area universities support Miami's development as an arbitral venue is the University of Miami's decision to provide full scholarships for the two judges assigned to the ICA Subsection to attend a one-week seminar on international arbitration held at its International Arbitration Institute. The seminar was taught by leading international arbitration scholars and greatly enhanced the judges' understanding and appreciation of this increasingly important field of law. Florida International University, a state-charted academic institution that is based in Miami, also has its own law school, which, true to its name, focuses extensively on international law, including international litigation and arbitration. The work of these and other local academic institutions is an invaluable resource and has helped to create a large local workforce of experienced and sophisticated international arbitration practitioners.

The work of professional organizations complements such efforts. For example, the International Law Section of the Florida Bar has held an annual international litigation and arbitration conference over the last decade in order to enhance the knowledge of local practitioners in this growing area of the law. The work of the International Law Section also includes reaching out to law students in Florida and helping to develop and support their interest in international arbitration. This is an important component of the overall effort. The thinking is that law students provide a vital pipeline of fresh ideas and energy necessary to sustain and develop Miami's stature in the field of international arbitration.

Accordingly, over the last ten years, the International Law Section has held a pre-moot for all of the Florida law schools competing in the Willem C. Vis international arbitration moot held each year in Vienna, Austria and Hong Kong. Not only does the International Law Section organize and operate the Vis pre-moot in Florida each year, it also provides a substantial stipend to each of the Florida law schools competing in this event. No other bar organization in the United States, and few, if any, bar organizations in the world, have developed such a comprehensive program. As a result, Florida sends at least six teams from different Florida law schools to the Vis moot each year. That is more than almost any other state in the United States and more than most countries send to the Vis competition. This investment in the future has paid and continues to pay huge dividends for Miami. For instance, Stetson University, one of the Florida law schools that participates in this program, won the Vis moot in Vienna several years ago and several of the Florida teams typically advance to the elimination rounds of the Vis moot each year. The success of these Florida law schools greatly enhances Miami's brand in the world of international arbitration. In addition, many of the law students in Florida who participate in the Vis become members of the International Law Section after they graduate and help to organize the various programs the Section runs to support the development of international arbitration in Florida.

Such outreach efforts also help to create an international buzz among young people about the international arbitration scene in Miami, which draws talented young lawyers from around the world who crave such an environment to Miami. These young practitioners have already begun to organize and work together and have created the group "Future of Arbitration: Miami!" (FA:M!). FA:M! is open to young professionals and law students who have an interest in developing a career in international arbitration and who want to work to continue to increase Miami's stature as a leading venue for international arbitration.

The Miami International Arbitration Society (MIAS), which was created over six years ago, is another important professional organization involved in this endeavor. MIAS was founded in order to promote the use of international arbitration and mediation and the selection of Miami as the situs for international arbitration proceedings related to the resolution of transborder commercial and investment disputes. MIAS works to maintain and enhance the extensive infrastructure developed to encourage international arbitration in Miami by supporting appropriate legislation, relevant academic programs at area universities, local international arbitration conferences, featuring distinguished practitioners as guest speakers, and providing training and legal updates to its members on the latest developments in international arbitration. The list of past speakers includes the following: Professor Albert Jan van den Berg, Former President, Netherlands Arbitration Institute; Gerold Herrmann, Former Secretary General, UNCITRAL; Professor Martin Hunter, Representative of ICCA at UNCITRAL; Professor George Berman, Chief Reporter, American Law Institute; Loretta Mallintoppi, Vice President, ICC Court of Arbitration; Doug Jones, President, Australian Centre for International Commercial Arbitration; and Prof. Jan Paulsson, Former President of ICCA. Presentations by these and many other distinguished speakers greatly enrich the international arbitration community in Miami and provide a forum where practitioners interested in international arbitration can network and exchange ideas and information about this practice area.

In addition, the United States Council for International Business (USCIB) based its Arbitration Sub-Committee for the Florida region in Miami. The USCIB is the US representative of the ICC. The ICC's International Court of Arbitration (ICA) maintains national arbitration committees throughout the world. The USCIB's Arbitration Committee is the national arbitration committee for the ICA in the United States The USCIB Arbitration Committee is divided into regions, of which Florida is the newest. Due to Florida's growing importance in the international arbitration world, particularly as it relates to arbitrations dealing with Latin America, the USCIB decided to make Florida its own region, with Miami as its seat. The Florida Arbitration Sub-Committee spearheads the ICC's efforts in Florida as it relates to educating corporations and lawyers based in Florida as to the benefits of international arbitration as a method of dispute resolution in general.

VI.   STATE-OF-THE-ART HEARING CENTERS

Miami is extremely fortunate to have two state-of-the-art hearing centers to conduct international arbitration proceedings. The centers are another important component of Miami's infrastructure geared towards this field. While parties are certainly free to rent facilities at a great number of fine hotels and office buildings in Miami to have hearings, use of the hearing centers avoids the often tedious and time consuming task of having to retrofit hotel facilities in order to make them suitable to conduct hearings.

Miami's two hearing centers are conveniently located in the heart of the city's business center. One is in the center of downtown and the other is in the adjacent Brickell international banking district. The downtown hearing center is operated by the AAA/ICDR, which located their regional offices for the southeastern United States in Miami. The Brickell hearing center is operated by JAMS, which recently opened in Miami in order to capitalize on Miami's growing importance in the international marketplace. These purpose-built state-of-the-art hearing centers offer excellent facilities equipped with the latest technology (Wi-Fi, video conferencing and fully-equipped office centers), including hearing rooms and breakout rooms, to conduct international arbitration and mediation proceedings, all while overlooking breathtaking views of the beautiful Miami skyline and Biscayne Bay. Due to a MIAS initiative, both of these centers are available to host any arbitration proceeding in Miami, regardless of whether that proceeding is administered by the AAA/ICDR, JAMS, or any other arbitral institution, such as the International Chamber of Commerce (ICC) or the London Court of International Arbitration (LCIA).

VII.   FAVORABLE CASE LAW

As all international practitioners know, case law is a critical part of the jurisprudence in a common law system such as the United States. Thus, any analysis of the desirability of a jurisdiction as a venue for international arbitration must include a review of the applicable case law and a comparison with the case law present in other relevant jurisdictions. Statistical information compiled by arbitral institutions such as the ICC and the ICDR show that New York and Miami are by far the most active venues for international commercial arbitration in the United States. What many practitioners are not aware of, however, is that the case law applicable to international arbitrations in Miami is generally more supportive of the institution of international arbitration than the applicable case law in New York.

Within the federal system in the United States, which divides appellate courts along regions of the country, Miami is in the Eleventh Circuit and New York is in the Second Circuit. A survey of cases from these two circuits dealing with issues involving the standard for vacatur, application of the defense of forum non conveniens, application of the defense of manifest disregard, and enforcement of the arbitration agreement, shows

845

that the case law in the Eleventh Circuit is more in line with the basic principles underlying international arbitration than the case law in the Second Circuit. This is an important point because no matter what local practitioners try to do to make their jurisdiction more attractive, there is no getting around the binding case law in your respective circuit.

1.   *Vacatur Standard*

In *Industrial Risk Insurers v. M.A.N. Gutehoffnungshutte GmbH*, 141 F.3d 1434 (11th Cir. 1998) the court was faced with the question of whether the seven defenses set out in Art. V of the 1958 New York Convention on the Recognition and Enforcement of Arbitral Awards (the Convention) are the only grounds available to contest the enforcement of an international arbitration award rendered in the United States. The case is instructive in that the arbitration at issue was seated in Florida and decided under Florida law but involved a foreign party.[14] As a result, the court concluded that the award constituted a non-domestic award (i.e., international award) and thus its enforcement was governed by Chapter 2 of the FAA, which is the US codification of the Convention.[15]

The parties seeking to vacate the award argued, among other things, that the award should be vacated on the ground that it was "arbitrary and capricious".[16] The court noted that such a defense was one of the recognized non-statutory defenses derived by courts from the list of the statutory defenses found in Chapter 1 of the FAA, which are applicable to domestic awards.[17] Because the award was a non-domestic award, however, the court held that it could not look to any of the defenses available under Chapter 1 of the FAA, and was limited to reviewing the defenses available under the Convention, codified in Chapter 2 of the FAA.[18] The Eleventh Circuit observed that "[t]he Convention does not, however, include a defense against enforcement of an award on the ground that the award is 'arbitrary and capricious'. The omission is decisive.... In short, the Convention's enumeration of defenses is exclusive."[19] The court proceeded to confirm the award indicating again that only the express grounds set out in the Convention can serve as a basis to challenge enforcement of an international arbitration award rendered in the United States under Chapter 2 of the FAA, and applied those same defenses to enforcement found in Art. V to the motion to vacate (applying Sect. 207 of Chapter 2).[20]

This decision in the Eleventh Circuit finding unequivocally that the defenses listed in Art. V of the Convention are the exclusive grounds available for challenging enforcement of international arbitral awards rendered in the United States, as well as to the motion to vacate, adheres to the spirit and letter of the Convention and promotes uniformity and finality in international arbitration proceedings. The Second Circuit takes a different

---

14. *Id*. at 1439.
15. *Id*. at 1439-1441.
16. *Id*. at 1445.
17. *Id*. 1445-1446.
18. *Id*. at 1446-1447.
19. *Id*. at 1446.
20. *Id*.

approach. In *Yusuf Ahmed Alghanim & Sons v. Toys "R" Us, Inc.*,[21] the Second Circuit addressed the issue of whether the FAA's implied grounds for setting aside arbitral awards apply to efforts to vacate non-domestic awards rendered in the United States. The parties in *Yusuf* agreed that the award at issue, which was rendered in the United States, was a non-domestic award covered by the Convention.[22]

The party challenging the award argued that the FAA's implied ground for vacatur should nonetheless apply to its motion to vacate.[23] The court held that while other grounds for vacatur could not be read in to Art. V of the Convention because that list of grounds was exhaustive, the court was free to apply the FAA's implied grounds under Art. V (1)(e).[24] The court reasoned that the language in Art. V(1)(e) which provides that "[t]he award ... has been set aside or suspended by a competent authority of the country in which, or under the law of which, that award was made", meant that it had the authority to apply domestic arbitral law, including the FAA's implied grounds for vacatur, to a non-domestic award rendered in the United States.[25] The court reached said conclusion despite noting that said ruling could potentially undermine some of the goals of the Convention.

> "The possible effect of this ground for refusal [Art. V(1)(e)] is that, as the award can be set aside in the country of origin on *all* grounds contained in the arbitration law of that country, including the public policy of the country, the grounds for refusal of enforcement under the Convention may indirectly be extended to include all kinds of particularities of the arbitration law of the country of origin. This might undermine the limited character of the grounds for refusal listed in Article V ... and thus decrease the degree of uniformity existing under the Convention."[26]

The Second Circuit eventually confirmed the award in question because it found that neither of the implied grounds at issue was proven.[27] However, its holding that Art. V(1)(e) of the Convention allows US courts to apply US "domestic arbitral law and its full panoply of express and implied grounds for relief" when analyzing a motion to vacate an international award rendered in the United States, remains the law of the Second Circuit today.[28] In contrast, the Eleventh Circuit limits review of such awards to the grounds expressly set out in Art. V.[29]

---

21. 126 F. 3d 15 (2nd Cir. 1997).
22. *Id.* at 18-19.
23. *Id.* at 18.
24. *Id.* at 18-23.
25. *Id.* at 20-23.
26. *Id.* at 21, (quoting Albert Jan VAN DEN BERG, *The New York Arbitration Convention of 1958: Towards a Uniform Judicial Interpretation* (Asser/Kluwer 1981) pp. 265, 355) .
27. *Id.* at 23-25.
28. *Id.* at 23.
29. *Industrial Risk Insurers,* 141 F.3d at 1446-1447.

2.   Recognition of Forum Non Conveniens Defense

The doctrine of forum non conveniens is a common-law doctrine whereby a court which would otherwise have jurisdiction to adjudicate a dispute may exercise its discretion not to do so whenever considerations of convenience, efficiency and justice indicate that a forum other than the one chosen by the plaintiff would be better suited to hear the case.[30] The Eleventh Circuit has never recognized the defense of forum non conveniens as a vehicle to deny enforcement of an international arbitration award. This of course makes sense. One of the primary purposes of the Convention is to facilitate the ability of parties to enforce international arbitral awards in any forum where the losing party may have assets. Oftentimes the losing party may have assets in a jurisdiction that has little or no connection to the underlying dispute, other than the fact that the losing party has assets there. If courts in such jurisdictions decline to enforce awards on the grounds of forum non conveniens, this severely restricts the ability of prevailing parties to seize assets to satisfy an award and contravenes one of the central objectives of the Convention. The Second Circuit, however, does recognize the defense of forum non conveniens in the context of enforcement proceedings dealing with international arbitration awards.

The Second Circuit first dealt with this issue in the case of *In re Arbitration Between Monegasque De Reassurances S.A.M. v. Nak Naftogaz of Ukraine.*[31] The case involved an attempt to enforce a Russian arbitration award in New York. The court rejected the petitioner's arguments that Art. V of the Convention contains the only grounds for refusing to enforce a foreign arbitral award and "that the application of the doctrine of forum non conveniens flouts the intent of the Convention and runs the risk of invalidating its purpose".[32] Instead, it reasoned that the language in Art. III of the Convention which provides that each signatory "shall recognize arbitral awards as binding and enforce them in accordance with the rules of procedure of the territory where the award is relied upon…", Convention Art. III, meant that proceedings involving enforcement of foreign arbitral awards are subject to the procedural rules in existence in the courts where enforcement is sought.[33]

The court went on to state that since the doctrine of forum non conveniens has historically been classified as procedural in nature, it had the authority, under the above-noted terms of Art. III, to apply that doctrine in the context of an enforcement proceeding involving a foreign arbitral award.[34] The Second Circuit proceeded to confirm the lower court's dismissal of the enforcement action based on the doctrine of forum non conveniens.[35] The Second Circuit subsequently extended its holding in *Monegasque* regarding the availability of the forum non conveniens defense in proceedings governed by the Convention, to efforts to enforce foreign arbitral awards under the

---

30. *Gulf Oil Corporation v. Gilbert*, 330 U.S. 501, 506-509 (1947).
31. 311 F.3d 488 (2nd Cir. 2002).
32. *Id.* at 496.
33. *Id.* 495-497.
34. *Id.*
35. *Id.* at 501.

Inter-American Convention on International Commercial Arbitration (the Panama Convention) as codified in Chapter 3 of the FAA.[36]

Following the reasoning explained in *Monegasque*, the Second Circuit in *Figueiredo Ferraz* noted that Art. 4 of the Panama Convention contained language similar to the language it relied on from Art. III of the New York Convention in *Monegasque*.[37] Specifically, the court stated that Art. 4 indicates that enforcement of international arbitral awards "may be ordered ... in accordance with the procedural laws of the country where it is to be executed...." and forum non conveniens is a procedural doctrine.[38] Accordingly, the Second Circuit applied the doctrine of forum non conveniens to the petition to confirm the foreign arbitral award under the Panama Convention and dismissed the petition based on said ground.[39] The dissent in *Figueiredo* aptly noted that the decision to apply the doctrine of forum non conveniens "in these circumstances would seem to dramatically undercut the treaty drafters' efforts to foster confidence in the reliability and efficiency of international arbitration" and "introduces a highly significant inconsistency into the international regime of reciprocal enforcement...".[40] No such precedent exists in the Eleventh Circuit.

3.   *Viability of Manifest Disregard Doctrine After Hall Street Assoc., LLC v. Mattel, Inc.*

The doctrine of manifest disregard of the law has been viewed as either an implied ground or as a judicial gloss on the enumerated grounds for vacatur under Chapter 1 of the FAA.[41] The manifest disregard standard historically authorized courts to vacate an award where there was "clear evidence that the arbitrator was conscious of the law and deliberately ignored it".[42]

The decision of the Supreme Court of the United States in *Hall Street* casts grave doubt on whether manifest disregard still exists as an implied ground or as a judicial gloss on the designated grounds for review under the FAA.

In *Hall Street*, the Court was asked to decide whether the parties could supplement the statutory basis for vacatur under Sect. 10 by agreeing through contract that any arbitration award could be vacated if the arbitrator's findings lacked evidentiary support or if the legal conclusions were clearly erroneous.[43] The Court held that the parties could not do so under the FAA because "Sects. 10 and 11 respectively provide the FAA's exclusive grounds for vacatur and modification."[44] The Court saw its reading of the text of the FAA "as substantiating a national policy favoring arbitration with just the limited review needed to maintain arbitration's essential virtue of resolving disputes

---

36. See *Figueiredo Ferraz E Engenharia de Projecto Ltda. v. Republic of Peru*, 665 F. 3d 384 (2nd Cir. 2011).
37. *Id.* at 393.
38. *Id.*, (quoting Panama Convention, Art. 4).
39. *Id.* at 392-394.
40. *Id.* at 397-398.
41. *Hall Street Assoc., LLC v. Mattel, Inc.*, 552 U.S. 576, 585 (2008).
42. *B.L. Harbert Int'l, LLC v. Hercules Steel Co.*, 441 F.3d 905, 910 (11th Cir. 2006).
43. *Hall Street*, 552 U.S. at 578-579.
44. *Id.* at 584.

straightaway. Any other reading [would] open[] the door to full-bore legal and evidentiary appeals....”[45] Thus, *Hall Street* made clear that the parties could not supplement the FAA's grounds for vacatur by contract and still travel under Sect. 10, and called into question the continued viability of judicially created extra-statutory grounds for vacatur, such as manifest disregard.

The Eleventh Circuit reached the issue of the continued viability of judicially-created grounds for vacatur after *Hall Street* in the case of *Frazier v. CitiFinancial Corp., LLC.*[46] The Eleventh Circuit concluded that the Supreme Court's categorical language in *Hall Street* meant that judicially created grounds for vacatur, such as manifest disregard, are no longer valid.[47] Thus, as applied to international arbitration matters in the Eleventh Circuit, it is no longer possible to set aside an award by incorporating manifest disregard, which is seen by some courts as a judicial gloss on Sects. 10 and 11 of Chapter 1 of the FAA, into Chapters 2 or 3 through the residual application of Chapter 1 in Sects. 208 and 307, respectively.

The Second Circuit takes a different view. In several decisions issued after *Hall Street*, the Second Circuit has held that the doctrine of manifest disregard survives the Supreme Court's decision in *Hall Street*. *T.Co Metals, LLC v. Dempsey Pipe & Supply, Inc.*;[48] *Schwartz v. Merrill Lynch & Co., Inc.*[49] The Second Circuit maintains that manifest disregard is not a judicially created extra-statutory ground for review but rather reads *Hall Street* as having reconceptualized manifest disregard as a judicial gloss on the specific grounds for vacatur enumerated in Sect. 10 of the FAA.[50] As such, the Second Circuit has held that the doctrine of manifest disregard is still a viable ground for review despite *Hall Street*.[51]

Thus, this comparison illustrates yet another area where the law in the Eleventh Circuit impacting international arbitration is more in line with the applicable public policy in that it supports a "national policy favoring arbitration with just the limited review needed to maintain arbitration's essential virtue of resolving disputes straightaway".[52]

---

45. *Id.* at 588.
46. 604 F.3d 1313 (11th Cir. 2010).
47. *Id.* at 1324.
48. 592 F.3d 329, 339-340 (2nd Cir. 2010).
49. 665 F.3d 444, 451-452 (2nd Cir. 2011).
50. *Id.*
51. *Id.*
52. *Hall Street*, at 588.

4. Enforcement of the Arbitration Agreement

In *Bautista v. Star Cruises*,[53], the Eleventh Circuit evaluated a defense to enforcement of an arbitral agreement based on the null and void clause of Art. II(3) of the Convention. The plaintiff was a crew member of a cruise ship who argued that the arbitration provision within his employment agreement with the cruise line should not be enforced because it was unconscionable under state law.[54] The court evaluated the plaintiff's defense under the null and void clause in Art. II(3) of the Convention. In doing so, the court noted that the Convention's null and void clause limits the basis for such challenges to standard breach-of-contract defenses.[55] The court further observed that the limited scope of this clause requires that it be interpreted to encompass only those defenses that are susceptible of neutral application on an international scale.[56]

The court stated that due to the unique policy considerations inherent in the area of international arbitration, such as international comity and the need for predictability in the resolution of international disputes, the domestic defenses to enforcement of an arbitration agreement that are transferable to a case under the Convention are limited.[57] In keeping with that philosophy, the court held that "[i]t is doubtful that there exists a precise, universal definition of the unequal bargaining power defense that may be applied effectively across the range of countries that are parties to the Convention, and absent any indication to the contrary, we decline to formulate one".[58] Thus, the court held that the plaintiff's unconscionability defense did not constitute a valid defense under the null and void clause in Art. II(3) and enforced the arbitration agreement.[59]

The *Bautista* decision is significant because it means that in the Eleventh Circuit, ordinary domestic defenses to arbitration are insufficient under the Convention unless they meet the heightened international standard of defenses that are universally accepted among the broad range of countries that are signatories to the Convention. There is no comparable decision in the Second Circuit.

VIII. CONCLUSION

Miami is blessed with many innate characteristics, including being the commercial center of the Americas, more non-stop daily flights from cities in Latin America than any other location in the region, a large multilingual professional workforce, and a magnificent climate, that make it an ideal seat for international arbitration disputes in the Americas. Additionally, Miami is a more convenient and affordable location to host proceedings relating to disputes originating in the Americas than traditional centers such as New

---

53. 396 F.3d 1289 (2005).
54. *Id.* at 1301-1302.
55. *Id.* at 1302.
56. *Id.*
57. *Id.*
58. *Id.*
59. *Id.* at 1302-1303.

York, London, or Paris. More importantly, local practitioners have built on these innate advantages and strategically pieced together the necessary infrastructure, incorporating the best practices in the field, to make Miami a leading world venue for international arbitration. Miami is also fortunate in that the case law in the Eleventh Circuit is generally more supportive of international arbitration than the case law in the Second Circuit, which applies to New York, Miami's only real competitor for international arbitration in the United States. While each of these individual factors is powerful in its own right, taken together they unquestionably demonstrate that Miami has arrived as a leading venue for international arbitration in the Americas.

Availability of Class Arbitration Under US Law

Rachael Kent* and Marik String**

I.   INTRODUCTION

Over the past several decades, there has been an explosion of class action litigation in the United States, particularly in connection with consumer disputes.[1] Not surprisingly, given the widespread inclusion of arbitration agreements in consumer contracts, class action litigation has been joined by so-called "class arbitrations", in which individual claimants assert claims in arbitration on behalf of a defined class of unnamed, similarly situated claimants.[2]

There has been considerable debate in the US courts about class arbitration. Among other questions, the courts have grappled with whether courts or arbitrators should have the role of determining whether particular arbitration agreements allow for class arbitration,[3] whether state or federal law governs that determination,[4] whether class arbitration must be expressly authorized by an arbitration agreement or can be inferred

---

* Partner in the International Arbitration Practice Group, Wilmer Cutler Pickering Hale and Dorr LLP.

** Associate in the International Arbitration Practice Group, Wilmer Cutler Pickering Hale and Dorr LLP.

The views expressed in this article are the views of the authors and do not necessarily reflect the views of Wilmer Cutler Pickering Hale and Dorr LLP or its clients.

1. See, e.g., Chris H. MILLER, "The Adaptive American Judiciary: From Classical Adjudication to Class Action Litigation", 72 Alb. L. Rev. (2009) p. 117 at p. 117 ("class action litigation has become one of the distinguishing features of our legal system and it remains one of the most politically controversial areas of law".).
2.   William H. BAKER, "Class Action Arbitration", 10 Cardozo J. Conflict Resol. (2009) p. 335 at p. 335 ("Class action arbitrations are a relatively recent phenomenon in the United States, but the number of such arbitrations is expanding at a rapid rate.").
3. See, e.g., *Stolt-Nielsen SA v. AnimalFeeds Int'l Corp.*, 559 U.S. 662 (2010) (analyzing the extent to which a court should review an arbitrator's decision on the availability of class arbitration).
4. See, e.g., *AT&T Mobility LLC v. Concepcion*, 563 U.S. 321 (2011) (assessing whether the Federal Arbitration Act (FAA) preempts state arbitration laws).

from a so-called "silent" clause,[5] and whether explicit waivers prohibiting class arbitration are valid.[6] Since 2003, the US Supreme Court has issued five key decisions addressing class arbitration.[7] Those decisions have failed to establish clear rules regarding several important aspects of class arbitration[8] and also strongly suggest that the Supreme Court has not yet said its last word(s) on the use of class arbitration in the United States.

In addition, and at least in part in response to the decisions of the Supreme Court, the United States Congress has also focused attention on the arbitration of consumer disputes and is considering legislation that would invalidate certain pre-dispute arbitration agreements in consumer contracts, which would likely lead to a sharp reduction in the use of class arbitration in the United States.[9] At the direction of Congress, the Consumer Financial Protection Bureau (CFPB), the agency established in the wake of the 2007 financial crisis to ensure the enforcement of federal consumer protection laws, has also turned its attention to mandatory arbitration agreements in consumer contracts, including the use of class arbitration waivers.[10]

This article discusses the status of class arbitrations in the United States. Part II provides background on the development of class arbitration. Part III discusses the Supreme Court's jurisprudence on class arbitrations. Part IV describes recent steps taken by Congress and the CFPB that may affect the arbitrability of consumer disputes, including through class arbitrations. Part V considers what questions regarding class arbitration remain unsettled under US law and what the Supreme Court's recent opinions suggest about the future of class arbitration in the United States.

---

5. See, e.g., *Green Tree Fin. Corp. v. Bazzle*, 539 U.S. 444 (2003) (examining whether an arbitrator can order class arbitration based on a silent arbitration clause).
6. See, e.g., *American Express Co. v. Italian Colors Restaurant*, 133 S.Ct. 2304 (2013) (assessing the validity of an express waiver of class arbitration in a contract of adhesion).
7. *American Express Co.*, 133 S.Ct. at 2304; *Oxford Health Plans v. Sutter*, 133 S.Ct. 2064 (2013); *AT&T Mobility LLC*, 563 U.S. at 321; *Stolt-Nielsen*, 559 U.S. at 662; *Green Tree Fin. Corp.*, 539 U.S. at 444 (examining whether an arbitrator can order class arbitration based on a silent arbitration clause).
8. One scholar commenting on the Court's decisions wrote:

   "Reading the various opinions in *Bazzle*, *Stolt-Nielsen* and now *Concepcion* makes one wish that the U.S. Supreme Court would stop deciding arbitration cases for a while – preferably, a long while. Preliminarily, the erratic course of ushering in class arbitration in *Bazzle*, followed by largely or entirely ushering it out again a decade later in *Stolt-Nielsen* and *Concepcion*, is both an institutional embarrassment and a profligate waste of resources – What was the point, and why must parties and taxpayers bear the costs, of the countless disputes, arbitrations and litigations over the past ten years provoked by the Court's shifting views? What happens now to the 300 or so AAA class arbitrations which are pending? What weight should parties and lower courts give to future Supreme Court pronouncements on the FAA – and for how long?"

   Gary BORN and Claudio SALAS, "United States Supreme Court and Class Arbitration: A Tragedy of Errors, The Symposium", 2012 J. Disp. Resol. (2012) p. 21.
9. See, e.g., S.878, 113th Cong. (2013) (Arbitration Fairness Act of 2013).
10. See Consumer Financial Protection Bureau, Arbitration Study Preliminary Results: Section 1028(a) Study Results to Date (12 December 2013), at <http://files.consumerfinance.gov/f/201312_cfpb_arbitration-study-preliminary-results.pdf> (CFPB Arbitration Study).

II.   ORIGIN OF CLASS ARBITRATION UNDER US LAW[11]

While there is a long history of collective actions in the civil courts of England and the United States,[12] the modern approach to "class action" litigation in the United States arose in the mid-1960s, with a major revision to Rule 23 of the Federal Rules of Civil Procedure.[13]

Under Rule 23, one or more "representative" members of a class may sue or be sued in US federal courts on behalf of all members of the class if: (1) the class is so numerous that joinder of all members is impracticable; (2) there are questions of law or fact common to the class; (3) the claims or defenses of the representative parties are typical of the claims or defenses of the class; and (4) the representative parties will fairly and adequately protect the interests of the class.[14] The final judgment in a class action litigation generally binds all members of the defined class, with the exception of individual members of the class who have affirmatively "opted-out" of the class.[15] The class action mechanism established by Rule 23 is intended to promote fair and efficient adjudication of disputes that affect a class of similarly situated class members and to avoid the risk of inconsistent or preclusive decisions with respect to individual class members.[16]

The Federal Arbitration Act (FAA), which governs arbitration in the United States, was enacted in 1925, long before modern class action litigation mechanisms.[17] The FAA therefore does not address the possibility of class arbitration. It simply provides that an arbitration agreement "shall be valid, irrevocable, and enforceable, save upon such grounds as exist at law or in equity for the revocation of any contract".[18] The FAA provides arbitration agreements with a strong presumption of enforceability: as the Supreme Court noted in the landmark 1967 case of *Prima-Paint Corp. v. Flood & Conklin*

---

11. See generally S.I. STRONG, "The Sounds of Silence: Are U.S. Arbitrators Creating Internationally Enforceable Awards when Ordering Class Arbitration in Cases of Contractual Silence or Ambiguity?", 30 Mich. J. Int'l L. (2009) p. 1017; Philip A. LACOVARA, "Class Action Arbitrations – The Challenge for the Business Community", 24 Arb. Int'l (2008) p. 541; William H. BAKER, "Class Arbitration in the United States: What Foreign Counsel Should Know", 1 Disp. Resol. Int'l (2007) p. 4; J. Maria GLOVER, "Beyond Unconscionability: Class Action Waivers and Mandatory Arbitration Agreements", 59 Vand. L. Rev. (2006) p. 1735.

12. Francisco VALDES, "Procedure, Policy, and Power: Class Actions and Social Justice in Historical and Comparative Perspective", 24 Ga. St. U. L. Rev. (2008) p. 627 at p. 630 ("we now know that the earliest uses of the thing now known generally as the class action were in England ...").

13. Fed.R.Civ.P. 23 (class actions).

14. *Ibid.* at 23(a). Most state court rules of civil procedure also include provisions allowing for class action litigation. In many cases, class actions that are initiated in state courts can be removed to federal courts on the motion of the defendant(s).

15. *Ibid.* at 23(c)(3).

16. See Tobias Barrington WOLFF, "Preclusion in Class Action Litigation", 105 Colum. L. Rev. (2005) p. 717 (describing preclusion issues in the class action context).

17. 9 U.S.C. Sect. 2.

18. 9 U.S.C. Sect. 2.

Manufacturing, the purpose of the FAA is to "make arbitration agreements as enforceable as other contracts".[19]

US courts have long recognized that arbitration is required only where the parties have freely agreed to submit their disputes to arbitration. Thus, historically, most US state and federal courts allowed arbitration to proceed only among the parties to a particular contract, thereby effectively barring class arbitrations because of a lack of privity.[20] While class action litigation became increasingly widely used throughout the second half of the twentieth century for a variety of consumer, environmental, civil rights and securities claims, most arbitrations continued to be conducted as individual actions, with only the parties to the specific contract participating in the arbitration. Eventually, some state courts, particularly in California, began to permit class-wide arbitrations on behalf of a defined class of unnamed claimants, all having identical arbitration agreements with the same defendant. For a time, class arbitration was, in the words of one commentator, a "mythical beast: half litigation, half arbitration and rarely seen".[21]

That all changed in 2003, following the Supreme Court's decision in *Green Tree Financial Corp. v. Bazzle*.[22] In *Bazzle*, two classes of homeowners asserted claims against Green Tree in South Carolina state court. Green Tree moved to compel arbitration pursuant to an arbitration agreement in the loan contracts with each member of the asserted class.[23] The lower court certified the class and ordered arbitration. The arbitrator then conducted a class arbitration and ultimately issued an award against Green Tree in favor of the claimant class. On appeal, the South Carolina Supreme Court upheld the arbitrator's award, holding that, while the arbitration agreements were silent as to the availability of class arbitration, "class-wide arbitration may be ordered when the arbitration agreement is silent if it would serve efficiency and equity, and would not result in prejudice".[24] The US Supreme Court granted certiorari.

In a plurality opinion on behalf of four of the Justices, Justice Breyer wrote that the South Carolina courts had erred in finding that the contracts were silent on the question of whether class arbitration was permitted, because that was a question of contract interpretation that should have been decided by the arbitrator, not the courts.[25] The four-member plurality reasoned that the question "whether the contracts forbid class arbitration" was not one of the narrow "gateway" issues that courts review de novo, but

---

19. *Prima Paint Corp. v. Flood & Conklin Mfg. Corp.*, 388 U.S. 395, 404 n. 12 (1967).
20. See, e.g., *Champ v. Siegel Trading Co., Inc.*, 55 F.3d 269, 275 (7th Cir. 1995); *Gammaro v. Thorp Consumer Discount Co.*, 828 F.Supp. 673 (D. Minn. 1993); *Steinberg v. Prudential-Bache Sec., Inc.*, 12 Del. J. Corp. L. 371, 380 (Del. Ch. 1986) (holding that class arbitration was impermissible as it constituted "rewriting the contract"); *Vernon v. Drexel Burnham & Co.*, 52 Cal.App.3d 706 (Cal. Ct. App. 1975) (denying claimants' request for class arbitration).
21. Kelly COCHRAN and Eric MOGILNICKI, "Current Issues in Consumer Arbitration", 60 Bus. Law. (2005) p. 785 at pp. 791-792; W.H. BAKER, *op. cit.*, fn. 2, p. 335 ("Class action arbitrations are a relatively recent phenomenon in the United States.").
22. *Green Tree Fin. Corp.*, 539 U.S. at 444.
23. *Ibid.* at 447-449.
24. *Bazzle v. Green Tree Fin. Corp.*, 569 S.E.2d 349, 360 (S.C. 2002).
25. *Green Tree Fin. Corp.*, 539 U.S. at 453.

was a matter that "concerns contract interpretation and arbitration procedures", which should be for an arbitrator to decide.[26] The plurality therefore held that the case must be remanded so that an arbitrator could interpret the parties' arbitration agreement.[27]

Justice Stevens, who issued a separate concurring opinion, disagreed that the case required remand, because the petitioner had not challenged the decision to allow class arbitration on the basis that it had been made by the wrong decision-maker. Rather, the petitioner had challenged that decision only on the merits.[28] Justice Stevens reasoned that "the decision to conduct class arbitration was correct as a matter of law" and said that he would simply have affirmed the judgment of the South Carolina Supreme Court upholding the arbitrator's decision.[29] Nevertheless, Justice Stevens concurred in the judgment written by Justice Breyer in order to avoid the outcome of having no controlling judgment of the Court.[30]

Although *Bazzle* did not result in a clear majority decision, it appeared that five of the nine Justices accepted that an arbitrator had the authority to interpret an arbitration agreement to determine whether it allowed class arbitration, even where the arbitration agreement did not expressly authorize class arbitration.[31] *Bazzle* was widely interpreted to mean that arbitrators could interpret arbitration agreements to allow class arbitration, even where the agreements were silent regarding the availability of class arbitration.[32]

Following *Bazzle*, two leading US arbitration institutions, the American Arbitration Association (AAA) and JAMS, issued new rules on class arbitration.[33] Almost immediately, there was a proliferation of class arbitrations, many of which were initiated under arbitration agreements that were silent as to the availability of class arbitration. The arbitrators in these cases generally interpreted silent arbitration agreements to

---

26. *Ibid.*
27. *Ibid.* at 454.
28. *Ibid.* at 455.
29. *Ibid.*
30. *Ibid.* at 446.
31. *Ibid.* at 453.
32. See Carole J. BUCKNER, "Due Process in Class Arbitration", 58 Fla. L. Rev. (2006) p. 185 (*Bazzle* "marked the beginning of a new era in class arbitration"); Meredith W. NISSEN, "AAA vs. JAMS: Different Approaches to a New Concept", 11 Disp. Resol. Mag. (2005, no. 4) p. 19 ("The recent growth in class arbitrations is the result of the U.S. Supreme Court's 2003 decision in *Green Tree Financial Corp. v. Bazzle*"); Peter J. KREHER and Pat D. ROBINSON III, "Substance, Process, and the Future of Class Arbitration", 9 Harv. Negot. L. Rev. (2004) p. 409 (noting that *Bazzle* had empowered arbitrators to decide on the availability of class arbitration).
33. See AAA Supplemental Rules for Class Arbitration (2003), at <www.adr.org/aaa/faces/rules/ searchrules/rulesdetail?doc=ADRSTG_004129&_afrLoop=4434361971835608&_afrWindo wMode=0&_afrWindowId=4z0f3v9wb_64#%40%3F_afrWindowId%3D4z0f3v9wb_64%26 _afrLoop%3D4434361971835608%26doc%3DADRSTG_004129%26_afrWindowMode%3D 0%26_adf.ctrl-state%3D4z0f3v9wb_120>; JAMS Class Action Procedures (2009), at <www. jamsadr.com/files/Uploads/Documents/JAMS-Rules/JAMS_Class_Action_Procedures- 2009.pdf>. The procedural mechanisms for class arbitration established under the AAA and JAMS rules are a hybrid of traditional arbitration procedures and class action civil litigation procedures. See Richard NAGAREDA, "The Litigation-Arbitration Dichotomy Meets the Class Action", 86 Notre Dame L. Rev. (2011) p. 1069.

permit class arbitration: according to one commentator, in the first sixty-seven class arbitrations administered by the AAA, the tribunals held that a silent arbitration clause permitted arbitration in every case but two.[34]

Most of the class arbitrations administered by these and other institutions have involved civil rights, securities, employment, consumer and environmental claims.[35] Although many class arbitrations have arisen out of domestic arbitration agreements entirely between US parties, class arbitrations have also been asserted against foreign companies, under arbitration agreements that do not refer to the possibility of class arbitration.[36]

While some consumer advocacy groups and plaintiffs' lawyers have welcomed the rise of class arbitration,[37] the business community and defense lawyers have generally been critical.[38] As with class action litigation, class arbitration is often seen as a means for plaintiffs' lawyers to assert low-value claims of questionable merit in order to force settlements that include large payments to plaintiffs' counsel.[39] Many companies include arbitration agreements in consumer contracts precisely to avoid the risks of US civil litigation, including the enormous exposure that is presented by class action litigation. The availability of class arbitration is therefore sometimes seen as eliminating much of the benefit of arbitration altogether.[40]

Following *Bazzle*, many companies that included arbitration agreements in their consumer or employment contracts thus began to include express prohibitions on class

---

34. See W.H. BAKER, *op. cit.*, fn. 2, p. 348.

35. *Ibid.* at p. 336.

36. See, e.g., *Stolt-Nielsen, SA v. Animalfeeds Int'l Corp.*, 435 F.Supp.2d 382 (S.D.N.Y. 2006) (involving class arbitration of an antitrust claim against a foreign shipping company).

37. See, e.g., Joshua LIPSCHUTZ, "The Court's Implicit Roadmap: Charting the Prudent Course at the Juncture of Mandatory Arbitration", 57 Stan. L. Rev. (2005) p. 1677 at pp. 1681-1682 ("other consumer advocates, and consumers themselves, argue that if consumers are not allowed to proceed on a classwide basis, then the arbitration agreement has effectively stripped them of substantive rights because some claims are simply too small to be worth pursuing individually, even in arbitration".).

38. See Myriam GILLES, "Opting Out of Liability: The Forthcoming, Near-Total Demise of the Modern Class Action", 104 Mich. L. Rev. (2005) p. 373 at p. 410 ("For corporate defendants, then, the *Bazzle* ruling alleviated the concern of judges ordering classwide arbitration."); Thomas J. CUNNINGHAM, "Class Actions in Arbitration", 92 Ill. B.J. (2004) p. 532 ("It is no surprise that corporate America would prefer not to be troubled by class action lawsuits, which are costly to defend and settle.").

39. Martin H. REDISH, "Class Actions and the Democratic Difficulty: Rethinking the Intersection of Private Litigation and Public Goals", 2003 U. Chi. Legal F. (2003) p. 71 at p. 77 ("what purports to be a class action, brought primarily to enforce private individuals' substantive rights to compensatory relief, in reality amounts to little more than private attorneys acting as bounty hunters, protecting the public interest by enforcing the public policies embodied in controlling statutes".).

40. See J. LIPSHUTZ, *op. cit.*, fn. 37, p. 1713 ("When surveyed, some attorneys who have participated in both class action litigation and class arbitration have concluded that class arbitration is not meaningfully different from class action litigation, involving approximately the same time and cost.").

arbitration.[41] However, state courts were often critical of these class arbitration waivers. In 2005, in the case of *Discover Bank v. Superior Court of Los Angeles*,[42] the California Supreme Court invalidated a class arbitration waiver, holding that it was unconscionable under California law. The California Supreme Court held that the FAA did not preempt the California rule, noting:

> "[W]hen the waiver is found in a consumer contract of adhesion in a setting in which disputes between the contracting parties predictably involve small amounts of damages, and when it is alleged that the party with the superior bargaining power has carried out a scheme to deliberately cheat large numbers of consumers out of individually small sums of money, then, at least to the extent the obligation at issue is governed by California law, the waiver becomes in practice the exemption of the party from responsibility for [its] own fraud, or willful injury to the person or property of another. Under these circumstances, such waivers are unconscionable under California law and should not be enforced."[43]

The so-called "*Discover Bank*" rule was applied to invalidate class arbitration waivers in California and was followed by similar rulings in numerous other states.[44]

III.   US SUPREME COURT JURISPRUDENCE ON CLASS ARBITRATION

In the ten years since *Bazzle*, the US Supreme Court has decided four more cases regarding the availability of class arbitration. Collectively, the Court's decisions have generally limited the reach of *Bazzle* and have allowed parties to exclude the possibility of class arbitration through the use of class arbitration waivers.[45] While the Court's

---

41. Samuel ESTREICHER and Steven C. BENNETT, "Using Express No-Class Action Provisions to Halt Class-Claims", N.Y. L.J. (10 June 2005) p. 3 ("In response to *Bazzle*, and the non-trivial risk that an arbitrator will entertain class or collective actions in the absence of such a clause, many employers have begun incorporating explicit 'no-class action' clauses into their employment alternative dispute resolution (ADR) programs.").

42. 36 Cal. 4th 148, 163-164 (2005).

43. *Ibid.* at 162-163.

44. See, e.g., *Omstead v. Dell, Inc.*, 594 F.3d 1081, 1086 (9th Cir. 2010); *Thibodeau v. Comcast Corp.*, 912 A.2d 874, 882-887 (Pa. Super. Ct. 2006); *Picardi v. Eighth Judicial Dist. Ct.*, 251 P.3d 723, 726-728 (Nev. 2011); *Dale v. Comcast Corp.*, 498 F.3d 1216, 1223-1224 (11th Cir. 2007) (Georgia law); *Skirchak v. Dynamics Research Corp.*, 508 F.3d 49, 58-60 (1st Cir. 2007) (Massachusetts law). See also Christopher R. DRAHOZAL, "Federal Arbitration Act Preemption", 79 Ind. L.J. (2004) p. 393.

45. See, e.g., "The Federal Arbitration Act and Access to Justice: Will Recent Supreme Court Decisions Undermine the Rights of Consumers, Workers, and Small Business, Hearing before the U.S. Senate Committee on the Judiciary" (17 December 2013) (henceforth "US Senate Judiciary Comm. Hearing") (Testimony of Prof. Myriam Gilles) ("Enter the Supreme Court of the United States, which has – in just a few decisions in recent terms – brought to life all my dire predictions [concerning the availability of class arbitration].").

decisions have provided clarity as to some issues related to the availability and use of class arbitration, other important questions remain unsettled.

1.   Stolt-Nielsen v. AnimalFeeds

In 2010, the Supreme Court took up the first case on class arbitration since its decision in *Bazzle*. Notably, the Court had undergone significant changes since 2003 when *Bazzle* was decided: Justice Souter (who joined the four-Justice plurality decision in *Bazzle*), and Justices Rehnquist and O'Connor (who dissented in *Bazzle*) had all left the Court and were replaced by Justices Roberts, Alito, and Sotomayor.

In *Stolt-Nielsen v. AnimalFeeds*, a class of purchasers of parcel tanker shipping services brought a class action litigation in the US federal courts asserting claims against Stolt-Nielsen and several other shipping companies under US antitrust laws.[46] The charters under which the plaintiffs had contracted for shipping services contained arbitration clauses, and the federal courts held that the plaintiffs' claims were subject to arbitration.[47] The plaintiffs then initiated a class arbitration. The parties selected a panel of arbitrators and stipulated that the arbitration clauses in their charters were "silent" as to the availability of class arbitration.[48] The arbitrators held that the arbitration agreements allowed for class arbitration.[49] The Supreme Court granted certiorari to determine "whether imposing class arbitration on parties whose arbitration clauses are 'silent' on that issue is consistent with the [FAA]".[50]

The majority (consisting of five Justices) said that *Bazzle* did not decide whether a court or the arbitrators generally have the authority to decide "whether a contract permits class arbitration", because only a plurality in *Bazzle* decided that it was a question for the arbitrators.[51] The Court concluded that, on the facts of the case before it, however, the parties had expressly assigned the issue to the arbitrators.[52] The Court therefore reviewed the arbitrators' decision under the deferential standard of Sect. 10 of the FAA.[53]

The Court held that the arbitrators had exceeded their authority by finding that the arbitration agreement allowed for class arbitration. The Court held that because the parties had stipulated that their arbitration agreement was "silent" as to the availability of class arbitration, the arbitrators could not have interpreted the parties' contract to allow class arbitration.[54] The Court held that the arbitrators had instead impermissibly imposed their "own conception of sound policy", thereby exceeding their authority.[55]

---

46. *Stolt-Nielsen SA*, 559 U.S. at 662.
47. *Ibid.* at 668.
48. *Ibid.* at 668-669.
49. *Ibid.* at 669.
50. *Ibid.* at 666.
51. *Ibid.* at 680.
52. *Ibid.*
53. *Ibid.* at 672.
54. *Ibid.* at 674.
55. *Ibid.* at 675.

The Court also held that it was unnecessary to remand the case to the arbitrators, because "there can be only one possible outcome on the facts".[56] The Court continued that "a party may not be compelled under the FAA to submit to class arbitration unless there is a contractual basis for concluding that the party *agreed* to do so".[57] The Court reasoned:

> "An implicit agreement to authorize class arbitration … is not a term that the arbitrator may infer solely from the fact of the parties' agreement to arbitrate. This is so because class-action arbitration changes the nature of arbitration to such a degree that it cannot be presumed the parties consented to it by simply agreeing to submit their disputes to an arbitrator. In bilateral arbitration, parties forgo the procedural rigor and appellate review of the courts in order to realize the benefits of private dispute resolution: lower costs, greater efficiency and speed, and the ability to choose expert adjudicators to resolve specialized disputes. But the relative benefits of class-action arbitration are much less assured, giving reason to doubt the parties' mutual consent to resolve disputes through class-wide arbitration."[58]

The Court's opinion in *Stolt-Nielsen* was generally viewed as limiting the reach of *Bazzle*.[59] The Court had expressly said that *Bazzle* did not decide the question whether it was generally for the courts or the arbitrators to decide if an arbitration agreement allowed class arbitration, and it had said that *Bazzle* did not establish any interpretative rule regarding when class arbitration should be allowed. Further, a majority of Justices in *Stolt-Nielsen* held that a party can be compelled to submit to class arbitration only if it affirmatively agreed to do so. Following *Stolt-Nielsen*, there was thus great uncertainty as to the availability of class arbitration under an arbitration agreement that did not specifically authorize it.

2. *AT&T Mobility LLC v. Concepcion*

A year later, in *AT&T Mobility LLC v. Concepcion*,[60] the Supreme Court took up the question of class arbitration again, this time addressing the validity of class arbitration waivers.

In that case, the Concepcions had filed a complaint against AT&T in US federal court, alleging that AT&T engaged in false advertising and fraud by charging a sales tax on

---

56. *Ibid.* at 663.

57. *Ibid.* at 664 (emphasis in original).

58. *Ibid.* at 685-686.

59. See Keerthi SUGUMARAN, "United States Supreme Court Sounds the Death Knell for Class Arbitration: *Stolt-Nielsen S.A. v. Animalfeeds Int'l Corp.*", 130 S.Ct. 1758, 16 Suffolk J. Trial & App. Advoc. (2011) p. 147; Terry F. MORITZ and Brandon J. FITCH, "The Future of Consumer Arbitration in Light of *Stolt-Nielsen*", 23 Loy. Consumer L. Rev. (2011) p. 265 at p. 277 ("Before *Stolt-Nielsen* it seemed that the Court would have to handle *Bazzle* carefully if it decided to reverse the Second Circuit. But the Court opted for force over finesse in its treatment of *Bazzle*.").

60. 131 S.Ct. at 1740.

mobile phones that were advertised as being free. The case was consolidated into a class action litigation in the federal courts. AT&T subsequently moved to compel individual arbitration with the Concepcions pursuant to an arbitration agreement in their phone service contract that provided that all claims must be brought in the parties' "individual capacity and not as a plaintiff or class member in any purported class or representative proceeding".[61] The trial court denied AT&T's motion to compel arbitration, and the US Court of Appeals for the Ninth Circuit affirmed, holding that under the *Discovery Bank* rule, the class arbitration waiver was unconscionable.[62] The Supreme Court granted certiorari to determine "whether the FAA prohibits States from conditioning the enforceability of certain arbitration agreements on the availability of classwide arbitration procedures".[63]

The majority (of five Justices) held that the *Discover Bank* rule, which had been established by California state law, was preempted by the FAA. The Court held that "[r]equiring the availability of classwide arbitration interferes with fundamental attributes of arbitration and thus creates a scheme inconsistent with the FAA".[64] Echoing its analysis in *Stolt-Nielsen*, the Court again drew a distinction between traditional bilateral arbitration and class arbitration and held that "the switch from bilateral to class arbitration sacrifices the principal advantage of arbitration – its informality".[65] The Court reasoned that arbitration is "poorly suited to the higher stakes of class litigation" and explained "[w]e find it hard to believe that defendants would bet the company with no effective means of review, and even harder to believe that Congress would have intended to allow state courts to force such a decision".[66] The Court held that the *Discover Bank* rule was therefore preempted by the FAA, and that California law could not invalidate a class arbitration waiver freely entered by the parties.

The Court's opinion was heavily criticized by the four dissenting Justices, who argued that the *Discover Bank* rule applied equally to any contract with a class action waiver, and not only to those contracts with arbitration clauses.[67] They argued that the *Discover Bank* rule was therefore precisely the kind of legal ground referred to in Sect. 2 of the FAA, which allows invalidation of arbitration agreements "upon such grounds as exist at law or in equity for the revocation of any contract".[68] The dissent disagreed with the Court's holding that class arbitration is inconsistent with the character of arbitration envisioned under the FAA, pointing out that arbitration procedures have evolved substantially since 1925, and argued that class arbitration may have significant advantages over class action litigation.

The Court's reasoning in *Concepcion* was also criticized by some arbitration scholars and practitioners, who took issue with the Court's characterization of the "character" and

---

61. *Ibid.* at 1744.
62. *Ibid.* at 1745.
63. *Ibid.* at 1744.
64. *Ibid.* at 1748.
65. *Ibid.* at 1751.
66. *Ibid.* at 1752.
67. *Ibid.* at 1757.
68. *Ibid.* at 1746.

"benefits" of arbitration.[69] These commentators argued that the Court's view of arbitration and its benefits was too narrow and failed to recognize that many widely used arbitration procedures go beyond the traditional "bilateral" model described by the Court and have benefits other than increased speed and lower costs.[70]

One scholar commenting on Justice Scalia's opinion for the majority in *Concepcion* wrote:

> "Justice Scalia's opinion is profoundly misconceived and fundamentally misunderstands the arbitral process. Most importantly, Justice Scalia's declarations about the supposed 'fundamental' character of arbitration, which is envisioned by the FAA, are both woefully inaccurate and dangerous: indeed, those declarations threaten the broader body of U.S. arbitration law by suggesting that the FAA only protects a particular type of arbitration, being the archetype that, in Justice Scalia's view, was envisioned by Congress in 1925. In fact, contrary to the Court's supposed archetype, arbitration has historically taken widely varying forms, in widely varying settings – ranging from institutional to ad hoc arbitration, from trade, commercial, religious, and international to investor-state arbitration, ranging from documents only, on-line or quality arbitrations to arbitrations resembling trial court litigations."[71]

In any event, following *Concepcion*, it was well established that class arbitration waivers are valid and that the FAA preempts broad state laws that categorically invalidate the use of class action waivers in arbitration agreements. As expected, the use of class arbitration waivers has since become widespread, and lower courts generally have recognized and upheld them. Over the long-term, *Concepcion* is likely to greatly reduce the number of new class arbitrations filed.

3.   *Oxford Health Plans v. Sutter*

In 2013, the Supreme Court returned to the question it had addressed in *Stolt-Nielsen*, again considering whether an arbitrator's decision to allow class arbitration exceeded his authority under Sect. 10 of the FAA.

In *Oxford Health Plans v. Sutter*, a doctor sought class arbitration against Oxford Health over its alleged failure to make prompt and accurate reimbursement payments for member services.[72] The parties agreed that the arbitrator should decide whether their

---

69. G. BORN and C. SALAS, *op. cit.*, fn. 8, p. 21; Frank BLECHSCHMIDT, "All Alone in Arbitration: *AT&T Mobility v. Concepcion* and the Substantive Impact of Class Action Waivers", 160 U. Pa. L. Rev. (2011-2012) p. 541 (arguing for reforms following the decision including amendment of the FAA, administrative regulations targeting class action waivers and a change in the Court's approach to class action waivers in the future).

70. G. BORN and C. SALAS, *op. cit.*, fn. 8, p. 39.

71. *Ibid.* at p. 21.

72. 133 S.Ct. at 2064.

contract allowed class arbitration.[73] The arbitrator analyzed the text of the parties' arbitration agreement, which did not expressly authorize class arbitration, and held that it required arbitration of everything that was prohibited from court process, reasoning that because the arbitration agreement precluded class action litigation, it thereby allowed class arbitration.[74]

In a unanimous decision, the Court upheld the arbitrator's decision interpreting the parties' agreement to allow class arbitration.[75] The Court reasoned that the parties had expressly assigned to the arbitrator the task of interpreting their arbitration agreement, which he did.[76] The Court held that the scope of its review of the arbitrator's decision was therefore limited and that there was no basis for finding that the arbitrator had exceeded his authority to interpret the arbitration agreement.[77]

The Court distinguished its holding in *Stolt-Nielsen*: in that case, the parties had specifically acknowledged that their agreement did *not* address the availability of class arbitration, leaving no room for an interpretation that the parties' agreement authorized class arbitration.[78] To the contrary, in *Oxford Health*, the parties had not agreed that their arbitration clause was silent, and the arbitrator therefore did not exceed his authority by finding that the clause was not silent, but rather did authorize class arbitration.

The Court expressly said that it was not endorsing the correctness of the arbitrator's interpretation of the parties' agreement.[79] Justice Kagan wrote for the Court:

> "Nothing we say in this opinion should be taken to reflect any agreement with the arbitrator's contract interpretation, or any quarrel with Oxford's contrary reading. All we say is that convincing a court of an arbitrator's error – even his grave error – is not enough.... The arbitrator's construction holds, however good, bad, or ugly."[80]

In their concurring opinion, Justices Alito and Thomas went even further, saying "[i]f we were reviewing the arbitrator's interpretation of the contract *de novo*, we would have little trouble concluding that he improperly inferred '[a]n implicit agreement to authorize class-action arbitration ... from the fact of the parties' agreement to arbitrate'".[81]

The Court's holding in *Oxford Health* seems, at first glance, to limit the application of the interpretative rule it set down in *Stolt-Nielsen*. Indeed, some commentators suggested

73. *Ibid.* at 2067.
74. *Ibid.*
75. *Ibid.* at 2069.
76. *Ibid.* at 2071.
77. *Ibid.* at 2068-2069.
78. *Ibid.* at 2069.
79. *Ibid.* at 2070.
80. *Ibid.* at 2070-2071.
81. *Ibid.* at 2071.

that *Oxford Health* "tentatively reopens the back door to class arbitration".[82] However, a footnote in the decision suggests that *Oxford Health* is likely not the Court's final word on the availability of class arbitration under an arbitration agreement that does not expressly authorize it. In footnote 2, the Court noted that it

> "would face a different issue if Oxford had argued below that the availability of class arbitration is a so-called 'question of arbitrability.' Those questions – which 'include certain gateway matters, such as whether parties have a valid arbitration agreement at all or whether a concededly binding arbitration clause applies to a certain type of controversy' – are presumptively for courts to decide.... *Stolt-Nielsen* made clear that this Court has not yet decided whether the availability of class arbitration is a question of arbitrability. But this case gives us no opportunity to do so because Oxford agreed that the arbitrator should determine whether its contract with Sutter authorized class procedures."[83]

This footnote leaves no doubt that the Court does not consider *Bazzle* to have resolved the question whether, absent agreement of the parties, it is for arbitrators or courts to consider whether an arbitration agreement authorizes class arbitration. It also seems to invite future parties to seek certiorari to resolve that question.

If the Court were to find that the availability of class arbitration is a "gateway" matter for the courts, and not arbitrators, then the Court could also elaborate on its holding in *Stolt-Nielsen* that class arbitration is available only where there is a contractual basis for finding that it has been authorized by the parties. A finding that the availability of class arbitration is a so-called "gateway" issue of arbitrability would seem to open the door to the Court setting out clear rules regarding the availability of class arbitration under arbitration agreements, like the one in *Oxford Health*, that do not expressly refer to class arbitration.

4.   *American Express Co. v. Italian Colors Restaurant*

Only ten days after it issued its decision in *Oxford Health*, the Supreme Court issued yet another decision on class arbitration, this time revisiting the validity of class arbitration waivers.

In *American Express Co. v. Italian Colors Restaurant*,[84] a group of merchants filed a class action lawsuit in US federal court against American Express, alleging that it violated antitrust laws by forcing merchants to accept its credit cards at rates that are approximately 30 percent higher than other cards.[85] The contracts between American Express and each of the merchants provided for all disputes to be resolved by arbitration

---

82. Steve VLADECK, "Opinion Analysis: Tentatively reopening the (back) door to class arbitration", Scotusblog (10 June 2013, 2:05pm), <www.scotusblog.com/2013/06/opinion-analysis-tentatively-reopening-the-back-door-to-class-arbitration/>.

83. 133 S.Ct. at 2068 fn. 2.

84. 133 S.Ct. at 2304.

85. *Ibid.* at 2308.

and contained a waiver of class claims. American Express sought to compel individual arbitrations under the contracts.[86]

The plaintiffs invoked the "effective vindication" doctrine,[87] arguing that the class arbitration waiver was invalid because the cost of the expert analysis necessary to prove the antitrust claims would exceed the recovery for an individual plaintiff. Enforcement of the class waiver would thereby deprive the plaintiffs of any effective remedy for violation of their federal statutory rights.[88] The United States filed an amicus curiae brief arguing that the class arbitration waiver should be unenforceable because "the practical effect of enforcement would be to foreclose respondents from effectively vindicating their Sherman Act claims in any forum".[89]

The Court rejected the plaintiffs' challenge to the class arbitration waiver. It reasoned that "[n]o contrary congressional command requires us to reject the waiver of class arbitration" because "antitrust laws do not guarantee an affordable procedural path to the vindication of every claim"[90] and do not demonstrate any intention to preclude class action waivers.[91] The Court went on to hold that the "effective vindication" rule was not applicable[92] because the "fact that it is not worth the expense involved in *proving* a statutory remedy does not constitute the elimination of the *right to pursue* that remedy".[93] The Court reasoned that:

> "The class-action waiver merely limits arbitration to the two contracting parties. It no more eliminates those parties' right to pursue their statutory remedy than did federal law before its adoption of the class action for legal relief.... Or to put it differently, the individual suit that was considered adequate to assure 'effective vindication' of a federal right before adoption of class-action procedures did not suddenly become 'ineffective vindication' upon their adoption."[94]

While there are undoubtedly a large number of existing contracts containing arbitration clauses that do not contain class waivers, the Court's holdings in *Concepcion* and *Italian*

---

86. *Ibid.* The contract stated that there "shall be no right or authority for any Claims to be arbitrated on a class action basis".

87. The "effective vindication" doctrine provides that arbitration agreements may be invalidated on grounds other than the savings clause of Sect. 2 of the FAA, where the arbitration agreement would prevent the vindication of other federal statutory rights. See, e.g., *Mitsubishi Motors v. Soler Chrysler-Plymouth*, 473 U.S. 614 (1985).

88. According to an expert analysis submitted by the plaintiffs, the costs necessary to prove the antitrust claims would be "at least several hundred thousand dollars, and might exceed $1 million", while the maximum recovery for an individual plaintiff would be US$ 12,850 or US$ 38,549 when trebled. *Ibid.* at 2308.

89. Brief for the United States as Amicus Curiae Supporting Respondents (January 2013), at 9, <www.justice.gov/osg/briefs/2012/3mer/1ami/2012-0133.mer.ami.pdf>.

90. 133 S.Ct. at 2309.

91. *Ibid.*

92. *Ibid.* at 2310-2311.

93. *Ibid.* at 2311 (emphasis in original).

94. *Ibid.*

Colors seem very likely to result in class arbitration waivers being included in the vast majority of all new consumer and employment contracts. Over the long-term, the use of class arbitration waivers may well have the effect of virtually eliminating class arbitration in the United States.

IV.   REGULATORY AND LEGISLATIVE INTEREST IN CLASS ARBITRATION

The US Supreme Court is not the only institution showing an interest in class arbitration. Over the past several years, the CFPB and Congress have also taken steps to examine the availability and use of class arbitration, particularly in consumer disputes, and to consider new rules regarding the arbitration of consumer disputes.

1.   Dodd-Frank Wall Street Reform and Consumer Protection Act

As part of the Dodd-Frank Wall Street Reform and Consumer Protection Act of 2010, Congress created the CFPB, which is authorized to implement the federal consumer financial laws.[95] Among other things, the Dodd-Frank Act specifically directed the CFPB to undertake a study on "the use of agreements providing for arbitration of any future dispute between covered persons and consumers in connection with the offering or providing of consumer financial products or services".[96]

On 12 December 2013, the CFPB released the preliminary findings of its study on the arbitration of consumer disputes. The December 2013 report included the study's statistical findings regarding the use of arbitration in consumer contracts but did not offer recommendations.[97] The CFPB explained that its December 2013 report included only "preliminary results reached in the Bureau's study to date" and that "[a]s our study effort continues, we will refine and place this work into fuller context".[98]

Among the CFPB's findings concerning class arbitration, the December 2013 report noted that 90 percent of consumer contracts with arbitration clauses include provisions excluding class arbitration.[99] Specifically, the report noted that:

> "93.9% of the clauses in our credit card sample, 88.5% of arbitration clauses in our checking account sample, and 96.1% of clauses in our prepaid sample did not allow arbitration to proceed on a class basis. The handful of clauses that did not include such no-class-arbitration terms tended to be from very small institutions. Thus, in our samples, class arbitration was unavailable for 99.9% of arbitration-

---

95. See Pub. Law 111-203, Title X.
96. Sect. 1028(a) requires the CFPB to "conduct a study of, and ... provide a report to Congress concerning, the use of agreements providing for arbitration of any future dispute between covered persons and consumers in connection with the offering or providing of consumer financial products or services". *Ibid*.
97. CFPB Arbitration Study, *op. cit.*, fn. 10.
98. *Ibid*. at p. 9.
99. *Ibid*. at p. 13.

subject credit card loans outstanding, 97.1% of arbitration-subject insured deposits, and essentially 100.0% of arbitration-subject dollar amounts loaded on prepaid cards."[100]

The CFPB noted that its December 2013 report focused "primarily [on] individual disputes" and that "although [the report] provides some initial data points about the interrelationship between individual and class proceedings ... later work will look further at consumer class actions".[101] Thus, it appears that the CFPB will continue to examine the availability and use of class arbitration in consumer disputes and will issue further reports and recommendations to Congress.

2.   *Congressional Initiatives*

On 7 May 2013, after *Oxford Health* and *Italian Colors* had been argued, but before the Supreme Court had issued its decisions, Senator Al Franken of Minnesota introduced Senate Bill 878, the Arbitration Fairness Act of 2013 (AFA).[102] On the same day, Representative Henry Johnson of Georgia introduced a parallel bill in the House of Representatives, H.R. 1844, with the same title.[103] The Act revives draft legislation that was introduced in prior sessions of Congress, most recently in 2011.[104]

The Act, which has the support of numerous Democrats in Congress,[105] would amend the FAA to invalidate any pre-dispute arbitration agreement covering an "employment dispute, consumer dispute, antitrust dispute, or civil rights dispute".[106] In addition, the Act would amend the FAA to provide that the validity of an arbitration agreement under this provision would be governed by federal law and that the "applicability of this chapter to an agreement to arbitrate and the validity and enforceability of an agreement to which this chapter applies shall be determined by a court, rather than an arbitrator, irrespective

---

100. *Ibid.* at p. 8.

101. *Ibid.* at p. 11.

102. Arbitration Fairness Act of 2013, S.878, 113th Cong. (2013).

103. See H.R. 1844, 113th Cong. (2013). A similar legislative initiative, the Investor Choice Act of 2013, has also been introduced in the US House of Representatives. The bill would amend the Securities Exchange Act of 1934 and the Investment Advisers Act of 1940 to revise the authority of the Securities and Exchange Commission (SEC) to limit the use of agreements that require customers or clients of any broker, dealer, or municipal securities dealer to arbitrate any future dispute arising under the federal securities laws. It would also declare it unlawful for a broker, dealer, funding portal, or municipal securities dealer to enter into, modify, or extend an agreement with customers or clients governing a future dispute between the parties that would mandate arbitration. H.R. 2998, 113th Cong. (2013).

104. None of the prior versions of the Arbitration Fairness Act have made it to the floor of the House of Representatives or the Senate for a vote.

105. As of 7 February 2014, twenty-five Members have co-sponsored the Senate version and seventy-two Members have co-sponsored the House version. See <www.congress.gov> (accessed 7 February 2014).

106. "Antitrust dispute" is defined to mean a dispute under the antitrust laws in which the plaintiff seeks certification of a class. "Civil rights dispute" is defined to mean that at least one party alleging a Constitutional violation is an individual.

of whether the party resisting arbitration challenges the arbitration agreement specifically or in conjunction with other terms of the contract containing such agreement".[107]

The Act would have a significant effect on the availability and use of class arbitration. By invalidating any pre-dispute arbitration agreement in a consumer contract, the Act would preclude arbitration of consumer disputes, on either an individual or a class-wide basis, sending these cases back into the civil courts. As noted above, the vast majority of disputes currently subject to the possibility of class arbitration arise from consumer contracts. In addition, by invalidating pre-dispute arbitration agreements in antitrust disputes where the plaintiffs seek to certify a class, the Act would also preclude class arbitration of antitrust disputes (such as that sought by the plaintiffs in *Stolt-Nielsen*).[108] Thus, the AFA would likely eliminate, or at least greatly reduce, the use of class arbitration in the United States (and would consequently increase the use of class action litigation).

The policy motivations behind the AFA are obvious from the section of the Act headed "Findings", which state:

> "(1) The Federal Arbitration Act (now enacted as chapter 1 of title 9 of the United States Code) was intended to apply to disputes between commercial entities of generally similar sophistication and bargaining power.
> (2) A series of decisions by the Supreme Court of the United States have interpreted the Act so that it now extends to consumer disputes and employment disputes, contrary to the intent of Congress.
> (3) Most consumers and employees have little or no meaningful choice whether to submit their claims to arbitration. Often, consumers and employees are not even aware that they have given up their rights.
> (4) Mandatory arbitration undermines the development of public law because there is inadequate transparency and inadequate judicial review of arbitrators' decisions.
> (5) Arbitration can be an acceptable alternative when consent to the arbitration is truly voluntary, and occurs after the dispute arises."[109]

These policy considerations were also evident in a hearing held by the US Senate Committee on the Judiciary and chaired by Senator Franken, entitled "The Federal Arbitration Act and Access to Justice: Will Recent Supreme Court Decisions Undermine the Rights of Consumers, Workers, and Small Businesses?"[110] The hearing, held in December 2013, examined the Supreme Court's decisions on class arbitration, and in particular, *American Express Co. v. Italian Colors Restaurant*. Among those providing oral

---

107. Arbitration Fairness Act of 2013, S.878, 113th Cong. (2013).

108. In addition, by expressly providing that the availability of arbitration in employment, consumer, antitrust and civil rights disputes is subject to determination by courts and not by arbitrators, the Act would preclude arbitrators from finding that arbitration agreements in consumer contracts allow for class-wide arbitration.

109. Arbitration Fairness Act of 2013, S.878, 113th Cong. (2013).

110. US Senate Judiciary Comm. Hearing, *op. cit.*, fn. 45.

testimony at the hearing was the owner of Italian Colors restaurant and a Deputy Assistant Attorney General from the Antitrust Division of the Department of Justice, who offered testimony explaining why the United States had submitted an amicus brief in favor of the plaintiffs in that case.[111]

During the hearing, Senator Franken made clear his views on the Supreme Court's jurisprudence regarding class arbitrations:

> "[In *AT&T v. Concepcion*] the Supreme Court said that corporations can use their arbitration clauses to prohibit class actions, even if applicable state law says that these class-action waivers are unconscionable. So under *Concepcion*, not only can a corporation force an individual into arbitration, with all of its shortcomings, but the corporation can force the individual to go it alone. Just the prospect of a class action gives corporations a real incentive to follow the law. They know that there will be real consequences if they don't. *Concepcion* removed that important check on corporate power.
>
> Not surprisingly, corporations are taking advantage of this new rule. Preliminary results from the Consumer Financial Protection Bureau's arbitration study indicate that nearly 100 percent of outstanding credit-card loans and insured deposits now are subject to class-action bans....
>
> And just when you thought it couldn't get any worse, it did when the Supreme Court decided *American Express v. Italian Colors* during its last term.
>
> Since at least the *Mitsubishi Motors* case in 1985, we've had something called the effective vindication rule, which says that an arbitration clause is invalid if it is so bad that it prevents an individual from enforcing his or her federal rights; in other words, the effective vindication rule prevented a corporation from drafting its arbitration clause in a way that implicitly forced consumers, workers and small businesses to waive their federal rights.
>
> But in the recent *Italian Colors* case, the court did away with that rule. And the court wasn't really shy about it either. Justice Scalia wrote that, quote, 'The FAA's command to enforce arbitration agreements trumps any interest in ensuring the prosecution of low-value claims,' end quote. In other words, in his opinion, corporate arbitration clauses simply are more important than the rights of consumers, workers and small businesses. I could not disagree more.
>
> The *Concepcion* and *Italian Colors* decisions stack the deck in favor of corporations and against consumers and workers, as if the deck weren't stacked enough already. Giant corporations now can use arbitration clauses to stifle enforcement of federal laws – the antitrust laws, the minimum-wage laws, the civil rights law; you name it.
>
> As the law has gotten worse, the need for reform has become more obvious and more urgent. I introduced the Arbitration Fairness Act to undo some of the damage that we've seen to the civil justice system."[112]

---

111. *Ibid.*
112. *Ibid.* (Statement of Senator Franken).

Opponents of the AFA have argued that it sweeps too broadly, and that it could have unintended negative consequences for the very people it is intended to help. They point out that arbitration can have significant advantages for individual claimants,[113] primarily by offering a "faster, more efficient and more cost-effective method of resolving disputes than court litigation".[114] They also criticize the legislation for taking to the opposite extreme the undifferentiated approach to arbitration agreements that the Act's proponents have criticized the Supreme Court's decisions for taking.[115]

The hearing of the Senate Judiciary Committee in December 2013 included testimony from two opponents of enacting the AFA, one of whom pointed out that recent research "generally has vindicated arbitration" as providing speedy and fair results for consumers and employees.[116] Professor Peter Rutledge counseled the Committee to bear in mind that the alternative to arbitration is court litigation, where individual consumers are often at a severe procedural disadvantage in comparison to large corporations, particularly in cases that cannot be asserted as class actions.[117] He also noted that there are procedural alternatives other than class actions available in arbitration that can safeguard the rights of individual consumers, such as multiple named claimants bringing joint proceedings against a respondent and sharing costs, using experts appointed by the arbitrator with costs shared between the parties or allocated to the respondent, and shifting to the respondent the arbitration and expert costs and potentially even the legal fees of the individual claimant.[118]

One of the co-sponsors of the AFA, Senator Richard Blumenthal from Connecticut, appeared to agree with Senator Franken's general sentiments about arbitration but noted the political challenges of enacting new legislation barring arbitration of consumer disputes:

---

113. See, e.g., Thomas J. STIPANOWICH, "Arbitration: The New Litigation", 2010 U. Ill. L. Rev. (2010) p. 1 at pp. 58-59 ("More than ever, 'arbitration' must be understood not as a unitary concept, but as a spectrum of possibilities and a realm of choice that demands more active participation by those who use, regulate, and comment on arbitration processes"); Keith N. HYLTON, "Arbitration: Governance Benefits and Enforcement Costs", 80 Notre Dame L. Rev. (2005) p. 489 at p. 490 ("[A]rbitration provides them the opportunity to appoint a different hammer-wielder, one who hits harder or perhaps more softly, or more or less frequently, than we see under the court regime.").

114. CFPB Arbitration Study, op. cit., fn. 10, p. 8 (quoting comments by the American Banker's Association, Consumer Bankers Association, and the Financial Services Roundtable).

115. Richard NAGAREDA, "The Litigation-Arbitration Dichotomy Meets the Class Action", 86 Notre Dame L. Rev. (2011) p. 1069 at p. 1126 ("[E]ven a casual observer cannot help but remark on how the undifferentiated exclusion from the FAA contemplated under the proposed legislation for wide swaths of arbitration clauses ... partakes of the same kind of undifferentiated approach that its proponents see in the Supreme Court's FAA case law.").

116. US Senate Judiciary Comm. Hearing, op. cit., fn. 45 (Statement of Peter Bowman Rutledge).

117. Ibid.

118. Ibid. He also advocated that "public enforcement authorities charged with the civil enforcement of certain statutory remedies", including attorneys general and other regulatory bodies, such as the CFPB, take responsibility for enforcing federal laws rather than relying on individual plaintiffs to do so through private litigation. Ibid.

"As you may have gathered, I think the majority of members of this panel who are here today agree that arbitration sometimes violates basic fairness, and sometimes even constitutional rights. But the members of the panel who are not here might not be part of that consensus. And likewise, members of the Senate may not be in agreement that we need to change the law to restrict arbitration, although I have been a long-time advocate of making sure that consumers are protected from arbitration clauses that may not be clear or conspicuous, hidden in the fine print, as one of you observed.

So I think we have political obstacles to overcome here, and not the least of them are the interests of corporations that are loathe to go to court, to be subjected to claims based on liability for violations of law relating to financial practices or product defects or a range of violations of consumer rights."[119]

Although the legislation faces substantial "political obstacles" to passage, it is significant that a group of Democrats in both houses of Congress appear to be focused on the effects of mandatory arbitration clauses in consumer contracts and are strongly critical of the Supreme Court's decisions upholding mandatory arbitration agreements and class action waivers in consumer contracts. They will undoubtedly be watching with keen interest as the CFPB continues its study of class arbitration in consumer disputes and as the Supreme Court returns to the questions surrounding class arbitration in future cases.

V.   STATUS OF CLASS ARBITRATION UNDER US LAW

At least until the Supreme Court or Congress speaks further on the subject of class arbitration, there is still some uncertainty regarding the availability of class arbitration in the United States. This section will attempt to summarize the current state of the law and to identify the questions on which further guidance is likely to be needed.

First, even after the Supreme Court's decisions over the past five years, class arbitration continues to be used. The AAA reports on its website that it is currently administering sixty-one active class arbitrations,[120] and more than twenty new class arbitrations were filed with the AAA in 2013.

Second, it appears well-settled that a provision in an arbitration agreement expressly providing for class arbitration will be enforceable. This is consistent with the pro-arbitration policies of the FAA, which generally give full effect to arbitration agreements as written,[121] as well as Supreme Court case law.[122]

Third, where an arbitration agreement is indisputably silent regarding class arbitration, such as in *Stolt-Nielsen* where the parties stipulated that their arbitration agreement did not address the availability of class arbitration, class arbitration will not

---

119. *Ibid.* (Statement of Senator Richard Blumenthal).
120. See <www.adr.org/aaa/faces/services/disputeresolutionservices/casedocket> (accessed 26 February 2014).
121. 9 U.S.C. Sect. 2.
122. See, e.g., *Prima Paint Corp.*, 388 U.S. at 404 n. 12.

be authorized because there is no contractual basis for concluding that the parties agreed to arbitrate on a class-wide basis.[123] If an arbitrator interprets an indisputably silent arbitration agreement as allowing class arbitration, she will have exceeded her authority under the FAA, and a court may vacate the arbitrator's decision.[124]

Fourth, where the parties do not agree on whether an arbitration agreement authorizes class arbitration, it is unsettled whether it is for an arbitrator or a court to interpret the parties' agreement to decide whether class arbitration is authorized. *Bazzle* appeared to hold that this was a question for the arbitrators, but subsequent decisions of the Supreme Court expressly held that *Bazzle* did not resolve this issue. If the parties assign this question to an arbitrator for decision, as did the parties in *Oxford Health*, then the courts must defer to the arbitrator's interpretation of the contract, "good, bad, or ugly".[125] If the parties have not agreed that this issue is assigned to the arbitrator, however, the Court may well be open to the argument that this is a "gateway" issue of arbitrability that is presumptively for the courts to decide. The Court's *Oxford Health* decision appears to invite submission of this precise question for resolution by the Court in a future case.

Fifth, express waivers of class arbitration are permissible, even in contracts of adhesion. In *Concepcion*, the Court held that the FAA preempts state laws providing that class arbitration waivers are unconscionable. Subsequently, in *Italian Colors*, the Court upheld a class arbitration waiver notwithstanding that it may have the effect of precluding a consumer from vindicating its federal statutory rights. The Court's decisions are likely to result in even more widespread use of class arbitration waivers in consumer contracts.[126]

While the Court's decisions in *Concepcion* and *Italian Colors* made clear that a state law categorically invalidating all class waivers is preempted by the FAA, the FAA is generally regarded not to preempt the application of general contract law principles which do not single out arbitration agreements but have general application to any contract.[127] There

---

123. *Stolt-Nielsen*, 559 U.S. at 683.

124. *Ibid.* at 676. Based on a survey of the AAA class arbitration docket since *Stolt-Nielsen* was decided, arbitrators appear less inclined to allow for class arbitration where the agreements do not expressly authorize class arbitration: out of thirty-one cases where an arbitrator interpreted such an agreement since 27 April 2010, the arbitrator allowed for class arbitration in only eighteen cases.

125. 133 S.Ct. at 2067.

126. See Myriam GILLES, "Procedure in Eclipse: Group-Based Adjudication in a Post-*Concepcion* Era", 56 St. Louis U. L.J. (2012) p. 1203 at p. 1208 ("Newly validated by Justice Scalia's majority opinion, class action waivers will soon seep into every contract – whether signed, clicked, mass-emailed, posted on a website, or otherwise 'consented to' – until aggregate litigation itself becomes a procedural relic examined only briefly in courses on the legal history of the twentieth century, that long-ago era when legal claims were actually adjudicated in public courts of law.").

127. See, e.g., *Doctor's Assocs. Inc. v. Casarotto*, 517 U.S. 681, 687 (1996) ("[G]enerally applicable contract defenses, such as fraud, duress, or unconscionability, may be applied to invalidate arbitration agreements without contravening Sect. 2 [of the FAA].."); see also *Marmet Health Care Ctr. v. Brown*, 132 S.Ct. 1201, 1204 (2012) ("On remand, the West Virginia court must consider whether, absent that general public policy, the arbitration clauses in Brown's case and Taylor's case are unenforceable under state common law principles that are not specific to arbitration and

is a substantial body of precedent in which courts have struck down arbitration agreements as unconscionable, for example, where they allow one party to appoint the arbitrator or require payment of unreasonably high upfront fees.[128] Justice Scalia noted in *Concepcion* that "Sect. 2's saving clause preserves generally applicable contract defenses".[129]

Following *Concepcion* and *Italian Colors*, consumers seeking to avoid arbitration have continued to invoke the unconscionability doctrine to challenge specific arbitration agreements containing class waivers. Lower courts applying *Concepcion* and *Italian Colors* have rejected arguments that class waivers are inherently unconscionable,[130] but they have still generally been willing to consider the terms of the arbitration agreement as a whole to determine whether those terms are unreasonably harsh, oppressive or one-sided.[131] It remains to be seen if a less categorical application of the unconscionability doctrine becomes a back-door route to invalidating arbitration agreements containing class waivers. In the words of one commentator, the lesson for corporations including arbitration agreements in consumer contracts is: "Do not overreach."[132]

---

pre-empted by the FAA.").
128. See, e.g., *Chavarria v. Ralph's Grocery Co.*, 733 F.3d 916 (9th Cir. 2013). See also Gary BORN, *International Commercial Arbitration* (Kluwer Law International 2009) pp. 727-729 (citing cases).
129. 131 S.Ct. at 1748 (emphasis added).
130. See *Muriithi v. Shuttle Express Inc.*, 712 F.3d 173, 180 (4th Cir. 2013) ("The Supreme Court's holding in *Concepcion* sweeps more broadly than [plaintiff] suggests. In *Concepcion*, the Supreme Court cautioned that the generally applicable contract defense of unconscionability may not be applied in a manner that targets the existence of an agreement to arbitrate as the basis for invalidating that agreement. Applying that principle to the *Discover Bank* "rule" at issue, the Court explained that state law cannot 'stand as an obstacle to the accomplishment of the FAA's objectives', by interfering with 'the fundamental attributes of arbitration'."); see also *Pendergast v. Sprint Nextel Corp.*, 691 F.3d 1224, 1234 (11th Cir. 2012) ("We need not decide whether the class action waiver here is unconscionable under Florida law ... because to the extent Florida law would invalidate the class action waiver, it would still be preempted by the FAA.").
131. See *Ocwen Loan Serv. v. Webster*, 232 S.E.2d 372 (W. Va. 2013) (examining an arbitration agreement containing a class waiver but finding it was not unconscionable); *Sonic-Calabasas, Inc. v. Moreno*, 311 P.3d 184 (Cal. 2013) ("[T]he FAA preempts our state-law rule categorically prohibiting waiver of a Berman hearing in a predispute arbitration agreement imposed on an employee as a condition of employment. At the same time, we conclude that state courts may continue to enforce unconscionability rules that do not 'interfere[] with fundamental attributes of arbitration'. Although a court may not refuse to enforce an arbitration agreement imposed on an employee as a condition of employment simply because it requires the employee to bypass a Berman hearing, such an agreement may be unconscionable if it is otherwise unreasonably one-sided in favor of the employer.... The fundamental fairness of the bargain, as with all contracts, will depend on what benefits the employee received under the agreement's substantive terms and the totality of circumstances surrounding the formation of the agreement."); *In re Checking Account Overdraft Litigation MDL No. 2036*, 685 F.3d 1269 (11th Cir. 2012) (finding that South Carolina's unconscionability doctrine, as applied to cost-and-fee-shifting provision that was applicable in arbitration between customer and bank, was not preempted by FAA).
132. Liz KRAMER, "Halloween Special: Scary Results if Employers Overreach in Arbitration Cases", Arbitration Nation (31 October 2013) <www.arbitrationnation.com>.

Finally, policymakers will likely continue to consider legislative changes to limit the use of class arbitration waivers and maybe to limit consumer arbitration more broadly. At one end of the spectrum of legislative possibilities would be a nearly complete ban on consumer arbitration, as proposed in the Arbitration Fairness Act of 2013, or on arbitration clauses in any contracts of adhesion.[133] Less sweeping alternatives might include legislation codifying the "effective vindication" doctrine for particular federal statutory rights, such as antitrust claims,[134] limiting or excluding the use of class action waivers, or requiring that companies using class arbitration waivers ensure that consumers are still able to pursue their claims by agreeing to pay the costs of the arbitration and allowing fee shifting to cover the consumer's legal fees.[135]

While commentators largely agree that the type of sweeping reforms contemplated by the AFA have little chance of passage by Congress in the near term, proponents of such changes may decide to take a more piecemeal approach to new legislation. For example, in the hearing of the Senate Judiciary Committee in December 2013, several Senators raised a particular concern about how consumer arbitration agreements and class arbitration waivers might affect members of the US military who are serving abroad.[136] These types of concerns may be addressed through narrower legislation targeted to specific types of transactions or specific consumer groups. It is also possible that further decisions of the Supreme Court or the further studies of the CFPB may be a catalyst for efforts to adopt new legislation affecting class arbitration.

VI.   CONCLUSION

The Supreme Court's recent decisions on class arbitration have made it unlikely that we will see widespread use of class arbitration in the years to come. Most businesses that include arbitration agreements in their consumer and employment contracts will include a class action waiver, thereby precluding arbitration on a class-wide basis. For those existing contracts that include arbitration agreements but do not expressly exclude class arbitration, it seems likely the Court will grant certiorari in a future case to decide whether it is for the arbitrator or the courts to determine whether the arbitration agreement authorizes class arbitration. If the availability of class arbitration is found to be a "gateway" issue for the courts to decide, it may be increasingly difficult for

---

133. See Andrea DONEFF, "Arbitration Clauses in Contracts of Adhesion Trap Sophisticated Parties Too", 2010 J. Disp. Resol. (2010) p. 235 at p. 269 ("Arbitration is being required in take-it-or-leave-it contracts by companies with disproportionate bargaining power against other companies with significantly less bargaining power, as well as against individuals with little or no bargaining power. In each instance, society suffers.").

134. *Italian Colors*, 133 S.Ct. at 2309.

135. See US Senate Judiciary Comm. Hearing, *op. cit.*, fn. 45 (question posed by Senator Charles Grassley of Iowa) ("Is it fair to say that at a minimum arbitration clauses prohibiting class actions must contain some mechanism for sharing or shifting costs? And if that's the case then the [D]epartment [of Justice] would agree that a claim can be effectively vindicated.").

136. See US Senate Judiciary Comm. Hearing, *op. cit.*, fn. 45 (Statement of Senator Richard Blumenthal and Statement of Vildan A. Teske).

consumers to bring class arbitrations under agreements that do not expressly authorize them.

In the meantime, when arbitrators are asked to determine whether class arbitration is available under a specific arbitration agreement, they will do so against the backdrop of the Court's decisions in *Stolt-Nielsen*, which establishes that class arbitration is allowed only where the parties have authorized it, and *Oxford Health*, where the arbitrator's interpretation of an arbitration agreement to allow class arbitration was sharply criticized. Arbitrators will approach so-called "silent" arbitration agreements carefully, and will likely hesitate before finding that a clause that does not clearly contemplate class arbitration nevertheless authorizes it. As a practical matter, even though the Court's decisions have left some important questions unanswered, they are likely to result in a decrease in the use of class arbitration.

Of course, to the extent that Congress and the CFPB continue to examine the use of arbitration in consumer disputes, and to consider the relative policy trade-offs between individual arbitration, class arbitration, and class action litigation, their efforts may result in new legislation or regulations that in turn affect the Court's analysis in future cases.

The bottom line seems to be that while the Supreme Court and the lower courts continue to develop the rules governing class arbitration in the United States, actual use of that mechanism may be on a decline. Perhaps the most important consideration for the Court in future cases, therefore, should be to do no harm to the broader legal framework governing arbitration in the United States. When it next considers whether the availability of class arbitration is an issue of arbitrability, the Supreme Court should carefully consider the implications of its decision, and equally importantly, its reasoning, on the principles underlying the broader legal framework for arbitration in the United States.

A Progress Report on the Restatement of the Law (Third) on the U.S. Law of International Commercial Arbitration

Jack J. Coe Jr.[*]

I. INTRODUCTION

In recent years the American Law Institute (ALI) has sponsored several projects with international facets. Among them is the Restatement (Third) of the U.S. Law of International Commercial Arbitration (ICA Restatement).[1] I have been asked to give a short introduction to the project and a progress report describing its current status.

The project's Chief Reporter is Professor George Bermann. Professor Chris Drahozal, Professor Catherine Rogers and I are the project's Associate Reporters. The first drafts for which we received comments were circulated on a limited basis in early 2009. Since then, the project has evolved to include about 400 pages. That material represents two completed chapters: Chapter 4, which is devoted to the courts' handling of international commercial arbitral awards; and Chapter 1, which contains nearly three dozen definitions relevant to the entire Restatement.[2] Together the two chapters contain thirty-seven sections. In the manner of all ALI Restatements, each section is made up of a "Black Letter" statement of a rule or rules, followed by "Comments", followed by "Reporters' Notes". The completed project will contain five chapters.[3]

As a formal matter, for the Reporters' work to represent the ALI's official views, it must be approved by the ALI's membership at large and by the ALI Council.[4] That

---

[*] Faculty Director of the LLM Concentration in International Commercial Arbitration and Professor of Law, Pepperdine University School of Law.

[1] See generally George A. BERMANN, Jack J. COE, Jr., Christopher R. DRAHOZAL and Catherine A. ROGERS, "Restating the U.S. Law of International Commercial Arbitration", 113 Penn State Law Rev. (2009) p. 1334.

[2] Having been approved by the relevant ALI organs, those two chapters now represent the positions of the ALI.

[3] The first chapter, which is largely complete, contains definitions relevant to all five chapters; Chapter 2 is a current work-in-progress and will address enforcement of international agreements to arbitrate; Chapter 3 will address US courts' involvement in the arbitration process; Chapter 4, which has been completed and approved, covers enforcement and set aside of international arbitral awards. The final chapter will address selective aspects of investor-State arbitration, with an emphasis on the distinctive ways in which that type of arbitration may interact with US courts.

[4] The Black Letter and Comments are the portions of a Restatement that the ALI ultimately approves.

approval, however, does not occur without the material having first undergone a drafting and comment regime involving many revisions and several textual iterations, facilitated by meetings between the Reporters and their two groups of peer advisors. Those two groups are the approximately three dozen persons that have been named as Advisors to the project and the much larger Members Consultative Group (comprised of volunteer ALI members).[5] Though time consuming,[6] the peer review process[7] has greatly enhanced the resulting product.

II.   SCOPE AND MISSION

The mission of the work is not exactly what some might have imagined. In particular, it is not the mandate of the Reporters to simply codify the majority view among courts in the United States, but rather to advance rules that represent the best ones among what are often several competing formulae. We take as our anchors – that is, the fixtures from which we cannot deviate – the 1958 New York and 1975 Inter-American (Panama) Conventions as implemented in the Federal Arbitration Act (FAA), and Supreme Court case law. Beyond that, the Reporters have been willing from time to time to depart from what may be majority positions adopted among the jurisdictions. When we do so, the result is typically a pro-arbitration rule. For example, the approved ALI texts holds that forum non conveniens should not be available to impede recognition and enforcement of a Convention award.[8] Similarly, the text rejects the notion that New York Convention's Art. XIV imposes a reciprocity requirement in addition to the basic one that the award be made in a Convention state.[9]

The approved text also posits that the set-aside grounds applicable to Convention awards made in the United States are the refusal grounds of Art. V of the New York Convention, rather than FAA Sect. 10's grounds.[10] We arrived at this result by construing the FAA itself,[11] and not the Convention in isolation; the Convention of course does not itself purport to supply set-aside grounds. Among courts in the United States, it is a minority view that the Convention's Art. V grounds apply in set-aside actions brought with respect to Convention awards rendered in the United States.[12]

---

5. The current list of Consultative Group Members contains approximately 200 names.
6. Those not familiar with ALI's peer-review process sometimes ask what is taking the four Reporters so long; those who know the drafting and peer comment processes of the ALI, however, often congratulate the Reporters on making so much progress.
7. The contribution of the peer groups is both editorial and substantive.
8. See ICA Restatement, Sect. 4-29 (Council Draft No.3, December 23, 2011 (henceforth Council Draft No. 3)).
9. See *id.*, Sect. 4-5.
10. See *id.*, Sect. 4-11.
11. We rely in particular on FAA, Sect. 207 (in pertinent part: "The court shall confirm the award unless it finds one of the grounds for refusal or deferral of recognition or enforcement of the award specified in [the New York] Convention.")
12. See, e.g., *Indus. Risk Insurers v. M.A.N. Gutehoffnungshutte, GmbH*, 141 F.3d 1435 (11th Cir. 1998), cert. denied, 525 U.S. 1068 (1998).

Nevertheless, that approach has positive by-products. For instance, under it, manifest disregard of the law is less likely to be raised.[13] The ALI position also replicates to a large extent the approach of the UNCITRAL Model Law on International Commercial Arbitration (the Model Law),[14] and accordingly might be more familiar to non-Americans than the FAA's Chapter 1 vacatur grounds (found in FAA Sect. 10), with their associated vagaries.[15]

III.   ENFORCEMENT OF AGREEMENTS

Our current work focuses on the enforcement of agreements. We are still in intermediate stages of drafting,[16] and several substantive issues remain under study. There is for example the question of the Conventions' writing requirements. At present, we are committed to implementing the New York Convention Art. II writing requirement in a flexible fashion, in the spirit of the Model Law and other UNCITRAL guidance. Additionally, despite the slightly different language to be found in the Panama Convention in comparison to the New York Convention, a single standard for the writing requirement will most likely be formulated, to apply whichever Convention governs.

The Reporters also wish to delineate restrictively the threshold issues that a court is authorized to decide to the relative exclusion of arbitral tribunals. In general, courts are authorized to consider the existence of the main agreement and the existence, scope and validity of the agreement to arbitrate.[17] The related questions that arise include the extent to which some of those questions can be delegated to the arbitral tribunal, and the showing that the agreement-enforcing party must make to shift the burden to the party resisting arbitration, who must then establish a defense to enforcement in order to prevail.

The role of public policy in the enforcement of arbitration agreements provides another example of the questions that have arisen in our formulation of Chapter 2. To what extent should public policy be a defense to the enforcement of such agreements under either the New York or Panama Convention? That is, is public policy subsumed under the formula "null and void, inoperative or incapable of being performed" as allowed by the New York Convention? The trend among courts is to reason that public

---

13. The New York Convention Art. V grounds and the corresponding Panama Convention grounds are exhaustively stated in those respective treaties.

14. See UNCITRAL Model Law on International Commercial Arbitration, Art. 34 (unchanged with the 2006 revisions).

15. Perhaps chief among FAA Sect. 10's challenges for Americans and non-Americans alike is ascertaining the precise status of the manifest disregard doctrine. See Jack J. COE, Jr., "The Curious Case of Manifest Disregard [of the Law]", Kluwer Arbitration Blog, 17 May 2010.

16. The current draft of Chapter 2 is styled as Preliminary Draft No. 6 (26 March 2013).

17. Cf. *BG Group v. Argentina*, decided March 5, 2014, 572 U. S. _____ (2014); see generally George A. BERMANN, The "Gateway" Problem in International Commercial Arbitration, 37 Yale J. Int'l L. (2013, no. 1).

policy is not a defense, but rather is available only with respect to awards.[18] The current draft is largely in accord with that trend, but holds that public policy may be invoked in rare and extreme circumstances.

A recurrent scope question is the degree to which we should formulate autonomous rules where those rules already exist in allied bodies of law. For example, should the Reporters set forth rules of estoppel and piercing the corporate veil to deal with the question of non-signatories or should we direct courts to the lex fori? At present, the proposed content of Chapter 2 does not include Black Letter treatment of estoppel, piercing the corporate veil and similar theories addressed to non-signatory situations;[19] those bodies of law seem already sufficiently well developed to guide courts and they are collateral to Chapter 2's main objective.[20]

The remainder of 2014 will be devoted to completing Chapter 2, on enforcing arbitration agreements, and to beginning Chapters 3 (court involvement in ongoing arbitrations) and 5 (investor-State arbitration).

---

18. See, e.g., *Lindo v. NCL (Bahamas)*, Ltd., 652 F.3d 1257, 1262-1283 (11th Cir. 2011) (neither unconscionability nor public policy is an available defense at the agreement enforcement stage).

19. Perhaps inconsistently, however, the current draft gives a rule on waiver of the agreement to arbitrate that takes a position on the role of prejudice. Contrary to what one finds in the cases, the current draft diminishes the importance of prejudice.

20. Nothing, however, precludes the Reporters from elaborating on the possibilities in the Reporters' Notes.

Enforcement of International Arbitral Awards in Florida and the United States: Judicial Consistency?

Daniel E. González* and María Eugenia Ramírez**

I. INTRODUCTION

This article was prepared in anticipation of the International Council for Commercial Arbitration (ICCA) Congress, held in Miami, Florida, on 6-9 April 2014. The fact that this historic ICCA Congress was held in Miami, Florida, is a reflection of at least three principle realities. First, International Commercial Arbitration continues to grow in popularity and demand. Second, as International Commercial Arbitration continues to grow, the demand for experienced counsel and arbitrators has also continued to grow. Third, among this growth, Miami has demonstrated that it is a key player in the worldwide scope of international arbitration, as well as an excellent choice to serve as the seat of an international arbitration, especially for arbitrations between Latin American parties. The fundamental reason for this continued success lies in the ability of a prevailing party to enforce an arbitral award.

The last time that the ICCA Congress was held in the United States was 1986, and that Congress was held in New York. In 1986, the world of international arbitration looked significantly different than today. In 1986, (i) the United States had the Federal Arbitration Act (FAA), which governs the enforcement of international arbitral awards in the United States; (ii) sixty-seven states had signed The Convention on the Recognition and Enforcement of Foreign Arbitral Awards (1958 New York Convention); (iii) nine states had signed the Inter-American Convention On International Commercial Arbitration (Inter-American Convention); (iv) Florida had a domestic arbitration code dating back to the 1950s that did not deal with international arbitration; and (v) lawyers had no cell phones, were barely starting to use standalone personal computers, with no emails, internet or other technology, which hindered lawyers' ability to truly transact business internationally or even communicate with each other about international arbitration matters that might be happening around the world or across the street.

---

* Global Head of the International Arbitration Practice Group and member of the Global Board, Hogan Lovells.

** Partner in the International Arbitration Practice Group, Hogan Lovells US LLP, Miami office.

Since then, there have been significant advancements in the field of international arbitration and the enforcement of international arbitral awards. For example, (i) Florida enacted the Florida International Commercial Arbitration Act (FICA); (ii) Miami-Dade County established a section of the court called the "International Commercial Arbitration" section, which will train certain judges in the complex business litigation section on the enforcement of international arbitral awards; (iii) eighty-two additional states signed the New York Convention, including sixteen of which are from the Americas and the Caribbean; (iv) ten more states signed the Inter-American Convention; and (v) the internet is used more than ever to streamline legal research.

These strides and advancements are all excellent news. However, for international arbitration to continue to progress, we need to overcome some of the challenges we face today in international arbitration. In particular, we face challenges with respect to the consistency of standards and rules regarding the enforcement of arbitral awards. In this context, "consistency" refers to the standards and rules that are applied when enforcing an arbitral award, not to consistently enforcing or refusing to enforce an international arbitral award.

For example, the standards and rules associated with service of process are inconsistent among the various state or federal jurisdictions in the United States. Service of process is a procedural mechanism that is governed by the rules of each state or by federal jurisdiction. This means that there is no uniform set of rules on service of process, and therefore when a prevailing party wants to enforce an award in multiple jurisdictions in the United States, the prevailing party must learn the service of process rules for each jurisdiction, whether state or federal, because service of process is a requirement when filing an application to enforce an international arbitral award. Notably, all of these inconsistencies arise before a prevailing party can even see the judge for the first time.

Once the prevailing party appears before the judge, there are additional inconsistencies that have arisen from jurisdiction to jurisdiction. Although arbitral decisions are typically entitled to judicial deference and can only be set aside in very specific circumstances, there have been or continue to be inconsistencies and confusion among Florida and federal courts with respect to certain grounds that are utilized or relied upon by parties seeking to enforce international awards.

Consistency in the enforcement of international commercial arbitral awards is important because it will further strengthen the trend towards selecting international arbitration as a preferred method of dispute resolution. In 2008, PriceWaterhouseCoopers conducted a six-month study that summarizes data from eighty-two questionnaires and forty-seven interviews with major corporations that are users of arbitration services.[1] Among its findings, the study showed that (1) when international arbitration cases proceed to enforcement, the process usually works effectively, (2) international arbitration remains companies' preferred dispute resolution mechanism for cross-border disputes, and (3) international arbitration is effective in practice.[2] With regard to enforcement of arbitral awards in particular, the study found

---

1. PriceWaterhouseCoopers, *International Arbitration: Corporate Attitudes and Practices* (2008) at p. 2.
2. *Ibid.*

that most corporations are able to enforce arbitral awards within one year from their issuance and usually recover more than 75 percent of the value of the award.[3]

Similarly, the International Chamber of Commerce (ICC) reports that requests for arbitration increased 30 percent from 1999 to 2012.[4] In 1999, the ICC received 529 requests for arbitration. And in 2012, the ICC received 759 requests for arbitration.

Given the increasing popularity of international commercial arbitration as a dispute resolution mechanism, and the need for consistency among the judiciary with respect to the enforcement of international arbitral awards, this article aims to analyze some of the inconsistencies (and some of the consistencies) among Florida and federal courts with respect to enforcement (and annulment) of arbitral awards. Sect. II will analyze the state of the law in Florida regarding the enforcement of arbitral awards pursuant to FICA. Sect. III will analyze the state of the law among the federal courts regarding the enforcement of arbitral awards pursuant to the FAA, which incorporates the Convention on the Recognition and Enforcement of Foreign Arbitral Awards (New York Convention)[5] and the Inter-American Convention on International Commercial Arbitration (Inter-American Convention).[6] Sect. III will also analyze the areas of inconsistencies (and consistencies) in both state and federal courts. This article concludes in Sect. IV that consistency from the judiciary is needed for international arbitration to continue to progress.[7]

II.   STATE OF THE LAW — FLORIDA

Since 1957, Florida has had an arbitration code.[8] In fact, Florida is one of the few states of the union that have enacted an arbitration code for domestic and international arbitration agreements. The arbitration code for domestic arbitration agreements is called the "Florida Arbitration Code" (FAC), and it applies to Florida agreements that do

---

3. *Ibid.*
4. Available at <http://www.iccwbo.org/Products-and-Services/Arbitration-and-ADR/Arbitra tion/Introduction-to-ICC-Arbitration/Statistics/>.
5. See generally 9 U.S.C. Sects. 201-208 (2013).
6. See generally 9 U.S.C. Sects. 301-307 (2013).
7. This article does not delve into each step of the process for enforcing an arbitral award. For an analysis of these particular steps, see Daniel E. GONZÁLEZ and María Eugenia RAMÍREZ, "International Commercial Arbitration: Hurdles When Confirming a Foreign Arbitral Award in the U.S.", 83 Fla. Bar. Int'l Sect. 10 (Nov. 2009).
8. See Fla. Stat. Sects. 682.01-682.25. The arbitration code has been modified throughout the years, including in 1967 and more recently in 2013.

not involve interstate commerce unless the agreement excludes the application of the FAC.[9] Florida's international arbitration code is called the "Florida International Commercial Arbitration Act" (FICA).[10]

In 2010, Florida became the seventh state to adopt an international arbitration code (i.e., FICA) that is based on the United Nations Commission on International Trade Law (UNCITRAL) Model Law on International Commercial Arbitration.[11] Since then, one additional state has also joined the list (i.e., Georgia).[12] Notably, however, Florida is the only state whose legislation is based on the text of the UNCITRAL Model Law on International Commercial Arbitration with amendments as adopted in 2006, which include an extensive scheme providing for ex parte orders and interim measures to be binding and enforceable.

In Florida, FICA is now considered the default to the rules employed the international arbitration institutions, which means that when the international arbitral rules are silent on an issue, FICA governs.[13] The goal of this legislation is to reduce the number of legal obstacles created by numerous foreign and international regulations. The law recognizes and enforces foreign arbitral awards, and promises uniform treatment for all awards regardless of international origin. The law also allows for court assistance with and supervision of international arbitrations, while at the same time explicitly authorizes an arbitral tribunal to rule on its own jurisdiction. There are also provisions that allow attorneys from other states or countries to participate more easily in arbitration.

FICA also allows certain previously unavailable challenges to the arbitrator due to bias or insufficient qualifications, sometimes even after the arbitrator's appointment. The law also grants the parties themselves the ability to unanimously terminate the arbitrator's mandate. The arbitrator is now able to enter preliminary orders, and there are procedures in place to enforce interim awards.

Additionally, FICA provides new restrictions on discovery. Previously, discovery in arbitration had been similar to broad, American-style, civil litigation. The new law is more restrictive and should result in less discovery and less expense, a primary reason parties choose arbitration in the first place. FICA, in conjunction with Florida's geographic location as well as the number of bilingual attorneys in the state, now makes Florida an ideal place for international arbitration for parties located in Central America, South America, and the Caribbean.

---

9. *Ibid.*, see also *Powertel, Inc. v. Bexley*, 743 So. 2d 570, 573 (Fla. 1st DCA 1999) (explaining that "[a]n arbitration clause in a contract involving interstate commerce is subject to the Federal Arbitration Act" and noting that the Florida Arbitration Code "applies in such cases only to the extent that it is not in conflict with federal law").

10. Fla. Stat. Sects. 684.0001-684.0049.

11. These states, and the years when they enacted the legislation, include: California (1988), Connecticut (1989), Texas (1989), Oregon (1991), Illinois (1998), Louisiana (2006), Florida (2010), and Georgia (2012).

12. <http://www.uncitral.org/uncitral/en/uncitral_texts/arbitration/1985Model_arbitration_s tatus.html>.

13. Jon POLENBERG, "Chapter 4: Commercial Arbitration" in *Business Litigation in Florida* (2012) Bar 4-1.

1.   Enforcing or Confirming an Award Pursuant to FICA

As stated above, the newly enacted FICA "applies to international commercial arbitration, subject to any agreement in force between the United States of America and any other country or countries".[14] The grounds for enforcing an award under FICA are similar to the grounds for enforcing an award under the FAA. The FAA will be discussed in more detail below.

Under FICA, "[a]n arbitral award, irrespective of the country in which it was made, shall be recognized as binding and, upon application in writing to the competent court, shall be enforced...".[15] Grounds for refusing recognition or enforcement of an award are set forth in Sect. 684.0048, Florida Statutes, which provides that a court may refuse to recognize or enforce an award only:

> "(a) At the request of the party against whom it is invoked, if that party furnishes the competent court where recognition or enforcement is sought proof that:
> 1. A party to the arbitration agreement was under some incapacity or the arbitration agreement is not valid under the law to which the parties have subjected it or, failing any indication thereon, under the law of the country where the award was made;
> 2. The party against whom the award is invoked was not given proper notice of the appointment of an arbitrator or of the arbitral proceedings or was otherwise unable to present its case;
> 3. The award deals with a dispute not contemplated by or not falling within the terms of the submission to arbitration, or it contains decisions on matters beyond the scope of the submission to arbitration;
> 4. The composition of the arbitral tribunal or the arbitral procedure was not in accordance with the agreement of the parties or, failing such agreement, was not in accordance with the law of the country where the arbitration took place;
> 5. The award has not yet become binding on the parties or has been set aside or suspended by a court of the country in which, or under the law of which, that award was made; or
> (b) If the court finds that:
> 1. The subject matter of the dispute is not capable of settlement by arbitration under the laws of Florida; or
> 2. The recognition or enforcement of the award would be contrary to the public policy of Florida.

---

14. Fla. Stat. Sect. 684.0002. An arbitration is "international" if (1) the parties to an arbitration agreement have, at the time of the conclusion of that agreement, their places of business in different countries; (2) one of the following places is situated outside the country in which the parties have their places of business (a) the place of arbitration if determined in, or pursuant to, the arbitration agreement; or (b) any place where a substantial part of the obligations of the commercial relationship are to be performed or the place with which the subject matter of the dispute is most closely connected; or (3) the parties have expressly agreed that the subject matter of the arbitration agreement relates to more than one country. See Fla. Stat. Sect. 684.0002(3).
15. Fla. Sat. Sect. 684.0047.

Given FICA's infancy, there are currently no Florida appellate court decisions that have specifically analyzed its provisions. Hopefully, Florida courts will find that the grounds set forth in FICA are the exclusive means for refusing to recognize and enforce an award. If so, we can expect consistent treatment and interpretation of this legislation.[16] From a practical standpoint, however, this legislation will likely be slow to develop in the Florida courts because when FICA applies, so does the FAA, which means that a defendant or defendants can remove the action to federal court.[17] In the meantime, FICA may serve as a guide for international arbitrations conducted in Florida pursuant to rules administered by private institutions, such as the International Court of Arbitration of the ICC or the International Centre for Dispute Resolution of the American Arbitration Association.

When Florida courts do begin to interpret the enforcement provisions of FICA, it is possible that the courts will turn to something they are more familiar with, such as Florida's domestic counterpart legislation on arbitration, the FAC, for guidance on how to apply FICA. Given the relative consistency in interpreting the enforcement provisions under FAC, this would be a welcomed sign.

Under the FAC, a court must enforce or confirm an arbitration award unless one of the parties moves to vacate the award within ninety days from when the parties receive the award.[18] Courts have consistently held that this requirement is "mandatory"[19] and unless the party opposing the enforcement or confirmation of the award seeks to vacate,

---

16. Currently, certain Florida judges are receiving training for a newly created section of the court called the International Commercial Arbitration Subsection (ICA), a subdivision of the Complex Business Litigation Section in the Circuit Civil Division of the Eleventh Judicial Circuit of Florida. See *In re: Creation of the International Commercial Arbitration Court, a Subsection of Section 40 ("Complex Business Litigation Section") in the Circuit Civil Division of the Eleventh Judicial Circuit of Florida and Procedures for the Assignment and Reassignment of Cases to this Subsection*, Administrative Order No. 13-08 (Companion AO to AO No. 11-04) (Dec. 3, 2013). With this specialized training, Florida judges will be particularly in tune with the issues that surround international commercial arbitration, including the enforcement of foreign arbitral awards.
17. See 28 U.S.C. Sects. 1441, 1446.
18. Fla. Stat. Sects. 682.12, 682.13. If the application to vacate the award alleges that the award was procured by corruption, fraud, or other undue means, the movant has ninety days after the ground is known or reasonably should have been known to file the motion to vacate. Fla. Stat. Sect. 682.12. The only two other exceptions to the requirement of enforcing or confirming the award are when a party files a motion to modify or correct the award. See Fla. Stat. Sects. 682.10, 682.14.
19. *Polley v. Gardner*, 98 So. 3d 648, 649 (Fla. 1st DCA 2012); see also SEIU Fla. Pub. Servs. Union, CTW, CLC v. City of Boynton Beach, 89 So.3d 960 (Fla. 4th DCA 2012) ("The language of section 682.12 is mandatory—the court must confirm the arbitration award unless a motion to vacate or modify has been filed within ninety days of delivery of the award.").

modify, or correct the award, "the trial court does not have any discretion and must confirm the award".[20] In fact, the court's obligation to enforce or confirm the award under these circumstances is nothing more than a ministerial act.[21]

Additionally, under the FAC, if a party opposing a motion to confirm or enforce the award files a motion to vacate the award, that party has the burden of proving one of six statutory grounds, each of which relate to fundamental unfairness in the proceedings or actions by the arbitrators that went beyond their authority.[22]

When interpreting the FAC, Florida courts have been consistent in holding that where the party moving to vacate fails to prove one of these statutory grounds, "neither a circuit court nor a district court of appeal has the authority to overturn the award".[23] To the extent that the award is contrary to law or legal principles, is wrong or incorrect on its merits, or there is no evidentiary support, the statutory framework does not allow these non-statutory grounds to vacate the award.[24] Indeed, "it is well settled that 'the award of arbitrators in statutory arbitration proceedings [in Florida] cannot be set aside for

---

20. *Moya v. Bd. of Regents, State Univ. Sys. of Fla.,* 629 So.2d 282, 284 (Fla. 5th DCA 1993) ("[T]he trial court does not have any discretion and must confirm the award unless one of the parties seeks to vacate, modify or correct the award within 90 days of delivery of the arbitrator's award, or unless there is an issue presented to the trial court in the motion to confirm which was not submitted to the arbitrator.").

21. *Polley v. Gardner*, 98 So. 3d 648, 649 (Fla. 1st DCA 2012) (holding that where the respondent's motion to set aside the arbitration award was untimely, "entry of final judgment confirming the arbitration award was a ministerial task, and there was no legal basis for the trial court to defer ruling on the petitioners' motion"); see also *Farmer v. Polen*, 423 So.2d 1035, 1036 (Fla. 4th DCA 1982).

22. These grounds include that: (1) the award was procured by corruption, fraud or other undue means; (2) there was evident partiality by an arbitrator appointed as a neutral or corruption or misconduct by an arbitrator that prejudiced the rights of a party to the arbitration proceeding; (3) an arbitrator refused to postpone the hearing upon showing of sufficient cause for postponement, refused to hear evidence material to the controversy, or otherwise conducted the hearing in an unfair manner that substantially prejudiced the rights of a party to the arbitration proceeding; (4) an arbitrator exceeded the arbitrator's powers; (5) there was no agreement to arbitrate; or (6) the arbitration was conducted without proper notice of the initiation of an arbitration so as to prejudice substantially the rights of a party to the arbitration proceeding. Fla. Stat. Sect. 682.13.

23. *Schnurmacher Holding, Inc. v. Noriega,* 542 So.2d 1327, 1328 (Fla.1989); see also *LeNeve v. Via S. Florida, L.L.C.*, 908 So. 2d 530, 534 (Fla. 4th DCA 2005).

24. *Schnurmacher Holding, Inc. v. Noriega*, 542 So. 2d 1327, 1328 (Fla. 1989); *Verzura Const., Inc. v. Surfside Ocean, Inc.*, 708 So. 2d 994, 996 (Fla. 3d DCA 1998) ("The law is clear that awards made by arbitration panels cannot be set aside for mere errors of judgment either as to the law or as to the facts; if the award is within the scope of the submission, and the arbitrators are not guilty of the acts of misconduct set forth in the statute, the award operates as a final and conclusive judgment."); *Cassara v. Wofford*, 55 So.2d 102, 105 (Fla. 1951); *District School Bd. v. Timoney*, 524 So.2d 1129 (Fla. 5th DCA 1988); *Prudential-Bache Securities, Inc. v. Shuman*, 483 So.2d 888 (Fla. 3d DCA 1986); *McDonald v. Hardee County School Bd.*, 448 So.2d 593 (Fla. 2d DCA 1984); *Newport Motel, Inc. v. Cobin Restaurant, Inc.*, 281 So.2d 234 (Fla. 3d DCA 1973).

mere errors of judgment either as to the law or as to the facts; if the award is within the scope of the submission, and the arbitrators are not guilty of the acts of misconduct set forth in the statute, the award operates as a final and conclusive judgment'".[25]

Notably, in 2013, the Florida legislature deleted a provision from the FAC statute that arguably assisted Florida courts in remaining consistent on the principle that the only grounds for vacatur are the statutory ones. The deleted provision read, "the fact that the relief was such that it could not or would not be granted by a court of law or equity is not ground for vacating or refusing to confirm the award.." It is yet to be seen whether Florida courts will find that, given this revision, a court sitting in equity could find non-statutory grounds for vacating an award.

III.   STATE OF THE LAW — FEDERAL

Originally enacted in 1925, the FAA governs domestic and international arbitration, though it may, under certain circumstances, be supplemented by state laws such as FICA or FAC.[26] As noted above, the FAA incorporates the New York Convention[27] and the Inter-American Convention.[28] In enacting the FAA, "Congress declared a national policy favoring arbitration and withdrew the power of the states to require a judicial forum for the resolution of claims which the contracting parties agreed to resolve by arbitration."[29] The United States Supreme Court has long recognized that "[t]he goal of the [New York] Convention, and the principal purpose underlying American adoption and implementation of it, was to encourage the recognition and enforcement of commercial arbitration agreements in international contracts and to *unify the standards* by which agreements to arbitrate are observed and arbitral awards are enforced in the signatory countries.."[30] As demonstrated below, however, the standards to enforce arbitral awards, whether foreign or domestic, have not been entirely uniform.

The FAA further provides separate mechanisms for enforcing foreign and domestic arbitral awards. Under both mechanisms, the court's role in reviewing the foreign or domestic arbitral award is strictly limited, and the court must confirm the award unless it finds that one of the grounds for refusal to enforce the award exists.[31] A review of instances where state and federal courts have applied these mechanisms, however, also reveals that courts have struggled to be consistent on at least three key standards, including (1) service of process, (2) personal jurisdiction to enforce a foreign arbitral

---

25. *Schnurmacher Holding, Inc. v. Noriega*, 542 So. 2d 1327, 1328 (Fla. 1989) (citing cases).

26. See generally 9 U.S.C. Sects. 1-16 (2013) (domestic arbitration); 9 U.S.C. Sects. 201-307 (2013) (international arbitration).

27. See generally 9 U.S.C. Sects. 201-208 (2013).

28. See generally 9 U.S.C. Sects. 301-307 (2013).

29. *Shotts v. OP Winter Haven, Inc.*, 86 So.3d 456, 462 (2011); see also *Gilman + Ciocia, Inc. v. Wetherald*, 885 So. 2d 900, 903 (Fla. 4th DCA 2004).

30. *Scherk v. Alberto-Culver Co.*, 417 U.S. 506, 520 n.15 (1974) (emphasis added).

31. See generally 9 U.S.C. Sects. 10-11 (2013) (domestic arbitration); 9 U.S.C. Sect. 207 (2013) (international arbitration).

award, (3) enforcing an international award that was issued in the United States, and (4) enforcing annulled foreign arbitral awards. These four areas are examined below.

1. Service of Process

First, there are inconsistencies before one can start the proceedings to enforce an international award. Service of process is a procedural mechanism that is governed by the rules of each state or federal jurisdiction. This means that there is no uniform set of rules on service of process, and in any given case where the prevailing party wants to enforce an award in multiple jurisdictions in the United States, the prevailing party must learn the service of process rules and application of the rules for each jurisdiction, whether state or federal, because service of process is a requirement when filing an application to enforce an international arbitral award. For example, under Federal Rule of Civil Procedure 4(f)(3) service of an extraterritorial individual may be made "by other means not prohibited by international agreement, as the court orders". Pursuant to this rule, district courts have wide discretion in determining what type of alternative service of process is appropriate in a particular case. Exercising this discretion, federal courts have endorsed many different combinations of methods of service as constitutionally permissible. For example, federal courts in Florida have approved service by email on the respondent plus service on local counsel; and service by courier/Federal Express on respondent plus email and US mail to respondent's local counsel.[32] In contrast, other federal courts have exercised their discretion under Rule 4(f)(3) to deny service of process by alternative means. For example, a federal court in New York refused to allow plaintiffs to serve foreign defendants via international courier.[33]

2. Personal Jurisdiction to Enforce a Foreign Arbitral Award

In the United States, federal courts must have personal jurisdiction over the respondent to be able to enforce an award. Personal jurisdiction can arise in the form of specific or general personal jurisdiction. "Specific jurisdiction" may be exercised over a respondent when the arbitrated issues "aris[e] out of or [are] related to the [respondent's] contacts with the forum."[34] By contrast, "general jurisdiction" may be exercised over a respondent when the respondent has "minimum contacts" with the forum, but the suit does not

---

32. See *U.S. Commodity Futures Trading Com'n v. Aliaga*, 272 F.R.D. 617, 620 (S.D. Fla. 2011); *Fru Veg Marketing, Inc. v. Vegfruitworld Corp.*, 896 F.Supp.2d 1175, 1183 (S.D. Fla. 2012).
33. See *Advanced Aerofoil Technologies, AG v. Todaro*, No. 11 Civ. 9505(ALC)(DCF), 2012 WL 299959 at *2-3 (S.D.N.Y. 31 Jan. 2012).
34. *U.S. S.E.C. v. Carrillo*, 115 F.3d 1540, 1542 n. 2 (11th Cir. 1997) (citing *Helicopteros Nacionales de Colombia v. Hall*, 466 U.S. 408, 414 n. 8 (1984)).

"aris[e] out of or relate[] to the [respondent's] contacts with the forum...."[35] Generally, this means that the defendant must have taken actions that were purposefully directed towards the forum state.[36]

When enforcing an arbitral award, the prevailing party will often file the enforcement action in a jurisdiction where the debtor has assets so that the assets can be seized to satisfy the award. In this context, personal jurisdiction is typically achieved through the fact that the assets reside within the forum state. For example, in *Base Metal Trading Ltd. v. OJSC "Novokuznetsky Aluminum Factory"*, Base Metal obtained a favorable award from the Moscow Chamber of Commerce and Industry against Novokuznetsky Aluminum Factory (NKAZ) regarding the manufacture and sale of aluminum.[37] After being unable to collect on the award, Base Metal learned that NKAZ was receiving an aluminum shipment in the port of the Baltimore Harbor, so it filed a motion with the District Court of Maryland to seize or attach the shipment to satisfy the arbitration award.[38] NKAZ never responded to receiving a copy of the summons and the complaint, and Base Metal was able to obtain a default judgment.[39] Upon learning of the default judgment, NKAZ moved to vacate it and to have the case dismissed for, among other reasons, lack of personal jurisdiction.[40] The District Court granted the motion to dismiss. On appeal, the Fourth Circuit affirmed the dismissal because the shipment that NKAZ was receiving at the Baltimore Harbor was not related to the issues in the arbitration.[41] The Fourth Circuit explained that "when the property which serves as the basis for jurisdiction is completely unrelated to the plaintiff's cause of action, the presence of property alone will not support jurisdiction".[42]

Base Metal appears to be at odds with the "[c]onsiderable authority" that supports the position that a prevailing party can enforce an arbitral award against the debtor's property in the forum "even if that property has no relationship to the underlying

---

35. *Ibid.* at 414 n. 9.

36. Determining whether jurisdiction is proper is normally a two-step process: (1) determining if the state's long-arm statute confers jurisdiction and (2) whether the exercise of jurisdiction, if authorized, is consistent with the Due Process requirements of the Fourteenth Amendment. See Fed.R.Civ. 4; see also *Touchcom, Inc. v. Bereskin & Parr*, 574 F.3d 1403, 1410 (Fed. Cir. 2009); *CFA Inst. v. Inst. of Chartered Fin. Analysts of India*, 551 F.3d 285, 292 (4th Cir. 2009); *see also Western Equities, Ltd. v. Hanseatic, Ltd.*, 956 F.Supp. 1232, 1237 (D.V.I. 1997), (citing *Eskofot A/S v. E.I. Du Pont De Nemours & Co.*, 872 F.Supp. 81, 87 (S.D.N.Y. 1995) (holding that defendant alleged to conduct no business, with no office or employees, and without license to conduct business in the United States by any state, was subject to general jurisdiction based on defendant's actions elsewhere having effect in terms of competition between business rivals and cash flows in the United States).

37. *Base Metal Trading Ltd. v. OJSC "Novokuznetsky Aluminum Factory"*, 283 F.3d 208 (4th Cir. 2002).

38. *Ibid.* at 211.

39. *Ibid.* at 212.

40. *Ibid.*

41. *Ibid.* at 213.

42. *Ibid.*

controversy between the parties".[43] In fact, the United States Supreme Court has explained that "[o]nce it has been determined by a court of competent jurisdiction that the defendant is a debtor of the plaintiff, there would seem to be no unfairness in allowing an action to realize on that debt in a State where the defendant has property, whether or not that State would have jurisdiction to determine the existence of the debt as an original matter".[44]

This is another area of inconsistencies or area where federal courts have struggled to be consistent. Given the importance of the underlying issue, i.e., using the debtor's assets to satisfy an arbitration award, this issue ranks high for arbitration users to determine whether arbitration is right for them. In fact, the 2008 PriceWaterhouseCoopers survey indicated that when asked to identify the main factors affecting corporate counsel's "decision on the place of enforcement, 27% considered first the country where the non-prevailing party has sufficient assets".[45]

3. Enforcing an International Award that Was Issued in the United States

There also are inconsistencies between the various Circuit Courts with regard to the standard of review for enforcing an international award issued in a US juridical seat as opposed to a foreign award. In this instance, the issue is whether the defenses in Art. V of the New York Convention are the exclusive defenses to an action seeking to enforce an international arbitration award that was issued in the United States or whether additional, judicially created defenses, including "manifest disregard of the law", are applicable to defend an enforcement action.[46]

---

43. *Glencore Grain Rotterdam B.V. v. Shivnath Rai Harnarain Co.*, 284 F.3d 1114, 1127 (9th Cir. 2002). This type of jurisdiction is sometimes referred to as *"quasi in rem* type II" jurisdiction, where a prevailing party "seeks to apply what he concedes to be the property of the [debtor] to the satisfaction of a claim against him". *Ibid.* at 1127 n. 8 (citing *Hanson v. Denckla*, 357 U.S. 235, 246 n. 12 (1958)).

44. *Shaffer v. Heitner,* 433 U.S. 186, 97 S.Ct. 2569, 53 L.Ed.2d 683 (1977); see also *Glencore Grain*, 284 F.3d at 1127; Joseph E. NEUHAUS, "Current Issues in the Enforcement of International Arbitration Awards", 36 U. Miami Inter-Am. L. Rev. (2004) p. 23.

45. PriceWaterhouseCoopers, *International Arbitration: Corporate Attitudes and Practices* (2008) at p. 11.

46. Art. V of the New York Convention provides:

"1. Recognition and enforcement of the award may be refused, at the request of the party against whom it is invoked, only if that party furnishes to the competent authority where the recognition and enforcement is sought, proof that:
(a) The parties to the agreement referred to an article II were, under the law applicable to them, under some incapacity, or the said agreement is not valid under the law to which the parties have subjected it or, failing any indication thereon, under the law of the country where the award was made; or
(b) The party against whom the award is invoked was not given proper notice of the appointment of the arbitrator or of the arbitration proceedings or was otherwise unable to present his case; or
(c) The award deals with a difference not contemplated by or not falling within the terms of the submission to arbitration, or it contains decisions on matters beyond the scope of the submission to arbitration, provided that, if the decisions on matters submitted to arbitration can be separated from those not so submitted, that part of the award which contains decisions on matters submitted

For example, inconsistencies have arisen in the Eleventh and Second Circuits. In the Eleventh Circuit, the Eleventh Circuit Court reads Art. V strictly and has held that the only defenses to an enforcement action are the ones listed in Art. V.[47] *Industrial Risk Insurers* involved an action arising out of two events where the tail gas expander installed in a nitric acid plant was damaged.[48] The case was first filed in state court, was removed to federal court, and then was ordered to arbitration in Tampa, Florida, pursuant to an arbitration provision in the contract regarding the design, manufacture, and purchase of the tail gas expander.[49] The arbitrators returned an award against a third-party claimant, Barnard and Burk, who was the designer and manufacturer of the pipes for the tail gas expander. Barnard and Burk then moved to vacate the award on the ground that the award was "arbitrary and capricious", but the district court denied the motion and confirmed the award.[50]

On appeal with the Eleventh Circuit, there was no question that the award was an international award and that the New York Convention applied. Barnard and Burk argued on appeal that the arbitral award should be vacated on the ground that it is "arbitrary and capricious".[51] The Eleventh Circuit rejected that argument, holding that "the Convention's enumeration of defenses is exclusive" and that "no defense against enforcement of an international arbitral award under Chapter 2 of the FAA [incorporating the New York Convention] is available on the ground that the award is 'arbitrary and capricious,' or on any other grounds not specified by the Convention".[52]

By contrast, in the Second Circuit, the court has held that where an international arbitration award has been issued in the United States, Art. V(1)(e) of the New York Convention authorizes the court to apply domestic law in determining whether to confirm the award; and under the domestic law of the United States, the FAA, courts can apply various judicially created standards for vacating an award, such as "manifest disregard of the law", "arbitrary and capricious", or "completely irrational" standards.[53]

---

to arbitration may be recognized and enforced; or

(d) The composition of the arbitral authority or the arbitral procedure was not in accordance with the agreement of the parties, or, failing such agreement, was not in accordance with the law of the country where the arbitration took place; or

(e) The award has not yet become binding on the parties, or has been set aside or suspended by a competent authority of the country in which, or under the law of which, that award was made.

2. Recognition and enforcement of an arbitral award may also be refused if the competent authority in the country where the recognition and enforcement is sought finds that:

(a) The subject matter of the difference is not capable of settlement by arbitration under the law of that country; or

(b) The recognition or enforcement of the award would be contrary to the public policy of that country."

47. See *Industrial Risk Insurers v. M.A.N. Gutehoffnungshutte*, 141 F.3d 1434, 1446 (11th Cir. 1998).
48. *Ibid.* at 1437-1438.
49. *Ibid.* at 1438-1439.
50. *Ibid.* at 1439.
51. *Ibid.* at 1445.
52. *Ibid.* at 1446.
53. See *Yusuf Ahmed Alghanim & Sons v. Toys "R" Us, Inc.*, 126 F.3d 15, 22 (1997).

In *Yusuf Ahmed Alghanim & Sons*, a foreign licensee filed a petition to confirm an arbitration award entered in the United States.[54] Neither of the parties seriously contested the applicability of the New York Convention to the arbitral award.[55] Instead, the respondent, Toys "R" Us, who was the non-prevailing party in the arbitration, argued that the award was "clearly irrational, in manifest disregard of the law, and in manifest disregard of the terms of the agreement".[56] The district court accepted Toys "R" Us' argument as valid, but it ultimately rejected the argument and confirmed the award.[57]

On appeal with the Second Circuit, the court explained that "[a]lthough Article V provides the exclusive grounds for refusing confirmation under the Convention, one of those exclusive grounds [Art. V(1)(e)] is where '[t]he award ... has been set aside or suspended by a competent authority of the country in which, or under the law of which, that award was made'."[58] The court read this provision to "allow a court in the country under whose law the arbitration was conducted to apply domestic arbitral law, in this case the FAA, to a motion to set aside or vacate that arbitral award".[59] Additionally, the court further explained that "[t]here is no indication in the Convention of any intention to deprive the rendering state of its supervisory authority over an arbitral award, including its authority to set aside that award under domestic law".[60] Under the domestic law of the United States (i.e., the FAA), awards may be vacated or modified where the arbitrator's award is in "manifest disregard of the terms of the agreement".[61] Having determined that "manifest disregard of the law" is a defense to an application to confirm an international award issued in the United States, the court considered the defense in this case and held that the arbitrators did not manifestly disregard the law.[62] Accordingly, the Second Circuit affirmed the district court's decision to confirm the award.[63]

Digging deeper into the application of the Second Circuit's opinion, there is yet another level of inconsistencies that is rooted in decades of confusion. Under domestic law, state and federal courts applying the FAA have inconsistently held that the statutory grounds are the exclusive grounds for vacating or modifying an arbitration award and have created non-statutory grounds to refuse to enforce an arbitration award.[64] Non-

---

54. *Ibid.* at 18.
55. The *Yusuf* Court explained, "The Convention's applicability in this case is clear. The dispute giving rise to this appeal involved two nondomestic parties and one United States corporation, and principally involved conduct and contract performance in the Middle East." *Id.* at 19.
56. *Ibid.* at 18.
57. *Ibid.*
58. *Ibid.* at 20.
59. *Ibid.* at 21.
60. *Ibid.* at 22.
61. *Ibid.* at 23.
62. *Ibid.* at 23-24.
63. *Ibid.* at 25.
64. State courts applying their own legislation on the enforcement of arbitral awards also struggle with deciding whether their respective state's laws on the statutory grounds for refusing to enforce the award are exclusive. For example, in Florida, when applying the FAC, "it is well settled that 'the award of arbitrators in statutory arbitration proceedings [in Florida] cannot be set aside for mere errors of judgment either as to the law or as to the facts; if the award is within the scope of the

statutory grounds are often traced back to the United States Supreme Court decision in *Wilko v. Swan*, which introduced the "manifest disregard of the law" standard for vacating awards.[65] Since then, courts have broadened the non-statutory bases for vacating awards.[66] Even state courts, like Florida, have applied similar non-statutory grounds to vacate awards when applying the FAA.[67]

The non-statutory ground that has received the most attention and been inconsistently applied is the "manifest disregard of the law" standard for vacating awards. In *Hall Street Assocs., L.L.C. v. Mattel, Inc.*, the United States Supreme Court was presented with the opportunity to clarify the validity of this non-statutory ground, as well as all other judicially created grounds.[68] There, Hall Street argued that the parties should be allowed to draft their own standards of review in their arbitration agreements, which would be enforced by a court.[69] Relying on *Wilko*, Hall Street reasoned that "if judges can add grounds to vacate (or modify), so can contracting parties".[70] The Court rejected Hall Street's argument and limited *Wilko* to its facts, stating that Hall Street's interpretation was "too much for *Wilko* to bear" and that *Wilko*'s phrasing was vague.[71] In dicta, the Court took the opportunity to comment on the exclusivity of the standards for vacating

---

submission, and the arbitrators are not guilty of the acts of misconduct set forth in the statute, the award operates as a final and conclusive judgment'". *Schnurmacher Holding, Inc. v. Noriega*, 542 So. 2d 1327, 1328 (Fla. 1989) (citing cases). But in New York, in addition to the statutory grounds in Art. 75 of New York's Civil Practice Law and Rules, a state court can refuse to enforce an arbitral award on the basis that the award is completely irrational. *Diana Joy Ingham derivatively on behalf of Cobalt Asset Management, L.P. v Charles L. Thompson, et al., Mark M. Thompson, et al., Cobalt Asset Management, L.P., Nominal Defendant*, 2014 NY Slip Op 00436 (23 Jan. 2014). Nevertheless, given that the "complete irrationality" standard is a difficult one to prove, both Florida law and New York law appear to be consistent in affording great deference to an arbitrator's decision, and short of corruption or fraud, partiality, or exceeding powers, an arbitral award should be enforced.

65. *Wilko v. Swan*, 346 U.S. 427, 436-437 (1953) ("While it may be true, as the Court of Appeals thought, that a failure of the arbitrators to decide in accordance with the provisions of the Securities Act would 'constitute grounds for vacating the award pursuant to section 10 of the Federal Arbitration Act, that failure would need to be made clearly to appear. In unrestricted submission, such as the present margin agreements envisage, the interpretations of the law by the arbitrators in contrast to manifest disregard are not subject, in the federal courts, to judicial review for error in interpretation.").

66. Other judicially created standards include: (1) conflict with public policy, (2) arbitrary and capricious, (3) completely irrational, or (4) failure to draw its essence from the parties' underlying contract. See Stephen L. HAYFORD, "Law in Disarray: Judicial Standards for Vacatur of Commercial Arbitration Awards", 30 Ga. L. Rev. (1996) p. 731 at pp. 763-797; see also Jon POLENBERG and Quinn SMITH, "Can Parties Play Games with Arbitration Awards? How *Mattel* May Put an End to Prolonged Gamesmanship", 83 Fla. B. J. (May 2009) p. 5.

67. See, e.g., *Wachovia Securities, LLC v. Vogel*, 918 So. 2d 1004, 1007 (Fla. 2d DCA 2006) (recognizing manifest disregard of the law standard); *World Invest Corp. v. Breen*, 684 So. 2d 221, 222-223 (Fla. 4th DCA 1996) (recognizing arbitrary and capricious standard).

68. *Hall Street Assocs., L.L.C. v. Mattel, Inc.*, 552 U.S. 576, 586 (2008).

69. *Hall Street*, 552 U.S. at 584.

70. *Ibid.* at 585.

71. *Ibid.*

or modifying arbitration awards. The Court acknowledged the split among the Circuits and held that "Sects. 10 and 11 respectively provide the FAA's exclusive grounds for expedited vacatur and modification."[72]

The Court was presented with another opportunity in *Stolt-Nielsen S.A. v. AnimalFeeds Int'l Corp.*, to clarify whether non-statutory grounds for vacating awards are permissible under the FAA.[73] The Court, however, did not directly address the issue and stated in a footnote that "[w]e do not decide whether 'manifest disregard' survives our decision in *Hall Street Associates*, as an independent ground for review or as a judicial gloss on the enumerated grounds for vacatur set forth at 9 U.S.C. Sect. 10".[74]

Since then, some courts have eliminated "manifest disregard of the law" from the grounds available to vacate an arbitral award.[75] But other courts have continued to rely on manifest disregard as an independent, non-statutory ground for vacating arbitral awards.[76] And some courts have retained the concept of manifest disregard but have re-conceptualized it as "judicial gloss" pursuant to section 10(a)(3) ("arbitral misconduct") or section 10(a)(4) ("excess authority") of the FAA.[77]

4.   *Enforcing Annulled Foreign Arbitral Awards Pursuant to the FAA*

Pursuant to Sect. 207 of the FAA and Art. V of the New York Convention and the Inter-American Convention, a court must enforce an arbitral award unless one of seven

---

72. *Ibid.* at 584.
73. *Stolt-Nielsen S.A. v. AnimalFeeds Int'l Corp.*, 559 U.S. 662, 673 (2010).
74. *Ibid.* at 672 n. 3.
75. Relying on *Hall Street*, the Fifth, Seventh, Eighth, and Eleventh Circuits have eliminated the manifest disregard standard as a basis to vacate an arbitral award. See *Air Line Pilots Ass'n Int'l v. Trans States Airlines, LLC*, 638 F.3d 572, 578 (8th Cir. 2011) ("*Hall Street* eliminated judicially created vacatur standards under the FAA, including manifest disregard for the law"); *Affymax, Inc.v. Ortho-McNeil-Janssen Pharma., Inc.*, 660 F.3d 281, 284-285 (7th Cir. 2011) ("This list is exclusive; neither judges nor contracting parties can expand it. Disregard of the law is not on the statutory list."); *Frazier v. CitiFinancial Corp.*, 604 F.3d 1313, 1324 (11th Cir. 2010) ("judicially-created bases for vacatur are no longer valid in light of *Hall Street*"); *Citigroup Global Mkts.*, 562 F.3d at 355 ("to the extent that manifest disregard of the law constitutes a non-statutory ground for vacatur, it is no longer a basis for vacating awards under the FAA").
76. *Wachovia Sec., LLC v. Brand*, 671 F.3d 472, 483 (4th Cir. 2012) (referring to footnote 3 in *Stolt-Nielsen*, 559 U.S. at 672 n. 3, the court held that "[w]e read this footnote to mean that manifest disregard continues to exist either 'as an independent ground for review or as a judicial gloss on the enumerated grounds for vacatur set forth at 9 U.S.C. Sect. 10.' Therefore, we decline to adopt the position of the Fifth and Eleventh Circuits that manifest disregard no longer exists."); *Ozormoor v. T-Mobile USA, Inc.*, 459 F. App'x 502, 505 (6th Cir. 2012) ("[T]he ability to challenge an arbitration award on the ground that it represents a "manifest disregard of the law" amounts to "a separate judicially created basis" for vacating an award.").
77. *T.Co Metals, LLC v. Dempsey Pipe & Supply, Inc.*, 592 F.3d 329, 340 (2d Cir. 2010) ("This Court recently made clear … that it reads *Hall Street* as 'reconceptualiz[ing]' manifest disregard 'as a judicial gloss on the specific grounds for vacatur' of arbitration awards under 9 U.S.C. Sect. 10."); *Comedy Club, Inc. v. Improv W. Associates*, 553 F.3d 1277, 1290 (9th Cir. 2009) ("[W]e conclude that, after *Hall Street Associates*, manifest disregard of the law remains a valid ground for vacatur because it is a part of Sect. 10(a)(4).").

specifically enumerated grounds is present.[78] Among these grounds, "[r]ecognition and enforcement of the award may be refused" if the party opposing enforcement of the award proves that "[t]he award has ... been set aside ... by a competent authority of the country in which, or under the law of which, that award was made".[79] In applying this particular ground, courts must determine what, if any, is the discretion of a court asked to confirm an arbitration award that has been nullified by a competent authority of a state in which the arbitration was held.[80] Two particular cases demonstrate the inconsistent results that US courts have reached in struggling with this question.[81]

In *Chromalloy Aeroservices v. The Arab Republic of Egypt*, an American company entered into a military procurement contract with the Air Force of the Republic of Egypt.[82] Due to certain disputes between the parties, the parties commenced arbitration proceedings pursuant to the arbitration clause of their contract.[83] An arbitral award was rendered in Egypt, under the laws of Egypt and in favor of the US corporation, and Egypt was ordered to pay damages to the American company.[84] While the American company sought enforcement of the award in the United States under the New York Convention, Egypt sought a nullification of the award before the Egyptian Court of Appeals.[85] Although the Egyptian Court of Appeals issued an order nullifying the arbitral award, the federal district court in the United States nevertheless confirmed and enforced the arbitral award.[86] The federal district court held that although under the Convention the "court may, at its discretion, decline to enforce the award" the court chose not to because it concluded that the arbitration agreement precluded an appeal in Egyptian courts, which meant that the award was final and should be enforced regardless of what happened in Egypt. The federal district court also noted that although Congress had not adopted the French version of the Convention, it still emphasized the extraordinary

---

78. A court may refuse to confirm and enforce an arbitral award only after finding proof of one of the following seven grounds: (1) the parties are under some incapacity with respect to the applicable arbitration agreement, or the agreement is otherwise invalid; (2) the party against whom the award is invoked was not given proper notice of the arbitration or appointment of an arbitrator or was otherwise unable to present its case; (3) the award exceeds the scope of the terms of the submission to arbitration; (4) the composition of the arbitral authority or the arbitral procedure was not in accordance with the parties' agreement; (5) the award has not yet become binding on the parties or has been set aside or suspended by a competent authority of the country in which, or under the law of which, that award was made; (6) the subject matter of the award is not capable of settlement by arbitration under the law of the court where confirmation and enforcement are sought; or (7) the confirmation or enforcement of the award would be contrary to public policy. See Inter-American Convention Art. V; New York Convention Art. V.

79. New York Convention Art. V(1)(e).

80. *Corporación Mexicana de Mantenimiento Integral, S. DE R.L. DE C.V. v. PEMEX-Exploración y Producción*, No. 10 Civ. 206(AKH), 2013 WL 4517225, at *14 (27 Aug. 2013).

81. *Compare Chromalloy Aeroservices v. The Arab Republic of Egypt*, 939 F.Supp. 907 (D. D.C. 1996), with *TermoRio S.A. E.S.P. v. Electranta, S.P.*, 487 F.3d 928 (D.C. Cir. 2007).

82. *Chromalloy Aeroservices*, 939 F.Supp. at 907.

83. *Ibid.*

84. *Ibid.*

85. *Ibid.*

86. *Ibid.*

nature of the refusal to recognize an award because it says, "Recognition and enforcement of the award will not be refused ... unless...."[87]

Eleven years later and at the other end of the spectrum is the case of *TermoRio S.A. E.S.P. v. Electranta, S.P.*, where the same federal district court faced a US$ 60 million award in a Colombian arbitration. There, a Colombian entity entered into a Power Purchase Agreement with a Colombian state-owned public utility for the generation and purchase of electricity.[88] When a dispute arose under the Power Purchase Agreement, the parties resorted to arbitration in Colombia pursuant to the Rules of Arbitration of the ICC in accordance to the agreement's dispute resolution clause.[89] Although the arbitral tribunal awarded TermoRio more than US$ 60 million in damages, the state-owned public utility defendant utilized its connections and obtained an "extraordinary writ" from a local Colombian court, which overturned and nullified the arbitral award because the agreement's arbitration clause allegedly violated Colombian law.[90] Around the same time, TermoRio commenced arbitral award enforcement proceedings in the United States to enforce the award pursuant to the FAA, the New York Convention, and the Inter-American Convention.[91] The US Court of Appeals for the District of Columbia Circuit affirmed the district court's dismissal of the enforcement proceedings on the grounds that Colombia – the country where the arbitral award was issued – lawfully nullified the award, thus, making it unenforceable in the United States.[92] The *TermoRio* court held, however, that the *TermoRio* case was clearly distinguishable from *Chromalloy* because in *Chromalloy* the parties' express contract provision concerning the non-appealability of the final arbitral award was violated when an appeal to vacate the final arbitral award was sought.[93]

To date, courts continue to struggle when asked to decide how much deference to give a foreign court's decision to annul an arbitration award. In one case, the district court confirmed an arbitral award that was annulled in the primary juridical seat.[94] In another case, a different district court confirmed an arbitral award that was annulled in a secondary juridical seat.[95]

---

87. *Ibid.*
88. *TermoRio*, 487 F.3d at 930.
89. *Ibid.* at 931.
90. *Ibid.*
91. *Ibid.*
92. *Ibid.* at 941.
93. *Ibid.* at 937.
94. *Corporación Mexicana de Mantenimiento Integral, S. DE R.L. DE C.V. v. PEMEX-Exploración y Producción*, No. 10 Civ. 206(AKH), 2013 WL 4517225 (27 Aug. 2013).
95. *Juan Castillo Bozo v. Leopoldo Castillo Bozo & Gabriel Castillo Bozo*, Case No. 1:12-cv-24174-KMW, D.E. 45 (Fla. S.D. 28 May 2013).

IV.   CONCLUSION

As noted above, there is currently a split among courts and inconsistency in enforcing arbitration awards. For arbitration to continue to progress in the United States, we need consistency among the judiciary. Consistency is an underlying principle in the basis for any country to adopt the New York and Inter-American Conventions. Indeed, as noted above, the Supreme Court has held that "the principal purpose underlying American adoption and implementation of [the New York Convention], was to ... *unify the standards* by which ... arbitral awards are enforced in the signatory countries."[96]

As analyzed above, to date, the Florida courts applying state legislation have generally been consistent in its application. When applying federal legislation, however, courts have not been so consistent. For example, as demonstrated in *Chromalloy*, *TermoRio*, *PEMEX*, and *Castillo Bozo*, courts have taken opposite views on the effect of an award that is nullified in the country where the award was issued. Additionally, as demonstrated in *Base Metal*, prevailing parties may have a difficult time enforcing an award in a jurisdiction where the debtor retains assets that are unrelated to the issues disputed in the arbitration.

On the domestic side of enforcing arbitration awards, the judicial landscape struggles with judicially created grounds for determining whether an award should be enforced. This landscape naturally influences corporate policy on whether to use arbitration, whether domestic or international.

The result of these inconsistencies is significant because it raises uncertainty about the possible enforcement of an arbitral award. Although arbitral decisions are typically entitled to judicial deference and can only be set aside in very specific circumstances, these inconsistencies cause confusion among Florida and federal courts with respect to certain grounds that are utilized or relied upon by parties seeking to enforce (and vacate) arbitral awards.

Although this is the current state of affairs, we remain hopeful that as arbitration becomes more popular, more consistency from the judiciary will develop. This consistency should further strengthen the trend towards selecting international arbitration as a preferred method of dispute resolution.

---

96. *Scherk v. Alberto-Culver Co.*, 417 U.S. 506, 520 n. 15 (1974) (emphasis added).

Breakout Sessions

Arbitral Legitimacy: The Users' and Judges' Perspectives

Report on the Breakout Sessions on
Arbitral Legitimacy: The Users' and Judges' Perspectives

Amanda Lees, Luis González García, L Andrew S. Riccio and Ruth Mosch

I.   NOTE GENERAL EDITOR

In four parallel Breakout Sessions, more conducive to dialogue than a plenary, panels of corporate counsel and judges armed with points collected in the eight Congress Panels offered observations and posed questions for discussion on the challenges confronting legitimacy in terms of both justice and precision. The Reports of the Panel Rapporteurs Amanda Lees, Luis González García, L Andrew S. Riccio and Ruth Mosch follow below.

II.   REPORT OF THE BREAKOUT SESSION ON "PROOF: A PLEA FOR PRECISION" AND "TREATY ARBITRATION: PLEADING AND PROOF OF FRAUD AND COMPARABLE FORMS OF ABUSE"[1]

Chaired by **Melanie van Leeuwen**, Partner, Derains & Gharavi, Paris, the panel comprising **Judge Rosemary Barkett**, Florida trial and appellate judge and judge at the Iran-U.S. Claims Tribunal, **Andrew Clarke**, General Counsel of Exxon Mobil International Limited and **David Brynmor Thomas**, counsel and arbitrator, discussed the need for precision in the standard of proof in both commercial and treaty arbitration with the active and lively participation of the floor. **Chief Justice Sundaresh Menon** of Singapore was unable to join the panel discussion in person but David Brynmor Thomas kindly delivered the thoughts and observations that Chief Justice Menon had provided in writing.

---

1. Report by Panel Rapporteur Amanda Lees, Of Counsel, Simmons and Simmons, Singapore.

Prior to the panel discussion **Andrew Clarke** reported on the outcome of the discussions held by the Corporate Counsel International Arbitration Group (CCIAG) at a joint conference with the International Chamber of Commerce in Paris in October 2013. In order to enhance the legitimacy of arbitration, the CCIAG considers that it is crucial that the users of arbitration participate in conferences and debates with arbitrators and counsel. Trust and confidence in the arbitrators are key factors in enhancing the legitimacy of arbitration and ensuring the efficacy of arbitration as a dispute resolution method. In this respect, Andrew Clarke highlighted the importance placed by the corporate users on arbitrators' reputations, the need for improvement in the process of arbitrator appointments, as well as the need for increased transparency in respect of the skills and capabilities of arbitrators.

The topics for discussion for the Breakout Session came from the propositions developed in Session A1 on "Proof: A Plea for Precision" and in Session A4 "Treaty Arbitration: Pleading and Proof of Fraud and Comparable Forms of Abuse".

1.   Proof

The topic of the plea for precision in proof was introduced with the comments of **Chief Justice Menon**, who is one of the proponents of the need for greater precision in the standard and burden of proof because of the absence of a common understanding in this respect between tribunals and parties, who operate in a cross-cultural and cross-systemic context. The differences between national systems, where issues of proof are sometimes treated as procedural issues and sometimes as substantive law issues, bear out the necessity of establishing a common understanding between the parties and the tribunal as to the standard and the burden that parties are held to in that particular arbitration. Failing such common understanding, parties may be unaware of what they are required to prove. For the losing party, it is unsatisfactory if it was unaware during the arbitral proceedings what the basis was upon which it was being judged, only to find out in the arbitral award what the test or standard was that the tribunal applied and that it failed to meet it. Justice Menon emphasized that greater precision in the tribunal's dealings with issues of proof would also enhance the quality of the reasoning of the award and thereby its legitimacy.

Judge Barkett introduced the proposition that "It is universally accepted that each party must prove the facts upon which it relies in support of its case." In her introductory remarks, Judge Barkett queried how this principle would apply if the respondent does not appear in the proceedings. Are the arbitrators required to undertake the type of questioning that the respondent would normally engage in?

Lively participation from the floor underscored the importance of the standard and burden of proof in the arbitrator's decision-making process. Some experienced arbitrators voiced their opinion that the standard of proof is rarely an issue because the test simply is "Do we feel satisfied?" In practice standards do not make any difference because it comes down to the question as to whether the tribunal believes a party's submission or not.

Others expressed the opinion that it is desirable for tribunals to clearly articulate expectations early in the process as this will assist the parties in conducting the arbitral process efficiently. If tribunals do not address the standard and burden of proof explicitly, they allow parties to proceed on assumptions that may turn out to be wrong. There was support from the floor for a best practice in which tribunals not only establish how the arbitral proceedings will be conducted early in the arbitration but also discuss with the parties the issues of standard and burden of proof.

Andrew Clarke introduced the proposition that "Arbitral tribunals should, at the earliest opportunity, ensure that the parties understand the burden of proof and who carries it with respect to each issue." The users would welcome guidance from the tribunal on issues of standard and burden of proof because it will assist the parties in understanding from the outset what evidence they will have to produce and in appreciating the standard they will have to meet in order to prevail. Andrew Clarke noted that for users more clarity on the direction that an arbitration is taking and the possible outcome would help in-house lawyers in managing expectations and advising management sensibly on the merits of a possible settlement, as early as possible in the process.

Overall the floor was split between those who thought it was desirable for tribunals to provide guidance to the parties about the standard and the burden of proof and those who thought that this was a myth.

David Brynmor Thomas introduced the proposition that "In order to reflect the intent of the parties, the standard of proof to be applied should be determined as a matter of substantive law and articulated by the arbitral tribunal at the earliest opportunity" by reference to **Justice Menon's** observations. As articulated in Jennifer Smith's paper (this volume, pp. 1033-1039), the parties have selected the applicable law to their contractual relations, which is the source of their rights and obligations. Given that the existence of such rights and obligations may turn on the standard of proof applied, should not that standard be the standard used by that applicable law system? More importantly, the tribunal should articulate which standard is being applied early in the process so as to take away any uncertainty stemming from the fact that different national systems treat these issues as substantive or procedural, thereby avoiding parties' proceeding in the arbitration on the basis of different understanding.

Several participants from the audience voiced the concern that this would overcomplicate an issue that did not even exist for lawyers coming from the civil law tradition. A practical suggestion was made to the effect that the list of issues should be drafted by the tribunal as a decision tree, showing logically how the issues were interrelated and how they would (or not) be outcome-determinative. Other participants commented that issues of standard and burden of proof only became an issue in the arbitration, once raised as such by one of the parties or when a party appeared to be on the wrong track. The majority of the floor considered it irrelevant whether the standard of proof is to be determined as a matter of procedural law or as a matter of substantive law.

2.   *Proof of Fraud and Corruption*

Subsequently, **Judge Barkett** introduced the propositions from the session on "Treaty Arbitration: Pleading and Proof of Fraud and Comparable Forms of Abuse." Judge Barkett reiterated the main themes from the session: first that fraud and corruption were wrong and should not be tolerated; second that there is still uncertainty as to what is the standard and burden of proof in relation to such allegations and whether it varies with the degree of wrongdoing; third there is debate as to the law to be applied, should it be the law of the host state or transnational standards; and finally whether arbitrators have sufficient tools to make findings in relation to such allegations. Turning to the proposition that "This is an appropriate maxim for all respondents: throw mud, it may stick, and if it does not, what matter," Judge Barkett stated that tribunals need to make clear that there will be cost consequences if a party makes unfounded allegations. Since research shows that decision-making is often intuitive, it is important for the decision-makers to be conscious of the occurrence of unconscious bias triggered by allegations of fraud and corruption that may later turn out to be unsubstantiated. As an arbitrator, one needs to be very careful to examine the precise reasons on which a decision is based, to ensure that it has not been tainted by unsubstantiated allegations.

A variety of anecdotes and comments were proffered from the floor. Certain participants pointed out that allegations of fraud, even if baseless, create a lot of additional work for the other party and have the potential of derailing or complicating the arbitration. In commercial arbitrations, allegations of fraud are often made to avoid contractual limitations (such as exclusion clauses or time limits for bringing a claim) or to void ab initio the contract whereas in investment treaty arbitrations allegations of fraud and corruption are often made by the host states to undermine the legality of the investment either ab initio or in the course of the investment project. There was broad consensus that allegations of fraud and corruption, whether in treaty or commercial arbitration, must be particularized by those making the allegations because of their serious nature and the potentially adverse effects on the integrity of the arbitral process and the legitimacy of its outcome. In light of the far-reaching legal consequences that fraud and corruption potentially have on a contract or an investment, there was support for the proposition that a higher standard of proof may be warranted for such allegations.

The proposition that "tribunals and counsel are not properly equipped to address the issue of corruption (both in terms of expertise, and the tools at their disposal)" was introduced by reference to the observations of **Chief Justice Menon**, who expressed concern that tribunals may not be properly equipped to address these issues because they do not have access to the apparatus of the state to investigate corruption; and they are not technically equipped to undertake such investigations.

There was broad consensus that the systematic and phased approach taken by the *Metal-Tech* tribunal in determining the issue of corruption in the recent ICSID arbitration against the Republic of Uzbekistan, was a model to be followed by other tribunals in their investigation of allegations of fraud and corruption.

One of the participants from the floor shared the impression that the arbitral process itself is sometimes used as a means of laundering money and noted that some countries are so notoriously rife with corruption that all parties to the arbitration may be participating towards that goal.

III.   REPORT OF THE BREAKOUT SESSION ON INTERIM MEASURES, DOCUMENT PRODUCTION AND MATTERS OF EVIDENCE[2]

Panel Chair **José Astigarraga**, of the Astigarraga Davis law firm in Miami, set the stage for interactive audience engagements with panelists **Judge Vance E. Salter**, Third District Court of Appeals in Florida, **Karl Hennessee**, Vice-President at Halliburton Energy Services, **Clyde Lea**, Deputy General Counsel at ConocoPhilips sharing with participants their experiences on the following topics: (1) document production; (2) interim measures and; (3) matters of evidence, in particular, witnesses and experts.

Judge Salter commenced the session by sharing his views on how arbitration is perceived by the judiciary, in particular in Florida. He stated that arbitration is seen by judges as an aid for the judicial system.

1.   Document Production

Mr. Lea stated that there are abuses in document production by parties in the arbitral process and that the real challenge is for arbitrators to exercise their authority. **Mr. Hennessee** agreed with Mr. Lea on this point. He stated that the question is not the result of a document request but how the process is handled by the arbitrators. Both agreed that the International Bar Association's IBA Rules on the Taking of Evidence in International Arbitration (the IBA Rules) provide a good balance in the document production process. The IBA Rules are seen by corporate counsel as a good restraint of document production. They also pointed out that what users want is courageous arbitrators willing to make an early intervention, to conduct the process expeditiously and willing to impose consequences/sanctions for non-compliance of the tribunal's orders. Mr. Hennessee emphasized that what users want is certainty. He stated that it is important that all issues in relation to disclosure are agreed by the parties with the tribunal at the outset of the proceedings.

Mr. Astigarraga asked the question on the cultural differences of arbitrators and how such differences may influence the way document production is handled in arbitration. It was agreed that arbitrators' views of document production are driven in part by the arbitrator's orientation on the role of finding the truth vs. efficiency driven in part by the different approaches under civil law and common law tradition.

2.   Interim Measures

Mr. Hennessee began by expressing that the frequency of interim measures is overestimated and raised some skepticism as to how useful they are in arbitration, finding them useful on only two issues: (i) the destruction of documents and (ii) security for costs. He stated that interim measures often delay the efficient resolution of disputes.

Mr. Lea agreed with **Mr. Hennessee**. He pointed out that interim measures should be used for very few occasions and that users do not seek interim measures often. **Mr. Astigarraga**, however, raised the question of whether an interim measures

---

2. Report by Panel Rapporteur Luis González García, Matrix Chambers, United Kingdom.

application may plant the seed of an idea into the arbitrator's mind. Would a request for an interim measure shape the arbitrator's mind? **Judge Salter** stated that interim measures as a tactic are not very effective in shaping the arbitrator's mind.

It was agreed by the three panelists that when interim measures are necessary, emergency arbitrators can provide relief. **Judge Salter** stated that that is true but only if the request is simple. It was also agreed that although the emergency arbitrator is helpful in obtaining interim relief, domestic courts can be faster. But then again, an emergency arbitrator's award is easier to enforce abroad than a domestic court order.

3. Matters of Evidence: Witnesses and Experts

The three panelists agreed that arbitrators should be hands-on in the management of the process but should be careful not to alter the balance and burdens of proof. **Mr. Lea** was of the view that in cases of complex issues, it is useful for arbitrators to call for experts. **Judge Salter** stated that appointing experts by judges is unusual. **Mr. Hennessee** stressed that it is more the parties' duty to assist the tribunal and that too much initiative on behalf of the arbitrators can be problematic. A distinction was made between commercial arbitration and investment treaty arbitration. It was agreed that in investment treaty cases, public policies could justify an arbitrator calling witnesses and experts *sua sponte*.

In commercial cases an arbitrator's desire to question a witness that parties are not calling or that a party has chosen not to cross-examine risks altering the burden of proof and reasoned decisions of the parties.

IV. REPORT OF THE BREAKOUT SESSION ON "WHO ARE THE ARBITRATORS" AND "UNIVERSAL ARBITRATION"[3]

The Panel consisted of two in-house counsel for international energy companies, **Janet Kelly** (ConocoPhillips) and **Eugene Silva** (ExxonMobil); a sitting Miami-Dade County Circuit Civil Court Judge of the Complex Business Litigation Section (and the new International Commercial Arbitration Subsection), **Judge John Thornton**; and a former Chief Justice of the New South Wales Supreme Court who now sits as arbitrator, **James Spigelman**. Needless to say, there was a diversity of opinions on the panel that led to some insightful discussion both among the panelists, and with the audience.

The objective of this panel was to discuss, from the practical perspective, the issues raised in Session B1: "Who Are the Arbitrators?" and in Session B4: "Universal Arbitration: An Aspiration Within Reach or a Sisyphean Goal?" The structure of this panel called for the Chair, **Joseph Matthews**, Of Counsel to Colson Hicks Eidson, to develop questions based upon the B1 and B4 presentations and pose them to the panelists.

---

3. Report by Panel Rapporteur L Andrew S. Riccio Associate, Assouline & Berlowe, P.A., Miami office; from December 2014: Associate, Baker & McKenzie LLP, New York.

1.   Who Are the Arbitrators?

This topic focused on gender diversity of the arbitrators. Gender diversity is relevant to the continued legitimacy of international arbitration; however, **Mr. Spigelman** believes it is not necessary. He stated that the world is not uniform. The relevant audience will determine legitimacy, so there is a clear distinction between private order (choice of parties) and public order (treaty regime). Though corporations *ought* to follow some social responsibility guideline that would increase gender diversity, it is only a relevant consideration in terms of legitimacy. In investment arbitration there are cultural issues, north-south issues, and religious issues that come to light, not just gender.

    Mr. Matthews turned to Ms. Kelly and Mr. Silva throughout to discuss the role of participants in the choice of the arbitrators. **Ms. Kelly** posed that the need for diversity relates to the need for more arbitrators. The pool of arbitrators is too small to achieve the efficiencies needed for arbitration. The mistake is to put too much reliance on the back of the individual user. One resolution offered by Ms. Kelly is that the users can get together and develop initiatives to enlarge the size of the pool.

    To **Mr. Silva** the overriding issue is that the client just wants to win. Thus, his or her first question in choosing an arbitrator will be: "How do we find someone who will help us win?" The corporate user is looking for an arbitrator that thinks exactly like the corporation, which does not exclude gender or nationality. Mr. Silva noted that the practicalities are very different for selecting an arbitrator in investment arbitration. The pool of arbitrators is smaller. Average age of the arbitrators is a serious factor, as people have died during a case. This concern is real because these cases can last a very long time. To Mr. Silva, the ability to appoint an arbitrator is very important to the party. It lends legitimacy to the process for the user, rather than detracting from it. A track record is a necessary prerequisite. Hypothetical rules are hard to sell to a client. The default thought is that the reason to enter into an arbitration agreement is to be able to control the process.

    Ms. Kelly noted that parties do not want to cede any control because they already feel powerless in arbitration. To her, the answer is non-party-appointed arbitrators, but this leaves to the institutions the responsibility of making it work.

    Mr. Matthews then turned the conversation to **Judge Thornton** to discuss the role of arbitrators in the international realm versus jurors in US courts. Judge Thornton responded that the rules on jury selection require non-discrimination. Participation of decision-makers from diverse backgrounds is important for arbitration, as it is for a jury. Judge Thornton proposed that the parties include a clause in their arbitral agreement instructing the parties to select a diverse panel.

    Mr. Silva expressed concern about a diversity clause in a contract as it could be used as basis for a challenge.

    Mr. Matthews asked the audience how they propose to change the status quo if no single participant will take it on. One member of the audience proffered that maybe patience is the solution. As far as investment arbitration is concerned, the institution is young so it is normal for the parties to flock to the most experienced. Over time, it will work itself out.

    Ms. Kelly and **Mr. Silva** agreed. Mr. Silva noted that simple demographics will work their way through. In 2034 we will still complain about a "mafia". They may look different, but will all have the same training. The client wants someone who looks at the world the way it looks at the world. You also want someone who works well with others. This is why the mafia wins sometimes.

Mr. Spigelman added that he is less patient and thinks there are ways of pushing it forward. He'd like to push it himself. Everyone has the capacity within the system to push it through.

Others in the audience added that patience always helps, but did not agree that no user is willing because change is already happening. Sometimes to win is not to have the most accurate decision. Diversity will be best achieved through the promotion of it by everyone. For this, the lawyer is also responsible. The client wants to win, so the lawyer will appoint the one he knows, likes, and trusts. Lawyers can offer their clients diverse options. It does not mean you are depriving your client of anything.

The audience also noted that the users alone will not drive the process, but the institutions play a big role. The nature of commercial arbitration is secret, so only the institutions know who the good arbitrators are.

2. *Universal Arbitration*

Mr. Spigelman started the discussion of the universal arbitration topic by acknowledging that arbitration can be applied to anything. Universality means that by reason of practice, over time, a uniform system around the world has developed. Arbitration has emerged as a compromise. It has been adopted throughout the world and will continue to be so.

Mr. Matthews noted that Stephan Schill's paper (this volume, pp. 789-827) identified three categories: consumer, employment and class arbitrations; business-to-business disputes where the outcome affects many people; and investor-state arbitration. Matthews asked if international arbitration can survive these three legitimacy attacks.

Mr. Silva commented that where there is a public overlay, you do not run into these issues. Though there is a lot of talk about a "crisis of legitimacy", arbitration is ultimately legitimate. Transparency is an issue in investor-state arbitration because of the public overlay. If additional standards are added, should an additional voice be added? What of the fact that the state is deemed to represent its people, is there really a need for this additional voice?

With this incisive question, the panel concluded. It was clear that the audience and panelists could have continued the discussion, but there was only so much time. The divergent perspectives of judges and users will always be insightful for the practitioner, and this panel accomplished its task of delivering practical observations to very real issues.

V.   REPORT OF BREAKOUT SESSION ON "CAN ARBITRAL INSTITUTIONS DO MORE TO
      FURTHER LEGITIMACY" AND "IS THE TREATY ARBITRATION PLAYING FIELD LEVEL?"[4]

Chaired by **Edna Sussman**, independent arbitrator and Distinguished ADR Practitioner
in Residence at Fordham University School of Law, the panelists **Justice Ellen Gracie
Northfleet**, former Chief Justice of the Federal Supreme Court, Brazil; **Judge
Dominique Hascher** of the French Supreme Judicial Court; and corporate counsel for
ConocoPhillips **Laura Robertson** discussed the legitimacy of the arbitral process with
the active participation and involvement of many participants from the floor.

Topics of the Breakout Session were the propositions "Arbitral Institutions Can Do
More To Further Legitimacy: True Or False" and "Treaty Arbitration: Is The Playing
Field Level and Who Decides Whether It Is Anyway?"

Laura Robertson commenced by introducing the recent report of the Corporate
Council International Arbitration Group (CCIAG). Similar to the subjects discussed
during the ICCA Miami 2014 Congress, the hot topics of the report were sources and
questions of legitimacy in international arbitration as well as possible solutions. The focus
was on the users' trust in the arbitral process and on the arbitrators' independence and
diversity.

Justice Northfleet continued in addressing the necessity for the arbitrator pool to
become more diverse and to provide easier access for newcomers. She further
emphasized that developing countries perceive investment arbitration as favouring the
investor. Repeated appointments of the same arbitrator by one party had to be avoided.

Judge Hascher focused on the financial independence of arbitral institutions. He
considered whether counsel working for an institution could be perceived as being biased
due to the fact that they often work in law firms before and after taking on the
institutional position.

Edna Sussman submitted the proposition that the pool of arbitrators is too small to
the audience for a vote. Two-thirds of the participants were of the opinion that there is
at least a perception that the pool is too small. Ms. Sussman pointed out that on earlier
panels, many had stated that it was the role of the institutions to advance diversity while
the institutions said they did not have the ability to do so because they only made
institutional appointments 20-30 percent of the time. The floor suggested that corporate
counsel had the responsibility to enlarge the pool by choosing newcomers as arbitrators.
Laura Robertson countered this suggestion by stating that corporate counsel usually
had to rely on outside counsel for choosing the arbitrator. Outside counsel had more
insights as to suitable candidates. She prefers knowing who is trying hard to make a name
for him- or herself as she believes he or she could be trusted to work diligently when
given the opportunity.

Ms. Sussman proposed for discussion two specific methodologies that could be
employed by the institutions to promote diversity. The first was the question of whether
or not sanitized arbitral awards should be published so as to create a body of work that
parties could look to in order to determine the capabilities of less well-known

---

4. Report by Panel Rapporteur Ruth Mosch, Member of the Executive Committee, German
   Institution of Arbitration.

arbitrators. There was a vigorous debate with both pros and cons expressed. **Justice Northfleet** expressed the view that the system should become more transparent especially through arbitral institutions publishing awards. The vote on this proposition showed that two-thirds of the participants in the room were in favour of a sanitized publication of awards.

Ms. Sussman then referred to the debate led by Brower and Paulsson about the party-appointed system and proposed various methodologies that institutions could discuss with parties for the appointment process as a mechanism for promoting diversity, without turning the selection process over for a unilateral institutional appointment. Again there was a vigorous discussion on the subject and an inconclusive vote.

After voting on the proposition that investor state arbitration is inherently biased towards investors it became apparent that there might be a disconnect between the statistics which do not demonstrate a bias and the perception, which as many previous panels had confirmed, was also of great importance. A discussion ensued as to why there was a discrepancy between the statistical results and the perception of bias as many of the participants did perceive investment arbitration as biased towards the investor. It was noted that the simple fact that investment treaties give rights to investors and not to states supports the perception.

The picture on whether investment arbitration has developed into an inconsistent body of jurisprudence did not become clear. Participants drew a comparison to litigation and expressed the opinion that domestic court decisions aren't consistent either nor can they be because of the many contours of the law and the differences in the facts. Similarly investor-state arbitrations are governed by bilateral investment treaties that are not identical and facts that vary. The proposition was deemed to be a myth by short majority.

Overall the discussions during the Breakout Session were very intensive and animated. They could have continued for a much longer time than ninety minutes. It showed the need for discussion fora and the benefit of exchange across different cultures and legal systems.

What developed during this Breakout Session was a true and open dialogue. My impression is that the format strengthened the intention of the Congress organizers: to further legitimacy in international arbitration and to divide certain myths from reality.

Lunch Seminar

Latin America: Hottest Issues, Country by Country

Report on the Lunch Seminar
Latin America: Hottest Issues, Country by Country

*Ricardo Dalmaso Marques**

I.   INTRODUCTION: WHY LATIN AMERICA (AGAIN)?

Few topics in international arbitration nowadays gather more interest than arbitral experiences had by practitioners in the most diverse regions of the globe. It is often especially interesting to hear and read about thrilling cases dealt with and superb challenges faced by arbitrators, counsel and clients in the most varied and peculiar parts of the world – triggering questions particularly with respect to those regions' legal orders, their local courts' attitudes and even these communities' views about foreign investment and international commercial relations.

Notwithstanding, this curiosity about "good" and "bad" incidents can perhaps be considered even more understandable when we consider Latin America, a region intensely marked by a number of political, economic and legal turnarounds in the past decades. The practice of law in Latin America, regardless of the area or specialty, is particularly inspiring – possibly to the same extent that it is complex and delicate. The diverse legal and social realities that can be encountered in the Latin American region, notably, make the legal profession challenging in any of its countries, either from a domestic or an international perspective. Most of us certainly have heard in the recent past "how exciting it must be to be a Latin American lawyer at the present time".

* Panel Rapporteur; Associate, Pinheiro Neto Advogados (São Paulo, Brazil); International Visiting
Associate at Skadden, Arps, Slate, Meagher & Flom (New York, United States).
    The author deeply thanks Caroline Cavassin Klamas, Pedro Martini and Estefanía San Juan for
their kind and crucial assistance in the drafting of this Report.

These are perhaps some of the explanations for why the Lunch Seminar titled "Latin America: Hottest Issues, Country by Country" was one of the best-attended panels at the 2014 ICCA Congress in Miami – these, and the fact that six leading practitioners in the region were assigned the tricky duty, during the lunchtime of the first event day, of enlightening the audience on the most recent trends in Latin American investment and international commercial arbitration. As summarized below, the panelists were meticulous in depicting novelties in the arbitration legal framework, case law developments and expected trends for the coming years in and pertaining to ten Latin American countries, these being: Argentina, Brazil, Chile, Colombia, Costa Rica, Ecuador, El Salvador, Mexico, Panama, and Peru.

II.   DOAK BISHOP (CHAIR OF THE PANEL): THE SUBSTANTIAL EVOLUTION OF INTERNATIONAL ARBITRATION IN LATIN AMERICA IN TERMS OF LEGAL FRAMEWORK, COURTS' ATTITUDE AND COUNSEL EXPERTISE

The chair of the panel, Doak Bishop, partner and co-chair of King & Spalding's international arbitration practice group in Houston, led the discussions by emphasizing the substantial evolution of arbitration that has distinguished Latin America, in his experience, in the past twenty-five years. Bishop made sure to remind the audience that many laws in the region have been written and rewritten over the past decades, reflecting a certain competition in this regard among Latin American countries. He also gave notable emphasis to the perceptible growth in the number of arbitral institutions, as well as to an increasing sophistication of the local courts in terms of acquaintance with and proficiency in international arbitration – also in dealing with the recognition of foreign arbitral awards.[1]

According to Bishop, however, the single most striking evolution seen in the past three decades in international arbitration in the region has been the growth of practitioners and of expertise in the "Latin American bar". A reflection and examples of this development, he said, were the creation in 2010 of *ALARB – Asociación Latinoamericana de Arbitraje* (the Latin-American Arbitration Association),[2] and the imminent establishment of *ITAFOR – ITA Foro de Arbitraje Latinoamericano* (ITA Latin-American Arbitration Forum),[3] a primarily Spanish-Portuguese language "listserv" created to foster discussion on arbitration and ADR topics pertinent to Latin America.

---

1. See R. Doak BISHOP and James E. ETRI, International Commercial Arbitration in South America, available at <www.kslaw.com/library/pdf/bishop3.pdf> (last visited on 8 May 2014).
2. See *Alarb – Asociación Latinoamericana de Arbitraje*, ALARB, <www.alarb.org> (last visited on 8 May 2014).
3. See *ITA Latin American Arbitration Forum (ITAFOR)*, Center for Am. & Int'l L., <www.cailaw.org/ Institute-for-Transnational-Arbitration/publications/itafor-listserv.html> (last visited on 8 May 2014).

III.   JONATHAN C. HAMILTON: THE MYTHICAL LEGENDS OF LATIN AMERICAN INVESTMENT
        ARBITRATION

The first panelist, Jonathan Hamilton, partner and head of Latin American arbitration at
White & Case LLP, based in Washington, D.C., and Mexico City, confronted "mythical
legends" (*los legados míticos*) of Latin American arbitration. Like Che Guevara, Latin
American arbitration has become laden with diverse and at times conflicting myths,
creating an alleged legitimacy crisis, particularly with respect to investment arbitration,
said Hamilton.

To assess the efficacy of Latin American arbitration, he emphasized the importance
of context, mentioning historical cycles between public and private control of natural
resources and the economies of Latin American states. Notably, he cited a leading
Peruvian lawyer who told him, at the outset of his legal career, during the momentous
legal changes in Latin America in the mid-1990s: "*Para entender inversión en América Latina,
necesitas entender La Brea y Pariñas*" – to understand investment in Latin America, you must
understand *La Brea y Pariñas*, an oil field in Peru. *La Brea y Pariñas* had significant legal,
political and economic ramifications including a notable ad hoc arbitration almost a
century ago, and was a source of domestic political upheaval in Peru in 1968. A
settlement agreement provoked controversy due to an apparent lack of transparency
regarding a compensation agreement, contributing to a change in governments and
subsequent renationalization of the oil fields.

In that historical context, the "Washington Consensus" of the 1990s was a watershed
moment, commented Hamilton.[4] The relationship between investors and States, and law
and economics, changed.[5] Economic models shifted toward private investment, but with
critical new additions: substantive promises under investment protection agreements,
together with international dispute mechanisms, including arbitration before the World
Bank.[6] More specifically, according to Hamilton, the adoption of modern arbitration
laws, the ratification of bilateral investment treaties and the adhesion to the ICSID
Convention put into place an entirely new legal framework in Latin America, which can
be seen as part of an overall political and macroeconomic change.[7]

Comparing this newer era to the past, Hamilton observed that history teaches lessons
about "the complications we used to live in" – a world that had no investment arbitration
system or international arbitration mechanisms as they exist today. Hamilton quoted
Winston Churchill's famous dictum, "democracy is the worst form of government,
except for all those other forms that have been tried", and commented that the same may
be said to apply to the current investment and international arbitration systems in Latin

---

4. See Jonathan C. HAMILTON, *International Arbitration as a Component of Latin American Reforms: The
   Case of Peru* (1997).
5. See Jonathan C. HAMILTON, et al., *Latin American Investment Protections: Comparative Perspectives on
   Laws, Treaties, and Disputes for Investors, States and Counsel* (2012).
6. See Jonathan C. HAMILTON, "A Decade of Latin American Investment Arbitration" in Mary H.
   MOURRA and Thomas E. CARBONNEAU, eds., *Latin American Investment Treaty Arbitration: The
   Controversies and Conflicts* (2008) p. 69.
7. See "Compendium of Latin American Arbitration Law" in Jonathan C. Hamilton, ed., *Latin
   Arbitration Law* (2014).

America – even in the face of limited steps away from the investment arbitration system by Bolivia, Ecuador and Venezuela. Hamilton pointed to a White & Case study finding that the outcomes of concluded Latin American cases before ICSID have been fairly balanced as a statistical matter, and noting that Peru, for example, had both maintained a pro-investment policy and also been a strong and successful respondent across varied investment cases.

To illustrate where the region stands today with respect to the legitimacy of investment arbitration, Hamilton focused on three paradigmatic areas related to economic and social development in Latin America.[8]

1. Sovereign Debt

Latin American development in contemporary history has been marked by various bouts involving sovereign debt. For Hamilton, the *Abaclat v. Argentina* ICSID case[9] – an arbitration in which the claimants, under the White & Case team's representation, alleged that Argentina's sovereign debt restructuring amounted to expropriation and violated the fair and equitable treatment standard established under the Argentina-Italy BIT – is reflective of how investment arbitration interacted with that reality. Thus, remembering that in the 1990s, Argentina was perhaps the most prolific issuer of sovereign bonds in the world, he noted that the bilateral investment treaties and the ICSID system marked the creation of a new forum for addressing sovereign default.

2. Infrastructure

Latin American development also required enhanced infrastructure. Hamilton focused on the *Quiport v. Ecuador* ICSID case,[10] a conflict that emerged from the denunciation of the ICSID Convention by Ecuador and expropriation of tariffs related to a concession to construct and operate Quito's new international airport. He highlighted that, after a long and intense negotiation period, the claimants (a multinational consortium), the Ecuadorian State and the Municipality of Quito entered into a "Strategic Alliance Agreement"[11] – an amicable solution taking into account the new Ecuadorian constitutional framework, concepts of strategic alliances under Ecuadorian law, and the security needed for the investors and lenders to inject the equity and debt required to finish the project. According to Hamilton, due to the successful renegotiation,

---

8. Based on cases in which Hamilton has acted as counsel to investors or States.
9. *Abaclat v. Argentine Republic* (ICSID Case No. ARB/07/5), filed 7 Feb. 2007, available at <www.italaw.com/cases/35> (last visited on 8 May 2014). See "A Brave New World?" Am. Lawyer (Focus Europe, June 2012) ("White & Case's Jonathan Hamilton argues … 'If you break treaty promises to tens of thousands of people, you can't be surprised when tens of thousands of people complain about it.'").
10. *Corporación Quiport S.A. v. Republic of Ecuador* (ICSID Case No. ARB/09/23), filed 30 Dec. 2009, available at <https://icsid.worldbank.org/ICSID>.
11. See *Corporación Quiport S.A. v. Republic of Ecuador* (ICSID Case No. ARB/09/23), Order of Discontinuance, 11 Nov. 2011, para. 5 available at <https://icsid.worldbank.org/ICSID/Front ServLet?requestType=CasesRH&actionVal=showDoc&docId=DC3492_En&caseId=C882>.

construction of the new airport resumed, bringing at least 2,500 jobs for contractors, subcontractors and skilled workers. The estimated impact of the airport as a new economic zone would be the creation of 10,000 jobs, he affirmed. The project has had a positive impact on Ecuador's local and national economy and major ramifications for foreign investment in Ecuador and international relations. Hamilton stated, "the new Quito international airport would not exist were it not for investment protections, access to arbitration and, critically, the affirmation of Ecuador's consent to ICSID arbitration during the course of the negotiations".[12]

3.   Energy

Energy and electricity are relevant to the economic development of the region as well. In this regard, Hamilton made reference to a trio of cases pertaining to the Peruvian energy sector, including *Peru v. Caraveli*, the first case registered at the World Bank by a Latin American State,[13] "an underutilized scenario in the ICSID system".[14] This case was resolved through an *Acuerdo Integral* ("Integral Agreement"), pursuant to which Peru, which made claims rising toward US$150 million, is being paid US$ 40 million with costs. Moreover, according to Hamilton, the agreement is transparent – "contrary to the *La Brea y Pariñas* story"– and available on the World Bank website.[15]

Based on these cases and experiences, Hamilton concluded that there is not *per se* a legitimacy crisis in Latin American arbitration: "We are in a different stage of this ongoing process of what investment arbitration means both procedurally and substantively," he stated. According to him, the *legados míticos* of Latin American arbitration portend less a legitimacy crisis than a potential to encourage stability and the rule of law, if nurtured accordingly.

---

12. See Jonathan C. HAMILTON, *Anatomy of a Deal: Expropriation, Denunciation, Arbitration, Negotiation and the Resolution of the Quito International Airport Project*, Latin Arb. Law, <http://latinarbitration law.com/anatomy-of-a-deal-expropriation-denunciation-arbitration-negotiation-and-the-resolution-of-the-quito-international-airport-project/> (last visited on 8 May 2014); LatinLawyer, Deal of the Year 2011, 4 May 2012 <http://latinlawyer.com/features/ article/43411/deal-year-2011/> ("Disputes category winner: resolution of the Quito international airport dispute") (last visited on 19 May 2014).

13. *Republic of Peru v. Caraveli Cotaruse Transmisora de Energía S.A.C.* (ICSID Case No. ARB/13/24), filed 19 Sept. 2013; Douglas THOMSON, "Peru Brings ICSID Claim Against Power Investor", Global Arb. Rev., 20 September 2013 <http://globalarbitrationreview.com/news/article/31907/peru-brings-icsid-claim-against-power-investor/>.

14. Andrew DE LOTBINIÈRE MCDOUGALL and Jonathan C. HAMILTON, "ICSID Growth Continues as Canada Ratifies and Cases Diversify", White & Case (6 Nov. 2013) <http://www.whitecase.com/alerts-11062013-1/#.U2vQaHe2Ff8>.

15. *Republic of Peru v. Caraveli Cotaruse Transmisora de Energía S.A.C.* (ICSID Case No. ARB/13/24), Procedural Order Taking Note of the Discontinuance of the Proceeding, 26 Dec. 2013), available at <https://icsid.worldbank.org/ICSID/FrontServlet?requestType=CasesRH&actionVal=viewCase&reqFrom=Home&caseId=C3084> (Spanish original).

IV.   DIEGO GOSIS: INVESTMENT ARBITRATION DEVELOPMENTS IN LATIN AMERICA

Dealing specifically with investment arbitration in Latin America, Diego Gosis, of counsel at Gomm & Smith in Miami, precisely described what he understands are the four major developments that the region has experienced in the past years in the field – submissions that he made in a "moot competition arguing format" in honor of Professor Eric Bergsten, the creator and for many years developer of the Willem C. Vis International Commercial Arbitration Moot, held annually in Vienna, Austria and Hong Kong, and who had just received the "ICCA Award for Lifetime Contribution to the Field of International Arbitration".

1.   Developments in Challenges to Arbitrators

"Who is deciding investment cases?" asked Gosis, bringing up, first, the recent cases in which challenges to arbitrators were upheld by the Chairman of the ICSID Administrative Council for the first time since the entering into force of the ICSID Convention: *Blue Bank v. Venezuela*,[16] and *Burlington v. Ecuador*.[17]

Furthermore, Gosis underscored that, similarly, ICSID tribunals have in the recent past considered and upheld challenges to arbitrators, such as in *Caratube v. Kazakhstan*,[18] in which the non-challenged arbitrators upheld the challenge filed by the claimants against one of the co-arbitrators; and in *Burlington v. Ecuador*,[19] in which the two non-challenged arbitrators (again, for the first time in ICSID history) failed to reach a decision on the challenge filed by Ecuador against one of the co-arbitrators – the reason why the final decision, upholding the challenge, was taken by the Chairman of the ICSID Administrative Council, as mentioned above, in accordance with Art. 58 of the ICSID Convention.[20]

---

16. *Blue Bank Int'l & Trust (Barb.) Ltd. v. Bolivarian Republic of Venez.* (ICSID Case No. ARB/12/20), Decision on the Parties' Proposals to Disqualify a Majority of the Tribunal, 12 Nov. 2013, available at <www.italaw.com/sites/default/files/case-documents/italaw3009.pdf>.

17. *Burlington Res., Inc. v. Republic of Ecuador* (ICSID Case No. ARB/08/5), Decision on the Proposal for Disqualification of Professor Francisco Orrego Vicuña, 13 Dec. 2013, available at <https://icsid.worldbank.org/ICSID/FrontServlet?requestType=CasesRH&actionVal=show Doc&docId=DC3972_En&caseId=C300>.

18. *Caratube Int'l Oil Co. v. Republic of Kaz.* (ICSID Case No. ARB/13/13), Decision on the Proposal for Disqualification of Bruno Boesch, 20 Mar. 2014, available at <www.italaw.com/sites/default/files/case-documents/italaw3133.pdf>.

19. *Burlington Resources v. Republic of Ecuador*, (ICSID Case No. ARB/08/5), Decision on the Proposal for Disqualification of Professor Francisco Orrego Vicuña, para. 16.

20. "The decision on any proposal to disqualify a conciliator or arbitrator shall be taken by the other members of the Commission or Tribunal as the case may be, provided that where those members are equally divided, or in the case of a proposal to disqualify a sole conciliator or arbitrator, or a majority of the conciliators or arbitrators, the Chairman shall take that decision. If it is decided that the proposal is well-founded the conciliator or arbitrator to whom the decision relates shall be replaced in accordance with the provisions of Section 2 of Chapter III or Section 2 of Chapter IV."

Convention on the Settlement of Investment Disputes between States and Nationals of Other

Gosis noted that challenges to arbitrators have also been upheld by arbitral tribunals constituted under the rules of other investment institutions, as in the case of *Devas v. India*.[21] All these cases, in Gosis' opinion, represent "a reflection of the massive increase in the number of cases, with only a limited pool of arbitrators available". Apparently, he affirmed, the pool of arbitrators has not expanded quickly enough, establishing a scenario that is "prone to create problems in the area of how we will cope with the conflicts of interest arising from these limitations".

2.   Developments in State Claims

"Who is claiming in investment arbitration?" was the second question asked by Gosis. Although the fact that States are regularly filing claims and counterclaims in investment cases is not necessarily new, he affirmed, emphasis must be given to the increasing number of arbitrations filed by States in the past twenty years, which have included, even, counterclaims filed by States after a decision on liability had already been issued by the tribunal (i.e., when the proceedings were about to move forward to a *quantum* determination stage).

3.   Growth of Latin American Arbitration Practice Groups

Gosis further corroborated Doak Bishop's observation of the growth of the number of Latin American lawyers specializing in arbitration, and stated that his experience has shown an active participation of teams coming mostly from "south of Miami", particularly Buenos Aires and Santiago. According to him, this trend will deserve further attention in the forthcoming decade for "what the advocacy looks like" in an international scenario. "This will certainly have an impact on the form of advocacy and then, of course, in the form and substance of the decisions," he asserted, highlighting that disparities may arise in practice depending on whether the arbitration practitioners and arbitrators were educated and trained in civil or common law jurisdictions.

4.   Transparency Expectations and Production of Evidence

Finally, for Gosis, not only has there been a very interesting move towards transparency in investment arbitration, but also a "corollary of this development has been a change of paradigm in the way that tribunals deal with 'things happening out there'". As an example, he mentioned experiences in which tribunals allowed submissions and evidence

---

States Art. 58, opened for signature 18 Mar. 1965, available at <https://icsid.worldbank. org/ICSID/StaticFiles/basicdoc/CRR_English-final.pdf>.

21. *CC/Devas (Mauritius) Ltd. v. Republic of India*, PCA Case No. 2013-09, Decision on the Respondent's Challenge to the Hon. Marc Lalonde as Presiding Arbitrator and Prof. Francisco Orrego Vicuña as Co-Arbitrator, Perm. Ct. Arb., 30 Sept. 2013), available at <www.italaw.com/sites/default/files/case-documents/italaw3161.pdf.pdf> (case administrated by the Permanent Court of Arbitration (PCA) and in which Judge Peter Tomka, President of the International Court of Justice (ICJ), as appointing authority, upheld a challenge filed by India against one of the co-arbitrators).

produced before other investment tribunals to be submitted in the form of evidence, with the purpose of assessing whether one of the parties was acting consistently with their position in other previous or parallel cases. A body of doctrine, techniques and theories, Gosis reported, have been developed around how parties should be prevented from adopting contradictory positions in different cases; and, according to him, this is a trend that may potentially give rise to accountability both for arbitrators (who may have decided a particular issue in a previous case) and for counsel (who may have argued a similar or identical position in the past).

V.   KATHERINE GONZÁLEZ ARROCHA: RECENT INTERNATIONAL COMMERCIAL ARBITRATION DEVELOPMENTS IN NORTHERN AND CENTRAL LATIN AMERICA

Katherine González Arrocha, Arbitration and ADR Director for Latin America at the ICC International Court of Arbitration, and based in Panamá, addressed the legislative and case law developments in northern and central Latin America, and started off by affirming that, finally, international arbitration has begun to find a comfortable place in Latin America. "In the recent years, we have seen more good news and advantages rather than setbacks," she contended.

According to González Arrocha, one of the biggest threats to international arbitration in Latin America traditionally consisted of the *amparos* actions, a very frequent topic in the arbitral practice in the region. The *amparos* were originally created to protect fundamental rights provided for by the national constitutions, and aim to require judges to ensure that laws and public authorities' acts are carried out in conformity with the constitutional framework. She explained that in arbitration, however, the *amparos* have been used to challenge the jurisdiction of the arbitral tribunal, or to challenge the arbitral award, based on purported violations to the constitution.

González Arrocha advised, in this regard, that for an *amparo* to be obtainable, "the arbitrator must be equal to the judge; to a public servant". She reported that, in her experience, unfortunately, it was very frequent that arbitrations were interrupted by a court's order issued in the context of an *amparo* action on the grounds of violations of constitutional rights – such as access to justice and due process of law (which are at the core of practically all national constitutions). Most local courts, she said, were not familiar with arbitration in the past and used *amparos* to halt the arbitral proceedings inappropriately.

The good news given by González Arrocha is that as the understanding of how arbitration works has spread through the region in the past decade, the courts have less frequently considered arbitrators to be equivalent to public servants for the purposes of *amparos* actions. "They have been considering that the arbitrators' authority is based on the parties' consent and not on the mandatory power of the State," she affirmed, conveying that in countries such as Mexico, Panamá and Costa Rica, it is nowadays less likely for a party to succeed in attempting to discontinue the proceedings through the filing of an *amparo* action.

To support these contentions, González Arrocha depicted the most recent arbitration-related legal developments coming from and pertaining to Mexico, El Salvador, Costa Rica, and, her home country, Panama.

1.   Mexico

a.   Public policy

According to González Arrocha, not all news has been positive in Mexico with regard to public policy issues in international arbitration, particularly in view of the annulment of an ICC award, in October 2011, in *Conmisa v. Pemex*. In this decision, which has been widely commented upon, the Mexican Eleventh Civil Appellate Court reasoned that the award violated public policy in large part on the grounds that a new Mexican law precluded the resolution through arbitration of administrative rescissions, deemed as acts of authority under the exclusive jurisdiction of the Mexican administrative courts.[22]

She pointed out, though, that most Mexican scholars have treated the decision as "an anomaly in regular Mexican practice", and that there are also very positive cases in the country that can be mentioned. For example, according to her, an encouraging decision was rendered by the Seventh Civil Appellate Court, in April 2012, stating that the concept of public policy must be assessed individually on a case-by-case basis, and that it was not sufficient for the party to prove that a mandatory provision was not taken into account by the arbitrators in the award. More precisely, she reported the court's reasoning that, to violate public policy, the violation must concern the validity of the award within the Mexican legal order, and that allegations of such violations should not be used for the purpose of reviewing or reassessing the reasoning of the arbitral tribunal.[23]

b.   Access to arbitration as a human right

González Arrocha noted that amendments to the Mexican Constitution in 2011 were written to encompass the right of access to alternative dispute resolution methods as a human right under the Mexican constitutional framework. According to her, this change has had a very positive impact on Mexican arbitration-related case law, as she illustrates with a case in which the Second Appellate Court of the Third District, in September 2012, rejected an *amparo* action and declared precisely that the access to arbitration is to

---

22. Eventually, however, the US District Court for the Southern District of New York confirmed and proceeded to enforce the annulled award, holding that it could decline to defer to a Mexican court decision that vacated an arbitration award. The reasoning was that the Mexican court decision violated basic notions of justice in that it applied a law that was not in existence at the time the parties' contract was formed, and left CONMISA without an apparent ability to litigate its claims. *Corporación Mexicana de Mantenimiento Integral S. de R.L. de C.V. v. Pemex-Exploración y Producción*, No. 10 Civ. 206 (AKH), 2013 WL 4517225 (S.D.N.Y. 27 Aug. 2013) (U.S.).

23. *Séptimo Tribunal Colegiado en Materia Civil del Primer Circuito. Amparo Directo 6/2012, Bergesen Worldwide Ltd. 19 de abril del 2012. Unanimidad de votos. Ponente:* Julio César Vázquez Mellado García. Secretario: Carlos Manríquez García. [Seventh Collegiate Civil Court of the First Circuit. Direct Appeal 6/2012, Bergesen Wordlwide Ltd., 19 April 2012. Unanimous vote. Reporter: Julio César Vázquez Mellado García. Secretary: Carlos Manríquez García.] 2001129. I.7o.C.17 C (10a.). *Tribunales Colegiados de Circuito. Décima Época.* Semanario Judicial de la Federación y su Gaceta. Libro X (July 2012) p. 1877 (Mex.).

be considered a human right.[24] Based on this decision and constitutional amendments, she emphasized, most Mexican scholars have acknowledged that to admit *amparos* against arbitrators would be a violation of this human right covered by the Constitution.

c. Amparo actions

As a final remark concerning Mexican law, González Arrocha mentioned that the Mexican *amparo* law was modified in its entirety in April 2012 to expand the definition of "authority" and to cover private individuals when they carry out acts equivalent to those of authorities – therefore raising doubts as to whether arbitrators are and should be covered by this provision. The majority of Mexican scholars, she said, consider that this provision "endangered what was already an accepted view in Mexico that arbitrators are not considered authorities, not even de facto authorities".

In effect, an *amparo* action was filed against an arbitration under this novel provision right after its enactment; however, in October 2013, a district judge rejected it, reasoning that "arbitration only affects the legal environment of those that voluntarily put themselves under the jurisdiction of the tribunal", and, therefore, "arbitrators could not be considered authorities under the terms of the Mexican *amparo* law".[25] This, according to González Arrocha, seems to be the prevailing position in Mexico, particularly because to admit *amparos* against arbitrators would result in a "twisted irony" of accepting that an action would have been designed to protect human rights but used to violate another human right.

2. *El Salvador*

González Arrocha further reported that, in May 2013, a new public-private association law (*Ley de Asocios Público Privados*) was enacted in El Salvador. This law, she advised, establishes that arbitrations concerning disputes arising between State-owned entities and infrastructure private contractors shall be decided by law, as opposed to ex aequo et bono, and that no recourse shall be admitted against the arbitral award.

Additionally, she explained that the Salvadorian Arbitration Law was amended in 2009 to establish that appellate recourses in arbitration should only be decided by law. According to González Arrocha, the constitutionality of this provision was contested in 2010, and, in 2012, the Salvadorian Constitutional Court ruled that it was in accordance with the Constitution, reasoning that the parties are free to waive their rights to any

---

24. *Segundo Tribunal Colegiado en Materia Civil del Tercer Circuito. Amparo en revisión* 278/2012. *Alfonso Ponce Rodríguez et al.*, *Unanimidad de votos. Ponente*: Gerardo Domínguez. *Secretario*: Enrique Gómez Mendoza 13 September 2012. [Second Collegiate Civil Court of the Third Circuit. Revision appeal 278/2012 Unanimous vote. Reporter: Gerardo Domínguez. Secretary: Enrique Gómez Mendoza] 2004630. III.2o.C.6 K (10a.). *Tribunales Colegiados de Circuito. Décima Época.* Semanario Judicial de la Federación y su Gaceta. Libro XXV, Octubre de 2013, p. 1723 (Mex.).

25. *Juzgado 6° Dtto Civil, Amparo indirecto* [Sixth Civil Court, Indirect appeal] 434/2013, decision of 23 October 2013 (Mex.).

appeal against the arbitration award.[26] She contended, however, that this decision may have confused the concepts of appeal and annulment of arbitral awards, and that this would be one of the reasons why it would not be considered by most local scholars as a very favorable decision.

3.   *Costa Rica*

González Arrocha focused on the new arbitration law enacted in Costa Rica in 2011, which governs international arbitration by particularly mirroring the UNCITRAL Model Law on International Commercial Arbitration (henceforth the UNCITRAL Model Law). She asserted that since the enactment of the new arbitration framework, the Costa Rican Constitutional Court has repeatedly ruled that *amparo* actions are not admissible against arbitrators, acknowledging that the courts are not to be deemed as a "legally controlling organ with regard to what was made and resolved in dispute resolution proceedings", and that the annulment action is the only available remedy to the contracting parties. She also mentioned the court's express reasoning that, "If the applicant considers that the actions taken by the arbitral tribunal violate its right to due process and defense, it may request ... the annulment of the arbitral award."

4.   *Panama*

A new arbitration law has also been enacted in Panama, on 31 December 2013, said González Arrocha. She advised that the new Panamanian arbitration framework regulates both domestic and international arbitration, and that "it was built on the favorable experiences of the previous law, which entered into force in 1999". The main additions, she explained, were the amendments brought by – and mirrored in – the UNCITRAL Model Law concerning the form of the agreement and the granting of provisional measures. She also emphasized some other improvements brought by the law, such as the prohibition of judicial intervention during the arbitration, and an express recognition that arbitrators and the arbitration institutions' employees are not equivalent to public servants. The competence-competence principle and the arbitrability of public disputes were already included in the Panamanian Constitution and were simply restated by the new arbitration law, she advised.

As an overall conclusion, González Arrocha emphasized that, although there is always room for improvement, the arbitration-related news is generally positive in northern and central Latin America, and more information exchanges between judges and arbitration practitioners would be a crucial and very welcome step in this direction. These exchanges, she stated, "have proved to be very successful in countries where they have

---

26. *Corte Suprema de Justicia, Sala de lo Constitucional, Sentencia del proceso de inconstitucionalidad*: 11-2010: *Apelación Judicial en el arbitraje*, 30 de noviembre de 2011 [Supreme Court of Justice, Constitutional Chamber, decision in unconstitutionality proceeding, 11-2010: Judicial appeal in arbitration 30 November 2011] (El Sal.), available at <www.csj.gob.sv/ResSalaConst.nsf/3904032ec36cbce60625767f000945eb/121b08a3795681fe0625771200621282/$FILE/11-2010.pdf>.

taken place because they have helped build consensus with regard to the content and also application of these new laws".

Furthermore, according to González Arrocha, it is perhaps not the time to stop talking about *amparos* yet, but a decisive step further would be to impose a higher cost on the parties that file these inadequate actions – costs that, in her opinion, should be determined not only from the perspective of the time wasted by the parties in the arbitration, but also from consideration of the time (unnecessarily) wasted by the public judges and other public servants financed by taxpayers.

VI.   CRISTIÁN CONEJERO ROOS: RECENT INTERNATIONAL ARBITRATION DEVELOPMENTS IN SOUTHERN LATIN AMERICA

Cristián Conejero Roos, now a partner at Philippi Abogados in Santiago, Chile, addressed the international commercial arbitration-related innovations, legal framework changes, and relevant national court judgments in some southern Latin American countries. And, "for a change", he noted, Conejero Roos chose to entertain the audience only with good news about the region.

1.   Colombia

For Conejero Roos, Colombia is "in the making" of a new and very robust arbitration regime with the enactment of Law No. 1563/2012. This law, advised Conejero Roos, was considered a major change in the Colombian legal framework, considering that, prior to its enactment, approximately six different bodies of law governed arbitration in Colombia and created a number of uncertainties, for instance, about how all of those legal texts interacted. Further, he clarified that the new arbitration regime establishes a dual system (i.e., provides for different norms for domestic and international arbitration), and closely follows the UNCITRAL Model Law, with some significant variations.

One of the key differences with the Model Law, he explained, consists of a broader definition of international arbitration provided for in the new law, which incorporates the French criterion when establishing that the arbitration will be international "if it affects the interests of international commerce". Also of great importance, Conejero Roos mentioned that the new Colombian arbitration law provides expressly for (i) a prohibition against States' invoking their own internal laws to object to their capacity to be subject to arbitration, and (ii) the possibility when neither of the parties is domiciled in Colombia, for the parties to agree on waiving their right to set aside the award.

Concerning the judicial trends, Conejero Roos focused on two cases pertaining to the recognition of foreign arbitral awards, particularly, he said, because of Colombia's historic understanding that the provisions of both the Colombian Code of Civil Procedure and the 1958 New York Convention governed the exequatur of arbitral awards in the country. According to Conejero Roos, this practice – which started with

Sunwards Overseas, dated November 1992[27] – lasted for two decades and established higher standards for recognition of foreign arbitral awards as compared to the standards applicable under the New York Convention, the Panama Convention and other treaties.[28]

As an indicator of a turnaround in this regard, however, Conejero Roos mentioned that, in *Drummond Ltda. v. Ferrovías en Liquidación and Ferrocarriles Nacionales de Colombia (FENOCO)*, the Colombian Supreme Court, in December 2011, for the first time held that the exequatur of a foreign arbitral award should be analyzed only under the regime provided for by Art. V of the New York Convention, and clarified that the terms of the Code of Civil Procedure were not applicable to foreign arbitral awards.[29] Similarly, he reported that, in *Poligráfica C.A.V. v. Columbia Tecnológica*, in November 2013, the Colombian Supreme Court confirmed this understanding that the threshold under the Code of Civil Procedure would not be applicable. In this last case, on the other hand, there was an apparent applicability conflict between the Panama and New York Conventions; and the Colombian Supreme Court rightly held that the more specific of the conflicting treaties should apply, and, accordingly, applied the Panama Convention.[30]

2.   Peru

Conejero Roos described Peru as an "advanced student" in international arbitration, considering that for years it has been a pioneer in implementing new arbitration laws, such as the current one (the Legislative Decree No. 1071/2008), which, for him, incorporates "very innovative provisions". The sources for the Peruvian arbitration framework, he affirmed, were mostly the Swiss Code of International Private Law, the Spanish Arbitration Act, some relevant case law from the French courts, and international arbitration rules, such as the ICC Rules.

Among the Peruvian Arbitration Law's most relevant provisions, Conejero Roos gave special attention to its Art. 14, which – unusually, if compared to other national laws –

---

27. *Corte Suprema de Justicia* [C.S.J.], *Sala Civil* [Supreme Court, Civil Chamber], 20 November 1992, M.P.: H. Marín Naranjo, No. 472 (Colom.), available at <http://190.24.134.121/webcsj/Documentos/Civil/Exequ%C3%A1tur%20V.%20Final/Providencias/SE%20%2820%202011%201992%29%20Estados%20Unidos.pdf>, reprinted in ICCA *Yearbook Commercial Arbitration* XX (1995) p. 651 (Colombia no. 2) .

28. See Cristián CONEJERO ROOS, "The New York Convention in Latin America: Lessons From Recent Court Decisions", Global Arb. Rev., <http://globalarbitrationreview.com/reviews/13/sections/50/chapters/499/the-new-york-convention-latin-america-lessons-recent-court-decisions/> (last visited 8 May 2014).

29. *Corte Suprema de Justicia* [C.S.J.], *Sala Civil* [Supreme Court, Civil Chamber], 19 December 2011, M.P.: F. Giraldo Gutiérrez, Case no. 2008-01760-00 (Colom.), available at <http://www.oas.org/es/sla/ddi/docs/Colombia%20-%20Drummond%20Ltd%20v%20Ferrovias%20en%20Liquidacion,%20Ferrocariles%20Nacionales%20de%20Colombia%20S.A..pdf>.

30. *Corte Suprema de Justicia* [C.S.J.], *Sala Civil* [Supreme Court, Civil Chamber], 19 November 2013, M.P.: A. Solarte Rodríguez, Case no. 2008-00317-00 (Colom.), available at <http://190.24.134.121/webcsj/Documentos/Novedades/Archivo/civil/2013/INFORMATIVO%20NOVIEMBRE%202013/INFORMATIVO%20SENTENCIAS%20NOVIEMBRE%202013/SENTENCIAS/S-%2019-11-2013%20(1100102030002008-00317-00).doc>.

provides expressly for the possibility of extending the effects of the arbitration agreement to non-signatory parties when, by applying the good faith principle, "one comes to the conclusion that those parties are indeed considered parties to the agreement, because of their active and decisive participation in the negotiation, execution, performance or termination of the underlying contract containing the arbitration clause". The same provision, according to Conejero Roos, also establishes the extension to parties who derive rights or benefit from the underlying contract.[31]

While describing some interesting court precedents, Conejero Roos highlighted the so-called *María Julia* case, in which the Peruvian Constitutional Tribunal, in his words, "put an end to the *amparo* recourses against arbitral awards in Peru".[32] In fact, he described the issue of the use of *amparos* in arbitration cases as a systemic discussion also encountered in other Latin American countries, such as Colombia, Venezuela and Chile (where another constitutional remedy, named *queja*, is also discussed). According to Conejero Roos, *Maria Julia* was the first Peruvian decision clearly stating that the *amparo* cannot be used by a party to attack arbitral awards, except in very rare circumstances that generally are not present in a commercial arbitration. One of the main criticisms brought up by the court, he asserted, was that the *amparo* was being used as a second stage to attack arbitral awards that had already been unsuccessfully attacked through annulment proceedings. "That door is now closed, and this deserves recognition," he said.

The second case addressed by Conejero Roos dealt precisely with the previously mentioned Art. 14 of the Peruvian Arbitration Law, and, more interestingly, involved the possibility of one of the parties' piercing the corporate veil of the counterparty to submit non-signatory parties to arbitration when these parties acted fraudulently, de facto exercised rights and obtained benefits that would have benefited the signatory parties. Conejero Roos reported that in this case, *Langostinera Caleta Dorada and others v. TSG Peru*, the Peruvian Superior Court of Justice rejected an action to set aside the award on the grounds that (i) the pertinent circumstances fell squarely within the scope of Art. 14 of the Peruvian Arbitration Law, and (ii) the arbitrators are empowered to decide which parties they are entitled to exercise jurisdiction against.[33]

3.   Chile

When dealing with his home country, Conejero Roos identified Chile as "a country with a solid arbitration culture", largely because it has been using arbitration in the domestic setting for more than a century now, and has implemented a well-tested international

---

31. See Cristián CONEJERO ROOS and René IRRA DE LA CRUZ, "*La extensión del acuerdo arbitral a partes no signatarias en la ley de arbitraje peruana: algunas lecciones del derecho comparado*", Lima Arb. (2012-2013, no. 5) at p. 56, available at <www.limaarbitration.net/LAR5/Revista.pdf>.

32. *Tribunal Constitucional de Peru* [Constitutional Court of Peru], *Sociedad Minera de Responsabilidad Ltda. Maria Julia*, STC 00142-2011-PA, 21 September 2011 (Peru), available at <www.tc.gob.pe/jurisprudencia/2011/00142-2011-AA.html>.

33. *Corte Superior de Justicia de Lima* [Superior Court of Justice of Lima], *Langostinera Caleta Dorada S.A.C. v. TSG Perú S.A.C*, Case no. 451-2009, 5 March 2013 (Peru), available at <www.forseti.pe/sites/default/files/19.pdf>.

arbitration law. He stressed that there are a good number of Chilean precedents in which the courts very restrictively applied the grounds to set aside an arbitral award, for instance. As an example of this approach, Conejero Roos mentioned that, in *Foods S.A. v. Domino's Pizza Internacional Inc.*, in 2012, the Santiago Appellate Court held that an "alleged erroneous application of the law is not a ground that allows a court to set aside the award, even if the court does not agree or concur with the reasoning provided in the award". According to Conejero Roos, the court also clarified that an alleged mistake in applying certain provisions of the Chilean Civil Code by a foreign sole arbitrator "would not amount to violation of Chilean public policy".[34]

Precisely concerning the application of the concept of public policy, Conejero Roos mentioned that the Chilean courts have interpreted such a notion very narrowly, as in *Pedro Vergara Varas Pedro v. Vasco Costa Ramírez*. In this case, according to him, in September 2013, the Santiago Appellate Court positively identified public policy "as referring only to violations of extreme gravity to principles and fundamental rules of Chilean law from a procedural standpoint, such as the right of due process and equal treatment, or substantive standpoint, such as the sanction of the abuse of rights or the respect to obligations undertaken by the State with other States or international organizations".[35]

4.   Argentina

Finally, Conejero Roos characterized Argentina as a country with "mixed realities" with respect to international arbitration, especially because, although arbitration therein is governed by outdated provisions of the Argentinean Commercial and Civil Procedure Codes, according to Conejero Roos, "yet, somehow Argentinean courts managed to build an arbitration case law that to a large extent is friendly to arbitration". He also contended that most practitioners have been "unfair" to Argentinean judges, and that it should be taken into consideration that Argentinean commercial arbitration has been "haunted by the ghost of the Argentinean State's experience in investment arbitration". This misconception with regard to the Argentinean approach towards international arbitration, said Conejero Roos, has led to several bad precedents in commercial cases

---

34. *Corte de Apelaciones* [C. Apel.] [Courts of Appeals], 9 October 2012, *Foods S.A. v. Domino's Pizza Internacional Inc.*, case no.: 1420-2010 (Chile) [unpublished].
35. *Corte de Apelaciones* [C. Apel.] [Courts of Appeals], 9 September 2013, *Vergara Pedro v. Ramírez Vasco*", case no.: 1971-2012 (Chile) [unpublished].

that involve State instrumentalities, such as in *Cartellone*,[36] *Yacyretá*,[37] and *Astilleros Santiago*.[38]

He noted, however, that recent Argentinean cases are in the majority very supportive to international arbitration, such as (i) *Oliva v. Disco*, dated March 2012,[39] in which the Appellate Court of Córdoba held, in the context of an action to set aside an award dealing with the 2001 Emergency Legislation, that the arbitrators are empowered to rule on constitutionality issues that may arise within the course of an arbitration, and (ii) *Aronna and Calcagno v. Petrobras Argentina*, dated November 2013,[40] in which the Buenos Aires Appellate Court ruled that "the lack of decision on certain issues raised by the parties does not render the award null, unless the tribunal has omitted issues that are essential for the proper adjudication of the dispute".

In a brief conclusion, Conejero Roos described arbitration practice in southern Latin America as a "real work in process", but one that also "gives us a great outlook for the future".

VII.   JOÃO BOSCO LEE: RECENT INTERNATIONAL ARBITRATION DEVELOPMENTS IN BRAZIL

The final panelist, João Bosco Lee, a partner at Lee Taube Gabardo Advogados and Professor at Positivo University in Curitiba, Brazil, portrayed international arbitration developments in the "Brazilian continent", as it was referred to by Cristián Conejero Roos. Lee devoted his presentation to the ongoing reform of the Brazilian Arbitration Law, which is in the process of being amended by a bill in progress before the Brazilian congress.

As an introduction, Lee emphasized the evolution of Brazil towards international and domestic arbitration, which is reflected, for instance, by the increasing number of arbitration specialists, more than a hundred of them attending the ICCA 2014 Miami Congress. "I am sure that at every table, you will find a Brazilian sitting beside you," he said. Lee also illustrated Brazil's "huge development" by referring to the Brazilian Arbitration Act enacted in 1996, the ratification of the New York Convention in 2002,

---

36. *Corte Suprema de Justicia de la Nación* [CSJN] [National Supreme Court of Justice], 1/6/2004, *José Cartellone Construcciones Civiles S.A. v. Hidroeléctrica Norpatagónica S.A. / proceso de conocimiento*" (Arg.), available at <www.limaarbitration.net/pdf/argentina/corte-suprema/cartellone-v-hidroelectrica.pdf>.
37. *Juzgado Nacional de Primera Instancia* [1a Inst.] [National Court of First Jurisdiction], 27 September 2004, *Entidad Binacional Yacyretá v. Eriday / proceso de conocimiento* (Arg.), available at <www.limaarbitration.net/pdf/argentina/yacireta-cuatelar.pdf>.
38. *Cámara Nacional de Apelaciones en lo Federal y Contencioso Administrativo de la Capital Federal* [CNFed.] [National Court of Appeals in Federal and Administrative Litigation of the Federal Capital], 30 August 2007, *Milantic Trans S.A. v. Ministerio de la Producción* (Arg.).
39. Tribunal Superior de Justicia de la Provincia de Córdoba [Trib. Sup. Cba.] [Superior Court of Justice of the Province of Córdoba], 13 March 2012, *Oliva, Oscar S. v. Disco, S.A.* (Arg.).
40. *Cámara Nacional de Apelaciones en lo Comercial de la Capital Federal* [CNCom.] [National Court of Commercial Appeals of the Federal Capital], 5 November 2013, *Alberto Angel, Aronna v. Petrobras Argentina SA* (Arg.).

and the ICC statistics indicating Brazil's solid position as the fourth-ranked country worldwide in terms of the most parties in ICC arbitrations.[41]

Then, triggering the core topic of his presentation, Lee asserted that, "[E]ven though arbitration in Brazil is doing pretty well, the Brazilian Arbitration Act is not perfect; nothing is perfect, of course." He indicated that there are some gaps and a number of specific provisions therein that could be improved, but that, in his opinion, "the Brazilian courts, especially the Superior Court of Justice, have filled the gaps and have interpreted the Arbitration Act according to the principle of *favor arbitrandum*". The question Lee put to the audience, therefore, was "[D]oes Brazil need a new arbitration law?", and the resounding answer he gave to this question was "No, we do not need a new law."

Lee reported, nevertheless, that the Brazilian authorities had decided that a new bill should be produced, and a twenty-one-member commission was created in 2011 for this purpose. He described the commission as "very eclectic," composed of judges, practitioners and government members. More importantly, he emphasized, "[W]e can see that half of the members of the commission are arbitration practitioners." The commission's decision, according to Lee, was not to enact a whole new arbitration law, but merely to review some very specific provisions, the core proposed changes of which he summarized in three main groups: (i) "filling the gaps", (ii) "consolidation of the case law and the practice", and (iii) "correction of mistakes and errors".

1. *"Filling the Gaps"*

Lee devoted great attention to the bill's suggested inclusion of an express provision authorizing the State and State-owned entities to participate in arbitration proceedings. According to him, Brazilian law currently does not establish a general rule in this regard, and this subject is apparently governed by the *Lage* case, ruled on by the Brazilian Supreme Federal Court in the 1970s,[42] and provisions established in the public concession and public-private partnership laws. He also mentioned that the Brazilian bill provides for new and specific norms to govern consumer and labor arbitrations, as well as the running of the statute of limitations in arbitration.

2. *"Consolidation of the Case Law and the Practice"*

With regard to the granting of interim and urgent measures, Lee explained that the bill intends to revoke the current controlling provision, which most consider rather confusing and misleading, and to create a new provision consolidating the threshold that

---

41. See 2012 *ICC Statistical Report*, ICC Int'l Court of Arb. Bulletin (2013) (report providing a statistical overview of ICC arbitration and ADR in 2012), available at <www.iccwbo.org/Products-and-Services/Arbitration-and-ADR/Articles/2013/New-release-from-the-ICC-International-Court-of-Arbitration-Bulletin/>.

42. *Supremo Tribunal Federal* (S.T.F.) [Federal Supreme Court], No. AI 52.181-GB, *Relator* [Reporting Justice]: Bilac Pinto, 14 November 1973, 68, Revista Trimestral de Jurisprudência [R.T.J.], 382 (Braz.), available at <www.stf.jus.br/portal/inteiroTeor/obterInteiroTeor.asp?id=22084>.

the Superior Court of Justice applied in *Itarumã*.[43] According to Lee, this proposed provision, in short, is aimed at confirming the current common understanding in Brazil in the sense that: (i) a party may resort to the national courts to request interim and urgent measures only before the constitution of the arbitral tribunal, and, (ii) after the constitution, the arbitral tribunal holds exclusive jurisdiction to decide on such requests. He also reported that the bill aims to create the "arbitration letter" (*carta arbitral*), a procedural instrument through which the arbitral tribunal would formally request the national courts to enforce an interim order that has been granted.

Moreover, for Lee, other positive consolidations intended by the new bill are the express authorization for tribunals to render partial awards (although, he contended, the practice in Brazil for years has already admitted this possibility), and the option for the parties to extend the deadline for requesting the tribunal to correct the arbitral award.

3.   *"Mistakes and Errors"*

Among others, a major mistake of the current Brazilian Arbitration Law, Lee asserted, consists of its Art. 25, which permits the tribunal to stay the proceedings and submit the dispute to the national courts if a non-arbitrable matter arises during the arbitration. He reported that this provision has been highly prejudicial in a number of cases and is intended to be revoked by the upcoming law.

Finally, he explained that the bill was approved by the Brazilian Senate in February 2014 and is now in progress before the House of Representatives, which has already made nine amendment propositions (most of them concerning the involvement of the State and State-owned entities in arbitration proceedings).

Lee predicted that in 2014 Brazil will probably have a new arbitration law modifying the current one, and advised the audience that it is most likely that every arbitration practitioner will eventually be involved in cases pertaining to Brazilian parties, seats or arbitrators. "Don't lose the opportunity to make a new Brazilian friend," he said, referring to the "almost certain" upcoming opportunities for arbitration practitioners worldwide to act in cooperation with or before Brazilian lawyers or other experts.

VIII.   CONCLUSION: NO NEWS IS GOOD NEWS?

The highlights of the panelists' presentations summarized above plainly reflect the confident spirit that marked each of the lectures. Despite tackling different realities – all of them from diverse standpoints – the panelists' satisfaction was evident regarding the major developments in the Latin American region in the past decades, as was their optimism regarding further short- and long-term improvements in most countries in the region.

---

43. *Superior Tribunal de Justiça* (S.T.J.) [Superior Court of Justice], Resp. [Appeal] No. 1,297,974-RJ, *Relator* [Reporting Justice]: Nancy Andrighi, 12 June 2012 (Braz.), available at <https://ww2.stj.jus.br/revistaeletronica/ita.asp?registro=201102409919&dt_publicacao=1 9/06/2012>.

"Bad news" may come from any part of the world, not only from developing regions. What these six leading practitioners successfully demonstrated in their presentations, however, is that an isolated unfavorable case in Latin America you may hear of in the future will not necessarily represent a setback, still less indicate that the region is an unsuitable atmosphere for foreign investment. This Report manifestly attests that, even though a great deal of work must still be done, the region has already built a very favorable and surprisingly resilient framework in respect of law enforcement, investment protection and healthy commercial relations. This scenario certainly will not be disrupted easily.

Lunch Seminar

Power of Arbitration to Fill Gaps in the Arbitration Agreement and Underlying Contract

"Gap Filling" by Arbitrators

Alan Scott Rau[*]

TABLE OF CONTENTS | Page

> *"[The arbitral tribunal] proceeded as if it had the authority of a common-law court to develop what it viewed as the best rule to applied in such a situation ... [and] the conclusion is inescapable that [it] simply imposed its own conception of sound policy."*[1]

I. THE NOTION OF "GAPS"

When I was first approached to talk on this topic – after of course the initial flush of pleasure at having been asked – there set in almost immediately a certain amount of uncertainty and indeed apprehension. I have in fact been trying – with incomplete success – to come to terms ever since with everything that lurks behind the announced title – and for that matter, with the entire subject matter.

For the notion of a "gap" is an evanescent one, one which can – and often does – mean everything and nothing.

• It could perhaps be said that the very notion of a "gap" is simply incoherent – that the very concept of "silence" or "lack of agreement" is problematical and somewhat naive – for once we are satisfied that the parties have entered into a "contract", there can by definition be *no "gaps"*. Indeed, "by its legal definition a 'contract' *cannot be incomplete*" (emphasis added).[2] As Justice Breyer bluffly remarked, there is "no such answer" that a contract is "truly silent" – for if "it doesn't say, you try to figure [it] out".[3]

---

[*] Mark G. and Judy G. Yudof Chair in Law, University of Texas at Austin.

1. *Stolt-Nielsen S.A. v. Animalfeeds Int'l Corp.*, 130 S.Ct. 1758, 1769 (2010).
2. That is, the existing contractual framework is necessarily all-encompassing, providing an answer to any question at all that may arise with respect to the rights of the parties: The Uniform Commercial Code (UCC), for example, defines *"contract"* as "the total legal obligation that results from the parties' agreement as determined by [the Code]", *"including all the gap fillers"*. Omri BEN-SHAHAR, "'Agreeing to Disagree': Filling Gaps in Deliberately Incomplete Contracts", 2004 WISC. L. REV. p. 389 at p. 399 n. 25.
3. The actual dialogue, a little less coherent given the constraints of oral argument, went like this:

   "Mr. WAXMAN [counsel for the petitioners]: There is a separate statutory question that arises if

• Or perhaps it could be said that, by contrast, there are *nothing but "gaps"* – that unless the parties have taken the pains to construct an infinite agreement, mapping onto every conceivable state of the world, likely or unlikely, known or unknown – a contract that stretches out to track the real world as if in a story by Borges – then courts must be free to reconstruct or interpolate.[4] "If contracts had to be complete, there would be no contracts at all."[5] For example:

> • Where invitations for bids to supply equipment contain detailed specifications of the goods – and notes that certain manufacturers are "approved sources" or that the goods "may be purchased" from them – have the parties said anything at all – or have they simply been silent – on the subject of whether the goods must actually be manufactured by the named firms so that identical components are excluded? If they failed to expressly address the issue, what are the consequences?[6]
> • Where the parties have entered into a contract granting a licensee the right to produce television shows based on a series of children's books, is there a "gap" in the agreement – that is, have the parties failed to tell the decisionmaker whether or not the licensee is permitted to produce and distribute videos – even if this is a technology that was "not in existence at the times the rights were given"? Have they failed to address the question?[7]

---

the answer to the contract question is [that] there is no meeting of the minds. It is truly silent –
JUSTICE BREYER: If there is no such answer –
MR. WAXMAN: Excuse me?
JUSTICE BREYER: I thought, in contracts, there is no such answer. When you interpret a contract and it doesn't say, you try to figure out – I used to be taught that; probably I am way out-of-date – you try to figure out what a reasonable party would have intended."

Oral Argument, Stolt-Nielsen S.A. v. Animalfeeds Int'l Corp., 2009 WL 4662509 at *5. Cf. *id.* at *17 (Justice Scalia: "I really don't understand what it means to say that the contract does not cover it … [I]f the contract is silent, either the court or the arbitrator has to decide, what is the consequence of that silence, in light of the background, in light of implied understandings.").

See also Charles FRIED, *Contract As Promise: A Theory of Contractual Obligation* (1981) p. 69 ("There is no bare flesh showing, as it were, when relations between persons are not covered by contractual clothing. These relations take place under the general mantle of the law").

4. "I once had a case in which the contract was 2000 pages long but did not cover the issue that the parties were litigating." Richard A. POSNER, "The Law and Economics of Contract Interpretation", 83 Tex. L. Rev. (2005) p. 1581 at p. 1606.
5. Daniel MARKOVITS, *Contract Law and Legal Methods* (2012) p. 667 ("to address every contingency precisely, would increase the costs of contracting so that they came to swamp whatever surplus the contractual exchange promised to generate"). See also POSNER, supra fn. 4 at p. 1583 ("perfect foresight is infinitely costly" and "even in a setting of perfect foresight, … parties may rationally decide not to provide for a contingency, preferring to economize on negotiation costs by delegating completion of the contract to the courts should the contingency materialize").
6. See *WPC Enterprises, Inc. v. U.S.*, 323 F.2d 874, 879 (Ct. Claims 1964).
7. See *Rey v. Lafferty*, 990 F.2d 1379 (1st Cir. 1993) ("ambiguous phraseology [may] mask an absence of intent rather than a hidden intent which the court simply must 'find'"); see also Robert HAMILTON, Alan Scott RAU and Russell WEINTRAUB, *Cases and Materials on Contracts* (2nd edn. 1992) p. 365 ("the occurrence of unexpected events or changes in circumstances usually places

• Where the parties have entered into a lease of rooms overlooking the planned route of a coronation procession, is there a "gap" in the agreement – that is, have the parties failed to tell the decisionmaker what to do – in the event that the King suddenly falls ill with an attack of appendicitis?[8] Have they failed to address the question?

• Where a father has made a support agreement for the benefit of his minor son, agreeing in 1937 to pay him US$ 1200 per year "until [the son] enters "into some college, university or higher institution of learning," is there a "gap" in the agreement – have the parties failed to tell the decisionmaker what to do – in the case where the son finishes high school and is (since the country is at war) immediately inducted into the army?[9] If there is a "blind spot" here, have the parties failed to address it?

• Where the parties entered into a "requirements" agreement by which the buyer would buy "solely" from the seller all his "requirements" of propane for use in its fleet of trucks, is there a "gap" in the agreement – have the parties failed to tell the decisionmaker what to do – if the buyer suddenly decides not to order any propane from the seller because he has decided not to convert its fleet to propane?[10]

• Where an agreement lacks any dispute resolution clause, is there a "gap" in the agreement with respect to arbitration – that is, have the parties failed to tell us whether they are committed anyway to submit future disputes to an arbitral tribunal? Is this a matter that the parties have failed to address? And if so, may we be justified in concluding that despite their "silence", the "gap" should be filled with an arbitration clause?[11] And if the answer is "yes", would this be as a result of

• an exercise of contractual "interpretation" grounded in their likely intent?[12]

---

great strain on language that was drafted with an entirely different (and often more modest) problem in mind").

8. *Krell v. Henry*, [1903] 2 K.B. 740 (C.A.).
9. *Spaulding v. Morse*, 76 N.E.2d 137 (1947).
10. *Empire Gas Corp. v. American Bakeries Co.*, 840 F.2d 1333 (7th Cir. 1988).
11. Obviously we leave to one side here any requirements touching on the formal validity of such an agreement, a subject that has nothing to do with the problem of interpretation. See "Explanatory Note by the UNCITRAL Secretariat on the 1985 Model Law on International Commercial Arbitration as amended in 2006", paras. 19-20 (the original Art. 7 of the Law "was amended in 2006 to better conform to international contract practices"; two options are now open to enacting states, both of which permit arbitration agreements to be "entered into in any form (e.g., including orally)").
12. Art. 2-207 of the UCC is suggestive here. In the common "battle of the forms" scenario, an offer may say nothing at all about arbitration – but the second form, which is assumed to be an "acceptance", contains an arbitration clause. The Code's contract-formation mechanism will lead to the conclusion that an arbitration agreement has nevertheless become part of the contract, at least where the arbitration clause is deemed not to be a "material alteration" of the offer. This question of "material alteration" will hinge on whether the clause will cause "unreasonable surprise" or "hardship" to the offeror – and that, in turn, will depend on whether arbitration would be outside the scope of usual "trade practice"; see, e.g., Alan Scott RAU, et al., *Processes of Dispute*

• the crafting of an alternative "default rule", grounded in the taken-for-granted nature of arbitration agreements in international transactions – a working presumption that would shift the burden to the objecting party to show that no such agreement exists?[13] Or by contrast, would it be

---

Resolution: The Role of Lawyers, 4th edn. (2006) p. 677 ("the idea seems to be that a clause which is sufficiently important and unusual that a party would expect to have his attention specifically directed to it, should not come into the contract by way of a form that is by hypothesis commonly unread"); *Aceros Prefabricados, S.A. v. TradeArbed, Inc.*, 282 F.3d 92, 102 (2d Cir. 2002) ("unrebutted evidence that arbitration is standard practice within the steel industry" "precludes" the buyer from demonstrating "surprise or hardship"; therefore the arbitration provisions in the seller's form became part of the contract); *Oceanconnect.com, Inc. v. Chemoil Corp.*, 2008 WL 194360 at *4, *5 (S.D. Tex.) ("numerous cases reflect the frequent use of arbitration in maritime contracts"; this "evidence of trade usage and the parties' course of dealing defeats a claim of surprise" and thus of "material alteration").

Note that when this becomes a plausible reading, the inference of the offeror's actual consent to arbitration, even though never made explicit, seems irresistible.

13. Cf. Gary BORN, *International Commercial Arbitration*, vol. 1 (2009) p. 653 ("because international arbitration is the natural and preferred means of resolving international business disputes", "there are very serious reasons to presume, as a general matter and absent contrary indications, that commercial parties are predisposed to enter into international arbitration agreements"). On whether as an empirical matter this suggestion should be treated as "majoritarian default", compare Theodore EISENBERG and Geoffrey P. MILLER, "The Flight from Arbitration: An Empirical Study of Ex Ante Arbitration Clauses in the Contracts of Publicly Held Companies", 56 Depaul L. Rev. (2007) p. 335 at pp. 351-352 (studying contracts contained as exhibits to Form 8-K filings with the Securities and Exchange Commission (SEC); while arbitration clauses do indeed appear more frequently in international contracts than in domestic ones, nevertheless, "the international contracts, like the domestic contracts, contain a low absolute rate of arbitration clauses: only about 20% of international contracts contain them"), with Christopher DRAHOZAL and Stephen J. WARE, "Why Do Businesses Use (or Not Use) Arbitration Clauses?", 25 Ohio St. J. Disp. Resol. (2010) p. 433 (the contracts studied by Eisenberg and Miller are not "a reasonable sample of what sophisticated parties specify ex ante regarding arbitration"; "regulations defining what contracts must be filed along with SEC filings effectively limit the Eisenberg and Miller sample to … unusual contracts unlikely to include arbitration clauses while excluding more typical contracts that are more likely to provide for arbitration").

See also Jack GRAVES, "Court Litigation Over Arbitration Agreements: Is It Time for a New Default Rule?", 23 Amer. Rev. Int'l Arb. (2012) p. 113 (since "arbitration is almost certainly the normative method of resolving disputes in the majority of international commercial transactions", "this normative reality should be recognized through a default legal rule providing for arbitration in the absence of any agreement to the contrary"; "parties to a particular contract may be deemed to have impliedly consented to certain majoritarian normative terms").

Professor Graves goes on to add that in fact, "as a practical matter", US courts "have already left consent far behind in deciding issues of arbitral jurisdiction" – pointing to the fact that "a party whose contractual consent is induced by fraud is deemed to have 'consented' to the arbitration clause within the main contract", *Id.* at p. 129. Now I have more or less abandoned, as futile, my longstanding practice of protesting common misunderstandings of *Prima Paint* – but perhaps just this one last time? All right: The notion of "separability" *does not in the slightest degree* suggest that consent to an arbitration clause is "implied"; all it does is to simply leave the matter open for a discrete inquiry – allocating *to the arbitrator* the question of the validity of the overall agreement, *but reserving to the court the question of consent to the process*; see Alan Scott RAU, "Everything You Really Need to Know About 'Separability' in Seventeen Simple Propositions", 14 Amer. Int'l

• the creation of a wholly new substantive right?[14]

(And does it really matter?)

When we are working through problems like this in the context of arbitration, the difficulties become far more acute – for

• there are our ordinary concerns aimed at giving effect to *contractual intention*, if we can locate it, and these intertwine with
• our concerns aimed at giving effect to *the choice of private decisionmakers* – that is, at preserving the powers that the parties, and thus the state, have entrusted to them.

I think that with respect to each of these, the values of private autonomy should be mutually reinforcing, and thus should tend to lead us in precisely the same direction – but as the epigraph to this paper suggests, not everyone sees it quite that way. Not long ago the US Supreme Court, in reviewing an arbitration award, performed an elaborate riff on the significance of "silence" (which I take to be a related metaphor), in an attempt to identify the outer limits of arbitral authority in "gap filling" – and with a lack of success that was quite dizzying.

Here by contrast is my "take" on the subject. I fear that it will be seen right away that the approach I take is inescapably that of a common-law lawyer, and what is worse, one tainted by, and cabined within, all the Legal Realist attitudes of the 1930s and 1940s. I have struggled against this tendency – I have tried to be a philosopher – but you may notice immediately how vain the struggle has been.[15]

Arb. (2003) p. 1 ("under any sensible reading of *Prima Paint,* a person is only bound to arbitrate a dispute if he has agreed to do so" and "'agreement' here has no meaning that is in any way different from the use of the term every day in the realm of Contract"; the point is that the possible invalidity of the container contract "will frequently", but "need not", affect the validity of the consent to arbitrate). See also Alan Scott RAU, "Arbitral Jurisdiction and the Dimensions of 'Consent'", 24 Arb. Int'l (2008) pp. 199, 200, 204-206 (despite "separability", the question of core consent "to arbitrate anything at all" is for the courts).

14. Cf. Giles CUNIBERTI, "Beyond Contract: The Case for Default Arbitration in International Commercial Disputes", 32 Fordham Int'l L.J. (2009) p. 417, who suggests that states could "amend their legislation in order to make arbitration available in the absence of any agreement on dispute resolution"; supposedly it is one virtue of this model that granting parties the right unilaterally to invoke arbitration, would cause arbitration to "lose its contractual foundation" altogether. But one consequence is that since the entire "contractual foundation of arbitration disappears", the proposed model "could not benefit from the New York Convention". *Id.* at p. 482. It is only at this point, as I have noted previously, that I begin to detect "considerable analytical confusion". Alan Scott RAU, "Understanding (and Misunderstanding) 'Primary Jurisdiction'", 21 Amer. Rev. Int'l Arb. (2010) p. 161 fn. 294; bargaining in the presence of known default rules can hardly be deemed non-consensual.

15. Dr. Johnson was once reunited with a boyhood friend whom he had not seen in many years. "I have tried too in my time," said his friend, "to be a philosopher, but I don't know how, cheerfulness was always breaking in." James BOSWELL, *The Life of Samuel Johnson* (Everyman 1992) p. 212.

II.   FATAL "GAPS" AND THE ROLE OF THE ARBITRATOR

Now there may exist cases where "gaps" may be so extensive, or so critical, that the very notion of private autonomy loses any possible legitimacy. These are the true "gaps": Here there is a failure of agreement that may be fatal in the sense that – as in some low-budget horror film – the cracks spread so widely as to swallow up any pretense of a contract.[16] Contracts students sometimes refer to such cases as exemplifying a lack of a "meeting of the minds" – but then have to be reminded that our "minds" are the least seemly thing that we should be talking about. The point is simply that in the event we should find it impossible to construct any story at all with respect to what the parties have agreed to – if there are inadequate manifestations of mutual assent – then neither has any right to impose duties on the other – and this may be true whether the lack of assent is caused by

• a "draftsman's blind spot" hidden by unconscious assumptions (concentrating on one problem to the point that no attention is paid to other potential problems);
• an unsuspected latent ambiguity leaving the parties at cross purposes;[17]

---

16. Cf. *WPC Enterprises, Inc.*, supra fn. 6 ("there was no subjective coming-together, it is true, but an enforceable agreement came into being nevertheless"; "it is a normal characteristic" of this class of cases that the "gap has not been permitted to swallow the whole contract except perhaps where the gulf is far closer to the bounds of the entire consensual perimeter than here").

17. See, e.g., Restatement of Contracts, Second, Sect. 20 ("There is no manifestation of mutual assent to an exchange if the parties attach materially different meanings to their manifestations and (a) neither party knows or has reason to know the meaning attached by the other; or (b) each party knows or each party has reason to know the meaning attached by the other."). Or, perhaps, putting them in the position of the proverbial "ships that pass in the night", as in the classic case of *Raffles v. Wichelaus*, [1864] EWHC Exch J19 ("contract" called for the delivery of cotton "to arrive ex Peerless from Bombay", but neither party apparently realized that there were two ships of that name, one departing in October and the other departing in December).
    Endless variations: One is presented by a case like *WPC Enterprises, Inc.*, supra fn. 6: Here, the parties' different interpretations had in fact surfaced prior to contracting – but a higher-level misunderstanding occurred; "compounding that confusion, they discussed the issue with each other in such a way that each thought, but this time without good reason, it had obtained the other's acquiescence in its chosen reading. The impasse became unmistakably plain when it was too late."
    And sometimes, by contrast, the parties may equally be at cross purposes when such "mutually-reinforced obscurity" is *absent* – that is, they may at all times remain painfully aware of their contradictory understandings of a contractual term. In such circumstances the Restatement seems to suggest that there is a lack of mutual assent and thus an absence of any enforceable contractual obligation. This was the fact pattern in *LCC v. Henry Boot & Sons*, [1959] 1 W.L.R. 1069 (H.L.): In a contract for the construction of apartment buildings, the question was presented whether an escalator clause calling for an increase in payments in the event of increases in the "rates of wages" included increases in the costs of "holiday stamps". The parties had entered into the contract "both perfectly aware of their opposing views on the subject", but the House of Lords bluffly rejected the assertion that on account of this difference of views "there was no consensus ad idem".

• a willingness to be content with amorphous, meaningless formulae expressive of nothing but a vague benevolent intention;[18]

• or, more troublingly, by a conscious preference to set aside remote but potentially troublesome contingencies in the hope that they will simply go away – or that if necessary, a court can be found to make the difficult choices that the parties themselves would rather avoid.[19]

These are all cases on the margins of contractual behavior, or indeed at its outer limits – and there are doubtless far fewer of such cases than there used to be. In any event a rather naive "contract/no contract" dichotomy is infinitely less interesting than two related points which are critical to our discussion:

(1) As a doctrinal matter, in normal discourse, a challenge on any of these grounds, if taken seriously, would suggest that there is simply "no agreement to which the parties could be bound" that "exists" – or so commentators regularly tell us.[20] But despite the continuing cackle that gravely insists on the formalistic and conceptual distinction

---

18. See, e.g., *Varney v. Ditmars*, 111 N.E. 822 (1916) ("if you boys will go on and continue the way you have been and get me out of this trouble and get these jobs started that were in the office three years, on the 1st of next January I will close my books and give you a fair share of my profits"; held, this is "not only uncertain, but [is] necessary affected by so many other facts that are in themselves indefinite and uncertain that the intention of the parties is pure conjecture"; "the courts cannot aid parties in such a case when they are unable or unwilling to agree upon the terms of their own proposed contract").

19. See, e.g., *Joseph Martin Jr. Delicatessen, Inc. v. Schumacher*, 417 N.E.2d 541 (N.Y. 1981) ("Tenant may renew this lease for an additional period of five years at annual rentals to be agreed upon"; held, tenant's action for specific performance dismissed; the renewal clause contains no "methodology for determining the rent", nor does it "invite recourse to an objective extrinsic event, condition, or standard on which the amount was made to depend"; "neither tenant nor landlord is bound to any formula").

I say these cases are more troubling because while courts are increasingly willing to enforce contracts despite the fact that material terms may have been left open, the fact that the *parties have expressly identified a possible hurdle to agreement* may suggest that they were unwilling to submit to a term supplied by some third party; cf. MARKOVITS, supra fn. 5 at p. 702 ("it is one thing for the parties to a negotiation simply to leave a term out on their way to agreement, it is quite another for them to agree to postpone negotiations concerning a term and to proceed to other facets of their negotiations, subject to subsequent agreement on the postponed matter"); BEN-SHAHAR, supra fn. 2 at p. 395 (with "agreements to agree" "it is not the materiality of the terms per se that prevents gap filling, but rather the fact that the parties explicitly identified them as the subject matter for further affirmative agreement", creating the possible inference that "they do not yet intend to be bound").

20. E.g., Marvin A. CHIRELSTEIN, *Concepts and Case Analysis in the Law of Contracts*, 3rd edn. p. 35 (Foundation Press 1998). Cf. G. RAU, et al., *Cours de Droit Civil Français* [Aubry and Rau]. 5th edn. (1897) p. 180 and fn. 3 ("We must not confuse transactions that are void [*nuls*] with those that are non-existent [*inexistants ou non avenus*].... If there are missing those factual elements that are presupposed by the very nature of the transaction – if it is logically impossible even to imagine the existence of the transaction in the absence of those elements – then we have a transaction that is not only void, but one that simply never existed.... So for example *one cannot conceive of a contract without the agreement of the parties, nor a sale without the goods sold or without a price*").

between notions of "existence" and of "validity"[21] – and despite ineradicable misunderstandings with respect to the implications of "separability" – such challenges *must not be taken to impair any contractual duty to arbitrate* – and so they should be entrusted *to the arbitrators themselves* for decision:

After all, parties who had repressed (or deferred consideration of) possible ambiguities, might still plausibly have gambled that should an ambiguity surface, they would be able to persuade the ultimate decisionmaker of the merits of their own interpretation – and might plausibly have preferred this decisionmaker to be an

---

21. I have written that "ingenious riffs on the metaphysical distinction between contract 'invalidity' and contract 'nonexistence' have long been a stable of Continental legal learning". "Its tendency to take metaphor for reality, its personification of legal concepts, its characterization of doctrine in terms of what is 'unthinkable' or 'impossible' – all of this exemplifies the worst excesses of formalism." Alan Scott RAU, "'Separability' in the United States Supreme Court", 1 Stockholm Int'l Arb. Rev. (2006) p. 1 at p. 18; see also *id.* at p. 19 ("the whole notion of 'nonexistence' is not only sterile and purely verbal – but what is worse, is completely unnecessary"). For examples, see Pieter SANDERS, "*L'autonomie de la clause compromissoire*" in *Hommage à Frédéric Eisemann* (1978) p. 31 at pp. 34-35 (one must distinguish between the "invalidity" [*nullité*] of the contract and the "complete absence [*inexistence*] of the contract"; "if there is no contract at all, any legal foundation for the powers of the arbitrators is equally lacking"); Eric LOQUIN, Note [to *Société Pia Investments v. Société L & B Cassia, Cour de Cassation*, 1990], 1992 J. Droit Int'l (Clunet) 170, 173 ("the arbitration clause [can] have no existence when the contract, which contains it, [is] itself non-existent"; "it is difficult to see how the parties could have bound themselves to arbitrate over a contract to which they had never consented"); *Sojuznefteexport v. Joc Oil Ltd.* (Bermuda), ICCA *Yearbook Commercial Arbitration* XV (1990) p. 384 at pp. 406, 430 (1990) (Ct. of App. Bermuda 1989) ("borrowing Prospero's language, was the sale contract the baseless fabric of a vision, insubstantial (i.e., non-existent) or was it in the more prosaic language of the law, something which mundane lawyers describe as an invalid contract?").

Happily, French jurisprudence and doctrine do seem in recent years to have retreated from such conceptualism. See *Société Omenex v. Hugon*, [2006] Rev. de l'Arb. 103, 105 (*Cour de Cassation*, 25 October 2005) (given the "autonomy" of the arbitration clause in international transactions, "neither the invalidity nor the inexistence of the container contract affect it"); Jean-Baptiste RACINE, Note, *id.* at pp. 106, 124 (a "turnaround" in the case law; it must now be considered a "given" [*acquise*] in French arbitration law that a claim alleging the non-existence of the main contract does not impair the jurisdiction of the arbitrator; "the non-existence of the main contract cannot automatically be thought to adversely affect the arbitration clause"). But then, curiously, we seem to find it resurfacing again, zombie-like, in the United States; see Restatement of the Law Third, The U.S. Law of International Commercial Arbitration Sect. 4-12(d) and *cmt. d* (Preliminary Draft No. 5, 1 September 2011), which lays down the rule that while "a court does not review the arbitral tribunal's determination of the *validity* of a contract that includes the arbitration agreement," nevertheless, "a court reviews de novo ... the *existence* of the contract that includes the arbitration agreement". "Such challenges necessarily implicate a party's assent to arbitration, and hence a court has the final say."

I must say that with all respect I disagree. It is just as facile to assume *a priori* that defects in the main agreement must vitiate the arbitration clause, as to assume that they cannot. In other words, "logic" – as usual – will take us precisely nowhere. See generally Alan Scott RAU, "Everything You Really Need to Know About 'Separability' in Seventeen Simple Propositions", supra fn. 13, p. 1 at pp. 27, 38-45 ("*void, schmoid*"). As the discussion in the text and in the following footnote demonstrates, *it is simply not true that a claimed lack of contract formation must always, and by definition, include a claim that the resisting party also did not agree to the arbitration clause.*

arbitrator. Contracting parties might have been willing to arbitrate – not only the existence of a breach of contract – but also whether the terms of the alleged contract *were too indefinite to give rise to a breach in the first place*. The only interesting question in any of these cases is the likely boundaries of contractual assent, and a claim that an enforceable agreement "was never concluded" need not prevent the inference that the parties would have wanted to entrust *that very question* to arbitrators chosen by them. In the words of Judge Easterbrook, *"if they have agreed on nothing else they have agreed to arbitrate"*.[22]

---

22. *Sphere Drake Ins. Ltd. v. All American Ins. Co.*, 256 F.3d 587, 591-592 (7th Cir. 2001); Judge Easterbrook was referring there to *Colfax Envelope Corp. v. Local No. 458-3M, Chicago Graphic Communications Int'l Union*, 20 F.3d 750 (7th Cir. 1994) (Posner, J.). In *Colfax* an employer and a union disagreed over the meaning of the term "4C 60 inches Press-3 Men" in a collective bargaining agreement; the employer believed the language meant – in contrast to past practice – that only 3 men would be required to man any of its 78-inch wide 4-color presses; the union interpreted the language to refer only to presses 60-inch *and under*. The employer sought a judicial declaration that no contract existed "because the parties never agreed on an essential term"; the union counterclaimed for an order to arbitrate. The court affirmed an order of summary judgment in favor of the union: *"Even if"* there was no *"meeting of the minds"* on the meaning of this critical term, at the least *"there was a meeting of the minds on the mode of arbitrating disputes between the parties"*.

Similarly, in *Bratt Enterprises, Inc. v. Noble Int'l Ltd.*, 99 F.Supp.2d 874 (S.D. Ohio 2000), *rev'd on other grounds*, 338 F.3d 609 (6th Cir. 2003), the contract provided that the purchase price of certain assets would be adjusted following the closing as a result of certain later expenditures, and "due to the uncertainty associated with this post-Closing adjustment, the Parties included an arbitration clause in the Purchase Agreement to resolve any disputes associated with this adjustment". One party later asserted a defense of "mutual mistake" regarding the drafting of this portion of the agreement; nevertheless the court pointed out that there was no claim at all "that there was any 'mutual mistake' in the negotiation of the arbitration clause itself".

Precisely the same analysis is applicable in related cases of indefiniteness or "agreement to agree". See, e.g., *Toray Industries Inc. v. Aquafil S.p.a.*, 17(10) Int'l Arb. Rep. Oct. 2002 at D-1 (Sup. Ct. N.Y. 2002) (parties signed a document that one party contends "was no more than agreement to agree and that the parties intended to negotiate further"; held, "the parties have agreed to arbitrate" – the parties "actively negotiated the choice of law and arbitration clause", which was not "inadvertently slipped in" – and so the arbitrators "will determine all questions including the meaning, effect, validity or enforceability of all other contract terms"); *Republic of Nicaragua v. Standard Fruit Co.*, 937 F.2d 469 (9th Cir. 1991) (in determining whether a "Memorandum of Intent" was a "binding contract for the purchase and sale of bananas, or merely an 'agreement to agree' at some later date", the trial court "improperly looked to the validity of the contract as a whole" and "ignored strong evidence in the record that both parties intended to be bound by the arbitration clause"; court should instead have "considered only the validity and scope of the arbitration clause itself"); W. Laurence CRAIG et al., *International Chamber of Commerce Arbitration* (3d edn. 2000) p. 165 (discussing case in which a "contract would have been null under French law if the price had not been specifically fixed or determinable by objective reference", but arbitration clause was unaffected by the alleged nullity; the arbitrators then went on to determine that the contract was invalid because the price was indeterminate).

In light of all this, Judge Easterbrook's earlier opinion in *Hill's Pet Nutrition, Inc. v. Fru-Con Construction Corp.*, 101 F.3d 63 (7th Cir. 1996) is puzzling and troubling. Here Fru-Con agreed to renovate and enlarge a pet food plant on a cost-plus basis, but the parties ultimately failed to agree on some fundamental issues, notably "how 'cost' would be defined". The district court concluded that the parties "never came to closure on all terms" of the agreement and they therefore "had not agreed on anything at all, precluding the possibility of arbitration". But the court of appeals did not

(2) A separate point is that *whoever the appropriate decisionmaker may be*, such challenges are increasingly unlikely to succeed, particularly where the putative defect is one of uncertainty and indefiniteness.

(a) At bottom, when you come to think about it, there is really nothing particularly *recherché* in the practice of creating entirely new contract terms through adjudication: When it is alleged that a failure of agreement has caused a deal to be insufficiently defined to be enforceable as a contract, judges, let alone arbitrators, will already and frequently do precisely that. The fact that they will often do so covertly, under the guise of interpretation – as an increasingly preferred alternative to allowing the gap to "swallow up" everything that has in fact been settled on – in no way changes the principle.

So despite the traditional wisdom familiar to every first-year student – to the effect that courts will not "make a contract for the parties" or enforce arrangements where they have merely "agreed to agree"[23] – we can see a growing judicial willingness to fill

---

agree, ruling instead that

- in circumstances where the parties have begun performance with some issues still to be resolved, *they do have an agreement* that
- at least "includes *all of the terms that have been mutually approved*".

So, there was indeed *an agreement to arbitrate*. Nevertheless the lower court's refusal to compel arbitration was affirmed: The disputed matters over which the lawsuit had been filed "were the very items over which negotiations [had] collapsed"; since "these were issues left open at the bargaining table", "the arbitration clause, although part of the parties' agreement, does not come into play". I could certainly use some help understanding this – please:

- Given the premise of an enforceable agreement to arbitrate, isn't the question whether "a contract had been formed in the first place" properly one that falls to be decided by the *arbitrators themselves*?
- If the arbitrators find that some contract has been entered into, isn't it for them to determine the precise terms?
- What can it possibly mean as a practical matter to allocate decisionmaking responsibility by saying respectively that "some terms" are indeed subject to arbitration – "the portions of the draft master agreement on which the parties agreed" – but that other terms – like those over which the negotiations happened to abort – are not arbitrable at all?
- Is the suggestion, then, that "*to the extent there has been a failure to agree,* the arbitrators are rendered impotent" – and if so, is this not an eerie precursor to *Stolt-Nielsen*?

23. See, e.g., *Joseph Martin, Jr. Delicatessen, Inc.*, supra fn. 19 at 543 ("Before the power of law can be invoked to enforce a promise, it must be sufficiently certain and specific so that what was promised can be ascertained. Otherwise, a court, in intervening, would be imposing its own conception of what the parties should or might have undertaken, rather than confining itself to the implementation of a bargain to which they have mutually committed themselves").

consensual gaps in an honest effort to uncover or even reconstruct the parties' original narrative.[24]

(b) But the challenge is far less likely to succeed – the challenge is a fortiori going nowhere – where we can make this further step: Perhaps we can conclude that if any "gap" appears – however fatal it would otherwise be – the parties contemplated that the defective agreement could be salvaged – the missing terms filled in – by the arbitral tribunal itself.

Let's begin at the beginning: The traditional reluctance of courts to enforce inadequately specified agreements – their traditional recital of their inability to "make a contract for the parties" – presumably serves certain functions and purposes, no? It certainly has to come from somewhere. An *a priori* assertion is not argument.[25] I think it must derive from policies like this: When courts continue to insist on a certain level of clarity and completeness in the terms of a contract, an economist would say that they are attempting to insure that the deal is "allocatively efficient" – roughly, that it serves to reallocate resources to higher-valued uses – and that they do so by assuring that the deal has been bargained out by the parties themselves, in terms of their own assessments of their own interests. They may also be trying to prevent parties from taking a "free

---

24. Compare *Sun Printing & Publishing Ass'n v. Remington Paper & Power Co.*, 139 N.E. 470 (N.Y. 1923) – a wooden mainstay of the Contracts curriculum of a generation ago – with *David Nassif Associates v. United States*, 557 F.2d 249 (Ct. Cl. 1977); see also UCC Sects. 2-204(3), 2-305). *Joseph Martin*, supra fn. 19, distinguished Sales cases decided both prior to and subsequent to the UCC on the grounds of "the more fluid sales setting in which [they] occurred"; by contrast, said the court, "stability is a hallmark of the law controlling" transactions in real estate.

Other legal cultures may in this respect be – if not indeed more adventuresome – at least more frank in openly acknowledging what they are doing. See, e.g., Sir Basil MARKESINIS, et al., *The German Law of Contract: A Comparative Treatise*, 2nd edn. (2006) pp. 59-60 ("the net of default rules is wider in German than it is in English law and one practical consequence of this is that the parties need not attempt to anticipate in the contractual drafts all eventualities"; even essential terms like price can be left to "be fixed at a later stage," and "the court is empowered to review the exercise of discretion of the contracting party ... and if necessary replace it with its own determination"); see also *id.* at pp. 140, 143 (the default rule of "good faith" "empower[s] the courts to imply into the contract a wide range of collateral obligations"; doing this work of implication "enabled the courts to transcend the actual intentions of the parties and imply terms, not which the parties would have included, but which they *should* have included in the contract") (emphasis in original); Stefan KRÖLL, "Contractual Gap-Filling by Arbitration Tribunals", 2 Int. Arb. L. R. (1999) p. 9 at p. 13 (so "fixing of a price at the judge's discretion must therefore be considered as dispute-settlement in the German legal system").

25. But see Pieter SANDERS, "Arbitration in Long-Term Business Transactions" in *Proceedings, Vth International Arbitration Congress* (New Delhi, 1975) at C.IV.b1, p. 2 (henceforth *Proceedings*) ("courts are ... nowhere, as far as I know, authorized to fill gaps and supplement the agreement of the parties by filling in ... open spots", and "many (national) arbitration laws of the world are based on the principle that the power of the arbitrators cannot reach further than the power of the Courts"; to complete the syllogism, then, this is not "arbitration proper").

ride" on the public court system by shifting onto the courts the burden of determining contract terms.[26]

But then, after all, none of these concerns applies with anything like their original force when the parties have chosen to entrust the power to fix terms to

• private decisionmakers – chosen by them, as their surrogates, with reference to their agents' training, background, experience, and presumed sensitivity to commercial realities;[27]
• and all this, of course, in a procedure for which they themselves have agreed to bear the costs.

In a sense then an arbitrator's decision, being itself an "instance of contractual gap-filling, just *is* a term of the parties' contract".[28]

It is thus a familiar proposition that what might otherwise be a fatal "uncertainty" of terms can be cured simply by adding an arbitration clause.[29] When the parties agree to

---

26. See generally Alan Scott RAU, "The Culture of American Arbitration and the Lessons of ADR", 40 Tex. Int'l L.J. (2005) p. 449 at pp. 476-477 (henceforth "The Culture of American Arbitration"). See also POSNER, supra fn. 4 at p. 1587 (interpolating a "reasonable term" is often rejected as too burdensome; "not only would the court incur the administrative cost of having to conduct an elaborate inquiry, but no matter how elaborate the inquiry, a substantial probability of error would remain, and an erroneous interpretation undermines the utility of contracting as a method of organizing economic activity").

27. One might also suppose that arbitrators – often chosen precisely for their familiarity with the commercial context of a dispute – are likely to be somewhat more attuned to the dangers of one party's opportunistic behavior in the wake of the other's change of position, and more inclined to police it. Cf. Juliet P. KOSTRITSKY, "Taxonomy for Justifying Legal Intervention in an Imperfect World: What To Do When Parties Have Not Achieved Bargains or Have Drafted Incomplete Contracts", Wisc. L. Rev. (2004) p. 323 at pp. 364, 368, 377 (in the presence of uncertainty, sunk costs, and opportunism, "it becomes difficult to solve problems by contract ex ante," and parties may instead "turn to private ordering and alternative mechanisms of private 'governance structures' as the most efficient means of solving their problems and maximizing the gains from trade"; "[t]he presence of a comprehensive structure of nonlegal sanctions lessens the reason for court intervention").

28. MARKOVITS, supra fn. 5 at p. 1346. See also *id.* at p. 1347 (arbitration "does not so much contractualize adjudication as replace adjudication and the adjudicatory process with contract *tout court*"; it "is not a *process* for deciding the content of independent legal entitlements at all, but rather a part of the *substance* of the contracts that create it, a means of fixing the content of contractual rights" (emphasis in original)). [Professor Markovits focuses his discussion here on what he terms "first-party arbitration", a formulation that I believe is intended to capture the idea of, "arbitration without third-party effects"].

29. See, e.g., *Lafayette Place Assocs. v. Boston Redevelopment Auth.*, 694 N.E.2d 820, 826-827 (Mass. 1998) (although the contract left undetermined "exactly what [was] to be included" in the parcel of land being sold as well as the price, it also specified that "'appropriate details of the purchase and sale ... shall be resolved be arbitration'" and thus "created a means for resolving disputes that might arise in the course of effecting the ultimate sale"; "[t]o borrow Justice Holmes's metaphor, the machinery was built and had merely to be set in motion"); see also *Leslie v. Leslie*, 24 A. 319 (N.J. Ch. 1892). Disputes between the two owners of a close corporation "became so bitter and dangerous to its prosperity" that they wished to separate, with one of them retiring from all

participate in this procedure, they may, even in commercial cases, be said to be taking part in a process that "involves not only the settlement of the particular dispute but also interstitial rule-making" – a process aimed at creating, refining, and elaborating for the future the rules which will govern their relationship.[30] At the same time, of course, such clauses – despite being labeled as "arbitration" – often exist precisely as a means of encouraging the parties' own voluntary efforts at renegotiation and readjustment. The right to invoke the arbitral process is there to make settlement more likely – as would indeed the right to force one's opponent into a game of Russian Roulette – that is, "as a spur toward a negotiated agreement", although inserted in the "fervent hope" that it will not ultimately be necessary to resort to it.[31]

---

participation in the company's affairs. "But which should sell – who should go out – was the point of difficulty about which they could not agree." So they "were willing to leave the question as to which one should retire by the sale of his stock, and what the other should pay him for his stock, to be settled by arbitration". *Id.* at 321. (The court ultimately vacated the award, though, because it had purported to decide matters not submitted to the arbitrators, and because it was "uncertain and inconclusive".)

The contrast suggested here is made abundantly explicit in a number of judicial decisions; e.g., *Walker v. Keith*, 382 S.W.2d 198, 199-200, 202, 204 (Ky. App. 1964) (lease provided that rental was to be fixed "as shall actually be agreed upon" by the parties and to be based on "comparative business conditions"; held, provision was too "indefinite and uncertain" to enforce; such provisions "have been the source of interminable litigation" and "courts sometimes must assert their right not to be imposed upon"; however, if the parties "had agreed upon a specific method of making the determination", such as the decision of an arbitrator, "they could be said to have agreed upon whatever rent figure emerged from utilization of the method"). More recently, see *1651 North Collins Corp. v. Laboratory Corp. of America*, 529 Fed. Appx. 628 (6th Cir. 2013) (option to renew lease at "the then market rent for similar space in the Louisville area, but not less than the immediately preceding five-year period"; held, the renewal option is not enforceable; the rental provision "is still too ambiguous to qualify as a definite objective standard"; the landlord "*could have solved this problem by submitting the question of what constituted a 'market rent' to arbitration, as the original lease agreement contemplates, but it did not do so*") (emphasis added).

30. Cf. David E. FELLER, "A General Theory of the Collective Bargaining Agreement", 61 Cal. L. Rev. (1973) p. 663 at p. 744 (labor arbitration).

This is not the principal subject of the present paper: But how often do we see arbitrators "*create a new term of the contract*" – *even a term inconsistent with the original agreement* – when liability has been determined, and such action can be spun (or framed) as an essential remedy needed in order *to preserve the overall framework – the overall allocation of risks – implicit in the deal?* See, e.g., *Timegate Studios, Inc. v. Southpeak Interactive, L.L.C.*, 713 F.3d 797 (5th Cir. 2013) (as a remedy for breach of contract and fraud committed by the publisher of a video game, the award provided that "the Publishing Agreement is hereby amended as a matter of law [so that the claimant has] a perpetual license for [the defendant's] intellectual property in the Game"; held, this was "a remedy that furthered the essence of the [agreement]", and "was permissible and rationally explainable as a logical means of furthering the aims of the underlying publishing agreement"); *Advanced Micro Devices, Inc. v. Intel Corp.*, 885 P.2d 994 (Cal. 1994) (arbitrator found that Intel had "breached the implied covenant of good faith and fair dealing" under a license agreement; AMD's actual damages were found to be "immeasurable", so the arbitrator gave AMD a permanent, royalty-free license to any of Intel's intellectual property that was embodied in AMD's competing chip).

31. See Lon FULLER, The Forms and Limits of Adjudication, 92 Harv. L. Rev. (1978) p. 353 at pp. 406-407 (in "complex long-term supply contracts" "obligations to negotiate under the threat of an exercise of adjudicative powers").

947

One common setting in which this problem arises is where the apparent need arises to "adapt" the terms of ongoing contracts to new and unforeseen conditions. Consider – dating back to 1975 – the *Georgia Power* case, in which a coal company entered into a ten-year contract to supply coal to a buyer company.[32] There was a base price per ton, and a provision for the calculation of adjustments upon changes in certain labor costs and in "governmental impositions". The agreement also provided that:

> "[A]ny gross proven inequity that may result in unusual economic conditions not contemplated by the parties at the time of the execution of this Agreement may be corrected by mutual consent. Each party shall in the case of a claim of gross inequity furnish the other with whatever documentary evidence may be necessary to assist in effecting a settlement."

And "any unresolved controversy between the parties arising under this Agreement" was to be settled by arbitration. Four years later, after a rapid escalation in prices, the open market price of coal of the same quality was more than three times the current adjusted base price under the agreement. The buyer predictably argued that in light of the contract language suggesting the need for "mutual consent", submitting the question of price adjustment to arbitration would be equivalent to empowering the arbitrator "to make a new contract for the parties". But arbitration was compelled nevertheless.

More recently, price-review mechanisms, "inserted in most long-term natural gas sales agreements", provide a conventional and familiar analogue – responsive to the well-known facts that in long-term commodity sales agreements a "fixed price for 15-20 years is usually unrealistic" and that even an agreed pricing formula may, if unaltered, "reflect a risk that is unacceptable to both of the parties".[33]

Now I suppose it is marginally more convenient – more reassuring for the timid – to find consent to arbitrate when the process is used

• as part of an ongoing, existing contract – to provide a "backup" for a failure of future assent in circumstances expressly contemplated by the parties – than when it is used

---

32. *Georgia Power Co. v. Cimarron Coal Corp.*, 526 F.2d 101 (6th Cir. 1975).

33. See Ben HOLLAND and Phillip SPENCER ASHLEY, "Natural Gas Price Reviews: Past, Present and Future", 30 J. of Energy & Natural Resources L. (2012) pp. 29-31. See also *id.* at p. 34: A clause suggested as a "typical price review clause" might provide:

"If a circumstance beyond the control of either party results in a significant change in the energy market of the Buyer compared to such energy market on [date], then either party may give notice for a price review.

If the parties fail to agree a revised price formula within 90 days after giving notice for a price review, the price formula shall be reviewed by arbitration. In any such arbitration the arbitrators shall review the price formula and shall decide whether it needs to be revised to reflect, as at the review date, the relevant significant change(s) in the energy market of the Buyer which affect the value of [the product] in the end user market of the Buyer as such value can directly or indirectly be obtained by a prudent and efficient buyer."

• to create an essential term of the contract in circumstances where there has been "no agreement" in the first place.

Only in the former case one can say (as the court did), that since the parties *"remain bound to continued operations under the contract"*, "the controversy over a claimed right to price adjustment must be settled somehow in the absence of mutual consent" (emphasis added). But note how neatly this conclusory formulation (the "right to price adjustment") begs the question – for the contractual foundation of any such "right" *is the very question that is up for grabs*. The case illustrates, then, how difficult it may be satisfactorily to distinguish

• a dispute over the scope of existing contract "rights" – asking the decisionmaker to do the necessary interpretive work of worrying the agreement, digging out what is already present in germ – and
• an "interest" dispute – asking the decisionmaker to devise the actual contract provisions by which the parties will henceforth be bound.[34]

And the lesson of course is how often the supposed distinction may be – as, after all, are most distinctions in the law – at best, and charitably, a mere question of emphasis or degree. A clause of the sort found in the contract in *Georgia Power* may render the question of arbitral authority marginally easier to resolve, but hardly provides a basis for a difference in principle – and matters of degree should not be turned into matters of principle without some compelling reason to do so.[35] Given a core consent to the process, and a sufficiently broad mandate, the role of the arbitrator is in both cases more or less identical.[36]

---

34. For a case quite similar to *Georgia Power* – although one that seems much closer along the line to the latter of these categories than to the former *and with absolutely no significance to be attributed to the distinction* – see *Aeronaves de Mexico, S.A. v. Triangle Aviation Services, Inc.*, 389 F.Supp. 1388 (S.D.N.Y. 1974), *aff'd per curiam*, 515 F.2d 504 (2nd Cir. 1975). Here a contract for the servicing of aircraft provided that if the changes in the "volume of flights, aircraft types, arrival/departure times, or cargo load factors" caused "additional manpower and equipment [to] be required", "an increase in the charges *will be negotiated to the satisfaction of both parties*" (emphasis added). Again the inevitable claim was made that an arbitrator under the arbitration clause "could not be expected to write a renewal contract for the parties". But the court noted that "it is precisely such questions in specialized commercial dealings of this sort that are especially adapted to resolution by commercial men as arbitrators". And so "a failure to agree would give rise to an arbitrable controversy" – or "[a]t least, the arbitrators could so conclude".
35. But cf. Emmanuel GAILLARD and John SAVAGE, *Fouchard, Gaillard, Goldman on International Commercial Arbitration* (1999) pp. 25-26 (apparently suggesting that the answer to the question should "depend on whether or not the contract submitted to the arbitrator contains a specific hardship clause").
36. The theme, in other words, is that "gap filling" and a semantic inquiry into "meaning" are both at bottom "interpretive"; see POSNER, supra fn. 4 at pp. 1586, 1589 (both "interpretive in the sense that they are efforts to determine how the parties would have resolved the issue that has arisen had they foreseen it when they negotiated their contract"; "disambiguation" cases "could be turned into 'gap' cases by redefining 'gap' to mean not just the omission of a term but a gap in meaning

(c) This notion of curing fatal "uncertainty" through arbitral discretion may not be viewed quite so complaisantly in legal cultures which are somewhat more reticent in accepting all the implications of arbitration as an expression of private autonomy – and where in consequence the potential of the arbitral process is cabined more tightly – the powers of arbitrators closely identified with, mapped upon, the sphere of action permitted to state courts.[37]

Indeed the authority of arbitrators in the United States to construe contracts so as to fill gaps in insufficiently specified agreements, may be treated as noteworthy and unusual in other states, where it is customary to indulge in sophisticated and rigorous exercises in taxonomy aimed at classifying just what an arbitration "really" "is".[38] A highly conceptual Continental jurisprudence frequently leads to the conclusion that someone who has been asked merely to supply a term in a contract just "can't be" an arbitrator at all.[39]

---

because the term the parties included is unclear with reference to the particular contingency that has materialized").

    Stefan Kröll notes that "in theory" arbitrators may not "create new obligations for the parties" but may only "determine existing rights" which – while perhaps not "immediately apparent" – "at least in theory already existed before the arbitrators intervened". KRÖLL, supra fn. 24 at p. 10. But the thrust of his argument seems to suggest – quite correctly – that such a "distinction" will not bear the weight of practical application. I return to this point at the end of this paper in my Conclusion; see text accompanying fns. 215-219 infra.

37. A good illustration of this point is *Société S.E.C.A.R. v. Société Shopping Décor*, 1986 Rev. de l'Arb. 263 (*Cour de Cassation*, 1984). Here a commercial lease provided for the rental to be fixed in terms of a construction cost index; if the index were no longer to be published, and if the parties could not agree on a substitute, it was provided that an alternative index could be chosen by an "arbitrator". A lower court vacated the award on the grounds of public policy, but was reversed by the *Cour de Cassation*. Professor Mayer doubts, however, whether this should have even been characterized as an "arbitration" in the first place:

"Courts – claiming to interpret the will of the parties – have assumed the power in such cases to determine the index that the parties would have adopted, if the one that has disappeared had never existed. But when [the parties explicitly provide for such a case in their contract, as they have here,] that excludes any possibility of discovering some implicit intention in the contract.... From that moment the role of the neutral is not to interpret, but to freely create, and this role cannot be taken on by a judge – *nor, as a consequence*, by an arbitrator."

Pierre MAYER, Note, Rev. de l'Arb. (1986) p. 267 at p. 270 (my translation, and my emphasis).

38. See, e.g., Charles JARROSSON, *La notion de l'arbitrage* (1987) p. 303; cf. Philippe FOUCHARD, et al., *Traité de l'arbitrage commercial international* (1996) p. 15 ("a comparative law study will indicate that the distinctions of French law [with respect to the question whether we 'are in the presence of a true arbitration'] are not observed with quite the same rigor in certain other legal systems").

39. I gather that in some legal systems, the law revolves around a dichotomy that I have already deprecated as largely formalistic and non-functional. In such cultures,

• it may be permissible for an arbitrator – at least one "appointed as such", or "whom [the parties] describe as such" – who has been charged with a general submission, to supply an omitted term as part of his overall mission; see Jean-Louis DELVOLVÉ, et al., *French Arbitration Law and Practice:*

A Dynamic Civil Law Approach to International Arbitration, 2nd edn. (2009) p. 24; cf. Giorgio BERNINI, "Techniques for Resolving Problems in Forming and Performing Long-Term Contracts" in *Proceedings*, supra fn. 25 at C.IV.a1, p. 11 at p. 15 (here the neutral is not "filling blanks" left open by the parties *"ab initio" but instead* "settl[ing] disputes arising from divergent party views over the exact impact the *rebus sic stantibus* clause will have" on the original contract; this is a function "which is strictly arbitral in nature").

• But at the same time, I gather, someone asked merely to come up with a term – *even in a binding fashion – in order to permit "a contract" to come into existence in the first place* – is simply not an arbitrator.

This is a familiar distinction; see, e.g., ICC Partial Award no. 7544 (1995), [1999] J.D.I. 1062 (adjustment of price in case of change order; contract provided that failing agreement by the parties, the price should be "provisionally fixed by the Engineer, then definitively fixed by an arbitral tribunal"); see *id.* at 1064, 1066 (note D.H.) ("the role of the arbitral tribunal was *not exercised in the context of contract formation*, in order to determine an essential element of the agreement, but *in the course of contractual performance*" (emphasis added).

This explains the *a priori* assumption in much Continental commentary that when a third party is asked to fix the price in a contract of sale, this "is absolutely not" arbitration – "not at all". Authorization for such a third-party determination is given, for example, in Art. 1592 of the French Code Civil: In a contract of sale "the price must be fixed and stated by the parties", although the price "can nevertheless be left to the determination [*arbitrage*] of a third party"; if the third party cannot or is not willing to fix the price, "there is no sale". Apparently such a third party is nothing but an "agent" whose task is "easily distinguishable" from arbitration; the difference lies in the fact that his setting of the price is necessary to the "formation of a contract" by fixing one of its "essential elements" – that is, "an element without which a contract cannot validly exist" – but which now "enables [the contract] to come into existence". See JARROSSON, supra fn. 38 at pp. 232, 287, 294-295, 364. So he makes a "simple finding of fact" – and thus "participates in the completion of the contract" – but without being authorized to draw the explicit consequences in terms of legal liability. By contrast, the arbitrator, "like the judge, exercises a jurisdictional function" – that is, the role of both arbitrator, just like the judge, is to "give a legal ruling" [*dire le droit]*. Jean Jacques DAIGRE, Note [to *Cour de Cassation*, 16 February 2010), [2010] Rev. de l'Arb. p. 506 at p. 510; see also DELVOLVÉ, supra at pp. 24-25 (the function of the third party "is not to render an award for the settlement of a dispute between the parties regarding ... their respective rights and obligations under the contract", but to fix a figure for the price of goods "which will become part of the contract for sale as one of its terms; the contract will thus be complete and capable of being performed"); Jean-François POUDRET and Sébastien BESSON, *Droit comparé de l'arbitrage international* (2002) p. 17 (the decision envisaged by Art. 1592 – as well as by similar provisions in Italian and German law – merely "determines an essential element of the contract without which the contract remains invalid" (my translation)); SANDERS, supra fn. 25 at C.IV.b2; Pieter SANDERS, *L'arbitrage dans les transactions commerciales à long terme*, Rev. de l'Arb. (1975) p. 83 at p. 85 ("can we expand the notion of arbitration in such a way as to include this kind of decision? It may be unfortunate, but that's really too much of a stretch [*il semble qu'on exagère un peu]*" (my translation)).

If we had to diagnose all this, we would note, at the same time,

• the residue of the same tired metaphysical trope of "existence";
• the failure, in consequence, to draw all the necessary functional implications from the canonical rule of "separability"; and
• the same culturally determined definition of the notion of arbitration – requiring it to be aligned ever-so-closely with the judicial model – a model in which claimant and respondent are presumed to

But I wouldsuggest that it will prove infinitely less interesting to hunt for the elements that make up "essential parts of the notion of arbitration",[40] than it is to acknowledge frankly how much a "single unitary model of arbitration" would be misguided – that "the process is sufficiently variable and flexible to accommodate instead a wide spectrum of potential forms".[41]

- have already staked out well-defined but irreconcilable positions, and
- to have exchanged contradictory pleadings, and
- to be seeking a judgment of liability founded on reasoning from legal texts.

40. Cf. KRÖLL, supra fn. 24 at p. 15; see also BERNINI, supra fn. 39 at C.Iva, p. 11 at p. 13 ("where no settlement of opposite claims is provided for", "we are clearly outside of the scope of rules aimed at governing arbitration *stricto sensu*"; "the machinery of international conventions can hardly be deemed applicable to *Arbitrage*"). Cf. Klaus Peter BERGER, "Power of Arbitrators to Fill Gaps and Revise Contracts to Make Sense", 17 Arb. Int'l (2001) p. 1 at p. 2 ("In his well-known study on hardship clauses published in 1976, Fontaine has asked the question that is still discussed today with respect to gap filling and contract revision by international arbitrators: 'Is this still arbitration?'");

I would suggest that the notion of a "dispute" – if this is, really and truly, essential to the definition of a valid arbitration process – is easily capacious enough to encompass the failure of an agreement on price. But compare *General Motors France v. societé Champs de Mars automobile*, [2011] Rev. de l'Arb. 436-438 (*Cour de Cassation*, 15 December 2010) (note Billemont) ("a dispute [*litige*] only exists in the presence of two contradictory *legal [juridiques]* claims"; by contrast, where the legal consequences "have already been stipulated in the contract at the outset [*en amont*]" we have nothing but a "purely factual disagreement") (emphasis in original); *Consorts Attali v. Lecourt*, [2001] Rev. de l'Arb. 151, 154 (*Cour d'appel* Paris 1998) (a partner and shareholder in a close corporation agreed to sell his shares to the others at a price to be fixed by two neutrals, in order to "put an end to the differences that had arisen" between them; held, the neutral's decision was not subject to vacatur as an award because there was, "after entering into the agreement which actually put an end to it, no longer any dispute between the parties, but simply a disagreement or a conflict of interests with respect to the price"); *Frydman v. Cosmair, Inc.*, 1995 WL 404841 (S.D.N.Y.) (dissatisfaction with an Art. 1592 valuation does not "relate to an arbitration" so as to allow removal to federal court; after all, the parties had informed the neutral that "his decision [would] form the parties' will" with respect to the price, and "[t]hat is hardly the language of dispute").

For an extended argument seeking to demonstrate the contrary, see the discussion in RAU, "The Culture of American Arbitration", supra fn. 26 at p. 494 (it is "beautifully circular" to say that "there can no longer be any 'dispute' [merely because] the very purpose of the submission agreement itself was to eliminate one!"), p. 495 (if "this is intended as a serious account of psychological realities [in the face of "conflicting interests, and aspirations"] it seems singularly impoverished"). If the neutral's determination is meant to be *binding on the parties* – which means, I take it, that it will be *enforceable at law* – then attaching importance to whether or not he actually "purported to draw a legal conclusion" is trivial and formulaic. Cf. *id*. at 492 fn. 169 (parties may ask for the resolution of issues of fact or may instead ask for something that "approximates a request for judicial relief," but *it is only the scope of the contractual submission that permits this distinction,*" and it is familiar ground that parties may choose to entrust a particularly broad – or particularly narrow – inquiry to neutrals whom they nevertheless consider "arbitrators").

41. RAU, "The Culture of American Arbitration", supra fn. 26 at p. 496.

III.   "SILENCE" IN THE COURT

"It's not the notes that you play, it's the notes that you don't play."[42]

Let's pass over now those rather unusual instances of contractual "failure" and let's assume that the decisionmaker, whoever he may be – whether court or arbitrator – is unwilling simply to leave the parties' losses where they lie – is unwilling to permit one of them simply to walk away from the other without facing the consequences – is satisfied that despite some level of failure to fully articulate the terms of the deal, their intention to form a binding agreement should be honored and that a reasonably certain basis for doing so can be found.[43] The problem presented to him then becomes: just what are the terms of the transaction to be? How is he to proceed given that the text is problematical – that the parties have not, unequivocally and completely, answered the question posed in the litigation?

Rather than discussing this in the abstract, I think it will be helpful to begin with some actual judgments – and I start with a line of cases, all quite similar, all posing more or less the same question, and all decided recently by the US Supreme Court. As Blake said, "To particularize is the alone distinction of merit."[44] It is sometimes striking to see the many things that one can learn if one sets out to deconstruct a line of decisions – teasing out from each concrete instance everything that has been assumed, everything that has been lost sight of, and everything that has been left unsaid.

The Court's decisions in *Bazzle*,[45] *Stolt-Nielsen*,[46] and *Oxford Health*[47] are interesting case studies: They not only underscore the difficulties inherent in the very notion of "gaps" or "silence", but reveal something else even more fundamental. If the following is the only "takeaway" from the discussion here, I'd be perfectly content:

> Whenever we are talking about "gaps" in agreements, we are in all probability talking about something else entirely. Tracking the Court's reasoning reveals that "silence" is frequently just a rhetorical trope, one that is responsive to – dependent on – the dialectics of adversarial argument. Implicit in the assertion that the

---

42. Commonly attributed to Miles Davis.
43. See, e.g., UCC Sect. 2-204(3) ("a contract for sale does not fail for indefiniteness if the parties have intended to make a contract and there is a reasonably certain basis for giving an appropriate remedy"); Sect. 3-305 (open price term; "a reasonable price at the time for delivery" if nothing is said as to price or the parties fail to agree; however, if "the parties intend not to be bound unless the price is fixed or agreed ... there is no contract").
44. William BLAKE, "Annotations to Sir Joshua Reynolds' Discourses", in Edwin John ELLIS and William Butler YEATS, eds., *Works of William Blake*, vol. 2 (1893) p. 323 (and "to generalize is to be an Idiot").
45. *Green Tree Financial Corp. v. Bazzle*, 539 U.S. 444 (2003).
46. *Stolt-Nielsen S.A. v. Animalfeeds Int'l Corp.*, 130 S.Ct. 1758 (2010).
47. *Oxford Health Plans LLC v. Sutter*, 133 S.Ct. 2064 (2013).

agreement is "silent", for example, is likely to be lurking an unexpressed premise[48] – perhaps a hidden assumption
(a) with respect to who has the burden of proof of demonstrating some critical procedural question, or
(b) with respect to just who the appropriate decisionmaker is to be.

1.   "Silence" as the Lack of a Textual Hook: Bazzle

It is best to start with *Bazzle*, which was the first of the Court's cases to worry the question whether it was congruent with the expressed intention of the parties for an arbitration to proceed on a class-wide basis. In the courts below the South Carolina Supreme Court, in the course of confirming a hefty class award,[49] had first found that the parties' agreement "was *silent* regarding class-wide arbitration"; it then asked whether in such circumstances of "silence" "class-wide arbitration is permissible".[50]

Now "silence" is in itself a curious and not particularly helpful construct. Presumably the state court meant to suggest nothing more than that

• the contractual text itself contained no particular semantic "hook" on which meaning could immediately be hung – or alternatively, perhaps, that
• no definitive meaning could be derived from the contractual text alone.

---

48. "Lurking" sometimes in the shadows to the point of invisibility: Thus it would elide a good share of the important work, for example, to assert that where the contract contains no clause expressly guarding against "unforeseen circumstances", arbitrators should be "reluctant to overrule the principle of *pacta sunt servanda* in favour of contract adaptation and gap filling" – and will tend to assume that "the parties have indicated that the principle of sanctity of contracts shall prevail". Cf. BERGER, supra fn. 40 at p. 8. That would be simply to assume the content of a default rule with respect to excuse (or shared responsibility) that may or may not be desirable, but whose legitimacy must in any case be demonstrated.

For precisely the same reason, it would elide a good deal of the important work to assert that an arbitrator is powerless to consolidate related arbitrations where the contract contains no clause expressly providing for this, since "if it had been the parties' intention to submit their disputes to a multiparty arbitration setting, they would have so provided in their contracts"; cf. "Note, Compulsory Consolidation of International Arbitral Proceedings: Effects on Pacta Sunt Servanda and the General Arbitral Process", 2 Tul. J. Int'l & Comp. L. (1994) p. 223 at p. 251 ("If the parties to a multi-party dispute have not explicitly agreed to submit their disputes to a consolidated tribunal, then they have chosen to submit their disputes to separate arbitral tribunals.... Under the doctrine of *pacta sunt servanda,* the parties are only bound by what is in the contract."). But see Alan Scott RAU and Edward F. SHERMAN, "Tradition and Innovation in International Arbitration Procedure", 30 Tex. Int'l L.J. (1995) p. 89 at p. 113 (this "is nothing more than an extravagant form of question begging").

49. In a class proceeding brought by the Bazzles, the arbitrator had awarded almost US$ 11 million in statutory penalties, and an additional US$ 3.6 million in attorneys' fees, for a lender's failure in violation of state law to notify the borrower of his right to select his own attorney or insurance agent. In a related proceeding the same arbitrator had awarded US$ 9.2 million in statutory penalties, and an additional US$ 3 million in attorneys' fees, to other claimants. There were no "actual damages". *Bazzle v. Green Tree Financial Corp.*, 569 S.E.2d 349 (S.C. 2002).

50. *Bazzle*, 569 S.E.2d at 351, 359 (emphasis in original).

Of course, if this were all there was to "silence", it would be the most trivial of preliminary steps – for it would be an impoverished view indeed of the interpretive enterprise to suppose that one could sensibly stop there; surely some sense of context, and some sort of purposive narrative, are necessary to tease out the parties' "framework of common understanding".[51]

(a) Once content with its finding of "silence", however – once it was satisfied the text "said nothing" – the South Carolina court did not pursue any further interpretative path. But it did not fail to perceive the need for what we would call "construction": So the lower court orders compelling class-wide arbitration were affirmed on the ground

(i) that "ambiguous" language must be construed against the drafter; and more fundamentally, on the ground
(ii) of what appears to be *a state-created default rule crafted for circumstances of "silence"*: In such cases, the court held, class-wide proceedings are permissible merely on the condition that they "would serve efficiency and equity, and would not result in prejudice".[52]

(b) By contrast, for the respondent, it was inappropriate even to go down the path of fashioning these rules of construction: This was because in its view, the agreements between the parties were really, ultimately, *not "silent" at all* – since a fair reading of the text would lead to the conclusion that by their terms they in fact *prohibited* any class-wide proceedings.[53]

But then, when the case reached the Supreme Court, this whole trope of "silence" largely disappeared: And the reason for this speaks volumes. Justice Breyer did begin his

---

51. Cf. UCC Sect. 1-303 *cmt.* 3 ("the commercial meaning of the agreement that the parties have made"; usage of trade, as well as the parties' "course of performance" and "course of dealing", "furnish the background and give particular meaning to the language used, and are the framework of common understanding controlling any general rules of law which hold only when there is no such understanding").

52. *Bazzle,* 569 S.E.2d at 360. The court was hardly unusual in claiming to reach this conclusion "under general principles of contract interpretation"; the common conflation of "interpretation" and "construction", which we will note later, was presumably beyond its ken.

53. See Brief for Petitioner [Green Tree], 2003 WL 721716 at *42-*43 ("the unlikely conclusion that the parties authorized class-action arbitration here is foreclosed by the language of their arbitration agreements"); Final Brief of Appellant [Green Tree Financial Corp.], in the Supreme Court of South Carolina, at 17 ("the fact that the clause limits the scope of arbitrable issues to 'disputes, claims or controversies arising from or relating to *this contract*' evinces an intent that *only* disputes concerning the contract to which the named plaintiffs were a party, *not* the contracts of absent third parties, were to be arbitrated") (emphasis in original).

This is of course precisely the tack taken in Chief Justice Rehnquist's dissent in the Supreme Court; see *Bazzle,* 539 U.S. at 455, 458-460 (Rehnquist, C.J., dissenting) – which argued that the Supreme Court of South Carolina had "imposed a regime that was contrary to the express agreement of the parties as to how the arbitrator would be chosen": since its holding "contravenes the terms of the contracts", the state courts had failed to enforce the agreement "according to [its] terms" in violation of Sect. 4 of the FAA.

opinion in *Bazzle* by posing the question in a rather puzzling way: Are the contracts in this case, he asked, "*silent, or do they forbid class arbitration?*"[54] But framing the question in that way was nothing more than a direct response to the dialectic of the parties' argument: This formulation thus neatly encapsulates the contending approaches – between,

- on the one hand, the claimant's invocation of *a state-law default rule* crafted to supplement a supposed textual indeterminacy ["(a)(ii)" above],
- and on the other, the respondent's claim rooted in a *supposed textual prohibition* ["(b)" above].

Writing for a plurality of four Justices, Justice Breyer rose above all that, and immediately pointed out that the question he had originally posed need not – and indeed, should not – be answered: Whichever of the two contending approaches was correct was simply not a matter that fell to be decided by any court at all, state or federal: Instead it "presents a disputed issue of contract interpretation" – a dispute about what the contract "*means*" (i.e., whether class-wide procedures were contemplated) – and was thus (within the language of the arbitration clause) a dispute "relating to this contract".[55] "The parties seem to have agreed that an arbitrator not a judge would answer the relevant question" and although the arbitrators – in going on to administer class-wide proceedings – may have acquiesced in the reading of the contract by the state courts, nevertheless the parties still had not "obtained the arbitration decision that their contracts foresee".

So this was a question that did not go to whether the parties had ever "agreed to arbitrate a matter" (that would have put us in the presence of what it is now customary to call a "gateway" question of "arbitrability").[56] Instead, the question went to "*what kind of arbitration proceeding the parties agreed to*". And Justice Breyer thus fashioned a rule by which, under the federal common law of arbitration, this question – a question, by the way, that "the arbitrators are well situated to answer" – is one presumptively entrusted to them by virtue of the standard "broad clause".[57] The state-court judgment was therefore vacated and the case remanded "so that the arbitrator may decide the question of contract interpretation".

It is striking that Justice Breyer reached out for this formula – as far as I can tell – with no particular urging from either party.[58] But to say that an agreement to class-wide

---

54. *Bazzle*, 539 U.S. at 447.

55. *Id.* at 447 ("we cannot ["resolve" the question whether the agreement was "in fact silent"] because it is a matter for the arbitrator to decide").

56. See, e.g., Alan Scott RAU, "Arbitrating 'Arbitrability'", 7 World Arb. & Med. Rep. (2013) p. 487.

57. *Bazzle*, 539 U.S. at 452-453 (emphasis in original).

58. The claimants – who had prevailed in seeking class-wide arbitration – would certainly have had no reason to urge vacatur and a remand to the arbitrators: Indeed the thrust of their argument was that the decision to order class-wide proceedings *had already been made by the arbitrators*. See Oral Argument, *Green Tree Financial Corp. v. Bazzle*, 2003 WL 1989562 at *37-38 (Justice Breyer suggests that "the correct resolution" is to "send it back to the arbitrator for that determination, not influenced by the South Carolina opinion", but counsel for the claimants demurs, "because the

arbitration involved "a matter of interpretation" is to minimize the significance as well as the likelihood of "silence": At least if the text is not as "clear" in excluding the possibility of class-wide proceedings as the dissent assumed[59] – at least, that is, if the matter is semantically "arguable" – then there presumably exists something here to "interpret". And to ask the arbitrators to decide how the contract should be read, means – if understood sympathetically, and with an eye to arbitration practice – that their work should encompass, at the same time,

• a semantic inquiry into the literal words of the text,
• an appreciation of circumstance and context, the "customs and practices which the parties have come to consider as settled patterns of conduct"[60] – all going to make up what was their "bargain in fact";[61] and, as well,
• the work of construction to determine what the text should be taken to "mean" – that is, its legal effect.

---

arbitrator already did look at this clause and decided that the language of the arbitration agreement allowed him to decide"); Brief for Respondents [Bazzles], 2003 WL 1701523 at *44 ("there is no reason ... to conclude that the arbitrator failed to appreciate that the decision was his to make").

For its part, the defendant wouldn't seem to have had much to gain by a remand to the arbitrators either: If anything, it took the position that the decision should be for the *court; see* Oral Argument at *20 (counsel for Green Tree: "whether the arbitrator has the authority to resolve the rights of unnamed third parties is not a question for the arbitrator to decide. That's a question for the court to decide"); Brief for Respondents [Bazzles], 2003 WL 1701523 at *44-*45 (remand to the arbitrator was "a remedy that [Green Tree] never sought here, could not now seek, and in any event does not want"); *Bazzle,* 539 U.S. at 455 (Stevens, J., concurring in the judgment) (defendant Green Tree "merely challenged the merits of the [state court] decision without claiming that it was made by the wrong decisionmaker").

59. *Bazzle,* 539 U.S. at 451 *(the Chief Justice, dissenting, argues that class-wide arbitration would be "contrary to the express agreement of the parties as to how the arbitrator would be chosen", but "we do not believe ... that the contracts' language is as clear as the Chief Justice believes").

60. *In re Standard Bag Corp. and Paper Bag, Novelty, Mounting, Finishing and Display Workers Union,* 45 Lab. Arb. 1149 (1965). See also, Jan PAULSSON, *The Idea of Arbitration* (2013) at Ch. 3 ("Inferences and counter-presumptions may also tip the scales, depending on the prior dealings of the parties, settled and notorious industry practices, and the like"); Lon FULLER, "Collective Bargaining and the Arbitrator", 18 Wisc. L. Rev. (1963) p. 3 at pp. 11-12, 17 (the problems in "complicated commercial litigation" "are not unlike those encountered in dealing with labor agreements"; both may involve "complex procedures that vary from industry to industry, from plant to plant, from department to department"; "though the terms of [its] vocabulary often seem simple and familiar, their true meaning can be understood only when they are seen as parts of a larger system of practice").

61. See UCC Sect. 1-201(3) ("agreement" is defined as "the bargain of the parties in fact, as found in their language or inferred from other circumstances, including course of performance, course of dealing, or usage of trade"). See also Omri BEN-SHAHAR, "The Tentative Case Against Flexibility in Commercial Law", 66 U. Chi. L. Rev. (1999, no. 3) p. 781 at pp. 782, 785 ("the Code recognizes that the rights and duties of contracting parties can be derived not solely from specified authoritative static forms, most notably the text of the bargain, but also from the dynamic, legally unformulated, fact patterns of common life"; nevertheless Ben-Shahar suggests that "the type of flexibility that the Code potentially promotes" will, because of factors like imperfect information and the randomness and imprecision of adjudication, often "make contractual parties worse off").

In resolving disputes over "meaning", no decisionmaker – not an arbitrator, and not the South Carolina Supreme Court, nor any common-law court – could be expected to divorce any of these from the others: All are within the sovereign appreciation of a "contract reader".[62]

And so,

• should the arbitrators conclude that class-wide proceedings were indeed permissible, the result would presumably be the same as that mandated by the South Carolina courts – that is, a final and definitive order to that effect – and remand would otherwise have been largely futile.[63]
• In the (virtually unimaginable) eventuality that the arbitrators should conclude that a proper construction of the agreement *forbids* class-wide arbitration, the result would presumably be to the contrary.[64]

While Justice Breyer write only for a plurality of the Court – and no rationale could command the assent of a majority – there was at the least, and clearly, a majority for the limited proposition that on the facts of *Bazzle* – and in the face of an allegation of "silence" – the FAA *did not foreclose a determination by somebody – whether court or arbitrator –* that class-wide proceedings were permissible.[65] So *Bazzle* was immediately taken to be

---

62. This is the canonical term in labor arbitration, where it is common to say that the arbitrator serves as "the parties' officially designated 'reader' of the contract. He (or she) is their joint *alter ego* for the purpose of striking whatever supplementary bargain is necessary to handle the anticipated unanticipated omissions of the initial agreement" (emphasis in original), Theodore ST. ANTOINE, "Judicial Review of Labor Arbitration Awards: A Second Look at Enterprise Wheel and Its Progeny", 75 Mich. L. Rev. (1977) p. 1137 at pp. 1140, 1142.
63. Hence Justice Breyer's stress on the fact that the arbitrators would be particularly "well situated to answer" the question posed, 539 U.S. at 453. Hence above all his invocation of his own earlier opinion in *First Options* – the true teaching of which is that *once a matter has been delegated to the arbitrators by agreement of the parties*, "courts would then be expected to defer *prospectively*, by refusing to rule on an issue that was entrusted to arbitral decisionmaking, and would be expected as well to defer *after the fact*, by limiting their review to narrow statutory grounds". See Alan Scott RAU, "The Arbitrability Question Itself", 10 Amer. Rev. Int'l Arb. (1999) p. 287 at p. 293 (emphasis in original).
64. Cf. David S. SCHWARTZ, "Claim-Suppressing Arbitration: The New Rules", 87 Ind. L. J. (2012) p. 239 at p. 257 fn. 89. Some understatement here: "It seems probable at this juncture that the arbitrator would construe the contract to allow class actions, since the alternative would entail vacating his own class arbitration awards."
      No third alternative could have been imagined: That is, it could not have been supposed that there would be some sort of bifurcated proceeding, in which the arbitrators must first decide whether the agreement is notionally "silent" – and if the answer is "yes", then their work of interpretation would be done, returning the legal implications of that conclusion, the question of the appropriate default rule, to the courts. Such a model would be at the same time unworkable, incoherent and naive.
65. Justice Stevens, who cast the deciding fifth vote in the case, agreed that "the decision to conduct a class-action arbitration was correct as a matter of law", *Bazzle*, 539 U.S. at 455 (Stevens, J., concurring in the judgment). So there's the majority for the proposition that *class-wide proceedings were permissible if ordered by someone*. Justice Stevens was however content to rely, without more,

an endorsement by the Court of a new norm of class-wide arbitrations.[66] Such an "endorsement" seemed overdetermined in light of the curious way that Justice Breyer had posed the question in the first place. (Does the parties' agreement actually "forbid class arbitration" or is it instead merely "silent"?) Such a formulation inevitably served to sow the seeds of future confusion: Eager claimants[67] and receptive arbitrators[68] would take up this frame in an unguarded and uncritical fashion; distinguished commentators, too, would come to speak as if Justice Breyer had somehow loaded the dice – as if the Court had wished to privilege class-wide arbitration to the extent that a reluctant party was required to affirmatively demonstrate that the parties had manifested an intent to *exclude* it.[69] But there is nothing whatever in Justice Breyer's statement of the problem –

---

were permissible if ordered by someone. Justice Stevens was however content to rely, without more, on the application by state courts of their own default rule. But leaving the decision to state courts would have led to an affirmance of the judgment below – and the plurality preferred to reverse, so that the question could be presented de novo to the arbitrators. So, conceding the essential, Justice Stevens concurred in the result and agreed that the matter of contractual interpretation "arguably" should have been made "in the first instance by the arbitrator", *Bazzle*, 539 U.S. at 455 (Stevens, J., concurring in the judgment)).

66. Cf. S.I. STRONG, "The Sounds of Silence: Are U.S. Arbitrators Creating Internationally Enforceable Awards When Ordering Class Arbitration in Cases of Contractual Silence or Ambiguity?", 30 MICH. J. INT'L L. (2009) p. 1017 at pp. 1022-1023 (where an international class arbitration is seated in the United States, "because the United States has already judicially approved of the class arbitration mechanism", a losing respondent will not be able to argue that the class-wide proceeding is "presumptively disfavored as a matter of international law or policy"); *Shroyer v. New Cingular Wireless Services, Inc.*, 498 F.3d 976, 991, 992 (9th. Cir. 2007) ("we read [*Bazzle*] as an implicit endorsement by a majority of the Court of class arbitration procedures as consistent with the Federal Arbitration Act"; since "class arbitrations further the FAA's purpose of encouraging alternative dispute resolution", our holding that a waiver of class proceedings is unconscionable cannot in consequence be preempted as in conflict with federal policy).

67. See *Stolt-Nielsen SA v. AnimalFeeds Int'l Corp.*, Clause Construction Hearing, Joint Appendix, 2009 WL 2777896 at *117a (attorney for claimant: prior arbitration cases "relied on a notion of a broad clause that does not expressly forbid class arbitration, that's permitting class arbitrations to move forward"); *Stolt-Nielsen*, 130 S.Ct. at 1772 (before the arbitral tribunal, claimant "argue[d] that *Bazzle* requires clear language that *forbids* class arbitration in order to bar a class action") (emphasis added).

68. E.g., *Flaxman v. Terminix, Inc.*, Partial Final Clause Construction Award, AAA No. 11 434 00701 07 (2008) at fn. 6 ("although it does not create an automatic presumption in favor of allowing class claims when the agreement is silent", nevertheless, "notably", the plurality in *Bazzle* "does consistently define the issue as whether there is any class action prohibition"); see also *Stolt-Nielsen SA v. AnimalFeeds Int'l Corp.*, 548 F.3d 85, 89-90 (arbitral tribunal ordered class-wide proceedings after noting that respondent "had been unable to cite any arbitration decision under [AAA Rules] in which contractual silence had been construed to prohibit class arbitration").

69. Cf. William G. WHITEHILL, "Class Actions and Arbitration Murky Waters", 4 World Arb. & Med. Rev. (2010) p. 1 at pp. 9-10 (the arbitrators in *Stolt-Nielsen* decided to proceed with a class arbitration "because the [respondent's] evidence did not *preclude* class arbitration" and so in effect "the Panel adopted *Bazzle's* approach of placing on the party opposing class treatment the burden to establish that the arbitration agreement affirmatively prohibits class arbitration") (emphasis in original); see also *Jock v. Sterling Jewelers, Inc.*, 725 F.Supp.2d 444, 448 (S.D.N.Y. 2010) (Arbitrator Roberts "devoted her analysis to determining whether there was any indication that

merely responsive, as we have seen, to the dialectic of party argument – that could justify any such assumption: A presumption to that effect may indeed have been the state-fashioned default rule in South Carolina – which is precisely what the plurality in *Bazzle set aside in favor of arbitral determination*. But this says nothing whatever about alternative background rules that might be preferred in litigation in other states,[70] or about the possible existence of a federal default rule, or – still less – about what would be a permissible uniform working rule for an arbitral tribunal.

So just four or five months after *Bazzle* was handed down, the American Arbitration Association (AAA) – in order to "prepare for an anticipated increase in demand for the administration of class arbitrations"[71] – published a set of "Supplementary Rules" for class-wide proceedings; these mirror in many respects Rule 23 of the Federal Rules, and create an elaborate framework for arbitral determinations of the sort envisaged by Justice Breyer: There is first to be an arbitral determination, "as a threshold matter", on the "construction" of the arbitration clause – to determine whether it permits the arbitration to proceed on behalf of a class. A party may move to confirm or vacate this "clause construction award" and after a stay for the purpose of seeking judicial review, the arbitrators are then to proceed to determine the question of class certification – that is, whether the case "*should* proceed as a class arbitration". So by virtue of the rules, incorporated as part of the parties' agreement, a contractual delegation of decisionmaking authority to the tribunal is clear[72] – although at the same time the rules caution that in "construing" the arbitration clause the arbitrator is not to "consider" the existence of the rules "to be a factor either in favor of or against permitting the arbitration to proceed on a class basis".[73]

---

the parties intended to preclude class arbitration, and ultimately concluded that the agreements 'do not prohibit' class arbitration").

70. Cf. *Green Tree Financial Corp. v. Bazzle*, Brief for Respondents [Bazzles], 2003 WL 1701523 at *28, *32, *38 ("although another state might apply a different default rule", Green Tree's own choice-of-law provision "incorporates the South Carolina default rule permitting class arbitration").

71. See *Stolt-Nielsen S.A. v. AnimalFeeds Int'l Corp.*, Brief of AAA as Amicus Curiae in Support of Neither Party, 2009 WL 2896309 at *9.

The AAA's searchable class arbitration "docket" of cases administered by the institution is available at its website at <www.adr.org>. As of 15 March 2014, it included 363 cases, including cases that were inactive because settled, withdrawn, or dismissed, and awards that had been vacated.

72. These supplementary class rules are to apply to any contract calling for arbitration under any body of AAA rules (although the AAA will not "administer class arbitrations where the underlying arbitration agreement explicitly *precludes* class procedures", Commentary to the American Arbitration Association's Class Arbitrations Policy, 18 February 2005).

73. R. 3. In short, mere agreement to the rules does not in itself amount to an "agreement to classwide arbitration" – is not even probative of any such agreement. There is a simple grant of authority to the arbitrators, but this does not in itself amount to expressing a preference for arbitral judgment to be exercised in any particular way.

Cf. STRONG, supra fn. 66 at pp. 1073-1074. Professor Strong criticizes the AAA rules for "apply[ing] the concept of implied consent to allow retroactive application" to parties whose contract may "dat[e] back to the 1970s or 1980s" when the rules were "not even in existence" – resulting in unfair "surprise". Does this suggest, by negative implication, that if the rules had

2. *"Silence" as the Failure of Agreement: Stolt-Nielsen*[74]

The trope of "silence" played a quite different, and far more problematical, role in another "class arbitration" case a few years later.

In *Stolt-Nielsen,* a number of charterers had brought antitrust suits against a shipping company, each purportedly on behalf of a class, and later consolidated. The respondent had successfully moved to compel arbitration, and the claimants then demanded a class-wide arbitration proceeding. The contract had not originally incorporated the rules of the AAA, but the parties – "in light of *Bazzle*"[75] – entered into a "supplemental agreement" by which the question of class arbitration was to be submitted to a panel of three arbitrators, who were to "follow and be bound by" the AAA's Supplementary Rules for Class Arbitrations; an arbitral tribunal was empanelled under those rules to render a "clause construction award". You will note immediately that this agreement of the parties rendered the jurisdictional holding of *Bazzle* largely irrelevant: We have here an express grant of power to the arbitrators that replaces the presumed allocation, found by the plurality in *Bazzle* to be implicit in the arbitral enterprise.

---

indeed been "in existence" at the time the contract was entered into, we would then be warranted in drawing the opposite conclusion – there had in fact been "consent" to class-wide proceedings? Precisely the same problem is lurking in her suggestion that there would be no problem in finding "implied consent to classwide proceedings" where parties have chosen as the seat of the arbitration a jurisdiction "that recognizes arbitrators' authority to order classwide proceedings", *id.* at pp. 1062-1067 and n. 209. Presumably to choose a lex arbitri is presumptively to choose the law in force at the seat *at the time the proceeding is instituted*, not the law that might have been in effect at the time when the contract was drafted.

All this highlights a far more fundamental problem: I confess that I still remain unsure whether the "implied consent" that Professor Strong is discussing, is in fact,

• "consent" to *empower the arbitral tribunal as the ultimate decisionmaker* [which will raise the question whether authority to order a class-wide proceeding was ever conferred on the tribunal in the first place], or
• "consent" *to the actual class-wide proceeding itself* [raising the question, for the tribunal, whether such a proceeding would be within the parties' expectations, and for a reviewing court, whether the undoubted jurisdiction of the tribunal has been exercised in an illegitimate manner].

Bazzle itself of course is a case that raised the former issue – where class arbitration rules did not exist at the time of contracting, but the existence of arbitral power was deduced from a general broad grant of decisionmaking authority. *Stolt-Nielsen* and *Oxford Health* are cases that raise the latter issue. The passage I quoted above (suggesting that if the chosen seat "recognizes arbitrators' authority to order classwide proceedings", then the parties may be said to have "impli[citly] consent[ed] to classwide proceedings"), shows how easily these two questions can be conflated – despite the earnest attempt by the AAA to keep them separate – shows how easily one can deduce the latter form of "consent" from the former – and so powerfully suggests that despite the caveat of R.3, the gravitational pull of these rules can be very intense indeed.

74. *Stolt-Nielsen S.A. v. Animalfeeds Int'l Corp.*, 130 S.Ct. 1758 (2010).
75. *Stolt-Nielsen SA v. AnimalFeeds Int'l Corp.*, Brief for Petitioners, 2009 WL2809359 at *7.

The arbitrators then went on to conclude that the arbitration clause did indeed authorize class-wide arbitration.[76] The respondents sought to have this "clause construction award" vacated, and in a most conventional analysis, the Second Circuit rebuffed the attempt: Repeating the mantra that "interpretation" is "an area we are particularly loath to disturb", it concluded that an arbitrator's "misapplication" of a contract's terms can hardly "rise to the stature of 'manifest disregard'" of the law – whatever that means – and that determinations of custom and usage, informing any reading of a contract, are themselves in any event "findings of fact" wholly immune to review on any such grounds.[77]

Now one would have thought that the next step could have been predicted with some confidence. The Court in *Bazzle* – after remanding for an arbitral exercise in construction – had seen no need to go further: That is, it saw no need to address what standards the arbitrators would be expected to use, or what sort of decision (if any) the FAA might require, or what level of scrutiny a court would be expected to deploy. But after all, the answers to all of these questions might reasonably have seemed implicit in the holding: The plurality there had pretty clearly taken the view that the availability of class-wide proceedings did not even rise to the level of what we have become accustomed in this country to call a "gateway question of arbitrability".[78] And what can

---

76. The arbitrators claimed to believe that the resolution of this issue was "controlled by the Supreme Court's decision in [*Bazzle*]" – but this betrays considerable misunderstanding and can't be taken at face value: However receptive to the notion of class-wide proceedings, and however deferential to arbitral competence, the Court in *Bazzle* provided no guidance at all with respect to how an arbitral tribunal should proceed.

77. *Stolt-Nielsen S.A.*, 548 F.3d at 98.

Nor could the court find any state or federal maritime "rule of construction" that "clearly governs" the issue here – that is, which governs whether a failure to address the question of class-wide arbitrations should be taken to be probative of an intent not to *allow* them, or of an intent not to *prohibit* them. *Id.* at 99. By contrast, as we have seen, a "rule of construction" with respect to this issue was precisely what the South Carolina courts had found and applied in *Bazzle* (although only Justices Stevens and Thomas thought that deference to this rule was necessary); see text accompanying fn. 52, and fn. 65, supra.

78. As it "concerns neither the validity of the arbitration clause nor its applicability to the underlying dispute between the parties". *Bazzle*, 539 U.S. at 452. See Alan Scott RAU, "'Consent' to Arbitral Jurisdiction: Disputes with Non-Signatories" in Belinda MACMAHON, ed., *Multiple Party Actions in International Arbitration: Consent, Procedure and Enforcement* (2009) p. 69 at p. 71:

"This 'question of arbitrability' – whether there is a 'duty for the parties to arbitrate' the dispute – whether the parties have consented to a final arbitral judgment on the issues – whether, in short, the arbitrators have 'jurisdiction' to decide – is undeniably an issue for judicial determination."

For one further contribution to the endless "gateway" discussion, see also Alan Scott RAU, "Arbitrating 'Arbitrability'", 7 World Arb. & Med. Rep. (2013) p. 487.

Yes, I appreciate that the terminology is highly fraught and that our usage is completely at odds with the way that the notion of "arbitrability" is used in other legal systems; see Jan PAULSSON, "Jurisdiction and Admissibility" in Gerald AKSEN, ed., *Global Reflections on International Law, Commerce and Dispute Resolution: Liber Amicorum in Honour of Robert Briner* (2005) p. 601 at p. 609 (our "persistent abuse" of this "vaporous locution" "has led to international disharmony, because

we possibly mean when we say that an issue is not one of "arbitrability"? Only this: that we are willing, *at the very outset*, to *presume* that the parties have consented to entrust it to the arbitrators, without any need for an express allocation. This must be true a fortiori when we can find such a delegation of authority in the form of the parties' express submission to the AAA rules. And if we are satisfied that the parties have in fact done this, then we would expect an arbitral award on the subject to command precisely the same degree of deference as would *any* decision "on the merits" resolving a dispute submitted by contract to the tribunal.

Nevertheless the Supreme Court reversed, mandating that the award should be vacated. While *Bazzle* itself could not be directly overruled,[79] the inevitable second thoughts, changes in the composition of the Court,[80] and the dreaded spectre for a business-oriented Court of an increased resort to class-wide proceedings, all meant that earlier confident predictions were to prove fruitless. For the Court in *Stolt-Nielsen*, there was no basis at all for the tribunal's endorsement of a class-wide proceeding. The holding can be broken down into two parts:

(1) Instead of making some "determination regarding the parties' intent"[81] – and instead of "identifying and applying a rule of decision" derived from state or federal law[82] – the arbitral tribunal had merely "imposed its view of sound policy"[83] – and by doing so, had "exceeded its powers" under Sect. 10(a)(4) of the FAA.[84]

---

elsewhere that word has an established meaning" referring to public policy limitations upon what it is legally permissible to arbitrate). I have in fact often suggested that the term "can easily be dispensed with". Alan Scott RAU, "Everything You Really Need to Know About 'Separability' in Seventeen Simple Propositions", supra fn. 13, p. 1 at p. 120.

79. The Court in *Stolt-Nielsen* acknowledged that *in light of the express agreement of the parties subjecting themselves to the AAA rules*, "we need not revisit" the question whether the permissibility of class-wide proceedings was otherwise reserved for the arbitral tribunal, *Stolt-Nielsen*, 130 S.Ct. at 1772.

80. The Court was divided 5-3. (Justice Sotomayor did not participate). Justice Kennedy, who had dissented in *Bazzle* on the ground that ordering class-wide arbitration was impermissible as a matter of federal law, naturally found himself in the majority here, as did Justice Alito and Chief Justice Roberts. Justice Thomas had also dissented in *Bazzle* – but on the basis of his customary and idiosyncratic position that state court arbitration rulings should not be interfered with by federal law; here, though, the absence of any overt Supremacy Clause concerns left him free to join the majority as well. The fifth vote of Justice Scalia – who had concurred in Justice Breyer's opinion in *Bazzle* – is considerably more difficult to rationalize. Justice Stevens, who had been willing to join the plurality in *Bazzle* – at least to the extent of remanding the case and preserving the issue of contract construction for the arbitrators – appropriately dissented in *Stolt-Nielsen* (as did of course Justice Breyer himself and Justice Ginsburg, both of whom were in the same position).

81. *Stolt-Nielsen*, 130 S.Ct. at 1768 n. 4.

82. *Id.* at 1770.

83. *Id.* at 1767-1768.

84. *Id.* at 1770; see also *id.* at 1767-1768.

This was the only invocation of any statutory ground for vacatur. I should mention that in the early proceedings below the district court had in fact vacated the award using a different formulation – relying on the assertion that the tribunal had "manifestly disregarded a well defined rule of governing maritime law". It is hard to know what to make of this; could it mean that the arbitrator is tasked with having *disregarded evidence with respect to the content of the prevailing custom*

(2) Nor was there any reason, after vacatur, to remand and "direct a rehearing by the arbitrators" under Sect. 10(b) – that would be pointless because "there can be only one possible outcome on the facts before us": Since there was no "contractual basis" to support a finding of consent to class-wide proceedings, the parties "cannot be compelled" to participate in one.[85]

a.   *"A determination regarding the parties' intent"*

"I used to teach Contracts, did you know that?"[86]

The first of these holdings has by far the most resonance for our present concerns: It is also by far the most inexplicable, and ultimately the least defensible. So naturally I will dwell on that here.

Now if a claimant is demanding that a court – or an arbitral tribunal – order "his" arbitration to proceed on a class-wide basis, what is the route to such a conclusion: What is the link between the demand and the order?

What is clearly the appropriate starting point is some sort of finding to the effect that this would be consistent with the "agreement of the parties".[87] The "threshold" inquiry

---

and usage? See *Stolt Nielsen,* 435 F.Supp.2d at 387 n. 3. ("silence" "simply opens the door to extrinsic evidence, which here strongly supports Stolt's position"); But see Alan Scott RAU, "The Culture of American Arbitration", supra fn. 26 at p. 526 (even in the Second Circuit the notion of "manifest disregard of the evidence" is "now treated as a mere sport in the law, having joined the choir invisible of discarded conceits"). The Supreme Court did touch on this matter briefly, in a rather curious footnote, *Stolt-Nielsen,* 130 S.Ct. at 1768 n. 4: Justice Alito remarked that "we do not decide" whether the "manifest disregard" ground still "survives" as an "independent ground for [judicial] review" – but added that "assuming, *arguendo,* that such a standard applies, we find it satisfied for the reasons that follow". All this is lazy and readily lends itself to ridicule; see Adam SAMUEL, "The U.S. Supreme Court's Undistinguished 2010 Trilogy: An English View", 66 DISP. RES. J., (Feb.-April 2011) p. 32 at pp. 33, 35 ("dodging issues"), 36 ("painful fence-sitting"). But I don't find the Court's footnote overly bizarre: For all the Court is really saying, at bottom, is that any notion of "manifest disregard" doesn't, and can't, matter much in the sensible resolution of any case – which must be arrived at on other grounds and for other reasons. And this is something we knew all along.

85. *Stolt-Nielsen,* 130 S.Ct. at 1770, 1776.

86. Oral Argument, supra fn. 3, 2009 WL 4662509 at *39 (Justice Scalia).

87. Sect. 4 of the FAA, as we know, mandates a court "order directing the parties to proceed to arbitration in accordance with the terms of the agreement". (For the use of Sect. 4 to rein in arbitrations that have not been authorized by contract, in the interest of preserving "freedom *from* arbitration", see the discussion at text accompanying fns. 165-166 infra). And after an award has been rendered, Sect. 10(a)(4) provides for vacatur where the arbitrators were "guilty" of "misbehavior by which the rights of any party have been prejudiced": It should hardly be surprising that this antique formulation does not expressly track Art. V(1)(d) of the New York Convention – which permits a refusal of recognition and enforcement where "the arbitral procedure was not in accordance with the agreement of the parties" – but it *would* be surprising indeed if the scope of Sect. 10 were held to be much narrower and not to encompass these Convention grounds as well; cf. Gary B. BORN, *International Commercial Arbitration,* vol 2 (2009) p. 2595 ("in jurisdictions where no statutory provision directly addresses the subject, courts have nonetheless held that

mandated by the AAA's "Supplementary Rules for Class Arbitration" is whether the arbitration clause "*permits* the arbitration to proceed on behalf of" a class. At oral argument, Justice Scalia complained that this "doesn't help me a lot. What does it mean, 'if it permits it'? ... [D]oes that mean whether the parties have agreed to it?"[88] Well, not quite: I would suggest that the proper answer to his question would have been this: The Rules simply envisage a "level 2" inquiry[89] into, "*whether the ability to order class-wide proceedings is within the scope of the powers granted by the parties to the arbitrators?*"

Before the arbitral tribunal, the parties in *Stolt-Nielsen* had apparently agreed that the arbitration clause said nothing particularly explicit on the issue of class-wide proceedings – but that it was instead "silent".[90] Before the case was over this trope of "silence" had come to mean something quite different from what it meant in Bazzle – but that such an offhand remark would ultimately assume such an outsized and outlandish importance must have been a considerable surprise to everyone.

At the outset, summoning up this notion of "silence" seemed to be little more than a rhetorical shorthand: For the claimant, "*because* the arbitration clauses were silent, arbitration on behalf of a class could proceed".[91]

(Here's the premise underlying that: Recall that Justice Breyer framed the problem faced by the Court in *Bazzle* as a choice between two "contending approaches" – between, on the one hand, a state law default rule deployed in the event of textual indeterminacy, and on the other hand, "the respondent's claim rooted in a supposed textual prohibition". So the claimant's obvious intent was to invoke Justice Breyer's dichotomy – and in doing so to point out the preferred alternative. In other words, to eliminate the latter prong – there could be no prohibition "because the arbitration clauses were silent" – would, it was hoped, necessarily open the door to choosing the former – that is, it would permit an arbitral choice of a default rule that would operate in his favor.)

For the respondent, by contrast, "*because* the arbitration clauses were silent, the parties intended not to permit class arbitration":[92]

(And here is the premise underlying that: The obvious purpose here was to invoke the many cases that, over the years, tended to assume – again, in the absence of some explicit authorization – that federal courts lack any power to order the consolidation of

---

arbitral awards are subject to annulment if the arbitrators fail to observe the procedures agreed by the parties"); cf. Alan Scott RAU, "The New York Convention in American Courts", 7 Amer. Rev. Int'l Arb. (1996) p. 213 at p. 236 ("as a practical matter [it is] highly unlikely – to put it mildly – that actual results in concrete cases will tend to diverge significantly depending on whether an award is scrutinized under Article V of the Convention or under § 10 of the FAA").

88. See Oral Argument, supra fn. 3, 2009 WL 4662509 at *52.
89. See RAU, "Everything You Really Need to Know About 'Separability' in Seventeen Simple Propositions", supra fn. 13 at pp. 92-94, 110-111 (elaborating a "conceptual framework" involving "three separate questions [that] will recur in connection with any arbitration").
90. Brief for Petitioners, supra fn. 75, 2009 WL 2809359 at *8.
91. *Stolt-Nielsen*, 548 F.3d at 89 (emphasis added).
92. *Id.*

related arbitrations. Reliance on this federal background law would, supposedly, explain and justify the lack of any more precise provision with respect to class proceedings.)[93]

So the conceit of "silence" here could not have been meant to carry much beyond the usefulness of such a frame in the dialectic of adversarial argument:[94] Nor did any supposed agreement along those lines prevent the parties from engaging in sustained and vigorous argument, both semantic and otherwise, with respect to what their "true intention" had been: A reading of the briefs and the transcript of the oral argument hardly suggests that they thought this question of interpretation had been stipulated away.[95] And neither the district court nor the court of appeals made the slightest

---

93. See generally RAU and SHERMAN, supra fn. 48 at p. 113 ("the dominant emerging tendency" has been a "presumption against consolidation in the absence of some affirmative evidence that the parties have consented to it, either in their original agreement or later at the time of submission").

  For this argument by the respondents, see *Stolt-Nielsen SA v. AnimalFeeds Int'l Corp.*, Clause Construction Hearing, Joint Appendix, supra fn. 67, 2009 WL 2777896 at *104a-*105a ("you have to know what the law said at the time you enter this agreement because you're not going [to] write down everything the law gives you anyway.... [T]hroughout this time period, they knew you couldn't consolidate."); Brief for Petitioners, supra fn. 75, 2009 WL 2809359 at *8 ("In the face of that silence, [respondents] cited federal case law prohibiting class or other consolidated arbitration without all parties' consent").

94. This insistence by the parties on mutually exclusive default rules triggered by "silence" also presumably explains their convergence on the proposition that the contract was "unambiguous" – with the apparent consequence that any need to consider "parol evidence" was obviated. See *id.* at *77a (counsel for claimant: "all the parties also agree that the arbitration clause is unambiguous"); *Stolt-Nielsen*, 130 S.Ct. at 1770.

  The continuing insistence by lawyers on the supposed lack of "ambiguity" – even in circumstances where it serves no particular function – that is, even in circumstances where there is no danger whatever of wayward fact finding on the part of a jury – continues to bemuse me. Cf. Restatement (Second) Contracts, Sect. 212 *cmt.* d. ("historically", "partly perhaps because of the fact that jurors were often illiterate, questions of interpretation of written documents have been treated as questions of law in the sense that they are decided by the trial judge rather than by the jury"). For the same reasons – while the concept of "an agreement that is silent" is challenging enough – the category of "an agreement that is *unambiguously* silent" is merely calculated to cause migraine. But cf. WHITEHILL, supra fn. 69 at p. 2.

  It is simply not our lot to escape doubt. I still remember an episode from my first-year Contracts class, when during a discussion of the Restatement First Sect. 31 ("In case of doubt it is presumed that an offer invites the formation of a bilateral contract"), our professor asked, "but what of the case where there is doubt as to whether there is doubt?" Even at the time, I think, I sensed that this could not have been intended to be taken seriously as a useful aid to taxonomy – although in the hands of the much- and appropriately-revered Jack Dawson it was certainly clever enough Socratically.

95. For the claimant in the arbitration (AnimalFeeds): Brief for Respondent, 2009 WL 3404244 at *33-*34 ("the contract's conferral on the arbitrators of power to decide '*any*' dispute is most reasonably read as not limited to the subset of disputes between a single parcel tanker owner and a single customer"; "so, too, the clause's use of the term 'dispute' is permissibly read to include disputes involving multiple parties, as here"); Oral Argument, supra fn. 3, 2009 WL 4662509 at *43-*44 (counsel for claimants: "that goes back to whether 'any disputes' can plausibly be read to encompass the class mechanism, because if it can, well then, by agreeing to that contract, you have, in effect, agreed to something that delegates to the arbitrator the ability to use that"); see also Clause Construction Hearing, Joint Appendix, supra fn. 92, 2009 WL 2777896 at *79a ("the

reference to it below: Indeed the award in *Stolt-Nielsen* did purport to proceed by divining contractual intent from the language of the agreement,[96] and the entire thrust of the Second Circuit's decision was deference to the arbitrators' own exercise in "interpretation" and to their "findings of fact" – finding their reading of the agreement to be "at least colorable".[97]

Nevertheless the Supreme Court took this putative stipulation and – with no particular urging from anyone – ran away with it. On the matter of "silence", the claimant had in fact gone on to concede that "when a contract is silent on an issue there's been no agreement that has been reached on that issue".[98] For the Court, this did not suggest merely that there had been no "express reference" to class-wide proceedings – it implied as well that the parties had had no understanding with respect to the matter whatever – that is, that *at least with respect to that particular term, there had been no "meeting of the minds" at all.*

And what are the implications of *that*, exactly?

Now as we have seen, there exists a weak account of what "silence", or "gaps" – we might prefer to talk instead of "omitted terms" – can mean: On this account the problem

---

arbitration clause here contains broad language and this language should be interpreted to permit class arbitrations"; "the term 'any' and 'all differences and disputes of whatever nature' ... would include class arbitrations").

    For the respondent: See *id.*, 2009 WL 2777896 at *92a-*93a ("you guys read the contract and you figure out the procedures that apply, whether we contemplated having a class action or not"); *id.* at *95a (Arbitrator Jentes: "What's the issue?"; counsel for respondents: "What do the parties intend in this contract. Basic contract interpretation. And it's for you to decide"); Brief for Petitioners, 2009 WL 2809359 at*21 (before the arbitrators, respondents argued "that in context, the [arbitration] clause should be construed to prohibit class arbitration as a matter of properly inferred intent"); Oral Argument, supra fn. 3, 2009 WL 4662509 at *15-*16 ("our position about the construction of the contract was that in fact, although there is no express provision one way or the other, this is a maritime contract, and the – and maritime law is ascertained by custom and practice, and we introduced evidence in the form of affidavits that were unrefuted ... since the days of Marco Polo....").

96. The arbitral award acknowledged that the arbitrators "must look to the language of the parties' agreement to ascertain the parties' intention whether they intended to permit or to preclude class action," see 548 F.3d at 97. And so on review, the claimants not only argued the point of interpretation, see fn. 94 supra, but in fact went further – suggesting that *they had actually submitted* this question of contract interpretation to the arbitrators, and that the arbitral award, ordering class-wide proceedings, had been rendered *precisely on that basis and in response to its arguments*; see Oral Argument, supra fn. 3, 2009 WL 4662509 at *30-*32 ("what they relied on was the broad language of the agreement, the language 'any disputes'"; "they are saying: We are not going to do this based on a default rule; we are going to do this based on the language and intent. Right?"); *id.* at *55 (counsel for claimants had previously made "the argument that we believe the arbitrators adopted, which is that the arbitration clause here contains broad language, and this language should be interpreted to permit class arbitrations").

97. *Stolt-Nielsen*, 548 F.3d at 99.

98. Clause Construction Hearing, Joint Appendix, supra fn. 67, 2009 WL 2777896 at *77a. But – once again – this can only be understood in the context and flow of the argument – as an attempt to underline that a favorable default rule remained available: "*Therefore*," the claimant went on, "there has been *no agreement to bar* class arbitrations." *Id.*

is merely this — that *the text of the agreement does not explicitly and immediately direct us to any conclusion* with respect to intent, or with respect to how a question of "meaning" should be resolved. In such cases ,whoever is charged with giving effect to the contract must begin by trying to tease out what the parties had wished to do, through recourse to the usual extrinsic methods for determining the content of the "bargain in fact" – either by

• "worrying the text of the agreement in order to discover some sort of underlying narrative",[99] or by
• looking to context and circumstances ("surrounding" by definition) to help determine the "commercial meaning" of the language and the "framework of common understanding."[100]

---

99. See RAU and SHERMAN, supra fn. 48 at p. 112 and fn. 124 (for example, a court might be able "to find some sort of 'implied' consent to consolidation" of related proceedings where it is presented with a vertical chain of related contracts and subcontracts).

   In doing this the "contract reader" will not disdain resort to marginal bits of homely "folk wisdom" that purport to tell him, as an empirical matter, how most people – draftsmen and legislators – are likely to deploy grammar and syntax. This includes, for example, many of the canons of construction; cf. *Circuit City Stores, Inc. v. Adams*, 121 S.Ct. 1302 (2000) (where Congress excluded from the reach of the FAA "contracts of employment of seamen, railroad employees, *or any other class of workers engaged in foreign or interstate commerce*", the italicized language must not be interpreted literally and in isolation from the rest – but must be understood in light of – and thus modified, qualified and restricted by, "controlled and defined by reference to" – the specific categories that precede it). Not all the canons, of course, can be described in that way; see, e.g., the dreaded canon *contra proferentem,* discussed at text accompanying fns. 156-160 infra.

100. See text accompanying fns. 51, 59-60 supra.

   This role of context in helping to determine the "framework of common understanding" assumed particular importance in the *Stolt-Nielsen* litigation. See *Stolt-Nielsen SA v. AnimalFeeds Int'l Corp.*, 435 F.Supp.2d 382, 385-386 (S.D.N.Y. 2006) ("in the maritime area ... the interpretation of contracts – and especially charter party agreements – is very much dictated by custom and usage", and "experts in international maritime arbitrations [testified] to the effect that sophisticated, multinational commercial parties ... would never intend that the arbitration clauses would permit a class arbitration"), *rev'd*, 548 F.3d 85, 97-98 (2d Cir. 2008) ("custom and usage is more of a guide than a rule"). In the Supreme Court, Justice Alito moved seamlessly from

   • noting the undisputed "expert opinion" with respect to the expectations of "sophisticated, multinational commercial parties" – summarizing, in a long footnote, extensive "expert evidence from experienced maritime arbitrators," "demonstrating that it is customary in the shipping business for parties to resolve their disputes through bilateral arbitration"; see *Stolt-Nielsen,* 130 S.Ct. at 1769 n. 6 ("in the view of the London Corps [sic] of International Arbitration, class arbitration is 'inconceivable'"),
   • to a conclusion that the tribunal has "simply imposed its own conception of sound policy", *Stolt-Nielsen,* 130 S.Ct. at 1769.

   This is either a non sequitur, or, more likely, a commentary to the effect that the tribunal had wantonly ignored the weight of the evidence.

Indeed the arbitral tribunal in *Stolt-Nielsen* had made gestures in this direction[101] – but for Justice Alito, it had been entirely illegitimate for it even to begin to go down this path. This suggests a much stronger version of "silence" – one asserting that the parties' "stipulation" of "no agreement" had necessarily barred, at the outset, *any of the traditional routes to contractual interpretation*: The arbitral tribunal, he wrote, had "had no occasion to 'ascertain the parties' intention'... because the parties were in complete agreement regarding their intent" – that is, presumably, that *they were in complete agreement that they had no intent at all*. In such circumstances, "any inquiry into that settled question would have been outside the [tribunal's] assigned task," and even the wording of the agreement itself "was quite beside the point". All that could be left, then, was not "interpretation" but the tribunal's own idiosyncratic "policy choice".[102]

Now a formal stipulation to the effect that the parties had not arrived at any common understanding with respect to a particular contractual issue – that on this issue, there were "no concordant wills"[103] – is surely uncommon. (Perhaps, though, the fact of expressly leaving a term open – in the form of an "agreement to agree" on it at some later time – may in the end amount to much the same thing?[104]) I have suggested in fact that in the procedural context of the *Stolt-Nielsen* litigation, the supposed "stipulation" was "largely fictive anyway", the Court's treatment of it "reek[ing] of disingenuousness": For "it seemed to operate here largely as a trap for the unwary claimant, who could hardly have imagined that he was conceding the very question of interpretation on which his case rested".[105] Nevertheless it is surely not unusual for the parties to enter into an agreement that purports to be a contract – that they believe to be a contract – without "agreement [having] been reached" on any number of terms, whether of price, or delivery, or conditions of financing – and this for any of a number of reasons that we have already canvassed.[106]

At the same time it could not seriously have been argued in *Stolt-Nielsen* that a finding of

• "no agreement" with respect to class-wide proceedings alone, could possibly suggest
• that the entire contractual process had aborted – that any "manifestation of mutual assent" to the exchange was lacking – that the "gap" had thereby swallowed up everything that *had* actually been agreed to, forcing us to conclude that the parties had never intended to be contractually bound at all. Nor was this argued.

---

101. See fn. 96 supra.
102. *Stolt-Nielsen*, 130 S.Ct. at 1770.
103. FRIED, supra fn. 3 at p. 60.
104. See fns. 19, 22 supra.
105. Alan Scott RAU, "Arbitral Power and the Limits of Contract: The New Trilogy", 22 Amer. Rev. Int'l Arb. (2011) p. 435 at p. 460.
    See also *Jock v. Sterling Jewelers, Inc.*, 646 F.3d 113, 129 fn. 2 (Winter. C.J., dissenting) ("If *Stolt-Nielsen* resolves only the effect of a *sui generis* and idiosyncratic stipulation of the parties, the case hardly meets [the criteria for granting a writ of certiorari (that "an important question of federal law" "has not been, but should be, settled by this Court")]).
106. See text accompanying fn. 17 supra.

For such a notion to come into play – for us to conclude that there was "no contract" – "the area of non-agreement would have to be considerably broader, and closer to the 'bounds of the entire consensual perimeter', than was the case in *Stolt-Nielsen*".[107]

In those circumstances, then, Justice Alito's reaching out to attribute significance to some supposed "stipulation" is especially telling – because it illustrates, I think, precisely where the Court went astray. The critical flaw lies in the limits that *Stolt-Nielsen* independently imposes on the process of contract construction when carried on by an arbitral tribunal – and in the cramped and cabined view of arbitral adjudication that the opinion reveals. For if we are really satisfied that the parties have "failed to manifest any type of inferable assent" with respect to a particular question,[108] then *the work of giving "meaning" to the contract hardly ends – really, it is just barely getting underway*.

An obvious, but modest, start is to look at the structure and purpose of the agreement, inquiring into the solution that would be most congruent with the "overall objectives of the parties".[109] Once we can identify the "sense of the transaction" – what the parties were about, and what they were trying to do – the question whether there has been a true "meeting of the minds" may begin to seem somewhat arid and abstract: Indefiniteness can often be cured by little more than an exercise of practical wisdom, striving to give content to the agreement by ensuring the "business efficacy" that the parties "must have intended" the transaction should have.[110]

To privilege a meaning towards which "most sensible people" would gravitate, may not, perhaps, always lead us directly to what the parties actually "had in mind when contracting" – but it is intended to coincide with "what a reasonable person would have understood under the circumstances".[111] More precisely, perhaps, it is intended to coincide with what a reasonable plaintiff believed and *had the right to believe* – as long as *a reasonable defendant ought to have realized* that such was the plaintiff's understanding. But *that*, of course, is precisely what the Orthodox "objective theory of Contracts" treats as the primarily relevant intention – or more properly, treats as the appropriate *definition*

---

107. RAU, supra fn. 105 at p. 462. Where the clause is marginal to the exchange, this must be true even where the "gap" was not the result of crossed signals – or a mere "blind spot" – but where the parties entered into the agreement despite the fact that they were "*at all times ... painfully aware of their contradictory understandings of a contractual term*", see fn. 17 supra.
108. BEN-SHAHIR, supra fn. 2 at p. 393.
109. RAU and SHERMAN, supra fn. 48 at p. 114.
110. The classic demonstration, if one is to take it at face value, is that of Justice Cardozo in *Wood v. Lucy, Lady Duff-Gordon*, 118 N.E. 214 (N.Y. 1917) ("A promise may be lacking, and yet the whole writing may be 'instinct with an obligation', imperfectly expressed"). Cf. POSNER, supra fn. 4 at pp. 1603-1604 (if "one of the rival interpretations proposed does not make commercial sense, the interpretation will be rejected because it probably does not jibe with what the parties understood when they signed the contract"); Ian R. MACNEIL, "Efficient Breach of Contract: Circles in the Sky", 68 Va. L. Rev. (1982) 947, 953 n.25 ("'Casual empiricism' is *not* a pejorative in my vocabulary; indeed, when used by wise people its other name is wisdom" (emphasis in original)).
111. Cf. Steven J. BURTON, *Elements of Contract Interpretation* (2009) p. 44.

of contractual intention – that is what "intention" *is*. We are never, after all, concerned about the viewpoint of the "reasonable fly on the wall".[112]

More broadly: In every long-term arrangement there are, in the immortal words of Donald Rumsfeld, known unknowns (suggesting the need for flexibility and adaptation in contract administration), and unknown unknowns (where the state of the world turns out somewhat differently from what we had taken for granted): But in either case – underlying both – the parties are likely to have shared certain tacit assumptions with respect to the nature of their common enterprise, and with respect to the scope of their cooperative venture. To inquire into these, leads us to an assessment of the ambit of the risks each party has undertaken.[113]

A tacit understanding with respect to the allocation of risk may for example be sought in any of *the other "dickered" terms of the deal*, for example, the agreed-upon price.[114] And merely to use *the overall framework of the agreement as a template* may make available any number of alternative devices: A total failure to agree on the conditions of financing may, for example, be bypassed if we imagine that the party seeking to enforce the deal is willing to concede to the other the best possible terms to which he would be entitled.[115]

---

112. Cf. *Davis v. Davis*, 175 A. 574 (Conn. 1934) ("plaintiff and defendant went on an automobile ride with several young people. It was a joyous occasion, and to add to the excitement the defendant dared the plaintiff to marry her"; "neither party intended at the time to enter into the marriage status"; held, although the ceremony had been performed by a justice of the peace – presumably a reasonable man – "no real contract [was] created" and "no marriage ever came into existence".)

Cf. Laurent LÉVY, *"L'interprétation arbitrale"*, Rev. de l'arb. (2013) p. 861 at p. 890 (distinguishing between an arbitrator's tendency to treat the matter from the point of view of the drafting parties themselves (attempting, in other words, to discover what it is that "they had meant to say"), and a judge's tendency to interpret a text in the way that "a reasonable person (himself)" would have understood it – but recognizing that the two methods converge in practice and "generally lead to the same result").

113. A textbook example, as you might expect, is Judge Posner's opinion in *Empire Gas Corp.*, supra fn. 10. The "gap" here consisted of the question – unaddressed by the parties – of "how much is the buyer obligated to buy in a requirements contract"? The court held that the buyer's decision, "for undisclosed reasons to order nothing at all, amounted to a lack of good faith – pointing to the fact that "the sudden termination of the contract midway through performance is bound to disrupt [the seller's] operations somewhat":

"The Illinois courts interpret a requirements contract as a sharing of risk between seller and buyer. The seller assumes the risk of a change in the buyer's business that makes continuation of the contract unduly costly [e.g., where there is a complete "lack of orders"], but the buyer assumes the risk of a less urgent change in his circumstances, perhaps illustrated by the facts of this case where so far as one can tell the buyer's change of mind reflected no more than a reassessment of the balance of advantages and disadvantages under the contract."

114. See, e.g., Restatement, Second, Contracts sec. 351 *cmt.* f (consequential damages; "an extreme disproportion between the loss and the price charged by the party whose liability for that loss is in question" "suggests that it was not intended to cover the risk of such liability").

115. See, e.g., Restatement, Second, Contracts Sect. 33 Ill. 2 (where part of the purchase price was to be in cash and part "on mortgage", but the terms of the loan were not stated, "the contract is too indefinite to support a decree of specific performance against [the buyer] – but [the buyer] may obtain such a decree if he offers to pay the full price in cash"); *Ontario Downs, Inc. v. Lauppe*,

In all these exercises of "interpretation" we are not, that is, "guessing at the hidden but determined content of some list of meanings in the speaker's head" – rather "our concerns particularize, *render concrete, inchoate meanings*" (emphasis added).[116] And – an overarching, but obvious point – the content of any merits-based contractual presumption with respect to *the proper allocation of risks* is a very different thing from any presumption that would foreclose *the decisionmaking authority of arbitrators*.[117]

Yet a further step – barely perceptible as anything different from what has gone before – would ask us to move from "interpretation" as commonly understood to the process of filling a gap in a responsible way. The law of Contracts is of course rife with "gap fillers" – it is rather hard to see how we could function without them – and much of the UCC in fact consists of presumptions to which we necessarily default in reading an agreement, where the parties have given us no particular indications to the contrary.[118] The most common tactic is to adopt a "mimicking" principle which seeks to align what the court does with a hypothetical consent (which is why we speak of "implied terms"). The search is for those terms "the parties would have agreed upon"[119] in a

---

192 Cal.App.2d 697 (2004) (parties entered into an agreement for the sale of 15.87 acres of land but did not specify *which* 15.87 acres within the seller's 450-acre lot were to be sold; held, if the buyer waived any right of selection he might have "and was willing to accept any 15.87-acre parcel, the court could require the [sellers] to select an appropriate parcel and upon [sellers'] refusal to so select, then allow [buyer] to designate a reasonable parcel"). See generally BEN-SHAHAR, supra fn. 2 at pp. 390, 411 (proposing that "a party who seeks enforcement of a deliberately incomplete agreement [should] be granted an option to enforce the transaction under the agreed-upon terms supplemented with terms that are the most favorable (within reason) to the defendant"; "if the parties recognize their deadlock and nevertheless draft a partial agreement, they are indicating that some assent has been obtained" and the remaining gap could be "decoupled" from the agreed-upon terms, allowing each party "to enforce upon her opponent a deal that, with respect to the contested issues, includes the opponent's favored terms").

116. FRIED, supra fn. 3 at p. 60 ("so when a person refers to all the even numbers between 10 and 1000, he intends to refer also to the number 946, although that number may not figure explicitly on some list in his head").

117. But cf. BERGER, supra fn. 40 at p. 8 ("the presumption of the professional competence of the parties to international business contracts" leads to a "yardstick" that "it is up to the parties to take precautions in their contract against unforeseen circumstances"; thus "in the absence of a special clause in the contract, the parties have indicated that the principle of sanctity of contracts shall prevail" so that "the risks of changed circumstances or discovery of gaps" is to be "borne by the parties"; "since the parties do not want an arbitration of that kind, adaption and supplementation may not be imposed on them by the arbitrators").

118. See RAU, "Everything You Really Need to Know About 'Separability'", supra fn. 13 at p. 29, fn. 71 ("sales law consists of little else but an abundant off-the-rack stock of background presumptions").

119. BEN-SHAHAR, supra fn. 2 at p. 397 ("the mimicking theory is based on a premise that there exists an underlying 'will' or hypothetical consent", or more precisely, that there are "specific definitive terms that the parties would have rationally agreed upon had they paid sufficient attention to the matter"); see also Clayton P. GILLETTE, "Cooperation and Convention in Contractual Defaults", 3 S. Cal. Interdisc. L.J. (1993) p. 167 at pp. 170-71("a default rule concerning risk of loss may reflect the objective that the parties would have achieved had they bargained fully about the matter, while allowing [them] to save the costs of achieving that bargain").

completely spelled-out agreement – or perhaps,[120] for the "bargain that most similarly situated parties would have chosen,[121] or that it would be rational for such parties to have chosen *ex ante*".[122]

I say this is a "barely perceptible" step because quite often, it is not acknowledged – or perhaps even realized – that a conscious choice of a default rule is being made.[123] Conventional commentary may insist on a doctrinal separation between mere questions of "interpretation" – necessarily focused on the search for the appropriate "intent" – and exercises in "gap filling"[124] – but after all, this is nothing but a matter of degree,[125] and conceptualism should not prevent us from appreciating that "gap filling" is equally "interpretive", *precisely to the extent that it represents an effort "to determine how the parties would have resolved the issue that has arisen had they foreseen it when they negotiated their contract".*[126] Conversely, given that there is often no true "intention" one way or the other, courts in a sense "make" contracts for the parties "almost every time they resolve an issue of contract interpretation" under the guise of deciphering the text:[127] Both

---

120. "[I]f the judicial task of identifying the hypothetical consent is more difficult, in light of the heterogeneity of contracting parties and the uncertainty concerning the circumstances," BEN-SHAHAR, supra fn. 2 at p. 398.

121. See also LÉVY, supra fn. 112 at p. 889 ("the views that people with characteristics similar to those of the parties in the suit, and placed in analogous circumstances, would have shared").

122. RAU and SHERMAN, supra fn. 48 at p. 115.

123. See the discussion at fn. 48 supra.

124. See, e.g., Margaret N. KNIFFIN, *Corbin on Contracts*, vol. 5 (rev. edn. 1998) Sect. 24.3 (a court's action in filling a gap "with respect to a matter which the parties did not have in contemplation and concerning which they therefore had no intention" "may be called construction" but "should not be called interpretation").

125. Cf. Restatement, Second, Contracts Sect. 204 *cmt.* a. ("the supplying of an omitted term is not technically interpretation, but the two are closely related"); *id. cmt.* c. (where there is "a common tacit assumption" or where "a term can be supplied by logical deduction from agreed terms and the circumstances", then "interpretation may be enough"; nonetheless "the supplying of an omitted term is not within the definition of interpretation").

126. See POSNER, supra fn. 4 at p. 1586; see also Eyal ZAMIR, "The Inverted Hierarchy of Contract Interpretation and Supplementation", 97 Colum. L. Rev. (1997) p. 1710 at p. 1719 ("when courts determine the meaning of a contract, they frequently resort to several sources at the same time", making the supposed distinction between interpretation of the contract and supplementation (or "gap filling"), "problematic"); cf. Eric A. POSNER, "There Are No Penalty Default Rules in Contract Law", 33 Fla. St. U. L. Rev. (2006) p. 563 at p. 579 ("one might plausibly argue that interpretive presumptions are analytically the same as default rules even if they are placed in a separate doctrinal category").

127. HAMILTON, RAU and WEINTRAUB, supra fn. 7 at pp. 366-367.
    Professor Nicklisch arrives, I think, at this conclusion – comes to realize it, it seems, almost in spite of himself – in Fritz NICKLISCH, "Agreement to Arbitrate to Fill Contractual Gaps", 5 J. Int'l Arb. (1988) p. 35 at p. 41. He writes there that a "course is often taken" to "regulate", "in the wording of the contract", "almost all areas and conceivable situations, using blanket clauses to cover those which are not foreseeable" – and in such a case an arbitral tribunal would not be "faced with the task of gap-filling, but rather with that of interpreting and applying the contractual regulations in an equitable manner". But of course, he ends with the obvious recognition that "materially speaking the concretization of blanket clauses is very near to gap-filling in the fuller

ambiguous and omitted terms can be recharacterized simply as terms that have failed to "fully specify obligations."[128]

From here there is often one further small, but significant step. A default rule that purports to mimic a hypothetical transaction may not after all make a great deal of sense once one concedes that really, there has been no agreement whatever with respect to the missing term.[129] As a consequence courts may think it best to bypass the exercise entirely – foregoing any pretense of conjecture about the bargaining process, or any attempt to reconstruct what the parties "would have chosen" – in favor of bringing to the surface what was probably latent all along: They may, in other words, proceed directly to select the solution which appears most economically efficient, or perhaps proceed to apply "a term which comports with community standards of fairness and policy".[130] We

---

sense".

128. POSNER, supra fn. 126 at p. 579.

At oral argument in *Stolt-Nielsen*, Justice Breyer posed this hypothetical:

"Imagine a worker who says: I have a right, permission, it's permissible for me to eat lunch next to the machine. The employer says no.... So the arbitrator or the judge reads the words [of the contract]. Nothing ... Then the judge or the arbitrator reads the rest of the contract. Hasn't a clue. Then the arbitrator or the judge goes and looks and sees: 'What's practice around here?' ... Then they might look to what happens in the rest of the industry."

Stolt-Nielsen, Oral Argument, supra fn. 3, 2009 WL 4662509 at *40.

It is obvious that in adjudicating such a case, whether one:

• looks at course of performance and custom and usage, or
• asks what seems most consistent otherwise with the overall structure of the agreement, or
• seeks to determine what is most likely to be consistent with the usual background presumption of employer control of physical arrangements in the workplace –

all will call for conducting a similar analysis and will tend to lead to a similar result.

It is striking that Justice Breyer doesn't stop there but continues: "Then they might look to what happens in foreign countries with comparable industries. Then they might look to public policy. They might look almost to anything under the sun they think is relevant." All of this goes to "*what, objectively read, those words in the contract mean*".

129. Cf. BEN-SHAHAR, supra fn. 2 at pp. 391-392, 414 (the premise that "a mutual will of the parties exists" is "problematic in incomplete contracts" and amounts to a "pure fiction").

130. Restatement, Second, Contracts Sect. 204 *cmt. d* ("where there is in fact no agreement, the court should supply a term which comports with community standards of fairness and policy rather than analyze a hypothetical model of the bargaining process"); see also *id.* at Sect. 351 *cmt. f* (consequential damages; "the fact that the parties did not attempt to delineate with precision all of the risks justifies a court in attempting to allocate them fairly"); cf. ZAMIR, supra fn. 126 at p. 1754 ("the judicial process of recognizing and developing 'implied terms' ordinarily produces rules that conform to prevailing conceptions of what is just, reasonable, and efficient in contractual relations"); Nicholas R. WEISKOPF, "*Wood v. Lucy*: The Overlap Between Interpretation and Gap-Filling to Achieve Minimum Decencies", 28 Pace L. Rev. (2008) p. 219 at pp. 226-227 ("the exhaustion of all interpretive steps is not needed to create a 'gap' designed to leave room for mandated observance of perceived minimum decencies in the course of performance").

can be pretty confident that a bluff and straightforward attempt to "supply" a term which is simply "reasonable in the circumstances"[131] is not likely to stray too far from what at the very least were the tacit assumptions of the contracting parties underlying the deal.[132] But in any event normative concerns will ineluctably play a role here, and a court which has no particular interest in camouflaging the route to its conclusion may well appeal to them explicitly.[133] Any number of default rules in our law of arbitration can already be understood in precisely this way.[134]

When courts act in this way, they are still remaining faithful to their usual role in formulating rules of general application – they are hardly at large, purporting to act as *amiables compositeurs* – nor could that be said of arbitrators who might follow their example.

131. Restatement, Second, Contracts Sect. 204.

132. See, e.g., Richard A. EPSTEIN, "Beyond Foreseeability: Consequential Damages in the Law of Contract", 18 J. Legal Stud. (1989) p. 105 at p. 106 ("what rational parties would have agreed to is ... strong evidence of what these parties did, in fact, agree to where there is silence or ambiguity"; there is accordingly "a complete congruence between the 'efficient' identification of the proper contract terms and honoring what the parties did, or would have agreed to do, under contract"); Randy E. BARNETT, "The Sound of Silence: Default Rules and Contractual Consent", 78 Va. L. Rev. (1992) p. 821 at pp. 827, 909(when "default rules are chosen to reflect the commonsense or conventional understanding of most parties", "enforcement may still be justified on the grounds of consent"; "abstract methods of analysis are simply presumptive surrogates for evidence of actual meaning").

133. Cf. David CHARNY, "Hypothetical Bargains: The Normative Structure of Contract Interpretation", 89 Mich. L. Rev. (1991) p. 1815 at pp. 1875-1877 (in the case of two unmarried persons living together, a court found "the existence of an agreement for property to be owned jointly"; this "strategy of imaginative reconstruction" – or in an alternative formulation, this "implicit paternalism" – might be justified on the ground that it "may help to change social attitudes about duties of men and women living in intimate relationships"; "the judicial standard of fair conduct may be one that persons will defer to").

134. For example, the time-honored doctrine of "separability" and our "presumption of arbitrability" [the former should be understood as just one aspect of the latter, an included case], are both probably best viewed as majoritarian defaults that impute to contracting parties a preference for "one- stop adjudication"; see RAU, "Everything You Really Need to Know About 'Separability'", supra fn. 13 at pp. 115-116 ("inevitably more economical, and thus likely to have been desired by both parties *ex ante*"; in addition, "questions of scope and questions going 'to the merits' are often so intertwined that we can expect similar arbitral competence to be relevant, and similar factual considerations to come into play"). At the same time, though, they might be thought to reflect a federal policy preference in favor of directing disputed issues to alternative fora. See, e.g., *Roadway Package System, Inc. v. Kayser*, 257 F.3d 287, 296-297 (3d Cir. 2001) ("any default rule is doomed to be inaccurate in some cases", but in light of the FAA's "*raison d'être*", it is worse to "wrongly conclud[e] that parties intended to opt out" of the FAA's standards of review, than to "wrongly conclud[e] that they did not").

Either way, the methodology – which is impeccable – has particular resonance for the cases we are discussing here. I say the methodology is "impeccable" because in any concrete case, as a response to a particular question, it supplies a presumptively applicable term on the basis either of

• an assessment of presumed intent, or
• an instrumental exercise of state policy.

So to review the bidding: Default rules in adjudication can be crafted by the decisionmaker as an attempt to "mimic" the contracting parties' hypothetical bargain, or to track their tacit assumptions – or such rules can be crafted, more simply and directly, in overt response to concerns of efficiency and fair play. But none of this – despite the suggestion of the Court – is remotely akin to suggesting that "mere silence" can itself *"constitute consent"* to class-wide proceedings:[135] That of course is not what the arbitrators did, nor is it what any reasonable arbitrator would do.

Now having reached this point, we pause and look around and find ourselves pretty clearly now in the realm of what would normally be termed, not "interpretation",[136] but "construction".[137] Nevertheless skepticism about the coherence, or stability, or utility, of any supposed dichotomy between the two seems abundantly justified, and growing –

The *Prima Paint* inquiry in particular has become so routine, so mechanical, so much a question of second nature to us, that we rarely notice the process we are going through. To courts, attorneys, and academics alike, *Prima Paint* does not really seem to be just a "presumption"—still less does it seem to be an individualized factual inquiry—it rather has the feel of a "doctrine," a "rule of law". But is in fact nothing but an "unremarkable and eminently sensible" *default rule "with respect to the likely boundaries of contractual consent", a "working presumption" that contracting* the parties did indeed wish the matter of contractual validity to be entrusted to arbitrators (emphasis added). This rule of thumb in the absence of explicit articulation, this allocation of the burden of proof, is no more a "fiction" than is our usual assumption that a seller has promised to deliver merchantable goods."

As a device allowing a court to "fill gaps" in the absence of an "agreement", a default rule is necessarily – at the same time – a presumption that allocates between the parties the burden of persuasion as to whether a particular term was included in the deal. And in assigning burdens in litigation, it is certainly a familiar enough phenomenon to see the choice made largely in the interest of handicapping a contention that happens to be socially disfavored. See, e.g., Edward W. CLEARY, "Presuming and Pleading: An Essay on Juristic Immaturity", 12 Stan. L. Rev. (1959) p. 5 at p. 11 (while "policy more obviously predominates at the stage of determining what elements are material, its influence may nevertheless extend into the stage of allocating those elements by way of favoring one or the other party to a particular kind of litigation"); Marshall S. SPRUNGE, Note, "Taking Sides: The Burden of Proof Switch in *Dolan v. City of Tigard*", 71 N.Y.U. L. Rev. (1996) p. 1301 at pp. 1309-1310(this rationale "reveals the link between the procedural device of the burden of proof and substantive legal concerns"; for example, "since some judges disliked that a negligent defendant could escape liability merely on the fortuity that a plaintiff had also been negligent, they assigned to the defendant the burden of proving contributory negligence").

135. *Stolt-Nielsen*, 130 S.Ct. at 1776.
136. See *Horan v. Danton*, 2005 WL 189733 (D. Del. 2005), *aff'd in part and vacated in part,* 2006 WL 859042 (3d Cir.2006) ("When a court engages in 'interpretation of language,' it determines what ideas the language induces in other persons").
137. See *id.* ("When a court engages in 'construction of the contract,' it determines the contract's legal operation – that is, its effect upon the action of courts and administrative officials").

whether it involves reading a will,[138] or even a constitution.[139] With respect to the reading of a contract – our particular concern – the two are routinely conflated.[140] And in any event it has never been thought that a court was foreclosed from going down this path; in all the cases I have mentioned there is a "gap" in the simple and straightforward sense that a conceded "contract" has failed to specify a result in all possible future states of the world.

So, at just what moment – just where in this gradual series of moves – are *arbitrators* now to be told to stop and to go no further? Note that the strategy of the Court in *Stolt-Nielsen* is to

• purport, somewhat disingenuously, to notice a supposed "stipulation" respecting a failure of "agreement" – and then

---

138. See Richard F. STORROW, "Judicial Discretion and the Disappearing Distinction Between Will Interpretation and Construction", 56 Case Western Res. L. Rev. (2005) p. 65 at pp. 82-83 (the American Law Institute "has decided that will interpretation and will construction are not discrete parts of a sequential process but are, in fact, simply components of a single process known as construction").

139. See, e.g., Laura A. CISNEROS, "The Constitutional Interpretation/Construction Distinction: A Useful Fiction", 27 Constitutional Commentary (2010) p. 71 at pp. 75, 80 (any line between the two is "artificial, as it defies all practical attempts to draw it consistently from case to case", and, "as an aid to the practice of judging", "unhelpful").

140. See *Corbin on Contracts*, supra fn. 124, Sect. 24.3 at 11 (the "overwhelmingly common practice" of courts is to use these terms "interchangeabl[y]").
    At most, perhaps, one might stake out some relevance for the distinction in the claim that "construction" (alone) is to be deemed a matter of "law" – if only in the precise sense that exercises in "construction" (alone), when engaged in by lower courts, are to be subject to a heightened standard of review on appeal; see *Horan*, supra fn. 136 ("Questions of contract interpretation are reviewed according to the clearly erroneous standard, while questions of contract construction are reviewed *de novo*"; nevertheless in this case, involving an "unambiguous written contract", it does not matter whether the Bankruptcy Court "construed" or "interpreted" the agreement, as under Delaware law "construction and/or interpretation" of such a contract "is a question of law").
    However doubtful we must be as to whether any of this is particularly manageable – for in disputes that turn on the meaning of a contract, questions of "fact" and "law" will be after all inextricably intertwined – it is very hard to see any purchase at all for such a notion in the context of attempts to vacate an award. The critical point is that an arbitration agreement makes arbitral tribunals plenary judges of fact and law without any sort of review remotely reminiscent of that exercised over a hierarchically inferior court; see *S.A. Wenger & Co., Inc. v. Propper Silk Hosiery Mills*, 146 N.E. 203 (N.Y.1924) ("Traders may prefer the decision of the arbitral tribunal to that of the courts" on "difficult questions of law as well as of fact"). The very fact that Americans (alone in the world) have to live with the civil jury – which after all sets the gold standard for unprincipled decisionmaking – may perhaps explain why we can be so tolerant of, and comfortable with, departures from legal norms in an arbitral process to which the parties have voluntarily submitted. For well over a century the cases have been full of reminders to the effect that "if an arbitrator makes a mistake either as to law or fact, it is the misfortune of the party and there is no help for it", *Patton v. Garrett*, 21 S.E. 679, 682-683 (N.C. 1895).

• to choose to draw the line right there – allowing a tribunal to go no further, on the ground that doing anything more – ordering class-wide proceedings in the absence of some "*contractual basis*" – would be to "impose *its own conception of sound policy*".[141]

This amounts to cabining our law of arbitration within an extraordinarily cramped view of adjudication:

• For one thing, as we have just seen, no designated "contract reader" operates this way.[142]
• For another, it is entirely ahistorical to insist on a constricted authority   not on the part of a lower court, but of an arbitral tribunal set in motion as the agent of the contracting parties – to fill gaps in an incomplete "non-agreement".[143]

That takes us, then, to what is for my money the most mystifying sentence to be found in any opinion ever written by the Supreme Court on the subject of arbitration: The award must be vacated, Justice Alito writes, because "the panel proceeded as if it had the authority of a common-law court to develop what it viewed as the best rule to be applied in such a situation".[144] But if an arbitral tribunal is really instructed to stop well short of all the usual work of construction that a common-law court would be expected to perform, then the resulting tension between our notions of arbitral and judicial adjudication becomes manifest.

The Court's remark that the arbitral tribunal had "exceeded its powers" by simply "impos[ing] its view of sound policy,", quickly gave rise to a vast amount of free-ranging

---

141. *Stolt-Nielsen*, 130 S.Ct. 1769, 1776 fn. 10.
142. The arbitrators in *Stolt-Nielsen* had in fact proceeded in precisely the same way as had the South Carolina courts in *Bazzle* – and the default rule chosen by the courts in *Bazzle*, had been unsuccessfully challenged by respondents on precisely the same grounds ultimately used to overturn the default rule chosen by the arbitrators in *Stolt-Nielsen*. See Brief for Petitioner [Green Tree], supra fn. 53, 2003 WL 721716 at *31 (South Carolina default rule "supplement[ed] the arbitration agreement, based", not on any attempt to "divine the intent of the parties", but solely on "its own views of public policy"; see also Oral Argument, supra fn. 58, 2003 WL 1989562 at *4, *26-*27 ("it wasn't anything with respect to the language or understanding of the parties"; the opinion of the South Carolina court "doesn't talk about anything that has to do with consent. It talks about equity and fairness and judicial economy, all factors that influence the rights of third parties who have nothing to do with the arbitration agreement that's before the arbitrator").
143. In fact the Uniform Arbitration Act has long warned that "the fact that the relief [granted by arbitrators] was such that it could not or would not be granted by a court of law or equity is not ground for vacating or refusing to confirm the award". Unif. Arb. Act Sect. 12(a) (1955); see also Revised Unif. Arb. Act Sect. 21(c) (2000). There are a number of possible implications of this language. Among other things, the text has been invoked to buttress our understanding that arbitral awards need not in substance track the course of official jurisprudence. At the same time it also serves to remind us that whatever policies underlie the traditional refusal of courts to take upon themselves the task of salvaging an excessively indefinite "agreement to agree," they have no particular relevance when the parties were content to have an arbitral tribunal do so. See also text accompanying fns. 25-30 supra.
144. *Stolt-Nielsen*, 130 S.Ct. at 1769.

speculation – much of which, it seems to me, misses the mark.[145] The Court could hardly have intended to suggest anything at all that would in the slightest call into question the power of arbitrators to adjudicate claims implicating the "public interest": For arbitrators may and indeed must decide questions of mandatory law in fidelity to the choice of the parties – once made – to entrust such matters to them. Nor, when the majority reminds us that arbitrators do not sit to "dispense [their] own brand of industrial justice", could it be thought that they were suddenly reaching out to appropriate some alien doctrine of review peculiar to our collective bargaining jurisprudence.[146]

No, I would think that what the Court was trying to say was undoubtedly much simpler – and it was even, marginally, to the point:[147] It seems that the intention was merely to invoke a conventional trope that has long been familiar to our law of arbitration – to the effect that what will provoke vacatur, is the arbitrator's frolic, his "flights of fancy"[148] – for this and only this "lies outside the perimeter of agreement". The

---

145. E.g., S.I. STRONG, "Does Class Arbitration 'Change the Nature' of Arbitration? *Stolt-Nielsen, AT&T,* and a Return to First Principles", 17 Harv. Negot. L. Rev. (2012) p. 201 at p. 240 (the Court's language seems "odd", given that in cases like *Mitsubishi* the Court "has indicated that the failure to consider relevant public policies can lead to the overturning of an award"); Margaret MOSES, "Did the U.S. Supreme Court, in its Stolt-Niesen [*sic*] Decision, Make it Easier for Courts to Vacate Arbitration Awards?, available at <http://kluwerarbitrationblog.com/blog/2010/12/14/did-the-u-s-supreme-court-in-its-stolt-niesen-decision-make-it-easier-for-court s-to-vacate-arbitration-awards/> (the Court's decision is "unusual and without precedent", since FAA Sect. 10(a)(4) "has never previously been interpreted as meaning that if arbitrators consider public policy, they have exceeded their powers"); Christopher R. DRAHOZAL and Peter B. RUTLEDGE, "Contract and Procedure", 94 Marquette L. Rev. 1103, 1155 (2011). 1148 n. 159 (if the "rationale" of *Stolt-Nielsen* is "that arbitrators lack the authority of common law courts to make decisions on the basis of public policy", does this suggest that parties by agreeing to arbitration might "be forgoing substantive rights" despite declarations to the contrary in cases like *Mitsubishi*?); Gerald AKSEN, "The Short Life of International Class Arbitration in the USA" in Laurent LÉVY, et al., eds., *Liber Amicorum en l'honneur de Serge Lazareff* (2011) p. 47 at p. 52 (*Stolt-Nielsen* "casts doubt regarding who decides 'public policy' issues", which is "particularly troubling – arbitrators decide questions of sound policy all the time"; while the New York Convention "allows a public policy defense in award review, here the decision arguably holds that the question does not even fall under the scope of a broad arbitration clause").

146. Cf. Thomas J. STIPANOWICH, "The Third Arbitration Trilogy: *Stolt-Nielsen, Rent-A-Center, Concepcion* and the Future of American Arbitration", 22 Amer. Rev. Int'l Arb. (2011) p. 323 at p. 342, n. 107 (the *Stolt-Nielsen* majority "borrowed, for the first time in a commercial arbitration decision by the Court, and somewhat anachronistically, [this] maxim from the collective bargaining realm" and so this "principle of labor arbitration must now be regarded as a part of the law surrounding FAA Section 10(a)(4)"); MOSES, supra fn. 145 ("the Court drew upon a standard from labor arbitration rather than from commercial arbitration"; this "labor arbitration standard" "does not appear to be very different from a finding that the arbitrator improperly applied the law").

147. Not the least of the "literary offenses of James Fenimore Cooper" in Mark Twain's delightful account, is that the conversations of Cooper's characters "consisted mainly of irrelevancies" – but "with here and there a relevancy, a relevancy with an embarrassed look, as not being able to explain how it got there". The essay is in Kenneth S. LYNN, ed., *The Comic Tradition in America* (1958) p. 328 at p. 338.

148. *Advest, Inc. v. McCarthy,* 914 F.2d 6, 10 (1st Cir. 1990).

"critical distinction" then has always been "between the arbitrators' imperfect ability to carry out the task entrusted to them, and their simple failure even to try".[149] That the award must in this sense "draw its essence" from the parties' agreement may seem a curious formulation, but it is also curiously satisfying, and manages to get the idea across quite adequately: And this is really all that "excess of power" (or "manifest disregard", for that matter) comes down to.[150]

Nevertheless: mere adjudication in the face of a lack of agreement is hardly tantamount to proscribed "faithlessness" – not as long as it remains within the authority of the parties' chosen arbitrators to devise appropriate default rules to help them construe the contract. It is only the arbitrator's failure to proceed as instructed[151] – or the defiance of some contractual mandate limiting his mission[152] – perhaps indeed to the

---

149. RAU, "The Culture of American Arbitration", supra fn. 26 at p. 531.

   To the same effect – although using the conventional language of "interpretation" – is *Hill v. Norfolk and Western Ry. Co.*, 814 F.2d 1192, 1194-1195 (7th Cir.1987) (Posner, J.) (the question "is not whether the arbitrator or arbitrators erred in interpreting the contract; it is not whether they clearly erred in interpreting the contract; it is not whether they grossly erred in interpreting the contract; it is whether they interpreted the contract"; a party can only complain if the arbitrators "disregard the contract and implement their own notions of what is reasonable and fair"); *Wise v. Wachovia Securities, LLC*, 450 F.3d 265, 269 (7th Cir. 2006) (Posner, J.) ("the issue for the court is not whether the contract interpretation is incorrect or even wacky but whether the arbitrators had failed to interpret the contract at all, for only then were they exceeding the authority granted to them").

150. The canonical "draws its essence" formula originated of course in the first, *"Steelworkers"* "trilogy" *United Steelworkers of America v. Enterprise Wheel & Car Corp.*, 363 U.S. 593, 597 (1960) ("an arbitrator is confined to interpretation and application of the collective bargaining agreement; he does not sit to dispense his own brand of industrial justice. He may of course look for guidance from many sources, yet his award is legitimate only so long as it draws its essence from the collective bargaining agreement"). But among the many non-labor cases that have since found it to be helpful, going back to the time immediately following *Steelworkers*, see *San Martine Compania de Navegacion, S.A. v. Saguenay Terminals Ltd.*, 293 F.2d 796, 801 (9th Cir. 1961) (charter party; "manifest disregard" "is the sort of thing the Court had in mind" in its language in *Steelworkers*); *Bosack v. Soward*, 586 F.3d 1096 (9th Cir. 2009) (claim of breach of fiduciary duty against former investment manager and general partner; arbitrators "exceed their powers" when they express a "manifest disregard of law" or when they issue an award that is "completely irrational" – and an award is "completely irrational" where it "fails to draw its essence from the agreement"); *Hoffman v. Cargill Inc.*, 236 F.3d 458, 461-462 (8th Cir. 2001) (proper price for delivered corn; "an award will only be set aside where it is completely irrational or evidences a manifest disregard for the law", and it "may only be said to be irrational where it fails to draw its essence from the agreement").

151. RAU, "The Culture of American Arbitration", supra fn. 26 at p. 531 ("suppose that an arbitrator has been entrusted with the task of valuing a party's shares in a close corporation, and that he has been told to value the business 'as a going concern in the light of past, present and prospective future earnings and the net worth of said business'"; however, "it can be shown that he did not even bother to obtain any operating figures or net earnings for the previous five years, and that he did not capitalize prospective earnings").

152. E.g., *Roadway Package System, Inc.*, supra fn. 134 (arbitrator was asked to determine "whether the termination of [an independent contractor] was within the terms of this Agreement,", but he instead framed the question as "whether the termination was wrongful or proper", and his award

point of saying, "to hell with" the applicable law[153] – that begins to endanger the paramount value of private autonomy. If there are indeed any outer "boundaries" to the process of construction, they are here.

In the very same sentence as its extraordinary rebuke of the arbitral tribunal for having "proceeded as if it had the authority of a common-law court to develop what it viewed as the best rule," the *Stolt-Nielsen* Court faulted the tribunal for failing to "[inquire] whether the FAA, maritime law, or New York law contains a 'default rule' under which an arbitration clause is construed as allowing class arbitration in the absence of express consent".[154] Such a "default rule", as we have seen, can indeed be found in the law of a number of jurisdictions, such as South Carolina – although of course in those jurisdictions the "rule" will only surface *in circumstances where it is assumed that the decision is not to be made by an arbitral tribunal in the first place, but instead by a court.*[155]

• Now the implication that the arbitrators were somehow obligated to expressly "identify" and articulate the basis of their award[156] – and that we are not permitted to deduce one circumstantially from the award itself – is surprising to begin with.[157]
• A further implication is more startling still – that if some textual hook, some "contractual basis" or "interpretive path", can't be found – then the arbitrators, in the absence of any well-established judicial "default rule", will be powerless to spin out one of their own. It is almost as if arbitrators were to be placed in a position analogous to

---

"makes crystal clear that [his] decision was based on the fact that he thought [the respondent's] procedures for notifying [claimant] of its dissatisfaction with his performance were unfair"; the arbitrator thus "ruled on an issue that was not properly before him").

153. See, e.g., *Edstrom Industries, Inc. v. Companion Life Ins. Co.*, 516 F.3d 546, 553 (7th Cir. 2008) (Posner, J.); see also *id.* at 552 ("if they tell him to apply Wisconsin law, he cannot apply New York law"). The arbitrator in *Edstrom* did not actually go quite so far – but although the contract directed that he "strictly apply Wisconsin law", it appeared to the court that "he seems not to have interpreted it at all but merely to have ignored it" – "it is unrealistic to think that the arbitrator was even *trying* to interpret Wisconsin law" (emphasis in original). So the award was vacated. See also *N.Y. Tel. Co. v. Communications Workers of Amer.*, 256 F.3d 89 (2d Cir. 2001) ("perhaps", the arbitrator had written, "it is time for a new court decision").

154. *Stolt-Nielsen*, 130 S.Ct. at 1768-1790; see also *id.* at 1770.

155. See text accompanying fn. 52 supra; cf. RAU and SHERMAN, supra fn. 48 at p. 114 (statutes permitting court-ordered consolidation in the interest of efficient case administration and in the absence of a contrary agreement).

156. *Stolt-Nielsen*, 130 S.Ct. at 1768 (because the agreement was "silent", "the arbitrators' proper task was to identify the rule of law that governs in that situation"); *id.* at 1770 ("instead of identifying and applying a rule of decision derived from the FAA or either maritime or New York law, the arbitration panel imposed its own policy choice and thus exceeded its powers").

157. Cf. *Robbins v. Day*, 954 F.2d 679, 684 (11th Cir. 1992) (the burden is on the party seeking to overturn the award to refute "every rational basis upon which the arbitrator could have relied"); see also RAU, "The Culture of American Arbitration", supra fn. 26 at pp. 513-514 (an arbitrator's ability to render a "naked award" may have "an important positive effect", maximizing "his freedom from overbroad rules or time-honored categories, which might otherwise appear to dictate a result he would prefer to avoid"; conversely, "any attempt to impose reasoned awards on arbitrators will be motivated at least in part by the desire to expand judicial supervision of the process").

federal courts in diversity cases, bound when embarking on an *Erie* exercise to defer to state law – but then, even so, federal courts in such circumstances are not really expected to end the process and turn off the lights should they be unable to identify a state-court rule of decision.

• And finally – and even more strikingly – any observer must be bewildered by what this passage does not take into account: An unexceptional "default rule" is after all readily to hand, if one only takes the trouble to look for it. For a "meta-default rule" informs every feature of our law of arbitration – I mean, of course, a background rule to the effect that by submitting to the process, the parties in cases of "silence" have presumptively entrusted *to their arbitrators* a wide-ranging power to determine just what form their proceeding will take.[158]

---

158. See Alan Scott RAU, "'Consent' to Arbitral Jurisdiction: Disputes with Non-Signatories", supra fn. 68, p. 69 at p. 139 (once there is "an agreement in which arbitrators have been selected and entrusted with the power to do *something*", the inquiry then turns to "what the parties could reasonably have expected to be within the authority of 'their' arbitrators", and "at the core of any mandate would naturally be matters touching on the appearance of the process and the conduct of the hearings"); Oral Argument, *Green Tree Financial Corp. v. Bazzle*, supra fn. 58, 2003 WL 1989562 at *25-*26 (Justice Scalia: "they don't consent to every jot and tittle of means by which the arbitration will be conducted; they consent in a gross kind of way to arbitration or nonarbitration, and – and that's – that's what their consent makes the difference between, but they don't consent to every consequent detail that enters into the actual conduct of the arbitration"); LCIA Arbitration Rules [Revised Working Draft, 18 February 2014], Arts. 14.4, 14.5 (tribunal "shall have the widest discretion to discharge [its] general duties", including "a duty to adopt procedures suitable to the circumstances of the arbitration ... so as to provide a fair, efficient, and expeditious means for the final resolution of the parties' dispute").

Note carefully that I am talking in the text about *the broad party-delegated authority of arbitrators to give meaning to contracts and to devise appropriate default rules (whether by means of "interpretation" or "construction").* This is the only question posed – the question is therefore *not,* as the Court phrased it, "whether the parties [actually] *agreed to authorize class arbitration*", *Stolt-Nielsen,* 1390 S.Ct. at 1776. *That,* by contrast, was precisely the question posed to *the arbitral tribunal itself.* To frame the matter as the Court did is thus to conflate questions going to the merits with questions going to the identity of the appropriate decisionmaker.

Of course, these two concepts – of "arbitral jurisdiction" and "unreviewable arbitral discretion" – are closely related – are tightly interdependent. An arbitral exercise of power delegated by the parties to the tribunal will after all routinely command the usual degree of deference that is extended to *any* decision "on the merits" – or at the very least will be subject to a judicial control substantially less intrusive than de novo review. Conversely, that a given outcome will be clearly illegitimate in arbitration, must cast considerable doubt on the willingness of the parties to entrust the matter to the arbitrator in the first place; see text accompanying fns. 175-181 infra. Still, the two represent separate analytic problems that should not be muddled.

Naturally, though, muddle is common. See, e.g., *Jock v. Sterling Jewelers Inc.,* supra fn. 105 at 122 (on facts similar to *Stolt-Nielsen,* arbitrator found that the agreement "cannot be construed to prohibit class arbitration" and construed it against the drafter ("construing the Agreement to contain a waiver of a significant procedural right would impermissibly insert a term for the benefit of one of the parties that it has chosen to omit from its own contract"); *held,* district court erred in vacating the award; "an arbitrator may exceed her authority first, by considering issues beyond those the parties have submitted for her consideration, or second, reaching issues clearly prohibited by law or by the terms of the parties' agreement"). See also text accompanying fn. 73

Here is one final test of the *Stolt-Nielsen* methodology: Suppose that an arbitrator were to issue a "clause construction award" holding that class-wide arbitration is permitted, and were to base his conclusion on a rule of applicable law to the effect that contracts are to be "construed against the drafter."[159] This *contra proferentem* canon is often marginalized as a technique of construction "of last resort":[160] Still it may do occasional useful service as a "penalty default" – setting the baseline *not at all at what the parties "probably wanted" (or "would have wanted"),* but precisely at what they would have wished to *avoid* – in the interest of discouraging strategic behavior, creating incentives for the more knowledgeable party to draft more explicitly in order to contract around the default.[161] And "interpreting" a contract against the drafter can above all serve an openly redistributive function, correcting for "an imbalance in the fairness of the exchange".[162] "It is chiefly a rule of policy, generally favoring the underdog."[163] *The one thing that this*

---

supra. For a mature attempt to grapple with the distinction, see Oral Argument, *Oxford Health Plans LLC v. Florida*, 2013 WL 1193215 (25 March 2013) at *21 (Justice Sotomayor: "I used to think that exceeding your powers was deciding an issue the parties hadn't agreed to arbitrate, but here you've conceded that you gave the issue to the arbitrator ... So what instead you're saying is that 'exceeded your powers' means that an error the arbitrator makes has to be of what quality?").

159. *Genus Credit Management Corp. v. Jones*, 2006 WL 905936, at *1-*3 (D. Md. 6 April 2006) (arbitrator determined that the agreement "was ambiguous as to class arbitration and should be interpreted against the drafter"; held, "it cannot be argued in any respect – as is plaintiff's burden – that [the arbitrator's] interpretation fails to draw its essence from the contract").

160. E.g., *Empire Rubber Mfg. Co. v. Morris*, 65 A. 450, 453 (N.J. Err. & App.1906) ("it is the last to be resorted to – a rule never to be relied upon except where other rules of construction fail").
   One could realistically go somewhat further and suggest that it serves most often as little more than a makeweight, wheeled out to bolster a result already reached and chosen for more functional purposes. This seems exemplified by *Mastrobuono v. Shearson Lehman Hutton, Inc.*, 514 U.S. 52, 62 (1995) (the strong "federal policy favoring arbitration" requires that arbitration agreements be "generously construed" and this requires "an unequivocal exclusion" of punitive damages; "moreover, respondents cannot overcome the common-law rule of contract interpretation that a court should construe ambiguous language against the interest of the party that drafted it").

161. The *locus classicus* is Ian AYRES and Robert GERTNER, "Filling Gaps in Incomplete Contracts: An Economic Theory of Default Rules", 99 Yale L.J. (1989) p. 87. On understanding *Hadley v. Baxendale* through this optic, see *id.* at pp. 101-104 (the *Hadley* default can "be understood as a purposeful inducement to the miller as the more informed party to reveal that information to the carrier", which "creates value because if the carrier foresees the loss, he will be able to prevent it more efficiently"). On understanding *contra proferentem* through this optic, see *Harnischfeger Corp. v. Harbor Ins. Co.*, 927 F.2d 974, 976 (7th Cir. 1991) (Easterbrook, J.), and BEN-SHAHAR, supra fn. 2 at pp.391, 398.

162. BURTON, supra fn. 111 at p. 188.

163. *Corbin on Contracts*, supra fn. 124 at 306. See also Restatement, Second, Contracts Sect. 206 *cmt. a.* (the drafting party is "more likely than the other party to have reason to know of uncertainties of meaning" and may indeed "leave meaning deliberately obscure"; "sometimes the result is hard to distinguish from a denial of effect to an unconscionable clause"); ZAMIR, supra fn. 126 at pp. 1724-1725 ("this established rule may be justified on grounds of personal responsibility, fairness, efficiency and redistribution"; "some of these ends, like the reallocation of power and wealth between the parties, represent distinctively social values").

"rule" is not, clearly, is an interpretive guide aimed at ferreting out what the true "intention" or "meaning" of the parties truly was. (If there *was* any "intention" at all, surely we can attribute to the drafting party the will to draft in a way as favorable as possible to *himself?*) While it remains commonplace for *courts* to conjure up notions of *contra proferentem*, are we now, after *Stolt-Nielsen*, to conclude that this can no longer be part of the tool box of the arbitral "contract reader"?

b.   "Only one possible outcome on the facts before us"
So one view of *Stolt-Nielsen,* then, is that it represents a censure of the arbitral tribunal for presuming to go about deciding the case *in the way it did*: If all that the award amounted to, was the arbitrators' attempt to "impose [their] own view of sound policy", then it seemed to follow that the requisite "contractual basis" for the award must be missing. This, as we have seen, has extremely troubling implications that extend far beyond the factual matrix of the case – implications for the way in which arbitrators are now to be expected to do their work of contract "construction" and implications for the way in which courts may now respond to demands for annulment. It does not seem too much to say that this analysis calls into question our traditional view of arbitration as an alternative forum for adjudication.

There is another way of looking at the holding, however, this somewhat more "substantive": It is that on the facts before the tribunal – and indeed on any view of the case – any award that would permit class-wide proceedings would be forever illegitimate. The starting point here is that "a party may not be compelled under the FAA to submit to class arbitration unless there is a contractual basis for concluding the party *agreed* to do so".[164] So the parties' supposed "stipulation" must mean precisely that the requisite affirmative showing of "consent" had not been made – therefore depriving the arbitral order of the requisite "contractual basis". On this view there was simply "no need" to send the case back to the arbitrators for a re-examination.

We need not dwell on the back story here, which is troubling enough but not our real concern today. Few legal issues are as deeply fraught for the modern US Supreme Court as the question of class-wide proceedings. This part of the holding is obviously responsive to the Supreme Court's predictable and result-driven agenda – captured as it has been by neo-liberal ideology and corporate interest – for it is clear enough that bilateral arbitration is valued by corporate users above all for "its promise to minimize the claim

---

Professor Horton has suggested an alternative rationale – that "the doctrine is better understood as encouraging uniformity of meaning in mass produced contracts", allowing firms to "reap the benefits of standardization" and consumers to "pay a price that reflects these savings"; without it, standardized terms would "mean different things to different consumers – a result that would tear the fabric of contract law". David HORTON, "Flipping the Script: Contra Proferentem and Standard Form Contracts", 80 U. Colo. L. Rev. (2009) p. 431 at pp. 438, 474. Whatever the merits of this approach it will be noted that it does not, any more than traditional notions, rest on any attempt to ascertain true "intention".

164. *Stolt-Nielsen,* 130 S.Ct. at 1775 (emphasis in the original).

facilitating and liability effects of all aggregate litigation".[165] So in our context of the "silent" arbitration clause, the premise from which everything follows is this – that class-wide proceedings would *"change the nature of arbitration* to such a degree that it cannot be presumed that the parties consented to it" – that is, the tribunal cannot be allowed to order it – merely because the underlying dispute is subject to arbitration.

(a) To say that an arbitral tribunal *may not "proceed as if it had the authority of a common-law court to develop what it viewed as the best rule to be applied"* is, as we have seen, a proposition that in the normal run of cases is unthinkable – but such a remark can perhaps be marginalized by how it plays out in context here: The Court is in fact saying that once the parties cannot be shown to have affirmatively agreed to class-wide proceedings, a new and overriding federal "default rule" comes into play – a default rule to which state law must yield and which state courts and arbitrators alike, in applying it, must honor: The technique is to spin out from the FAA a federal policy privileging party autonomy – not only to preserve the freedom to arbitrate but equally in the interest of protecting the parties' *freedom from having to arbitrate* in any particular manner. So what will be considered to be "in accordance with the terms of the agreement" must apparently be evaluated, not by the state law of contracts, but by a federal common law grounded in Sect. 4; to "enforce arbitration as agreed" apparently means that neither state courts nor arbitrators may impose any form of proceeding alien to the parties' expectations. Under this "default rule" the absence of an acceptable "agreement" necessarily means that recourse to the AAA class procedures is foreclosed.[166]

---

165. See RAU, "Arbitral Power and the Limits of Contract", supra fn. 105 at pp. 543, 527. In a case handed down one year to the day after *Stolt-Nielsen* – and relying heavily on the earlier decision – the Court held that state law may not invalidate as "unconscionable" contractual provisions in which the drafting party attempts to insist on bilateral arbitration and to exclude class-wide proceedings. The state rule, Justice Scalia wrote, would impermissibly "interfere with arbitration". And he added candidly that:

> "[C]lass arbitration greatly increases risks to defendants. ... [W]hen damages allegedly owed to tens of thousands of potential claimants are aggregated and decided at once, the risk of an error will often become unacceptable. Faced with even a small chance of a devastating loss, defendants will be pressured into settling questionable claims. Other courts have noted the risk of 'in terrorem' settlements that class actions entail, and class arbitration would be no different."

AT&T Mobility, LLC v. Concepcion, 131 S.Ct. 1740, 1752 (2011).

166. Earlier remarks in which the Court reproached the arbitral tribunal for its failure to have considered the "New York default rule" [cf. text accompanying fns. 154-155] have to be considered disingenuous (or are perhaps just a case of running up the score?) – because

- whatever purchase state-law rules may have in informing the interpretation of contracts generally,
- they have none here.

In his decision, Justice Alito intimated strongly that federal courts even in diversity cases had no reason to defer to any contrary state-law default rule with respect to class-wide proceedings, see *Stolt-Nielsen*, 130 S.Ct. at 1773 ("while the interpretation of an arbitration agreement is generally

(b) And to say that class-wide proceedings would necessarily *"change the nature of arbitration"* can also readily be misunderstood. The Court is saying nothing in particular about whether a given process "qualifies" as arbitration, or about how to "define" the true "'nature' of arbitration", or about what arbitration "really" "is"[167] – an inquiry that has a conceptual, essentialist – dare I say, "Continental" – air to it. As we have seen – and thankfully – the quest for the "true essence" of the concept of "arbitration" has not, in this country, been conducted with anything like the ingenuity and obsessiveness devoted to the task in some other legal cultures.[168] Rather, the Court need only be taken as saying this: That the arbitrators' imposition of a class-wide proceeding,

- was (a matter of degree) so far outside the scope of the probable expectations of the contracting parties, and in consequence
- would (a matter of degree) so drastically alter the cost/benefit calculus of their original decision to arbitrate,

that (as a consequence) their agents should not have taken it upon themselves to do so – not, at least, without some further indicia of the parties' consent.[169]

Now this is in fact an attractive and measured argument. It has considerable appeal when we are looking at commercial parties, particularly in the maritime context in

---

a matter of state law, the FAA imposes certain rules of fundamental importance, including the basic precept that arbitration is a matter of consent, not coercion"). And remember *Bazzle?* True, no single rationale emerged there to command the approval of five Justices, and nothing much seems to remain, these days, of *Bazzle's* insistence on deference to arbitral determinations: But as we have seen, there was nevertheless an overwhelming majority there for the proposition that *the FAA controls the question of when class-wide proceedings could be ordered* – to the point that the courts of South Carolina would be expected to abandon their state-crafted default rule. See text accompanying fn. 64 supra.

And then there is *AT&T Mobility, LLC,* supra fn. 165: If, as the Court put it there, the FAA "prohibits states" from insisting on class-wide proceedings as a condition of enforcement – if state law to that effect is "preempted" because this would somehow denature arbitration – then "I should think it most unlikely that state courts remain free instead to 'nudge' the parties in the direction of class proceedings, by prescribing a similar 'default rule' in cases of 'silence'"; see RAU, "Arbitral Power and the Limits of Contract", supra fn. 105 at p. 484 fn. 173.

167. Cf. STRONG, supra fn. 145 at pp. 246-262 (attempting "to identify a universally acceptable definition of arbitration that can be used ... to determine whether class arbitration does, in fact, 'change the nature of arbitration'").

168. See generally the discussion at text accompanying fns. 38-39 supra.

169. Among the "fundamental changes brought about by the shift from bilateral arbitration to class-action arbitration", the court pointed to the fact that

- the arbitrator "no longer resolves a single dispute between the parties to a single agreement, but instead resolves many disputes between hundreds or perhaps even thousands of parties";
- under the AAA rules the "presumption of privacy and confidentiality" no longer applies, and
- the award "no longer purports to bind just the parties to a single arbitration agreement, but adjudicates the rights of absent parties as well".

Stolt-Nielsen, 130 S.Ct. at 1776.

which *Stolt-Nielsen* itself arose.[170] It also has some appeal – of a different sort, perhaps, but still real – in the context of contracts of adhesion with consumers and employees – where concededly the drafter may have had reason to be aware of the possibility of class-wide proceedings – but also, at the same time, where he had the motivation (and the probable desire) to structure the transaction in such a way as to avoid them. Whatever the systemic benefits of aggregate litigation,[171] the very fact that contracting parties will rarely structure their transactions so as to subject themselves to class-wide liability – and can be expected, if permitted to do so, to immediately opt out of any general background rule that does carry this danger – suggests that the Court's may be a "majoritarian default". Even the notorious "stickiness" of default rules does not seem to have prevented strenuous attempts to "contract around" *Bazzle*.

The delicate point rather lies elsewhere. This new "default rule" may in the abstract seem sane enough. Nevertheless – however sensible it may be – it does not come to us as mere counsel to guide the exercise of arbitral discretion – but instead, as a limitation imposed by the state from outside the system entirely, and intended to demarcate the outer boundaries of arbitral "power". It is thus remarkably blind to the considerations of context and policy that usually inform the arbitrator's process of contract construction: Apparently we are asked to accept that our practice of leaving judgments with respect to the parties' expectations in the hands of their chosen arbitrators – a conventional assumption – must now be overridden by

- the unusual nature of class-wide proceedings, coupled perhaps with
- the particularly acute danger of distortion through arbitral self-interest.

While default rules pervade so much of our law of arbitration,[172] this is their first appearance in the form of rules that are said to govern *the determinations of the arbitrators themselves, on pain of vacatur.* Indeed, one would have to invest a good deal of time and effort before being able to identify cases – which in the end amount only to a trivial number – in which the Supreme Court has been willing to mandate or approve the annulment of an arbitral award. (And before now these have been strictly outliers, grounded either on the lack of any agreement at all,[173] or on some impropriety in the composition of the arbitral tribunal).[174] But then we come to *Stolt-Nielsen*: It can hardly

170. See fn. 100 supra.
171. Cf. STRONG, supra fn. 66 at pp. 1048-1049 (identifying the advantages of "efficiency", extending also to "unnamed claimants" and to "society as a whole", as well as of "promoting social justice").
172. See fn. 134 supra. For other examples, see RAU, "Arbitral Power and the Limits of Contract", supra fn. 105 at fn. 168.
173. *First Options of Chicago, Inc. v. Kaplan*, 514 U.S. 938 (1995) (company president argued that he had never consented in his individual capacity to allow arbitrators to determine the merits of the dispute; the Court held that he had not "submitted" this "arbitrability" challenge to the arbitrators merely by arguing the point before them).
174. *Commonwealth Coatings Corp. v. Continental Cas. Co.*, 393 U.S. 145 (1968).
In *Bazzle*, as we have seen, the Court did vacate a state court's confirmation of the award, but only because – with respect to the critical question of whether class-wide proceedings were

be accidental that the specter of class relief in arbitration is just about the only feature of the arbitration process that has been anathema to the business community – or that this rare decision restrictive of arbitral power happens, wonder of wonders, to be one in which a business-oriented court manages more or less to relieve it of any such anxiety.

The dangers this seemed to pose in breathing new vigor into the mysterious prohibition of "excess of powers" – of forcing open widely "the door of vacatur" – were obvious, and immediately perceived.[175] The risk does seem to have receded considerably in recent months, a point I will turn to in a minute when we discuss the third case in this triptych, *Oxford Health*.

Before we go further, though, it might be appropriate to pause for just a moment to ask what was left, after all this, of the *Bazzle* case – which had been decided after all just a few years previously. As we remember, *Bazzle* was all about reserving the question of interpretation for the tribunal – and so the validity of the actual holding there could not directly be called into question – given that in *Stolt-Nielsen* the parties' adoption of the AAA Rules had amounted instead to an *express delegation* to the arbitrators of the authority to do so.[176]

Still, the Court in *Stolt-Nielsen* went out of its way to suggest that the premise underlying *Bazzle* – the notion that arbitrators had presumptive competence to construe a contract in order to ask whether class-wide proceedings were authorized – has not survived (at least in the absence of an express delegation of the sort contained in the Rules). What else can one conclude from the Court's flat assertion that "an implicit agreement to authorize class-action arbitration ... is not a term that the arbitrator may infer solely from the fact of the parties' agreement to arbitrate"?[177] That it is not enough for parties to be properly before the arbitrators – that the arbitrators may not presume to order class-wide proceedings in the absence of some demonstrable "consent" to the arrangement – that their mission must terminate once the lack of some "contractual basis" for the order is noted – all must cast considerable doubt on whether the matter could be properly submitted to them in the first place.[178] And all of that comes very close

---

authorized – "the parties have not yet obtained the arbitral decision that their contracts foresee"; the case was remanded "so that the arbitrator may decide the question of contract interpretation". Efforts to characterize a measure as "pro-arbitration" or "anti-arbitration" are as often as not simplistic and naive, see Alan Scott RAU, "The UNCITRAL Model Law in State and Federal Courts: The Case of 'Waiver'", 6 Amer. Rev. Int'l Arb., p. 223 at pp. 270-271 ("waiver"; do courts "favor" the arbitration process "by staying litigation and moving the parties into arbitration whenever they have a chance to do so? Or do they 'favor' arbitration by creating incentives for the parties to initiate the process at the earliest possible moment, rather than allowing litigation to proceed?"). But it is not seriously open to argument that *Bazzle* falls securely in the former category.

175. See STIPANOWICH, supra fn. 146 at p. 342; AKSEN, supra fn. 145 at p. 53 (*Stolt-Nielsen* "contains enough dictums to jeopardize the finality of commercial arbitration awards in general").

176. See text accompanying fns. 75-76 supra.

177. That is, "it cannot be presumed the parties consented to it by simply agreeing to submit their disputes to an arbitrator". *Stolt-Nielsen,* 230 S.Ct. at 1775.

178. When Justice Ginsburg in dissent noted in passing that the issue of class-wide proceedings merely concerned "the procedural mode available for presentation of [the claimant's] antitrust claims," *Stolt-Nielsen*, 130 S.Ct. at 1781-1782, she seemed to be channeling the *Howsam/Bazzle*

to saying that this issue of construction is now one where it is the *court* that is charged with monitoring entrance through the "gateway"[179] – a conclusion made explicit in later jurisprudence[180] and one which – while rejected by the plurality in *Bazzle* itself[181] – was already adumbrated in Justice Rehnquist's dissenting opinion there.[182]

Still, it seems excessive to say flatly that as a result, *Bazzle* "has been left with essentially no remaining effect".[183] If indeed the avoidance of class relief is the engine driving the *Stolt-Nielsen* machine,[184] the holding might be cabined as something of a "one

---

jurisprudence under which such "procedural" questions were presumptively confided to arbitrators "well situated" to answer them. See *Bazzle*, 539 U.S. at 452 ("the question here" "does not fall into [the] narrow exception", the "limited circumstances" in which "the parties intended courts, not arbitrators, to decide a particular arbitration-related matter"; such "gateway matters" include the question "whether the parties have a valid arbitration agreement at all or whether a concededly binding arbitration clause applies to a certain type of controversy", but neither is at stake here). However, the *Stolt-Nielsen* majority simply brushed this aside: "If the question were that simple," wrote Justice Alito, "there would be no need to consider the parties' intent with respect to class arbitration." *Stolt-Nielsen*, 130 S.Ct. at 1776. I find that a most puzzling comment: In the first instance the relevant "intention" at stake would appear to concern *the parties' willingness to submit to an arbitral determination;* if indeed it is only the proper "procedural mode" of adjudication that is implicated, then party intention remains critical in yet a second sense – in the sense that it would then become a matter for the arbitrators themselves to go on to tell us, with the statutory degree of finality, *what the parties' manifestation of intention in their contract "means"*. See also the discussion at text accompanying fn. 78, and fn. 158, supra.

179. See text accompanying fn. 56, and fn. 78 supra.
180. See *AT&T Mobility, LLC*, supra fn. 165 at 1751-1752: Here, on its way to holding that states may not condition the enforceability of an arbitration agreement in a consumer case on the availability of class-wide relief, the Court closely tracked the argument of *Stolt-Nielsen* and went on to conclude: "We find it unlikely that in passing the FAA Congress meant to leave the disposition of [the] procedural requirements [of class arbitration] to an arbitrator"; since "arbitration is poorly suited to the higher stakes of class litigation", "we find it hard to believe that defendants would bet the company with no effective means of review". See also the discussion of *Oxford Health* at text accompanying fn. 197 infra.

    In the lower courts, see, e.g., *Anwar v. Fairfield Greenwich Ltd.*, 950 F.Supp.2d 633 (S.D.N.Y. 2013) ("whether a case may proceed as a class action" is "a gateway dispute about whether the parties are bound by a given arbitration clause", and is thus "a question of arbitrability for a court to decide"; a mere generic broad agreement to arbitrate "any and all disputes" "does not in and of itself authorize class arbitration if there is no provision in the contract which contemplates class arbitration").

181. See fns. 56-57 supra. Of course, as the opinion in *Stolt-Nielsen* was quick to point out, *Bazzle* had only been decided by a plurality of the Court and thus "did not yield a majority decision" on this question, *Stolt-Nielsen*, 130 S.Ct. at 1172; see text accompanying fn. 65 supra.
182. See *Bazzle*, 439 U.S. at 456-457 (Rehnquist, C.J., dissenting) "the parties' agreement as to how the arbitrator should be selected is much more akin to the agreement as to what shall be arbitrated, a question for the courts under *First Options*", than it is to questions that are "for the arbitrator under *Howsam*"; "just as fundamental to the agreement of the parties as to *what* is submitted to the arbitrator is to *whom* it is submitted") (italics in original).
183. Christopher R. DRAHOZAL, "Error Correction and the Supreme Court's Arbitration Docket", 29 Ohio St. J. on Disp. Resol. (2014) p. 1 at p. 18.
184. See text accompanying fns. 165-169 supra.

off" – that is, it may be seen as largely responsive to the unusual and dramatic feature of class proceedings. The Court's aversion to class-wide proceedings may thus be the impetus for *Stolt-Nielsen* and, at the same time, its limiting principle.[185] And even more importantly, remember that *Bazzle* retains a sting in its tail: The decision there was after all the impetus for the elaborate class-arbitration mechanism contained in the AAA Rules – which contain an express delegation of authority to arbitrators – and, at least where the stronger party has not drafted around it, these continue and flourish.

3.   *The Arbitrator at Large: Oxford Health*

> *"JUSTICE SCALIA: But ... he has to have come to a plausible construction. It's not enough that he said, I'm construing the contract; I have looked at the terms of the contract and what the parties said, and my construction of the contract is X. That's not enough. It has to be plausible.*
> *MR. KATZ [counsel for the claimants]: Yes.*
> *JUSTICE SCALIA: Now, why is this plausible?*
> *MR. KATZ: Well, with all due respect, Justice Scalia, I don't think plausibility comes into play."[186]*

---

185. For example, *Stolt-Nielsen* might plausibly be read as falling short of a prohibition of arbitral orders of consolidation: If indeed such orders do not implicate to the same degree the concerns expressed by the Court [see fn. 169 supra], then *Bazzle* is left intact – that is to say, everything said in *Bazzle* with regard to the interpretative power of arbitrators in cases of "silence" still has purchase – even, I would suggest, where the parties have been naive enough to make a "stipulation" concerning their "lack of agreement".

    See, e.g., *Safra Nat'l Bank of N.Y. v. Penfold Investment Trading, Ltd.*, 2011 WL 1672467 (S.D.N.Y.) ("joinder and consolidation remain distinct procedural issues of the sort parties would intend for the arbitrator to decide"); *Medicine Shoppe Int'l, Inc. v. Bill's Pills, Inc.*, 2012 WL 1660958 (E.D. Mo.) ("whether the arbitration clause authorizes joinder is a procedural question for the arbitrator"; "while class arbitration may be included among the gateway issues for courts to decide under *Stolt-Nielsen*, "joinder and consolidation remain distinct procedural issues of the sort parties would intend for the arbitrator to decide"; "the concerns pertaining to class arbitration do not apply to consolidation proceedings where only three claimants are asserting their individual claims in the underlying arbitration"); *The Rice Co. v. Precious Flowers Ltd.*, 2012 WL 2006149 (S.D.N.Y.) (two arbitration proceedings arising out of a single shipment of wheat from Texas to Peru; "consolidation does not fall within the narrow exception reserved for gateway matters that the parties would likely have expected a court to resolve"; "the question of consolidation "concerns the nature of the arbitration proceeding agreed to, not whether the parties agreed to arbitrate" and therefore "presumptively falls to the arbitrator"). At the very least – the bare minimum – the differences may be such as to affect the calculus of "likelihood of success on the merits" for the purpose of evaluating requests for preliminary injunctions against arbitral proceedings. E.g., *Anwar v. Fairfield Greenwich Ltd.*, 728 F.Supp.2d 462, 477-478 (S.D.N.Y. 2010) ("only twenty-four investment accounts held by thirty-eight parties are at stake in the arbitration; the usual rules of privacy and confidentiality apply; and no parties are absent").

186. Oral Argument, *Oxford Health Plans LLC v. Florida*, 2013 WL 1193215 (25 March 2013) at *34.

Inevitably, in a common-law system, the matter could not rest there. Right after *Stolt-Nielsen* was decided I speculated, in print, as to what might be expected to happen in the future – in a lower court

• which has been presented with a case that seems identical to *Stolt-Nielsen* in every way,
• where the parties have also both consented to an arbitral determination on whether class-wide proceedings were permitted by the contract,
• where they both are making the same and inevitable arguments with respect to the text of the arbitration agreement – an agreement conventionally drafted, encompassing in "broad" language "any dispute, claim or controversy" and empowering the tribunal to award "any types of legal or equitable relief" that would be available in court – but necessarily indeterminate on the subject of class-wide proceedings,
• but where there has been no comparable stipulation by the claimant with respect to a "lack of agreement" – no concession, that is, that could be seized upon and exploited.[187]

One would have thought that in order to remain true to the spirit of *Stolt-Nielsen,* the inevitable conclusion was that in these circumstances, the text alone – even in the absence of any "stipulation" – would be insufficient to justify an arbitral order of class-wide proceedings. This was in fact a view shared by a number of thoughtful observers.[188] But the world in fact turned out somewhat differently.

Sutter v. Oxford Health Plans was a putative class action in which primary care physicians accused a managed care network of improperly denying, underpaying, or delaying reimbursement of their claims for the provision of medical services to the plan's members. The agreement's arbitration clause provided that

---

187. RAU, *Arbitral Power and the Limits of Contract*, supra fn. 105 at p. 458.
188. See, e.g., DRAHOZAL and RUTLEDGE, supra fn. 145 at p. 1155 (to reason that "any dispute" would sweep in disputes being arbitrated on a class basis "does not satisfy *Stolt-Nielsen*", for according to that case "a general arbitration clause … does not authorize class arbitration because class arbitration differs too much from individual arbitration"; the authors do not, however, address the possible relevance to this question of any party "stipulation" regarding a "lack of agreement"); RAU, "Arbitral Power and the Limits of Contract", supra fn. 105 at p. 460 ("the mere failure to locate any 'stipulation' with respect to 'silence' (coupled with the canonical 'broad' clause) is unlikely to provide any stable equilibrium for understanding and applying the Court's holding"; "the text alone, even in the absence of any 'stipulation,' to justify an order of classwide proceedings"); *Jock v. Sterling Jewelers, Inc.*, supra fn. 69. 725 F.Supp.2d at 449 (Rakoff, J.) (after all, "the clauses at issue in *Stolt-Nielsen* contained similarly broad wording"; "at most the record supports a finding that the agreements do not *preclude* class arbitration, but under *Stolt-Nielsen*, this is not enough"), *rev'd*, 646 F.3d 113 (2nd Cir. 2011); *Reed v. Fla. Metropolitan University, Inc.*, 681 F.3d 630, 642 (5th Cir. 2012) (the "any dispute" clause "is a standard provision that may be found, in one form or another, in many arbitration agreements" and "merely reflects an agreement between the parties to arbitrate their disputes").
  Professor Park was somewhat more prescient; see 5 Global Arbitration Rev. (2010, no. 5) p. 33 at p. 34 (since the *Stolt-Nielsen* holding "was based" on a supposed "stipulation" – but since "in the future [no] party in the position of AnimalFeeds [is] going to agree to" such a thing – then despite the case we may in fact even see class-wide arbitration "increase in the US".

"No civil action concerning any dispute arising under this Agreement shall be instituted before any court, and all such disputes shall be submitted to final and binding arbitration in New Jersey, pursuant to the Rules of [the AAA]."

Immediately following the *Bazzle* case, "at a conference with the parties it was agreed that under [*Bazzle*], [the arbitrator] must determine whether the parties' Agreement allows for class action" and "the parties ... agreed that [the arbitrator] should proceed to make the determination"[189] – so again, as in *Stolt-Nielsen,* an express delegation of authority to the arbitrators had clearly occurred.

The arbitrator found that the clause I quoted above was not even "ambiguous"—but that "on its face" it "expresses the parties' intent that class action arbitration can be maintained". The award authorizing class-wide proceedings was confirmed by the lower courts.

Now if I were a "liberal" member of the Supreme Court, eager to preserve the possibility of class-wide proceedings in contracts of adhesion against the encroachments of a neo-liberal majority, I would certainly have voted to grant a writ of certiorari and accept review of this case.[190] For the Court had in fact painted itself into a difficult corner in *Stolt-Nielsen:* Surely it could not have been envisaged that federal courts were now to go wholesale into the business of second-guessing awards – spinning out a jurisprudence aimed at developing detailed legal standards intended to govern arbitral construction of contracts – monitoring how arbitral tribunals are expected to deal with the problem of "silence"?

Still, *Oxford Health* itself was not perhaps the vehicle in which the Court could best announce its intention to back away from such an enterprise. For the award in fact was facially preposterous. Consider the wonderfully brazen sleight-of-hand in this arbitral "syllogism":

(a) "No civil action" must mean "no civil action of any kind whatsoever".
(b) To say that "all such disputes shall be submitted" to arbitration means that the clause sends to arbitration "all such disputes which ... could have been brought in the form of any conceivable civil action".
(c) "Since there can be no dispute in any court without a civil action of some sort, the disputes that the clause sends to arbitration are the same universal class of disputes the clause prohibits as civil actions before any court."
(d) "A class action is plainly one of the possible forms of civil action that could be brought in a court."
(e) "Therefore [sic], because all that is prohibited by the first part of the clause is vested in arbitration by its second part, I find that the arbitration clause must have been intended to authorize class actions in arbitration."
Q.E.D.

---

189. Memorandum and Order, *Sutter v. Oxford Health Plans, Inc.*, AAA 18-193-20593-02 (23 September 2003).
190. The votes of only four members of the nine-member Court are necessary for the writ to be granted.

In addition, said the arbitrator, any conclusion to the contrary would mean that a class action, prohibited in litigation by the first phrase of the clause, could not be brought in arbitration under the second – leading to the result that class actions would not be "possible in any forum" – a "bizarre result" that could not have been intended in the absence of some "clear expression".[191]

It is, I hope, obvious that "reasoning" of this sort – had it been indulged in by a district judge – would never have been tolerated by a hierarchically superior court. Naturally I recognize that the standard on review of an arbitral award is not and should not be in any way comparable, and I am hardly suggesting the contrary – but surely noting this fact should give us some insight into just what it is that we mean by "the process of engaging in interpretation"? It is rather hard to escape the conclusion that all the preceding rigmarole was little more than pretextual – the thinnest "textual" veneer applied to an outcome-driven award.[192]

• Although the arbitrator claimed to believe that this arbitration clause was "much broader even than the usual arbitration clause", it reads to me pretty much like the most conventional of boilerplate: "No civil action" means nothing more than this – that no party is allowed to institute a lawsuit on a matter "arising under the Agreement,," but must instead go to arbitration – a provision that is actually relatively narrow, as these things go, and a conclusion that was in any event not contested. Is the arbitrator's "reasoning" really any different from inferring an agreement to class-wide proceedings "solely from the fact of the parties' agreement to arbitrate"?[193]
• And to find that it would be "bizarre" to read the contract so as to completely foreclose the possibility of class-wide proceedings, is either

> • grotesquely naive – after all that's rather the point, isn't it?
> • a reversal of the federal default rule imposed by *Stolt-Nielsen*, or
> • a policy decision on an issue of "unconscionability".

Or, perhaps, all three.

Nevertheless the Court unanimously affirmed: The opinion by Justice Kagan consisted of little but a single litany: The award may have been in "grave error", may have been "mistaken",[194] but it holds nevertheless, "however good, bad, or ugly", as long as the arbitrator had not "strayed from his delegated task of interpreting a contract" – as long,

---

191. Memorandum and Order, supra fn. 189 at *18-*19.
192. Allowing for the hyperbole of adversarial argument, counsel for the respondents in *Oxford Health* was nevertheless on to something when he characterized the award as "a ruse", "a "cover up", "dissembling", "post hoc rationalization", "pretense" and "pretext". See *Oxford Health Plans LLC v. Sutter*, Brief [by Respondent] in Opposition to Writ of Certiorari, 2012 WL 5838439 at *18-*19.
193. See text accompanying fn. 177 supra; see also RAU, "Arbitral Power and the Limits of Contract", supra fn. 105 at p. 460 fn. 89 ("not indeed from 'the mere fact of an agreement to arbitrate', for that would be expressly proscribed by *Stolt-Nielsen* – but apparently from the next best thing (and functionally identical to it) – the terms of a boilerplate 'broad' clause").
194. The *New Yorker* used to run a recurring column headed, "Department of Understatement"; *Oxford Health Plans LLC v. Sutter*, 2013 WL 2459522 (U.S.) at *4-*5.

that is, as he stopped short of what *Stolt-Nielsen* had expressly proscribed. And here the award revealed that he had indeed "focused on the arbitration clause's text", and his "decisions" were, "through and through, interpretations of the parties' agreement". A rather curious concurring opinion by Justice Alito warned nevertheless that even should a class be certified, the *absent* members of the putative class might not be bound by the arbitrator's ultimate resolution of the dispute because unlike the named members, they had "never conceded" that the contract authorizes him to make the class determination in the first place.[195] The point of this concurrence is superficially difficult to understand[196] and, if taken uncritically and at face value, can readily lend itself to misunderstanding[197] – but it is at bottom of extremely limited significance.[198]

---

195. *Id.* at *7 ("the absent members of the plaintiff class have not submitted themselves to this arbitrator's authority in any way"; in consequence "it is far from clear that they will be bound" – indeed "it is difficult to see how an arbitrator's decision to conduct class proceedings could bind absent class members who have not authorized the arbitrator to decide" on a class-wide procedure).

196. *All class members, absent or present*, signed "materially identical" arbitration agreements that provided for arbitration *under AAA rules*. Under these rules, as we have seen, agreeing to arbitration "pursuant to any of the rules of the AAA" means that "the Supplementary Rules for Class Arbitration" "apply" wherever a dispute is submitted on behalf of a purported class, and in such a case, the arbitrator is empowered to "determine as a threshold matter, in a reasoned, partial final award on the construction of the arbitration clause", whether the clause permits the arbitration to proceed on behalf of the class. That's what happened. So how can it be plausibly, sensibly, said that "absent" members "didn't consent to this exercise of authority"?

197. See, e.g., Linda MULLENIX, "The Court's 2012 Class Act: A Little Bit of This, a Little Bit of That", 40 Preview of United States Supreme Court Cases (10 August 2013, no. 8) p. 328 at p. 332 (Justice Alito "oddly sounded a precautionary note protective of absent class members").

198. Nobody seems to have talked about this, although Justice Alito asked a question to the same effect (and without getting much of an answer) in oral argument. Oral Argument, supra fn. 155, 2013 WL 1193215 *35-*40. He speaks as if some principle of general application is involved, but the apparent explanation is far less interesting:

   The arbitrator's clause construction award – in which he decided that the agreement did indeed authorize class-wide proceedings – was dated 23 September 2003, and so the arbitration had presumably been initiated some time prior to that. But the AAA's rules for class arbitrations were promulgated only on *8 October 2003*, as a "supplement" to the other rules. And the Commercial Arbitration Rules (presumably otherwise applicable) provide that "these rules and any amendment of them shall apply in the form in effect at the time the administrative requirements are met for a Demand for Arbitration or Submission Agreement received by the AAA". R. 1(a) (version in effect as of 1 July 2003, but the current rules are identical). So the Supplementary Class Rules, with their express delegation of decisionmaking power to the arbitral tribunal, were for this reason presumably not applicable to the *Oxford Health* arbitration.

   Thus Justice Alito's point is an extremely narrow one:

   (a) While the AAA's "Supplementary Class Rules" may not have governed the *Oxford Health* arbitration, they will of course apply *in any AAA arbitration that will have been initiated later*, even only a few weeks later – on the (generous) assumption, that is, that the drafting party has not insisted by contract on a bilateral arbitration. Cf. *President & Fellows of Harvard College v. JSC Surgutneftegaz*, Partial Final Award on Clause Construction (AAA 11-168-T-01654-04, 1 Aug. 2007) at *7 fn. 5 ("the Supplementary Rules became effective about eight months before this arbitration was commenced"; "since the AAA rules apply here … the Supplementary Rules also

Now given the obvious defects in the *Oxford Health* award – in which the Court readily acquiesced – it might well be wondered what has become of the federal "default rule" so critical to *Stolt-Nielsen*. (This default rule, as we remember, was imposed there by the Court on an arbitral tribunal that was not even allowed to inquire into the text of an agreement conceded to be "silent".) It would certainly have been consistent with the thrust of *Stolt-Nielsen* to say – even in the absence of any "stipulation" – that at the very least, a thumb is to be placed on the scales. Surely, to base an argument on the assertion that class-wide proceedings would necessarily *"change the fundamental nature of arbitration"*– to claim that such proceedings were so far outside the scope of the probable expectation of the contracting parties, that arbitrators should not have taken it upon themselves to order such proceedings in the absence of some indicia of consent – would have seemed to invite some requirement of explicit statement.[199]

That indeed would have left the holding of *Stolt-Nielsen* as at least a shot across the bow – requiring arbitrators henceforth to think twice and work strenuously at justifying any construction that would favor class-wide proceedings. For a while that is precisely the effect it had on the more earnest arbitrators who were gamely trying to follow along

---

apply").

(b) If one assumes that the "express delegation" in the AAA rules do not apply to bind the absent class members in *Oxford Health*, then the only thing that could possibly bind them is the *Bazzle*-plurality-presumption that under a "broad" clause this question (a question of "what sort of proceeding has been agreed to") falls to the arbitral tribunal for decision. If Justice Alito reasoned this far, then for him to assert that they will nevertheless not be bound, is necessarily to assert that *Bazzle* has not survived. Indeed, in his concurrence he invokes the critical language in *Stolt-Nielsen* to this effect, remarking that "if we were reviewing the arbitrator's interpretation of the contract *de novo*, we would have little trouble concluding that he improperly inferred "[a]n implicit agreement to authorize class-action arbitration ... from the fact of the parties' agreement to arbitrate". See my discussion of this language at text accompanying fn. 177 supra. That this aspect of *Bazzle* has not survived is thus consistent with my reading of *Stolt-Nielsen*. To the extent that the Court purports to leave open the question whether "the availability of class arbitration is a so-called 'question of arbitrability'", 2013 WL at *4 fn. 2, the only explanation is unnecessary coyness.

199. On "changing the nature of arbitration", see text accompanying fns. 167-169 supra.

On the inference of a heightened standard of proof, see Oral Argument, supra fn. 158, 2013 WL 1193215 at *5, *15-*16 (counsel for respondent: "we are asking that that generally applicable standard of review be applied to a question with a very strong empirical presumption that the FAA has attached to it"; "what you held in *Stolt-Nielsen* was not simply that parties who have stipulated can't be forced into class arbitration. What you held was that you cannot have class arbitration in the absence of affirmative agreement that is not evidenced by an all-disputes clause; and ... that background – that strong presumption must as a matter of Federal law inform the arbitrator's decision"). See also RAU, "Arbitral Power and the Limits of Contract", supra fn. 105 at p. 477 ("at the very least, the proponent will now need to make a strong affirmative showing – a showing (in text or context) that this was in fact the intention of the contracting parties – in order to overcome the contrary presumption. The formula that such a showing must be 'clear and unmistakable' – not being used so much anymore elsewhere – will presumably be available, and would certainly be consistent with the spirit of Justice Alito's opinion").

with the twists and turns of Supreme Court jurisprudence.[200] But we can only glean from *Oxford Health* that while arbitrators are still presumably bound to place the burden of proof on the proponent of any agreement, the *Stolt-Nielsen* "default rule" doesn't have much more sting than that: It does not function like the presumption of arbitrability – it does not even function as a rule of "clear statement" like the fraught and hollow *First Options* requirement of the "clear and unmistakable"[201] – it is far more easily overcome.

A glance at the arbitral case law in the wake of *Oxford Health* certainly confirms this impression – and suggests that arbitrators are finding very little difficulty in scooping up something more than "silence" to throw in the eyes of potential reviewing courts. Between the date that *Oxford Health* was decided and the date this is being written (15 March 2014), AAA arbitrators issued fourteen "clause construction awards". *In all but one*, the arbitrator found that class-wide proceedings had been agreed upon by the parties[202] – and in most of these, the putative "interpretative path" was one that would

---

200. See, e.g., *Rivera v. Sequoia Education, Inc.*, Award on Motion to Reconsider Clause Construction Award, AAA 11-434-1075-08 (22 September 2011) (in 2009 the arbitrator determined that the agreement "permitted class arbitration based upon applicable California law"; however, *Stolt-Nielsen*, decided subsequently, "has caused me to conclude that where an arbitration agreement ... does not explicitly contain language permitting class arbitration, class arbitration is not permitted"; both *Stolt-Nielsen* and *Concepcion* make clear that "class arbitration is so fundamental a structural shift that it is not to be ordered in the absence of an express and explicit agreement"); *Maslo v. Oak Pointe Country Club, Inc.*, AAA 11-181-02243-06, Amended Clause Construction Award (15 June 2010) (in 2007 the arbitrator rendered a Clause Construction Award finding that the agreements "permit the action to proceed as a class"; however, *Stolt-Nielsen* "compels a reconsideration" of this award; Justice Breyer's dissent, concluding that the majority opinion was "establishing an affirmative-authorization requirement in contracts for class arbitrations", allows us "to determine the full impact" of the case; "being unable to presume [an] intent [to "affirmatively agree to class arbitration"] from the broad language of the arbitration clause", "the reasoning set forth in the original Clause Construction Award is no longer tenable as a matter of law and must be reversed").

   I do not know if these cases are still pending or if yet another motion could now be entertained to reconsider, yet again, in light of *Oxford Health*.

201. See Alan Scott RAU, "Arbitrating 'Arbitrability'", 7 World Arb. & Med. Rep. (2013) p. 487 ("On the 'Clear and Unmistakable': 'This is All One Big Overblown Latke'").

202. This is in fact a somewhat more positive track record than the outcomes in the arbitral case law in the years *prior* to *Stolt-Nielsen*: According to the AAA, in the first six years that the AAA's Class Rules were in effect, 135 clause construction awards were rendered, and of these only 5% held that "the arbitration clause did not permit the arbitration to proceed on behalf of a class"). *Stolt-Nielsen S.A. v. AnimalFeeds Int'l Corp.*, Brief of AAA as Amicus Curiae in Support of Neither Party, 2009 WL 2896309 at *9.

   Is a tribunal's decision to "construe" an agreement so as to permit class-wide proceedings likely to be skewed by the nature of arbitral incentives? The reader may possibly think so, although I couldn't possibly comment.

   The only exception to date in the post-*Oxford Health* period has been *Alam v. Charter College, LLC*, AAA 73 160 00378 12 (26 September 2013). In this barely reasoned award the arbitrator noted simply that "the relevant language of the arbitration clause in this case is substantially the same as the contractual language" in *Stolt-Nielsen*, and that "there is no dispute that the parties in this case, like those in *Stolt-Nielsen*, have come to 'no agreement'". It is not clear just what the "no agreement" claim was based on – the claimants did after all argue that "there was no way for

make a first-year law student blush: I do not know if the awards are truly disingenuous, but they are by and large (in Judge Posner's term) "wacky".[203]

For the moment, the principal "interpretative techniques" *du jour* appear to be:

• reliance on the generic "broad" arbitration clause" (i.e., precisely the same clause that was in issue in *Stolt-Nielsen* itself);[204]

• reliance on the very fact of "silence" – apparently deploying a presumption to the effect that the mere failure to address the matter in the contract implies the parties' willingness to arbitrate on a class-wide basis (i.e., a discredited interpretation of *Bazzle* itself and a move explicitly foreclosed by *Stolt-Nielsen*);[205]

[them] to have known that their agreement to the language 'all disputes' would not include class claims", and I take this to be an interpretive argument based on their apparent intention. But the proponents of class-wide proceedings had equally argued the interpretive point in *Stolt-Nielsen* itself, see text accompanying fns. 94-97 supra, and so the award seems faithful enough to Supreme Court authority.

203. See *Wise v. Wachovia Securities*, supra fn. 149 (Posner, J.); cf. *Tice v. American Airlines, Inc.*, 373 F.3d 851, 854 (7th Cir. 2004) (Posner, J.) ("As long as what the arbitrators did can fairly be described as interpretation, our hands are tied").

204. See, e.g., Partial Final Clause Construction Award, *Harding v. Midsouth Bank, N.A.*, AAA 69-516-Y-00219-12 (29 August 2013) (language requiring the arbitration of "any controversy or claim ... that arises out of or relates to this agreement" permits arbitration of the class-action claims; "the word 'claim' clearly includes class claims"; "the word 'controversy' is even broader than the word 'claim'" and the word "any" "is the broadest possible modifier that could have been chosen, and leaves no doubt that the clause was intended to cover representative claims"); Clause Construction Award, *Betts v. Fastfunding The Company, Inc.*, AAA 33-516-00012-13 (21 August 2013) ("the 'broad' arbitration clause language leads the arbitrator to the conclusion that the Agreement was intended by the parties to operate as a plenary diversion of all disputes between them 'arising from or relating to' the Transactions to arbitration"; "under the plain language of the Agreement" "the parties agreed to submit all disputes to arbitration, including claims for class relief"); Partial Final Clause Construction Award, *McCullough v. Terminal Trucking Co., LLC*, AAA 31-160-00371-12 (17 September 2013) (a commitment to arbitrate "any controversy or claim", "with no distinction drawn between (a) those claims involving the treatment of just one person or (b) those under a statute like the Worker Adjustment and Retraining Notification Act, which expressly creates representational authority as part of a cause of action for Claimant to sue on behalf of other employees affected by the same alleged violation").

See also fn. 188 supra; Oral Argument, *Stolt-Nielsen S.A. v. Animalfeeds Int'l Corp.*, 2009 WL 4662509 at *36: (Justice Scalia: "so the only language you can point to is ... that 'any dispute' language?"; "you are hanging ... your whole assertion that these arbitrators ... found that the contract positively authorized class action, upon that language"?).

205. On *Bazzle*, see text accompanying fns. 54-67 supra; on *Stolt-Nielsen*, cf. 130 S.Ct. at 1776 ("the differences between bilateral and class-action arbitration are too great for arbitrators to presume, consistent with their limited powers under the FAA, that the parties' mere silence on the issue of class-action arbitration constitutes consent to resolve their disputes in class proceedings").

But nevertheless, see, e.g., Clause Construction Award, *Gonzales v. Brand Energy & Infrastructure Services, Inc.*, AAA 70-160-000270-13 (15 October 2013) (same arbitrator as in *Betts*, supra fn. 204; "there is no suggestion [in the agreement] of any truncation in arbitration of procedural devices or substantive rights available in court"; the agreement's "silence in regard to what [the respondent] now asserts the parties intended to foreclose is deafening in context", and the fact that the agreement "does not hint that [class-wide] procedures are foreclosed strongly suggests

997

• reliance on the clearly noninterpretive canon *contra proferentem*[206] and, most commonly,
• reliance on a variety of supposedly "textual" elements which, however ingenious, appear from out of deep left field and are unqualifiedly irrelevant.[207]

---

that under the terms of the agreement, the parties intended that they be available in arbitration"); Clause Construction Award, *Grande v. Lawrence Recruiting Specialists Inc.*, AAA 57-160-00080-13 (20 December 2013) ("LRS could have made this interpretive task easy by inserting or amending this contract and clause to preclude class arbitration by using clear language," but "did not avail itself of this opportunity," despite the fact that "the development of the case law relating to class actions arbitrations ... raised 'red flags' about how arbitration clauses were being construed"; *Stolt-Nielsen* "was a signal that if a Party to a contract wanted to avoid class arbitration they [sic] could write a clause precluding class arbitration"; the case "gave employers an open invitation to write contracts that would clearly foreclose class arbitrations"). Apparently, then, here the "interpretive basis" for class-wide proceedings is to be found in the drafting party's very failure to exclude them.

A variation on the "presumption from silence" – equally making something out of nothing, equally reversing the default rule of *Stolt-Nielsen* – can be found in the occasional recourse to the canon *expressio unius*. See, e.g., Clause Construction Award, *Guzman v. AIMCO River Club, LLC*, AAA 18-526-Y-000120-13 (4 December 2013) (the agreement "provides a 'carve out' for certain actions the parties intended not to be arbitrable" [such as actions for eviction or to collect past due rent]; "having turned its attention to enumerating the various claims, actions, and proceedings to be excluded, the Landlord certainly could have added class arbitration claims or proceedings to the list of excluded claims. It did not," and this then is "more than 'mere silence'"); cf. Partial Final Clause Construction Award, *Benson v. CSA-Credit Solutions of America, Inc.*, AAA 11-160-M-02281-08 (6 July 2010) (since the parties had ruled out arbitration for *trade secret disputes*, they "knew how to exclude certain disputes from the scope of the arbitration agreement, but apparently chose not to exclude collective and class arbitrations" – despite the fact that it was "not uncommon" for other parties to do so in other agreements).

206. See, e.g., Partial Final Clause Construction Award of Arbitrator, *Price v. NCR Corp.*, AAA 51-160-908-12 (24 October 2013) ("the Agreement was entirely drafted by Respondent and presented to Claimant as a condition of his being hired without opportunity for negotiation. As such, it is a contract of adhesion and must be construed against the draftsman"). On *contra proferentem*, see text accompanying fns. 159-163 supra.

207. See, e.g.,

• *Grande*, supra fn. 205. Here the clause required arbitration of "any claim or controversy between the parties to this Agreement which arises out of or relates to the Agreement, *the business of the Company*, [Employee's] employment with Company, or any other relationship between [Employee] and the Company"; for the arbitrator, "*surely*" this language empowers the employee to bring claims that "[raise] questions about a pattern or practice by which the business of the company is conducted", a category "broad enough to involve more than one employee where that claim questions a pattern or practice of the business". As I tell students, "surely" – like underlining and raising one's voice – is usually a bad sign in an argument. *Quaere* whether (a) the scope of the substantive claims that are stipulated to be "arbitrable" is really the same question as (b) the identity of the parties to the proceeding.

• Partial Final Clause Construction Award, *Kissel v. Sirius XM Radio Inc.*, AAA 13-516-00198-13 (6 December 2013). Here the clause called for arbitration "if we cannot resolve a Claim informally, including any claim between us, and any claim by any of us against any agent, employee, successor, or assign of the other, *including, to the full extent permitted by applicable law, third-parties who are not a party to this Agreement*"; for the arbitrator, the italicized language was "broad enough to contemplate incorporating class claims into the arbitration clause". *Quaere*

Other moves, equally unprincipled, have something of a history but do not seem for the moment to have reappeared in the recent arbitral case law – doubtless they are being held in reserve. For example: In purporting to assess the "intentions" of contracting parties, might it perhaps be relevant to point to the fact that class actions happen to be commonplace in cognate litigation – say in employment discrimination claims?[208] Might the prevalence of class litigation, then – given its comforting familiarity – bespeak the acceptability of the mechanism of aggregation – and thus give us some assurance that it was within the expectation of the contracting parties – at the same time permitting

---

though whether the italicized language, plainly subject to the word "against", does anything more than extend the benefit of the arbitration clause to potential defendants.

    Precisely the same move – and the same error – is regularly found in other recent awards, e.g., Partial Final Award on Clause Construction, *Cordova v. United Education Institute*, AAA 73-516-Y-000065-13 (21 August 2013) (respondent "inserted language extending the student's obligation to arbitrate any 'controversy' or 'claim' the student might have *against any of a laundry list of other persons and entities affiliated with [respondent,]* all of whom are non-signatories" to the agreement; given the extension of the agreement "for the benefit of a broad range of persons and entities related to [the respondent], the reasonable expectation of [claimants] … is that there would likewise [sic] be class arbitration of claims such as those they seek to raise on behalf of other students"); Partial Final Award on Clause Construction, *Baer v. TruGreen Limited Partnership*, AAA 14-160-01482-12 (22 July 2013) ("Clearly [sic], the concern for absent parties raised by the Supreme Court in *Stolt-Nielsen* is not an impediment here as the Plan, by its express terms, includes as a Party on Respondent's side non-employees, such as Respondents' directors, as well as potentially vendors, such as agents of their benefit plans"; this "supports the view" that the agreement "did not intend to limit the adjudication of Disputes to bilateral arbitrations").
    • *McCullough*, supra fn. 204 (under the AAA Employment Rules the "arbitrator may grant any remedy or relief that would have been available to the parties had the matter been heard in court"; the arbitrator reasoned that if the Worker Adjustment and Retraining Notification Act "expressly allows an individual in court to seek a statutory remedy and relief on behalf of himself and other employees … does it not follow that he has authority to do the same in this arbitration?" *Quaere* though whether even in employment cases, the federal procedural rules for aggregate litigation can fairly be deemed to amount to delegated "remedies". *Quaere* also whether characterizing a class-wide proceeding in this way – as "the same remedy" that would be available in a court of law – can truly be deemed an "interpretive" move – as opposed to a surreptitious policy judgment to the effect that any holding to the contrary would be "unconscionable" as against "public policy", cf. *American Express Co. v. Italian Colors Restaurant*, 133 S.Ct. 2304, 2313, 2318 (2013) (Kagan, J., dissenting) ("an arbitration clause may not thwart federal law" by preventing "the effective vindication of federal statutory rights" by making such vindication "impossibly expensive").
    • Still, even these recent cases must be considered marginal improvements over prior awards that were occasionally willing to attribute significance to whether the object of a preposition is singular or plural; see *Sidhu v. GMRI, Inc.*, AAA 11-160-02273-04 (10 June 2005) (terms in the agreement "which infer [sic] that a class arbitration is permitted" include the provision that the agreement "applies to the '*claims* of *Employees* … for wages or the compensation due'") (emphasis added by arbitrator).

208. See *United Airlines, Inc. v. McDonald*, 432 U.S. 385, 394 n. 13 (1977) ("Title VII actions are by their very nature class complaints").

arbitrators to bootstrap themselves into a desirable job?[209] ("Or might it rather represent *the precise motivation for the parties' desire to avoid it*, through an escape into arbitration?" (emphasis added).)[210]

IV.   SOME CONCLUSIONS

What, then, are we to make of this dizzying series of twists and turns? Where has the Supreme Court left us in our attempt to assess the power of arbitral tribunals to "fill gaps" in apparently "silent" agreements? One may well be forgiven for thinking that the result-oriented "reading" indulged in by the arbitrator in *Oxford Health* – in which the Court apparently saw itself obligated to acquiesce – has set courts on the path of leaving future arbitrators quite at large. Has the Supreme Court then just climbed all the way up the hill in *Stolt-Nielsen* just to placidly walk down it again a year or two later?

A number of things, though, can be asserted with at least some degree of confidence.

(1) The results reached by the arbitral tribunals in *Oxford Health* – and by those in succeeding cases – seem to be perfectly in line with the expansive "gap filling" authority that I have argued earlier should be presumptively attributed to arbitrators. This is at least as broad as – and indeed considerably exceeds – the authority that a "common-law court" is assumed to possess. After all, the power that an arbitral tribunal may be given

• to supply the appropriate default rule – whether a "majoritarian" rule that purports to "mimic" the parties' hypothetical bargain or to track their tacit assumptions – or a rule "crafted, more simply and directly, in overt response to concerns of efficiency and fair play"[211] –

is not, when you come to think about it, fundamentally different from

• the power given to an "interest" arbitrator to determine what "contract rights ought to be" – at least to the extent he defines his task as an inquiry into what the parties "should,

---

209. For the argument that this is relevant to an arbitral determination, cf. WHITEHILL, supra fn. 69 at pp. 14-15 (imagine a price-fixing claim arising from a commercial supply contract "with the same broad arbitration agreement"; since "class action antitrust suits invariably follow the related criminal proceedings," "it could fairly be argued that the parties understood that an antitrust class arbitration of that type could arise and be covered by" the agreement); *Smith & Wollensky Restaurant Group, Inc. v. Passow*, 831 F.Supp.2d 390 (D. Mass. 2011) (arbitrator noted that "wage and hour claims like those in play here are frequently pursued as class or collective actions, and both [parties] must be deemed to understand that"; in consequence class-wide arbitration was "contemplated and permitted by the agreement" and the arbitrator subsequently "affirmed [his] initial Clause Construction Award as consistent with *Stolt-Nielsen*"; held, award was "the result of a reasonable interpretation" of the agreement).
210. RAU, "Arbitral Power and the Limits of Contract", supra fn. 105 at p. 459 fn. 85.
211. See the discussion at text accompanying fns. 118-135 supra.

by negotiation, have agreed upon": "What should the parties themselves, as reasonable men, have voluntarily agreed to?"[212]

But however the cases are characterized, at least one thing should be clear: Even a cursory look at the current state of arbitral jurisprudence makes it impossible to believe that the outcomes at which tribunals arrive are truly the results of exercises in anything like "textual interpretation": To accept any such thing amounts to nothing but willful blindness, the technique of Nelson at Copenhagen.

(2) The Court's refusal in *Stolt-Nielsen* to allow arbitrators themselves to devise appropriate default rules in the absence of some demonstrable "agreement" may perhaps have rested on considerations peculiar to class-wide proceedings – concerns that seemed to justify the intrusion of some supervening federal common-law default rule that arbitrators are bound to respect.[213] But whether in that context or otherwise, there is inherent in the Court's opinion a vision of arbitral adjudication that is cramped indeed – and which in consequence creates obvious incentives for private decisionmakers to be somewhat less than candid with respect to the true rationale of their awards, in the interest of avoiding the risk of vacatur. This cabined view of what is permissible (a "contractual basis") and what is not ("sound policy") promotes disingenuousness and denatures the arbitral task, which – *precisely as is true for state tribunals themselves* – should embrace both.

Of course, *Oxford Health* suggests that the prevailing standard of review will be easy enough for any but the most unwary, clumsy, or naive of arbitrators to satisfy: In some jurisdictions we already see *Stolt-Nielsen's* intrusive insistence on "interpretation" reformulated, so that nothing more is required than that a court assure itself that it "cannot *say with certainty* that the *arbitrator's own words demonstrate* that he failed to interpret the [agreement]" (emphasis added).[214] And at least with respect to class-wide proceedings, drafting parties can be counted on – with the Court's blessing – increasingly to create a "new normal" by drafting around – forestalling – the foreseeable propensities of arbitrators to parrot the *Oxford Health* analysis.[215]

---

212. *Twin City Rapid Transit Co.*, 7 Lab. Arb. 845 (1947) (collective bargaining agreement provided that "if at the end of any contract year the parties are unable to agree upon the terms of a renewal contract, the matter shall be submitted to arbitration"). See the discussion at text accompanying fns. 23-36 supra.

213. See the discussion at text accompanying fns. 164-174 supra.

214. *Archer-Daniels-Midland Co. v. Paillardon*, 944 F.Supp.2d 636, 645 (C.D. Ill. 2013) (a very easy case, however, in which the losing respondent claimed that the arbitrator had "exceeded his authority" by concluding that it had breached the agreement because the agreement "did not require it to make sales through the joint venture" – something that indicated that the award was "not based on the contract but rather the Arbitrator's 'own sense of equity'").

215. Allowing a drafting party to prevent even nominal exercises in "interpretation" by means of contractual provisions barring class-wide proceedings outright, was a move sanctioned by the Court in *AT&T Mobility, LLC,* supra fn. 165 (upheld against state challenges on the ground of "unconscionability"); and in *American Express Co.,* supra fn. 207 (upheld against federal challenges on the ground that a class-wide proceeding was necessary to effectively "vindicate" plaintiff's rights under the antitrust laws); see generally RAU, *Arbitral Power and the Limits of Contract,* supra fn. 105 at p. 523 et seq.

(3) I suggested earlier that it simply will not do to try to demarcate the "gap filling" authority of arbitrators by purporting to distinguish between their power to "determine existing rights", and their inability to "create new obligations": This, as I said – nothing especially original here – is essentially question-begging, involves characterization after the fact, and really is little more than rhetoric.[216] More fundamentally, Lon Fuller's seminal work reminds us that this common assumption – that it is the "proper province" of courts and arbitrators, the proper "limits of adjudication", solely to make authoritative determinations of "claims of right" – is at bottom nothing but circular: For "it is not so much that adjudicators decide only issues presented by claims of right or accusations. The point is rather that *whatever* they decide, or *whatever* is submitted to them for decision, tends" by the institutional framework in which they function "to be converted into a claim of right or an accusation of fault" (emphasis in original).[217]

So, for example, in the case of unforeseen events having arisen in the course of a long-term relationship, a claim

• of "excuse" grounded in doctrines of "mistake" or "impracticability" – and equally,
• a claim for readjustment and reformation of the transaction –

are both claims that might be justified as appeals to an arbitrator to "work out all the implications of the original deal". This is true without regard to how they are characterized, and without regard to whether they are ultimately found to have any

---

216. See text accompanying fns. 33-36 and fn. 36 supra.

    Cf. KRÖLL, supra fn. 24 at p. 12. Here Dr. Kröll gives an account of the frequent objections made to the "gap-filling power of the arbitrator" – summarizing arguments to the effect that the arbitrator's task is normally restricted to the determination of "pre-existing rights" – but that when arbitrators engage in gap filing in the sense of "adding provisions to the contract at their discretion,", they instead "take up the creative task of rule-making ... and create at their discretion new obligations for the parties which did not exist before their intervention, not even in a hidden form". But it is striking that so often, and with but a little ingenuity, much that is latent, or lurking beneath the surface, or inherent in the structure, of a cooperative venture can be teased into "existence" – revealing implications to be explored and possible ways of giving effect to the parties' original objectives. See, e.g., fn. 30 supra; text accompanying fn. 113 supra. And in the same vein see the highly convincing demonstration in MARKOVITS, supra fn. 5 at p. 703. Here Professor Markovits discusses the leading case of *Joseph Martin, Jr. Delicatessen, Inc.*, supra fn. 19 – in which the court refused to enforce a renewal term in a commercial lease by which, after an initial five-year term, the annual rentals were "to be agreed upon". He points out that over the course of the initial term the "the shopping habits and travel patterns" of the tenant's customers likely "made its business much more valuable in its current location than in any other"; conversely, for the landlord, this "developed customer base made the site more valuable when occupied by the existing firm than it would be when occupied by any other". In consequence both parties had "a great deal to gain from maintaining their relationship" – and "insofar as the parties could have anticipated this contingency when they signed their initial lease, they had good reason ... to allow a third party to divide the gains from their co-dependence between them, and hence relieve them of the transaction costs that any negotiated solution would impose on them".

217. FULLER, supra fn. 31 at pp. 368-369.

merit.[218] An employee's demand for a raise, if made not to his boss but before an

---

218. Cf. *Aluminum Co. of Amer. v. Essex Group, Inc.*, 499 F.Supp. 53 (W.D. Pa. 1980). Under the parties' contract, Essex was to supply ALCOA with alumina which ALCOA would then convert by a smelting process into molten aluminum, which Essex in turn would pick up for further processing. The contract contained an escalation formula, designed with the aid of Alan Greenspan, by which the price paid to ALCOA would vary with changes in the Wholesale Price Index; by this means ALCOA sought to achieve "a stable net income of about $.04 per pound of aluminum converted", with a "range of foreseeable deviation [of] roughly $.03". But ALCOA claimed that in the period following execution of the contract, its production costs (mostly the cost of electricity) had risen greatly "beyond the foreseeable limits of risk" under the contract's index formula, and it sought relief under the Contract-law doctrines of "impracticability and frustration of purpose". The court held for ALCOA – and what is particularly interesting, the relief it granted took the form of "reformation or equitable adjustment" or "equitable modification" of the contract. The price calculation derived from the contract was to be "changed" according to a formula devised by the court itself in order to "reduce ALCOA's disappointment to the limit of risk the parties expected in making the contract" – Essex was thus to pay prices that would ensure to ALCOA for all the aluminum it delivered a profit of $.01 per pound. Merely to decree rescission would be "to grant ALCOA a windfall gain in the current aluminum market"; "a remedy modifying the price term of the contract in light of the circumstances which upset the price formula will better preserve the purposes and expectations of the parties". In a learned "Appendix" the court surveyed the remedies resorted to by courts in other legal systems "when beset with contracts that are no longer deemed 'fair' in light of changed circumstances", and observed that the prevailing approaches were to "try to establish the original economic position and intent of the parties; to try to distribute the consequences of the unforeseen burden equally between the parties; [or to] try to determine what the parties would have agreed to had they been aware of what was going to happen".

Note that I am certainly making no claim that the *ALCOA* case was "correctly decided" under US law – for it has always been much criticized and remains very much an outlier. (Professor Dawson has described the decision there as "bizarre," and "a lonely monument on a bleak landscape," John P. DAWSON, "Judicial Revision of Frustrated Contracts: The United States", 64 B.U.L. Rev. (1984) p. 1 at pp. 28, 35). Nor is there any reason why the choice posed to an adjudicator must be (as the court in ALCOA seemed to assume) binary; for intermediate and provisional positions are conceivable: For example, the adjudicator might encourage the parties to salvage the transaction themselves by providing them an interlude for renegotiation, and then by saying, should a reasonable offer of modification have been rejected, "you should have accepted this reasonable proposal, so we will treat you as though you did". Cf. *id.* at 29-30. Nor, finally, am I making any claim whatever to the effect that an arbitrator in all these cases will be expected to proceed in precisely the same way, regardless of whether he is asked

- to devise a remedy for an alleged breach,
- to make the "yes/no" decision of
- excuse that justifies rescission as opposed to
- plenary enforcement, or instead
- to undertake to readjust the terms of a transaction in light of changed circumstances.

The point being made is infinitely simpler: It is just that the question under the applicable law of the "*merits*" of reformation, like the merits of excuse, is *not at all the same thing as the question of power.* If, as St. Paul writes in Corinthians, "all things are lawful", "not all things are expedient. All things are lawful, but not all things edify."

Under German law, cf. MARKESINIS, supra fn. 24 at p. 336 (doctrine of the "disturbance of

arbitrator, would have to be supported "by a principle of some kind, and a demand supported by principle is the same thing as a claim of right".[219]

(4) If there is any limiting principle to an arbitrator's adjudicative authority, it may be one that Fuller himself suggested – cases where the ethic of reasoned argument no longer has any purchase at all – cases where the objectives of an enterprise would not be served if it were to be organized at the outset around the notion of formally defined rights. The canonical examples are those problems that he called "polycentric" (or "many-centered"): A bequest to two museums of paintings "in equal shares", for example, or the assignment to a particular position of players on a football team, may lie outside the province of adjudication because any particular choice (the disposition of a single painting, the shift of any one player) will necessarily have implications and repercussions for all the others: The task of the judge – or arbitrator – would require him to coordinate "mutually interacting variables"; "the only way to solve the problem is to take account of all the variables at once, in other words, to consider the situation as a whole".[220] The case then doesn't call for a decision of "yes" or "no", or "more" or "less," but the available solutions are "scattered in an irregular pattern across a checkerboard of possibilities".[221]

In such cases, Fuller suggests, an optimal solution can only be arrived at by vesting the decisionmaker, whoever he is, with the power of "managerial direction".[222]

---

the foundation of the transaction" in German law; in the case of a "very exceptional transformation of circumstances", courts are not limited to terminating the contractual relationship, "but will adjust it", substituting new terms, at least if: "both parties wish to continue with the contractual relationship"); DAWSON, supra at p. 2 (a "preferred" solution at least if the court-ordered revision will produce "an imitation 'contract' that the parties could perform and that would bear a recognizable resemblance to the transaction it replaced").

219. FULLER, supra fn. 31 at p. 369.("he may argue the fairness of the principle of equal treatment and call attention to the fact that Joe, who is no better than he, recently got a raise").

220. See Robert G. BONE, "Lon Fuller's Theory of Adjudication and the False Dichotomy between Dispute Resolution and Public Law Models of Litigation", 75 B.U. L. Rev. (1995) p. 1273 at p. 1314.

221. See Lon FULLER, *Collective Bargaining and the Arbitrator*, Proceedings, 15th Annual Meeting, National Academy of Arbitrators (1962) p. 8.

Professor Eisenberg would add another category of cases in which adjudication might not be appropriate – cases where decisions cannot be reached through an application of authoritative standards, that is, where among multiple possible criteria for decision, "no criterion would be authoritative in the sense that it would trump other criteria, or even in the sense that it carried an objective weight in relation to others. One football coach may legitimately emphasize one kind of ability, a second another kind, and a third experience." Melvin Aron EISENBERG, "Participation, Responsiveness, and the Consultative Process: An Essay for Lon Fuller", 92 Harv. L. Rev. (1978) p. 410 at pp. 424-425. This is a subtly different analysis from Fuller's: Unlike selection of players on a football team, for example, choosing members of *a college golf team* "may involve multiple criteria but not polycentricity, because golf is played on an individual basis and selection of the team therefore entails little or no interaction between choices". *Id.*

222. FULLER, supra fn. 31 at p. 398 ("the manner in which managerial direction solves polycentric problems is exemplified by the baseball manager who assigns his players to their positions, decides when to take a pitcher out, when and whom to pinch-hit, when and how far to shift the infield and outfield for a particular batter, etc.").

Now: Such power is not inevitably and in all cases outside the realm of private ordering: At least I know of no policy – nothing other than a rigid and a priori insistence on what "arbitration" necessarily "is" – that would place it irrevocably beyond the pale.[223] With a small amount of research one can readily find cases where "arbitrators" have been entrusted with the open-ended task of exercising business judgment in the running of a collaborative venture.[224] But here – and only here – we are so far from the modal adjudication in terms of what is expected of parties by way of proof and reasoned argument,[225] that a court will naturally require a certain level of specificity and explicit contractual direction before subjecting the parties to any arbitration regime. And putative arbitrators will equally shrink from construing the agreement so as to give them that role.

---

223. Cf. the discussion at text accompanying fns. 37-41 supra.

224. See, e.g., *Ringling v. Ringling Bros. Barnum & Bailey Combined Shows, Inc.*, 49 A.2d 603, 605 (Del. Ch. 1946), modified, 53 A.2d 441 (Del. 1947): Here shareholders agreed to "consult and confer" with each other and to "act jointly" in exercising their voting rights, and that if they failed to agree, the disagreement would be submitted to arbitration "to the end of assuring ... good management"; the court held the agreement enforceable. The rationale contains much rich irony and somehow manages to get things completely backward: State law at the time did not provide for the specific enforcement of arbitration agreements, but the court conveniently concluded that this agreement "does not possess the characteristics which go to make up an arbitration Agreement" since the "so-called arbitrator is not called upon to resolve a conflict which would otherwise be decided by a court". See also *Vogel v. Lewis*, 268 N.Y.S.2d 237 (App. Div. 1966), aff'd, 224 N.E.2d 738 (N.Y. 1967): Here an agreement between the two owners of a close corporation provided that "in the event of a dispute, or difference, arising between them in the course of their transaction with each other", the dispute would be settled by arbitration; the court held that a dispute over whether the company should exercise an option to purchase the warehouse where the business was carried on, was arbitrable. The precise legal issue posed was somewhat different from what we have been discussing – it was whether the agreement violated the state Business Corporation Law requiring that a corporation "shall be managed by its Board of Directors" – but the court held that there was "no reason why arbitrators may not be useful in resolving issues which involve *some business judgment* so long as they are not required to assume a *continuing burden of management*". And, inter alia, see Application of DeCaro, 25 N.Y.S.2d 849 (App. Div. 1941) ("the chief controversy submitted for arbitration related to the management of the business of a corporation"; the "arbitrators applied the only feasible remedy to a situation which, if continued, would have ruined the business of the corporation, and acted well within their powers").

Some years ago, among various "hypotheticals" to "illustrate the use of arbitration to fill 'gaps' in long-term international commercial transactions", Howard Holtzmann posed the case of a joint venture agreement under which disagreements between the owners "on such matters as the amount to be spent for advertising, or the choice of the managing director, or whether [the company] should pay a dividend rather than keeping the money to finance its future growth", were to be resolved by arbitration. He concluded that at least in the United States "the use of arbitration for this purpose is well recognized". Howard HOLTZMANN, "Powers of Arbitrators Under United States Law to Fill 'Gaps' Arising Under Long-Term Commercial Contracts" in *Proceedings*, supra fn. 25 at C.IV.h1, C.IV.h10.

225. "An adjudicative board might well undertake to allocate one thousand tons of coal among three claimants; it could hardly conduct even the simplest coal-mining enterprise by the forms of adjudication." FULLER, supra fn. 31 at p. 371.

Filling the Gaps: A Civil Law Tradition

*Cristiano de Sousa Zanetti**

"*A vida ali não é completamente boa nem completamente má.*" [Life over there is neither completely good nor completely bad.][1]

I.   INTRODUCTION

Everything that is perfect is comprised of all its parts.[2] Perfect literally means done until the end. Nothing exceeding. Nothing missing. The elements relate to each other with harmony and without flaws, leaving no space for disorder, questions or doubts. By definition, perfection should be acknowledged, not discussed. All the parts are already there. One has just to realize it.

Unfortunately, perfection is not easily found among human societies and their creations. This is certainly the case of the law. Disorder, questions and doubts are frequent, for the rules are not perfect. A major effort is then required to find coherence and to construct a set of rules that could be deemed fair and reasonable altogether.

Gaps are a sign of the imperfection of the law. Although they have always been acknowledged by Civil Law tradition, they have never been welcome. The struggle to codify the law throughout the centuries shows how hard civil lawyers have fought against

---

*   Associate Professor of Private Law at the Law School of the University of São Paulo – USP (2009). J.D. from the University of São Paulo (1999); LL.M in Private Law from the University of São Paulo – USP (2003); LL. M. in Roman Legal System, Unification of Law and Integration Law from Università degli Studi di Roma Tor Vergata (2006); Ph.D in Private Law from the University of São Paulo – USP (2007); Habilitation in Private Law from the University of São Paulo – USP (2011). Listed as Arbitrator of the Chamber of Ciesp/Fiesp (2011). Lawyer in São Paulo (2000). Former Assistant Executive Vice President for Administration of the University of São Paulo (December 2012 – January 2014).

1. Machado de Assis, Joaquim Maria, *Quincas Borba* (Garnier, Rio de Janeiro 1891) p. 5, available at <www.brasiliana.usp.br/>.

2. "*[I]n omnibus rebus animadverto id perfectum esse, quod ex omnibus suis partis constaret*" (D. 2,1,1).

gaps. The story of codification can be retraced to Roman Law and shows an impressive development both of the rules and its organization.[3]

The Civil Code of France, of 1804, is a milestone in this never ending process. It is one of the most precious monuments ever built by Civil Law tradition. Its rules are clear and precise, aimed to be understood by its mere reading. Compared to the prior attempts of codification, the French Civil Code represents a major development. The rules were never before so well written or better organized.

Thus, it is no surprise that the Civil Code of France has caught the attention of the Civil Law tradition during the entire 19th Century. It has even led some enthusiastic scholar to state that he did not care about Private Law, for it was enough to teach what was in the French Civil Code. There was a whole movement dedicated to studying every detail of its rules. It was labeled school of exegesis and its devotion to the text of the Civil Code was total.[4]

Yet, not even the most faithful member of the school of exegesis could deny that the Civil Code of France contained gaps. The Code says it itself. Its Art. 4 states that a judge who refuses to rule under the pretext of silence, obscurity or insufficiency of the law, could be pursued for denial of justice.[5] This Article reveals that the Civil Code does not have every answer. Sometimes, gaps should be filled to decide a given case.

The simple recognition of gaps in the law did not suffice to solve legal issues that are not specifically regulated by Civil Codes. It is necessary to go further and to define how a gap can be filled. With this purpose, the Introductory Law of Brazil from 1942 uses a widespread formula that is worth mentioning. In case a specific provision is missing in the law, gaps can be filled by resorting to analogy, to customs or to the general principles of law.[6]

Considering that most Civil Codes contain thousands of articles, analogy is a very important tool to fill gaps. It is based on resemblance and allows applying the rule designed for a similar situation to a case that is not specifically regulated. The method of analogy is the most frequently used and allows filling the majority of the gaps of the law.

If analogy fails, gaps can be filled with rules extracted from customs. Customs may be defined as the conjunction of two elements. The first is the behavior constantly observed by the people during a relevant period of time. The second is the belief that such behavior is right and should be respected.[7] Customs are easy to identify and also help to fill gaps. Still, most customs are already incorporated in the law, meaning that this source is not as fruitful as analogy.

---

3. See Sandro SCHIPANI, *La codificazione del diritto romano comune* (Giappichelli, Torino 1999).

4. See John GILISSEN, *Introdução histórica ao direito,* [translated by A.M. Hespanha and L.M. Macaísta Malheiros], 3rd edn. (Calouste Gulbenkian, Lisboa 2001) pp. 515-518. The saying is usually attributed to a Professor Bugnet.

5. *"Art. 4. Le juge qui refusera de juger, sous prétexte du silence, de l'obscurité ou de l'insuffisance de la loi, pourra être poursuivi comme coupable de déni de justice."*

6. *"Art. 4 Quando a lei for omissa, o juiz decidirá o caso de acordo com a analogia, os costumes e os princípios gerais de direito."*

7. See Caio Mário da SILVA PEREIRA, *Instituições de Direito Civil,* v. I, 23rd edn., [reviewed and updated by Maria Cristina Bodin de Moraes] (Forense, Rio de Janeiro 2010) pp. 56-57.

In case analogy and customs are not available, gaps can be filled with the rules extracted from the general principles of law. Such principles are not necessarily expressed but may be inferred by the consideration of rules that share a common ground. It is a method that operates through induction, revealing the guidelines that govern the entire spectrum of a branch of law in a given country.

By recognizing and facing the challenges posed by the gaps of the law, civil lawyers have gradually built a whole library on such matter. There are indeed several books and innumerable articles that deal with this issue, discussing the related questions almost to exhaustion. Such books and articles can be found in almost every country affiliated to the Civil Law tradition.

This fortunate circumstance barely hides the fact that the questions raised by gaps are not exclusively related to the legal rules created by the legislator. Most of the countries that belong to the Civil Law tradition can also be qualified as Private Law societies, for they acknowledge their citizens' powers to create rules to govern their own relationships. In fact, one of the main characteristics of a Private Law society is party autonomy, which gives its citizens the freedom to enter into transactions that are legally binding, provided that some limits are respected. In a Private Law society, the citizens are free to make their own choices, but they also have to live with the consequences of their decisions.[8]

Contracts are the main instrument of party autonomy. In a Private Law society, they appear in several forms and shapes. They bring into life all kinds of economic transactions. Because contracts are binding, they must be drafted carefully. Ideally, all aspects of a legal transaction should be covered by its clauses, leaving no room for disorder, questions or doubts.

However, contracts are also a product of human society. As much as the law, they are far from perfect, no matter how well prepared and dedicated their drafters could be. Gaps will possibly occur. There will be disorder, questions and doubts that have to be faced in order to understand and correctly apply the clauses crafted by the parties.

Historically, contractual gaps have not received the same attention as those related to the law itself. It is generally perceived as a very important and intriguing problem, but not many books or articles deal specifically with the issue. Its library is considerably smaller. Since contemporary economies are often distinguished by long-term agreements, gaps are always more frequent, for no one is able to foresee all the implications that such a contract may have over time. That means that academic contributions are not just welcome, but necessary.

This is particularly true regarding international arbitration. This kind of dispute is frequently related to long-term agreements executed between foreign parties, adding complexity to the economic transactions and leading to the appearance of contractual gaps. Experience also shows that even an arbitration clause may present gaps that should be filled to solve a dispute in a given case.

---

8. See Claus-Wilhem CANARIS, "*A liberdade e a justiça contratual na sociedade de direito privado*", in A. PINTO MONTEIRO, eds., *Contratos: actualidade e evolução* (Universidade Católica Portuguesa, Porto 1997) pp. 49-66.

To meet the intellectual challenge posed by contractual gaps, it is wise to proceed in an orderly manner. That is why this paper is divided into four sections. The first will deal with the concept of contractual gaps. The second will examine the methods developed by Civil Law tradition to fill gaps contained in contracts in general, dedicating special attention to the results achieved by using good faith and analogy. The third will address the same issue, but specifically related to the arbitration agreement. The fourth will examine the boundaries of the gap-filling process. The results obtained throughout this reasoning will be summarized in a conclusion.

Having set the aim and the structure of the path to be followed, it is time to try to better understand what a contractual gap is.

II.   CONTRACTUAL GAPS

Gaps are a sign of contractual imperfection. They are usually unwanted and they are certainly not welcomed. It is always better to deal with a contract the clauses of which regulate all the relevant aspects of a given transaction. Still, such contract is not free from discussions. As practitioners know, there could be a dispute related to the exact meaning of its wording, with important consequences for the development of the relationship between the parties.

In this case, it is necessary to interpret the contract. The aim of interpretation is to acknowledge the deepest sense of contractual clauses. To interpret a contract is to clarify what was actually agreed between the disputing parties, as interpretation seeks to reconstruct their common intent. Several elements could help to interpret a contract, such as the parties' prior relations, the negotiations and the performance of the agreement. Nevertheless, the point of departure and arrival is always the text. Interpretation enlightens the meaning of the clauses, but does not add anything to the agreement.

By definition, in case of contractual gaps, there is no text to rely on. Interpretation is no longer available, for it is necessary to provide what was left out by the disputing parties. In other words, integration is required. This a very complex task to be performed, because the aim of integration is to fill gaps without changing the balance of risks agreed by the parties.

To move towards integration, it is necessary to define how a gap in an agreement can be identified. This question leads directly to the problem of contractual completeness.

There are two perspectives from which we can distinguish contracts in accordance to their completeness. The first emerged from the law and refers to the formation of a contract. The second originates from economics and considers the range of subjects covered by a contract.

From the first perspective, all contracts are complete. Either the parties have reached an agreement about all the essential terms or there is no contract. The essential terms of a sales contract, e.g., are well known to every student: object, price and agreement. There can be no sales contract if there is no agreement regarding the object and the price.

From the second perspective, all contracts are incomplete. Time and resources are limited, meaning that the parties cannot or will not agree on every single aspect that could be relevant for their relationship. Instead, they will concentrate on what is most important to them, trying to obtain the maximum profit within the shortest amount of time. Traditionally, the agreement to exchange an object for a sum of money is enough to generate a sales contract, but it does not imply that all relevant issues are covered by its clauses. There could be several unattended aspects, such as the transfer of risk or the guarantee for payment.

The same could be said about the arbitration agreement. From the first perspective, it is enough to empower the arbitrators to deal with the case, provided that the parties have agreed to submit their conflict to arbitration and also have defined the object of the dispute. From the second perspective, not all issues are covered. There could be gaps relating to the institution responsible for handling the procedure or even doubts about the extension of the powers granted to the Arbitral Tribunal.

This means that the different perspectives of law and economics do not bring enough insight to identify contractual gaps. Either all contracts are complete, in accordance with the law, or all contracts are incomplete, in accordance with economics.

To prevent such dilemma, it is necessary to create another definition. The key to doing that would be to find an appropriate distinction, which should be based upon the relevance of incompleteness. If the clauses crafted by the parties allow the contract to be regularly performed, it can be deemed as complete. On the other hand, if the missing clause is relevant to defining their relationship, the contract should be taken as incomplete. A gap is a relevant omission. Therefore, incomplete contracts can be defined as those contracts distinguished by a relevant omission, which has to be filled to allow its regular performance.[9]

In accordance with such a concept, relevant omissions are always related to the performance of the agreement. This should be emphasized. Every contract should be performed exactly as agreed. Yet, sometimes the terms of the agreement are not sufficient to define what each party should do to fulfill its obligation. In this case, integration is mandatory; not with the aim to change a contract, but in order to preserve the distribution of risks agreed by the parties.

Both contracts in general and, specifically, the arbitration agreement, may contain relevant omissions. For centuries, civil lawyers have dealt with this problem with respect to several types of contracts. In light of that, it is worth to consider the methods developed by tradition to fill gaps in contracts in general, in order to later examine the particular issues raised by the arbitration agreement.

III.   GAPS IN UNDERLYING CONTRACTS

In case of contractual incompleteness, it is necessary to provide what was left out by the disputing parties. The first option is legislation, as Civil Codes provide a conspicuous number of default rules to fill contractual gaps. In the lack of default rules, scholars debate about the best method to promote integration. Practices and usages are often

---

9. Luciano de Camargo PENTEADO, *Integração de Contratos Incompletos* (USP, Tese de Livre-Docência, São Paulo 2014) passim.

mentioned in this context, but they are not always present, so there must be other methods available. With respect to the Civil Law tradition, at least two resources should be considered: good faith and analogy. Because of their importance, each one of them will be treated as a separate topic.

1.   Good Faith

Good faith is at the core of contract law. It requires both parties to be loyal and to honor the trust generated by their behavior over the course of their contractual relationship. This is the objective sense of good faith: a standard to be observed by the parties, to preserve the values of loyalty and trust.[10] It is this objective sense that allows labeling someone as acting in accordance or in deviation of good faith.

There is also a subjective sense of good faith. It is more related to the law of property than to the law of obligations. It is only mentioned here for the sake of contrast. In a subjective sense, good faith is the belief in acting according to the law. This belief is at the basis of several legal rules related to property, as those concerning acquisition of fruits and adverse possession reveal.[11] Based on the subjective sense, it is possible to establish if someone acts with or without good faith.

In its objective sense, good faith is strictly connected to the commitment undertaken by the parties to perform their obligations. The Roman jurist Ulpian, who lived during the third century, said that the correct performance of a contract was the utmost protection of good faith.[12]

He also made the remarkable argument that, sometimes, even with the aid of the agreement, it is not possible to define what is to be performed by the parties. In this case, he said, the parties were obligated to perform what was required by good faith.

This is a statement full of meaning, as it implies that a contract contains not only what is expressly agreed in it, but also what results from good faith. By adding what is necessary to preserve the values of loyalty and trust that are at the basis of every agreement, good faith enhances the content of the contract.

---

10. See Judith MARTINS-COSTA, *A boa-fé no direito privado* (RT, São Paulo 1999) pp. 410-427, distinguishing both senses of good faith.
11. Once again, the Civil Code of Brazil can be used as an example of rules widespread in the whole Civil Law tradition:

    "*Art. 1.214. O possuidor de boa-fé tem direito, enquanto ela durar, aos frutos percebidos*"

    and

    "*Art. 1.242. Adquire também a propriedade do imóvel aquele que, contínua e incontestadamente, com justo título e boa-fé, o possuir por dez anos.*"

12. "*Et in primis sciendum est in hoc iudicio id demum deduci, quod praestari convenit: cum enim sit bonae fidei iudicium nihil magis bonae fidei congruit quam id praestari, quod inter contrahentes actum est. Quod si nihil convenit, tunc ea praestabuntur, quae naturaliter insunt huius iudicii potestate*" (D. 19,1,11,1).

With that in mind, it should come to no surprise that contracts that are important to every economy were firstly legally protected to preserve the good faith of the parties. This is the case of sales, lease, mandate and partnership contracts, all protected in Roman Law because of good faith.[13] In the Civil Law tradition, party autonomy and good faith are connected from the very beginning.

Nowadays, the very same idea can be found in several Civil Codes. This is the case of the Civil Codes in France,[14] Germany[15] and Italy[16] in Europe, and Argentina,[17] Peru[18] and Brazil[19] in South America. Yet, the Roman rule is better preserved in the Codes of Chile and Spain.

Both the Civil Code of Chile[20] and the Civil Code of Spain[21] clarify that a contract must be performed in accordance with the requirements of good faith, thus obliging the

---

13. See José Reinaldo LIMA LOPES, *O direito na história*, 3rd ed. (Atlas, São Paulo 2008) p. 364.
14. In France, two articles are worth mentioning in this regard:

> *"Art. 1134. Les conventions légalement formées tiennent lieu de loi à ceux qui les ont faites. Elles ne peuvent être révoquées que de leur consentement mutuel, ou pour les causes que la loi autorise. Elles doivent être exécutées de bonne foi"*

and

> *"Art. 1135. Les conventions obligent non seulement à ce qui y est exprimé, mais encore à toutes les suites que l'équité, l'usage ou la loi donnent à l'obligation d'après sa nature."*

15. *"§ 242. Leistung nach Treu und Glauben. Der Schuldner ist verpflichtet, die Leistung so zu bewirken, wie Treu und Glauben mit Rücksicht auf die Verkehrssitte es erfordern."*
16. There are two related articles in the Italian Civil Code:

> *"Art. 1374. Integrazione del contratto. Il contratto obbliga le parti non solo a quanto è nel medesimo espresso, ma anche a tutte le conseguenze che ne derivano secondo la legge, o, in mancanza, secondo gli usi e l'equità"*

and

> *"Art. 1375. Il contratto deve essere eseguito secondo buona fede (1337,1358,1366, 1460)."*

17. *"Art. 1198. Los contratos deben celebrarse, interpretarse y ejecutarse de buena fe y de acuerdo con lo que verosímilmente las partes entendieron o pudieron entender, obrando con cuidado y previsión."*
18. *"Art. 1362. Buena Fe. Los contratos deben negociarse, celebrarse y ejecutarse según las reglas de la buena fe y común intención de las partes."*
19. *"Art. 422. Os contratantes são obrigados a guardar, assim na conclusão do contrato, como em sua execução, os princípios de probidade e boa-fé."*
20. *"Art. 1546. Los contratos deben ejecutarse de buena fe, y por consiguiente obligan no sólo a lo que en ellos se expresa, sino a todas las cosas que emanan precisamente de la naturaleza de la obligación, o que por la ley o la costumbre pertenecen a ella."*
21. *"Art. 1258. Los contratos se perfeccionan por el mero consentimiento, y desde entonces obligan, no sólo al cumplimiento de lo expresamente pactado, sino también a todas las consecuencias que, según su naturaleza, sean conformes a la buena fe, al uso y a la ley."*

parties not only to what is already agreed, but also to what emerges from the nature of the contract itself. Party autonomy and good faith are strictly and explicitly connected.

By using good faith, civil lawyers can solve quite a number of cases. Good faith requires the parties to cooperate, to act coherently during the performance, to avoid contractual uncertainty and, under the condition that this does not lead to relevant sacrifice, even to protect the other party's interest.[22]

Some examples help to clarify the point. If the seller delivers more merchandise than what was agreed upon, the buyer is not allowed to refuse performance. Instead, he has to retain the outstanding merchandise and invite the seller to withdraw it as soon as possible. Such measure does not depend upon an explicit agreement, because it is required by good faith. It is the same good faith that demands the principal to confirm, to an interested third party, the power granted through a mandate contract. The principal could not leave the third party uncertain and speculate about the fate of the contract concluded with his representative.

Good faith also defines the content of a contract by controlling the behavior of the parties during its performance. The Civil Codes of Portugal[23] and Brazil[24] determine that the rights that arise from a contract must be exercised in accordance with the requirements of good faith. By considering this role of good faith, scholars have created several legal figures to protect the values of loyalty and trust. *Venire contra factum proprium, tu quoque, Verwirkung* and *Erwirkung* are examples of those legal figures, all forged by German legal science.[25]

Those figures are especially useful while dealing with the termination of long-term contracts. Even if termination is allowed by the contract, it does not mean that the party is entitled to do it as it pleases. Prior notice may be required, especially in case of an already long-standing relationship, in which one of the parties depends economically on the other. The making of investments during the contractual relationship could also play a role on integration, if they were acknowledged and stimulated by the party now interested in terminating the agreement. The sudden termination of such contract could lead to deviation of the values of loyalty and trust, therefore violating the requirements of good faith.

Furthermore, good faith is helpful while dealing with the change of circumstances between the execution and the performance of a contract that provokes hardship to one of the parties. The Civil Code of Portugal establishes that a contract may be adapted, if

---

22. See Vincenzo ROPPO, *Il contratto* (Giuffrè, Milano 2011) pp. 467-470, also the source of the examples in the following paragraph.
23. "*Art. 334. É ilegítimo o exercício de um direito, quando o titular exceda manifestamente os limites impostos pela boa fé, pelos bons costumes ou pelo fim social ou económico desse Direito.*"
24. "*Art. 187. Também comete ato ilícito o titular de um direito que, ao exercê-lo, excede manifestamente os limites impostos pelo seu fim econômico ou social, pela boa-fé ou pelos bons costumes.*"
25. See António Manuel da Rocha MENEZES CORDEIRO, *Da boa-fé no direito civil* (Almedina, Coimbra 2001) passim.

such measure is required by good faith and does not change the balance of risks originally agreed to by the parties.[26]

In this case, good faith is called to fill gaps that could not be foreseen by the parties. However, if the change of circumstances was foreseeable, there could be no integration, for good faith does not allow interfering with the division of risks agreed to by the parties. Since the reform of 2002, the German Civil Code is clear on such matter, by asserting that every modification has to respect the distribution of the risks already agreed to by the parties.[27] A similar provision can be found in the Civil Code of Italy, although it considers the question in relation to the problem of termination of a contract.[28]

Practice shows that construction contracts are a field in which the change of circumstances is usually relevant. Construction contracts are designed to last in time. That means that they are subject to change of circumstances, which could lead to different economic outcomes. This is particularly evident regarding the situation of the soil. Because it is not possible to entirely predict its characteristics before the excavation, the result of the performance of the contract remains uncertain until it begins. The calculation of the price to be paid to the builder takes this into consideration. The outcome will be to his advantage if there are no surprises. Yet, things could go otherwise, if a major inconsistency of the available rocks is found, which would require much more effort to achieve the result agreed upon.

Whether it is possible to intervene in such contract depends on the division of the risks agreed to by the parties. If they have foreseen such possibility and deliberately accepted the risk, there is no room to fill a supposed gap. By contrast, if the event is left untreated because it was unforeseeable, adaptation may be required.

In Civil Law tradition, good faith helps to integrate a contract, by adding what is necessary to protect the values of loyalty and trust that emerge from a given agreement.

---

26. *"Art. 437. 1. Se as circunstâncias em que as partes fundaram a decisão de contratar tiverem sofrido uma alteração anormal, tem a parte lesada direito à resolução do contrato, ou à modificação dele segundo juízos de equidade, desde que a exigência das obrigações por ela assumidas afecte gravemente os princípios da boa-fé e não esteja coberta pelos riscos próprios do contrato".*

27. *"§ 313. Störung der Geschäftsgrundlage*
   (1) Haben sich Umstände, die zur Grundlage des Vertrags geworden sind, nach Vertragsschluss schwerwiegend verändert und hätten die Parteien den Vertrag nicht oder mit anderem Inhalt geschlossen, wenn sie diese Veränderung vorausgesehen hätten, so kann Anpassung des Vertrags verlangt werden, soweit einem Teil unter Berücksichtigung aller Umstände des Einzelfalls, insbesondere der vertraglichen oder gesetzlichen Risikoverteilung, das Festhalten am unveränderten Vertrag nicht zugemutet werden kann.
   (2) Einer Veränderung der Umstände steht es gleich, wenn wesentliche Vorstellungen, die zur Grundlage des Vertrags geworden sind, sich als falsch herausstellen.
   (3) Ist eine Anpassung des Vertrags nicht möglich oder einem Teil nicht zumutbar, so kann der benachteiligte Teil vom Vertrag zurücktreten. An die Stelle des Rücktrittsrechts tritt für Dauerschuldverhältnisse das Recht zur Kündigung."

28. *"Art. 1467. Contratto con prestazioni corrispettive. Nei contratti a esecuzione continuata o periodica ovvero a esecuzione differita, se la prestazione di una delle parti è divenuta eccessivamente onerosa per il verificarsi di avvenimenti straordinari e imprevedibili, la parte che deve tale prestazione può domandare la risoluzione del contratto, con gli effetti stabiliti dall'art. 1458 (att. 168). La risoluzione non può essere domandata se la sopravvenuta onerosità rientra nell'alea normale del contratto. [...]"*

It helps to deal not only with congenital gaps, but also with those that appear throughout the parties' relationship. As important as it is, good faith is not the only available source to fill gaps. There is another very profitable method, which is the next topic to be examined.

2. Analogy

The second method to fill a gap is analogy. Justice requires equal situations to be considered in the same manner. The aim of analogy is to identify similar situations, which should be treated in the same way, in order to ensure the application of a given rule.[29]

In Civil Law countries, analogy is frequently used to fill gaps in contracts performed without an agreement on the amount of money to be paid by one of the parties. With respect to sales contracts, in countries such as Italy,[30] Portugal[31] and Brazil,[32] it is established that, in the lack of an agreement, a price must be determined considering similar situations. In such case, there is no doubt that a contract was concluded. Yet, it could not be regularly performed without the definition of the amount of money to be paid, which is the aim of the above-mentioned provisions, all related to integration.

---

29. "*Non possunt omnes singillatim aut legibus aut senatus consultis comprehendi: sed cum in aliqua causa sententia eorum manifesta est, is qui iurisdictioni praeest ad similia procedere atque ita ius dicere debet. Nam, ut ait pedius, quotiens lege aliquid unum vel alterum introductum est, bona occasio est cetera, quae tendunt ad eandem utilitatem, vel interpretatione vel certe iurisdictione suppleri*" (D. 1,3,12-13).

30. "*Art. 1474. Mancanza di determinazione espressa del prezzo. Se il contratto ha per oggetto cose che il venditore vende abitualmente e le parti non hanno determinato il prezzo, né hanno convenuto il modo di determinarlo, né esso è stabilito per atto della pubblica autorità o da norme corporative, si presume che le parti abbiano voluto riferirsi al prezzo normalmente praticato dal venditore. Se si tratta di cose aventi un prezzo di borsa o di mercato, il prezzo si desume dai listini o dalle mercuriali del luogo in cui deve essere eseguita la consegna, o da quelli della piazza più vicina. Qualora le parti abbiano inteso riferirsi al giusto prezzo, si applicano le disposizioni dei commi precedenti; e, quando non ricorrono i casi da essi previsti, il prezzo, in mancanza di accordo, è determinato da un terzo, nominato a norma del secondo comma dell'articolo precedente (1561).*"

31. "*Art. 883. 1. Se o preço não estiver fixado por entidade pública, e as partes o não determinarem nem convencionarem o modo de ele ser determinado, vale como preço contratual o que o vendedor normalmente praticar à data da conclusão do contrato ou, na falta dele, o do mercado ou bolsa no momento do contrato e no lugar em que o comprador deva cumprir; na insuficiência destas regras, o preço é determinado pelo tribunal, segundo juízos de equidade.*

    2. Quando as partes se tenham reportado ao justo preço, é aplicável o disposto no número anterior."

32. "*Art. 488. Convencionada a venda sem fixação de preço ou de critérios para a sua determinação, se não houver tabelamento oficial, entende-se que as partes se sujeitaram ao preço corrente nas vendas habituais do vendedor. Parágrafo único. Na falta de acordo, por ter havido diversidade de preço, prevalecerá o termo médio.*"

Similar rules regarding contracts of mandate,[33], service contracts,[34] business and commission agreements,[35] brokerage,[36] lease,[37] deposit,[38] agency,[39] supply of work and

---

33. This is the case of the Civil Codes of Italy and Brazil:

Civil Code of Italy:
"*Art. 1709. Presunzione di onerosità. Il mandato si presume oneroso. La misura del compenso, se non è stabilita dalle parti, è determinata in base alle tariffe professionali o agli usi; in mancanza è determinata dal giudice.*"

Civil Code of Brazil:
"*Art. 658. O mandato presume-se gratuito quando não houver sido estipulada retribuição, exceto se o seu objeto corresponder ao daqueles que o mandatário trata por ofício ou profissão lucrativa. Parágrafo único. Se o mandato for oneroso, caberá ao mandatário a retribuição prevista em lei ou no contrato. Sendo estes omissos, será ela determinada pelos usos do lugar, ou, na falta destes, por arbitramento.*"

34. This is the case of the Civil Codes of Italy and Brazil.

Civil Code of Italy:
"*Art. 2233. Compenso. Il compenso, se non è convenuto dalle parti e non può essere determinato secondo le tariffe o gli usi, e determinato dal giudice, sentito il parere dell'associazione professionale a cui il professionista appartiene. In ogni caso la misura del compenso deve essere adeguata all'importanza dell'opera e al decoro della professione.*"

Civil Code of Brazil:
"*Art. 596. Não se tendo estipulado, nem chegado a acordo as partes, fixar-se-á por arbitramento a retribuição, segundo o costume do lugar, o tempo de serviço e sua qualidade.*"

35. Civil Code of Brazil. "*Art. 701. Não estipulada a remuneração devida ao comissário, será ela arbitrada segundo os usos correntes no lugar.*"
36. This is the case of the Civil Codes of Germany and Brazil.

Civil Code of Germany:
"*§ 653. Mäklerlohn. (1) Ein Mäklerlohn gilt als stillschweigend vereinbart, wenn die dem Mäkler übertragene Leistung den Umständen nach nur gegen eine Vergütung zu erwarten ist.*
(2) Ist die Höhe der Vergütung nicht bestimmt, so ist bei dem Bestehen einer Taxe der taxmäßige Lohn, in Ermangelung einer Taxe der übliche Lohn als vereinbart anzusehen."

Civil Code of Brazil:
"*Art. 724. A remuneração do corretor, se não estiver fixada em lei, nem ajustada entre as partes, será arbitrada segundo a natureza do negócio e os usos locais.*"

37. Such is the case of the Civil Code of Brazil:

"*Art. 569. O locatário é obrigado: […] II - a pagar pontualmente o aluguel nos prazos ajustados, e, em falta de ajuste, segundo o costume do lugar; […].*"

38. Such is the case of the Civil Code of Brazil:

"*Art. 628. O contrato de depósito é gratuito, exceto se houver convenção em contrário, se resultante de atividade negocial ou se o depositário o praticar por profissão. Parágrafo único. Se o depósito for oneroso e*

materials,[40] and labor contracts,[41] appear in several legislations. The German Commercial Code even has a general article on the matter, allowing the Court to fix an appropriate amount of money for measures taken on the interest of the other party.[42] Part of the rules herein mentioned refers to customs and practices and not directly to analogy. Nevertheless, there is no doubt that their rationale is always based on comparing similar situations, which is key to the definition of the analogy technique itself.

Analogy is a powerful method to fill contractual gaps. If integration is mandatory, comparing the case at hand with similar situations could offer a response that allows defining the object of the performance without altering the distribution of risks originally agreed upon by the parties.

Analogy is a technique based on resemblance and should only be used when it is not possible to fill a gap by considering the particularities of the contract actually executed

---

a retribuição do depositário não constar de lei, nem resultar de ajuste, será determinada pelos usos do lugar, e, na falta destes, por arbitramento."

39. Such is the case of the Civil Code of Brazil:

"*Art. 721. Aplicam-se ao contrato de agência e distribuição, no que couber, as regras concernentes ao mandato e à comissão e as constantes de lei especial.*"

40. This is the case of the Civil Codes of Germany and Italy.

Civil Code of Germany:
"*§ 632. Vergütung. (1) Eine Vergütung gilt als stillschweigend vereinbart, wenn die Herstellung des Werkes den Umständen nach nur gegen eine Vergütung zu erwarten ist.*
(2) Ist die Höhe der Vergütung nicht bestimmt, so ist bei dem Bestehen einer Taxe die taxmäßige Vergütung, in Ermangelung einer Taxe die übliche Vergütung als vereinbart anzusehen.
(3) Ein Kostenanschlag ist im Zweifel nicht zu vergüten."

Civil Code of Italy:
"*Art. 1657. Determinazione del corrispettivo. Se le parti non hanno determinato la misura del corrispettivo né hanno stabilito il modo di determinarla, essa è calcolata con riferimento alle tariffe esistenti o agli usi; in mancanza, è determinata dal giudice.*"

41. Such is the case of the Civil Code of Germany:

"*§ 612. Vergütung. (1) Eine Vergütung gilt als stillschweigend vereinbart, wenn die Dienstleistung den Umständen nach nur gegen eine Vergütung zu erwarten ist.*
(2) Ist die Höhe der Vergütung nicht bestimmt, so ist bei dem Bestehen einer Taxe die taxmäßige Vergütung, in Ermangelung einer Taxe die übliche Vergütung als vereinbart anzusehen."

42. "*§ 354. (1) Wer in Ausübung seines Handelsgewerbes einem anderen Geschäfte besorgt oder Dienste leistet, kann dafür auch ohne Verabredung Provision und, wenn es sich um Aufbewahrung handelt, Lagergeld nach den an dem Ort üblichen Sätzen fordern.*
(2) Für Darlehen, Vorschüsse, Auslagen und andere Verwendungen kann er vom Tag der Leistung an Zinsen berechnen."

by the parties. This means that one should only resort to analogy when no answer can be constructed based on good faith.

The difference between these two methods is that good faith allows defining terms that are directly related to the common intentions already expressed by the parties, while analogy could only provide an approximated answer, based on relations established among third parties. Considering the exceptional character of integration and the aim to respect at most the balance of risks specifically agreed to by the parties, it is clear that good faith precedes analogy as a method to fill contractual gaps.

Along with default rules, practices and usages, good faith and analogy are methods that historically have helped filling contractual gaps. With that in mind, it is worth to look at some questions specifically related to the integration of the arbitration agreement.

IV.   ARBITRATION AGREEMENT

Gaps in arbitration agreements are more frequent than one would think. This is probably due to two main reasons. First, the arbitration agreement is almost never at the heart of the discussion between the parties, which sometimes leads to a pathological clause. Second, the choice of arbitration and the definition of the object of the dispute are usually enough to bind the parties, which could leave important aspects unregulated, such as the seat, the applicable law, the language of the procedure, the institution that is responsible for handling the procedure and even the extension of the powers granted to the Arbitral Tribunal.

Those issues certainly have to be defined at the start of the arbitral procedure. They are relevant omissions that have to be filled, in order to allow the regular performance of the arbitration agreement. The seat establishes the Law that will govern the validity of the arbitration agreement itself. The definition of applicable law is necessary to examine the merits of the case. The language is mandatory to start the procedure. It is also fundamental to decide whether it will be an institutional or an *ad hoc* arbitration. Lastly, in every case it is extremely important to establish the boundaries to the extension of the Arbitral Tribunal's powers.

To fill those gaps it is worth remembering that the arbitration agreement can be seen as a special type of contract. In that respect, it is interesting to analyze its history in Brazil. The Civil Code of 1916 regulated the arbitration agreement within the general framework of the law of obligations. By then, the legal authorities already acknowledged the special characteristics of the arbitration agreement and questioned its qualification as a contract.[43] The Arbitration Law of 1996 revoked the Civil Code, as it established a separate and specific set of rules for arbitration, further to emphasizing its peculiarities. Nevertheless, the Civil Code of 2002 included the arbitration agreement among the nominate contracts, reinforcing its ties with the law of obligations.

---

43. See Clóvis BEVILAQUA, *Código Civil dos Estados Unidos do Brasil,* vol. IV (Francisco Alves, Rio de Janeiro 1938) p. 200.

As a concept whose grounds are clearly based on consensus, the integration of the arbitration agreement can benefit from the solutions provided by the Civil Law tradition concerning contractual gaps in general. This means that good faith and analogy are methods that may also help to fill gaps contained in the arbitration agreement.

A case from Switzerland might illustrate the point. Two foreign parties had drafted a pathological arbitration clause, by, among other issues, referring to an institution that did not exist. The clause was so poorly written that there were even doubts as to the parties' intentions to have the case decided by an Arbitral Tribunal or to have only the arbitrators helping them to settle the case.[44]

In the case of a clause that refers to a non-existent institution, the arbitrators could have concluded that it had been an *ad hoc* arbitration, allowing them to define all the rules applicable to the procedure. Instead, they decided that both parties had expressed their intentions to have their dispute decided by an arbitration institution in Geneva. Hence, they determined that it would be the most prominent institution of that location, which was the Geneva Chamber of Commerce and Industry.[45]

---

44. The case is described in the 19 ASA Bulletin (2001, issue 2) pp. 265-275. The text is available at <www.kluwerarbitration.com> and was last consulted on 23 March 2014. The arbitration clause reads as follows:

   "All disputes arising in connection with this [agreement] shall be settled in accordance with the laws of conciliation and arbitration of the Geneva Chamber of Commerce. In case of non-settlement, the dispute will be submitted for a final decision to the arbitrators of the Geneva Court of Justice. The rules of conciliation and arbitration of the said court will be binding for both parties."

45. "Once admitted that the Parties have agreed on arbitration, they also appear to have agreed on Geneva as the place of arbitration. This conclusion may be drawn from their reference first to a conciliation under the rules of the Geneva Chamber of Commerce, then to a final decision to be rendered under the *rules of conciliation and arbitration* of the *Geneva Court of Justice*. This intention of the Parties to choose Geneva as the place where their disputes were to be settled was confirmed by their agreement to appear in Geneva for the conciliation hearing and especially, on the Defendant's side, by the fact that while contesting the existence of an arbitration clause, the defendant admitted that *'the dispute should be settled judicially by the courts of Geneva'* (Statement of Defense p. 4). The next question is what kind of Geneva arbitration the Parties were contemplating. One could argue that they were thinking to an *ad hoc* arbitration by arbitrators appointed by the Geneva Court of Justice. That could appear like a reasonable interpretation of the words *'arbitrators of the Geneva Court of Justice'*, especially in view of the fact that at the time the clause was drafted, the appointing authority was the Geneva Court of Justice pursuant to Art. 3 of the 1969 Intercantonal Arbitration Convention. But this interpretation, which has not been proposed by any of the Parties, is inconsistent with the last paragraph of the [agreement] under which *'the rules of conciliation and arbitration of the said court will be binding for both parties'*, which shows that for the signatories of the agreement, the Court of Justice was an arbitration institution. From the erroneous reference in the [agreement] to the Geneva Court of Justice and its rules of conciliation and arbitration, one should draw the conclusion that the Parties agreed to an institutional rather than *ad hoc* arbitration. Since they referred to a (non existent) Geneva institution, their intention was certainly not to submit the arbitration to an institution having its seat in another city or country, such as the ICC. Is it possible to go further and interpret their reference to the Court of Justice as relating to any other specific institution? A reasonable

Although the award does not mention it, this decision was based on good faith and best preserved the common intentions of the parties, by leading them to discuss their dispute before the institution that had the closest connection to what they had expressed in their agreement. The parties were obliged to do what was required by loyalty and trust on the given case.

Moreover, the Arbitral Tribunal decided that its intervention was not limited to the attempt of conciliating the parties, as it also had power to judge the case. The arbitrators considered relevant that it was a dispute related to the payment of a consultation fee in connection with the settlement of a conflict between a foreign company and a government. It was a dispute that, for a number of reasons, including the confidentiality of the procedure, is typically submitted to arbitration.[46]

By comparing the case at hand with similar situations, the Arbitral Tribunal used the method of analogy to fill the gap represented by the pathological clause and ensured the same treatment to situations that are equal in the eyes of the Law.

This example shows that the methods of good faith and analogy can be a valuable resource to fill contractual gaps not only in general, but also within the particularities of an arbitration agreement.

However, sometimes integration is forbidden, for a reason that is common both to contracts, in general, and to the arbitration agreement, in particular. As we will see in the next topic, integration could never change the agreement and is consequently prohibited if the events that are not specifically regulated on the contract fall within the risks taken by the parties.

---

interpretation, which the Arbitral Tribunal will adopt, is to consider that the Parties have shown their intention to refer to the prominent arbitration institution of the place of arbitration. This broad interpretation is justified by the *favor arbitri* which prevails in the interpretation of arbitral clauses in Switzerland, and under which: '*Ut res magis valeat quam pereat*, an arbitration clause must be interpreted in such a way that the purpose that the parties wanted to achieve is as nearly realized as possible' (Pierre A. KARRER, 'Pathological Arbitration Clauses, Malpractice, Diagnosis and Therapy', in *The International Practice of Law, Liber Amicorum for Thomas Bär and Robert Karrer* (Basel, Frankfurt, 1997) pp. 109 ff., 118-119). In the case of Geneva, the prominent arbitration institution is the Geneva Chamber of Commerce and Industry (P.A. KARRER, *op. cit.*, p. 123)."

46. "The context of the contractual relations between the parties and the usages of international trade also are in favour of the interpretation of the clause as referring to arbitration. The [agreement] relates to the payment of a consultancy service fee by a German Company to [a citizen of country W resident in country Y] in connection with the settlement of a dispute between the German Company and the [W] Government. This is typically the kind of matter which the parties usually agree to submit to arbitration for a number of reasons, in particular the need for confidentiality, the need for flexible and prompt settlement of the disputes, the wish to avoid translating documents into the judge's language, etc. This context reinforces the likelihood of an agreement to arbitrate which has been seen to result from a literal and systematic interpretation of the clause wording. The Arbitral Tribunal is therefore of the opinion that the Parties have agreed to submit their disputes to arbitration".

V.   BOUNDARIES

Every contract involves risks. By pursuing an opportunity, one must leave several other alternatives behind. Power and responsibility are two sides of the same coin. The parties are free to engage themselves in a legally binding contract, but they have to support the consequences of their decisions.

That means the outcome of a contract could vary immensely. The contract could benefit both parties, only one of them and, unfortunately, even none of them. The projections of the parties can be very accurate or full of flaws. Irrespective of that, the parties will remain obliged to comply with what they have agreed to do, unless they jointly decide otherwise.[47]

To assure the regular performance of a given contract, it is usually enough to carefully consider its clauses and the elements left by the parties to interpret them. Again, the rule is that a contract is to be performed exactly as agreed. Clarification is required in several cases, but its aim is only to define the correct meaning of the clauses, for the parties have provided everything that was necessary to preside over their relationship.

The fact that sometimes integration is necessary does not concede disregarding party autonomy. Integration is directed to allowing the regular performance of the agreement. Gaps should be filled in order to allow the parties to achieve their common objective that justified the execution of the contract in the first place. Integration is designed to support, and not to conflict with, party autonomy.

That means that the process of filling gaps cannot interfere on the balance of risks already agreed to by the parties. It implies that there are two boundaries that should not be crossed while dealing with integration. First, there is no room for contract improvement. Second, the parties cannot be released from the risks that they decided to take. If the parties have consciously accepted some risk, they have to bear its consequences, regardless of whether or not those are in accordance with their expectations at the time they executed the agreement.

This proposes the problem of identifying the extension of the risks taken by the parties. It goes without saying that the risk is different for every contract. Nevertheless, there are some criteria that could help to establish the risks involved, hence allowing to verify whether there is a gap to be filled.

The first criterion to be considered is the nature of a contract. Broadly speaking, there are contracts that involve greater risks than others. Usually, the distribution agreement is riskier than agency, for the distributor has to buy and sell the merchandise, while the agent only intermediates businesses. Coherently, the profits of a dealer are often bigger than those of an agent.

The second is the market conjuncture. Some markets are characterized by frequent oscillations, some are not. A contract executed between two local companies is subject to less risk than a joint venture concluded between two foreign parties, aiming to

---

47. See Cristiano de Sousa ZANETTI, *"O risco contratual"*, in T. ANCONA LOPEZ, P. FAGA IGLECIAS RAMOS and O.L. RODRIGUEZ JR., eds., *Sociedade de risco e direito privado* (Atlas , São Paulo 2013) pp. 455-468. The text is also the source of the following criteria.

promote the reconstruction, for instance, of a country that still has to cope with civil war.

The third is the qualification of the parties. It is directly related to foreseeability. The more expert the parties are, the wider the range of possibilities they could foresee. Construction contracts executed between two neighbors are different from those executed between large entrepreneurs. This should also be taken into consideration while setting the risks that are congenital to a certain economic operation.

The fourth is the length of the contract. The longer the time, the greater the risk involved. The present is never equal to the past, so contracts of long duration necessarily have to deal with the change of circumstances. In a long-term agreement, a variation could be compensated by another, leaving no room for gap-filling. Things could be different in a short-term agreement, in which adaptation may be required in order to allow both parties to regularly perform their obligations.

The fifth and final criterion is external to a contract, as it is related to the change of circumstances that could reveal the existence of gaps. The rarer the event, the more likely it is to be outside the risks taken by the parties. A war in a conflict zone is expected. By contrast, if a historically peaceful country suddenly engages in battle, there will probably be a gap to be filled, for such event could not have been foreseen by the parties when they executed the agreement.

Once the risk is defined, it is easier to verify if there is a gap to be filled. If the events are within the risks that have been undertaken, there is no need for integration. On the contrary, if the events are outside the risk that was undertaken, adaptation may be required to preserve the originally agreed-upon relation of equivalency.

The same could be said about the arbitration agreement itself. If the parties failed to correctly appoint the institution that is responsible for handling the procedure, there could be a gap to be filled, as has happened in the Switzerland case above mentioned. Things would be entirely different had the arbitration clause not contained any reference to an institution. In this case, there would be no gap, for the parties would have chosen an *ad hoc* arbitration, giving powers to the Arbitral Tribunal to define everything that is necessary to make the procedure move forward. The parties would have consciously accepted the risks of attributing greater power to the arbitrator compared to an institutional arbitration. Arbitration agreements are binding and cannot be changed under the guise of gap-filling.

Integration is a last resource, to be used only when necessary. On the one hand, it could be very helpful. On the other, it could be dangerous. Party autonomy implies party responsibility and does not allow intervention to protect the parties from their own decisions. Integration is an extreme measure and should not be used unless necessary. That being said, it is time to conclude.

VI.   CONCLUSION

The Civil Law tradition is struggling against imperfection for centuries. The imperfection of Law is better known. Even a monument as the French Civil Code must admit that it does not contain answers for every problem. Integration is necessary and there are very-well-developed methods to deal with questions that remain outside the legislation.

Analogy, customs and the general principles of Law have proven to be very helpful. Of course, there could be discussions on a given case, but the instruments to deal with it are well developed and known to every civil lawyer.

Yet, in Private Law societies not all rules come from the legislators. The recognition of party autonomy implies that citizens may engage themselves in legally binding agreements. They have the power to execute contracts, therefore creating rules that they, themselves, should observe, irrespective of whether they change their minds after execution of the agreement. Power and responsibility are necessarily linked.

Being drafted even in the most peculiar situations, contracts are not perfect and gaps are frequent; this is all the more so in contemporary economics, characterized by long-term contracts. This is particularly evident in the domain of international arbitration, where the fact that the parties belong to different countries adds more difficulty to predicting everything that will happen during the life of a contract. Nevertheless, the amount of work produced by scholars in this context is relatively small, meaning that further efforts are required to deal with the issue technically .

Keeping that in mind, perhaps some proposals may be advanced and hopefully considered of some use.

The first is the identification of an incomplete contract and the subsequent concept of contractual gaps. Incomplete contracts are those distinguished by a relevant omission. This means that there is a gap that must be filled in order to allow its regular performance. A gap is then a relevant omission.

The second regards the methods to fill those gaps. Default rules are indisputably the best option. If they are not present, available practices and usages could be very helpful. Furthermore, the Civil Law tradition has developed two other methods that can also lead to profitable results: good faith and analogy. Good faith is based on the values of loyalty and trust. Analogy seeks to treat similar situations accordingly. They both help to solve several cases on contracts, by filling gaps that should not be there or could not be avoided at the time of the execution of the agreement.

The legacy of Civil Law tradition can also be profited from when it comes to the arbitration agreement. This is the third proposal. Along with practices and usages, good faith and analogy can help to integrate an incomplete arbitration clause, leading to the definition of a content that is in close connection to the common intentions of the parties.

The fourth proposal concerns the boundaries to which the integration is subjected. The aim of integration is to allow the regular performance of a given agreement. That implies that integration could not conflict with what was already agreed to by the parties. The process of gap-filling must always respect two limits. It can neither lead to an improvement of a contract, nor can it alter the balance of risks agreed to by the parties. Party autonomy implies party responsibility. In Private Law societies, citizens are allowed to engage themselves in binding contracts, but they also have to bear the consequences of doing so.

The Civil Law tradition is a rich source for dealing with gap-filling. Its methods have survived for centuries because they have been useful to generations of jurists. This is a legacy that is worth considering while dealing with the complex problems of contemporary economies. There certainly is a lot of work to be done. Nevertheless, one can be sure that good faith and analogy still have something to tell us in the twenty-first century. They remain important allies in the battle against imperfection, which characterizes the struggle for justice in human societies. Before such a challenge, jurists can neither renounce the battle, nor win it completely, but only perform their task: duly consider every case, find the best possible solution and hope for it to be right.

Closing Plenary

Legitimacy:
Examined Against Empirical Data

Report on the Closing Plenary Session

James Freda [*] *and Tobias Lehmann* [**]

I.   PRELIMINARY RESULTS OF THE ICCA EXPERIMENT AND SURVEY

Ms. Meg Kinnear, Secretary-General of the International Centre for Settlement of Investment Disputes, began the Closing Plenary Session. She re-introduced Professor Susan Franck of Washington & Lee University School of Law, Professor Anne van Aaken of the University of St. Gallen, and James Freda of Freshfields Bruckhaus Deringer from the Opening Plenary. This team, along with Tobias Lehmann of the University of St. Gallen, had conducted a study on arbitral decision-making at the opening plenary session. Their study also included a separate short survey based on the Congress' themes of Legitimacy, Justice and Precision.

Professor Franck, Professor van Aaken and Mr. Freda presented the preliminary results of the survey to a highly distinguished panel. The panel was moderated by Professor Jan Paulsson of the University of Miami Law School and Three Crowns LLP, Donald Donovan of Debevoise & Plimpton, Makhdoom Ali Khan, Senior Advocate at the Supreme Court of Pakistan and the former Attorney-General of Pakistan, Wolfgang Peter of Python & Peter, and Professor Catherine Rogers of Penn State Law and Queen Mary University of London.

Mr. Freda first described the results of the thematic survey. The results of the survey and the arbitral decision-making study were presented on a preliminary basis at the Congress. As such, they will not be reproduced here and the report on the discussion of the panel will necessarily be limited. The formal results of the survey can be found at pp. 33-122 of this volume. The formal results of the arbitral decision-making study will be presented in a forthcoming publication.

Commenting on the survey questions regarding diversity, Professor Rogers noted that there was substantial discussion at the Congress of party autonomy versus concerns about increasing diversity. She thought that the problem could, in part, be addressed by increasing information about new arbitrators (or those arbitrators who were not well known outside of insider groups). Mr. Donovan stated that the great challenge of

---

[*]   Panel Rapporteur; Senior Associate, Freshfields Bruckhaus Deringer US LLP.
[**] Panel Rapporteur; Doctoral candidate, University of St. Gallen.

The following is their Report of the ICCA Closing Plenary Session and any mistakes, misstatements or misimpressions should be attributed to them and not to the speakers.

international arbitration was to be international, and to reflect the constituencies that arbitral decisions impact. Mr. Ali Khan stated that there is a strong perception that institutions and major arbitral players need to do more to encourage diversity. As to the survey's other qualitative questions unrelated to issues of diversity, Mr. Peter expressed skepticism about their reliability and asked whether they portrayed an overly optimistic portrait of international arbitration and the arbitrators themselves.

Professor Paulsson then introduced Professors Franck and van Aaken to present the preliminary results of the experimental study on arbitral decision-making. Professor Rogers responded to some of the data by stating that there was often a myth of "non-humanness" surrounding international arbitrators and judges, and that arbitrators should attempt to understand their own biases. Mr. Peter noted that although it is normal to have an intuitive answer to a legal question, there is a strong need to check that answer through deliberation. Mr. Donovan stated that an understanding of the issues tested in the experiment could not only could improve decision-making, but could also lead to changes in advocacy. Mr. Ali Khan echoed Mr. Peter by stating that the experimental subject matter demonstrated how there was no substitute for looking at the evidence and doing the hard work of decision-making.

II.   REPORT ON THE PANEL PROPOSITIONS

Ms. Lucy Reed of Freshfields Bruckhaus Deringer continued the session after the break. She re-introduced the chairs of the eight "Precision" (A) and "Justice" (B) Stream Panels.[1] Each panel's ultimate conclusions on the propositions that were created for the Congress are presented at the Annex to the Report on the Opening Plenary Session, which is located at pp. 22-29 of this volume. What follows here is a brief note on the remarks given by each panel chair at the closing plenary.

1.   Precision Stream

Panel A-1, "Proof: A Plea for Precision": Dr. David Brynmor Thomas of Thirty-Nine Essex Street Chambers noted that although ICCA participants stated that the burden and standard of proof were frequently outcome determinative in their cases, parties were frequently surprised to realize that issues of proof were indeed determinative. He called for greater clarity on these issues at the outset of an arbitration.

Panel A-2, "Early Stages of the Arbitral Process: Interim Measures and Document Production": Mr. John Barkett of Shook, Hardy & Bacon reflected on the conference theme of legitimacy. His overall conclusion was that "self policing and tireless training preserve legitimacy, [and] complacency destroys legitimacy".

Panel A-3, "Matters of Evidence: Witness and Experts": Dr. Nathalie Voser of Shellenberg Wittmer recounted the findings of her panel, which are reproduced in this volume, pp. 297-430.

---

1. For a greater description of the structure of the ICCA Congress, see the Report on the Opening Plenary Session located at pp. 15-29 of this volume.

Panel A-4, "Treaty Arbitration: Pleading and Proof of Fraud and Comparable Forms of Abuse": Mr. Klaus Reichert SC of Brick Court Chambers stated that the major problem regarding investor misconduct is that of proof. He stated that there needed to be greater exposition regarding the burden and standard of proof of serious investor misconduct in investment treaty arbitration.

2. Justice Stream

Panel B-1, "Who Are the Arbitrators?": Ms. Adriana Braghetta of L.O. Baptista – SVMFA stated that her panel concluded that there was a limited pool of arbitrators and those arbitrators share a common profile. It also concluded that diversity enhances legitimacy. She stressed that users want more options with regard to nationality, especially with respect to the chairs of arbitral panels.

Panel B-2, "Premise: Arbitral Institutions Can Do More To Further Legitimacy. True or False?": Mr. Salim Moollan of Essex Court Chambers stated that the general consensus of his panel was that there was a real concern regarding legitimacy, although arbitral institutions are somewhat constrained by the parties' choices. He noted that there is a perception outside of arbitration that under the guise of procedure, the substantive law of international arbitration can favor one camp. He called for "radical thinking in [the] area" that could "lead to significant change".

Panel B-3, "Treaty Arbitration: Is the Playing Field Level and Who Decides Whether It Is Anyway?": Ms. Anna Joubin-Bret of Cabinet Joubin-Bret described the results of her panel. Of note, her panel concluded that whether investment treaty arbitration was inherently imbalanced toward investors was both a reality and a myth. It was a reality because the law is based on investment treaties, which give rights to an investor vis-à-vis states, but it was also a myth due to the fact that empirical analysis of jurisprudence tended to show that the playing field was more balanced than perceived. She stated that this latter finding was enhanced by greater transparency in the investment arbitration process.

Panel B-4, "Universal Arbitration: An Aspiration Within Reach or a Sisyphean Goal?": The rapporteur Ms. Belinda McRae of 20 Essex Street Chambers, presented the conclusions of the panel on behalf of its chair, Mr. Dushyant Dave. Ms. McRae noted that universal arbitration did not mean uniform arbitration, but related to the convergence of practice in arbitration in diverse locations in fundamentally the same manner. She stated that the panel agreed that users could safeguard the arbitral system by questioning its founding principles, including from the perspective of those outside the system who are affected by it.

With the closing of Ms. McRae's remarks, the portion of the Plenary relating to the panel propositions was complete.

III. LOOKING BACK, AND MOVING FORWARD

Sundaresh Menon, Chief Justice of the Republic of Singapore, was then introduced. He presented a "report card" of international arbitration's progress after his Keynote

Address at the XXI ICCA Congress in Singapore in 2012. A copy of his remarks are available at pp. 6-27 of the Singapore Congress Book.[2]

The XXII Congress then held its Closing Ceremonies. Burton Landy of Akerman and chair of the Host Committee thanked the Congress participants, sponsors, volunteers and guests. He hoped that Miami, Florida, would become a greater venue for international arbitration and international law in general as a result of the Congress. ICCA subsequently presented Mr. Landy with an award for his work on the Host Committee.

Professor Albert Jan van den Berg of Hanotiau & van den Berg assumed the ICCA Presidency taking over the post from the outgoing President, Professor Jan Paulsson. Professor van den Berg stated that he would apply four guiding principles during his ICCA presidency:

(i) *cooperation* with other organizations active in the field of international arbitration;
(ii) *expansion* and continued outreach to parts of the world where international arbitration was new or developing;
(iii) *mentorship* of younger practitioners in the field; and
(iv) *inclusiveness* in order to make ICCA as diverse as international arbitration should be.

Professor van den Berg then thanked Ms. Reed and the Program Committee for their work on the XXII Congress.

Finally, Mr. Salim Moollan looked forward to the XXIII ICCA Congress to be held in Mauritius in 2016. Mr. Moollan described the importance of Mauritius as a commercial and legal hub. He also noted the necessity for ICCA and its members to have a presence in Africa. A short video on behalf of ICCA Mauritius was shown to the Congress.

The Plenary Session, and the work of the Program Committee, was then concluded.

---

2. *International Arbitration: The Coming of a New Age?* ICCA Congress Series no. 17 (2013). The text of the Keynote Address is also available online at <http://www.arbitration-icca.org/AV_Library/AV_Library_textformat/ICCA_2012_Singapore_Keynote_Menon.html>.

Closing Plenary

Where We Have Been,
Where We Should Go

Where We Have Been, Where We Should Go

Sundaresh Menon[*]

I.   INTRODUCTION

I feel extraordinarily privileged to have been asked to address the closing plenary of this magnificent conference. I must first thank and congratulate the organizing committee, the host committee and the very many others who have worked very hard indeed to give all of us a conference that sets yet a new standard for excellence in organisation, hospitality and programming.

When I was asked if I would accept this invitation, I was of course delighted to do so. I had the privilege of delivering the keynote address at the ICCA Congress 2012.[1] On that occasion, the approach path was straightforward: I worked on the premise that never again would I have the opportunity to address such a distinguished audience of those who are involved with and care so deeply about international arbitration. And so, I said all that I thought needed to be said; and perhaps the indicia of some success, is that it was acclaimed and derided in almost equal measure.

As we come to the closing of this Congress, how have things moved on? The theme for this Congress was an ambitious one – Legitimacy: Myths, Realities and Challenges. Over the course of eight breakout sessions and the opening and closing plenaries, we have pored over this theme by examining it from the vantage point of several different perspectives. In particular the A-stream sessions examined the question of legitimacy by reference to whether there was a need for greater precision in the context of a number of vitally important areas, while the B-stream sessions examined whether there was a threat to the legitimacy of arbitration by reason of issues that seemingly affect the quality of justice.

The focus on precision was in many respects a focus on whether there was consistency, if not common ground in our understanding of the concepts and rules affecting four important areas of arbitration. But let me just touch on one for illustrative purposes: the question of proof – do we have a common understanding of who generally

---

[*] Chief Justice of of Singapore; ICCA Governing Board Member.
1. See Sundaresh MENON, "International Arbitration: The Coming of a New Age for Asia (and Elsewhere)", Opening Plenary Session at ICCA Congress 2012 (henceforth *"Coming of a New Age"*); available online at <http://www.arbitration-icca.org/media/0/13398435632250/ags_opening_speech_icca_congress_2012.pdf>.

carries the burden of proof, and of what the appropriate standard of proof is? Should these be raised and fleshed out by the parties or by the arbitrators?

I think it is fair to say that the one thing that most participants in the room agreed upon was that there is no consistent understanding on these questions in international arbitration. From differences over the approach towards evaluating oral evidence, to the standard of proof applicable in cases, to the obligation to produce documents and whether an adverse inference may be drawn as a matter of proof in weighing the evidence, there was, and is, room for divergence. This divergence can be of critical importance because it can exist within a case where the parties are coming to these questions from different perspectives with different understandings and approaches. The Panel suggested a number of propositions which were directed at enhancing precision and consistency so that in each case, the parties would be encouraged to address their minds to the issue and the arbitrators could clarify the issue early in the process.

On the face of it, this seemed to promise enhanced legitimacy. But the majority of speakers from the floor seemed opposed to such an idea. Some from the floor suggested that there was no need to spell this out because there is a shared understanding on these issues — a view which I respectfully disagree with, and a view which I believe is likely to be challenged even more in the years to come, as the diversity of the international arbitration community increases.

This brings me to my first point. International arbitration today features an incredible and unprecedented richness and diversity of intellectual viewpoints and debate across an extremely wide range of issues. The number of books and publications on arbitration readily evidences this. It is also noteworthy that this diversity of viewpoints, perhaps even ideologies, emanates from a large and rapidly growing group of people who share two traits: first, they are passionate in what they believe because they care so deeply about it; and second, the group to a very large extent consists of smart lawyers.

This mix of concern and intelligence that characterizes this community leads me to conclude that it would be unrealistic and perhaps unwise as yet to expect or even to seek consensus on many of these issues. For those who suggest that we need to have a measure of regulation in this vast field of growing importance, there will be others who say that regulation will destroy arbitration. For those who say that we need a consensus on ethical standards, there will be others who say "no, not yet another statement or code of practice". For those who advocate practices that could promote consistency and precision, there will be others who say that it would be wiser to retain a significant degree of flexibility on these matters.

I believe that being such a large field and featuring such a large array of thinkers and practitioners, arbitration is perhaps better suited to evolution rather than to revolution. On this footing, the task before us is perhaps not to agree on solutions; indeed, it might not even be to definitively identify the problems because to do so would require agreement that there are some issues in need of solutions. There are, after all, many among us who passionately believe that all is well. The task before us is perhaps better couched as a forward-looking one that calls for us to recall where we have come from, understand where we are and anticipate what might prove to be the defining issues in the coming years. And if I may say so, I think this is precisely what this Congress has set out to accomplish, and I dare say, has achieved; to examine and table the likely issues on which will hang the legitimacy of arbitration in the coming years — from issues concerning proof and evidence to issues concerning expert evidence and witness statements; to issues concerning the selection of arbitrators, the role of the institutions and the prospect of universal arbitration. Inevitably, as the dust settles we will conclude that some of these issues rest on myths; many others on realities which require our attention; while nearly all of them will be challenging in some way or the other. Indeed, this much emerges from the careful summaries just presented by the panel moderators.

I believe arbitration will evolve over time to adapt to these issues as they emerge and that evolution will ultimately be driven by what is best for arbitration, in particular, for its users – and I have intentionally put them first – the parties who depend on arbitration to a very large extent; and then for its practitioners who must confront a reality that their numbers have swelled and will continue to swell exponentially in the coming years. I highlight this last point because I believe that this is the essential challenge of this age – we are moving very rapidly from a time when the key players knew one another; when they often looked similar and spoke similarly; and when they had a common legal, cultural and social background; to a period in which there is unprecedented growth in numbers and in diversity.

This diversity also extends to the number and the experience of the Judges who will hear enforcement applications under the 1958 New York Convention legislation or recourse applications under the Model Law. The fact that ICCA recognizes this explains why we have a Judiciary Committee, which is devoted to outreach to Judges, to provide training and resources to enhance the prospects of consistency in outcomes.

Let me pause to make one further observation here, which might shape the way we look at these issues: the future of arbitration is not in the hands of the grand men and women of the past decades. It is in the hands of younger practitioners whose numbers are burgeoning. This is a welcome development; but it helps bring into focus the importance of preparing for the surge in diversity that we can expect will continue.

II.   FURTHER ISSUES FOR CONSIDERATION

I have been invited to offer a brief retrospective on the issues and challenges as I saw them two years ago and since. The last couple of years have seen a great deal of debate and discussion on some of the issues that have been raised. It is much too soon to say how these will be resolved; but the fact of the debate is important in its own right. The organizers of this immensely successful Congress anticipate producing a Congress Book that will be a lasting reference work. This will undoubtedly collate all the many ideas, propositions and reactions that we have seen over the past three days. But I do feel extremely optimistic about our future because we care so deeply about this that we have brought a thousand of us together for three days to discuss the issues, and I am certain that the discussions will carry on after Miami.

Let me touch on three issues that relate to international commercial arbitration, which were not directly dealt with in this Congress. These are: (1) rising costs, (2) third-party funding, and (3) ethical standards.

1. Rising Costs

Why is the cost of arbitration likely to be a hot-button issue in the years to come? My first response is because it already is. But more deeply, it is because in a single generation the tables have been turned. Arbitration staked its claim to legitimacy in the fact that it was a cheaper, more informal alternative to litigation. But today, courts in many jurisdictions offer their services as the cheaper alternative to arbitration. Surveys of the users of arbitration tell us that they are forced to consider arbitration in spite of its cost rather than, as it once was, because of it. There are many reasons for the rising costs of international arbitration: greater complexity, much larger sums of money, the "one-shot" nature of arbitration resulting in protracted proceedings, and so forth. But aside from the tale of the absolute numbers, there is also the important and sometimes overlooked angle of transnational access to justice.

As part of the modern order of transnational commerce, trade and investment by multinational corporations are facilitated by the assurance that many transnational commercial disputes will be decided by competent and neutral arbitral tribunals. Parties from capital-importing countries, while benefiting directly or indirectly from such trade, often forsake their access to domestic courts and agree to accept justice dispensed by arbitral tribunals. Is there not a risk, given the rising cost of arbitration, that parties might prevail by virtue of the depth of their pockets rather than of the merits of their cases? If arbitration is to retain the mantle of being a primary dispenser of justice in transnational commerce, must we not ensure that the users of this system have effective access to justice? And must we not pay heed to the woes of our primary clients, the users of arbitration?

At the Singapore International Arbitration Forum 2013, a smaller group of distinguished arbitration thinkers and practitioners got together for a day of reflection about what we might do differently if we started over. Among the views most widely held was that arbitrators should be actively involved in cases from an early stage, pursue "active case management" during the lifetime of the case and tailor ideal solutions and even encourage settlements, instead of issuing a fairly standardized Procedural Order No. 1 and then waiting until the hearing dates to really come to grips with what the case is about. Other ideas included encouraging arbitrators to have greater regard to the *pareto* principle, encouraging parties to focus on the real issues in the case by imposing page limits or limiting the scope of document production, and adopting inquisitorial processes more readily where these are appropriate. These all seem perfectly sensible but I wonder if we will see their increasing deployment in international arbitration in the years to come. This segues nicely into the second point.

2. Third-Party Funding

The rising complexity and cost of arbitration, amongst other factors, has contributed to the phenomenon of third-party funding. We have witnessed a substantial increase in such funding since the turn of the century.[2]

While this might facilitate access to justice in some cases, recognizing that it is a new phenomenon, it might be unwise to leave it unaddressed without active study of the issues raised. In the international arbitration context, counsel and arbitrators are often drawn from the same pool. Where a financier funds multiple claims, situations of conflict might arise. Are there disclosure standards that apply in this context? Where the financier has had prior and perhaps ongoing commercial relationships and contacts with counsel or the arbitrators, would or should these be disclosed?

It is certainly heartening that arbitral institutions and think tanks are taking the lead in studying the implications of third-party funding in international arbitration. This is an essential precursor towards any sort of regulatory stitch, which if made in time might well save nine.

3. Ethical Standards

Let me finally touch on ethical standards. Why is this an issue? Because we have come such a long way from where we began that the premises on which we operated in the past can no longer hold.

In days long gone, arbitration was a small industry governed by implied norms, peer standards and shared values. Today, the practice of international arbitration has fundamentally changed. It is now a global industry, with a multitude of new entrants. The number of cases has increased exponentially, as has the number of discrete international arbitral institutions. It is impossible to rely on implied understandings or shared values to continue shaping, influencing or even regulating conduct since there are no such shared norms.[3] The problem is not the lack of any ethical standards or guidance;

---

2. It has been noted that the "first and most obvious reason for [the increase in third party funding in international arbitration] lies in the heavy costs associated with the conduct of usually lengthy proceedings in international investment arbitration": see Eric DE BRABANDERE and Julia LEPELTAK, "Third Party Funding in International Investment Arbitration", Grotius Centre Working Paper No. 2012/1 (<http://ssrn.com/abstract=2078358>) at p. 6. For example, in 2012, a European gas company announced that a Luxembourg fund would finance its €1 billion ICSID claim (see Wolfgang RAUBALL, *EuroGas AG: European Investment-Fund Financed Billion-Lawsuit of EuroGas Group against the Slovak Republic*, Business Wire (6 November 2012), (<www.businesswire.com/news/home/20121106005568/en/EuroGas-AG-European-Investment-Fund-Financed-Billion-Lawsuit-EuroGas#.UwQWtqL_Ajw>)). Again, in 2013, a third-party funder agreed to cover the costs of a Canadian mining company's multi-billion arbitration claim brought against Bolivia (see Leo SZOLNOKI, "Miner Secures Funding for Bolivia Claim" (28 May 2013) Global Arbitration Review).
3. Sundaresh MENON, "Some Cautionary Notes for an Age of Opportunity", Chartered Institute of Arbitrators International Arbitration Conference (22 August 2013) (henceforth "*Cautionary Notes*"); available online at <www.ciarb.org.sg/images/courses/Some_cautionary_notes_for_an_age_of_opportunity.pdf>, at para. 5.

it is the lack of *common* ethical standards to guide a great diversity of practitioners that poses serious difficulties and might even create uneven and unpredictable battlegrounds.[4]

A few weeks ago, I was sent an advanced draft of Catherine Rogers' forthcoming work *Ethics in International Arbitration* for comment. I welcome this work with great enthusiasm because, quite aside from its magisterial scale, it sets about discussing the issue of ethics on the premise that it is a legitimate and discrete subject in its own right within the broad field that is arbitration. Ethics in arbitration should be approached as such, by having regard to what the contesting viewpoints might be and then considering how these might be resolved, rather than by throwing one's hands up and saying that it is all pointless.

Of course there are cultural differences that make it a challenge to find a consensus. But these differences are precisely the *raison d'être* for the need to migrate towards consensus. Legend has it that the game of rugby started when William Webb Ellis used his hands to pick up the ball during a game of football and then ran forward with it.[5] My point is that it was quickly recognized that if you want to play according to different rules, then you must opt for a different game because it is ultimately not possible to play a game where there is no consensus as to what the rules of engagement are. The search for such a consensus is not an impossible dream for arbitration. As a starting point, the values of impartiality and independence appear to find almost universal acceptance within the international arbitration community. There are also instances of cross-cultural agreements on extensive sets of ethical guidelines, such as the IBA Guidelines on Conflicts of Interest in International Arbitration and on Party Representation in International Arbitration. We can be cautiously optimistic that such guidelines can be created, if only we apply our minds and efforts to this task.

III.   CONCLUSION

My keynote address two years ago seemed to evoke fairly robust reactions: some believed that I had made serious and valid observations on the challenges ahead; others believed that there might be serious and valid reasons to suspect that I had lost my mind. But as the dust settles, I think that we have collectively begun to recognize that adopting polarized positions does not advance our dialogue on the important issues that face our industry. I believe that there is perhaps a subtle shift in the tone of the debate from whether anything needs to be done, gently towards *what* precisely should be done and *why*.

In many areas, it is encouraging that international arbitral think tanks, institutions and even states have stepped up to engage in the dialogue over what could be done to steer the development of international arbitration in a sustainable direction.

The international arbitration industry is vast and increasingly amorphous; but there is every reason to believe that our community, with all its undoubted brainpower and

---

4. *Cautionary Notes,* supra fn. 3, at para. 6.
5. This is, in some quarters, regarded as a myth.

talent, can and will apply its energies to identify the issues, to debate them, and then to imagine fresh solutions to them.

As I noted two years ago, the sun has indeed risen over this "glorious, golden age of arbitration".[6] But bathed in its light, we should take note of the pitfalls that might lie ahead. We should not turn from them. Far from it, we should tackle them head on and strengthen this industry we all care so deeply about.

---

6. Sundaresh MENON, *Coming of a New Age*, supra fn. 1, at para. 81.

ICCA MIAMI CONGRESS LIST OF PARTICIPANTS

Argentina

Capparelli, Santiago
Baker & McKenzie LLP
Avenida Leandro N. Alem 1110, 13th Floor
C1001AAT Buenos Aires

De Luca, Juan Pablo
Rattagan Macchiavello Arocena &
Peña Robirosa
Avenida Leandro N. Alem 855, 8th Floor
C1001AAT Buenos Aires

Rivera, Julio Cesar
Rivera & Asociados
Uruguay 750, 8th Floor
C1015ABP Ciudad de Buenos Aires

Tawil, Guido
Governing Board Member of ICCA
M. & M. Bomchil
Suipacha 268
C1008 AAF Buenos Aires

Australia

Baykitch, Alexander
King & Wood Mallesons
Level 61, Governor Phillip Tower,
1 Farrer Place
Sydney, NSW 2000

Bonnell, Max
King & Wood Mallesons
Level 61, Governor Phillip Tower
1 Farrer Place
Sydney, NSW 2000

Easton, Graham
DRBF
Level 26, 1 Bligh Street
Sydney, NSW 2065

Freeman, Christopher
Culwulla Chambers
Level 11, 67 Castlereagh Street
Sydney, NSW 2000

Griffith, Gavan
Barrister

205 William Street
Melbourne, VIC 3000

Jones, Doug
Clayton Utz
1 Bligh Street
Sydney, NSW 2000

Little, Graeme
Elizabeth Street Chambers
Level 16
179 Elizabeth Street
Sydney, NSW 2000

Martignoni, Andrea
Allens
Deutsche Bank Place
126 Phillip Street
Sydney, NSW 2000

Morrison, James
Allens
Deutsche Bank Place
126 Phillip Street
Sydney, NSW 2000

O'Donahoo, Ian Peter
Allens
101 Collins Street
Melbourne, VIC 3000

Spigelman, James
One Essex Court
22 Darling Point Road
Darling Point
Sydney, NSW 2027

Stephenson, Andrew
Corrs Chambers Westgarth
GPO Box 9925
Brisbane, QLD 4000

Waincymer, Jeffrey
Monash University
45 Victoria Road North
Malvern
Melbourne, VIC 3144

Wakefield, Samantha
Australian Centre for International
Commercial Arbitration

1 Bligh Street
Sydney, NSW 2000

Austria

Baier, Anton
Vienna International Arbitral Centre (VIAC)
Kärntner Ring 12
1010 Vienna

Bergsten, Eric
Pace Law School
Schimmelgasse 16/16
1030 Vienna

Dorda, Christian
Dorda Brugger Jordis Rechtsanwälte GmbH
Universitätsring 10
1010 Vienna

Haugeneder, Florian
Wolf Theiss
Schubertring 6
1010 Vienna

Hauser, Wulf Gordian
Hauser Partners Rechtsanwälte GmbH
Seilerstätte 18-20
1010 Vienna

Heider, Manfred
Vienna International Arbitral Centre (VIAC)
Wiedner Hauptstrasse 63
1045 Vienna

Horvath, Guenther
Freshfields Bruckhaus Deringer LLP
Seilergasse 16
1010 Vienna

Klein, Peter
Petsch Frosch Klein Arturo
Rechtsanwälte OG
Esslinggasse 5
1010 Vienna

Klochenko, Lilia
Law Firm AKP Consulting
Guepferlingstrasse 39/2
1170 Vienna

Montineri, Corinne
United Nations
Vienna International Centre
PO Box 500
1400 Vienna

Pitkowitz, Nikolaus
Graf & Pitkowitz
Stadiongasse 2
1010 Vienna

Sekolec, Jernej
Jernej Sekolec
Formanekgasse 63/3
1190 Vienna

Zeiler, Gerold
Schönherr Rechtsanwälte GmbH
Tuchlauben 17
1014 Vienna

Bahamas

Woods, Phylicia
Ministry of Financial Services
Manx Corporate Centre
PO Box N 8975
Nassau

Bahrain

Mutaywea, Aysha
Bahrain Chamber for Dispute Resolution
(BCDR-AAA)
Park Plaza, Suite 401
Road 1704, Building 247
Diplomatic Area
Manama

Ziadé, Nassib
Bahrain Chamber for Dispute Resolution
(BCDR-AAA)
Park Plaza, Suite 401
Road 1704, Building 247
Diplomatic Area
Manama

Belgium

van den Berg, Albert Jan
President of ICCA
Hanotiau & van den Berg
IT Tower, 9th Floor
480 Avenue Louise, B9
1050 Brussels

Dal, Georges Albert
Dal Et Veldekens
Avenue Louise 81
1050 Brussels

García Gallardo, Ramón
King & Wood Mallesons
Square de Meeûs 1
1000 Brussels

van Houtte, Hans
Iran-US Claims Tribunal
Schoonzichtlaan 17
3020 Herent

Villeneuve, Charlotte
Hanotiau & van den Berg
IT Tower, 9th Floor
480 Avenue Louise, B9
1050 Brussels

Bermuda

Elkinson, Jeffrey
Conyers Dill and Pearman
Clarendon House
2 Church Street
Hamilton, HMCX

Bolivia

Aguirre, Fernando
Bufete Aguirre Soc. Civ.
Avenida Los Alamos 322, La Florida
La Paz

Anaya Leigue, Leonardo Alejandro
Bolivia General Attorney's Office, Division of
International Investment Arbitration
Rosendo Gutierres #694
La Paz, 2403

Fernandez, Marcelo
Bolivia General Attorney's Office, Division of
International Investment Arbitration
Avenida 20 de Octubre No. 2151
La Paz, 2403

Moreno Gutierrez, Andres
Moreno Baldivieso Estudio de Abogados
Calle Capitan Ravelo No. 2366
La Paz, 830

Wayar Ocampo, Bernardo
Wayar & von Borries Abogados
Avenida 20 de Octubre Edfi. Topater of. 801
Sopocachi
La Paz

Botswana

Fashole-Luke, Edward
Luke & Associates
PO Box 301097
Tlokweng
Gaborone

Brazil

Amaral, Guilherme
Souto Correa Advogados
Avenida Carlos Gomes 700, 13th Floor
Porto Alegre 90480-000

Aprigliano, Ricardo
Godoi Aprigliano Zambo Advogados
Rua Bela Cintra 1149, 11th Floor
Cerqueira Cezar
São Paulo, 01415-003

Araújo, Mariana
Centro de Arbitragem e Mediação da
Câmara de Comércio Brasil-Canadá
(CAM - CCBC)
Rua do Rocio 220
12th Floor - cj.122
São Paulo, 04552-000

Baraldi, Eliana
De Vivo, Whitaker e Castro Advogados
Rua Dr. Renato Paes de Barros 1017, 7th
Floor
São Paulo, 04530-001

Benetti Timm, Luciano
Carvalho, Machado, Timm & Deffenti
Avenida Carlos Gomes 1340, Room 602
Porto Alegre, 90480-001

Berezowski, Aluisio
Tepedino, Migliore e Berezowski Advogados
Avenida Paulista 283, 9th Floor
São Paulo, 01311-000

Berni, Vinícius
Tozzini Freire Advogados
Avenida Carlos Gomes 222, 5th Floor
Porto Alegre, 90480

Bianco, Rogerio
Lilla, Huck, Otranto e Camargo Advogados
Avenida Brig Faria Lima 1744, 6th floor
São Paulo, 01451-910

Bittar, Flávia
Grebler Advogados
Avenida Raja Gabaglia 1400, 8th Floor
Belo Horizonte – Minas Gerais, 30441-194

Bondioli, Andressa
BM&FBOVESPA
Rua XV de Novembro 275, 5th Floor
São Paulo, 01013-001

Braghetta, Adriana
Vice President of ICCA
LOBaptista - SVMFA
Avenida Paulista 1294, 8th Floor
São Paulo, 01310-100

Brasso, Maristela
Centro de Arbitragem e Mediação da
Câmara de Comércio Brasil-Canadá
(CAM - CCBC)
Rua do Rocio 220
12th Floor - cj.122
São Paulo, 04552-000

Bucker, Fatima Cristina Bonassa
Bonassa Bucker Advogados
Rua Afonso Bras 864, cj 112
São Paulo, 04011-001

Cardoso, Christiana
Centro de Arbitragem e Mediação da
Câmara de Comércio Brasil-Canadá
(CAM - CCBC)

Rua do Rocio 220
12th Floor - cj.122
São Paulo, 04552-000

Carneiro, Cristiane
Fiaux & Jraige Advogados
Avenida Paula Souza 351-303
Rio de Janeiro, 22260-020

Catarucci, Douglas
Pinheiro Neto Advogados
Rua Hungria 1100
São Paulo, 01455-906

Celidonio, Luciana
Tauil & Chequer Advogados Associados a
Mayer Brown LLP
Avenida Juscelino Kubitschek 1455, 5th & 6th
Floor
São Paulo, 04543-011

Coelho, Eleonora
Castro, Barros, Sobral, Gomes, Advogados
Rua do Rócio 291, 11th Floor
São Paulo, 04552-000

Correa, Fabio
Lilla, Huck, Otranto e Camargo Advogados
Avenida Brig Faria Lima 1744, 6th floor
São Paulo, 01451-910

Correa, Leonardo
Brandão Couto Wigderowitz e Pessoa
Advogados
Rua Dom Gerardo 35, 4th Floor
Rio de Janeiro, 20090-905

Costa, Caroline
Centro de Arbitragem e Mediação da
Câmara de Comércio Brasil-Canadá
(CAM - CCBC)
Rua do Rocio 220
12th Floor - cj.122
São Paulo, 04552-000

Costa, Pedro
Barbosa, Müssnich & Aragão Advogados
Avenida Almirante Barroso 52, 29th Floor
Rio de Janeiro, 20031-000

de Araujo, Nadia
Nadia de Araujo Advogados

Rua Igarapava 14, Apt 401
Rio de Janeiro, 22450-200

Del Gallo, Silvia
Centro de Arbitragem e Mediação da
Câmara de Comércio Brasil-Canadá
(CAM - CCBC)
Rua do Rocio 220
12th Floor - cj.122
São Paulo, 04552-000

Fernandes, Gustavo
Tauil & Chequer Advogados Associados a
Mayer Brown LLP
Rua Teixeira de Freitas 31 & 9
Rio de Janeiro, 20021-350

Fernandes, Luisa
Cascione Pulino Boulos e Santos
Avenida Brigadeiro Faria Lima 3015, 10th
Floor
São Paulo, 01452-000

Ferro, Marcelo Roberto
FCDG - Ferro, Castro Neves, Daltro &
Gomide Advogados
Avenida Rio Branco 85, 13th Floor
Rio de Janeiro, 20020-080

Figueiredo, Gabriel
Souza, Cescon, Barrieu & Flesch Advogados
Avenida Tancredo Neves 620, cj. 1522/1523
Salvador, Bahia 41820-020

Finkelstein, Claudio
Finkelstein Advogados
Praça Amadeu Amaral, 27 - Conj. 112
São Paulo, 01327-010

Fonseca, Rodrigo
Osorio e Maya Ferreira Advogados
Rua General Urquiza 114 Ap 501
Leblon
Rio de Janeiro, 22431-040

Fontes, Marcos
Cunha Ricca Advogados
Rua Jesuino Arruda 131, Apt. 1B
São Paulo, 04532-080

Forbes, Carlos
Centro de Arbitragem e Mediação da
Câmara de Comércio Brasil-Canadá

(CAM - CCBC)
Rua do Rocio 220
12th Floor - cj.122
São Paulo, 04552-000

Gagliardi, Rafael
Demarest Advogados
Avenida Pedroso de Moraes 1201, 3rd Floor
Centro Cultural Ohtake
São Paulo, 05419-001

Galindez, Valeria
Uria Menendez
Avenida Paulista 1079
São Paulo, 01311-200

Gama, Lauro
Binenbojm, Gama & Carvalho Britto
Advocacia
Rua Primeiro de Março 23, 23rd Floor
Rio de Janeiro, 20010-904

Gandelman, Marcelo
Barbosa, Müssnich & Aragão Advogados
Avenida Almirante Barroso 52, 29th Floor
Rio de Janeiro, 20031-000

Giusti, Gilberto
Centro de Arbitragem e Mediação da
Câmara de Comércio Brasil-Canadá
(CAM - CCBC)
Rua Hungria, 1100
São Paulo, 01455-000

Goldberg, Karina
FCDG - Ferro, Castro Neves, Daltro &
Gomide Advogados
Rua Ramos Batista 198, 8th Floor
São Paulo, 04552-020

Gonçalves, Eduardo
Mattos Filho, Veiga Filho, Marrey Jr. E
Quiroga Advogados
Avenida Joaquim Eugenio de Lima, 447
São Paulo, 01403-001

Gondinho, Andre
Doria, Jacobina e Gondinho - Advogados
Rua da Assembleia 98, 13th Floor
Centro
Rio de Janeiro, 20011-000

Guimarães Pessoa, Carlos Alexandre
Brandão Couto Wigderowitz e Pessoa
Advogados
Rua Dom Gerardo 35, 4th Floor
Rio de Janeiro, 20090-905

Huck, Hermes Marcelo
Lilla, Huck, Otranto e Camargo Advogados
Avenida Brig Faria Lima 1744, 6th Floor
São Paulo, 01451-910

Junior, Roberto
Escritório de Advocacia Sergio Bermudes
Avenida Frei Caneca 1380, 6th Floor
São Paulo, 01307-002

Kobayashi, Patrícia
Centro de Arbitragem e Mediação da
Câmara de Comércio Brasil-Canadá
(CAM - CCBC)
Rua do Rocio 220
12th Floor - cj.122
São Paulo, 04552-000

Lee, Joao Bosco
Lee Taube & Gabardo
Avenida Anita Garibaldi 850
Torre C, cj 310
Curitiba, 80540-180

Luiz Menezes Lino, Wagner
Finkelstein Advogados
Praça Amadeu Amaral, 27 - Conj. 112
São Paulo, 01327-010

Mannheimer, Sergio
Andrade & Fichtner Advogados
Avenida Almirante Barroso 139, 4th Floor
Rio de Janeiro, 20031-005

Marques, Ricardo T. Dalmaso
Pinheiro Neto
Rua Hungria, 1.100
São Paulo, 01455-906

Martins, Andre
Sergio Bermudes Advogados
Praça XV de Novembro n° 20
8th Floor, Contro
Rio de Janeiro, 20010

Mason, Paul Eric
Paul Eric Mason

Caixa Postal 95454
Itaipav
Rio de Janeiro, 25750-970

Melo, Leonardo
FCDG - Ferro, Castro Neves, Daltro &
Gomide Advogados
Avenida Rio Branco 85, 13th Floor
Rio de Janeiro, 20040-004

Mizrahi Lamas, Natália
FCDG - Ferro, Castro Neves, Daltro &
Gomide Advogados
Avenida Rio Branco 85, 13th Floor
Rio de Janeiro, 20040-004

Monteiro, Vitor
Morata, Galafassi, Nakaharada, Serpa e
Monteiro Advogados
Avenida Paulista n. 1.048
10th Floor, cj. 102
São Paulo, 01310-100

Monteiro da Silva Filho, Antonio Carlos
Tess Advogados
Avenida Brasil 471
Jardim Paulista
São Paulo, 01431-000

Monteiro de Barros, Vera Cecília
Selma Lemes Advogados
Rua Alves Guimarães 518, Apt. 194
Pinheiros
São Paulo, 05410-000

Morato, Leonardo
Tauil & Chequer Advogados Associados a
Mayer Brown LLP
Avenida Juscelino Kubitschek 1455
5th & 6th Floor
São Paulo, 04543-011

Moreira Franco, Alice
FCDG - Ferro, Castro Neves, Daltro &
Gomide Advogados
Avenida Rio Branco 85, 13th Floor
Rio de Janeiro, 20040-004

Muniz, Joaquim
Trench, Rossi e Watanabe Advogados
Avenida Rio Branco, 01 19°, Sector B
Rio de Janeiro, 20090-003

Nanni, Giovanni Ettore
Tozzini Freire Advogados
Rua Borges Lagoa
1328 Vila Clementino
São Paulo, 04038-904

Northfleet, Ellen Gracie
Ellen Gracie Advogados
Avenida Rui Barbosa 566/301
Rio de Janeiro, 22250-020

Pasqualin, Roberto
PLKC Advogados
R. Henrique Schaumann 600
São Paulo, 05413-011

Passaro, Rafael
Stocche Forbes Advogados
Rua Pais de Araujo 59, Apt. 192
São Paulo, 04531-090

Pastore, Guilherme
Stocche Forbes Advogados
Avenida Magalhães de Castro 4800
18th Floor
Torre 2 - Edifício Park Tower
São Paulo, 05676-120

Pecoraro, Eduardo
FCDG - Ferro, Castro Neves, Daltro &
Gomide Advogados
Rua Ramos Batista 198, 8th Floor
São Paulo, 04552-020

Pereira, Cesar
Justen, Pereira, Oliveira & Talamini
Rua Padre Agostinho 1667, Apt. 401
Curitiba, 80710-000

Poppa, Bruno
Tepedino, Migliore e Berezowski Advogados
Avenida Paulista 283, 9th Floor
São Paulo, 01311-000

Pucci, Adriana Noemi
Adriana Noemi Pucci Sociedade de
Advogados
Rua Afonso Braz 473/143
Vila Nova Conceição
São Paulo, 04511-011

Pugliese, Antonio Celso
Vella Pugliese Buosi Guidoni Advogados

Rua Sao Tome 86, 17th Floor
São Paulo, 04551-080

Ranzolin, Ricardo
Silveiro Advogados
Rua Dom Pedro II 1240 - 601
Porto Alegre, 90550-141

Rebouças Mendes, Deise
Centro de Arbitragem e Mediação da
Câmara de Comércio Brasil-Canadá
(CAM - CCBC)
Rua do Rocio, 220
12th Floor - cj.122
São Paulo, 04552-000

Ribeiro de Oliveira, Pedro
Sacha Calmon Misabel Derzi LLP
Rua Sao Paulo 2189, Apt. 602
Belo Horizonte, 30170-132

Robalinho Cavalcanti, Fabiano
Sergio Bermudes Advogados
Praça XV de Novembro No. 20
8th Floor, Contro
Rio de Janeiro, 20010-010

Salles, Marcos Paulo de Almeida
Centro de Arbitragem e Mediação da
Câmara de Comércio Brasil-Canadá
(CAM - CCBC)

Rua Boa Vista 280, 16th Floor
São Paulo, 01014-000

Sampaio Carvalho, Antonio Luiz
Centro de Arbitragem e Mediação da
Câmara de Comércio Brasil-Canadá
(CAM - CCBC)
Rua do Rocio 220, 12th Floor
São Paulo, 04552-000

Serec, Fernando Eduardo
Tozzinifreire Advogados
Rua Borges Lagoa
1328 Vila Clementino
São Paulo, 04038-904

Silva, Luis Renato
Tozzini Freire Advogados
Avenida Carlos Gomes 222, 5th Floor
Porto Alegre, 90480-000

Soares Maciel, Pedro
Veirano Advogados
Avenida Brigadeiro Faria Lima 3477
16th Floor
São Paulo, 04538-133

Sobrinho, Washington
Company Melhoramentos São Paulo
Avenida Jabiru 578, Cond. Vista Alegre Café
Vinhedo, 13280-000

Souza, Marcelo Inglez
Demarest Advogados
Avenida Pedroso de Moraes 1201
3rd Floor
Centro Cultural Ohtake
São Paulo, 05419-001

Straube, Frederico
Centro de Arbitragem e Mediação da
Câmara de Comércio Brasil-Canadá
(CAM - CCBC)
Rua do Rocio 220
12th Floor - cj.122
São Paulo, 04552-000

Tannuri, Rodrigo
Escritório de Advocacia Sergio Bermudes
Avenida Frei Caneca 1380, 6th Floor
Consolação
São Paulo, 01307-002

Teixeira, Eliane
Machado Meyer Sendacz e Opice Advogados
Avenida Brigadeiro Faria Lima 3144
5th Floor
Itaim Bibi
São Paulo, 01451-000

Tepedino, Ricardo
Tepedino, Migliore e Berezowski Advogados
Avenida Paulista 283, 9th Floor
São Paulo, 01311-000

Tess, Eduardo
Tess Advogados
Avenida Brasil 471, Jardim Paulista
São Paulo, 01431-000

Tortorelli, Mauro
Vieira Rezende Advogados
Avenida Brigadeiro Faria Lima 3355
São Paulo, 04538-133

Verçosa, Fabiane
Brandão Couto Wigderowitz e Pessoa
Advogados
Rua Dom Gerardo 35, 4th Floor
Rio de Janeiro, 20090-905

Verona, Carlo
Veirano Advogados
Avenida Brigadeiro Faria Lima 3477
16th Floor
São Paulo, 04538-133

Visconte, Debora
José Carlos de Magalhães Advogados
Rua da Consolação 3367, 7th floor
São Paulo, 01416-001

Wigderowitz, Walter
Brandão Couto Wigderowitz e Pessoa
Advogados
Rua Dom Gerardo 35, 4th Floor
Rio de Janeiro, 20090-905

Zanetti, Cristiano de Sousa
University of São Paulo
Rua Batataes, 460
cjs. 31/32
São Paulo, 01423-010

British Virgin Islands

Smith, Dawn
BVI Financial Services Commission
PO Box 418
Pasea Estate, Road Town
Tortola, VG 1110

Canada

Barin, Babak
Barin Avocats
76 Arlington Avenue
Westmount, QC H3Y2W4

Bienvenu, Pierre
Norton Rose Fulbright
1 Place Ville Marie, Suite 2500
Montréal, QC H3B 1R1

Casey, J. Brian
Bay Street Chambers

Suite 2700
161 Bay Street
Toronto, ON M5J 2S1

Cherniak, Earl A.
Lerners LLP
Suite 2400,
130 Adelaide Street West
Toronto, ON M5H 3P5

Chiasson, Craig R.
Borden Ladner Gervais LLP
1200 Waterfront Centre
200 Burrard Street
Vancouver, BC V7X 1T2

Cunningham, Douglas
Cunningham Dispute Resolution
Services Ltd.
Neeson Chambers
141 Adelaide Street West
Toronto, ON M5H 3L5

Fortier, L. Yves
Advisory Board Member of ICCA
Cabinet Yves Fortier
1 Place Bille Marie, Suite 2822
Montréal, QC H3B 4R4

Haigh, David
BD&P LLP
2400, 525 - 8th Avenue South-West
Calgary, AB T2P 1G1

Heald, Fiona
IT Expert Reports
Suite 1901
3230 Yonge
Toronto, ON M4N 3P6

Heintzman, Thomas
Heintzman ADR
Arbitration Place, Bay Adelaide Centre
Suite 900
333 Bay Street
Toronto, ON M5H 2T4

Judge, John
Thirty Nine Essex Street Chambers
Suite 900
333 Bay Street
Toronto, ON MSH 2T4

Lalonde, Marc
Advisory Board Member of ICCA
Suite B-1
1155 René-Lévesque Boulevard West
Montréal, QC H3B 3V2

Leon, Barry
Perley-Robertson, Hill & McDougall LLP
340 Albert Street, Suite 1400
Ottawa, ON K1R 0A5

McCutcheon, David
Dentons Canada, LLP
77 King Street West
Toronto, ON M5K 0A1

McDougall, John Lorn
Dentons Canada, LLP
77 King Street West
Toronto, ON M5K 0A1

McEachern, Sarah
Borden Ladner Gervais LLP
1200 Waterfront Centre
200 Burrard Street
Vancouver, BC V7X 1T2

Michell, Paul
Lax O'Sullivan Scott Lisus LLP
145 King Street West, Suite 2750
Toronto, ON M5H 1J8

Mizrahi, Neal
FTI Consulting
79 Wellington Street West
Suite 2010
Toronto, ON M5K 1G8

Newcombe, Andrew
Faculty of Law, University of Victoria
1149 Victoria Avenue
Victoria, BC V8S4P3

Palazzo, Franca
Toronto Commercial Arbitration Society
19 Idlewilde Lane
Mount Hope, ON L0R 1W0

Richler, Joel
Blake, Cassels & Graydon LLP
199 Bay Street, Suite 4000
Toronto, ON M5L 1A9

Rosen, Howard
FTI Consulting
79 Wellington Street West
Suite 2010
Toronto, ON M5K 1G8

Rowley, J. William
20 Essex Street Chambers
Suite 4400, Brookfield Place
181 Bay Street, Bay Wellington Tower
Toronto, ON M5J 2T3

Seers, Myriam
Torys LLP
79 Wellington Street West
Box 270, TD Centre
Toronto, ON M5K 1N2

Smith, Murray
Smith Barristers
1008 Beach Avenue, Suite 105
Vancouver, BC V6E 1T7

Taylor, Richard
Deloitte Financial Advisory Services LLP
181 Bay Street, Suite 1400
Toronto, ON M5J 2V1

Walker, Janet
Arbitration Place
104-40 Glen Road
Toronto, ON M4W 2V1

Weiler, Todd
University of Western Ontario
2014 Valleyrun Boulevard, Unit 19
London, ON N6G 5N8

Woods, Seumas
Blake, Cassels & Graydon LLP
199 Bay Street, Suite 4000
Toronto, ON M5L 1A9

Yore, Richard
Business Events Sydney
248-970 Burrard Street
Vancouver, BC V6Z 2R4

Chile

Conejero Roos, Cristian
Philippi Yrarrazaval Pulido Brunner

Avenida El Golf No. 40, 20th Floor
Las Condes
Santiago 7550107

Figueroa, Juan Eduardo
Figueroa, Illanes, Huidobro, Salamanca
Apoquindo 3669, 11th Floor
Santiago

Gil, Rodrigo
Bofill Mir & Alvarez Jana Abogados
Avenida Andres Bello 2711, 8th Floor
Las Condes
Santiago 7550611

Jana Linetzky, Andres
Bofill Mir & Alvarez Jana Abogados
Avenida Andres Bello 2711, 8th Floor
Las Condes
Santiago 7550611

Klein Kranenberg, Johanna
Bofill Mir & Alvarez Jana Abogados
Avenida Andres Bello 2711, 8th Floor
Las Condes
Santiago 7550611

Orrego Vicuña, Francisco
Governing Board Member of ICCA
20 Essex Street Chambers
Avenida El Golf 40, 6th Floor
Santiago 7550117

China PR

Dong, Xiao
An Jie Law Firm
Level 26, Tower D, Central International
Trade Center
No. 6A Jiangguomenwai Avenue
Chaoyang District
100022 Beijing

Horrigan, Brenda
Herbert Smith Freehills LLP
No. 222 Yan An Road East
Room 3805, Bund Centre
200002 Shanghai

Li, Hu
China International Economic and Trade
Arbitration Commission

(CIETAC)
Level 6, CCOIC Building,
No. 2 Huapichang Hutong
Xicheng District
100035 Beijing

Li, Xiaoguang
China International Economic and
Trade Arbitration Commission
(CIETAC)
Level 6, CCOIC Building,
No. 2 Huapichang Hutong
Xicheng District
100035 Beijing

Ning, Fei
Hui Zhong Law Firm
One Indigo 20 Jiuxianqiao Road, Chaoyang
District
Room 2304
100016 Beijing

Ren, Sijiu
China International Economic and
Trade Arbitration Commission
(CIETAC)
Level 6, CCOIC Building,
2 Huapichang Hutong
Xicheng District
100035 Beijing

Sun, Wei
Beijing Arbitration Commission
Level 16, China Merchants Tower
No. 118 Jian Guo Road
100022 Beijing

Wang, Yingmin
China International Economic and
Trade Arbitration Commission
(CIETAC)
Level 6, CCOIC Building,
No. 2 Huapichang Hutong
Xicheng District
100035 Beijing

Xing, Yun
Beijing Arbitration Commission
Level 16, China Merchants Tower
No. 118 Jian Guo Road
100022 Beijing

Zhang, Haoliang
Beijing Arbitration Commission
Level 16, China Merchants Tower
No. 118 Jian Guo Road
100022 Beijing

Zheng, Rungao
Clifford Chance LLP
Level 33, China World Office 1
No. 1 Jianguomenwai Dajie
100004 Beijing

Zhou, Wen
China International Economic and
Trade Arbitration Commission
(CIETAC)
Level 6, CCOIC Building,
No. 2 Huapichang Hutong
Xicheng District
100035 Beijing

Colombia

Benavides Galvis, Claudia
Baker & McKenzie LLP
Avenida 82 No. 10-62, 6th Floor
Bogotá, 8

Cortes, Edwin
Cuberos Cortes Gutierrez Abogados S.A.S.
CRA. 12 No. 71-33
Bogotá, 57

De La Pava, Alonso
Baker & McKenzie LLP
Avenida 82 No. 10-62, 6th Floor
Bogotá, 11001000

Zuleta, Eduardo
Governing Board Member of ICCA
Gomez-Pinzon Zuleta Abogados
Calle 67 No. 7-35 Of.1204
Bogotá

Costa Rica

Diaz, Christian
LLM Attorneys
Meridiano Tower
Suite 12, 3rd Floor
San Rafael, Escazu, 1251

Czech Republic

Dubovsky, Miroslav
Hogan Lovells LLP
Na Prikope 22
110 00 Prague

Hodgson, Matthew
Allen & Overy LLP
V Celnici 4, 5th Floor
110 00 Prague

Lokajova, Maria
Squire Sanders
Vaclavske namesti 57
110 00 Prague

Mareš, Alexandr
Arbitration Court attached to the Economic
and Agricultural Chambers of the Czech
Republic
Dušní 10
110 00 Prague

Pekar, Rostislav
Squire Sanders
Vaclavske namesti 57
110 00 Prague

Skopovy, Pavel
Hogan Lovells LLP
Na Prikope 22
110 00 Prague

Denmark

Lett, Jesper
Lett Lawfirm
Rådhuspladsen 4
1306 Copenhagen

Pihlblad, Steffen
The Danish Institute of Arbitration
Kronprinsessegade 28, 3rd Floor
1306 Copenhagen

Spiermann, Ole
Bruun & Hjejle
Nørregade 21
1165 Copenhagen

Dominican Republic

Contreras, Leidylin
Office of the Legal Advisor to the Presidency
of the Dominican Republic
Avenida Mexico Esq. Dr. Delgado
Palacio de la Presidencia
10204 Santo Domingo

Moquete Pelletier, Luis
FONPER
Avenue Gustavo Mejia Ricart No. 73,
Edificio Gubernamental Dr. Rafael Kasse
Acta
Santo Domingo

Pantaleon, Jose
Office of the Legal Advisor to the Presidency
of the Dominican Republic
Avenida Mexico Esq. Dr. Delgado
Palacio de la Presidencia
10205 Santo Domingo

Ecuador

Coronel Jones, Cesar
Coronel & Pérez
Avenida 9 de Octubre No. 100 y Malecon
24th Floor
090103 Guayaquil

Coronel Ortega, César
Coronel & Pérez
Avenida 9 de Octubre No. 100 y Malecon
24th Floor
090103 Guayaquil

Perez Loose, Hernan
Coronel & Pérez
Avenida 9 de Octubre No. 100 y Malecon
Ed. La Previsora p24 of 2401
090103 Guayaquil

Egypt

Abdel Raouf, Mohamed
Vice President of ICCA
Cairo Regional Centre for International
Commercial Arbitration
1 Alsaleh Ayoub Street, Zamalek
11211 Cairo

Abdel Wahab, Mohamed
Faculty of Law, Cairo / Zulficar & Partners
Law Firm
Nile City Building,
South Tower, 8th Floor
2005 A Cornich El Nil
Ramlet Beaulac
11221 Cairo

El Kosheri, Ahmed Sadek
Advisory Board Member of ICCA
Kosheri, Rashed & Riad
16A Maamal El Sokkar
Garden City
11451 Cairo

Riad, Tarek
Kosheri, Rashed & Riad
16A Maamal El Sokkar
Garden City
11451 Cairo

El Salvador

Ponce, José
PROCEDE
Urbanizacion Cumbres de Cuscatlan
Calle Xochiquetzal No. 61 Poligono M
01502 Antiguo Cuscatlan

Finland

Wallgren-Lindholm, Carita
Lindholm Wallgren, Attorneys Ltd.
Aleksanterinkatu 48 A
00100 Helsinki

France

Beechey, John
ICC International Court of Arbitration
33-43, avenue du Président Wilson
75116 Paris

Bensaude, Denis
Bensuade
12, rue Déodat de Séverac
75017 Paris

Bevilacqua, Thomas
Foley Hoag LLP
153, rue du Faubourg Saint-Honoré
75008 Paris

Blumrosen, Alexander
Bernard-Hertz-Béjot
8, rue Murillo
92200 Paris

Bonnard, Sébastien
Brown Rudnick LLP
29, rue de Bassano
75008 Paris

Cabrol, Emmanuelle
Herbert Smith Freehills LLP
66, avenue Marceau
75008 Paris

Carducci, Guido
Carducci Arbitration
29, rue montagne esperou
75015 Paris

Carlevaris, Andrea
ICC International Court of Arbitration
33-43, avenue du Président Wilson
75116 Paris

Castellane, Beatrice
CCA Cabinet Castellane Avocats
14, rue des Sablons
75116 Paris

Craig, W. Laurence
Orrick, Herrington & Sutcliffe LLP
31, avenue Pierre Ier de Serbie
75782 Paris

Danis, Marie
AuguStreet& Debouzy
6-8, avenue de Messine
75008 Paris

de Boisséson, Matthieu
Linklaters LLP
25, rue de Marignan
75008 Paris

Degos, Louis
K&L Gates LLP

116, avenue des Champs-Elysées
75008 Paris

Derains, Yves
Advisory Board Member of ICCA
Derains & Gharavi
25, rue Balzac
75008 Paris

Dupeyron, Carine
August & Debouzy
6-8, avenue de Messine
75008 Paris

Duprey, Pierre
Linklaters LLP
25, rue de Marignan
75008 Paris

Flower, Andrew
Deloitte
185, avenue Charles de Gaulle
92200 Neuilly Sur Seine

Garde, Anne
International Arbitration Institute (IAI)
114, avenue des Champs Elysées
75008 Paris

Grierson, Jacob
McDermott, Will & Emery LLP
23, rue de l'Université
75007 Paris

Hascher, Dominique
Governing Board Member of ICCA
Supreme Judicial Court (France)
Paris

Hertzfeld, Jeffrey
5, boulevard Malesherbes
75008 Paris

Honlet, Jean-Christophe
Dentons
Salans FMC SNR Denton
5, boulevard Malesherbes
75008 Paris

Jaeger, Laurent
Orrick Rambaud Martel
31, avenue Pierre Ier de Serbie
75116 Paris

Joubin-Bret, Anna
Cabinet Joubin-Bret
4bis, rue du Colonel Moll
75017 Paris

Kessedjian, Catherine
Universite Pantheon-Assas
19, villa Seurat, Boite B
75014 Paris

Khayat, Dany
Mayer Brown International LLP
20, avenue Hoche
75008 Paris

Le Bars, Benoit
Lazareff Le Bars
22, rue du Général Foy
75008 Paris

Leboulanger, Philippe
Leboulanger & Associés
5, rue de Chaillot
75116 Paris

Lécuyer-Thieffry, Christine
Thieffry & Associés
29, rue de Lisbonne
75008 Paris

Legum, Barton
Dentons Europe
5, boulevard Malesherbes
75008 Paris

Leleu-Knobil, Nanou
International Arbitration Institute (IAI)
114, avenue des Champs Elysées
75008 Paris

Maffei, Antoine
de Pardieu, Brocas, Maffei
57, avenue d'Léna
75116 Paris

Mantilla-Serrano, Fernando
Shearman & Sterling LLP
114, avenue des Champs Elysées
75008 Paris

Marquardt, Alexander
Kramer Levin Naftalis & Frankel LLP

47, avenue Hoche
75008 Paris

Michou, Isabelle
Herbert Smith Freehills LLP
66, avenue Marceau
75008 Paris

Najar, Jean-Claude
Curtis, Mallet-Prevost, Colt & Mosle
6, avenue Velasquez
75008 Paris

Obadia, Eloise
Derains & Gharavi
25, rue Balzac
75008 Paris

Peterson, Patricia
Linklaters LLP
25, rue de Marignan
75008 Paris

Petrochilos, Georgios
Three Crowns LLP
7, rue de la Paix
75002 Paris

Rosell, José
Hughes Hubbard & Reed LLP
8, rue de Presbourg
75116 Paris

Savoie, Pierre-Olivier
Freshfields Bruckhaus Deringer LLP
2, rue Paul Cézanne
75008 Paris

Seraglini, Christophe
Betto Seraglini
43, avenue Hoche
75008 Paris

Stern, Brigitte
University of Paris 1 Panthéon Sorbonne
7, rue Pierre Nicole
Code B3804
75005 Paris

Thieffry, Patrick
Thieffry & Associés
29, rue de Lisbonne
75008 Paris

Thorp, Peter
12, rue du Caire
75002 Paris

van Hooft, Annet
Bird & Bird AARPI
Centre d'Affaires Edouard VII
3, Square Edouard VII
75009 Paris

van Leeuwen, Melanie
Derains & Gharavi
25, rue Balzac
75008 Paris

Wetmore, Todd
Shearman & Sterling LLP
114, avenue des Champs Elysées
75008 Paris

Yates, George
Orrick, Herrington & Sutcliffe LLP
31, avenue Pierre Ier de Serbie
75016 Paris

Ziade, Roland
Linklaters LLP
25, rue de Marignan
75008 Paris

Zivkovic, Lidia
ICC International Court of Arbitration
33-43, avenue du President Wilson
75116 Paris

Georgia

Gotsiridze, Mariam
Ministry of Justice of Georgia
24 Gorgasali Street
0133 Tbilisi

Injia, Beka
Georgian Chamber of Commerce and
Industry/Georgian International Arbitration
Center
15/27 A. Katalikosi Street
0114 Tbilisi

Tsertsvardze, David
Georgian Chamber of Commerce and
Industry

1055

30, Ts. Dadiani Street
0180 Tbilisi

Germany

Berger, Klaus Peter
German Institution of Arbitration (DIS)
Hölderlinstrasse 38
50968 Cologne

Bietz, Hermann
Bietz Law Office
Schillerstrasse 12
10625 Berlin

Böckstiegel, Karl-Heinz
Advisory Board Member of ICCA
Independent Arbitrator
Parkstrasse 38
51427 Bergisch Gladbach

Broedermann, Eckart
Broedermann Jahn RA GmbH
Neuer Wall 71
20354 Hamburg

Busse, Daniel
Allen & Overy LLP
Haus am OpernTurm
Bockenheimer Landstrasse 2
60306 Frankfurt

Elsing, Siegfried H.
Orrick Herrington and Sutcliffe
Heinrich-Heine-Allee 12
40213 Düsseldorf

Gantenberg, Ulrike
Heuking Kuhn Luer Wojtek
Georg-Glock-Strasse 4
40474 Düsseldorf

Hanfland, Philipp
Hengeler Mueller
Bockenheimer Landstrasse 24
60323 Frankfurt

Hirth, Rene-Alexander
Luther RA GmbH
Augustenstrasse 7
70178 Stuttgart

Kreindler, Richard
Cleary Gottlieb Steen & Hamilton LLP
Main Tower
Neue Mainzer Strasse 52
60311 Frankfurt

Maurer, Anton
CMS Hasche Sigle
Schoettlestrasse 8
70597 Stuttgart

Mazza, Francesca
German Institution of Arbitration (DIS)
Beethovenstrasse 5-13
50674 Cologne

Mosch, Ruth
German Institution of Arbitration (DIS)
An der Schanz 2, Apt. 3.3
50735 Cologne

Pickrahn, Guenter
Baker & McKenzie LLP
Bethmannstrasse 50-54
60311 Frankfurt

Pörnbacher, Karl
Hogan Lovells LLP
Karl-Scharnagl-Ring 5
80539 Munich

Sachs, Klaus
CMS Hasche Sigle
Nymphenburger Strasse 12
80335 Munich

Schäfer, Erik
Cohausz & Florack
Bleichstrasse 14
40411 Düsseldorf

Schill, Stephan
Max Planck Institute for Comparative Public
Law and International Law
Im Neuenheimer Feld 535
69120 Heidelberg

Sharma, Daniel Harish
DLA Piper UK LLP
Isartorplatz 1
80331 Munich

Trittmann, Rolf
Freshfields Bruckhaus Deringer LLP
Bockenheimer Anlage 44
60322 Frankfurt

Wiegand, Nicolas
CMS Hasche Sigle
Nymphenburger Strasse 12
80335 Munich

Ghana

Goka, Emmanuel
Selsen Consult
PO Box. C. T 5175, Cantoments
Accra

Greece

Tsavdaridis, Antonios
Rokas Law Firm
Voukourestiou 25A
106 71 Athens

Vassardani, Aphrodite
A. Vassardanis & Partners
340, Kiffissias Avenue
154 51 Psychiko, Athens

Guatemala

Mata, Estuardo
QIL Abogados, Guatemala
Diagonal 6, 10-01, Zona 10
Centro Gerencial Las Margaritas
Torre II, Nivel 14, Oficina 1402 A
Guatemala

Haiti

LaFortune, David
Haitian Chamber of Conciliation and
Arbitration
13 imp. oseille delmas 89
Delmas, NC

Hong Kong

Bao, Chiann
Hong Kong International Arbitration Centre
38/F, Two Exchange Square
8 Connaught Place
Hong Kong

Bateson, David
King & Wood Mallesons
13/F, Gloucester Tower
The Landmark
Hong Kong

Budge, John
Hong Kong International Arbitration Centre
6/F, Prince's Building
10 Chater Road
Hong Kong

Cheng, Teresa
Governing Board Member of ICCA
Des Voeux Chambers
38/F, Gloucester Tower
The Landmark, Central
Hong Kong

D'Agostino, Justin
Herbert Smith Freehills LLP
15 Queens Road Central
23/F, Gloucester Tower
Hong Kong

Denton, Gavin
Arbitration Chambers Hong Kong
Chinachem Hollywood Centre Suite 801
1 Hollywood Road
Midlevels
Hong Kong

Gearing, Matthew
Allen & Overy LLP
9/F, Three Exchange Square
Hong Kong

Hasofer, Menachem
Mayer Brown International LLP
18/F, Prince's Building
10 Chater Road
Hong Kong

1057

Kaplan, Neil
Governing Board Member of ICCA
9/F, Gloucester Tower
The Landmark
Hong Kong

Lane, Chris
HKIAC
38/F, Two Exchange Square
8 Connaught Place
Hong Kong

Lee, Tin Yan
Department of Justice
4/F, High Block Queensway
Government Offices
Admiralty

Pandjaitan, Jelita
Linklaters LLP
101F Alexandra House
Hong Kong

Poon, Ying Kwong Frank
Department of Justice
4/F, High Block Queensway
Government Offices
Admiralty

Sanghera, Kiran
Hong Kong International Arbitration Centre
38/F, Two Exchange Square
8 Connaught Place
Hong Kong

Tan, Karen
Hong Kong International Arbitration Centre
38/F, Two Exchange Square
8 Connaught Place
Hong Kong

Tan, May Ling
Hong Kong International Arbitration Centre
38/F, Two Exchange Square
8 Connaught Place
Hong Kong

Wong, Hing Hong Peter
Department of Justice
4/F, High Block Queensway
Government Offices
Admiralty

Yeoh, Friven
O'Melveny & Myers
31/F, AIA Central
1 Connaught Road
Central

Zadkovich, John
Vinson & Elkins
10/F, Gloucester Tower
The Landmark, 15 Queen's Road
Central

Hungary

Kecskés, László
Arbitration Court attached to the Hungarian
Chamber of Commerce and Industry
Szabadság tér 7
Budapest, H-1054

India

Agarwal, Sanjay
The Institute of Chartered Accountants
of India
ICAI Bhawan
Indraprastha Marg
New Delhi, 110002

Barot, Rajendra
AZB & Partners
Express Towers
23/F, Nariman Point
Mumbai, 400021

Baya, Madhur
LexArbitri
Suite No. FF50, Regus Business Centre
Ismail Building
Flora Fountain, D. N. Road
Mumbai, 400001

Dave, Dushyant
Governing Board Member of ICCA
Supreme Court of India
43 Prithviraj Road
New Delhi, 110011

Garg, Shashank
Suri and Company, Law Firm
Flat 10 & 12, Golf Apartments

Sujan Singh Park
New Delhi, 110003

Kapoor, Sanjeev
Khaitan & CO LLP
Ashoka Estate Barakhama Road
New Delhi, 110001

Karia, Tejas
Amarchand & Mangaldas & Suresh A. Shroff
& Co.
Amarchand Towers
216, Okhla Industrial Estate Phase-III
New Delhi, 110020

Khambata, Darius
501 White House
off Navroji Gamadia Road
Mumbai, 400026

Mathur, Dinesh
Dua Associates
B-115 Neeti Bagh
New Delhi, 110049

Mukherjee, Sitesh
Trilegal
A-38,
Kailash Colony
New Delhi, 110048

Naik, Rajiv
Trilegal
One Indiabulls Centre
14/F, Tower One, Elphinstone Road,
New Delhi, 400013

Rautray, Dharmendra
Kachwaha & Partners
1/6 Shanti Niketan
Delhi, 110021

Sachdeva, Neeti
Economic Laws Practice
109 Dalamal Tower
Free Press Journal Marg Nariman Point
Mumbai, 400021

Suri, Suruchi
Suri and Company, Law Firm
Flat 10 & 12, Golf Apartments
Sujan Singh Park
New Delhi, 110003

Vajani, Kunal
Wadia Ghandy & Co.
N. M. Wadia Buildings, 1st Floor
123, M. G. Road, Fort
Mumbai, 400001

Ireland

Collins, Michael M.
Bar of Ireland
4 Arran Square
Arran Quay
Dublin, 7

Ó hOisín, Colm
Bar of Ireland
Law Library Building
158/159 Church Street
Dublin, 7

Italy

Azzali, Stefano
Chamber of Arbitration of Milan - Italy
Via Meravigli 9/b
Milan, 20123

Cicogna, Michelangelo
De Berti Jacchia Law Firm
Via San Paolo 7
Milan, 20121

Crivellaro, Antonio
Bonelli Erede Pappalardo
via Michele Barozzi 1
Milan, 20122

Paradell Trius, Luis
Freshfields Bruckhaus Deringer LLP
Piazza del Popolo 18
Rome, 00187

Radicati di Brozolo, Luca G.
Arblit - Radicati di Brozolo Sabatini
Via Alberto Da Giussano n. 15
Milan, 20145

Japan

Goto, Shigehiko
1-6-7-708
Atago
Tokyo, 105-0002

Lingard, Nicholas
Freshfields Bruckhaus Deringer LLP
Akasaka Biz Tower 36F
5-3-1 Akasaka, Minato-ku
Tokyo, 107-6336

Naito, Junya
Momo-o, Matsuo & Namba
Kojimachi Diamond Building
4-1, Kojimachi
Chiyoda, 102-0083

Oghigian, Haig
Baker & McKenzie LLP
Ark Hills Sengokuyama Mori Twr. 28F
1-9-10 Roppongi
Minato-ku, Tokyo, 106-0032

Takatori, Yoshihiro
Orrick, Herrington & Sutcliffe LLP
Izumi Garden Tower, 28th Floor
6-1 Roppongi 1-Chome
Minato-ku, Tokyo, 106-6028

Tezuka, Hiroyuki
Nishimura & Asahi
ARK Mori Bldg 1-12-32
Akasaka Minato-ku
Tokyo, 107-6029

Yokokawa, Hiroshi
The Japan Commercial Arbitration
Association
3-17, Kanda Nishiki-cho,
Chiyoda-ku,
Tokyo, 1010054

Kazakhstan

Toktarov, Bolat
LLP Olympex Advisers
8/2 Turkestan Street
Astana

Yereshev, Diyar
LLP Olympex Advisers
8/2 Turkestan Street
Astana

Kenya

Karanja, Elizabeth
JMiles & Co.
ALN House, Eldama Ravine Gardens
Off Eldama Ravine Road, Westlands
Nairobi, 200-00606

Miles, John
JMiles & Co.
ALN House, Eldama Ravine Gardens
Off Eldama Ravine Road, Westlands
Nairobi, 200-00606

Korea, Republic of

Bang, John P.
Bae, Kim & Lee LLC
133 Teheran-ro, Gangnam-gu
Seoul, 135-723

Christensen, Matthew
Bae, Kim & Lee LLC
133 Teheran-ro, Gangnam-gu,
Seoul, 135-723

Chung, Liz Kyo-hwa
Kim & Chang
39, Sajik-ro 8-gil
Jongno-gu
Seoul, 110-720

Kim, Beomsu
Shin & Kim
8th Floor, State Tower Namsan
100-Toegye-ro, Jung-gu
Seoul, 100-052

Kim, Kap-You (Kevin)
Governing Board Member of ICCA
Bae, Kim & Lee LLC
133 Teheran-ro, Gangnam-gu
Seoul, 135-723

Kim, Min-Kyoo
Korean Commercial Arbitration Board
Trade Tower No. 4301
Samseong-dong, Gangnam-gu
Seoul, 135-729

Kwon, Daisoo
Korean Commercial Arbitration Board
Trade Tower No. 4301
Samseong-dong, Gangnam-gu
Seoul, 135-729

Lee, Young Seok
Yulchon LLC
Textile Center 12F, 518 Teheran-ro,
Daechi-dong, Gangnam-gu,
Seoul, 135-713

Schwing, Mel
Yulchon LLC
No. 2002, Michelan 107 Bldg.
602, Yeongdong-daero, Gangnam-gu
Seoul, 135-873

Shin, Hi-Taek
Seoul National University School of Law
599 Gwanak-ro
Gwanak-ku
Seoul, 151-743

Yang, David H.
Yulchon LLC
Textile Center 12F, 518 Teheran-ro,
Daechi-dong, Gangnam-gu,
Seoul, 135-713

Yeum, June Junghye
Lee & Ko
Hanjin Building
63 Namdaemun-ro, Jung-gu
Seoul, 100-770

Yi, Kellie
Hyundai Heavy Industries, Co., LTD
1000, Bangeojinsunhwan-doro
Dong-gu
Ulsan, 682-792

Malaysia

Abraham, Cecil
Governing Board Member of ICCA

Zul Rafique & Partners
D3-3-8 Solaris Dutamas
No. 1 Jalan Dutamas 1
Kuala Lumpur, 50480

Abraham, Sunil
Zul Rafique & Partners
D3-3-8 Solaris Dutamas,
No. 1 Jalan Dutamas 1
Kuala Lumpur, 50480

Nadarajah, Sundra Rajoo
Kuala Lumpur Regional Centre
for Arbitration
Bangunan Sulaiman
Jalan Damansara
Kuala Lumpur, 50676

Noble, Roderick
Thirty Nine Essex Street Chambers
A-19-2 Hampshire Park,
6 -8 Persiaran Hampshire
Kuala Lumpur, 50450

Quah, Ean Lin, Ann
Kuala Lumpur Regional Centre
for Arbitration
Bangunan Sulaiman
Jalan Damansara
Kuala Lumpur, 50676

Malta

Delia, Adrian
Aequitas Legal
Valletta Buildings, South Street
Valletta, VLT 1103

Hyzler, George M.
Malta Arbitration Centre
33, Palazzo Laparelli
South Street
Valletta, VLT 1100

Paris, Matthew
Aequitas Legal
Valletta Buildings, South Street
Valletta, VLT 1103

Mauritius

Bagshaw, Duncan
LCIA-MIAC Arbitration Centre
Level 3, Unit B3
Cybertower 1
Ebene, 72201

Jeetah, Nirmala
Board of Investment Mauritius
10th Floor, One Cathedral Square
16 Jules Koenig Street
Port Louis, 11328

Lefebure, Fabien
Solis Indian Ocean
Old Pailles Road
Pailles
Port Louis

Valere, Marie Joelle Sandrine
Prime Minister's Office,
Republic of Mauritius
c/o Prime Minister's Office
7th Level, New Government House
Port Louis, 11319

Mexico

Brown de Vejar, Kate
Curtis, Mallet-Prevost, Colt & Mosle S.C.
Ruben Dario 281, Piso 9
Bosque de Chapultepec, 11580

Fonseca, Salvador
Baker & McKenzie LLP
Boulevard Manuel Avila Camacho No. 1
Piso 12
Álvaro Obregó, DF 11009

González de Cossío, Francisco
González de Cossío Abogados, S.C.
Bosques de Acacias 61B
Bosques de las Lomas
Mexico, 11700

Llano Oddone, Rafael
White & Case LLP
Boulevard Manuel Avila Camacho 24 - PH
Lomas de Chapultepec
Mexico, 11000

Navarro Velasco, Javier L.
Baker & McKenzie LLP
1884 PTE P. 10
Santa Maria
Monterrey, 64650

Rodríguez, José Antonio
Bufete Rodriguez Marquez SC
Socrates 128-602
Mexico, 11560

Wöss, Herfried
Wöss & Partners, S.C./PLLC
Torre Esmeralda I, Boulevard Manuel Ávila
Camacho 40-1606
Col. Lomas de Chapultepec
Mexico, 11000

Morocco

Skalli, Allia
Allen & Overy LLP
Anfaplace, Centre d'Affaires
Immeuble A Boulevard de la Corniche
Casablanca, 20000

Netherlands

Ameli, Koorosh
Ameli Arbitration
New Babylon
Anna van Buerenplein 41
The Hague, 2595 DA

Barkett, Rosemary
Iran-US Claims Tribunal
Parkweg 13
The Hague, 2585 JH

Bartolone, David
Wolters Kluwer Law & Business
Zuidpoolsingel 2
Alphen aan den Rijn, 2408 ZE

Bier, Lyda
Dr. L. Bier B.V.
Baroniesingel 32
Vught, 5262 KB

Bingham, Lisa
ICCA-PCA
Peace Palace
Carnegieplein 2
The Hague, 2517 KJ

Borelli, Silvia
ICCA Publications
Peace Palace
Carnegieplein 2
The Hague, 2517 KJ

Bosman, Lise
Executive Director of ICCA
ICCA-PCA
Peace Palace
Carnegieplein 2
The Hague, 2517 KJ

Brower, Charles N.
Iran- Claims Tribunal
Parkweg 13
The Hague, 2585 JH

Daly, Brooks
Permanent Court of Arbitration
Peace Palace
Carnegieplein 2
The Hague, 2517 KJ

De Ly, Filip
Erasmus University Rotterdam
Johan Buziaulaan 33
Utrecht, 3584 ZT

Doe, Martin
Permanent Court of Arbitration
Peace Palace
Carnegieplein 2
The Hague, 2517 KJ

Grimmer, Sarah
Permanent Court of Arbitration
Peace Palace
Carnegieplein 2
The Hague, 2517 KJ

Johnson, O. Thomas
Iran-US Claims Tribunal
Parkweg 13
The Hague, 2585 JH

Kemshaw, Amanda
De Brauw Blackstone Westbroek N.V.
Claude Debussylaan 80
Amsterdam, 1082 MD

Kjos, Hege Elisabeth
University of Amsterdam
Faculty of Law
PO Box 1030
Amsterdam, 1000 BA

Kuscher, Matthias
De Brauw Blackstone Westbroek N.V.
Claude Debussylaan 80
Amsterdam, 1082 MD

Lee, Hyun Jung
Permanent Court of Arbitration
Peace Palace
Carnegieplein 2
The Hague, 2517 KJ

Levine, Judith
Permanent Court of Arbitration
Peace Palace
Carnegieplein 2
The Hague, 2517 KJ

Meerdink, Eelco
De Brauw Blackstone Westbroek N.V.
Claude Debussylaan 80
Amsterdam, 1082 MD

Pincombe, Michelle
ICCA-PCA
Peace Palace
Carnegieplein 2
The Hague, 2517KJ

Pulkowski, Dirk
Permanent Court of Arbitration
Peace Palace
Carnegieplein 2
The Hague, 2517 KJ

Rivers, Joyce
Kluwer Law International
Zuidpoolsingel 2
Alphen aan den Rijn, 2408 ZE

Schofield, Garth
Permanent Court of Arbitration
Peace Palace

Carnegieplein 2
The Hague, 2517 KJ

Siegel, Alice
ICCA-PCA
Peace Palace
Carnegieplein 2
The Hague, 2517 KJ

Smith, Fedelma Claire
Permanent Court of Arbitration
Peace Palace
Carnegieplein 2
The Hague, 2517 KJ

van Baren, Willem
Allen & Overy LLP
Apollolaan 15
Amsterdam, 1077 AB

van Haersolte-van Hof, Jackie
HaersolteHof B.V.
Delistraat 27
The Hague, 2585 VX

van Hooijdonk, Marieke
Allen & Overy LLP
Apollolaan 15
Amsterdam, 1077 AB

Verschoor, Vincent
Kluwer Law International
Zuidpoolsingel 2
Alphen aan den Rijn, 2408 ZE

Vloemans, Natalie
Ploum Lodder Princen
Blaak 28
Rotterdam, 3011 TA

de Vries, Gwen
Kluwer Law International
Zuidpoolsingel 2
Alphen aan den Rijn, 2408 ZE

New Zealand

Butler, Petra
Victoria University of Wellington
Victoria University Law Faculty
55 Lambton Quay
Wellington, 6011

Hart, Deborah
Arbitrators' and Mediators' Institute of
New Zealand
PO Box 1477
Wellington, 6021

Johnston, Derek
Thorndon Chambers
PO Box 1530
Wellington, 6140

Walton, John
Bankside Chambers
88 Shortland Street
Auckland, 1010

Williams, David
Governing Board Member of ICCA
David A R Williams QC
PO Box 405
Shortland Street
Auckland, 1140

Nigeria

Adekoya, Olufunke
Aelex Legal Practitioners & Arbitrators
PO Box 52901
Ikoyi
Lagos

Ogundipe, Babajide
Sofunde, Osakwe, Ogundipe & Belgore
7th Floor, St. Nicholas House
Catholic Mission Street
Lagos

Oyekunle, Tinuade
Honorary Vice President of ICCA
Sonotina Chambers
17 Olujobi Street
Gbagada Phase 1
Lagos

Tayo-Oyetibo, Mofesomo
Tayo Oyetibo & Co
Plot A15, A2 Street
NIcon Town
Lekki

Ufot, Dorothy
Dorothy Ufot & Co

2nd Floor, Okoi Arikpo House
5, Idowe Taylor Street
Victoria Island, Lagos

Pakistan

Ali Khan, Makhdoom
Governing Board Member of ICCA
Fazleghani
F-72/1, Block 8, KDA 5,
Clifton
Karachi, 75600

Panama

Correa, Agenor
Panama Canal Authority
ACP Administration Building
Altos de Balboa
Balboa

González Arrocha, Katherine
ICC International Court of Arbitration
Torres de las Américas, Torre A, 15th Floor
Panama, 0832-0588

Peru

Amado, Jose Daniel
Miranda & Amado Abogados
Avenida Jose A. Larco 1301, Piso 20
Miraflores
Lima

Cuba Copello, Yvo
Estudio Echecopar, A Member Firm of Baker
& McKenzie International
Avenida De la Floresta 497
San Borja
Lima

Rubio, Roger
Lima Chamber of Commerce - International
Arbitration Centre
Avenida Giuseppe Garibaldi 396
Lima

Soto, Carlos A.
Instituto Peruano de Arbitraje
Avenida San Felipe No. 540

Dpto. 1503 – Jesús María
Lima

Philippines

Calimon, Donemark Joseph
Quisumbing Torres (Baker & McKenzie)
12/F Net One Center, 26th Street crn. 3rd
Avenue
Crescent Park West, Bonifacio Global City
Taguig City, 1634

Khan, Rebecca
Office of the Solicitor General of the
Republic of the Philippines
201 Asian Mansion 1, 109 Dela Rosa Street
Makati Central Business District
Makati City, 1221

Ongkiko, Ricardo
SyCip Salazar Hernandez & Gatmaitan
SyCip Law Center
105 Paseo de Roxas
Makati City, 1226

Salvador III, Tranquil
Romulo, Mabanta, Buenaventura, Sayoc and
de los Angeles
21/F, Philamlife Tower
Paseo de Roxas
Makati City, 1100

Teehankee, Manuel A.J.
Center for the Rule of Law
Ateneo Law School
4/F Floor Integritas Room
Makati City, 1200

Tumangan, Daniel Kendrick
Romulo Mabanta Buenaventura Sayoc & de
los Angeles
Romulo Mabanta Buenaventura Sayoc & de
los Angeles
21/F, Philamlife Tower, 8767 Paseo de
Roxas
Makati City, 1226

Portugal

Barrocas, Manuel
Barrocas Advogados

1065

Amoreiras Torre 2, 15th Floor
Lisbon, 1070-274

Gouveia, Mariana
SRS Legal
Rua Francisco Manuel de Melo, 21
Lisbon, 1070-085

Júdice, José-Miguel
PLMJ
Avenida da Liberdade 224
Lisbon, 1250-148

Lousa, Nuno
Linklaters LLP
Avenida Fontes Pereira de Melo,
14-15th Floor
Lisbon, 1050-121

Martins, Sofia
Miranda Correia Amendoeira & Associados
Rua Soeiro Pereira Gomes, 1st Floor
Lisbon, 1600-196

Pinto Cardoso, Miguel
Vieira de Almeida & Associados
Avenida Duarte Pacheco, 26th Floor
Lisbon, 1070-110

Vaz Pinto, Filipe
MLGTS
Rua Castilho No. 165 - 8.°
Lisbon, 1070-050

Romania

Dragos-Alexandru, Sitaru
Faculty of Law
University of Bucharest, Romania
Bulevardul Ion Ionescu de la Brad, No. 5,
Etaj 3
Ap. 9, Sector 1, Sector 1
Bucharest, 013813

Russian Federation

Bednova, Ekaterina
Expocentre
14 Krasnopresnenskaya nab.
Moscow, 123100

Komarov, Alexander
Governing Board Member of ICCA
International Commercial Arbitration Court
Pudovkin Street 4a
Moscow, 119285

Muranov, Alexander
Muranov, Chernyakov & Partners
23 Denisovsky Lane
Building 6
Moscow, 105005

Pakerman, Galina
CDR Litigation Boutique, LLC
Moscow Region, Khimki, Podrezkovo
Microdistrict
Jarinova Street, 10-37
Khimki, 141446

Rwanda

Gakuba Thierry, Ngoga
Kigali International Arbitration Centre
(KIAC)
PO Box 695
Kigali

Uwicyeza, Bernadette
Kigali International Arbitration Centre
(KIAC)
PO Box 695
Kigali

Singapore

Ang, Roy
Singapore International Arbitration Centre
32 Maxwell Road
#02-01
Singapore, 069115

Ban, Jiun Ean
Maxwell Chambers
32 Maxwell Road
#03-01
Singapore, 069115

Bull, Cavinder
Drew & Napier LLC
10 Collyer Quay

#10-01 Ocean Financial Centre
Singapore, 049315

Chan, Calvin
Skadden Arps Slate Meagher & Flom LLP
6 Battery Road
Suite 23-02
Singapore, 049909

Dulac, Elodie
King & Spalding LLP
9 Raffles Place, Level 31
Republic Plaza
Singapore, 048619

Dunbar, Simon
King & Spalding LLP
9 Raffles Place, Level 31
Republic Plaza
Singapore, 048619

Holmes, Emerson
Nabarro LLP
12 Marina Boulevard #35-01
Marina Bay Financial Centre Tower 3
Singapore, 018982

Hwang, Michael
Honorary Vice President of ICCA
Michael Hwang Chambers
8 Marina Boulevard #06-02
Marina Bay Financial Centre Tower 1
Singapore, 018981

Janssen, Joan
Ministry of Law
100 High Street, #08-02
The Treasury,
Singapore, 179434

Jhangiani, Sapna
Clyde & Co Clasis Singapore Pte. Ltd.
12 Marina Boulevard
Marina Bay Financial Centre Towers, #30-03
Singapore, 018982

Khoo, Shem
Focus Law Corporation
105 Cecil Street #07-01
The Octagon
Singapore, 257720

Lau, Christopher
Maxwell Chambers
32 Maxwell Road Hex 02-04
Singapore, 069115

Lees, Amanda
Simmons & Simmons Asia LLP
#38-04 Marina Bay Financial Centre
Tower 3
12 Marina Boulevard
Singapore, 018982

Lim, Seok Hui
Singapore International Arbitration Centre
32 Maxwell Road
#02-01
Singapore, 069115

Lim, Shiqi
Ministry of Law
100 High Street, #08-02
The Treasury
Singapore, 179434

Menon, Sundaresh
Governing Board Member of ICCA
Supreme Court Singapore
1 Supreme Court Lane
Singapore, 178879

Pryles, Michael
Governing Board Member of ICCA
Singapore International Arbitration Centre
32 Maxwell Road
#02-01
Singapore, 069115

Reed, Lucy
Governing Board Member of ICCA
Freshfields Bruckhaus Deringer LLP
10 Collyer Quay 42-01
Ocean Financial Centre
Singapore 049315

Teh, Lawrence
Rodyk & Davidson LLP
80 Raffles Place
#33-00 UOB Plaza 1
Singapore, 048624

Yeo, Justin
Supreme Court Singapore

1 Supreme Court Lane
Singapore, 178879

Zhao, Huili
Singapore International Arbitration Centre
32 Maxwell Road
#02-01
Singapore, 069115

Slovakia

Magal, Martin
Allen & Overy LLP
Pribinova 4
Eurovea Central 1
Bratislava, 81109

South Africa

McKenzie, Sarah
Webber Wentzel
PO Box 61771
Marshalltown
Johannesburg, 2107

Movshovich, Vladislav
Webber Wentzel
PO Box 61771
Marshalltown
Johannesburg, 2107

Wild, Duncan
Webber Wentzel
PO Box 61771
Marshalltown
Johannesburg, 2107

Spain

Allan, Virginia
Uria Menendez Abogados SLP
C Principe de Vergara, 187
Plaza Rodrigo Uria
Madrid, 28002

Alonso, José María
Baker & McKenzie LLP
Paseo de la Castellana, 92
Madrid, 28046

Conthe, Manuel
Bird & Bird LLP
Jorge Juan, 8
Madrid, 28001

Cremades, Bernardo
Governing Board Member of ICCA
B. Cremades y Asociados
Calle de Goya, 18
2nd Floor
Madrid, 28001

de Los Santos, Carlos
J&A Garrigues, S.L.P.
Hermosilla, 3
Madrid, 28001

de Luis y Lorenzo, José Félix
Legal 21 Abogados
Bolivia 5, 8-E
Madrid, 28016

Fernández-Ballesteros, Miguel Ángel
Miguel Ángel Fernández-Ballesteros
& Associates
Serrano, 22
Madrid, 28001

Gómez-Acebo, Alfonso
Baker & McKenzie LLP
Paseo de la Castellana, 92
Madrid, 28046

Guerrero Righetto, Alfredo
King & Wood Mallesons
Claudio Coello, 37
Madrid, 28001

López Ortiz, Alejandro
Hogan Lovells LLP
Paseo de la Castellana, 51
Madrid, 28046

Málaga, Francisco
Linklaters S.L.P
Almagro, 40
Madrid, 28010

Montero, Félix
Pérez-Llorca
Paseo de la Castellana, 50
Madrid, 28034

Rodríguez-Sastre, Iñigo
Olleros Abogados
Plaza Lealtad, 3-4
Madrid, 28014

Sweden

Altamirano Jimenez, Frida Paola
Stockholm University
Karins Alle 3-1107
Stockholm, 181 45

Bagner, Hans
MAQS
Norrmalmstorg 1
Stockholm, 103 86

Campbell-Wilson, Kristin
Stockholm Chamber of Commerce
PO Box 16050
Stockholm, 103 21

Eklund, Jonas
Advokatfirman Vinge KB
PO Box 1703
Smålandsgatan 20
Stockholm, 111 87

Franke, Ulf
Honorary Secretary General of ICCA
Stockholm Arbitrator
Norr Malarstrand 68 LGH 1502
Stockholm, 112 35

Herdenberg, Ida
Advokatfirman Urban Olson AB
Engelbrekitsgatan 9-11
Stockholm, 11432

Isaksson, Therese
Advokatfirman Lindahl KB
PO Box 1065
Stockholm, 101 39

Lettius, Carin
Advokatfirman Glimstedt
PO Box 1027
Helsingborg, 25110

Lettius, Michael
Advokatfirman Glimstedt

PO Box 1027
Helsingborg, 25110

Lundblom, Fredrik
Advokatfirman Vinge KB
PO Box 1703
Smålandsgatan 20
Stockholm, 111 87

Magnusson, Annette
Arbitration Institute of the
Stockholm Chamber of Commerce
PO Box 16050
Stockholm, 103 21

Mörnholm, Terje
Advokatfirman Urban Olson AB
Engelbrekitsgatan 9-11
Stockholm, 114 32

Nilsson, Bo
Lindahl
PO Box 1065
Stockholm, 101 39

Sidklev, Johan
Roschier
Roschier Advokatbyrå AB
Blasieholmsgatan 4 A
Stockholm, 103 90

Soderlund, Christer
Advokatfirman Vinge KB
PO Box 1703
Smålandsgatan 20
Box 1703
Stockholm, 111 87

Tiberg, Jesper
Advokatfirman Lindahl KB
PO Box 1065
Stockholm, 101 39

Widjeskg, Niclas
Linklaters LLP
Regeringsgatan 67
Stockholm, 103 98

Wiwen-Nilsson, Tore
Advokat Tore Wiwen-Nilsson AB
Pålsjövägen 24
Lund, 22363

Switzerland

Baertsch, Philippe
Schellenberg Wittmer Ltd
15Bis, rue des Alpes
Geneva 1, 1211

Baizeau, Domitille
LALIVE
35, rue de la Mairie
Geneva 6, 1207

Bangert, Jan
Boeckli Bodmer & Partners
St. Jakobs-Strasse 41
Basel, 4052

Blessing, Marc
Bär & Karrer
Brandschenkestrasse 90
Zurich, 8027

Boisson de Chazournes, Laurence
University of Geneva
40, Boulevard du Pont d'Arve
Geneva, 1211

Dasser, Felix
Homburger AG
Prime Tower
Hardstrasse 201, PO Box 314
Zurich, 8037

Ehle, Bernd
LALIVE
35, rue de la Mairie
Geneva 6, 1207

Favre-Bulle, Xavier
Lenz & Staehelin
Route de Chêne 30
Geneva 17, 1211

Geisinger, Elliott
Schellenberg Wittmer Ltd
15Bis, rue des Alpes
Geneva 1, 1211

Heiskanen, Veijo
LALIVE
35, rue de la Mairie
Geneva 6, 1207

Hirsch, Laurent
Hirsch Kobel
8, rue Eynard
Geneva, 1205

Jermini, Cesare
Bär & Karrer SA
Via Vegezzi 6
Lugano, 6901

Kaufmann-Kohler, Gabrielle
Governing Board Member of ICCA
Levy Kaufmann-Kohler
3-5, rue du Conseil-General
PO Box 552
Geneva 4, 1211

Lehmann, Tobias
University of St. Gallen
Guisanstrasse 36
St. Gallen, 9000

Marzolini, Paolo
Patocchi & Marzolini
5, rue Pedro-Meylan
Geneva, 1208

Mazuranic, Alexandre
Schellenberg Wittmer Ltd
15Bis, rue des Alpes
Geneva 1, 1211

McLin, Alexander
Swiss Arbitration Association
Boulevard du Theatre 4
Geneva, 1211

McQuillen, Monika
Eversheds AG
Stadelhoferstrasse 22
Zurich, 8001

Meyer, Bernhard F.
MME Partners
Kreuzstrasse 42
Zurich, 8008

Peter, Wolfgang
Python & Peter
9, rue Firmin-Massot
Geneva, 1206

Radjai, Noradèle
LALIVE
35, rue de la Mairie
Geneva 6, 1207

Schlaepfer, Anne Véronique
Schellenberg Wittmer Ltd
15Bis, rue des Alpes
Geneva 1, 1211

Schneider, Michael E.
LALIVE
35, rue de la Mairie
Geneva 6, 1208

Stutzer, Hansjoerg
Thouvenin Rechtsanwälte & Partner
Klausstrasse 33
Zurich, 8034

Tercier, Pierre
Governing Board Member of ICCA
Chemin Guillaume-Ritter 5
Fribourg, 1700

Triebold, Claudius
Eversheds Ltd.
Stadelhoferstrasse 22
Zurich, 8001

van Aaken, Anne
University of St. Gallen
Guisanstrasse 36
St. Gallen, 9010

Veit, Marc
LALIVE
Stampfenbachplatz 4
PO Box 212
Zurich, 8042

Vock, Dominik
MME Partners
Kreuzstrasse 42
Zurich, 8044

von Segesser, Georg
Schellenberg Wittmer LTD
Löwenstrasse 19
PO Box 1876
Zurich, 8021

Voser, Nathalie
Schellenberg Wittmer LTD
Löwenstrasse 19
PO Box 1876
Zurich, 8021

Wiebecke, Martin
Anwaltsbüro Wiebecke
Kohlrainstrasse 10
Küsnacht, 8700

Wiegand, Wolfgang
University of Berne
Choisystrasse 7
Berne, 3008

Wolfe Martin, Suzanne
Suzanne Wolfe Martin Law Offices
15, rue de Cendrier
Geneva, 1201

Yasseen, Rabab
Mentha
4, rue de l'Athénée
Geneva, 1205

Zenhäusern, Urs
Baker & McKenzie LLP
Holbeinstrasse 30
Zurich, 8008

Tanzania, United Republic of

Mbwambo, Rosan
Law Associates Advocates
CRDB Building, 6th Floor, Azikiwe Street
PO Box 11133
Dar Es Salaam,

Turkey

Coşar, Utku
Coşar Avukatlik Burosu
Inonu Cad. No. 18/2
Taksim
Istanbul, 34437

Uganda

Rukidi-Mpuuga, Elijah Paul
Rukidi-Mpuuga
PO Box 137
Fort Portal, 52306

Ukraine

Kliuchkovskyi, Markiyan
Egorov Puginsky Afanasiev & Partners LLC
38 Volodymyrska Street
Kiev, 01030

United Arab Emirates

Al Mulla, Habib
Baker & McKenzie LLP
O14 Tower
Business Bay
Dubai, 2268

Al Tamimi, Essam
Al Tamimi & Company
DIFC, Building 4 East
Level 6
Dubai, 9275

BouMalhab, Nassif
Clyde & Co LLP
PO Box 7001
Rolex Tower, Sheikh Zayed Road
Dubai

Chadwick, Adrian
Hadef & Partners
PO Box 37172
Emaar Square Building 3
Dubai, 37172

Chaykhouni, Jamal
AlMarsat Projects Developments
503 Warsan Building, Tecom
Dubai, 357620

Nassar, Rana
Dubai International Arbitration Centre
(DIAC)
PO Box 1457
Deira
Dubai, 1457

Saoud, Ritta
Dubai International Arbitration Centre
(DIAC)
PO Box 1457
Deira
Dubai, 1457

United Kingdom

England and Wales

Aboim, Luiz
Freshfields Bruckhaus Deringer LLP
65 Fleet Street
London, EC4Y 1HS

Abrahams, Anthony
Chartered Institute of Arbitrators
12 Bloomsbury Square
London, WC1N 2LP

Abu-Manneh, Raid
Mayer Brown International LLP
201 Bishopsgate
London, EC2M 3AF

Ashford, Peter
Fox Williams LLP
Ten Dominion Street
London, EC2M 2EE

Azpiroz, Maddi
ClaimTrading
39-40 St. James's Place
London, SW1A 1NS

Baloch, Tariq
3 Verulam Buildings
Gray's Inn
London, WC1R 5NT

Barnes, David
Thirty Nine Essex Street Chambers
39 Essex Street
London, WC2R 3AT

Baruti, Rukia
AILA
1 Bream Close
London, N17 9DF

Beeley, Mark
Vinson & Elkins LLP
CityPoint, 33rd Floor
One Ropemaker Street
London, EC2Y 9UE London, EC2Y 9UE

Bellamy, Jonathan
Thirty Nine Essex Street Chambers
39 Essex Street
London, WC2R 3AT

Black, Michael
XXIV Old Buildings Barristers' Chambers
24 Old Buildings
Lincoln's Inn
London, WC2A 3UP

Borrelli, Matteo
Berkeley Research Group
15th Floor
6 New Street Square
London, EC4A 3BF

Bradfield, Michelle
Dentons UKMEA LLP
One Fleet Place
London, EC4M 7WS

Brekoulakis, Stavros
Queen Mary, University of London
67-69 Lincoln's Inn Fields
London, WC2A 3JB

Brennan, Daniel
Matrix Chambers
6 Caroline Terrace
London, SW1W W8JS

Bruton, Leilah
Freshfields Bruckhaus Deringer LLP
65 Fleet Street
London, EC4Y 1HS

Burn, George
Vinson & Elkins LLP
CityPoint, 33rd Floor
One Ropemaker Street
London, EC2Y 9UE

Burrington, Katie
Thomson Reuters Legal UK & Ireland
100 Avenue Road
London, NW3 3PF

Cameron, Peter
Centre for Energy, Petroleum & Mineral Law
& Policy
CEPMLP, University of Dundee
1-3 Perth Road
Dundee, DD1 4HN

Capper, Phillip
White & Case LLP
5 Old Broad Street
London, EC2N 1DW

Caron, David D.
King's College London
Dickson Poon School of Law, King's College
Somerset House EW 2.20, The Strand
London, WC2R 2LS

Carroll, Ben
Linklaters LLP
One Silk Street
London, EC2Y 8HQ

Clarke, Andrew
Governing Board Member of ICCA
ExxonMobil International Limited
ExxonMobil House
Ermyn Way
Leatherhead, KT22 8UX

Clegg, Richard
Selborne Chambers
10 Essex Street
London, WC1X 0AH

Collins, Alys
TransPerfect Legal Solutions
5th Floor, 45 Moorfields
London, EC2Y 9AE

Daele, Karel
Mishcon de Reya
Red Lion Square 12
London, WC1R 4QD

Davies, Kate
Allen & Overy LLP
One Bishops Square
London, E1 6AD

Dhar, Siddharth
Essex Court Chambers

24 Lincoln's Inn Fields
London, WC2A 3EG

Drake, James
7 King's Bench Walk
Temple
London, EC4Y 7DS

Dunn, Susan
Harbour Litigation Funding
1 Conduit Street
1st Floor, Kendal House
London, W1S 2XA

Falach, Alon
Global Legal Group
59 Tanner Street
London, SE1 3PL

Ferrigno, Joe
Essex Court Chambers
24 Lincoln's Inn Fields
London, WC2A 3EG

Finizio, Steven
Wilmer Cutler Pickering Hale and Dorr LLP
49 Park Lane
London, W1K 1PS

Foden, Timothy
Quinn Emanuel Urquhart & Sullivan
One Fleet Place
London, EC4M 7RA

Fraser, John
Shook Hardy & Bacon LLP
25 Cannon Street
London, EC4M 5SE

Freeman, James
Allen & Overy LLP
One Bishops Square
London, E1 6AD

Gill, Judith
Allen & Overy LLP
One Bishops Square
London, E1 6AD

Goldberg, David
White & Case LLP
5 Old Broad Street
London, EC2N 1DW

Goldsmith, Peter
Debevoise & Plimpton LLP
65 Gresham Street
London, EC2V 7NQ

González García, Luis
Matrix Chambers
Griffin Building
Gray's Inn
London, WC1R 5LN

Graham, Helena
Capital Business Events
CBE
5 Olliffe Street
London, E14 3NL

Grief, David
Essex Court Chambers
24 Lincoln's Inn Fields
London, WC2A 3EG

Hall, Doug
Smith & Williamson LLP
25 Moorgate
London, EC2R 6AY

Heilbron, Hilary
Brick Court Chambers
7-8 Essex Street
London, WC2R 3LD

Herlihy, David
Skadden Arps Slate Meagher & Flom LLP
40 Bank Street
Canary Wharf
London, E14 5DS

Hickman, Damian
IDRC
70 Fleet Street
London, EC4Y1EU

Hunter, Ian
Essex Court Chambers
24 Lincoln's Inn Fields
London, WC2A 3EG

Hunter, Martin
Advisory Board Member of ICCA
Essex Court Chambers
24 Lincoln's Inn Fields
London, WC2A 3EG

Ivanenko, Galina
Buzachi Operating
CBE
5 Olliffe Street
London, E14 3NL

Jackson, Rhodri
Oxford University Press
Great Clarendon Street
Oxford, OXF-A314

Jagusch, Stephen
Quinn Emanuel Urquhart & Sullivan
One Fleet Place
London, EC4M 7RA

Johnson, Colin
Grant Thornton
33 Kingsmead
London, AL4 9JG

Kaytaz Eker, Bihter
Queen Mary, University of London
Old Palace Guest House
7 Madeira Place
Brighton, BN2 1TN

Kelly, Richard
Shearman & Sterling LLP
Baljinder Matharu
Broadgate West, 9 Appold Street
London, EC2A 2AP

Key, Paul
Essex Court Chambers
24 Lincoln's Inn Fields
London, WC2A 3EG

Kostin, Aleksei
MKAS
CBE
5 Olliffe Street
London, E14 3NL

Kyriacou, Emily
Thomson Reuters Legal UK & Ireland
100 Avenue Road
London, NW33PF

Lamb, Sophie
Debevoise & Plimpton LLP
65 Gresham Street
London, EC2V 7NQ

Lapuerta, Carlos
The Brattle Group
Halton House
20-23 Holborn
London, EC1N 2JD

Leathley, Christian
Herbert Smith Freehills LLP
Exchange House
Primrose Street
London, EC2A 2EG

Leaver, Peter
One Essex Court Chambers
One Essex Court
Temple
London, EC4Y 9AR

Levy, Mark
Allen & Overy LLP
One Bishops Square
London, E1 6AD

Lidstrom, Tom
Linklaters LLP
One Silk Street
London, EC2Y 8HQ

Lifely, Adrian
Osborne Clarke
One London Wall
London, EC2Y 5EB

McAlpine, Rory
Skadden Arps Slate Meagher & Flom LLP
40 Bank Street
Canary Wharf
London, E14 7FX

McRae, Belinda
20 Essex Street Chambers
20 Essex Street
London, WC2R 3AL

Miles, Wendy
Boeis, Schiller & Flexner LLP
25 Old Broad Street
London, EC2N 1HQ

Mistelis, Loukas
Queen Mary, University of London
67-69 Lincoln's Inn Fields
London, WC2A 3JB

Moollan, Salim
Essex Court Chambers
24 Lincoln's Inn Fields
London, WC2A 3EG

Moore, Christopher
Cleary Gottlieb Steen & Hamilton LLP
City Place House
55 Basinghall Street
London, EC2V 5EH

Nadtochiy, Mikhail
Collector Partner LLP
CBE
5 Olliffe Street
London, E14 3NL

Nairn, Karyl
Skadden Arps Slate Meagher & Flom LLP
40 Bank Street
Canary Wharf
London, E14 7FX

Narancio, Victoria
Wilmer Cutler Pickering Hale and Dorr LLP
49 Park Lane
London, W1K 1PS

Nesbitt, Simon
Hogan Lovells LLP
Atlantic House
50 Holborn Viaduct
London, EC1A 2FG

Nkontchou, Adebimpe
Addie & Co Advisory
44 Maiden Lane
London, WC2E 7LN

Norton, Patrick
Steptoe & Johnson LLP
99 Gresham Street
London, EC2R 7NJ

Partasides, Constantine
Three Crowns LLP
64 Highgate WestHill
London, N6 6BU

Poulton, Edward
Baker & McKenzie LLP
100 New Bridge Street
London, EC4V 6JA

Rawding, Nigel
Freshfields Bruckhaus Deringer LLP
65 Fleet Stree
London, EC4Y 1HS

Reichert, Klaus
Governing Board Member of ICCA
Brick Court Chambers
7-8 Essex Street
London, WC2R 3LD

Sarkodie, Kwadwo
Mayer Brown International LLP
201 Bishopsgate
London, EC2M 3AF

Schwarz, Franz
Wilmer Cutler Pickering Hale and Dorr LLP
49 Park Lane
London, W1K 1PS

Sebastian, Thomas
Monckton Chambers, London
11C Ockendon Road
London, N1 3NN

Shperchuk, Natalya
Merkusheva & Partners
CBE
5 Olliffe Street
London, E14 3NL

Sinclair, Anthony
Quinn Emanuel Urquhart & Sullivan
One Fleet Place
London, EC4M 7RA

Singh, Saira
Thomson Reuters Legal UK & Ireland
19 Hatfields
London, SEI 8DJ

Smith, Mick
Calunius Capital LLP
11 Haymarket
London, SW1Y 4BP

Sprange, Thomas
King & Spalding LLP
125 Old Broad Street
London, EC2N 1AR

Stephens, Michael
Chartered Institute of Arbitrators
12 Bloomsbury Square
London, WC1N 2LP

Tazhgaliyeva, Kosmagul
Chevron Munaigas Inc.
5 Olliffe Street
London, E14 3NL

Templeman, Mark
Essex Court Chambers
24 Lincoln's Inn Fields
London, WC2A 3EG

Tevendale, Craig
Herbert Smith Freehills LLP
Exchange House
Primrose Street
London, EC2A 2EG

Thomas, David Brynmor
Thirty Nine Essex Street Chambers
39 Essex Street
London, WC2R 3AT

Tout, Liz
Dentons UKMEA LLP
One Fleet Place
London, EC4M 7WS

Veeder, V.V.
Governing Board Member of ICCA
Essex Court Chambers
24 Lincoln's Inn Fields
London, WC2A 3EG

Virdee, Jivan
Global Arbitration Review
87 Lancaster Road
London, W11 1QQ

Vorobjova, Natalia
UkrOboron Service
CBE
5 Olliffe Street
London, E14 3NL

Welsh, Angeline
Allen & Overy LLP
One Bishops Square
London, E1 6AD

Winstanley, Adrian
LCIA
70 Fleet Street
London, EC4Y 1EU

Zakirov, Elnar
Arbitral Tribunal Union of
Enterpreners Russia
CBE
5 Olliffe Street
London, E14 3NL

Zamaziy, Alexander
Arbitral Tribunal Union of
Enterpreners Russia
CBE
5 Olliffe Street
London, E14 3NL

Scotland

Cameron, Peter
Centre for Energy, Petroleum & Mineral Law
& Policy
CEPMLP, University of Dundee
1-3 Perth Road
Dundee, DD1 4HN

Mackenzie, Andrew
Scottish Arbitration Centre
Dolphin House
4 Hunter Square
Edinburgh, EH1 3NX

Malone, Brandon
Scottish Arbitration Centre
Dolphin House
4 Hunter Square
Edinburgh, EH1 1QW

United States of America

Aedo, Rolando
Greater Miami Conventions & Visitors
Bureau
701 Brickell Avenue
Suite 2700
Miami, FL 33131

Aguilar-Alvarez, Guillermo
Treasurer of ICCA

King & Spalding LLP
1185 Avenue of the Americas
New York, NY 10036

Ahee, Linda
Global Financial Analytics
PO Box 2629
Fairfax, VA 22031

Alberro, Jose
BRG
1919 M Street N.W.
Suite 800
Washington, DC 20036

Ali, Arif
Weil, Gotshal & Manges LLP
1300 Eye Street N.W.
Suite 900
Washington, DC 20005

Allen, Ray
TransPerfect Legal Solutions
700 6th Street, N.W.
Washington, DC 20001

Allison, Matthew
Baker & McKenzie LLP
300 E. Randolph Street
Suite 5000
Chicago, IL 60601

Altieri, Peter
Epstein Becker Green P.C.
250 Park Avenue
New York, NY 10177

Amirfar, Catherine
Office of the Legal Adviser
US State Department
2430 E Street N.W.
Washington, DC 20005

Andersen, Steve
International Centre for Dispute Resolution
(ICDR)
1108 E. South Union Avenue
Midvale, UT 84047

Anzola, Jose Eloy
JEA DR

3625 Bougainvillea Road
Miami, FL 33133

Arango, Maria Elisa
Holland & Knight LLP
31 West 52nd Street
New York, 10019

Armas, Oliver J.
Hogan Lovells LLP
875 Third Avenue
New York, NY 10022

Ashby, Patrick
Linklaters LLP
1345 Avenue of the Americas
New York, NY 10105

Astigarraga, José I.
Astigarraga Davis Mullins & Grossman, P.A.
1001 Brickell Bay Drive
9th Floor
Miami, FL 33131

Atkins, Alden L.
Vinson & Elkins LLP
2200 Pennsylvania Avenue N.W.
Suite 500 West
Washington, DC 20037

Bailey, Jennifer
U.S. Civil Court, 11th Judicial Circuit
73 West Flagler Street
Miami, FL 33157

Barkett, John
Shook Hardy & Bacon LLP
201 South Biscayne Boulevard
Suite 3200
Miami, FL 33131

Barrena, Alexandra
PwC LLP
1441 Brickell Avenue
Suite 1100
Miami, FL 33131

Bassler, William
William G. Bassler & Associates
130 Bodman Place
Suite 15
Red Bank, NJ 07701

Bedard, Julie
Skadden Arps Slate Meagher & Flom LLP
Four Times Square
New York, NY 10036

Berry, Erica
PwC LLP
1441 Brickell Avenue
Suite 1100
Miami, FL 33131

Bianchi, Jaime A.
White & Case LLP
200 South Biscayne Boulevard, Suite 4900
Miami, FL 33131

Birnberg, Gary
Global Resolution
1395 Brickell Avenue
Suite 800
Miami, FL 33131

Bishop, Doak
King & Spalding LLP
1100 Louisiana
Suite 4000
Houston, TX 77002

Blackaby, Nigel
Freshfields Bruckhaus Deringer LLP
700 13th Street N.W.
10th Floor
Washington, DC 20005-3960

Borrasso, Ava J.
Astigarraga Davis Mullins & Grossman, P.A.
1001 Brickell Bay Drive
9th Floor
Miami, FL 33131

Bouchenaki, Amal
Herbert Smith Freehills
450 Lexington Avenue
14th Floor
New York, NY 10017

Brennan, Lorraine M.
JAMS
620 Eighth Avenue
34th Floor
New York, NY 10018

Briz, Brian
Holland & Knight LLP
701 Brickell Avenue
Suite 3300
Miami, FL 33131

Brower, Chip
Wayne State Law School
471 West Palmer Street
Detroit, MI 48202

Burd, Gene
Arnall Golden Gregory LLP
1775 Pennsylvania Avenue N.W.
Suite 1000
Washington, DC 20006

Burr, Scott
Chartered Institute of Arbitrators
255 Aragon Avenue
2nd Floor
Coral Gables, FL 33134

Calderon, Ines
1200 Anastasia Avenue
Suite 213
Coral Gables, FL 33134

Caplan, Lee
Arent Fox
1717 K Street N.W.
Washington, DC 20036

Cardenas, Maria Cristina
Astigarraga Davis Mullins & Grossman, P.A.
1001 Brickell Bay Drive
9th Floor
Miami, FL 33131

Cardozo, Camilo
DLA Piper LLP
1251 Avenue of the Americas
New York, NY 10020

Carson, Derrick
Locke Lord LLP
600 Travis Street
Suite 2800
Houston, TX 77002

Cartagena, Jose W.
Jose W. Cartagena

701 Ponce de Leon Suite 401
San Juan, PR 00907-3248

Carter, Janet
Wilmer Cutler Pickering Hale and Dorr LLP
7 World Trade Center
250 Greenwich Street
New York, NY 10007

Cassidy, William
Cassidy & Black, P.A.
7700 North Kendall Drive
Suite 505
Miami, FL 33156

Cheskin, Mark
Hogan Lovells US LLP
600 Brickell Avenue
Suite 2700
Miami, FL 33131

Childs, Thomas
King & Spalding LLP
1185 Avenue of the Americas
New York, NY 10036

Chirinos, Ricardo
Freshfields Bruckhaus Deringer LLP
700 13th Street N.W.
10th Floor
Washington, DC 20005-3960

Cibelli, Emma
Akerman LLP
666 Fifth Avenue
20th Floor
New York, NY 10103

Claussen, Kathleen
Office of the U.S. Trade Representative
Washington, DC

Coe, Jack
Straus Institute, Pepperdine Law School
Pepperdine University School of Law
Malibu, CA 90263

Cohen, Paul
Perkins Coie LLP
30 Rockefeller Plaza
22nd floor
New York, NY 10112

Collins, Michael
Crandall, Hanscom & Collins PA
9304 Belmart Road
Potomac, MD 20854

Concepcion, Carlos
Concepcion Martinez & Bellido
255 Aragon Avenue
2nd Floor
Coral Gables, FL 33134

Cope, Gerald
Akerman LLP
One S.E. Third Avenue
25th Floor
Miami, FL 33134

Courtney, William
PwC LLP
1441 Brickell Avenue
Suite 1100
Miami, FL 33131

Coyne, Joanna
Crowell & Moring LLP
1001 Pennsylvania Avenue N.W.
Washington, DC 20004

Crook, John
George Washington University Law School
10610 Belfast Place
Potomac, MD 20854

Cruz-Alvarez, Frank
Shook Hardy & Bacon LLP
201 South Biscayne Boulevard
Suite 3200
Miami, FL 33131

Cuneo, Jose
Kaufman, Rossin & Co.
2699 South Bayshore Drive
Suite 300
Miami, FL 33133

Davidson, Gary
Diaz Reus & Targ, LLP
100 S.E. 2nd Street
Suite 3400
Miami, FL 33131

Davis, Thomas W.
University of Miami School of Law

1311 Miller Drive
Suite G366
Coral Gables, FL 33146

Day, Peter
Mercer Island Arbitration Chambers Int'l
LLC
6915 S.E. 33rd Street
Mercer Island, WA 98040-3323

de Gramont, Alexandre
Weil, Gotshal & Manges LLP
1300 Eye Street N.W.
Suite 900
Washington, DC 20005

Delgado, Eddie
Akerman LLP
One S.E Third Avenue
25th Floor
Miami, FL 33131

Delgado, Juan José
DLA Interjuris
200 S. Biscayne Boulevard
Suite 2500
Miami, FL 33131

Dellepiane, Santiago
Compass Lexecon
156 West 56th Street
19th Floor
New York, NY 10019

Desierto, Diane
University of Hawaii William S. Richardson
School of Law
2515 Dole Street
Room 210
Honolulu, HI 96822

Digon, Rocio
International Court of Arbitration
1212 Avenue of the Americas
9th Floor
New York, NY 10036

Donovan, Donald
Honorary Vice President of ICCA
Debevoise & Plimpton LLP
919 Third Avenue
39th Floor
New York, NY 10022

Dosman, Alexandra
New York International Arbitration Center
(NYIAC)
150 E. 42nd Street
17th Floor
New York, 10017

Doyle, Thomas
Baker & McKenzie LLP
300 E. Randolph Street
Suite 5000
Chicago, IL 60601

Elkin, Michael
Kaufman, Rossin & Co.
2699 South Bayshore Drive
Suite 300
Miami, FL 33133

Elul, Hagit
Hughes Hubbard & Reed LLP
One Battery Park Plaza
New York, NY 10004

Engle, Philip
Chartered Institute of Arbitrators
230 Axworth Ct
Roswell, GA 30075

Enix-Ross, Deborah
Debevoise & Plimpton LLP
919 Third Avenue
39th Floor
New York, NY 10022

Ferrer, José
Bilzin Sumberg Baena Price & Axelrod
1450 Brickell Avenue
23rd Floor
Miami, FL 33131

Fields, Richard
Juridica Asset Management
6801 Collins Avenue
#1106
Miami Beach, FL 33141

Figueroa, Kenneth
Foley Hoag LLP
1717 K Street N.W.
Suite 1200
Washington, DC 20006

Fowler, Jordan
Vinson & Elkins LLP
1001 Fannin Street
Suite 2500
Houston, TX 77002

Franck, Susan
Washington and Lee University School of
Law
Sydney Lewis Hall
Lexington, VA 24450

Freda, James
Freshfields Bruckhaus Deringer LLP
601 Lexington Avenue
31st Floor
New York, NY 10022

Freedberg, Judith
3530 S.W. 22nd Street
Unit 516
Miami, FL 33145

Freedman, Velvel
Boies, Schiller & Flexner LL
100 S.E. 2nd Street
Suite 2800
Miami, FL 33131

Friedman, Elliot
Freshfields Bruckhaus Deringer LLP
601 Lexington Avenue
31st Floor
New York, NY 10022

Friedman, Mark
Debevoise & Plimpton LLP
919 Third Avenue
39th Floor
New York, NY 10022

Fuchs, Jeffrey
Delta Consulting Group, Inc.
4330 Prince William Parkway
Suite 301
Woodbridge, VA 22192

Galindo, Alvaro
Dechert LLP
1900 K Street N.W.
Washington, DC 20006

Gardiner, John
Skadden Arps Slate Meagher & Flom LLP
Four Times Square
New York, NY 10036

Gardner, Christa
University of Miami School of Law
3500 Coral Way
Apt. 1009
Miami, FL 33145

Garfinkel, Barry
Skadden Arps Slate Meagher & Flom LLP
Four Times Square
New York, NY 10036

Gastrell, Lindsay
International Centre for Settlement
of Investment Disputes
(ICSID)
1818 H Street N.W.
MSN J 2-200
Washington, DC 20433

Gearhart-Serna, Terra
Debevoise & Plimpton LLP
919 Third Avenue
39th Floor
New York, NY 10022

George, Scott
KPMG LLP
1676 International Drive
McLean, VA 22102

Gill, Samantha
Strut Legal, Inc.
49 North Federal Highway
#354
Pompano Beach, FL 33062

Gimblett, Jonathan
Covington & Burling LLP
1201 Pennsylvania Avenue N.W.
Washington, DC 20004

Glick, Ruth
Dispute Resolution Section, ABA
1325 Howard Avenue
No. 512
Burlingame, CA 94010

Gluck, George
2 William Street
Suite 200
White Plains, NY 10601

Goldstein, Marc
Marc J. Goldstein Litigation & Arbitration
Chambers
One Rockefeller Plaza
11th Floor
New York, NY 10020

Gomez, Manuel
Florida International University College of
Law
11200 S.W. 8th Street, RDB 2043
Miami, FL 33199

González, Analia
Foley Hoag LLP
1717 K Street N.W.
Suite 1200
Washington, DC 20006

González, Daniel
Hogan Lovells LLP
600 Brickell Avenue
Suite 2700
Miami, FL 33131

Gonzalez, Ricardo
Greenberg Traurig
333 S.E. 2nd Avenue
Miami, FL 33131

Goodman, Ronald
Foley Hoag LLP
1717 K Street N.W.
Suite 1200
Washington, DC 20006

Gorskie, Jennifer
Chaffetz Lindsey LLP
505 Fifth Avenue
4th Floor
New York, NY 10017

Gosis, Diego Brian
Gomm & Smith
175 South-West 7th Street
Suite 2110
Miami, FL 33130

Grachova, Julia
Chartered Institute of Arbitrators
8700 West Flagler St, Suite 355
Miami, FL 33174

Grigera Naon, Horacio
5224 Elliott Road
Bethesda, MD 20816

Grubbs, Shelby
Miller & Martin, PLLC
1170 Peachtree Street N.E.
Suite 800
Atlanta, GA 30309

Gutchess, Jeffrey
Bilzin Sumberg Baena Price & Axelrod
1450 Brickell Avenue
23rd Floor
Miami, FL 33131

Guttman, Jaime
Private Advising Group, P.A.
600 Brickell Avenue
Suite 1607
Miami, FL 33180

Haber Kuck, Lea
Skadden Arps Slate Meagher & Flom LLP
Four Times Square
New York, NY 10036

Hackell, Matthew
Paduano & Weintraub LLP
1251 Avenue of the Americas
9th Floor
New York, NY 10020

Hadaway, Brant
Diaz Reus & Targ, LLP
100 S.E. 2nd Street
Suite 3400
Miami, FL 33131

Hamilton, Jonathan C.
White & Case LLP
701 13th Street N.W.
Washington, DC 20005

Hanessian, Grant
Baker & McKenzie LLP
452 Fifth Avenue
New York, NY 10018

Haridi, Samaa
Weil, Gotshal & Manges LLP
767 Fifth Avenue
New York, NY 10153

Hayden, Don
Berger Singermon
1450 Brickell Avenue Suite 1900
Miami, FL 33131

Hellmann, Betsy
Skadden Arps Slate Meagher & Flom LLP
Four Times Square
New York, NY 10036

Hendrix, Glenn
Arnall Golden Gregory LLP
171 17th Street, N.W.
Suite 2100
Atlanta, GA 30319

Hennessee, Karl
Halliburton Energy Services
3000 North Sam Houston Parkway East
Bldg J4
Houston, TX 77032

Hernandez, Jessica
JURIS
71 New Street
Huntington, NY 11743

Herrmann, Gerold
Honorary President of ICCA
1021 Hillsboro Mile, No. 806
Hillsboro Beach, FL 33062

Hille, David
White & Case LLP
1155 Avenue of the Americas
New York, NY 10036

Hodgson, Melida
Foley Hoag LLP
1717 K Street N.W.
Suite 1200
Washington, DC 20006

Hosking, James
Chaffetz Lindsey LLP
505 Fifth Avenue
4th Floor
New York, NY 10017

Huckstep, Charles
KBR
601 Jefferson
KT 3706
Houston, TX 77006

Hunnefeld, Angelika
Greenberg Traurig
333 S.E. 2nd Avenue
Suite 4400
Miami, FL 33131

Infantino, Christopher
JURIS
71 New Street
Huntington, NY 11743

Jayson, Melinda
Melinda G. Jayson, P.C.
5445 Caruth Haven Lane
Suite 2015
Dallas, TX 75225

Jemison, Jonathan
Dentons US LLP
101 JFK Parkway
4th Floor
Short Hills, NJ 07078

Jeong, Sang Eun
Washington and Lee University School of
Law
2 Tucker Street
Apartment 2
Lexington, VA 24450

Jimenez, Adolfo
Holland & Knight LLP
701 Brickell Avenue
Suite 3300
Miami, FL 33131

Johnson, India
American Arbitration Association
120 Broadway
21st Floor
New York, NY 10271

Kahn, Sherman
Mauriel Kapouytian Woods
27 W. 24th Street
Suite 302
New York, NY 10010

Kalicki, Jean
Arnold & Porter LLP
555 Twelfth Street, N.W.
Washington, DC 20004

Kantor, Mark
110 Maryland Avenue, N.E.
Suite 311B
Washington, DC 20002

Kelly, Janet
ConocoPhillips
600 North Dairy Ashford
PE 3034
Houston, TX 77079

Kent, Rachael
Wilmer Cutler Pickering Hale and Dorr LLP
1875 Pennsylvania Avenue N.W.
Washington, DC 20006

Kessler, Judd L.
Porter Wright
4907 Brookeway Drive
Bethesda, MD 20816

Kiefer, David W.
Dentons US LLP
101 JFK Parkway
Fourth Floor
Short Hills, NJ 07078

Kilani, Imad
Alkilani Law Firm
4106 North Narragansett Avenue
Apartment 410
Chicago, IL 60634

Kinnear, Meg
Governing Board Member of ICCA
International Centre for Settlement
of Investment Disputes
(ICSID)
1818 H Street N.W.
MSN J 2-200
Washington, DC 20433

Kitzen, Michael
JURIS
71 New Street
Huntington, NY 11743

Knull, William
Mayer Brown International LLP
700 Louisiana Street
Suite 3400
Houston, TX 77002

Kostadinova, Milanka
International Centre for Settlement
of Investment Disputes
(ICSID)
1818 H Street N.W.
MSN J 2-200
Washington, DC 20433

Kozai, Satoshi
Sojitz Corporation of America
1120 Avenue of the Americas
7th Floor
New York, NY 10036

Krasuk, Javier
9th Insight, Inc
PO Box 848
Fairfax, VA 22030

Krigelski, Aaron
Strut Legal, Inc.
49 North Federal Highway
No. 354
Pompano Beach, FL 33062

Kurtz, Birgit
Crowell & Moring LLP
590 Madison Avenue
20th Floor
New York, NY 10022

La Chuisa, Jenelle
Astigarraga Davis Mullins & Grossman, P.A.
1001 Brickell Bay Drive
9th Floor
Miami, FL 33131

Laeuchli, Urs
United-ADR
PO Box 20361
Palo Alto, CA 94309

Lahlou, Yasmine
Chaffetz Lindsey LLP
505 Fifth Avenue
4th Floor
New York, NY 10017

1085

Laird, Ian A.
Crowell & Moring LLP
1001 Pennsylvania Avenue N.W.
Washington, DC 20004

Lamm, Carolyn
Governing Board Member of ICCA
White & Case LLP
701 13th Street N.W.
Washington, DC 20005

Landy, Burton
Akerman LLP
One S.E. Third Avenue
25th Floor
Miami, FL 33131

Lavion, Didier
PricewaterhouseCoopers LLP
300 Madison Avenue
New York, NY 10017

Lawson, Bernadette
Shook Hardy & Bacon LLP
2555 Grand Boulevard
Kansas City, MO 64108

Lazic, Djurdja
American Society of International Law
2223 Massachusetts Avenue N.W.
Washington, DC 20008

Lazzarini, Shannon
Skadden Arps Slate Meagher & Flom LLP
Four Times Square
New York, NY 10036

Lea, Clyde
ConocoPhillips
600 North Dairy Ashford
Houston, TX 77079

Leonardo, Giselle
One East Broward Boulevard
Suite 700
Ft. Lauderdale, FL 33301

Levetown, Andrew
Levetown & Jenkins, LLP
1439 Woodhurst Boulevard
McLean, VA 22102

Lewis-Gruss, Ayanna
Orrick, Herrington & Sutcliffe LLP
51 West 52nd Street
New York, NY 10019

Lindsay, Alvin
Hogan Lovells US LLP
600 Brickell Avenue
27th Floor
Miami, FL 33131

Lindsey, David
Chaffetz Lindsey LLP
505 Fifth Avenue
4th Floor
New York, NY 10017

Litt, Greg
Skadden Arps Slate Meagher & Flom LLP
Four Times Square
New York, NY 10036

Llamzon, Aloysius
King & Spalding
1185 Avenue of the Americas
New York, NY 10036

Loftis, James
Vinson & Elkins LLP
1001 Fannin Street
Suite 2500
Houston, TX 77002

Lopez, Guadalupe
Freshfields Bruckhaus Deringer LLP
700 13th Street N.W.
10th Floor
Washington, DC 20005-3960

Lorenzo, Richard
Hogan Lovells LLP
600 Brickell Avenue
Suite 2700
Miami, FL 33131

Maher, Stephen
Shutts & Bowen LLP
201 South Biscayne Boulevard
Suite 1500
Miami, FL 33131

Mahoney, C.J.
Williams & Connolly LLP

725 12th Street N.W.
Washington, DC 20005

Mamounas, Joseph
Bilzin Sumberg Baena Price & Axelrod
1450 Brickell Avenue
23rd Floor
Miami, FL 33131

Maniatis, Alexis
The Brattle Group
1850 M Street N.W.
Suite 1200
Washington, DC 20036

Marinelli, Marisa
Holland & Knight LLP
31 W. 52nd Street
New York, NY 10019

Marmolejo, Matthew
Mayer Brown LLP
350 South Grand Avenue
25th Floor
Los Angeles, CA 90071

Marriott, David
Cravath, Swaine & Moore LLP
825 Eighth Avenue
Worldwide Plaza
New York, NY 10019

Martinez, Luis
International Centre for Dispute Resolution
(ICDR)
150 East 42nd Street
New York, NY 10017

Martínez-Betanzos, Carlos E.
Hogan Lovells US LLP
875 Third Avenue
New York, NY 10022

Matthews, Joseph
Colson Hicks Eidson, P.A.
255 Alhambra Circle
Penthouse
Coral Gables, FL 33134

Matthews, Joseph
University of Miami School of Law
11511 S.W. 80th Terrace
Miami, FL 33176

McCauley, John (Jay)
J. McCauley & Associates LLC
3001 N.E. 102nd Terrace
Kansas City, MO 64155

McGovern, Francis
Duke Law
210 Science Drive
Durham, NC 27708

Mechelli, Stefano
McDermott Will & Emery LLP
340 Madison Avenue
New York, NY 10173

Menaker, Andrea
White & Case LLP
701 13th Street N.W.
Washington, DC 20005

Mencio, George
Holland & Knight LLP
701 Brickell Avenue
Suite 3300
Miami, FL 33131

Michaelson, Peter
Michaelson ADR Chambers, LLC
590 Madison Avenue
18th Floor
New York, NY 10022

Moarbes, Charbel
American Society of International Law
2223 Massachusetts Avenue N.W.
Washington, DC 20008

Moore, Allan
Covington & Burling LLP
1201 Pennsylvania Avenue N.W.
Washington, DC 20004

Moore, Richmond
Williams & Connolly LLP
725 12th Street N.W.
Washington, DC 20005

Moreno-Baldivieso, Ramiro
Moreno Baldivieso Estudio de Abogados
Capitan Ravelo 2366
2000 North Ocean Boulevard
Boca Raton, FL 33431

Morkin, Michael
Baker & McKenzie LLP
300 E. Randolph Street
Suite 5000
Chicago, IL 60601

Morril, Mark
MorrilADR
413 W. 53rd Street
New York, NY 10019

Morris, Tiff'ny
Akerman LLP
One S.E. Third Avenue
25th Floor
Miami, FL 33131

Moxley, Charles
MoxleyADR LLC
850 Third Avenue
14th Floor
New York, NY 10022

Naimark, Richard
International Centre for Dispute Resolution
(ICDR)
120 Broadway
21st Floor
New York, NY 10271

Nelson, Timothy
Skadden Arps Slate Meagher & Flom LLP
Four Times Square
New York, NY 10036

Neufeld, Paul
Fulbright & Jaworski LLP
1301 McKinney Street
Suite 5100
Houston, TX 77010

Neuhaus, Joseph
Sullivan & Cromwell LLP
125 Broad Street
New York, NY 10004

Newman, Lawrence
Baker & McKenzie LLP
452 Fifth Avenue
New York, NY 10018

Norgaard, Thomas
Debevoise & Plimpton LLP

919 Third Avenue
39th Floor
New York, NY 10022

Nyer, Damien
White & Case LLP
1155 Avenue of the Americas
New York, NY 10036

Ocariz, Humberto
Shook Hardy & Bacon LLP
201 South Biscayne Boulevard
Suite 3200
Miami, FL 33131

O'Connor, Ciara
Oxford University Press
198 Madison Avenue
New York, NY 10016

Oliveau, Maidie
Arent Fox LLP
555 West Fifth Street
48th Floor
Los Angeles, CA 90013

Oliveira, Gustavo
8 Cartorio Notas-RJ
200 Sunny Isles Boulevard
Apt. 2-1603
Sunny Isles, FL 33160

O'Malley, Nathan
Gibbs Giden Locher Turner Senet
& Wittbrodt
1880 Century Park East
Los Angeles, CA 90067

O'Naghten, Luis
Akerman LLP
One S.E. Third Avenue
25th Floor
Miami, FL 33131

Owens, Debra
PortMiami
1015 North America Way
2nd Floor
Miami, FL 33132

Pagliery, Sergio
Shook Hardy & Bacon LLP
201 South Biscayne Boulevard

Suite 3200
Miami, FL 33131

Palmer, Eduardo
Eduardo Palmer, P.A.
255 Aragon Avenue
2nd Floor
Coral Gables, FL 33134

Parker, Chris
Herbert Smith Freehills LLP
450 Lexington Avenue
14th Floor
New York, NY 10017

Parmelee, Brian
JAMS
500 North State College Boulevard
Suite 1400
Orange, CA 92673

Paulsson, Jan
Honorary President of ICCA
Three Crowns LLP/University of Miami
School of Law
1311 Miller Drive
Suite G366
Coral Gables, FL 33146

Paulsson, Marike
University of Miami School of Law
1311 Miller Drive
Suite G366
Coral Gables, FL 33146

Pearsall, Patrick W.
U.S. State Department
2200 C Street N.W.
Suite 6422
Washington, DC 20037

Pena, Ruben
Vinson & Elkins LLP
1001 Fannin Street
Suite 2500
Houston, TX 77002

Pereira, Diogo
Freshfields Bruckhaus Deringer LLP
700 13th Street N.W.
10th Floor
Washington, DC 20005-396

Perez, Angelina
Akerman LLP
One S.E. Third Ave
25th Floor
Miami, FL 33131

Perez, Luis
Akerman LLP
One S.E. Third Avenue
25th Floor
Miami, FL 33131

Pettibone, Peter
Hogan Lovells LLP
875 Third Avenue
New York, NY 10022

Pieper, Thomas N
Hogan Lovells LLP
875 Third Avenue
New York, NY 10022

Pierce, John
Wilmer Cutler Pickering Hale and Dorr LLP
7 World Trade Center
250 Greenwich Street
New York, NY 10007

Pierz, Kathleen
JAMS
620 Eighth Avenue
34th Floor
New York, NY 10018

Pinsky, David
Covington & Burling LLP
620 Eight Avenue
New York, NY 10013

Polasek, Martina
International Centre for Settlement
of Investment Disputes
(ICSID)
1818 H Street N.W.
MSN J 2-200
Washington, DC 20433

Polášek, Petr
White & Case LLP
701 13th Street N.W.
Washington, DC 20005

Pollock, Peter
Siemens Energy, Inc.
4400 North Alafaya Trail, MC Q2-480
Orlando, FL 32826

Posner, Theodore R.
Weil, Gotshal & Manges LLP
1300 Eye Street N.W.
Suite 900
Washington, DC 20005

Prager, Dietmar
Debevoise & Plimpton LLP
919 Third Avenue
39th Floor
New York, NY 10022

Puente, Ricardo
Concepcion Martinez & Bellido
255 Aragon Avenue
2nd Floor
Coral Gables, FL 33134

Ramirez, Juan
Diaz Reus & Targ, LLP
100 S.E. 2nd Street
Suite 3400
Miami, FL 33131

Ramirez, Maria
Hogan Lovells LLP
600 Brickell Avenue
Suite 2700
Miami, FL 33131

Rau, Alan
University of Texas at Austin
727 East Dean Keeton Street
Austin, TX 78705

Reid, Natalie
Debevoise & Plimpton LLP
919 Third Avenue
39th Floor
New York, NY 10022

Reyes, Ana C.
Williams & Connolly LLP
725 12th Street N.W.
Washington, DC 20005

Reyna, Manuel
Akerman LLP

One S.E. Third Ave
25th Floor
Miami, FL 33131

Ribeiro, Rafael
Bilzin Sumberg Baena Price & Axelrod
1450 Brickell Avenue
23rd Floor
Miami, FL 33131

Riccio, L Andrew
Baker & McKenzie LLP
452 Fifth Avenue
New York, NY 10018

Richardson, Patrick
JURIS
71 New Street
Huntington, NY 11743

Riviere-Badell, Adriana
Kobre & Kim LLP
2 South Biscayne Boulevard
Miami, FL 33131

Robertson, Laura
ConocoPhillips
600 North Dairy Ashford
ML 1048
Houston, TX 77079

Rodriguez, Francisco
Akerman LLP
One S.E. Third Ave
25th Floor
Miami, FL 33131

Roesser, John
Alston & Bird LLP
90 Park Avenue
12th Floor
New York, NY 10708

Rogers, Catherine
Penn State Law/Queen Mary
Penn State Law
324 Katz Building
State College, PA 16801

Rooney, John
John H. Rooney, Jr., P.A.
175 S.W. 7th Street

Suite 2110
Miami, FL 33130

Roppolo, William
Baker & McKenzie LLP
1015 S.E. 6th Street
Ft. Lauderdale, FL 33301

Rostov, Eugene
E. Rostov & Associates LLC
2601 South Bayshore Drive
Suite 605
Miami, FL 33133

Rowe, Samantha
Debevoise & Plimpton LLP
919 Third Avenue
39th Floor
New York, NY 10022

Russo, Louis
Alston & Bird LLP
90 Park Avenue
12th Floor
New York, NY 10016

Sabater, Anibal
Norton Rose Fulbright
666 Fifth Avenue
New York, NY 10103

Saccani, Zel
SLBT
36 Sam Perl Boulevard
No. 150
Brownsville, TX 78520

Salas, Claudio
Wilmer Cutler Pickering Hale and Dorr LLP
7 World Trade Center
250 Greenwich Street
New York, NY 10007

Salter, Vance
Third District Court of Appeal
2001 S.W. 117 Avenue
Miami, FL 33175

Samra, Harout Jack
DLA Piper LLP
200 S. Biscayne Boulevard
Suite 2500
Miami, FL 33131

Sanchez, Ernesto
Law Offices of Ernesto J. Sanchez
1530 Catalonia Avenue
Coral Gables, FL 33134

Sanchez, Margarita
Arnold & Porter LLP
555 Twelfth Street, N.W.
Washington, DC 20004

Santens, Ank
White & Case LLP
1155 Avenue of the Americas
New York, NY 10036

Santos, José
Florida International University College
of Law
200 South Biscayne Boulevard
Suite 2790
Miami, FL 33131

Santos, Mauricio
Gomm & Smith
175 S.W. 7th Street
Suite 2110
Miami, FL 33130

Sblendorio, Jessica
University of Miami School of Law
6001 S.W. 70 Street
Apt. 140
South Miami, FL 33143

Schimmel, Daniel
Kelley Drye & Warren LLP
101 Park Avenue
New York, NY 10178

Schwebel, Stephen
1501 K Street N.W.
Suite 410
Washington, DC 20005

Shannon, Victoria
Washington and Lee University School of
Law
204 West Washington Street
445 Sydney Lewis Hall
Lexington, VA 24450

Sharpe, Jeremy
US State Department

2430 E Street N.W.
Suite 203
Washington, DC 20005

Shore, Laurence
Herbert Smith Freehills LLP
450 Lexington Avenue
14th Floor
New York, NY 10017

Sicard-Mirabal, Josefa
ICC International Court of Arbitration
1212 Avenue of the Americas
9th Floor
New York, NY 10036

Sills, Robert L.
Orrick, Herrington & Sutcliffe LLP
51 W. 52nd Street
New York, NY 10019

Silva, Effie
McDermott, Will & Emery, LLP
333 Avenue of the Americas
Suite 4500
Miami, FL 33131

Silva, Eugene
Exxon Mobil Corporation
800 Bell Street
EMB 1686K
Houston, TX 77002

Slate, William
Governing Board Member of ICCA
547 Island Walk West
Mt. Pleasant, SC 29464

Slater, Matthew
Cleary Gottlieb Steen & Hamilton LLP
2000 Pennsylvania Avenue N.W.
Washington, DC 20006

Slifkin, Daniel
Cravath, Swaine & Moore LLP
670 West End Avenue
No. 15F
New York, NY 10025

Smit, Robert
Simpson Thacher & Bartlett LLP
425 Lexington Avenue
New York, NY 10017

Smith, Jennifer
Baker Botts LLP
910 Louisiana Street
One Shell Plaza
Houston, TX 77002

Smith, Quinn
Gomm & Smith
175 S.W. 7th Street
Suite 2110
Miami, FL 33130

Smith, Stephen
Sherman and Howard
400 E. Third Avenue
Apt. 1002
Denver, CO 80203

Smutny, Abby Cohen
White & Case LLP
701 13th Street N.W.
Washington, DC 20005

Snider, Thomas
Greenberg Traurig
2101 L Street, N.W.
Suite 1000
Washington, DC 20037

Sobota, Luke
3C
3406 Rodman Street N.W.
Washington, DC 20008

Sotelo, Luis
DLA Piper LLP
200 S. Biscayne Boulevard
Suite 2500
Miami, FL 33131

Spahn, Eva
Greenberg Traurig
333 S.E. 2nd Avenue
Miami, FL 33131

Stapleton, Lee
Baker & McKenzie LLP
1111 Brickell Avenue
Suite 1700
Miami, FL 33131

Storrow, Rebecca
American Arbitration Association

6076 S.E. Woodfield Court
Stuart, FL 34997

Suarez Anzorena, Ignacio
Clifford Chance US LLP
2001 K Street N.W.
Suite 1040
Washington, DC 20006

Sussman, Edna
Fordham Law School
20 Oak Lane
Scarsdale, NY 10583

Sutton, Ralph
Bentham IMF
712 Fifth Avenue
14th Floor
New York, NY 10019

Swerdloff, Nicolas
Hughes Hubbard & Reed LLP
201 South Biscayne Boulevard
Suite 2500
Miami, FL 33131

Tan, Dan
Dan Tan Law
175 Varick Street
New York, NY 10014

Tancula, James
Mayer Brown International LLP
71 South Wacker Drive
Chicago, IL 60606

Taylor, Greig
FTI Consulting
3 Times Square
11th Floor
New York, NY 10036

Taylor, Kimberly
JAMS
620 Eighth Avenue
34th Floor
New York, NY 10018

Teitelbaum, Ruth
Freshfields Bruckhaus Deringer LLP
601 Lexington Avenue
31st Floor
New York, NY 10022

Tejera, Victorino
Florida International University College of Law
11325 N.W. 52nd Lane
Doral, FL 33178

Thornton, John
U.S. Civil Court, 11th Judicial Circuit
73 West Flagler Street
Room 1017
Miami, FL 33130

Tobon, Camila
Shook Hardy & Bacon LLP
201 South Biscayne Boulevard
Suite 3200
Miami, FL 33131

Torrealba, Jose
Hoet Pelaez Castillo & Duque
PO Box 025323
Miami, FL 33102 5323

Torterola, Ignacio
Foley Hoag LLP
1717 K Street N.W.
Suite 1200
Washington, DC 20006

Townsend, John
Hughes Hubbard & Reed LLP
1775 I Street N.W.
Suite 600
Washington, DC 20006-2401

Trevino, Clovis
Gomm & Smith
175 S.W. 7th Street
Suite 2110
Miami, FL 33130

Tumpovskiy, Anna
Tumpovskiy Law Group, P.A.
21204 Harbor Way
Miami, FL 33180

Tyler, Timothy
Vinson & Elkins LLP
1001 Fannin Street
Suite 2500
Houston, TX 77002

Uran Bidegain, Mairee
International Centre for Settlement
of Investment Disputes
(ICSID)
1818 H Street N.W.
MSN J 2-200
Washington, DC 20433

Van Tassel, Karyl
PwC LLP
1201 Louisiana
Suite 2900
Houston, TX 77002

Veliz, Yoly
Akerman LLP
One S.E. Third Ave
25th Floor
Miami, FL 33131

Ventrone, Thomas
International Centre for Dispute Resolution
(ICDR)
120 Broadway
21st Floor
New York, NY 10271

Vielleville, Daniel
Assouline & Berlowe, P.A.
3250 Mary Street
Suite 100
Miami, FL 33133

Volsky, George
Akerman LLP
One S.E. Third Ave
25th Floor
Miami, FL 33131

Walck, Richard
Global Financial Analytics
PO Box 2629
Fairfax, VA 22031

Wang, Sheng Chang
Advisory Board Member of ICCA
Beijing Hui Zhong Law Firm
21921 Providence Forge Drive
Ashburn, VA 20148

Warnot, James
Linklaters LLP

1345 Avenue of the Americas
New York, NY 10017

Weisburg, Henry
Shearman & Sterling LLP
599 Lexington Avenue
New York, NY 10022

Whitesell, Anne Marie
Georgetown University Law Center
1900 K Street N.W.
Washington, DC 20006

Whittaker, Janet
Simpson Thacher & Bartlett LLP
1155 F Street N.W.
Washington, DC 20004

Wilkinson, Phoebe
Hogan Lovells LLP
875 Third Avenue
New York, NY 10022

Williams, Kathleen
US Court of Appeal, Eleventh Circuit
400 North Miami Avenue
Suite 11-3
Miami, FL 33128

Witthoft, Carolyn
Libretto Group LLC
24 Linden Road
Suite 707
Ridgefield, CT 06877

Witthoft, Charles
Libretto Group LLC
24 Linden Road
Suite 707
Ridgefield, CT 06877

Wojtkowski, Jo
Oxford University Press
198 Madison Ave
New York, NY 10016

Yanos, Alex
Freshfields Bruckhaus Deringer LLP
601 Lexington Avenue
31st Floor
New York, NY 10022

Zaslowsky, David
Baker & McKenzie LLP
452 Fifth Avenue
New York, NY 10018

Venezuela

Betancourt C., Milagros
Centro Empresarial de Conciliación
y Arbitraje-CEDCA
2a. Avenida de Campo Alegre
Torre Credival. Piso 6
Caracas, 1060

Droulers, Diana
Centro Arbitraje Camara de Caracas
Calle Andres Eloy Blanco
Edif Camara de Comercio
Los Caobos Caracas, 1050

Torrealba L., Henry
Baker & McKenzie LLP
Centro Bancaribe, Av, PPAL de Las Mercedes
Cruce C Calle Paris
Caracas, 1060

Vietnam

Le, Net
LNT & Partners
Level 21 Bitexco Financial Tower
Ho Chi Minh, PBN Q1 HCMC

INTERNATIONAL COUNCIL FOR COMMERCIAL ARBITRATION (ICCA)

Correspondence address:
ICCA Bureau
Peace Palace, Carnegieplein 2
Phone:+ 31 70 302 2834
Fax:+ 31 70 302 2837
E-mail: bureau@arbitration-icca.org

LIST OF ICCA OFFICERS AND GOVERNING BOARD MEMBERS

MARCH 2015

OFFICERS

President

PROF. DR. ALBERT JAN VAN DEN BERG (Netherlands)
Partner, Hanotiau & van den Berg (Brussels, Belgium); General Editor, ICCA *Yearbook Commercial Arbitration* and ICCA *Congress Series*; Past President, Netherlands Arbitration Institute; Professor of Arbitration Law, Erasmus University, Rotterdam; Visiting Professor, Tsinghua University in Beijing; Member, Amsterdam and Brussels Bars

Vice Presidents

DR. MOHAMED ABDEL RAOUF (Cairo, Egypt)
Director, Cairo Regional Centre for International Commercial Arbitration (CRCICA); Lecturer, Institute of International Business Law (IDAI), Cairo University – Université Paris 1 Panthéon-Sorbonne; Vice President, International Federation of Commercial Arbitration Institutions (IFCAI); Member of the Board, Arbitration

Institute of the Stockholm Chamber of Commerce (SCC); CEDR Accredited Mediator; Editorial Board Member, Journal of Arab Arbitration

MS. ADRIANA BRAGHETTA (São Paulo, Brazil)
Co-Head of the arbitration group, LOBaptista-SVMFA; Professor of Arbitration Law, Instituto Internacional de Ciências Sociais (IICS), São Paulo; former President, Comitê Brasileiro de Arbitragem – CBAr; Past Vice President and Co-Founding Member, CBAr;. Member, International Law Association (ILA) International Arbitration Committee; Member, International Chamber of Commerce (ICC) Arbitration Commission; Member, ICC Latin-American Arbitration Commission; Member, International Centre for Dispute Resolution/American Arbitration Association (ICDR/AAA) Board for Latin America; Member, Editorial Council, CBAr Journal

Treasurer

MR. GUILLERMO AGUILAR-ALVAREZ (New York, USA)
Past General Counsel, ICC International Court of Arbitration; Principal Legal Counsel for the Government of Mexico for the Negotiation and Implementation of NAFTA; Visiting Scholar, Yale Law School; Partner, King & Spalding

Executive Director

MS. LISE BOSMAN (The Hague, The Netherlands)
Senior Legal Counsel, Permanent Court of Arbitration; Executive Director and Executive Editor, ICCA; Acting General Editor, ICCA *International Handbook on Commercial Arbitration*; Adjunct Professor, University of Cape Town; Fellow, Association of Arbitrators (Southern Africa); Editorial Board, Tijdschrift voor Arbitrage; Series Editor, PCA Award Series

GOVERNING BOARD MEMBERS

MR. CECIL ABRAHAM (Kuala Lumpur, Malaysia)
Fellow, Chartered Institute of Arbitrators; Fellow, Malaysian Institute of Arbitrators; Fellow, Singapore Institute of Arbitrators; Fellow, Australian Centre for International Commercial Arbitration Limited; Member, International Chamber of Commerce (ICC) Commission on Arbitration; Member, Advisory Panel of the Kuala Lumpur Regional Centre for Arbitration; Past Chairman, Chartered Institute of Arbitrators Malaysia Branch; Past Member, LCIA; Past President, Inter-Pacific Bar Association;

Past Vice President, Asia Pacific Regional Arbitration Group (APRAG); Past Deputy President Malaysian Institute of Arbitrators; Past Vice Chair, Committee D, International Bar Association (IBA); Head of Dispute Resolution Practice Group, Zul Rafique & Partners

MS. TERESA CHENG, GBS, SC, JP (Hong Kong)
Senior Counsel; Chair of Hong Kong International Arbitration Centre; Past President of the Chartered Institute of Arbitrators; Past Vice President of ICC International Court of Arbitration; Visiting Professor, Law School of Tsinghua University, Beijing

MR. ANDREW CLARKE (Surrey, United Kingom)
General Counsel, ExxonMobil International Limited; Steering Committee Member and Past Chair, Corporate Counsels' International Arbitration Group; Member, Past Director and Past Court Member, London Court of International Arbitration; Member, Advisory Council to the Centre for Commercial Law Studies at Queen Mary University of London; Member, Advisory Board for the Turkish Commercial Law Review; Bencher, Middle Temple (London)

PROF. BERNARDO M. CREMADES (Madrid, Spain)
Professor, Faculty of Law, Madrid University; Member of the Madrid Bar

MR. DUSHYANT DAVE (New Delhi, India)
Senior Advocate at the Supreme Court of India; Member of the Board, American Arbitration Association; former Member, LCIA; former Vice Chair, Arbitration Committee, International Bar Association (IBA); former Member, National Legal Services Authority of India (NALSA)

MR. DONALD FRANCIS DONOVAN (New York, USA)
Co-Head, International Disputes Group, Debevoise & Plimpton LLP; Adjunct Professor, New York University School of Law; Alternate US Member, ICC International Court of Arbitration; former President, American Society of International Law;former Chair, Institute for Transnational Arbitration; former Chair, US National Committee, ICC International Court of Arbitration; Member of the Board of Directors and Chair of the Litigation Committee, Human Rights First

PROF. DR. EMMANUEL GAILLARD (Paris, France)
Professor of Law, University of Paris XII; Chairman, International Arbitration Institute; Past Member, LCIA Court; Past Chairman, International Arbitration Committee, International Law Association (ILA)

PROF. DR. BERNARD HANOTIAU (Brussels, Belgium)
   Member, Brussels and Paris Bars; Professor Emeritus of International Dispute
   Resolution, University of Louvain; former Vice-President, LCIA; former
   Vice-Chairman, Institute of Transnational Arbitration; former Vice-Chairman, The
   Belgian Centre for Arbitration and Mediation (CEPANI)

JUDGE DOMINIQUE HASCHER (Paris, France)
   Judge, Supreme Judicial Court (France); Adjunct Professor of Law, University
   Panthéon-Sorbonne; Past General Counsel and Deputy Secretary General,
   International Court of Arbitration of the International Chamber of Commerce (ICC);
   Hon. Bencher of Gray's Inn, London

DR. GEROLD HERRMANN (Vienna, Austria)
   Former Secretary, United Nations Commission on International Trade Law
   (UNCITRAL); Honorary Professor, University of Vienna

DR. MICHAEL HWANG, SC (Singapore)
   Former High Court Judge (Fixed Term), Singapore; Senior Counsel, Singapore;
   former Member, Permanent Court of Arbitration; Chartered Arbitrator; former
   Adjunct Professor, National University of Singapore; former Vice Chair Committee
   D, International Bar Association (IBA); former Vice Chair, ICC International Court
   of Arbitration; Council Member, International Council of Arbitration for Sport
   (ICAS); former Member, LCIA; Chief Justice, Dubai International Financial Centre
   Courts; former Trustee, Dubai International Arbitration Centre (DIAC); Member of
   Advisory Boards, Singapore International Arbitration Centre (SIAC), Hong Kong
   International Arbitration Centre (HKIAC); former President, Law Society of
   Singapore; former Non-Resident Ambassador of Singapore to Switzerland

MR. NEIL KAPLAN, CBE, QC (Hong Kong)
   Former Judge, High Court, Hong Kong; Past Chairman, Hong Kong International
   Arbitration Centre (HKIAC); Past President, The Chartered Institute of Arbitrators;
   Member, ICC Court; Honorary Professor, City University of Hong Kong

PROF. DR. GABRIELLE KAUFMANN-KOHLER (Geneva, Switzerland)
   Professor, Geneva University Law School; Director, Geneva LL.M. in International
   Dispute Settlement (MIDS); Partner, Lévy Kaufmann-Kohler; Honorary President,
   Swiss Arbitration Association (ASA)

DR. FATHI KEMICHA (Tunis, Tunisia)
Avocat à la Cour, Member of the Bars of Paris and Tunisia; former Member, International Law Commission of the United Nations; former Chair and Member, World Bank Group Sanctions Board; Member, Board of Trustees, Dubai International Arbitration Centre; First appointed Secretary General, Constitutional Court of the Kingdom of Bahrain; former Vice President, LCIA; former Vice President, ICC Commission on Arbitration

MR. MAKHDOOM ALI KHAN (Karachi, Pakistan)
Senior Advocate, Supreme Court of Pakistan; former Attorney General, Pakistan (2001-2007); former Member, Court of the London Court of International Arbitration; Member of the Board, American Arbitration Association (AAA) and Dubai International Arbitration Centre (DIAC); Member, Panel of arbitrators, Singapore International Arbitration Centre (SIAC) and Kuala Lumpur Regional Centre for Arbitration (KLRCA); designated as an arbitrator, ICSID panel

MR. KAP-YOU (KEVIN) KIM (Seoul, Korea)
Head of Arbitration Group, Bae, Kim & Lee LLC; Senior Advisor and Arbitrator, Korea Commercial Arbitration Board (KCAB); Secretary General, Seoul International Dispute Resolution Center (Seoul IDRC); Chair, International Arbitration Committee of ICC Korea; Court Member, ICC International Court of Arbitration; Board Member, American Arbitration Association (AAA); Panel of Arbitrators, International Centre for Settlement of Investment Disputes (ICSID), Singapore International Arbitration Centre (SIAC), Hong Kong International Arbitration Centre (HKIAC), Japan Commercial Arbitration Association (JCAA), Beijing Arbitration Commission (BAC) & South China International Economic and Trade Arbitration Commission (SCIA); Editorial Board Member, Global Arbitration Review; Part-time Professor, Judicial Training and Research Institute, Supreme Court of Korea and Yonsei Law School

MS. MEG KINNEAR (Washington, DC, USA)
Secretary-General, International Centre for Settlement of Investment Disputes (ICSID); former Senior General Counsel and Director General, Trade Law Bureau of Canada; former Executive Assistant to the Deputy Minister of Justice of Canada and Counsel, Civil Litigation Section, Department of Justice Canada

PROF. ALEXANDER S. KOMAROV (Moscow, Russian Federation)
Honorary Chairman, ICC Russia National Committee, Arbitration Commission; Professor, Head of International Private Law Chair, Russian Academy of Foreign Trade; Member of the Presidium, International Commercial Arbitration Court at the Russian Federation Chamber of Commerce and Industry

MS. CAROLYN LAMM (Washington, DC, USA)

Partner, White & Case LLP; Co-Chair, International Arbitration Americas; former President of the District of Columbia Bar and the American Bar Association; Chair of the Board of the American-Uzbekistan Chamber of Commerce; Member of the Board, American-Turkish Council and American Indonesian Chamber of Commerce; Member of ICSID Panel of Arbitrators (appointed by Uzbekistan); Member, ICDR International List; former member of the American Arbitration Association Executive Committee and Board; US member of the NAFTA 2022 Committee; Member of the American Law Institute's (ALI) Council and its Advisory Committee on Restatement on International Arbitration and a Counselor on the ALI Restatement Fourth on Public International Law; Counselor to the Executive Board of the American Society of International Law (ASIL); Visiting Professor teaching International Investment Arbitration, University of Miami, School of Law

MR. ARTHUR MARRIOTT, QC (London, United Kingdom)

Barrister

CHIEF JUSTICE SUNDARESH MENON (Singapore)

Chief Justice, Supreme Court of Singapore; former Attorney-General, Singapore; former Judicial Commissioner, Supreme Court of Singapore; former Deputy Chairman, Singapore International Arbitration Centre

PROF. FRANCISCO ORREGO VICUÑA (Santiago, Chile)

Professor of Law, Heidelberg University Center for Latin America; Director, LL.M. on Investments, Trade and Arbitration offered jointly with the University of Heidelberg and the Max Planck Institute; former Judge *Ad-Hoc*, International Court of Justice; former Judge and President, Administrative Tribunal of the World Bank; Judge, International Monetary Fund Administrative Tribunal; former Vice President, LCIA; Arbitrator, 20 Essex Street Chambers, London and Singapore

PROF. WILLIAM W. PARK (Cohasset, MA, USA)

Professor of Law, Boston University; General Editor, Arbitration International; President, LCIA; Past Chairman, American Bar Association (ABA) Committee on International Commercial Dispute Resolution

PROF. DR. MICHAEL PRYLES (Melbourne, Australia and Singapore)

President, Singapore International Arbitration Centre (SIAC) Court of Arbitration; former Chairman, SIAC Board of Directors; President, Australian Centre for International Commercial Arbitration; Member, Board of Trustees of the Dubai International Arbitration Centre; Chairman, ICC Australia; Foundation President,

Asia Pacific Regional Arbitration Group; Member, LCIA Court; Commissioner, United Nations Compensation Commission

MS. LUCY REED (Hong Kong)
Head, Freshfields Global International Arbitration Group; Member, ICC Governing Body; Member, LCIA Court; Panel of Arbitrators, ICSID; former Chair, Institute for Transnational Arbitration; former President, American Society of International Law (ASIL)

MR. KLAUS REICHERT, SC (London, England)
Barrister, Irish and English Bars

DR. ANKE SESSLER (Frankfurt am Main, Germany)
Partner, Skadden, Arps, Slate, Meagher & Flom & Affiliates (1 September 2014); former Chief Counsel Litigation, Siemens AG; Member, German Institution of Arbitration (DIS) Advisory Board; Member ICC Commission on Arbitration; Member, ICC National Committee for Germany; Member, American Arbitration Association (AAA) Board of Directors; Member, Swiss Arbitration Association (ASA) Board; former Member, International Bar Association (IBA) Arbitration Committee; former Panel of Conciliators, ICSID

MR. WILLIAM K. SLATE II (Washington, DC, USA)
Arbitrator and ADR consultant; Senior Visiting Fellow, Duke University Law School; Past President and Chief Executive Officer, American Arbitration Association; Founder, International Centre for Dispute Resolution; for fourteen years was an invited member of the United Nations Commission on International Trade Law (UNCITRAL) Arbitration Working Group, and a member of the Secretary of State's Advisory Committee on Private International Law; authored forty-two published articles on arbitration, mediation, data, and culture in international conflict management

PROF. DR. GUIDO SANTIAGO TAWIL (Buenos Aires, Argentina)
Professor, University of Buenos Aires School of Law; Chairman, Latin American Arbitration Association (ALARB); former Co-Chair, International Bar Association (IBA) Arbitration Committee; Council Member, IBA Legal Practice Division; former Court Member, LCIA; Member, Institute for Transnational Arbitration Academic Council; Member, ICC Latin American Arbitrators Committee; Member, ICC Institute of World Business Law; Attorney at Law, Partner, M. & M. Bomchil

PROF. DR. DR. HC. PIERRE TERCIER (Fribourg, Switzerland)
Honorary Chairman, International Court of Arbitration of the International Chamber of Commerce; Professor Emeritus, Law Faculty, University of Fribourg; former Chairman, Swiss Antitrust Commission; Member, Board of the Swiss Arbitration Association; Panel of Arbitrators, International Centre for Settlement of Investment Disputes (ICSID) (Chairman list)

MR. V.V. VEEDER, QC (London, United Kingdom)
Vice President, LCIA; Council Member, ICC Institute of World Business Law; Board Member, Dubai International Arbitration Centre (DIAC); Visiting Professor on Investment Arbitration, King's College, University of London

THE HON. S. AMOS WAKO, F.C.I.ARB, SC (Nairobi, Kenya)
Former Attorney General, Republic of Kenya; former Chairman, Arbitration Tribunal, Kenya Chamber of Commerce and Industry; Arbitrator, Vienna Convention on the Law of Treaties, Centre for Settlement of Investment Disputes; former Vice President, LCIA-Africa Region; former Chairman, Law Society of Kenya; former Member, International Advisory Committee of World Intellectual Property Organization (WIPO) Centre for Settlement of Disputes; former Commission Member, International Commission of Jurists; former Deputy Secretary General, International Bar Association (IBA); former Secretary General, African Bar Association; former Senior Partner, Kaplan & Stratton; former President, Asian-African Legal Consultative Organisation; former Member, International Law Commission (ILC)

MR. DAVID A.R. WILLIAMS, QC (Auckland, New Zealand)
Barrister, Member of New Zealand and English Bars; Chartered Arbitrator; former Judge of the High Court of New Zealand; former Chief Justice of the Cook Islands; President of the Cook Islands Court of Appeal; former Judge, Court of Dubai International Financial Centre; Past President, Arbitrators and Mediators Institute of New Zealand; former Member, ICC Court of International Arbitration; former Member, LCIA; Board of Directors, American Arbitration Association; Honorary Professor of Law, University of Auckland, New Zealand

MS. ARIEL YE (Beijing, People's Republic of China)
Partner, King & Wood Mallesons Beijing office; Member of the China Bar Association; Member of the Court of the Singapore International Arbitration Centre (SIAC); Member of the Court, LCIA; Arbitrator of China International Economic and Trade Arbitration Commission (CIETAC),Hong Kong International Arbitration Centre (HKIAC), SIAC and International Centre for Dispute Resolution (ICDR); Co-chair of the Arbitration Committee of International Defence Counsel Association; Member of the working group of the Asia Pacific Arbitration Group of the

International Bar Association (IBA); Lecturer, LLM program for International Arbitration of the Law School of Tsinghua University.

MR. EDUARDO ZULETA (Bogota, Colombia)
Co-Chair, International Bar Association (IBA) Arbitration Committee; Vice-Chair Institute for Transnational Arbitration (ITA); Member, London Court of International Arbitration (LCIA); Panel of Arbitrators, International Centre for Settlement of Investment Disputes (ICSID) (Chairman's List); Vice-Chair Latin American Arbitration Association (ALARB); Member ICC Latin American Arbitration Group

Honorary Presidents

THE HON. GIORGIO BERNINI (Bologna, Italy)
Former Minister of Foreign Trade and Member of Parliament; former Member, Italian Antitrust Authority; Professor, University of Bologna, Chair of Arbitration and International Commercial Law; President, Association for the Teaching and Study of Arbitration and International Trade Law (AISA); Member, Executive Committee, Italian Arbitration Association; Senior Partner, Studio Bernini e Associati

DR. GEROLD HERRMANN (Vienna, Austria)
Former Secretary, United Nations Commission on International Trade Law (UNCITRAL); Honorary Professor, University of Vienna

MR. FALI S. NARIMAN (New Delhi, India)
President Emeritus, Bar Association of India; Honorary Member, International Commission of Jurists; Past President, Law Association for Asia and the Pacific (LAWASIA); Member, Court of the LCIA; Past Vice Chairman, International Court of Arbitration of the International Chamber of Commerce (ICC); Past Co-Chair, Human Rights Institute of the International Bar Association (IBA); Senior Advocate, Supreme Court of India

PROF. JAN PAULSSON (Miami, USA)
Michael Klein Distinguished Scholar Chair, University of Miami School of Law; Partner, Three Crowns LLP; Visiting Professor of Law, London School of Economics; Past Vice-President, ICC Court; Past President, LCIA

Honorary Vice Presidents

MR. DONALD FRANCIS DONOVAN (New York, USA)
Co-Head, International Disputes Group, Debevoise & Plimpton LLP; Adjunct Professor, New York University School of Law; Alternate US Member, ICC International Court of Arbitration; former President, American Society of International Law;former Chair, Institute for Transnational Arbitration; former Chair, US National Committee, ICC International Court of Arbitration; Member of the Board of Directors and Chair of the Litigation Committee, Human Rights First

DR. MICHAEL HWANG, SC (Singapore)
Former High Court Judge (Fixed Term), Singapore; Senior Counsel, Singapore; former Member, Permanent Court of Arbitration; Chartered Arbitrator; former Adjunct Professor, National University of Singapore; former Vice Chair Committee D, International Bar Association (IBA); former Vice Chair, ICC International Court of Arbitration; Council Member, International Council of Arbitration for Sport (ICAS); former Member, LCIA; Chief Justice, Dubai International Financial Centre Courts; former Trustee, Dubai International Arbitration Centre (DIAC); Member of Advisory Boards, Singapore International Arbitration Centre (SIAC), Hong Kong International Arbitration Centre (HKIAC); former President, Law Society of Singapore; former Non-Resident Ambassador of Singapore to Switzerland

PROF. SERGEI LEBEDEV (Moscow, Russian Federation)
Former President, Maritime Arbitration Commission; Member of the Presidium, International Commercial Arbitration Court of the Russian Federation Chamber of Commerce and Industry; Professor, Moscow Institute of International Relations (University); former Commissioner, UN Compensation Commission; Member, United Nations Commission on International Trade Law (UNCITRAL) Working Group on Arbitration; Vice-president in the two Russian Associations: International Law and Maritime Law

DDR. WERNER MELIS (Vienna, Austria)
Honorary President, International Arbitral Centre of the Austrian Federal Economic Chamber, Vienna; Past Vice President, LCIA

MS. TINUADE OYEKUNLE (Lagos, Nigeria)
Barrister and Solicitor, Supreme Court of Nigeria; Arbitrator and Notary Public; Member, Association of Arbitrators of Nigeria; Fellow, Chartered Arbitrator of the Chartered Institute of Arbitrators, London; Member, Arbitration Committee of the Lagos Chamber of Commerce; Member, Panel Membership Group (PMG), Chartered Institute of Arbitrators, London; former Chairman, Education & Training

Committee of the Chartered Institute of Arbitrators, London; former Member, Board of Management of the Chartered Institute of Arbitrators, London; Regional Representative for Promotion of Arbitration in the West African Region; Past Chairman, Chartered Institute of Arbitrators, Nigeria Branch, and current member of the Executive Committee of the Branch; former Member, London Court of International Arbitration; Correspondent, UNIDROIT; Member, Board of Directors, Kigali International Arbitration Centre

Honorary Secretaries General

MR. ULF FRANKE (Stockholm, Sweden)
Chairman, Arbitration Institute of the Stockholm Chamber of Commerce (SCC); Past Secretary General, ICCA; Past Secretary General, SCC; Past President, International Federation of Commercial Arbitration Institutions (IFCAI)

MR. ANTONIO R. PARRA (Washington, DC, USA)
Past Secretary General, ICCA; Past Deputy Secretary-General and Legal Adviser, International Centre for Settlement of Investment Disputes (ICSID); Fellow, Chartered Institute of Arbitrators; Consultant, World Bank

Advisory Members

PROF. PIERO BERNARDINI (Rome, Italy)
Former Member of the Court of the London Court of International Arbitration (LCIA); designated by Italy as an arbitrator, International Centre for Settlement of Investment Disputes (ICSID) panel; Member of the Advisory Board, ASA Bulletin; Member Comité Scientifique, Revue de l'arbitrage; past Professor of Arbitration Law, LUISS University, Rome; President, Italian Arbitration Association; past Vice-President, ICC International Court of Arbitration

PROF. DR. KARL-HEINZ BÖCKSTIEGEL (Bergisch-Gladbach, Germany)
Professor Emeritus of International Business Law, University of Cologne; Honorary Chairman and Past Chairman, German Institution of Arbitration (DIS); Past Patron, Chartered Institute of Arbitrators; Past President, International Law Association (ILA); Past President, London Court of International Arbitration (LCIA); Past President, Iran-United States Claims Tribunal, The Hague; Past Panel Chairman, United Nations Compensation Commission

PROF. DR. NAEL G. BUNNI (Dublin, Ireland)
Past President, Chartered Institute of Arbitrators; Past Member, Board of Trustees and Past Chairman, Executive Committee, Dubai International Arbitration Centre; Past Member, LCIA Board of Directors; Visiting Professor in Construction Law and Contract Administration, Trinity College, Dublin; Chartered Engineer and Chartered Registered Arbitrator

M^E YVES DERAINS (Paris, France)
Partner, Derains & Gharavi; former Chairman, Comité Français de l'Arbitrage and Co-Chairman of the ICC Working Group on the Reduction of Costs and Time in International Arbitration; past Secretary General, ICC International Court of Arbitration; Chairman, ICC Institute of World Business Law; Member of the Paris Bar

PROF. DR. RADOMIR DJUROVIČ (Belgrade, Serbia)
Former President, Arbitration Court of Yugoslavia; Professor of International Commercial Law, Belgrade University

DR. MAURO FERRANTE (Rome, Italy)
Former Secretary General, Italian Arbitration Association; former Managing Director, ICC-Italy

MR. L. YVES FORTIER, PC, CC, OQ, QC (Montréal, Canada)
Sole practitioner, Cabinet Yves Fortier, Montréal; former Chairman Emeritus and Senior Partner, Ogilvy Renault Montréal; Past President, The London Court of International Arbitration (LCIA); former Ambassador and Permanent Representative of Canada to the United Nations; former Judge *Ad Hoc*, International Court of Justice (ICJ); Chairman, Sanctions Board of the World Bank; Member, Security and Intelligence Review Committee of Canada; Resident Arbitrator, Arbitration Place, Toronto; Member, 20 Essex Court Chambers

MR. ULF FRANKE (Stockholm, Sweden)
Past Secretary General, ICCA; Past Secretary General, Arbitration Institute of the Stockholm Chamber of Commerce (SCC); Past President, International Federation of Commercial Arbitration Institutions (IFCAI)

PROF. MARTIN HUNTER (London, United Kingdom)
Barrister, Essex Court Chambers, London; former solicitor and partner, Freshfields (1967-1994); former Chairman, Dubai International Arbitration Centre (DIAC) (2005-2012); former member, ICC International Court of Arbitration; former member, LCIA Court; Emeritus Professor, Nottingham Trent University

PROF. AHMED S. EL-KOSHERI (Cairo, Egypt)
Former Professor of International Economic Law and former President, International University for African Development (Université Senghor, Alexandria); Member, *l'Institut de Droit International*; former Judge *Ad Hoc*, International Court of Justice; Partner, Kosheri, Rashed & Riad Law Firm

THE HON. MARC LALONDE (Montréal, Canada)
Former Judge *Ad Hoc*, International Court of Justice; former Minister of Justice and Attorney General; former Minister of Energy, Mines and Resources; former Minister of Finance; former President, LCIA North American Users Committee; Member, Institute of International Business Law and Practice

MR. MARK LITTMAN, QC (London, United Kingdom)
Barrister

DDR. WERNER MELIS (Vienna, Austria)
Honorary President, International Arbitral Centre of the Austrian Federal Economic Chamber, Vienna; Past Vice President, LCIA

Mᴱ CARLOS NEHRING NETTO (São Paulo, Brazil)
Founder, Nehring & Associados – Advocacia; former Member, ICC International Court of Arbitration; Member, London Court of International Arbitration

MS. TINUADE OYEKUNLE (Lagos, Nigeria)
Barrister and Solicitor, Supreme Court of Nigeria; Arbitrator and Notary Public; Member, Association of Arbitrators of Nigeria; Fellow, Chartered Arbitrator of the Chartered Institute of Arbitrators, London; Member, Arbitration Committee of the Lagos Chamber of Commerce; Member, Panel Membership Group (PMG), Chartered Institute of Arbitrators, London; former Chairman, Education & Training Committee of the Chartered Institute of Arbitrators, London; former Member, Board of Management of the Chartered Institute of Arbitrators, London; Regional Representative for Promotion of Arbitration in the West African Region; Past Chairman, Chartered Institute of Arbitrators, Nigeria Branch, and current member of the Executive Committee of the Branch; former Member, London Court of

International Arbitration; Correspondent, UNIDROIT; Member, Board of Directors, Kigali International Arbitration Centre

THE HON. ANDREW JOHN ROGERS, QC (Sydney, Australia)

Former Chief Judge, Commercial Division, Supreme Court of New South Wales; Adjunct Professor, University of Technology, Sydney; Chairman, National Dispute Centre, Sydney

DR. JOSÉ LUIS SIQUEIROS (Mexico City, Mexico)

Past President, Mexican Academy of International Commercial Arbitration; Past President, Inter-American Bar Association; Past Chairman, Inter-American Juridical Committee (OAS)

PROF. TANG HOUZHI (Beijing, People's Republic of China)

Honorary Vice Chairman, CIETAC; Vice Chairman, CCPIT/CCOIC Beijing Conciliation Centre; Professor, Law School of the People's University of China; Visiting Professor, Amoy University School of Law; Arbitration Adviser, UN International Trade Centre; Fellow and Chartered Arbitrator, Chartered Institute of Arbitrators; former Court Member, LCIA; Honorary Professor, Hong Kong City University School of Law; Vice President, International Federation of Commercial Arbitration Institutions (IFCAI)

DR. WANG SHENG CHANG (Beijing, People's Republic of China)

Past Vice Chairman and former Secretary General, China International Economic and Trade Arbitration Commission (CIETAC); Past Vice Chairman, China Maritime Arbitration Commission (CMAC); Senior Consultant, Beijing Hui Zhong Law Firm, China

PROF. YASUHEI TANIGUCHI (Tokyo, Japan)

Former Member, Appellate Body of the World Trade Organization Dispute Settlement Body; Special Advisor, Japan Commercial Arbitration Association; Professor Emeritus, Kyoto University; former President, Japan Association of Arbitrators; Of Counsel, Matsuo & Kosugi

ICCA Membership
n o w o p e n

Membership of ICCA is now open to all law graduates specializing in dispute resolution.

Membership benefits include:

- Listing in a fully searchable electronic membership directory on the ICCA website
- Listing in a hard-copy membership directory, to be distributed to members once per year
- 10% discount on the purchase price of the Yearbook Commercial Arbitration
- 10% discount to attend biennial ICCA Congresses and Conferences
- Regular electronic and hard copy newsletters
- Advance notice of ICCA-sponsored events and activities

How to apply:

- On-line via www.arbitration-icca.org
- Via email to membership@arbitration-icca.org

www.arbitration-icca.org